AMERICAN DEFENSE POLICY

AMERICAN
DEFENSE POLICY
Third Edition

Edited by

RICHARD G. HEAD   ERVIN J. ROKKE
Assistant Professor   *Associate Professor*

With a Foreword by

RICHARD F. ROSSER
Professor and Head

*Department of Political Science
United States Air Force Academy
Colorado*

The Johns Hopkins University Press, Baltimore and London

The Johns Hopkins University Press, Baltimore, Maryland 21218
The Johns Hopkins University Press Ltd., London

Library of Congress Catalog Card Number 72-12357
ISBN 0-8018-1486-3 (clothbound edition)
ISBN 0-8018-1487-1 (paperback edition)
Manufactured in the United States of America

Originally published, 1965
Second edition, 1968
Third edition, 1973
Johns Hopkins Paperbacks edition, 1968, 1973
Second printing, third edition, 1973

Contents

FOREWORD: THE STUDY OF AMERICAN DEFENSE POLICY

Every citizen should be concerned with American defense policy. No subject today is ultimately more vital to the people of the United States. Never has the defense of the nation been a more urgent task, and never a more complex problem. The military power of the United States is immense, yet security of the vital interests of our nation is increasingly difficult to achieve. To see why this is so we must examine the fundamental changes in the international environment since World War II.

The first change is technological. The twilight of World War II saw the dawn of the nuclear era and the primitive prototypes of nuclear delivery systems—jet aircraft and ballistic missiles. In the midst of the last great wartime conference at Potsdam, President Truman received a cryptic message on July 16, 1945, announcing the first atomic test at Alamogordo, New Mexico: "Operated on this morning. Diagnosis not yet complete but results seem satisfactory and already exceed expectations." In a few weeks the atomic bomb would be ready for Hiroshima. The full implications of this revolutionary weapon, however, could not be imagined. The hydrogen bomb, still to be developed, would have a hundred times the destructive force of the crude atomic device. And once perfected, the new weapons could not be forgotten, no matter how horrible they proved to be. Technological change is not reversible.

One week after news of Alamogordo, Truman privately informed Stalin of the new weapon. Stalin was delighted—what a bit of luck! Churchill thought Stalin had not understood the significance, for he failed to ask one question about the experiment. Molotov later claimed that Stalin understood this to be a "super bomb," the like of which had never been seen, but not an "atomic" bomb. Some were ready to believe Stalin was this naive, and Russia this backward. The Russians would not have their "bomb" for a hundred years, it was predicted. In reality, Stalin would soon launch a crash program to develop nuclear weapons and their delivery systems. On September 23, 1949, President Truman announced that an atomic explosion had been detected in the Soviet Union. The United States could no longer rest comfortably with its nuclear monopoly. If we soon could destroy an aggressor with one climactic stroke, the time would come when we could face the same fate.

The second great change in the international environment was the radical alteration of the distribution of power in the international political system. Gaping holes were left in Europe and the Far East with the defeat of the Third Reich and the Japanese Empire. Britain and France, kingpins of the interwar security system, could no longer assume the burden of maintaining the peace. Although Churchill was loath to admit it, the sun was setting on the British Empire. The French nation then seemed to reside mainly in the obstinate and visionary General de Gaulle.

Perhaps the fundamental alteration in the balance of power was the appearance of a new kind of nation-state, the superpower. There were two—the United States and the Soviet Union. Before World War II, America had been isolationist, Russia had been isolated. Now their armies had met on the Elbe in the heart of Europe. Because of their new world interests, neither state could ignore the other.

America's new role, which she accepted with some hesitation, required profound changes in American defense policy. For over 150 years the United States had been a reluctant participant in world politics. Except for a brief foray abroad in the latter days of World War I "to make the world safe for democracy," Americans lived a relatively secure and tranquil life. The rape of Ethiopia and Czechoslovakia was deplorable but not our concern. Our security supposedly was not involved. Two huge oceans protected us from invasion. We tended to forget that other nations were carrying the burden of opposing aggression. We were lucky to have England and Churchill. On December 7, 1941, we found that the Pacific was not quite the barrier we supposed.

After World War II, American national security clearly depended on American military power. Allies were helpful, but they relied on us for economic and military aid. More important, the tremendous cost of nuclear weaponry dictated that only the United States could provide the ultimate military power of the Western world. The primary threat to the security of the United States could come only from the other superpower, the Soviet Union. The USSR, as should all nations, worried first about its own security. But its leaders were dedicated followers of an ideology called Marxism-Leninism. This ideology predicted the inevitable transformation of country after country to communism, and the Soviet leaders had a moral duty to support such transformations. The confrontation between the two superpowers thus seemed preordained. A fundamental conflict of interest was involved because the United States opposed an extension of the communist system. The Cold War resulted.

Even in the darkest days of the Cold War, neither nation appeared to seriously consider a frontal attack on the other. Each soon realized the power of nuclear weapons and the probable effect of a nuclear exchange on their countries. Each was concerned with perfecting its deterrent, which it hoped never to use. The primary conflict therefore would not take place between the two superpowers, but in the area now called the "Third World."

The third fundamental change in the international political system after World War II was the emergence of this Third World, composed of the so-called developing nations. For centuries, Europe had been the center of the world political system. European powers controlled vast empires and dominated the few independent countries of Africa and Asia.

As Western power disintegrated after World War II, colony after colony gained independence. But freedom did not usher in the land of plenty. Economically, politically, and socially the new states—they were not yet really "nations"—lived essentially as they had for centuries.

The process of political and economic development inevitably created profound strains on each society. Opportunities appeared for leftist, sometimes communist, parties to gain power under the guise of "national liberation" movements. In the West, such movements were often seen as extensions of the Soviet Empire, and Soviet communism had to be "contained."

Yet, in the period since World War II, one fact has been obvious. Change has not stopped. Indeed, the world of today and of the foreseeable future is more complex, the challenges to United States national security more serious, and American defense policy more vital a subject than ever before.

To begin with, the military-technological revolution has not ceased. The primitive device dropped in 1945 bears little relation to the sophisticated intercontinental missile with its multiple, separately targetable, thermonuclear warheads. At the same time, the knowledge and technology needed to build the simpler nuclear weapons is widely diffused. Moreover, these weapons can be built more cheaply than ever. It is entirely possible that the world will soon have not five nuclear powers but twenty.

Delivery systems also have undergone drastic change. The German V-2 flew several hundred miles and sometimes hit London. Today, the intercontinental ballistic missile can travel thousands of miles and hit its target with amazing accuracy. Moreover, the present balance in favor of offensive weapons is being challenged. The United States and the Soviet Union are developing antiballistic missile systems. To counteract such systems, each nation must in turn increase the sophistication of its missile delivery systems and their warheads. The technological race seems endless. New weapons systems are obsolescent before they become operational.

The political dominance of the superpowers also is in question. The so-called Soviet Empire —"monolithic" communism—no longer exists. (Even in its heyday, the bloc was never fully under Moscow's control.) Communist China is Russia's main competitor for leadership in the socialist camp. But Yugoslavia has held an independent course for twenty years.

Because the Soviets today have so little direct control—indeed, little influence in some cases—over other communist states and parties, it is misleading to talk of a general "communist" threat. In addition, it is incorrect to assume that communist-inspired activity in any given country is directly influenced by one communist state. Within most parties there are now Soviet and Chinese wings, and, in Latin America, Castroite factions. All this does not mean, of course, that the threat of "communism" no longer exists. It is merely diffused and much more complex. In response, American policymakers must create a defense policy to meet a series of diverse and constantly changing threats from the many strains of communism.

Similarly, the Western alliance is in disrepair. In effect, France has left NATO. Other NATO members question the continuing relevance of this defense organization. The threat is not as evident since the USSR appears to accept the status quo in Europe. Meanwhile, Western Europe is making steady progress toward economic, and perhaps eventually political, integration. The resulting political unit would almost certainly be a third superpower. America's defense relationship with a United Europe inevitably would differ from the present NATO system. The new superpower might acquire a nuclear arsenal and weapons delivery systems which match the sophistication of those held by the United States and the USSR.

Finally, developments in the Third World have not always matched predictions. The Western powers and the communist states have given much economic and military aid to the developing countries. The influence of the donor states on the recipients, however, has not been in direct proportion to this support. The developing countries are eager for aid from wherever it may come, as long as they can avoid foreign domination. They do not want to be pawns in the East-West struggle. The so-called national liberation movements, even where communist influence is significant, generally are more nationalist than communist. American defense policy must adapt to this possibility.

In summary, the threats to American security today and in the future will be diverse and of complex composition. To be successful, the defense policy of the United States must be carefully attuned to the constantly changing face of international conflict. Perhaps the most difficult challenge in this respect will be the accurate determination of whether or not an international crisis directly threatens the vital interests of the United States.

Meanwhile, the ultimate hope is that all states someday will settle conflicts without the use of force, that leaders and peoples will find satisfactory and peaceful alternatives to military power in their respective national interests. The final result may not be general and complete disarmament, long the goal of those who would replace the state system with a world government, but any lowering of the level of tension is desirable—provided peace with justice results. To this end, American policymakers must develop a defense policy which provides satisfactory national security at each progressive step in arms control negotiations.

Having set the international stage, it is now appropriate to discuss the specific field of American defense policy. For many years Americans wrote on international politics, on foreign policy, on military strategy, but not on the unique ground where these subjects meet—American defense policy. Strategy was treated separately from foreign policy objectives. Once at war, America fought for victory and then worried about the political settlement. (The "unconditional surrender" formula of World War II is the most recent reminder.) In peacetime, United States policymakers shunned the limited use of military force to achieve foreign policy objectives. This in turn reflected the inability of Americans to understand the realities of international politics and America's responsibility to fight for international peace with justice.

After World War II, it became painfully evident that much thinking was needed to devise theoretical guidance for American policymakers in their attempts to insure national security in an entirely new international environment. The old simplistic prewar (and wartime) approach to national-security questions would not suffice. American defense policy, a new field of study integrating the concepts and approaches of international politics, foreign policy, and military strategy, was born. The theoreticians were scholars from the traditional disciplines generally writing in direct response to government request, or military staff officers attempting to meet the new challenges of their profession. The questions were so serious, and policymakers were so concerned, that government could not wait for academe to discover the new field of study.

Today, political scientists are heavily represented in the field of defense policy, but the breadth and seriousness of the questions involved concern scholars from many disciplines: economics, psychology, sociology, history, and physics, to name a few. And each discipline has something to contribute to the study of defense policy, given the ramifications of the subject for all phases of national and international life.

In addition to the central concerns of the new subject, interest has developed in the process by which defense policy is formulated and in the institutions involved in the process. It is evident that sound policy is generally the result of careful consideration and full analysis of all alternatives. The integration of relevant organizations in the decisionmaking process therefore is a critical ingredient in the formulation of a successful defense policy. The budgetary process is of particular interest because decisions about weapons systems involve staggering costs and the efficient allocation of scarce resources. The proper organization of the Department of Defense also is of special concern. The result of the interest in process and institutions is another facet in the study of defense policy.

In the last several years, the vital importance of the military and its relationship with society —usually called "civil-military relations"—has received increased recognition. Indeed, in the coming decades there may be no more vital concern for defense decisionmakers. Trends already evident in American society indicate declining defense budgets (after increases to account for inflation are subtracted) and fewer voluntary recruits. The primary problem of the military may be to exist as an effective organization in a society which is basically apathetic to the military and its requirements.

The subject of American defense policy in all its ramifications is of vital interest to the military profession. Members of the armed forces wield the weapons, the ultimate sanction of military power. Yet the responsibility of the professional soldier today does not end on the battlefield. President Kennedy told the graduating class of the United States Air Force Academy on June 5, 1963:

Your major responsibilities, of course, will relate to the obligations of military command. Yet, as last October's crisis in the Caribbean so aptly demonstrated, military policy and power cannot and must not be separated from political and diplomatic decisions. . . . We needed in October—and we shall need in the future—military commanders who are conscious of the enormous stakes involved in every move they make—who are aware of the fact that there is no point where a purely political problem becomes a purely military problem—who know the difference between vital interests and peripheral interests—who can maneuver military forces with judgment and precision as well as courage and determination—and who can foresee the effects of military moves on the whole fabric of international power.

The armed services need soldiers who are also scholars. Learning can never cease, because the military profession in the twentieth century is infinitely complex and the parameters of defense are constantly changing.

There is tension, of course, in the character of the soldier-scholar. The soldier must function in a disciplined and highly structured organization. The scholar must constantly question the most sacred dogmas of his profession in the endless search for truth. Yet the roles can be compatible. The soldier-scholar searches for new answers to defense problems, but ultimately acquiesces in the decision of his civilian and military superiors. The role of the soldier always must prevail.

The education of the soldier-scholar in the complexities of defense policy should begin early, preferably during his undergraduate education. This requirement has been particularly obvious to leading military educators at the service academies.

At the United States Military Academy, Colonel George A. Lincoln, Professor and Head of the Department of Social Sciences (now Director of the Office of Emergency Preparedness), was long a driving force in the development of the soldier-scholar concept. His work, in turn, was an inspiration to other military educators. Brigadier General Robert F. McDermott, the first permanent Dean of the Faculty of the United States Air Force Academy, in particular saw the potentialities of American defense policy as a new academic subject and quickly introduced it into the basic curriculum at the new Academy. The subsequent development of defense policy as a field of interest was a constant concern of Wesley W. Posvar, the first permanent Professor and Head of the Department of Political Science at the Air Force Academy. For ten years, until his retirement in 1967 to become Chancellor of the University of Pittsburgh, Colonel Posvar led his colleagues in a continual effort to collect the latest and best materials in defense policy, and to develop a conceptual framework for the presentation of this complex subject.

The first edition of this book, published in 1965, was the direct result of the efforts of Colonel Posvar and his colleagues to present the subject of defense policy in a logical framework. Colonel Posvar and Captain John C. Ries (now Professor of Political Science at the University of California at Los Angeles) were the editors of the first edition. They in turn had built upon the work of earlier directors of the Academy's required course in defense policy: John J. Boyne; John W. Carley; Donald W. Galvin; William F. Lackman, Jr.; Larry J. Larsen; and Thomas C. Pinckney. Colonel William G. McDonald and Brigadier General Brent Scowcroft (currently military assistant to the President of the United States) also played a vital role in the production of the first edition while serving as acting chairmen of the Academy's Department of Political Science in 1963 and 1964, respectively.

The second edition, printed in 1968, was essentially a new book. Because of the rapidly developing field of defense policy, 90 percent of the articles had not appeared in the first edition. Almost three-fourths of those articles were written between 1965 and 1968. Moreover, the book was expanded by some 20 percent. The editors of the second edition were Major Mark E. Smith III, and Lt. Colonel Claude J. Johns, Jr.

The present edition also is basically a new book. Only three of the fifty-four articles were in the second edition. Thirty-nine were published after that edition appeared. A major departure from the earlier editions is the inclusion of a section on civil-military relations.

The editors of the present edition are Majors Richard G. Head (D.P.A., Syracuse) and Ervin J. Rokke (Ph.D., Harvard). These young officers, both Air Force Academy graduates, epitomize the soldier-scholar concept. The editors received invaluable help from other members of the Department of Political Science at the Air Force Academy. The third edition, like the earlier two, has built on the hard work of a generation of soldier-scholars—teaching, researching, and writing in the field of defense policy. The present volume therefore is a corporate product of the military profession. We hope that it will be of aid to all who are interested in the subject of American defense policy.

Richard F. Rosser

August 1972
U.S. Air Force Academy, Colorado

INTRODUCTION TO THE THIRD EDITION

Since the first edition of *American Defense Policy* was published in 1965, there have been a multitude of changes in the international political system and in American domestic politics. At the same time, there has been a considerable expansion of theoretical tools and concepts useful for analyzing the changing scene of policy. The second edition of *American Defense Policy* (1968) included many of these changes, but events of the past five years have surfaced critical issues and analytical techniques not apparent from the perspective of 1968. These events include the following:

1. Decreased concern among both the general public and defense intellectuals about the threat of a general nuclear war. The perceived danger of a nuclear holocaust has diminished with the evolving nature of the international system. Early strategists like Thomas C. Schelling and Herman Kahn are now involved with environmental studies, Japanese political culture, and prognoses of the future. The intellectual stimulus of the nuclear revolution which yielded a host of highly sophisticated strategic theories and concepts has given way, at least temporarily, to the law of diminishing returns.

2. Increased interest in arms control. Strategic asymmetry between the Soviet Union and the United States has been replaced with approximate equality. Both sides give evidence of wanting to reduce the costs and dangers of a spiraling arms race; phase I of the Strategic Arms Limitation Talks (SALT) is now history.

3. The war in Vietnam. The tragic war in Vietnam has produced a crisis not only in the study of national security problems but also in the American response to the challenges of international politics. The study of war and strategy has become for many scholars an emotionally repulsive and unattractive endeavor. More important, perhaps, is the emergence of a general ambiguity about international politics which threatens to turn American interests almost exclusively inward.

4. Public disenchantment. At a time when the challenges and opportunities have never been greater, those agencies of the "establishment" tasked with achieving national security are faced with threats to their legitimacy from substantial portions of the populace they serve. Current debates over proper roles for the military in American society are but one manifestation of this phenomenon.

The purpose of this edition is to provide a basic set of readings which examines American defense policy as it emerges from these disparate factors of the international and domestic political environments.

SCOPE OF THIS EDITION

Previous editions of *American Defense Policy* have been used in undergraduate and graduate level curricula at various institutions, including the Air Force Academy. The organization of the current edition reflects not only the changing context of American defense policy but also those issues and approaches perceived by instructors and students to be most useful in an academic environment. Like the first two editions, this volume emphasizes the substance of defense strategy and the process by which it is formulated. A major change, however, is the inclusion of a third primary topic, the role of the military in American society. These three areas —strategy, policymaking, and civil-military relations—are the core of the book. The first chapter, on international and domestic constraints, provides an introduction to this core and describes the context of our study.

"Strategy and the Use of Force" (Part II) is conceptually the most rigorous section. The first chapter in this part contains a series of readings which outlines the evolution of defense strategy from Massive Retaliation through Realistic Deterrence and the Nixon Doctrine. The next three chapters present a typology of force levels which has proved useful in teaching and analysis. These include general war and arms control, limited war and the concept of tacit bargaining, and wars of rural and urban insurgency. Space limitations caused us to omit lengthy discussions concerning the more unlikely variations of nuclear war, several classic writings on guerrilla warfare, arguments for and against SALT, and examinations of comparative defense policies. It is hoped that most of these deficiencies might be minimized by use of the topical bibliography following Part II. *Comparative Defense Policy*, a forthcoming companion reader being edited by Squadron Leader Tony Rogerson and Majors Frank B. Horton and Edward L. Warner III of the Academy's Political Science Department, also will be useful in this regard.

"American Defense Policymaking" (Part III) is based upon the conceptual framework developed in the early seventies by scholars such as Professor Graham Allison and Dr. Morton Halperin. The first two chapters are concerned with the theory and organization of defense decisionmaking; the last chapter contains case studies that illustrate this theory.

"The Military and American Society" (Part IV) begins with a theoretical section on the military as a professional institution and discusses alternative models of civil-military relations. Articles on the Truman-MacArthur controversy, the assault on ROTC, and the types of individuals entering the military officer corps through the ROTC and service academies also are included in this section. The concluding chapter presents a series of critical issues facing the professional military in today's society. Among these are the revolution in public opinion concerning military expenditures, charges of a "military-industrial complex," military racism, and the implications of an all-volunteer military. Again, space limitations precluded coverage of the drug issue, war and morality, military justice, and public relations; the reader will find these and other current issues referenced in the annotated bibliography that follows Part IV.

ALTERNATIVE WAYS TO USE THIS VOLUME

The introductory essays, articles, and annotated bibliographies presented in this volume were designed for upper division college and university students who are interested in a single, interdisciplinary examination of the field.

Previous editions have been used successfully as basic readers in defense policy courses and as supplementary readers in government, international politics, public administration, sociology, and contemporary history courses. Since many of the contributors have considerable experience in the national security policy process, it is hoped that this work will also be useful to the defense policymaker and practitioner.

The logic behind the organization for each of the specific parts of this book is explained in the introductory essays. While considerable effort was made to order the articles in a meaningful manner, individual readers will no doubt have unique reasons for choosing their own. We strongly recommend, however, that three series of articles be read in the published sequence. These are:

1. Chapter 2 ("Evolution of Strategy"), wherein articles were arranged chronologically to reflect the historical evolution of defense strategy.

2. Part III ("American Defense Policymaking"), wherein the theory of bureaucratic decisionmaking is developed prior to the empirical studies related to it.

3. Chapter 9 ("The Military as a Socializing Institution"), wherein the Huntington and Bradford/Murphy articles present the traditional alternatives to civil-military relations, and the Moskos article integrates the two.

Instructors and students using this book in a classroom environment might benefit from experiences gained at the Air Force Academy, where courses in American defense policy have been offered since 1958. During this time, it has become the consensus of instructors and cadets concerned that the study of major strategic issues should precede the study of policymaking and process. This insures that the student will be familiar with the objectives and topics under discussion by the bureaucratic actors. We also recommend that strategy and policymaking be covered prior to civil-military relations. The theoretical underpinnings of the latter area are less well developed, and the multitude of controversial civil-military issues provide a welcome acceleration of interest near the end of the academic term.

Finally, we recommend that the undergraduate instructor complement this volume by assigning to the students articles and books such as those cited within the annotated bibliographies. In this regard, we have found Adam Yarmolinsky's *The Military Establishment* (1971) and Ward Just's *Military Men* (1970) to be extremely well received by students.

PARTICIPANTS

This volume is the product of many minds whose common goal was to provide a basic reader in defense policy. At every stage in the development process we received inputs from Army, Navy, Air Force, and civilian sources to insure we were not guilty of myopia. We would especially like to thank the Air Force ROTC, represented by Lt. Colonel Melvin G. Cooper, Major Charles W. Haney, and Major Louis J. Samelson, who spent many hours going over the outline and topics with us. In the United States Army we would like to thank Lt. Colonels Zeb Bradford, Jr., and Rick Brown for their assistance, advice, and professional guidance, and, in the Army ROTC, Lt. Colonel W. L. Portteus. At the Naval Academy we would like to thank Professor Charles Cochran for his advice on the outline.

In its early stages the book benefited from the lively discussions at the First Inter-Service Defense Policy Conference held at the Air Force Academy, May 10–12, 1972. This conference was supported, as was the entire book project, by the members of the Department of Political Science, and we owe a debt of gratitude to them.

Particular thanks go to the Department Chairman, Colonel Richard F. Rosser, and his Deputy, Lt. Colonel Perry M. Smith. Without their support and encouragement, this edition would not have been possible. Other members of the Department, including Lt. Colonel Richard J. Daleski, Squadron Leader Anthony C. Rogerson (RAF), Majors Richard L. Kuiper, Owen W. Lentz, and Charles A. May, Jr., and Captains Donald J. Alberts, Frank B. Horton, George C. Gibson, Bard E. O'Neill, Robert C. Stine, and Edward L. Warner III, critiqued the manuscript at various stages and wrote introductory and bibliographic materials. Lt. David K. Hall served as an able member of the editing team during the difficult stages of indexing and proofing.

We would especially like to thank our wives, whose understanding sustained us throughout. Many thanks go to the Political Science Department secretarial staff, Mrs. Nellie Dykes, Jackie Mignolet, Denise Pfalzgraf, and our chief typist, Mrs. Carol Rivard, for their efficiency and patience. Finally, we would like to thank the entire staff at The Johns Hopkins University Press, and particularly Penny James, our copy editor.

R.G.H.
E.J.R.

September 1972
U.S. Air Force Academy, Colorado

Part I · The Context of American Defense Policy

Introduction

ERVIN J. ROKKE

A nation needs many qualities, but it needs faith and confidence above all. Skeptics do not build societies; the idealists are the builders. Only societies that believe in themselves can rise to their challenges. Let us not, then, pose a false choice between meeting our responsibilities abroad and meeting the needs of our people at home.—President Richard M. Nixon, June 1969

So went the challenge from a new President to the graduating class of the Air Force Academy in 1969. Years have passed; the twofold quest for domestic and international tranquillity continues. In an age when the search for a just peace is paramount, conflict and war remain bitter realities of the human condition. Men of peace find themselves compelled to prepare for war. Men fight and realize too frequently the Pyrrhic nature of their victories. Like Sisyphus' stone, tranquillity rises and falls—but refuses to surmount the challenge of dissension.

CAUSES OF WAR

With universal consistency, men of good will wonder why their firm choices for peace are negated by an apparent necessity for conflict. The answers are manifold. Seventeenth-century British philosopher Thomas Hobbes wrote: "in the nature of man, we find three principal causes of quarrel. First, competition; secondly, diffidence; thirdly, glory."[1] Hans Morgenthau, a modern scholar of international politics, also argues that war results from man's biological desire for power.[2]

Not everyone is willing to accept human nature as the prime explanation for war, however. The French philosopher Jean-Jacques Rousseau, for example, believed man's actions and nature were primarily determined by the society in which he lived.[3] The Marxist view that capitalist states cause war is consistent with this perspective. Even President Eisenhower blamed the nation-state for war when he commented: "Now people don't want conflict—people in general. It is only, I think, mistaken leaders that grow too belligerent and believe that people really want to fight."[4]

Finally, war among nation-states is explained as a necessary result of an anarchical international setting. Proponents of this theory generally point out that the world is organized into a number of competing nation-states which recognize no superior power or international law. Over two thousand years ago, Thucydides considered the "real but unavowed cause" of the Peloponnesian War between Athens and Sparta "to have been the growth of the power of Athens, and the alarm which it inspired in Lacedaemon."[5] In short, nations often feel compelled to fight when their military advantage is threatened by another. War occurs because there is nothing to stop it.

THE INTERNATIONAL PERSPECTIVE

The question of whether war results primarily from the nature of man, the nation-state, or the international setting has been discussed elsewhere.[6] Our interests are somewhat different. Rather than concentrate on the causes of

---

[1] Thomas Hobbes, *Leviathan*, ed. Michael Oakeshott (Oxford: Basil Blackwell, n.d.), p. 80.

[2] Hans J. Morgenthau, *Politics Among Nations*, 3rd ed. (New York: Alfred A. Knopf, 1961), p. 4.

[3] Jean-Jacques Rousseau, *Discourse upon the Origin and Foundation of the Inequality among Mankind* (1761).

[4] Robert J. Donovan, "Eisenhower Will Cable Secret Geneva Reports," *New York Herald Tribune*, July 13, 1955, p. 1.

[5] Thucydides, *The History of the Peloponnesian War*, trans. R. W. Livingstone (London: Oxford University Press, 1949), p. 46.

[6] For example, see Kenneth N. Waltz, *Man, the State, and War* (New York: Columbia University Press, 1959).

international conflict, we will examine the American response to such conflict as it occurs in the modern environment. From this perspective, the fundamental causes of war as outlined above become multiple constraints operating on those responsible for national security. The articles in Part I by Stanley Hoffmann and Henry Kissinger describe the nature of these constraints and suggest a range of choices open to American defense strategists.

Professor Hoffmann's article deals with the current international political system. Briefly defined, an international political system refers to any collection of independent entities—be they nation-states or empires—that interact with considerable frequency and according to regularized processes.[7] The current international political system encompasses the planet earth.

From Professor Hoffmann's perspective, the relationships among nations are determined to an important extent by the structure of the political system in which they find themselves. He specifically addresses the question of whether international politics is currently a struggle for existence between two intensely competitive power blocs (led by the United States and the Soviet Union) or a multitude of more independent actors, including not only the Superpowers but also the long-established nations of lesser capabilities and the emerging Third World.

The answer to this problem is relevant to the student of American defense policy for several reasons. It establishes, first of all, the outer limits of the United States' capability to accomplish its own objectives. The most important of these, of course, is survival. Second, it gives an indication of whether we live in a stable, peaceful world or in a revolutionary international system with tendencies toward self-destruction. Finally, it offers a basis for prescription. If the structure of the international political system significantly determines the degree of comfort in which we exist, a prime challenge becomes that of developing a structure conducive to tranquillity.

Significantly, Professor Hoffmann does not provide a concise, monolithic description of the current international political system. He suggests, on the contrary, a rapidly changing world exhibiting traits of bipolarity and multipolarity. The United States and the Soviet Union are at once powerful and muscle-bound. More important, the current system tends toward both violence and peace. The complexities of reality, according to Professor Hoffmann, would seem to preclude clear-cut prescriptions. As the student reads Part I, it is important that he consider whether these same complexities preclude stability and peace.

THE DOMESTIC PERSPECTIVE

The logic of Professor Hoffmann's emphasis upon the international political system is compelling. Total reliance upon this perspective, however, can be dangerously misleading. Nation-states are not like billiard balls rebounding from interactions with identical and predictable movements. They are, as Professor Hoffmann and Dr. Kissinger suggest, fundamentally different, not only with regard to objectives, but also with regard to methods of operation. Domestic structure, then, becomes an important corollary of the international structure when one examines defense policy.

Nation-states have tended to view international affairs through a divergent spectrum of ideological lenses. Of particular interest to students of defense policy are those situations in which ideologies or traditional national interests reflect differing conceptions of what is just and desirable. The perceptions and prescriptions of Marxism-Leninism do not correspond with those of the United States. Many of the emerging nations present still other outlooks. The result can be only a considerable challenge to the emergence of international tranquillity.

Equally significant are the decisionmaking styles employed by the nation-states. Later portions of this volume will discuss the bureaucratic politics of the American system in considerable detail.[8] At this point, however, it should be remembered that no significant actor within the current international system can totally avoid the constraints imposed by the politics of increasingly massive bureaucracies and unique styles employed by individual statesmen. Program execution diverges from program concep-

---

[7] For a more detailed explanation of the international political system, see K. J. Holsti, *International Politics: A Framework for Analysis* (Englewood Cliffs, N.J., 1967), pp. 27–96.

[8] For example, see Part III.

tion, and objectivity within the bureaucracy merges with advocacy. In the summer of 1952, President Truman summarized the problems of his potential successor by musing: "He'll sit here and he'll say, 'Do this! Do that!' *And nothing will happen. Poor Ike*—it won't be a bit like the Army. He'll find it very frustrating."[9] President Truman was correct in his assessment. As Dr. Kissinger's article demonstrates, the flexibility of foreign and defense policies is hampered by domestic as well as international political structures.

CONCLUSION

The international and domestic perspectives provide an all-inclusive framework for analyzing the essence of American national security. Unfortunately, the framework's complexity and scope are such that few scholars of defense policy can hope to master it entirely. One apparent solution to this dilemma is for those who teach or study in the field to concentrate on those aspects of the framework suggested by their expertise or inclination. An economist, for example, may want to examine the economic factors of military potential or mobilization. A student of American government might be inclined toward the bureaucratic aspects of defense decisionmaking. The international relations specialist will no doubt be more concerned with the process of interaction among nations. In short,

[9] As quoted in Richard E. Neustadt, *Presidential Power* (New York: John Wiley & Sons, 1960), p. 22.

the framework provides a multitude of entry perspectives for scholars from all disciplines.

If used properly, however, the framework will provide more than a map for the specialist in search of a "pure" study in his area of interest. Just as maps suggest relationships among various routes, so also can a framework encompassing international and domestic perspectives demonstrate the degree to which national security has become interrelated with politics at every level. Events of the past decade have demonstrated conclusively that American defense policy can no longer be legitimized or explained in terms of single-level analysis. For example, the decisions concerning deployment of an anti-ballistic missile (ABM) were constrained by local interests within the smallest units of the domestic system as well as by considerations of the international strategic equation. Arguments for and against deployment of this weapon were offered by experts from the natural and social sciences, politicians, the professional military, ordinary laymen, and theologians. Such a diversity of interest is not unique to the ABM debate.

One might conclude, then, by suggesting that President Nixon's caution to avoid choosing only domestic or international priorities is sound. Both our responsibilities abroad and those at home must be satisfied. The challenge facing the student and practitioner of American defense policy involves optimizing the simultaneous pursuit of these potentially conflicting objectives.

CHAPTER 1

International and Domestic Constraints

THE INTERNATIONAL SYSTEM TODAY

STANLEY HOFFMANN

Professor Hoffmann describes the structure of the current international political system and suggests its implications for stability. He notes that the present system is characterized by three levels. The fundamental level is one of "muted bipolarity," with the United States and the Soviet Union assuming a preponderance of force within their respective blocs. Neither Superpower is anxious to put its devastating nuclear capabilities to an ultimate test, however. Trading upon this reluctance, lesser powers have become more willing to use their subnuclear and nonmilitary capabilities to effect their own international goals and objectives. This phenomenon brings about what Professor Hoffmann refers to as the second, or "polycentric," level within the international system. Finally, he cites the rise of independent nuclear capabilities as evidence of a third level— emergent "multipolarity." From this milieu are derived several prescriptions for American foreign and defense policies. Professor Hoffmann is currently Professor of Government at Harvard University. His books include Contemporary Theory in International Relations *(1960) and* The State of War *(1965).*

REVOLUTIONARY OR MODERATE?

At first sight, the international milieu of the 1960s is almost a textbook example of a revolutionary system. If we examine its main *elements*, we find:

1. Bipolarity, i.e., the existence of the United States and the Soviet Union, whose power far exceeds that of other units and which are sufficiently matched to be placed in the same top league, if one applies to the present system the customary yardstick of power, namely, the capacity to wage war and to inflict damage on an enemy. Whether this yardstick is still decisive in the nuclear age, whether a bipolar structure means an actual dual hegemony in interstate relations, whether indeed the *structure* of the system (i.e., the distribution and hierarchy of power) can be called bipolar, are matters that

will have to be explored later. But we can expect the present international system to be marked, as all previous bipolar systems have been, by a tendency toward instability, due to the dialectic of reciprocal fear, and inflexibility, due to the dialectic of opposed interests.

2. An unprecedented heterogeneity in the structure of the system. For the first time, the international system covers the whole planet, but it now includes ingredients of widely different origins and vintage. What Raymond Aron calls the "unity of the diplomatic field" is a fiery unity. Even though the basic unit of modern world politics is the nation-state, this over-all term conceals an extraordinary diversity. For one thing, modern nation-states differ in their degree of integration. Some are states still in search of a nation, marked by serious discontinuities among tribes, ethnic groups, or classes.

Others are nations in a formal, but not in a substantive, sense—i.e., although they have national consciousness, authoritative central power, and social mobility across regional, ethnic, or social lines, there is no consensus on political purposes and institutions. Others are national communities in a substantive sense as well. They also differ in their historical dimensions. Some (well integrated or not) have had an independent existence and an institutional framework for generations or centuries, others are new and ramshackle. Finally, they differ in size, ranging from tiny units that are little more than dots on the map, to traditional territorial states, to what might be called empire-states, huge and often ethnically heterogeneous. Because of this heterogeneity, the distribution of power between and around the United States and the Soviet Union is highly discontinuous and uneven. Consequently the "relation of major tension," the opposition of the two great powers, breeds a permanent danger of conflict through aspiration, expansion, or escalation in the various "soft underbellies" that lie between or within the two camps.

3. Extreme variety in the domestic political systems. Verbal agreement on the two principles of self-determination and self-government conceals fundamental differences over the meaning of democracy, and there are many uncertainties about where the limits of self-determination must be placed and about its relevance in racially or ethnically mixed situations. The variety of regimes is so dazzling that political scientists cannot even begin to agree on classificatory schemes. As for the economic regimes, they range from the most backward societies, where governments have no effective control over economies that are still at subsistence level and/or in foreign hands, to modern societies of mass consumption, heavily regulated by the state. As Henry Kissinger puts it: "When the domestic structures are based on fundamentally different conceptions of what is just, the conduct of international affairs grows more complex. . . . Statesmen can still meet, but their ability to persuade has been reduced, for they no longer speak the same language."[1]

4. Sharp ideological clashes: communism versus the so-called free world; anticolonial na-

tionalisms of Asia, Africa, and Latin America versus the West. These are doubly asymmetrical: in each case, one side is heavily ideological and the other rather pragmatic; in each case, the ideological side is on the offensive.

5. A technological revolution contributes to instability both because it proceeds so fast and because it aggravates the unevenness among nations. There is a technological race among the powerful or would-be powerful, and an increasing gap between the "haves" and the "have nots." And there is a race between what might be called the technological factors of equalization (the revolution in communications which makes of the world an echo chamber, spreads information all over the globe, and equalizes concern) and the countless disparities and inequalities—military, economic, political, ethnic, ideological—which distort this revolution and often put it at the service of the most powerful and of the most dissatisfied.

If we turn to the *relations* of the units within the system, we can see why such a milieu is likely to be immoderate in ends and means. All the factors mentioned above contribute to the inflation of objectives, to the rise of universal claims. In a bipolar contest, prestige, power, and security are rolled into one; moderate compromises are made difficult (because the contest is acted out in apocalyptic fashion, since any local move may affect the entire field, any hole in the tapestry may lead to its total destruction). When this contest is ideological as well, the distinction between a threat to the physical existence of the foe and a threat to his moral integrity becomes blurred. And the unprecedented heterogeneity of states, political regimes, and economic stages creates total insecurity, in which leaders try to consolidate their power by making enormous demands on the outside world.

The immoderation of means is due to the proliferation of conflict situations. A bipolar contest implies the risk of clashes at any point of contact between the two great powers and elsewhere in the search for supporters. And the heterogeneity of the system makes it likely that border clashes between "empire-states," imperial wars of extension and disintegration, and traditional international wars all will occur. The variety of principles of domestic legitimacy invites clashes between rival conceptions and makes it possible to invoke one of the princi-

[1] "Domestic Structure and Foreign Policy," p. 20 of this volume.

ples as a cover for national ambitions. The un-evenness of economic development condemns the poor to do their best to control their re-sources, and this may be at the expense of the wealthy. Lastly, the ideological substance of the contest leads to generalized intervention in international conflicts and in civil wars. "Total diplomacy" thus requires virtuosity over a range that goes from mere propaganda to the use of force.

This immoderation in ends and means of course results in instability. Both the United States and the Soviet Union, out of reciprocal fear and opposed interests, try to court neutrals, win friends and keep them (hence the prolif-eration of alliances), and detach the friends of the rival. This need for support from lesser powers (whether for strategic, diplomatic, or symbolic reasons) tends to make the Americans and Russians dependent on their clients; the latter want to safeguard their independence and exploit every possible asset in their posi-tion, and this subverts the hierarchy. (The United Nations contributes to this trend.)

One would thus expect each of the "poles" to enjoy a position very close to that which the model of revolutionary systems suggests. One would expect, as a bitter effect of total insecu-rity, that each would search for at least partial hegemony and full exploitation of its power in order to marshal support, to protect its areas of influence, to stop penetration by the rival, and to penetrate his domain in turn. One would ex-pect that these efforts would lead to a kind of *de facto* partition of the world or to conflagra-tion; at any rate, the likelihood should be a pres-suring of all third parties to choose sides—"total diplomacy" in a vertical dimension and omi-nous deadlock on the horizontal level.

But reality has not gone so far. The present system is also one of relative moderation. Whereas the dynamics have by and large been those of a revolutionary system, the actual re-sults have not differed so much from those of moderate ones. The most important factor here has been moderation in the use of force. The international milieu is saturated with conflicts and violence, and the list of armed conflicts be-tween and within states from 1945 to the Mid-dle Eastern war of 1967 is long and varied. But, on the whole, the use of "brute force" to take and to hold, and the use of force as a means of "coercive violence" to hurt and to punish,[2] has been kept at low levels and within limits. In the past, multipolarity and homoge-neity led to moderation in ends and means; today, relative moderation in means seems to bring back some features of multipolar systems, including some moderation in ends. Demonic or global ends, while maintained intact in proc-lamations, are pursued only piecemeal. As in the nineteenth century, the great powers have resorted more to threats and confrontations than to war.[3] There is a modicum of flexibility. The system has outlived countless conflicts and confrontations and has accommodated drastic changes in the distribution of power; there are some signs of a return to flexibility in align-ments and to neutral acceptance of a variety of regimes; an erosion of ideology has begun. The two main rivals are beginning to temper their hostility, not just with prudence, but with co-operation: as in balance-of-power systems, the notion of mixed interests of the great powers spreads.

Do these transformations improve the situa-tion of the great power? Do they decrease its insecurity, giving it greater freedom of choice? Do they at the same time preserve the advan-tage of hegemony? That is, do they unblock the "horizontal" level while maintaining the effectiveness in the vertical dimension?

THE THREE LEVELS OF THE SYSTEM

We can find the answer by analyzing the present international system as a three-level one. The fundamental level—the foundation—is bipolar. But there are two more levels, which we will call *polycentric* and *multipolar*, corre-sponding to two trends in present world poli-tics: a dominant one that modifies bipolarity, and a secondary, derivative one that challenges it.

MUTED BIPOLARITY

I refer to muted bipolarity in order to sug-gest, first, that the bipolar level remains; sec-ond, that the bipolar conflict has been damp-ened; and, third, that the two poles have not

[2] A distinction made, with his usual relentless virtu-osity, by Thomas C. Schelling, *Arms and Influence* (New Haven: Yale University Press, 1966), chap. 1.

[3] Robert E. Osgood and Robert W. Tucker, *Force, Order, and Justice* (Baltimore: The Johns Hopkins Press, 1967), pp. 89–90.

been willing or able to switch from a full bi-polar conflict to a full bipolar partnership.

Causes

The dominant modification of bipolarity is caused by the convergence of two separate features in the contemporary system: the consecration of the nation-state, and new conditions in the use of force. Those two features emerged only gradually, during the first decade after World War II. Since 1955, the triumphs of decolonization and the nuclear stalemate between Russia and the United States have brought out fully the meaning of these two new developments in international politics.

Virtually the entire globe is now covered with independent states, most of which are, or aspire to be, nation-states. Sixty years ago, the international landscape was, in cadastral terms, dominated by the big landlords. Today, it resembles those European countrysides so remarkable to the traveler who observes them from the air, with every piece of land cultivated and marked out, with the fields divided into countless strips. This fragmentation has occurred at a time when all the factors of conflict we mentioned before, as well as developments in military technology, have rendered the notion of the "impermeable territorial state"[4] obsolete. Still, the very existence of more than a hundred sovereign units poses formidable obstacles to open, free, and easy penetration of national borders. A border is like a burglar alarm, in that it has value only if there are *other* factors that deter the burglar, such as policemen, or the burglar's sensitivity to noise, or scruples that a ringing alarm would heighten. This is the case today.

First, there is the *nation's* legitimacy in most parts of the world. (It is tempting, yet misleading, to analyze international politics at a level so abstract that one forgets what stuff the units of international relations are made of, for their nature shapes their goals and the stakes of the contest.) The collapsing colonial empires learned the hard way what resistance to an irresistible claim for national self-determination entails. A world of nations in which most political leaders are engaged in one way or another in the "social mobilization" of their followers is

a world in which even the most ruthlessly brutal and expansionist rulers cannot afford to be *too* crude. For, as Hitler's fate showed, any great power that embarks on a policy of destruction of other nations provokes a decisive countervailing response. A would-be conqueror in a world of nonnational states did not worry too much about the attitudes of the conquered; but in a world of nation-states, even the cynic will acknowledge that, however much "world public opinion" may be an empty cliché, a statesman's means must be appropriate to his end when the support of other powers is at stake. The burglar himself must pretend that he respects the jeweler's integrity.

Moreover, the nature of the contest between the United States and the Soviet Union makes the formally independent nation-state a point of saliency and a beneficiary of the rivalry. Here again, we are dealing not with *any* bipolar competition but with a *specific* struggle. National self-determination is one of the principles of the United States and one of the cornerstones of its conception of world order. We are thus inclined to use it as a weapon against the Soviet Union; but, *ipso facto*, we are also obliged to take it into account or be embarrassed when we do not, for we cannot afford to blunt a needed tool. And, whereas Communist ideology devotes little attention to the idea of the independent nation and certainly does not rank it as an integral part of its creed, it has used the aspiration to national independence as a club against its enemies. Thus, this fundamentally equalitarian kind of legitimacy, which tends to impart to every nation, whatever its size and resources, a right to existence, obliges both powers to define their competition as one for the "voluntary" support (or nonhostility) of other nations, rather than as one for the enslavement of other territories; the rivalry of Athens and Sparta could afford to be blunter. This does not mean that they are devoid of means of influence, but only that the means are altogether changed. The present contest is well described by the familiar vocabulary: each leading power wants "friends," or clients, or "satellites"—terms that maintain a distinction between actual dependence, which is sought, and formal independence, which is preserved.

Lastly, the effect of the United Nations must not be ignored in this connection. On the one hand, membership in the United Nations has

[4] See John Herz, *International Politics in the Atomic Age* (New York: Columbia University Press, 1959).

become a concrete symbol of national independence, one of the foundation stones of the Charter. On the other hand, the deadlock between Russia and America and the tendency of each to fan the flames of independence for its own purposes have aided in the well-known increase in the power of smaller nations in the General Assembly.

We may well ask how long and how well the distinction between "friends," or "clients," and "servants" would have lasted, how long and how well the fences between the various plots of land, while frequently crossed or damaged, would have formally persisted if the second great change had not occurred: the appearance of new conditions in the use of force. Here again, we are dealing with an objective and a subjective factor. The new attitude toward force reflects both a change of heart and a change in costs.

The change of heart can best be described as a growing sense that resort to force is an illegitimate instrument of national policy. In the West, the horrors of the last world war, the new implications of national legitimacy, the traditional American dislike of the use of force —all explain the thorough discredit of Darwinian theories, in whatever form, applied to politics. The strength of this feeling is such that even the Communists, in their more pugnacious statements, have adopted it to the point of saying that, if or when war comes, it will be due to imperialism's inevitable resort to violence, not to their own preferences.

But even the most sincere repudiation of aggressive war is usually marked by equally sincere qualifications, which pierce the mental barrier to war with holes through which entire armies could pass. No one, of course, repudiates defensive war, and, in a situation of protracted conflict in which contenders thrust and parry across contested borders and arbitrary partition lines, or around shaky regimes, each belligerent convinces himself that he is on the defensive, or he cleverly tries to put himself there.[5] Nor

does the repudiation of violence extend to so-called liberation wars waged on behalf of the sacred principle of self-determination. Here again, one can easily imagine war provoked by diametrically opposed interpretations of "national liberation" and of aggression or defense; consider Hungary in 1956 if the United States had chosen to act, or Cuba in 1961 if the United States had intervened more openly and the Soviet Union had reacted more vigorously. No, I would not stress the deterrent power of this subjective change of heart, were it not reinforced and supplemented by more tangible evidence. The reason these wars did not occur is to be found in the realm of fact, not thought.

The evidence is that the costs of using force have become excessive in two kinds of cases. First, if the aim is to subjugate (or to continue to subjugate) people who are determined to resist and who have the capacity to organize protracted revolutionary warfare (a capacity which tends to entail outside support), the cost in suppressive military measures will probably be so high as to make statesmen prefer the costs of secession. It may still be too early to celebrate the end of conquest: poor but militarily strong nations may still be tempted by the fruits of conquest; a nation stronger than its neighbors and threatened in its very existence by them may still attempt to buy security, or time, through conquest; and developed nations, which know that economic exploitation and territorial sovereignty can be separated, and that the costs of maintaining sovereignty over reluctant foreigners exceed the economic benefits, may still be tempted to conquest for purely strategic reasons, or to subjugate a rebellious partner so as not to lose face. However, the chances of this kind of conquest being attempted are minimal when the prospects of liquidating the rebel in one fell swoop are also minimal or nil.[6]

Second, and more important, there is blinding evidence that nuclear war is, for antagonists

---

[5] The Middle East crisis of 1967 is particularly interesting in this respect. As was shown by the failure of the emergency session of the UN General Assembly to pass any meaningful resolution, Egypt's acts of May 1967 (whether they were deliberately aimed at provoking a war or merely represented a risky bluff that boomeranged) were judged by a majority of states to have been rash enough to legitimize, or at least to redeem, Israel's resort to preventive war. The Arab

argument that Israel's very existence is an act of aggression that deserves and requires violent suppression (assuredly a major exception to the "change of heart" described here) has obviously failed to convince even many of the Arabs' supporters.

[6] The preceding remarks apply only to wars of conquest or to attempts to safeguard conquest against rebellion. So-called wars of national liberation, in which each side sees itself as a champion of freedom, are a different problem.

capable of inflicting intolerable devastation on one another, a suicidal policy to follow for any purpose whatsoever. Between the United States and the Soviet Union, the two poles of power, fear of nuclear war inhibits the use of force at any level above that of subversion; United States armed forces have never fought Soviet soldiers. Leaving aside American attempts to "communicate" (with some success) to the enemy the message that limited war is the only practicable alternative to the dilemma of humiliation or holocaust in a "hot" test, the residual uncertainty about employing nuclear weapons has itself effectively prevented any confrontation from becoming "hot." Between each of the two main antagonists and the allies, or clients, of its rival, the fear of provoking a full-fledged (including possibly nuclear) intervention by the rival, in what has been called war by proxy, has also kept the limits of violence low (although much less so than between America and Russia directly). In conflicts between third parties, or in civil wars in which the chief antagonists are not directly involved, the fear of a general war with unpredictable consequences has often led the United Nations, with the tacit consent of the two superpowers, to request and obtain an early end to violence.

Thus, the effect of nuclear weapons so far has certainly not been to compel nations to renounce force (how could they, given the absence of any compelling supranational authority and the proliferation of conflicts among and within states). Rather, it has compelled them to adhere to a considerable amount of both deterrence and self-deterrence in the use of force, and to make the two chief rivals behave at times exactly like partners in a balance-of-power system—i.e., associates with a common interest in not having world peace upset by lesser powers.[7]

In balance-of-power systems, each major power must curtail its ambitions and moderate its means so as not to bring upon itself a damaging response from its rivals. There are important differences in the system today. The margin of deterrence and self-deterrence has increased enormously. Whereas in the balance-

of-power system a state that failed to be deterred by the prospect of a coalition against it paid a relatively small and temporary price for its mistake, the cost of miscalculations today could be final. Then too, the hierarchy of big and small states is more complex today. In fact, the United States and the Soviet Union are in a unique situation, both with regard to each other and with regard to the lesser powers. In order to clarify this situation, we must first look at the modern revolution in the nature of power, and at its effects on the structure of the international system.

POLYCENTRISM

The Distribution of Power

The distribution of power among units is, as we know, of great importance in defining the nature of the system. And a system's moderation or immoderation could, in the past, be measured by examining the goals of the major units. Traditionally, a moderate system was a homogeneous, multipolar one, the logic of which led to each unit having restraints on both its ends and means; a revolutionary system was either multipolar (when the great powers had revolutionary ends and means) or bipolar. The very reasons given by Kenneth Waltz for our system's relative stability[8]—the intensity, certainty, and scope of a bipolar contest with, so to speak, no loose ends—are ordinarily reasons for instability and war. Today, for the first time, stability is achieved *despite* revolutionary aims and *despite* apparent bipolarity.

In terms of ultimates, there are today only two poles of power, only two states whose military and economic capabilities permit them to be "present" more or less overtly all over the globe, whose resources as well as policies involve them more or less discreetly in the affairs of all other nations. They exceed all other states in the supply of the power to reward. Only they have full reservoirs of coercive power from which they can draw; only they can destroy each other completely and almost instantly. Only these two states could embroil the world in a general nuclear war; and no important settlements can be reached without their consent.

[7] See my *The State of War* (New York: Praeger, 1965), chap. 8; and "Nuclear Proliferation and World Politics," in *A World of Nuclear Powers?* ed. Alastair Buchan (Englewood Cliffs, N.J.: Prentice-Hall, for the American Assembly, 1966).

[8] See "The Stability of a Bipolar World," *Daedalus*, Summer 1964, pp. 881–909.

Now this means that in terms of the capacity to incite a "moment of truth"—i.e., the aptitude to use fully the coercive power for general war —there is a *latent* bipolar system (latent because of the hesitancy to use this power). Second, this means that, while the weight of the two powers is theoretically preponderant and their voice is essential in all matters in which both are involved and power can talk (Germany, disarmament, and outer space; Cuba, the Near East, and Southeast Asia), in practical terms the meaning of this preponderance is reduced by their competition, and their achievements are essentially negative. Each one is able to prevent the other (as well as, *a fortiori*, all others) from achieving goals sought by force or through diplomacy; each one is therefore likely to preserve his preponderance in areas that are, so to speak, on the firing line—such as the two Germanies, each of whose security and political future depends on the effectiveness of its protector's power. *Denials* prevail; *gains* are few. Due to nuclear weapons, the two "poles" enjoy an exceptionally high negative productivity but suffer from a low positive productivity of power. In their mutual relations they are frustrated not only, as in past bipolar contests, by their very competition, which prevents a moderated duel from becoming a condominium, but also because they cannot freely resort to coercion in order to force each other into either agreement or submission. In relation to lesser powers, each is able to use his superiority only when those lesser powers have made the mistake of resorting to large-scale force themselves.

Thus we come to the notion of an international system in which the bipolarity is a *latent* one of *potential* ultimates. The actual manifestations of these ultimates are moments when everyone's heart misses a beat while the superpowers "confront" each other. No one else much matters then. But these confrontations have been, when direct, nonmilitary. When they are violent, they are so indirect or at such low levels of violence that the final outcome has not been determined by the ratios of the military strength.[9]

As a result, a kind of *de facto polycentrism* occupies the forefront of the stage, on which almost anyone who wants to can play. Old-fashioned multipolarity resulted from the distribution of coercive power, but this polycentrism results from the devaluation of coercive power. The "centers" are states, many of which lack the traditional ingredients of military might, but which are well supplied in the new factors of power and are eager to play the game. Because the fullest use of modern coercive power is for mutual deterrence, these lesser centers can push their pawns between the deadlocked giants. Because the new factors of power are complex and varied, their playing has a flexibility that seems to defy analysis.

This is the most novel element of today's international system. As long as international affairs were dominated by a contest between two rivals, either of which was thought ready to use its military power in order to reach its goal, all other participants were reduced to being anxious dependents or frightened spectators, who hoped that their abstention from the game would help them escape the holocaust. Once it became clear that neither of the two rivals wanted to use (or could easily use) precisely that supply of power which made it one of the "superpowers," once it became clear that, being in a bottle, the two scorpions had lost some of their sting, other beasts decided they had had their chance.

The Fate of the International Hierarchy

Nuclear bombs have not "equalized" the big and the small. Since there is no "military obsolescence," differences among states in the supply of military power—both in capabilities and in the skill with which they can be used defensively or offensively—continue to matter, even in the intervals between the great confrontations, when the bipolar conflict obliterates the polycentric game. So, of course, do differences in economic resources. But, if "equalization" is absurd, the coexistence of bipolarity and poly-

---

[9] The mistake made by Kenneth Waltz in his analysis of the international system (see *ibid.*) lies in his failure to distinguish between the supply of power and its uses and achievements, and in his analysis of the supply in traditional terms. If the supply of full coer- cive power were (still) the decisive criterion of the system's structure, Waltz would be right in analyzing the system as bipolar and in charging critics with confusing the structure of the system and relations in the system. But what make the relations different from those of a typical bipolar system are the diversification of the supply of usable power and the consecration of the nation-state, i.e., the two features discussed above, which greatly affect even the structure of the system.

centrism plays havoc with the international hierarchy. For one thing, it moderates the usually exaggerated hierarchy of a purely bipolar system, since the two superpowers restrain themselves from using force to discipline misbehaving partners or ill-behaving neutrals, out of fear of how the rival could exploit such a deed in a competition that is necessarily more psychological than military. (The importance of the United Nations in this is not negligible.) For another, the usual possibilities open to small powers in a bipolar system to subvert the hierarchy are enhanced by the new conditions in the use of force. There are certain new limitations here. Any overt resort to force on their part is likely to re-create a hierarchy at their expense; and, as in any bipolar system, for reasons of history or geography, many of the smaller powers are strategically, politically, or economically utterly dependent on one of the superpowers' protection and aid, and are thus unable to exploit the basic rivalry or to challenge the power to which they cling. Within those limits, however, there are many new vistas open to middle and even small powers. Let us examine some of them.

In a pure bipolar system, opportunities for the small states are both created and curtailed by the drive of the two great powers for allies and resources. As Thucydides so clearly showed, a small power too close to one of the rivals and beyond the reach of the other's help was in a tragically determined situation. Opportunities existed only in two cases: when a state submitted to inevitable domination but then subtly blackmailed its leader; and when a state was so luckily located in the field of tension that each "pole" would prefer its neutrality to a conflict for its allegiance. Such opportunities were defensive, precarious, and few. As John Burton correctly puts it,[10] they were "part of the strategy of conflict"; today the opportunities are "part of the strategy of avoiding conflict," and they are better.

One reason is that the transformation of power has strengthened the *defensive* position of smaller states. The inhibitions that now restrict the use of force by the two superpowers protect many more of them from the super-

powers' military might. And the deadlock of deterrence assures that a superpower will refrain from overtly threatening their integrity, lest the other intervene and start the machine of escalation ticking. Even when the rival superpower is unlikely to help, the smaller nations feel somewhat reassured by their own aura of national legitimacy, which the United Nations reinforces. Moreover, because of the relative security that mutual deterrence gives to the superpowers, these feel the need for satellites less desperately than in past bipolar systems. Also, the compression of the use of force to lower levels and diversion from open coercion serve the smaller nations well, since their capacity to resist at those levels and in those realms is often considerable. Since the basic bipolar contest is not a direct military confrontation, what the smaller powers have to offer (and defend) is likely to be something less than territory and men (diplomatic strength, for instance)—i.e., something that it is easier to defend, and whose defense will not inevitably trigger military action on the part of the pressuring superpower. In such a contest, purely diplomatic support may matter more to a superpower than anything more tangible; the weakest of states still has one kind of useful power—the power of its mere existence. These smaller states, whether allies or neutrals, are the real, if relatively peaceful, battlefields; an uncommitted state that threatens to move toward a superpower's enemy, a minor ally who threatens to obstruct an alliance, is obviously not a military threat; its defection would not be a disaster in the traditional terms of power. But in the new contest it is the psychological and diplomatic chessboard that matters. In short, by a remarkable paradox, what conditions the defensive power of the small state is *at the same time* the intensity of the contest between the two larger powers, and its predominantly nonmilitary aspect.

This defensive power is largely provided by internal factors. A small state frequently shows a considerable capacity to resist—indeed, to integrate and flourish—under threat, and thus disposes of an increased potential to inflict pain, should the threat be carried out. Tito benefited from Stalin's pressure; Albania has survived Khrushchev's displeasure; France survived America's; and South Africa has not crumbled. Consider in this regard the contrast

---

[10] For a fascinating mixture of insights and wishful thinking, see his *International Relations* (Cambridge: Cambridge University Press, 1966), p. 115.

of the two Cubas. When Cuba briefly became a Soviet military base, the potential bipolar system suddenly became actual; in the naked confrontation between the two powers, the United States won, because of its over-all strategic superiority and because it superbly turned the tables. What prevented the confrontation from escalating was, at heart, the fear of nuclear war. Now it is this new, rational recoil before the use of force that explains why, when faced with a hostile Cuba acting *on its own*, the United States has hesitated to apply heavy pressure and why it has failed when it has done so. The Soviet Goliath defied the American Goliath and lost; the Cuban David continues to defy the American Goliath. And the North Vietnamese David has been defying him despite all the bombings.

This example tells us something more. Prevented from open coercion by the conditions of their rivalry, the Soviet Union and the United States, each in its own way, try to find ways to reassert their mastery over the smaller states. The Soviet Union does this by encouraging subversion, but this "indirect aggression" is a form of Russian roulette. Whether communism will ultimately triumph in the subverted state without the help of the Red Army is a gamble. Unwilling to provide such help, the Soviets have therefore switched more and more from covert coercion to seduction. The United States, interestingly enough, has more often resorted to what could be called conspicuous force (Cuba in 1961, Lebanon in 1956, the Dominican Republic, Vietnam), but it has always done so with inhibitions (both internal and external) that limited its effectiveness. Often, the United States has tried to use the United Nations as an instrument of policy (as in the Congo), but this has obliged the United States to submit to the influence of small states, who skillfully exploit the power given them in the voting regulations of the General Assembly.

Second, the transformation of power increases the *offensive* power of smaller states. If they remain nonaligned and act cautiously, they are assured of a modicum of impunity, not merely to avoid subservience to the great, but also to realize ambitions of their own. Nations "may now be imperialist on a shoestring."[11]

11 Andrew M. Scott, *The Revolution in Statecraft* (New York: Random House, 1965), p. 162.

They can exploit their less tangible elements of power, particularly their diplomatic potential, in fronts and organizations. They can exploit each rival's interest in keeping them out of the other's orbit in order to get economic aid from both. Moreover, within each camp, the blackmail of weakness is no longer the only form of self-assertion; a restive ally can risk a test of strength (if not of military force).

Thus, the opportunities open to the lesser powers in the present bipolar contest both result from its muffling and contribute to it, for they fill the air with clamors different from the familiar noises of the dominant conflict. These nations enjoy a considerable negative productivity of power—i.e., military safety from the great powers—unless they imprudently overreach the limits of permissible violence, and they can achieve such safety at considerably lower costs than the superpowers, which have to spend astronomical sums on the weaponry, research, and development of mutual denials. The lesser powers also have a small but respectable productivity of power, not through overt coercive uses, not in achieving tangible territorial gains, but often, through skillful bargaining, in achieving economic gains and gains in prestige.

We can see, then, why earlier models of international systems have become less than relevant. The bipolar systems of the past led inevitably to war, because the costs of using force were deemed bearable. Today, the rivals tend to move away from the points at which they confront each other directly, to avoid the dilemma of "humiliation or holocaust," and the contest therefore moves toward lower levels and grayer areas—a dilution that gives more of a chance to the smaller states. Multipolar systems of the past, in which rivalries among the strong were similarly muffled and diverted to "frontiers," were marked by a continuing series of moments of truth. In the relations between the weak and the strong, disproportion was more effective; and in the relations among the strong, since there was a greater possibility both of resort to force and of accommodation, the positive productivity of their power was much higher. But such moderate systems came to fiery ends—either when (as before 1914) the conditions for a favorable balance of power deteriorated so badly that the major powers divided into groups, between which the fatal process of rigidity and escalation would occur, or when (as in 1792 and in the 1930s) one major power tried to disrupt the balance by forcibly imposing its ideas and ambitions on others. In today's system, both bipolar and polycentric, one major power's capacity to destroy without expecting to be destroyed has vanished.

Another change in the international hierarchy is apparent in the hierarchy of *concerns* of smaller and greater states. The smaller states, feeling stronger in their defenses against threats from the superpowers, are often able and willing to pursue goals beyond mere survival and security. Conversely, the superpowers, encumbered by their nuclear power, must concentrate as never before on the requirements of security and survival. For, while mutual deterrence provides for survival and security at far lower levels of applied coercion than in the past, the energy and resources spent on *avoiding* the application of massive (nuclear) coercion divert the superpowers from other goals. The might of the strong used to be like the commander's statue appearing at the feast of the puny. Today, it is a brooding presence at the meals of the mighty. (These contrasting trends make terrible mischief, of course, in alliances. The small powers take offense at the preoccupation of the mighty patron with his own security and use it as a pretext to pursue their own ambitions.)

Thus, in the present international system, the superpowers suffer from an acute case of what Raymond Aron calls the impotence of power.[12] In a pure bipolar system, small states enjoyed a kind of vicarious power to coerce and destroy, thanks to their capacity for embroiling larger states in inexpiable rivalries—the kind of power so well described by Thucydides. But in a moment of truth they stood naked before the armed might of the only states that finally mattered. Athens' warning to Melos rang true: the strong do what they can, the weak what they must. Today, by contrast, the great powers' capacity to destroy is to some extent annulled by its very nature. So the strong do what they must (and can do only a little more), and the weak do a little better than they must.

[12] "Macht, power, puissance," in *Archives européennes de Sociologie*, 5, no. 1 (1964): 44.

THE EMERGENCE OF MULTIPOLARITY

The survival of the nation-state is not just the by-product of what I have called muted bipolarity, the basis for the polycentric level of international relations. The nation-state can also be the elevator to a multipolar nuclear world. The "nuclear revolution" explains why the bipolar system is now more latent than manifest, and why the world appears polycentric at the same time; but the uncertainty of this revolution explains a secondary trend, that which leads to nuclear proliferation. This trend is both a reaction against the fragility of the limits on force and a consequence of the persistence of force.

For the balance of terror is fragile in two ways. For one thing, it could always collapse; hence the other powers' desire to consolidate it by complicating the would-be aggressor's calculations. Yet, to the degree to which it is stable, it both undermines the nuclear protection of third parties and requires a re-evaluation of nonnuclear force; hence the other powers' desire to plug the nuclear hole and to deter the threat of a return to classical war. The persistence of the trappings of force in an armed world, the mileage its possessors can still get out of it, at least in preventing other states from reaching a desired goal, and the consequences of the "balance of terror" in lessening the protection of the lesser powers incite the states that can afford it to seek power themselves in the traditional way and to try to become nuclear powers. They use the freedom created by the "impotence of power" to build up their own.

At first sight, this appears paradoxical, not only because the costs of acquiring nuclear weapons are high, but because they are compounded by the risks of eventual application. Why invest so much in getting equipment that it is then almost impossible to operate? First, since the two major nuclear powers are capable of annihilating each other, the plausibility of their accepting suicide to protect a lesser power decreases, and the lesser power is tempted to buy an insurance policy of its own. If "peril parity" strengthens mutual nuclear deterrence between the superpowers at the cost of weakening the indirect nuclear deterrence that protects their allies (as well as third parties whose safety is vital to the superpowers), it is the duty of the now less protected state to shore up its position. Second, since in a polycentric world teeming with sources of conflict there are acute tensions at the "subsystemic" (i.e., regional) level, and since force, while muted, is not banned, one side in an international dispute is sorely tempted to acquire nuclear weapons so as either to deny its opponent any gains or to do at the local level what "peril parity" precludes at the top—exploit a nuclear monopoly or first-strike advantage for offensive purposes. The only development that would thwart such reasoning would be a joint agreement by the superpowers not only to denounce but also to prevent the proliferation of nuclear weapons by joint measures of disarmament, by joint punitive action, or by joint guarantees to the potential nuclear power or its rival—something the competing superpowers have not been able to devise. Third, this trend toward the proliferation of nuclear weapons is a precaution, indeed a reaction, against polycentrism. The pattern of many new "centers" of power is felt to be fragile, since it results from circumstances that would disappear if the two major powers suddenly moved from deadlock to duel or duopoly; to a middle (or would-be middle) power, it is felt as a nuisance, since it distorts the hierarchy. If polycentrism is unstable and unhealthy, like inflation, then multipolarity, paradoxically enough, is a deflationary remedy.

Thus, the spread of nuclear weapons exploits *and* reacts against the muted bipolar contest and the rise of polycentrism. As long as there is no change in the basic structure of the international milieu, the possession of the *ultima ratio*, nuclear weapons, increases a nation's power of inflicting death and makes it virtually inevitably a party to any settlement of issues in which it has a stake.

Today, the attempt to acquire weapons that a nation could not easily use and may not want ever to have to use is a way of exploiting the present polycentric system so as to turn latent bipolarity into emergent multipolarity. It expresses the desire to increase the negative productivity of one's power. At present, the uncertainty of the balance of terror—the fact that no one knows whether a conventional fuse can be stopped from setting off the nuclear detonator—keeps the use of force repressed at very low levels. If the balance of terror became

much more stable, so that the superpowers' inhibitions against the use of force at higher levels disappeared, then the negative productivity of the power of small states, which they owe to the restraints kept on the power of the two poles, would decrease, unless they too become nuclear possessors.[13]

The drive toward multipolarity also corresponds to a desire to increase the positive productivity of one's power, by more aggressively exploiting one's new strength or by helping to force the superpowers to make settlements in which their challengers participate.

In the present phase of world politics, the mere threat to become a nuclear power (or a state sharing in the nuclear capabilities of a possessor) or the mere fact that one is known to be capable of becoming one—what might be called the power of holding back—is an asset in the game. While it obviously does not provide a state with all the advantages of being a nuclear power, holding back on the threshold saves the costs and risks of actual nuclear weapons and delivery systems, yet enhances the capacity to extract concessions, guarantees, or support from the superpowers (due to their interest in preventing proliferation) or to prevent issues in which one has a stake from being settled by the superpowers alone. Being on the thin line that separates the polycentric from the multipolar level increases the productivity of one's power.[14]

What is difficult to know at this stage is whether the emergent multipolar system would be latent, like the present bipolar one, or actual. If it should consolidate the freeze on force—which the stability of the balance of nuclear power on top threatens to crack at the conventional level, and which the uncertainty of this balance threatens to crack at the nuclear level—then the system would still be predominantly polycentric. The new nuclear powers would simply share the bittersweet fruits of that impotence of power which now affects mainly two nations. If, on the other hand, the proliferation of nuclear weapons leads to *more* rather than less widespread use of force, or to a new hierarchy tied more directly to the military

---

[13] See General André Beaufre, *Dissuasion et Stratégie* (Paris: Armand Colin, 1965).

[14] West Germany's case is an exception.

component of power, then the new multipolar system would be the actual one.

AN IMPERIAL SYSTEM?

In the preceding analysis I have tried to explain the relative moderation of the international system. Yet another explanation is conceivable, has indeed gained some popularity, and deserves discussion. Some American officials, as well as political scientists, have developed the notion of the United States as the preponderant world power; according to them, the international system is no longer bipolar, but not for the reasons I have suggested. To be sure, there is a latent bipolarity at the "apocalyptic" level of ultimate military might. But what is apocalyptic—like what is exaggerated, according to Talleyrand—does not matter; at the level of manifest international politics, what matters is not polycentrism and the trend toward multipolarity, but "imperial America." This thesis has been accepted by a number of French commentators. But, whereas they tend to fear the effects of American world hegemony, the American writers attribute the relative moderation and stability of the international system to America's combination of firmness (in resisting the forces of disruption) and self-restraint.

Powerful arguments can be made for this thesis. First, in terms of "usable" coercive power, the United States not only has provided capabilities for limited war to match those of the U.S.S.R. but also, as already mentioned, has shown a greater willingness to use them— even by attacking the territory of an ally of the Soviet Union, North Vietnam, thus far without incurring Soviet retaliation. American naval and air superiority is unquestioned. American soldiers, military bases, and military advisers can be found in more than forty countries. America's huge power to reward has been used through military assistance and economic aid to three-fifths of the world's nations. The Soviet record, in all these respects, is much less impressive.

Second, if we look not at the uses but at the achievements of power, we find that the United States, through the skillful use of the power to reward and through more or less subterranean

uses of coercive power (for instance, the power to threaten the end of rewards), has succeeded in preserving or establishing friendly or at least nonhostile regimes in all of Latin America except Cuba, most of Africa, and a great part of Asia, not to mention Western Europe. Moreover, in the great nonviolent confrontations with the Soviet Union—direct ones, as in Berlin from 1948 to 1961, in Cuba in 1962, or "by proxy," as in the Middle East in 1967—the United States has prevailed, either (in 1967) because its opponent happened to back the losing side and chose to accept defeat rather than risk escalation, or else (Berlin and Cuba) because American resolve even more than the balance of military forces (unfavorable in Berlin) gave the United States a decisive edge in "the balance of interests as manifested in the relative capacity of opponents to convince each other that they will support their positions with war, if necessary."[15] Third, if, as George Liska has suggested, an imperial power is characterized by the scope of its interests and involvements and by its sense of task, then the United States does indeed wage "the international politics of primacy"; for, whereas its chief rival assuredly has a sense of universal task, the breakup of its camp and the scope of American success have sharply curtailed its effective involvements.

A case can be made to show that what has muffled the bipolar conflict and reintroduced moderation in ends and means into the system is the assertion of American primacy. Both the early American nuclear monopoly and the later nuclear stalemate have encouraged the Communist states to use all forms of power except full coercion in the pursuit of their goals. This could have led to violent instability, had it not been for America's ability to meet and thwart them at every level, and thus to oblige them to recognize, either in their doctrinal statements or in their actual conduct, the failure or limits of offensive violence. It is America's primacy that has led to the disintegration of the enemy's camp. As for the troubles in its own, they mark both a futile attempt by lesser powers to challenge American preponderance and a decline in the strategic and economic importance of other areas for the United States. Thus, stability and

---

[15] Osgood and Tucker, *op. cit.*, p. 152.

primacy can be seen as synonymous: like all empires, America is said to have "a great margin for error," to face only "differences in kinds" and timing of success, but not "alternatives that [spell] the difference between conspicuous success and total failure."[16]

In my opinion, the thesis of "Pax Americana" (seen as the nature of the international system rather than as merely a tendency in American foreign policy) is an optical illusion. What this thesis suffers from is not, as in the case of the bipolar interpretation, a confusion between the military supply, on the one hand, and the uses and achievements of power, on the other, but a confusion between the kinds of purposes for which power is used and between the kinds of achievements of power—gains versus denials. It neglects the asymmetries between the two great powers: diplomatic-strategic asymmetry (one side is on the ideological and political offensive; the United States is on the defensive) and geographic-strategic asymmetry (the Soviet Union is a land mass; the United States, so to speak, is an island-continent).[17]

Thus, what is interpreted as evidence of primacy is merely the success of the United States in *denying* its adversaries the establishment of bases close to the United States, or the conquest of areas challenged by them, or the dislodgment of Western economic and political influence in areas once controlled by the West but now politically independent, or the establishment of regimes ideologically allied to the main adversaries of the United States. Now, in order to deny such achievements to its foes, the United States has indeed had, first, to show superior resolve, so as to make them back down, even when the local balance of force was in their favor; second, to maintain naval and air supremacy in order to protect communications with other continents and to be able to strike at enemy forces coming outside their land mass, and also to spread its own forces and bases abroad, so as to deter piecemeal aggression by assuring American involvement; third, to strive for strategic superiority in "nonusable" nuclear power, so as to deter eventual nuclear first strikes against America's allies as

well as against itself, and to discourage major Communist nonnuclear military attacks by posing a credible threat of an American first strike. In other words, what appears as "primacy" is largely a superiority in the supply and uses of defensive power. Given the nature of the challenges it has faced—either, as in Korea, massive military aggression; or, as in the Middle East in 1958 or in the Congo since 1960–62, political anarchy exploitable by Communist forces or powers; or, as in Greece in 1947, economic and social chaos; or, as in the eastern Mediterranean in the spring of 1967, a risk of active Soviet support to its anti-Western Arab friends—it is not surprising that America has had to use its huge economic power to reward and to develop and use (albeit in limited ways) its military power.

A more widespread use of superior or comparable supplies of power is one thing; world primacy is quite another. For, if the negative productivity of American power has been high, three sets of factors make it quite different from primacy. First, the celebrated achievements have often been obtained not merely because of the array of American advantages but also because of independent factors. Those factors—the proliferation of nation-states and nationalisms and the new conditions in the use of force—hinder the U.S.S.R. and Red China as offensive powers more than they hinder the United States, yet they also restrict both the uses and the achievements of American power.[18]

Second, in the defensive struggle against Moscow and Peking, American power has not always achieved the denials sought. Military force has not proved a panacea, either in Cuba or, so far, in Vietnam, any more than the combination of economic aid and military supplies proved effective in China in 1949.

Third, the barrier between denials and gains remains. On the one hand, no Communist nation has been decommunized, and, while the Soviet bloc has cracked, the United States is now faced with two major challengers instead of one. To be sure, the fear of a major military clash with the United States has led the Soviets to dampen revolutionary violence in many parts

[16] George Liska, *Imperial America: The International Politics of Primacy* (Baltimore: The Johns Hopkins Press, 1967), pp. 29–30.

[17] For further elaboration, see Hoffmann, *The State of War*, p. 165.

[18] In one instance—the 1967 Middle Eastern crisis—the Soviet defeat was clearly due not so much to America's actions as to the defeat of the Arab "proxies" by a nation endowed with superior national fervor and the willingness to use force.

of the world; but their preference for dealing with governments rather than revolutionaries is not unrelated to their continuing hope of exploiting those governments' own grievances against Western influence. In the non-Communist parts of the world, the United States has won all the major confrontations except Vietnam, thanks to that "favorable balance of interests." But then the United States has never chosen to stage a confrontation within the enemy's domain: there was no East-West crisis over Hungary. On the other hand, while the non-Communist nations assisted by the United States have, on the whole, been kept out of communism, they have not, *ipso facto,* served the other purposes and interests of American foreign policy. The existence in many countries of "American parties," "economic ties converging at the center,"[19] and military programs directed from Washington does not annihilate the assets which the transformations of the map and of power give to the smaller states; nor does this existence provide the United States with effective means of making others do what we would want them to do, or refrain from doing what we dislike.

The United States has indubitably contributed to moderating the international system by obliging its enemies to delay and fragment the pursuit of their ends and to restrict the scope of the means they could use with some chance of success. The United States' failure in "containment" would have led either to some desperado American escalation that would have brought World War III, or to the primacy of the U.S.S.R., victorious in its search for positive achievements. But America's own "margin for error," while large, may not be so huge as to keep the system safe from potentially immoderate disruptions. These could be caused either by American mistakes, especially in the use of force in situations where the sword opens wounds but does not heal them, or by too unbroken a series of successes in denial, for the Soviet Union can hardly afford to be rebuffed everywhere without trying to snatch some success of its own even at great risks. Room for error stems less from America's imperial primacy than from the transformations of the map and of force, which leave the great powers

more serene about local fiascoes, and seem to provide many powers—not only the United States and the Soviet Union, but, say, France in the Algerian drama, or China in its present turmoil—with a comfortable margin for mistakes. Indeed, only the superpowers face the peril of crossing the brink.

Finally, the moderating impact of the United States has merely resulted, first, in keeping the international system latently bipolar in terms of general war or essential settlements, and, second, in allowing the spread of polycentrism and multipolarity. If America were serene in her primacy, and the Soviet Union had resigned itself to it, would each of the superpowers show so much of an interest in the *other's* preponderance within its coalition?[20] If order in an imperial system "rests in the last resort on the widely shared presumption of the ultimately controlling power of the imperial state . . . even if the manifestation of the controlling power is only intermittent,"[21] then we are wide of the mark, for the world seems to have at present two "controlling" powers, each in a different sphere, and wide areas in which neither exercises control, although one may try to score some gains at the other's expense, while the other succeeds in denying control to its rival.

Raymond Aron has argued that, for the West to achieve survival and peace—deterring one's adversaries from destroying the West, making them accept moderate objectives and means—would be tantamount to achieving victory.[22] Even if one agreed that victory has been won (a statement that would ignore the uncertainties of the nuclear balance, the risks created by polycentrism, and the perils of multipolarity), one would have to distinguish such a victory from imperial primacy. It may be that, in the nuclear age, only a world empire could assure peace, but the limited "victory" won in the past twenty years leaves the world exposed to major hazards, the great powers embroiled in dizzying dilemmas of control, and the international system in a state that bears little resemblance to past configurations.

[19] Liska, *op. cit.*, p. 24.

[20] Osgood and Tucker, *op. cit.*, p. 171.
[21] Liska, *op. cit.*, p. 37.
[22] See *Peace and War* (New York: Doubleday, 1966), pt. II.

DOMESTIC STRUCTURE AND FOREIGN POLICY

HENRY A. KISSINGER

*Dr. Kissinger describes the impact of domestic factors on the foreign policies
of nation-states. Among the factors he discusses are national ideologies,
governmental structures, and the nature of national leaderships. Each is
susceptible to a profound cleavage in philosophical perspective and
style of policy. As Dr. Kissinger persuasively argues, these cleavages can
present an unprecedented challenge to the emergence of a stable
international order. Dr. Kissinger, formerly Professor of Government at
Harvard University, was appointed Special Assistant for National Security
Affairs in the White House under President Nixon. His writings include*
Nuclear Weapons and Foreign Policy *(1957),* The Necessity for Choice
(1961), and The Troubled Partnership *(1965).*

THE ROLE OF DOMESTIC
STRUCTURE

In the traditional conception, international relations are conducted by political units treated
almost as personalities. The domestic structure
is taken as given; foreign policy begins where
domestic policy ends.

But this approach is appropriate only to stable periods, because then the various components of the international system generally
have similar conceptions of the "rules of the
game." If the domestic structures are based on
commensurable notions of what is just, a consensus about permissible aims and methods of
foreign policy develops. If domestic structures
are reasonably stable, temptations to use an
adventurous foreign policy to achieve domestic
cohesion are at a minimum. In these conditions,
leaders will generally apply the same criteria
and hold similar views about what constitutes
a "reasonable" demand. This does not guarantee agreement, but it provides the condition
for a meaningful dialogue, that is, it sets the
stage for traditional diplomacy.

When the domestic structures are based on
fundamentally different conceptions of what is
just, the conduct of international affairs grows
more complex. Then it becomes difficult even
to define the nature of disagreement, because

what seems most obvious to one side appears
most problematic to the other. A policy dilemma arises because the pros and cons of a
given course seem evenly balanced. The definition of what constitutes a problem and what
criteria are relevant in "solving" it reflects to a
considerable extent the domestic notions of
what is just, the pressures produced by the
decisionmaking process, and the experience
which forms the leaders in their rise to eminence. When domestic structures—and the
concept of legitimacy on which they are based
—differ widely, statesmen can still meet, but
their ability to persuade has been reduced, for
they no longer speak the same language.

This can occur even when no universal claims
are made. Incompatible domestic structures can
passively generate a gulf, simply because of the
difficulty of achieving a consensus about the
nature of "reasonable" aims and methods. But,
when one or more states claim universal applicability for their particular structure, schisms
grow deep indeed. In that event, the domestic
structure becomes not only an obstacle to understanding but one of the principal issues in
international affairs. Its requirements condition
the conception of alternatives; survival seems
involved in every dispute. The symbolic aspect
of foreign policy begins to overshadow the
substantive component. It becomes difficult to

Reprinted by permission and with minor changes from "Conditions of World Order," Daedalus, Journal
of the American Academy of Arts and Sciences, Boston, Mass., no. 2 (Spring 1966).

consider a dispute "on its merits" because the disagreement seems finally to turn not on a specific issue but on a set of values as expressed in domestic arrangements. The consequences of such a state of affairs were explained by Edmund Burke during the French Revolution:

I never thought we could make peace with the system; because it was not for the sake of an object we pursued in rivalry with each other, but with the system itself that we were at war. As I understood the matter, we were at war not with its conduct but with its existence; convinced that its existence and its hostility were the same.[1]

Of course, the domestic structure is not irrelevant in any historical period. At a minimum, it determines the amount of the total social effort which can be devoted to foreign policy. The wars of the kings who governed by divine right were limited because feudal rulers, bound by customary law, could not levy income taxes or conscript their subjects. The French Revolution, which based its policy on a doctrine of popular will, mobilized resources on a truly national scale for the first time. This was one of the principal reasons for the startling successes of French arms against a hostile Europe which possessed greater over-all power. The ideological regimes of the twentieth century have utilized a still larger share of the national effort. This has enabled them to hold their own against an environment possessing far superior resources.

Aside from the allocation of resources, the domestic structure crucially affects the way the actions of other states are interpreted. To some extent, of course, every society finds itself in an environment not of its own making and has some of the main lines of its foreign policy imposed on it. Indeed, the pressure of the environment can grow so strong that it permits only one interpretation of its significance; Prussia in the eighteenth century and Israel in the contemporary period may have found themselves in this position.

But for the majority of states the margin of decision has been greater. The actual choice has been determined to a considerable degree by their interpretation of the environment and by their leaders' conception of alternatives. Napoleon rejected peace offers beyond the

dreams of the kings who had ruled France by "divine right" because he was convinced that *any* settlement which demonstrated the limitations of his power was tantamount to his downfall. That Russia seeks to surround itself with a belt of friendly states in Eastern Europe is a product of geography and history. That it is attempting to do so by imposing a domestic structure based on a particular ideology is a result of conceptions supplied by its domestic structure.

The domestic structure is decisive finally in the elaboration of positive goals. The most difficult, indeed tragic, aspect of foreign policy is how to deal with the problem of conjecture. When the scope for action is greatest, knowledge on which to base such action is limited or ambiguous. When knowledge becomes available, the ability to affect events is usually at a minimum. In 1936, no one could know whether Hitler was a misunderstood nationalist or a maniac. By the time certainty was achieved, it had to be paid for with millions of lives.

The conjectural element of foreign policy—the need to gear actions to an assessment that cannot be proved true when it is made—is never more crucial than in a revolutionary period. Then, the old order is obviously disintegrating, while the shape of its replacement is highly uncertain. Everything depends, therefore, on some conception of the future. But varying domestic structures can easily produce different assessments of the significance of existing trends and, more important, clashing criteria for resolving these differences. This is the dilemma of our time.

Problems are novel; their scale is vast; their nature is often abstract and always psychological. In the past, international relations were confined to a limited geographic area. The various continents pursued their relations essentially in isolation from one another. Until the eighteenth century, other continents impinged on Europe only sporadically and for relatively brief periods. And, when Europe extended its sway over much of the world, foreign policy became limited to the Western Powers, with the single exception of Japan. The international system of the nineteenth century was for all practical purposes identical with the concert of Europe.

The period after World War II marks the first era of truly global foreign policy. Each

---

[1] Edmund Burke, *Works* (London, 1826), 8: 214–15.

major state is capable of producing consequences in every part of the globe by a direct application of its power, or because ideas can be transmitted almost instantaneously, or because ideological rivalry gives vast symbolic significance even to issues which are minor in geopolitical terms. The mere act of adjusting perspectives to so huge a scale would produce major dislocations. This problem is compounded by the emergence of so many new states. Since 1945, the number of participants in the international system has nearly doubled. In previous periods the addition of even one or two new states tended to lead to decades of instability until a new equilibrium was established and accepted. The emergence of scores of new states has magnified this difficulty many times over.

These upheavals would be challenge enough, but they are overshadowed by the risks posed by modern technology. Peace is maintained through the threat of mutual destruction based on weapons for which there has been no operational experience. Deterrence—the policy of preventing an action by confronting the opponent with risks he is unwilling to run—depends in the first instance on psychological criteria. What the potential aggressor believes is more crucial than what is objectively true. Deterrence occurs above all in the minds of men.

To achieve an international consensus on the significance of these developments would be a major task even if domestic structures were comparable. It becomes especially difficult when domestic structures differ widely and when universal claims are made on behalf of them. A systematic assessment of the impact of domestic structure on the conduct of international affairs would have to treat such factors as historical traditions, social values, and the economic system. But this would far transcend the scope of an article. For the purposes of this discussion we shall confine ourselves to sketching the impact of two factors only: administrative structure and the formative experience of leadership groups.

THE IMPACT OF THE ADMINISTRATIVE STRUCTURE

In the contemporary period, the very nature of the governmental structure introduces an element of rigidity which operates more or less independently of the convictions of statesmen or the ideology which they represent. Issues are too complex and relevant facts too manifold to be dealt with on the basis of personal intuition. An institutionalization of decisionmaking is an inevitable by-product of the risks of international affairs in the nuclear age. Moreover, almost every modern state is dedicated to some theory of "planning"—the attempt to structure the future by understanding and, if necessary, manipulating the environment. Planning involves a quest for predictability and, above all, for "objectivity." A deliberate effort is made to reduce the relevant elements of a problem to a standard of average performance. The vast bureaucratic mechanisms that emerge develop a momentum and a vested interest of their own. As they grow more complex, their internal standards of operation are not necessarily commensurable with those of other countries or even with other bureaucratic structures in the same country. There is a trend toward autarky. A paradoxical consequence may be that increased control over the domestic environment is purchased at the price of loss of flexibility in international affairs.

The purpose of bureaucracy is to devise a standard operating procedure which can cope effectively with most problems. A bureaucracy is efficient if the matters which it handles routinely are, in fact, the most frequent and if its procedures are relevant to their solution. If those criteria are met, the energies of the top leadership are freed to deal creatively with the unexpected occurrence or with the need for innovation. Bureaucracy becomes an obstacle when what it defines as routine does not address the most significant range of issues or when its prescribed mode of action proves irrelevant to the problem.

When this occurs, the bureaucracy absorbs the energies of top executives in reconciling what is expected with what happens; the analysis of where one is overwhelms the consideration of where one should be going. Serving the machine becomes a more absorbing occupation than defining its purpose. Success consists in moving the administrative machine to the point of decision, leaving relatively little energy for analyzing the merit of this decision. The quest for "objectivity"—while desirable theoretically—involves the danger that means and ends are confused, that an average standard of performance is exalted as the only valid one. Attention tends to be diverted from the act of choice— which is the ultimate test of statesmanship—to the accumulation of facts. Decisions can be avoided until a crisis brooks no further delay, until the events themselves have removed the element of ambiguity. But at that point the scope for constructive action is at a minimum. Certainty is purchased at the cost of creativity.

Something like this seems to be characteristic of modern bureaucratic states, whatever their ideology. In societies with a pragmatic tradition, such as the United States, there develops a greater concern with an analysis of where one is than with where one is going. What passes for planning is frequently the projection of the familiar into the future. In societies based on ideology, doctrine is institutionalized and exegesis takes the place of innovation. Creativity must make so many concessions to orthodoxy that it may exhaust itself in doctrinal adaptations. In short, the accumulation of knowledge of the bureaucracy and the impersonality of its method of arriving at decisions can be achieved at a high price. Decisionmaking can grow so complex that the process of producing a bureaucratic consensus may overshadow the purpose of the effort.

While all thoughtful administrators would grant in the abstract that these dangers exist, they find it difficult to act on their knowledge. Lip service is paid to planning; indeed, planning staffs proliferate. However, they suffer from two debilities. The "operating" elements may not take the planning effort seriously. Plans become esoteric exercises which are accepted largely because they imply no practical consequence. They are a sop to administrative theory. At the same time, since planning staffs have a high incentive to try to be "useful," there is a bias against novel conceptions which are difficult to adapt to an administrative mold. It is one thing to assign an individual or a group the task of looking ahead; this is a far cry from providing an environment which encourages an understanding of deeper historical, sociological, and economic trends. The need to provide a memorandum may outweigh the imperatives of creative thought. The quest for objectivity creates a temptation to see in the future an updated version of the present. Yet true innovation is bound to run counter to prevailing standards. The dilemma of modern bureaucracy

is that, while every creative act is lonely, not every lonely act is creative. Formal criteria are of little help in solving this problem, because the unique cannot be expressed "objectively."

The rigidity in the policies of the technologically advanced societies is in no small part due to the complexity of decisionmaking. Crucial problems may—and frequently do—go unrecognized for a long time. But, once the decisionmaking apparatus has disgorged a policy, it becomes very difficult to change it. The alternative to the *status quo* is the prospect of repeating the whole anguishing process of arriving at decisions. This explains to some extent the curious phenomenon that decisions taken with enormous doubt and perhaps with a close division become practically sacrosanct once adopted. The whole administrative machinery swings behind their implementation as if activity could still all doubts.

Moreover, the reputation, indeed the political survival, of most leaders depends on their ability to realize their goals, however these may have been arrived at. Whether these goals are desirable is relatively less crucial. The time span by which administrative success is measured is considerably shorter than that by which historical achievement is determined. In heavily bureaucratized societies all pressures emphasize the first of these accomplishments.

Then, too, the staffs on which modern executives come to depend develop a momentum of their own. What starts out as an aid to decisionmakers often turns into a practically autonomous organization whose internal problems structure and sometimes compound the issues which it was originally designed to solve. The decisionmaker will always be aware of the morale of his staff. Though he has the authority, he cannot overrule it too frequently without impairing its efficiency; and he may, in any event, lack the knowledge to do so. Placating the staff then becomes a major preoccupation of the executive. A form of administrative democracy results, in which a decision often reflects an attainable consensus rather than substantive conviction (or at least the two imperceptibly merge). The internal requirements of the bureaucracy may come to predominate over the purposes which it was intended to serve. This is probably even more true in highly institutionalized Communist states—such as the U.S.S.R.—than in the United States.

When the administrative machine grows very elaborate, the various levels of the decisionmaking process are separated by chasms which are obscured from the outside world by the complexity of the apparatus. Research often becomes a means to buy time and to assuage consciences. Studying a problem can turn into an escape from coming to grips with it. In the process, the gap between the technical competence of research staffs and what hard-pressed political leaders are capable of absorbing widens constantly. This heightens the insecurity of the executive and may thus compound either rigidity or arbitrariness or both. In many fields—strategy being a prime example—decisionmakers may find it difficult to give as many hours to a problem as the expert has had years to study it. The ultimate decision often depends less on knowledge than on the ability to brief the top administrator—to present the facts in such a way that they can be absorbed rapidly. The effectiveness of briefing, however, puts a premium on theatrical qualities. Not everything that sounds plausible is correct, and many things which are correct may not sound plausible when they are first presented; and a second hearing is rare. The stage aspect of briefing may leave the decisionmaker with a gnawing feeling of having been taken—even, and perhaps especially, when he does not know quite how.

Sophistication may thus encourage paralysis or a crude popularization which defeats its own purpose. The excessively theoretical approach of many research staffs overlooks the problem of the strain of decisionmaking in times of crisis. What is relevant for policy depends not only on academic truth but also on what can be implemented under stress. The technical staffs are frequently operating in a framework of theoretical standards, while in fact their usefulness depends on essentially psychological criteria. To be politically meaningful, their proposals must involve answers to the following types of questions: Does the executive understand the proposal? Does he believe in it? Does he accept it as a guide to action or as an excuse for doing nothing? But, if these kinds of concerns are given too much weight, the requirements of salesmanship will defeat substance.

The pragmatism of executives thus clashes with the theoretical bent of research or planning staffs. Executives as a rule take cognizance of a problem only when it emerges as an administrative issue. They thus unwittingly encourage bureaucratic contests as the only means of generating decisions. Or the various elements of the bureaucracy make a series of nonaggression pacts with one another and thus reduce the decisionmaker to a benevolent constitutional monarch. As the special role of the executive increasingly becomes to choose between proposals generated administratively, decisionmakers turn into arbiters rather than leaders. Whether they wait until a problem emerges as an administrative issue or until a crisis has demonstrated the irrelevance of the standard operating procedure, the modern decisionmakers often find themselves the prisoners of their advisers.

Faced with an administrative machine which is both elaborate and fragmented, the executive is forced into essentially lateral means of control. Many of his public pronouncements, though ostensibly directed to outsiders, perform a perhaps more important role in laying down guidelines for the bureaucracy. The chief significance of a foreign policy speech by the President may thus be that it settles an internal debate in Washington (a public statement is more useful for this purpose than an administrative memorandum because it is harder to reverse). At the same time, the bureaucracy's awareness of this method of control tempts it to short-cut its debates by using pronouncements by the decisionmakers as charters for special purposes. The executive thus finds himself confronted by proposals for public declarations which may be innocuous in themselves—and whose bureaucratic significance may be anything but obvious—but which can be used by some agency or department to launch a study or program which will restrict his freedom of decision later on.

All of this drives the executive in the direction of extrabureaucratic means of decision. The practice of relying on special emissaries or personal envoys is an example; their status outside the bureaucracy frees them from some of its restraints. International agreements are sometimes possible only by ignoring safeguards against capricious action. It is a paradoxical aspect of modern bureaucracies that their quest for objectivity and calculability often leads to impasses which can be overcome only by essentially arbitrary decisions.

Such a mode of operation would involve a great risk of stagnation even in "normal" times. It becomes especially dangerous in a revolutionary period. For then the problems which are most obtrusive may be least relevant. The issues which are most significant may not be suitable for administrative formulation and even when formulated may not lend themselves to bureaucratic consensus. When the issue is how to transform the existing framework, routine can become an additional obstacle to both comprehension and action.

This problem, serious enough *within* each society, is magnified in the conduct of international affairs. While the formal machinery of decisionmaking in developed countries shows many similarities, the criteria which influence decisions vary enormously. With each administrative machine increasingly absorbed in its own internal problems, diplomacy loses its flexibility. Leaders are extremely aware of the problems of placating their own bureaucracy; they cannot depart too far from its prescriptions without raising serious morale problems. Decisions are reached so painfully that the very anguish of decisionmaking acts as a brake on the give-and-take of traditional diplomacy.

This is true even *within* alliances. Meaningful consultation with other nations becomes very difficult when the internal process of decisionmaking already has some of the characteristics of compacts between quasi-sovereign entities. There is an increasing reluctance to hazard a hard-won domestic consensus in an international forum.

What is true within alliances—that is, among nations which have at least some common objectives—becomes even more acute in relations between antagonistic states or blocs. The gap created when two large bureaucracies generate goals largely in isolation from each other and on the basis of not necessarily commensurable criteria is magnified considerably by an ideological schism. The degree of ideological fervor is not decisive; the problem would exist even if the original ideological comment had declined on either or both sides. The criteria for bureaucratic decisionmaking may continue to be influenced by ideology even after its élan has dissipated. Bureaucratic structures generate their own momentum which may more than counterbalance the loss of earlier fanaticism. In the early stages of a revolutionary movement, ideology is crucial and the accident of personalities can be decisive. The Reign of Terror in France was ended by the elimination of a single man, Robespierre. The Bolshevik Revolution could hardly have taken place had Lenin not been on the famous train which crossed Germany into Russia. But, once a revolution becomes institutionalized, the administrative structures which it has spawned develop their own vested interests. Ideology may grow less significant in creating commitment; it becomes pervasive in supplying criteria of administrative choice. Ideologies prevail by being taken for granted. Orthodoxy substitutes for conviction and produces its own form of rigidity.

In such circumstances, a meaningful dialogue across ideological dividing lines becomes extraordinarily difficult. The more elaborate the administrative structure, the less relevant an individual's view becomes—indeed, one of the purposes of bureaucracy is to liberate decisionmaking from the accident of personalities. Thus, while personal convictions may be modified, it requires a really monumental effort to alter bureaucratic commitments. And, if change occurs, the bureaucracy prefers to move at its own pace and not be excessively influenced by statements or pressures of foreigners. For all these reasons, diplomacy tends to become rigid or to turn into an abstract bargaining process based on largely formal criteria such as "splitting the difference." Either course is self-defeating: the former because it negates the very purpose of diplomacy; the latter because it subordinates purpose to technique and because it may encourage intransigence. Indeed, the incentive for intransigence increases if it is known that the difference will generally be split.

Ideological differences are compounded because major parts of the world are only in the first stages of administrative evolution. Where the technologically advanced countries suffer from the inertia of overadministration, the developing areas often lack even the rudiments of effective bureaucracy. Where the advanced countries may drown in "facts," the emerging nations are frequently without the most elementary knowledge needed for forming a meaningful judgment or for implementing it once it has been taken. Where large bureaucracies operate in alternating spurts of rigidity and catastrophic (in relation to the bureaucracy) upheaval, the new states tend to take decisions on the basis of almost random pressures. The excessive institutionalization of one and the inadequate structure of the other inhibit international stability.

THE NATURE OF LEADERSHIP

Whatever one's view about the degree to which choices in international affairs are "objectively" determined, the decisions are made by individuals who will be above all conscious of the seeming multiplicity of options. Their understanding of the nature of their choice depends on many factors, including their experience during the rise to eminence.

The mediating, conciliatory style of British policy in the nineteenth century reflected, in part, the qualities encouraged during careers in Parliament and the values of a cohesive leadership group connected by ties of family and common education. The hysterical cast of the policy of Imperial Germany was given impetus by a domestic structure in which political parties were deprived of responsibility while ministers were obliged to balance a monarch by divine right against a Parliament composed of representatives without any prospect of ever holding office. Consensus could be achieved most easily through fits of national passion which in turn disquieted all of Germany's neighbors. Germany's foreign policy grew unstable because its domestic structure did little to discourage capricious improvisations; it may even have put a premium on them.

The collapse of the essentially aristocratic conception of foreign policy of the nineteenth century has made the career experiences of leaders even more crucial. An aristocracy—if it lives up to its values—will reject the arbitrariness of absolutist rule; and it will base itself on a notion of quality which discourages the temptations of demagoguery inherent in plebiscitarian democracy. Where position is felt to be a birthright, generosity is possible (though not guaranteed); flexibility is not inhibited by a commitment to perpetual success. Where a leader's estimate of himself is not completely dependent on his standing in an administrative

structure, measures can be judged in terms of a conception of the future rather than of an almost compulsive desire to avoid even a temporary setback. When statesmen belonged to a community which transcended national boundaries, there tended to be consensus on the criteria of what constituted a reasonable proposal. This did not prevent conflicts, but it did define their nature and encourage dialogue. The bane of aristocratic foreign policy was the risk of frivolousness, of a self-confidence unrelated to knowledge, and of too much emphasis on intuition.

In any event, ours is the age of the expert or the charismatic leader. The expert has his constituency—those who have a vested interest in commonly held opinions; elaborating and defining its consensus at a high level has, after all, made him an expert. Since the expert is often the product of the administrative dilemmas described earlier, he is usually in a poor position to transcend them. The charismatic leader, on the other hand, needs a perpetual revolution to maintain his position. Neither the expert nor the charismatic leader operates in an environment which puts a premium on long-range conceptions or on generosity or on subordinating the leader's ego to purposes which transcend his own career.

Leadership groups are formed by at least three factors: their experiences during their rise to eminence; the structure in which they must operate; the values of their society. Three contemporary types will be discussed here: (1) the bureaucratic-pragmatic type; (2) the ideological type; and (3) the revolutionary-charismatic type.

BUREAUCRATIC-PRAGMATIC LEADERSHIP

The main example of this type of leadership is the American elite—though the leadership groups of other Western countries increasingly approximate the American pattern. Shaped by a society without fundamental social schisms (at least until the race problem became visible), and the product of an environment in which most recognized problems have proved soluble, its approach to policy is *ad hoc*, pragmatic, and somewhat mechanical.

Because pragmatism is based on the conviction that the context of events produces a solution, there is a tendency to await developments. The belief is prevalent that every problem will yield if attacked with sufficient energy. It is inconceivable, therefore, that delay might result in irretrievable disaster; at worst it is thought to require a redoubled effort later on. Problems are segmented into constituent elements, each of which is dealt with by experts in the special difficulty it involves. There is little emphasis or concern for their interrelationship. Technical issues enjoy more careful attention, and receive more sophisticated treatment, than political ones. Though the importance of intangibles is affirmed in theory, it is difficult to obtain a consensus on which factors are significant, and even harder to find a meaningful mode for dealing with them. Things are done because one knows how to do them and not because one ought to do them. The criteria for dealing with trends which are conjectural are less well developed than those for immediate crises. Pragmatism, at least in its generally accepted form, is more concerned with method than with judgment; or rather it seeks to reduce judgment to methodology and value to knowledge.

This is reinforced by the special qualities of the professions—law and business—which furnish the core of the leadership groups in America. Lawyers—at least in the Anglo-Saxon tradition—prefer to deal with actual rather than hypothetical cases; they have little confidence in the possibility of stating a future issue abstractly. But planning by its very nature is hypothetical. Its success depends precisely on the ability to transcend the existing framework. Lawyers may be prepared to undertake this task; but they will do well in it only to the extent that they are able to overcome the special qualities encouraged by their profession. What comes naturally to lawyers in the Anglo-Saxon tradition is the sophisticated analysis of a series of *ad hoc* issues which emerge as problems through adversary proceedings. Insofar as lawyers draw on the experience which forms them, they have a bias toward awaiting developments and toward operating within the definition of the problem as formulated by its chief spokesmen.

This has several consequences. It compounds the already powerful tendencies within American society to identify foreign policy with the solution of immediate issues. It produces great refinement of issues as they arise. But it also encourages the administrative dilemmas described earlier. Issues are dealt with only as the pressure of events imposes the need for resolving them. Then, each of the contending factions within the bureaucracy has a maximum incentive to state its case in its most extreme form because the ultimate outcome depends, to a considerable extent, on a bargaining process. The premium placed on advocacy turns decisionmaking into a series of adjustments among special interests—a process more suited to domestic than to foreign policy. This procedure neglects the long-range because the future has no administrative constituency and is, therefore, without representation in the adversary proceedings. Problems tend to be slighted until some agency or department is made responsible for them. When this occurs—usually when a difficulty has already grown acute—the relevant department becomes an all-out spokesman for its particular area of responsibility. The outcome usually depends more on the pressures or the persuasiveness of the contending advocates than on a concept of over-all purpose. While these tendencies exist to some extent in all bureaucracies, they are particularly pronounced in the American system of government.

This explains in part the peculiar alternation of rigidity and spasms of flexibility in American diplomacy. On a given issue—be it the Berlin crisis or disarmament or the war in Vietnam—there generally exists a great reluctance to develop a negotiating position or a statement of objectives except in the most general terms. This stems from a desire not to prejudge the process of negotiations and above all to retain flexibility in the face of unforeseeable events. But, when an approaching conference or some other pressures make the development of a position imperative and some office or individual is assigned the specific task, a sudden change occurs. Both personal and bureaucratic success are then identified with bringing the particular assignment to a conclusion. Where so much stock is placed in negotiating skill, a failure of a conference may be viewed as a reflection on the ability of the negotiator rather than on the objective difficulty of the subject. Confidence in the bargaining process causes American negotiators to be extremely sensitive to the tactical requirements of the conference table—sometimes at the expense of longer-term considerations. In internal discussions, American negotiators—generally irrespective of their previous commitments—often become advocates for the maximum range of concessions; their legal background tempts them to act as mediators between Washington and the country with which they are negotiating.

The attitudes of the business elite reinforce the convictions of the legal profession. The American business executive rises through a process of selection which rewards the ability to manipulate the known—in itself a conciliatory procedure. The special skill of the executive is thought to consist in coordinating well-defined functions rather than in challenging them. The procedure is relatively effective in the business world, where the executive can often substitute decisiveness, long experience, and a wide range of personal acquaintance for reflectiveness. In international affairs, however —especially in a revolutionary situation—the strong will which is one of our business executives' notable traits may produce essentially arbitrary choices. Or unfamiliarity with the subject matter may have the opposite effect of turning the executive into a spokesman of his technical staffs. In either case, the business executive is even more dependent than the lawyer on the bureaucracy's formulation of the issue. The business elite is even less able or willing than the lawyer to recognize that the formulation of an issue, not the technical remedy, is usually the central problem.

All this gives American policy its particular cast. Problems are dealt with as they arise. Agreement on what constitutes a problem generally depends on an emerging crisis which settles the previously inconclusive disputes about priorities. When a problem is recognized, it is dealt with by a mobilization of all resources to overcome the immediate symptoms. This often involves the risk of slighting longer-term issues which may not yet have assumed crisis proportions and of overwhelming, perhaps even undermining, the structure of the area concerned by a flood of American technical experts proposing remedies on an American scale. Administrative decisions emerge from a compromise of conflicting pressures in which accidents of personality or persuasiveness play a crucial role. The compromise often reflects the maxim that "if two parties disagree the truth is usually somewhere in between." But the pedantic application of such truisms causes the various contenders to exaggerate their positions for bargaining purposes or to construct fictitious ex-

tremes to make their position appear moderate. In either case, internal bargaining predominates over substance.

The *ad hoc* tendency of our decisionmakers and the reliance on adversary proceeding cause issues to be stated in black and white terms. This suppresses a feeling for nuance and makes it difficult to recognize the relationship between seemingly discrete events. Even with the perspective of a decade there is little consensus about the relationship between the actions which culminated in the Suez fiasco and the French decision to enter the nuclear field; or about the inconsistency between the neutralization of Laos and the step-up of the military effort in Vietnam.

The same quality also produces a relatively low valuation of historical factors. Nations are treated as similar phenomena, and those states which present similar immediate problems are treated similarly. Since many of our policymakers first address themselves to an issue when it emerges as their area of responsibility, their approach to it is often highly anecdotal. Great weight is given to what people say and relatively little to the significance of these affirmations in terms of domestic structure or historical background. Agreement may be taken at face value and seen as a reflection of more consensus than actually exists. Opposition tends to produce moral outrage, which often assumes the form of personal animosity—the attitude of some American policymakers toward President de Gaulle is a good example.

The legal background of our policymakers produces a bias in favor of constitutional solutions. The issue of supranationalism or confederalism in Europe has been discussed largely in terms of the right of countries to make independent decisions. Much less weight has been given to the realities which would limit the application of a majority vote against a major country, whatever the legal arrangements. (The fight over the application of Article 19 of the United Nations Charter was based on the same attitude.) Similarly, legal terms such as "integration" and "assignment" sometimes become ends in themselves and thus obscure the operational reality to which they refer. In short, American leadership groups show high competence in dealing with technical issues, and much less virtuosity in mastering historical process. And the policies of other Western countries exhibit variations of the American pattern. A lesser pragmatism in continental Europe is counterbalanced by a smaller ability to play a world role.

The Ideological Type of Leadership

As discussed above, the impact of ideology can persist long after its initial fervor has been spent. Whatever the ideological commitment of individual leaders, a lifetime spent in the Communist hierarchy must influence their basic categories of thought—especially since Communist ideology continues to perform important functions. It still furnishes the standard of truth and the guarantee of ultimate success. It provides a means for maintaining cohesion among the various Communist parties of the world. It supplies criteria for the settlement of disputes both within the bureaucracy of individual Communist countries and among the various Communist states.

However attenuated, Communist ideology is in part responsible for international tensions. This is less because of specific Marxist tactical prescriptions—with respect to which Communists have shown a high degree of flexibility—than because of the basic Marxist-Leninist categories for interpreting reality. Communist leaders never tire of affirming that Marxism-Leninism is the key element of their self-proclaimed superiority over the outside world; as Marxist-Leninists they are convinced that they understand the historical process better than the non-Communist world does.

The essence of Marxism-Leninism—and the reason that normal diplomacy with Communist states is so difficult—is the view that "objective" factors such as the social structure, the economic process, and, above all, the class struggle are more important than the personal convictions of statesmen. Belief in the predominance of objective factors explains the Soviet approach to the problem of security. If personal convictions are "subjective," Soviet security cannot be allowed to rest on the good will of other statesmen, especially those of a different social system. This produces a quest for what may be described as absolute security—the attempt to be so strong as to be independent of the decisions of other countries. But absolute security for one country means absolute insecurity for all others; it can be achieved only by reducing other states to impotence. Thus an es-

sentially defensive foreign policy can grow indistinguishable from traditional aggression.

The belief in the predominance of objective factors explains why, in the past, periods of détente have proved so precarious. When there is a choice between Western good will or a physical gain, the pressures to choose the latter have been overwhelming. The wartime friendship with the West was sacrificed to the possibility of establishing Communist-controlled governments in Eastern Europe. The spirit of Geneva did not survive the temptations offered by the prospect of undermining the Western position in the Middle East. The many overtures of the Kennedy Administration were rebuffed until the Cuban missile crisis demonstrated that the balance of forces was not in fact favorable for a test of strength.

The reliance on objective factors has complicated negotiations between the West and the Communist countries. Communist negotiators find it difficult to admit that they could be swayed by the arguments of men who have, by definition, an inferior grasp of the laws of historical development. No matter what is said, they think that they understand their Western counterpart better than he understands himself. Concessions are possible, but they are made to "reality," not to individuals or to a bargaining process. Diplomacy becomes difficult when one of the parties considers the key element to negotiation—the give-and-take of the process of bargaining—as but a superstructure for factors that are not part of the negotiation itself.

Finally, whatever the decline in ideological fervor, orthodoxy requires the maintenance of a posture of ideological hostility to the non-Communist world, even during a period of coexistence. Thus, in a reply to a Chinese challenge, the Communist party of the U.S.S.R. declared: "We fully support the destruction of capitalism. We not only believe in the inevitable death of capitalism but we are doing everything possible for it to be accomplished through class struggle as quickly as possible."[2]

The wariness toward the outside world is reinforced by the personal experiences which Communist leaders have had on the road to

[2] "The Soviet Reply to the Chinese Letter," open letter of the Central Committee of the Communist party of the Soviet Union as it appeared in *Pravda*, July 14, 1963, pp. 1–4; *The Current Digest of the Soviet Press*, 15, no. 28 (August 7, 1963): 23.

eminence. In a system where there is no legitimate succession, a good deal of energy is absorbed in internal maneuvering. Leaders rise to the top by eliminating—sometimes physically, always bureaucratically—all possible opponents. Stalin had all individuals who helped him into power executed. Khrushchev disgraced Kaganovich, whose protégé he had been, and turned on Marshal Zhukov six months after being saved by him from a conspiracy of his other colleagues. Brezhnev and Kosygin owed their careers to Khrushchev; they nevertheless overthrew him and started a campaign of calumny against him within twenty-four hours of his dismissal.

Anyone succeeding in Communist leadership struggles must be single-minded, unemotional, dedicated, and, above all, motivated by an enormous desire for power. Nothing in the personal experience of Soviet leaders would lead them to accept protestations of good will at face value. Suspiciousness is inherent in their domestic position. It is unlikely that their attitude toward the outside world is more benign than that toward their own colleagues or that they would expect more consideration from it.

The combination of personal qualities and ideological structure also affects relations *among* Communist states. Since national rivalries are thought to be the result of class conflict, they are expected to disappear wherever socialism has triumphed. When disagreements occur they are dealt with by analogy to internal Communist disputes: by attempting to ostracize, and then to destroy, the opponent. The tendency to treat different opinions as manifestations of heresy causes disagreements to harden into bitter schisms. The debate between Communist China and the U.S.S.R. is in many respects more acrimonious than that between the U.S.S.R. and the non-Communist world.

Even though the basic conceptual categories of Communist leadership groups are similar, the impact of the domestic structure of the individual Communist states on international relations varies greatly. It makes a considerable difference whether an ideology has become institutionalized, as in the Soviet Union, or whether it is still impelled by its early revolutionary fervor, as in Communist China. Where ideology has become institutionalized a special form of pragmatism may develop. It may be just as empirical as that of the United States, but it will operate in a different realm of "reality." A different philosophical basis leads to the emergence of another set of categories for the settlement of disputes, and these in turn generate another range of problems.

A Communist bureaucratic structure, however pragmatic, will have different priorities from ours; it will give greater weight to doctrinal considerations and conceptual problems. It is more than ritual when speeches of senior Soviet leaders begin with hour-long recitals of Communist ideology. Even if it were ritual, it must affect the definition of what is considered reasonable in internal arguments. Bureaucratization and pragmatism may lead to a loss of élan; they do not guarantee convergence of Western and Soviet thinking.

The more revolutionary manifestations of Communism, such as Communist China, still possess more ideological fervor, but, paradoxically, their structure may permit a wider latitude for new departures. Tactical intransigence and ideological vitality should not be confused with structural rigidity. Because the leadership bases its rule on a prestige which transcends bureaucratic authority, it has not yet given so many hostages to the administrative structure. If the leadership should change—or if its attitudes were modified—policy could probably be altered much more dramatically in Communist China than in the more institutionalized Communist countries.

THE CHARISMATIC-REVOLUTIONARY TYPE OF LEADERSHIP

The contemporary international order is heavily influenced by yet another leadership type: the charismatic-revolutionary leader. For many of the leaders of the new nations the bureaucratic-pragmatic approach of the West is irrelevant because they are more interested in the future which they wish to construct than in the manipulation of the environment which dominates the thinking of the pragmatists. And ideology is not satisfactory, because doctrine supplies rigid categories which overshadow the personal experiences that have provided the impetus for so many of the leaders of the new nations.

The type of individual who leads a struggle for independence has been sustained in the risks and suffering of such a course primarily by a commitment to a vision which enabled him to override conditions that had seemed overwhelmingly hostile. Revolutionaries are rarely motivated primarily by material considerations—though the illusion that they are persists in the West. Material incentives do not cause a man to risk his existence and to launch himself into the uncertainties of a revolutionary struggle. If Castro or Sukarno had been principally interested in economics, their talents would have guaranteed them a brilliant career in the societies they overthrew. What made their sacrifices worthwhile to them was a vision of the future—or a quest for political power. To revolutionaries the significant reality is the world which they are striving to bring about, not the world they are fighting to overcome.

This difference in perspective accounts for the inconclusiveness of much of the dialogue between the West and many of the leaders of the new countries. The West has a tendency to believe that the tensions in the emerging nations are caused by a low level of economic activity. To the apostles of economic development, raising the gross national product seems the key to political stability. They believe that it should receive the highest priority from the political leaders of new countries and that it should supply their chief motivation.

But, to the charismatic heads of many of the new nations, economic progress, while not unwelcome, offers too limited a scope for their ambitions. It can be achieved only by slow, painful, highly technical measures which contrast with the heroic exertions of the struggle for independence. Results are long-delayed; credit for them cannot be clearly established. If Castro were to act on the advice of theorists of economic development, the best he could hope for would be that after some decades he would lead a small progressive country—perhaps a Switzerland of the Caribbean. Compared to the prospect of leading a revolution throughout Latin America, this goal would appear trivial, boring, perhaps even unreal to him.

Moreover, to the extent that economic progress is achieved, it may magnify domestic political instability, at least in its early phases. Economic advance disrupts the traditional political structure. It thus places constant pressures on the incumbent leaders to re-establish the legitimacy of their rule. For this purpose a dramatic foreign policy is particularly apt. Many leaders of the new countries seem convinced that an adventurous foreign policy will not harm prospects for economic development and may even foster it. The competition of the superpowers makes it likely that economic assistance will be forthcoming regardless of the actions of the recipient. Indeed, the more obtrusive their foreign policy, the greater is their prospect of being wooed by the chief contenders.

The tendency toward a reckless policy is magnified by the uncertain sense of identity of many of the new nations. National boundaries often correspond to the administrative subdivisions established by the former colonial rulers. States thus have few of the attributes of nineteenth-century European nationalism: common language, common culture, or even common history. In many cases, the only common experience is a century or so of imperial rule. As a result, there is a great pressure toward authoritarian rule, and a high incentive to use foreign policy as a means of bringing about domestic cohesion.

Western-style democracy presupposes that society transcends the political realm; in that case, opposition challenges a particular method of achieving common aims but not the existence of the state itself. In many of the new countries, by contrast, the state represents the primary, sometimes the sole, manifestation of social cohesion. Opposition can therefore easily appear as treason—apart from the fact that leaders who have spent several decades running the risks of revolutionary struggle or who have achieved power by a coup d'état are not likely to favor a system of government which makes them dispensable. Indeed, the attraction of communism for many of these leaders is not Marxist-Leninist economic theory but the legitimacy for authoritarian rule which it provides.

No matter what the system of government, many of the leaders of the new nations use foreign policy as a means to escape intractable internal difficulties and as a device to achieve domestic cohesion. The international arena provides an opportunity for the dramatic measures which are impossible at home. These are often cast in an anti-Western mold because this is the easiest way to re-create the struggle against imperial rule, which is the principal unifying element for many new nations. The incentive is particularly strong because the rivalry of the nuclear powers eliminates many of the risks which previously were associated with an adventurous foreign policy—especially if that foreign policy is directed against the West, which lacks any effective sanctions.

Traditional military pressure is largely precluded by the nuclear stalemate and by respect for world opinion. But the West is neither prepared nor able to use the sanction which weighs most heavily on the new countries: the deliberate exploitation of their weak domestic structures. In many areas the ability to foment domestic unrest is a more potent weapon than traditional arms. Many of the leaders of the new countries will be prepared to ignore the classical panoply of power, but they will be very sensitive to the threat of domestic upheaval. States with a high capacity for exploiting domestic instability can use it as a tool of foreign policy. China, though it lacks almost all forms of classical long-range military strength, is a growing factor in Africa. Weak states may be more concerned with a country's capacity to organize domestic unrest in their territory than with its capacity for physical destruction.

Conclusion

Contemporary domestic structures thus present an unprecedented challenge to the emergence of a stable international order. The bureaucratic-pragmatic societies concentrate on the manipulation of an empirical reality which they treat as given; the ideological societies are split between an essentially bureaucratic approach (though in a different realm of reality than the bureaucratic-pragmatic structures) and a group which uses ideology mainly for revolutionary ends. The new nations, insofar as they are active in international affairs, have a high incentive to seek in foreign policy the perpetuation of charismatic leadership.

These differences are a major obstacle to a consensus on what constitutes a "reasonable" proposal. A common diagnosis of the existing situation is hard to achieve, and it is even more difficult to concert measures for a solution. The situation is complicated by the one feature all types of leadership have in common: the premium put on short-term goals and the domestic need to succeed at all times. In the bureaucratic societies policy emerges from a compromise which often produces the least common denominator, and it is implemented by individuals whose reputation is made by administering

the *status quo*. The leadership of the institutionalized ideological state may be even more the prisoner of essentially corporate bodies. Neither leadership can afford radical changes of course, for they result in profound repercussions in administrative structure. And the charismatic leaders of the new nations are like tightrope artists—one false step and they will plunge from their perch.

DOMESTIC STRUCTURE AND FOREIGN POLICY: THE PROSPECTS FOR WORLD ORDER

Many contemporary divisions are thus traceable to differences in domestic structure. But are there not countervailing factors? What about the spread of technology and its associated rationality, or the adoption on a global scale of many Western political forms? Unfortunately, the process of "Westernization" does not inevitably produce a similar concept of reality. For what matters is not the technology or the institutions but the significance which is attached to them. And this differs according to the evolution of the society concerned.

The term "nation" does not mean the same thing when applied to such various phenomena as India, France, and Nigeria. Similarly, technology is likely to have a different significance for different peoples, depending on how and when it was acquired.

Any society is part of an evolutionary process which proceeds by means of two seemingly contradictory mechanisms. On the one hand, the span of possible adaptations is delimited by the physical environment, the internal structure, and, above all, by previous choices. On the other hand, evolution proceeds not in a straight line but through a series of complicated variations which appears anything but obvious to the chief actors. In retrospect, a choice may seem to have been nearly random or else to have represented the only available alternative. In either case, the choice is not an isolated act but an accumulation of previous decisions reflecting history or tradition and values, as well as the immediate pressures of the need for survival. And each decision delimits the range of possible future adaptations.

Young societies are in a position to make radical changes of course which are highly impractical at a later stage. As a society becomes more elaborate and as its tradition is firmly established, its choices with respect to its internal organization grow more restricted. If a highly articulated social unit attempts basic shifts, it runs the risk of doing violence to its internal organization, to its history and values as embodied in its structure. When it accepts institutions or values developed elsewhere, it must adapt them to what its structure can absorb. The institutions of any political unit must therefore be viewed in historical context, for that alone can give an indication of their future. Societies—even when their institutions are similar—may be like ships passing in the night which find themselves but temporarily in the same place.

Is there then no hope for cooperation and stability? Is our international system doomed to incomprehension and its members to mounting frustration?

It must be admitted that, if the domestic structures were considered in isolation, the prognosis would not be too hopeful. But domestic structures do not exist in a vacuum. They must respond to the requirements of the environment. And here all states find themselves face to face with the necessity of avoiding a nuclear holocaust. While this condition does not restrain all nations equally, it nevertheless defines a common task which technology will impose on even more countries as a direct responsibility.

Then, too, a certain similarity in the forms of administration may bring about common criteria of rationality as Professor Jaguaribe has pointed out.[3] Science and technology will spread. Improved communications may lead to the emergence of a common culture. The fissures between domestic structures and the different stages of evolution are important, but they may be outweighed by the increasing interdependence of humanity.

It would be tempting to end on this note and to base the hope for peace on the self-evidence of the need for it. But this would be too pat. The deepest problem of the contemporary international order may be that most of the debates which form the headlines of the day are peripheral to the basic division described in this article. The cleavage is not over particular political arrangements—except as symptoms—but between two styles of policy and two philosophical perspectives.

The two styles can be defined as the political as against the revolutionary approach to order or, reduced to personalities, as the distinction between the statesman and the prophet.

The statesman manipulates reality; his first goal is survival; he feels responsible not only for the best conceivable outcome but also for the worst. His view of human nature is wary; he is conscious of many great hopes that have failed, of many good intentions that could not be realized, of selfishness and ambition and violence. He is therefore inclined to erect hedges against the possibility that even the most brilliant idea might prove abortive and that the most eloquent formulation might hide ulterior motives. He will try to avoid certain experiments, not because he would object to the results if they succeeded, but because he would feel himself responsible for the consequences if they failed. He is suspicious of those who personalize foreign policy, for history teaches him the fragility of structures that depend on individuals. To the statesman, gradualism is the essence of stability; he represents an era of average performance, of gradual change and slow construction.

By contrast, the prophet is less concerned with manipulating than with creating reality. What is possible interests him less than what is "right." He offers his vision as the test and his good faith as a guarantee. He believes in total solutions; he is less absorbed in methodology than in purpose. He believes in the perfectibility of man. His approach is timeless and does not depend on circumstances. He objects to gradualism as an unnecessary concession to circumstance. He will risk everything because his vision is the primary significant reality to him. Paradoxically, his more optimistic view of human nature makes him more intolerant than the statesman. If truth is both knowable and attainable, only immorality or stupidity can keep man from realizing it. The prophet represents an era of exaltation, of great upheavals, of vast accomplishments, but also of enormous disasters.

The encounter between the political and the prophetic approach to policy is always somewhat inconclusive and frustrating. The test of

[3] Helio Jaguaribe, "World Order, Rationality, and Socioeconomic Development," *Daedalus*, no. 2 (Spring 1966): 607–26.

the statesman is the permanence of the international structure under stress. The test of the prophet is inherent in his vision. The statesman will seek to reduce the prophet's intuition to precise measures; he judges ideas on their utility and not on their "truth." To the prophet, this approach is almost sacrilegious because it represents the triumph of expediency over universal principles. To the statesman, negotiation is the mechanism of stability because it presupposes that maintenance of the existing order is more important than any dispute within it. To the prophet, negotiations can have only symbolic value—as a means of converting or demoralizing the opponent; truth, by definition, cannot be compromised.

Both approaches have prevailed at different periods in history. The political approach dominated European foreign policy between the end of the religious wars and the French Revolution, and then again between the Congress of Vienna and the outbreak of World War I. The prophetic mode was in the ascendant during the great upheavals of the religious struggles and the period of the French Revolution, and in the contemporary uprisings in major parts of the world.

Both modes have produced considerable accomplishments, though the prophetic style is likely to involve greater dislocations and more suffering. Each has its nemesis. The nemesis of the statesman is that equilibrium, though it may be the condition of stability, does not supply its own motivation; that of the prophet is the impossibility of sustaining a mood of exaltation without the risk of submerging man in the vastness of a vision and reducing him to a mere figure to be manipulated.

As for the difference in philosophical perspective, it may reflect the divergence of the two lines of thought which since the Renaissance have distinguished the West from the part of the world now called underdeveloped (with Russia occupying an intermediary position). The West is deeply committed to the notion that the real world is external to the observer, that knowledge consists of recording and classifying data—the more accurately the better. Cultures which escaped the early impact of Newtonian thinking have retained the essentially pre-Newtonian view that the real world is almost completely *internal* to the observer.

Although this attitude was a liability for centuries—because it prevented the development of the technology and consumer goods which the West enjoyed—it offers great flexibility with respect to the contemporary revolutionary turmoil. It enables the societies which do not share our cultural mode to alter reality by influencing the perspective of the observer—a process which we are largely unprepared to handle or even to perceive. And this can be accomplished under contemporary conditions without sacrificing technological progress. Technology comes as a gift; acquiring it in its advanced form does not presuppose the philosophical commitment that discovering it imposed on the West. Empirical reality has a much different significance for many of the new countries than it has for the West because in a certain sense they never went through the process of discovering it (with Russia again occupying an intermediary position). At the same time, the difference in philosophical perspective may cause us to seem cold, supercilious, lacking in compassion. The instability of the contemporary world order may thus have at its core a philosophical schism which makes the issues that produce most political debates seem largely tangential.

Such differences in style and philosophical perspective are not unprecedented. What is novel is the global scale on which they occur and the risks which the failure to overcome them would entail. Historically, cleavages of lesser magnitude have been worked out dialectically, with one style of policy or one philosophical approach dominating one era, only to give way later to another conception of reality. And the transition has rarely been free of violence. The challenge of our time is whether we can deal consciously and creatively with what in previous centuries was adjusted through a series of more or less violent and frequently catastrophic upheavals. We must construct an international order *before* a crisis imposes it as a necessity.

This is a question not of blueprints but of attitudes. In fact, the overconcern with technical blueprints is itself a symptom of our difficulties. Before the problem of order can be "dealt" with—even philosophically—we must be certain that the right questions are being asked.

We can point to some hopeful signs. The

most sensitive thinkers of the West have recognized that excessive empiricism may lead to
stagnation. In many of the new countries—
and in some Communist ones as well—the second or third generation of leaders is in the
process of freeing itself from the fervor and
dogmatism of the early revolutionary period
and of relating their actions to an environment
which they helped to create. But these are as
yet only the first tentative signs of progress on
a course whose significance is not always understood. Indeed, it is characteristic of an age
of turmoil that it produces so many immediate
issues that little time is left to penetrate their
deeper meaning. The most serious problem
therefore becomes the need to acquire a sufficiently wide perspective so that the present
does not overwhelm the future.

BIBLIOGRAPHY: PART I

Claude, Inis L., Jr. *Power and International Relations*. New York: Random House, 1962. 285 pp.
    The management of power is a central issue of
our time. Professor Claude deals with this problem in terms of three basic concepts: balance of
power, collective security, and world government. The utility of each for reducing conflict is
examined in light of considerable historical evidence. An understanding of Claude's book is essential to the student interested in prescriptions
for world peace.

de Rivera, Joseph. *The Psychological Dimension of
Foreign Policy*. Columbus, Ohio: Charles E.
Merrill Publishing Co., 1968. 434 pp.
    Professor de Rivera's work is concerned with
the individual as an actor in the formulation of
foreign policy. Specifically, he demonstrates how
contemporary psychology can be meaningfully
applied to such individuals' perceptions, values,
and interpersonal relations. This psychological
approach, when used in conjunction with traditional political and historical techniques for
analysis, can provide a more detailed picture of
the forces that shape policy.

Deutsch, Karl W., and Singer, David J. "Multipolar
Power Systems and International Stability."
World Politics, 16 (1964): 390–406.
    This article examines the proposition that, as
the international system moves away from bipolarity toward multipolarity, the frequency and
intensity of wars should diminish. The authors
suggest that while the proposition may be affirmed for the short term, the long-run prospects
for a stable, multipolar world are dubious.

Farrell, R. Barry. "Foreign Policies of Open and
Closed Political Societies." In *Approaches to
Comparative and International Politics*, edited
by R. Barry Farrell, pp. 167–206. Evanston, Ill.:
Northwestern University Press, 1966.
    The articles by Dr. Kissinger and Professor
Hoffmann in Part I of the present volume suggest
that domestic politics play important roles in the
formulation of foreign and defense policies. Professor Farrell examines some hypotheses about
the impact of "open" and "closed" domestic political systems on such elements of foreign policy
as information derivations, time of decision, revisionist versus status quo orientation, and scope
of diplomatic instruments comprehended by
policies.

Haas, Ernst B. "The Balance of Power: Prescription, Concept, or Propaganda?" *World Politics*,
5 (1953): 442–77.
    Numerous attempts have been made to use
"balance of power" as the key for explaining relations among states. Professor Haas examines
the concept and shows how it has been used in
a variety of ambiguous ways. After reading his
article, one might reasonably conclude that the
balance-of-power concept lacks sufficient precision to explain or prescribe international relations.

Herz, John H. *International Politics in the Atomic
Age*. New York: Columbia University Press,
1959. 357 pp. Cloth and paper.
    This volume represents an early attempt by
Professor Herz to examine the implications of
modern technology for the nature and role of
the nation-state. He suggests that nuclear missiles have destroyed the "hard-shell imperme-
ability" of the nation-states. This in turn renders
them incapable of serving their main function—
the protection of the citizenry. The important
question facing the student of national security
is whether the nation-state can retain its role as
the major source of protection for the individual.

————. "The Territorial State Revisited: Reflections on the Future of the Nation-State." *Polity,
the Journal of the Northeastern Political Science
Associations*, 1 (1968): 12–34.

In 1959, Professor Herz forecast that nuclear missiles would significantly reduce the role of the nation-state in international politics (see entry above). This article represents a reversal of his earlier thesis. The careful reader will determine for himself whether Professor Herz's estimate of the continued viability of the nation-state can be supported by empirical evidence.

Hoffmann, Stanley. "Restraints and Choices in American Foreign Policy." *Daedalus*, 91 (Fall 1962): 668–704.

This article describes international and domestic constraints which limit the options available to American foreign policy strategists. Although his article was done over a decade ago, it retains relevance today. The section on domestic constraints is a particularly useful adjunct to the more internationally oriented selection by Hoffmann contained in Part I of the present volume.

Holsti, K. J. *International Politics: A Framework for Analysis.* 2d ed. Englewood Cliffs, N.J.: Prentice-Hall, 1972. 514 pp.

This is a basic text in international politics which addresses the questions of how and why states conduct foreign policies as they do. The constraints imposed by the international and domestic systems are readily apparent in Professor Holsti's explanations. The relative utility of military actions is also demonstrated vis-à-vis diplomatic bargaining, propaganda, and economic tools of foreign policy.

Holsti, Ole R. "The Belief System and National Images: A Case Study." *The Journal of Conflict Resolution,* 6 (1962): 244–52.

Individuals view international politics through unique sets of ideological lenses. Professor Holsti demonstrates considerable evidence to support his hypothesis that Secretary of State Dulles' personality resulted in his viewing Soviet actions as inherently bad. The implication of his study is that the Cold War may have resulted in part from images held by foreign policy elites rather than from actual conflicts of interest.

Jervis, Robert. *The Logic of Images in International Relations.* Princeton: Princeton University Press, 1970. 276 pp.

The image one state holds of another is frequently as important as the objective power relationship between the two. In this volume, Professor Jervis shows how states try to get others to accept desired images of themselves. He differentiates between easily controlled signals and more substantive acts that are taken as indices of a nation's intent; he explores the uses of ambiguity; and he examines the coupling and decoupling of signals and indices by nations. His last chapter applies the analysis to the Vietnam War.

Knorr, Klaus. *Military Power and Potential.* Lexington, Mass., 1970. 150 pp. Paper.

In this classic treatise, Professor Knorr succeeds in erasing considerable ambiguity associated with the concept of power by specifying which factors in a nation-state produce potential for international military effectiveness. Among the factors he describes are the economic, technological, political, and bureaucratic. The book is particularly useful for those tempted to equate military potential solely with the quantity and quality of weapons systems.

McClelland, Charles A. *Theory and The International System.* London: Collier-Macmillan Ltd., 1966. 138 pp. Paper.

The utility of the systems approach as a framework for understanding the actions of nation-states has been the topic of considerable debate. Charles McClelland both describes what the systems approach entails and discusses how it can be used by students of international affairs. It is significant to note his argument that analysis of the international system does not introduce a requirement for either traditional or behavioral modes of research. As he convincingly demonstrates, historical, comparative, statistical, and simulative approaches can be used in the work of system analysis one at a time or in combination.

Morgenthau, Hans J. *Politics among Nations.* 4th ed. New York: Alfred A. Knopf, 1966. 575 pp. (See especially pp. 1–82.)

The "realist" theory of international politics has provided the source for considerable debate among scholars. Professor Morgenthau's development of this theory is perhaps the most famous. Students of national security should examine the fundamental assumptions underlying his hypothesis and determine whether they are in fact realistic assessments of the various actors in international politics.

Pruitt, Dean G., and Snyder, Richard C., eds. *Theory and Research on the Causes of War.* Englewood Cliffs, N.J.: Prentice-Hall, 1969. 279 pp. Cloth and paper.

An increasing number of scholars from a widening variety of disciplines have become involved in the study of the causes and possible cures for war. This reader presents a series of articles that discuss research methods currently used in the field, the forces which impel states into war, military and nonmilitary constraints on war, and statistical correlates of war.

Rosecrance, Richard N. "Bipolarity, Multipolarity, and the Future." *The Journal of Conflict Resolution,* 10 (1966): 314–27.

Professor Rosecrance is concerned with which type of international political system is most conducive to stability. He summarizes the arguments for and against the traditional bipolar and multipolar systems. Neither appears ideally suited to promoting stability. Professor Rosecrance then suggests a structure which draws from the stabilizing elements of both the bipolar and multipolar alternatives.

Rosenau, James N., ed. *Domestic Sources of For-*

eign Policy. New York: The Free Press, 1967. 331 pp.

This book of readings examines the impact of public opinion on foreign policy formulation. Among the "domestic" variables considered are personality and attitude dynamics operating upon individual citizens, as well as group and organizational processes that are operative at the grosser levels of society and politics. The clash of interests among individuals and larger aggregates and the roles of leaders who represent the larger aggregates are constant themes throughout the articles.

Singer, J. David. "The Level-of-Analysis Problem in International Relations." In *The International System: Theoretical Essays,* edited by Klaus Knorr and Sidney Verba, pp. 77–92. Princeton: Princeton University Press, 1961.

Professor Singer differentiates between the international and domestic political systems as models for analyzing the interactions of nation-states. He does not prescribe one perspective over the other; rather, he suggests advantages and disadvantages for each, depending upon the issue at hand. He concludes with the recommendation that students of a particular issue might avoid having to shift their orientation in the midst of a study if they carefully chose the proper level of analysis in advance.

Waltz, Kenneth N. *Man, the State, and War.* New York: Columbia University Press, 1954. 238 pp. Cloth and paper.

The questions of why wars occur and how they might be controlled or eliminated have fascinated scholars for centuries. Professor Waltz has chosen to investigate the contributions made to these problems by classical political theorists. His book is more than a historical exegesis, however. As the careful reader will come to realize, the descriptions and prescriptions of the classical theorists provide most of the fundamental assumptions that underlie current attempts to promote national security.

————. "The Stability of a Bipolar World." *Daedalus,* 93 (Summer 1964): 892–907.

Professor Waltz suggests that a major factor promoting stability in the postwar era is East-West bipolarity. His argument serves as an interesting rejoinder to the Deutsch/Singer article cited above, as well as to the Hoffmann article included in Part I of the present volume. The student should carefully examine the assumptions that underlie Waltz's position to determine whether they have been sufficiently verified.

Part II · Strategy and the Use of Force

Introduction to Strategy

CHARLES A. MAY, JR.

Nuclear weapons generated a renaissance in strategic thinking throughout the Western world. During the years since World War II an enormous quantity of academic research has been conducted in an attempt to understand the implications of this new technology. The primary goal of this scholarship has consistently been to reduce the probability that a thermonuclear war will ever be fought. Because of the excellent foundation which has been laid, a great deal of light has been shed on the parameters of the nuclear age as they affect nation-states in the international system. But much work remains to be done; many difficult and perplexing questions have not been answered.

In the years prior to Hiroshima, military men dominated the study of strategy and the use of force.[1] Because of the nonmilitary aspects of strategy, civilians contributed, but always to a lesser extent. In the United States, for example, only two men had received international recognition as strategists—Admiral Mahan and General Mitchell. Today, however, civilians dominate the field which they entered either because they feared nuclear weapons or possessed vital technical skills, or both. Dozens of American scholars have earned fame for their efforts to develop a viable strategy in the nuclear age.[2]

Opinions vary as to the precise nature of the impact of these theorists on actual policy. One school of thought argues that there is a direct cause-effect relationship. This is the conservative view that American policy since World War II has been overresponsive to liberal ideas. Another point of view is that the thinkers themselves, rather than their ideas *per se*, influenced American behavior. This occurred because these individuals were given high-level positions in the national government, especially during the early Kennedy years but also today.[3] There are other points of view, but a full examination of the debate is beyond our present purpose. Nevertheless, the irrefutable conclusion seems to be that these strategic studies have influenced both the planning and use of force in the international system since 1945. For this reason, it is imperative that the student of national security policy have a working knowledge of the conceptual foundation of modern strategy. The objective of this part of the present volume is to satisfy that need.

STRATEGY

What is strategy? According to the dictionary, the word is derived from the Greek word *strategos*, which means "the art of the general." The definition offered is very broad, including not only military forces of a nation but also political, economic, and psychological resources. When these forces, either alone or in combination, are employed by "a nation or group of nations to afford the maximum support of adopted policy in peace or war," then the sci-

---

[1] One of the excellent books on prenuclear strategy is Edward Meade Earle, ed., *Makers of Modern Strategy: Military Thought from Machiavelli to Hitler* (Princeton: Princeton University Press, 1943).

[2] In addition to the authors included in this section, interested readers can consult the annotated bibliography at the end of Part II for the names and works of the more prominent American strategists.

[3] Colin S. Gray, "What Rand Hath Wrought," *Foreign Policy*, Fall 1971, pp. 111–29.

Major Charles A. May, Jr. (USAF), wrote this introduction while he was an Assistant Professor of Political Science at the USAF Academy.

ence and art of strategy are involved. Writers throughout the centuries have examined this basic concept, but the term itself did not appear in the literature until the latter part of the eighteenth century.

For our purposes, a narrower definition of strategy seems appropriate. It is provided by Michael Howard in his article which appears in Chapter 2. Howard argues that the crucial variable in strategy is the element of force. In ordering its priorities, each nation must answer for itself the perennial questions of national interest and national security. How can its limited, finite resources be optimally allocated so as to maximize the possibility of achieving these goals, however defined? If the answer involves *the use of force*, then that nation is implementing the kind of strategy we will be discussing here.

Before examining substantive strategy, it is useful to consider briefly the elements of national policy formulation on the national level. It is not necessary to go into the institutional procedures that are followed in the United States or any other nation-state. But it is important, as a point of departure, that we look at some of the variables which must be taken into account by any national command authority when it devises a national strategy. The most prominent of these variables are goals and purposes, resources, public opinion, and the threat.

GOALS AND PURPOSES

First of all, the leadership of the nation-state should determine what its goals and purposes are vis-à-vis the other members of the international community. According to rational theory, each new leadership group starts with a *tabula rasa* and builds a new foundation for all of the planning done by subordinate echelons of government. The latter then carefully digest this new guidance and prepare new programs to carry out their individual responsibilities. Not only does this model assume rationality, but it also rejects the concept of feedback, which implies a circular rather than a linear planning process.

In reality, the process is neither wholly rational nor linear. It is a very complex operation which ultimately provides some type of guidance to the subordinate planner. But the planner still faces a difficult, if not impossible, task

in trying to formulate reasonable programs based on goals that are frequently idealistic and therefore unattainable. This situation occurs when the national leadership fails to take into account real-world constraints such as those discussed by Kissinger and Hoffmann in Chapter 1. Broad generalities do not provide meaningful political guidance but serve as points of departure for justifying almost any imaginable proposal. Nevertheless, the strategic planner seeks and must have guidance, and it is a continuing challenge for the political leadership to communicate its intentions and to maintain command and control over its own institutions.

RESOURCES

Second, what resources does the nation-state have to carry out its goals and purposes? This is a major qualification on "pie in the sky" schemes, and it is the traditional "guns versus butter" issue. Unlike the previous variable, this one has more obvious quantifiable limits. Between the extremes of "all guns" or "all butter" lies an arbitrary division of resources which must be determined by the national command authority. Each nation-state has its own constitutional procedures for making this determination. In the United States, the decision is ostensibly made by the executive and legislative branches working together, although the charge of executive predominance has been raised frequently since 1945. The result of this bargaining process is the percentage of GNP allocated to defense spending: 42 percent during World War II; 5 percent just prior to the Korean War; and less than 8 percent today. To illustrate how the economic factor impinges on strategic policy, recall that the Kennedy Administration adopted a Flexible Response posture and set out to procure forces to fight "2 and ½" wars simultaneously.[4] The requisite force levels were never met. President Nixon revised that strategy to a "1 and ½" wars posture. In many respects, this decision can be viewed as an acknowledgment that we will allocate only suf-

---

[4] "A *local war* (½) is defined as a war in which the United States and the Soviet Union (or China) see themselves on opposite sides but in which no attacks are made on the homelands of the two superpowers." Morton H. Halperin, *Contemporary Military Strategy* (Boston: Little, Brown & Co., 1967), p. 15.

ficient resources to prepare for this less costly option. Flexible Response can be very cogently argued by strategic theorists, but reality demands that fiscal constraints be incorporated early in the planning cycle.

PUBLIC OPINION

A third factor is public opinion. This has been an important issue since the Napoleonic reforms from professional to citizen armies in the eighteenth century. It has come into the foreground in this country with the internal debate over our participation in the Korean and Vietnam wars. With regard to the latter, one might criticize the Kennedy Administration for establishing a military capability to fight an insurgency in the jungles of Asia without adequately preparing the American people for the sacrifices involved. His Administration did not convince, nor did it seriously attempt to convince, the average man in the street that this was an exigency which would demand substantial quantities of blood, sweat, and tears over an extended period of time. In fairness, there were few, if any, policymakers who believed that American involvement would demand such a level of commitment. On the other hand, public opinion in a nondemocratic state is not as important to the policymaker as it is in a democracy, where relatively wide public support is a prerequisite for the maintenance of long-term policy. However, military planners in all states undermine their credibility and effectiveness if they do not take into account the sentiments of the nation's population. Despite numerous research projects, no scholar has been able to operationalize this concern and measure public sentiment conclusively on a particular issue. The likelihood of this being done in the foreseeable future is small. Therefore, the policymaker and planner are forced to rely on judgment and intuition with all of their inherent weaknesses, especially their vulnerability to hindsight.

THE THREAT

Still another major factor influencing national strategy is the threat. The perception of a new threat should reasonably be expected to produce a new strategy, or at least some modifications in the previous design. As we know, events do not always follow the rational model, either immediately or over a period of time. Today, most Americans would agree that our relationships with the Soviet Union and the People's Republic of China have evolved from unquestioned hostility and animosity to a new pattern best exemplified by the 1972 visits of President Nixon to Moscow and Peking. Under these new circumstances, should the United States modify its strategy with respect to these former implacable enemies, or should it continue to do business as usual? The latter position is based on the premise that U.S. military strength and national strategy have induced this behavioral change on the part of the Communist powers. A continuation of the old, hardline approach may solidify gains and prevent a return to the condition of maximum tension. Another school of thought argues that this country should modify its stance in light of changing circumstances and should relax its guard on a *quid pro quo* basis. This new approach may lead to a further reduction in the level of hostility and a corresponding reduction in the world's inventory of armaments. At the present time, the Nixon Administration is still debating the issue.

Hanoi's strategic dilemma of the 1960s and 1970s is an example of the problems faced by a national command authority in analyzing a threat. In this case, the United States imperiled North Vietnam's goals in Southeast Asia. In dealing with American intervention, General Giap and his fellow strategists should not be accused of blindly following a preplanned battle strategy, whether or not it fit the unfolding situation. But one can ponder why they did not return to Phase I of the Maoist three-phase insurgency in the face of increasing military opposition in the late 1960s. According to this scenario, the foreigners would soon tire of garrison duty, probably because of mounting domestic discontent and unacceptable financial burdens. Then the insurgents could return to the battlefield and win an easy victory. Hanoi perceived the threat differently and for reasons no one seems to understand fully, although they probably relate to ideological and historical interpretations made by the North Vietnamese leadership. In the final analysis, threat perception is idiosyncratic—a verity which explains much of the tension and insecurity in the relations among nation-states.

A SEAMLESS WEB

The list of factors could also include ideology, geography, leadership, and so on. But hopefully the four primary variables discussed above make it clear that an efficacious strategy is not formulated in a vacuum and that its disciples cannot afford to practice scholasticism. As Michael Howard reminds us, strategy is best thought of as an art which has produced broad principles. These must be adapted to immediate and foreseeable situations. But they must never be allowed to evolve into dogmatic and inflexible proclamations, for, "even when these principles appear self-evident, it may be extraordinarily hard to apply them."[5]

Another point is that the variables outlined above do not exist independently. In fact, it is impossible for the student of national security policy to ascertain the beginning or end of this seamless web. To study the subject efficiently, one must make simplifying assumptions, a fundamental operation which is not always made clear, but which should be kept in mind throughout the reading of Part II. Graham Allison, whose work appears later in this volume, has theorized about a common practice of simplification, calling it the "rational policy model." Two basic assumptions underlie his model: the use of a logical reasoning process and a decision based on a cost-benefit analysis. This paradigm allows the strategic thinker to deal intelligently with a complex subject, albeit with more precision than is probably applicable. To put it another way, what is the exact relationship between the rational model and the decisionmaking process used by national command authorities? Consider the following caveat:

When war is seen as determined by rational laws, it is only logical to leave nothing to chance and to expect that the adversary will throw his hand in when he has been brought into a position where the game is rationally lost. The result of considering war as a mere science or at least of overvaluing the rational element in military affairs leads easily to the view that war can be decided quite as well on paper as on the battlefield.[6]

WHY THEORY?

Having defined strategy and discussed some of the variables that are germane to its formulation, it seems appropriate to address a common complaint of undergraduate students. In their opinion, courses spend too much time on theory and not enough on more practical or relevant matters. Recognizing the frequent validity of this accusation, the editors have exerted considerable effort to present only that theory which is essential for understanding national security policy. To have eliminated theory altogether would have been a disservice to the student for several reasons. First, the student needs a conceptual framework in order to organize and comprehend the immense amount of current-events data. Even more noteworthy, theory has an amazingly persistent way of affecting national policy. On occasion, policy originates from political or economic rationale, such as the Massive Retaliation doctrine of John Foster Dulles. It had no foundation in academic research *per se* and was almost immediately subjected to intense scholarly criticism. To a lesser extent, the same comment can be made about the Realistic Deterrence doctrine of President Nixon, although many of the bits and pieces can be culled from various scholarly publications. A celebrated case on the other side of the ledger is the *Foreign Affairs* article written by Mr. X (George Kennan) in 1947 in which he argued the case for the containment policy subsequently adopted by the Truman Administration. There are numerous other examples to be found of the interplay between scholarship and policymaking during the post–World War II years.[7] In essence, the argument is that a student must understand strategic theory and its corollaries if he is going to appreciate the present and anticipate the future.

STAGNATION IN STRATEGIC THEORY?

Some observers have suggested that the renaissance in strategic thinking which took place in the 1950s under the ominous shadow of nuclear weapons became stagnant in the 1960s

---

[5] Michael Howard, "The Classical Strategists," p. 48 of this volume.
[6] Felix Gilbert, "Machiavelli: The Renaissance of the Art of War," in *Makers of Modern Strategy*, p. 25.

[7] For an excellent account of this interplay, see Gray, *op. cit.*, pp. 111–29, and a rebuttal by Bernard Brodie, "Why Were We So (Strategically) Wrong?" *Foreign Policy*, 5 (Winter 1971):151–62.

because the international climate began to improve markedly after the Cuban missile crisis of 1962. Another explanation for the quiescent state is that all which needed to be said was published. The world will have to wait for new technology or additional intellectual digestion before the Schellings, Brodies, Kahns, Snyders, and the like are replaced by a new crop of original thinkers. A third point of view is that the academic, political, and military communities have not begun to explore together the labyrinth of strategy in the nuclear age. It is a basic premise of this book that the third point of view is essentially correct, especially in view of the May 1972 SALT Treaty and accompanying executive agreements. Hopefully, some of the readers of this book will accept and conquer the implicit challenge.

There are numerous examples to support the contention that we have only scratched the surface in thinking about strategy in the nuclear age. Contemplate the often repeated argument that the capability to win a total war has been replaced as a national goal by the capability to deter attacks. Academically, this may be a very rational hypothesis. On the other hand, deterrence may ultimately rest on the ability of a nation to *win* a nuclear war. This relationship between deterrence and war-fighting capability has been inadequately examined in the literature. During a period in which the Soviet Union has more than doubled its deployed ICBM strength so that by the early 1970s it has more ICBMs on station than the United States, the issue of parity should have been, and now must be, studied in greater depth and detail.[8] Furthermore, it is one thing to announce from the presidential pulpit a doctrine of Strategic Sufficiency and quite another to change the outlook of a people socialized in a very competitive environment which has institutionalized winning. In fact, deterrence may someday be accepted by world leaders as being more important than winning or fighting. A necessary precondition is the acceptance and use of this criterion by a country's citizens when they evaluate their leader's performance in office.

[8] For an excellent seminal effort, see Walter Slocombe, "The Political Implications of Strategic Parity," *Adelphi Papers*, no. 77, May 1971.

UNIVERSALITY

Another inadequately investigated aspect of strategic thinking during the postwar period is its lack of universality. Does strategic thinking apply to all nation-states—large or small, rich or poor, aggressive or passive, nuclear or conventional? Almost all published strategic thinking has been done by Western scholars, the majority of whom are citizens of the United States, Great Britain, and France. Very little original work has emanated from the Soviet Union. That which has come from China has dealt exclusively with "people's wars of national liberation." This state of affairs is deficient because the promulgated principles are culturally biased and generally are relevant only to relations among superpowers and their allies. Little of what Van Cleave, Snyder, Lambeth, and Gray have to say about general war in Chapter 3 is pertinent to the issues facing the leadership of the Third World, except tangentially as a result of superpower acts. Yet these nations and their long-suffering people can and do experience total war, with all of its destructive ramifications, using only conventional weapons. In other words, to derive universal maxims, the scholar must take into account nonsuperpowers and their security dilemmas as well. In addition, if strategic theory is insufficiently catholic, one must question whether or not it is adequate for the needs of American decisionmakers whose problems frequently involve worldwide parameters.

MILITARY THINKING

Many commentators have noted inquisitively that the American military establishment has produced very few strategic thinkers who compare to the greats like Clausewitz, Jomini, and Liddell-Hart—all of whom made the military a career. With the exception of General Maxwell Taylor, the prominent American strategists since the end of World War II have been civilians. No attempt will be made in this essay to explain why this is so, but the normative view that it should not be so will be briefly argued.

Career military men should contribute to the strategic debate along with individuals who are proficient in related fields of study because strategic thinking cannot be comprehensive unless it is interdisciplinary in nature. The only one who can adequately present the military variable is a military man schooled in the art of managing the application of force. On the other hand, it is mandatory that the national decision-maker be exposed to the views of economists, politicians, moralists, and so on. When the EXCOM deliberated over the proper American response to the placement of Soviet IRBMs in Cuba, only a professional military man could advise President Kennedy as to the feasibility of a "surgical airstrike" to destroy the offensive threats. But the need for a military contribution goes beyond the staff meetings, interagency panels, and other institutional ways the military point of view is normally interjected into the policy process. It should be represented in the strategic literature because of the unique insights which professional military men possess. Too often other scholars have attempted to articulate the military view, and with less than satisfactory results.

The RAND Corporation has produced many outstanding studies of strategic issues since 1946. This success, in no small way, is attributable to the interface and interchange these brilliant scholars have enjoyed with the military. Ideas, frequently born in military minds, were nurtured and matured by civilian pencils. This is one solution to the problem of the military contribution to the debate. But it is not the only one, nor is it necessarily the optimum one. More and more military men are earning advanced degrees in the social sciences. Many of them are publishing while on active duty, and many will continue to study the issues after retirement. A casual perusal of this body of literature should convince the skeptic that very few "military minds" are in evidence, whatever that pejorative term really means. The articles by O'Neill and Bradford in Chapter 5 of this vol-

ume clearly represent views that are firmly in the mainstream of modern academic research. The latter article, especially, provides the debaters with insights that could come only from one who is a professional manager of force. This nascent community of military writers, founded by General George Lincoln and continued by Colonel Amos Jordan at the United States Military Academy, Colonels Wesley Posvar and Richard Rosser at the Air Force Academy, and Professor John Probert at the Naval Academy, must continue to grow so that the field of strategic inquiry can be truly comprehensive in its analyses and conclusions.

OVERVIEW

In organizing Part II, the editors have been forced to make some very difficult and somewhat arbitrary choices. They have included several classical works, such as Snyder's discussion of the differences between deterrence and defense; Schelling's views on bargaining as it applies to limiting warfare, and Kaufmann's description of McNamara's early years in the Pentagon. But the majority of the selections are the most current writings on strategy and the use of force. Some of the authors are public figures; others are renowned scholars contributing new insights—men like Osgood and Halperin. Finally, a large number of articles are written by young scholars who are just beginning to make their presence known and felt among strategic thinkers. This group includes Colin Gray, Ben Lambeth, Jean Baechler, and Robert Moss. Two other members of this group —Bard O'Neill and Zeb Bradford—are also professional military officers. Hopefully, these young scholars will continue to write, publish, and clarify the enormously complex issues that constitute this intellectual discipline.

CHAPTER 2

The Evolution of Strategy

THE CLASSICAL STRATEGISTS

MICHAEL HOWARD

Strategy is an art, involving the outline of broad principles, and the unique factor in strategy is the element of force. Howard uses a British perspective to trace the development of strategy from World War II to the present. The essential concepts for study include deterrence, counterforce, countervalue, second-strike forces, multipolarity, limited war, revolutionary war, and the doctrine of indirect strategy. He stresses that the quality of military strategy is strictly dependent upon the dual understanding of international relations and weapons technology. Michael Howard is a Fellow in Higher Defense Studies, All Souls College, Oxford.

I

It may help to begin with a definition of "classical" strategy. Liddell-Hart has provided us with one which is as good as any, and better than most: "the art of distributing and applying military means to fulfil the ends of policy."[1] Whether this remains adequate in the nuclear age is a matter of some controversy. André Beaufre, for example, has adumbrated the concept of an "indirect strategy," to be considered later, which embraces more than purely military means;[2] but even he still gives as his basic definition of the term "the art of the dialectic of two opposing wills using force to resolve their dispute."[3] It is this element of *force* which distinguishes "strategy" from the purposeful planning in other branches of human activity to which the term is often loosely applied. When other elements, such as economic pressure, propaganda, subversion, and diplomacy, are combined with force, these elements may also be considered as "strategic"; but to apply this adjective to activities unconnected with the use, or threatened use, of force would be to broaden it to such an extent that it would be necessary to find another word to cover the original meaning of the term as defined by Liddell-Hart, and as considered in this paper.

It need hardly be said that students of strategy have generally assumed that military force is a necessary element in international affairs. Before World War I, there were few who questioned even whether it was desirable. After 1918, many regretted its necessity and saw their function as being to ensure that it should be used as economically, and as rarely, as possible. After 1945, an even greater proportion devoted themselves to examining not how wars should be fought but how they could be prevented, and the study of strategy merged into that of arms control, disarmament, and peace-keeping. There the "classical strategists" found themselves working with scholars of a different kind: men who believed that the element of force was *not* a necessary part of inter-

[1] B. H. Liddell-Hart, *Strategy: The Indirect Approach* (London: Faber, 1967), p. 335.
[2] André Beaufre, *An Introduction to Strategy* (London: Faber, 1965), *passim*, esp. pp. 107–30.
[3] *Ibid.*, p. 22.

Reprinted by permission and with minor changes from Problems of Modern Strategy, *pt. 1, Adelphi Papers, no. 54, February 1969, pp. 18–32. Copyright © 1969 by the Institute for Strategic Studies, 18 Adam Street, London, WC2.*

national intercourse, but could be eliminated by an application of the methodology of the social sciences. This paper, therefore, will concern itself solely with the thinkers who assume that the element of force exists in international relations, that it can and must be intelligently controlled, but that it cannot be totally eliminated. Further, it is confined to the men who have primarily used the methodology of history or traditional political science, though it includes such figures as Schelling and Morgenstern, who have made considerable contributions in the newer disciplines as well.

The art[4] of strategy remains one of such complexity that even the greatest contributors to its study have been able to do little more than outline broad principles, principles which nevertheless must often be discarded in practice if the circumstances are inappropriate, and which must never be allowed to harden into dogma. Even when these principles appear self-evident, it may be extraordinarily hard to apply them. In World War II "command of the sea," as advocated by Mahan, and "command of the air," as advocated by Douhet, were certainly necessary preliminaries to the military victory of the Western powers. The problem was how to obtain them with resources on which equally urgent calls were being made for other purposes. The academic strategist could not help the Chiefs of Staff much, for example, in deciding how to allot a limited number of long-range aircraft among the conflicting needs of the strategic offensive against Germany, the war against German submarines, interdiction bombing of German railways, the requirements of the Pacific theater, and support for guerrilla activities in occupied Europe. Operational research and systems analysis could simplify the problem without ever eliminating it. In the last resort the quality termed by Blackett "the conventional military wisdom"[5] remained the basic factor in making the decision; and that decision was determined by what could be done rather than by what ideally should be done. The military commander is always primarily conscious of the constraints under which he operates, in

terms both of information and of resources. He is therefore likely to be impatient with the advice of the academic strategist, which may appear to him either platitudinous or impracticable. His decisions must be based at best on educated guesses.

But the academic strategist does have one vital role to play. He can see that the guesses *are* educated. He may not accompany the commander to battle, as Clausewitz expressed it, but he forms his mind in the schoolroom, whether the commander realizes it or not. In World War II the Allied High Command did operate in accordance with certain very definite strategic principles. It is tempting to link these principles with the names of specific theorists: General Marshall's desire for concentration against the enemy army with Clausewitz; General Brooke's desire to enforce dispersal on the enemy with Liddell-Hart; the doctrine of the Allied air forces with Douhet. It is tempting, but difficult to prove. The name of Douhet was virtually unknown in the Royal Air Force.[6] The most eminent thinkers sometimes do no more than codify and clarify conclusions which arise so naturally from the circumstances of the time that they occur simultaneously to those obscurer, but more influential, figures who write training manuals and teach in service colleges. And sometimes strategic doctrines may be widely held which cannot be attributed to any specific thinkers, but which represent simply the consensus of opinion among a large number of professionals who had undergone a formative common experience.

Of this kind were the doctrines which were generally held in the armed forces of the Western world in the mid-1940s as a result of the experiences of World War II. It was considered, first, that the mobilization of superior resources, together with the maintenance of civilian *morale* at home, was a necessary condition for victory, a condition requiring a substantial domestic "mobilization base" in terms of industrial potential and trained manpower. It was agreed that, in order to deploy these resources effectively, it was necessary to secure command of the sea and command of the air. It was agreed that surface and air operations

---

[4] The term seems appropriate. Strategy deals with too many imponderables to merit the description "science." It remains, as Voltaire described it two hundred years ago, "murderous and conjectural."

[5] P. M. S. Blackett, *Studies of War* (London: Oliver & Boyd, 1962), p. 128.

[6] Sir John Slessor, "Air Power and the Future of War," *Journal of the Royal United Service Institution*, August 1954.

were totally interdependent. And it was agreed that strategic air power could do much— though *how* much remained a matter of controversy—to weaken the capacity of the adversary to resist. The general concept of war remained as it had been since the days of Napoleon: the contest of armed forces to obtain a position of such superiority that the victorious power would be in a position to impose its political will. And it was generally assumed that in the future, as in the immediate past, this would still be a very long-drawn-out process indeed.

II

The advent of nuclear weapons, in the eyes of the layman, transformed the entire nature of war. But certain eminent professionals suggested that they made remarkably little difference, at least in a conflict between two powers the size of the United States and the Soviet Union. These weapons obviously would make it possible to inflict with far greater rapidity the kind of damage by which the strategic bombing offensive had crippled Germany and Japan. But the stockpiles of bombs were small—how small is still not known. The bombs were vulnerable to interception, and they had to operate from bases which had to be protected by land armies, which in turn would have to be supplied by sea. All this was pointed out to the general public by, among others, two scientists with long experience in military planning—the British professor P. M. S. Blackett and the American Dr. Vannevar Bush. Blackett, on the basis of careful calculations from unclassified material, concluded in 1948 that "a long-range atomic bombing offensive against a large continental Power is not likely to be by itself decisive within the next five years."[7] Bush, a figure closely associated with the American military establishment, described in 1949 a conflict barely distinguishable from the last.

The opening phases would be in the air soon followed by sea and land action. Great fleets of bombers would be in action at once, but this would be the opening phase only . . . They could undoubtedly devastate the cities and the war potential of the enemy and its satellites, but it is highly

doubtful if they could at once stop the march of great land armies. To overcome them would require a great national effort, and the marshaling of all our strength. The effort to keep the seas open would be particularly hazardous, because of modern submarines, and severe efforts would be needed to stop them at the source. Such a war would be a contest of the old form, with variations and new techniques of one sort or another. But, except for greater use of the atomic bomb, it would not differ much from the last struggle.[8]

It was along these lines that planning went forward when the framework of the North Atlantic Treaty Organization was established at the end of the 1940s. Such ideas were legitimate deductions from the then "state of the art." NATO planners had to think what could be done with the weapons they had available, not with those which might or might not be developed in ten years' time. But many scientists and academic strategists, particularly in the United States, were already thinking ahead. Because their views appeared to have no immediate relevance, or because of the pressures of interservice politics, they had little immediate influence on Western policy; and they were usually set out in papers or articles which enjoyed only a limited circulation within the academic world.[9] An adequate account of these seminal discussions would require a separate paper. We can, however, salvage and admire the shrewd insights shown by two thinkers who had already established their reputation in the prenuclear era: Bernard Brodie and Sir Basil Liddell-Hart. Both of them, in works published in 1946, made prophecies which twenty years later were to be commonplaces of strategic thinking.

In the final chapter of *The Revolution in Warfare*,[10] Liddell-Hart suggested that, failing

---

[7] P. M. S. Blackett, *The Military and Political Consequences of Atomic Energy* (London: The Turnstile Press, 1948), p. 56.

[8] Vannevar Bush, *Modern Arms and Free Men* (New York: Simon and Schuster, 1949), pp. 115–16.

[9] As, for example, Jacob Viner's paper on "The Implications of the Atomic Bomb for East-West Relations," the influence of which is acknowledged by Brodie and many others. Albert Wohlstetter gave an impromptu account, at the ISS Conference, of the main lines along which these discussions ran. Some account will also be found in Richard G. Hewlett and Oscar E. Anderson, *The New World* (vol. 1 of *The History of the United States Atomic Energy Commission* [University Park: Pennsylvania State University, 1962]), and in the early issues of the *Bulletin of the Atomic Scientists*.

[10] B. H. Liddell-Hart, *The Revolution in Warfare* (London: Faber, 1946), p. 87.

disarmament, attempts should be made "to revive a code of limiting rules for warfare—based
on a realistic view that wars are likely to occur
again, and that the limitation of their destructiveness is to everybody's interest." "Fear of
atomic war," he wrote, "might lead to indirect
methods of aggression, infiltration taking civil
forms as well as military, to which nuclear retaliation would be irrelevant. Armed forces
would still be required to fight "sub-atomic
war," but the emphasis should be on their
mobility, both tactical and strategic."

The great armies of the past would be irrelevant to the needs of the nuclear age. Liddell-
Hart did not, at this stage, consider the problems
and contradictions of limited war, including the
possibility which emerged fifteen years later,
that it might be necessary to have large conventional forces precisely in order to keep war
limited.

Neither did he explore the implications and
requirements of deterrence. Brodie, however,
with his collaborators in the Yale Institute of
International Studies' publication *The Absolute
Weapon*, did exactly this, and with remarkable
prescience. Much that he wrote was to become
unquestionably valid only with the development of thermonuclear weapons, but his insights were nonetheless remarkable. He rejected, for example, the whole concept of a
"mobilization base." "The idea," he wrote,
"which must be driven home above all else is
that a military establishment which is expected
to fight on after the nation has undergone
atomic bomb attack must be prepared to fight
with the men already mobilized and with the
equipment already in the arsenals."[11] More important, he outlined the concept of a stable
balance of nuclear forces.

If the atomic bomb can be used without fear of
substantial retaliation in kind, it will clearly encourage aggression. So much the more reason,
therefore, to take all possible steps to assure that
multilateral possession of the bomb, should that
prove inevitable, be attended by arrangements to
make as nearly certain as possible that the aggressor who uses the bomb will have it used against
him. . . .
    . . . Thus, the first and most vital step in any
American programme for the age of atomic bombs
is to take measures to guarantee to ourselves in

case of attack the possibility of retaliation in kind.
The writer in making that statement is not for the
moment concerned about who will *win* the next
war in which atomic bombs are used. Thus far the
chief purpose of our military establishment has
been to win wars. From now on its chief purpose
must be to avert them. It can have almost no other
useful purpose.[12]

Not until thermonuclear weapons had been
developed and the Soviet Union had shown itself to possess an intercontinental delivery system did the U.S. Joint Chiefs of Staff accept
Brodie's logic; it is significant, however, that
shortly after the publication of this work Brodie
joined the newly formed RAND Corporation,
where with the support of the U.S. Air Force
the full implications and requirements of his
ideas, and others current in the United States
academic community, were to be exhaustively
studied. The first Western government to adopt
the concept of "deterrence" as the basis of its
military policy was that of the United Kingdom
in 1952; very largely thanks to the thinking of
Marshal of the Royal Air Force Sir John Slessor, the then Chairman of the Chiefs of Staff.[13]

Giving a late account of his stewardship at
Chatham House in 1953, Slessor was to say:

The aim of Western policy is not primarily to be
ready to win a war with the world in ruins—
though we must be as ready as possible to do that
if it is forced upon us by accident or miscalculation. It is the prevention of war. The bomber holds
out to us the greatest, perhaps the only hope of
that. It is the great deterrent.[14]

This doctrine of "the great deterrent" was to
unleash within the United Kingdom a debate
which foreshadowed that set off in the United
States by the comparable "New Look" strategy
which Mr. Dulles was formally to unveil there
in January 1954. Among its earliest and ablest
critics were the men who, four years later, were
to be primarily responsible for the foundation
of the Institute for Strategic Studies: Rear Admiral Sir Anthony Buzzard, Mr. Richard Goold-

---

[11] Bernard Brodie, ed., *The Absolute Weapon* (New
York: Harcourt, Brace, 1946), p. 89.

[12] *Ibid.*, pp. 75–76. He did not, however, deal with
the problem of vulnerability of retaliatory forces, and
the consequent dependence of stability on an effective
second-strike capability.
[13] Richard N. Rosecrance, *The Defense of the
Realm* (New York and London: Columbia University
Press, 1967), p. 159.
[14] "The Place of the Bomber in British Policy," reprinted in *The Great Deterrent* (London: Cassell,
1957), p. 123.

Adams, Mr. Denis Healey, and Professor P. M. S. Blackett. In its public presentation by ministers and senior officers, the doctrine of "massive retaliation" provided its critics in England with an even easier target than it did in the United States. No official distinction was made between the use of Bomber Command as a first-strike force in response to a Soviet "conventional" invasion of Western Europe and as a second-strike force to retaliate after a Soviet nuclear attack. In the face of the growing strength of Soviet nuclear strike forces, the first role appeared to lack political, the second technical, credibility. Liddell-Hart had already pointed out in 1950 that defense against nuclear weapons would be credible only if accompanied by massive civil defense measures of a kind which no government showed any sign of being prepared to carry out.[15] Indeed, Britain's military leaders at first assumed that the civilian population might be induced to grin and bear the nuclear holocaust as cheerfully as they had endured the German blitz. The inhabitants of areas which contained no protected installations, suggested Slessor, "must steel themselves to risks and take what may come to them, knowing that thereby they are playing as essential a part in the country's defence as the pilot in the fighter or the man behind the gun."[16] This attitude presumably remained the basis of British official thinking until the acquisition of the Polaris missile system gave the United Kingdom a second-strike weapon which was technically, if not politically, credible. The validity of this thesis, however, gave rise to widespread doubts, and not only among the members of the Campaign for Nuclear Disarmament. In a famous lecture to the Royal United Service Institution in November 1959, after Mr. Duncan Sandys had, in two Defense White Papers, laid yet greater stress on the importance of "the deterrent," Lieutenant General Sir John Cowley was to ask a question unusual for a senior serving officer:

The choice of death or dishonour is one which has always faced the professional fighting man, and there must be no doubt in his mind what his answer must be. He chooses death for himself so that

his country may survive, or on a grander scale so that the principles for which he is fighting may survive. Now we are facing a somewhat different situation, when the reply is not to be given by individuals but by countries as a whole. Is it right for the Government of a country to choose complete destruction of the population rather than some other alternative, however unpleasant that alternative may be?[17]

As a coherent theory of strategy in the traditional sense, the doctrine of deterrence by the threat of massive retaliation, in the simple form in which it was set out by the British and American governments in the early 1950s, is not easy to defend, and its exponents tended at times to use the vocabulary of exhortation rather than that of rational argument in their attempts to justify it. But three points should be noted if we are to appreciate their standpoint. First, the British Chiefs of Staff from the beginning saw Bomber Command as a supplement to, rather than a substitute for, the United States Strategic Air Command, with its task being to strike at targets of particular significance for the United Kingdom. Its strategic utility and its credibility as a deterrent were thus to be judged within the context of the Western deterrent force as a whole.[18]

Second, it was an attempt, like the American "New Look" two years later, to solve the problem—and one far more difficult for the United Kingdom than for the United States—of maintaining an effective military force in a peacetime economy. The burden of rearmament assumed in 1950 had proved not only economically crippling but politically unacceptable; and, since the political objective of the United Kingdom was the maintenance, *virgo intacta*, of the *status quo* in Europe, a policy which imposed the maximum penalty for *any* violation of that *status quo* was not so irrational as it appeared. For the United Kingdom, not one inch of Western Europe could be considered negotiable.

Third, as British officials repeatedly said later in the decade, "the Great Deterrent" existed not to fight but to deter war: "If it is used, it

[15] B. H. Liddell-Hart, *The Defence of the West* (London: Cassell, 1950), pp. 97, 134, 139, 140.
[16] Sir John Slessor, *Strategy for the West* (London: Cassell, 1954), p. 108.
[17] Lt. Gen. Sir John Cowley, "Future Trends in Warfare," *Journal of the Royal United Service Institution,* February 1960, p. 13.
[18] This, of course, begs the whole question so carefully examined by Stephen Maxwell in Adelphi Paper No. 50: *Rationality in Deterrence* (London: ISS).

will have failed." This argument was open to the rejoinder that a strategy which was not militarily viable was not politically credible, but this rejoinder is by no means conclusive. The concept of "deterrence" takes us out of the familiar field of military strategy into the un-mapped, if not unfamiliar, territory of political bargaining, where total rationality does not in-variably reign supreme. Schelling and others were only then beginning their studies of "the strategy of conflict"; but even without the help of game-theory techniques, it could be reason-ably argued that, even if there were only one chance in a hundred that a political move would really be met by the threatened nuclear response, that chance would be an effective de-terrent to any responsible statesman.[19] "The most that the advocates of the deterrent policy have ever claimed for it," said Slessor in 1955, "is that it will deter a potential aggressor from undertaking total war as an instrument of pol-icy, as Hitler did in 1939, or from embarking upon a course of international action which ob-viously involves a serious risk of total war, as the Austrian Government did in 1914."[20]

Certainly the British advocates of the "deter-rent policy" in the 1950s did not underrate the continuing importance of conflicts which would *not* be deterred by nuclear weapons. Liddell-Hart repeatedly pointed out that nuclear stale-mate would encourage local and indirect ag-gression which could be countered only by conventional forces, a lesson which British armed forces, tied down in operations from Cyprus to Malaya, had no need to learn. Faced with the double burden of deterring total war and fighting small ones, it was natural enough for British strategists to adopt the doctrine later termed "minimal deterrence." This was stated with uncompromising clarity by Blackett in 1956:

I think we should act as if atomic and hydrogen bombs have abolished total war and concentrate our efforts on working out how few atomic bombs and their carriers are required to keep it abolished. In the next few years I see the problem not as how many atomic bombs we can afford but as how few we need. For every hundred million pounds spent on offensive and defensive preparations for global war, which almost certainly will not happen, is so much less for limited and colonial wars, which well may.[21]

British strategic thinkers in fact—even Sles-sor after his retirement—tended to take the existence of stable deterrence very much for granted. In view of the highly classified nature of all information relating to Bomber Command and the absence of any serious intercourse at that time between Ministry of Defence officials and free-lance strategic thinkers, this was not altogether surprising. It enabled them to con-centrate not only on problems of limited wars (Liddell-Hart) but on graduated deterrence and restraints on war (Buzzard) and, in the atmosphere of détente which followed the Geneva summit meeting of 1955, on "disen-gagement," disarmament, and arms control (Blackett and Healey). When a few years later American thinkers questioned the validity of the doctrine of "minimal deterrence," they evoked from Blackett a forceful rejoinder[22] in which he expressed the fear that to depart from such a policy would only lead to an endless and increasing arms race. But by the end of the 1950s it was becoming clear that any doctrine of deterrence depended for its validity on tech-nical calculations which stretched far beyond the orthodox boundaries of strategic thinking, and on which it was difficult for thinkers who did not enjoy access to the facilities available in the United States to pronounce with any degree of authority.

III

Within the United States the controversy was now well under way. It had been got off to an excellent start by Mr. John Foster Dulles, whose definition of the doctrine of "massive retaliation" in January 1954 had been far more precise and dogmatic than the statements to the same effect which had emanated from Whitehall during the past two years. This, it

---

[19] Rosecrance, *op. cit.*, pp. 160–61.
[20] Sir John Slessor, lecture at Oxford University, April 1955, reprinted in *The Great Deterrent*, p. 181.

[21] P. M. S. Blackett, *Atomic Energy and East-West Relations* (Cambridge: Cambridge University Press, 1956), p. 100.
[22] P. M. S. Blackett, "Critique of Some Contem-porary Defence Thinking." First published in *Encoun-ter* in 1961, this article is reprinted in *Studies of War*, pp. 128–46. See also Blackett's dissenting note in Alastair Buchan, *NATO in the 1960's* (London: Chatto & Windus, 1960).

will be remembered, announced the intention of the United States administration to place its military dependence "primarily upon a great capacity to retaliate, instantly, by means and at places of our own choosing," thereby gaining "more basic security at less cost."[23] The rationale behind this policy was of course political and economic: American weariness with the Korean War, and the desire of the Republican party to return to financial "normalcy" after what they regarded as the ruinous spending spree of the last four years.[24] It should perhaps be judged not as a coherent strategic doctrine but as a political expedient—or even as a diplomatic communication, itself a maneuver in a politico-military strategy of "deterrence." By these criteria the policy must be pronounced effective. But its logical fallacies were too glaring to be overlooked. The assumption of American invulnerability to a pre-emptive or a retaliatory strike was unconvincing in the year in which the Soviet Union first unveiled her intercontinental bombers. Even when that assumption had been justifiable four years earlier, American nuclear monopoly had not deterred the Korean conflict; and in that very year American nuclear power was to prove irrelevant to the conflict in Indochina. These, and other points, were rapidly made with force and relish by Democratic politicians and sympathizers out of office, by academic specialists, and by members of the armed services, which were being cut back to provide greater resources for the Strategic Air Command.

There has perhaps never been a strategic controversy which has not been fueled by political passions and service interests. It is entirely understandable, and for our purposes quite unimportant, that the U.S. Air Force should have sought every argument to justify the doctrine of massive retaliation while the U.S. Army powerfully supported its opponents. What is significant, however, is that the latter included every strategic thinker of any consequence in the United States; and the failure of the present writer to find any serious academic defense of the doctrine may not be entirely due

to unfamiliarity with the literature. Among the first critics was that pioneer of deterrence theory, Bernard Brodie, who published in November 1954 one of the earliest analyses of the place of "limited war" in national policy;[25] but the first really formidable public broadside was fired by a group of scholars at the Princeton Center of International Studies under the leadership of William W. Kaufmann, in a collection of essays published in 1956 under the innocuous-sounding title *Military Policy and National Security*. In this work Kaufmann himself stressed the need for the United States to have the capacity to meet, and therefore deter, Communist aggression at every level;[26] that "spectrum of deterrence," in fact, was to be developed by Mr. Robert McNamara, not without some assistance from Dr. Kaufmann himself, when he became Secretary of Defense four years later. In the same work Dr. Roger Hilsman discussed the actual conduct of nuclear war, both making the distinction between counterforce and countervalue targets in total war, and considering the tactics of war with nuclear weapons fought on the ground.[27] Professor Klaus Knorr gave one of the earliest published estimates of the kind of civil defense policy which might be feasible and necessary if the United States were really to employ the kind of nuclear strategy implied in Mr. Dulles' statement.[28] Finally, Mr. Kaufmann emphasized the necessity for ensuring that military force be tailored to the actual requirements of foreign policy, a point which was to be expanded more fully in two important books published the following year.

These were Dr. Robert Osgood's study *Limited War* and Dr. Henry Kissinger's *Nuclear Weapons and Foreign Policy*.[29] Neither

23 Text in the *New York Times*, January 13, 1954.

24 See the analysis " 'The New Look' of 1953," by Glenn H. Snyder, in Warner R. Schilling, Paul Y. Hammond, and Glenn H. Snyder, *Strategy, Policy, and Defense Budgets* (New York: Columbia University Press, 1962), pp. 379–524.

25 Bernard Brodie, "Unlimited Weapons and Limited War," *The Reporter*, November 18, 1954. For an indispensable annotated bibliography of the whole controversy, see Morton H. Halperin, *Limited War in the Nuclear Age* (New York and London: John Wiley, 1963).

26 William W. Kaufmann, ed., *Military Policy and National Security* (Princeton: Princeton University Press, 1956), pp. 28, 38, 257.

27 *Ibid.*, pp. 53–57, 60–72.

28 *Ibid.*, pp. 75–101.

29 Robert E. Osgood, *Limited War: The Challenge to American Strategy* (Chicago: University of Chicago Press, 1957); Henry A. Kissinger, *Nuclear Weapons and Foreign Policy* (New York: Houghton Mifflin, 1957).

author had any significant experience of military operations or operational research. Their intellectual training was in the disciplines of history and political science. But with the shift of strategic thinking from the problem of waging war to that of its prevention, this background was at least as relevant as any more directly concerned with military affairs. Both analyzed the traditional rigidity of the American attitude toward war and peace, contrasting it with the flexibility of Communist theory and, as they saw it, practice. Both emphasized the irrelevance of strategic nuclear weapons to the conduct of foreign policy in peripheral areas. Both stressed, as had Kaufmann, the need to provide the appropriate forces for the fighting of limited wars; and both considered that tactical nuclear weapons should be regarded as appropriate for this purpose—a view shared by Mr. Dulles himself[30] and by the Joint Chiefs of Staff under the chairmanship of Admiral Radford.

Osgood based his belief in the need to use nuclear weapons in limited wars largely on the difficulty of preparing troops to fight with both nuclear and conventional weapons.[31] Kissinger, whose study developed out of panel discussions at the Council on Foreign Relations in which a number of professional soldiers took part, went into the question more deeply, discussing both the possible *modus operandi* of tactical nuclear forces and the kind of limitations which might be agreed to by two belligerents anxious not to allow their military confrontation to get out of hand.[32] In doing so he aligned himself with the views of Rear Admiral Sir Anthony Buzzard, who was energetically canvassing before British audiences both the value of tactical nuclear weapons in making possible graduated deterrence at acceptable cost and the feasibility of negotiating limitations on the conduct of war.[33] But Buzzard's views were hotly contested in England. Slessor gave them general support, but Liddell-Hart was highly skeptical (believing the capabilities of conventional forces to be

unnecessarily underrated), and Blackett, after some hesitation, came out flatly against them.[34] In the United States the same controversy blew up. Brodie, writing in 1959, was prepared to admit only that there might be *some* circumstances in which tactical nuclear weapons might be appropriate, but considered that "the conclusion that nuclear weapons *must* be used in limited wars has been reached by too many people, too quickly, on the basis of too little analysis of the problem." Schelling the following year suggested that the break between conventional and nuclear weapons was one of the rare "natural" distinctions which made tacit bargaining possible in limiting war.[35] By this time Kissinger himself had had second thoughts, and agreed that, though tactical nuclear weapons were a necessary element in the spectrum of deterrence, they could not take the place of conventional forces.[36] Within a year Mr. McNamara was to take the debate into the council chambers of NATO, where the advocates of tactical nuclear weapons had already found staunch allies among officials grimly conscious of the unpopularity and expense of large conventional forces. Throughout the 1960s the debate was to continue, in three major languages, about the place of tactical nuclear weapons in the defense of Europe.[37] Only the sheer exhaustion of the participants keeps it from continuing still.

It will be seen that the major American contributions to strategic thinking published in 1956–1967 were distinguished by two main

---

[30] J. F. Dulles, "Challenge and Response in United States' Policy," *Foreign Affairs*, October 1957.

[31] Osgood, *op. cit.*, p. 258.

[32] Kissinger, *op. cit.*, pp. 174–202.

[33] Anthony Buzzard *et al.*, *On Limiting Atomic War* (London: Royal Institute of International Affairs, 1956); and Anthony Buzzard, "The H-Bomb: Massive Retaliation or Graduated Deterrence," *International Affairs*, 1956.

[34] Sir John Slessor, "Total or Limited War?" in *The Great Deterrent*, pp. 262–84; Liddell-Hart, *Deterrent or Defence: A Fresh Look at the West's Military Position* (London: Stevens, 1960), pp. 74–81; Blackett, "Nuclear Weapons and Defence," *International Affairs*, October 1958.

[35] Bernard Brodie, *Strategy in the Missile Age* (Princeton: Princeton University Press, 1959), p. 330; Thomas C. Schelling, *The Strategy of Conflict* (Cambridge: Harvard University Press, 1960), pp. 262–66. But the debate continued. Brodie, in *Escalation and the Nuclear Option* (Princeton: Princeton University Press, 1966), was to argue strongly against what had by then become known as the "firebreak" theory, and to emphasize the deterrent value of tactical nuclear weapons.

[36] Henry A. Kissinger, *The Necessity for Choice* (London: Chatto & Windus, 1960), pp. 81–98.

[37] The literature is enormous, but three outstanding contributions are Helmuth Schmidt, *Verteidigung oder Vergelrung* (Stuttgart, 1961); Alastair Buchan and Philip Windsor, *Arms and Stability in Europe* (London: Chatto & Windus, 1963); and Raymond Aron, *Le Grand Débat* (Paris: Calmann-Lévy, 1963).

characteristics. They attempted to reintegrate military power with foreign policy, stressing, in contradiction to the doctrine of massive retaliation, the need for "a strategy of options." And they tended to be the work of academic institutions: Kaufmann's group at Princeton; Osgood from Chicago; Kissinger working with the Council on Foreign Relations. Their authors were thus concerned less with the technicalities of defense (Hilsman at Princeton, a former West Pointer, was an interesting exception) than with its political objectives. Over what those objectives should be, they had no quarrel with John Foster Dulles. Although British thinkers, like British statesmen, had been exploring possibilities of détente ever since 1954, in the United States the cold war was still blowing at full blast. The Soviet Union was still, in the works of these scholars, considered to be implacably aggressive, pursuing its objective of conquest in every quarter of the globe, its machinations visible behind every disturbance which threatened world stability. As Gordon Dean put it in his introduction to Kissinger's book, "Abhorrent of war but unwilling to accept gradual Russian enslavement of other peoples around the world, which we know will eventually lead to our own enslavement, we are forced to adopt a posture that, despite Russian military capabilities and despite their long-range intentions, freedom shall be preserved to us."[38] The strategy of options which they urged had as its object not the reduction of tensions but the provision of additional and appropriate weapons to deal with a subtle adversary who might otherwise get under the American guard.

IV

Two years later, in 1959–1960, the major works on strategy in the United States showed a slight but perceptible change of emphasis. As it happened, the most significant of these were the work not of full-time academics in universities but of men drawn from a wide variety of disciplines—physicists, engineers, mathematicians, economists, and systems analysts—who had been working in defense research institutes on classified information, particularly at RAND Corporation. As a result they analyzed the tech-

nical problems of deterrence with an expertise which earlier works had naturally lacked. These problems appeared all the more urgent to the general public after the 1957 launching of the Sputnik satellite, which revealed the full extent of the challenge which the United States had to meet from Soviet technology. For the first time in its history the United States felt itself in danger of physical attack, and the question of civil defense, which had for some time agitated academic specialists, became one of public concern. Yet at the same time there was beginning to emerge in some quarters a new attitude toward the Soviet Union. This saw in that power not simply a threat to be countered but a partner whose collaboration was essential if nuclear war through accident or miscalculation was to be avoided. It recognized that Soviet policy and intentions might have certain elements in common with those of the United States, and that its leaders faced comparable problems. This attitude was by no means general. For scholars such as Robert Strausz-Hupé and William Kintner the conflict still resembled that between the Archangels Michael and Lucifer rather than that between Tweedledum and Tweedledee. But the concept of a common interest between antagonists and a joint responsibility for the avoidance of nuclear holocaust became increasingly evident after the new administration came into power in 1961.[39]

The view which commanded growing support among American strategic thinkers was, therefore, that the "balance of terror" was a great deal less stable than had hitherto been assumed, but that, if it could be stabilized (which involved a certain reciprocity from the Soviet Union), there would be reasonable prospects of lasting peace. The technical instability of the balance was discussed by Albert Wohlstetter in the famous *Foreign Affairs* article which described, on the basis of his classified studies at RAND Corporation, the full requirements of an invulnerable retaliatory force: a stable "steady-state" peacetime operation within feasible budgets; the capacity to survive enemy attacks; to make and communicate the decision to retaliate; to reach enemy territory, penetrate all defenses, and destroy the target; with each

[38] Kissinger, *Nuclear Weapons*, p. vii.

[39] For an analysis of the various attitudes of American strategic thinkers to the question of détente, see Robert A. Levine, *The Arms Debate* (Cambridge: Harvard University Press, 1963), *passim*.

phase demanding technical preparations of very considerable complexity and expense.[40]

The following year the mathematician Oskar Morgenstern was to suggest, in *The Question of National Defense*, that the best answer to the problem as defined by Wohlstetter, and the best safeguard against accidental war, was to be found in the development of seaborne missiles; and that it would be in the best interests of the United States if such a system could be developed by both sides. "In view of modern technology of speedy weapons-delivery from any point on earth to any other," he wrote, "it is in the interest of the United States for Russia to have an invulnerable retaliatory force and vice versa."[41] Whether Morgenstern reached this conclusion entirely through applying the game-theory, in which he had made so outstanding a reputation, is not entirely clear. Professor Thomas Schelling, who also brought the discipline of game-theory to bear on strategy, reached the same conclusion at approximately the same time;[42] but even by cruder calculations its validity seemed evident, and the concept of a "stable balance" was central to Bernard Brodie's *Strategy in the Missile Age*, which also appeared in 1959.[43] This study pulled together all the threads of strategic thinking of the past five years and set them in their historical context. Brodie reduced the requirements of strategy in the missile age to

three: an invulnerable retaliatory force; "a real and substantial capability for coping with local and limited aggression by local application of force"; and provision for saving life "on a vast scale" if the worst came to the worst.[44] About how, if the worst did come to the worst, nuclear war should be conducted, he did not attempt to offer any guidance, beyond suggesting that the most important problem to study was not so much how to conduct the war as how to stop it.

Not all of Brodie's colleagues at the RAND Corporation were so modest. The following year, 1960, saw the publication of Herman Kahn's huge and baroque study *On Thermonuclear War*,[45] the first published attempt by any thinker with access to classified material to discuss the action which should be taken in case deterrence *did* fail. The horrible nature of the subject, the broad brush strokes with which the author treated it, his somewhat selective approach to scientific data, and the grim jocularity of the style all combined to ensure for this study a reception which ranged from the cool to the hysterically vitriolic. Many of the criticisms, however, appear to arise rather from a sense of moral outrage that the subject should be examined at all than from serious disagreement with Kahn's actual views. In fact, Kahn basically made only two new contributions to the strategic debate. The first, based on the classified RAND *Study of Non-Military Defense*, for which he had been largely responsible, was that a substantial proportion of the American population could survive a nuclear strike, and that this proportion might be considerably increased if the necessary preparations were made. The second was that the United States should equip itself with the capacity to choose among a range of options in nuclear, as well as in nonnuclear, war; that, rather than rely on a single spasm reaction (von Schlieffen's *Schlacht ohne Morgen* brought up to date), the United States should be able to conduct a controlled nuclear strategy, suiting its targets to its political intentions—which would normally be not to destroy the enemy but to "coerce" him.[46] Kahn in fact reintroduced the concept of an operational strategy,

---

[40] Albert Wohlstetter, "The Delicate Balance of Terror," *Foreign Affairs*, January 1958. The article is reprinted in Henry A. Kissinger, ed., *Problems of National Strategy* (New York and London: Praeger and Pall Mall, 1965).

The principal relevant studies were *Selection and Use of Air Bases* (R-266, April 1954) and *Protecting US Power to Strike Back in the 1950s & 1960s* (R-290, April 1956) by Albert Wohlstetter, F. S. Hoffman, and H. S. Rowen. Wohlstetter, in a private communication to the present writer, has stressed also the significant part played in these studies by experts in systems analysis such as J. F. Pigby, E. J. Barlow, and R. J. Lutz.

[41] Oskar Morgenstern, *The Question of National Defence* (New York: Random House, 1959), p. 75.

[42] See particularly his "Surprise Attack and Disarmament," in *NATO and American Security*, ed. Klaus Knorr (Princeton: Princeton University Press, 1959). Schelling's whole work on the problem of dialogue in conflict situations is of major importance. His principal articles are collected in *The Strategy of Conflict* (Cambridge: Harvard University Press, 1960).

[43] Brodie, *Strategy in the Missile Age*, chap. 8. Brodie and Schelling, like Wohlstetter, were at the time working at RAND Corporation, as also was Herman Kahn. All have' acknowledged their mutual indebtedness during this formative period in their thinking.

[44] *Ibid.*, pp. 294–97.

[45] Herman Kahn, *On Thermonuclear* War (Princeton: Princeton University Press, 1960).

[46] *Ibid.*, pp. 301–2.

which had been almost entirely missing, at least from public discussion, since the thermonuclear age had dawned ten years earlier. For smaller nuclear powers any such notion, as applied to a conflict with the Soviet Union, was self-evidently absurd. Between the superpowers it was—and remains—a perfectly legitimate matter for analysis. Kahn may have exaggerated the capacity of the social and political structure of the United States to survive a nuclear holocaust; certainly many of his comments and calculations were oversimplified to the point of naiveté. But it is hard to quarrel with his assumption that that capacity, whatever its true dimensions, could be increased by appropriate preliminary measures, while the position adopted by some of his critics, that even to contemplate the possibility of deterrence failing might increase the possibility of such failure, is hardly one that stands up to dispassionate analysis.

At the beginning of 1961 President Kennedy's Administration took office and Mr. Robert McNamara became Secretary of Defense. Not entirely coincidentally, the great period of American intellectual strategic speculation came to an end, after five astonishingly fruitful years. The military intellectuals either were drawn, like Kaufmann and Hilsman, into government or returned to more orthodox studies on university campuses. Most of them continued to write. Kahn has produced two further works refining some of the views he expounded in *On Thermonuclear War*.[47] Kissinger has remained a sage observer of, and a prolific commentator on, the political scene, and is, at the moment of writing, President Nixon's adviser on international security affairs. Osgood, Wohlstetter, and Brodie have all produced notable works of synthesis or criticism. Perhaps the most interesting work has been that of Knorr and Schelling, who have broadened their studies to embrace the whole question of the role of military power in international relations,[48] a remarkably little-explored field in which a great deal of work remains to be done. It would be absurdly premature to suggest that

any of these scholars—many of them still comparatively young men—have no more substantial contributions to make to strategic studies; but they are unlikely to surpass the intellectual achievement for which they were individually and jointly responsible in the 1950s. Together they have done what Clausewitz and Mahan did in the last century during times of no less bewildering political and technological change; they have laid down clear principles to guide the men who have to take decisions. Like Clausewitz and Mahan they are children of their time, and their views are formed by historical and technological conditions whose transformation may well render them out of date. Like those of Clausewitz and Mahan, their principles are likely to be misunderstood, abused, or applied incorrectly, and must be subjected by each generation to searching examination and criticism. Debate will certainly continue; but at least we now have certain solid issues to debate about.

The principles established by the thinkers of the 1950s were to guide Mr. McNamara in his work of remolding American defense policy during the eight years of his period of office in the Department of Defense. "The McNamara Strategy" had a logical coherence—almost an elegance—which may have commanded rather more admiration among academics than it did in the world of affairs.[49] An invulnerable second-strike force was built up on a considerably larger scale than that considered adequate by the believers in "minimal deterrence." These forces were endowed with the capability, even after a surprise attack, of retaliating selectively against enemy forces rather than against his civilian population, so that "a possible opponent" would have "the strongest imaginable incentive to refrain from striking our own cities."[50] Forces for "limited wars" at all levels were created, armed with nuclear and conventional weapons. This involved an increase in expenditure, but it was an increase which was not grudged by congressmen alarmed by an alleged "missile gap" and happy to see fat defense con-

[47] *Thinking about the Unthinkable* and *On Escalation: Metaphors and Scenarios* (London: Pall Mall, 1965).

[48] Klaus Knorr, *On the Uses of Military Power in the Nuclear Age* (Princeton: Princeton University Press, 1966). Thomas C. Schelling, *Arms and Influence* (New Haven: Yale University Press, 1966).

[49] William W. Kaufmann, *The McNamara Strategy* (New York: Harper & Row, 1964), provides a useful, if uncritical, account. It should be read in association with Bernard Brodie's dry commentary "The McNamara Phenomenon," *World Politics*, July 1965.

[50] McNamara speech at the University of Michigan at Ann Arbor, June 16, 1962; Kaufmann, *op. cit.*, p. 116.

tracts being placed within their home states; the techniques of systems analysis which had also been developed at RAND Corporation were employed to keep this increase within bounds.[51] Overtures were made, official and unofficial, to the Soviet Union to establish arms-control agreements based on the principle of a stable balance resting on invulnerable second-strike forces on either side. And plans were put in hand for civil defense projects on a massive scale.

McNamara was able to carry out much of his program, but not all of it. The Russians were remarkably slow to absorb the reasoning which appeared so self-evident to American academics. The American public was even slower to cooperate in the sweeping measures necessary to provide effective insurance against holocaust. The ideal of a second-strike counterforce strategy seemed to many critics to be one almost intrinsically impossible to realize. And America's European allies flatly refused McNamara's requests that they should increase their conventional forces to provide the necessary "spectrum of deterrence." The Germans saw this as a diminution of the deterrent to any invasion of their own narrow land, and besides had their own, not particularly enjoyable memories of "conventional war." The British, struggling to maintain a world presence on their obstinately stagnant economy, could not afford it, while the French had ideas of their own. None of them, perhaps, could produce a coherent theoretical framework to sustain them in their arguments, but they remained unconvinced. Several of Mr. McNamara's emissaries received, in consequence, a somewhat grueling introduction to the refractory world of international affairs.

For the American strategic program was based on two assumptions which were not accepted by all the major allies of the United States: first, that America was the leader of "the Free World" and had both the right and the power to shape its strategy; and, second, it was in the interests of the world as a whole that

the United States and the Soviet Union should enter into an ever-closer dialogue. Neither of these assumptions was challenged by the British, though not all their countrymen admired the assiduity with which successive British Prime Ministers set themselves up as "honest brokers" between the superpowers the moment they set foot inside 10 Downing Street. Indeed, the most substantial British contribution to the strategic debate in the early 1960s, John Strachey's *On the Prevention of War*, quite explicitly advocated a Russo-American diarchy as the best guarantee of world peace.[52] But, on the Continent, reactions were different. The Chancellor of the Federal German Republic took a glum view of a Russo-American détente, which could only, in his view, confirm the division of his country and might even threaten the position of Berlin. And, long before Mr. McNamara appeared on the scene, the President of the Fifth French Republic had made clear his own attitude toward the American claim to act as the leader and spokesman of "the Free World."

V

Too much should not be made of the personality of General de Gaulle in shaping the French contribution to the strategic debate which began to gain in importance toward the end of the 1950s. French military experience during the past twenty years had been distinctive and disagreeable. They had their own views on the reliability of overseas allies as protectors against powerful continental neighbors —neighbors who might in the future comprise not only Russia but a revived Germany or, in moments of sheer nightmare, both. The decision to develop their own nuclear weapons had been taken before de Gaulle came into power, though perhaps it took de Gaulle to ensure that they would not be integrated, like the British, in a common Western targeting system. General Pierre Gallois, the first French writer to develop a distinctive theory of nuclear strategy,[53] advanced the thesis that nuclear weapons rendered traditional alliance systems totally out of date since no state, however powerful, would

[51] See Charles Hitch and Roland McKean, *The Economics of Defense in the Nuclear Age* (Cambridge: Harvard University Press, 1960), for the promise. The performance was examined in U.S. Senate, *Planning—Programming—Budgeting: Hearings before the Subcommittee on National Security and International Operations of the Committee on Government Operations,* 90th Cong., 1st sess., 1967.

[52] John Strachey, *On the Prevention of War* (London: Macmillan, 1962).

[53] Pierre Gallois, *Strategie de l'Age nucléaire* (Paris: Calmann-Lévy, 1960).

risk nuclear retaliation on behalf of an ally when it really came to the brink. In a world thus atomized (in the traditional sense of the word), the security of every state lay in its capacity to provide its own minimal deterrence. Indeed, the more states that did, the greater the stability of the international system was likely to be.

Extreme as Gallois' logic was, it probably reflected the sentiments of a large number of his countrymen and a substantial section of the French armed forces. In spite of innumerable official expressions to the contrary, there is every reason to suppose that many influential members of the British governing establishment felt very much the same about their own nuclear force. A more subtle variant of this doctrine was presented by General André Beaufre, who argued powerfully in his work *Deterrence and Strategy* that a multipolar nuclear balance in fact provided greater stability than a bipolar balance, since it reduced the area of uncertainty which an aggressor might exploit. So, far from atomizing alliances, argued Beaufre, independent nuclear forces cemented them, "necessarily covering the whole range of their vital interests."[54] He was careful to distinguish between multipolarity and proliferation. "The stability provided by the nuclear weapon," he argued, "is attainable only between *reasonable* powers. Boxes of matches should not be given to children"[55] (a sentiment which one can endorse while wondering what Beaufre would define, in international relations, as the age of consent). As for the Russo-American diarchy welcomed by Strachey, Beaufre specifically identified this as a danger to be avoided. "The prospect of a world controlled by a *de facto* Russo-American 'condominium' is one of the possible—and menacing—results of nuclear evolution," he wrote. "Looked at from this point of view, the existence of independent nuclear forces should constitute a guarantee that the interests of the other nuclear powers will not be sacrificed through some agreement between the two superpowers."[56]

The doctrine of "multipolarity" was thus one of the French theorists' distinctive contributions to the study of strategy in the nuclear age. The second was their analysis of revolutionary war, a subject virtually ignored by American strategic thinkers until the Vietnam involvement brutally forced it on their attention. For the French it had been inescapable. For nearly ten years after World War II the flower of their armies had been involved, in Indochina, in operations of far larger scope than the various "imperial policing" activities which absorbed so much of the attention of the British armed forces, and one which imposed on the French nation a longer and perhaps even more severe strain than the Korean War imposed on the United States. The war in Indochina was lost. It was followed by six years of struggle in Algeria which ended, for the French armed forces, no less tragically. The outcome of these wars significantly altered the balance of power in the world, but the strategic concepts being developed in the United States appeared as irrelevant to their conduct as had those which guided—or misguided—the French armies during the two world wars. The concepts which *were* relevant, of course, were those of Mao Tse-tung; those precepts evolved during the Sino-Japanese struggles of the 1930s and developed into a full theory of revolutionary warfare whereby a strongly motivated cadre operating from a position of total weakness could defeat a government controlling the entire apparatus of the state.

The theories of Mao lie outside the scope of this study, though there is little doubt that he is among the outstanding strategic thinkers of our day. Certainly the French paid him the compliment of trying to imitate him. The literature on the subject is so considerable that it may be only by hazard that the earliest French study to receive widespread recognition was Colonel Bonnet's historical analysis, *Les guerres insurrectionnelles et révolutionnaires.*[57] In this work Bonnet gave a definition which has since been generally accepted: "Guerre de partisans + guerre psychologique = guerre révolutionnaire." "Poser cette équation," he went on to claim, "c'est formuler une loi valable pour tous les mouvements révolutionnaires qui, aujourd'hui,

---

[54] André Beaufre, *Deterrence and Strategy* (London: Faber, 1965), p. 93.

[55] *Ibid.*, p. 97.

[56] *Ibid.*, p. 140. Beaufre's experience as commander of the French land forces in the Suez operation of 1956 may have had some bearing on his views on this point.

[57] Gabriel Bonnet, *Les guerres insurrectionnelles et révolutionnaires de l'antiquité à nos jours* (Paris: Payot, 1955). Important unpublished studies by Colonel Lacheroy were in circulation at the same time.

agitent le monde."[58] On the basis of this definition and their own experiences, French military
thinkers, true to their national intellectual traditions, attempted to formulate *une doctrine*.
(It is interesting to note that the pragmatic
British, whose cumulative experience in counterinsurgency campaigning was certainly no
less than that of the French, thought more
modestly in terms of "techniques."[59]) As
worked out by such writers as Bonnet himself,
Hogard, Lacheroy, Nemo, and Trinquier,[60] this
doctrine set out the object of both revolutionary and counterrevolutionary war as the gaining of the confidence and support of the people
by a mixture of violent and nonviolent means
directed at both "military" and "nonmilitary"
targets. It was not enough to suppress guerrillas; it was necessary to destroy the basis of
their support among the population by eliminating the grievances which they exploited, by
giving protection against their terrorist activities, and, insisted the French writers, by a
process of intensive indoctrination to combat
that of the revolutionary cadres themselves.

It would be painful to record in detail where
and why these excellent recommendations went
wrong. The use of undifferentiated violence by
legitimate authority undermines the basis of
consent, which is its strongest weapon against
revolutionary opponents. Indoctrination of a
population can be done only by men who are
themselves indoctrinated; and, since the essence
of the "open societies" of the West is virtually
incompatible with the concept of ideological
indoctrination, the men thus indoctrinated
rapidly found themselves almost as much at
odds with their own society as the revolutionaries they were trying to combat. In Algeria the
French army applied its doctrines with a fair
measure of at least short-term success, but in so
doing it alienated the sympathies of its own
countrymen. The main fault of its theorists—
and of their imitators in the United States—
was to overlook the element of simple *national-*

ism, which provided such strength for the
insurgent forces—a curious failing in the country which was the original home of that im-
mensely powerful force. They accepted the
propaganda of their adversaries and saw the
conflict simply in terms of a global struggle
against the forces of world Communist revolution. Marxist categories of thought make it impossible for their theorists even to consider
that the most potent revolutionary force in the
world may be not the class struggle but old-
fashioned "bourgeois" nationalism. The French
theorists were no doubt equally unwilling to
take into account a consideration which boded
so ill for their own side. But there is good reason to suppose that the FLN won in Algeria
not because they were Marxist but because
they were *Algerian*, and the French were not.
Mutatis mutandis, the same applied—and applies still—in Indochina. Marx and Lenin may
provide the rationale of insurgency warfare;
Mao Tse-tung may provide the techniques; but
the driving power is furnished by the ideas of
Mazzini. It is therefore difficult for foreign
troops, however well intentioned, to apply
counterinsurgency techniques with any chance
of success among a people which has awoken to
a consciousness of its national identity.

In addition to the doctrines of multipolarity
and revolutionary war, France has produced
yet a third contribution to strategic thinking:
the doctrine of indirect strategy. This was not
totally novel. A group of American thinkers
based at the Center for Foreign Policy Research at the University of Pennsylvania had
long been working on the assumption that "the
Free World" and the Communists were locked
in a protracted conflict which could end only in
the victory of one side or the other and in
which force was only one element of many
which might be used.[61] It was an assumption
that could certainly be justified by reference to
the works of Marxist-Leninist theoreticians. But
the publications of these writers tended to be
as emotional and tendentious as those of the
Marxists themselves. Certainly they had never
formulated their theories with the clarity, reasonableness, and dispassionate precision of

58 *Ibid.*, p. 60.
59 See, for example, Julian Paget, *Counter-Insurgency
Campaigning* (London: Faber, 1967), and Sir Robert
Thompson, *Defeating Communist Insurgency* (London: Chatto & Windus, 1966).
60 For a good select bibliography see the excellent
and highly critical study by Peter Paret, *French Revolutionary Warfare from Indo-China to Algeria* (London: Pall Mall, 1964).

61 Robert Strausz-Hupé *et al.*, *Protracted Conflict:
A Challenging Study of Communist Strategy* (New
York, 1959), and *A Forward Strategy for America*
(New York, 1961).

General André Beaufre and his colleagues at the Institut d'Études Stratégiques in Paris.[62] For Beaufre the whole field of international relations constituted a battlefield in which the Communist powers, thwarted in the use of force by the nuclear stalemate, were attacking the West by indirect means. Strategy had progressed from the "operational" (Clausewitz and Jomini) through the "logistic" (the great build-ups of World War II) to the "indirect." Political maneuvers should therefore be seen as strategic maneuvers. The adversary attacked, withdrew, feinted, outflanked, or dug in, using direct force where he could and infiltration where he could not. The West should respond accordingly, devise a single over-all political strategy and use economic, political, and military means to implement it.

The trouble with this is that it is not simply a theory of strategy but also a theory of international relations. If it is correct, Beaufre's recommendations follow naturally enough; but Beaufre states his assumptions rather than argues them, and to most students of international relations they are not self-evident. Such a view leaves too many factors out of account. The world is not really polarized so simply. Communist leaders do not control events so firmly. Whatever the ideologues may say, in practice, interests are not so implacably opposed. Strategy must certainly be shaped by the needs of policy; but policy cannot be made to fit quite so easily into the Procrustean concepts of the professional strategist.

Perhaps the most significant conclusion to be drawn from this survey is the extent to which the quality of strategic thinking in the nuclear age is related to an understanding of interna-

tional relations, on the one hand, and of weapons technology, on the other. There is, of course, nothing new in this dependence. Clausewitz emphasized the first, though he never fully adjusted his purely strategic thinking to take account of the political environment, whose overriding importance he quite rightly stressed. The second has been evident, particularly in naval and air operations, at least since the beginning of the twentieth century. But strategic thinkers, from the pioneers of the eighteenth century to Liddell-Hart in his earlier writings, have been able to assume a fairly simple model of international relations within which armed conflict might occur, as well as a basically stable technological environment. Neither assumption can now be made. No thinking about deterrence is likely to be of value unless it is based on a thorough understanding of "the state of the art" in weapons technology. Any thinking about limited war, revolutionary war, or indirect strategy must take as its starting point an understanding of the political—including the social and economic—context out of which these conflicts arise or are likely to arise. Inevitably the interaction works both ways. Strategic factors themselves constitute an important element in international relations: the statesman can never be a purely despotic law-giver to the strategist. Similarly, strategic requirements have inspired scientists and technologists to achievements they would normally consider impossible. Increasingly the three fields overlap. That is why strategic studies owe at least as much to the work of political scientists at one end of the spectrum, and to that of physical scientists, systems analysts, and mathematical economists at the other, as they do to the classical strategist. One may indeed wonder whether "classical strategy," as a self-sufficient study, has a valid claim to exist any longer.

[62] André Beaufre, *An Introduction to Strategy* (London: Faber, 1965), *Deterrence and Strategy* (London: Faber, 1965), and *Strategy of Action* (London: Faber, 1967).

THE DOCTRINE OF MASSIVE RETALIATION

JOHN FOSTER DULLES

This speech on January 12, 1954, marked the beginning of the "New Look" policy in which the United States employed a defense strategy known as Massive Retaliation. In conjunction with a foreign policy of Containment and Collective Security, Massive Retaliation threatened an aggressor with overwhelming force at a point and time of U.S. choosing. The strategy was strongly influenced by U.S. disenchantment with the limited war in Korea and economics—the need to maintain an effective military force on a peacetime economy. At the time of this speech, Mr. Dulles was the Secretary of State.

It is now nearly a year since the Eisenhower administration took office. During that year I have often spoken of various parts of our foreign policies. Tonight I should like to present an over-all view of those policies which relate to our security.

First of all, let us recognize that many of the preceding foreign policies were good. Aid to Greece and Turkey had checked the Communist drive to the Mediterranean. The European Recovery Program had helped the peoples of Western Europe to pull out of the postwar morass. The Western powers were steadfast in Berlin and overcame the blockade with their airlift. As a loyal member of the United Nations, we had reacted with force to repel the Communist attack in Korea. When that effort exposed our military weakness, we rebuilt rapidly our military establishment. We also sought a quick build-up of armed strength in Western Europe.

These were the acts of a nation which saw the danger of Soviet communism; which realized that its own safety was tied up with that of others; which was capable of responding boldly and promptly to emergencies. These are precious values to be acclaimed. Also, we can pay tribute to congressional bipartisanship, which puts the nation above politics.

But we need to recall that what we did was, in the main, emergency action, imposed on us by our enemies.

. . . .

We live in a world where emergencies are always possible, and our survival may depend upon our capacity to meet emergencies. Let us pray that we shall always have that capacity. But, having said that, it is necessary also to say that emergency measures—however good for the emergency—do not necessarily make good permanent policies. Emergency measures are costly; they are superficial; and they imply that the enemy has the initiative. They cannot be depended on to serve our long-time interests.

THE NEED FOR LONG-RANGE POLICIES

This "long time" factor is of critical importance.

The Soviet Communists are planning for what they call "an entire historical era," and we should do the same. They seek, through many types of maneuvers, gradually to divide and weaken the free nations by overextending them in efforts which, as Lenin put it, are "beyond their strength, so that they come to practical bankruptcy." Then, said Lenin, "our victory is assured." Then, said Stalin, will be "the moment for the decisive blow."

In the face of this strategy, measures cannot be judged adequate merely because they ward off an immediate danger. It is essential to do this, but it is also essential to do so without exhausting ourselves.

. . . .

From a speech given before the Council on Foreign Relations, January 12, 1954. Reprinted and edited from the Department of State Bulletin, *30, no. 791 (January 25, 1954).*

A MAXIMUM DETERRENT AT A BEARABLE COST

We want, for ourselves and the other free nations, a maximum deterrent at a bearable cost.

Local defense will always be important. But there is no local defense which alone will contain the mighty landpower of the Communist world. Local defenses must be reinforced by the further deterrent of massive retaliatory power. A potential aggressor must know that he cannot always prescribe battle conditions that suit him. Otherwise, for example, a potential aggressor who is glutted with manpower might be tempted to attack in confidence that resistance would be confined to manpower. He might be tempted to attack in places where his superiority was decisive.

The way to deter aggression is for the free community to be willing and able to respond vigorously at places and with means of its own choosing.

So long as our basic policy concepts were unclear, our military leaders could not be selective in building our military power. If an enemy could pick his time and place and method of warfare—and if our policy was to remain the traditional one of meeting aggression by direct and local opposition—then we needed to be ready to fight in the Arctic and in the tropics; in Asia, the Near East, and in Europe; by sea, by land, and by air; with old weapons and with new weapons.

The total cost of our security efforts, at home and abroad, was over $50 billion per annum, and involved a projected budgetary deficit of $9 billion for 1953 and $11 billion for 1954. This was on top of taxes comparable to wartime taxes; and the dollar was depreciating in effective value. Our allies were similarly weighed down. This could not be continued for long without grave budgetary, economic, and social consequences.

But before military planning could be changed, the President and his advisers, as represented by the National Security Council, had to take some basic policy decisions. This has been done. The basic decision was to depend primarily upon a great capacity to retaliate, instantly, by means and at places of our choosing. Now the Department of Defense and the Joint Chiefs of Staff can shape our military establishment to fit . . . *our* policy, instead of having to try to be ready to meet the enemy's many choices. That permits . . . a selection of military means instead of a multiplication of means. As a result, it is now possible to get, and share, more basic security at less cost.

. . . [In] April [1953] . . . , the United States put forward a new concept, now known as that of the "long haul." That meant a steady development of defensive strength at a rate which will preserve and not exhaust the economic strength of our allies and ourselves. This would be reinforced by the striking power of a strategic air force based on internationally agreed positions.

.   .   .   .

THE HOPE

In the ways I outlined we gather strength for the long-term defense of freedom.

We do not, of course, claim to have found some magic formula that insures against all forms of Communist successes. It is normal that at some times and at some places there may be setbacks to the cause of freedom. What we do expect to insure is that any setbacks will have only temporary and local significance, because they will leave unimpaired those free world assets which in the long run will prevail.

If we can deter such aggression as would mean general war, and that is our confident resolve, then we can let time and fundamentals work for us. We do not need self-imposed policies which sap our strength.

The fundamental asset, on our side, is the richness—spiritual, intellectual, and material—that freedom can produce and the irresistible attraction it then sets up. That is why we do not plan . . . to shackle freedom to preserve freedom. We intend that our conduct and example shall continue, as in the past, to show all men how good can be the fruits of freedom.

If we rely on freedom, then it follows that we must abstain from diplomatic moves which would seem to endorse captivity. That would, in effect, be a conspiracy against freedom. I can assure you that we shall never seek illusory security for ourselves by such a "deal."

We do negotiate about specific matters, but only to advance the cause of human welfare.

.   .   .   .

If we persist in the courses I outline we shall confront dictatorship with a task that is, in the long run, beyond its strength. For, unless it changes, it must suppress the human desires that freedom satisfies—as we shall be demonstrating.

If the dictators persist in their present course, then it is they who will be limited to superficial successes, while their foundation crumbles under the tread of their iron boots.

Human beings, for the most part, want simple things.

They want to worship God in accordance with the dictates of their conscience. But that is not easily granted by those who promote an atheistic creed.

They want to think in accordance with the dictates of their reason. But that is not easily granted by those who represent an authoritarian system.

They want to exchange views with others and to persuade and to be persuaded by what appeals to their reason and their conscience. But that is not easily granted by those who believe in a society of conformity.

They want to live in their homes without fear. But that is not easily granted by those who believe in a police-state system.

They want to be able to work productively and creatively and to enjoy the fruits of their labor. But that is not easily granted by those who look upon human beings as a means to create a powerhouse to dominate the world.

We can be sure that there is going on, even within Russia, a silent test of strength between the powerful rulers and the multitudes of human beings. Each individual no doubt seems by himself to be helpless in this struggle. But their aspirations in the aggregate make up a mighty force.

There are signs that the rulers are bending to some of the human desires of their people. There are promises of more food, more household goods, more economic freedom.

That does not prove that the Soviet rulers have themselves been converted. It is rather that they may be dimly perceiving a basic fact . . . : that there are limits to the power of any rulers indefinitely to suppress the human spirit.

In that God-given fact lies our greatest hope. It is a hope that can sustain us. For, even if the path ahead be long and hard, it need not be a warlike path; and we can know that at the end may be found the blessedness of peace.

FLEXIBLE RESPONSE: A NEW NATIONAL MILITARY PROGRAM

MAXWELL D. TAYLOR

*The so-called missile gap and other questions relating to American
defense strategy were important issues in the presidential campaign of
1960. When this book was written the Air Force was getting 47 percent of
the Defense budget, and General Taylor had just resigned as the Army
Chief of Staff. He recommended that the U.S. increase missile production,
deploy an ABM system, provide more limited war forces, and increase
their mobility and striking power. When John F. Kennedy was elected he
adopted many of General Taylor's recommendations as official policy.
Kennedy appointed Taylor as his special assistant and later to the position of
Chairman of the Joint Chiefs of Staff. Taylor was appointed Ambassador
to South Vietnam under President Johnson, and has served as the
President of the Institute for Defense Analysis. He is the author of*
Responsibility and Response *(1967) and an autobiography,* Swords and
Plowshares *(1972).*

At the outset of this reappraisal, we should
recognize and accept the limitations of our
atomic retaliatory forces. Under the conditions
which we must anticipate in the coming years,
it is incredible to ourselves, to our allies, and to
our enemies that we would use such forces for
any purpose other than to assure our national
survival. When would our survival be at stake?
Two clear cases would be an atomic attack on
the continental United States or the discovery
of indisputable evidence that such an attack
was about to take place. A third possible case
would be a major attack upon Western Europe,
since the loss of that area to communism would
ultimately endanger our national survival.
These seem the only situations imaginable in
which our atomic retaliatory forces might be
deliberately used. Hence, they are the only
situations to which their deterrence applies.

Having recognized the limitations of our
atomic deterrent forces, we should, in consist-
ence, redefine general war as being synonymous with a nuclear exchange between the
United States and the USSR. Limited war

would then be left to cover all other forms of
military operations. The question of using
atomic weapons in limited wars would be met
by accepting the fact that primary dependence
must be placed on conventional weapons while
retaining the readiness to use tactical atomic
weapons in the comparatively rare cases where
their use would be to our national interest.

*The National Military Program of Flexible
Response should contain at the outset an unqualified renunciation of reliance on the strategy
of Massive Retaliation.* It should be made clear
that the United States will prepare itself to respond anywhere, any time, with weapons and
forces appropriate to the situation. Thus, we
would restore to warfare its historic justification
as a means to create a better world upon the
successful conclusion of hostilities.

These broad, fundamental decisions as to the
objectives and nature of our strategy, the use of
atomic weapons, and the definitions which indicate the kinds of war which we must prepare
to fight should be taken by the President on the
recommendation of the National Security

Edited from pp. 145–47 and 158–61 of The Uncertain Trumpet *(New York: Harper & Row, 1960); italics
added. Copyright © 1959, 1960 by Maxwell D. Taylor. Reprinted by permission of the author and Harper
& Row, Publishers, Inc.*

Council. When approved, they would serve as the basis for action by the Joint Chiefs of Staff in determining the type, size, and priority of the military forces required to execute the approved strategy.

In a field where costs are staggering, it is essential that our new Military Program put first things first and know why the priority is right. *In my judgment, the first priority of our Military Program is a double-barreled extension of our "quick fixes"—to modernize and protect the atomic deterrent force and to build up our limited-war, counterattrition forces to offset the present preponderant Soviet forces on the ground.* Thereafter, I would make carefully selective provision for continental air defense, for the requirements of full mobilization, and for survival measures to hedge against the failures of deterrence.

.   .   .   .

To tabulate the conclusions of the foregoing discussion, the new military program should provide for the following forces and resources in the indicated order of priority.

Priority I

Kind	Size and Composition
1. Atomic deterrent forces	A few hundred reliable and accurate missiles, supplemented by a decreasing number of bombers capable of destroying a sufficient number of vital Soviet targets to assure destruction of enemy warmaking capability. To be mobile, concealed, and dispersed.
a. Offensive retaliatory	
b. Active defensive	Enough Nike-Zeus, Nike-Hercules, and Hawk missile batteries to protect the offensive retaliatory forces. Sophisticated early warning service capable of timely reporting of incoming missiles.
2. Counterattrition	Size to be based on studies of hypothetical limited wars. Modernized in weapons, equipment, air and sea lift. To carry very small yield atomic weapons but to be prepared to fight with conventional weapons alone.
3. Overseas deployments	Generally, same unit composition as now, but modernized like the other counterattrition forces and moderately increased in numerical size to achieve better internal balance.
4. Mobile reserve forces and supplies	A partial mobilization to assure a back-up of units, trained individuals, supplies, and equipment necessary to support at least the first six months of combat.
5. Air and sea lift to move and support the foregoing categories of forces	Progressively modernized through introduction of cargo jet land and sea planes and roll on–roll off shipping.
6. Antisubmarine warfare forces	Those necessary for surveillance of USSR submarine fleet and for defense of the atomic retaliatory force against missile-launching submarines.

Priority II

Kind	Size and Composition
1. Continental air defense	Emphasis on defense against missiles. Weapons comprise principally Nike-Zeus, Nike-Hercules, and Hawk missiles. Size sufficient to give _____ percent probability of protection to _____ percent of U.S. population and industry. (JCS to determine percentages from specific studies.)
2. Antisubmarine warfare forces	Those necessary to protect foregoing U.S. targets from attack by submarine-launched missiles, especially civilian targets (if there is a requirement beyond forces in Priority I-6 above).

Priority III

Kind	Size and Composition
1. Hedges against the failure of deterrence	Size and character of these programs indeterminable. Depends largely on resources left over for these purposes after requirements in higher priorities have been met.
a. Requirements of general mobilization	
b. Remaining	

Kind	Size and Composition	Kind	Size and Composition
needs of air defense		antisubmarine warfare	
c. Civil defense		e. Stockpiling against bomb damage	
d. Remaining needs for			

THE McNAMARA STRATEGY

WILLIAM W. KAUFMANN

*The Kennedy defense program, as designed and implemented by
Secretary of Defense Robert S. McNamara, is described in this article.
The major issues discussed include those of general nuclear war strategy,
limited war policy for NATO, and military assistance for the underdeveloped
world. Together the policies became known as the strategy of Flexible
Response. Dr. Kaufmann served in the U.S. Army Air Forces in World
War II, worked for the RAND Corporation from 1956 to 1961, and
is currently Professor of Political Science at the Massachusetts Institute
of Technology. His publications include* British Policy and the Independence
of Latin America *(1951) and* Military Policy and National Security *(1956).*

The task that awaited McNamara when he entered the office of Secretary of Defense in the deep snows of January 1961, had two major dimensions. He needed to redeem the President's campaign pledges to reduce the missile gap. At the same time, he had to start providing a detailed blueprint of the Kennedy defense program. The President set him a rapid pace. He had already alluded to defense matters in his inaugural address when he said: "Only when our arms are sufficient beyond doubt can we be certain beyond doubt that they will never be employed." Ten days later, in his State of the Union message, he made abundantly clear his expectations.

We are moving into a period of uncertain risk and great commitment in which both the military and diplomatic possibilities require a Free World force so powerful as to make any aggression clearly futile. Yet in the past, lack of a consistent, coherent military strategy, the absence of basic assumptions about our national requirements and the faulty estimates and duplication arising from inter-service rivalries have all made it difficult to assess accurately how adequate—or inadequate—our defenses really are.

I have, therefore, instructed the Secretary of Defense to reappraise our entire defense strategy—our ability to fulfill our commitments—the effectiveness, vulnerability, and dispersal of our strategic bases, forces, and warning systems—the efficiency and economy of our operation and organization—the elimination of obsolete bases and installations—and the adequacy, modernization and mobility of our present conventional and nuclear forces and weapons systems in the light of present and future

Edited from "The Search for Options," The McNamara Strategy *(New York: Harper & Row, 1964), pp. 47–
56, 60–63, 65–67, 71, 72, 87, 88; italics added. Copyright © 1964 by William W. Kaufmann. Reprinted by
permission of Harper & Row, Publishers, Inc. Footnotes have been omitted.*

dangers. I have asked for preliminary conclusions by the end of February.

In addition, McNamara received two other instructions: "Develop the force structure necessary to our military requirements without regard to arbitrary or predetermined budget ceilings. And secondly, having determined that force structure, . . . procure it at the lowest possible cost." It was a tall order, but McNamara, facing his first press conference, seemed unperturbed. He said: "The President in the State of the Union message referred in one point to the American Eagle and the fact that in its talons it held an olive branch and a bundle of arrows. We propose to give equal attention to each."

McNamara's apparent calm probably stemmed from several sources. The Eisenhower defense budget for fiscal year 1962 (running from July 1, 1961, to June 30, 1962) was already before the Congress, and it gave him a basis for determining what further action needed to be taken. At hand, in addition, were the staffs of the armed services and of the Joint Chiefs to advise him about prospective changes; and he had already set in motion four task forces to explore for him the requirements for strategic nuclear war, limited war, research and development, and military installations. Furthermore, he was rapidly acquiring an understanding of the techniques by which military planning is done. There was good reason why he should be able to do so. Military planning deals with numbers: of dollars in the budget; of men and weapons; of ships sunk, aircraft and missiles destroyed, casualties suffered, prisoners taken, and so forth. Many of the numbers come from experience in previous wars. Others are derived from force exercises, maneuvers, and the hypothetical experience of detailed war games in which forces with known attributes are tested against an enemy in simulated combat. The costs of alternative forces can also be determined, and the expected effectiveness of these alternatives can be measured to some degree in the laboratory of the war game. The best buy for a given budget can thus be defined; or, what amounts to the same thing, it is possible to find the force with the lowest cost to achieve a given set of objectives. That, in essence, is what peacetime military planning is all about. The practice of it is, of course, extremely complex, and many subtleties enter

into it. Nevertheless, McNamara found in it much that was similar to his own mode of thought and experience.

McNamara is notorious for his habit of immersing himself in the details of staff reports, annotating them in his left-handed script, and locking away the summaries in his personal safe at the Pentagon. It is doubtful that he has in there a set of rules for policymaking. But it is possible to surmise what are major parts of his code. He likes to see objectives concretely defined. He abhors the thought that there is only one way of doing something; he is intensely interested in alternatives. And he is a restless seeker of ways to measure the effectiveness of the alternatives. Several of McNamara's operating principles are in the highest tradition of military planning. He dislikes having programs out of balance; he sees no point in calling up soldiers when there is no ammunition for them to shoot. He is an economizer of resources, always on the alert for ways of determining how much is enough to perform a given mission. He is an advocate of taking out insurance against the failure of a program or an action. Above all, he recognizes that the world is an uncertain place, and he believes in plans that take the uncertainty specifically into account. One way to deal with uncertainty is to buy options, and that is what he seeks. As he told a congressional subcommittee, "I do not believe we should embark upon a course of action that is almost certain to destroy our Nation when that course of action can be avoided without substantial penalty to us." That spirit dominated his approach to his two great tasks.

Among his first acts was to inform himself on the nature of the missile gap. Whether or not a gap still existed, he found the deterrent itself in working order, although in need of urgent repair in order to survive a future surprise attack. He was reported to have said as much at a press briefing. Two days later the President took the position that it would be premature to say whether the gap was still there. Judgment would have to be reserved until the Defense Department had completed its review of the problem. Some months later, a reporter twitted McNamara about the gap.

Question: The [House Appropriations] Committee suggested that there might be, if you will pardon the expression, a gap in the Polaris program if you did not have long lead-time items.

Secretary McNamara: Yes. We did not request funds for Polaris submarines beyond Boat 29. I will pass by without commenting on the gap. (Laughter.)

Exactly why the gap did not materialize remains something of a mystery. Responsible officials in the Eisenhower Administration and other knowledgeable students of the problem were deeply concerned about the prospective state of the strategic nuclear balance. The reaction of the Eisenhower Administration, in strengthening SAC, reducing its vulnerability, and accelerating the missile program, goes part of the way toward explaining why the situation in 1961 looked less ominous than had been expected. Crying wolf for once had had a salutary effect. But the greater part of the explanation lies with what the Soviets had not done. In a word, they had not built as many ICBMs as they were thought to be capable of doing. Everyone had reason to be thankful.

McNamara, however, was responsible not only for the here-and-now but also for the future. And, if the present looked less gloomy than he had anticipated, the future remained uncertain and precarious. He owed it to the country to prevent the specter of the gap from arising again. But what precisely did that mean? The school of thought which was labeled *Minimum Deterrence* had already made its case to McNamara that numerical superiority, or even equality, was meaningless as a deterrent to strategic nuclear war. What the nation required, rather, was a small, well-protected force—perhaps several hundred Polaris missiles —aimed at Soviet cities. That would provide a sufficient deterrent. It would also contribute to a slowing down of the arms race, reduce the possibility of provoking the Soviets into an attack, and free resources for other purposes.

An alternative would have been to continue with the existing strategy and program of the optimum mix: buying the forces necessary to crush Soviet society and knock out enemy bombers and missiles on the ground in one great spasm. But it was not at all clear what one was buying with this kind of approach other than the terrifying ability to make sure that in a war more Russians than Americans would end up dead. The third major contender for McNamara's attention went variously under the war-fighting, *Flexible Response*, and counterforce labels. It argued that deterrence was not the only function of strategic nuclear forces and that, in any event, the best deterrent was the ability to establish military superiority in a war. Accordingly, the proponents of the strategy of Flexible Response, led by General Thomas D. White, Air Force Chief of Staff, recommended a posture which would be so designed and controlled that it could attack enemy bomber and missile sites, retaliate with reserve forces against enemy cities, if that should prove necessary, and also exert pressure on the enemy to end the war on terms acceptable to the United States. The recommendations specifically stated that the posture should be designed not for the case of a first strike against the Soviet Union but for the retaliatory role, especially since important military targets would remain for attack in the second strike.

The strategy of Flexible Response rested upon several premises. The first was that there were circumstances in which deterrence might not work. The second was that the number of lives lost in a thermonuclear war would vary significantly, depending, among other factors, on the types of targets attacked by the belligerents. The third was that limiting damage to the United States and its allies would constitute a major wartime objective, and that it could best be done by attacking the enemy's bombers and missiles, and by providing active and civil defenses for American and Allied populations. The fourth and related premise was that the combination of avoiding enemy cities and holding forces in reserve would provide the enemy with incentives to confine his own attacks to American and Allied military targets and thus contribute further to the limitation of damage. Whether or not the incentives would prove powerful enough, it would be foolish, according to this argument, automatically to destroy cities at the outset of the war when they could always be taken under attack by reserve forces at some later stage, if that should seem necessary. Finally, there was the premise that even a thermonuclear conflict would not totally erase the interest of the United States in the postwar world; hence, sufficient forces should be available to eliminate or neutralize residual enemy capabilities, bring the war to a conclusion, and provide a measure of protection thereafter. Proponents of Flexible Response answered the argument that a shift in strategy would weaken deterrence by asking whether the enemy would be any more willing to go to strategic nuclear war if he faced the prospect of being thwarted in his objectives and of suffering substantial damage than if the outcome was likely to be mutual civil devastation. As for the arms race, they questioned whether unilateral American restraint would really slow it down, and pointed out that under the concept of Flexible Response there were limits to the numbers of offensive forces that it would be necessary to procure, owing simply to the combination of high costs and the law of diminishing returns.

As McNamara surveyed these alternatives, several points became apparent. All three concepts possessed certain features in common: they stressed second-strike forces of high survivability and emphasized the importance of command-control to guard against unleashing the holocaust in the face of accidents and unauthorized acts. Where they differed was in the size and composition of the offensive forces, the role of active and passive defenses, and the targets to be attacked. The concept of minimum deterrence was the most extreme in these respects. It rested on the assumption that the Soviets could not find ways to counter a small offensive force by such measures as antisubmarine warfare, antimissile defenses, and the pressure of superior nuclear power; it also tended to ignore the overseas commitments of the United States and the role that strategic nuclear forces might have to play in their fulfillment. What was involved, therefore, was a choice between a deterrent capability of high quality with a range of options built into it, and a deterrent of lesser quality, greatly dependent on Soviet restraint for its effectiveness, with essentially one strategy open to its commander in the event that deterrence should fail. *McNamara, naturally, was predisposed toward the alternative of Flexible Response* with the options that it contained. As early as February 1961, therefore, he set in place a major building block in his strategic concept.

He made a typically cautious statement about it to the House Armed Services Committee. "So long as the adversaries of freedom continue to expand their stockpiles of mass destruction weapons," he explained,

the United States has no alternative but to ensure that at all times and under all circumstances it has the capability to deter their use. In this age of nuclear-armed intercontinental ballistic missiles, the ability to deter rests heavily on the existence of a force which can weather a massive nuclear attack, even with little or no warning, in sufficient strength to strike a decisive counterblow. This force must be of a character which will permit its use, in event of attack, in a cool and deliberate fashion and always under the complete control of the constituted authority.

McNamara's first step toward implementing the new concept was to accelerate the existing Polaris program by nine or ten months. A month later he recommended a more elaborate program which would add ten more Polaris submarines to the number planned by the Eisenhower Administration, double the production capacity for the Minuteman ICBM, place one-half of SAC's bombers on a quick-reaction ground alert (as against the previous one-third), complete the capability for maintaining an eighth of SAC's B-52s on an airborne alert in a crisis, strengthen the air defenses of the country against bomber attack, and improve the critically important command-control and communications system for the strategic nuclear forces. As McNamara was to explain later: "In the short term, that is to say, between 1961 and 1962, we have simply taken the steps that were within our capability to increase the megatonnage as rapidly as possible in the alert force. And that involved expending the funds to raise the percentage of bombers in the alert force, plus accelerating certain delivery schedules."

This was the technique of the quick fix: doing those things which would add measurably to combat strength in a relatively short period of time. In what was to become a typical McNamara tactic, he recommended simultaneously a series of reductions in what appeared to be superfluous aspects of the Eisenhower program so as to hold down the costs of the proposed improvements. Among the projects which suffered from this economizing approach were two squadrons of heavy ballistic missiles, the obsolete Snark air-breathing missiles which the Air Force had installed in Maine, the mobile Minuteman program, the atomic-powered airplane, and the famed and controversial B-70.

At the same time, McNamara put additional funds into a number of major development projects, including the Skybolt air-to-surface ballistic missile, the Midas early warning satellite, and such esoteric programs as Dynasoar, Advent, Defender, and Discoverer—all of which concerned military activities in space. In total, the new changes required an addition of $1.5 billion to the proposed Eisenhower budget.

McNamara explained the rationale for the program to a Senate subcommittee in these words:

Today our strategic forces are fully adequate to carry out their assigned tasks. But as our principal antagonists acquire a large and ready force of ICBM's which could be launched with little or no warning, the problem of preventing the destruction of our forces on the ground becomes much more difficult. Essentially, there are two major approaches available to us: (1) develop forces which can be launched within the expected period of tactical warning; (2) develop forces which can ride out a massive ICBM attack.

The feasibility of the first approach is heavily dependent on timely and unambiguous warning. While we can be reasonably sure of timely warning, we cannot in the present state of the art be wholly sure of unambiguous warning. In the case of the manned bomber, this uncertainty presents some serious, but not necessarily critical, problems. The bomber can be launched under positive control and then ordered to attack its target only after the evidence of an attack is unmistakable. But, a ballistic missile once launched cannot be recalled. Yet, unless it is deployed in a mode which gives it a good chance to survive an attack, it too must be launched before the attacker strikes home (i.e., within the relatively brief tactical warning time) or risk destruction on the ground. I need not elaborate on the dangers of this situation.

Accordingly, in re-evaluating our general war position, our major concern was to reduce our dependence on deterrent forces which are highly vulnerable to ballistic missile attack or which rely for their survival on a hair-trigger response to the first indications of such an attack. Conversely, we sought to place greater emphasis on the second approach—the kind of forces which could ride out a massive nuclear attack and which could be applied with deliberation and always under the complete control of the constituted authority.

To make the strategy of Flexible Response meaningful, it was clearly necessary to provide the kind of strategic offensive forces and active defense systems that McNamara was now advocating. But that, by itself, was not sufficient. If planning was to proceed on the basis that thermonuclear war might occur, and if it became a prime objective to limit damage to the United States and its allies, something had to be done about the problem of fallout. If the enemy confined his attack to military targets, the fallout from his bombs would still cause tremendous devastation. If he acted irrationally and struck cities, the damage would be more appalling still. But, in both cases, large numbers of people could be saved from fallout, if not from blast, provided they could find adequate shelter and stay protected for days or possibly even several weeks. Strategic offensive forces and active defenses could do only so much in destroying enemy weapons and limiting damage. Fallout shelters were an essential component of Flexible Response.

.   .   .   .

. . . There was one area, in addition to strategic nuclear deterrence, where McNamara, following the President's lead, had determined to institute a major change. That was with respect to the defense of the underdeveloped countries. In justification of the change, he cited two sources. The first was a major declaration of policy by Khrushchev on January 6, 1961, just before the Kennedy Administration had come into office. McNamara quoted the declaration at some length.

With respect to world wars, Mr. Khrushchev maintains that: "Communists are the most resolute opponents of world wars, as they are of wars among states in general." He then goes on to describe the terrible death and destruction such a war would wreak on all mankind, and concludes that world wars are not needed for the victory of Communism. Local wars are also rejected since a small war "might develop into a world thermonuclear rocket war." Communists, Mr. Khrushchev proclaims, "must wage a struggle both against world wars and against local wars." There is, however, a third type of conflict, which we know as subversion and covert aggression, but which he calls "wars of national liberation" or "popular uprisings." "What attitude do Marxists have toward such uprisings?" he asks; "The most favorable," he replies. Such conflicts, "Communists fully and unreservedly support."

McNamara's second source was the President

himself. Kennedy, upon his return from a somber meeting with Khrushchev in Vienna at the beginning of June 1961, told the nation:

In the 1940's and early '50's the great danger was from Communist armies marching across free borders. . . . Now we face a new and different threat. We no longer have a nuclear monopoly. Their missiles, they believe, will hold off our missiles, and their troops can match our troops should we intervene in these so-called wars of liberation.

Thus the local conflict they support can turn in their favor through guerrillas or insurgents or subversion. A small group of disciplined Communists could exploit discontent and misery in a country where the average income may be $60 or $70 a year and seize control, therefore, of an entire country without Communist troops ever crossing any international frontier.

Castro had already taken power in Cuba in this manner, and both Laos and South Vietnam stood in imminent danger of being reduced to complete chaos by guerrilla attacks. The answer to the threat, in these circumstances, lay not in nuclear weapons or even in large conventional forces, but in a battery of political, economic, and military measures. To fulfill the responsibility of the Defense Department for counterinsurgency, McNamara repeated the request of the previous Administration for over $1.8 billion in military assistance funds. In doing so, he spelled out to the Senate Foreign Relations Committee the approach he proposed to take.

From the President's messages to Congress you will have noted the new emphasis on strategic forces which can ride out a nuclear attack, on command and control of nuclear weapons, on increased and more mobile non-nuclear forces, and on the problem of how best to assist those jeopardized by internal aggression. Our projected military assistance programs are a necessary, integral part of this conceptual framework. Through the assistance planned we anticipate an improvement in our ability to deal with aggression in its incipient phases, to furnish help for friends and allies which will be more consistent with the kind of threat they face, and to maintain the facilities abroad required for the quick and effective deployment of appropriate U.S. forces.

McNamara divided the threatened countries into two major categories.

In the first category, which may be called the single-threat countries, belong the underdeveloped nations of Asia, the Middle East, Africa and Latin America that are not contiguous to the Sino-Soviet Bloc but which Communist words and actions have shown to be targets for indirect aggression. In these areas we recognize as the primary requirement the need for economic and social progress and the cooperation of governments and peoples in striving for a better life. Through economic programs we seek to contribute to this development. An essential component of their progress, however, is the maintenance of internal stability, and in this function the role of the military establishment and other security forces is essential. Military aid to such countries involves primarily the provision of small arms, transport, communications and training. Our objective here is to provide the means for local military establishments, with the support and cooperation of local populations, to guard against external covert intrusion and internal subversion designed to create dissidence and insurrection.

McNamara also pointed out, in the President's words, that military assistance to these countries could, "in addition to its military purposes, make a contribution to economic progress. The domestic works of our own Army Engineers are an example of the role which military forces in the emerging countries can play in village development, sanitation and road building."

The problem in the countries of the first category was complicated enough. It was still worse elsewhere.

In the second category, which may be called the double-threat countries, belong those nations contiguous to or near the Sino-Soviet Bloc that face a direct threat from without and an indirect threat from within. Vietnam today is a classic example of how these threats feed on and reinforce each other. The two-fold threat requires dual-purpose forces in terms of arms, equipment and personnel. Our military assistance programs play an essential role in furnishing arms and equipment and in teaching troops to operate, maintain and use them. Because of this two-fold threat the military aid we plan to give them is proportionally high. We recognize the inadequacy of their forces to cope with an outright Communist invasion, yet with our assistance we count on their courage and ability to deal with large-scale guerrilla warfare. Should they suffer an open attack across their borders, we look for local forces to resist the initial thrust until such time as Free World forces may come to their support. In these areas the capability of our own forces to deploy quickly against aggression is heavily dependent upon the development and maintenance of base facilities or military infrastructure on the spot or in the vicinity. Military assistance is a key factor in constructing new facilities, improving existing facilities and ensuring their availability when required.

McNamara's objective here was to create a system of defense for what used to be called the gray areas—the Far East, South Asia, and Latin America—that would be responsive to the threats without having to depend on nuclear weapons. The military assistance program was one way of fostering this development. . . . But there remained the difficult problem of what to do about Europe.

An alternative would have been to rely exclusively on the nuclear deterrent, as the Eisenhower Administration had seemed to do. It was becoming evident at this juncture not only that the missile gap had evaporated, but also that the United States had a far greater strategic nuclear power at its disposal than the Soviet Union. Indeed, in October, Deputy Secretary of Defense Gilpatric was to be quite explicit on that score. He advised his audience that "the total number of our nuclear delivery vehicles, tactical as well as strategic, is in the tens of thousands; and of course, we have more than one warhead for each vehicle." American nuclear retaliatory power, in his estimation, had "such lethal power that an enemy move which brought it into play would be an act of self-destruction on his part." Despite this, however, the President was determined "to have a wider choice than humiliation or all-out nuclear war." McNamara, for his part, was skeptical that the strategic nuclear deterrent would be any more effective in this kind of situation than it had been in the past. And he was more than doubtful that anyone would actually be willing to use nuclear weapons at the outset of a conflict over Berlin. In fact, he informed the Senate Armed Services Committee precisely to this effect.

Believing that the Western World will be very reluctant to invoke the use of nuclear weapons in response to anything short of a direct threat to its survival, the Kremlin leaders hope to create divisive influences within the Alliance by carefully measured military threats in connection with the Berlin situation. In order to meet such threats with firmness and confidence and to provide us with a greater range of military alternatives, we will need more non-nuclear strength than we have today.

Nonnuclear strength, however, in the quantities that were likely to become available during the critical period, would not necessarily suffice to overcome the supposed Soviet advantage in conventional capabilities. Therefore, the question remained as to what purpose any additional nonnuclear forces would serve. The answer came in the form of the strategy of escalation. The idea here bore some similarity to a poker game. Presumably, the nonnuclear chips were the easiest ones to play; NATO therefore should have a sufficient supply of them to make a substantial ante in the event that the Soviets started the game. Not only would this be a believable step; it would also commit the United States irrevocably to the play. As such, it might well act as a deterrent to Soviet action. If not, it might suffice to cause a Soviet withdrawal from the game. However, if the Soviets persisted, the United States would then have to resort to nuclear weapons, at first on the tactical level, and, if that did not work, on the strategic level. The threat of a graduated use of force, in which nonnuclear capabilities would be the leading elements, thus was the only technique that seemed applicable to the threat in Europe.

. . . .

In 1961, McNamara had applied the quick fix to the existing force structure; he had removed major imbalances and had accelerated programs of obvious importance. He had also put the armed forces into the business of counterinsurgency with a vengeance. As a result of the improvements in airlift and sealift, and the expansion of the Army, Marine Corps, and tactical air forces, he was approaching a position from which the nation could handle one medium-sized local conflict with conventional means and still have the reserves to meet the full American commitment to NATO or deal with another small-scale local threat. Although the character of a tactical nuclear engagement remained obscure, and the question mark of escalation loomed over it, McNamara commanded a powerful and still-growing tactical nuclear capability. And, contrary to the expectations of 1960, he had acquired a strategic nuclear capability which was superior to that of the Soviet Union in numbers, in quality, and in survivability. All in all, the country was obtaining a greater number of options—achieving more flexibility—in its military posture.

. . . .

While McNamara no doubt saw the creation

of multiple options as the answer to the President's demand for a choice between humiliation and holocaust, he also regarded it as the only appropriate method of dealing with the uncertainties of the future. But multiple options said very little about how the United States would actually fight in the event of aggression. The Eisenhower Administration had provided a measure of guidance on this score by announcing a policy of main but not sole reliance on nuclear weapons. The military establishment looked eagerly to McNamara to furnish comparable direction. Stubbornly, he refused to do so. Instead, he immersed himself in the details of future force structure. There could be no question, in these circumstances, about the nature of the capabilities that he wanted to have at the disposal of the country; to that degree he removed the ambiguities that accompanied the BNSP and budgetary ceilings of the Eisenhower era. But could satisfactory contingency planning proceed on the basis of clear direc-

tives about force structure and the concept of multiple options? The Joint Chiefs and the armed services thought not; they wanted further guidance. McNamara remained unpersuaded. He disliked being tied down to any rigid doctrine about when and how the different types of forces should be employed. There was something dangerous and ridiculous about the dogma, for example, that any direct Soviet-American confrontation meant general nuclear war. His experience with the Berlin crisis, and more recently with the Soviet missiles in Cuba, convinced him—if he needed any convincing—that the best strategy was to let the circumstances determine the choice of weapons and to make sure that there was a plentiful supply in each major category. Despite this wariness, he made no secret about his preferences. He wanted to have the capabilities for all the modern types of warfare and, if forced to commit himself, he wanted to place main but not sole reliance on nonnuclear weapons.

UNITED STATES FOREIGN POLICY FOR THE 1970s

RICHARD M. NIXON

*President Nixon proclaims a "new era" for American foreign policy
and describes several of the changes that have occurred in the international
system since World War II. He then sets out three principles as guides
for foreign policy in his administration: partnership, strength, and a
willingness to negotiate.*

A nation needs many qualities, but it needs faith and confidence above all. Skeptics do not build societies; the idealists are the builders. Only societies that believe in themselves can rise to their challenges. Let us not, then, pose a false choice between meeting our responsibilities abroad and

meeting the needs of our people at home. We shall meet both or we shall meet neither.—*From the President's remarks at the Air Force Academy commencement, June 4, 1969*

When I took office, the most immediate prob-

Edited from A Report to the Congress *by Richard Nixon, President of the United States, February 18, 1970, pp. 1–13.*

lem facing our nation was the war in Vietnam. No question has more occupied our thoughts and energies during this past year.

Yet the fundamental task confronting us was more profound. We could see that the whole pattern of international politics was changing. Our challenge was to understand that change, to define America's goals for the next period, and to set in motion policies to achieve them. For all Americans must understand that, because of its strength, its history, and its concern for human dignity, this nation occupies a special place in the world. Peace and progress are impossible without a major American role.

This first annual report on U.S. foreign policy is more than a record of one year. It is this Administration's statement of a new approach to foreign policy, to match a new era of international relations.

A NEW ERA

The postwar period in international relations has ended.

Then, we were the only great power whose society and economy had escaped World War II's massive destruction. Today, the ravages of that war have been overcome. . . .

Then, new nations were being born, often in turmoil and uncertainty. Today, these nations have a new spirit and a growing strength of independence. . . .

Then, we were confronted by a monolithic Communist world. Today, the nature of that world has changed—the power of individual Communist nations has grown, but international Communist unity has been shattered. Once a unified bloc, its solidarity has been broken by the powerful forces of nationalism. . . .

Then, the United States had a monopoly, or an overwhelming superiority, of nuclear weapons. Today, a revolution in the technology of war has altered the nature of the military balance of power. . . .

Then, the slogans formed in the past century were the ideological accessories of the intellectual debate. Today, the "isms" have lost their vitality—indeed, the restlessness of youth on both sides of the dividing line testifies to the need for a new idealism and deeper purposes.

This is the challenge and the opportunity before America as its enters the 1970s.

THE FRAMEWORK FOR A DURABLE PEACE

In the first postwar decades, American energies were absorbed in coping with a cycle of recurrent crises, whose fundamental origins lay in the destruction of World War II and the tensions attending the emergence of scores of new nations. Our opportunity today—and our challenge—is to get at the causes of crises, to take a longer view, and to help build the international relationships that will provide the framework for a durable peace.

I have often reflected on the meaning of "peace," and have reached one certain conclusion: peace must be far more than the absence of war. Peace must provide a durable structure of international relationships which inhibits or removes the causes of war. Building a lasting peace requires a foreign policy guided by three basic principles.

Peace requires *partnership*. Its obligations, like its benefits, must be shared. This concept of partnership guides our relations with all friendly nations.

Peace requires *strength*. So long as there are those who would threaten our vital interests and those of our allies with military force, we must be strong. American weakness could tempt would-be aggressors to make dangerous miscalculations. At the same time, our own strength is important only in relation to the strength of others. We—like others—must place high priority on enhancing our security through cooperative arms control.

Peace requires a *willingness to negotiate*. All nations—and we are no exception—have important national interests to protect. But the most fundamental interest of all nations lies in building the structure of peace. In partnership with our allies, secure in our own strength, we will seek those areas in which we can agree among ourselves and with others to accommodate conflicts and overcome rivalries. We are working toward the day when *all* nations will have a stake in peace, and will therefore be partners in its maintenance.

.   .   .   .

Peace Through Partnership— The Nixon Doctrine

This is the message of the doctrine I announced at Guam—the "Nixon Doctrine." Its central thesis is that the United States will participate in the defense and development of allies and friends, but that America cannot—and will not—conceive *all* the plans, design *all* the programs, execute *all* the decisions, and undertake *all* the defense of the free nations of the world. We will help where it makes a real difference and is considered in our interest.

. . . .

AMERICA'S STRENGTH

The second element of a durable peace must be America's strength. Peace, we have learned, cannot be gained by good will alone.

In determining the strength of our defenses, we must make precise and crucial judgments. We should spend no more than is necessary. But there is an irreducible minimum of essential military security; if we are less strong than necessary, and if the worst happens, there will be no domestic society to look after. The magnitude of such a catastrophe, and the reality of the opposing military power that could threaten it, presents a risk which requires of any President the most searching and careful attention to the state of our defenses.

. . . .

The last twenty-five years have also seen an important change in the relative balance of strategic power. From 1945 to 1949, we were the only nation in the world which possessed an arsenal of atomic weapons. From 1950 to 1966, we possessed an overwhelming superiority in strategic weapons. From 1967 to 1969, we retained a significant superiority. Today, the Soviet Union possesses a powerful and sophisticated strategic force which approaches our own. We must consider, too, that Communist China will deploy its own intercontinental missiles during the coming decade, thereby introducing new and complicating factors for our strategic planning and diplomacy.

. . . .

WILLINGNESS TO NEGOTIATE— AN ERA OF NEGOTIATION

Partnership and strength are two of the pillars of the structure of a durable peace. Negotiation is the third. For our commitment to peace is most convincingly demonstrated in our willingness to negotiate our points of difference in a fair and businesslike manner with the Communist countries.

We are under no illusions. We know that there are enduring ideological differences. We are aware of the difficulty in moderating tensions that arise from the clash of national interests. These differences will not be dissipated by changes of atmosphere or dissolved in cordial personal relations between statesmen. They involve strong convictions and contrary philosophies, necessities of national security, and the deep-seated differences of perspectives formed by geography and history.

The United States, like any other nation, has interests of its own, and will defend those interests. But any nation today must define its interests with special concern for the interests of others.

. . . .

This is the spirit in which the United States ratified the Non-proliferation Treaty and entered into negotiations with the Soviet Union on control of the military use of the seabeds, on the framework of a settlement in the Middle East, and on the limitation of strategic arms. This is the basis on which we and our Atlantic allies have offered to negotiate on concrete issues affecting the security and future of Europe, and on which the United States took steps last year to improve our relations with nations of Eastern Europe. This is also the spirit in which we have resumed formal talks in Warsaw with Communist China. No nation need be our permanent enemy.

NATIONAL SECURITY STRATEGY OF REALISTIC DETERRENCE

MELVIN R. LAIRD

President Nixon's first Secretary of Defense builds on the Nixon Doctrine and describes guidelines for Realistic Deterrence, including the concepts of "total force planning" and "net assessment." He goes on to discuss four primary constraints on defense planning—strategic, political, fiscal, and manpower—and concludes with a definition of "strategic sufficiency." Melvin Laird was Secretary of Defense from 1969 to 1973.

THE STRATEGY IN BRIEF

President Nixon, in his January 1969, inaugural address, committed this nation to the pursuit of something we have not known in this century—an enduring peace.

At Guam, six months later, he enunciated the Nixon Doctrine.

In his first Foreign Policy Report to the Congress in early 1970, the President explained in detail his new strategy for peace. He insisted that attainment of lasting peace requires a foreign policy guided by three basic principles— strength, partnership, and a willingness to negotiate. The President noted that sustained American strength remains crucial, but related this strength to a new order of partnership under the Nixon Doctrine—a partnership in which "the United States will participate in the defense and development of allies and friends, but . . . cannot—and will not—undertake all the defense of the free nations of the world."

In my Defense Report to the Congress last year, I described a national security strategy of Realistic Deterrence based upon the strength and partnership principles of the President's strategy for peace and designed to implement the Nixon Doctrine. Strength and partnership also provide an essential foundation for the third principle, a willingness to negotiate.

To set the stage for a comprehensive discussion of our follow-on plans, programs, and actions for this year, I will briefly review this strategy of Realistic Deterrence and its basic relationship to President Nixon's strategy for peace.

The Nixon Doctrine calls for a new approach to security planning. It means changing the allocation of responsibilities among Free World nations by providing a new emphasis on shared strength. This approach has been incorporated in our national security strategy.

The ultimate goal of the strategy of Realistic Deterrence is to discourage—and ultimately to eliminate—the use of military force as a means by which one nation seeks to impose its will upon another. Military power in the hands of nations that wish to preserve peace and freedom is an essential part of this strategy, although military power alone cannot achieve the objective. As long as the threat of aggression against the independence and territorial integrity of nations with whom we share common interests exists, our country and our friends and allies must maintain strong military forces to deter conflict. Further, our strategy must provide the defense capability necessary to protect our nation and its interests should deterrence fail.

The task before us is not easy. Successful implementation of the strategy of Realistic Deterrence is, I believe, the most difficult and challenging national security effort this country has ever undertaken. This is so because we must move forward in an environment of virtual balance in the strategic nuclear field, and in a

Edited from Statement of Secretary of Defense Melvin R. Laird before the House Armed Services Committee on the FY 1973 Defense Budget and FY 1973–1977 Defense Program, *February 17, 1972, pp. 21–23, 25–27, 30–32, 34–35, 65–66, 80–81.*

period of vigorous Soviet military expansion at sea, on the land, in the air, and in space. In addition, we must pursue our goal with due regard for the influences of today's other constraining realities—realities which I will discuss at some length.

Success will require deep understanding and strong support, both from Congress and from the American people. For, without understanding of our national objectives, and without support for the means we adopt to reach them, no strategy pursued by the representative leaders of a free and open society can possibly succeed for long when contested by a powerful, closed society. Free nations must measure the ultimate strength of their defense policies in proportion to the willing support their citizens give to those policies. A closed society is not dependent on such popular support.

Approach to Defense Planning

Our defense strategy is based on the three key elements of the Nixon Doctrine:

First, the United States will keep all of its treaty commitments.

Second, we shall provide a shield if a nuclear power threatens the freedom of a nation allied with us or of a nation whose survival we consider vital to our security.

Third, in cases involving other types of aggression we shall furnish military and economic assistance when requested and as appropriate. But we shall look to the nation directly threatened to assume the primary responsibility of providing the manpower for its defense.

From these elements, and after a thorough review of the situation as it existed at the time this Administration took office, we established the following basic criteria for national security planning for the decade of the seventies:

1. Preservation by the United States of an adequate strategic nuclear capability as the cornerstone of the Free World's nuclear deterrent.

2. Development and/or continued maintenance of Free World forces that are effective and that minimize the likelihood of requiring the employment of strategic nuclear forces should deterrence fail.

3. An international security assistance program that will enhance self-defense capabilities throughout the Free World, and, when coupled with diplomatic and other actions, will encourage regional cooperation and/or security agreements among our friends and allies.

Last year I reported that these defense planning criteria, which reflect the imperatives of the Nixon Doctrine, would be implemented in harmony with the following four guidelines:

1. In deterring *strategic nuclear warfare* primary reliance will continue to be placed on U.S. strategic deterrent forces.

2. In deterring *theater nuclear warfare* the U.S. also has primary responsibility, but certain of our allies are able to share this responsibility by virtue of their own nuclear capabilities.

3. In deterring *theater conventional warfare* —for example, a major war in Europe—U.S. and allied forces share responsibility.

4. In deterring *subtheater or localized warfare,* the country or ally which is threatened bears the primary burden, particularly for providing manpower, but when U.S. interests or obligations are at stake we must be prepared to provide help as appropriate.

.   .   .   .

Net Assessment, Total Force, and Long-Range Planning

The three national security planning criteria for the decade of the 1970s, based on the Nixon Doctrine, have established the basic parameters within which we must do our planning. As previously noted, there are four categories of potential conflict with which we, our allies, and our friends, must be prepared to cope: strategic nuclear, theater nuclear, theater conventional, and subtheater. This means that our force planning must be focused on deriving the most realistic mixture of forces and supporting assistance possible in order to carry out the necessary tasks.

We seek to accomplish this through the process of *Total Force Planning,* which I described in detail in last year's report and which calls for the use of all appropriate resources for deterrence—U.S. and Free World—to capitalize on the potential of available assets.

But force planning, no matter how effective, will rest on an uneasy base if it disregards a host of influences either largely or wholly beyond our ability to control, such as the nature of a potential enemy's capabilities and his likely strategy to the extent that we can perceive it. Acceptable force planning, therefore, must be based not only on a definition of our *objectives* but also on a sophisticated analysis of the nature and relative importance of the various impediments and *obstacles* to the achievement of our objectives—be they economic, political, technological, or military.

We intend to accomplish this through a more coordinated emphasis on *Net Assessment* in my immediate office and throughout the Department of Defense. Net Assessment is a comparative analysis of those factors—military, technological, political and economic—which impede, or have a potential to impede, our national security objectives with those factors available or potentially available to enhance the accomplishment of those objectives. Through this process, we are able to determine how to apply our resources most effectively in order to improve our total capability to accomplish our national security goals.

It is important to bear in mind, however, that Total Force planning must be carried out in terms of immediate as well as longer-range, phased objectives. Our approach to Vietnamization illustrates this. As it has been with Vietnamization, however, this will be a difficult task, since the apparent demands of the moment may sometimes have an adverse impact on what we hope to accomplish in the future.

In order to minimize this often troublesome problem, my Director of Net Assessments will be supported by and work closely with the office of my Assistant for Long-Range Planning, whose task it will be to assure effective coordination of the Net Assessment and Total Force planning functions of the Secretary of Defense.

Through our net assessment effort to date we have a better understanding of the difficulties that lie ahead, an understanding that I will share with you in the following section.

We have made substantial progress in achieving our objectives over the past year; we have moved closer to peace through effective implementation of the Nixon Doctrine. Our budget and our proposed programs for FY 1973 are designed to continue this movement.

As a former member of the Congress, I am confident that our new approach, with its emphasis on Net Assessment and Total Force planning, will permit the Department of Defense in coming months and years to be even more responsive to the Congress as we share

the responsibility for assuring our national security. The appropriate committees of the Congress will receive more meaningful information in a form more useful to the members than ever before. As we continue to develop and refine these new comprehensive approaches to national security planning, there will undoubtedly be additional changes in the way that I utilize the resources available to the Department. I will keep you fully informed of such changes.

While there are many difficulties ahead—difficulties that we can and must overcome—our policy for the future is clear. It was summarized by President Nixon before the Congress on January 20, 1972.

We will maintain a nuclear deterrent adequate to meet any threat to the security of the United States or of our allies.

We will help other nations develop the capability of defending themselves.

We will faithfully honor all of our treaty commitments.

We will act to defend our interests whenever and wherever they are threatened any place in the world.

But where our interests or our treaty commitments are not involved our role will be limited.

—We will not intervene militarily.

—But we will use our influence to prevent war.

—If war comes we will use our influence to try to stop it.

—Once war is over we will do our share in helping to bind up the wounds of those who have participated in it.

.   .   .   .

THE STRATEGIC, POLITICAL, FISCAL, AND MANPOWER REALITIES

Strategic Reality

The discussion and assessment of the threats we and our allies face—from strategic nuclear to subtheater, from communist military assistance to the Soviet challenge to U.S. technological superiority—will be the major focus of this chapter. In combination, these threats represent the more obvious dimensions of the strategic reality.

Developments in the Soviet threat have brought the strategic reality into sharper focus during the past year. The Soviet build-up is showing even greater momentum than I projected in last year's Defense Report:

The Y-class ballistic missile submarine force

of the Soviet Union could be as large as our Polaris/Poseidon force by the end of next year, rather than in 1974 as I predicted last year.

The new Soviet supersonic dash bomber, the Backfire, could be operational by the mid-1970s.

Nearly 100 new ICBM silo sites have been identified, for new or modified ICBM systems. The possibility of such a new deployment program was mentioned in my Defense Report last year.

Construction of the Moscow ABM system has resumed, and testing of an improved missile continues.

Ongoing Soviet naval ship construction programs include production of nuclear-powered torpedo attack and cruise-missile submarines, and at least one large new cruiser, armed with multiple missile systems.

New Soviet fighter aircraft, especially the high speed Foxbat, as well as the Flogger and Fitter B, are entering the inventory.

Two new Soviet tanks, one a light tank and the other a new main battle tank, are probably in production.

Political Reality

The President in his Foreign Policy Report, and the Secretary of State in his annual Report on U.S. Foreign Policy, discuss in detail the national and international political realities that confront the United States.

As Secretary of Defense, I also must take explicit account of both international and domestic political realities. From my perspective as a defense planner, these include:

1. The political and psychological effects of the growing Soviet military capabilities and presence around the world, such as in the Mediterranean, the Middle East, the Indian Ocean, and the Caribbean.

2. Allied concerns that we maintain substantial forward-deployed U.S. forces.

3. Countervailing congressional concerns to bring about a withdrawal of substantial portions of our forward-deployed forces.

4. The possible effect potential agreements controlling or reducing arms could have on the need for U.S. military forces.

5. The difficulty of maintaining broad domestic public support for those programs necessary to assure national security.

Fiscal Reality

The fiscal reality is simply stated. Resources are limited, yet there is an increasing need to commit greater resources to urgent domestic demands. This reality is apparent from the allocation of resources in this Administration's federal budgets. In 1968 the Department of Defense received about 39 percent of the federal budget; in 1973 it will be about 30 percent. Over the same periods the human resources share of the budget went from some 32 percent to 45 percent. While these numbers express a fiscal reality, they must also be considered in the context of the internal factors that impact on the DOD budget and the external factors of change in the Soviet Union's budget. For example: 53 percent of FY 1972 outlays in the DOD budget were people-related costs, a figure that will rise to 56 percent in the FY 1973 budget. By comparison, only about 30–35 percent of the Soviet defense budget is devoted to such costs. As a result, when we estimate Soviet personnel expenditures relative to U.S. prices, the U.S.S.R. starts with a significant advantage in purchasing power available for weapons-related programs, given roughly comparable total defense budgets. This built-in Soviet advantage has been greatly enhanced at our expense since 1965 because of the costs of the war in Vietnam.

. . . .

Manpower Reality

The manpower reality has become an increasingly important factor in defense planning, particularly as we move toward a restructured and revitalized defense force without resort to the draft. It is not easy to obtain and retain the manpower needed in quality and quantity under voluntary enlistment.

Military manpower in the last few years has become considerably more expensive. The average annual pay for military personnel and civilian employees has been significantly improved in the past few years. Since 1964, average military basic pay rates have more than doubled (125 percent growth). Average civilian salaries have increased by 70 percent since 1964.

Furthermore, when comparing our general purpose forces with those of the Soviet Union,

we have to face the hard reality that the Soviets can field more men than the U.S. can at
equal over-all costs.

Among the factors which account for higher
manpower costs in U.S. forces are the following: the growing demand for highly skilled
people; the increasing level of technical sophistication of U.S. weaponry, which, in turn, requires highly skilled people; and the continued
need for a high state of readiness, which requires extensive training and calls for a high
level of maintenance for our weapon systems.

The collective impact of all these pressures
is great. The costs of our personnel will constitute 56 percent of our budget outlays in FY
1973, compared with 43 percent in FY 1964.
The obvious implication is that we must place
greater emphasis in our reduced force on modernized and technically capable forces.

These four realities must be carefully considered in determining our military requirements and planning our forces to meet these
requirements. We need to know the full dimension of the strategic reality if correct requirements are to be formulated. In meeting the
threat, we must consider the fiscal reality to
bring maximum efficiency in the use of scarce
resources for defense, to claim for defense no
more of the nation's resources than needed, and
to minimize economic dislocations influenced
by defense spending. Also, we need to take
account of the political realities, including the
feasibility of obtaining legislative approval and
public support for our programs.

Finally, the manpower reality—in conjunction with the fiscal reality—has generated
powerful pressures for smaller forces. Given
these realities, our forces must have the most
modern and effective equipment practicable
and must be supported by a vigorous research
and development program that can assure our
continued technological superiority in the future. In addition, our intelligence activities take
on greater importance. In the face of an increasing and complex threat, we need to know
more about what is going on. We need fore-
knowledge of attacks against us or our allies,
and we need to know enough about each
major threat to be able to counter it as necessary.

.   .   .   .

STRATEGIC NUCLEAR FORCES FOR DETERRENCE

Our forces must be maintained at a level sufficient to make it clear that even an all-out surprise
attack on the United States by the USSR would
not cripple our capability to retaliate. Our forces
must also be capable of flexible application. A simple "assured destruction" doctrine does not meet
our present requirements for a flexible range of
strategic options. No President should be left with
only one strategic course of action, particularly that
of ordering the mass destruction of enemy civilians
and facilities.—*From the President's Foreign Policy
Report to Congress, 1972*

Strategic Sufficiency and the Implications for Force Planning

In deterring strategic nuclear warfare—i.e.,
enemy use of nuclear weapons involving a direct attack on the U.S.—primary reliance will
continue to be placed on U.S. strategic deterrent forces.

In planning these forces, we have certain
objectives derived from the sufficiency criteria.
As explained last year these include:

1. Maintaining an adequate second-strike
capability to deter an all-out surprise attack on
our strategic forces.

2. Providing no incentive for the Soviet
Union to strike the United States first in a
crisis.

3. Preventing the Soviet Union from gaining
the ability to cause considerably greater urban/
industrial destruction than the United States
could inflict on the Soviets in a nuclear war.

4. Defending against damage from small
attacks or accidental launches.

I want to note, however, that these criteria
are under intensive review in light of the
changing strategic conditions, including the
momentum of Soviet and Chinese nuclear capabilities and potential outcomes in the Strategic
Arms Limitation Talks (SALT).

As the President has stated, sufficiency includes maintaining forces adequate to prevent
our allies, as well as the U.S., from being co-
erced. Therefore, we also plan our strategic nuclear forces so that they will enhance our
theater nuclear capabilities and the nuclear
capabilities of our allies to deter attacks on
them by strategic or other nuclear forces.

In order to maintain needed flexibility, we

design our forces so that we have strategic alternatives available for use depending on the
nature or level of provocation. This means
capabilities that enable us to carry out an appropriate response without necessarily resorting to mass urban and industrial destruction.

.   .   .   .

CONVENTIONAL FORCES FOR
DETERRENCE

To serve as a realistic deterrent, our general purpose forces, together with those of our allies, must
be such as to convince potential enemies that they
have nothing to gain by launching conventional
attacks.

To deter conventional aggression, we and our
allies together must be capable of posing unacceptable risks to potential enemies. We must not
be in a position of being able to employ only strategic weapons to meet challenges to our interests.
On the other hand, having a full range of options
does not mean that we will necessarily limit our
response to the level or intensity chosen by an
enemy. Potential enemies must know that we will
respond to whatever degree is required to protect
our interests. They must also know that they will
only worsen their situation by escalating the level
of violence.

It is our policy that future guerrilla and subversive threats should be dealt with primarily by the
indigenous forces of our allies. Consistent with the

Nixon Doctrine, we can and will provide economic
and military assistance to supplement local efforts
where our interests are involved.

Our forces will be developed and deployed to
the extent possible on the basis of a common
strategy with our allies and a common sharing of
the defense burden.—*From the President's Foreign
Policy Report, 1971*

In deterring theater conventional warfare—
i.e., a major nonnuclear war involving the
U.S.S.R. or P.R.C., such as a major conventional
war in Europe—U.S. and Allied forces share
the responsibility.

Under our Total Force Concept for Force
Planning, U.S. general purpose forces include
assets applicable to theater nuclear, theater
conventional, and subtheater roles.

.   .   .   .

National Guard and Reserve forces have a
key role to play under the Total Force Concept
in implementing the strategy. Reserve components will be the initial and primary source of
augmentation of the active forces during a
contingency. This increased reliance on the Reserves requires much higher readiness than
they have had in the past, however, and we
are continuing to emphasize the three key elements of combat readiness—equipping, man-
ning, and training. . . .

THREE FIGURES: THE EISENHOWER STRATEGY,
THE KENNEDY-JOHNSON STRATEGY, AND
THE NIXON STRATEGY FOR PEACE

DEPARTMENT OF DEFENSE

The following figures are reprinted from Toward a National Security
Strategy of Realistic Deterrence: Statement of Secretary of Defense
Melvin R. Laird before the Senate Armed Services Committee on the
FY 1972 Defense Budget and the FY 1972–1976 Defense Program,
March 15, 1971, pp. 155, 157, 161.

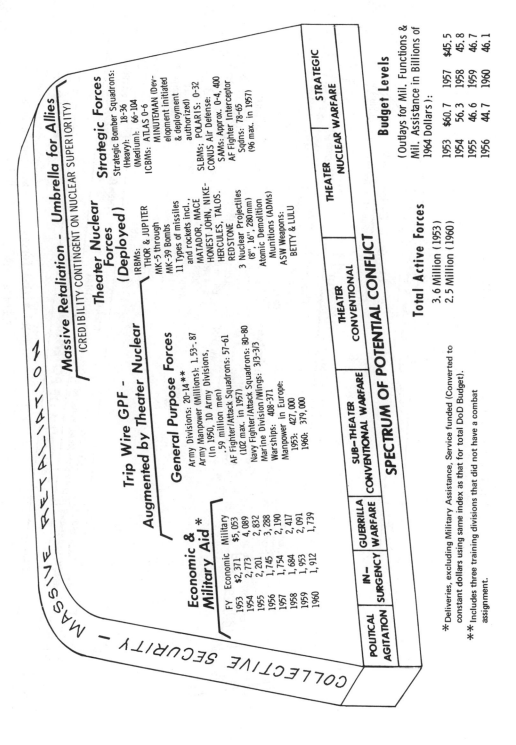

THE KENNEDY-JOHNSON STRATEGY, 1961–1968

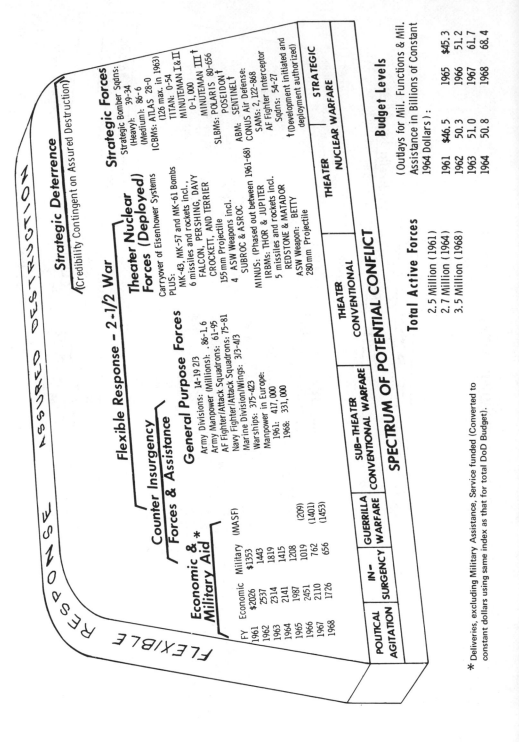

Strategic Deterrence
(Credibility Contingent on Assured Destruction)

Flexible Response – 2-1/2 War

Counter Insurgency
Forces & Assistance

Economic & Military Aid *

General Purpose Forces

Army Divisions: 14-19 2/3
Army Manpower (Millions): .86-1.6
AF Fighter/Attack Squadrons: 61-95
Navy Fighter/Attack Squadrons: 75-81
Marine Division/Wings: 3/3-4/3
Manpower in Europe:
1961: 417,000
1968: 331,000

Theater Nuclear Forces (Deployed)

Carryover of Eisenhower Systems
PLUS:
MK-43, MK-57 and MK-61 Bombs
6 missiles and rockets incl.:
  FALCON, PERSHING, DAVY
  CROCKETT, AND TERRIER
155 mm Projectile
4 ASW Weapons incl.
  SUBROC & ASROC
MINUS: (Phased out between 1961-68)
IRBMs: THOR & JUPITER
5 missiles and rockets incl.
  REDSTONE & MATADOR
ASW Weapon: BETTY
280 mm Projectile

Strategic Forces

Strategic Bomber Sqdns:
  (Heavy): 39-34
  (Medium): 86-6
ICBMs: ATLAS 28-0
  (126 max. in 1963)
  TITAN: 0-54
  MINUTEMAN I & II
  0-1,000
  MINUTEMAN III †
SLBMs: POLARIS 80-656
  POSEIDON †
ABM: SENTINEL †
CONUS Air Defense:
  SAMs: 2, 122-868
  AF Fighter Interceptor
  Sqdns: 54-27
† (Development initiated and
  deployment authorized)

FY	Economic	Military (MASF)		IN-SURGENCY	GUERRILLA WARFARE	SUB-THEATER CONVENTIONAL WARFARE	THEATER CONVENTIONAL	THEATER NUCLEAR WARFARE	STRATEGIC NUCLEAR WARFARE
1961	$2026	$1353							
1962	2537	1443							
1963	2314	1819							
1964	2141	1415							
1965	1987	1208							
1966	2451	1019	(209)						
1967	2110	762	(1401)						
1968	1726	656	(1453)						

POLITICAL AGITATION | IN-SURGENCY | GUERRILLA WARFARE | SUB-THEATER CONVENTIONAL WARFARE | THEATER CONVENTIONAL | THEATER NUCLEAR WARFARE | STRATEGIC NUCLEAR WARFARE

SPECTRUM OF POTENTIAL CONFLICT

Total Active Forces

2.5 Million (1961)
2.7 Million (1964)
3.5 Million (1968)

Budget Levels

(Outlays for Mil. Functions & Mil.
Assistance in Billions of Constant
1964 Dollars):

1961	$46.5
1962	50.3
1963	51.0
1964	50.8
1965	$45.3
1966	51.2
1967	61.7
1968	68.4

FLEXIBLE RESPONSE ASSURED DESTRUCTION

* Deliveries, excluding Military Assistance, Service funded (Converted to
  constant dollars using same index as that for total DoD Budget).

THE NIXON STRATEGY FOR PEACE: STRENGTH, PARTNERSHIP, NEGOTIATIONS

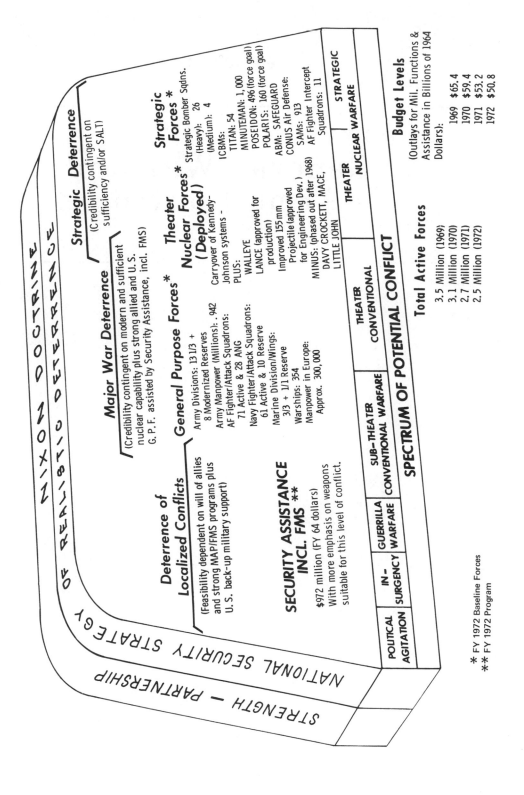

CHAPTER 3

General War and Arms Control

THE NUCLEAR WEAPONS DEBATE

WILLIAM R. VAN CLEAVE

*A "schools of thought" approach is taken here to introduce the key
issues and concepts in general war thinking. People are divided according
to their answers to three critical questions: (1) What is the role and utility of
nuclear weapons? (2) What is the likelihood of future nuclear warfare,
and what forms will this warfare take? and (3) What is emphasized as the
primary danger or the primary objective? Dr. Van Cleave served in
the Marine Corps from 1953 to 1957, received an M.A. in Government and
International Relations at Claremont Graduate School, worked as a political
scientist in the Strategic Studies Center, Stanford Research Institute,
and served in International Security Affairs, DOD.*

In his testimony before the House Armed
Services Committee on the 1965 defense budget,
Secretary of Defense Robert S. McNamara
commented upon the public debate concerning
nuclear forces and the proper strategies American nuclear forces should be designed to support. The Secretary remarked that "at one extreme there are the proponents of the 'overkill'
theory," and at the other extreme "there are the
proponents of what one might call the 'full
first strike' theory." In fact, a careful survey of
the literature pertaining to nuclear weapons
and strategies reveals that those are not the
correct boundaries of the debate at all.

The simultaneous development of the Cold
War and of nuclear weaponry has generated a
complex intellectual response. The number of
commentators or "experts" on nuclear defense
problems has increased; more and more agencies for strategic studies have emerged, and an
enormous, new body of literature has been
spawned. An examination of this mass of literature discloses a very wide range of competing
viewpoints on nuclear weaponry and the Cold
War, a range that should be understood by
those involved in national security matters.

In order to structure and present in a clear
manner the full range of views on nuclear
weapons, it seems useful to employ a logical
spectrum of "schools of thought" based upon
the most important issues in the debate. Certain key issues and questions emerge from the
literature as the most important for identifying
different positions.

*The role and utility of nuclear weapons: Is
there any rational or necessary use for nuclear
weapons, and, if so, what?* At one end of the
spectrum, a loud and clear "no" is coupled with
the advocacy of nuclear disarmament—unilateral if necessary; at the other end, a certain
impression of nuclear weapons and of the Cold
War leads to the advocacy of virtually unlimited nuclear forces.

This issue seems the most important for distinguishing different positions concerning nuclear forces and strategies, especially since it
encompasses other questions that facilitate the
identification of views and the refinement of
schools of thought. For example: (1) Are nuclear weapons qualitatively different from conventional weaponry, or are they primarily a
more efficient packaging of destructive energy?

Reprinted by permission and with minor changes from U.S. Naval Institute Proceedings, *May 1966, pp.
26–38. Copyright © 1966 by U.S. Naval Institute.*

(2) Can a distinction be made among different types of nuclear weapons useful for different purposes? (3) Should the emphasis of defense policy be on the need for disarmament, the control of arms, or the increase of arms, and to what extent in each case? (4) If nuclear weapons have utility for deterrence, what types of deterrence (i.e., of attack on the United States, on Europe, on more peripheral areas) and what strategies of deterrence should be adopted? (5) How much nuclear force is enough?

The last question is closely related to the question of utility. If the utility of nuclear forces is seen merely for the deterrence of nuclear attack on the United States, a minimum survivable countercity force may be adequate. If the nuclear force is also considered to have a prominent role in deterring transgression against other interests, or perhaps in limiting damage to the United States through a counterforce capability, more sophisticated and higher levels of weaponry are necessary. Or, if nuclear weapons are seen to have utility for battlefield purposes, an even more varied arsenal is needed.

What is the likelihood of future nuclear warfare, and what form will this warfare take? Commentators such as C. P. Snow have postulated a mathematical certainty of general nuclear war if nuclear disarmament is not accomplished, and have furthermore insisted that such warfare will inevitably be cataclysmic. Herman Kahn, Thomas Schelling, and others, while admitting a substantial possibility of general nuclear warfare, carefully distinguish among various levels of warfare and uses of nuclear weapons and refuse to rule out the possibility of a limited, rationally conducted nuclear war, even on the strategic level.

This question involves the issue of the conventional-nuclear firebreak and its significance, escalation, and the controlled use of nuclear weapons. Other related issues include the feasibility or desirability of defense measures and the efficacy of damage-limitation efforts.

What is emphasized, explicitly or implicitly, as the paramount danger or the primary objective? For example, is the primary danger seen as the existence of nuclear weaponry, or the continuing arms race, or Soviet ambitions, or communism per se? Is the main objective that of ridding the world of nuclear weaponry, ar-

resting the arms race, thwarting infringements upon concrete national interests, or destroying the menace of communism?

It is not always possible to identify clearly the values or assumptions that form the basis of a position, or to separate clearly the normative and descriptive components of a position. This need not be a matter of concern here, since the structuring of the nuclear debate depends upon the articulated views that result from the correlation between values and analysis. Whether a position is based upon an analysis of threat or upon a personal value structure may be an important consideration, but, unless the answer is made quite clear (and usually it is not clear to the person himself), it is not necessary to make the distinction.

An important component of the threat assessment related to nuclear weaponry is the issue of the nature of communism and the motivations of the Soviet Union and Communist China, or, a little less specifically, the view taken of the nature of international relations. The position taken on this issue obviously conditions the position taken on defense and nuclear matters. Toward the right end of the spectrum of views there is a preoccupation with the threat of communism per se, and little discrimination among Communist states, or between Communist behavior and behavior due to traditional national interest. Toward the left end of the spectrum there is a tendency to disparage the threat posed by either communism or the Soviet Union, at least as it relates to the assessment of dangers presented by nuclear weaponry and the arms race. Between those two poles there is less tendency to focus on communism and more tendency to analyze threats presented by antagonistic states, or by the coupling of nuclear weapons with normal international conflicts.

Based upon the foregoing issues, but primarily upon the question of the utility of nuclear weapons, it is possible to construct a model of the spectrum of positions on nuclear weapons. A useful model is one in the form of a nearly closed circle such as is commonly used to present a range of policy positions and similar to the "horse-shoe" model employed by Robert Levine to present a range of opinions from "antiwar" to "anticommunism."[1] Among

[1] *The Arms Debate* (Cambridge, Mass., 1963), p. 45.

the advantages of such a model over a linear spectrum is the visual emphasis it gives to the similarities between the two poles. Both extremes deal in the black and white of "either-or" alternatives, highly dramatized definitions or problems, and the pursuit of single, overriding goals at the expense of other objectives.

In developing the spectrum of positions on nuclear weaponry, the basic question of the utility of nuclear weapons was first used to produce a range of opinion from no-use-whatsoever, through various positions emphasizing the passive or deterrence use, to views that contemplate various types of physical use. The circle can be divided into four quadrants (Figure 1). In the lower left quadrant is a group of positions that deny the possibility of any rational or necessary use for nuclear weapons. Positions in the second quadrant emphasize the deterrent use of nuclear weapons—the *threat* to use them in order to deter major aggression. As the second quadrant merges into the third, the deterrent role of nuclear weapons is broadened and there appears a willingness to contemplate the physical use of nuclear weapons in the waging of warfare. And, as the final quadrant is approached, the contemplated use of nuclear weapons covers a progressively greater number of contingencies, or approaches a more total usage. The final pole would logically include the advocacy of preventive nuclear war; however, there is no significant extant literature that espouses this position.

This model can be refined by adding other important questions discussed above and correlating them with views on the utility of nuclear weapons (Figure 2). Thus, positions on the possibilities of defense and control are added. Control refers both to control over the use of nuclear weapons, and thus involves questions concerning escalation and the tactical use of nuclear weapons, and control over the nuclear arms race. There are four general recommendations concerning nuclear arms: disarm, limit arms, control arms, increase arms. The "types" of deterrence follow the usage of Herman Kahn, with Type I referring to the deterrence of nuclear attack on the United States; Type II, the extension of our nuclear deterrent to other important areas, such as Western Europe; and Type III, the extension of nuclear deterrence to less important areas of interest and to lower levels of conflict. The Roman numerals refer to the characteristic view of the paramount danger: I, the paramount danger is seen to be the existence of nuclear weaponry; IV, the primary threat is deemed to emanate from communism; II and III tend to balance multiple threats, with II assigning more weight to dangers involved in the nuclear arms race and III assigning relatively more weight to threats posed by the Soviet Union, Communist China, and other national enemies.

Keeping in mind the spectrum defined by the above models, various schools of thought can now be identified and located on the spectrum (Figure 3). To this model a chart has been added suggesting individuals representative of positions associated with the respective schools and also listing organized groups and periodicals that seem to emphasize one position more frequently than others. It should be noted that any model, while useful for generalization, necessarily involves simplification and should not be interpreted too rigidly. Schools of thought are not clearly divided but overlap and shade into each other. Many individuals may justifiably be included in two different schools of thought. The inclusion of individuals was made on the basis of their *primary emphasis on those issues used as criteria* for the spectrum, and is more a means to illustrate the views of the defined school than an attempt to classify an individual.

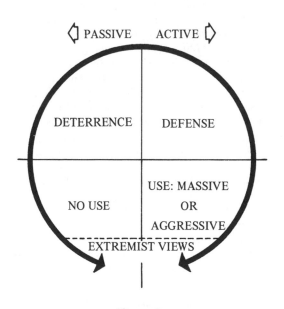

Figure 1

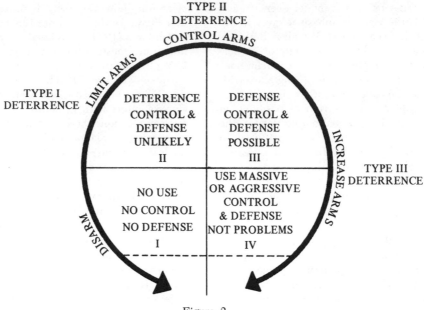

Figure 2

The division of the circle into four quadrants, three broad categories, and eight schools of thought emphasizes the overlapping of positions. It is important not only to show the differences among schools of thought but also to point out similarities between adjoining schools.

The first broad category, labeled the "Peace Movement—Disarmers," itself encompasses substantially different views and approaches, ranging from pacifists who advocate immediate and unilateral nuclear disarmament to spokesmen who accept minimum deterrence as a temporary necessity and advocate unilateral measures to reduce Cold War tensions and arrest the nuclear arms race. Essentially, the common characteristic of this category is a concentration on methods to "ban the bomb." Whatever the differences among representatives of this category, all agree that nuclear armaments should be destroyed—either immediately, and unilaterally if necessary, or progressively and in guarded concert with other nuclear powers.

Two main groups can be singled out within this general category: the extreme pacifists, who subordinate all other considerations to their goal of accelerated nuclear disarmament, and the "unilateral initiative" groups, who advocate various unilateral actions to reduce tension and lead toward ultimate nuclear disarmament. The latter group includes the "peace

researchers," who look to the tools of social and behavioral science to isolate the causes of international tensions in order to resolve conflict peacefully.

There are two separate schools of thought within the extreme pacifist group: the "Radical Pacifists," who are pacifist due to religious or moral conviction, and the "Nuclear Pacifists," whose assessment of the nuclear threat leads them to the position that nuclear weaponry is an intolerable danger that must be eliminated. Professor Mulford Sibley reflects the pacifist-on-moral-grounds position in his arguments for unilateral disarmament: "In the end, rejection of deterrence and adoption of unilateralism depend upon certain propositions about morality." Even though Professor Sibley admits there might be dangers in unilaterally disarming, this still remains the only acceptable course of action. "If we carry through on unilateral disarmament it is possible that we die, but at least we do not kill."[2]

On the other hand, Bertrand Russell is a nuclear pacifist because his assessment of the danger of a nuclear holocaust leads him to maintain that the risks unilateral nuclear disarmament might entail are worth taking to

[2] Mulford Sibley, *Unilateral Initiatives and Disarmament* (Philadelphia, 1962).

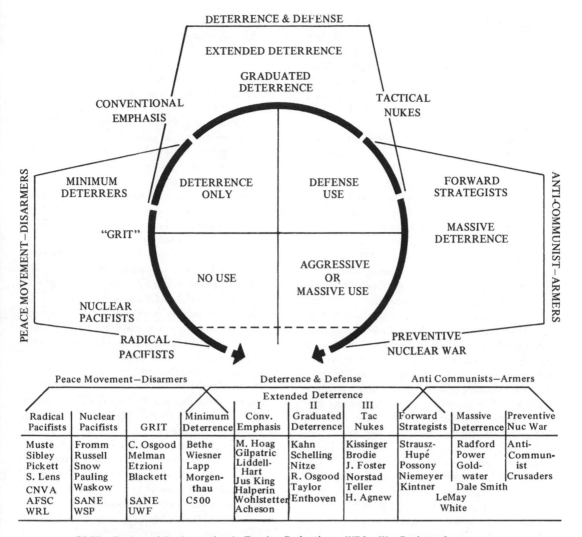

DETERRENCE & DEFENSE			
CONVENTIONAL EMPHASIS		TACTICAL NUKES	
EXTENDED DETERRENCE			
GRADUATED DETERRENCE			

DETERRENCE & DEFENSE

EXTENDED DETERRENCE

GRADUATED DETERRENCE

CONVENTIONAL EMPHASIS   TACTICAL NUKES

MINIMUM DETERRERS   DETERRENCE ONLY   DEFENSE USE   FORWARD STRATEGISTS

"GRIT"   MASSIVE DETERRENCE

NO USE   AGGRESSIVE OR MASSIVE USE

NUCLEAR PACIFISTS

RADICAL PACIFISTS   PREVENTIVE NUCLEAR WAR

PEACE MOVEMENT–DISARMERS

ANTI-COMMUNIST–ARMERS

Peace Movement–Disarmers			Deterrence & Defense				Anti Communists–Armers		
			Extended Deterrence						
				I	II	III			
Radical Pacifists	Nuclear Pacifists	GRIT	Minimum Deterrence	Conv. Emphasis	Graduated Deterrence	Tac Nukes	Forward Strategists	Massive Deterrence	Preventive Nuc War
Muste	Fromm	C. Osgood	Bethe	M. Hoag	Kahn	Kissinger	Strausz-Hupé	Radford	Anti-Communist Crusaders
Sibley	Russell	Melman	Wiesner	Gilpatric	Schelling	Brodie	Possony	Power	
Pickett	Snow	Etzioni	Lapp	Liddell-Hart	Nitze	J. Foster	Niemeyer	Gold-water	
S. Lens	Pauling	Blackett	Morgen-thau	Jus King	R. Osgood	Norstad	Kintner	Dale Smith	
CNVA	Waskow			Halperin	Taylor	Teller		LeMay	
AFSC	SANE	SANE	C500	Wohlstetter	Enthoven	H. Agnew		White	
WRL	WSP	UWF		Acheson					

GRIT: Graduated Reciprocation in Tension Reduction   WRL: War Resisters League
CNVA: Committee for Non-Violent Action   SANE: Committee for a Sane Nuclear Policy
AFSC: American Friends Service Committee   UWF: United World Federalists
WSF: Women Strike for Peace   C500: Committee of 500

Figure 3

avoid the danger of a nuclear war he believes might destroy Western civilization.

Evident in the views of the pacifists, and even of most representatives of the unilateral initiatives position, is a single image of nuclear war as an unmitigated disaster, and, consequently, the viewpoint that nuclear weapons are completely unacceptable and of no beneficial use. Virtually no distinction is made among nuclear weapons in terms of yield or usage, and there is very little precision about levels of warfare. According to these positions, nuclear weapons—visualized primarily as multimegaton bombs—have made war obsolete, irrational, or morally indefensible. Even conventional warfare must be ended because of the great danger (or virtual inevitability) of escalation to nuclear war. No control is possible over the use of nuclear weaponry, and perhaps not over the dynamism of the arms race. The nuclear arms race is perceived as the root of the Cold War, as well as a guarantee of future nuclear holocaust. Thus, the only rational policy is to eliminate all nuclear weaponry. The apocalyptic definition of dangers and alternatives is obvious in this part of the spectrum. C. P. Snow has asserted the certainty of a nuclear holocaust *unless* nuclear disarmament is accomplished. In the 1955 "Mainau Declaration," fifty-two Nobel Laureates issued the statement: "All nations must renounce the use of force or they will cease to exist."

A more moderate and intellectual approach to the Cold War and nuclear weaponry, but an approach that still reflects the views noted above, is found in the concept of "unilateral initiatives" as the solution to the Cold War and the arms race. Since Dr. Charles Osgood, Professor of Psychology at the University of Illinois and past president of the American Psychological Association, advocated his GRIT (Graduated Reciprocation in Tension-Reduction) strategy, adherents to this approach have increased and coalesced sufficiently to be regarded as a distinct school. According to this school, international conflict is based upon misunderstanding and artificial fears, generated primarily by reaction to falsely perceived actions of others. Nuclear weapons and the arms race are tension-*inducing* rather than tension-*reflecting*. The way to peace is to correct the misunderstanding between the West and the Communist world (a "mirror-image" phenomenon), reduce tension through unilateral peace initiatives, and arrest the arms race. The Soviet Union will be bound to reciprocate the peaceful initiatives and, as Charles Osgood and Seymour Melman assert, the "peace race" will be on. Obviously, quite a sanguine view is taken of the Soviet Union and communism, although different representatives of this school reflect varying degrees of optimism, as reflected in the specific unilateral initiatives they advocate. Spokesmen such as Seymour Melman, Erich Fromm, David Riesman, and Arthur Waskow advocate substantial unilateral measures such as overseas disengagement, cutbacks to low levels of nuclear forces, and large reductions in the defense budget. Other representatives of the unilateral initiatives approach, such as the sociologist Amitai Etzioni, emphasize caution and advocate phased and initially symbolic initiatives that depend upon Soviet reciprocation for further implementation. (Etzioni terms his approach "gradualism.")

The unilateral initiative school is similar to the more pacifistic schools in its fear of nuclear war and the arms race, in its optimistic view of Soviet behavior, and in its advocacy of nuclear disarmament. However, this school couples some concern for the immediate requirements of defense with its long-range goal of nuclear disarmament. Thus, at least some short-run utility in terms of Type I strategic deterrence is ascribed to a low level of nuclear force. Unilateral disarmament is not advocated; disarmament is to be achieved by negotiated stages. The acceptance of a minimum nuclear deterrent force, however, is a reluctant concession. Ultimately, nuclear weaponry must be eliminated or mankind is doomed. This position has been expressed, for example, by Professor Hans Morgenthau, who has argued that (1) "a mere deterrent function" is "the only rational function" a nuclear arsenal can possibly have; (2) a minimum force of strategic weapons is all that is necessary for that function; and (3) "if the nuclear armaments race cannot be brought under control . . . we have in all likelihood sealed our and mankind's doom, and the only issue remaining to be settled will be how and when we shall be doomed."[3]

An integral part of this minimum deterrence position is the concept of "overkill," associated widely with Dr. Seymour Melman of Columbia University. Melman's thesis is that the American nuclear arsenal is so huge that the United States has the capacity to "overkill" the Soviet Union—and, indeed, the entire world—several times. Melman bases his argument on the "Hiroshima unit" (i.e., a 20-kiloton bomb produces 100,000 deaths; thus, every kiloton kills 5,000 people, and every megaton 5,000,000, in this vastly oversimplified approach). In addition, Melman uses inaccurate force estimates and generally neglects many important strategic and targeting considerations. On this basis, he concludes that the American nuclear arsenal, as presently constituted, is senseless, dangerous, and wasteful. The United States needs far less military power to deter a strategic attack; the oversized arsenal and continuing arms race will lead to a nuclear holocaust; and the money wasted on nuclear forces can best be diverted to domestic improvements. Dr. Melman advocates an immediate two-fifths reduction in the defense budget, and an ultimate total defense budget of approximately nine billion dollars,

[3] Hans J. Morgenthau, *The Restoration of American Politics* (Chicago, 1962), p. 162.

which is claimed to be sufficient to maintain a minimum deterrent force.[4] This thesis of "overkill" is intimately connected with the concept of unilateral initiatives, and with the notions of technological plateau, weapons surfeit, and minimum deterrence associated with spokesmen such as Ralph Lapp, Jerome Wiesner, and Herbert York.

It is clear from the foregoing discussion that the GRIT school and the Minimum Deterrence school merge in the overlap between the Peace Movement category and the Deterrence and Defense category. The main distinction between them is one of emphasis: on unilateral initiatives as the means to end the Cold War, or on nuclear force levels and strategies. Of course, many individuals bridge the two schools—for example, George Kennan, Kenneth Boulding, Hans Bethe, and J. David Singer.

The category labeled "Deterrence and Defense" includes views ranging from the short-run acceptance of minimum deterrence to the reliance upon an extensive, sophisticated military establishment that would include counterforce and damage-limiting capabilities. Nuclear deterrence is accepted as a premise of U.S. policy. The differences in this category concern the best posture and strategies to assure deterrence and to prevail should deterrence fail.

In the Extended Deterrence school, minimum deterrence is rejected as insufficient to service a range of American interests, including the "assured deterrence" of a nuclear attack on the United States. Individuals in this group are concerned about both nuclear weapons and the Soviet Union or communism, and tend to reflect a "pessimistic realism" about nuclear problems and the dynamics of international politics. Within this category, disarmament is dismissed as either a Utopian goal or a dangerous delusion. In either case, disarmament is deemed unfeasible, and the concept of arms control is preferred. The best way to prevent unwanted warfare and perhaps ultimately to bring about peace is through an adequate defense posture and the mutual deterrence of a stable, military confrontation. Still, individuals in this category do not concentrate solely on improving deter-

[4] See Seymour Melman's pamphlet *A Strategy for American Security: An Alternative to the 1964 Military Budget* (1963) and his book *The Peace Race* (New York, 1961).

rence and stability, but recognize the likelihood of continual limited conflict and the possibility of a failure of nuclear deterrence. Thus, this category includes views on forces and strategies for waging various levels of warfare and for limiting damage to American values.

Although it is possible to identify an Extended Deterrence school of thought, the differences within this school on matters of force postures, weapons selection, and strategic policies make further distinction useful. These differences constitute the subject matter of a continuing debate within the defense community, a debate that is no less significant and intense because the different positions may be based on differences in emphasis, priority, or timing. An important point of contention relevant to this study is the comparative role of conventional and nuclear forces in extended deterrence and in fighting local-limited wars. Differences arise over the issues of what forces constitute "effective local defense capabilities" in various areas (especially Europe), the role of tactical nuclear weapons in these capabilities, and the extent or duration of reliance upon such capabilities.

Prominent in this general issue is the question of the use of nuclear weapons in local-limited engagements, and thus the extent to which the United States should develop and deploy tactical nuclear weapons. Technological developments and an emphasis on the discriminate utility of nuclear weapons have led some analysts to include low-yield nuclear weapons in their own definition of an effective limited-war capability. Other analysts are not convinced of the efficacy and safety of nuclear weapons in local-limited conflicts, or at least regard the conventional-nuclear firebreak as something that should be preserved if at all possible.

On the basis of these differences, the Extended Deterrence school has been subdivided into three groups labeled "Conventional Emphasis," "Graduated Deterrence," and "Tac Nukes." Except for Graduated Deterrence, which primarily signifies a middle ground between emphasizing conventional weapons and utilizing tactical nuclear weapons for local deterrence and defense, the labels are self-explanatory. Certainly, graduated deterrence is accepted by all three groups, and many of the representative individuals listed (see Figure 3) could just as well have been included in two groups. But distinguishing a middle position provides a place for those who emphasize neither conventional nor nuclear weapons in their writings so much as the need for a flexible defense capability, whatever it requires for various contingencies, and it also helps emphasize the distinction between the other two groups.

The Conventional Emphasis position is based on the degree of desirable importance assigned to the conventional-nuclear firebreak, on skepticism about the utility of tactical nuclear weapons in peripheral local war situations, and on the importance assigned to conventional forces for deterrence and defense in NATO Europe. The RAND economist Malcolm Hoag and the military strategist B. H. Liddell-Hart particularly typify this position, and many other names could be added: Gilpatric, King, Wohlstetter, and Halperin as examples.

Certain other civilian analysts, weapons scientists, and military leaders concern themselves with the possible role and utility of small-yield nuclear weapons as instruments of usable military power. There is a sufficiently identifiable group of positions on the tactical use of nuclear weapons to justify the inclusion of a Tac Nuke position within the Extended Deterrence school. Representatives of this position are more inclined to see utility in tactical nuclear weapons, or less inclined to accept the conventional–tactical nuclear firebreak, than are the schools to its left, but there is a significant range of views within the Tac Nuke position itself. Bernard Brodie has argued against what he deems an overemphasis on conventional options in Europe and has commented:

I see no basis in experience or logic for assuming that the increase in level of violence from one division to thirty is a less shocking and less dangerous form of escalation than the introduction of any kind of nuclear weapons. A galloping consensus has developed among some like-minded people around the entirely unfounded assumption that it is not size of conflict but use of nuclear weapons that would make all the difference.[5]

Some Tac Nuke advocates emphasize the deterrence contribution of a tactical nuclear capability; others focus upon the necessity for a tactical nuclear response to aggression in Europe;

[5] Bernard Brodie, "What Price Conventional Capabilities in Europe?" *The Reporter*, May 23, 1963, p. 32.

still others envisage the use of low-yield nuclear weapons on military targets in conflicts such as Vietnam. Perhaps the most extreme viewpoint in this school is that of Dr. Harold Agnew, who is quoted in the July 19, 1965, issue of *Newsweek* as stating, "If you want to take out a bridge, what difference does it make whether you use one nuclear weapon or axes and shovels?"

The more accepted position on the utility of tactical nuclear weapons (and a view that reflects a more general attitude of the Extended Deterrence school) was voiced by Secretary McNamara in his February 1963 testimony before the House Committee on Department of Defense Appropriations:

. . . While it does not necessarily follow that the use of tactical nuclear weapons must inevitably escalate into global nuclear war, it does present a very definite threshold, beyond which we enter a vast unknown. This does not mean that the NATO forces can or should do without tactical nuclear weapons. On the contrary, we must continue to strengthen and modernize our tactical nuclear capabilities to deal with an attack where the opponent employs such weapons first, or any attack by conventional forces which puts Europe in danger of being overrun.

Such a statement of tactical nuclear weapons policy for NATO Europe is specific enough to distinguish this position from stronger conventional emphasis positions, as well as from advocacy of broader utility for tactical nuclear weapons, but it is also general enough to gain concurrence from spokesmen who then differ on the precise meaning and application of such a statement. For example, General Lauris Norstad would probably subscribe to the statement but differ in his emphasis sufficiently to justify his inclusion in the Tac Nuke group. To Norstad, conventional forces in Europe have the primary function of enforcing a "pause" after the initiation of nonnuclear conflict and before tactical nuclear weapons are used, rather than of defending against conventional attacks up to those that threaten to "overrun" Europe. Thus, according to Norstad, a little more emphasis should be placed on preparing for tactical nuclear warfare, and tactical nuclear weapons should be dispersed and deployed down the chain of command a little more than pronounced government policy admits.

The general Deterrence and Defense category is characterized *more than the other categories* by a strategic-analytical-pragmatic mode of thought rather than by an ideological or Utopian one. The existing environment is both the starting point and the framework for foreign and military policy. An analysis of this environment, not the single-minded pursuit of Utopias, is the main criterion for policy. There is a greater tendency in this category to recognize the ambiguities of competing objectives, complex risks, and uncertain analyses. Overriding value cannot be assigned to a single goal such as peace or war-avoidance per se. There are dangers other than nuclear war, and the security of the United States is an objective at least as important as avoiding nuclear war. In fact, the sometimes incompatible goals of peace and security can be optimized best through balanced military capabilities rather than through disarmament. The prevention of nuclear war and the protection of American interests lies neither in disarmament nor in an all-out military effort, but somewhere in between. Henry Kissinger expressed this approach in his book, *The Necessity for Choice*:[6]

The choice is not between a complete counterforce capability or none at all nor between a strategy of pure devastation or a strategy which guarantees victory in all circumstances. Between these limiting conditions many other possibilities exist, each with its own implications for deterrence and for strategy should deterrence fail.

Nuclear war is not considered an unlikely event by representatives of this portion of the spectrum; indeed, it is considered very likely. But the notion that future nuclear warfare is, *a priori*, predetermined to be a cataclysmic event is rejected. Careful thought and careful planning can contribute to the limitation and rational conduct of even a general nuclear war.

As the middle Deterrence and Defense category merges with the final group of schools of thought, there is a greater tendency to perceive at least low-yield nuclear weapons primarily as a more efficient weapon rather than as a qualitatively different form of destructive energy. Nuclear weapons can be vastly improved and adapted to a wide range of possible uses.

In the final category on the spectrum, however, the continual improvement of nuclear weaponry and the struggle against communism

[6] (New York, 1961), p. 29.

become closely correlated in policy recommendations. The over-all view of individuals in this category is that communism is a threat which far outweighs the threat posed by nuclear weaponry. Nuclear weapons provide an important means not only to defend American interests but, to some spokesmen, also to "roll back" and destroy communism. To many representatives of this category, especially those of the "Forward Strategy" school, nuclear weapons are to be used not directly to roll back communism but indirectly to support or promote rollback by other means. Thus, nuclear weaponry is seen as a protective umbrella that enables the forward strategy to be carried out by conventional, or even nonmilitary, methods.

As in the other categories there is a wide range of views within this group. As the right pole is approached, ideological considerations gain weight at the expense of analysis or calculation, and—similar to approaches near the left pole—extreme policies are advocated in accordance with extreme definitions of the problem.

The Forward Strategy school is the anti-Communist counterpart to the unilateral initiatives (GRIT) group of the Peace Movement category. Both schools mark the transition of their respective categories from the Deterrence and Defense community, and both schools are characterized by their advocacy of American initiatives in the Cold War. The GRIT school recommends pacifistic initiatives to reduce tension and end the arms race; the Forward Strategy school advocates strategic initiatives to enhance tension in the Communist world and ultimately to produce victory over communism.

The Forward Strategy school, most widely associated with Dr. Robert Strausz-Hupé and the Foreign Policy Research Institute, links the defense community with the anti-Communist movement and can be included in both. Much of its analysis and many of its policy recommendations are accepted widely within the defense community and may even be reflected in official policy. The primary difference between this school and the schools in the Deterrence and Defense category lies in the differing conceptions of the Soviet/Communist threat and of the purposes of American policy and strategy.

The Forward Strategy school is related to the anti-Communist movement because of the ideological orientation of its viewpoints and its tendency to think in terms of threat manifested in a single-purpose *Communist plan* for a "protracted conflict" with non-Communist societies. According to this view, the Soviet Union, by its very Communist-totalitarian nature, cannot give up its international goals, and the proper response is an equally determined and pervasive Western struggle to eliminate the danger. As Dr. Strausz-Hupé remarked in an interview published in *U.S. News and World Report*, "The struggle with Communism is an all-out struggle." Furthermore, according to this view, ideology, not traditional national interest, is the ultimate motivation of the Soviet leaders. Dr. Gerhart Niemeyer argued during a recent Georgetown Center for Strategic Studies conference that it is the Communist world view more than practical considerations which motivates Communist decisionmakers, and the West should "focus the objectives of the Cold War on measures against Communists anywhere in the world, rather than on warfare against Russia or China or other countries."

The "hard" anti-Communist approach of the "Forward Strategists" entails a recommendation to fight fire with fire, to take the initiative with a "forward strategy." This strategy, while designed to apply pressure upon the Soviet Union, stops well short of recklessness. Strategic recommendations are tempered by a regard for the danger and destructiveness of nuclear weapons. The struggle with communism is not to be waged directly with nuclear weaponry unless the West is forced into it; however, the implications of the analyses and recommendations of this school show that it attributes considerably less danger to nuclear weapons and the arms race than do other defense schools, and perceives a protean utility for nuclear weapons.

The qualitative arms race must continue because (1) no stable balance based on existing capabilities is possible, due to "incessant technological change;" (2) a "win second strike" strategy requires arms superiority; and, somewhat different from other analysts, (3) the arms race itself is a means for waging the protracted conflict.

The "Forward Strategists" tend to agree with certain representatives of the Tac Nuke School that nuclear weapons can and should be used as required in a tactical or battlefield role. Dr. Strausz-Hupé has stated, "In modern war, nu-

clear weapons are as 'conventional' as any other lethal weapon."

A prominent part of this school of thought is the emphasis on "forward technology." Dr. Edward Teller and the weapons scientists differ greatly from the rest of the scientific community, which is generally disarmament-oriented, in their emphasis upon technological change and the need to pursue the qualitative arms race relentlessly. To Teller there is very little danger in the testing of nuclear weapons, the active (or, perhaps more accurately, the aggressive) continuance of the arms race, and even the physical use of nuclear weapons for military purposes if that becomes necessary. (Teller emphasizes low-yield nuclear weapons used tactically.) At least there is *relatively* little danger as compared to the dangers entailed in not doing so. The emphasis of Dr. Teller and the weapons scientists on technology supplements the emphasis on strategy of the rest of the Forward Strategy school.

In our spectrum, the "Forward Strategists" merge with positions to their right that tend to be even more inclined to rely upon the use of nuclear power, or more ideologically oriented, or both. Since the spectrum is based primarily upon views concerning nuclear weapons, and schools are arranged further to the right primarily in terms of the positions taken on the utility and role of nuclear weapons, the school to the right of the "Forward Strategists" is the Massive Deterrence school. Representatives of this school may be—and generally are, as in the cases of Barry Goldwater and General Thomas S. Power—even more ideologically anti-Communist than many representatives of the Forward Strategist school, but the main distinguishing characteristic of this school is the emphasis upon massive strategic nuclear deterrence.

The Massive Deterrence school emphasizes the need for continual strategic nuclear superiority and rejects the notions of strategic stalemate or nuclear parity with the Soviet Union. General Curtis LeMay has stated flatly in reference to a possible nuclear stalemate: "I don't believe in stalemates. I don't think there is such a thing." The late General Thomas White, in the February 24, 1964, issue of *Newsweek*, argued strongly against the concepts of stalemate and mutual deterrence: "I deplore a tendency . . . to accept 'mutual deterrence' as a blessing.

. . . Next to unilateral disarmament, stalemate is the most misleading and misguided military theme yet conceived."

The school is characterized by a pronounced confidence in the efficacy and utility of strategic nuclear air and missile power, and by the tendency to rely upon this type of force for deterrence against a broad range of possible threats. Accordingly, deterrence by the threat of massive punishment is strongly emphasized over deterrence by the capability to meet a wide range of attacks on their own level. Offensive forces are given priority over defensive capabilities. High-yield strategic nuclear weapons are emphasized over low-yield tactical nuclear capabilities, and the concern for damage limitation and for "deliberate, selective, and controlled" uses of force which characterizes Extended Deterrence groups is not a prominent feature of the Massive Deterrence school. Since a large part of this school is comprised of SAC-oriented individuals, it is understandable that strategic air delivery systems are given priority over other forms of military force and that representatives of this school argue the continued need for improved manned bombers.

Just as in the other schools of thought, there is a noticeable range of thought, or at least of emphasis, among representatives of this school. In Figure 3, Generals LeMay and White are placed to the left of the Massive Deterrence school, between it and the Forward Strategist school, to illustrate this point. The published writings of neither are as strongly ideologically oriented as the works of General Thomas S. Power or Barry Goldwater, nor is the emphasis on the massive use of strategic nuclear power as closely connected with anti-Communist crusading.

The more extreme view of the utility and efficacy of strategic air power and of massive retaliation bears similarity both to the view of air power voiced by men like Douhet and de Seversky and to the historical isolationist movement in America. The combination of these two traditions produces the notions that American interests can be safeguarded and that America can win wars cheaply and cleanly from a detached "Fortress America" position— a theory which Roger Hilsman has referred to as the idea of the "immaculate war." This strategic airpower view is commonly coupled with rather extreme ideological views to produce a crusading implication that seems further to imply a relatively unrestrained or aggressive use of nuclear power.

Barry Goldwater argued in his article "A Foreign Policy for America" that it is America's mission to establish its system and values throughout the world, but that it cannot do so without "the prior defeat of world Communism. . . . It follows that victory over Communism is the dominant, proximate goal of American policy. . . . Where conflicts in policy objectives arise they must always be resolved in favor of achieving the indispensable condition for a tolerant world—the absence of Soviet Communist power." Coexistence is not the proper goal and containment is not the proper policy: "Since Communism is organically expansive, it follows . . . that we cannot succeed by attempting merely to hold on to what we have. American policy must be geared to the offensive. Our appetite for Communist territory must be every bit as keen as theirs for non-Communist territory."[7] Such a statement obviously carries the idea of a forward strategy to its logical conclusion.

Similar views have been stated by the recently retired commander of SAC, General Thomas S. Power. According to General Power, peaceful coexistence cannot work, and any agreements with the Communists are meaningless. While the Soviets deceive us with talk about coexistence, the Communist threat continues to mount:

> The Soviet leadership is irrevocably committed to the achievement of the ultimate Communist objective, which is annihilation of the capitalist system and the establishment of Communist dictatorship over all nations of the world. . . . The Soviets realize they cannot achieve their ultimate objective unless and until they succeed in eliminating the major hurdle in their path, the United States. They are determined to resort to any means at their disposal in order to remove that hurdle.[8]

With the expression of views such as these, an anti-Communist crusade fervor is added to the view that nuclear weaponry should be constantly improved and increased, and to the belief in a protean utility of nuclear weapons. As stated earlier, there are no prominent spokes-

[7] *National Review*, 10, no. 11 (March 25, 1961): 177–81.
[8] General Thomas S. Power, *Design for Survival* (New York, 1965), p. 43.

men for the preventive nuclear war school of thought, but views such as those quoted above tend to lend themselves to the conclusion that the catonic strategy should be implemented with thermonuclear weapons. The extreme anti-Communist spokesmen in the United States have provided no clear answer to the question. However, even more than the statements by Goldwater and Power, their views of the Cold War seem to approach a preventive-war strategy by implication. An example is the following statement by Clarence E. Manion: "For twenty years our government has been paying the Soviet blackmailer with one concession after another. It is obvious now that the extortioner will be satisfied with nothing short of the complete and unconditional surrender of our national life. To 'kill' the blackmailer might or might not require a nuclear war. . . ." The only alternative, though, according to Mr. Manion, is an "official proclamation of the truth about Communists" by the government of the United States. This proclamation presumably would "open the door to the destruction of Communism by its own oppressed victims" and would thus obviate the need for a preventive nuclear strike.[9] However, if this remarkable panacea failed to accomplish its objective, it seems we are left with the choice between killing communism or being killed. The circle is almost complete. The apocalyptic choices are "disarm or be killed," "kill or be killed."

These are the ranges of the debate concerning nuclear weapons. Such extreme alternatives are rejected by national strategic policymakers, defense analysts of the middle category, and the mass public. They are likely to continue to be rejected for the foreseeable future. A stigma on the physical employment of nuclear weapons remains, but there is a consensus that a substantial nuclear arsenal is essential for the protection of important national interests. Nuclear weapons have utility at least for deterrence, and the possibility of their use in deliberate, controlled warfare should not be rejected off hand.

[9] Clarence E. Manion, *The Conservative American* (New York, 1964), pp. 200–201.

DETERRENCE AND DEFENSE:
A THEORETICAL INTRODUCTION

GLENN H. SNYDER

*Snyder defines the two central concepts of general war strategy. He notes
that deterrence works on the enemy's intentions, while defense reduces his
capabilities. He further introduces the concepts of strategic value,
deterrent value, and political value and elaborates on the differences
between the balance of terror and the balance of power. Professor Snyder
is Professor of Political Science at the State University of New York, Buffalo.
He was formerly associated with the Princeton University Center for
International Studies, and is the author of* Stockpiling of Strategic
Materials *(1966) and other works.*

National security still remains an "ambiguous symbol," as one scholar described it almost a decade ago.[1] Certainly it has grown more ambiguous as a result of the startling advances made since then in nuclear and weapons technology, and since the advent of nuclear parity between the United States and the Soviet Union. Besides such technological complications, doctrine and thought about the role of force in international politics have introduced additional complexities. We now have, at least in embryonic form, theories of limited war, of deterrence, of "tactical" versus "strategic" uses of nuclear weapons, of "retaliatory" versus "counterforce" strategies in all-out war, of "limited retaliation," of the mechanics of threat and commitment-making, of "internal war," "protracted conflict," and the like. Above all, the idea of the "balance of terror" has begun to mature, but its relation to the older concept of the "balance of power" is still not clear. We have had a great intellectual ferment in the strategic realm, which of course is all to the good. What urgently remains to be done is to tie together all of these concepts into a coherent framework of theory so that the end goal of national security may become less ambiguous, and so that the military means available for pursuance of this goal may be accumulated, organized, and used more efficiently. This article can claim to make only a start in this direction.

The central theoretical problem in the field of national security policy is to clarify and distinguish between the two central concepts of *deterrence* and *defense*. Essentially, deterrence means discouraging the enemy from taking military action by posing for him a prospect of cost and risk which outweighs his prospective gain. Defense means reducing our own prospective costs and risks in the event that deterrence fails. Deterrence works on the enemy's *intentions;* the *deterrent value* of military forces is their effect in reducing the likelihood of enemy military moves. Defense reduces the enemy's *capability* to damage or deprive us; the *defense value* of military forces is their effect in mitigating the adverse consequences for us of possible enemy moves, whether such consequences are counted as losses of territory or war damage. The concept of "defense value," therefore, is broader than the mere capacity to hold territory, which might be called "denial capability." Defense value is de-

[1] Arnold Wolfers, " 'National Security' as an Ambiguous Symbol," *Political Science Quarterly*, 67, no. 4 (December 1952): 481ff.

nial capability plus capacity to alleviate war damage.

It is a commonplace, of course, to say that the primary objectives of national security policy are to deter enemy attacks and to defend successfully, at minimum cost, against those attacks which occur. It is less widely recognized that different types of military force contribute in differing proportions to these two objectives. Deterrence does not vary directly with our capacity for fighting wars effectively and cheaply; a particular set of forces might produce strong deterrent effects and not provide a very effective denial and damage-alleviating capability. Conversely, forces effective for defense might be less potent deterrents than other forces which were less efficient for holding territory and which might involve extremely high war costs if used.

One reason why the periodic "great debates" about national security policy have been so inconclusive is that the participants often argue from different premises—one side from the point of view of deterrence, and the other side from the point of view of defense. For instance, in the famous "massive retaliation" debate of 1954, the late Secretary of State Dulles and his supporters argued mainly that a capacity for massive retaliation would deter potential Communist mischief, but they tended to ignore the consequences should deterrence fail. The critics, on the other hand, stressed the dire consequences should the threat of massive retaliation fail to deter and tended to ignore the possibility that it might work. The opposing arguments never really made contact, because no one explicitly recognized that considerations of reducing the probability of war and mitigating its consequences must be evaluated simultaneously, that the possible consequences of a failure of deterrence are more or less important depending on the presumed likelihood of deterrence. Many other examples could be cited.

Perhaps the crucial difference between deterrence and defense is that deterrence is primarily a peacetime objective, while defense is a wartime value. Deterrent value and defense value are directly enjoyed in different time periods. We enjoy the deterrent value of our military forces prior to the enemy's aggressive move; we enjoy defense value after the enemy move has been made, although we indirectly profit from defense capabilities in advance of

war through our knowledge that if the enemy attack occurs we have the means of mitigating its consequences. The crucial point is that *after* the enemy's attack takes place, our military forces perform different functions and yield wholly different values than they did as deterrents prior to the attack. As deterrents they engaged in a psychological battle—dissuading the enemy from attacking by attempting to confront him with a prospect of costs greater than his prospective gain. After the enemy begins his attack, while the psychological or deterrent aspect does not entirely disappear, it is partly supplanted by another purpose: to resist the enemy's onslaught in order to minimize *our* losses or perhaps maximize *our* gains, not only with regard to the future balance of power, but also in terms of intrinsic or nonpower values. That combination of forces which appeared to be the optimum one from the point of view of deterrence might turn out to be far inferior to some other combination from the point of view of defense should deterrence fail. In short, maximizing the enemy's cost expectancy may not always be consistent with minimizing our own. Thus we must measure the value of our military forces on two yardsticks, and we must find some way of combining their value on *both* yardsticks, in order accurately to gauge their aggregate worth or "utility" and to make intelligent choices among the various types of forces available.

Before launching into a theoretical analysis of the concepts of deterrence and defense, it may be useful to present a sampling of policy issues involving a need to choose between deterrence and defense; the examples will be treated in more detail later.

EXAMPLES OF CHOICES AND CONFLICTS BETWEEN DETERRENCE AND DEFENSE

A strategic retaliatory air force sufficient to wreak only minimum, "unacceptable" damage on Soviet cities—to destroy, say, twenty cities —after this force had been decimated by a surprise Soviet nuclear attack would have great value for deterring such a surprise attack and might be an adequate deterrent against that contingency. But, if deterrence were to fail and the Soviet attack took place, it would then not be rational to *use* such a minimum force in massive retaliation against Soviet cities, since this would only stimulate the Soviets to inflict further damage upon us and would contribute nothing to our "winning the war." If we are interested in defense—i.e., in winning the war and in minimizing the damage to us—as well as in deterrence, we may wish to have (if technically feasible) a much larger force and probably one of different composition—a force which can strike effectively at the enemy's remaining forces (thus reducing our own costs) and, further, either by actual attacks or the threat of attacks, force the enemy to surrender or at least to give up his territorial gains.

The threat of massive nuclear retaliation against a major Soviet ground attack in Western Europe may continue to provide considerable deterrence against such an attack, even if actually to carry out the threat would be irrational, because of the enormous costs we would suffer from Soviet counterretaliation. Strategic nuclear weapons do not provide a rational means of defense in Western Europe unless they not only can stop the Russian ground advance but also, by "counterforce" strikes, can reduce to an acceptable level the damage we would suffer in return. We may not have this capability now, and it may become altogether infeasible as the Soviets develop their missile technology. For a means of rational defense, therefore, NATO may need enough ground forces to hold Europe against a full-scale attack by Soviet ground forces. This does not mean, however, that we necessarily must maintain ground forces of this size. If we think the probability of attack is low enough, we may decide to continue relying on nuclear deterrence primarily, even though it does not provide a rational means of defense. In other words, we might count on the Soviet uncertainties about whether or not nuclear retaliation is rational for us, and about how rational we are, to inhibit the Soviets from attacking in the face of the possible damage they *know* they would suffer if they guessed wrong.

An attempt to build an effective counterforce capability, in order to have both a rational nuclear defense and a more credible nuclear deterrent against ground attack in Europe, might work against the *deterrence* of direct nuclear attack on the United States. Since, by definition, such a force would be able to eliminate all but a small fraction of the Soviet strategic

nuclear forces if it struck first, the Soviets might, in some circumstances, fear a surprise attack and be led to strike first themselves in order to forestall it.

Tactical nuclear weapons in the hands of NATO forces in Europe have considerable deterrent value because they increase the enemy's cost expectation beyond what it would be if these forces were equipped only with conventional weapons. This is true not only because the tactical weapons themselves can inflict high costs on the enemy's forces but also because their use (or an enemy "pre-emptive" strike against them) would sharply raise the probability that the war would spiral to all-out dimensions. But the defense value of tactical nuclear weapons against conventional attack is comparatively low against an enemy who also possesses them, because their use presumably would be offset by the enemy's use of them against our forces, and because in using such weapons we would be incurring much greater costs and risks than if we had responded conventionally.

For deterrence, it might be desirable to render automatic a response which the enemy recognizes as being costly for us, and to communicate the fact of such automation to the enemy, thus reducing his doubts that we would actually choose to make this response when the occasion for it arose. For example, a tactical nuclear response to conventional aggression in Europe may be made semi-automatic by thoroughly orienting NATO plans, organization, and strategy around this response, thus increasing the difficulty of following a nonnuclear strategy in case of a Soviet challenge. But such automation would not be desirable for defense, which would require flexibility and freedom to choose the least costly action in the light of circumstances at the time of the attack.

The continental European attitude toward NATO strategy is generally ambivalent on the question of deterrence versus defense; there is fear that, with the Soviet acquisition of a substantial nuclear and missile capability, the willingness of the United States to invoke massive retaliation is declining, and that therefore the deterrent to aggression has weakened. Yet the Europeans do not embrace the logical consequence of this fear: the need to build up an adequate capacity to defend Europe on the ground. A more favored alternative, at least in

France, is the acquisition of an independent strategic nuclear capability. But, when European governments project their imaginations forward to the day when the enemy's divisions cross their borders, do they really envisage themselves shooting off their few missiles against an enemy who would surely obliterate them in return? One doubts that they do, but this is not to say that it is irrational for them to acquire such weapons; they might be successful as a deterrent because of Soviet uncertainty as to whether they would be used and Soviet unwillingness to incur the risk of their being used.

Further examples easily come to mind. For the sake of deterrence in Europe, we might wish to deploy the forces there as if they intended to respond to an attack with nuclear weapons; but this might not be the optimum deployment for defense once the attack has occurred, if the least costly defense is a conventional one. For deterrence of limited aggressions in Asia, it might be best to deploy troops on the spot as a "plate-glass window." But, for the most efficient and flexible defense against such contingencies, troops might better be concentrated in a central reserve having transport facilities for moving them quickly to a threatened area.

As Bernard Brodie has written,[2] if the object of our strategic air forces is only deterrence, there is little point in developing "clean" bombs; since deterrence is to be effected by the threat of dire punishment, the dirtier the better. But, if we also wish to minimize our own costs once the war has begun, we might wish to use bombs that produce minimum fallout, in order to encourage similar restraint in the enemy.

For deterrence, it might be desirable to disperse elements of the Strategic Air Command to civilian airfields, thus increasing the number of targets which the enemy must hit if he is to achieve the necessary attrition of our retaliatory power by his first strike. However, this expedient might greatly increase the population damage we would suffer in the enemy's first strike, since most civilian airfields are located near large cities, assuming that the enemy would otherwise avoid hitting cities.[3]

THE TECHNOLOGICAL REVOLUTION

The need to *choose* between deterrence and defense is largely the result of the development of nuclear and thermonuclear weapons and long-range airpower. Prior to these developments, the three primary functions of military force—to *punish* the enemy, to *deny* him territory (or to take it from him), and to *mitigate damage* to oneself—were embodied, more or less, in the same weapons. Deterrence was accomplished (to the extent that military capabilities were the instruments of deterrence) either by convincing the prospective aggressor that his territorial aim was likely to be frustrated or by posing for him a prospect of intolerable costs, or both, but both of these deterrent functions were performed by the *same* forces. Moreover, these same forces were also the instruments of defense if deterrence failed.

Long-range airpower partially separated the function of punishment from the function of contesting the control of territory, by making possible the assault of targets far to the rear, whose relation to the land battle might be quite tenuous. Nuclear weapons vastly increased the relative importance of prospective *cost* in deterring the enemy and reduced (relatively) the importance of frustrating his aggressive enterprise. It is still true, of course, that a capacity to deny territory to the enemy, or otherwise to block his aims, may be a very efficient deterrent. And such denial *may* be accomplished·by strategic nuclear means, though at high cost to the defender. But it is now conceivable that a prospective aggressor may be deterred, in some circumstances at least, solely or primarily by threatening and possessing the capability to inflict extreme punishment on his homeland assets and population, even though he may be superior in capabilities for contesting the control of territory. Nuclear powers must, therefore, exercise a conscious choice between the objectives of deterrence and defense,

---

[2] Bernard Brodie, *Strategy in the Missile Age* (Princeton: Princeton University Press, 1959), p. 205.

[3] This particular choice between deterrence and war costs has been analyzed by Thomas C. Schelling, "Arms Control Will *Not* Cut Defense Costs," *Harvard Business Review*, 39, no. 2 (April 1961): 6–12.

since the relative proportion of "punishment capacity" to "denial capacity" in their military establishments has become a matter of choice.

This is the most striking difference between nuclear and prenuclear strategy: the partial separation of the functions of preattack deterrence and postattack defense, and the possibility that deterrence may now be accomplished by weapons which might have no rational use for defense should deterrence fail.

DETERRENCE

Deterrence,[4] in one sense, is simply the negative aspect of political power; it is the power to dissuade, as opposed to the power to coerce or compel. One deters another party from doing something by the implicit or explicit threat of applying some sanction if the forbidden act is performed, or by the promise of a reward if the act is not performed. Thus conceived, deterrence does not have to depend on military force. We might speak of deterrence by the threat of trade restrictions, for example. The promise of economic aid might deter a country from military action (or any action) contrary to one's own interests. Or we might speak of the deterrence of allies and neutrals, as well as of potential enemies, as Italy, for example, was deterred from fighting on the side of the Dual Alliance in World War I by the promise of substantial territorial gains. In short, deterrence may follow, first, from any form of control which one has over an opponent's present in terms of his prospective "value inventory"; second, from the communication of a credible threat or promise to decrease or increase that

[4] Other treatments of the theory of deterrence include Bernard Brodie, "The Anatomy of Deterrence," *World Politics*, 11, no. 2 (January 1959): 173–92; Morton A. Kaplan, "The Calculus of Deterrence," *ibid.*, no. 1 (October 1958): 20–44; William W. Kaufmann, "The Requirements of Deterrence," in *Military Policy and National Security*, ed. William W. Kaufmann (Princeton: Princeton University Press, 1956); Thomas W. Milburn, "What Constitutes Effective Deterrence?" *Conflict Resolution*, 3, no. 2 (June 1959): 138–46; Glenn H. Snyder, *Deterrence by Denial and Punishment*, Research Monograph no. 1, Center of International Studies, Princeton University, January 2, 1959; and *idem*, "Deterrence and Power," *Conflict Resolution*, 4, no. 2 (June 1960): 163–79. See also Robert E. Osgood, "A Case for Graduated Unilateral Disengagement," *Bulletin of the Atomic Scientists*, 16, no. 4 (April 1960): 127–31 and "Rational Defense: Nuclear Displacement," *ibid.*, 18, no. 6 (June 1962): 21–24.

inventory; and, third, from the opponent's degree of confidence that one intends to fulfill the threat or promise.

In an even broader sense, however, deterrence is a function of the *total* cost-gain expectations of the party to be deterred, and these may be affected by factors other than the apparent capability and intention of the deterrer to apply punishments or confer rewards. For example, an incipient aggressor may be inhibited by his own conscience, or, more likely, by the prospect of losing moral standing, and hence political standing, with uncommitted countries. Or, in the specific case of the Soviet Union, he may fear that war will encourage unrest in, and possibly dissolution of, his satellite empire, and perhaps disaffection among his own population. He may anticipate that his aggression would bring about a tighter welding of the Western alliance or stimulate a degree of mobilization in the West which would either reduce his own security or greatly increase the cost of maintaining his position in the arms race. It is also worth noting that the benchmark or starting point for the potential aggressor's calculation of costs and gains from military action is not his *existing* value inventory, but the extent to which he expects that inventory to be changed if he refrains from initiating military action. Hence, the observation is commonly made that the Russians are unlikely to undertake overt military aggression, because their chances are so good for making gains by "indirect" peaceful means. Conceivably the Soviets might attack the United States, even though they foresaw greater costs than gains, if the alternative of not attacking seemed to carry within it a strong possibility that the United States would strike them first and, in doing so, inflict greater costs on the Soviet Union than it could by means of retaliation after the Soviets had struck first. In a (very abstract) nutshell, the potential aggressor presumably is deterred from a military move not simply when his expected cost exceeds his expected gain but when the net gain is less, or the net loss is more, than he can expect if he refrains from the move. But this formulation must be qualified by the simple fact of inertia: deliberately to shift from a condition of peace to a condition of war is an extremely momentous decision, involving incalculable consequences, and a government is not likely to make this decision unless it foresees a very large advantage in doing so. The great importance of *uncertainty* in this context will be discussed below.

In a broad sense, deterrence operates during war as well as prior to war. It could be defined as a process of influencing the enemy's *intentions*, whatever the circumstances, violent or nonviolent. Typically, the outcome of wars has not depended simply on the clash of physical capabilities. The losing side usually accepts defeat somewhat before it has lost its physical ability to continue fighting. It is deterred from continuing the war by a realization that continued fighting can only generate additional costs without hope of compensating gains, this expectation being largely the consequence of the previous application of force by the dominant side.[5] In past wars, such deterrence usually has been characteristic of the terminal stages. However, in the modern concept of limited war, the intentions factor is more prominent and pervasive; force may be threatened and used partly, or even primarily, as a bargaining instrument to persuade the opponent to accept terms of settlement or to observe certain limitations.[6] Deterrence in war is most sharply illustrated in proposals for a strategy of limited retaliation, in which initial strikes, in effect, would be *threats* of further strikes to come, threats designed to deter the enemy from further fighting. In warfare limited to conventional weapons or tactical nuclear weapons, the strategic nuclear forces held in reserve by either side may constitute a deterrent against the other side's expanding the intensity of its war effort. Also, limited wars may be fought in part with an eye to deterring future enemy attacks by convincing the enemy of one's general willingness to fight.

The above observations are intended to suggest the broad scope of the concept of deterrence, its nonlimitation to military factors, and its fundamental affinity to the idea of political power. In the discussion which follows, we shall use the term in a narrower sense, to mean the discouragement of the *initiation* of military aggression by the threat (implicit or explicit)

of applying military force in response to the aggression. We shall assume that, when deterrence fails and war begins, the attacked party is no longer "deterring" but rather "defending." Deterrence in war and deterrence, by military action, of subsequent aggressions will be considered as aspects of defense.

. . . .

DEFENSE

The deterrer, in choosing his optimum military and threat posture in advance of war, must estimate not only the effectivenes of that posture for deterrence but also the consequences for himself should deterrence fail. In short, he is interested in defense[7] as well as in deterrence; his security is a function of both of these elements. Capabilities and threats which produce a high level of deterrence may not yield a high degree of security, because they promise very high costs and losses for the deterrer should war occur. We turn now to a discussion of the factors which go into the deterrer's estimate of the consequences of the failure of deterrence and into his evaluation of the defense effectiveness of his military forces. . . .

THE COMPONENTS OF DEFENSE VALUE

As already pointed out, military forces affect not only the probabilities of various enemy moves but also the potential costs which the defender would suffer should the enemy undertake aggressive moves. We will assume, for simplicity, that the consequences of aggression are always net costs to the defender. This does not mean, of course, that aggression should not be resisted, for much greater losses might be entailed in not resisting. The extent to which given military forces potentially can mitigate the defender's costs and losses of all kinds is the measure of the "defense value" of those forces in various contingencies. It is assumed that, to all possible enemy moves, the most rational response will be made—i.e., the response which the defender thinks will minimize his ag-

---

[5] For an excellent extended discussion of this point, with case studies, see Paul Kecskemeti, *Strategic Surrender* (Stanford: Stanford University Press, 1959).

[6] See Thomas C. Schelling, *The Strategy of Conflict* (Cambridge: Harvard University Press, 1969), chap. 3.

[7] The reader is reminded that I am using the word "defense" in a rather special sense, which is narrower than one ordinary usage of the term and broader than another. Obviously it is narrower than the usage which makes "defense" synonymous with all military preparedness. It is broader, however, than the "capacity to hold territory in case of attack," which I would prefer to call "denial capability."

gregate loss during, and as a result of, the ensuing war.

The potential costs of enemy moves—followed by one's own optimum responses—are counted in two categories of value: intrinsic value and power value.

Intrinsic values are "end values"; they are valued for their own sake rather than for what they contribute to the power relations between the protagonists. They include such things as the value we place upon our own independence (including all the subsidiary values which flow from this independence), the value we attach to the independence (or noncommunization) of other countries with which we feel a cultural or psychic affinity (apart from what their independence contributes to our own security), the economic values we find in trading with other free countries (to the extent that these values would be lost should these countries fall under Communist control), and moral values such as self-respect, honor, and prestige. Some of these intrinsic values obviously attach to the continued independence either of our own country or of other countries; others are inherent in the response or lack of response rather than in the political entity or territory attacked. Other intrinsic values are the material assets and lives (again as valued for their own sake rather than for their contribution to the power equation) which would be lost in the act of resisting aggression.

Power values are "instrumental values," not end values. That is, they are valued not for their own sake but for what they contribute to the security of intrinsic values. It might be more precise to say that the "assets" at stake in international conflict are valued on two scales —a power scale and an intrinsic scale—and that the aggregate value of any given asset is the sum of its valuation on both scales. "Assets," of course, may be either tangible, like raw materials and productive resources, or intangible, like prestige or a set of enemy expectations concerning one's willingness to fight in future contingencies. The "defense value" of given military forces includes both the power values and the intrinsic values which can be preserved by using the forces in various contingencies.

Power values are of three major kinds: strategic value, deterrent value, and political value. Strategic value is the potential contribution of the territorial prize to the military capabilities of either side; it includes such familiar elements of power as population, industrial capital, natural resources, and strategic location, valued as war potential. More precisely, the strategic value of any country or territory is the probable effect of its loss on increasing the chances that the aggressor would be able to take other areas, or on increasing the costs to the defender of holding other areas.

While strategic value is entirely a function of the warmaking potential inherent in the contested territory, deterrent value is an attribute primarily of the *act of responding* to aggression. Deterrent value may be described as the effect of a response in reducing the probability of enemy attacks against other areas in the future—i.e., reducing it below what it would be if no resistance were offered to the immediate aggression. The enemy may be discouraged from making future attacks either if (1) his territorial gains from his present move are limited or denied entirely or if (2) the costs we inflict upon him by our response are greater than he had expected. In the main, deterrent value stems from the evidence which our response provides to the enemy concerning our future intentions.

Political value is the effect of a response, and of its direct consequences, on the alignment or attitudes of third countries. Although we have classified political value under the rubric of "power values," it is really a mixture of intrinsic and power effects. In its power dimension, political value may be subsumed under either strategic value or deterrent value. That is, the political loss of an ally to the other side may increase the enemy's capability to make future conquests, or it may reduce our own capability to prevent such conquests. It may also increase the enemy's inclination to attempt future aggression and reduce our own capacity to deter it. It may reduce the cohesion of our own alliances. All of these are power effects. However, we also place an intrinsic value on "having friends" abroad, on keeping democratic countries out of the Communist sphere of influence, on economic relations which might be disrupted by a transfer of political allegiance or the adoption of a "neutralist" stance. Political value is the sum of all such considerations.

A net loss in power value means an increase in the probability and/or the potential adverse consequences of *future* aggressive enemy moves after completion of the "first" enemy move and the ensuing war (if the move is resisted). A strategic loss is an increase in the potential estimated loss as a result of such future attacks. A deterrent loss is an increase in the probability of future enemy moves. A political loss may affect either the probabilities or the costs of future attacks, or both.

Power values, especially strategic value, may be lost as a result of losses of lives and attrition of military capabilities and future war potential in the process of fighting. More subtle strategic forms of war cost might include such things as a weakening of the population's willingness to sacrifice in future wars or its willingness to stand up to enemy threats in future political crises. This, in other words, along with the intrinsic value of the lives and economic assets sacrificed in the war, offsets the power and intrinsic values which may be gained or saved by fighting.

In summary, the total value of a response (and the defense value of the military forces available for making the response) is the sum of the power values and intrinsic values which can be saved or gained by the response, minus the power values and intrinsic values lost as the result of war casualties and damage.

Strategic Value and Deterrent Value

Much of the inconclusiveness of the recurring "great debates" about military policy might be avoided if the concept of "strategic value" could be clarified and clearly separated from the deterrent effects of military action. The strategic value of a particular piece of territory is the effect which its loss would have on increasing the enemy's *capability* to make various future moves, and on decreasing our own capacity to resist further attacks. The deterrent value of defending or attempting to defend that piece of territory is the effect of the defense on the enemy's *intention* to make future moves. The failure to recognize this distinction contributed to the apparent about-face in United States policy toward South Korea, when we decided to intervene after the North Korean attack in June 1950. Earlier, the Joint Chiefs of Staff had declared that South Korea had no strategic value—apparently meaning that its

loss would have no significant effect on the United States' capacity to fight a general war with the Soviet Union. This determination was thought to justify—or at least was used as a rationalization for—the withdrawal of U.S. combat forces from the Korean peninsula in 1948 and 1949. Secretary of State Dean Acheson strengthened the impression that "no strategic value" meant "no value" when, in a speech early in 1950, he outlined a U.S. "defense perimeter" in the Far East which excluded Korea. Then, when the North Koreans, perhaps encouraged by these high-level U.S. statements, attacked in June 1950, the United States government suddenly discovered that it had a deterrent interest, as well as strong political and intrinsic interests, in coming to the rescue of South Korea. The dominant theme in the discussions leading up to the decision to intervene was that, if the Communists were "appeased" this time, they would be encouraged to make further attacks on other areas.[8] The chief motive behind the intervention was to prevent such encouragement from taking

[8] As former President Truman has stated: "Our allies and friends abroad were informed through our diplomatic representatives that it was our feeling that it was essential to the maintenance of peace that this armed aggression against a free nation be met firmly. We let it be known that we considered the Korean situation vital as a symbol of the strength and determination of the West. Firmness now would be the only way to deter new actions in other portions of the world. Not only in Asia but in Europe, the Middle East, and elsewhere the confidence of peoples in countries adjacent to the Soviet Union would be very adversely affected, in our judgment, if we failed to take action to protect a country established under our auspices and confirmed in its freedom by action of the United Nations. If, however, the threat to South Korea was met firmly and successfully, it would add to our successes in Iran, Berlin and Greece a fourth success in opposition to the aggressive moves of the Communists. And each success, we suggested to our allies, was likely to add to the caution of the Soviets in undertaking new efforts of this kind. Thus the safety and prospects for peace of the free world would be increased." Harry S. Truman, *Years of Trial and Hope* (New York: Doubleday & Co., 1956), pp. 339–40.

The primary political value of the intervention, as U.S. decisionmakers saw it, was that it would give other free nations confidence that they could count on U.S. aid in resisting aggression. The most salient intrinsic values were moral value in opposing the aggressive use of force, support for the "rule of law" in international affairs, support for the collective security system embodied in the United Nations Charter, and the special responsibility the United States felt for the Republic of Korea, whose government it had played a major role in establishing. "Support for the collective security system," of course, had deterrent and political, as well as moral, overtones.

place, and positively to deter similar attempts in the future.

. . . .

THE NEW BALANCE OF POWER

The separation of the functions of punishment and denial, and especially the enormous magnification of the capability to inflict punishment, has profoundly affected the traditional concept of "balance of power."[9] In effect, nuclear weapons, long-range aircraft, and missiles have superimposed a new balance upon the old. These weapons have not simply added higher levels of potential destructiveness to the traditional balancing process; they have changed the very nature and meaning of "balance." Two balancing systems—the strategic balance of terror and a truncated tactical balance of power—now operate simultaneously, each according to different criteria, but interacting in various ways which are not yet thoroughly understood.

The "power" that was balanced in the prenuclear balancing process was essentially the military power to take or hold territory. Moreover, territory, and the human and material resources on it, was the predominant source of power. The motive for engaging in the balancing process was to prevent any single state or bloc from becoming so powerful that it could make territorial conquests with impunity and eventually achieve hegemony over the other states in the system. The objectives were, first, to *deter* the potential disturber from initiating war, by forming alliances and building up armaments sufficient to defeat him; and, second, if deterrence failed, to *defend* or restore the balance by engaging in war. Whether or not a balance existed depended essentially on whether the states interested in preserving the *status quo* were able to *deny* territorial gains to the expansion-minded state or states.

The balance of terror centers on a different form of power—not the power to contest the control of territory directly, but the power to inflict severe punishment, to prevent the enemy from inflicting punishment on oneself, and to deter by the threat of punishment. In its pure deterrent form, a balance of terror exists between two nuclear powers when neither can strike first at the other without receiving a completely intolerable retaliatory blow in return. A balance does not exist when one power, in striking first, can eliminate all but a tolerable portion of the opponent's capacity to strike back.

. . . .

Differences between the Balance of Terror and the Balance of Power

The traditional balancing process continues to operate as a balance between conventional forces (and the potential for building such forces) in all situations in which there is no significant possibility that nuclear weapons will be used. Hereafter, we shall refer to this balance as the "tactical" balance of power, differentiating it both from the strategic balance of terror and from an over-all balance of power involving interactions between the strategic balance and the tactical balance. Some significant differences between these two balancing systems in their "pure" forms are worth noting.[10]

One difference is that, in the strategic balance, quantitatively matching the enemy's capabilities is virtually irrelevant as a criterion for balance. A balance of terror exists when neither side can eliminate enough of the other's forces in striking first to avoid an unacceptable retaliatory blow. Depending chiefly on technological conditions, especially the degree of vulnerability of the opposing forces, a potential attacker may be balanced with a force only a fraction of the size of the attacker's forces; or balance may require having more forces than the potential attacker. The proper criterion is to be able to inflict unacceptable retaliatory damage.

By contrast, in the modern tactical balance centering on conventional ground forces, as in the traditional balancing process, simply equaling the strength of the enemy's forces is still the most plausible balancing criterion, although, of course, a sophisticated calculation would re-

[9] This section essentially is a condensation of my article, "Balance of Power in the Missile Age," *Journal of International Affairs*, 14, no. 1 (1960): 21–35.

[10] The term "tactical balance of power" refers chiefly to the balance of conventional capabilities; "strategic balance of terror" refers to the balance of long-range nuclear air and missiles forces. Tactical nuclear weapons fall somewhere in between, but I am inclined to consider them principally as components of the balance of terror. Presently, I shall discuss the "mixed" balance—i.e., the over-all balance of power when the strategic and tactical balances interact.

quire that it be modified to take account of factors such as a possible advantage of the defense over the offense, possibilities for postattack mobilization, geography, asymmetries in supply capabilities, and so on.

The balance of terror is primarily a *deterrent* balance, rather than a *defensive* balance. That is, a "balance" is said to exist when a potential aggressor faces the prospect of retaliatory damage sufficient to deter him, not when he faces the prospect of defeat or frustration of his aims. Conceivably, a balance of terror could exist in the defensive sense, if the forces on both sides were so invulnerable that the side which absorbed the first blow could still retaliate with sufficient force to destroy or prostrate the attacker. But the forces required for winning the war after being attacked would be considerably larger in number and probably different in kind from the forces required to deter the attack.

The tactical balance of power, on the other hand, centers primarily on the function of defense. A balance of power exists when the defending side has enough forces to defeat the attacker or at least to prevent him from making territorial conquests. Deterrence is the consequence of this defensive capability, not of a capacity to inflict unacceptable costs. In the tactical balance, the requirements for deterrence and for effectively fighting a war more or less coincide; this is not the case in the balance of terror.

Another difference concerns the strategic value of territory and of territorial boundaries. In the tactical balance, the strategic value of territory and of the human and material assets associated with territory continues to be high. The traditional elements of national power, such as manpower, natural resources, industrial strength, space, geographic separation, command of the seas, and so on, remain the primary sources of power, and they are important criteria for determining the existence or nonexistence of a tactical balance.

These territorially based elements are also a source of power in the balance of terror, but their significance is less and is considerably different from that in the tactical balance. Strategic nuclear weapons have reduced the importance of geographical separation of the opponents in the balance of terror, since ICBMs can reach from continent to continent. However, distance still retains some significance in the strategic balance of terror. An aggressor can reduce the required range and hence increase the accuracy and possible payload of his missiles by obtaining control of territory between himself and his prospective nuclear opponent. He may also increase the points of the compass from which he can attack, thus complicating the opponent's warning and air defense problem. He may increase the space available for dispersal of his striking forces, and he may obtain useful staging bases and postattack landing points for his long-range aircraft.

The acquisition of industrial and resource assets by conquest may increase a nuclear power's capability to produce additional strategic weapons. While "raw" manpower is not a significant source of power in the balance of terror, an aggressor may turn to his own uses the scientific brainpower of a conquered nation. On balance, however, the strategic value of territory and its associated assets is probably smaller in the balance of terror than in the tactical balance.

Overconcentration on the strategic balance and on the contingency of all-out war has caused us, in recent years, to downgrade excessively the importance of industrial potential for war. War potential continues to be a source of power in the tactical balance, not only prior to war, but also after the war has begun. Stockpiles of raw materials, stand-by war production plants, and the like can be translated into actual military power during the progress of a limited war, provided, of course, that the forces ready in advance of the attack can hold off the enemy until the additional power can be mobilized. However, in the balance of terror, industrial potential provides only preattack power, not postattack power. Once the war has started, if such potential were not destroyed, its usefulness probably would be limited to survival and reconstruction. Even in a very restrained war, involving only counterforce attacks on military installations, with minimum damage to economic assets, a decision probably would be reached before industrial potential could be brought into play.

In the tactical balance, alliances are useful for both deterrence and defense, in roughly equal proportions; the costs of war are low enough, and the incentives to prevent the conquest of an ally are high enough, that allies are likely to see a net advantage in coming to each other's aid. The conquest of an ally means a very serious erosion of one's own power and security position, and such erosion may be prevented at bearable intrinsic costs if the necessary forces are available. Since the potential aggressor is aware of this, the credibility of alliance obligations tends to be high.

In a world of many nuclear powers—i.e., in a "multipolar" balance of terror—alliances are likely to have less utility and credibility for protection against nuclear attack. Obviously, a country which could mount a completely unacceptable retaliation to a nuclear attack on itself would not need allies for security against this contingency. (It might, of course, enter into an alliance for security against nonnuclear attack.) Countries which doubted their individual capacity to deter a nuclear attack might feel they could gain security by combining. In combination, they might be able to muster enough retaliatory power to deter either an attack on the whole alliance simultaneously or an attack on a single member.

The alliance's capacity to deter attack on a single member would depend critically on the amount of his forces the aggressor would have to use up in attacking the first victim. It is conceivable that the attacker would so deplete his own forces that the other members of the alliance could strike without fear of serious retaliation; at least the prospect of this would limit the amount of force the attacker could use against the initial victim and might deter the attack. But, if the aggressor could retain substantial and invulnerable forces while successfully attacking a single member, the supporting allies would feel powerful incentives to renege. Fulfilling the alliance obligation would mean accepting severe destruction. These costs might be suffered in vain, for there would be little chance of saving the attacked ally by nuclear retaliation. And, in retaliating, the supporting allies would be using up forces which they would need for their own future protection. Thus the alliance pledge may not seem very credible to a prospective nuclear aggressor.

Nevertheless, alliances might have some deterrent value in a multipolar balance of terror because of the aggressor's uncertainties, because an alliance would limit the amount of force an aggressor would be free to apply against a single victim, and because deterrence does not depend on absolute credibility. A nuclear attack on a single country would be a very momentous act which might stimulate enough emotional reaction and irrationality among the victim's allies to trigger retaliation on their part. The aggressor would have to realize that the *possible* damage he might suffer at the hands of the whole alliance would be very much higher than the value he placed on conquest of a single member. The magnitude of the possible retaliatory damage might very well offset in his mind the low credibility of an alliance response.

INTERACTION BETWEEN THE BALANCE OF TERROR AND THE BALANCE OF POWER

The strategic and tactical balancing processes do not function independently, but impinge on each other in various ways. In its pure form, the balance of terror operates only to deter an all-out nuclear attack by the Soviet Union against the United States and Great Britain, or by the latter countries against the Soviet Union. The traditional, or tactical, balancing process operates independently only in conflict situations which involve no possibility of the use of nuclear weapons. Thus it operates between nonnuclear countries and blocs with respect to issues in which the nuclear powers are not significantly interested, and in minor conflicts between nuclear powers. But between the two balancing processes in their pure forms is a wide range of situations in which they are interdependent.

For example, since the end of World War II, the United States has used its dominant position in the balance of terror to deter a considerably wider range of contingencies than a direct nuclear attack on itself. The *means* of the balance of terror—the threat and capability of inflicting punishment—have been applied to the furtherance of certain *ends* in the tactical balance of power, notably the deterrence of a large-scale Soviet ground attack in Western Europe. Consequently, in U.S. and Western policy, the scope of the tactical balancing process has shrunk to the deterrence and defense of limited aggression, primarily outside Western Europe. The validity of this concept became increasingly questionable after 1953 and 1954, when the Russians exploded a hydrogen bomb and then demonstrated that they had a modern, long-range delivery capability. These and further Russian advances in missilery since 1957 have tended to reduce the plausible scope of our threat of a "first strike" and to increase the scope of the tactical balancing process.

However, it is not likely that the scope of the balance of terror will narrow to its pure form or that the tactical balance will widen to its prenuclear dimensions. In other words, some form of nuclear response remains a possibility whenever the interests of one of the superpowers are challenged militarily—especially if challenged directly by the other superpower. In some circumstances, and with appropriate capabilities, the threat of massive retaliation may retain some significant credibility. Even if a nuclear response takes only a limited form, there is always the chance—and a conservative aggressor must consider it a good chance—that the war will escalate to severe levels of destruction, perhaps to all-out war. Thus the modern balance of power takes a "mixed" form. Any conventional military attack by one nuclear power (or its adherent) against the interests of another nuclear power creates a risk of nuclear reprisal of some kind; whether a balance exists with respect to *that act* depends not only on the defender's "denial" forces but also on the attacker's appreciation of the risk that punishment will be imposed and of the possible severity of that punishment. The greater the severity of the provocation, the greater the relative importance of the punishment component.

The idea of a mixed balance can be extended and elaborated in terms of a "spectrum of violence." The pole of least violence would be "peaceful competition"—the use of economic aid, propaganda, infiltration of subversive agents, and the like—to affect the internal political complexion of a country. Such competition shades into lower-keyed forms of violence like sabotage and the fomenting of rebellion. The next-higher stage would be military (matériel) aid to rebellious or potentially rebellious groups or to the established government for use against such groups. Successively higher stages would be covert assistance in manpower to either side in a civil war—e.g., by military missions, advisers, and "volunteers"—then limited interstate conventional conflict, then limited or tactical nuclear warfare, then limited strategic warfare involving the territories of the super-

powers, and, finally, all-out nuclear warfare. The word "spectrum" is appropriate because it suggests a gradual shading or progression from one intensity to another and gets away from a common tendency to think of the dimensions of warfare as sharply defined categories such as "limited war" and "all-out war." One suspects that such sharp delineation does not correspond to the realities of human behavior.

At each shading of the spectrum—i.e., for each possible aggressive act—an over-all balance of power either does or does not exist, depending on the potential aggressor's image of the defender's capabilities and intentions. A balance of capabilities would exist at any level if the defender had sufficient forces to deny gains to the aggressor or could impose such high costs as to offset any possible gains. But true balance requires an additional condition: that the aggressor recognizes a will or intent on the part of the defender to use his capabilities. This might be recognized only as a "likelihood" or "probability," rather than as a certainty, and still present a prospect of defeat, or high costs, sufficiently serious to deter attack.

A potential aggressor is "balanced" at each level of violence if his objectives can be denied him at that level, if his costs of fighting at that level would be higher than his expectation of gain, or if, by attacking at that level, he would exceed a certain critical threshold of risk that the defender would "up the ante" to a higher level, at which either the aggressor's aims would be frustrated or he would suffer unacceptable costs. In both a deterrent and a defensive sense, a balance exists at any level when the aggressor knows he would not be able to make gains in attacking at that level. A balance exists only in a deterrent sense when the aggressor can make territorial gains but foresees too great a risk of suffering war costs incommensurate with the gains. For example, should the Russians attack conventionally in Europe, they would be balanced or deterred either if the NATO "shield" could contain their attack or if, in attacking with sufficient force to break through the shield, they incurred too serious a risk that NATO would respond with tactical nuclear weapons or make some other nuclear response which would either frustrate the Soviets' objectives or produce excessive costs for them.

An over-all balance of power depends on the

existence of a balance at all possible levels of violence, in the sense described above. The potential disturber would not be balanced in an over-all sense if there were one or more weak links—i.e., levels of conflict at which he could achieve his goal at tolerable cost and risk. The defender, or *status quo* power, can achieve a balance at some levels by having forces which can frustrate the enemy's aims, and, at other levels, by threatening to impose unacceptable costs on the aggressor.

There are feedbacks between the various levels. For example, if we were to use nuclear weapons in response to a North Vietnamese attack on South Vietnam, we might alienate other Asian countries to the extent that our position in the balance of "peaceful competition" would be grievously weakened. Consideration of this might deter us from using nuclear weapons; also, if the North Vietnamese were to discover or suspect strongly that we would not use nuclear weapons for this reason, they would be less likely to be deterred. For some years, the Soviets have been making gains in the balance of peaceful competition more or less as a by-product of their strengthening position in the balance of terror. Also, the Soviets have attempted to use their new missile force to strengthen their position in the tactical balance by making threats of rocket attacks on various NATO members which are clearly intended to weaken the cohesion of the alliance.

As the above discussion has implied, nuclear technology has increased the importance of *intentions*, relative to *capabilities*, in the balancing process. Intentions have always been important, of course. In the prenuclear balance, the balancing process was set in motion by the perception of the disturber's aggressive intent, as well as by his military capabilities and war potential. And the adequacy of the balance as a deterrent rested in part on the aggressor's being clear about the intentions of the states which would eventually oppose him. But both sides could be fairly sure that, once the conflict was joined, all states which did participate would do so to the full extent of their military power. An important calculation for each side, therefore, concerned the balance of total capabilities.

The relation between total capabilities is still important at the level of the balance of terror —i.e., in the deterrence and fighting of all-out war. But, for conflicts beginning at lower levels, the balance between over-all capabilities is less important, and a new dimension has been added to the factor of intentions—namely, each side's assessment of the other's intent regarding what portion of its destructive power will be used. Each knows that the other can inflict costs that far outweigh the value of any political objective if it cares to do so. Total capabilities establish the bounds of what is possible, but what is probable depends on a reciprocal assessment of wills, which in turn depends on each side's appraisal of the values the other has at stake in each particular issue, of his gambling propensities, his tendencies toward irrationality, his ideological or organizational commitments to certain responses, and his image of the other's characteristics in these respects.

Such estimates are, of course, highly subjective and uncertain, and the pervasive uncertainty adds an important element of stability to the over-all balance of power. Each side is driven to think in terms of probabilities, and, when even the smallest military action *may* eventuate in nuclear war and totally unacceptable costs, small probabilities are likely to be important. Consequently, there is considerable deterrent value in making threats which the threatener knows, and the threatened party suspects, it would be irrational to carry out; if the threat increases the probability of unacceptable costs to the other side by only a few percentage points, it may be sufficient to deter.

This is to say that the existence of a balance of power, or the capabilities requirements for balancing, can hardly be determined without attempting to look into the "mind" of the enemy. One might say that a subjective "balance of intentions" has become at least as important as the more objectively calculable "balance of capabilities."

A corollary of the increased relative importance of intentions is that methods of communicating intent have become more important *means* in the balancing process than they have been in the past. First, nations are becoming more sensitive to what they say to each other about their intentions; the psychological importance of threats and other declarations is on the increase. Second, the function of military forces themselves may be shifting in the direction of a demonstrative role: toward the signaling of future intentions to use force in order to influence the enemy's intentions, as opposed to being ready to use, or using, force simply as a physical means of conquest or denial. Hence we have the enhanced importance of *deterrence* in the modern balance of power as compared with *defense*. We are likely to see more imaginative and subtle uses of "force demonstration" in time of peace—the Russians have given the lead with such acts as the U-2 incident, the test-firing of missiles in the Pacific near U.S. territory, and the shooting down of the U.S. RB-47 in the summer of 1960. Warfare itself may in the future become less a raw physical collision of military forces and more a contest of wills, or a bargaining process, with military force being used largely to demonstrate one's willingness to raise the intensity of fighting and thus to induce the enemy to accept one's terms of settlement. While direct conflict or competition is going on at a low level of the spectrum of violence, selective force demonstrations, using means appropriate to higher levels, may take place as threats to "up the ante."

DETERRENCE IN THE MIRV ERA

BENJAMIN S. LAMBETH

Lambeth traces the evolution of the U.S.-Soviet strategic relationship and discusses the important concepts of mutual deterrence, strategic superiority, and arms control. Lambeth examines crisis behavior to determine what role nuclear weapons play and whether strategic superiority is functionally useful. He then outlines five arguments used to justify arms control measures: (1) to avoid an arms race that would not add to security; (2) to save money; (3) to avoid nuclear proliferation; (4) as a medium of superpower dialogue; and (5) to aid in tension reduction. Lambeth has worked for the Institute for Defense Analyses and is a Teaching Fellow in Government and a Graduate Research Associate of the Center for International Affairs at Harvard University. He is co-author of The Soviet Union and Arms Control: A Superpower Dilemma *(1970), and is currently editing a symposium on* The Dynamics of Soviet Defense Policy.

INTRODUCTION

In one of the landmark contributions to the strategic literature of the late 1950s, Albert Wohlstetter advanced the disquieting thesis that the vulnerability of our strategic retaliatory force (which then consisted largely of overseas-based manned bombers and rather primitive, unhardened IRBMs) to a well-orchestrated Soviet surprise attack had come to suggest worri-

Reprinted by permission and with minor changes from World Politics, *24, no. 2 (January 1972): 221–42. Copyright © 1972 by Princeton University Press.*

The views expressed in this article are solely the author's and should not be interpreted as necessarily reflecting the official view of the Institute for Defense Analyses or of any of its governmental or private research sponsors. I would like to thank Fritz Ermarth, Stanley Hoffmann, Robert Jervis, and Joshua Menkes for their helpful comments on an earlier draft.

some implications for continued U.S. security.[1] The credibility of a deterrent posture, he pointedly emphasized, presupposed the ability of the deterring power to convey to its opponent an absolute certainty that any attack, however massive, would be answered by an unacceptably devastating reprisal. In view of the appreciable possibility that a combined Soviet bomber and missile strike, clandestinely mounted and targeted against our retaliatory forces, might succeed in decimating those forces to a point of virtual uselessness, he went on to argue, the generally accepted notion that our deterrent capacity was a fact to be taken for granted had, in reality, become a dangerously fallacious assumption. Under the right conditions, he suggested, the Soviets could make an entirely rational decision to start a nuclear war and could stand a good chance of carrying it off with impunity.

That article, along with the elaborate RAND Corporation analysis upon which it was based,[2] had a revolutionary impact on the prevailing pattern of American strategic thought. Its assertion of the existence of a "delicate balance of terror" between the two superpowers inspired searching reassessments of the traditional assumptions that underlie our defense policy and, in short order, led strategic analysts of diverse persuasions to conclude that the American deterrent posture was in need of some drastic revisions. The ultimate outcome of this conceptual ferment, needless to say, was the far-reaching decision to expand, disperse, and protect the American retaliatory force, a decision made during the latter years of the Eisenhower era and carried through under the aegis of the Kennedy Administration.[3]

By the mid-point of the 1960s, the attainment of an invulnerable deterrent posture by the United States and the gradual development of a similar posture by the Soviet Union had changed things a great deal. Despite the repeated political crises and conflicts which beset it at lesser thresholds, the U.S.-Soviet relationship had come to assume a remarkable degree of stability at the strategic level. The mainspring of that stability was the mechanism of mutual deterrence, created and maintained by the existence of credible second-strike nuclear forces in the strategic arsenals of each superpower. These forces, in the form of hardened land-based ICBMs and submarine-deployed medium-range missiles, conferred upon both countries the assured ability to ride out a premeditated nuclear first strike with enough residual arms to guarantee a crippling reprisal against the attacker. The paradoxical result was that each country, though totally vulnerable as never before, now assumed an unprecedented degree of security from its opponent's certitude that starting a general nuclear war would be consummately suicidal. As a consequence, nuclear weapons had become both self-negating and substantially devoid of political exploitability, setting new limits on each country's range of permissible action and imparting new "rules of the game" to the international system. East-West disagreements had become modulated by the superpowers' shared fear of nuclear war, and both countries acquired expectations that their adversary's behavior would remain rational and circumspect in the crisis arena.

The recent advent of ABM and MIRV[4] technology and the continued expansion of the Soviet ICBM force throughout the past half-decade, however, have aroused widespread fears among many American observers that a new "delicate balance of terror" may be about to materialize. At the same time, precisely how we should interpret these developments and what we should do to accommodate them have remained subjects of considerable disagree-

---

[1] Albert J. Wohlstetter, "The Delicate Balance of Terror," *Foreign Affairs*, 37 (January 1959): 211–34.

[2] A. J. Wohlstetter, F. S. Hoffman, R. J. Lutz, and H. S. Rowen, *Selection and Use of Strategic Air Bases*, The RAND Corporation, R-266 (April 1954). A summary of this study may be found in E. S. Quade, "The Selection and Use of Strategic Air Bases: A Case History," in *Analysis for Military Decisions*, ed. E. S. Quade (Chicago, 1964), pp. 24–63. For an analysis of its impact on U.S. defense policy, see Bruce L. R. Smith, *The RAND Corporation: Case Study of a Non-Profit Advisory Corporation* (Cambridge, Mass., 1966), pp. 195–240; and *idem*, "RAND Case Study: Selection and Use of Strategic Air Bases," pp. 446–65 of this volume.

[3] The Eisenhower phase of this policy shift is discussed in Samuel P. Huntington, *The Common Defense: Strategic Programs in National Politics* (New York, 1961), pp. 88–122. On the Kennedy-McNamara phase, see William W. Kaufmann, *The McNamara*

Strategy (New York, 1964), pp. 47–101, and Alain C. Enthoven and K. Wayne Smith, *How Much Is Enough? Shaping the Defense Program, 1961–1969* (New York, 1971), pp. 165–96.

[4] MIRV is an acronym for "Multiple Independently Targetable Re-entry Vehicle," a system which has the effect of multiplying the number of warheads deliverable by a single booster to separate aiming points.

ment. Some individuals, particularly within the official American defense policy community, have expressed deep-seated concern over what they consider to be an active Soviet drive for strategic "superiority." In its more alarmist variations, this argument maintains that the Soviet Union is once again moving dangerously close to achieving a nuclear first-strike capability against the United States, that Moscow's avowed interest in the ongoing Strategic Arms Limitation Talks (SALT) may simply be a ruse to lull us into a false sense of security, and that, if we fail to move quickly in deploying our own ABMs and MIRVs, our entire deterrent capacity may well become compromised.[5] Other commentators, predominantly among the academic, scientific, and "defense intellectual" communities, have propounded the opposite thesis: that Moscow merely seeks to equalize the East-West strategic balance, that the Soviets recognize the futility of seeking "superiority" in an era of mutual deterrence, and that the current prospect for arms control offers an unprecedented opportunity for both superpowers which must not be relinquished. Their central concern, unlike that of their conservative counterparts, is not that the Soviets may achieve a first-strike capability against the United States (something they consider impossible), but that a new round of Soviet-American arms competition would severely disrupt the stability of mutual deterrence which has heretofore protected *both* superpowers from a nuclear cataclysm.[6] They maintain, in other words, that a successful conclusion to SALT is not merely a diplomatic nicety which we can easily take or leave, but that, indeed, it constitutes a *sine qua non* for continued international security.

Despite their vast epistemological and normative differences, both of these arguments derive from a number of questionable common premises. Both assume that there are certain inherent qualities in MIRVs and ABMs which make them fundamentally different from existing weapons systems. Both maintain that the familiar parameters of the U.S.-Soviet strategic relationship would be drastically changed if either or both superpowers deployed such weapons in significant numbers. And each harbors a more or less apocalyptic vision of the consequences which would flow from a failure to heed its counsel. In doing so, it may be argued, each tends both to exaggerate the strategic implications of ABMs and MIRVs and to underestimate the extent to which deterrence stability can sustain technological "system shocks."

In practical terms, as we shall seek to demonstrate in the following discussion, this suggests (1) that the balance of terror is substantially less "delicate" than either school in the arms debate has been willing to allow; (2) that the United States need not be too concerned over a Soviet quest for "superiority"—in the unlikely event Moscow should indeed prove to have such a goal; (3) that, *mutatis mutandis*, we should not be misled by the false confidence that "superiority" in our favor would provide any political returns over and beyond those accruing from our existing nuclear forces; and (4) that, insofar as a new round of arms competition would not significantly destabilize the East-West nuclear balance, we must find other than strategic reasons to justify the case for arms limitation measures.

THE DURABILITY OF MUTUAL DETERRENCE

The asserted first-strike (or, alternatively, destabilizing) potential of ABM-MIRV deployment combinations stems from what deterrence theorists would term the "damage-limiting" or "war-fighting" potential of these weapons. Traditional forms of strategic weaponry—namely, hardened single-warhead ICBMs—are merely useful for deterring an attack. They do not possess enough accuracy, reliability, or (as presently deployed) numerical strength to destroy an opponent's similar force in a surprise attack. MIRVs and ABMs, however, tend to complicate matters a great deal. The important quality of MIRV systems is that they promise to multiply almost overnight each superpower's

---

[5] On this last count, Secretary of Defense Laird has gone so far as to assert that U.S. security is "literally at the edge of prudent risk." See Bernard Nossiter, "Laird Warns of Risks in Missile Delay," *The Washington Post*, April 21, 1970. For a somewhat more measured statement of concern over the integrity of our deterrent, see also Albert J. Wohlstetter, "The Case for Strategic Force Defense," in *Why ABM? Policy Issues in the Missile Defense Controversy*, ed. John J. Holst and William Schneider (New York, 1969), pp. 119–42.

[6] See, for example, Herbert F. York, *Race to Oblivion: A Participant's View of the Arms Race* (New York, 1970).

supply of targetable destructive power. Once installed on existing missiles, MIRVs will provide their possessors with at least a fourfold increase in the available number of deliverable warheads.[7] The theoretical military advantage which this development will immediately bestow upon the side that would contemplate striking first is readily deducible. With reasonable confidence in the aiming precision of its warheads, that side could well consider itself capable of almost completely disarming its opponent's land-based missile force by saturating it with a skillfully planned MIRV barrage. It might further hope, with an effective ABM system, to blunt a retaliatory strike by the few enemy missiles that escaped destruction in the initial blow. It would then have but a short step between adding these two calculations and discovering that a nuclear surprise attack against its adversary might just be an option to consider.

The possibility of *both* superpowers' acquiring such a capability is the underlying concern of arms control advocates, who perceive a threatened re-emergence of mutual first-strike incentives similar to those which purportedly dominated the strategic balance of the late 1950s. The possibility of the Soviet Union's acquiring such a capability if the force posture of the United States remains static is the dominant nightmare of many American defense planners. This latter concern has been most clearly reflected in Secretary of Defense Laird's declared belief that, should the Soviets "go on with the development of MIRV's and install them in a new version of their SS-9 type ICBM," and "should they also greatly improve the accuracy of their small ICBM's, which the intelligence community considers possible, the serviceability of our Minuteman force as presently deployed would be virtually nil by the mid- to late-1970s."[8]

There is a deceptive simplicity to both of these arguments, however, which begs for qualifications. Admittedly, the interactions among alternative configurations of U.S.-Soviet ABM and MIRV postures can get to be an intricate business, and this is not the place to go into a detailed examination of targeting scenarios and weapons trade-offs.[9] We can safely suggest, however, that legitimate concerns over either a threat to our deterrent credibility or an impending U.S.-Soviet "delicate balance of terror" must be based on factors other than merely the asserted vulnerability of land-based ICBM forces to MIRV attack.[10]

The U.S. retaliatory capability consists of a good deal more than just the land-based Minuteman force. It also includes a sizeable number of manned bombers on continuous, quick-reaction alert status and a fleet of forty-one nuclear submarines, each of which carries sixteen medium-range Polaris missiles, and over half of which remain constantly on operational

---

highly suspect even on its own terms. The U.S. Minuteman force consists of 1,000 missiles. The Pentagon's standard "worst-case" assumption is that 95 percent of those missiles would be destroyed in a Soviet counterforce first strike using MIRVed SS-9s. If we accept that assumption as valid, then presumably 50 Minutemen would survive the attack. If we further accept the Pentagon's assumption that each of the surviving Minutemen would be 80 percent reliable, then we could count on retaining a serviceable retaliatory force of 40 ICBMs (and of anywhere from 40 to 120 deliverable warheads)—hardly an overkill capability, but one large enough to wreak considerable destruction and, in any event, one clearly larger than Mr. Laird's statement would have us believe.

[9] See, however, Jerome B. Wiesner, "Some First-Strike Scenarios," in *ABM: An Evaluation of the Decision to Deploy an Anti-Ballistic Missile*, ed. Abram Chayes and Jerome B. Wiesner (New York, 1969), pp. 70–83. Wiesner persuasively argues that, even following the worst conceivable Soviet first strike between now and 1980, the United States could still retaliate with upward of 2,500 megatons.

[10] Leaving those other factors aside for the moment, it is not unreasonable to ask just how vulnerable such ICBM forces would stand to become in a MIRV environment. The greater the total number of warheads in any given MIRV package, the smaller each one of those warheads must become in terms of nuclear explosive yield. The smaller each warhead becomes, moreover, the greater its accuracy must be in order to provide reasonable assurance of being able to destroy a hardened target. Consequently, it is far from certain that MIRVs will automatically provide a disarming capability against enemy land-based missiles. They will have to be highly accurate and their delivery systems will have to be consistently reliable. For some useful charts and figures which show the full enormity of these requirements, see Institute for Strategic Studies, *Strategic Survey, 1969* (London, 1970), pp. 30–33.

---

[7] This "fourfold" figure is a rough deduction from available data on U.S. MIRV deployment plans. The land-based Minuteman III ICBM is to be fitted with a MIRV package containing three individual warheads. The MIRV being developed for the submarine-launched Poseidon medium-range missile will carry up to ten warheads. However, not all of the delivery vehicles are to be MIRVed, and not all of those which will be MIRVed are to have the maximum possible number of warheads.

[8] Quoted in "Reflections on the Quarter," *Orbis*, 13 (Summer 1969): 401. This argument, incidentally, is

patrol.[11] Each of these additional force categories complicates the Soviet war-planning effort enormously. The B-52 bomber contingent has the capability of being launched on sufficiently short warning notice to stand a good chance of evading destruction on the ground by any incoming missile attack.[12] Moreover, as much as the missile age has appeared to relegate manned bombers to the status of outmoded relics, these aircraft still possess a respectable capability for penetrating Soviet air defenses and getting through to their assigned targets.[13] The Polaris submarine fleet, for its part, is virtually invulnerable to attack and will remain so until the Soviets can acquire a credible antisubmarine warfare capability. Since most defense planners consider such a development to lie far beyond the foreseeable technological horizon, the Soviet Union's accommodation of the Polaris threat would have to depend solely on ABMs to sustain the brunt of retaliation. Given both the massiveness of which the retaliation would surely be capable and the highly questionable ability of even the most extensive Soviet ABM system to cope with it, that would seem to be an almost insurmountable task.[14] Finally, even though the U.S. has

consistently rejected the launch-on-warning option in its declaratory policy, the Soviets could never be absolutely assured that an eleventh-hour change of mind would not occur in the panic of a nuclear crisis, and their uncertainty on this score would, even aside from all the other factors, give them more than ample reason to think twice before committing themselves to a first strike.

To be sure, this analysis has reduced a complicated problem to some rather sweeping general propositions and, in the process, has necessarily by-passed many of the detailed, technical objections which might be raised. Its primary intent, however, has not been to address technical arguments on technical grounds.[15] Rather, it has been to point out both the profound potical uncertainties which would have to be overcome before a meaningful first strike could rationally be considered and the equally profound technical difficulties which would have to be overcome before such a consideration could even become strategically feasible. Defense Secretary Laird has been widely quoted as having said of the Soviets that "they are going for our missiles and they are going for a first-strike capability. There is no question about that."[16] In point of fact, there is a great deal of question about it—if not about whether they would prefer such a capability, then certainly about whether it lies within their universe of attainability.[17]

---

[11] On this count, moreover, George Quester has pointed out the important and frequently overlooked fact that although improved warhead accuracies and the advent of MIRV systems indeed cast doubts on the long-term reliability of our land-based ICBMs as second-strike weapons, the same developments promise to increase the target coverage of our submarine-launched ballistic missile force by as much as a factor of ten. See his "Missiles in Cuba, 1970," *Foreign Affairs*, 49 (April 1971): 495–96.

[12] Some concern has been expressed that the Soviet FOBS, or "fractional orbital bombardment system," would dangerously reduce the reaction time available to the bomber force by combining a depressed-trajectory flight path with a back-door entry through the southern approach corridor to the United States, where our early warning system is least concentrated. The planned introduction of over-the-horizon radar facilities and advanced missile-launch detection satellites into the United States' early warning network, however, is expected to accommodate the FOBS threat adequately.

[13] We might note in passing that the Soviet Union's persistent statements of concern in the SALT talks over U.S. forward-deployed fighter-bombers in Europe and aboard aircraft carriers may be read, among other things, as authoritative confirmation of the continued deterrent effectiveness of manned aircraft.

[14] In what one is strongly tempted to regard as a classic technological *reductio ad absurdum*, the Defense Department has gone on record with the argument that the Soviet Union could conceivably upgrade its extensive anti-aircraft missile network to ballistic-missile intercept capability, and that these Soviet air

defense missiles would consequently have to be included in any ABM limitation agreement. In private conversations, various Soviet spokesmen have tended to view this argument as a transparent attempt on the part of the Pentagon to complicate the SALT talks unnecessarily. Indeed, it stretches credulity to accept the notion that the Soviets could impart to an obsolete weapon—one which has shown a remarkably poor performance record even against U.S. fighter aircraft in the Vietnam War—a capability which many experts doubt the considerably more sophisticated U.S. ABM could provide. The Pentagon concedes its case to be "hypothetical." See John W. Finney, "Dispute on Soviet Missiles Hampers U.S. Arms Stand," *New York Times*, January 11, 1970.

[15] For an informed and sophisticated survey of technical issues in the current arms debate, see B. T. Feld, T. Greenwood, G. W. Rathjens, and S. Weinberg, eds., *Impact of New Technologies on the Arms Race* (Cambridge, Mass., 1971).

[16] Quoted in Ralph E. Lapp, *Arms Beyond Doubt* (New York, 1970), p. 58.

[17] The U.S. intelligence community, for example, has been anything but unanimous in its appraisal of the Soviet strategic threat. Using the same intelligence data available to Secretary Laird, Director of the Central Intelligence Agency Richard Helms made the un-

The United States and the Soviet Union have long since reached a plateau in their strategic relationship. The terms "mutual deterrence," "qualitative parity," and "nuclear stalemate" all describe it appropriately. Until military technology can devise a truly effective and credible means of neutralizing an adversary's deterrent force, the persistence of residual second-strike capabilities in the possession of each superpower, the continued uncertainty of both regarding the probability of success a first strike would have, and the continued unwillingness of either to place its society's livelihood on the scale in an attempt to find out, will all tend to preserve stability as a "systemic" characteristic of the East-West nuclear balance. Let us now turn to some of the implications of this thesis for U.S. strategy and arms control policy.

THE "SUPERIORITY" FALLACY

The notion that the United States should maintain strategic "superiority" over the Soviet Union (or, in a somewhat muted variant, that we should at least aim to deny such superiority to the Soviets) has for years enjoyed an almost mystical fixation in American strategic folklore. This fixation may perhaps be partly explained simply by the natural psychological and chauvinistic satisfaction that Americans traditionally have drawn from being "stronger than," "better than," or "ahead of" their Communist adversary. For the most part, however, it seems to have derived from a genuine belief that superiority somehow confers political advantages on its possessor that a lesser strategic posture would be unable to provide. Indeed, it is quite amazing how quick strategic analysts have consistently been to assume that our "superiority" was the determining factor in various American foreign policy successes against the Soviet Union. More often than not, such assumptions have been advanced uncritically, and they deserve a closer examination.

In principle, nuclear weapons serve two functions. First of all, they deter a premeditated attack directly on one's own homeland.

As we have just argued at some length, this is a rather undemanding function. The weapons do not have to do anything but merely exist in sufficient quantity and quality to guarantee an "assured destruction" retaliation against any conceivable first strike. And for this, relative numbers in the strategic balance are, by and large, unimportant. All one needs for deterrence is "enough" strength, even if that strength is less, in quantitative terms, than that of the adversary.

Second, many observers have argued that nuclear weapons also underwrite their possessor's foreign policy objectives by threatening his adversary with undesirable sanctions should he attempt to interfere with those objectives. This function seeks to extract some "marginal strategic utility" from nuclear weapons, over and beyond their primary role of deterring an attack on one's homeland, by maximizing the adversary's fear that, in seeking limited objectives at his opponent's expense, he might subject himself to ultimate losses from massive retaliation or uncontrolled crisis escalation, either of whose consequences would be out of all proportion to the original values sought. Here, however, unlike the case of simple deterrence, the credibility and force-level requirements are much more exacting. The adversary must be really convinced that his own contemplated action would in fact trigger the threatened response, and that such a response could be carried off according to promise. During the early postwar years, when the United States enjoyed a nuclear monopoly, this sort of "marginal strategic utility" could possibly have been wielded with some degree of success. Under conditions of mutual deterrence, however—in which even a strategically inferior power could deliver a devastating second strike—any threat to resort to nuclear war that was implied by the political invocation of strategic superiority would quite probably be met with incredulity.[18] To

---

precedented move, in the spring of 1969, of allowing himself to become publicly identified with the view that Defense Department projections of a Soviet first-strike capability were exaggerated. See Peter Grose, "U.S. Intelligence Doubts Soviet First-Strike Goal," *New York Times*, June 18, 1969.

[18] A critic might protest that, while this argument indeed holds for threats of cold-blooded nuclear attacks "out of the blue," it does not consider the possibility that a country could credibly threaten a preemptive nuclear strike against its adversary during an acute crisis in which its core values were at stake, and thereby reap bargaining advantages from its strategic nuclear forces which, under calmer conditions, would be unavailable. More specifically, he might accuse it of a "minimum deterrence" monism, which overlooks the possible utility of those "Type II Deterrence" concepts advanced by Herman Kahn in *On Thermonuclear*

be sure, there have been many occasions when the Soviet Union has backed away from crises when confronted with American diplomatic and military pressure. The question, however, is whether superiority or other factors were the deciding elements in our favor. Since our success in the Cuban missile crisis has most frequently been cited as proof of the value of superiority,[19] it might be helpful to seek an answer there.

In his nationwide television address inaugurating the Cuban crisis, President Kennedy did indeed state that "it shall be the policy of this nation to regard any nuclear missile launched from Cuba against any nation in the Western hemisphere as an attack by the Soviet Union on the United States, requiring a full retaliatory response on the Soviet Union."[20] He plainly did not, however, promise the Soviets a nuclear retaliation if they failed to remove the missiles from Cuba, a fact generally overlooked by the superiority advocates. On the contrary,

he threatened such retaliation only in the event that the missiles were fired, and concern that the Soviets would actually use them militarily was hardly the major element in the crisis. For what it literally promised, Kennedy's threat was perhaps not altogether unbelievable. The important point, however, is that it was not addressed to the main objective of getting the Soviet missiles physically removed from Cuba. Moreover, had the threat of a direct U.S. nuclear attack against the Soviet Union in fact been resorted to as an instrument for inducing Soviet cooperativeness, it would most likely have been patently unconvincing to Khrushchev. However superior the American strategic capability may have been numerically, it could not have met the preconditions for a successful first strike. The Soviet Union, though quantitatively inferior, still possessed an appreciable counterdeterrent in the form of its "not-incredible"[21] second-strike capability, a fact which was no doubt hardly lost on President Kennedy. Why, then, did Khrushchev back down?

Aside from our numerical missile superiority over the Soviets, there were several other factors of relevance to the Cuban crisis. First of all, the crisis was played out within an arm's reach of the United States and fully half a globe away from the Soviet Union. We had a preponderance of conventional power at the point of contact, and there was no guarantee that we would not use it to remove the missiles from Cuba forcibly in the event of a Soviet refusal to withdraw them peacefully. Second, we had a distinct margin of resolve working in our favor. U.S. policy had made it unambiguously evident that the presence of Soviet offensive weaponry in the Western hemisphere posed a direct threat to our vital interests, and Moscow —knowing from the outset that it was fishing in troubled waters—could not persuasively articulate an equally convincing counterclaim. Since it was the Soviets who had chosen to alter the status quo, it was they who had to bear the burden of responsibility. Third, the United States' imposition of a naval quarantine around Cuba, and its threat to launch an air strike against the missiles already on station

---

War (Princeton, 1960), pp. 126–60. In anticipation of such criticism, two points may be made. First, while the force-level requirements of Kahn's Type II Deterrence (i.e., the deterrence of provocative acts other than a direct Soviet attack on the U.S.) are substantially greater than those of mere deterrence against premeditated attacks "out of the blue," they do not necessarily in any way depend on strategic "superiority" over the adversary. It is theoretically possible for a state to have Type II Deterrence without being superior, and equally possible for it to have superiority but not Type II Deterrence. (Indeed, it is noteworthy that Kahn never even mentions superiority in his discussion of the preconditions for Type II Deterrence.) Second, Type II Deterrence requires a credible first-strike capability, something we have already seen to be unattainable under conditions of stable nuclear stalemate. Even Kahn admits—in *Thinking about the Unthinkable* (New York, 1962), p. 113—that under such conditions "the use by a rational (or at least rational-appearing) decisionmaker of Type II Deterrence will not be feasible."

[19] A report by the Georgetown University Center for Strategic Studies, for example, maintains that our Cuban victory constituted "a particularly vivid example of the political utility of military superiority based on advanced technology." *The Soviet Military Technological Challenge* (Washington, D.C., 1967), p. 6. See also Raymond L. Garthoff's assertion that, as a result of Khrushchev's forced removal of the missiles from Cuba, "the American strategic superiority was doubly confirmed: his ploy proved his need for such . . . missiles, and its failure not only denied them but bore impressive witness to the American superiority that compelled him to capitulate." "Military Power in Soviet Policy," in *The Military-Technical Revolution: Its Impact on Strategy and Foreign Policy*, ed. John Erickson (New York, 1966), p. 255.

[20] Quoted in Elie Abel, *The Missile Crisis* (New York, 1966), p. 106.

[21] The qualification is an important one. Whether or not the Soviets in fact had a guaranteed retaliatory capability, the uncertainty on our part obliged us to act as though they did.

there, left the onus of a decision to escalate or back off on the Soviets. Any Soviet ship attempting to run the blockade would have had to face the possibility of being sunk by American naval forces, and, while Khrushchev may have had good reasons for wanting the missiles in Cuba in the first place, he certainly was under no obligation to commit himself to the risk of armed conflict in order to keep them there.

It is among these factors, it seems, that the most plausible explanation of Moscow's retreat from Cuba is to be found. The United States reacted with a degree of alacrity totally unexpected by Khrushchev,[22] displayed consistently pre-eminent resolve throughout the crisis, and skillfully manipulated the risks in such a way that the Soviets had to double or fold.[23] Its strategy, moreover, was dominated not by a direct threat of "massive retaliation" but rather by a calculated management of uncertainty. Thomas Schelling has described the mechanics of such bargaining processes quite impressively. Rejecting the simplistic notion that "the two sides just measure up to each other and one bows before the other's superiority and acknowledges that he was only bluffing," he has pointed out the important (and often overlooked) fact that, "if war tends to result from a process, a dynamic process in which both sides get more and more deeply involved, more and more expectant, more and more concerned not to be a slow second in case the war starts, it is not a 'credible first strike' that one threatens but just plain war."[24]

It was the specter of "just plain war" that essentially caused Khrushchev to reconsider, and that specter had little to do with the American preponderance of ICBM strength. For those who continue to exalt the American success in Cuba as "the classic example of strategic superiority snatching a partial victory from the jaws of political disaster,"[25] two additional points are worth mentioning. First, if the imputed political persuasiveness of U.S. superiority had been as compelling as they assume, it is highly unlikely that the Soviets would have attempted the Cuban missile gamble in the first place, for fear of a preordained failure. Second, the actual behavior of the United States during the crisis suggested anything but confidence that our superiority would bring us through unscathed. The whole affair, on the contrary, was a bewildering encounter with the uncertainties of nuclear brinkmanship in which our own fears and doubts were quite probably no less than those of the Soviets. The self-congratulatory Monday morning quarterbacking displayed by many American strategists in the aftermath of the crisis had little in common with President Kennedy's more judicious postcrisis reflection that, while the Soviets "were in the wrong and . . . had to back down, . . . this doesn't mean at all that they would back down when they felt they were in the right and had vital interests involved."[26]

---

[22] A fair case can be made that the Soviet missile gamble in Cuba was the product of a wholly rational decision, given the evidence and beliefs which Khrushchev had to go on. His expectation of success was no doubt heavily conditioned by a calculation that the United States, having been badly burned once in Cuba during the Bay of Pigs debacle, would not risk a similar failure by opposing his deployment of the missiles. It may also have been enhanced by a belief on his part, reinforced by his earlier confrontation with President Kennedy in Vienna, that the American President was, at bottom, a callow youth who could be easily manipulated by the more wily Soviet ruler. If Khrushchev had had any reason to believe otherwise, he probably would not have made his move at all. As it was, the American response was in all likelihood totally unexpected by him. Rather than ask the standard question of why the Soviets put their missiles in Cuba in the first place, we might usefully consider an alternative question: What did we do (or not do) that led them to believe they could get away with it? In this regard, Bernard Brodie has pointedly observed that "our having made a bad prediction does not itself justify our calling the Russians 'unpredictable.'" *Escalation and the Nuclear Option* (Princeton, 1966), p. 49.

[23] As Oran R. Young has aptly put it, "the United States succeeded in achieving 'escalation dominance' by placing the Soviets in a situation in which they could not improve their bargaining position by raising the level of conflict." *The Politics of Force: Bargaining during International Crises* (Princeton, 1968), p. 388.

[24] Thomas C. Schelling, *Arms and Influence* (New Haven, 1966), pp. 98–99.

[25] William R. Kintner, *Peace and the Strategy Conflict* (New York, 1967), pp. 222–23.

[26] Quoted in Arthur M. Schlesinger, Jr., *A Thousand Days: John F. Kennedy in the White House* (Greenwich, Conn., 1965), p. 759. Indeed, practically all of the published memoirs of the Kennedy era point out President Kennedy's uncertainty during the crisis and his humility in victory. On the first count, Robert F. Kennedy related the President's statement that, "if anybody is around to write after this, they are going to understand that we made every effort to find peace and every effort to give our adversary room to move. I am not going to push the Russians an inch beyond what is necessary." *Thirteen Days: A Memoir of the Cuban Missile Crisis* (New York, 1969), p. 127. On the second count, Theodore Sorensen observes that, while many of the President's advisers felt—after the crisis had abated—that the U.S. victory would make

It is precisely this factor of asymmetrical interests, commitments, and levels of resolve,
rather than the mere presence of asymmetrical
strategic nuclear forces, which seems to have
been the controlling variable in nuclear-age
crisis resolution. We came out ahead in the
Cuban episode because we were able to demonstrate that our interest in getting the missiles
removed was manifestly greater than the Soviet interest in keeping them there. Moreover,
the event occurred close enough to home that
we could quickly mobilize the required local
preponderance of force to give our commitment credibility. Had the crisis been played
out in an area closer to the Soviet Union's
sphere of influence, the odds would have been
much less disproportionately balanced in our
favor. To underscore this point, we need only
recall that the Soviet Union succeeded in occupying Hungary in 1956 and in erecting the
Berlin Wall in 1961, despite the fact that at
both times it was strategically "inferior" to the
United States in at least the same degree that
supposedly determined its defeat in Cuba.
During those crises, the East-West distribution
of bargaining power was essentially reversed
from that which prevailed during the Cuban
missile affair, and the Soviets clearly had more
to lose than we had to gain. In none of the
three cases, however, did the strategic nuclear
balance play any significant role in shaping the
outcome of events. In each, the winner prevailed not because he was willing to go to nuclear war in defense of his interests (which, in
fact, he probably was not) but because the
loser was clearly unwilling to *risk* such a war
in order to stay in the game. The lesson of
these examples thus seems to be that the over-
all nature of the objective, rather than strategic
"superiority," ultimately determines which pro-

tagonist will prevail in a crisis.[27] As Brent
Scowcroft has put it, "the criticality of the
issue at stake for each side in any crisis is a
factor too often overlooked by those who advocate force 'superiority' as a panacea for the
resolution of conflicts with the Soviet Union,"
and, though superior military forces may occasionally "assist in bolstering resolve, . . . one
should never imagine that they somehow constitute 'instant courage.' "[28]

A NONSTRATEGIC CASE FOR ARMS CONTROL

On balance, we come to several interim conclusions. In our earlier discussion of the durability of mutual deterrence, we argued that,
given the foreseeable limits of future military
technology, a credible first-strike capability
(the only meaningful form of strategic "superiority") remains permanently denied to both
superpowers. In analyzing the Cuban missile
crisis, we also maintained that any sort of strategic advantage short of a first-strike capability
offers virtually nothing in the way of direct
coercive utility. Together, these arguments
suggest both the fallaciousness of prescriptions
for U.S. superiority and the groundlessness of
fears that the Soviets may be seeking superiority. Paradoxically, however, they also suggest

---

Kennedy look "ten feet tall" in the eyes of the rest of
the world (including, presumably, those of the Soviets),
the President realistically maintained: "That will wear
off in about a week, and everybody will be back to
thinking of their own interests." Kennedy was, in fact,
so convinced that his success was a narrow and fortuitous one that he subsequently laid down a firm line
against his administration's gloating over the victory.
Theodore Sorensen, *Kennedy* (New York, 1965), pp.
808–9. The notion that "nothing succeeds like success" seems to have had a compelling influence on the
proponents of superiority. By every account, however,
the outcome of the missile crisis was a close one, and
our eventual victory was hardly foreordained. What
would they have said if we had failed?

[27] For further discussion on this point, see the excellent study by Alexander L. George, David K. Hall,
and William E. Simons, *The Limits of Coercive Diplomacy: Laos, Cuba, Vietnam* (Boston, 1971).

[28] Brent Scowcroft, "Deterrence and Strategic Superiority," *Orbis,* 13 (Summer 1969): 450, 453. There
is, it should be pointed out, a serious counterargument
to this view that holds that, "if both sides believe . . .
the side with more missiles has more useable military
power and can prevail in more situations, then the
number of missiles each side has does affect the outcome of political bargaining." Robert Jervis, *The Logic
of Images in International Relations* (Princeton,
1970), p. 231. In theory, this argument is hard to disagree with. In practice, however, it is only as good as
its assumption is valid, and there is little evidence to
suggest that such a constellation of beliefs has ever in
fact existed in the East-West relationship. On the contrary, as we have seen, the United States has frequently been circumspect and the Soviet Union adventurous, even though the prevailing asymmetries of the
nuclear balance would have suggested that the reverse
should have been the case. Indeed, it is perhaps one
of the notable ironies of the nuclear age, that while
both Washington and Moscow have often lauded superiority as a military force-posture goal, neither has
ever behaved as though it really believed superiority
significantly mattered in the resolution of international
conflicts.

that there exists little compelling *strategic* reason for either of the superpowers to engage in arms control negotiations.[29] If it is true that asymmetries in the nuclear balance are irrelevant to the functioning of mutual deterrence, that superiority is worthless as an instrument of policy, and that the stability of deterrence is likely to remain intact whether an arms race ensues or not, then what difference should it make whether the SALT talks succeed or fail? Indeed, why should the "arms problem" be a cause for concern at all?

THE "RATIONALIST" ARGUMENT

Perhaps the most compelling indictment against continued arms competition between the United States and the Soviet Union is that its ultimate offspring, for each country, would almost certainly be stillborn. In Lewis Carroll's *Through the Looking Glass*, the Red Queen confronts Alice with a perplexing inversion of conventional logic that neatly captures the essence of this indictment. "Now here, you see," the Red Queen points out, "it takes all the running you can do to keep in the same place. If you want to get somewhere else, you must run at least twice as fast as that!"[30] There could hardly be a more appropriate metaphor to describe the current pace of East-West strategic interaction. The technological dynamism displayed by this interaction has bordered on the bedazzling. Yet, like Alice's race on the treadmill of Wonderland, it seems to have been just as unyielding of tangible progress. As each superpower has sought new levels of security through new breeds of weaponry, it has invariably provoked its opponent—equally driven by the imperative of security—to counteract in kind. The resultant exercise in strategic one-upmanship has thus been essentially a competition in countervailing frustration, imparting high costs to both countries and, in the end, advantages to neither. Former Defense Secretary McNamara once likened it to a "mad mo-

mentum,"[31] and other observers have been equally moved to ask whether this seemingly mindless scramble for ABMs, MIRVs, and more advanced forms of strategic gadgetry is really a product of rational policy or merely the outgrowth of some blind technological determinism with a life of its own.[32]

The "rationalist" argument for arms control derives not so much from fear of the dangers of a new arms race as from the conviction that such an arms race cannot serve the security interests of either superpower. It holds that both the United States and the Soviet Union have already gained as much security as life in the deterrence arena will allow, that the point of diminishing returns from new weapons deployments has long since been passed, and that the SALT talks offer both countries every incentive and opportunity to get off the treadmill and relax.

THE ECONOMIC ARGUMENT

A logical corollary to the "rationalist" argument holds that, if new strategic weapons have nothing to offer, then it is patently wasteful to expend the gargantuan amounts of resources necessary to produce and maintain them. Modern weapons systems are enormously costly to create, develop, and deploy. While a turn down in their production rate would hardly eliminate defense spending entirely, it would certainly allow for substantial savings which could possibly be redirected to other sectors of society. It would probably be fair to assert that no two countries are in greater need of a radical shift in economic priorities than the United States and the Soviet Union. Arms control, while certainly no panacea in itself, would clearly seem to provide each country with a considerable share of the economic preconditions for a step in the right direction.

---

[29] Among the few analyses that have recognized and sought to deal with this paradox are Robert Jervis, "Bargaining and Bargaining Tactics," in *Coercion*, ed. J. Roland Pennock and John W. Chapman, Nomos 15 (New York, 1971), and Herbert Scoville, Jr., *Toward a Strategic Arms Limitation Agreement*, Carnegie Endowment for International Peace (New York, 1970).

[30] Lewis Carroll, *The Annotated Alice* (New York, 1960), p. 210.

[31] Robert S. McNamara, *The Essence of Security* (New York, 1968), p. 166.

[32] Indeed, an argument can be made that the hypervigilance induced by this "mad momentum" often forces each superpower into what amounts, in effect, to an arms race with itself. The paradigm of this phenomenon is the case where superpower *A* develops weapon *Y* to counteract its weapon *X*, which it assumes superpower *B* also will have eventually. More often than not, the net result is to provoke the adversary into actually deploying the weapon which such anticipatory countermeasures are intended to check. For discussion on this point, see Robert L. Rothstein, "The Scorpions in the Bottle," *Washington Monthly*, 1 (January 1970): 31.

ARMS CONTROL AND NUCLEAR PROLIFERATION

If the two superpowers had only each other to worry about, then the question of their international "image," leadership, and responsibility might hardly arise. Indeed, there was a time when East-West bipolarity was so all-pervasive that the two nuclear giants could blithely dismiss lesser states as merely minor irritants. The nuclear stalemate, however, has changed matters profoundly and irretrievably. Caught up in a deadlock of mutual deterrence, the Soviets and Americans alike have watched the political relevance of their strategic power decline steadily. Encumbered and frustrated by the essential unusability of their nuclear-missile strength, they have paradoxically also found themselves increasingly vulnerable to the pressures of other states, whose interests have now come to demand accommodation.

Today, both the United States and the Soviet Union confront a revolutionary international system dominated by fluidity, incipient tension, and often virulent and explosive forms of assertive nationalism. Moreover, nuclear weapons technology has become virtually a free-market commodity, raising the disquieting possibility that world politics in the years ahead will be intensified by a profusion of lesser nuclear states crowding one another and the superpowers for a measure of international stature and influence.

Concern over such a possibility has been explicitly acknowledged by the superpowers in their eager acceptance of the nuclear nonproliferation treaty. Along with that concern, however, have come new responsibilities. The various nuclear "threshold" countries have made it abundantly clear that a precondition to their acceptance of nonproliferation must be a demonstrated willingness on the part of the superpowers to modulate their own nuclear arms race. In signing the nonproliferation treaty, the United States and the Soviet Union rhetorically acceded to that precondition, and are now obliged to follow through with it by action.[33] To do otherwise—preaching the virtues of nonproliferation while at the same time more

firmly securing their own nuclear duopoly—would be to convey an image of transparent double-dealing, which could serve only to aggravate the probability of eventual nuclear-weapons acquisition by the present "threshold" powers.

ARMS CONTROL AS A MEDIUM OF SUPERPOWER DIALOGUE

Another possible contribution of arms control negotiations (and one often overlooked in many Western strategic writings) would be simply the opportunity afforded to each of the two superpowers to get to know the other better.[34] Not nearly enough attention has been paid, either in scholarly analyses or in official government circles, to the persistent mutual misperceptions and misunderstandings which have continually plagued Soviet-American relations.[35] More often than not, these misperceptions and misunderstandings have been substantially due to distorted images generated by insufficient information. "Intelligence gaps" on the part of both countries (particularly regarding each other's strategic intentions) have been characteristic obstacles to effective policymaking, enhancing fears of the worst, and fueling continued arms increases by each side. American Sovietologists in particular have labored under immense difficulties in trying to winnow out the mainstream of Soviet thinking, policies, and concerns from the limited clues provided by the available documentary evidence.

Much of this groping in the dark would stand to be significantly reduced in the course of a serious U.S.-Soviet arms control dialogue. The perceptual, political, and strategic problems which would have to be addressed in such a dialogue could not long sustain an exchange of generalities. Weapons interactions, implications, and trade-offs in the contemporary strategic milieu are highly intricate

---

[33] For elaboration on the relationship between the proliferation issue and SALT, see Benjamin S. Lambeth, "Nuclear Proliferation and Soviet Arms Control Policy," *Orbis*, 14 (Summer 1970): 298–325.

[34] Discussion of this possibility and of its potential value may be found in Jerome H. Kahan, "Strategies for SALT," *World Politics*, 23 (January 1971): 171–79. See also Jeremy Stone, *Strategic Persuasion: Arms Limitations through Dialogue* (New York, 1968).

[35] See, however, Ole Holsti, "Cognitive Dynamics and Images of the Enemy," *Journal of International Affairs*, 21, no. 1 (1967): 16–39; Robert Jervis, "Hypotheses on Misperception," *World Politics*, 20 (April 1968): 454–79; and Anatol Rapoport, *The Big Two: Soviet-American Perceptions of Foreign Policy* (New York, 1971). See also Adam B. Ulam, *The Rivals: America and Russia since World War II* (New York, 1971).

technical matters which sooner or later would require specific and precise examination by both negotiating partners. In the process, each side would almost certainly come to learn a great deal about the fears, calculations, and motivations which inform its adversary's security policies.

ARMS CONTROL AND TENSION REDUCTION

Finally, it seems self-evident that a negotiated arms limitation agreement would provide a welcome degree of psychic relief from the breathtaking pace of nuclear weapons competition which has heretofore dominated the nuclear age. Notwithstanding our contention that, in terms of the technical mechanics of mutual deterrence, a continued U.S.-Soviet arms race would most likely not be seriously destabilizing, we must remember that political leaders are not necessarily "rational strategic men." They view the world darkly, like most ordinary people, through the filter of their own subjective values and fears. To them, a reasoned argument that deterrence was in good shape might be difficult to accept calmly in the context of a reality in which their opponents were building ever-increasing levels of nuclear destructive power. Perceptions of security, at bottom, are rooted in obscure cognitive processes rather than in the austere and logical deductive schemes of strategic theoreticians. Consequently, it is altogether probable that political decisionmakers would find a rapid pace of strategic arms development and deployment on the part of their avowed enemy quite unnerving, even though the objective technical evidence and the rules of "strategic logic" would suggest that there was plainly nothing to fear. In the narrow sense that an arms race would tend to maximize each side's inner feeling of insecurity and to heighten its perceived need to be "vigilant," therefore, it could legitimately be argued that such an arms race would be "destabilizing." Arms control, by eliminating the sources of such perceived insecurity, would go a long way toward providing for a more livable world. Disagreements, conflicts, and even occasional crises would doubtlessly persist, but they could be considerably less enervating if the superpowers were able to act upon them with the measured confidence a nuclear *modus vivendi* would permit.

CONCLUSION

The history of the nuclear age has traditionally been dominated by an almost dialectical process of technological change and conceptual readjustment. Repeatedly over the past two decades, developments in weaponry by the two superpowers have produced qualitative shifts in the nature of their strategic relationship, adding new limits and corollaries to the international "rules of the game," and forcing each country, in consequence, to recast its old strategic doctrines and policy formulas in order to accommodate these changing imperatives. The result has been a marked periodicity in the U.S.-Soviet arms competition, a competition driven by the relentless advance of military technology and characterized by a progression of evolutionary phases, revolutionary "turning points," and concomitant "agonizing reappraisals" on the part of both superpowers.[36]

Moscow's initial acquisition of an airdeliverable nuclear capability in the early 1950s marked the beginning of this pattern by irretrievably eliminating our brief atomic monopoly and invalidating in one stroke all the enshrined military verities of a simpler past. The enormous destructive potential of atomic weaponry and the new certainty that "a major unrestricted war would begin with a disaster . . . of absolutely unprecedented and therefore unimaginable proportions" for both superpowers led a distinguished American strategist to reflect the changed temper of the time by calling for a "comprehensive pursuit of the new ideas and procedures necessary to carry us through the next two or three dangerous decades."[37]

This "comprehensive pursuit" soon became beset by the task of accommodating the perceived insecurities of the "delicate balance of terror," a second quantum stage in the nuclear relationship introduced by Moscow's attainment of sufficient strategic capabilities to place our vulnerable retaliatory forces in possible danger of being destroyed by a surprise first strike. Sparked by this concern over the security of our deterrent, American defense policy-

[36] For a detailed account of these developments, see George Quester, *Nuclear Diplomacy: The First Twenty-Five Years* (New York, 1970).
[37] Bernard Brodie, "Strategy Hits a Dead End," *Harper's*, October 1955, pp. 33, 37.

makers moved to harden and disperse the strategic arsenal of the United States during the early 1960s so as to provide for a guaranteed nuclear second-strike capability. The Soviet Union followed suit shortly thereafter with a similar hardening and dispersal program of its own, and the nuclear era entered upon its third and present phase of stable mutual deterrence.

The heightened activity of recent American and Soviet weapons-development programs has led many American strategists to conclude that the East-West nuclear equation is once again on the verge of a qualitative shift. While these strategists, as we have seen, are polarized in their respective attitudes regarding the proper response we should take, they share a common belief that the present trend in the nuclear arms race seriously threatens to endanger our continued security if we let it go on unattended.

Contrary to this widespread belief, our central contention here has been that the "dialectic" of the Soviet-American strategic relationship has become firmly immobilized—at least for the foreseeable future—by the durability of mutual deterrence, and that, while new weapons deployments by either or both superpowers may induce numerical fluctuations in the strategic balance, neither the stability of that balance nor the security it provides will be significantly affected in the process.

If we view the arms race in this light, it should follow that the dominant cause of the ongoing American arms debate has been not so much a legitimate concern over the dangers of technological change as a fundamental crisis of traditional strategic ideas. The United States today stands at a crossroads of choice between serious pursuit of an arms limitation dialogue with the Soviets and continued deployment of strategic weaponry. That the choice remains unmade is clear testimony both to the magnetic appeal held out by the prospect of arms control and to the simultaneous reluctance on the part of U.S. policymakers to make the radical conceptual departure which that prospect requires. The psychological underpinnings of this reluctance are, of course, readily understandable. It is easy enough for intellectuals and analysts to advance sweeping proposals for change: they are far from the wellspring of political power and are accountable only to the moral canons of their calling. Presidents and policymakers, on the other hand, must be more circumspect because of the responsibilities they shoulder for the well-being of their constituents. Consequently, there is a strong tendency on their part to adhere to the familiar pattern of the status quo rather than to experiment with new policies that bear a high uncertainty of outcome.

Yet, occasions emerge periodically in which conventional wisdom becomes inappropriate to prevailing realities. Under such conditions, adherence to the outmoded dogmas of the past can only have a corrosive effect on the health of the nation. We have long since reached a point in the evolution of the nuclear age where traditional strategic theories have outlived their applicability. Mutual deterrence has deprived nuclear weapons of any coercive utility, rendered strategic "superiority" both a worthless instrument of foreign policy and a false guarantee of national security, and, in the process, made numerical comparisons of forces altogether useless as means for measuring relative strategic power.

Until recently, American policymakers had no need to face up to these facts, both because there was no tangible prospect for arms control available to provoke a choice among alternatives, and because doubts about the adequacy of American security could be assuaged by seeking confidence in the belief that our numerical missile superiority held the key to nuclear deterrence. Today's crisis in traditional strategic thought stems from our traumatic loss of that superiority and from our confusion over whether we ought to try to recapture it. It is not by any means a novel sort of crisis in American political history. Alluding to the profound moral indecision which preceded our entry into World War I, the American essayist Randolph Bourne described such "crises of confidence" with remarkable incisiveness and perceptivity. "Mental conflicts," he observed more than a half-century ago, "end either in a new and higher synthesis . . . or else in a reversion to more primitive ideas which have been outgrown but to which we drop when jolted out of our attained position."[38] The pre-eminent question of contemporary American strategic life is whether we shall seek the "new and higher synthesis" of accommodation to nuclear parity and accept-

[38] Randolph S. Bourne, *War and the Intellectuals: Collected Essays, 1915–1919* (New York, 1964), p. 10.

ance of arms control—perhaps taking on some small but necessary risks in the process—or whether we shall fall back on the "primitive ideas" of security through nuclear superiority and thus submit to the arms race which would inevitably result.

In the course of this essay, we have tried systematically to lay out a case in favor of arms control, a case dominated not by apocalyptic warnings of the dire consequences which would flow from a failure to accept it but by a more modulated suggestion that it would merely defy common sense to do otherwise. It clearly follows from our argument that, if we really wish to achieve a negotiated arms limitation accord with the Soviets, we must openly abandon our pursuit of "superiority" and assimilate into our image of strategic reality the recognition that East-West nuclear equality can be the only basis for fruitful arms control discussions. A promising step in this direction seems to have been made by President Nixon's articulation of the concept of "sufficiency" as the proper premise upon which U.S. strategic policy should be developed.[39] Unlike "superiority," "sufficiency" is a term with enough semantic ambiguity to allow the United States the satisfaction that its security is protected and, at the same time, to avoid bruising the *amour-propre* of the Soviet Union. It is a relatively value-free slogan that both superpowers can easily live with.

We cannot, however, have our cake and eat it too. On the very heels of President Nixon's embrace of the "sufficiency" construct, Secretary Laird was quoted as having inserted the qualification that the use of the term should in no way be taken to suggest that we have given up "the idea of superiority."[40] At the risk of lecturing the Secretary of Defense on the delicate art of strategic communication, we must

plainly note that this sort of approach will simply not be good enough. Superiority, by any other name, will remain superiority in the eyes of the Soviets, and our continued pursuit of it will only drive them to a vigorous counteraction in kind. Indeed, the rearguard effort of many American defense policymakers to beat the superiority drum while others in the government are trying to smooth a path through the SALT negotiations brings to mind Santayana's remark about fanatics who redouble their efforts as they lose sight of their goals.

A rational defense policy must meet the imperatives of national security, but it must not do so at the unnecessary sacrifice of other important social values. A continued drive by the United States to outmatch the Soviets in numbers of nuclear missile weapons would be doubly injurious: along with the economic deprivation it would impose upon other sectors of society and the hypertension it would perpetuate in the American strategic "psyche," it would also, in the end, contribute nothing to its primary goal of enhancing the military protection of the country. Arms control, on the other hand, has a great deal to offer on all counts and deserves a place of particular priority in the hierarchy of U.S. objectives. If, for any reason, the Soviet Union should change its position in the future and combine accelerated strategic arms build-ups with a militant and aggressive foreign policy, the primacy of political expediency over strategic logic would make it impossible to justify total American inaction. For the moment, however, our first imperative should be to continue exploring the possibility of an arms-limitation accord which might well eliminate the causes of such reflexiveness altogether. The price of that possibility is our acceptance of the Soviet Union as an equal in the exclusive community of superpowers. It is a price which we can safely afford to pay, and one which we owe to the next generation of American policymakers, who would inherit the consequences of our failure to do so.

---

[39] For a useful background discussion on the genealogy of the "sufficiency" concept, see I. F. Stone, "Nixon and the Arms Race: How Much is 'Sufficiency'?" *New York Review of Books*, 12 (March 27, 1969): 6–18.

[40] Quoted in Michael E. Sherman, "Nixon and Arms Control," *International Journal*, 24 (Spring 1969): 335. A similarly Kafkaesque example of this sort of rhetorical sleight-of-hand may be found in Hanson Baldwin's statement that, while "the first and absolute requirement for any grand strategy tomorrow is 'sufficiency' in strategic weapons, . . . 'sufficiency,' in this context, must mean a clear-cut and visible U.S. qualitative and quantitative superiority. Equivocation on this issue risks the life of the nation." *Strategy for Tomorrow* (New York, 1970), p. 295. In the face of

such blatant cases of disregard for the meaning of words, one is almost tempted, out of despair, to agree with the candid and undoubtedly revealing remark made by Deputy Secretary of Defense Packard when pressed by reporters for a definition of sufficiency: "It means," said Packard, "that it's a good word to use in a speech. Beyond that, it doesn't mean a God-damned thing." "Arms Sufficiency Defined," *Washington Post*, June 16, 1969.

THE ARMS RACE PHENOMENON

COLIN S. GRAY

Arms races are the product of "two or more parties who, perceiving themselves to be in an adversary relationship, increase or improve their armaments at a rapid rate." This article attempts a systematic investigation of the subject by providing: (1) an extensive review of the types of arms races; (2) their strategies; (3) possible outcomes; and (4) their dynamics. It also gives a timely discussion of two vital concepts, sufficiency and stability. Colin S. Gray is a staff member (Strategic Studies) of the Canadian Institute of International Affairs and a Visiting Associate Professor of Political Science at the University of British Columbia. He is the author of Canadian Defense Priorities: A Question of Relevance *(1972).*

DEFINITIONS AND FUNCTIONS

Since the 1850s there has been intermittent but always renewed interest on the part of politicians, academics, and journalists in the particular aspect of interstate rivalry generally termed an "arms race." Despite the longevity of concern and the eclecticism of approach, the prime impetus behind the inquiry that has resulted in this article is the sad truth that, aside from somewhat banal and highly questionable hypotheses, we really know very little about arms race phenomena. This analysis will attempt a systematic investigation of some of the most important aspects of the subject.

It is organized for inquiry into the following areas: typology, strategies, outcomes, and hypothetical explanations of the dynamic elements driving the phenomenon.

Two observations must preface an attempt at definition. It should be noted that arms races do not occur only between states or coalitions of states. Those whose eyes are firmly fixed on the great issues of interstate politics tend to neglect intrastate violence and preparations for violence. This is probably the mundane yet correct explanation for the interstate focus of practically all writing related to arms races. The concurrent arming of the Ulster and Irish

volunteers between 1910 and 1914 would appear to be as clear a case of a competitive arms relationship as we could wish for. Second, in practice it is extremely difficult to distinguish between decisions taken primarily to have effect upon the external, competitive arms situation of a state and those decisions that are taken primarily for domestic reasons.[1] However, these decisions, whether externally or internally induced, may properly be regarded as being of importance to the arms race. An arms race competitor, seeking a particular state of military balance, will probably not be able to ignore an opponent's activity, on the ground that he believes it to be inward- as opposed to outward-looking.[2]

At this juncture it is sensible to make a very

[1] This complication is explored in Bruce M. Russett, *What Price Vigilance? The Burdens of National Defense* (New Haven, 1970), particularly on pp. 13, 178.

[2] This point refers to the classic dilemma of intentions versus capability. It would seem to me that, in the current superpower arms race, defense decisions taken to appease domestic lobbies may have the same consequences as they would if they were unambiguously competitive in the arms race context. A somewhat more optimistic view is provided by N. Petersen, "The Arms Race Implications of Anti-Ballistic Missile Defences," in *Implications of Anti-Ballistic Missile Systems*, ed. C. F. Barnaby and A. Boserup, Pugwash Monograph no. 2 (London, 1969), p. 40.

Reprinted by permission and with minor changes from World Politics, 24, no. 1 (October 1971): 39–79. *Copyright © 1971 by Princeton University Press.*

For their helpful comments on an earlier draft of this article, I would like to express my thanks to my former colleagues at Lancaster University, England, particularly to Martin Edmonds, David Holloway, Peter Nailor, and David Travers.

minimal condition for the existence of an arms race relationship; notably, that there should be two or more parties who, perceiving themselves to be in an adversary relationship, increase or improve their armaments at a *rapid* rate and structure their respective military postures with a *general* attention to the past, current, and anticipated military and political behavior of the other parties.[3] In short, actors may march to the beat of their own drums and pursue a logic of military development and deployment that is strictly domestic; but this activity may serve as an arms race "trigger" for other actors. Indeed, it can be argued that a competition may be sustained at a high level and accelerated by the fact that the parties do not share a common strategic logic.

Today the superpowers are locked into a deterrent relationship, the stability of which depends upon their both maintaining a sufficiency of military preparation. However, the Soviet notion of sufficiency may include the deployment of MIRV and ABM technologies for the missions of pre-emption and homeland defense. American doctrine does not currently list these missions as being desirable. As indicated in the definition, the military preparations of an arms "racing" state will be conducted with a general concern for the activities of certain preselected parties. A rigid pattern in the action-reaction of competitive armament as a limiting definition of the arms race phenomenon should not be implied; such a hypothesis is simply one explanation of the possible reasoning behind arms expenditure.[4]

There is so much confusion attached to arms race definitions that it may be helpful to clarify the broad definition offered above by listing the basic conditions for an arms race.

1. There must be two or more parties who are conscious of their antagonism.
2. They must structure their armed forces with attention to the probable effectiveness of the forces in combat with, or as a deterrent to, the other arms race participants.
3. They must compete in terms of quantity (men, weapons) and/or quality (men, weapons, organization, doctrine, deployment).
4. There must be rapid increases in quantity and/or improvements in quality.

All four of these factors must be present for there to be any valid assertion that a particular relationship is an arms race.

The question of the genesis of arms races is one that merits some attention. Leaving aside the option of a disarmed neutrality, in seeking national security a state will either pursue supporting alliances or it will seek to amass armaments, essentially within its own territory. This simple ideal typology must allow for two qualifications. First, the choice of roads to the national security is, by and large, a forced one; second, state policy will probably be mixed— that is to say, there will be a measure both of alliance acquisition and of armaments increase. Naturally, this discussion refers to a group of decisionmakers who perceive an adversary and decide that measures for defense must be taken. At least in theory, we can conceive of a ruling elite deciding upon the pursuit of a competitive arms policy in order to attain glory, prestige, domestic political tranquillity, or the

---

[3] Alternative definitions may be found in *ibid.*; Samuel P. Huntington, "Arms Races: Pre-Requisites and Results," in *Public Policy, 1958*, ed. Carl S. Friedrich and Seymour E. Harris (Cambridge, Mass., 1958), p. 41; Arthur L. Burns, "A Graphical Approach to Some Problems of the Arms Race," *Journal of Conflict Resolution*, 3 (December 1959): 326; Urs Schwarz and Laszlo Hadik, *Strategic Terminology: A Trilingual Glossary* (New York, 1966), p. 35; Stockholm International Peace Research Institute, *SIPRI Yearbook of World Armaments and Disarmament, 1968/69* (Stockholm, 1969), p. 44 (hereafter cited as *SIPRI Yearbook*). The definitions of these authors are all too exclusive: Huntington and Burns stress the interstate nature of arms race phenomena, Schwarz and Hadik require participants to endeavor to stay ahead in the race, and the SIPRI authors equate an arms race with the "action-reaction phenomenon."

[4] The debate over the various ABM decisions announced by the U.S. government since September 1967 has drawn attention to the possible role of different kinds of Soviet-American interactive patterns in strategic armaments. The strongest statement endorsing an action-reaction interpretation of the superpower arms race is to be found in George W. Rathjens, "The Dynamics of the Arms Race," *Scientific American*, April 1969, particularly the diagram on p. 24. On the other side, considerable skepticism concerning the action-reaction cycle may be found in Laurence W. Martin, *Ballistic Missile Defence and the Alliance*, The Atlantic Papers (Paris, 1969), p. 25; William T. Lee, "The Rationale Underlying Soviet Strategic Forces," in *Safeguard: Why the ABM Makes Sense*, ed. William R. Kintner (New York, 1969), pp. 142–78; Richard B. Foster, "The Safeguard BMD Proposal and Arms Control Prospects for the 1970's," *ibid.*, pp. 242–77; Jeremy J. Stone, "When and How to Use 'SALT,' " *Foreign Affairs*, 48 (January 1970): 262–73.

enrichment of domestic industrial allies. The problem that is in need of empirical investigation is why states have in fact offered and accepted arms race challenges.

It is possible that an arms race might develop without there being any driving political antagonisms. A quite autonomous arms increase may be matched by a fairly disinterested party, solely as a precautionary move, and hence a cycle of close or intermittent armament interactions and previously unappreciated political antagonisms may ensue. Prior to the opening rounds of an arms race, the eventual competitors are not in a situation of zero armaments. Every arms race opens with a particular ratio of military forces. The importance of existing disparities in arms levels for the decision to engage in a race must await further investigation.

On those many occasions when reliable allies are not available, states have been encouraged either to issue an arms race challenge, or to accelerate previously low-gear arms race activity, following upon an apparent military-technological opportunity. This opportunity may take the form of diminished activity by the rival or, more likely, the successful development of a technology that offers to negate, or render less significant, an existing quantitative or qualitative imbalance. As examples of this, we could cite France versus England in the 1840s and 1850s; Germany versus England after 1906; and the Soviet Union's missile development and procurement policy in the middle 1950s and from 1963 to 1970.

This last example is a very contentious one. It has been argued that the great increase and improvement in the Soviet ICBMs and SLBMs (submarine-launched ballistic missiles) apparent in the late 1960s reflected decisions taken in the period 1961–1965.[5] Thus, the building programs have reflected a sustained determination to match and perhaps to outbuild the United States. A different interpretation would be that the Soviet Union was encouraged to challenge the American lead by the quantitative restraint shown by the Americans after 1964. This latter view is a direct repudiation

of the idea that an arms race may be restrained by the operation of a "sympathetic parallelism."[6]

With regard to the functions of a competition, we may choose to view an arms race as an alternative to war, to be planned, waged, and then won or lost—with due reward or punishment. A more apocalyptic view would be that an arms race is not an alternative to war, but is a preparation for war. Thus, instead of an arms race being a bloodless ritual of preparation,[7] it is a race for that measure of military superiority which would allow for the exploitation of arms race victory in war-waging success.

The choice of an overall view of an arms race is directly dependent upon the major empirical referents. The introduction of nuclear weapons has made a very considerable difference to the conduct of an arms race. Indeed, one leading interpreter of Lewis Richardson's theory of arms races has developed Richardson's idea of submissiveness, originally applied to the interwar period, with the argument that nuclear weapons have introduced an unprecedented fear factor into the post-1945 nuclear arms race.[8] However, even if we grant the quantum jumps in the time scale of contem-

---

[5] See Lee, op. cit., pp. 168–71; and Thomas W. Wolfe, Soviet Power and Europe, 1945–1970 (Baltimore, 1970), chap. 16.

[6] Wolfe, op. cit., pp. 503–4; Lee, op. cit., p. 147; Foster, op. cit., pp. 259–60.

[7] Paul Smoker, "Fear in the Arms Race: A Mathematical Study," in International Politics and Foreign Policy, ed. James Rosenau (New York, 1969), p. 579.

[8] Ibid., p. 573. Arms races comprise a single class of phenomena in international relations and (with due caution) a comparative analysis of different arms races will yield a measure of general wisdom. With respect to the empirical base of the article, most of the historical illustrations refer to the following arms races: England-France and Russia (naval, 1884–1904, with Italian, German, and Austro-Hungarian complications); England-Germany (naval, Phase I, 1898–1905; Phase II, 1906–1914); England–United States–Japan (naval, 1918–1922, with many complications—principally respecting France and Italy; also, it could be argued that the nature of the Washington Treaty restrictions caused a redirection rather than a termination of the race); Soviet Union–United States (all categories of armaments, from 1946 to the present, with Chinese complications after 1964). Other races are very briefly mentioned in the text. A detailed inventory of arms races, by type, awaits the attention of a further study. As may be deduced from the breadth of the definition offered in the text, the arms race phenomenon is far more prevalent than many students of politics will commonly allow. See Huntington, op. cit., and Quincy Wright, A Study of War (Chicago, 1942), 2: 690. Itemization is dependent upon definition. Huntington's "duel" focus for arms races and Wright's insistence upon the "general" nature of recent races renders the empirical bases of both works somewhat suspect to me.

porary war and the destruction that could be imposed by nuclear weapons, it would still be a gross oversimplification to assert that, prior to 1945, arms races were more often than not serious preparations for war, whereas, since 1945, arms races involving nuclear powers have been essentially a form of diplomatic activity, remote from considerations of the conduct and termination of war. Two vital complications must be noted. First, competition in missiles, since at least 1959, bears an important resemblance to races between land forces prior to 1945. Both kinds of races are what can be termed "damped" or "non-self-aggravating" arms races.[9] In other words, the needed ratio of offense to defense is such that a strategy of militarily exploitable superiority is prohibitively expensive.[10] The traditional ratio required for offensive land force success was 3:1, and the requirement for a successful nuclear first strike has, since the mutual Soviet and American deployments of second-strike missiles, been equally difficult to attain. The relatively low cost to the defense of offsetting an offensive build-up has been a stabilizing factor in the superpower arms race.

The second complication is related to uncertainty concerning the arms race views of the Soviet leadership. In the current superpower arms race, the idea of its being more a ritual than a preparation for war has been steadfastly resisted by the Soviet military and also, inferentially, by Soviet politicians. This point is indicated by the kinds of defense preparation the military has been permitted to develop and maintain, and reflects the fact that, if the arms race is largely a ritual competition governed by such factors as military-industrial interests and possibly unforeseen technical advances and mutual misperception, then this entire field of endeavor must be labeled wasteful and irrelevant or, at worst, positively harmful to the national security. Consciously or unconsciously,

Soviet arms race strategy has stressed preparation for war, even to the extent of pursuing lines of development, procurement, and doctrine that, according to Western theory, could only aggravate the arms race. Examples of this point have been the apparent Soviet indifference to America's "assured-destruction" requirements by the pursuit of active-missile and passive-population defenses. Also, there is no evidence that Soviet leaders are reluctant to develop and deploy multiple warheads on the grounds of arms race "instability." The basic Soviet position would appear to be that the almost exclusively offensive deterrence doctrine of the United States in the 1960s was a great mistake, comparable with similarly mistaken strategies in the past that stressed a single combination of arms (for example, *Blitzkrieg*). Soviet military doctrine holds that as long as nuclear war is possible, indeed we might say probable, then only a balanced offensive-defensive strategic-force posture can hope to insure the survival of Soviet society. It is not too extreme to maintain that the Soviet military leadership has never convincingly denied the possibility of victory in a nuclear war.

It may perhaps be granted that the Soviet Union plans to employ its strategic forces only in a defensive mode, that is, in a pre-emptive or a second strike. However, the ritual view of the arms race does not exclude the possibility that crisis behavior may be influenced by individual perceptions of relative strategic positions, calculated possibly in crude arithmetic, or by feelings that are quite unrelated to prospective success in war. In short, the ritual of war preparation, though (at least in the West) distant from considerations of the conduct of war, may be far from meaningless.

AN ARMS RACE TYPOLOGY

The term "typology" may be the source of some confusion. I do not suggest that there are ten types of arms race. My argument is that every arms race is capable of being analyzed in terms of each category of distinction. Thus the potential number of types of arms race is the number of different combinations of features that can be extracted from the ten categories. This number of types of arms race is greatly enlarged by the certainty that some competi-

---

[9] See Malcolm W. Hoag, "On Stability in Deterrent Races," *World Politics*, 13 (July 1961): 515.

[10] Provided the word "exploitable" is qualified, it presents no problems. However, a Senate report in 1968 referred to the unqualified and mystifying notion of "exploitable superiority." See U.S. Senate, Committee on Armed Services, Preparedness Investigating Subcommittee, *Status of U.S. Strategic Power*, 90th Cong., 2nd sess., 1968, p. 3 (hereafter cited as *Status of U.S. Strategic Power*).

tors will have distinctive features in their arms race behavior. For example, one competitor may be racing in only a single weapon category, and another competitor may decide that prudence indicates the value of acquiring a mix of quite distinct types of weapon.

NUMBERS: BILATERAL/MULTILATERAL/ BILATERAL "CONNECTED" (OPEN SYSTEM)/UNILATERAL

An argument given considerable prominence by Samuel Huntington was that there could be no such thing as a general arms race; that, in fact, all races are duels.[11] This line of thinking holds that any appearance of mutilateral complexity disguises a series of duels. The course of post–World War II international relations, down to the explosion of China's first atomic bomb in October 1964, inclines the contemporary analyst to a position of sympathy for the bilateral argument. However, the prospect for the 1970s is that the international system will have to accommodate an increasingly tripolar nuclear balance.[12] Donald Watt has demonstrated convincingly, from the evidence of the 1920s and 1930s, that all arms races are not necessarily bilateral.[13] Even if we use Samuel Huntington's empirical base, the evidence of Britain's naval relations with France and Russia, and the naval relations of France with Italy and Germany in the early 1890s, suggests a complexity of naval building standards that defies an exclusively bilateral interpretation.[14]

The possibility of a bilateral "connected," or open system, arms race refers to a situation in which there are only two adversaries, each of which builds in the relevant categories of weapons only against the other, whose bilateral competition may be stimulated by a series of trigger events originating quite beyond the system of their arms competition. This view is easier to sustain if we are analyzing some gross and undifferentiated measure of defense preparedness (for example, the percentage of GNP allocated to, or expended upon, defense functions) rather than one or several categories of major weapon systems. It should be noted that no set of arms race adversaries can conduct their external and domestic policies as if they lived in a "two-person" world. Other conflicts may trigger a preparedness reaction. An interesting development of this argument is the widely acknowledged budgetary phenomenon of "fair shares." Thus it is conceivable that for the sake of bureaucratic harmony the Air Force might receive a "compensation package" (possibly of arms race relevance) because the Army and the Navy have expanded to fight a distant limited war.

The final possibility among these distinctions of numerical arms race participation is the apparent absurdity of a unilateral arms race. This possibility could refer to a situation in which one side was "spurting" toward a level of strength proclaimed by the other to be sufficient. The unilateral nature of the race would of course be spurious. For a time the party currently ahead could eschew quantitative competition, but might, and probably would, be pursuing a qualitative competition so as to secure a favorable technological and industrial position for the next round. Also, there have been situations in which a power felt bound to compete with an adversary who built to a legally predetermined rhythm and who consistently denied that it was racing. The fixed tempo of building provided by the German Navy Laws of 1898 and 1900 and the Supplementary Laws of 1906, 1908, and 1912 placed Great Britain, at least superficially, in the position of conducting a unilateral arms race against an adversary not susceptible to "panics" or "holiday" proposals.[15]

QUANTITATIVE/QUALITATIVE/ QUALITATIVE-QUANTITATIVE

Logic requires that the distinction be sharply drawn in theory between quantitative and qualitative races.[16] However, for an analysis to

11 Huntington, op. cit., p. 42.

12 This possibility has been well-explored by Harry Gelber, "The Impact of Chinese ICBM's on Strategic Deterrence," in Kintner, op. cit., pp. 179–206.

13 Donald C. Watt, "The Possibility of a Multilateral Arms Race: A Note," International Relations, 2 (October 1962): 372–77, 397.

14 See Sir Herbert Richmond, Sea Power in the Modern World (London, 1934), p. 123.

15 Among the most helpful guides to Anglo-German naval rivalry are Jonathan Steinberg, Yesterday's Deterrent: Tirpitz and the Birth of the German Battle Fleet (London, 1965); E. L. Woodward, Great Britain and the German Navy (orig. pub. 1935; London, 1964); and Arthur Marder, From the Dreadnought to Scapa Flow, vol. 1: The Road to War, 1904–1914 (London, 1961).

16 See Huntington, op. cit., pp. 65–79.

have any contemporary relevance it must be stated clearly that all arms races have had both quantitative and qualitative aspects.[17] A race between rival research and development communities would be no arms race. The 1968 Senate report *Status of U.S. Strategic Power* made this point very forcefully. "Forces in being are required to deter a potential aggressor. Pursuit of R and D to develop options and hedges against future threats is a logical and economical approach to the problem, but such options are only the raw material for the hard decisions on deployment."[18]

The definitions of arms race phenomena that stress the minimum condition of there being a competitive increment in armaments are committing an important error. For example, although a state's ICBM inventory might show no increment over a period of years, as a result of "product improvement," the capability of this inventory might have been very substantially enhanced. This comment is applicable to an analysis of the succession of models of the Minuteman and Polaris missiles. In practice, the quantitative and qualitative aspects of an arms race interact in an intricate manner. It might be argued that a race marked by a rapid succession in generations of weapons is not a qualitative race, but is a series of reasonably distinct quantitative races.[19] However, such an assertion would be misleading in its attempt to understate the importance of technical improvement.

One's view as to the dominance of the quantitative or qualitative element in arms races is a direct result of the empirical base selected. The belief of Samuel Huntington that most arms races are likely to be single-weapon races[20] rests upon the fact that there are periods, perhaps lasting several years, in which the design of the most advanced weaponry is in a state of flux, followed by relatively long periods of quantitative competition based upon the qualitative plateau attained. This argument would term Anglo-German naval rivalry from 1905 to 1914 an essentially quantitative race, despite the introduction of the Dreadnought and super-Dreadnought, with their greater displacement, heavier caliber of main armament, different fuel (oil instead of coal), and greater speed. Similarly, notwithstanding the disruptive undercurrents of multiple-warhead and ABM technologies, the period from 1961 to 1970 might be characterized as a period of competitive quantitative increase in the second and third generations of the ICBM. Such a lofty disdain for improvements of models and such a one-dimensional view would do considerable violence to history.

A footnote of practical relevance here is that, although it may not stand out in traditional measures of arms race progress, competition in strategic doctrine, and the changes in organization and equipment to which it can lead, has been an almost totally neglected aspect of qualitative rivalry.

A possibility that incorporates features of both quantitative and qualitative rivalry is that of an extended-deployment race. In other words, the overall size of the rival arsenals may remain static and the models may not have been improved, but there may be a race to establish, initially, a "presence" in a region, and eventually there may be competitive regional increases in quantities of weapons.

PARTICIPANTS: INTERADVERSARY/INTERALLIED/ INTERSERVICE/INTERGROUP

One of the most fruitful questions to ask is, "Between whom are arms races run?" The obvious and standard answer is, "Between mutually perceived potential enemies." It is worth noting that arms race behavior is also discernible in the relations among formal allies, among "sister" services, and among organized groups within the same society.

For the inputs of manpower and treasure required by arms competition, the outputs of goal satisfaction in competition between allies may be enhanced authority within the alliance, or attractiveness (as opposed to rival, less well-armed contenders) to potential ally-recruiters.

It may be argued that the most unambiguous example of qualitative weapons competition lies not in interstate relations but in the rela-

17 "Today's 'arms race' is qualitative rather than quantitative." This comment by Dr. Edward Teller would be endorsed by most contemporary strategic analysts. U.S. Senate, Committee on Foreign Relations, Subcommittee on International Organization and Disarmament Affairs, *Strategic and Foreign Policy Implications of ABM Systems*, Hearings, pt. 2, 91st Cong., 1st sess., 1969, p. 517 (hereafter cited as *Strategic and Foreign Policy Implications of ABM Systems*). See also *SIPRI Yearbook*, chap. 2.
18 *Status of U.S. Strategic Power*, p. 2.
19 Huntington, *op. cit.*, p. 71.
20 *Ibid.*, p. 52.

tions of the development programs of "sister" armed services. In such a competition, the quality of the weapon, admittedly among other, less reputable criteria, should result in a budgetary victory reflected in favorable decisions about procurement and operating responsibility.[21] Even a brief glance at the relations between the United States Army and Air Force since 1955 provides an abundance of illustration for this argument.

Finally, we should not ignore intrasocietal arms competition, although the data on armaments for this area of inquiry are extremely elusive and difficult to interpret. Interesting examples of competitive arms relationships are discernible in the contemporary United States. Militant Black Power groups and the police have been arming and counterarming for urban guerrilla warfare for several years. Indeed, one study has gone so far as to refer to a racial arms race.[22]

EXPENDITURE: ANNUAL ARMAMENTS
EXPENDITURE AS A PERCENTAGE OF
GNP INCREASING/ANNUAL INCREASE IN
ARMAMENTS EXPENDITURE INCREASING/
ANNUAL ARMAMENTS EXPENDITURE
STABLE/ANNUAL ARMAMENTS
EXPENDITURE DECREASING

These distinctions offer a different view to the focus upon weapons in most historical studies of arms race behavior. They derive, in part, from the mathematical theory of arms races developed by Lewis F. Richardson. Fundamental to the Richardson argument are the propositions that each side increases its armaments in proportion to the absolute level of the other side (that level being taken as the measure of that state's hostility), and that there will be no time-lag between the perception of hostility and the reaction to it. The effect of perceived hostility upon the rate of increase of armaments will be reinforced by a constant "grievance" factor. In other words, there is an assumption of the interlocking nature of weapons decisions. It may be useful to expand upon

the writings of Gustave Le Bon and Harold Lasswell and to characterize Richardson's arms race theory as being descriptive of a form of "crowd behavior."[23] In the Richardson theory, gross, undifferentiated defense statistics—the level of hostility—and trade statistics—the measures of friendliness—are both taken as reflecting predictable psychological reactions to the activities of the adversary.

Richardson's achievements include a series of writings that display both a paramount concern for the scientific, quantitative investigation of the behavior of large numbers of individuals (crowds) and a profound moral concern for the unintended consequences of blind psychological reactions. More specifically, he developed a series of equations that have inspired the inquiries and methodology of a large number of devoted, though critical, followers. Also, he made explicit in his model the basic interdependence of arms expenditures, a premise that underlies all writings on arms races—though there is argument regarding the directness and the nature of the reciprocity. Furthermore, he both developed an explicitly dynamic model and sought to cut through the potential looseness of verbal identification and analysis of the variables and parameters by concentrating upon those elements he believed could be quantified.

The theoretically separable categories of arms races identified in this section may be useful for countries whose official statistics are reliable, but they are obviously of far less utility for any analysis concerning the Soviet Union.[24] Furthermore, the action-reaction basis for the Richardson equations is highly questionable as an exclusive explanation of arms

---

[21] For a case study of just such an example, see Michael H. Armacost, *The Politics of Weapons Innovation: The Thor-Jupiter Controversy* (New York, 1969).

[22] Martin Oppenheimer, *Urban Guerrilla* (orig. pub. 1969; London, 1970), chap. 7.

[23] Gustave Le Bon, *The Crowd* (orig. pub. 1895; New York, 1960); Harold Lasswell, *World Politics and Personal Insecurity* (orig. pub. 1935; New York, 1965), p. 63, n. 10.

[24] See the Institute for Ştrategic Studies, *The Military Balance, 1969–1970* (London, 1969), p. 5; *SIPRI Yearbook*, pp. 198–99; William T. Lee, "Calculating Soviet National Security Expenditures," in U.S. Congress, Joint Economic Committee, Subcommittee on Economy in Government, *The Military Budget and National Economic Priorities*, pt. 3: *The Economic Basis of the Russian Military Challenge to the United States*, Hearings, 91st Cong., 1st sess., 1969, pp. 932–34; Russett, *op. cit.*, pp. 8–10, 193–94. For an overview of this problem area, see Pertti Joenniemi, "Aspects on the Measurement of Armament Levels," *Cooperation and Conflict*, 3 (1970): 141–51.

races. It would seem that the analysis of total defense statistics is far too blunt an instrument of inquiry to be very useful.[25] It may be interesting to note, for a particular set of arms race adversaries, the facts concerning the total increase of armaments and the percentage of GNP expended upon defense or per capita military expenditure, but a large segment of the defense budget may be quite irrelevant to the arms race. In other words, "internal" or imperial policing duties may distort a budget that, according to the theory, should be a reflection of popular "major adversary-directed" hostility.

Behind the first two distinctions looms the Richardsonian identification of stable, as opposed to unstable, arms races. An unstable race is one in which the parties move, at an accelerating rate, away from a point of defense-expenditure equilibrium. "The two great European arms races of 1909–1914 and 1933–39 have been called unstable because, the more the contestants spent, the more rapidly they increased their expenditure."[26]

Richardson believed that it is in arms races in which the annual increase in armaments expenditure is increasing that the risk of war approaches the level of a certainty. He "proves" this conclusion by means of a presentation of the arms race statistics for 1909–1914 and 1933–1939.

As indicators of threat perception, the level of expenditure and its rate of change are useful though imprecise guides, but there is no substitute for a detailed investigation of the tangled skeins of defense politics. For example, of the three major increases in American defense expenditure made since 1945—the Korean rearmament, the Kennedy build-up, and the Vietnam expansion—only the Korean rearmament increase can unequivocally be assigned to a major reassessment of the threat apparently presented by the Soviet Union. The basic inadequacy of the Richardsonian equations and their developments is the fundamental assumption of a close expenditure interdependence—or, in contemporary jargon, action-reaction.

25 Note the comments on this point in Thomas C. Schelling, "War without Pain, and Other Models," *World Politics*, 15 (April 1963): 474.
26 Lewis F. Richardson, *Arms and Insecurity* (London, 1960), pp. 74–75.

The arms competition was expressed by Richardson as follows:

$$\frac{dx}{dt} = ky - ax + g \quad \text{and} \quad \frac{dy}{dt} = lx - by + h[27]$$

In response to the new conditions imposed by nuclear weapons, Lewis Richardson modified his basic equations so as to take account of the submissiveness or fear factor mentioned above. The new submissiveness coefficients (s and r) would work to dampen the explosive potential of an otherwise unstable arms race. Richardson's new, post-1945 equations took the following form.

$$\frac{dx}{dt} = ky \, (l - s[y - x]) - ax + g$$

$$\frac{dy}{dt} = lx \, (l - r[x - y]) - by + h[28]$$

The two possibilities identified as stable or decreasing arms race expenditures serve to expose the dangers of a concentration upon expenditure as a tool for the measurement of the velocity of an arms race. For the United States, the 1960s show a pattern of greatly diminishing expenditure on strategic forces (followed, admittedly, by an increase toward the end of

27 Where t is time and x and y are the respective armaments of two sides, k and l being positive constants or defense coefficients, a and b being positive constants or fatigue and expense coefficients, g and h representing the unchanging level of grievance held by each state against the other. For the basic and comprehensive statement of the Richardson theory of arms interdependence, see *ibid.*, particularly chap. 2. Important critical analyses of the Richardsonian world view may be found in Anatol Rapoport, "Lewis Fry Richardson's Mathematical Theory of War," *Journal of Conflict Resolution*, 1 (September 1957): 249–99; *idem, Fights, Games, and Debates* (Ann Arbor, 1960), chap. 1; Kenneth Boulding, *Conflict and Defense* (New York, 1962); Paul Smoker, "Trade, Defense, and the Richardson Theory of Arms Races: A Seven Nation Study," *Journal of Peace Research*, 2 (1965): 161–76; William R. Caspary, "Richardson's Model of Arms Races: Description, Critique, and an Alternative Model," *International Studies Quarterly*, 11 (March 1967): 63–90; Martin C. McGuire, *Secrecy and the Arms Race* (Cambridge, Mass., 1965), pp. 33–38. Excellent overviews of the whole field of mathematical arms race modeling are provided by Peter Busch's appendix in Russett, *op. cit.*, pp. 193–233, and by Thomas L. Saaty, *Mathematical Models of Arms Control and Disarmament* (New York, 1968).
28 See Paul Smoker, "The Arms Race as an Open and Closed System," paper presented at the 4th Peace Research Conference, Chicago, November 7–8, 1968, p. 13.

the decade). This pattern does not reflect a loss of momentum in arms race activity; instead, it reflects an increasing attention to "product improvements." The anticipation of the eventual procurement of these improved products, it may be argued, had a considerable effect upon the Soviet Union.

It is probable that most arms race participants will pass through all, or some, of these distinct expenditure phases. The important point is that an apparent quiescence of arms race activity, as reflected in budget figures, may signify only the comparatively low cost of system maintenance and intense research and development activity.

SINGLE WEAPON/MULTIWEAPON

It is possible to assert that most arms competitions, at most times, have had as their focus the contemporary dominant weapon, or, in General J. F. C. Fuller's words, "the weapon of superior reach or range."[29] There is certainly much justification for the view that simple, easily quantifiable standards of comparison have long been in demand—inventory comparison of a single class of weapons is thus attractive to the analyst.

We might assert that Anglo-German rivalry after 1905 was a single-weapon race; similarly, Soviet-American competition can be presented as a series of races in the latest generation of strategic weapons. There has been a series of qualitative, or development, races; what is less certain is whether the superpowers have raced to deploy the latest generation of weapons. One of the complications, in any analysis that seeks to present Soviet-American competition as a series of finite races, is the fact that these two states have not had a common strategic doctrine. The Soviet Union has sought a balanced posture containing significant offensive and defensive components, whereas the United States has been less constrained in its racing efforts in offensive weapons by the great expense of very extensive air defenses. A further complication, in a study seeking to identify those categories of weapons in which the superpowers have competed, is that the Soviet Union chose, in the mid-1950s, to deploy a very significant continental or regional I/MRBM

force, to which the United States has not chosen to respond in kind or in mirror fashion. The particular mix of offensive and defensive strategic forces and the composition of general-purpose forces may be viewed in the single-weapon perspective, but the potential trade-offs between different systems contributing to one strategic mission render a multiweapon approach more appropriate to contemporary Soviet-American competition.

Another example of multiweapon rivalry is provided by the contemporary Arab-Israeli arms competition. Any analysis of this competition would have to examine the balances of both the air (offensive and defensive) and the armored forces; however, we must admit that a limited trade-off between these two categories of armament is possible.[30]

HIERARCHY: SINGLE-TIERED/TWO-TIERED, "PROXY"/TWO-TIERED, INDEPENDENT/ MULTITIERED

This section draws attention to the distinctions made among different degrees of third-party involvement in arms rivalry. It is possible to imagine a number of superficially similar, yet distinct, variants of the two-tiered arms race. First, we may identify a situation in which two or more client-states or dependent groups compete in pursuit of their own objectives. In this context the senior security partners are, probably somewhat reluctantly, compelled to maintain a dynamic local equilibrium.

Second, we might hypothesize an "arms race by proxy," wherein the client-states provide a useful, though perhaps fairly dispensable, outlet for the ambitions of the arms race "parents." The present arms race in the Middle East displays features of both two-tiered arms race models; Israeli-American and Egyptian-Soviet relations provide examples of very different degrees of independence of clients.

An example which offers greater complexity of clients, suppliers, and motives is that of the India-Pakistan arms competition. In this case, the United States, Britain, and the Soviet Union either have supplied or are about to supply both India and Pakistan with major

---

[29] J. F. C. Fuller, *Armament and History* (London, 1946), p. 21.

[30] A good exploration of Arab-Israeli rivalry (and one that is explicitly concerned with the structure of the regional arms race) is to be found in J. C. Hurewitz, *Middle East Politics: The Military Dimension* (New York, 1969), chaps. 24–25.

weapon systems. China has provided lesser forms of military assistance to Pakistan. Of the four interested parties beyond the subcontinent, only China has had any interest in the success of one of the competitors, and this interest has been disciplined by a lack of modern weapon systems to supply.

The final point relates to the possibility of there being a multitiered arms race. This applies very clearly to intrasocietal conflicts such as those in the Congo and in Biafra, for which the arms supply links may be long, tortuous, and very often apparently anonymous.

ACTIONS: OFFSET/IMITATIVE/INDEPENDENT

Action-reaction is commonly invoked as the all-purpose, or at least dominant, model for explaining the arms race logic of actions that would offset the latest or anticipated moves of the adversary. However, action-reaction will serve equally well, though often with less apparent internal arms race logic, as an explanation of those aspects of arms race behavior whose result is the often futile emulation of adversary action rather than its neutralization.

An example of such imitative behavior, by one interpretation, would be the increased production rates the United States ordered in 1955 and 1956 for the B-52 in response to the prognoses of a "bomber gap," an activity that may be labeled as foolishly imitative, in that it reflected only a concern for the respective preattack inventory quantities of strategic bombers.

The relevance of the distinction between offsetting and imitative behavior rests upon the availability of a "menu" of military-technical alternatives.[31] There may be periods in a single-weapon arms race in which an offsetting action is simultaneously an imitative action, but for the Soviet-American competition, the roads to security are so diverse that decisions can be roughly identified and allocated as appropriate within these categories of action. However, there are some complications. On occasions a reaction may have been intended to be offsetting, whereas in truth it was imitative with no, or very little, neutralizing effect. Second, imitation may be a temptation of differing attractiveness to the two sides.

With regard to the Soviet-American competition, there is no doubt that military-technical development has had a logic of its own—a logic that, within limits, has been equally compelling to both sides.[32] Some of the major limits referred to here are basic doctrinal preferences for a particular balance of offense and defense, available economic resources, and the military posture indicated by geographical location. Thus, it may appear that in most categories of weapons the Soviet Union has been imitating the United States, whereas a fairer interpretation would be that very often similar advantages beckoned to each side in turn. This discussion does some violence to the historical record, in that, although the two sides have a closely comparable record of the kinds of systems developed, the decisions about sizable arsenal acquisition have been very different indeed.

The third possibility in this section, identified as "independent" actions, is that of arms race moves that may well be reactive, yet neither offset, in a direct way, an adversary's actual or anticipated capability nor emulate his activities. An example in this category might have been the Soviet stress upon high megatonnage in the early 1960s.[33]

EMBRYONIC/ONGOING

Lewis F. Richardson identified the period 1945–1946 as one in which Soviet-American arms competition was in embryonic form.[34] The dilatoriness of Soviet demobilization and the secrecy with which the United States surrounded its atomic program were both unannounced and possibly unrealized bases for an arms competition that would very soon be widely visible. The date taken by Richardson and his followers as marking the opening of the Soviet-American arms race is 1948.

---

[31] See C. B. Joynt, "Arms Races and the Problem of Equilibrium," in *The Yearbook of World Affairs, 1964* (London, 1964), pp. 34–35.

[32] By way of analogy, it should be recalled that Clausewitz wrote of war: "It has certainly a grammar of its own, but its logic is not peculiar to itself." Carl von Clausewitz, *On War* (orig. pub. 1832; London, 1966), 3: 122.

[33] An excellent theoretical analysis of the arms race significance of high-yield weapons is contained in Colonel Glenn A. Kent, *On the Interaction of Opposing Forces under Possible Arms Agreements*, Occasional Paper no. 5, Center for International Affairs, Harvard University (March 1963).

[34] Lewis F. Richardson, "Could an Arms Race End without Fighting?" *Nature*, September 20, 1951, pp. 567–68.

There is much sense in labeling a period of rising political tensions and military moves (in their widest meaning), preparatory to a burst of arms competition, one of arms race "in embryo." An arms race may not begin with the public announcement of an ambitious weapons-building program—a program that both at the time and in retrospect may be seen as an unambiguous arms race challenge, marking the opening of the competition. Instead, in the words of Quincy Wright's *A Study of War*, there will be "acceleration in all countries involved of the rate of armament growth. A larger proportion of the productive energy of states is devoted to military affairs . . . though the boundaries either in time or in space could not be very clearly defined."[35]

Despite the great uncertainty which attaches to an embryonic period, further research may indicate that for many races there was a last clear chance for averting the competition. I discuss this possibility of an arms race in embryo because it should be emphasized that, in the same way that acute international crises and wars do not occur without previous storm warnings, neither do arms races.

Primitive/Sophisticated[36]

In the recent ABM debate in the United States, the primitive arms race model has been advanced by opponents of the Nixon Administration as best characterizing the decisions for Sentinel and Safeguard deployments. A primitive arms race is one in which each participant reacts to the move of an adversary without giving thought to the probable effect this reaction will have upon the future moves of the adversary; hence, the likelihood of positive feedback is ignored. In contemporary terminology, a primitive action reflects the "fallacy of the last move."[37]

A sophisticated arms race would be one in which all participants recognized that they were in a non-zero-sum game situation. They would realize that the arms race strategies likely to be pursued by adversaries in the next round will depend in part upon the strategies selected for the current round. Among the diffi-

culties that present themselves for consideration are the following: (1) apparently primitive arms race behavior may not be proof of the folly of the adversary, but may reflect an irresistible domestic logic; (2) behavior planned within a sophisticated framework may, in its consequences, turn out to be primitive, because its rationale is insufficiently clear to the adversary. Finally, we should note that the appropriate frame of reference for considering arms race behavior need not necessarily be that of a game situation in which the competitors have common motivations. A sophisticated slackening of military effort (a move guided by the theory of sympathetic parallelism) might be rewarded by a grave military imbalance in favor of the adversary.

Damped/Undamped[38]

The principle in this category may be stated as follows: to some important degree, the nature of the weapon(s) in terms of which the competitors are racing will determine the velocity of the race. However, the importance of the damping factor will rest not only upon the nature of the weapon, but also upon the objectives of the competitors.

In a damped arms race any attempt at superiority should be discouraged because of its exorbitant cost. In other words, as long as the competitor who is behind must be outnumbered by three or four or more to one in order for him to stand little chance of survival in war, then the cost of the offense will rise exponentially by comparison with the cost of the defense. Competition in the categories of land forces and ICBMs without individually targetable multiple warheads may be offered as examples of damped arms races. For the purposes of theory, the forces are assumed to be of an approximate competence. In practice, faulty strategic and/or tactical doctrine or a catastrophic failure in command and control might totally upset the expected outcome.

Undamped arms races, in which the required ratio of forces for military victory would not be prohibitively expensive, might be expected to be those involving naval forces and ballistic missiles carrying individually targetable multiple warheads.

[35] Wright, *op. cit.*, 2: 690–91.
[36] Schelling, *op. cit.*, p. 476.
[37] Herbert F. York, "Military Technology and National Security," *Scientific American*, August 1969, p. 26.

[38] Hoag, *op. cit.*, pp. 508, 515.

ARMS RACE STRATEGIES

Every arms race must involve a process of interaction, either continuous or intermittent, among a number of arms race strategies.[39] We cannot necessarily infer the intended strategies of participants from the consequent dynamic military balance. One side may aim for a certain ratio of forces favorable to itself and yet be compelled, in the event, to make the best of a definite margin in favor of the adversary.

The strategies pursued by each or some of the competitors may vary over time, not solely as a choice forced by unforeseen circumstances, but also because perceptions may alter, and hence the state of the balance identified as desirable may change.

Two terms, above all, have dominated recent arms race discussion: sufficiency and stability. Both are employed very freely and defy satisfactorily precise definition. The determination of how much is enough should include considerations of rival geostrategic responsibilities, the inferred intentions of the adversary, compensating advantages in other areas important to the national security, and, perhaps preeminently, certain domestic preferences for a particular state and composition of the arms balance.

Stability has several unambiguous, though restricted, definitions. For example, in Richardson's inquiry, an unstable arms race is one which suffers exponential annual increments of expenditure. In a narrow American military definition, stability may be understood to be the state of a strategic relationship in which the "first-strike bonus" was either nonexistent or extremely low. This definition holds that stability is the product of the maintenance of mutual assured-destruction capabilities. Thus, to link the two terms of the discussion, a sufficiency of assured destruction capabilities insures stability. Unfortunately, as I noted above, the Soviet notion of stability appears to rest upon the maintenance of strategic forces suffi-

cient not only to assure considerable destruction but also to disrupt an intended surprise attack in a pre-emptive manner and to defend the homeland in the event of war.[40] Arms race strategies are not devised in a political vacuum; hence, even if both superpowers maintained the doctrine of assured destruction through hostage cities, the military-technical logic of a sufficient deterrent would be unacceptable. The very high level of urbanization in the United States should mean that what would be enough to the Soviet Union would be far less than the United States would need to maintain her level of assured destruction. Apart from the counterforce potential of a great American numerical superiority in missiles, it is inconceivable that the Soviet Union would find a gross numerical asymmetry politically tolerable.

A wider interpretation of the term would hold that stability refers to the current beliefs regarding the proximity of war. Thus, quite apart from any armament "improvements," interstate tension might be low following political consultation or good-will gestures. Clearly, such a stability would be extremely fragile. Finally, it might be held that a rapid succession of weapon generations is inherently destabilizing, in good part because the known and familiar military environment would be changing faster than would the strategic or tactical views of military planners and politicians.

As an interesting addition to the above comments upon sufficiency and stability, we cannot but notice the fact that much contemporary arms race theorizing is conditioned by some aspects of deterrence theory. In the West, at least, there is a very wide consensus to the effect that by engaging in a nuclear arms race one is doing so solely with the objective of continuing an effective deterrence of inimical military and diplomatic actions. In short, there is no question of racing to "win" or to avoid the worst consequences of a nuclear war. This means that sufficiency may be identified as that size and configuration of the arsenal which will guarantee unacceptable damage; any margin above the sufficient-for-deterrence level may thus be labeled wasteful and possibly even pro-

---

[39] A dimension of arms race strategy that (on grounds of space) I have not singled out for separate investigation is the question of the effect on an arms race of the possible different *knowledge-states* of each arms race participant concerning the strategies of rivals. Explicit and vigorous attention to this question may be found in Knut Midgaard, "Arms Races, Arms Control, and Disarmament," *Cooperation and Conflict*, no. 1 (1970), pp. 34–40; and McGuire, *op. cit.*

[40] Note the speculation on the pre-emption point in one recent and excellent analysis, Wolfe, *op. cit.*, p. 437, n. 45.

vocative. Because one important school of deterrence theorists (finite or minimum) has persuaded many that deterrence is a comparatively
simple exercise that may be conducted with
small and invulnerable forces, the task of those
charged with the continuing conduct of the nuclear arms race has been rendered extremely
difficult.

The dominant strain of contemporary comment upon the nuclear arms race stresses the
folly of the whole enterprise rather than the
need for continued armed vigilance. This opinion might be traced to the justification of the
race in the West as deterrence rather than as
war or even crisis-waging scenarios.

The terms employed in the succeeding para-
graphs are intended to reflect a composite
measure of both quantity and quality in categories of weapons. Furthermore, the strategies
outlined are meant to refer to the intended
direction of increase in armaments to an intended proportional relationship. I suggest that,
in theory, the following five distinct strategies
may be applied in an arms race: clear inferiority; marginal inferiority; parity; marginal superiority; and clear superiority.

Essential prefatory remarks are, first, that
different strategies may be followed in different categories of weapons and, second, that
each participant may pursue different strategies toward different adversaries. Third, a participant may not be thinking or planning in
such oversimplified terms as parity or superiority. The motive underlying the development of a particular military posture might be
to provide for as many contingencies as possible, compatible with alternative resource-
allocation demands and the interactive potential of certain kinds of capability. It is possible
that no overall judgment upon the relative strategic positions of two arms racing rivals can be
given; hence, the rivals do not deliberately
race to attain a particular relative position.[41]

CLEAR INFERIORITY

A state or group may prepare as best it can,
even though, in the test of actual war, it must
be defeated. Orthodox arms race thinking
would exclude this situation, but by most tests
an arms race situation would obtain. Each side
—say, the Soviet Union, and Yugoslavia in the

1970s, or the Soviet Union and Finland in
1939—would prepare against the other, each
structuring all or a portion of its forces so as to
capitalize upon the perceived weaknesses of
the other. Preparation for apparent national
suicide may not be a common trait, but it may
not be as illogical as it would appear at first
sight. The greater power may be deterred by
the prospect of resistance, such resistance perhaps being likely to prove embarrassing; futile
national resistance may stir some support from
states that would otherwise stand aside.

As a historical footnote, it should be remembered that Tirpitz's "risk theory" held that
Great Britain could be blackmailed into concessions by the prospect that the probable cost
of Britain's naval victory over Germany would
render her vulnerable to the combined fleets of
France and Russia.[42] The contemporary relevance of "risk-theory" thinking has been outlined by the current American administration.
"A very difficult problem that would face us if
the Chinese launched or threatened to launch
a nuclear attack on the United States has to do
with the need for maintaining our deterrent
against the Soviet Union. Obviously, if we un-
loaded most or all of our Minuteman missiles
against China, we would be leaving ourselves
relatively naked as far as the Soviet threat is
concerned."[43]

MARGINAL INFERIORITY

It is conceivable that, in an arms race between two states of unequal economic strength,
the weaker may choose to remain behind, but
within reach of, the war-waging power of the
stronger. The advantage of this strategy could
be, first, that the stronger state would be less
likely to accelerate its military preparations
than it would if parity were sought; although,
second, should political relations deteriorate,
should the adversary slacken his arms race
efforts, or should a temporary military-technical
advantage appear, then a lead and possibly a
diplomatic or war-waging success might be
within reach.

41 See Lee, op. cit., p. 175.

42 Woodward, op. cit., vol. 2.
43 U.S. House, Committee on Appropriations, Sub-
committees on Department of Defense and on Military
Construction, Safeguard Antiballistic Missile System,
Hearings, 91st Cong., 1st sess., 1969, p. 59 (Mr.
Laird, May 22, 1969).

It must be admitted that it is extremely difficult to furnish clear and unambiguous examples of the pursuit of a strategy of marginal inferiority. It may be that Imperial Germany was
hoping to attain a marginally inferior position
to Great Britain in capital ships, once the risk
theory was rendered inoperable by the Anglo-
French and Anglo-Russian ententes. It is possible that the Soviet Union today is seeking a
state of military balance that, on the one hand,
can be denied as being a bid for superiority,
though, on the other hand, it insures that a
temporary measure of superiority might be attainable should any of the conditions obtain
that are suggested above. In the long run the
Soviet Union might aspire to parity, but the
continuing, though currently heavily qualified,
stress upon a measure of superiority by some
important sections of the American defense
community renders a Soviet posture of marginal inferiority less provocative.

Parity

Between nuclear powers, the deficiencies of
active and passive defenses make a mockery of
attempts to identify, with any confidence, advantages attaching to any arms race quantities.[44]
In the triangular Soviet-American-Chinese nuclear relationship, a gross disparity in the numbers of weapons and a not inconsiderable disparity in their quality might be belied by an
apparent parity of deterrent effect. In one particular view of the risk-taking propensity of the
Chinese, it is probable that the American capability for the assured destruction of China as a
functioning society is soon to be balanced by a
Chinese capability for the destruction of a
handful of cities.[45] The crisis-instability potential inherent in such an imbalance of capability
requires no further comment. Should China
acquire a substantial arsenal of nuclear delivery
vehicles, then a Sino-Soviet or a Sino-American
war might seriously erode the prewar parity
that existed between the United States and the
Soviet Union. However, as Dr. Harry Gelber
has argued, the consequences for superpower
deterrent stability that might follow such a war
with China would be more important in the
realms of popular psychology and governmen-

tal determination than in the realm of an
eroded weapons arsenal.[46]

Between states conducting an arms race with
the continued deterrence of war the objective,
parity offers a number of attractions. First, it
may serve to appease those domestic critics
who measure security by comparing inventories. Second, parity should deter any arms
race acceleration by the adversary, being in
itself a declaration of intent that no measure of
inferiority will be accepted.[47] Third, parity
may facilitate balanced measures of arms control; indeed, the common acceptance of parity
may in itself have the effect of limiting armaments. If each party were to define parity as
being its goal, were to identify the precise
quantitative and qualitative meaning it was
currently giving to the term, and were to state
the dependence of these numbers and characteristics of forces upon certain features of the
strategic forces of the other side, then parity
could be a norm used to promote "sophisticated" arms race behavior.

In practice it is difficult to give a precise
meaning to parity, even within the narrow context of the quantity and quality of weapons.
We might argue that the Soviet-American military balance today is best described as being in
a state of parity. It could be stated that both
parties have pursued similar military technologies and that numerical differences among the
relative sizes of particular components of their
arsenals are unimportant. On the other hand,
we might hold that the United States maintains
an important qualitative edge in multiple warhead technology, in missile accuracy, possibly
in ABM technology, and certainly in numbers
of separate deliverable warheads. Furthermore,
it is necessary to recognize that different states
acquire their strategic forces with different
ends in mind. A weapons parity is not necessarily a parity of diplomatic effect. In other
words, the United States, as a conservative,
status quo power, may feel the need for a
measure of superiority in order to counterbalance the perceived (or misperceived) ambitions of more active adversaries.

Marginal Superiority

Although marginal inferiority, parity, and
marginal superiority are analytically distin-

---

[44] A radically different view is to be found in
Foster, *op. cit.*, pp. 254–55.
[45] *Strategic and Foreign Policy Implications of
ABM Systems*, pt. 1, pp. 189–90.

[46] Gelber, *op. cit.*, p. 186.
[47] See Richmond, *op. cit.*, p. 209.

guishable as separate, intended states of a military balance, in practice these distinctions may be blurred beyond recognition. Industrial lead-time delay, domestic politics, and faulty intelligence, among a myriad of other contributory factors, might serve to render an intended parity either marginally inferior or marginally superior.

The introduction of the term "marginal" is intended to identify a short lead as opposed to a long lead, or, as some Cold War warriors would have it, a nonexploitable lead as opposed to an exploitable lead. Also, it must be admitted that today a long lead may be of no more military significance than a short lead. In prenuclear arms races, such distinctions as these were more significant. For example, Lanchester's Square Law holds that a conflict between firing points should conclude with the victor's preserving the number of bases equal to the square root of the difference between the squares of the numbers engaged on each side.[48] Hence, marginal superiority should result in disproportionately light damage in war.

Clearly the law is of no relevance to a nuclear conflict, in which it is possible that even a very small number of weapons could inflict disproportionate damage. Indeed, the dominant French school of nuclear deterrence has adhered to the so-called doctrine of proportional deterrence. This doctrine recognizes the absolute difference between the destruction that might be visited upon France by a Soviet strike and the destruction that the *force de frappe* might effect upon the Soviet Union, but it concludes that the small French assured-destruction capability would be disproportionate to the "worth" of France as a destroyed wartime target to the Soviet Union. The contrast to Lanchester's prenuclear arithmetic could not be clearer.

A state may prefer to be slightly ahead in an arms race so that, if a promising line of military-technical development were to beckon, it would be in the best position to gain an advantage and obtain a lead that could be turned either to diplomatic or to war-waging advantage. So difficult is the task of relative strategic assessment, that it is not inappropriate to comment that marginal inferiority, parity, or marginal superiority exist essentially in the eye of the beholder.

CLEAR SUPERIORITY

Statesmen may feel that, although unacceptable damage would be visited upon their country in the event of war, an undeniably large military margin could be of diplomatic utility. In the first place, it might be reasoned that politicians and their attentive publics are impressed with naked arithmetic. Military superiority is much despised in contemporary strategic literature as being illusory or meaningless, but for those fairly unsophisticated in strategic matters the effect of feeling behind or ahead should not be dismissed too readily. Second, it may not be true that any large measure of superiority is bound to prove only temporary; indeed, this may be a clear case of the self-fulfilling prophecy. Undoubtedly the most sufficient of arms race positions is to be comfortably and permanently ahead of all rivals.

Analogies between different pairs of states at different periods are bound to be perilous, but it may be instructive to note that some observers believed that German Dreadnought construction tended to "increase or decrease in inverse ratio to that of Great Britain."[49] Similarly, one interpretation of Soviet-American competition in the late 1960s might be that the Soviet Union was encouraged to make her successful bid for numerical superiority in land-based ICBM-launchers by the determination, on November 5, 1964, of a cutoff figure of 1,000 for American Minutemen.[50] A development of this argument would be that the economically stronger power would be well advised to state, unequivocally, that it will maintain a clear numerical superiority in the most advanced military hardware. Such a declaratory policy might serve, in the long run, to reduce the costs of the competition for all parties.

However, many assumptions are implicit in

---

[48] In a battle between two naval forces of twelve and nine ships, the larger side should emerge with both a meaningful victory and with seven or eight ships undamaged (or only slightly damaged). F. W. Lanchester, *Aircraft in War* (London, 1916), pp. 28, 36. A useful discussion of Lanchester's ideas is offered by Malcolm W. Hoag, "Increasing Returns in Military Production Functions," in *Issues in Defense Economics*, ed. Roland McKean (New York, 1967), pp. 12–14.

[49] Woodward, *op. cit.*, p. 242, n. 1.

[50] *Status of U.S. Strategic Power*, p. 12; Wolfe, *op. cit.*, pp. 432–33.

this argument, and the notion of cost is multi-dimensional. The basic assumption of this section is that clear superiority is the desired state of the military balance—in which case, resting upon a favorable asymmetry of economic resources, the state that is ahead might be able to restrain the competition, and also to reduce the risks inherent in a military environment of very active competition, by an unambiguous public adherence to a continuing doctrine of superiority. The disadvantages of such a doctrine might take some of the following forms: (1) the adversary grows desperate at its inability to attain even parity, and hence is induced to try a high-risk shortcut to a better military balance (Khrushchev's Cuban missile gamble); (2) the political cost of clear inferiority to the adversary is so high, both domestically and internationally, that no option is believed open other than to strain all resources to attain a better military balance; (3) in a situation characterized by widespread disapproval of "wasteful" expenditure related to the arms race, in which the security advantages of superiority cannot convincingly be demonstrated, a strategy of clear superiority provides much ammunition to critics at home and abroad.

As an arms race strategy, striving for an unambiguous superiority of numbers in strategic weapons is defensible on very traditional grounds. First, such a strategy should provide a wide range of damage-limiting options for central war; second, on the one hand, there is a great deal of uncertainty respecting the intentions of the arms race adversary, and, on the other hand, strategic intelligence, though vastly improved by satellite reconnaissance since 1961, is still less than perfect. Thus, a comfortable margin of superiority may serve as a hedge against the unforeseen. For illustration of these two points I quote the thoughts of Secretary of Defense Melvin Laird in 1969 and Lord Grey of Falloden in 1909:

They [Speakers Rayburn and McCormack] cautioned me, that if I were to make any mistakes while I was on that committee that I err on the side of the national security of this country. I thought that was pretty good advice.[51]

While we pay every regard to declaration of in-

tention . . . we cannot build upon them . . . we are obliged by the most simple and elementary requirements of precaution to act as though the present intention of Germany may peradventure be subsequently modified.[52]

The record of Soviet-American strategic interaction since 1957 shows that the difficulties of guessing the future rate of deployment of weapons, the requirements of domestic politics, and the opportunities thrown up by technology have all served to confound the arms race intentions of both sides. Even in the unlikely event of both sides deciding (1) upon complementary strategies (for example, parity/parity; marginal inferiority/marginal superiority), and (2) upon identical definitions, in both qualitative and quantitative respects, of such terms as parity or marginal inferiority, it is equally improbable that the military-industrial establishments of the two sides would actually produce a close approximation of the intended forces on the predetermined dates. Therefore, a slippage or unexpected ease in research, development, testing, evaluation, or full-scale production in only one of the competing countries will place both in unintended arms race positions.

ARMS RACE OUTCOMES

Much journalistic alarmism concerning the details of arms race termination might be avoided if a systematic investigation were undertaken of the ways in which history demonstrates arms races to have ended and logic deduces arms races could end. This section analyzes five possible arms race outcomes.

WAR

"Above all, it [the arms race] kept alive the anachronistic idea that wars were inevitable."[53]

"The most dangerous result of the arms race [is] the mounting fear or 'tension' which it creates."[54]

There is no proven relationship between arms races and wars. However, the *Study of War* investigators were convinced that the broad, single races of modern times were "gen-

[51] U.S. Senate, Committee on Foreign Relations, *Intelligence and the ABM*, Hearing, 91st Cong., 1st sess., 1969, p. 63 (June 23, 1969).

[52] Quoted in Woodward, *op. cit.*, p. 235.
[53] Philip Noel-Baker, *The Arms Race* (London, 1958), p. 74.
[54] *Ibid.*, p. 78.

erally" terminated by a balance-of-power war. We suspect that this conclusion was induced by the very broad scope of Wright's understanding of the nature of recent arms races.[55] A more restrictive view, both as to dates and as to participants, does not yield this broad conclusion.

The baleful effects of an arms race would seem to fall in the following areas. First, heavy and sustained expenditure on armaments by rival parties will result in a fueling of existing predilections to impute hostile motives. In short, suspicions will mount, the tension will grow, and instability will result—instability being defined as the believed proximity of war.

In this connection, the following comment upon the arms race and the tension-war nexus by Lewis Richardson is appropriate: "There is some evidence that diplomatic relations become, during the tacit mutual threats of an arms race, such a strain that the outbreak of war is felt as a relief."[56] Harold Lasswell also has subscribed to this argument: "Dangers to the safety, the material claims, and the deference demands of the 'we' group can be tolerated no longer; these interminable provocations must cease; the incessant alarms of recent years must come to an end."[57]

"Relief" on the outbreak of war, however, does not prove that by some mysterious process the desire for such relief was the immediate cause of war.

Second, an arms race may result in war because of the belief of one party that the military balance will move against it in the future; this is known as the "now-or-never," preventive-war syndrome. A slight variation upon this theme is the possibility that a state will choose war rather than risk the domestic economic and political consequences of continued competition. In this connection, we might with advantage recall the Russian rationale for the installation of the Doomsday Machine as a cut-price deterrent in *Dr. Strangelove.*

Third, a rather simple-minded view of the contemporary superpower competition is that the risk of technical accident is increasing with every succeeding weapons generation.[58] There is no steady increase in risk over time; indeed, Samuel Huntington's argument that war is most likely in the opening, nervous rounds of an arms competition, though not particularly convincing, is at least as tenable a hypothesis as its journalistic alternative.[59] Common sense suggests that armaments in themselves are only part of the decision to go to war. The contribution of armaments to the likelihood of an outbreak of war will (by the narrow American definition) be a function of the contemporary "first-strike bonus"; this will vary over time, but it will not necessarily vary in the direction of a steady, or even an intermittent, increase.

BANKRUPTCY-EXHAUSTION

This is a strictly hypothetical possibility; I could find no example of one, two, or more parties recoiling in economic ruin from an armaments competition, a conclusion also reached by Lewis Richardson.[60] To the extent that an arms race raises tensions and focuses public attention upon an adversary, the boundary of toleration of taxation can prove remarkably elastic. The years 1949 through 1953 in the United States showed a bewildering succession of authoritative statements upon the subject of "what the economy can stand."[61]

Arms race competitors are rarely in a position of approximate equality regarding the resources that may be invested in the military dimension of the national security. Each competitor will have different domestic circumstances and different foreign commitments. For example, despite an approximate equality in national incomes, Germany spent roughly only half as much as did Great Britain on her navy from 1910 to 1914:[62] Britain did not have two land frontiers to defend. With regard to the contemporary nuclear arms race, the estimated GNPs of the United States and the Soviet Union for 1968 were $861 billion and $430 bil-

---

[55] Wright, *op. cit.*, pp. 690–91. Single, general arms races were identified as occurring between the following dates: 1787–1815; 1840–1871; 1886–1919; and 1932–1941 (date of writing).

[56] Richardson, *op. cit.*, p. 61.

[57] Lasswell, *op. cit.*, p. 64.

[58] Albert Wohlstetter has replied to this view very effectively in U.S. Senate, Committee on Government Operations, Subcommittee on National Security and International Operations, *Planning-Programming-Budgeting, Defense Analysis: Two Examples*, 91st Cong., 1st sess., 1969, p. 5 (September 10, 1969).

[59] Huntington, *op. cit.*, pp. 63–65.

[60] Richardson, *op. cit.*, p. 61.

[61] See the three studies in Warner Schilling, Paul Hammond, and Glenn Snyder, *Strategy, Politics, and Defense Budgets* (New York, 1962).

[62] Wright, *op. cit.*, 1: 670–71 (Tables 58 and 59).

lion respectively. For 1968 the respective estimated defense expenditures were $79,576 million and $39,780 million.[63] The American figure is inflated by approximately $25 billion because of Vietnam; the Soviet figure refers only to declared defense expenditure and is questionable because of the uncertainty regarding the proper exchange rates of rubles for dollars. Furthermore, there is some evidence that, in the category of strategic delivery systems, the Soviet Union was, by 1968–1969, spending twice as much as was the United States.[64] The important point here is that, although a particular idea of sufficiency, hopes for a sympathetic parallelism, and competing military and nonmilitary demands have served to depress America's strategic-forces budget, severe economic strain should occur first in the Soviet Union if both sides decide upon a great acceleration in their strategic-forces programs.

In general, it is likely that, short of a situation of great mutual alarm, one side will have more to spend or one side will be prepared to spend more. In either event the probable outcome would be an arms race victory for one side or a war launched by the prospective arms race loser.[65] These dramatic possibilities will be heavily dependent upon the nature of the competition. In a qualitative-quantitative race, defeat in one phase might be avenged by victory in the next.

Victory/Defeat

In the same way that wars and crises can be won or lost, so arms races can be won or lost. However, history provides very few examples of a party's being unambiguously defeated and then sinking back into a position of sullen and near-permanent inferiority. Indeed, the conventional notion of victory or defeat must really be adapted to the particular strategies being followed. I mention the possibility of clear vic-

tory or defeat because it provides a limiting case, one not frequently encountered. Anglo-German naval relations from 1898 to 1914 would appear to provide a good example of an arms race victory: the German navy never succeeded in passing through its "danger zone."[66] Some members of the American defense community were persuaded that the failure of Premier Khrushchev's Cuban gamble and the "three environments" Nuclear Test Ban Treaty of 1963 marked a decisive and possibly enduring arms race victory for the United States. The statistics of ICBM and SLBM deployment since 1966 have demonstrated the premature nature of such a belief.

There is no evidence that the Soviet Union accepted the victory/defeat labels. However, the Soviets' post-1963 build-up in ICBMs (SS-9, SS-11, SS-13) and SLBMs (deployed in the new "Y" class nuclear submarine) would suggest that they did not deem the 1964 missile imbalance tolerable. The 1964 ICBM comparison was as follows: U.S.A., 834; Soviet Union, 200.[67] An unambiguous example of American convictions regarding the state of the arms race was provided early in 1965 by Secretary of Defense Robert McNamara: "[The Soviet leaders] have decided that they have lost the quantitative race, and that they are not seeking to engage us in that conflict. . . . There is no indication that they are catching up or planning to catch up. . . . There is no indication that they are in a race at this time."[68]

Arms race victory and defeat may be recognized either tacitly or formally. A tacit recognition might take the shape, as did the German one after 1912, of a denial of any competitive relationship, or it might take the shape of a treaty. A somewhat ambiguous example of the latter possibility would be the 1922 Washington Naval Treaty, which fixed the capital ship tonnage ratios of the great powers. Force-ratio agreements may, on occasion, be intended as preventive measures as opposed to termination measures; the Anglo-German treaty of 1935 might be seen in this light.[69]

[63] Institute for Strategic Studies, *op. cit.*, pp. 1, 5, 57. See also Joenniemi, *op. cit.*

[64] See Johan Hölst and William Schneider, Jr., eds., *Why ABM?* (Elmsford, N.Y., 1969), chap. 7; Lee, *op. cit.*, p. 173; Foster, *op. cit.*, p. 248; Thomas W. Wolfe, "Soviet Approaches to SALT," *Problems of Communism*, 19 (September–October 1970): 1–3.

[65] The imagery of bankruptcy continues to stalk the halls of arms race rhetoric: "If we do not adopt more discrimination in choosing these many weapon systems we are going to bankrupt the country." So said Senator Symington in *Strategic and Foreign Policy Implications of ABM Systems*, pt. 1, p. 57.

[66] Woodward, *op. cit.*, p. 431.

[67] Institute for Strategic Studies, *op. cit.*, p. 55.

[68] Quoted in *Status of U.S. Strategic Power*, p. 2.

[69] Sir Herbert Richmond, *Statesmen and Sea Power* (London, 1946), p. 293. It is only fair to assert that for Germany this treaty was more a "hunting license" than a restraint.

If one state challenges another that is already powerfully armed, an appropriate definition of victory might be to secure a position that is (1) not greatly inferior or (2) not inferior when in combination with another state. Finally, it is a near certainty that over time the aims of each arms race participant will alter, and that what constitutes victory will be redefined.

AGREED TERMINATION AT PARITY

Even if two or more states wanted to halt or severely restrict their competition, an appropriate definition of parity would be extremely difficult to reach. The background to this difficulty has found no better expression than that by Admiral Sir Herbert Richmond: "Parity in the instruments which constitute naval strength is a mathematical possibility but a strategical absurdity since it does not take into consideration the conditions under which those instruments have to be used, or the facilities which subserve their needs and without which they cannot be used."[70]

Arms race termination at parity is possible, provided that a very restricted definition is maintained concerning the military instruments that are to be precisely balanced. For example, the Anglo-American equality of tonnage agreed upon in Washington in 1922 may be taken as the outstanding, if not totally happy, example of the "one-power standard." Parity, as a likely arms race outcome, has attracted considerable attention as a result of accelerated Soviet missile deployment in the late 1960s and the American arms race move of deploying a limited ABM screen. Indeed, it is probable now that the Soviet Union will negotiate an arms limitation package on the basis of nothing short of an acknowledged parity. For the negotiation of an agreed freeze upon numbers of nuclear delivery vehicles, the rival delegations to the Strategic Arms Limitation Talks would have to consider, as best they could, the performance parameters and growth potential of each separate delivery system. Also, they would have to be informed of the missions that each side desires its various systems to be able to accomplish. The difficulty with mathematical parity, as suggested above by Admiral Richmond, is

that it must ignore such disturbing parameters as geostrategic location, asymmetry of dislike, and imbalance of strategic-intelligence provision.

RESOLUTION OF POLITICAL DIFFERENCES

Like an old soldier, an arms race may simply fade away. Historically, the classic example of the outcome of political resolution is provided by the Anglo-French and Anglo-Russian ententes of 1904 and 1907. To lay great stress upon this highly desirable outcome, however, is to deny one of the central paradoxes of contemporary international relations—namely, that an arms race is not necessarily very sensitive to a lessening of interstate tensions. The other side of the coin is that an arms race may not be accelerated by an increase in tensions.[71]

Soviet-American relations have outgrown their Cold War phases and are now in a state of typical great-power rivalry. However, although great-power rivals must always be watchful of the military preparations of others, not all great-power rivalry reaches the pitch of intensity in military preparation that would warrant its definition as an arms race. Here it should be stressed that there is no clear dividing line between a situation of attention or concern and one of arms race. The "atmospherics" of détente in the 1960s do not constitute, or even approach, such a resolution of political differences as was exemplified by the "diplomatic revolution" of 1904. It might be held that arms control must precede and contribute to a lessening of tensions, leading to a further braking of the arms race and thence to more fundamental political agreement. This question of "arms first" or "tensions first" has been well attacked by Philip Noel-Baker and J. David Singer.[72]

ARMS RACE DYNAMICS

Despite the thin trickle of arms race speculation that may be traced to Kant and certainly

---

[70] Richmond, *Sea Power in the Modern World*, pp. 257–58.

[71] See the comments of Marshall Shulman on the desirability of decoupling political relations from the issues of strategic confrontation, in "The Effect of ABM on US-Soviet Relations," in *ABM: An Evaluation of the Decision to Deploy an Antiballistic Missile System*, ed. Abram Chayes and Jerome Wiesner (New York, 1969), p. 158.

[72] See Noel-Baker, *op. cit.*, chaps. 6–7; J. David Singer, "Threat Perception and the Armament-Tension Dilemma," *The Journal of Conflict Resolution*, 2 (March, 1958): 90–105.

to the nineteenth-century English liberals of the Cobdenite school, post-1945 interest in arms race workings has been minimal and has only recently been galvanized by the debate over the ABM in the United States. Most scholars, politicians, and journalists have been content with the sure knowledge that there is a superpower arms race. It is only in the debate over the ABM, in which the liberal opposition has been compelled to make explicit its assumptions concerning the logic of superpower interaction, that analysts have begun to realize that we are certain of remarkably little in the region of arms race dynamics. This comment applies particularly to the principles that are believed to underpin Soviet decisions concerning strategic forces.

There are a considerable number of hypotheses regarding arms race dynamics that contend for analytical priority. Broadly, the hypotheses fall into two distinguishable, though far from mutually exclusive, doctrinal camps. These camps are here labeled action-reaction and domestic process.

ACTION-REACTION

At the basis of action-reaction thinking is the belief that an arms race situation constitutes a system—that is, "a set of components with identifiable attributes, among which patterned relationships persist over a period of time."[73] By contrast, those skeptical of the systemic nature of the arms race phenomenon are both unconvinced that many of the attributes have been adequately identified or understood, and convinced that the relationships are far from being patterned. One crisp example of the action-reaction world view is that offered by Paul Smoker when he says that an arms race is "a cybernetic set of interacting sub-systems."[74] The action-reaction model may be termed either "tight" or "loose," depending upon the assumption made respecting the nature of the system, whether it is open or closed. This is not an abstruse distinction, for central to any investigation of a particular arms race, within the action-reaction framework, is the question of what triggers a reaction.

It is important to remember that any study of the action-reaction mechanism must be informed

of the theoretical possibility of two temporally distinct forms of action and of four identifiable classes of triggering, or fueling, events. The temporal distinction has been labeled sequential/anticipatory by Johan Hölst.[75] He proceeds to demonstrate the considerable contemporary relevance of this distinction. The sequential reaction is simply that which succeeds an adversary action to which some counter is felt to be appropriate, either of an offset or of an emulative nature. The anticipatory reaction has prompted some observers to comment that the superpower arms race works by means of an action-overreaction dynamic.

The four distinguishable classes of triggering events may be briefly listed as follows: (1) a military-technological trigger *internal* to the arms race system; (2) a political trigger *internal* to the arms race system; (3) a military-technological trigger *external* to the arms race system; (4) a political trigger *external* to the arms race system.

To date, for the contemporary superpower arms race, attention has focused upon the military-technological triggers both internal to the arms race system and relevant to the configuration of the strategic-force postures of the adversaries. Indeed, an extreme development of this view would hold to an interpretation of the arms race that would emphasize the technological autonomy of strategic interaction.[76] The high priest of action-reaction by superpower military-technological trigger has been Robert McNamara:

> Whatever be their intentions—whatever be our intentions, actions—or even realistically potential actions—on either side relating to the build-up of nuclear forces, be they either offensive or defensive weapons, necessarily trigger reactions on the other side. . . . It is precisely this action-reaction phenomenon that fuels an arms race.[77]

It would seem prudent for the student of arms races to investigate the possibility of po-

---

[73] Andrew Scott, *The Functioning of the International Political System* (New York, 1967), p. 27.
[74] Smoker, *op. cit.*, p. 173.

[75] Hölst and Schneider, *op. cit.*, p. 162.
[76] See Milton Leitenberg, "The Present State of the World's Arms Race," *Cooperation and Conflict*, no. 3 (1970), pp. 188–89.
[77] Remarks before United Press International Editors and Publishers, San Francisco, Calif., September 18, 1967, Appendix 4 in U.S. Congress, Joint Committee on Atomic Energy, Subcommittee on Military Applications, *Scope, Magnitude and Implications of the United States Antiballistic Missile Programs*, Hearings, 90th Cong., 1st sess., 1967, p. 107.

litical trigger-events as well. For example, a change or prospective change in leadership might alter one side's view of the strategic-force posture desirable for the future; diplomatic activity might prompt a revision in the estimate of the policy guidelines being followed by the adversary.

The action-reaction triggering potential of activities filtering into the arms race system from its environment must be given some attention. The question arises as to whether the allies of the arms race principals should be considered as being internal or external to the arms race.[78] No general answer is possible. Allies may, by their own behavior, stimulate the arms program of the adversary. Also, allies might successfully generate demands for arms that are additional to those believed to be essential by the principals. In these ways the actions of allies should be viewed as being external to the arms race system. Allied contributions may also be substitutes for armaments that would otherwise have to be found by the principals; to that extent it is reasonable to view them as being internal to the system.

One side or the other may feel compelled to develop and deploy weapons and devise organizations that, primarily, are responsive to threats perceived in diverse parts of the world, quite apart from any direct machination by the rival. These developments might serve to improve a state's arms race position. Such external threats from beyond the system could be of a military or of a political nature, probably of both.

DOMESTIC PROCESS

It seems fair to suggest that those persuaded of the reality of a reasonably tight pattern of reciprocal interaction are likely to find it. Persistent, though variable, time-lags in reactions can be explained away as being the product of an inevitable bureaucratic inertia.[79] It may well be that the United States is more prone to the anticipatory reaction or overreaction than is the Soviet Union, in good part because of the asymmetry of information available to the adversaries respecting each other's weapons development and deployment intentions. However, the action-reaction interpretation of America's arms race behavior has been overstressed. Similar interpretation has been made of some Soviet activities—largely because of the paucity of reliable knowledge regarding the Soviet defense decisionmaking process. A model of tight strategic reciprocity has the advantage of a comprehensible and familiar strategic logic, and it cannot easily be challenged. Whichever view of the superpower arms race is the more accurate, it is apparent that more detailed studies are urgently required of the defense politics of both countries. This is a task for the political scientist rather than for the strategic analyst.

If taken to the extreme, the domestic process hypothesis would deny the existence of an arms race. One statement of this hypothesis would be that to understand the progress of a particular arms race, we should focus attention not upon threat perception—that is, upon triggers beyond the states in question—but upon domestic processes, strategic doctrines, moods, bureaucracies, and interests that interact to produce defense decisions.[80] Once an adversary has been identified, a close watch will be kept upon his shifting capabilities and intentions, but the major pressures for change in force structure will be internally derived. This hypothesis holds that interstate interaction is bound to occur, but that the majority of interstate arms races will involve states of roughly parallel technology and with bases of resources adequate for most phases and levels of expenditure.[81] The participants will be almost certain to be following, or at least considering, similar lines of military-technical development. Furthermore, belief in a close pattern of action-reaction would underrate the significance of the different responsibilities, world views, and problems of the participants.

The most important domestic influences on arms race behavior may be identified as (1) inertia, (2) technological momentum, (3) interest, (4) epidemiology, (5) absolute plan-

---

[78] Note Watt's criticism of Huntington on this question, *op. cit.*, p. 374. See also Russett, *op. cit.*, chap. 4.

[79] Shulman, *op. cit.*, pp. 154–55.

[80] One of the most persuasive statements of this view is provided by Steinberg, *op. cit.*, Introduction. Steinberg's comment upon Anglo-German naval rivalry is applicable to the 1960s. "The treadmill aspect of the Anglo-German arms race was not caused by the technology but by the politics of the participants" (p. 24).

[81] Any resource disparity may prove significant if all competitors are equally alarmed. However, the evidence would suggest that alarm is unlikely to persist. Thus, economically weaker states are not necessarily priced out of a competition.

ning, (6) strategic doctrine, (7) government, its structure, and the balance of power among its agencies, and (8) geographical location.

The inertia factor refers to the explanation that activity related to the arms race will be pursued by political and military bureaucracies as an ongoing and expected aspect of their daily lives, that is, until there is some dramatic change in the world view, and eventually in the basic policies, of the incumbent administration.

Technological momentum refers to the fact that scientists and engineers will produce a new generation of weapons, regardless of their contemporary arms race relevance, simply because it is their task and because the frontiers of knowledge beckon the inquisitive. In other words, expensive research and development activity may, by "sunk costs" and dependent-industry arguments, foreclose upon nondeployment decisions. As long as modernity in weapons is favored and research activity is well funded, weapons scientists will continue to develop new and improved models. Decisions about timing and size of production-run may bear no precise relationship to the contemporary activity of the rival. It will be sufficient to know, probably in a general way, that the adversary is working along similar lines of technical development.

The argument of interest states that necessary arms race reaction rationales for many major defense decisions are merely rationalizations for the domestic interests of the decisionmakers. These interests could be the health of a political constituency, the prestige of an armed service, or the continued vitality of a center of industrial excellence.

The epidemiological argument holds that an arms race should be seen as two or more nationwide diseases.[82] Once aroused to an external danger, irresponsible politicians, soldiers, industrialists, and journalists can tap the national "preparedness syndrome." Naval scares and bomber, missile, and security gaps can be invoked for electoral advantage. The inherent uncertainty regarding adversary intentions, and the difficulty of predicting the scale of weapons deployment over time, lends a certain plausibility to every identification of a future year of maximum danger.

Another factor worthy of attention is the one I identify as absolute planning. We may suppose that a state observes the probable course of military policy of its rival, identifies an appropriate force structure, and then builds according to its own blueprint—insensitive even to fairly large changes in the rival's programs.[83] Economy of production should be facilitated, a sense of stability engendered, and possibly an ease of annual parliamentary approval of expenditure assured. Furthermore, regularity of building tempo might discourage rivals. Such an interpretation could not explain the totality of a single state's behavior in an arms race, but it does contain more than a germ of truth for some phases of most arms races.

Those who believe that an approximate symmetry of military forces, both qualitative and quantitative, is required before an arms race can seriously be restrained must confront the fact that each party will hold to different notions concerning the best deterrent to war and the most effective way to conduct military operations. Strategic dialogue may lead not to a convergence of doctrines but rather to a recognition of different strategic principles. The ideology of one party might lead it to expect a surprise attack by the warmongering "adventurists"; such a belief could be a parameter for military preparation. Hence, a pre-emptive capability, despite its effect on positive feedback to the adversary, might appear to be a necessary precaution. Historical experience, in combination with a strong belief in the probability of war, might cause a party to seek a balanced offensive-defensive structure in its strategic forces. This preference could be impervious to technological developments, to periods of détente, or to warnings concerning instability in the arms race.

There can be no question but that defense decisions are influenced in their substance by the organizational structure and the decisionmaking processes involved in their consideration.[84] The degree of autonomy of the armed services, and even the traditional supremacy of

---

[82] See Rapoport, *Fights, Games, and Debates*, pt. 1, chap. 3; Lasswell, *op. cit.*, chaps. 3–4.

[83] See Huntington, *op. cit.*, pp. 50–54.

[84] Russett draws attention to the difficulty of controlling military expenditures in a political system that ensures a wide dispersion of authority. The degree of Cabinet or Politburo control of expenditure is limited in any executive structure by the plurality of strong vested interests. However, the U.S. government offers an extreme example of how an institutionalized balance of power may frustrate attempts to brake arms racing activity. *Op. cit.*, pp. 184–91.

one particular branch of them, might direct the verdict on a particular issue. A somewhat extreme view of the superpower arms race might be that bomber and artillery emphases are to be detected, respectively, in American and Soviet strategic doctrines. Civil-military relations are another aspect of the domestic process that might influence the substance of decisions important to an arms race. Civilian command over the scale and direction of defense expenditure will differ from country to country and from time to time. The degree and nature of such control is a crucial variable influencing arms race behavior.

The final domestic factor to be considered is that of geographical location. Location will influence, though not determine, choice of allies, and is very likely to offer quite distinct strategic opportunities. The continental location of the Soviet Union has profoundly conditioned its strategic doctrine and has allowed for the deployment of medium-range weapon systems that could exploit the close proximity of areas whose territorial integrity the rival believed to be vital. The geographical consideration could be expanded so as to include the distinct resource base of an arms race competitor, its population distribution, and the defense problems that such distribution imposes.

It must be understood that these domestic factors will interact to produce a stimulation to the arms racing incentives perceived to be imperative because of the external threat. The factors most commonly linked are technological momentum, the competition in funds and prestige among the armed services, and the interest of defense corporations in the selling of their products. As a subject for comment, the arms race offers much material for a polemic. I hope that the complexity presented in this article will serve to discipline the very narrow focus of much contemporary criticism—for example, that the superpower arms race is an instrument of "outdoor relief" for an amorphous but sinister "military-industrial complex."

Thus far I have suggested two broad theses concerning arms race dynamics, action-reaction and domestic process. However, if our understanding of the arms race phenomenon is to improve, synthesis is needed. It is unfortunate that many American politicians and academics seem to have taken their stand upon the issues of ABM and multiple-warhead deployments and then have adhered to the appropriate

thesis concerning the dynamics of the arms race. The majority of those who spoke upon national security affairs in the Johnson Administration, and the liberal opposition to the Nixon Administration's ABM decisions, have adhered overwhelmingly to a fairly exclusive action-reaction interpretation of the arms race. On the other hand, the Nixon spokesmen on national security and the more conservative strategic analysts are far less satisfied with action-reaction.

There must be a measure of action-reaction, or there would be no arms race at all. In other words, arms race participants must maintain a general attention to the developing military posture of their rivals. The argument between an autonomy of separate military development and a close reciprocity of action-reaction must be resolved in an understanding that action-reaction can be either close or distant. The arms race rival(s) provide(s) vital, though possibly intermittent, flows of data that serve to trigger arms race reactions.

However, the domestic processes of a state will determine whether there are to be reactions or not, whether there is any available reaction that would be both expedient and relevant, and also the scale and timing of a reaction. Each state will have its own problems and its preferences as to the best way of solving those problems. Thus, it can be said that the American Sentinel and Safeguard decisions were of a category that would be considered by the Soviet Union as potentially requiring an arms race reaction; but, to predict the Soviet reaction or nonreaction, an analyst would have to have mastered more detail concerning contemporary Soviet defense politics than would appear currently to be available in the West.

Most of those convinced of the pre-eminence of action-reaction give passing reference to the fact that there are also other factors driving the arms race. Having given a passing reference, they then offer little serious or prolonged analysis that might substantiate the claims for the priority accorded action-reaction. For example, George Rathjens, in his excellent study "The Dynamics of the Arms Race," records both that there is "a considerable debate" concerning the role of action-reaction and that action-reaction has been "a major stimulant" to the arms race.[85] Both of these statements are

---

[85] Rathjens, *op. cit.*, p. 19.

appropriate and beyond question, but it is reasonable to wonder what the other major stimulants have been and how important a role they have played.

The argument of this article is that there has been so little systematic study of arms race behavior that we cannot reasonably assume the dominance either of action-reaction or of domestic process explanations. We cannot refer to "the basic laws" of the arms race,[86] because it is almost certain that different factors have been of pre-eminent importance to each competitor during different phases of the race and that different factors are accorded different weights in each country.

ARMS RACE STUDY: THE WAY FORWARD

Apart from the requirement for refinement and revision of a structure for inquiry such as that outlined in this article, the way forward to a more complete and useful understanding of arms races should be marked by the following steps: (1) a full and critical guide to the relevant literature; (2) a series of case studies of particular arms races; (3) a comparative analysis of arms races. Although the separate

[86] One group of authors has referred to such "laws." See Union of Concerned Scientists, *ABM: ABC*, in U.S. House, Committee on Armed Services, *Hearings on Military Posture, FY 1970*, 91st Cong., 1st sess., 1969, pp. 2140–54.

case studies should be concerned with asking very general questions, the following questions should be the explicit concern of a comparative analysis of arms races. This list is by no means exhaustive, and some particular questions have already been raised and briefly discussed above.

Genesis. Why have there been arms races? What have been believed to be the attractions of this particular road to security?

Function. Once an arms race is begun, regardless of the original motives, what functions has the conduct of such a race performed, both for the participants and for the international system?

Typology. What kind of arms races have there been?

Strategy. What arms race objectives have guided competitors? What is the relationship between the nature of the weapons and the strategies pursued? What impact have different "knowledge states" concerning the programs of rivals had upon the subsequent course of an arms race?

Outcome. How have arms races ended?

Dynamics. How have arms races "worked"? What has been the balance between external and domestic driving factors? To what extent have these factors been mutually supporting?

These studies should be pursued by, or in concert with, students of the domestic politics of the countries concerned—not solely by those fascinated by the logic of strategic interaction.

SALT ABM TREATY

Treaty between the United States of America and the Union of Soviet Socialist Republics on the Limitation of Anti-Ballistic Missile Systems, May 26, 1972.

The United States of America and the Union of Soviet Socialist Republics, hereinafter referred to as the Parties,

Proceeding from the premise that nuclear war would have devastating consequences for all mankind,

Considering that effective measures to limit anti-ballistic missile systems would be a substantial factor in curbing the race in strategic offensive arms and would lead to a decrease in the risk of outbreak of war involving nuclear weapons,

---

The SALT ABM Treaty, the SALT Interim Agreement, and the Protocol to the SALT Interim Agreement are reprinted from Weekly Compilation of Presidential Documents, June 5, 1972, pp. 925–29.

Proceeding from the premise that the limitation of anti-ballistic missile systems, as well as certain agreed measures with respect to the limitation of strategic offensive arms, would contribute to the creation of more favorable conditions for further negotiations on limiting strategic arms,

Mindful of their obligations under Article VI of the Treaty on the Non-Proliferation of Nuclear Weapons,

Declaring their intention to achieve at the earliest possible date the cessation of the nuclear arms race and to take effective measures toward reductions in strategic arms, nuclear disarmament, and general and complete disarmament,

Desiring to contribute to the relaxation of international tension and the strengthening of trust between States,

Have agreed as follows:

ARTICLE I

1. Each Party undertakes to limit anti-ballistic missile (ABM) systems and to adopt other measures in accordance with the provisions of this Treaty.

2. Each Party undertakes not to deploy ABM systems for a defense of the territory of its country and not to provide a base for such a defense, and not to deploy ABM systems for defense of an individual region except as provided for in Article III of this Treaty.

ARTICLE II

1. For the purpose of this Treaty an ABM system is a system to counter strategic ballistic missiles or their elements in flight trajectory, currently consisting of:

(a) ABM interceptor missiles, which are interceptor missiles constructed and deployed for an ABM role, or of a type tested in an ABM mode;

(b) ABM launchers, which are launchers constructed and deployed for launching ABM interceptor missiles; and

(c) ABM radars, which are radars constructed and deployed for an ABM role, or of a type tested in an ABM mode.

2. The ABM system components listed in paragraph 1 of this Article include those which are:

(a) operational;

(b) under construction;

(c) undergoing testing;

(d) undergoing overhaul, repair or conversion; or

(e) mothballed.

ARTICLE III

1. Each Party undertakes not to deploy ABM systems or their components except that:

(a) within one ABM system deployment area having a radius of one hundred and fifty kilometers and centered on the Party's national capital, a Party may deploy: (1) no more than one hundred ABM launchers and no more than one hundred ABM interceptor missiles at launch sites, and (2) ABM radars within no more than six ABM radar complexes, the area of each complex being circular and having a diameter of no more than three kilometers; and

(b) within one ABM system deployment area having a radius of one hundred and fifty kilometers and containing ICBM silo launchers, a Party may deploy: (1) no more than one hundred ABM launchers and no more than one hundred ABM interceptor missiles at launch sites, (2) two large phased-array ABM radars comparable in potential to corresponding ABM radars operational or under construction on the date of signature of the Treaty in an ABM system deployment area containing ICBM silo launchers, and (3) no more than eighteen ABM radars each having a potential less than the potential of the smaller of the above-mentioned two large phased-array ABM radars.

ARTICLE IV

The limitations provided for in Article III shall not apply to ABM systems or their components used for development or testing, and located within current or additionally agreed test ranges. Each Party may have no more than a total of fifteen ABM launchers at test ranges.

ARTICLE V

1. Each Party undertakes not to develop, test, or deploy ABM systems or components which are sea-based, air-based, space-based, or mobile land-based.

2. Each Party undertakes not to develop,

test, or deploy ABM launchers for launching more than one ABM interceptor missile at a time from each launcher, nor to modify deployed launchers to provide them with such a capability, nor to develop, test, or deploy automatic or semi-automatic or other similar systems for rapid reload of ABM launchers.

ARTICLE VI

To enhance assurance of the effectiveness of the limitations on ABM systems and their components provided by this Treaty, each Party undertakes:

(a) not to give missiles, launchers, or radars, other than ABM interceptor missiles, ABM launchers, or ABM radars, capabilities to counter strategic ballistic missiles or their elements in flight trajectory and not to test them in an ABM mode; and

(b) not to deploy in the future radars for early warning of strategic ballistic missile attack except at locations along the periphery of its national territory and oriented outward.

ARTICLE VII

Subject to the provisions of this Treaty, modernization and replacement of ABM systems or their components may be carried out.

ARTICLE VIII

ABM systems or their components in excess of the numbers or outside the areas specified in this Treaty, as well as ABM systems or their components prohibited by this Treaty, shall be destroyed or dismantled under agreed procedures within the shortest possible agreed period of time.

ARTICLE IX

To assure the viability and effectiveness of this Treaty, each Party undertakes not to transfer to other States, and not to deploy outside its national territory, ABM systems or their components limited by this Treaty.

ARTICLE X

Each Party undertakes not to assume any international obligations which would conflict with this Treaty.

ARTICLE XI

The Parties undertake to continue active negotiations for limitations on strategic offensive arms.

ARTICLE XII

1. For the purpose of providing assurance of compliance with the provisions of this Treaty, each Party shall use national technical means of verification at its disposal in a manner consistent with generally recognized principles of international law.

2. Each Party undertakes not to interfere with the national technical means of verification of the other Party operating in accordance with paragraph 1 of this article.

3. Each Party undertakes not to use deliberate concealment measures which impede verification by national technical means of compliance with the provisions of this Treaty. This obligation shall not require changes in current construction, assembly, conversion, or overhaul practices.

ARTICLE XIII

1. To promote the objectives and implementation of the provisions of this Treaty, the Parties shall establish promptly a Standing Consultative Commission, within the framework of which they will:

(a) consider questions concerning compliance with the obligations assumed and related situations which may be considered ambiguous;

(b) provide on a voluntary basis such information as either Party considers necessary to assure confidence in compliance with the obligations assumed;

(c) consider questions involving unintended interference with national technical means of verification;

(d) consider possible changes in the strategic situation which have a bearing on the provisions of this Treaty;

(e) agree upon procedures and dates for destruction or dismantling of ABM systems or their components in cases provided for by the provisions of this Treaty;

(f) consider, as appropriate, possible proposals for further increasing the viability of this Treaty, including proposals for amendments in accordance with the provisions of this Treaty;

(g) consider, as appropriate, proposals for further measures aimed at limiting strategic arms.

2. The Parties through consultation shall establish, and may amend as appropriate, Regulations for the Standing Consultative Commission governing procedures, composition and other relevant matters.

ARTICLE XIV

1. Each Party may propose amendments to this Treaty. Agreed amendments shall enter into force in accordance with the procedures governing the entry into force of this Treaty.

2. Five years after entry into force of this Treaty, and at five-year intervals thereafter, the Parties shall together conduct a review of this Treaty.

ARTICLE XV

1. This Treaty shall be of unlimited duration.

2. Each Party shall, in exercising its national sovereignty, have the right to withdraw from this Treaty if it decides that extraordinary events related to the subject matter of this Treaty have jeopardized its supreme interests. It shall give notice of its decision to the other Party six months prior to withdrawal from the Treaty. Such notice shall include a statement of the extraordinary events the notifying Party regards as having jeopardized its supreme interests.

ARTICLE XVI

1. This Treaty shall be subject to ratification in accordance with the constitutional procedures of each Party. The Treaty shall enter into force on the day of the exchange of instruments of ratification.

2. This Treaty shall be registered pursuant to Article 102 of the Charter of the United Nations.

Done at Moscow on May 26, 1972, in two copies, each in the English and Russian languages, both texts being equally authentic.

For the UNITED STATES OF AMERICA
RICHARD NIXON
President of the United States of America

For the UNION OF SOVIET SOCIALIST REPUBLICS
LEONID I. BREZHNEV
*General Secretary of the Central
Committee of the CPSU*

SALT INTERIM AGREEMENT

---

*Interim Agreement between the Union of Soviet Socialist Republics and
the United States of America on Certain Measures with respect to the
Limitation of Strategic Offensive Arms, May 26, 1972.*

The Union of Soviet Socialist Republics and the United States of America, hereinafter referred to as the Parties,

Convinced that the Treaty on the Limitation of Anti-Ballistic Missile Systems and this Interim Agreement of Certain Measures with respect to the Limitation of Strategic Offensive Arms will contribute to the creation of more favorable conditions for active negotiations on limiting strategic arms as well as to the relaxation of international tension and the strengthening of trust between States,

Taking into account the relationship between strategic offensive and defensive arms,

Mindful of their obligations under Article VI of the Treaty on the Non-Proliferation of Nuclear Weapons,

Have agreed as follows:

ARTICLE I

The Parties undertake not to start construction of additional fixed land-based intercontinental ballistic missile (ICBM) launchers after July 1, 1972.

ARTICLE II

The Parties undertake not to convert land-based launchers for light ICBMs, or for ICBMs of older types deployed prior to 1964, into land-based launchers for heavy ICBMs of types deployed after that time.

ARTICLE III

The Parties undertake to limit submarine-launched ballistic missile (SLBM) launchers and modern ballistic missile submarines to the numbers operational and under construction on the date of signature of this Interim Agreement, and in addition launchers and submarines constructed under procedures established by the Parties as replacements for an equal number of ICBM launchers of older types deployed prior to 1964 or for launchers on older submarines.

ARTICLE IV

Subject to the provisions of this Interim Agreement, modernization and replacement of strategic offensive ballistic missiles and launchers covered by this Interim Agreement may be undertaken.

ARTICLE V

1. For the purpose of providing assurance of compliance with the provisions of this Interim Agreement, each Party shall use national technical means of verification at its disposal in a manner consistent with generally recognized principles of international law.

2. Each Party undertakes not to interfere with the national technical means of verifica-

tion of the other Party operating in accordance with paragraph 1 of this Article.

3. Each Party undertakes not to use deliberate concealment measures which impede verification by national technical means of compliance with the provisions of this Interim Agreement. This obligation shall not require changes in current construction, assembly, conversion, or overhaul practices.

ARTICLE VI

To promote the objectives and implementation of the provisions of this Interim Agreement, the Parties shall use the Standing Consultative Commission established under Article XIII of the Treaty on the Limitation of Anti-Ballistic Missile Systems in accordance with the provisions of that Article.

ARTICLE VII

The Parties undertake to continue active negotiations for limitations on strategic offensive arms. The obligations provided for in this Interim Agreement shall not prejudice the scope or terms of the limitations on strategic offensive arms which may be worked out in the course of further negotiations.

ARTICLE VIII

1. This Interim Agreement shall enter into force upon exchange of written notices of acceptance by each Party, which exchange shall take place simultaneously with the exchange of instruments of ratification of the Treaty on the Limitation of Anti-Ballistic Missile Systems.

2. This Interim Agreement shall remain in force for a period of five years unless replaced earlier by an agreement on more complete measures limiting strategic offensive arms. It is the objective of the Parties to conduct active follow-on negotiations with the aim of concluding such an agreement as soon as possible.

3. Each Party shall, in exercising its national sovereignty, have the right to withdraw from this Interim Agreement if it decides that extraordinary events related to the subject matter of this Interim Agreement have jeopardized its supreme interests. It shall give notice of its decision to the other Party six months prior to

withdrawal from this Interim Agreement. Such notice shall include a statement of the extraordinary events the notifying Party regards as having jeopardized its supreme interests.

Done at Moscow on May 26, 1972, in two copies each in the Russian and English languages, both texts being equally authentic.

For the UNION OF SOVIET SOCIALIST REPUBLICS
LEONID I. BREZHNEV
General Secretary of the Central Committee of the CPSU
For the UNITED STATES OF AMERICA
RICHARD NIXON
The President of the United States

PROTOCOL TO THE SALT INTERIM AGREEMENT

Protocol to the Interim Agreement between the United States of America and the Union of Soviet Socialist Republics on Certain Measures with respect to the Limitation of Strategic Offensive Arms, May 26, 1972.

The United States of America and the Union of Soviet Socialist Republics, hereinafter referred to as the Parties,

Having agreed on certain limitations relating to submarine-launched ballistic missile launchers and modern ballistic missile submarines, and to replacement procedures, in the Interim Agreement,

Have agreed as follows:

The Parties understand that, under Article III of the Interim Agreement, for the period during which that Agreement remains in force:

The U.S. may have no more than 710 ballistic missile launchers on submarines (SLBMs) and no more than 44 modern ballistic missile submarines. The Soviet Union may have no more than 950 ballistic missile launchers on submarines and no more than 62 modern ballistic missile submarines.

Additional ballistic missile launchers on submarines up to the above-mentioned levels, in the U.S.—over 656 ballistic missile launchers on nuclear-powered submarines, and in the U.S.S.R.—over 740 ballistic missile launchers on nuclear-powered submarines, operational and under construction, may become operational as replacements for equal numbers of ballistic missile launchers of older types deployed prior to 1964 or of ballistic missile launchers on older submarines.

The deployment of modern SLBMs on any submarine, regardless of type, will be counted against the total level of SLBMs permitted for the U.S. and the U.S.S.R.

This Protocol shall be considered an integral part of the Interim Agreement.

For the UNITED STATES OF AMERICA
RICHARD NXION
The President of the United States of America

For the UNION OF SOVIET SOCIALIST REPUBLICS
LEONID I. BREZHNEV
The General Secretary of the Central Committee of the CPSU

CHAPTER 4

Limited War

THE REAPPRAISAL OF LIMITED WAR

ROBERT E. OSGOOD

Limited war is here defined as "war fought for ends far short of the complete subordination of one state's will to another's and by means involving far less than the total military resources of the belligerents, leaving the civilian life and the armed forces of the belligerents largely intact and leading to a bargained termination." This article presents a classic review of limited-war concepts and objectives while admitting that Vietnam fits none of the strategic models. Osgood concludes that limited-war theory will not lead to predictable, universal rules of the game, but that it can inculcate a novel respect for the deliberate control and limitation of warfare. Robert E. Osgood is the Director of the Washington Center of Foreign Policy Research and Professor of Political Science at The Johns Hopkins University School of Advanced International Studies. His publications include Limited War *(1957),* Force, Order and Justice, *with Robert W. Tucker (1967), and* America and the World, *with Tucker et al. (1970).*

I

One of the most significant developments in international politics since World War II is the change of attitude toward armed force in the advanced Western countries. Between the two world wars total warfare was commonly viewed as virtually the only kind of warfare relevant to military preparedness and strategy. In such a war, victory would depend on destroying in the most thorough way the enemy's capability and will to fight. But in the cold war quite a different view has become widespread—the view that the principal objective of military policies is the avoidance of general war and the limitation and control of lesser wars according to political ends short of traditional military victory. One aspect of this change of attitude is the great attention devoted to limited-war strategy and preparedness in the United States, especially in the last ten or twelve years.[1]

[1] One symptom of the increased acceptance of the concept of limited war is the increased ambiguity of

To an extent that must amaze early proponents of limited war, who sought to over-

the term, since the concept of controlling war within rational limits relevant to specific political objectives has come to be applied to *any* kind of war, even one involving a nuclear exchange. A limited war is generally conceived to be a war fought for ends far short of the complete subordination of one state's will to another's and by means involving far less than the total military resources of the belligerents, leaving the civilian life and the armed forces of the belligerents largely intact and leading to a bargained termination. Although a war between nuclear states might conform to this definition, the term "limited war" is generally applied to relatively more likely, local, nonnuclear wars in which the interests and deliberately restricted means of the superpowers are involved on opposite sides, if only indirectly. The term "local war" is now often reserved for the great number of local conventional wars in which neither of the superpowers is directly or indirectly involved. The difficulty of defining limited war arises partly because the relevant limits are matters of degree and partly because they are a matter of perspective, since a war that is limited for one side might be virtually total from the standpoint of the other, on whose territory the war is fought. Furthermore, a limited war may be carefully restricted in some respects (e.g., geographically) and much less so in others (e.g., in weapons, targets, or political objectives).

Reprinted by permission and with minor changes from Problems of Modern Strategy, *pt. 1,* Adelphi Papers, *no. 54 (London, 1969), pp. 41–54. Copyright © 1969 by the Institute for Strategic Studies.*

come the formidable antipathy toward the concept during the Korean War and the Eisenhower-Dulles Administration, the rationale of limited war has gained widespread acceptance in the United States and, to a somewhat lesser degree, in allied countries. In the 1960s the United States went far in implementing the concept with strategies, weapons, and organization. Among research, academic, and military analysts the concept of limited war inspired a great outpouring of strategic doctrine. In the Kennedy Administration limited war became official doctrine and achieved something approaching popularity.

But now the war in Vietnam, which has called so much into question, raises doubts about some limited-war concepts and the premises upon which they were based. It is not just Vietnam, however, that raises these doubts; it is the conjunction of Vietnam with basic changes in the international environment within which limited-war concepts arose and flourished. It is time, therefore, to reappraise limited-war thinking and experience during the past two decades, and such a reappraisal must take into account the international context in which limited war has come to command such unprecedented attention.

However, the reappraisal should start with the antecedents of this attention, which lie in international developments before World War II. The concept and practice of limited war are as old as war itself; but the consciousness of limited war as a distinct kind of warfare, with its own theory and doctrine, has emerged most markedly in contrast and reaction to three major wars, wars waged between several major states, in behalf of popular national and ideological goals, by means of mass conscription and massive firepower: the Napoleonic Wars, World War I, and World War II. The contemporary interest in limited war springs partly from a determination to avoid World War III.

The relevance of limited war to contemporary international politics is manifest in the occurrence of more than fifty internationally significant local wars of various kinds since World War II, during which time there have been no general wars, and the armed forces of the most powerful states have come no closer to fighting each other than the American-Soviet confrontation in the Cuban missile crisis of 1962. The great majority of these wars, however, did not directly involve a nuclear, or even a major, power. Most of them were insurgent or civil wars; none of them (except the Hungarian intervention in 1956) was fought between advanced industrial states or on the territory of an advanced state.[2] They were limited, as before World War II, by such factors as the restricted fighting capacity of the belligerents, the one-sided nature of the contest, or the inherent limits of internal war. With the diffusion of power and the intensification of local conflicts, such wars in the Third World may become an increasingly disturbing element in international politics, if only because they could involve major powers. But the kinds of wars that have occasioned the systematic concern with strategies and weapons of limited war are wars that the United States has fought, wars that might have expanded into much wider and more violent conflicts, but that remained limited because the United States and its adversaries deliberately refrained from conducting military operations with their full capacities. Equally important, the concern has arisen from the desire to deter or limit hypothetical wars, wars that have not occurred—especially wars that might have resulted from limited aggressions impinging on America's vital interests abroad.

The detailed elaboration of a strategic doctrine of limited war, the formulation of specific plans for carrying out this doctrine, and the combined efforts of government, the military establishment, and private analysts and publicists to translate the doctrine into particular weapons and forces are developments peculiar to the nuclear age. They are products of the profound fear of nuclear war and the belief that the limitation of war must be carefully contrived rather than left to inherent limitations upon military capabilities. But they are also products of American foreign policy in a particular period of history. Reappraising limited-war strategy as, in part, a function of American policy in the cold war will help us to distinguish between those aspects of limited-war thinking that are obsolescent or of only transitory relevance, because they reflect vanishing or short-run circumstances, and those that are likely to remain valid or become in-

[2] For a useful list and classification of armed "conflicts," see David Wood, *Conflict in the Twentieth Century*, Adelphi Papers, no. 48 (London, 1968).

creasingly relevant, because they reflect fundamental conditions or significant international developments.

II

On the most general grounds the conception of limited war surely remains relevant—indeed, imperative. On grounds of morality and expediency alike, it is essential that states—especially nuclear states—systematically endeavor to control and limit the use of force where force is unavoidable. The fact that American public officials and spokesmen now generally take this for granted, while little over a decade ago high government officials commonly asserted that once war occurs it has no limits save those determined by the capacity to gain a military victory, must be regarded as a major and, hopefully, lasting triumph of reason over viscera.

But little about the feasibility and utility of particular limitations in specific conflicts, whether with respect to deterring or fighting a war, can be deduced from the general rationale of limited war. Nor can feasibility and utility be deduced simply by applying the logic derived from abstract models of conflict, although these may sometimes aid rational calculation. Judgments about the feasibility and utility of particular methods of limitation must, of course, take account of objective technical and physical facts, but these facts do not speak for themselves in strategic terms. Such judgments must depend largely on disciplined intuitions, informed and qualified by experience, about the way states actually behave when they are faced with war or the threat of war.

Yet experience is likely to be an inconclusive and misleading guide. If the test of a particular strategy lies in the results of actual warfare, how can one be sure whether the outcome is due to the characteristics of that strategy, to the way it was carried out, or to factors unrelated to strategy? If the test is deterrence, how can one know whether either the occurrence or nonoccurrence of the act that one intended to deter was due to the strategy or to other circumstances? At best, experience is a partial representation of the full range of circumstances that might affect the feasibility and utility of strategies of limited war. Neverthe-

less, because strategy has no self-contained logic like mathematics, experience of one kind or another has been, and must be, the primary shaper of strategy in thought and action.

It is significant, in this respect, that limited-war thinking has been conditioned by the perspectives common to a particular phase of the cold war, when the cold war expanded to Asia, and the Soviet Union achieved the capacity to inflict terrible damage on the United States in any nuclear exchange. Limited-war strategy first blossomed in response to the Korean War (although the implications of nuclear weapons had led Bernard Brodie, Sir Basil Liddell-Hart, and a few others to adumbrate concepts of limited war before). It flourished, especially among those out of office, during the Eisenhower-Dulles Administration. The appeal of limited-war strategy in this period was basically twofold: on the one hand was the desire to mitigate the danger of nuclear war; on the other hand was the desire to support the policy of containment more effectively. The underlying disposition in both respects was to bring force under control as a rational instrument of policy, but the motive for control has been a combination of fear and determination in different admixtures at different times and in different minds.

In the course of applying the concept of limited war to changing international circumstances, it has become apparent that these two objectives may lead to different policy conclusions, depending on whether one emphasizes effective containment or the avoidance of nuclear war. They may lead to different conclusions, not only about particular strategies, which had been copiously examined and discussed, but also about two issues that have scarcely been discussed at all by proponents of limited war: (1) when or whether to intervene in a local war; and (2) the proper intensity and scale of intervention within existing restrictions.

But even more important than the two objectives of limitation in shaping views on these questions are certain premises about the international and domestic political environment which have been relatively neglected in limited-war thinking. These premises concern (1) the nature of the Communist threat and its bearing upon American security; (2) the willingness of the American government and people to sustain the costs of fighting aggression; and (3) the identity and behavior of potential adversaries.

It is not difficult to understand why the issues of intervention and the premises about the objectives and the political environment of limited warfare have received far less attention than strategies of limited war. The explanation lies partly in the familiar limits to man's ability to foresee basic changes in his environment or to imagine how new events and conditions might affect his outlook. Strategies, on the other hand, are adaptations to foreign policy in the light of realities and trends that are perceived at the moment. They are frequently rationalizations of existing military capabilities and domestic constraints. Man's political imagination is constrained by what is familiar, but his strategic imagination is relatively free to draw its inferences and to design its plans until some unforeseen war tests its propositions; fortunately, most strategic propositions remain untested in the nuclear age.

But the explanation for the relative neglect of political premises in strategic thought also lies in the propensity of American civilian strategists to propound their ideas, often with brilliant ingenuity, as revelations of an esoteric body of learning (which to some extent they have been) that would rescue military thinking from conventional wisdom and put it on a rational basis. In this respect, however, the deference of the uninitiated, overawed by the secrets and rituals of the strategic priesthood, has been more important than the pretensions of the priests.

III

Limited-war thinking has been conditioned by a period in which the overriding objective of American policy was to contain international communism by preventing or punishing external and internal aggression. According to the prevailing consensus, a local Communist aggression, even in an intrinsically unimportant place, could jeopardize American security by encouraging further aggressions in more important places, thereby leading to a chain of aggressions that might eventually cause World War III. This view, fortified by the lessons of fascist aggression, did not, as critics contended, depend on the assumption that international communism was under the monolithic control of the Soviet Union—an assumption that the proponents of the consensus qualified as soon as did its critics—but it did depend on an assumption that amounted to the same thing in practice: that a successful aggression by one Communist state would enhance the power of the Soviet Union, China, and other Communist states vis-à-vis the United States and the Free World. By this reasoning American security interests were extended from Western Europe to Korea and, by implication, to virtually anyplace where aggression threatened.

Proponents of the limited-war strategy sought to strengthen containment. They hoped to make deterrence more credible and to bolster Allied will and nerve in crises, such as the one arising over access to Berlin. They argued their case as strategic revisionists seeking to save American military policies from the thralldom of misguided budgetary restrictions imposed at the expense of security needs. Conscious of America's superior economic strength and military potential, they rejected the thesis of the Eisenhower-Dulles Administration that the United States would spend itself into bankruptcy if it prepared to fight local aggression in places and with weapons of the enemy's choosing.

With the advent of the Kennedy Administration the revisionists came into office. Responding to a dominant theme in Kennedy's campaign, they were determined to fill the military gaps in containment. The United States, according to this theme, was in danger of losing the cold war because the government had not responded to new conditions—particularly to the rise of Soviet economic power and nuclear strength, but also to the shift of Communist efforts to the Third World. The most dramatic evidence of America's threatened decline of power and prestige was the Soviet Union's prospect of gaining the lead in long-range missile striking power, but the missile gap was thought to be part of a wider threat encouraged by misguided American political and military policies that had allegedly alienated potential nationalist resistance to Communist subversion in the Third World and forfeited America's capacity to deter or resist local aggression. To safeguard American security and restore American prestige it would be necessary, among other measures (reinvigorating the domestic base of American power, adopting policies better suited to the aspirations of the underdeveloped countries, and ensuring America's strategic nuclear superiority), to build up the United States' capacity to fight limited wars without resorting to nuclear weapons. If the Communists could be contained at the level of strategic war and overt local aggression, the new administration reasoned, the Third World would be the most active arena of the cold war, and guerrilla war would be the greatest military threat.

In office, the Kennedy Administration not only increased the United States' lead in long-range missile power; it also built up her capacity to intervene quickly with mobile forces against local aggression at great distances, and it emphasized a strategy of "controlled and flexible response." Identifying the most dangerous form of Communist expansionism as "wars of national liberation," it created special forces to help combat aggression by guerrillas and concerned itself intensively with methods of counterinsurgency.

By 1964, after the Cuban missile crisis and before large numbers of American forces got bogged down in Vietnam, the United States looked so powerful that not only some Americans but others too (particularly Frenchmen) began to think of the world as virtually monopolar and of America's position in the world as comparable to that of a global imperial power. The only remaining gap in military containment might be closed if the United States could demonstrate in Vietnam that wars of national liberation must fail. To achieve that demonstration was America's responsibility to world order as well as to its immediate interests. In this atmosphere of confidence and determination there was no inducement to question the premises about the wisdom and efficacy of intervention that underlay the prevailing American approach to limited war. The tendency was rather to complete the confirmation of a decade of limited-war thinking by proving the latest and most sophisticated conceptions in action.[3]

[3] Beyond proving the efficacy of any particular strategy, a successful war in Vietnam would demonstrate America's psychological and political capacity

We shall return to the impact of the adversities of Vietnam on American conceptions of limited war, but first let us review the development of limited-war thinking that had taken place in the meantime.

IV

Apart from the fascination with counterinsurgency in the early 1960s, the great outpouring of strategic imagination in the United States was inspired by efforts to deter or fight hypothetical conflicts in Western Europe. But these conflicts, in contrast to wars in the Third World, seemed less and less likely as détente set in. So in this area it was not the discipline of war that impinged upon strategic thought but rather the discipline of restrictions on defense expenditures and changes in the international political atmosphere. Moreover, in the absence of war, merely the passage of time caused a certain attrition of ambitious strategic ideas, as the inherent implausibility of limited war in Europe and the difficulty of gaining agreement on how to meet such unlikely contingencies dampened successive sparks of strategic innovation.

In Europe, as in the Third World, the dominant objectives of limited-war strategy were, first, to enhance the credibility of deterrence; second, to strengthen conventional resistance to local nonnuclear aggression; and, no less important, to bolster the West's bargaining position in crises on the brink of war. These three objectives were integrally related. But the objective of effective resistance was far more difficult to achieve in Europe because of the greater physical and political obstacles to limitation and the greater strength of potential adversaries.

The effort to formulate a strategy that would combine effective resistance with reliable limitations reached its logical extreme in 1957

to cope with limited war. As Secretary McNamara put it: "If you read Toynbee, you realize the importance of a democracy learning to cope with a limited war. The greatest contribution Vietnam is making—right or wrong is beside the point—is that it is developing in the United States an ability to fight a limited war, to go to war without the necessity of arousing the public ire. In that sense, Vietnam is almost a necessity in our history, because this is the kind of war we'll most likely be facing for the next fifty years." Quoted by Douglas Kiker, "The Education of Robert McNamara," *Atlantic Monthly*, March 1967, p. 53.

with the theories of limited tactical nuclear war propounded by Henry Kissinger, Admiral Sir Anthony Buzzard, and others. But these strategies soon died from indifference and incredulity. The difficulty of settling upon a convincing strategy for integrating tactical nuclear weapons into limited warfare in Europe evidently remains overwhelming, and the interest in doing so has declined as the credibility of the West using any kind of nuclear weapons first, except in circumstances warranting the risks of general war, has declined.

While the cold war was still relatively warm the search for a strategy of limited war in Europe enriched the postwar history of military strategy with ingenious ideas, some of which now seem strangely irrelevant. Strategies for fighting large-scale limited wars (endorsed by Alain Enthoven and, apparently, by McNamara in the early 1960s) were condemned to irrelevance by the unwillingness of an ally to support them with the necessary expenditures and manpower, by the unlikelihood that a war involving such powerful adversaries in such a vital area would remain limited, and by the fear of allied governments that emphasizing large-scale conventional resistance would undermine the efficacy of nuclear deterrence. That left strategies (1) to enforce short conventional pauses and raise the threshold between conventional and nuclear war (first publicized by General Norstad); (2) to combine static with mobile, and conventional with tactical nuclear, resistance in limited wars resulting from accident and miscalculation (most notably formulated by F. O. Miksche and Malcolm Hoag); and (3) to control escalation as a bargaining process using nonnuclear and nuclear reprisals and demonstrations (chiefly identified with Herman Kahn and Thomas Schelling).

All of the latter three strategies were attempts to accommodate the logic of limited war to the realities of limited conventional means. They were also responses to perceived security needs in an international political environment in which it was assumed that the threat of Soviet-supported limited aggression was undiminished—and even rising, according to many who foresaw the Soviet achievement of virtual parity with the United States in the capacity to inflict unacceptable second-strike damage. But this assumption became much less compelling or was abandoned altogether with the onset of détente, although the conception of raising the threshold of conventional resistance continued to gain adherents and in 1967 was finally embodied in NATO's official strategic position. Consequently, although the logic of flexible and controlled response prevailed on paper and in strategic pronouncements, the means to withstand anything more than the most limited attack for longer than a week were not forthcoming. France's withdrawal from most arrangements for collective defense only made this predicament more conspicuous.

Only the French government rejected the objective of avoiding an automatic nuclear response to a local nonnuclear incursion; but for all governments the objective of deterrence increasingly overshadowed the objective of defense. Yet, despite the declining concern with strategies of limited resistance, the Allies were less worried than ever about their security. This was not because nuclear deterrence was more credible. Indeed, one might suppose that Secretary of Defense McNamara's open admission that the United States could not prevent the Soviet Union from devastating the United States, even if the United States struck first, would have undermined confidence in America's will to use the ultimate deterrent to defend its European allies. The Allies felt secure because even a low degree of credibility was regarded as sufficient for deterrence under the new political conditions of détente.

In this atmosphere there was a tendency for strategic thought to revert to the conceptions of the Eisenhower-Dulles period. Proponents of the limited-war strategy now took comfort in pointing to the deterrent effect of the danger that any small conflict in Europe might escalate out of control. Considering the nature of Soviet intentions, the value of the stakes, and the integration of tactical nuclear weapons into American and Soviet forces, they were prepared to rely more on this danger and less on a credible capacity to fight a limited war effectively. It is symptomatic that this view found support from Bernard Brodie, an outstanding former champion of local conventional resistance in Europe who now saw the official emphasis on stressing the conventional-nuclear "firebreak" and increasing conventional capabilities as unfeasible, unnecessary, and politically disadvantageous in America's relations with its allies.[4]

In one respect, the limited-war strategy of the Kennedy-McNamara Administration underwent a modification that was tantamount to official abandonment. The most far-reaching application of the idea of contrived reciprocal limitation of warfare was the counterforce, or no-cities, strategy, which was intended to make possible the option of a controlled and limited Soviet-American nuclear exchange by holding America's assured-destruction forces (that is, the forces capable of delivering unacceptable damage on a retaliatory strike) in reserve and inducing the Soviets reciprocally to confine nuclear strikes to military targets.[5] When McNamara first publicly announced this strategy at Ann Arbor in June 1962, critics charged that it was intended to enhance the credibility of extended deterrence. This inference was not unwarranted, since McNamara's statement did reflect his view at the time that a strategic deterrent, to be useful, had to be rational to use. In a few years, however, McNamara came to view the strategy as no more than an option for keeping as limited as possible a nuclear war that might result from accident or miscalculation, not as a means of deterring or fighting such a war more effectively. In subsequent statements McNamara explained the objective of a counterforce strategy as exclusively damage limitation. He also explained the difficulties of inducing the Soviets to fight a limited strategic war in such a way as to cast doubt upon its feasibility.[6] Finally, in successive annual reports on the nation's defense posture he indicated that cost-effectiveness considerations dictated a relatively increased allocation of money and resources to maintaining a capability for assured destruction, as compared to the objective of damage limitation.

Summing up the fortunes of limited-war strategy with respect to Europe and central war, we can say that the basic rationale of limited war seems firmly established in the United States and in allied countries, with the possible exception of France, and that this rationale is to some extent implemented in operational plans, military policies, and weapons. But the highpoint of limited-war theory—in terms of the inventiveness, thoroughness, and energy with which it was carried out in strategic thought and actual policies—was roughly the period from 1957 to 1963. Since then, economic restrictions and diminished fear of Soviet military action, together with the inroads of time upon novel plans for hypothetical contingencies that never occur, have nullified some of the most ingenious strategies and have eroded others, so that limited-war thinking is left somewhere between the approach of the Eisenhower-Dulles Administration and the initial Kennedy-McNamara views.

In military affairs, as in international politics, one senses that an era has ended but finds little intimation of the era that will replace it. Meanwhile, strategic imagination seems to have reached a rather flat plateau surrounded by a bland atmosphere in which all military concerns tend to dissolve into the background.

V

This was the state of limited-war thinking in 1965, when American forces became the dominant element in fighting Communist forces in Vietnam. At that time the only really lively ideas were counterinsurgent warfare and controlled escalation.

Some regarded the war as a testing ground for strategies of counterinsurgency. When the

---

[4] See Bernard Brodie, *Escalation and the Nuclear Option* (Princeton: Princeton University Press, 1966). Brodie's differences with the official position (which, incidentally, he exaggerated in attributing to it the objective of resisting conventionally a large-scale Soviet aggression) were no less significant for being differences of degree. For they were intended as an antidote to a strategic tendency, just as his earlier advocacy of preparedness for limited conventional defense was intended as an antidote to the Eisenhower-Dulles emphasis on nuclear deterrence in Europe. See, for example, Bernard Brodie, *Strategy in the Missile Age* (Princeton: Princeton University Press, 1959), pp. 335ff.

[5] An even more radical, but not necessarily less plausible, strategy for limited strategic nuclear war, based on striking cities selectively rather than sparing them had already attracted some academic attention. Klaus Knorr and Thornton Read, eds., *Limited Strategic War* (New York: Praeger, 1962).

[6] On the one hand, he explained, the Soviet Union would be unlikely to withhold its countercity capability as long as its missiles were relatively scarce and vulnerable; but, on the other hand, he acknowledged that, as Soviet missiles became more numerous and less vulnerable, the prospects of confining retaliatory damage from them would vanish completely. In any event, in each annual "posture statement" he stated in progressively more categorical terms that there was no way the United States could win a strategic nuclear war at a tolerable cost.

United States began bombing selected targets in North Vietnam, ostensibly in retaliation for attacks on American units at Pleiku and elsewhere in the South, some regarded this as a test of theories of controlled escalation. When American forces in South Vietnam engaged regular units of the North Vietnamese army in large numbers, a host of new strategic-tactical issues arose, such as the issue, which was surely oversimplified by polemics, between search-and-destroy and seize-and-hold methods and the equally overdrawn issue between a mobile and an enclave strategy.

The war in Vietnam should have been a great boon to strategic innovation, since it fitted none of the existing models of limited war, although it contained elements of several. But the lessons derived from the strategies that were tried have been either negative or inconclusive, and it is not apparent that alternative strategies would have worked any better. Some critics of the conduct (as opposed to the justification) of the war assert that different political or military strategies and tactics, executed more skillfully, might have enabled the United States to gain its political objectives—primarily, the security of an independent non-Communist government in South Vietnam—more readily. Others assert that those objectives were either unattainable because of the lack of a suitable political environment in South Vietnam or attainable only at an unacceptable cost, no matter what methods had been adopted.

If it is difficult to make confident judgments about the efficacy of various strategies and tactics in Vietnam, it is even more difficult to draw lessons applicable to other local wars in which the United States may become involved, since the war in Vietnam is almost surely unique in its salient characteristics: the large size and effectiveness of North Vietnam's combat forces, the organizing genius of Ho Chi Minh, the North's appeal to the South on nationalist grounds stemming from the postwar independence movement, and the weak and fragmented nature of South Vietnam. Yet lessons will, and probably must, be drawn. Many have already been offered.

The most general lessons concern the political and other conditions under which the United States should intervene in revolutionary or quasi-revolutionary wars, and the proper scale of intervention. It is asserted, for example, that the lesson of Vietnam is that no regime too weak to defend itself against revolution or subversion without American military intervention will be able to defend itself with American intervention.[7] This may turn out to be true in Vietnam, although it is too early to tell. But, even so, can one conclude from this single, sad experience that no kind of American intervention under any circumstances, regardless of the nature of external support for revolutionary forces and the characteristics of the defending government and nation, could provide the margin of assistance needed to enable a besieged regime to survive? No such categorical rule is warranted. And, if it were, what would be its utility? The rule does not tell one how to determine whether a regime can defend itself, and it may be impossible to tell in time for American assistance to be useful.

Rejecting any such sweeping rules of abstention, Hanson Baldwin draws a no less sweeping lesson of intervention. Future interventions against insurgency, he says, must be undertaken "under carefully chosen conditions and at times and places of our own choosing," and they must avoid the sin of "gradualism" by applying overwhelming force (including tactical nuclear weapons, if necessary) at an early stage.[8] Walter Lippmann, on the other hand, sees the lesson of Vietnam in such negative terms as virtually to preclude successful intervention in wars of insurrection under any circumstances. Impressed by the unsuitability of such wars for American genius and power, he asserts that Vietnam simply demonstrates that elephants cannot kill swarms of mosquitoes.[9]

Given the general disaffection with the war, Lippmann's conclusion is likely to be more persuasive than Baldwin's. Indeed, although overstated, it contains an important kernel of truth.

[7] Former Ambassador Edwin O. Reischauer reaches the following "simple rule of thumb" on the basis of the Vietnam experience: "Any regime that is not strong enough to defend itself against its internal enemies probably could not be defended by us either and may not be worth defending anyway." See *Beyond Vietnam: The United States and Asia* (New York: Alfred A. Knopf, 1967), p. 188.
[8] "After Vietnam—What Military Strategy in the Far East?" *New York Times Magazine*, June 9, 1968.
[9] "Elephants Can't Beat Mosquitoes in Vietnam," *Washington Post*, December 3, 1967.

Once the United States becomes involved in any local war with its own troops, it will tend to use its modern military logistics, organization, and technology (short of nuclear weapons) to whatever extent is needed to achieve the desired political and military objectives, as long as its military operations are consistent with the localization of the war. For every military establishment fights with the capabilities best suited to its national resources, experience, and ethos. In practice, this means that American armed forces (and the large nonfighting contingents that accompany them), when engaged in a protracted revolutionary war on the scale of the Vietnamese War, tend to saturate and overwhelm the country they are defending. If the war were principally an American operation, as the long counterinsurgency war in Malaya was a British operation, the elephant might nevertheless prevail over the mosquitoes in time, even if it had to stamp out in the crudest way every infested spot and occupy the country. But the war in Vietnam, like every other local war in which the United States has or will become engaged, has been fought for the independence of the country under siege— in this case the country nominally represented by various South Vietnamese governments. Therefore, despite South Vietnam's great dependence on the United States, the United States is also dependent on South Vietnam. The chief trouble with this situation is that, in some of the most crucial aspects of counterinsurgency, South Vietnamese forces and officials have been ineffective, and the United States could do nothing about it. Moreover, where American pressure on South Vietnam might have been useful, the very scale of the United States' involvement has deprived it of leverage, since its direct involvement gave it a stake in the war which militated against the sanctions of reducing or withdrawing assistance.

In one respect Lippmann's metaphorical proposition may understate the difficulty the United States must encounter in trying to apply containment to a situation like the Vietnam conflict. If South Vietnam lacks the minimum requisites of a viable polity, then no amount of leverage or control could succeed in establishing the independence of a country, even if the organized insurrection and its external support were defeated. In this case, the incapacity of the elephant would be more profound than its inability to kill mosquitoes. In this case, when the adversary was defeated, the task of establishing an independent country would have just begun.

The lesson—although it is not universally applicable—seems to be that, if a country cannot defend itself from insurrection with assistance short of American regular forces, the United States probably can defend it only at a level of involvement that will contravene its objective of securing the sovereignty of that country; thus, even if the United States should defeat the insurgents, it will be burdened with an unviable protectorate. To oversimplify the proposition: either the United States, under these internal circumstances, must virtually take over the country and run the war itself at the risk of acquiring a troublesome dependent, or it must keep its role limited at least to guerrilla operations, and probably to technical and staff assistance, at the risk of letting the besieged country fall.

Hanson Baldwin is probably right in thinking that an early massive intervention can, in some circumstances, achieve a limited objective more effectively than a sustained war of gradually increasing scale, but following this generality as a rule of action would entail great risks of overinvolvement in quasi-revolutionary wars. Consequently, to condition American support of a besieged country on its ability to survive at a low threshold of direct American involvement seems like the more prudent strategy. This proposition, however, like others concerning the conduct of local wars, implicitly contains a consideration more basic than strategy and tactics: how important are the interests for which the United States may intervene? If they are truly vital, a high-risk strategy is justified, and even under the most unpromising conditions intervention may be imperative.

America's intervention in Vietnam has suffered from ambiguity on this question of interests. South Vietnam was evidently not considered important enough to justify the costs and risks of a scale of intervention that, if undertaken early enough, might (or might not) have led to a more successful outcome. Indeed, probably no American leader would have considered the eventual scale of war worth the costs had he known the costs in advance. The reason the United States got so heavily involved in Vietnam lies not in its estimate of South Vietnam's importance to America's vital interests but in the United States' inability to limit an expanding involvement after it had drifted beyond a certain scale of intervention. Hence, the United States found itself fighting a small version of World War II without undertaking a commensurate mobilization of its resources and manpower—or of its moral energy. In this sense, the scale and costs of the war were greater than the nation was prepared to sustain.

If the larger lessons of Vietnam concerning the efficacy and scale of intervention are ambiguous, the validity and utility of subordinate lessons concerning the strategy of limited warfare are no less inconclusive. Perhaps the strategy that has come closest to a clear-cut failure is controlled escalation, as applied by means of selective bombing in North Vietnam. But even in this case it would be misleading to generalize about the efficacy of the same methods under other conditions. Controlled escalation is a strategy developed principally to apply to direct or indirect confrontations between the United States and the Soviet Union.[10] It envisages influencing the adversary's will to fight and his willingness to settle a conflict by means of a process of "bargaining" during a "competition in risk-taking" on ascending—and, hopefully, on the lower—levels of violence, which would culminate in a mutually unacceptable nuclear war at the top of the escalation "ladder." In the spring of 1965 the American government, frustrated and provoked by Hanoi's incursions in the South and anxious to strike back with its preferred weapons, put into effect a version of controlled escalation, borrowing language and style from the latest thinking on the subject.[11] Through highly selective and gradually intensified bombing of targets on lists authorized by the President—incidentally, a notable application of one of the tenets of limited-war theory is strict political control of

military operations—the United States hoped to convince Hanoi that it would have to pay an increasing price for aggression in the South. By the graduated application of violence, the government hoped through tacit "signaling" and "bargaining" to bring Hanoi to reasonable terms. But Hanoi, alas, did not play the game.

Perhaps the experiment was not a true test of escalation, since the punitive purpose of the bombing was ambiguous. Indeed, in deference to public protests throughout the world, the United States explicitly stressed the purely military nature of the targets, as though to deny their bargaining function. Perhaps the escalation was not undertaken soon enough or in large enough increments, thereby sparing the North Vietnamese a decisive dose of punishment and enabling them to make material and tactical adjustments. But it seems more likely that the failure of controlled escalation lay in inherent deficiencies of bombing as a punitive device. In any case, there are special difficulties in applying to an underdeveloped country a strategy that presupposes a set of values and calculations found only in the most advanced countries. Yet even in an underdeveloped country there must be some level of bombing damage that would bend the government's will to fight. Perhaps controlled escalation exerts the desired political effect only when there is a convincing prospect of nuclear war at the top of the ladder. Or perhaps it works only against a country that is fighting for limited objectives. Hanoi had unlimited ends in the South, but the United States had quite limited ends in the North. Whatever the explanation, controlled escalation failed to achieve its intended political effect; and that should be sobering to its enthusiasts, if any remain. Nonetheless, the experience does not prove much about the efficacy of a different strategy of escalation against a different adversary in different circumstances.

Nor does the war carry any clear lesson about the wisdom of granting or denying impunity from attack to a country supporting insurrection in an adjacent country. Critics con-

---

[10] The concept and strategy of controlled escalation are set forth most fully in Herman Kahn, *On Escalation* (New York: Praeger, 1967), and Thomas C. Schelling, *Arms and Influence* (New Haven: Yale University Press, 1966), although both authors developed the idea in earlier writings. Needless to say, neither author believes that controlled escalation was properly applied in Vietnam.

[11] Punitive bargaining, however, was only one of the objectives of the bombing. Two other principal objectives were to raise the morale of the South Viet-

namese and to impede the infiltration of men and supplies to the South. See General Maxwell D. Taylor, *Responsibility and Response* (New York: Harper & Row, 1967), pp. 26–28; Thomas C. Schelling, *Arms and Influence* (New Haven: Yale University Press, 1966), pp. 170ff.; and Tom Wicker, "The Wrong Rubicon," *Atlantic Monthly*, May 1968, pp. 81ff.

tend that carrying the war to the North violated one of the few clear-cut rules of the game on which limitation might be reliably based, alienated world and domestic opinion, fortified North Vietnam's determination to fight for an unconditional victory, and distracted attention from the real war—the civil war—in the South, without substantially affecting that war. But advocates of carrying the war to the North argue that the attrition against North Vietnamese units and logistics was significant and might have been decisive but for self-imposed restrictions that were unnecessarily confining, that these operations were necessary to South Vietnamese morale and provided a valuable bargaining counter for mutual de-escalation, and that the denial of sanctuary is a valuable precedent for avoiding disadvantageous rules of the game in the future and may be a useful deterrent against other states who may contemplate waging wars against their neighbors. Moreover, it can be argued that, when a local war cannot be won at a tolerable cost within the country under attack, the only reasonable alternative to a dishonorable withdrawal is to engage the source of external support directly, and charge it with a greater share of the costs, in order to secure a satisfactory diplomatic termination of hostilities.

Both the Korean and the Vietnamese Wars indicate that the particular restrictions on military operations will be determined by such a variety of conditions and considerations that it is almost fruitless to try to anticipate them. In some conceivable future circumstances, one can even imagine a sensible case being made for crossing the threshold that bars the United States from using tactical nuclear weapons. It is unlikely, however, that the prevailing reaction to Vietnam will be in the direction that Hanson Baldwin advocates when he condemns the constraints of gradualism and the "cult" of self-imposed limitations. For Vietnam does at least indicate that the United States will go a long and frustrating way to observe significant self-imposed restrictions on a war rather than insist on obtaining a military victory by all means available.[12] It indicates that, even when

the nation is "locked in" to an unpromising local war with its own troops, it will prefer to follow the rule of proportionate response to enemy initiatives rather than incur the immediate risks of massive escalation.

It is significant how weak and ineffectual American all-or-nothing sentiment has been in Vietnam, as compared to the Korean War. The idea of the United States confining itself to a limited war, which was novel and antithetical in Korea, has been widely taken for granted in Vietnam. Indeed, the most influential American critics have urged more, not less, stringent restrictions on combat, despite the fact that the danger of nuclear war or of Chinese or Russian intervention never seemed nearly so great as they did during the Korean conflict.[13] Those (including some prominent conservative senators and congressmen) who took the position that the United States ought either to escalate the war drastically in order to win it or else disengage, clearly preferred the latter course. But their frustration did not manifest a general rejection of the concept of limited war; rather, it manifested opposition to the particular way of applying that concept in Vietnam.

Thus the popular disaffection with the Vietnam War does not indicate a reversion to pre-Korean attitudes toward limited war. Rather, it indicates serious questioning of the premises about the utility of limited war as an instrument of American policy, the premises that originally moved the proponents of the limited-war strategy and that underlay the original confidence of the Kennedy Administration in America's power to cope with local Communist

---

[12] One indication of the magnitude of self-imposed restrictions is the number and kinds of military actions the United States refrained from taking that it might have taken to defeat Communist forces. In Vietnam, as in Korea, a major restriction was on the number of

armed forces mobilized and deployed. In both wars the United States reached an upper limit on these forces—higher in Vietnam than in Korea—beyond which it would not go, even if it meant ending the war on less advantageous terms. Perhaps the most obvious restrictions—such as not bombing civilian targets and not invading the enemy's homeland—were in North Vietnam. Correspondingly, the most obvious limitations of political objectives have applied to North, not to South, Vietnam. Of North Vietnam the American government has asked, essentially, only that it stop supporting the war in the South materially and with its regular units. But in the South, too, the American government has become willing to settle for something considerably less than a total victory without arousing popular protest in the nation.

[13] It should be noted, however, that one of the reasons the danger of nuclear war did not seem so great was that the United States refrained from taking actions, like bombing Haiphong, which seemed to carry too great a risk of Chinese or Soviet intervention compared to their military or political value.

incursions of all kinds. In Vietnam the deliberate limitation of war has been accepted by
Americans simply from the standpoint of keeping the war from expanding, or from the standpoint of de-escalating it, whereas in Korea the
desire to keep the war limited had to contend
with a strong sentiment to win it for the sake
of containment. In Korea the principal motive
for limitation was the fear that an expanding
war might lead to general war with China or
nuclear war with the Soviet Union, but in Vietnam the limits were motivated as much by the
sense that the political objective was not sufficiently promising to warrant the costs of expansion. This change of emphasis reflects more
than the unpopularity of the war in Vietnam.
It reflects also the domestication, as it were, of
limited war—that is, of the deliberate, calculated restriction of the ends and means of
fighting—as an operational concept in American foreign policy.

Some of the reasons for the strength of
sentiment for keeping the war limited, however, bear upon the political question of
whether to intervene in local wars at all. They
suggest that the specific lessons about the strategy and constraints of limited war that one
might derive from Vietnam are likely to be less
important than the war's impact on the political premises that underlay American intervention.

VI

The political premises that Vietnam has
called into question are more profound, yet
more limited, and at the same time less explicit
than the sentiment embodied in the popular
refrain "no more Vietnams." If Vietnam exerts
a fundamental impact on American policy with
respect to limited-war interventions, it will not
be merely because of the national determination to avoid future Vietnams and to restrict
American commitments to a scope more compatible with American power and the will to
use it. The whole history of the expansion of
American commitments and involvements is
pervaded with the longing to avoid new commitments and involvements. Yet a succession of
unanticipated crises and wars has led the nation to contravene that longing. Sometimes the
desire to avoid the repetition of unpleasant involvements has led only to a further extension

of commitments, which in turn has led to
further involvements. That is what happened
when the Eisenhower-Dulles Administration
formed deterrent alliances (including SEATO)
to avoid another Korean War.

The reason for this contradiction is not really
a sublimated national longing for power—at
least not power for its own sake—but rather
the nation's persistent pursuit of a policy of
containment, which under the prevailing international conditions has repeatedly confronted
it with predicaments in which the least objectionable course has seemed to be the exercise
and extension, rather than the abstention or re-
traction, of American power. If a fundamental
change in America's use of limited-war strategy
as an instrument of policy takes place, it will
be because the premises of containment are no
longer convincing to the nation and because
Vietnam has acted as the catalyst to enforce
this realization.

In effect, the United States has equated
Communist aggression with a threat to American security. Although the relationship of
Communist aggression in Asia or Africa to
American security is quite indirect and increasingly far-fetched, this equation was plausible
enough if one assumed—as Americans generally did assume until after the Korean War
and the Sino-Soviet split in the late 1950s—
that the cold war was essentially a zero-sum
contest between the two superpowers and that
a successful aggression by any small Communist state would shift the world balance of
power toward the Communist bloc. Moreover,
there was no need to question this view of
American security as long as American efforts
to counter aggression were successful at a
tolerable cost.

But détente with the Soviet Union and the
increasing divergencies of interest among Communist states and parties are changing the
American view of international reality, and of
the nature and intensity of the Communist
threat in particular. Thus, a gain for China or
even North Vietnam is not automatically seen
as a gain for the Soviet Union or a loss for the
United States, and opportunities for limited cooperation with the Soviet Union occasionally
appear attractive. Moreover, the accentuation
of national and subnational particularism outside the Communist world may have diminished what capacity the Soviet Union or China

ever had to extend their control and influence through diplomacy, subversion, or revolution. In Africa, most notably, Americans are becoming accustomed to a great deal of disorder and Communist meddling without jumping to the conclusion that the balance of power or American security is jeopardized. To some extent China emerges as a new object of containment; but, despite the long strand of American obsession with China, the Chinese do not yet—and may never—have the strength to pose the kind of threat to Asia that the Soviet Union could have posed to Western Europe, and Asia is simply not valued as highly on the United States' scale of interests as Western Europe.

American involvement in the Vietnam War began on a limited scale at a time of national self-confidence and self-assertion in the Third World. The United States applied forceful containment there according to familiar premises about America's general interest in stopping Communist aggression and without questioning the precise relevance of the war to the balance of power and American security.[14] The scope of American involvement grew in an effort to defeat North Vietnam's "war of national liberation" and to establish a secure non-Communist government in the South. But during this period the familiar American image of the Communist world and its threat to American security was changing. Furthermore, in contrast to the Korean War, the Vietnam War never seemed to pose a threat to the security of Western Europe or Japan.

Nonetheless, if American objectives could have been achieved with no greater pain and effort than were expended in the Korean War (which also was unpopular, but not beyond being resolved on satisfactory terms), the nation might have accepted the Vietnam War as another vindication of containment—troublesome and frustrating, but not so costly or unsuccessful as to call into question the premises of American intervention. In reality, however,

the war became so costly and unpromising that, given its remote relationship to American security, Americans began to doubt the validity of the premises on which the government intervened. So, whereas the "never-again" reaction against the Korean War fostered the effort of the Eisenhower-Dulles Administration to apply containment more effectively to Asia at less cost by strengthening deterrence, the "no-more-Vietnams" spirit seems to challenge the necessity, if not the basic rationale, of strengthening military containment in any way that would increase American commitments.

At the least, these doubts seem likely to lead to a marked differentiation of interests in the application of containment—a downgrading of interests in the Third World and a greater distinction between these interests and those pertaining to the security of the advanced democratic countries. Possibly, they will lead to abandonment of containment in Asia altogether, insofar as containment requires armed intervention against local aggression on the mainland. More likely, they will simply lead to a sharper distinction in practice between supporting present security commitments and not forming new ones, and between supporting present commitments with American armed forces when aggression is overt, and abstaining from armed intervention in largely internal conflicts. What they seem to preclude, at least for a while, is any renewed effort to strengthen military deterrence and resistance in the Third World by actively developing and projecting the United States' capacity to fight local wars.

VII

On the other hand, it is misleading to reach conclusions about future American limited-war policies and actions on the basis of the nation's desire to avoid quasi-revolutionary wars like the one in South Vietnam, since the threat of local wars impinging on American interests could arise in many different forms. Thus, while the war in Vietnam seems to be waning and the prospect of similar wars of national liberation in Asia is uncertain, the capacity, and perhaps the incentive, of the Soviet Union to support local wars that might spring from quite different circumstances is increasing. The Soviet will to exploit this capacity will depend, in part, on the American position. If Soviet

14 One indication of the generalized and unquestioned anti-Communist purpose of America's intervention is that, according to Bill Moyers, President Johnson's special assistant and White House Press Secretary, the containment of China was rarely discussed even as late as the deliberations about the escalation decisions of 1965. Rather, these decisions were taken simply to prevent a Communist (that is, Viet Cong) victory. See "Bill Moyers Talks about LBJ, Power, Poverty, War, and the Young," *Atlantic Monthly*, July 1968, pp. 30–31.

leaders were to gain the impression that the United States is firmly set upon a course of neo-isolationism and the absolute avoidance of intervention in local wars, they might become dangerously adventurous in the Middle East and elsewhere. The United States would almost surely regard Soviet exploitation of local conflicts more seriously than it would regard another war like Vietnam. So one of the military-political issues facing the United States in the late 1960s is how to respond to the growing capacity of Soviet mobile overseas forces.

Current trends seem destined to provide the Soviet Union with a significantly enlarged capacity to intervene in local conflicts overseas, a capacity of which the United States has heretofore enjoyed a virtual monopoly.[15] The build-up of Soviet naval, amphibious, air, and land forces in this direction has been accompanied by a substantial expansion of Soviet arms deliveries and technical assistance to Middle Eastern countries, as well as to North Vietnam, and the acquisition of technical facilities (although not permanent bases) in several Mediterranean ports. The experience of observing America's large-scale support of South Vietnam and of providing North Vietnam with weapons and logistics support has given Soviet leaders a new appreciation of overseas local-war forces. At the same time, Soviet strategic doctrine has assigned a greater role to supporting Soviet interests overseas, both on the sea and in local wars on land.

These developments do not portend a mobile overseas capacity that can compete with America's capacity in an armed conflict, but they do provide Soviet leaders with new options for intervening in local wars. They provide new

levers of influence in the Middle East and elsewhere. And they impose new constraints on American intervention. The greatest danger they pose is that the superpowers will unintentionally become involved in competitive interventions in local conflicts where they lack control and where the *modus operandi* of avoiding a direct clash has not been established.[16]

VIII

The history of limited-war thought and practice in the last decade or so provides little basis for confidently generalizing about the feasibility and utility of particular strategies. Many strategies have never really been put to the test; and, where they have been tested, either in deterrence or war, the results have been inconclusive. Moreover, strategies are very much the product of particular circumstances—not only of technological developments, but also of domestic and international political developments. This political environment is always changing. Developments that have made some strategies seem obsolete—for example, the impact of détente, domestic constraints, and the balance of payments on strategies of conventional resistance in Europe—might change in such a way as to revive abandoned strategies or evoke new ones. The limited-war strategies appropriate to the international environment of the 1970s—especially if there should be a significant increase in the number and severity of local wars, a more active Soviet policy of intervention in local wars, a more aggressive Chinese military posture, or new nuclear powers—might contain some interesting variations on strategic notions that were born in past periods of intense concern with military security. Changes in military technology, such as forthcoming increases in long-range air- and sea-lift capabilities, also will affect the strategies and political uses of limited-war capabilities.[17]

Yet one has the feeling, which may not

---

[15] Thomas W. Wolfe, "The Projection of Soviet Power," *Survival*, May 1968, pp. 159–65 (reprinted from *Interplay*, March 1968); Curt Gasteyger, "Moscow and the Mediterranean," *Foreign Affairs*, July 1968, pp. 676–87; Claire Sterling, "The Soviet Fleet in the Mediterranean," *Reporter*, December 14, 1967, pp. 14–18. Since the Cuban missile crisis the Russians have made new investments in large long-range air transports and have built up their naval, infantry, and amphibious forces, enlarged their merchant marine (including ships configured for military cargo) to put the Soviet Union among the two or three leading maritime powers, and have established a greatly augmented naval presence in the Mediterranean, including two helicopter carriers for support of landing operations or antisubmarine warfare. There are no signs, however, that the Soviet government intends to create what the United States regards as a balanced naval force capable of coping with American naval forces.

[16] Gasteyger, *op. cit.*, p. 687.

[17] In particular, the C-5A air transports, now coming into operation, and fast-deployment logistics ships, not yet appropriated, will greatly increase the amount of troops, equipment, and supplies that can be lifted from the United States overseas in a short time. Such improvements in air- and sea-lift will provide increased capabilities and flexibility in supporting many different

spring entirely from a lack of imagination, that, in the nature of international conflict and technology in the latter half of the twentieth century, only a limited number of basic strategic ideas pertain to limited war, and that we have seen most of these emerge in the remarkable strategic renaissance of the past decade or so. These ideas can be combined in countless permutations and combinations and implemented by a great variety of means, but we shall still recognize trip wires, pauses, reprisals, denials, thresholds, sanctuaries, bargaining, demonstrations, escalation, Mao's three stages, enclaves, seize-and-hold, search-and-destroy, and all the rest.

What we are almost certain not to witness is the perfection of limited-war conceptions and practice in accordance with some predictable,

---

kinds of military tasks in remote places, at all levels of conflict, and in varied physical and political conditions. By reducing or eliminating the need for a standing American presence overseas they will enable the United States to be more selective in establishing and maintaining bases and commitments. See Robert E. Osgood, *Alliances and American Foreign Policy* (Baltimore: The Johns Hopkins Press, 1968), pp. 137–43.

rational calculus and reliable, universal rules of the game. The conditions and modalities of international conflict are too varied, dynamic, and subjective for limited war to be that determinate. Any search for the strategic equivalent of economic man on the basis of which a grand theory of military behavior might be erected is bound to be ephemeral and unproductive. On the other hand, I think it is equally clear that military conceptions and practices among the advanced states are not going to revert to romantic styles of the past that glorified the offensive spirit, war *à l'outrance*, the national will to victory, and overwhelming the enemy. If counterparts of the stylized limited warfare of the eighteenth century are unrealistic, counterparts of the total wars of the following centuries would be catastrophic.

The nuclear age has not made armed conflict obsolete, nor has it excluded the possibility of catastrophic war. It has, however, inculcated a novel respect for the deliberate control and limitation of warfare. That respect is a more significant and enduring achievement of limited-war strategists than any of their strategies.

BARGAINING, COMMUNICATION, AND LIMITED WAR

THOMAS C. SCHELLING

The theme of this article is "tacit bargaining"—bargaining in which (explicit) communication is incomplete or impossible. The fundamental problem of tacit bargaining is coordination of actions, whereas the fundamental problem of explicit bargaining is the coordination of expectations. Schelling notes that tacit coordination is most successful around points of prominence characterized by: (1) uniqueness, (2) avoidance of ambiguity, (3) qualitative differences, and (4) simplicity. Similarly, solutions emerging from explicit bargaining display characteristics which include: precedent, simplicity, the specific suggestion, and the status quo ante. *Dr. Schelling is Professor of Economics at Harvard University and a former director of its Center for International Affairs. He has written extensively on economics and game theory and is the author of* Strategy and Arms Control, *with Morton H. Halperin (1961), and* Arms and Influence *(1966).*

Limited war requires limits; so do strategic maneuvers if they are to be stabilized short of war. But limits require agreement or at least some kind of mutual recognition and acquiescence. And agreement on limits is difficult to reach, not only because of the uncertainties and the acute divergence of interests, but because negotiation is severely inhibited both during war and before it begins and because communication becomes difficult between adversaries in time of war. Furthermore, it may seem to the advantage of one side to avoid agreement on limits, in order to enhance the other's fear of war; or one side or both may fear that even a show of willingness to negotiate will be interpreted as excessive eagerness.

The study of tacit bargaining—bargaining in which communication is incomplete or impossible—assumes importance, therefore, in connection with limited war, or, for that matter, with limited competition, jurisdictional maneuvers, jockeying in a traffic jam, or getting along with a neighbor that one does not speak to. The problem is to develop a modus vivendi when one or both parties either cannot or will not negotiate explicitly or when neither would trust the other with respect to any agreement explicitly reached. The present article will examine some of the concepts and principles that seem to underlie tacit bargaining and will attempt to draw a few illustrative conclusions about the problem of limited war or analogous situations. It will also suggest that these same principles may often provide a powerful clue to understanding even the logically dissimilar case of explicit bargaining with full communication and enforcement.

The most interesting situations and the most important are those in which there is a conflict of interest between the parties involved. But it is instructive to begin with the special simplified case in which two or more parties have identical interests and face the problem not of reconciling interests but only of coordinating their actions for their mutual benefit, when communication is impossible. This special case brings out clearly the principle that will then serve to solve the problem of tacit "bargaining" over conflicting preferences.

TACIT COORDINATION (COMMON INTERESTS)

When a man loses his wife in a department store without any prior understanding on where

---

to meet if they get separated, the chances are good that they will find each other. It is likely that each will think of some obvious place to meet, so obvious that each will be sure that the other is sure that it is "obvious" to both of them. One does not simply predict where the other will go, since the other will go where he predicts the first to go, which is wherever the first predicts the second to predict the first to go, and so ad infinitum. Not "What would I do if I were she?" But "What would I do if I were she wondering what she would do if she were I wondering what I would do if I were she . . . ?" What is necessary is to coordinate predictions, to read the same message in the common situation, to identify the one course of action that their expectations of each other can converge on. They must "mutually recognize" some unique signal that coordinates their expectations of each other. We cannot be sure they will meet, nor would all couples read the same signal; but the chances are certainly a great deal better than if they pursued a random course of search.

The reader may try the problem himself with the adjoining map (Figure 1). Two people parachute unexpectedly into the area shown, each with a map and knowing the other has one, but neither knowing where the other has

dropped nor able to communicate directly. They must get together quickly to be rescued. Can they study their maps and "coordinate" their behavior? Does the map suggest some particular meeting place so unambiguously that each will be confident that the other reads the same suggestion with confidence?

The writer has tried this and other analogous problems on an unscientific sample of respondents; and the conclusion is that people often can coordinate. The following abstract puzzles are typical of those that can be "solved" by a substantial proportion of those who try. The solutions are, of course, arbitrary to this extent: any solution is "correct" if enough people think so. The reader may wish to confirm his ability to concert in the following problems with those whose scores were recorded in the writer's sample.[1]

1. Name "heads" or "tails." If you and your partner name the same, you both win a prize.

2. You are to meet somebody in New York City. You have not been instructed where to meet; you have no prior understanding with the person on where to meet; and you cannot communicate with each other. You are simply told that you will have to guess where to meet and that he is being told the same thing and that you will just have to try to make your guesses coincide.

3. You were told the date but not the hour of the meeting in No. 2; the two of you must guess the exact minute of the day for meeting. At what time will you appear at the meeting place that you elected in No. 2?

4. You are to divide $100 into two piles, labeled A and B. Your partner is to divide another $100 into two piles labeled A and B. If you allot the same amounts to A and B, respectively, that your partner does, each of you gets $100; if your amounts differ from his, neither of you gets anything.

These problems are artificial, but they illus-

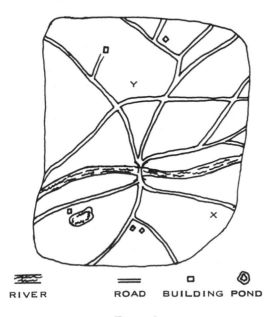

RIVER   ROAD   BUILDING   POND

Figure 1

[1] In the writer's sample, 36 persons concerted on "heads" in problem 1, and only 6 chose "tails." Problems 2 and 3, which may reflect the location of the sample in New Haven, Connecticut, showed an absolute majority managing to get together at Grand Central Station (information booth), and virtually all of them succeeded in meeting at twelve noon. Problem 4 caused no difficulty to 36 out of 41, who split the total 50-50. On a map like the one reproduced here (Figure 1), 7 out of 8 respondents managed to meet at the bridge.

trate the point. People *can* often concert their intentions or expectations with others if each knows that the other is trying to do the same. Most situations—perhaps every situation for people who are practiced at this kind of game —provide some clue for coordinating behavior, some focal point for each person's expectation of what the other expects him to expect to be expected to do. Finding the key, or rather finding *a* key—any key that is mutually recognized as the key becomes *the* key—may depend on imagination more than on logic; it may depend on analogy, precedent, accidental arrangement, symmetry, aesthetic or geometric configuration, casuistic reasoning, and who the parties are and what they know about each other. Whimsy may send the man and his wife to the "lost and found"; or logic may lead each to reflect and to expect the other to reflect on where they would have agreed to meet if they had had a prior agreement to cover the contingency. It is not being asserted that they will always find an obvious answer to the question; but the chances of their doing so are ever so much greater than the bare logic of abstract random probabilities would ever suggest.

A prime characteristic of most of these "solutions" to the problems—that is, of the clues or coordinators or focal points—is some kind of prominence or conspicuousness. But it is a prominence that depends on time and place and who the people are. Ordinary folk lost on a plane circular area may naturally go to the center to meet each other; but only one versed in mathematics would "naturally" expect to meet his partner at the center of gravity of an irregularly shaped area. Equally essential is some kind of uniqueness; the man and his wife cannot meet at the "lost and found" if the store has several. The writer's experiments with alternative maps indicated clearly that a map with many houses and a single crossroads sends people to the crossroads, while one with many crossroads and a single house sends most of them to the house. Partly this may reflect only that uniqueness conveys prominence; but it may be more important that uniqueness avoids ambiguousness. Houses may be intrinsically more prominent than anything else on the map; but if there are three of them, none more prominent than the others, there is but one chance in three of meeting at a house, and the

recognition of this fact may lead to the rejection of houses as the "clue."[2]

TACIT BARGAINING
(DIVERGENT INTERESTS)

A conflict of interest enters our problem if the parachutists dislike walking. With communication, which is not allowed in our problem, they would have argued or bargained over where to meet, each favoring a spot close to himself or a resting place particularly to his liking. In the absence of communication, their overriding interest is to concert ideas; and, if a particular spot commands attention as the "obvious" place to meet, the winner of the bargain is simply the one who happens to be closer to it. Even if the one who is farthest from the focal point knows that he is, he cannot withhold his acquiescence and argue for a fairer division of the walking; the "proposal" for the bargain that is provided by the map itself—if, in fact, it provides one—is the only extant offer; and, without communication, no counter-proposal can be made. The conflict gets reconciled—or perhaps we should say is ignored—as a by-product of the dominant need for coordination.

"Win" and "lose" may not be quite accurate, since both may lose by comparison with what they could have agreed on through communication. If the two are actually close together and far from the lone house on the map, they might have eliminated the long walk to the house if they could have identified their locations and concerted explicitly on a place to meet between them. Or it may be that one "wins" while the other loses more than the first wins: if both are on the same side of the house and walk to it, they walk together a greater distance than they needed to, but the closer one may still have come off better than if he had had to argue it out with the other.

This last case illustrates that it may be to the advantage of one to be unable to communicate. There is room here for a motive to destroy communication or to refuse to collaborate in advance on a method of meeting if one is

[2] That this would be "correct" reasoning, incidentally, is suggested by one of the author's map experiments. On a map with a single house and many crossroads, the eleven people who chose the house all met, while the four who chose crossroads all chose different crossroads and did not even meet one another.

aware of his advantage and confident of the "solution" he foresees. In one variant of the writer's test, A knew where B was, but B had no idea where A was (and each knew how much the other knew). Most of the recipients of the B-type questionnaire smugly sat tight, enjoying their ignorance, while virtually all the A-questionnaire respondents grimly acknowledged the inevitable and walked all the way to B. It may be better still to have the power to send but not to receive messages: if one can announce his position, state that his transmitter works but his receiver does not, and say that he will wait where he is until the other arrives, the latter has no choice. He can make no effective counteroffer, since no counteroffer could be heard.[3]

The writer has tried a sample of conflicting-interest games on a number of people, including games that are biased in favor of one party or the other, and, on the whole, the outcome suggests the same conclusion that was reached in the purely cooperative games. All these games require coordination; they also, however, provide several alternative choices over which the two parties' interests differ. Yet, among all the available options, some particular one usually seems to be the focal point for coordinated choice, and the party to whom it is a relatively unfavorable choice quite often takes it simply because he knows that the other will expect him to. The choices that cannot coordinate expectations are not really "available" without communication. The odd characteristic of all these games is that neither rival can gain by outsmarting the other. Each loses unless he does exactly what the other expects him to do. Each party is the prisoner or the beneficiary of their mutual expectations; no one can disavow his own expectation of what the other will expect him to expect to be expected to do. The need for agreement overrules the potential disagreement, and each must concert with the other or lose altogether. Some of these games are arrived at by slightly changing the problems given earlier, as we did for the map problem by supposing that walking is onerous.

1. A and B are to choose "heads" or "tails" without communicating. If both choose "heads," A gets $3 and B gets $2; if both choose "tails,"

A gets $2 and B gets $3. If they choose differently, neither gets anything. You are A (or B); which do you choose? (Note that if both choose at random, there is only a 50-50 chance of successful coincidence and an expected value of $1.25 apiece—less than either $3 or $2.)

2. You and your partner (rival) are to be given $100 if you can agree on how to divide it without communicating. Each of you is to write the amount of his claim on a sheet of paper; and if the two claims add to no more than $100, each gets exactly what he claimed. If the two claims exceed $100, neither of you gets anything. How much do you claim?

3. Two opposing forces are at the points marked X and Y in a map similar to the one in Figure 1. The commander of each force wishes to occupy as much of the area as he can and knows the other does too. But each commander wishes to avoid an armed clash and knows the other does too. Each must send forth his troops with orders to take up a designated line and to fight if opposed. Once the troops are dispatched, the outcome depends only on the lines that the two commanders have ordered their troops to occupy. If the lines overlap, the troops will be assumed to meet and fight, to the disadvantage of both sides. If the troops take up positions that leave any appreciable space unoccupied between them, the situation will be assumed "unstable" and a clash inevitable. Only if the troops are ordered to occupy identical lines or lines that leave virtually no unoccupied space between them will a clash be avoided. In that case, each side successfully obtains the area it occupies, the advantage going to the side that has the most valuable area in terms of land and facilities. You command the forces located at the point marked X (Y). Draw on the map the line that you send your troops to occupy.

The outcomes in the writer's informal sample are given below.[4] In those problems where there is some asymmetry between "you" and

---

[3] This is an instance of the general paradox that what is impotence by ordinary standards may, in bargaining, be a source of "strength."

[4] In the first problem, 16 out of 22 A's and 15 out of 22 B's chose "heads." Given what the A's did, "heads" was the best answer for B; given what the B's did, "heads" was the best answer for A. Together they did substantially better than they would have by a random method; and, of course, if each had tried to win $3, they would all have scored a perfect zero. In problem 2, 36 out of 40 chose $50. In problem 3, 14 of 22 X's and 14 of 23 Y's drew their boundaries exactly along the river. The "correctness" of this

"him," that is, between A and B, the A formulations were matched with the B formulations in deriving the "outcome." The general conclusion, as given in more detail in footnote 4, is that the participants can "solve" their problem in a substantial proportion of the cases; they certainly do conspicuously better than any chance methods would have permitted, and even the disadvantaged party in the biased games permits himself to be disciplined by the message the game provides for their coordination.

The "clues" in these games are diverse. "Heads" apparently beat "tails" through some kind of conventional priority. Roads might seem, in principle, as plausible as rivers, especially since their variety permits a less arbitrary choice. But, precisely because of their variety, the map cannot say *which* road; so roads must be discarded in favor of the unique and unambiguous river. (Perhaps in a symmetrical map of uniform terrain, the outcome would be more akin to the 50-50 split in the $100 example—a diagonal division in half, perhaps—but the irregularity of the map rather precludes a geometrical solution.)

In each of these situations the outcome is determined by something that is fairly arbitrary. It is not a particularly "fair" outcome, from either an observer's point of view or the points of view of the participants. Even the 50-50 split is arbitrary in its reliance on a kind of recognizable mathematical purity; and, if it is "fair," it is so only because we have no concrete data by which to judge its unfairness, such as the source of the funds, the relative need of the rival claimants, or any potential basis for moral or legal claims. Splitting the difference in an argument over kidnap ransom is not particularly "fair," but it has the mathematical qualities as problem 2.

If we ask what determines the outcome in these cases, the answer again is in the coordination problem. Each of these problems requires coordination for a common gain, even though there is rivalry among alternative lines of common action. But, among the various choices, there is usually one or only a few that can serve as coordinator.

EXPLICIT BARGAINING

The concept of "coordination" that has been developed here for tacit bargaining does not seem directly applicable to explicit bargaining. There is no apparent need for intuitive rapport when speech can be used; and the adventitious clues that coordinated thoughts and influenced the outcome in the tacit case revert to the status of incidental details.

Yet there is abundant evidence that some such influence is powerfully present even in explicit bargaining. In bargains that involve numerical magnitude, for example, there seems to be a strong magnetism in mathematical simplicity. A trivial illustration is the tendency for the outcomes to be expressed in "round numbers"; the salesman who works out the arithmetic for his "rock-bottom" price on the automobile at $2,507.63 is fairly pleading to be relieved of $7.63. The frequency with which final agreement is precipitated by an offer to "split the difference" illustrates the same point, and the difference that is split is by no means always trivial. More impressive, perhaps, is the remarkable frequency with which long negotiations over complicated quantitative formulas or *ad hoc* shares in some costs or benefits converge ultimately on something as crudely simple as equal shares, shares proportionate to some common magnitude (gross national product, population, foreign exchange deficit, and so forth), or the shares agreed on in some previous, but logically irrelevant, negotiation.

Precedent seems to exercise an influence that greatly exceeds its logical importance or legal force. A strike settlement or an international debt settlement often sets a "pattern" that is followed almost by default in subsequent negotiations. Sometimes, to be sure, there is a reason for a measure of uniformity, and sometimes there is enough similarity in the circumstances to explain similar outcomes; but more often it seems that there is simply no heart left in the bargaining when it takes place under the shadow of some dramatic and conspicuous precedent.[5] In similar fashion, mediators often display a power to precipitate agreement and a power to determine the terms of agreement;

---

solution is emphatically shown by the fact that the other 15, who eschewed the river, produced 14 different lines. Of 8 × 7 possible pairs among them, there were 55 failures and 1 success.

[5] This and the preceding paragraph are illustrated by the speed with which a number of Middle Eastern oil-royalty arrangements converged on the 50-50 formula a few years after World War II.

their proposals often seem to be accepted less by reason of their inherent fairness or reasonableness than by a kind of resignation of both participants. "Fact-finding" reports may also tend to draw expectations to a focus, by providing a suggestion to fill the vacuum of indeterminacy that otherwise exists: not the facts themselves but the creation of a specific suggestion seems to exercise the influence.

There is, in a similar vein, a strong attraction to the *status quo ante* as well as to natural boundaries. Even parallels of latitude have recently exhibited their longevity as focal points for agreement. Certainly there are reasons of convenience in using rivers as the agreed upon stopping place for troops or in using old boundaries, whatever their current relevance; but often these features of the landscape seem less important for their practical convenience than for their power to crystallize agreement.

These observations would be trivial if they meant only that bargaining results were *expressed* in simple and qualitative terms or that minor accommodations were made to round off the last few cents or miles or people. But it often looks as though the ultimate focus for agreement did not just reflect the balance of bargaining powers but provided bargaining power to one side or the other. It often seems that a cynic could have predicted the outcome on the basis of some "obvious" focus for agreement, some strong suggestion contained in the situation itself, without much regard for the merits of the case, the arguments to be made, or the pressures to be applied during the bargaining. The "obvious" place to compromise frequently seems to win by some kind of default, as though there is simply no rationale for settling anywhere else. Or, if the "natural" outcome is taken to reflect the relative skills of the parties to the bargain, it may be important to identify that skill as the ability to set the stage in such a way as to give prominence to some particular outcome that would be favorable. The outcome may not be so much conspicuously fair or conspicuously in balance with estimated bargaining powers as just plain "conspicuous."

This conclusion may seem to reduce the scope for bargaining skill, if the outcome is already determined by the configuration of the problem itself and by where the focal point lies. But perhaps what it does is shift the locus

where skill is effective. The "obvious" outcome depends greatly on how the problem is formulated, on what analogies or precedents the definition of the bargaining issue calls to mind, on the kinds of data that may be available to bear on the question in dispute. When the committee begins to argue over how to divide the costs, it is already constrained by whether the terms of reference refer to the "dues" to be shared or the "taxes" to be paid, by whether a servicing committee is preparing national-income figures or balance-of-payments figures for their use, by whether the personnel of the committee brings certain precedents into prominence by having participated personally in earlier negotiations, by whether the inclusion of two separate issues on the same agenda will give special prominence and relevance to those particular features that they have in common. Much of the skill has already been applied when the formal negotiations begin.[6]

If all this is correct, as to the writer it seems frequently to be, our analysis of tacit bargaining may help to provide an understanding of the influence at work; and perhaps the logic of tacit bargaining even provides a basis for believing it to be correct. The fundamental problem in tacit bargaining is that of *coordination*; we should inquire, then, what has to be coordinated in explicit bargaining. The answer may be that explicit bargaining requires, for an ultimate agreement, some coordination of the participants' expectations. The proposition might be as follows.

Most bargaining situations ultimately involve some range of possible outcomes within which each party would rather make a concession than fail to reach agreement at all. In such a situation any potential outcome is one from which at least one of the parties, and probably both, would have been willing to retreat for the sake of agreement, and very often the other party knows it. Any potential outcome is therefore one that either party could have improved by insisting; yet he may have no basis for insisting, since the other knows or suspects that he would rather concede than do without

---

[6] Perhaps another role for skill is contained in this general approach. If one is unsuccessful in getting the problem so formulated that the "obvious" outcome is near his own preferred position, he can proceed to confuse the issue. Find multiple definitions for all the terms and add "noise" to drown out the strong signal contained in the original formulation.

agreement. Each party's strategy is guided mainly by what he expects the other to accept or insist on; yet each knows that the other is guided by reciprocal thoughts. The final outcome must be a point from which neither expects the other to retreat; yet the main ingredient of this expectation is what one thinks the other expects the first to expect, and so on. Somehow, out of this fluid and indeterminate situation that seemingly provides no logical reason for anybody to expect anything except what he expects to be expected to expect, a decision is reached. These infinitely reflexive expectations must somehow converge on a single point, at which each expects the other not to expect to be expected to retreat.

If we then ask what it is that can bring their expectations into convergence and bring the negotiation to a close, we might propose that it is the intrinsic magnetism of particular outcomes, especially those that enjoy prominence, uniqueness, simplicity, precedent, or some rationale that makes them qualitatively differentiable from the continuum of possible alternatives. We could argue that expectations tend not to converge on outcomes that differ only by degree from alternative outcomes, but that people have to dig in their heels at a groove in order to make any show of determination. One has to have a reason for standing firmly on a position; and along the continuum of qualitatively undifferentiable positions one finds no rationale. The rationale may not be strong at the arbitrary "focal point," but at least it can defend itself with the argument "If not here, where?"

There is perhaps a little more to this need for a mutually identifiable resting place. If one is about to make a concession, he needs to control his adversary's expectations; he needs a recognizable limit to his own retreat. If one is to make a finite concession that is not to be interpreted as capitulation, he needs an obvious place to stop. A mediator's suggestion may provide it, as may any other element that qualitatively distinguishes the new position from surrounding positions. If one has been demanding 60 percent and recedes to 50 percent, he can get his heels in; if he recedes to 49 percent, the other will assume that he has hit the skids and will keep sliding.

If some troops have retreated to the river on our map (Figure 1), they will expect to be expected to make a stand. This is the one spot to which they can retreat without necessarily being expected to retreat farther, while, if they yield any more ground, there is no place left where they can be expected to make a determined stand. Similarly, the advancing party can expect to force the other to retreat to the river without having his advance interpreted as an insatiable demand for unlimited retreat. There is stability at the river—and perhaps nowhere else.

This proposition may seem intuitively plausible; it does to the writer, and in any event some kind of explanation is needed for the tendency to settle at focal points. But the proposition would remain vague and somewhat mystical if it were not for the somewhat more tangible logic of tacit bargaining. The latter provides not only an analogy but the demonstration that the necessary psychic phenomenon—tacit coordination of expectations—is a real possibility and in some contexts a remarkably reliable one. The "coordination" of expectations is analogous to the "coordination" of behavior when communication is cut off; and, in fact, they both involve nothing more nor less than intuitively perceived mutual expectations. Thus the empirically verifiable results of some of the tacit-bargaining games, as well as the more logical role of coordinated expectations in that case, prove that expectations can be coordinated and that some of the objective details of the situation can exercise a controlling influence when the coordination of expectations is essential. *Something* is perceived by both parties when communication is absent; it must still be perceptible, though undoubtedly of lesser force, when communication is possible. The possibility of communication does not make 50-50 less symmetrical or the river less unique or A B C a less natural order for those letters.

If all we had to reason from were the logic of tacit bargaining, it would be only a guess, and perhaps a wild one, that the same kind of psychic attraction worked in explicit bargaining; and, if all we had to generalize from were the observation of peculiarly "plausible" outcomes in actual bargains, we might be unwilling to admit the force of adventitious details. But the two lines of evidence so strongly reinforce each other that the analogy between tacit and explicit bargaining seems a potent one.

To illustrate, consider the problem of agreeing explicitly on how to divide $100: 50-50 seems a plausible division, but it may seem so for too many reasons. It may seem "fair"; it may seem to balance bargaining powers; or it may, as suggested in this paper, simply have the power to communicate its own inevitability to the two parties in such a fashion that each appreciates that they both appreciate it. What our analysis of tacit bargaining provides is evidence for the latter view. The evidence is simply that, *if* they had to divide the $100 without communicating, they could concert on 50-50. Instead of relying on intuition, then, we can point to the fact that in a slightly different context—the tacit-bargaining context—our argument has an objectively demonstrable interpretation.

To illustrate again, the ability of the two commanders in one of our problems to recognize the stabilizing power of the river—or, rather, their inability not to recognize it—is substantiated by the evidence that, if their survival depended on some agreement about where to stabilize their lines *and communication were not allowed*, they probably could perceive and appreciate the qualities of the river as a focus for their tacit agreement. So the tacit analogy at least demonstrates that the idea of "coordinating expectations" is meaningful rather than mystical.

Perhaps we could push the argument further still. Even in those cases in which the only distinguishing characteristic of a bargaining result is its evident "fairness," according to standards that the participants are known to appreciate, we might argue that the moral force of fairness is greatly reinforced by the power of a "fair" result to focus attention, if it fills the vacuum of indeterminacy that would otherwise exist. Similarly, when the pressure of public opinion seems to force the participants to the obviously "fair" or "reasonable" solution, we may exaggerate the "pressure" or at least misunderstand the way it works on the participants unless we give credit to its power to coordinate the participants' expectations. To put it differently, it may be the power of *suggestion*, working through the mechanism described in this paper, that makes public opinion or precedent or ethical standards so effective. Again, as evidence for this view, we need only to suppose that the participants had to reach ultimate agreement without communicating, and to visualize public opinion or some prominent ethical standard as providing a strong suggestion analogous to the suggestions contained in our earlier examples. Finally, even if the force of moral responsibility or sensitivity to public opinion truly constrains the participants, and not the "signal" they get, we must still look to the source of the public's own opinion; and there, the writer suggests, the need for a simple, qualitative rationale often reflects the mechanism discussed in this paper.

But, if this general line of reasoning is valid, any analysis of explicit bargaining must pay attention to what we might call the "communication" that is inherent in the bargaining situations, the signals that the participants read in the inanimate details of the case. And it means that tacit and explicit bargaining are not thoroughly separate concepts, that the various gradations from tacit bargaining up through types of incompleteness or faulty or limited communication to full communication all show some dependence on the need to coordinate expectations. Hence, all show some degree of dependence of the participants themselves on their common inability to keep their eyes off certain outcomes.

This is not necessarily an argument for expecting explicit outcomes as a rule to lean toward exactly those that would have emerged if communication had been impossible; the focal points may certainly be different when speech is allowed, except in some of the artificial cases we have used in our illustrations. But what may be the *main* principle in tacit bargaining apparently may be at least *one* of the important principles in the analysis of explicit bargaining. And, since even much so-called explicit bargaining includes maneuver, indirect communication, jockeying for position, or speaking to be overhead, or is confused by a multitude of participants and divergent interests, the need for convergent expectations and the role of signals that have the power to coordinate expectations may be powerful.

TACIT NEGOTIATION AND LIMITED WAR

What useful insight does this line of analysis provide into the practical problems of tacit bargaining that usually confront us, particularly the problems of strategic maneuver and limited war? It certainly suggests that it is *possible* to find limits to war—real war, jurisdictional war, or whatever—without overt negotiation. But it gives us no new strong sense of *probability*. War was limited in Korea, and gas was not used in World War II; on the possibility of limited war these two facts are more persuasive than all the suggestions contained in the foregoing discussion. If the analysis provides anything, then, it is not a judgment of the probability of successfully reaching tacit agreement but rather a better understanding of where to look for the terms of agreement.

If there are important conclusions to be drawn, they are probably these: (1) tacit agreements or agreements arrived at through partial or haphazard negotiation require terms that are qualitatively distinguishable from the alternatives and cannot simply be a matter of degree; (2) when agreement must be reached with incomplete communication, the participants must be ready to allow the situation itself to exercise substantial constraint over the outcome; specifically, a solution that discriminates against one party or the other or even involves "unnecessary" nuisance to both of them may be the only one on which their expectations can be coordinated.

Gas was not used in World War II. The agreement, though not without antecedents, was largely a tacit one. It is interesting to speculate on whether any alternative agreement concerning poison gas could have been arrived at without formal communication (or even, for that matter, with communication). "Some gas" raises complicated questions of how much, where, under what circumstances; "no gas" is simple and unambiguous. Gas only on military personnel; gas used only by defending forces; gas only when carried by vehicle or projectile; no gas without warning—a variety of limits is conceivable; some may make sense, and many might have been more impartial to the outcome of the war. But there is a simplicity to "no gas" that makes it almost uniquely a focus for agreement when each side can only conjecture at what rules the other side would propose, and when failure at coordination on the first try may spoil the chances for acquiescence in any limits at all.

The physical configuration of Korea must have helped in defining the limits to war and in making geographical limits possible. The area was surrounded by water, and the principal northern political boundary was marked dramatically and unmistakably by a river. The thirty-eighth parallel seems to have been a powerful focus for a stalemate; and the main alternative, the "waist," was a strong candidate, not just because it provided a shorter defense line, but because it would have been clear to both sides that an advance to the waist did not necessarily signal a determination to advance farther and a retreat to the waist did not telegraph any intention to retreat farther.

In Korea, weapons were limited by the qualitative distinction made between atomic and all other types; it would surely have been much more difficult to stabilize a tacit acceptance of any limit on size of atomic weapons or selection of targets. No definition of size or target is so obvious and natural that it goes without saying, except "no size, on any target." American assistance to the French forces in Indochina was persuasively limited to material, not people; and it was appreciated that an enlargement to include, say, air participation could be recognized as aid limited to the air, while it would not be possible to establish a limited *amount* of air or ground participation. One's intentions to abstain from ground intervention can be conveyed by the complete withholding of ground forces; one cannot nearly so easily commit *some* forces and communicate a persuasive limit to the *amount* that one intends to commit.

The strategy of retaliation is affected by the need to communicate or coordinate on limits. Local aggression defines a place; with luck and natural boundaries, there may be tacit acceptance of geographical limits or limits on types of targets. One side or both may be willing to accept limited defeat rather than take the initiative in breaching the rules, and to act in a manner that reassures the other of such willingness. The "rules" may be respected because, once broken, there is no assurance that any new ones can be found and jointly recognized in time to check the widening of the conflict. But, if retaliation is left to the method and place of the retaliator's own choosing, it may be much more difficult to convey to the victim what the proposed limits are, so that he has a chance to accept them in his counterretaliation. In fact, the initial departure of retaliation from the locality that provokes it may be a kind of declaration of independence that is not conducive to the creation of stable mutual expectations. Thus the problem of finding mutually recognized limits on war is doubly difficult if the definition implicit in the aggressor's own act is not tolerable.

In sum, the problem of limiting warfare does not involve a continuous range of possibilities from most favorable to least favorable for either side; it is a lumpy, discrete world that is able to recognize qualitative differences better than quantitative differences, that is embarrassed by the multiplicity of choices, and that forces both sides to accept some dictation from the elements themselves. The writer suggests that the same is true of restrained competition in every field in which it occurs.

PRIOR ARRANGEMENTS

While the main burden of this paper has been that tacit bargaining is possible and is susceptible of systematic analysis, there is no assurance that it will succeed in any particular case or that, when it succeeds, it will yield to either party a particularly favorable outcome compared with alternatives that might have been available if full communication had been allowed. There is no assurance that the next war, if it comes, will find mutually observed limits in time and of a sort to afford protection, unless explicit negotiation can take place. There is reason, therefore, to consider what steps can be taken, before the time for tacit bargaining occurs, to enhance the likelihood of a successful outcome.

Keeping communication channels open seems to be one obvious point. (At a minimum, this might mean making sure that a surrender offer could be heard and responded to by either side.) The technical side of this principle would be identification of who would send and receive messages, upon what authority, over what facilities, using what intermediaries if intermediaries were used, and of who stood in line to do the job in what fashion if the indicated parties and facilities were destroyed. In the event of an effort to fight a restrained nuclear war, there may be only a brief and busy instant in which each side must decide whether limited war is in full swing or full war has just begun; and twelve hours' confusion over how to make contact might spoil some of the chances for stabilizing the action within limits.

Thought should be given to the possible usefulness of mediators or referees. To settle on influential mediators usually requires some prior understanding, or at least a precedent or a tradition or a sign of welcome. Even if we rule out overt arrangements for the contingency, evidences by each side of an appreciation of the role of referees and mediators, even a little practice in their use, might help to prepare an instrument of the most extreme value in an awful contingency.

But all such efforts may suffer from the unwillingness of an adversary to engage in any preparatory steps. Not only may an adversary balk at giving signs of eagerness to come to agreement; it is even possible that one side in a potential war may have a tactical interest in keeping that war unrestrained and in aggravating the likelihood of mutual destruction in case it comes. Why? Because of the strategy of threats, bluffs, and deterrents. The willingness to start a war or take steps that may lead to war, whether aggression or retaliation to aggression, may depend on the confidence with which a nation's leaders think a war could be kept within limits. To be specific, the willingness of America to retaliate against local aggression with atomic attack depends—and the Russians know that it depends—on how likely we consider it that such retaliation could itself remain limited. That is, it depends on how likely it is in our judgment that we and the Russians, when we both desperately need to recognize limits within which either of us is willing to lose the war without enlarging those limits, will find such limits and come to mutually recognized acquiescence in them. If, then, Russia's refusal to engage in any activity that might lead to the possibility of limited war deters our own resolution to act, the Russians might risk foregoing such limits for the sake of reducing the threat of American action. One parachutist in our example may know that the other will be careless with the plane if he is sure they can meet and save themselves; so, if the first abstains from discussing the contingency, the other will have to ride quietly for fear of precipitating a fatal separation in the terrain below.

Whether this consideration or just the usual inhibitions on serious negotiation make prior discussion impossible, a useful idea still emerges from one of our earlier games. It is that negotiation or communication for the purpose of coordinating expectations need not be reciprocal: unilateral negotiation may provide the coordination that will save both parties. Furthermore, even an unwilling member cannot necessarily make himself unavailable for the receipt of messages. If one of our parachutists, just before the plane failed and while neither of them dreamed of having to jump, idly said, "If I ever had to meet somebody down there, I'd just head for the highest hill in sight," the other would probably recall and know that the first would be sure he recalled and would go there, even though it had been on the tip of his tongue to say "How stupid," or "Not me, climbing hurts my legs," when the plane failed. When some signal is desperately needed by *both* parties and both parties know it, even a poor signal and a discriminatory one may command recognition, in default of any other. Once the contingency is upon them, their interests, which originally diverged in the play of threats and deterrents, substantially coincide in the desperate need for a focus of agreement.

ESCALATION AND LIMITATION IN WARFARE

EDWARD L. WARNER III

Captain Warner discusses the dimensions of military conflict and develops a classification scheme for distinguishing various levels of conflict and analyzing the process of escalation. The conflict parameters are: (1) its geographic scope; (2) the weapons employed; (3) targeting differences; and (4) the tempo of military operations. His discussion of the escalation process includes a number of basic definitions, as well as an analysis of the importance of highly visible thresholds, as a possible basis for the successful limitation of warfare between distrustful adversaries. A number of capabilities factors that appear to be prerequisites for successful limitation are noted, and some recent examples of limited warfare are discussed. Captain Warner received his M.A. from Princeton University in 1967 and is presently a member of the Department of Political Science at the USAF Academy. He has served as an intelligence officer with the Strategic Air Command and as a consultant for the National Security Council and the Office of Doctrine, Concepts, and Objectives, HQ USAF.

INTRODUCTION

In recent years the term "escalation," broadly defined as an action that raises the level of a particular variable, has enjoyed immense popularity. We have witnessed escalation in student demands on college campuses, escalation in political rhetoric on a number of contentious issues, and economic escalations in a variety of salary demands and prices, to name but a few examples. A more narrow international political usage of the term identifies escalation as an in-

Reprinted by permission and with minor changes from A Guide to Strategic Concepts, *ed. B. Lambeth, L. Satori, V. Teplitz, and E. Warner (Princeton: Princeton University Press, forthcoming).*

crease in the level of conflict within international crises. Escalations have been noted and discussed in the political-military interactions of the Indochina War, the conflict in the Middle East, and during the Soviet-Czechoslovakian confrontation of 1968.

Discussions of escalation in terms of contemporary strategic analysis are concerned with specifically military aspects of the international "levels of crisis" usage of the term. Military escalation involves increases in the intensity of a particular conflict through threats of force, or applications of force employed, by one participant or both. These increases may occur along a number of dimensions and at various tempos.

Escalation may be viewed as a deliberate strategy. As such, it consists of the conscious manipulation of force or threats of force in pursuit of specific objectives. From this perspective, the expansion of conflict may become a highly competitive process as the adversaries seek to coerce one another in the face of the pervasive threat of further intensification of conflict, perhaps into the realm of large-scale nuclear exchange when nuclear powers are involved.

Since escalation involves increases in the level of conflict, its discussion entails delineation of a spectrum of the levels of warfare. For our purposes, the desired spectrum describes the range of possible conflicts between the United States and the Soviet Union. With appropriate adjustments for the reduced capabilities of lesser powers, the scheme may be applied in analyzing escalation moves between other states as well.

In elaborating such a classification scheme, one must be concerned not only with definitional precision and clarity but, more important, with the extent to which the major political actors can and will recognize the distinctions developed in actual practice. Consequently, concern about the problems of mutual recognition of the prominent thresholds of limitation in military conflict and the role of these thresholds in promoting conflict stability has been a central focus of escalation studies.

In today's world, uncontrolled warfare between the superpowers would be catastrophic. Accordingly, despite the existence of significant areas of conflict, the Soviet Union and the United States share a fundamental interest in avoiding this eventuality. Their mutual awareness of this cooperative interest should provide a continuing basis for prudent restraint even during (*especially* during) periods of intense crisis. In an escalating confrontation, the activities of both sides are likely to involve a variety of coercive initiatives in pursuit of their opposing objectives, as well as conscious efforts to restrain the conflict short of mutually destructive nuclear holocaust.

Escalation crises are likely to occur in situations in which there is incomplete verbal communication between the adversaries, which thus produces a rather prominent element of communication-through-action or tacit bargaining. Under these circumstances, rather gross distinctions in operational patterns will be necessary if these are to be reliably recognized and honored as a basis for reciprocal limitation and restraint. A useful classification scheme should reflect this vital consideration. Special attention should be focused upon those points of obvious and distinct discontinuity along the various parameters of conflict which hold promise as possible limitation thresholds.

PARAMETERS OF CONFLICT

In the development of a classification of conflict, a number of significant dimensions are subject to variation. These include the geographic scope of the conflict, the nature of the weapons employed, the patterns of weapons employment or targeting doctrines, and the temporal pace of combat operations. Differentiations along these dimensions may serve as the basis for separating and identifying major classes of conflict.

The most destructive warfare scenario envisioned is that of a massive thermonuclear exchange. This would involve large volleys of strategic nuclear weapons, fired nearly simultaneously, which could produce widespread and indiscriminate destruction of military, political, and population-industrial targets in the homelands of the adversaries. All threat and action contingencies short of this extreme and mutually disastrous case involve important *limitations* and *restraints* in word and deed. Thus there is a large spectrum of possible "limited" wars, ranging from peripheral confrontations between conventional military forces through a variety of symbolic shows-of-force to high-intensity, but less than total, strategic nuclear exchanges.

Geographic Scope

In terms of geographic scope, the fundamental classificatory distinction turns on the involvement of the homelands of the major adversaries as targets of military operations. Conflicts that include such attacks on the territory of the superpowers are called "central wars," while all other military confrontations are called "noncentral" wars.

Within either central or noncentral engagements, there are possible geographic limitations. The initial phase of military engagements may serve to define a theater of operations. The emergence of an identifiable battle zone is most probable when some prominent boundaries, either topographical (rivers, mountain ranges, and so on) or legalistic (particularly an international boundary), are available to provide a visible basis for mutual restraint. Once a theater stabilizes geographically, any subsequent extension of its scope may be properly viewed as an escalation.

A particular kind of geographic expansion, the initiation of threats or military actions in a separate noncontiguous area during an ongoing crisis, is called compound escalation. Such an expansion may be carried out in order to bring to bear unique military or political advantages in the newly opened theater, thus greatly complicating the balance of political and military forces within the compounded crisis. During the Cuban missile crisis of 1962, grave American concern that the Soviets might initiate a countering crisis in Berlin led President Kennedy to warn the Russians in his momentous October 22 speech that such actions would not be tolerated.

The escalation of a local crisis into central warfare represents the most serious form of compound escalation.

Weapons Distinctions

Important differences among the types of weapons employed in war may serve as a basis for classifying levels of conflict. These distinctions may be made in terms of the type of delivery vehicles used or the means of destruction employed. A wide choice of vehicles may be utilized, including aircraft, missiles, a variety of land vehicles, and naval craft. However, such differences by themselves do not offer a basis for meaningful escalation classification. While differing operational characteristics in terms of range, accuracy, and visibility may offer tactical employment advantages, escalation significance stems from the geographic scope of, and targeting practices in, their application rather than from the nature of the delivery vehicle itself.

The nature of the means of destruction has more intrinsic significance. The paramount distinction in this area is between "conventional" ordinance and the "unconventional" means—nuclear, some chemical, and bacteriological weapons. Expert and popular opinion identify these unconventional means as weapons of mass destruction and view their use with considerable alarm.

Categorizing weapons within these two groups is not entirely straightforward. In the field of chemical warfare in particular, difficulties are encountered. While various incendiaries have acquired conventional status, there is persisting disagreement on the proper identification of tear gas and chemical defoliants. A number of nerve gases and toxic chemicals are by consensus recognized and stigmatized as unconventional. Bacteriological weapons are universally condemned and thus present no definitional difficulties.

The most important unconventional weapons are nuclear and thermonuclear. Although modern weapons technology has produced very small tactical nuclear devices with the explosive power of conventional explosives, fundamental qualitative differences remain in terms of radiation and thermal effects. More important, in light of the enormous destructiveness of the larger weapons, *all* nuclear weapons have acquired a generalized stigma in the eyes of the general public which starkly separates them from even the largest conventional explosives. These shared perceptions, reinforced by the tradition of nonuse since 1945, underlie the extreme significance attached to the threshold that separates conventional and nuclear weapons.

The conventional-use versus nuclear-use distinction is frequently referred to as a "firebreak" separating qualitatively different levels of warfare. This term emphasizes that the threshold is an easily perceived basis for mutual restraint. Also, it strongly conveys the judgment that it may be very difficult to locate a further viable and recognizable limitation point along the weapons parameter should the nuclear barrier be breached. Much discussion has also been heard regarding a firebreak separating tactical and strategic nuclear weapons, but, in this case, the existence of a discrete and obvious dividing line between the two types is practically impossible to define and reliably locate.

TARGETING DISTINCTIONS

Important differences in the level of conflict are linked to varying patterns of weapons employment or targeting doctrine. These distinctions may be quantitative with respect to the numbers of weapons directed against a given type of target or series of targets. Qualitatively, the fundamental distinction is between *counterforce* strikes—those directed against the elements of the enemy's military capabilities (military forces, logistic reserves, warning and surveillance systems, as well as command and control facilities)—and *countervalue* attacks, which are designed to punish the enemy by destroying his industrial capacity and population. The latter attack mode, with its attendant toll in noncombatant civilian casualties, is considered in general to be the more serious of the two targeting doctrines.

The ability to make these qualitative distinctions in practice will depend on the geographic proximity of force and value targets as well as on the combination of destructive power and accuracy of the weapons systems employed. Given the proximity of the two target types, the problem of collateral-value destruction may blur the distinctiveness of an intended counterforce attack and thus represents a significant obstacle to the establishment of a counterforce-only exchange.

A third targeting variant is also available. Military forces may be employed in a highly visible *demonstration role* by means of the detonation of weapons (probably nuclear) in operationally insignificant areas. This could serve to communicate the high level of concern and resolve of the initiating party and to heighten mutual awareness of the possibility of undesired nuclear conflict. Possible "targets" of such exemplary operations include explosions in outer space, over international waters, and on or above a desolate land area. This communications function may be accomplished at a higher level of intensity using controlled and selective assaults on either force or value targets of varying importance.

TEMPO OF CONFLICT

The tempo of military operations may prove important in defining the seriousness of a particular crisis. Along the time dimension there is no starkly obvious discontinuity such as those which separate nuclear from conventional weapons, or central from noncentral zones of military operations. Nevertheless, the time period between initiations of major military actions is significant. Time variation may involve the interval between the launches of one's own strikes as well as the pace of reciprocal operations: that is, the pause intervals between adversary retaliatory exchanges.

While the qualitative nature of the military operations themselves along the previously discussed dimensions is of dominant significance, timing variation can also be important. Thus, extended strategic bargaining by means of the controlled destruction of selected urban centers over a period of days, so-called city-swapping, is considered a less severe form of warfare than a more time-compressed version of the same basic strategy, which would destroy these same targets by closely spaced salvo attacks.

By combining the various distinctions within the parameters discussed above, one can construct a rough typology of warfare along an ascending scale of conflict intensity (see Figure 1). This classification scheme could be expanded further by integrating within it a number of threat activities and mobilization-preparedness measures, thus producing an elaborate model of possible political-military actions. Such is the nature of Herman Kahn's renowned escalation ladder.

Thus military escalation, whether viewed descriptively or as a conscious conflict strategy, involves increases in the intensity of conflict along any of the enumerated parameters. The dynamics of this intensification process may be broadly described in terms of two general patterns. On the one hand, escalation may occur as a series of discrete, gradual, and incremental increases in conflict intensity. This pattern is called *expansion*. Alternatively, military interactions may produce a sudden jump in the level of violence, skip past a number of available intermediate courses of action, and arrive at a relatively high level of military activity.

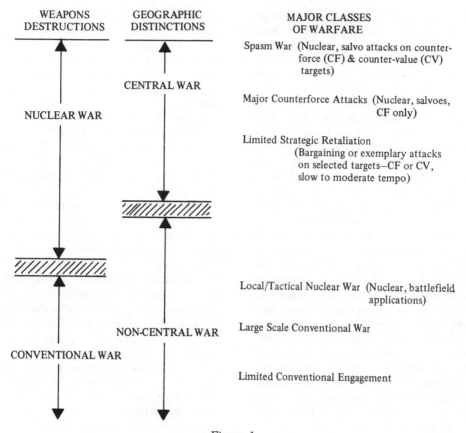

WEAPONS
DESTRUCTIONS

GEOGRAPHIC
DISTINCTIONS

MAJOR CLASSES
OF WARFARE

Spasm War (Nuclear, salvo attacks on counterforce (CF) & counter-value (CV)
targets)

CENTRAL WAR

Major Counterforce Attacks (Nuclear, salvoes,
CF only)

NUCLEAR WAR

Limited Strategic Retaliation
(Bargaining or exemplary attacks
on selected targets—CF or CV,
slow to moderate tempo)

Local/Tactical Nuclear War (Nuclear, battlefield
applications)

NON-CENTRAL WAR   Large Scale Conventional War

CONVENTIONAL WAR

Limited Conventional Engagement

Figure 1

Such escalation, particularly when the leap transports the conflict into the dangerous area of central warfare operations, is called *eruption* or *explosion*.

THE DYNAMICS OF ESCALATION

Any act of military escalation in a crisis entails change in two important ways. On the one hand, the new activity will breach the existing pattern of operational restraints, thus serving to legitimize a discretely expanded level of combat activity between the adversaries. This creates a new pattern of military operations judged by the initiator to be to his military and political advantage. At the same time, such escalation is significant in that, by disrupting the existing battle, it invites further escalation beyond the tentative limits set by the actions of the initial disrupter. As a result, a spiral of action-reaction moves or a sudden eruption or explosion to a much higher level of conflict

may occur. Judgments concerning the simultaneous interplay of these factors, the quest for military or political advantage, and the concurrent risks of precipitating even greater escalation lie at the heart of any escalation decision.

In many situations one can imagine a calculation of the risks of further escalation being the crucial factor in the decision to forgo a specific escalatory act. This might be particularly true in regard to the decision to employ nuclear weapons. In light of their enormous destructive power, these weapons may be militarily attractive for the efficient destruction of either opposing force or of value targets. Yet, given the grave stigma attached to their use, their potential for touching off an uncontrolled explosion-eruption could well be judged to be sufficiently great to warrant forgoing these apparent increases in tactical coercive efficiency.

In another situation, however, this question of the shared risks of disaster might serve as the causative agent, rather than as the restrainer, of escalation. National decisionmakers faced with a highly unfavorable situation in an ongoing conflict, and enjoying no apparent prospect for favorably altering the military balance through deliberate escalation, might nevertheless threaten or indulge in escalation tactics. This could be done as a means of manipulating the shared risks of mutual suicide in order to persuade the stronger party to limit his military and political gains. Such a tactic would clearly be of a rather desperate nature. Nevertheless, it clearly demonstrates the manner in which the uncertainties concerning further escalation might be manipulated in order to bring about a cessation of hostilities.

Thus an escalating confrontation may be perceived by the participants as a competition in risk-taking. The adversaries deliberately employ their military and political resources to coerce one another in pursuit of their differing objectives. If one side enjoys pronounced superiority within the upper levels of conflict activity, it is said to possess "escalation dominance." That side may threaten or actually move the crisis to this advantageous level in order to produce a favorable outcome. The mere existence and recognition of such dominance may prove adequate to encourage settlement by the inferior power at the lower crisis level.

Today's relative strategic nuclear parity between the superpowers denies escalation dominance to either. Consequently, both must be prepared to exercise restraint during crises in order to avoid undesired eruption-explosions. Superpower crises should be marked by the operation of both intrawar deterrence—that is, avoidance of particularly provocative actions for fear of explosion—and deliberate coercion or constraint as military forces are maneuvered, brandished, and even employed in a tense period of bargaining.

In superpower confrontations, a number of factors would acquire significance. From a capabilities standpoint, flexibility of military forces can provide the decisionmakers with a wide range of usable options. This flexibility may be based upon diverse conventional and strategic-force postures and supportive contingency planning. Precision in mission execution and a high degree of responsiveness to political-military command and control also are important. Additionally, effective surveillance systems that can monitor and evaluate both the results of one's own operations and the damage inflicted by the enemy can play a vital role. The enormous and diversified arsenals of the Soviet Union and the United States appear capable of meeting these requirements and thus of supporting a wide variety of escalation strategies.

Even with the possession of versatile force capabilities and a shared sensitivity to the nature of the escalation process, the dangers inherent in the employment of such strategies remain formidable. Crisis confrontations between the superpowers are bound to involve enormous intrinsic and instrumental stakes. Furthermore, the tacit bargaining process relies heavily upon communication through action and thus provides ample opportunity for the misreading of both the underlying intentions and the actual operation undertaken. At the upper levels of crises, particularly nuclear crises, problems of misperception, precision in execution, and predictability of responses become especially acute. Decisionmakers will be placed under enormous emotional stress. In this state, they may tend to fixate upon punishing, retaliatory responses rather than upon the cold and calculating bargaining patterns often prescribed in abstract strategic theory.

Concern about these problems and their impact on the potential for control of serious crises has moved many commentators to place strong value on the nuclear firebreak and thus to oppose the initiation of nuclear operations, either locally or at the strategic level, except in the direst circumstances.

.   .   .   .

Escalation strategies are by no means confined to superpower confrontations. Other nations may become involved in crises of increasing intensity, including the reciprocal recourse to a variety of military activities. Furthermore, the superpowers may confront less powerful states and resort to military measures in their disagreement. In the latter case, the respective repertories of political and military capabilities will be decidedly asymmetrical, although alliance patterns may superimpose the possibility of the emergence of direct superpower conflict, thus restoring a semblance of capabilities balance.

Two contemporary international crises have produced similar escalation scenarios, and with them criticism of escalation theory. Both in Indochina and in the Middle East in the wake of the June 1967 war, gradually expanding aerial bombardment campaigns were waged.

The air war over North Vietnam which lasted from February 1965 until November 1968 was said to be highly controlled throughout. It was marked by a series of discrete expansions (in types and numbers of targets, in the quantitative intensity of attacks, in the geographic areas subjected to attack) as well as by continuing restraints (avoidance of both major urban countervalue targeting and the use of nuclear weapons). The inability of the air campaign to compel the Democratic Republic of Vietnam to cease all assistance and support for the war in the South has been cited by several critics as a failure caused by the "gradualism" induced by the excessive prudence of escalation-conscious politicians.

Such criticisms draw one's attention to the multiple objectives that were apparently sought in that American bombing campaign. Among many goals, the campaign appears to have been aimed at impeding the logistic flows of men and material to the South. These interdiction efforts inevitably produced widespread collateral destruction within North Vietnam. It was apparently hoped that this devastation, combined with attacks upon the air defense system and selected industrial targets within the North, would produce a cumulative effect that would coerce Hanoi into abandoning its efforts in the South. Thus, what amounted to a strategy of indirect constraint was employed, and the possibility of a more direct punishment campaign was at least implicitly threatened. Additionally, the bombing campaign was intended to bolster morale in the South by demonstratively and directly subjecting the people of the North to the privations and rigors of war.

It is noteworthy that a maximally pain-inflicting, value-directed compellent campaign was *not* employed against North Vietnam. In retrospect, one can easily elaborate such a plan. However, if one is to make reasonable estimates concerning the possible results of such an alternative, one must be prepared to take into account the possible responses of the American public and interested great powers, especially Russia and China. In addition, the relative vulnerability of North Vietnam to such

a campaign, given its level of economic development and the historical experience of its leaders in their prolonged independence struggle, is a matter of some doubt.

Nevertheless, both the accomplishments and difficulties encountered during the 1965–1968 air war itself are relevant to the question of deliberate escalation. It appears clear that the gradual intensification of the campaign over a period of months, while avoiding the precipitation of major intervention by Russia and China, had other consequences. It also provided time for the build-up of sizable air defenses, the diversification of logistic lines and techniques, the dispersal of industrial capacity and population, and produced, if anything, solidified popular support of the North Vietnamese government and greater determination on the part of its leaders to persist in and intensify their war effort. Yet again the probable outcomes of hypothetical alternatives remain moot.

In the Middle East, from 1968 until 1970 the Israelis conducted an air campaign against the UAR which was designed primarily to limit Egyptian military capabilities along the Suez Canal and additionally to compel the Cairo leadership to enter into serious political negotiations. As in Vietnam, the asymmetry of military capabilities in the area initially permitted relatively undisputed Israeli air superiority in the prosecution of the campaign. Similarly, the strictly operational objectives were for the most part successfully accomplished.

However, Israeli offensive operations were paralleled by a massive Soviet-supported and -directed series of defensive measures, particularly in the area of air defense. Thus the campaign produced a limited military success, but at the price of a number of countering political and military responses. These included a greatly increased Soviet role in the area, with the attendant dangers of more probable Russian participation in any major new round of fighting, and a significant increase in the radicalism and solidarity of the popular masses of the UAR.

Instead, a number of possible costs associated with a drawn-out, incremental pattern of conventional escalation with respect to operational effectiveness and unintended political effects, both internationally and in the target country, have become more clear.

At this point in time, a number of theoretical

studies have produced a sizable body of literature dealing with the various aspects of international political escalation. In addition, the
politicians themselves, in both the East and
the West, have exhibited an acute sensitivity
to these problems and have demonstrated considerable skill in the practice of deliberate escalation tactics. In an era of continuing international instability, it seems probable that crisis
confrontations will frequently arise and that
the various participants, great powers and
small, will continue to employ coercive political
and military strategies. It is hoped that an
awareness of the difficulties and dangers inherent in such situations will encourage prudence
and caution on the part of the decisionmakers.

THE KOREAN WAR

MORTON H. HALPERIN

*This article is a case study in which the reader may apply the several
propositions of limited-war theory presented previously. The author uses
both international and domestic political pressures to analyze the limitations
placed on objectives, weapons, targets, and the area of combat. Halperin
critiques five different interpretations of Soviet intentions, four reasons for
the nonuse of nuclear weapons, and three factors which may have influenced
the Chinese to exercise restraint in the use of their air forces. The author
is a Senior Fellow at The Brookings Institution in Washington, was
formerly a member of the Senior Staff of the National Security Council
and a Deputy Assistant Secretary of Defense. His writings include* Strategy
and Arms Control, *with Thomas C. Schelling (1961),* China and the Bomb
(1965), Contemporary Military Strategy *(1967), and* Defense Strategies
for the Seventies *(1971).*

FOREIGN POLICY OBJECTIVES

Prior to the outbreak of the Korean War,
the United States believed that a major objective of the Soviet Union was to expand the
area under its control. Thus, in responding to
the North Korean attack—which had not been
anticipated—American objectives were developed in the framework of the belief that the
attack was part of a general plan for expansion and perhaps a prelude to general war.
The United States sought to prevent the success of this Communist attempt to expand by
the use of force in the belief that allowing the
Soviets to succeed in Korea would encourage
aggression elsewhere. General Omar Bradley
expressed this purpose at the MacArthur hearings in describing Korea as "a preventive limited war aimed at avoiding World War III."[1]

[1] U.S. Senate, Committee on Armed Services and
Committee on Foreign Relations, *Military Situation in
the Far East*, Hearings, 82nd Cong., 1st sess., 1951,
p. 154 (hereafter cited as *Military Situation in the
Far East*).

President Harry Truman later described his objectives in intervening in the Korean War in similar terms:

Communism was acting in Korea just as Hitler, Mussolini, and the Japanese had acted ten, fifteen, and twenty years earlier. I felt certain that if South Korea was allowed to fall Communist leaders would be emboldened to override nations closer to our own shores. If the Communists were permitted to force their way into the Republic of Korea without opposition from the free world, no small nation would have the courage to resist threats and aggression by stronger Communist neighbors. If this was allowed to go unchallenged it would mean a third world war, just as similar incidents had brought on the second world war.[2]

The defense of Korea was partly motivated by the feeling that the action was necessary to convince the West Europeans that the United States would come to their aid. The Administration was wary of committing its military power, thereby leaving itself exposed to Soviet aggression in Europe. During the latter stages of the Korean War, in fact, the major American build-up occurred in Europe and not in the Far East. The Administration was also aware of the danger of splitting the NATO alliance in a dispute over Far Eastern policy. A major objective throughout the war was to prevent adverse repercussions in Europe while using the episode to strengthen NATO and build up its military capability. America's NATO allies, particularly the British, constantly applied pressure on the United States to prevent expansion of the war and to bring it swiftly to a conclusion. Following an almost inadvertent reference by President Truman at a press conference to the possibility of using atomic weapons, British Prime Minister Clement Attlee flew to the United States to confer with Truman and to propose the seeking of a cease fire in Korea to be followed by the admission of Communist China to the United Nations. Partly because the defense effort in Korea was carried on under UN auspices, the United States felt obliged constantly to consult its allies on policy and was influenced by their continuous efforts to halt the expansion of the war and to bring about its conclusion.

Soviet objectives were more closely related to the situation in the Far East. The Soviets were interested in the capture of South Korea for its own sake and probably expected a relatively quick and easy North Korean victory. In addition, the Soviets probably hoped to prevent Japan's alignment with the Western powers. Allen Whiting has suggested the nature of the Soviet Far Eastern objective:

In view of the multiple pressures directed at Japanese foreign policy, the Communist leaders may have conceived the Korean War as serving ends beyond the immediate control of the peninsula. Military victories in Taiwan and Korea could be heralded as ushering in the Communist era in Asia, and as demonstrating the impotence of America's "puppets," Chiang Kai-shek and Syngman Rhee. The resultant effect upon Japan might swing opportunistic groups behind existing neutralist opposition to Yoshida and prevent his supporting American policy.[3]

This interpretation of Soviet strategy in the Korean War was offered by John Foster Dulles right after the North Korean attack. Dulles, who was at the time the State Department planner for the Japanese Peace Treaty, suggested that the Korean attack may have been motivated in part by a desire to block American efforts to make Japan a full member of the Free World. He conjectured also that the attack may have been ordered because the Communists could not tolerate the "hopeful, attractive Asiatic experiment in democracy" that was under way in South Korea.[4]

The Chinese objectives in entering the Korean War were also based on general political considerations, but of a defensive nature. According to Whiting, the Chinese also hoped to influence the course of United States–Japanese relations. Moreover, they were worried about the loss of prestige they would suffer if they allowed the Western "imperialists" to march unhindered to their borders. And they were perhaps most concerned with the beneficial effects of a United Nations success in Korea on the many opponents of the Communist regime still active in China and on Taiwan. Whiting concluded:

In sum, it was not the particular problems of safeguarding electric-power supplies in North

---

[2] Harry S. Truman, *Memoirs*, vol. 2: *Years of Trial and Hope* (Garden City, N.Y.: Doubleday & Co., 1956), p. 333.

[3] Allen S. Whiting, *China Crosses the Yalu: The Decision to Enter the Korean War* (New York: Macmillan Co., 1960), p. 37.

[4] *New York Times*, July 2, 1950.

Korea or the industrial base in Manchuria that aroused Peking to military action. Instead, the final step seems to have been prompted in part by general concern over the range of opportunities within China that might be exploited by a determined, powerful enemy on China's doorstep. At the least, a military response might deter the enemy from further adventures. At the most, it might succeed in inflicting sufficient damage to force the enemy to compromise his objectives and to accede to some of Peking's demands. Contrary to some belief, the Chinese Communist leadership did not enter the Korean War either full of self-assertive confidence or for primarily expansionist goals.[5]

The Chinese apparently entered the war with the aim of saving at least some of North Korea. Their minimal objective was to preserve the identity of Communist North Korea rather than its total territorial integrity.

In an effort to secure the political effects discussed, American battlefield objectives and war-termination conditions underwent considerable fluctuation during the course of the war. When the United States first intervened, its objective was simply to restore peace and the South Korean border. Very early in the war and after the Chinese intervention, the United States considered a total withdrawal from Korea.[6] Later its battlefield objective was expanded to include the unification of Korea. But, in the end, the United States accepted a truce line which closely approximated the *status quo ante*. As Richard Neustadt has pointed out, Truman's original decision to seek the unification of Korea failed to take into account the political-effects objectives that the United States was pursuing, and in the end the recognition of this forced the abandonment of the unification effort.

Had the unification of Korea been Truman's dearest object, its announcement as a war aim would have been another matter. But it was among the least of the objectives on his mind. In July and August 1950, in December after Chinese intervention, in his struggles with MacArthur, and thereafter through his last two years of office, his behavior leaves no doubt about the many things he wanted more than that. He wanted to affirm that the UN was not a League of Nations, that aggression would be met with counterforce, that "police

actions" were well worth their cost, that the "lesson of the 1930's" had been learned. He wanted to avoid "the wrong war, in the wrong place, at the wrong time," as General Bradley put it—and any "War," if possible. He wanted NATO strengthened fast, both militarily and psychologically. He wanted the United States rearmed without inflation, and prepared, thereafter, to sustain a level of expenditure for military forces and for foreign aid far higher than had seemed achievable before Korea.[7]

Once the Soviets recognized that they could not easily secure their objective of demonstrating American weakness and unwillingness to use force, they seemed to abandon the battlefield objective of capturing all of Korea. They may have been willing to accept an end to the war with part, or perhaps even all, of North Korea in Western hands, and ultimately settled for a virtual restoration of the *status quo ante*.

RISK OF CENTRAL WAR

The Korean War was fought before the era of intercontinental ballistic missiles and fusion weapons. Thus, while both sides could have expanded the war quickly and decisively, there was not the danger that now exists of a sudden unleashing of nuclear missiles which within an hour could destroy a large part of both the United States and the Soviet Union.

Even without this threat of a mutually devastating strategic exchange, the danger of a world war was nevertheless present, and both sides seem to have been determined to prevent its occurrence. Truman has reported that the major American aim in Korea was to prevent a third world war. The Russian decision to remain out of the war seemed to be partly motivated by a fear of igniting a global war. In this situation, where neither side could gain a decisive advantage by going first, both sides seemed to recognize that, no matter who started the global war, both would suffer major losses. Though the United States could have attacked the Soviet Union with its very limited stockpile of atomic weapons, it probably could not have prevented a Soviet ground attack in Western Europe, which might have resulted in Communist domination of the European con-

5 Whiting, *op. cit.*, p. 159.
6 Courtney Whitney, *MacArthur: His Rendezvous with History* (New York: Alfred A. Knopf, 1956), pp. 429–31, 438.

7 Richard E. Neustadt, *Presidential Power: The Politics of Leadership* (New York: John Wiley & Sons, 1960), p. 126.

tinent. The Soviets had almost no capacity to attack the United States and could not have prevented an American attack on the Soviet Union. Though both sides avoided forcing the other into starting a global war, neither was constantly concerned with the possibility of "pre-emption" by its adversary.

The United States, however, was concerned that the Korean War should not lead it to expend those military capabilities which were considered an important deterrent to general war. In Korea the United States was employing the troops and the matériel which it felt were necessary to deter general war. At the MacArthur hearings, Air Force General Vandenburg rejected a senator's suggestion that the United States should commit a major part of the American Air Force to the Korean War effort. He argued instead that the United States must get a cease fire

without endangering that one potential that we have which has kept the peace so far, which is the United States Air Force; which, if utilized in a manner to do what you are suggesting, would [sic], because of attrition and because the size of the Air Force is such and the size of the air force industry is such that we could not still be that deterrent to [general] war which we are today.[8]

Soviet action during the war, including the failure to commit combat forces, suggests that they shared with the United States the desire to avoid a global war.

IMAGES OF THE ROLE OF FORCE

The North Korean attack on South Korea suggested the willingness of the Communists to seek a limited objective by a limited use of force. The Soviets probably intended to seize South Korea with the use of North Korean forces and then to halt their military operations. When the United States intervened, the Soviets recognized their miscalculation of American intentions, but proceeded on the assumption that American intervention need not lead to world war. The attack on South Korea, moreover, seems to have been motivated by the Soviet compulsion to fill power vacuums. In view of the specific United States declaration that South Korea was outside its defense perimeter, the Soviets reasonably could have

counted on a quick and easy victory by the North Koreans. But, while Communist conduct during the war reflected a doctrine that included the limited use of military force and limited objectives, neither the Chinese nor the Russians seemed to have any idea of the optimum methods of communicating intentions and capabilities to the other side in the course of such a war.

American images of the role of force, on the other hand, seem to have been much less hospitable to the limitation of warfare. It would appear that the United States had not foreseen the possibility of Soviet military action in South Korea or any other local area unconnected with a general Soviet military offensive. The result was the American decision not to prepare for the defense of South Korea, in view of the low estimate of its value in a general war. Thus the decision of June 1950 to defend South Korea was not based on a re-estimate of South Korea's military importance but on a recognition that something had occurred for which American military doctrine had not been prepared. In making its policy decisions throughout the war, the United States was operating without any general theoretical notions of the nature of local war in the atomic age, and its decisions were probably affected by the lack of such theory.

Each side's image of the other's intentions influenced its decisions. The Soviets clearly underestimated the likelihood of American intervention. In the Soviet view America's action in withdrawing its troops from Korea and its declarations that it would defend South Korea only as part of its United Nations obligations had meant that the United States would not, in fact, defend South Korea. The Soviets failed to anticipate the partly moral and partly political American reaction to aggression. They were insensitive to the importance that the United States would attach to repelling "illegal" aggression, as opposed to less clear-cut violations of international law.

The American decision to intervene in Korea and subsequent decisions were also based on, and influenced by, estimates of Soviet intentions.[9] In assessing the motives of the North

---

[8] *Military Situation in the Far East*, p. 1385.

[9] This discussion of the American image of Soviet doctrine is based on Alexander L. George, "American Policy-Making and the North Korean Aggression," *World Politics*, 7 (January 1955): 209–32.

Korean attack, American policymakers gave consideration and, to some extent, credence to five different interpretations, as follows:

1. The "diversionary move" interpretation. In view of the number of other areas, particularly Western Europe, that appeared more militarily significant than South Korea, the North Korean attack was seen as a diversionary move aimed to draw American resources away from the areas where they were most important. Truman reports that he shared this view in part and was determined not to leave Europe vulnerable to Soviet aggression.

2. The "soft-spot probing" interpretation. By this image of Soviet doctrine, the Soviet compulsion to fill power vacuums had led to the attack on South Korea, which had been abandoned by the United States and which was clearly incapable of defending itself.

3. The "testing" interpretation. This was the view that seemed to influence most Truman's image of the North Korean attack. It recalled the progress of Hitler's aggressive moves and asserted that the North Korean attack should be seen as a prelude to attacks in other areas if that aggression were allowed to succeed. This view differed from the "soft-spot probing" interpretation in its assumption that the Communists' success in Korea would encourage them to attempt aggression in the other areas where Western defense capabilities were far stronger. In short, the purpose of the Korean attack was to probe the firmness of Western intentions, and not simply to fill a power vacuum.

4. The "demonstration" interpretation. By this interpretation, the Soviets were mainly concerned with demonstrating their own strength and American weakness in order to promote, on a long-term basis, important shifts in political allegiance throughout the world.

5. The "Soviet–Far East strategy" interpretation. This interpretation put emphasis on the idea, already discussed, that the Soviets hoped to prevent the entrance of Japan into the Western camp and to pave the way for further Communist expansion in the Far East.

. . . The inclination of American policymakers toward the "testing" interpretation of Soviet doctrine—in which the Korean attack was equated with Hitler's early expansionist moves —may have reinforced the likelihood that the United States would intervene in Korea. If the "soft-spot probing" interpretation of Soviet con-

duct had been accepted instead, the United States might have been more prone to cede South Korea while taking steps to prevent the existence of power vacuums elsewhere. The belief that successful aggression would embolden the Soviets made the defense of South Korea seem crucial.

DOMESTIC POLITICAL PRESSURES

During the Korean War the Truman Administration continued to pursue its domestic political goals. Despite the war there was politics-as-usual on both sides of the political fence. The President was constantly concerned with promoting his Fair Deal program, consolidating the position of the Democratic party, strengthening his northern and western liberal support in Congress, and calming the political crises raised by such men as Senator Joseph McCarthy. Nor was the Administration immune to criticism from the Republican party, which felt that it was possible, necessary, and desirable to attack the Administration's conduct as well as to question the basic concept of limiting war.

After the MacArthur hearings, a Republican minority report declared:

We believe that a policy of victory must be announced to the American people in order to restore unity and confidence. It is too much to expect that our people will accept a limited war. Our policy must be to win. Our strategy must be devised to bring about decisive victory.[10]

These few sentences suggest a number of important assumptions about the nature of wartime politics. The first is the notion that the unity of the American people can be achieved only with a declaration that victory is the goal. A further implication is that, after such a declaration, the method of achieving a battlefield victory becomes a "military" problem that is beyond the realm of partisan domestic politics. On the other hand, once the government admits that there are other political considerations that affect and moderate the goal of a strictly military victory, then, according to this Republican statement, it is legitimate to criticize the particular policy adopted. Unity will come only when the country is asked to back an absolute goal. If there is no such goal, then the

---

[10] *Military Situation in the Far East*, p. 3590.

opposition has a duty to examine and critically appraise the war effort.

Congress, as a whole, also felt itself free to criticize. The hearings into the firing of General Douglas MacArthur were striking in that they required the Administration, *during the war*, to justify its conduct and to explain what it hoped to accomplish in the war and how the war was being conducted, as well as to explicate a host of particulars which must have been of as much interest to the Communists as they were to the senators across the table. Actually the hearings provided a unique and invaluable opportunity for the Administration to communicate what it wanted to communicate to the Chinese and the Russians. However, the senators' questions at this hearing did not have that motivation. Congress forced the Administration to discuss its strategy and objectives during the war without any apparent consideration of the effect this would have on the American war effort.

The quotation from the report of the Republican senators also reflects the then still strong American opposition to fighting a local war. The senators stated flatly that the American people would not accept a strategy of limiting war, and indicated their rejection of the strategy as well. The implication is that during a local war the American government will be subjected to attacks from the political opposition, from Congress, and from public citizens on two grounds: the legitimacy of fighting such a war and the particular strategy employed in the war.

The general public seems to have shared the Republican senators' dissatisfaction with the course of the Korean War, at least in its later stages. On the other hand, the public apparently approved the decision of the Eisenhower Administration to end the war short of victory as it had approved the initial decision to intervene. The public's frustration with the continuing war probably added to the margin of Eisenhower's victory in 1952; his ending the war enhanced the Republican image as the party of peace and increased the Eisenhower plurality in 1956. The Korean War does not seem to have had a major or lasting impact on popular political attitudes.[11] In this respect,

American political leaders seem to have overestimated the effect of the war on the voting public. Korea is taken as demonstrating—as to some extent it did—that extended local wars which cannot be decisively won are not popular with the American public. Leading the United States into a major local war or expanding the war without securing a clear victory is likely to be perceived as a political liability; ending a war on almost any terms may be a political asset.

All these domestic pressures undoubtedly influenced the manner in which the Truman Administration conducted its Korean operations, both by hampering its freedom of action and by increasing the costs of various actions.

ATOMIC WEAPONS

The most dramatic limit on the Korean War was that neither side used its atomic weapons. According to Brodie, there were four reasons why these weapons were not used by the United States:[12]

1. The Joint Chiefs of Staff and civilian policymakers continued to feel that the war in Korea was basically a Soviet feint. There was, therefore, a strong case for conserving the then relatively limited stockpile of atomic weapons for the principal war which, they thought, would come in Europe. Their fear was not that the employment of nuclear weapons would lead to an expansion of the war and a Soviet attack on Europe but rather that Korea was deliberately designed as a decoy to get the United States to exhaust its nuclear stockpile and conventional military resources so that the Soviets could later attack with impunity in Europe. It was, then, the desire to save resources and not the fear of provoking the enemy which was one of the main causes of the American decision not to use nuclear weapons in Korea.

2. American policy was also affected by the reports of local Air Force commanders that there were no suitable targets for atomic weapons in Korea. While the impact of this view was considerable, it apparently reflected an uninformed attitude about the possible uses of atomic weapons. Commanders in the field came to think, for example, that atomic bombs

---

[11] Angus Campbell *et al.*, *The American Voter* (New York: John Wiley & Sons, 1960), pp. 49, 50, 527, 546, 555.

[12] Bernard Brodie, *Strategy in the Missile Age* (Princeton: Princeton University Press, 1959).

were of little use against bridges, a belief which Brodie explained as follows:

> This odd idea probably resulted from a misreading of the results at Hiroshima and Nagasaki. Some bridges were indeed badly damaged at those places and some were not, but for the latter it was generally forgotten that a bridge only 270 feet from ground zero at Hiroshima was actually 2,100 feet from the point of explosion, and also that it received its blast effect from above rather than from the side.[13]

Nuclear weapons were still relatively new and had not been extensively tested, and it is probable that commanders in the field were too busy to search out potential targets for nuclear weapons.

3. America's allies, particularly the British, were strongly and emotionally opposed to the use of atomic weapons in the Korean War. This pressure from its allies strengthened America's own anxieties and moral doubts about again using these weapons.

4. A subsidiary reason for the failure to use atomic weapons in the Korean War was fear of the retaliatory employment by the Soviets of the few atomic weapons in their possession against Pusan or Japan, despite America's near-monopoly of these weapons. Brodie doubts, however, whether this fear played a conscious part in the relevant decisions.

The first two motives just discussed will not be important in the future. The American stockpile of tactical nuclear weapons is now so great that military commanders may urge their use precisely because they are a non-scarce military resource, and certainly no argument can be made that they should not be used because they are scarce. Military officers now have a much better understanding of the capabilities of nuclear weapons, which, moreover, now come in much smaller packages. Thus it will be clear to military commanders that there would be suitable targets for their use in any conceivable future major limited war. While we can expect continued pressure from our allies against the use of nuclear weapons, certain allies might advocate their use in some situations. There will, however, be other international political pressures—for example, from the uncommitted or neutral states— against nuclear weapons, and the possibility of

a Soviet nuclear response will be a much more important determinant of the decision.

We know much less about the details of the Russian decision not to use atomic weapons in Korea. The Russians seemed determined not to supply any matériel to the forces fighting in Korea which could clearly be labeled as having been supplied by them after the war began. This would certainly be the case with atomic weapons.[14] In addition, the Soviet stockpile of such weapons was so small that its use in a localized military encounter might have seemed wasteful.

The limit observed by both sides seems not to have resulted from an attempt—or even an awareness of the need—to bargain with the enemy. However, the Soviets were probably more restrained than the United States by the fear that the initiation of nuclear attacks would be met by a response in kind.[15]

The Chinese Communists seem genuinely to have feared the possibility of the American use of atomic weapons when they intervened in the Korean War. According to Whiting, the Chinese felt that a nuclear response was a real possibility; intervention was considered risky, and every effort was made to delay it and to minimize its consequences. The extent of this Chinese concern was reflected both in its shelter-building program and in domestic Chinese Communist propaganda. But Peking was reassured by the three-week testing period of relatively small Chinese intervention which revealed that United States aircraft, though authorized to bomb the Korean ends of the Yalu bridges, were forbidden to venture into Chinese territory.

The background of the limit on the use of atomic weapons in the Korean War, then, suggests a failure of both sides to understand what the other side was likely to do and what the other side's fears and goals were. It also suggests that, to a large extent, the determination of limits is based on considerations other than those that result from the battlefield interaction. Some of the other limiting points established in the war reveal the same pattern.

---

[13] *Ibid.*, p. 319n.

[14] It was also true, however, of the MIGs the Soviets supplied, probably with Russian pilots.

[15] However, if the use of atomic weapons had been confined to the Korean theater—that is, if the decision to use these weapons was not coupled with a decision to expand the war in some other way—it is not clear who would have gained from an atomic exchange.

CHINESE INTERVENTION

One of the major expansions of the Korean War was the decision of the United Nations Command to cross the thirty-eighth parallel. This decision was based partly on the military consideration that one could not stand by and allow the enemy forces to regroup for renewed attack just beyond the border, but also on political grounds—when the battlefield conditions changed in its favor, the United States decided to pursue the unification of Korea by military means. In crossing the parallel the United States was aware of the risk that it might trigger Chinese Communist intervention, and tried by reassuring statements to prevent it. But it apparently underestimated the Chinese reaction and, at the same time, failed to develop a concurrent strategy which, by retaliatory threats or other sanctions, could succeed in preventing Chinese intervention. As Whiting has suggested, the threat to use atomic weapons on the Chinese mainland if the Chinese intervened might have been a much more effective deterrent than the attempt to reassure them that a march to the border did not presage an attack on mainland China.[16] The threat to use atomic weapons would have involved major political costs for the United States, and the American government might not have threatened to launch an atomic attack even if it had recognized that the threat might be effective. Had the Administration been aware of the fact that the fear of greater expansion might have deterred Chinese intervention, an alternative course might have been to threaten to expand the war to China with conventional weapons. But even this was not done. In fact, a decision was made before the intervention that Chinese intervention would not lead to conventional bombing beyond the Yalu. MacArthur reportedly believed that this decision had been leaked to the Chinese.[17]

In choosing, instead, to inform the Chinese of its limited objectives, the United States also considered it important to reassure the Chinese that their hydroelectric plants would not be jeopardized by a march up to the Yalu. But, as Whiting has pointed out:

It was widely believed in Western circles that a determining factor in Chinese Communist concern over North Korea was the reliance of Manchurian industry upon power supplies across the border as well as along the Yalu River. This belief prompted explicit reassurances from Western spokesmen, both in Washington and at Lake Success, concerning "China's legitimate interests" near the frontier. Yet we have seen that Peking ignored this issue completely in its domestic as well as its foreign communications. The absence of propaganda about the protection of the hydroelectric installations, despite the need to maximize popular response to mobilization of "volunteers," suggests that this consideration played little if any role in motivating Chinese Communist intervention.[18]

In its advance through North Korea, then, the United Nations Command was attempting to communicate two points to the Chinese Communists: first, that it was prepared to go up to but not beyond the Yalu; and, second, that it was prepared to respect China's legitimate interests in the northern regions of North Korea. The United States sought, therefore, to establish its limited objectives: that United Nations forces would take all North Korea; that the North Korean government would cease to exist; but that China's legitimate industrial interests would be protected. An effort was made to assure the Chinese that the capture of North Korea would not be used as a springboard for an attack into China. The United States assumed that the limits were ones that the Chinese were interested in, and that these limits would serve to keep the Chinese out of the war. But Chinese interests were different and could be satisfied only by different boundary conditions to the war.

Neustadt argues that the Chinese were not in any way affected by the announcement of the United Nations' aim to destroy the North Korean government.

To judge from what the Chinese said, and later did, Peking's concern was with MacArthur's military progress, never mind its foreign policy objective. Chinese concern was not confined to anything so simple as a buffer zone along the border; an entity called North Korea, not the border, was at stake (perhaps in roughly the same sense that South Korea, under reverse circumstances, was

---

[16] Whiting, *op. cit.*, p. 162. Panikkar, the Indian ambassador in Peking, reported that the Chinese expected an atomic attack, but were nontheless prepared to intervene.

[17] Whitney, *op. cit.*, pp. 455–56.

[18] Whiting, *op. cit.*, pp. 151–52.

for Washington). Even had the UN promised restoration of an independent North once all resistance ceased—which, naturally, no one proposed —I know of nothing to suggest that Peking would have withheld intervention. The communist world does not take kindly, it appears, to the dismantling of a member state's facilities for governance: the party and the army. MacArthur's military progress threatened both, no matter what came after. In short, the military risks and diplomatic dangers usually associated with MacArthur's march across the parallel existed independent of the words used in the UN resolution. MacArthur's march was authorized before the words were seen, much less approved, at Lake Success.[19]

Washington was apparently convinced, even in retrospect, that its declarations did not influence the Chinese decision to enter the war and that no other declaratory policy could have altered the Chinese decision. American policymakers concluded that, once the decision was made to cross the thirty-eighth parallel, nothing could be done to affect the Chinese decision. In fact, the State Department reportedly argued in December of 1950 that the Chinese decision to intervene was made prior to the crossing of the thirty-eighth parallel. In one sense, at least, this conclusion may be wrong: the Chinese position might have been altered by threats to expand the war with the use of atomic weapons against China. Moreover, it is by no means certain that the Chinese were concerned with the preservation of the total territorial integrity of North Korea. As Whiting suggests, an American commitment to advance only part way up the peninsula—that is, to permit the maintenance of the North Korean government in some part of its territory—might have been sufficient to deter China's entrance into the war.

Neither before nor during the first three months of war [Whiting wrote] did the degree of interest in Pyongyang evinced by Peking warrant acceptance at face value of its concern for a "just" peace, based upon the *status quo ante bellum*.
This is not to say that the Chinese Communist leadership was prepared to accept with equanimity the total defeat of North Korea. As a minimal goal, intervention must have been attempted to preserve an entity identifiable as the DPRK, and to prevent unification of all Korea under U.N. supervision. The late date of Chinese Communist entry into the war suggests that it was the political importance of the North Korean government, rather than its territorial integrity, that was at stake. Although intervention was officially predicated upon U.N. crossing of the thirty-eighth parallel, no Chinese People's Volunteers and Democratic People's Republic of Korea defense lines were established during the August–October period, not even to protect Pyongyang. To Peking, a "just" Korean peace was not an end in itself but rather a means towards fulfilling other related goals of policy.[20]

Thus, even after the crossing of the thirty-eighth parallel, Chinese intervention might have been prevented had the United States acted differently. Although trying to impose limits on expansion, the United States failed to grasp adequately either the reasons why the Chinese felt intervention was necessary or the threats that might have deterred their intervention. Both sides expanded the war—the United Nations by crossing the thirty-eighth parallel, and the Chinese by entering the war. Each side failed to convey to the other the kind of counteraction to be expected which might have deterred expansion. China attempted to prevent the crossing of the thirty-eighth parallel by declaring her intention to intervene, but this intention, relayed by the Indian ambassador, was not taken seriously by the United Nations Command. The United Nations sought to prevent the Chinese entrance, not by threatening a further expansion, but by attempting to satisfy the Chinese security interests that, it was assumed, might lead her to enter the war.

PORTS AND TROOPS

Despite the fact that United States planes, taking off from airfields in South Korea and Japan and from aircraft carriers, consistently bombed targets in North Korea, the Communists engaged in almost no bombing south of the thirty-eighth parallel. This was one of the major asymmetries of the war, both from a legalistic point of view and in terms of interfering with the military operations of the enemy. Both sides apparently devoted considerable attention to the question of what targets to attack, and a variety of motives affected the relevant decisions.

The American decision to bomb targets in North Korea was made prior to the commit-

[19] Neustadt, *op. cit.*, p. 125.   [20] Whiting, *op. cit.*, pp. 155–56.

ment of American ground troops in June 1950. A month later permission was given to bomb industrial targets in North Korea, but the use of incendiary bombs was not allowed, because of the civil damage that would have resulted. The United States Air Force was not authorized to bomb areas close to the Soviet and Chinese borders. Rashin was the single industrial center within the forbidden area, and it was the only industrial target in North Korea which was not destroyed by mid-September, when an end to strategic bombing was ordered by the Joint Chiefs. Not until June 1952 were attacks on the hydroelectric plants in North Korea authorized; within two weeks almost 90 percent of North Korea's power capacity was destroyed.[21]

American attacks on targets in North Korea steadily expanded. The attacks were aimed at affecting the immediate military situation. The restraints observed had several motives: (1) to avoid extensive civilian destruction considered undesirable on both humanitarian and propaganda grounds; (2) to avoid a spillover of the war into China or the Soviet Union (the spillover into China prior to her entry into the war probably did not have a major impact on Chinese policy, but the incursion did create propaganda and political difficulties); (3) to avoid damaging, in the case of the hydroelectric plants, targets considered vital to the Chinese so as to avoid their entrance into the war, presumably in retaliation.

The Communists exercised far greater restraint on their air forces. Except for a few night "heckling" attacks from small biplanes in the spring of 1951, no air attacks were made on any targets in South Korea. The Communists' restraint was not the result of the absence of inviting military targets. The port of Pusan was an extremely inviting target for bombardment and mining. It was the key to the American logistic effort and frequently was lighted up all night. American logistic convoys and troops in the field also could have been hampered by air attacks. A number of factors seem to have influenced the Communist decision not to respond in kind to United Nations air attacks on North Korea:

1. The Communists might have believed

that it would have been very difficult, if not impossible, for the United Nations to continue its operations in Korea if Pusan came under heavy attack, and that, once the United Nations committed itself to the defense of South Korea, it was no longer in a position to accept complete withdrawal. Therefore, if attacks on logistic lines made impossible the continued conduct of an effective ground war in Korea, the United States might have been forced to engage in strategic strikes against the Chinese, if not the Russian, homeland.[22] If the Communists found this supposition credible, they may have concluded that, once their initial grab for South Korea failed, they could not afford to do anything that would lead to their complete control over South Korea.[23] They may have recognized that American confinement of the war to the Korean peninsula was dependent on her ability to fight there effectively.

2. In order to avoid attacks on Chinese air bases just north of the Yalu, Red airmen were not allowed to attack United Nations positions from these bases. Although the Communists were permitting the United States the sanctuary of bases in Japan and on aircraft carriers, they apparently were afraid that they would not be granted a similar sanctuary for bombing operations. United States planes managed to keep the North Korean airfields out of commission almost continuously throughout the war. Thus, given that the Chinese limited the use of their fields to staging operations and to fighter planes, the Communists were incapable of bombing operations.

3. There is some evidence to suggest that Soviet pilots constituted a significant part of the "Chinese" air force during the Korean War.[24] If this is true, the explanation for target restraint may have been the desire to avoid the capture of Soviet airmen. This proof of direct Soviet involvement in the war would at

---

[21] Robert Frank Futrell, *The United States Air Force in Korea, 1950–1953* (New York: Duell, Sloan & Pearce, 1961), pp. 449–52.

[22] The United States had secured British concurrence to bomb bases in China in the event of heavy air attacks from Chinese bases on United Nations troops (Great Britain, *Parliamentary Debates* [Commons], 5th ser., 496 (1952): 970) and this was probably communicated to the Chinese. However, Truman reported that he was convinced that Russia would come in if Manchurian bases were bombed.

[23] This thesis implies that the Chinese would not have driven the United Nations forces off the Korean peninsula by ground action even if they had had the capability. There is no evidence to substantiate or invalidate this point.

[24] Futrell, *op. cit.*, pp. 370, 651–52.

the least have been politically damaging, and, from the Soviet point of view, might have created an intolerable risk of American retaliation.

By the end of the war the United States was exercising almost no target restraint in North Korea, and the Communists were doing no bombing in South Korea. Each side was guided by a complex series of motives and incentives. However, despite the asymmetry of the actions, there is nothing to suggest that either side treated its decisions on targeting as being closely related to, affected by, or likely to affect, the opponent's decisions on these questions.

EXPANSION AND LIMITATION

Decisions on expanding the United Nations operations resulted from the rejection or approval of the field commanders' proposals by the Joint Chiefs of Staff or civilian officials. In some cases, particularly on the question of using atomic weapons, the military never made the request, and so, in some sense, no decision was made. On three occasions General MacArthur was refused his requests: to employ Chinese Nationalist troops, to impose a naval blockade on China, and to bomb bases and supply lines in China. But a number of MacArthur's requests for permission to expand the war were approved. These included the commitment of American ground forces, the Inchon offensive, and the crossing of the thirty-eighth parallel.

President Truman states that the National Security Council recommended the consideration of three factors relevant to the decision of whether to go on the offensive: action by the Soviet Union and the Chinese Communists, the views of friendly members of the United Nations, and the risk of general war.[25] These and other decisions were also influenced by American doctrine as well as by domestic political pressures. The balancing of the factors varied from decision to decision, but all played a role in the major decisions to limit or expand the war.

Much less is known about the Communist decisionmaking process or the factors which influenced their decisions to limit or expand the war. The initial decision to keep the Chinese out of the war seems to have been based largely on domestic conditions in China, particularly the desire of the Chinese to implement their program of economic growth and development, and their desire to avoid military entanglements at a time when they had not yet consolidated their hold over their own country.[26] The reasons for the Russians' abstention from open intervention in the war are less clear. The Soviets were determined not to do anything that would directly label them as participants; they did not publicize the participation of any Russian "volunteers" in the war; nor did they provide any atomic capability, although they did supply large amounts of conventional military equipment. One likely explanation is the Russian fear that intervention would lead to general war. The United States had the capability of inflicting great destruction on the Soviet homeland with its stock of atomic weapons, while the Soviets had no capability of directly attacking the United States, although they might have been able to capture a large part of Western Europe with ground forces. Thus the Soviets, aware of their inferior strategic position, were probably determined to keep out of the war and to provide no excuse for a direct American attack on the Soviet Union.

Each side apparently made its decisions to limit the war for different reasons and with minimal attention to the battlefield interaction. In addition, the two sides observed very different limits. What the United States did in North Korea was quite different from what the Communists did in South Korea, and the Chinese used a much greater percentage of their gross national product than the United States did. Nevertheless, while the United States used naval vessels and airplanes to bomb troops and airfields within Korea, the Communists did not. The United States engaged in logistical interdiction; the Communists did not. Each side, then, observed its own series of limits and restraints, which only in some very general way were related to, and dependent on, the limits of the other side.

At least a few of the limits were symmetrical. Both sides restricted their military opera-

25 Truman, op. cit., p. 359.

26 It was probably based also on the belief that the United States would not intervene and that the North Korean army would capture all of South Korea.

tions almost entirely to Korea, and neither used nuclear weapons. There was lack of symmetry in that all the military targets in North Korea were attacked but most in South Korea were not. The United States attacked the Chinese points of entry—the Yalu bridges; but the Chinese did not attack the United States' points of entry—the ports. Both sides observed a number of what Schelling has called "legalistic" limitations.[27] The United Nations carefully observed both the Chinese and Russian borders and tried to avoid crossing them inadver-

tently. There was symmetry in the absence of an official declaration of war. The United Nations troops participated in the war in a "police action" capacity, and none of the countries involved, including the United States, declared war. The Chinese used "volunteers," and the Russians supplied equipment and presumably technicians, but little manpower for the battle.

In some cases the limits represented a recognition of the battlefield interaction. But the origin of many of the limits observed, and part of the explanation for others, lay not within the dynamics of the war itself but within the domestic and international context in which the war was fought.

[27] Thomas C. Schelling, *Nuclear Weapons and Limited War*, RAND P-1620, February 20, 1959, p. 1.

CHAPTER 5

Wars of Insurgency

INSURGENCY: A FRAMEWORK FOR ANALYSIS

BARD E. O'NEILL

Captain O'Neill discusses the major factors involved in the analysis of insurgency-type warfare. The key variables in the scheme are: (1) the government's response, (2) popular support, (3) organization, (4) external support, and (5) environment. As the article points out, each factor can be important in determining the outcome of insurgency warfare. The salience of a given factor, however, will vary from case to case, and, in order to understand the variations, one must focus on the linkages among the major variables. As Captain O'Neill argues, the government's response and the environment have a particularly important effect on the progress of an insurrection and the performance requirements placed on insurgents in terms of popular support, organization, and external support. Captain O'Neill received his Ph.D. from the Graduate School of International Studies, University of Denver, in 1972 and is presently a member of the Department of Political Science at the USAF Academy. He has served in Vietnam with the Third Tactical Fighter Wing and as a consultant for the Office of Doctrine, Concepts, and Objectives, HQ USAF.

INTRODUCTION

The period since World War II has often been characterized as an era of revolutionary warfare, a description that is not surprising, given the recurrence of insurgent conflicts in such places as Malaya, the Philippines, Vietnam, China, Burma, Sarawak, Greece, Cyprus, Bolivia, the Sudan, Ethiopia, Chad, Algeria, and Thailand, to name but a few. Indeed, the significance of the insurgency phenomenon over the past twenty-six years has been mirrored by a plethora of books, articles, government studies, and scholarly monographs devoted to the study of both insurgency and counterinsurgency, the majority of which have been descriptive case studies either of an insurrection as a whole or a part thereof.[1] While

many such works have proven to be insightful and informative, they have often suffered from insufficient attention to generalization. That is to say, there was little attempt to identify, formulate, and test propositions about insurgency.

In order to offset the case studies' tendency to focus on the unique, a few scholars oriented their research efforts toward a search for variables that might be used to assess and compare a number of insurgencies. Unhappily, the variables they enumerated were not comprehensive, nor were they given in-depth consideration in specific cases. Instead, what the authors tended to do was first to posit a number of criteria and then to research the literature on insurgency to obtain supportive examples for each factor. Moreover, both the number of variables identified and the operational indicators of each were often incomplete

---

[1] An example of a general case study is Bernard B. Fall, *The Two Viet-Nams*, rev. ed. (New York: Praeger, 1967); an excellent partial study would be Douglas

Pike, *Viet Cong* (Cambridge: M.I.T. Press, 1966). The focus of the latter is on organization.

This is an original article written for this volume.

or underdeveloped, and the linkages among them were either overlooked or underemphasized.[2] In short, what has been lacking in the scholarship on insurgency is a study which (1) sets forth in an explicit, systematic, and comprehensive fashion the criteria for assessing insurgency warfare and (2) applies those criteria in given cases. The summary which follows is an *initial* attempt to deal with the first aspect of this problem—the need to devise a framework for the analysis and comparison of insurgencies.[3] Although the framework presented below was tested in a lengthy study of the Palestinian Resistance Movement, the exigencies of space preclude presentation of the empirical segment herein. Nevertheless, many of the findings in the case study have influenced the analytical framework in that they led to confirmation, nonconfirmation, modifications, and elucidation of the propositions therein.

Hopefully, by using the framework set forth below, the student of a given insurgency can arrive at a more comprehensive understanding of its status and some general conclusions regarding its prospects for success or failure. What the framework seeks to do, in other words, is to alert the researcher to a number of salient variables and questions which should be investigated when analyzing a particular insurgency, especially one that is of a protracted nature.

THE MAJOR ANALYTICAL VARIABLES

For the purposes of this paper, the term "insurgency" is used to denote a violent conflict between a government (colonial or indigenous) and an outgroup in which the latter uses some or all of the resources at its disposal to seize political power.[4] Within the general framework of insurgency warfare two types of political violence can be identified. The first, conspiracy, is characterized by low-level but highly organized violence which has limited popular participation, including organized political assassinations, small-scale guerrilla warfare, coups d'état, and mutinies. The second, internal war, is highly organized violence which has widespread popular participation, is designed to overthrow the regime or dissolve the state, and is accompanied by extreme violence, including large-scale terrorism and guerrilla wars, civil wars, and revolutions.[5] While internal war is more closely related to conventional notions of insurgency, conspiracy cannot be ignored, for there have been several insurrections which more closely approximated the conspiracy end of the continuum. The Castro revolution, in contrast to the Chinese and Viet Minh revolutions, for example, did not require widespread popular participation or prolonged and steadily intensifying terrorism and guerrilla warfare in order to bring down the Batista government. Instead, the Cuban insurgency was a highly organized short-term conflict in which psychological pressure combined with low-level guerrilla attacks to bring success;

---

[2] See, for example, Virgil Ney, "Guerrilla Warfare and Modern Strategy," in *Modern Guerrilla Warfare*, ed. Franklin Mark Osanka (New York: The Free Press, 1962).

[3] Given the demands of space and the fact that the intended readership of this article goes beyond the social sciences, the discussion of the analytical framework has eschewed the use of the technical jargon of political science. Nevertheless, the reader should be aware that the topic is amenable to an approach that uses the concepts, methods, and tools of political science. For example, a model could be devised in which the likelihood of success is the dependent variable and the five success criteria are the independent variables. Following that, the operational indicators of each variable would be outlined, techniques for measuring them would be set forth, and explicit hypotheses which link the variables would be postulated (e.g., the degree of external support varies moderately with the cohesion of the insurgent organization). However, since such an undertaking would no doubt be quite lengthy, it is impractical for this article.

[4] Those conducting an insurgency may have, *inter alia*, revolutionary aims (restructuring the political-economic-social order) or restorational aims (reestablishing a pre-existing system). Examples of the first would be the Chinese and Cuban revolutions, while examples of the second would be the noncommunist partisan movements of World War II.

[5] This breakdown is based on the distinctions made by Ted Robert Gurr, *Why Men Rebel* (Princeton: Princeton University Press, 1970), pp. 10–11. Many writers identify insurgency with protracted internal war and analyze it in terms of the Maoist model or a variant thereof. See John Pustay, *Counterinsurgency Warfare* (New York: The Free Press, 1965), p. 5. Pustay uses a typical Maoist stage approach when he defines insurgency as "a cellular development of resistance against an incumbent political regime . . . which expands from the initial stage of subversive infiltration through intermediate stages of overt resistance by small bands and insurrection to final fruition in civil war." The trouble with such a definition, of course, is that not all insurgencies have proceeded in such a manner. Castro's revolution, for instance, succeeded at an early stage, and even then it did not follow the Maoist sequence, which calls for organization to precede military activity. Castro began military action prior to the development of a strong political organization.

hence, there was no need to mobilize or organize a substantial section of the population for prolonged conflict.

Whether a given insurgency can succeed by confining itself to activity more akin to conspiracy or will have to take on the dimensions of a prolonged internal war is largely determined by the nature of the government and its response to the incipient actions of the insurgents. Thus, the first major variable to be examined when assessing an insurgency is the government's will and capability to resist the insurgents. Following that, four additional major variables to be considered are popular support, organization, external support, and environment.

THE GOVERNMENT'S RESPONSE: THE COUNTERINSURGENCY DIMENSION

Four Threats

Governments facing an insurrection are confronted with a political-military challenge which usually includes: (1) *terrorism*—assassination, torture, kidnapping, mutilation, bombings, and so on; (2) *guerrilla warfare*—hit-and-run attacks by small armed units against military, economic, and political installations or personnel; and (3) attempts to detach the people from the government through a combination of *propaganda appeals* and *organizational techniques*. Yet a fourth type of threat that governments have to deal with is *mobile-conventional warfare*—attacks against large government military units or important political targets (e.g., a provincial capital) by guerrilla forces that have been transformed into conventional formations (e.g., regiments). When this occurs, the insurgent is usually confident that by inflicting heavy losses on the enemy he will undercut the last vestiges of his will to resist. How the government responds to the first three types of threat will be a major factor in determining whether or not the fourth type of threat will ever be posed, and the eventual outcome of the conflict. As Professor Walter Sonderlund put it:

"as soon as the challenge is in the open the success of the operation depends not primarily on the development of insurgent strength, but more importantly on the degree of vigor, determination

and skill with which the incumbent regime acts to defend itself, both politically and militarily.[6]

Since a government can be confronted with four types of threats, it must carefully differentiate among them if it is to devise relevant solutions.[7] In other words, each type of threat requires a different reaction and series of measures on the part of the government.

Basic Strategy

Underlying the use of political, terror, and guerrilla warfare tactics by insurgents is an essential strategy which conceives of a target country as being divided into three zones: bases controlled by the revolutionary forces; bases controlled by the government; and contested areas. Within this context the insurgent aim is to expand the revolutionary movement's bases and area so as to reduce government control. In contrast to conventional warfare's method of achieving political objectives by defeating enemy forces in the field, the insurgent seeks to arrive at his aim by first gaining control of the population or a significant segment thereof. The government counterstrategy, as John McCuen has persuasively argued, should be to reverse the insurgent formula by extending from its secure areas and converting contested regions into government bases, an undertaking which requires that the government convince and organize the uncommitted people to support its cause.[8]

Coordination

A basic requisite for the initiation of an effective counterinsurgency program is a coordinated political, administrative, military,

[6] Walter C. Sonderlund, "An Analysis of the Guerrilla Insurgency and Coup d'État as Techniques of Indirect Aggression," *International Studies Quarterly*, 14 (December 1970): 345.

[7] Some writers assess the four types of threats in terms of models based on the Chinese and Viet Minh experience. In such schemes the four types of threat represent four stages of revolutionary warfare, each of which is emphasized in a given phase. However, as noted, not all insurgencies follow the organization–terror–guerrilla warfare–mobile-conventional warfare sequence.

[8] John J. McCuen, *The Art of Counter-Revolutionary War* (Harrisburg, Pa.: Stackpole Books, n.d.), pp. 50–56, 78–80; Franklin A. Lindsay, "Unconventional Warfare," in *Problems of National Strategy*, ed. Henry A. Kissinger (New York: Praeger, 1965), pp. 344–45. The section on counterinsurgency closely follows the scheme outlined by McCuen.

police, and intelligence effort, preferably under civilian control. This is essential if the various counterinsurgency agencies are to minimize working at cross-purposes.[9] In order to have a common sense of direction which will facilitate cooperative behavior among the various counterinsurgency sectors, the government must arrive at an overall program for the future of the country.[10]

National Program

Since the national program should also serve as a basis for gaining the support of the population, the government must ascertain the people's aspirations, which vary from one insurrection to another and from one region to another within the same country. Land reform, for instance, may be a basic grievance in some circumstances but not in others. History provides a number of cases which sustain the thesis that benevolent treatment of the population and reforms designed to meet the basic needs of the people can go a long way toward undermining the support of the insurgents. Arthur Campbell calls attention to the fact that as long ago as the Spanish guerrilla war against Napoleon the guerrillas had great difficulty in getting aid from the people of Huesca because of the material benefits provided by the French and the lack of exactions by the latter's forces. Likewise, he cited the kindness, administrative reform and good management of General Souchet in Aragon as a factor that made it difficult for the guerrillas to get popular support. In contrast, the repression of General Augereau in Catalonia is credited with playing into guerrilla hands and facilitating their quest for popular backing.[11]

The actions of the German administration in the Ukraine during World War II were a striking example of the government being its own worst enemy, especially since the Ukrainians had no love for Stalin and seemed ready to help the Germans. As it happened, the German exactions and repression against the Ukrainians eventually turned the latter against the Third Reich. Benevolent administration and effective reforms, such as those carried out by Colonel General Schmidt, which proved effective in harnessing popular support, were few and far between and were undercut by general Nazi policies.[12]

A classic case of the government righting itself and gaining popular support would be the actions of the Philippine regime against the Huks. In that instance the election of Ramon Magsaysay to the presidency led to a number of social and military reforms which mobilized popular support and combined with the use of ruthless force against the insurgents to bring victory.[13] In contrast, the Batista government in Cuba provides an example of a repressive government that did not mend its ways and hence further alienated the people and turned them toward Castro.

Devising a program to satisfy the economic grievances of the population is, of course, no easy undertaking for a developing nation, given the latter's poor resource capabilities. In light of this, it may be necessary for the governments of such states to seek economic assistance from external sources. Demands for redistribution of existing economic or political power, on the other hand, are largely internal matters that can be accommodated by the government from within.[14]

The most difficult demand for a government to meet is the demand that it abdicate in favor of insurgent rule at the central level. However, since popular support for an insurgent organi-

---

[9] The importance of a unified government effort has been stressed by a number of writers. See McCuen, *op. cit.*, pp. 71, 182–91. McCuen suggested that the civil-military effort in Malaya was a model that was worth emulating. Yet he also conceded that conditions in other areas may not be as good, since, unlike the British situation, there may be no effective administration in existence, no tradition of civilian primacy, and a shortage of good leaders.

[10] McCuen, *op. cit.*, pp. 58–59, 96.

[11] Arthur Campbell, *Guerrillas* (New York: The John Day Co., 1968), pp. 10–17.

[12] Campbell, *op. cit.*, pp. 73–89; Fredrick Wilkins, "Guerrilla Warfare," in *Modern Guerrilla Warfare*, pp. 10–11; Walter D. Jacobs, "Irregular Warfare and the Soviets," *ibid.*, p. 61; Brooks McClure, "Russia's Hidden Army," *ibid.*, pp. 96–97; Ernst von Dohnanyi, "Combatting Soviet Guerrillas," *ibid.*, pp. 102–5.

[13] On this point see Kenneth M. Hammer, "Huks in the Philippines," in *Modern Guerrilla Warfare*, p. 182; Boyd T. Bashore, "Dual Strategy for Limited War," *ibid.*, pp. 193–96, 199–201; Tomas C. Tirona, "The Philippine Anti-Communist Campaign," *ibid.*, pp. 206–7; Campbell, *op. cit.*, pp. 129–32. On Batista see Dickey Chapelle, "How Castro Won," in *Modern Guerrilla Warfare*, pp. 328–29.

[14] The decision of the Sudanese government to meet some of the demands of the rebels from the three southern provinces for greater autonomy is an example of a regime terminating an insurrection by agreeing to reallocate political power. See *New York Times*, February 28, 1972.

zation with such a totalistic objective is usually based on lesser socioeconomic demands, the government must seek to undercut the basis of insurgent support by eliminating the concrete grievances of the masses. In other words, the lesser demands of the people must be distinguished from the political power aims of the insurgent leadership. While the government cannot accommodate the latter, it may well be able to deal with the former and by so doing deprive the insurgent movement of its main source of strength and resources—the people.

Obviously, it will be more difficult to design an effective counterinsurgency program in colonial situations, where not only the insurgent leadership but the people are motivated by the nationalist aim of independence. In some colonial insurgencies, however, it may be possible for the government to control the situation by improving the well-being of the population. The regime's aim will be to provide concrete benefits for the populace in the hope that the latter will support the existing political order in return for short-term benefits.[15] In cases where the population is divided into rival ethnic groups, the government may also seek to sustain or exacerbate primordial societal cleavages in order to keep the insurgent movement divided (the well-known strategy of divide and rule).[16]

Administration

Once the government has ascertained the needs of the people and has devised a general program to deal with them, it must create an effective administration—staffed by local personnel if possible—in order to provide the necessary and relevant services.[17] History is replete with cases wherein governments forfeited

their presences in the villages to insurgent forces, which were quick to exploit the administrative vacuum by establishing their own organizational apparatus, however rudimentary it might have been. The initial British inattention to the Chinese squatters in areas bordering the jungles during the Malayan Emergency is a case in point.

As part of its organizational efforts, the government must seek to create a sense of loyalty and friendship between itself and the people. To facilitate this task, potential groups and leaders that can serve the government and provide personnel for auxiliary police and militia forces must be identified and organized.[18] The role of the police and militia is to keep infiltrators away from the people, to prevent exactions from being made on the people by the insurgents, and to provide security against terrorism and low-level guerrilla operations. Since personal security is one of the strongest human drives, it is imperative that it be accommodated from the earliest possible moment if the government expects to benefit from the cooperation of the people.[19]

Security Measures

Along with the political and administrative action outlined above, the government must be prepared to invoke a number of security measures—detention without trial, resettlement of sections of the population, control of the distribution of food, curfews, restrictions on movement, the issuance and checking of identification cards, and the imposition of severe penalties for the carrying of unauthorized weapons—in order to separate the population from the insurgents.[20] While collective sanctions are not desirable from an ideal standpoint, they can be, and have been, effective, but only when applied consistently, fairly, and judiciously.[21]

[15] Campbell, *op. cit.*, p. 311.

[16] The tribal divisions in both South Africa and Rhodesia, for example, are welcomed and encouraged by the governments because they keep the black populations divided.

[17] In situations where installation of the regular administrative apparatus is impossible in the short run because of a paucity of resources and trained persons, the government should use civic action teams to help meet the needs of the population and to establish a government presence. On civic action see Otto Heilbrunn, *Partisan Warfare* (New York: Praeger, 1962), p. 157; Julian Paget, *Counter-Insurgency Campaigning* (New York: Walker & Co.), p. 178; Douglas Hyde, *The Roots of Modern Guerrilla Warfare* (Chester Springs, Pa.: Dufour Editions, 1968), pp. 44–45.

[18] The advantages of using local people for administration, police work, and military functions have been discussed by Heilbrunn, *op. cit.*, p. 36; Campbell, *op. cit.*, pp. 34, 218, 320; and Roger Trinquier, *Modern Warfare* (New York: Praeger, 1964), p. 75.

[19] McCuen, *op. cit.*, pp. 98–105, 107–13.

[20] *Ibid.*, pp. 143–58. At this point, isolating the insurgents from the population is more important than establishing a positive attitude toward the government.

[21] In other words, each law must be enforceable, fairly applied, and avoid falling unfairly on particular groups in the population. For a discussion of a regime's coercive measures see Gurr, *op. cit.*, pp. 236–59; Sir Robert Thompson, *Defeating Communist Insur-*

Resettlement of portions of the population, for example, may become necessary if the government is to sever the links between the insurgents and the populace. Though it is not a desirable course of action, resettlement may be required if terror and/or guerrilla attacks persist and are attributed, at least partially, to the support rendered the insurgents by certain segments of the population. In the event that the government decides to relocate sections of the population, the move should be explained to those affected, and every effort must be made to see that the material benefits of the new locale supersede those of the old one. Civic action and political organization become extremely important during resettlement; in fact, they should be considered concomitants of that technique. The Briggs Plan for relocating the Chinese squatters in Malaya, the Kitchener resettlement scheme during the Boer War, and the relocation program during the Mau Mau uprising were examples where moving segments of the population was instrumental in denying the insurgents the support of the population. Conversely, the resettlement carried out by the regime of Ngo Dinh Diem in South Vietnam failed, largely because it was too fast, overextended, and characterized by poor regulatory procedures, ineffective local government, inadequate police forces (both quantitatively and qualitatively), and a lack of attention to alternate ways of earning a living.[22]

Intelligence

If the security measures suggested above are to be applied fairly, the government must have accurate information about the insurgent organization, including the identification and location of its members and its intended activities. This will require establishment of an effective intelligence apparatus which extends to the rural areas. Moreover, if the information obtained therefrom is to be properly exploited, there must be institutional procedures for its exchange at every level among the police, administrative, and military sectors.[23]

Military-Political Actions and the Four Threats

Military dispositions designed to deal with insurgent *organizational* activities, low-level terrorism, and sporadic guerrilla attacks must be oriented toward population contact. Thus, military units should be located in a large number of small posts that parallel the civil administration and allow for the protection of, and mixing with, the local people. If there is a small-scale guerrilla threat, the territorial defense force must make extensive use of ambushes and patrols in an effort to intercept insurgent bands. In addition, the government should provide backup mobile air, naval, and ground forces, which can be used to assist ambush patrols that engage the enemy and to conduct harassment operations against insurgent units in underpopulated hinterland areas. In no case should the mobile forces be considered a substitute for the territorial defense forces.[24]

In situations where the insurgent movement has been able to mount a substantial *terrorist* campaign the government must consolidate its own areas and then, operating from these secure bases, seek to destroy the political-military structures of the insurgent organization by locating and detaining members of the insurgent infrastructure. For this task the government should use police forces which have received quasi-military training for operations in the contested areas and the hinterland. Lesser

---

gency (New York: Praeger, 1966), p. 53; Charles Wolf, Jr., "Insurgency and Counterinsurgency: New Myths and Old Realities" (Santa Monica, Calif.: The RAND Corporation, July 1965), p. 22. Thompson argued that harsh security measures could be followed only in areas within the scope of government control. If they were sporadically applied in the areas under insurgent control, the people would have little choice but to support the insurgents. Arguing along similar lines, others have suggested that if collective sanctions are to be morally acceptable they must be implemented in a context within which the government can provide security against insurgent reprisals. See Heilbrunn, *op. cit.*, pp. 151–58; Paget, *op. cit.*, p. 169; Campbell, *op. cit.*, pp. 232–33; and Trinquier, *op. cit.*, pp. 43–50.

22 On the question of resettlement and its successes and failures see Richard L. Clutterbuck, *The Long, Long War* (New York: Praeger, 1966), pp. 56–63, 66–72; Campbell, *op. cit.*, pp. 36, 148, 218; Paget, *op. cit.*, p. 36; Heilbrunn, *op. cit.*, pp. 36, 153; and McCuen, *op. cit.*, pp. 231–34.

23 Trinquier, *op. cit.*, pp. 23–27, 35–38; Campbell, *op. cit.*, pp. 300–323; Paget, *op. cit.*, p. 164; McCuen, *op. cit.*, pp. 113–19; Clutterbuck, *op. cit.*, pp. 95–100.

24 McCuen, *op. cit.*, pp. 119–24, 166–84. The French mobile operations in the Atlas Mountains in Algeria are cited by McCuen as a model that might be emulated. Moreover, he suggested that counterorganization using native tribes could prove useful in some underpopulated areas, the French experiences with the Moi and Thai tribes in Indochina being examples.

duties can be performed by the auxiliary police so that the regular police can concentrate on the destruction of the insurgent apparatus.[25]

If the insurgents have begun to conduct large-scale *guerrilla* actions, the government will face a greater threat. In response, it must first consolidate the area it does hold and then gradually expand therefrom with the objective of gaining control of the population, food, and other resources.[26]

When the government forces are ready to venture forth from their own base areas, their primary objective should be to neutralize the insurgent's political apparatus while at the same time inflicting losses on guerrilla units and defending vital lines of communication (the French in Indochina mistakenly tried to defend all lines of communication and thus ended up with a large static defense force). An essential component of the antiguerrilla campaign should be a nomadic territorial offensive that will make use of patrols, attacks, and ambushes by small dispersed units during both day- and nighttime hours. Once an area has been cleared of guerrilla bands, it is important that it be reorganized by military civic action teams which are prepared to play a defensive role in conjunction with the nomadic offensive or territorial defensive forces operating in the region.[27]

In order to further deprive the guerrillas of the initiative, the government should use its mobile forces, commandos, airpower, and artillery to harass insurgents in remote and thinly populated hinterland areas where they are likely to have established bases. Eventually this area should also be organized by the government. If forbidden zones (i.e., areas that

can be fired into at will) are to be created, great care must be taken to assure that innocent civilians are not located therein; otherwise such military actions may prove to be counterproductive in that they risk creating more insurgents than are eliminated.[28]

If the government finds itself confronted by *mobile-conventional* warfare, it is near defeat, a reality that may require a call for outside assistance.[29] McCuen argues that the first countermove by the government should be to consolidate a base area, even if this means sacrificing large areas of the country. This is necessary to avoid the type of overextension which marked the French and Chinese Nationalist reactions to mobile-conventional warfare. One aspect of the French operations in Indochina which might serve as an example of what should be done, however, was the Tassigny campaign in the Red River delta, which used strike forces behind the cover of territorial units organized in depth. After securing base areas and expanding from them, mobile strike forces should be used against guerrilla bases in much the same manner that the assaults were made on the Greek guerrilla stronghold during the Greek civil war. If the government is lucky, the guerrillas may choose, as the Greek guerrillas did, to defend their bases, thus violating a cardinal guerrilla principle which warns against engaging a superior force. In the event the revolutionaries decide to revert to guerrilla warfare the government should respond likewise, taking the appropriate steps summarized above.[30]

If the government ascertains that sanctuaries across the border are playing an important role in sustaining the insurgent activities at any point in time, it can attempt to create a *cordon sanitaire*.[31] Should jungle and mountain terrain

[25] McCuen, *op. cit.*, pp. 128–42.

[26] *Ibid.*, pp. 195–205. The failure of the French to heed General Latour's advice that they consolidate their own bases before searching for Viet Minh had disastrous consequences.

[27] *Ibid.*, pp. 205–31; Hyde, *op. cit.*, pp. 94–95; Clutterbuck, *op. cit.*, p. 176. Examples of costly failures to organize the population after an area had been cleared were the French Odine operations in Indochina (cited by McCuen) and Operation Hammer in Sarawak (cited by Hyde). The importance of active day and night patrols cannot be stressed enough. The success of the Israelis between 1969 and 1972 is notable in this regard. A review of *Arab Report and Record's* issues during that period reveals continuous clashes between Israeli patrols and Arab guerrillas, with the latter usually coming out second-best.

[28] McCuen, *op. cit.*, pp. 235–45.

[29] In situations where external help is required the outsider's role should be confined to combatting regular guerrilla units or carrying out civic action. Outside forces should not be used for applying security measures against the population. See *ibid.*, p. 66.

[30] Heilbrunn, *op. cit.*, p. 51; McCuen, *op. cit.*, pp. 258–309.

[31] Sanctuaries may be important early in the insurgency, especially if the government is effective in dealing with insurgent activity within the target country. In Sarawak, for example, insurgent forces were forced to depend on bases in Indonesia during the early stages. The operations of the Palestinian guerrillas after 1969 also were dependent upon sanctuaries in the border states, particularly Jordan.

make this task impossible or difficult, the government may choose to establish forbidden zones, conduct a nomadic territorial offensive, build barriers, infiltrate counterguerrillas across the border, or directly strike the sanctuary country. However, since the last-mentioned tactic can be a *casus belli* that might widen the conflict, the government must weigh its aims, the possible costs, and the risks carefully.[32] In any event, while military neutralization of the sanctuary is important, the government must not neglect follow-up organization of the population if it is to achieve permanent success.

While the government must realize that the insurgent threat is largely a political-administrative one, this does not mean that military success is unimportant. Indeed, besides inflicting material and personnel losses on the insurgent movement and in some cases forcing the guerrillas from familiar operating terrain, military victories can bolster government morale, tarnish the insurgent image, and impress the population.

Although the insurgents are trying to establish an image of strength in order to convince the people that they will succeed, their propaganda is effective in the long run only when backed by concrete deeds such as military successes. When most of the victories go to the government side, the credibility of the insurgents suffers. In sum, military success, while not the primary concern in an insurgency, is nonetheless important.

One caveat should be mentioned here, however. If military victories are achieved at the expense of the local population—in terms of casualties and property losses—they may prove to be counterproductive in the sense that the alienation engendered will create revolutionaries among the affected group. This leads to the inescapable conclusion that all military operations must be planned and executed in such a way as to minimize civilian losses, since

one misplaced bomb or artillery shell can undo countless hours of political effort.[33]

Summary

To sum up, the government faced with an insurrection must be prepared to combat four different types of threats with four different types of responses. Insurgent organizational and propaganda efforts must be countered by government counterorganization and psychological warfare actions as well as by police operations designed to uncover insurgent political cadres; terrorism must be countered by the invocation of security measures and intensified police and intelligence operations; guerrilla warfare must be countered by low-level military action (the nomadic territorial offensive) that puts a premium on small-unit patrolling, mobile operations against hinterland guerrilla bases, and the defense of vital lines of communication; and mobile-conventional warfare must be countered by conventional military operations on the part of the government's mobile units. One important qualification here is that the government must be prepared to deal with each of these threats simultaneously. Thus, while a government faced with mobile-conventional warfare must combat regimental- or divisional-sized units, it must also be prepared to deal with guerrilla activity, terrorism, and insurgent political actions in certain sectors. In the past, some counterinsurgency efforts have been faulted for relying solely on conventional forces when faced with mobile-conventional warfare, the Westmoreland strategy in Vietnam between 1966 and 1968 being a case in point. The problem with the Westmoreland approach was not so much the use of search-and-destroy operations against large enemy units (such operations appeared necessary, since sending small units or civic-action pacification teams into sectors with divisional-sized North Vietnamese forces would have been suicidal) as it was the frequent failure to follow up by effectively organizing and securing the cleared areas.

In short, since there is no single panacea for dealing with the various threats posed by insurgent forces, the counterinsurgent must have a sophisticated strategy that differentiates among the types of threats posed in various

---

32 McCuen, *op. cit.*, pp. 240–49; Trinquier, *op. cit.*, pp. 101–3. Trinquier favored using counterguerrillas drawn from the population of the sanctuary country. That he may have overestimated the possibilities here was suggested by Bernard Fall in the Foreword to Trinquier's book. Israel found that direct strikes against guerrilla bases in Jordan and Lebanon were feasible. However, Israel had such marked military superiority over the two states that they did not choose to retaliate, because of the high losses that might result.

33 Clutterbuck, *op. cit.*, p. 161.

regions and coordinates responses in such a way that they are not working at cross-purposes. For instance, search-and-destroy operations in areas threatened with terrorism would not only be of limited value but could be damaging to the overall effort if they involved substantial human or material losses to the local population. The simple fact is that air, artillery, and regimental-sized units are not required to deal with terror networks, and they are far from being cost effective when used against terrorists.

No matter how one looks at it, the effort required by a counterinsurgency program is substantial. The demands in terms of morale, patience, and determination become greater as the guerrilla movement progresses. In order to succeed, the counterinsurgency forces need the firm backing of their government and people. Whether or not such support is forthcoming will be partially determined by the strategy the regime uses and the way in which it is implemented. Signs that things are not going well are serious dissent that supports the guerrilla objective (explicitly or implicitly) by calling for an end to hostilities, desertions from the army, a general lack of combativeness, a poor job of local law enforcement, guerrilla operations carried out by increasingly larger units, a lack of information from the people, and a low surrender rate. Conversely, the opposite of each of these indicators would signify the government is succeeding.

If the government has been able to devise and apply the types of programs suggested above, the insurgents will have little chance of success. Even if the government does a mediocre job, it may still succeed, depending upon how the insurgents perform in relation to the other major criteria for successful insurgency, a point to which we now turn.

Popular Support

Both practitioners and scholars of insurgency warfare have stressed the vital importance of *popular support*,[34] the second major variable involved in the analysis of insurgencies. Com-menting on the importance of the population, for example, the Viet Minh manual for guerrilla warfare states:

> Without the "popular antennae" we would be without information; without the protection of the people we could neither keep our secrets nor execute quick movements; without the people the guerrillas could neither attack the enemy nor replenish their forces and, in consequence, they could not accomplish their missions with ardour and speed. . . .

> The population helps us to fight the enemy by giving us information, suggesting ruses and plans, helping us to overcome difficulties due to lack of arms, and providing us with guides. It also supplies liaison agents, hides and protects us, assists our actions near posts, feeds us and looks after our wounded. . . . Cooperating with the guerrillas it has participated in sabotage acts, in diversionary actions, in encircling the enemy, and in applying the scorched earth policy. . . . On several occasions and in cooperation with the guerrillas it has taken part in combat.[35]

Echoing the views of the practitioners, one of the foremost students of contemporary insurgency, the late Bernard Fall, concluded that the evidence amassed on the guerrilla battlefields of three continents over three decades had demonstrated that popular support was the essential element of successful guerrilla operations.[36]

Although scholars and practitioners have agreed that popular support is important in insurgencies, they have often been vague about what constitutes popular support and how much is necessary for success. For the purposes of this article, popular support is divided into two categories: verbal and active. Verbal support denotes a sympathetic attitude toward the insurgent movement, whereas active support refers to a willingness on the part of individuals to make sacrifices for the insurgents. In the latter category one can place not only active insurgent fighters and those who supply the movement with food, concealment, medical aid, and information, but also those who respond to insurgent calls for strikes, demonstrations, boycotts, and acts of civil disobedience, since all of these actions are undertaken at the risk of punishment by the government. Although active supporters are the most

---

[34] The importance of popular support has been reflected in several well-known aphorisms and clichés, such as Mao's famous statement that "the people are to the guerrillas as water is to fish," and the American characterization of insurgency as a battle "to win the minds and hearts of the people."

[35] Cited in Heilbrunn, *op. cit.*, p. 87.
[36] Fall, *op. cit.*, p. 345.

important in sustaining an insurgency, verbal supporters also are significant, for, if nothing else, they are not apt to betray the insurgents.

Since circumstances vary from one insurgency to another, the amount of popular support necessary for success will differ. For instance, in situations such as Cuba, where the government proves to be very weak and its army is demoralized, the creation of widespread support may not be necessary; on the other hand, if, as in the French–Viet Minh conflict, the government persists and its army continues to resist the insurgents, the creation of broad support may be required. Given the variations from case to case, it seems neither wise nor appropriate to deal with percentages of popular support that would be presumed to apply in all cases.[37] Instead, the investigator should focus upon the questions of whether or not the population is providing the kinds of assistance suggested above and whether or not the population is exposing the guerrillas.

In order to obtain active popular support, insurgent organizations must direct their efforts at the intellectuals as well as the masses, since the former are necessary for the crucial political leadership and cadre roles. Indeed, as David Wilson has pointed out, purely peasant rebellions in all eras have been extremely ineffective.[38]

Generally, the revolutionaries will employ five methods to gain the desired support and recruits: (1) esoteric appeals; (2) exoteric appeals; (3) terror; (4) provocation of government counterterror; and, (5) demonstration of potency. All of these, in one way or another, aim at convincing the people to render support because the insurgent's goal is both just and achievable.

Esoteric Appeals

Esoteric appeals are primarily directed at the intellectuals and focus on ideological ex-

planations of the situation. Ideological appeals are often attractive to the intellectuals because they offer answers to a number of questions that the latter are apt to be concerned with. As Gabriel Almond has noted, ideology imputes a particular structure to political action, defines who or what the main initiators of action are (whether they be individuals, status groups, classes, nations, magical forces, or deities), attributes specific roles to these actors, describes their relationships with one another, and defines the arena in which actions occur.[39] In short, ideology provides an ordering and interpretation of political phenomena that appeals to many intellectuals who are searching for definite, complex, and coherent answers.

Even though the esoteric appeal is primarily directed at the intellectuals, it is not totally unrelated to the support of the masses, because the latter often need to have their discontent focused on a real villain if they are to be mobilized for action. One of the functions of ideology, the identification of friend and foe, fulfills this need.[40] Indeed, identifying the source of frustration and grievances is important because "discontented people act aggressively only when they become aware of the supposed source of frustration, or something or someone with whom they associate frustration."[41]

Thus, while the ideological-esoteric appeal is usually directed at the intelligentsia, its partial relevance to the masses should not be overlooked. Moreover, doctrinal justifications for violence can themselves increase discontent by increasing and raising expectations and defending violence as a means to their attainment. This, of course, presupposes that there are existent grievances—the exoteric feature—because "men's susceptibility to these beliefs is a function of the intensity of their discontent."[42]

Exoteric Appeals

Exoteric appeals are those which center on the concrete grievances held by the intellec-

[37] For a study which does deal with percentage figures see Andrew R. Molnar, James M. Tinker, and John D. LeNoir, "Human Factors Considerations of Undergrounds in Insurgencies" (Washington, D.C.: Center for Research in Social Systems, The American University, December 1966), p. 64.

[38] David A. Wilson, "Nation Building and Revolutionary War" (Santa Monica, Calif.: The RAND Corporation, September 1962), p. 7; see also Gil Carl Alroy, "The Involvement of Peasants in Internal Wars," Research Monograph no. 24 (Princeton: Center for International Studies, Princeton University, 1966), pp. 16–19; Gurr, *op. cit.*, p. 337.

[39] Gabriel Almond, *The Appeals of Communism* (Princeton: Princeton University Press, 1954), p. 66; for a similar scheme see Morris Watnick, "The Appeal of Communism to the Underdeveloped Peoples," in *Political Change in Underdeveloped Countries*, ed. John H. Kautsky (New York: John Wiley & Sons, 1962).

[40] Gurr, *op. cit.*, p. 205.
[41] *Ibid.*, p. 199.
[42] *Ibid.*, p. 198.

tuals, by the masses, or by both. Examples of intellectuals' complaints are unemployment, underemployment, and lack of political or economic power. Grievances of the masses vary from situation to situation and may involve such matters as poverty, lack of jobs, medical services and other social benefits, and land reform. For the revolutionary leadership it is important that the popular grievances be discerned and exploited, even if they deviate from long-range goals. In Mao's words:

In all practical work of our party, correct leadership can only be developed on the principle of "from the masses to the masses." This means summing up (i.e., co-ordinating and systematizing after careful study) the views of the masses (i.e., views scattered and unsystematic), then taking the resulting ideas back to the masses, explaining and popularizing them until the masses embrace the ideas as their own, stand up for them and translate them into action by way of testing their correctness.[43]

It is likely that the grievances of the intellectuals and the masses will overlap at certain points, since both groups may be frustrated by such matters as lack of jobs, denial of land, and repressive measures undertaken by the government. In these instances the successful insurgent movement will emphasize the grievances, blame the regime, and argue that they will be redressed if the revolution succeeds.

Nationalism is often a key factor related to grievances that can be employed to attract mass and intellectual support and to solidify the two. After reviewing several insurgencies, Paul Kecskemeti of the RAND Corporation noted that

all the populations in question experienced either the denial of their aspirations to national independence or an extreme threat to their national existence and integrity. Nationalist motivations, then, seem intimately connected with the phenomenon of "subversive insurgency," although the role they have played has varied from one case to another.[44]

Terror

Where the esoteric and exoteric appeals are not sufficient to convince the people to support the revolution, terror can be employed to obtain the required support, or at least the acquiescence, of the population. Furthermore, terror can function to keep the guerrillas themselves loyal and to demoralize the government by demonstrating its weaknesses as compared to guerrilla strength. All of this has led some scholars to argue that terror is the most powerful weapon for establishing community support.[45] Roger Trinquier, for example, called it the principal weapon of modern warfare (revolutionary warfare) and suggested that by making the people feel insecure it causes them to lose confidence in the government and to be drawn to the guerrillas for protection.[46]

In contrast to Trinquier, others have argued that, since terror is generally employed in situations where the terrain is insufficient for guerrilla warfare and/or authorities exercise effective control over an entire area, it is a weapon of weakness.[47] A third school of thought on terror is represented by Jerry Silverman and Peter Jackson, who argue that, while terror should be de-emphasized as the revolutionary war proceeds, it can be used in an early stage of the insurgency to arouse potential support and sympathy.

One factor that can be decisive in determining the people's attitude is the target of terror. If terror is aimed at individuals or groups despised by the people, it can facilitate the identification of the revolutionaries with the suppressed and exploited elements. By manipulating resentment (based on grievances) and using selective terror against hated individuals and groups, the insurgents may well be able to increase popular support. Such was the case in the Cypriot insurrection against the British. On the other hand, if, at the outset, potential support is low, terror can create hostility.[48]

Terrorist actions directed at the majority of the population will bring into question the effectiveness of terrorism. As Silverman and Jackson contend:

The level of toleration for sabotage and bru-

[43] Mao Tse-tung, "On Methods of Leadership," *Selected Works*, vol. 4 (New York: International Publishers, 1958), p. 113.

[44] P. Kecskemeti, "Insurgency as a Strategic Problem" (Santa Monica, Calif.: The RAND Corporation, February 1967), pp. 15–16; reprinted in *American Defense Policy*, ed. Mark E. Smith III and Claude J. Johns, Jr., 2nd ed. (Baltimore: The Johns Hopkins Press, 1968), pp. 279–93.

[45] See, for example, Ney, *op. cit.*, pp. 32–33.
[46] Trinquier, *op. cit.*, pp. 16–17.
[47] McCuen, *op. cit.*, p. 32; Paget, *op. cit.*, p. 28.
[48] Jerry M. Silverman and Peter M. Jackson, "Terror in Insurgency Warfare," *Military Review*, October 1970, pp. 62–64.

tality is reduced as terrorism upsets the traditional life patterns of the population and renders that life increasingly miserable. To maintain what support they have, terrorists employ a program of harassment and discriminatory murder directed at known informants and uncooperative officials.[49]

Time may be an important consideration here, for the failure to replace terror with regular operations can create the impression that the guerrillas have lost the initiative and thus can diminish support for the revolutionary movement. Likewise, excesses in terror may prove counterproductive to the primary aim of terror—obtaining verbal or active popular support.

Counterterror

A fourth means which the insurgent utilizes in winning popular support lies in "catalyzing and intensifying counterterror which further alienates the enemy from the local population."[50] In other words, the guerrillas seek to provoke the government into carrying out reprisals against the people, which, in turn, will increase resentment and win the insurrectionary forces more adherents and support. While ruthless methods by the government may restore law and order in the short run, their long-term effect may be to provide the seeds for further insurgency.[51] The treatment of the Bengali population in East Pakistan by the Pakistani army in 1971 exemplifies the latter.

Demonstrations of Potency

The final but by no means least significant means the guerrilla employs to establish popular support, demonstration of potency, has two dimensions: retaining the military initiative and meeting the needs of the people through social services and a governing apparatus. The latter aspect clearly impresses the people because it demonstrates not only the reality of the guerrilla presence but the corresponding government failure to deal with shadow government political cadres. Besides governing, guerrilla political operators will seek to meet

some of the people's basic needs and to cooperate with them in such mundane affairs as accomplishing the daily chores.[52] Quite often the extension of such aid to the people will be the first step in involving them with the revolutionary movement, either actively or passively. This would seem to be especially true in those contexts where the regime has been delinquent in meeting the people's needs or is repressive.

The second feature of demonstration of potency is gaining the military initiative, by which the insurgent seeks to create the impression that the revolution has momentum and will succeed. A number of writers have stressed the importance of initiative to the guerrillas because, in addition to winning adherents for the movement, it boosts and sustains morale within the revolutionary organization itself. "Units that are active and successful in the accomplishment of assigned missions build a high esprit de corps and attract followers; success is contagious," writes George B. Jordan. Putting it another way, Paget suggests that "no guerrilla movement in the field can afford to remain inactive for long; by so doing it loses its morale and sense of purpose."[53]

Military initiative will require continuous local victories. Since the guerrilla is usually weak at the outset of hostilities, these may be only small successes, but such tactical self-sacrifice at the beginning may be necessary for eventual victory.[54] Local victories in a guerrilla war, however, are heavily dependent upon popular support; hence initiative and popular support are mutually reinforcing.

ORGANIZATION

Achievement of popular support is closely related to another major factor, organization. When examining an insurgent organization three structural dimensions—scope, complexity, and cohesion—and two functions—provision of

---

[49] *Ibid.*, p. 64; see also Gurr, *op. cit.*, p. 355.

[50] J. K. Zawodny, "Unconventional Warfare," in *Problems of National Strategy*, pp. 340–41; see also Paget, *op. cit.*, p. 23; Fall, *op. cit.*, pp. 348–52; and Brian Crozier, "The Study of Conflict" (London: The Institute for the Study of Conflict, October 1970), p. 9.

[51] Clutterbuck, *op. cit.*, pp. 178–79.

[52] Molnar, Tinker, and LeNoir, *op. cit.*, p. 109; see also Vo Nguyen Giap, *People's War, People's Army* (New York: Bantam Books, 1968), p. 50.

[53] George B. Jordan, "Objectives and Methods of Communist Guerrilla Warfare," in *Modern Guerrilla Warfare*, pp. 404, 409; Paget, *op. cit.*, p. 22; McCuen, *op. cit.*, p. 20; Hyde, *op. cit.*, p. 123; Heilbrunn, *op. cit.*, pp. 60–61, 67, 68.

[54] Edward L. Katzenbach, Jr., and Gene Z. Hanrahan, "The Revolutionary Strategy of Mao Tse-tung," in *Modern Guerrilla Warfare*, pp. 144–45.

instrumental services and channels for expressive protest—are of primary interest.[55]

Scope

Scope refers to the proportion of the population which participates in the insurgent organization. As suggested earlier, the greater the participation, the more the insurgency takes on the character of an internal war as opposed to a conspiracy. The essential point to remember here is that organizational institutions or structures must be created if potential supporters in the population are to be mobilized to assist the insurgent effort.[56]

Complexity

If the organization is to increase its membership, it must, through the efforts of its political operators, penetrate the hamlets, villages, and cities, especially in the contested areas. In so doing it seeks to create a parallel hierarchy that rivals government institutions. The parallel hierarchy can take two forms: the use of existing administrative structures through the infiltration of subversive individuals; or the creation of new clandestine structures designed to take over full administrative responsibility when military-political conditions are appropriate.[57] Moreover, the insurgent movement may go beyond the government structures that it seeks to imitate and increase the complexity of the organization by creating functional units in order to involve more people in the movement. Examples of such additions would be youth groups, peasant associations, workers' groups, women's organizations, and so forth.[58] The aim is to widen the participation in the movement by integrating these auxiliaries with the main organizational structures and terming the new entity a front. The effectiveness of winning adherents by increasing the differentiation of the organization was manifested in the Philippines, where many joined the Huks through front organizations, often without even knowing party aims.[59]

In addition to the differentiation of political structures, the insurgent movement must also diversify its military organization by creating logistical units, terrorist networks, and guerrilla forces, with the last-mentioned being divided into full-time and part-time fighters. The former, operating from secure bases, carry out attacks against government military units and installations on a continuous basis and will form the nucleus of a regularized force if the movement progresses to mobile-conventional warfare. The part-time or local guerrillas, on the other hand, stay in their communities and provide a number of invaluable services, such as collecting intelligence, storing supplies, and providing a coercive arm to protect the political organizers. In addition, the local guerrillas can attach themselves to main-force units for local attacks, either as combatants or in the capacity of scouts and guides.[60]

The continual functioning of both the parallel hierarchies and the military units may itself convert people by simply demonstrating the insurgents' ability to control an area in defiance of the government (a linkage between demonstration of potency and organization). Such differentiation is particularly important in situations where the regime is reasonably strong.

Cohesion

Cohesion, the third structural aspect of organization, refers to the extent of goal consensus and cooperative interaction among members of an insurgent movement.[61] While unity is an important consideration in an insurgency—some writers treat it as a separate

[55] While the above categorization is Gurr's, a number of other writers have discussed these aspects. See, for example, the already cited Molnar, Tinker, and LeNoir study.

[56] Gurr, op. cit., pp. 279–84. The importance of organization is reflected in two hypotheses suggested by Gurr: (1) the likelihood of internal war increases as the level of dissident to regime institutional support reaches equality; and (2) dissident institutional support varies strongly with the proportion of the population belonging to dissident organizations.

[57] See Fall, op. cit., pp. 130–38; McCuen, op. cit., pp. 31, 33–35; Clutterbuck, op. cit., p. 22, 56, 87–88; Heilbrunn, op. cit., pp. 26–29; Paget, op. cit., pp. 20–21; and Hyde, op. cit., pp. 92, 126.

[58] For commentaries on auxiliary organizations see Fall, op. cit., p. 134; McCuen, op. cit., pp. 34–35; and, especially, Pike, op. cit., chap. 10.

[59] Tirona, op. cit., p. 204; Hyde, op. cit., pp. 90–91.

[60] On the question of military differentiation see Ney, op. cit., pp. 35–36; Heilbrunn, op. cit., p. 25; James E. Dougherty, "The Guerrilla War in Malaya," in Modern Guerrilla Warfare, p. 302; and Pike, op. cit., chap. 13. For a discussion of several possibilities of the relationship between the civilian and military wings of insurgencies see Heilbrunn, op. cit., pp. 24–27.

[61] Gurr, op. cit., p. 285.

major factor[62]—disunity has not always been an insuperable obstacle to success. Despite ideological divisions and internecine violence between the FLN and MNA in Algeria and the Tito and Mihailovitch factions in Yugoslavia, both the FLN and Tito achieved their political goals. However, in each case other major developments offset the lack of cohesion. In Algeria it was the lack of French resolve to stay on, despite the fact that the military aspect of the insurrection was brought under control, that enabled the FLN to succeed, while in Yugoslavia it was the thrust of the Allied armies (an external support input) that defeated the Germans and created a power vacuum in the country.[63] It seems, therefore, that, if the regime loses its will or if outside forces intervene in a substantial way, insurgent disunity need not be a critical failing. On the other hand, where the regime is strong, the insurgents court disaster by fighting among themselves and failing to coordinate their efforts.[64]

Besides providing a clear sense of direction for the insurgents and a basis for coordinating the political and military aspects of strategy, cohesion is also important if segments of the movement are to avoid working at cross-purposes, if the movement is to avoid the loss of valuable human and material resources as a result of internecine conflict, and if the movement is to avoid jeopardizing its needs vis-à-vis other major factors such as popular and external support.

A striking example of the deleterious and far-reaching effects of disunity has been provided by the Palestine Liberation Movement (PLM) in the Middle East.[65] In that case ideological, personal, and tactical differences among the guerrilla groups resulted in the diversion of resources and attention from the principal enemy, Israel, and seriously damaged the PLM's image in the eyes of both the local Arab population and the leaders of potential external support states. No doubt more significant was the fact that the ideological hostility of left-wing groups toward the regimes of vital sanctuary states—Syria, Lebanon, and especially Jordan—led these countries to restrict guerrilla activities severely and, in the case of Jordan, to inflict serious military and material losses on the PLM. All of this, of course, alleviated the burden on the Israeli counterinsurgency forces. In short, disunity not only resulted in substantial losses of existing resources and precluded the PLM from having a sense of direction but it also undercut efforts to weaken the target regime and to obtain popular and external support.

In situations where rival organizations do exist, the achievement of cohesion becomes more difficult, although not theoretically impossible. Three possibilities for cooperative interaction exist: a unified command for a particular operation, division of labor among the organizations, and a general unified command.[66] Of the three, the last appears to be the most promising, since it is more conducive to giving the regime a sense of strategic direction and for dealing with the ideological, tactical, and personal differences which divide the movement in the first place. For a unified command to be successful, however, the rival organizations must agree to subordinate their parochial interests to the overall interests of the movement, as defined by the unified command. If the unified command's decisions are to be considered authoritative and legitimate, the rival groups must reach a consensus on the mechanics of the decisionmaking process and on methods for invoking sanctions against de-

---

[62] Ney, *op. cit.*, p. 30, treats unity as a separate issue.

[63] The Zionists in Israel succeeded in achieving their aims despite splits within their ranks. However, it was Britain's loss of will to retain its mandate in Palestine that offset the divisiveness.

[64] The importance of unity has been noted by a number of scholars and practitioners of insurgency. See, for example, Jordan, *op. cit.*, pp. 403, 407; Campbell, *op. cit.*, p. 85; Regis Debray, *Revolution in the Revolution?* trans. Bobbye Ortiz (New York: Monthly Review Press, 1967), pp. 73–74, 79–80; and McCuen, *op. cit.*, pp. 69–73.

[65] The aim of the Palestinian guerrillas (*fedayeen*), which is constantly reiterated in their documents, is to destroy Zionism. To achieve this goal *fedayeen* documents call for a protracted people's war. Inspiration for their strategy comes from the Cuban, Algerian, Viet Minh, and Chinese revolutionary wars. State-

ments of *fedayeen* aims can be found in *Free Palestine*, 1, no. 1 (September 1970); editorial in *Fatah* (Beirut), November 28, 1971; interview of Abu Ammar (Yasir Arafat) in *Free Palestine*, 2, no. 1 (February 1971). On the strategy of protracted insurgency and the influence of the experiences cited above see the following pamphlets from the Fatah series "Revolutionary Lessons and Trials": *The Chinese Experience* (n.p., August 1967); *The Cuban Experience* (n.p., August 1967); and *The Vietnamese Experience* (n.p., August 1967).

[66] Heilbrunn, *op. cit.*, p. 30.

viationists. As the PLM found out from 1967 to 1972, the creation of supraorganizational structures (the Palestine Armed Struggle Command, the Unified Command of the Palestine Resistance, the Central Committee of the Palestine Resistance, and the present Palestine Liberation Organization Executive Committee) did not provide a sufficient remedy for its lack of unity, because there was an unwillingness on the part of some groups to subordinate their interests to those of the movement as a whole.[67] The Popular Front for the Liberation of Palestine, for example, was never satisfied with the decisionmaking mechanism, because it felt underrepresented, and thus, while it retained nominal membership in the Central Committee, it proceeded to take actions which were contrary to the policies of the Central Committee and which cost the movement heavily.

While the insurgent movement must achieve cohesion and a significant degree of differentiation because of the losses that can result from their absence, the two structural requirements are also important if the insurgent organization is to perform the instrumental and expressive functions that attract adherents.

Functions

The most direct instrumental function of an insurgent organization is to provide members with successful courses of action for direct value satisfaction. Participation can provide intrinsic interpersonal satisfactions, such as comradeship, self-definition, and reinforcement of shared beliefs, provided that members follow the normative prescriptions for conduct in the organization. Membership can also provide for the attainment of power values, in the sense that in stable, effective organizations members can achieve security from external interference. Finally, if the organization has the resources, it can provide welfare values for members. Although material external support and control of base areas by dissidents facilitates the servicing of material needs, most dissident organizations lack the capability to meet economic demands. To compensate, great stress is placed on the psychosocial needs for status, communality, and ideational coherence.[68]

For a discontented individual the immediate instrumental function of joining an organization is to increase his value opportunities—that is, the courses of action open to him for attaining his desired value position. If the new means fail to provide a sense of progress and also fail to give such compensatory satisfactions as status, communality, and participation, organizational conflict, division, and desertion are likely.[69] A lack of progress in toppling the regime, however, need not have such results, because most members of dissident groups are intensely hostile to the government and hence intrinsically value opposition to it. Provision for means of expressing hostility is thus an important function for rebel organizations.[70]

EXTERNAL SUPPORT

External support, another factor which has often been important in insurgencies, has three dimensions: (1) material aid; (2) sanctuaries; and (3) intangible moral and political support.

Material Support

Material support consists of such things as weapons, medical supplies, and food. It becomes especially important as the insurgency progresses toward mobile-conventional warfare, a development which usually necessitates greater logistical inputs.[71] While prior to this period the guerrilla may rely on the populace or on items captured from the enemy for his sustenance, the advent of large-unit warfare usually renders these sources inadequate. The North Vietnamese decision to move into mobile-conventional warfare in 1965–1966, for example, required the establishment of an elaborate logistical system stretching through Cambodia and Laos to North Vietnam and substantial Russian and Chinese economic and military assistance. Although the greatest volume of aid may come from distant states, it is important that a state or states adjacent to the territory being contested be friendly enough to allow the supplies to reach the insurgents

---

[67] All the *fedayeen* organizations agree with the general aim of liberating all of Palestine—including Israel—from Zionist control. When it comes to the structural and ideological basis of the new Palestine, however, there is sharp disagreement between the left wing and the moderates.

[68] Gurr, *op. cit.*, pp. 297–300.
[69] *Ibid.*, p. 301.
[70] *Ibid.*, pp. 303–4.
[71] It stands to reason that larger units, which fight longer and bigger battles, will require more supplies than guerrilla formations.

through their territory. The fact that the Philippines were an island nation was one reason why the Huks could not get substantial Chinese and Russian assistance.[72]

Sanctuary Support

In addition to being a supply funnel, contiguous states may be important as sanctuaries in which the revolutionaries can be trained, arms stockpiled, operations planned, leadership secured, and perhaps a provisional government established.[73] Indeed, Fall, in his most celebrated book, *Street Without Joy*, wrote that, "in brutal fact, the success or failure of all rebellions since World War II depended entirely on whether the active sanctuary was willing and able to perform its expected role."[74]

While both aid and sanctuaries are usually more important in the later stages of an insurgency, the insurgents' failure to establish a secure base in the target country and a lack of popular support may make these factors indispensable early in the struggle. With such an inauspicious start the insurgents are literally forced to rely on adjacent countries, since, at a minimum, security and freedom of movement must be guaranteed if the revolutionaries are ever to set up bases, organize the people, and obtain popular support in the target country.[75]

Besides allowing its territory to be used by the insurgents for logistical and sanctuary

needs, the host country may directly help the insurgents. This help can include the provision of intelligence, fire support, use of advisers, and deployment of ground forces in support of the insurgents. However, since the last possibility runs the risk of transforming the war from a revolutionary type to an interstate type, host states are likely to avoid such a commitment.

Moral and Political Support

In addition to aid and sanctuaries the insurgents may also seek to gain moral (acknowledgment of the legitimacy of the insurgency) and political (backing of the insurgents' political aims in the diplomatic arena) support from the states that comprise the international system. The search for such support may also extend to groups within nations—including the target state—that are perceived to have the potential to influence their government's position on the conflict. An example would be the Viet Minh propaganda efforts aimed at the French Left during the first Indochina war.

As experience has demonstrated, it would be a great mistake to underestimate the importance of intangible external support. In a long, tiresome struggle against a wavering regime, particularly a colonial one, it may be the straw that breaks the camel's back and impels the government to give up the struggle. In such a case a colonial regime may withdraw to the *metropole* rather than face a chorus of international criticism. Algeria is a case in point.

If the insurgent movement is to obtain external support, it must first gain the attention of outside states. While dramatic gestures such as skyjacking may be used, they need to be followed by more substantial and rewarding actions if the movement is to gain respectability. This, in turn, puts a premium on guerrilla successes against the regime, good organization, and demonstrable popular support.

While the types of external support discussed thus far are very often important to the fortunes of insurgent movements, there have been cases in which only low-level outside help has been sufficient. In these instances one usually finds that the guerrillas have benefited from a favorable position vis-à-vis the other success criteria, such as a weak regime or substantial popular support. Such a case was the Castro revolution in Cuba, during which the

---

[72] On the importance of external support see Ney, *op. cit.*, pp. 31–32; Campbell, *op. cit.*, p. 21; Paget, *op. cit.*, p. 25; Gurr, *op. cit.*, pp. 269–70; Bernard B. Fall, *Street Without Joy* (Harrisburg, Pa.: Stackpole, 1963), p. 294.

[73] On the importance of sanctuaries see Ney, *op. cit.*, p. 29; McCuen, *op. cit.*, p. 37; Trinquier, *op. cit.*, pp. 97–98; Clutterbuck, *op. cit.*, p. 7; Heilbrunn, *op. cit.*, pp. 60–61.

[74] Fall, *Street Without Joy*, p. 294; for a different view see J. J. Zasloff, "The Role of the Sanctuary in Insurgency: Communist China's Support to the Vietminh, 1946–1954" (Santa Monica, Calif.: The RAND Corporation, May 1967), p. 80. For cases in which the denial of sanctuary privileges was credited as being a key factor in the defeat of the insurgents see McCuen, *op. cit.*, p. 302; Trinquier, *op. cit.*, p. 98; Campbell, *op. cit.*, p. 80; and J. C. Murray, "The Anti-Bandit War," in *The Guerrilla—And How to Fight Him*, ed. T. N. Greene (New York: Praeger, 1964), p. 74.

[75] Sarawak is a case in point. See Hyde, *op. cit.*, pp. 86–88. The Israelis' ability to contain terrorism and to force guerrillas out of the occupied areas by late 1969 meant that the *fedayeen* were forced to rely on sanctuaries in the adjacent states, especially the "pillar" base in Jordan.

insurgents did not have a contiguous friendly country that could function as a sanctuary or logistics area, although they did receive some arms via flights from Mexico, Venezuela, and the United States.[76] Given the inept, corrupt, and indecisive government and a demoralized army, however, this level of aid was sufficient to help topple the Batista regime and to obviate the need for a protracted guerrilla war along the lines of the Chinese and Vietnamese models.

ENVIRONMENT

The fifth major variable used to assess an insurgency is environment. This includes terrain, the road and communications network, ethnicity, religion and culture, the size of the country, and the quantity and distribution of the people.

Terrain

Rugged terrain—vast mountains, jungles, swamps, forests, and the like—is usually related to successful guerrilla operations because it hinders movement by government forces and provides inaccessible hideouts for the guerrillas' main bases. As A. H. Shollom aptly put it:

One of the main factors contributing to the development of a partisan movement was the presence of suitable terrain in which to operate. We include in such terrain: swamps, mountains and forests where mobility is limited to movements on foot and in light vehicles. The fact that the partisan operates in such terrain will be to his advantage for in an environment of this nature the regular forces lose the use of their vehicles and artillery as well as the ability to mass superior members. In essence, the terrain reduces the better equipped, better trained, and better armed regular force to a level where the partisan is its equal. It has been estimated that approximately 5,000 communist partisans in Malaya were being hunted by 230,000 popular soldiers and police, a seemingly overwhelming majority, but the jungle is the equalizer. In this jungle it took 1,000 man-hours of patrolling to make one contact with the partisans and 1,500 man-hours for each partisan killed. In open terrain the future of these partisans would be something less than secure.[77]

Deserts have in the past proven to be advantageous areas for guerrilla operations, one such case being the Arab revolt led by the legendary T. E. Lawrence from 1916 to 1918.[78] However, with the advent and development of air surveillance and attack, the guerrilla has become susceptible to detection and destruction in open desert areas.[79]

Size

Along with the make-up of the terrain one must consider its extensiveness. If favorable areas for guerrilla operations and bases are small, they can be easily isolated and penetrated; if, on the other hand, the area is vast and the guerrillas take advantage of this by expanding the space their operations cover, regime administration will be complicated, fire-power concentration reduced, and supervision of the populace made more difficult.[80]

The importance of terrain is further accentuated by the fact that geography is a key consideration in the establishment of the guerrilla bases that are so important in protracted conflicts.[81] As noted earlier, it is in the base areas that the guerrillas first establish the parallel hierarchy that rules the population, and from these the insurgents seek to expand into areas partially controlled by the government.

Transportation-Communications System

Another aspect of the environment that can have an important bearing on the fortunes of an insurgency is the state of the transportation-communications system. Suffice it to say that, if this system is highly developed and extensive, the government forces are favored because they can move about expeditiously and make better use of their technological superiority.

Demography

The size and distribution of the population will also have an impact on the insurgency. Where the number of people is small and they are concentrated, it will be easier for the government to control the populace and sever

---

[76] Chapelle, *op. cit.*, pp. 333–34.

[77] A. H. Shollom, "Nowhere Yet Everywhere," in *Modern Guerrilla Warfare*, p. 19. Others have also cited the importance of rugged terrain for guerrilla operations. See, for example, Ney, *op. cit.*, p. 28; Trinquier, *op. cit.*, pp. 63–65; Paget, *op. cit.*, p. 21; and Heilbrunn, *op. cit.*, pp. 46–47.

[78] Campbell, *op. cit.*, p. 49.

[79] Campbell, *op. cit.*, p. 283.

[80] C. E. S. Dudley, "Subversive Warfare: Five Military Factors," *The Army Quarterly and Defence Journal*, July 1968, p. 209.

[81] On the question of bases see Heilbrunn, *op. cit.*, p. 45; McCuen, *op. cit.*, p. 30; Jordan, *op. cit.*, p. 406.

its links with the insurgents. In the case of a large and dispersed population, the government will have to either undertake extensive resettlement or use a large force to prevent the guerrillas from establishing themselves.[82]

Linking topography and demography, Gurr has argued that it is important that the inaccessible rugged areas contain a population that either supports the insurgent cause or is neutral.[83] All this, of course, relates to the earlier point about the importance of popular support. The importance of population concentrations in rugged hinterland areas lies in the fact that government control is hampered there while insurgent control is facilitated.

The location of the bulk of the people in cities is not favorable to the development of a guerrilla threat, since government control is easier and the establishment of guerrilla bases next to impossible. Nevertheless, cities are conducive to terrorism, and, in situations where the government is wavering and the insurgents have international support, that is all that may be required for the achievement of insurgent aims (e.g., Cyprus, Ulster?).

Societal Cohesion

Societal cleavages such as ethnicity, race, religion, and language may also be helpful to insurgents. This would seem to be especially true where the majority of the population is from the same group as the insurgents, while the regime members are not. Although colonial governments are classical examples of this, it may also be true in independent states ruled by minority factions. Even where this dichotomy exists, however, the insurgents will be required to undertake a substantial political effort to actualize the potential support.

SUMMARY

As the above discussion indicates, insurgency is a complicated and multifaceted phenomenon, the success of which depends on a number of interrelated factors. Thus, if an interested student wishes to arrive at a comprehensive understanding and some meaningful conclusions about a given case, he must be prepared to assess the problem in its totality— that is, in light of the five variables identified in this essay. Since both the government and environmental variables have a determinative effect on the length of the insurgency and on the insurgents' needs vis-à-vis the popular support, organizational, and external support factors, they should receive careful attention at the outset. In situations where the government is very strong and the environment is not conducive to guerrilla warfare, the insurgents must do an excellent job in relation to popular support, organization, and external support. Whether such excellence can be achieved in such a context is doubtful, however. On the other hand, in cases where the government is very weak at the outset of hostilities (e.g., Cuba), the insurgents' needs may not be very substantial.

Occupying the middle of the spectrum are a number of cases, such as the Sudan, Burma, Ethiopia, and Vietnam, wherein the government response is uneven and at least part of the environment is conducive to the various forms of insurgency warfare. Although the potential for eventual success clearly exists in these situations, it will take a great deal of effort on the part of the insurgents (in relation to popular support, organization, and external support) to actualize such potential.

For the analyst, the third general type of situation is the one which poses the greatest intellectual challenge, given the dynamic relationships among all five factors and their subfactors. The investigator must be prepared to assiduously examine each dimension and to ascertain the effects that the various dimensions have on one another at specific points in time. Hopefully, this essay, by orienting the reader toward the most significant issues to be investigated, will facilitate such an undertaking.

---

[82] Dudley, op. cit., p. 208; Campbell, op. cit., p. 283.

[83] Gurr, op. cit., pp. 264–65.

REVOLUTIONARY AND COUNTERREVOLUTIONARY WAR: SOME POLITICAL AND STRATEGIC LESSONS FROM THE FIRST INDOCHINA WAR AND ALGERIA

JEAN BAECHLER

Baechler presents an integrated examination of two insurgency cases and analyzes them from the perspectives of political goals and military strategies. He stresses that the prime objectives of the insurrection are the quests for sovereignty and legitimacy, while the established government seeks to maintain moral authority and a unified political objective. The insurgent in a colonial country knows that the center of gravity of the enemy is not the expeditionary force but the mother country; the government must know that the center of gravity of the enemy is not the insurgent army but the entire indigenous population. Professor Baechler received his degree in history at the University of Paris in 1962, and in 1966 he joined the National Scientific Research Center (Sociological Section). His principal publications include The Politics of Trotsky *(1968) and* Revolutionary Phenomena *(1970).*

As is true of all discrete historical occurrences, the French experiences with revolutionary war in Indochina and in Algeria have their own uniqueness.[1] These wars, however, also illustrate well-known, generally applicable maxims systematized by Clausewitz. Three of his concepts appear particularly relevant to our analysis of revolutionary war:

1. War is a duel between two protagonists,

but within each camp one must distinguish three levels of interaction: the combatant forces, the domestic politics of the antagonists, and the actions and reactions of the international community. This distinction means that political dynamics are much more operative in revolutionary wars than in classical conventional wars.

2. Two grand strategies are possible: the attack, which aims at winning the war; and the defense, which seeks not to lose it. In revolutionary war, the defense enjoys a decisive superiority over the attack.

3. War is the continuation of policy by other means; and one must carefully distinguish the political end from the military objective. In revolutionary wars especially, the political goal must *always* determine the military objective.

Revolutionary wars, in contrast to classical conventional wars, are wholly social phenomena, and analysis requires some consideration of the social systems of the antagonists. As in all wars, the strategies of the antagonists are dialectically linked; the strategy of the one de-

[1] There is an extensive bibliography for the two wars: Yves Courrière, *La Guerre d'Algérie*: vol. 1, *Les Fils de la Toussaint* (Paris: Fayard, 1968); vol. 2, *Le Temps des Leopards* (1969); vol. 3, *L'Heure des Colonels* (1970). I have consulted the following sources for Viet Minh accounts: Nguyen Giap, *L'Armée Populaire de Liberation du Viet Nam* (Hanoi, 1952); *Dien Bien Phu* (Hanoi, 1959); *Guerre du Peuple, Armée du Peuple* (Hanoi, 1961). For the French point of view, see M. Bigeard, *Contre-Guerrilla* (Algiers: Bacconnier, n.d.); L. Bodard, *La Guerre d'Indochine*, 3 vols. (Paris: Gallimard, n.d.); G. Bonnet, *Les Guerres Insurrectionelles et Révolutionnaires* (Paris: Payot, 1958); Bernard Fall, *Guerres d'Indochine* (Paris: Robert Laffont, 1970); P. Langlais, *Dien Bien Phu* (Paris: Empire, 1963); P. Rolland, *Contre Guerrilla* (Paris: Louvois, 1956); J. Roy, *La Bataille de Dien Bien Phu* (Paris: Juilliard, 1963); and R. Trinquier, *La Guerre Moderne* (Paris: Table Ronde, 1961).

termines that of the other. Because of the three levels of interaction, however, the revolutionary battlefield is much more complex. Yet, the most persistent error of the French authorities in the field was to disregard the strategy of the other side or, worse, to sneer at it. The purpose of this article is to analyze the military and political strategies of the insurgents and of the established authorities. We begin with insurrection, for it is insurrection which decides the stakes of war and establishes the ground rules of the struggle.

INSURRECTION: THE POLITICAL GOALS

THE QUEST FOR SOVEREIGNTY

The quest for sovereignty and legitimacy is the logical cause and end of the whole insurrectional movement. Indeed, the mainspring of the process of decolonization has been the will to reconquer or to define a national or ethnic identity. Such an identity, however, is guaranteed only from the moment the former colony has the advantage of full and complete sovereignty. Internally, sovereignty is defined by the possibility of establishing a legitimate political, economic, and social system without foreign interference; externally, it is defined by the possibility of freely choosing a place in the international system. Whatever the initial level of demands—equal rights with the French, internal autonomy, independence with special ties, or total independence—and regardless of whether the mother country yields to or represses these demands with force, the quest for sovereignty is inevitable. Therefore, it is wrong to believe that the eventual fulfillment of certain Indochinese or (especially) Algerian demands would have enabled the French to keep these people under their control. It is certain that these colonies would have achieved sovereignty anyway.

The pursuit of sovereignty in no way prejudices the nature of the socio-political system that will be set up, or the international alignment of the new political unit. The choices are open, and consequently are determined by other factors. The principal factor is war itself; what is probable is that the longer and harsher the war, the more *extremist* the regime which will finally take over from the colonialists will be.

THE CONQUEST OF THE PEOPLE

Conquest of the people will result, at best, in the active support, at worst, in the neutrality, of most of the population. This conquest is a technical necessity imposed by the initial disproportion of the contending forces. Lest they perish from logistical asphyxiation or be limited to sporadic blows, the insurgents must be able to rely on the complicity of the majority of the people and on the rallying of activists. The neutrality of the population poses no problem. Aside from minorities and the assimilated (for example, the Algerian veterans of the two world wars and the Algerian and Indochinese social strata which were completely Francophile), the population constitutes a source of implicit support for the insurgents.

Indeed, even if we were to suppose that a population could ever be induced to identify with its conqueror, French colonization was too short and too superficial to achieve this empathy. Consciousness of the difference of the Other and of his menacing character never fades away. The intermittent reappearance of insurrections from the earliest days of colonization proves that colonization is the imposition of an order which is essentially unstable. As a result, the apparent neutrality of the population has every chance of transforming itself into active support from the moment the insurgents successfully convince the people that they are able to win. From this point on, revolutionary vocations will multiply (especially among the youth and students) and a snowball phenomenon of activism will occur. Participation in the liberation movement begins in the ranks of the elite inherited from the old regime as well as in the ranks of the new elite born from contact with the West. Together these elites suffer most directly from the limitations of colonialization but are in the best position to determine opportunities to construct a strategy for liberation.

The mobilization of the masses—composed essentially of the traditional peasantry—poses more difficult problems. With important exceptions—for example, on the plantations—the masses do not suffer directly from colonialization. On the contrary, the masses were probably dissatisfied with the prevailing order even before colonialization. This is particularly valid in reference to Indochina, where the political and social system rested on the subjugation and exploitation of an overabundant and miserable peasantry. The insurgents are therefore confronted with the enormous task of convincing the masses that the struggle is social as well as national. And for the peasantry social combat means a struggle for land. This is why the essential point of the insurgents' program is agrarian land reform and why a war for national liberation necessarily becomes a revolutionary war.

Armed insurrection is constantly accompanied by intense *political* agitation among the masses, with all that this signifies: a deepening of social cleavages in the countryside, violent elimination of opponents, rigorous mobilization of the population by activists, and—where the absence of the colonialists allows it—the setting up of a politico-administrative infrastructure that foreshadows the future regime and competes with the incumbents for political legitimacy and control of the people. These activities, however, lead directly to a fundamental socio-political choice which has divisive repercussions among the leaders of the insurrection. Indeed, as long as the goal is simply national independence, unanimity can exist. From the moment the insurgent program adopts political and social aims, ideological and social cleavages will appear and threaten unity. This in turn provides the colonial authorities with the possibility of exploiting these divisions and of trying to gain the support of the most acceptable factions. A group of loyalist ralliers will form, composed for the most part of men who have everything to fear from a social revolution and who will resist any attempt by the insurgents or by the established authorities to impose a social upheaval aimed at mobilizing the masses. Struggles among rebel factions and the settling of accounts among the insurgents also will take place. It is very likely that in this struggle the extremists will finally triumph, and consequently a radicalization of the insurgent movement will take place. This dialectical result is obviously not endogenous, but is entirely determined by the reactions of the established authorities. The longer and harsher the war, the more the consequences of this radicalization reveal themselves.

THE INTERNATIONAL ENVIRONMENT

The Indochinese and Algerian insurgents benefited from direct and indirect outside support, both of which were equally important. Direct help was provided by the bordering countries—China on the one hand, Morocco and especially Tunisia on the other. The insurgents had the opportunity of establishing bases outside the country in order to train, regroup, and form units. They also received, through their sanctuary bases, arms and logistical support which came from all over the world.[2] Indirect support is more subtle and entails, broadly speaking, two strategies. First, it is necessary to insert a wedge between the mother country and its allies. This can be done by convincing them of the illegitimacy of the counterrevolutionary war or by showing them that its pursuit can lead to issues which threaten the international balance of power.[3] Second, it is necessary to alert international public opinion so that its awakening might bring pressure to bear on the adversary: no country, especially a democratic one, can indefinitely neglect the condemnation of world public opinion. For example, the main objective of the blind and bloody attacks in Algiers in 1955 and 1956 was to publicize the existence of the Algerian revolution. An attack carried out in the center of the city of Algiers had a far greater repercussion than a successful ambush deep in the Aures region. Most international public opinion is essentially anticolonialist; but, even if it were not, the natural tendency is to side with the underdog.

Insurrection aims at a clear and simple end toward which it is possible to channel all energies and around which one can hope to rally world opinion. The clarity of the political goal is essential, for politics determine the outcome

[2] To have a powerful and active ally on one's doorstep is essential. Indeed, it enables one to avoid asphyxiation and poses the problem for the established authorities of whether to expand the conflict. The French army set up between Tunisia and Algeria an extremely effective barrier, but this did not prevent the insurrection from spreading.

[3] The first argument was used by Ho Chi Minh with the Americans; for many years, the Americans were convinced that France was engaged in the criminal attempt to keep Indochina within the French Empire. The second argument convinced the Americans that the Algerian War would lead to the Sovietization of the Maghreb.

of the war; a bad or imprecise policy results in an unsuccessful war. As Clausewitz has stated:

Under all circumstances War is to be regarded not as an independent thing, but as a political instrument; and it is only by taking this point of view that we can avoid finding ourselves in opposition to all military history. . . . Now, the first, the grandest, and most decisive act of judgment which the Statesman and General exercises is rightly to understand . . . the War in which he engages and not to take it for something, or to wish to make of it something, which by the nature of its relations it is impossible for it to be. This is, therefore, the first, the most comprehensive, of all strategic questions.[4]

This advice applies to both antagonists, but the insurgents in their exploitation of political advantages establish the ground rules which determine the nature of the revolutionary war.

INSURRECTION: THE MILITARY STRATEGY

THE CENTER OF GRAVITY OF THE ENEMY

The goal of military operations is to disarm the enemy; this is accomplished (materially and/or morally) when his center of gravity is destroyed. The center of gravity varies according to the political regime involved and the type of war. According to Clausewitz:

Alexander had his centre of gravity in his Army, as had Gustavus Adolphus, Charles XII, and Frederick the Great, and the career of any one of them would soon have been brought to a close by the destruction of his fighting force: in States torn by internal dissensions, this centre generally lies in the capital; in small States dependent on greater ones, it lies generally in the Army of these allies; in a confederacy, it lies in the unity of interests; in a national insurrection, in the person of the chief leader, and in public opinion. Against these points the blow must be directed.[5]

In a revolutionary war, the counterinsurgent's center (in these cases that of the French) *is not* the expeditionary force. Indeed, in a revolutionary war the disproportion of forces in favor of the established authorities is such that the destruction of the expeditionary corps is almost impossible. But, in the unlikely event

that this should happen, it would mean that one type of war had been lost; it would still be possible to start another one with new forces from the mother country.[6] France has never waged total war, even in Algeria. An expeditionary corps, which represented only a small proportion of the mobilizable armed forces, was always used.

It is clear that the center of gravity of the counterinsurgent lies in the mother country, and more precisely in the national will to fight. In a pluralistic political system, however, there is inevitably a party which favors negotiation and peace. Consequently, the prime strategy of the insurgents is to try to turn this party into a majority. In order to accomplish this, the insurgents must hold out militarily long enough for war-weariness to develop in the mother country, or else they must inflict enough casualties so that the costs incurred seem disproportionate to the stakes. Using systematic propaganda to take advantage of the natural divisiveness inherent in pluralistic polities, the insurgents must convince a majority in the mother country that two nations are not struggling, but rather that an aspiring nation is resisting an imperialist war faction in the mother country. An appropriate measure is the refusal to bring terrorism into the mother country, for this would then result in the defeat of the peace party. The Algerian FLN found it difficult to accept this principle; some wanted to put France to fire and sword with the help of immigrant workers. There were, for example, several spectacular attacks against the oil installations in Marseilles. Of course, these incidents turned people almost unanimously *against* the FLN.

In the case of a nonhegemonical power like France, its allies represent a secondary center of gravity. The insurgents strive to erode alliance support or transform it into opposition. They can accomplish this by carefully avoiding interference with the interests of the allies and by using diplomatic blackmail.

---

[4] Carl von Clausewitz, *On War*, ed. Anatol Rapoport (London: Pelican Books, 1968), p. 121.
[5] *Ibid.*, p. 389.

[6] Dien Bien Phu was an absurdity from all points of view—especially on the political level, for it meant a double-or-nothing situation. Thus defeat meant the loss of North Vietnam through a war fought by a limited number of professionals and volunteers who did not have the moral support of the mother country. A national awakening to the situation would have been expressed by a massive dispatchment of troops and the start of a new war.

The Strategy of Defense, or the Prevention of Defeat

Because of its initial matériel and numerical inferiority, the insurrection must assume a strategic defensive posture to shield itself and to conserve its offensive capability. As Clausewitz has noted, strategic defense does not mean mere passivity, but a shrewd attempt to extend the offense spatially and temporally:

The idea of wearing out the enemy in a struggle amounts in practice to *a gradual exhaustion of the physical powers and of the will by the long continuance of exertion.*

Now, if we want to overcome the enemy by the duration of the contest, we must content ourselves with as small objects as possible, for it is in the nature of the thing that a great end requires a greater expenditure of force than a small one; but the smallest object that we can propose to ourselves is simple passive resistance, that is a combat without any positive view. In this way, therefore, our means attain their greatest relative value, and therefore the result is best secured. How far now can this negative mode of proceeding be carried? Plainly not to absolute passivity, for mere endurance would not be fighting; and the defensive is an activity by which so much of the enemy's power must be destroyed that he must give up his object. . . . If then the negative purpose, that is the concentration of all the means into a state of pure resistance, affords a superiority in the contest, and if this advantage is enough to *balance* whatever superiority in numbers the adversary may have, then the mere *duration* of the contest will suffice gradually to bring the loss of force on the part of the adversary to a point at which the political object can no longer be an equivalent, a point at which, therefore, he must give up the contest. We see then that this class of means, the wearing out of the enemy, includes the great number of cases in which the weaker resists the stronger.[7]

This defensive strategy of revolutionary war corresponds to several simple maxims of guaranteed efficacy. First, never accept combat with an enemy attacking in force, but retreat before superior force. To illustrate this point one can cite the example in Indochina of the offensive along la Route Coloniale No. 4, along the Chinese border in 1949, or the Battle of the Black River and Hoa Binh (November 14, 1951–February 24, 1952). Any offensive necessarily reaches a climax, after which time plays against the attacker: he must administer occupied territory, disperse his troops, and maintain logistics lines; or he must retreat and risk ambush. The evacuation of the garrison at Cao Bang on la Route Coloniale No. 4 (October 1951) became a disaster. Second, attack only when assured of an absolute superiority. This maxim presupposes that the counterinsurgent has dispersed his forces and that the insurgents can concentrate forces rapidly at any given place. It also implies mobility, freedom of movement, and patience. From it comes the decisive importance to the insurgents of the complicity of the people, a rugged terrain, and dense vegetation. Third, never engage all of one's strength in a single battle. Fourth, break off the combat as soon as it appears that losses are excessive. General Giap ordered a retreat as soon as the losses reached 50 percent of the combatants, no matter what the situation was on the battlefield.

These maxims hold true for the defenders, whatever the level of forces involved. In the adaptation of available forces and armament to the terrain, and in response to the conventional superiority of the counterinsurgents, the defending insurgent has at his disposal a whole gamut of operations, from isolated acts of terrorism, through guerrilla warfare, to mobile warfare using a regular army.[8] One is vanquished only when one recognizes his own defeat; a single active will is all that is needed for the war to continue.

On the whole, the systematic implementation of these rules for the strategic defense compensates for the insurgents' inferiority of means and numbers. Besides, since bravery, skill, and enthusiasm make up for any lack of the characteristic military qualities of a professional army, and since the insurgents know why they are fighting and dying, the insurrection benefits from a decisive superiority in the conduct of the defense.[9] Add this to the insurgents' political advantages. Does this mean they can hope for the same superiority in the attack?

---

[7] Clausewitz, *op. cit.*, p. 128.

[8] In Indochina there were two kinds of war, and they were radically different: in Cochinchina there were terrorist acts and surprise attacks (guerrilla warfare in the strictest sense of the word); in Tonkin, Giap maneuvered regular army divisions. On the other hand, in Algeria, where the disproportion of forces was incomparably greater, only the first type of war was put into effect by the insurgents.

[9] This Clausewitzian truth was completely ignored by the French command.

The Strategy of the Attack, or the Attempt to Win

The strategy of the attack is to take the offensive with the aim of destroying the expeditionary forces of the colonial authorities. To gain victory several conditions must be satisfied. First, it is necessary to assemble insurgent guerrilla forces and to incorporate them into a regular army for the final mobile-war phase. Second, massive outside help in the form of heavy and light weapons must be assured. Third, sanctuaries (mountains, forests) which offer protection from attack, especially from air power, are necessary. Fourth, one must have immediate superior strength to engage in pitched battles, although miscalculation can bring catastrophe. For example, Giap committed a serious error in judgment, which he recognized, by going on the offensive in Tonkin. The battles of Vinh Yen (January 13–17, 1951), of Dong Trieu (March 23–28, 1951), and of Day (May 29–July 18, 1951) resulted in such great slaughters within the ranks that the outcome of the war was put off for several years. For their part, the French disdain of the fighting qualities of the fellahs and the Viet Minh was widespread and led to tragic miscalculations, especially in Indochina. Fifth, the colonial authorities may accept combat for stakes of "double or nothing" in a single battle, but it is unreasonable to assume that the colonialists will stake the outcome of the entire war on a single battle. (The counterinsurgent forces must, from the moment they have lost the initiative, assume in their turn the defensive strategy and avoid decisive combat.) Finally, it is necessary to insure that, if the incumbent has engaged in a double-or-nothing battle and lost, he should not have the will to send another strengthened expeditionary corps. The outcome of the revolutionary war hinges on an imponderable factor—national pride. (Some hegemonical powers have never experienced defeat, and do not realize that defeat is a relative thing.)

It follows from all the above conditions that a decisive victory in a single classical battle is highly improbable (Dien Bien Phu being not a model but an aberration). This is explained by the fact that the counterinsurgent's center of gravity is not the expeditionary corps but the will of the mother country to continue fighting. The logic of the conflict leads the insurgents not to destroy the enemy's army but to convince the politicians that the cost exceeds the stakes. This is difficult when the only stake in the war is prestige, for the defeated counterinsurgent has to find the means to disengage from a futile war without further tarnishing his prestige.

THE ESTABLISHED AUTHORITIES: POLITICAL GOALS

The Political Objective

In Indochina, France was willing initially to grant broad autonomy within the framework of the French Union, and planned to grant independence later—provided it would not benefit a communist regime. In Algeria there was a much greater diversity of objectives. For example, the slogan *Algérie Française* had at least two entirely different meanings: for some it meant a return to the *status quo ante* and the maintenance of colonial privileges; for others it meant that the Moslems were Frenchmen—equals—possessing indefeasible rights.

In general, when the colonial status quo is challenged, there are three possible responses: one merely desires military victory followed by a return to the status quo ante or else a military victory followed by reforms designed to prevent another upheaval; the third answer would be to seek a stalemate by asking for a cease-fire. The latter would be followed by elections and negotiations in order to bring out the various points of view and to reach a compromise. This was the official position of the French government in Algeria from 1956 on. These three alternatives are inevitable, whoever the antagonists might be. If an authoritarian political system were to engage in counterrevolutionary war, one of the above alternatives would be chosen and imposed as the political objective. In contrast, under a pluralistic system, where, by definition, freedom of opinion, expression, and organization is guaranteed, each of these alternatives would be adopted by political parties or pressure groups. The divergences among these contradictory alternatives become all the more accentuated as the moral authority of the government becomes weak or collapses. Indeed, the executors of the pluralistic government's policy are able to implement their own political strategy in the field instead of the one chosen by the government. In Indochina several policies were used by different factions, especially by the military. In Algeria political incoherence reached such a high level that the Fourth Republic finally collapsed in May of 1958. Thus, the diversity of political objectives which is unavoidable in pluralistic governments will be all the more apparent in actual practice as the strategy of the regime falters and the government itself loses authority.

The military consequences of this chaotic political situation are very serious, for the situation produces incoherence in the military strategy. If the objective is the maintenance of colonial sovereignty or military victory pure and simple, then all means are justified and the colonial authorities will blindly massacre and thereby alienate the population. If the objective is the establishment of relationships of trust and equality with the population, repression will be carried out on a selective basis and will respect the rights of men and the laws of war. Consequently, repression will be weak and will encourage the insurrection. The situation becomes inextricable if these two strategies are applied simultaneously by divergent elements of the established authorities. Thus, political incoherence and contradictions have profound repercussions on military operations and lead necessarily to confusion and catastrophe in the field or to upheaval in the *métropole* in an effort to impose one and only one policy on the conduct of the war.

This confused situation has grave consequences for the counterinsurgent combatants. In fact, it becomes difficult or impossible for a soldier to know why he fights or why he risks his life. Without profound motivation, a country has only spiritless and passive troops, and therefore an ineffective instrument. Those who are drafted probably oppose the war. Lacking enthusiasm and the proper training for this type of war, a conscript army will be mediocre. Sending professionals, who have a stronger taste for war and military glory, limits the size of the army and risks seeing it cut off from the country, and this may embitter the troops who find themselves abandoned. Public opinion, which is directly influenced by the risks run by its sons, will probably be profoundly divided. In short, counterrevolutionary war brings about a political polarization in the mother country; this can be very dangerous, for it weakens the regime and challenges its legitimacy.

Finally, political uncertainty has repercussions upon the rationalizations used to justify the war. Three of these rationalizations have been used. First, the war could be interpreted as a fight to uphold the integrity of the French Empire. In fact, this argument has been little used, undoubtedly because most Frenchmen have always been indifferent toward their colonies. There was, therefore, no hope of convincing the French people that it was urgent to make sacrifices or to die for an imperial cause. A second rationalization represented the objective of the war as the desire to spare the indigenous population a socio-political regime judged unbearable. In other words, it was necessary to convince the French that their sacrifice would save the Indochinese or the Algerians from communism. At the very best, this rationalization is insufficient. The third justification for the war has been called the "domino theory." It affirms that if France surrenders one colony, then it must surrender all the others. This statement is certainly true, but it brings us back to the first point: there was no hope of arousing the majority of the French people by using such a threat. If by the domino theory, however, one means that defeat in one place will bring about a series of communist regimes in the entire area under consideration, many sound objections arise. The first one is that the intensification of the war is, itself, the surest guarantee of victory for the insurgent extremists. It is the cure which kills the patient. In the second place, the domino theory cannot be proven; there is no evidence that a communist regime in Algeria would lead *ipso facto* to communist regimes in Tunis and Rabat; political conditions vary so much from country to country that the domino theory has no predictive value. In the third place, even assuming the validity of the domino theory, the question is: what happens afterwards? The final result can be interpreted only as a catastrophe if one postulates the monolithic unity of the communist bloc. One can just as well accept the opposite postulate, that the more political units there are in a bloc, the more its internal tensions compromise its cohesion and create polycentrism. In a pluralist regime, these rationalizations ineluctably reinforce division in public opinion and in the ruling elite, further compromising the unity of the policy being followed and bringing indecision into the conduct of military operations.

On the whole, these rationalizations can rally only impassioned minorities, those still nostalgically longing for imperial grandeur and those longing for counterrevolutionary crusades. Imperialists have no chance of predominating, because of the complex international situation which resulted from the two world wars. The counterrevolutionaries could gain the ascendancy, however, provided the crusade could be undertaken by the whole Western camp. This would presuppose a movement toward political unity, a conviction of the deadly character of the threat posed by the communist bloc, and the exalted monopoly of Truth and Good. France was indeed far from fulfilling these conditions.

THE PROBLEM OF THE COLONIAL POPULATION

The attitudes toward the colonial population are necessarily as diverse and contradictory as the political goals of the counterinsurgents. Three basic modes of behavior accompany these attitudes. First, a realistic and logical attitude deems that the entire population is composed of actual or virtual enemies. Consequently, all military operations would be carried out without consideration for the civilian losses of the adversary; only military victory would count. Such a ruthless solution poses certain difficult technical and diplomatic problems. Furthermore, it is incompatible with the social, political, and ethical values of a pluralistic country. It is inconceivable that a democratic system nurtured through centuries should have recourse to mass terrorism. It would first be necessary for democracy to have died and given way to a totalitarian system.

Second, an unrealistic and illogical attitude tries to make a clear distinction between national war and social war. The underlying arguments for this strange attitude can be summarized in the following fashion. The retrieval of national identity is for the insurgents only an ideological pretense which conceals real claims; these are of a socio-economic nature. Consequently, it is enough to grant agrarian reforms, to launch a bold program of economic development, and to insure the process of democratization by suppressing the old elite

class and creating a new one. This new elite class will presumably emerge from a democratic system of education open to all. Thus, the people and the majority of the insurgents will quit fighting and docilely return to the bosom of the mother country. A variation, which should take its place in the museum of ideological drollery, states that the substance of the insurgents' demands is purely imaginary and is the result of an exogenous indoctrination. An intensive counterpropaganda campaign will suffice to win over the population and thereby put an end to the insurgency. This strategy resulted in the "psychological action" in Algeria, which was based on the hypothesis that one could convince anyone of everything. It is not certain that such stupidity belongs only to France. This argument, which is so widespread in France and elsewhere, seems so strange because it does not take into account the importance of strong national passions. It assumes that man lives by bread alone. It also assumes that an aspiring people seeking redress of long-standing grievances will have more confidence in foreigners than in its own sons. All these opinions are based on such primitive psychology that they would not deserve mention if they were not so widespread.

Finally, there is the pragmatic attitude which recognizes that colonialism is anachronistic, and that its costs outweigh its benefits. The solution is to support a moderate political faction in the colony in order to undermine the extremist insurgents. This was the most widespread attitude within the expeditionary forces, at least in Algeria. Soldiers of all ranks had only mixed feelings toward the French settlers in Algeria and tended to recognize the legitimacy of the economic and social demands of the Moslems. Let us also remember that the Constantine speech of General de Gaulle, in which he announced that huge investments would be poured into the Algerian economy, corresponds to the argument just outlined. This solution is possible so long as there is no war and national passions are not exacerbated. Once war breaks out, the decolonization solution becomes less and less possible as the war goes on. Indeed, those indigenous leaders who support this nonrevolutionary solution are recruited from the social strata which have the most to lose from the revolution, since the national revolution is gradually transformed into a social revolution. They are the propertied classes, the traditional elite, and the corrupt native bureaucracy, which thrives on the economic opportunities that are available during a state of war. On the whole, revolutionary war produces a result which is the diametrical opposite of the desired one: the war definitely isolates the puppet political faction from the people; it furnishes the insurgents with wonderful arguments for their propaganda and thereby accelerates the momentum of the social revolution. Thus, the established authorities find themselves cornered in an untenable position, which is the result of the contradiction inherent in seeking forcibly to convince a people to choose freely a noncommunist regime.

THE INTERNATIONAL MILIEU

What is to the international advantage of the insurrection is to the international disadvantage of the colonial authorities. France, not being a hegemonical power, and finding herself in a system of alliances, was forced to rely upon her allies for matériel and political support. Even supposing that she had the means and the will, France could not have pursued a war of extermination without encountering overwhelming international opposition; this would have forced reconsideration. Furthermore, the consensus of international feeling favors decolonization and the liberation of oppressed peoples. Thus, in Indochina and Algeria, France appeared to be engaged in anachronistic wars. There was no chance of any country enthusiastically supporting her. In Indochina, probably because of the Korean War, France was successful in convincing the American government that she was fighting for freedom, and from that came a huge amount of American aid in the form of money and matériel. However, this aid resulted in dubious relations. It was improbable that the United States, financing the French, would indefinitely allow France to wage the war as it saw fit.

General de Gaulle's accession to power introduced a new factor. He visualized France at the head of a coalition of countries which would not accept the Soviet-American duopoly; but the continuation of the Algerian war was a nullifying obstacle which had to be removed before France could again venture into the delights of great power politics. It took de

Gaulle four years to convince others that the war could not be won. It was to his credit that he successfully transformed a defeat into victory.

THE ESTABLISHED AUTHORITIES: THE MILITARY STRATEGY

THE ENEMY'S CENTER OF GRAVITY

From what has been said about revolutionary warfare, it is clear that the insurgents' center of gravity is not the insurgent army (regular or guerrilla) but the entire indigenous population. This has at least two very important consequences. Even if repression is effective enough to eliminate the armed insurgents, and even if few people are won over to the revolution, the insurrection will always be able to reconstitute its strength and be capable of acts of terrorism and guerrilla surprise attacks. Thus, there is no hope that repression might lead to a permanently imposed peace. It is also obvious that a classical military "vision" of the revolutionary war—i.e., the conviction that the enemy will be defeated by the strategy and tactics learned in the conventional school of war drawn from European experiences—leads to catastrophe.

As the established authorities must soon realize, the people constitute the center of gravity, and they must direct their efforts toward the winning of the population. Four basic strategies are possible and have been used in succession or simultaneously. The first can be called the winning of the hearts. By introducing or promising radical reforms (accompanied by propagandistic psychological action), the counterinsurgents try to win the population over to their side. As pointed out, such a policy is of rather dubious efficacy. Besides, it has the disadvantage of accentuating tensions within the counterinsurgent camp, because some segments refuse categorically to consider reforms.[10]

---

[10] In Algeria the important colonists, and after them the "small whites," were violently opposed to reform of any kind, since they believed that to yield on one point would eventually mean giving in on everything. They succeeded in aborting all inclinations to reform. One interpretation of this currently heard circulating in France is that it is this obstinacy which led them to the catastrophic re-embarkment of 1962. A more conciliatory attitude would have led to the same result, but without war and its atrocities—and by means of an orderly withdrawal.

A second strategy consists of the large-scale mobilization of the population by the counterinsurgents and of the systematic elimination not only of the militants but of all groups which might be capable of being insurgent cadres. In short, it is a strategy designed to atomize the population, making it incapable of opposition. This implies an enormous conscription of troops from the mother country and the use of terrorist methods in the field. In order to hold down the number of troops required and to provide an easier and less bloody surveillance, it is necessary to displace the population to "centers of regroupment" or "shelters." In this way one hopes to isolate the insurrection from its breeding ground, the people. If such an evacuation is effected, one can be sure that it will completely fail to attain its goal. Indeed, the suffering connected with these deportations serves as excellent propaganda material for the insurgents. Because it is impossible to prevent contact between the centers and the outside, they become an excellent culture medium for the recruitment of revolutionaries. Certainly, the consciences of those in the mother country will revolt against what would look like an embarrassing reappearance of concentration camps. This policy was followed in Algeria, without much success in the field, but with violent opposition in France.

A third strategy involves the systematic utilization of cleavages which divide the population. Thus, in Indochina, a traditional enmity exists between the ethnic Vietnamese (Annamites) and the Montagnards (the Moi, Muong, and Thai tribes, etc.). The French mobilized, armed, and organized the latter in an effort to use them against the insurgents. They also used the religious minorities: the Catholics, Cao Dai, and Hoa Hao. But it is impossible for the established authorities to use residual or marginal groups to build a new order that can be imposed on the majority, or to divide and rule. In Algeria, tribal conflicts were used in the same manner, but with the same limitations. For example, in the Aures region an age-old hatred separated the Ouled Abdi from the Touabas. The latter having participated in the insurrection on November 1, 1954, the former, *ipso facto*, fell in with forces of the established authorities.

There remains a final strategy, which is simply to annihilate the population. Aside from the moral and political problems involved, this strategy meets with technical obstacles which a country such as France would find difficult to overcome. In sum, since the center of gravity is the population itself, the logical alternatives which the counterinsurgent is forced to face are eventual surrender or genocide. This logic determines the conduct of the operations.

THE STRATEGY OF ATTACK, OR THE ATTEMPT TO WIN

If we start with the hypothesis that there is no alternative to victory, four types of war are possible. The first is *the classical war of movement* inspired by World War II. According to the best tradition, one sets up huge mechanized operations with infantry, armor, artillery, and aircraft with the intent of dealing a mortal blow to the adversary. If this strategy is used by the counterinsurgents in a revolutionary war, their defeat is assured and constant. Indeed, on the strength of the logic of the defense, the adversary will usually refuse to fight and will disappear into the countryside and into the population. On the whole it will be like beating the air. An operation of this type launched in the Aures region in 1955 did not encounter a single one of the enemy. Since "mistakes" are inevitable, to the detriment of the civilian population, atrocities resulting from conventional fire power and tactics are good propaganda for the insurgents and are an excellent source of recruitment.

Next comes *the war of territorial security* (*quadrillage*), which involves systematic occupation of the country with garrisons in each populated area. These outposts are linked to larger installations capable of sending reinforcements and tanks and of providing artillery support. Each post guards a limited sector and hunts down the insurgents. Such a strategy meets with insurmountable difficulties. The requirement for large numbers of troops would necessitate massive mobilization in the mother country—and political difficulties would inevitably arise. In addition, it is physically impossible to interdict all of the natural sanctuaries where the insurgents find refuge. Because of his mobility, the insurgent is able to concentrate relatively invincible forces against this or that outpost, destroy it, and set up ambushes against the reinforcements sent in by the "supporting" outpost. The nibbling and the loss of matériel finally exhaust the occupation troops.[11] Therefore, unless millions of troops are used, this strategy does not lead to victory.

At first glance, *counterguerrilla war* bears the closest resemblance to the correct solution. It is based on a simple truth, which finally becomes evident to a few: the only way to win is to learn from the insurgent and to practice the same kind of tactics he does. The insurgent bases his strength on small but extremely mobile groups, which are almost self-sufficient and always on the lookout for an ambush or surprise attack. All that is necessary, therefore, is to form small but highly trained units made up of volunteers and professionals, who have a perfect knowledge of the terrain and who are ready to lead a life of sacrifice and danger for weeks and months. By the systematic use of intelligence, obtained by the usual methods (torture, owing to the lack of cooperation by the population), and constant mobility, these counterguerrilla units will give chase in order to surprise and destroy the insurgent. Tested locally and rather spontaneously in Indochina and more systematically in Algeria, this strategy has proven to be remarkably effective.

However, the counterguerrilla war has its limitations. The main one is the number and quality of troops required. In a far-away war with dubious or incoherent political goals, one can hope to find men qualified for this type of war only among those who have fighting in their blood and who enjoy it without worrying about the moral or political justifications for their actions. Such men can be found in every country, but they are an infinitesimal minority. Therefore, the effectiveness of an army of commandos will be inversely proportional to the extent and intensity of the insurrection. In contrast, nationalist and revolutionary passion multiplies the number of insurgent guerrillas greatly. Counterguerrilla warfare can thus be effective and lead to victory only as long as the insurrection remains localized. Using this method, however, the British succeeded in eliminating the Malaysian guerrillas, and this method can be particularly effective in big cities. On the condition that the population of the *métropole* does not object to the means employed, such as the systematic use of torture (the *style-para*), the forces of the established authorities can in principle hold the cities indefinitely. The Battle of Algiers (1957) is a perfect example of this. In six months the paratroopers completely cleaned out the Casbah.

One must also keep in mind a second limitation. Counterguerrilla war employs means that inevitably infringe upon human rights and the laws of war. Domestic and foreign consciences cannot help but be moved by such a war and an international campaign will be launched in order to denounce it. In a pluralist regime this campaign has an irresistibly logical appeal, for it is based upon an irrefutable argument: why continue a struggle which can no longer be associated with democratic and humanitarian ideals, but which moves the nation to horror and perhaps to authoritarianism? What is the meaning of victory if its price is the loss of the national soul? A fatal split can result between the army—for whom victory is now an end in itself and not a means to a political end—and the nation, which recoils at the means used for such a victory. This formula can help to define an absurd war, a war which has become insane because it has broken loose from the control of political objectives. A counterrevolutionary war, because of its inherent logic, at any moment runs the risk of turning into madness.

A third limitation is set by the outside bases of the insurrection. A counterguerrilla war cannot stop at the borders. Should it cross them, it lends to the struggle an international dimension which might escape the control of the political leaders and arouse reactions which will destroy national and international stability. Finally, there is a limitation within the army itself. Traditional military leaders do not like restless and rebellious soldiers, either conscripts or commandos. They feel them slipping out from under their supervision and distrust their subversive potential. This distrust is transformed into hatred of political men, whom they regard as having played the sorcerer's apprentice by meddling in military affairs.

A final possible strategy is the *war of annihilation*. By the massive use of firepower, one aims to break not the will but the living forces

---

[11] Thousands of soldiers disappeared in this manner in Cochinchina. Lucien Bodard, among others, has told of the atrocious character of this war. It was guerrilla war in the strictest sense which claimed even Roland as its victim at Roncevaux.

of the adversary: war turns into a wholesale massacre. This poses technical problems. The record proves that the classical means (bombs and shells) are ineffectual over wide areas which have effective, camouflaged defense. After the experiences of World War II, one is surprised that there should still exist military men and politicians who think that massive bombing could bring the adversary to his knees. Constant experience and simple psychology would indicate the certain result to be a strengthening of the will to resist and to fight. The colonial power is inevitably led to consider more radical means: the systematic destruction of crops and irrigation systems in order to starve the population.[12] If this is insufficient—for outside help can compensate for the destruction—one goes a step further into the horrors of war and uses atomic or bacteriological weapons. When it was becoming apparent that the battle of Dien Bien Phu was turning into a disaster, certain French leaders were hoping that the United States would consent to make use of atomic weapons to reverse the situation. It goes without saying that such a strategy would arouse reactions—such as intervention by a third power—which would make its application unthinkable. International indignation would be so great that the colonial power would have to capitulate quickly or risk being discredited forever in the eyes of the world. Finally, the inevitable internal unrest would bring the regime to a state of paralysis and dissolution. On the whole, it was absolutely impossible for France to resort to such extremes. On the other hand, a hegemonical power with a totalitarian regime might not hesitate to do so.

The Strategy of the Defense, or the Prevention of Defeat

Having been persuaded of the fact that they cannot win without killing everyone, the established authorities can completely reverse their policy and decide not to lose—that is, to hold on indefinitely in the hope that weariness will finally rally large numbers of the population to

a moderate solution. But protracted revolutionary war can only benefit the insurgents. Despite its futility, the first rule that governs the counterinsurgent's defensive strategy is to avoid at any cost a double-or-nothing battle such as Dien Bien Phu, and to refuse all engagements in which absolute superiority is not certain. Second, the counterinsurgent must hold the big cities (by exercising police control) and the main lines of communication and establish impregnable bases in strategic areas. Third, an effective and sustained counterguerrilla war must be conducted in order to wear down the insurgents and prevent them from organizing. Finally, the counterinsurgent must launch massive and unexpected strikes to prevent the insurgent from concentrating his forces and consolidating his hold on the countryside. There is no need to add that in this case the established authorities must forgo the idea of winning the hearts of the people. It is clear that such a strategy allows the war to continue indefinitely in stalemate, for insurrection has no chance of prevailing from a military point of view. It can win politically only as the war is transformed into a political struggle in the mother country; the war will continue as long as the will to fight exists. However, a war of attrition cannot last indefinitely in the pluralistic mother country. Aside from the weariness and the burdensome costs which arise from a war whose end is not in sight, those who oppose the war can have a decisive political argument when they claim that the war has entered the absurd phase: it has become its own end, and the military objective has replaced the political goal. It is unthinkable, in a pluralist regime, that those in power will indefinitely continue their course into the absurd. Sooner or later common sense will prevail.

CONCLUSION

The principal lesson of this analysis—aside from the fact that the organic relationship between politics and war is never so clear as in revolutionary war—can be summarized with one simple formula: all an insurrection needs in order eventually to win politically is not to lose militarily. Because of the strategic defensive advantages of the insurgents, the established authorities cannot win a counterrevolu-

---

[12] In a country which is primarily agricultural, the destruction of the industrial infrastructure cannot have decisive consequences; all the less since there is a defense: the dispersion into small production units. As for the complete destruction of the lines of communication, it is simply impossible.

tionary war; they can only lose the war or pervert their political ideals. It would have been wiser never to have become involved in a struggle which was futile and unjustified.[13]

[13] The situation just outlined is the situation reached in the Algerian War. At no time was the French army on the verge of defeat. But, on the other hand, it could not win. At that stage, the resolution of the conflict required a political decision, and this was effected in the *Accords d'Evian*.

But if, in spite of everything, revolutionary war breaks out, and its suppression is attempted, what can be done? The problem of disengagement reveals, at least as much as military operations, the diabolical nature of revolutionary wars. How can defeat be transformed into victory? The answer to this question depends on the art of politics, not on the science of the analysts.

THE LESSONS OF THE VIETNAM EXPERIENCE

ZEB B. BRADFORD, JR.

The purpose of this article is to analyze the tactics of U.S. forces in Vietnam, compare them with the tactics of the enemy, and draw some conclusions about the U.S. role in wars of insurgency. The author notes a common criticism that the only way to defeat a guerrilla is on his own terms, but he does not agree. On the contrary, he suggests that the true difference between the U.S. Army in Vietnam and the French experience was the widespread use of the helicopter. This permitted a tactical innovation—the accelerated rate of reinforcement—for which Communist military doctrine had no answer. Lt. Colonel Zeb B. Bradford, Jr. (USA), is a graduate of West Point, earned a master's degree in public administration from Harvard, and served as a Fellow of the Woodrow Wilson International Center for Scholars in Washington, D.C. He has also served in Vietnam with the First and Ninth Infantry Divisions, and is working on a book with Lt. Colonel Frederic J. Brown on the policy implications of American ground power after Vietnam.

OVERVIEW

Realistic military policies for the future must take into account the impact of the Vietnam experience. We need to absorb the military lessons of that difficult conflict as they bear upon our capabilities. Unfortunately, however, the contention and discord over our *goals* in Vietnam often tend to inhibit an honest appraisal of the *means* employed in support of policy. This has been particularly true with regard to the ground war, which has been viewed principally in terms of either scandalous vignettes or dramatic atypical episodes such as the foray into Cambodia in 1970. General public understanding of the more typical

Reprinted by permission and with minor changes from "U.S. Tactics in Vietnam," Military Review, February 1972, pp. 63–76. Copyright © 1972 by the U.S. Army Command and General Staff College, Fort Leavenworth.

operational features remains obscure. Deceptively simple terms such as "search and destroy" or "search and clear" explain little about the actual tactical employment of our forces, which was far from simple.

In order to evaluate our tactics in Vietnam, we must assess them against the situation facing our forces on the ground when we entered the conflict in force—both from our own point of view and from that of the enemy. His view was consistent with his previous experiences, convictions, and doctrines.

COMMUNIST THREE-STAGE WARFARE

From the point of view of the enemy, success in conventional battle was essential to winning the war in South Vietnam. The Communists, at least initially, did not believe that success in guerrilla war could by itself lead to victory. They entered the conflict in South Vietnam with a formula for victory which had been tried and tested successfully against the French, and had resulted in a stunning victory on the battlefield, culminating in the fall of the French fortress of Dien Bien Phu in 1954. This formula identified three main phases of conflict: "guerrilla war," "local war," and finally "mobile war."

Theoretically these phases run sequentially, with each phase paving the way for the one to follow. Actually, all of these phases have existed concurrently within South Vietnam, varying from place to place. The geographic compartmentalization and the primitive communications of Vietnam have contributed to this. The result has been a conflict in Vietnam which has been a virtual kaleidoscope of apparently unrelated actions, actions that are bewildering to many observers.

There is an enduring interdependence between these phases which remains throughout the course of a struggle. The organizational apparatus necessary for each phase is a key fixture of the succeeding one as well. For example, the local infrastructure constructed in the "guerrilla war" stage of the movement is needed to secure and maintain lines of communication and provide logistics support for the "local war" and "mobile war" operations which occur later. In fact, a unique feature of Communist operations in Vietnam has been that military lines of communication are placed in *front* of the attacking main force— laid out in advance by the "guerrilla war" infrastructure and "local war" guerrilla forces. But also to be noted is the fact that, because of this organizational depth, the theoretically sequential phases are to some extent reversible. Conflict can be de-escalated by the insurgent high command when necessary, to a lower and perhaps less risky phase, provided the struggle has not seriously weakened the political apparatus. This helps to explain the resilience and persistence of the insurgent movement in Vietnam.

Reversion to a "lower profile," however, is a temporary expedient to the insurgents according to classical doctrine. Final victory requires successful progression to mobile warfare. Seizure of political power lies beyond the grasp of a movement which cannot prosecute conventional battle as a prelude to seizure of the reins of government. All activities which go before are necessary but insufficient ingredients. The willingness of Hanoi to suffer repeated disasters on the conventional battlefield against American main-force units cannot be explained without reference to this doctrine.

A succinct description of the Viet Minh scenario for victory over the French and of the enduring philosophy which motivates the Communist forces was given up by General Giap in early 1950:

Our strategy early in the course of the third stage is that of a general counter-offensive. We shall attack without cease until final victory, until we have swept the enemy forces from Indochina. During the first and second stage, we have gnawed away at enemy forces; now we must destroy them. All military activities of the third stage must tend to the same simple aim—the total destruction of French forces.

When we shall have reached the third stage, the following tactical principle will be applied: mobile warfare will become the principal activity, positional warfare and guerrilla warfare will become secondary.[1]

There is room for argument over whether or not this abbreviated version of Giap's formulation encompassed the Communist approach in all of its complexity. But there can be no doubt that enemy actions and troop deployments

---

[1] Bernard S. Fall, *Street Without Joy* (Harrisburg, Pa.: Stackpole Co., 1964), pp. 34, 35.

have been consistent with this conceptual approach. No more dramatic demonstration of the importance placed upon conventional success can be imagined than the massive invasion of South Vietnam by virtually the entire North Vietnamese Army in overt conventional fashion in April of 1972.

THE PHASES OF THE VIETNAM WAR

The very large conventional component of the war is shown by the figure below, which makes a comparison over time of opposing maneuver battalions (Figure 1). While there were always important features of guerrilla warfare present, from the time the U.S. entered in force in 1965 until the aftermath of the 1968 Tet offensive, the war in South Vietnam was primarily one of big units fighting each other.

Prior to the intervention of U.S. ground combat forces in 1965, the Communist high command clearly sensed victory in South Viet-

nam. A long period of Communist preparation and chronic South Vietnamese political instability was now to culminate with a straight-forward defeat of the Army of the Republic of South Vietnam (ARVN). To execute the final stages of the campaign, Hanoi deployed a great number of large units into South Vietnam beginning in late 1964. Some eight regiments infiltrated the South in 1965, joining a large number of Viet Cong units already present or being formed within South Vietnam. By mid-1965 the Communists could field considerably more maneuver battalions than could the ARVN. It was at this point that the U.S. entered in force. The conflict had, therefore, *already* reached its final stages, as far as Hanoi was concerned, when the U.S. intervened and began its build-up of regular forces. The ARVN was at the point of collapse, losing a battalion a week in the early months of 1965. Our escalation of forces was matched by Hanoi for an extended period as Figure 1 clearly illustrates. In 1966 some fifteen more

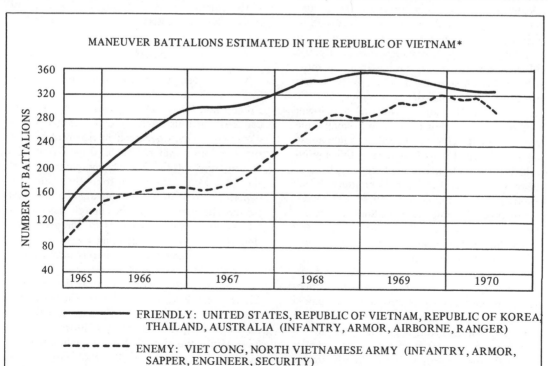

Figure 1

communist regiments infiltrated or formed within South Vietnam. Therefore, contrary to widespread American public misconceptions about the nature of the war, the task faced by U.S. forces upon arriving in Vietnam was one not mainly of tracking down guerrillas but of defeating an enemy field army on the threshold of victory.

Our units initially used more-or-less conventional tactics because they had to in order to hold off disaster. In the spring and summer of 1965 our forces served chiefly in a reaction role, to assist South Vietnamese units being attacked. It was some time before we could move against the enemy in his own base areas within South Vietnam. But by the spring of 1966 this was possible; large-unit warfare continued, but with the U.S. forces on the offensive. After having taken heavy losses, the enemy was forced to reassess his entire approach to the war. He could not get at the vitals of South Vietnam—the populated areas—without exposing his large units to disastrous defeat by U.S. firepower. Yet, if he stayed in his secure sanctuaries, his local forces and infrastructure could be neither reinforced nor protected from increasingly active Vietnamese forces. By the end of 1966 the enemy had withdrawn most of his main-force units into relatively secure base areas or cross-border sanctuaries, and the war within South Vietnam reverted to a lower level of conflict, mostly involving small-scale fighting. Both U.S. and South Vietnamese forces were relatively free during this period to devote their attention to attempting to neutralize local forces and the Communist infrastructure. The summer and fall of 1967 were a comparatively quiet time in South Vietnam. The enemy had virtually vanished from the battlefield. This was the calm before the storm of the Tet offensive of 1968.

While the Tet offensive was a historic turning point in the war, and may in the perspective of history be viewed as a psychological success for the Communists, it did not produce what *they* planned and hoped it would in the short run—a general uprising of the people, large-scale disintegration of the ARVN, and a dramatic defeat of U.S. units. Instead, staggering losses were suffered by both Viet Cong and North Vietnamese units and by the political infrastructure which had surfaced to support them in taking the cities.

The Tet offensive may well have been the beginning of wisdom for both the United States and Hanoi with regard to the nature of the war and their respective limitations. Certainly, we had not envisioned such ambition and capability by an enemy who had virtually none of the technical resources of modern war. For his part, the enemy apparently put aside his hopes for victory on the pattern of Dien Bien Phu against U.S. ground forces. From the Tet offensive until the spring of 1972, when Vietnamization was tested by massive conventional attack, the war changed in character. It became increasingly that of small-unit actions and devolved to a far greater extent to South Vietnamese local forces as U.S. forces withdrew under the Vietnamization program. We may correctly say, then, that the large-unit stage of the war was over after mid-1968—at least as far as U.S. ground forces were concerned—and that the United States had innovated tactical means which successfully thwarted the original Phase III military goals of the enemy during that period. The scope of this analysis is limited to that earlier period.

ANALYSIS

We succeeded against Communist main-force units in a tactical arena where the French had failed. The reasons for our success can best be illustrated by comparing two engagements which occurred in different eras of the Vietnam conflict. One is drawn from the closing days of the French campaign against the Viet Minh, the other from the American experience in South Vietnam against the Viet Cong. The actions contain enough basic similarities to permit an analysis of some of their details. In both, the opposing forces were attempting to exploit their inherent advantages, and both sides were seeking combat.

The first action, remembered as the battle of Mang Yang Pass, occurred near Pleiku in the central highlands in the early part of 1954. In an effort to gain tactical superiority over the Viet Minh, the French had reorganized many of their best combat units into *"Group Mobiles."* These elite task forces were designed to maximize mobility and heavy firepower to offset the advantages of cross-country mobility and flexibility possessed in abundance by the guerrilla forces. The force in this action was

"*Group Mobile* 100," formed in November of 1953 and dispatched to the highlands in December to prevent a Communist takeover of the area. Further north the historic battle of Dien Bien Phu was beginning to take shape. History has therefore cast the men of *Group Mobile* 100 and their opponents into the shadows of the greater battle.

For the first few months of 1954, *Group Mobile* 100 was in almost continuous movement throughout the highlands attempting to counter Viet Minh attacks on widely dispersed French strongholds. On April 1 it was ordered to An Khe to assume the defense of this vital sector endangered by Communist reinforcements.

The task force had already suffered 25 percent casualties from repeated contacts with the enemy by late June, when it was ordered to evacuate An Khe and fall back to Pleiku—the key center in the highlands. Dien Bien Phu had fallen on May 8. The *Group* started on the eighty-kilometer road march on June 24. As a viable combat unit, the force never completed the move.

Group Mobile 100 consisted of about 2,600 men at the time of the battle. Its basic combat units were three veteran French infantry battalions. These were the famed First and Second Korean Battalions, which had served under the UN flag with great distinction prior to coming to Indochina, and the Bataillon de Marche (B.M.) of the Forty-third Colonial Infantry. A Vietnamese infantry battalion, the 520th, was attached. Accompanying these units was a formidable array of firepower in support—three battalions of 105 millimeter artillery of the Tenth Colonial Artillery Regiment, the Third Squadron of the Fifth Armored Cavalry, an armored-car platoon, and limited air support on call from the French field at Nha Trang. *Group Mobile* 100 was fully mounted on wheeled or tracked vehicles—no one had to walk.

The enemy this potent force was destined to oppose was the 803rd Viet Minh Regiment, manned at about the same strength. It was made up of four light infantry battalions, and its fire support consisted only of 60 and 81 millimeter mortars and an unknown number of hand-held rockets. It had no vehicles of any type, either tracked or wheeled, no artillery support, and, needless to say, no air support.

One would assume from comparing these forces in terms of equipment and weaponry that any engagement would be heavily in favor of the French. Yet *Group Mobile* 100 was virtually annihilated by the 803rd Regiment on its eighty-kilometer road march in the highlands.

As the French task force moved along Highway 19 from An Khe toward Pleiku in late June, it was ambushed by elements of the 803rd only fifteen kilometers outside of An Khe. Pinned down on the road, and trapped amid the wreckage of its own burning vehicles, *Group Mobile* 100 lost all of its artillery, almost of all of its vehicles, and half of its men. The Viet Minh had attacked the column from the front and rear, making movement impossible for the French. They then destroyed the Frenchmen trapped on the road. The survivors lived by abandoning their equipment and taking to the jungle in small groups. A schematic picture of the disaster is shown in Figure 2.

The best that military technology could then provide had not been enough for the French. The mobility and fire power marshaled at such great effort had been rendered impotent in the face of a skillful but lightly armed force. All that remains today of *Group Mobile* 100 is a simple marker in the Mang Yang Pass. The 803rd Viet Minh Regiment had turned the tide in the highlands. In the words of Bernard Fall, "This was the moment they had been waiting for, the battle which was going to repay them for hundreds of their own dead, and which was going to give them control of the plateau area."[2]

More will be said about this vignette from the earlier stage of the Indochina war after a brief look at another operation which took place some twelve years later—the battle of Minh Thanh Road in South Vietnam. This action took place in the dense jungle area north of Saigon, several kilometers northeast of the vast Michelin rubber plantation. The opposing forces this time were American and Viet Cong. On the American side was the First Brigade of the First Infantry Division. Their enemy was the 272nd Viet Cong Regiment. Employed eventually by the First Division were four infantry battalions, and an armored cavalry squadron. These units were supported by five

[2] *Ibid.*, p. 213.

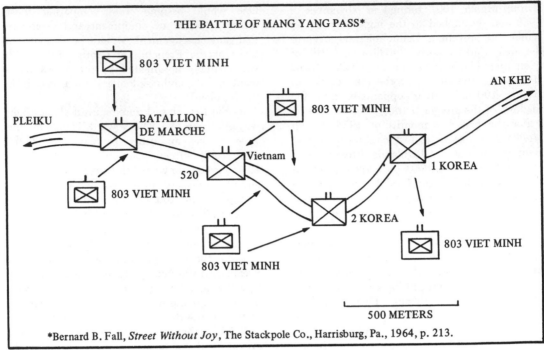

THE BATTLE OF MANG YANG PASS*

803 VIET MINH

803 VIET MINH

PLEIKU

BATALLION DE MARCHE

AN KHE

Vietnam

520

1 KOREA

803 VIET MINH

2 KOREA

803 VIET MINH

803 VIET MINH

500 METERS

*Bernard B. Fall, *Street Without Joy*, The Stackpole Co., Harrisburg, Pa., 1964, p. 213.

Figure 2

batteries of artillery and, significantly, by some sixty troop-lift assault helicopters and massive air support both from helicopter gunships and fighter-bombers.

In this action, a successful effort was made by the Americans to entice the enemy into ambushing an American convoy—to lure him into attacking our forces in a situation which on the surface appeared similar to that which had spelled the end of *Group Mobile* 100. This was done by the simple expedient of preparing a bogus convoy plan and insuring that it was leaked to the Viet Cong. At 0700 on July 9, 1966, an armored column departed Quan Loi bound for Minh Thanh, some twenty-five kilometers away along a narrow dirt road through the jungles of War Zone C. This column was comprised of most of an armored cavalry squadron (First Squadron, Fourth Cavalry) with its tanks and heavy firepower. At 1110 hours, the 272nd Viet Cong Regiment attacked, immediately inflicting a substantial number of casualties on the U.S. column. Here the similarity with the Mang Yang Pass affair ended. Within minutes, reinforcing battalions of infantry were en route by helicopter from First Division bases to attack the Viet Cong

from his flanks and rear, and to block his escape. The commander of the First Division airlifted four air-mobile infantry battalions from bases from ten to twenty kilometers distant from the scene of initial combat in order to encircle the enemy. What had begun, as far as the Viet Cong were concerned, as a carefully prepared ambush, turned into a larger-scale counterambush—a "vertical ambush" by air. Once pinpointed and fixed in position, the 272nd Regiment was hit by nearly one hundred air strikes over a period of several hours, as well as by continuous ground and artillery fire. It is estimated that about half of the 272nd Regiment died in this holocaust, as compared to some twenty-four Americans. A sketch of the battle appears in Figure 3.

These two engagements are taken as examples not because they had a large impact on the outcome of the war but because they are typical of the kind of combat which had evolved during the French campaign in Indochina in the 1950s and of that developed in South Vietnam more than a decade later. In the interim, a key factor had been altered by technology, and it was a factor for which Communist military doctrine had no answer—

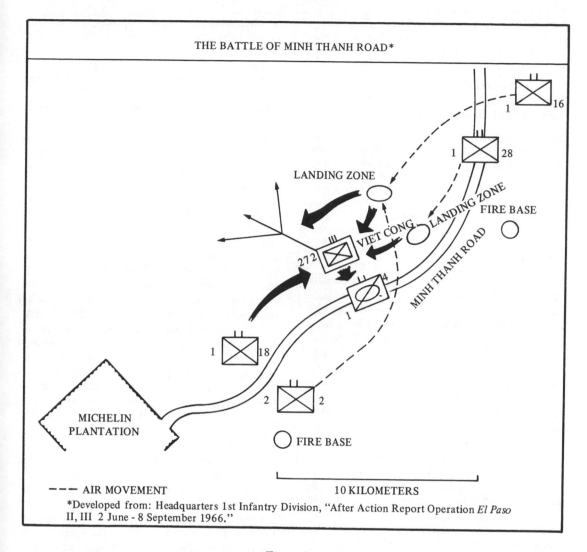

THE BATTLE OF MINH THANH ROAD*

LANDING ZONE

VIET CONG

LANDING ZONE

FIRE BASE

272

MINH THANH ROAD

MICHELIN
PLANTATION

FIRE BASE

--- AIR MOVEMENT　　　　　10 KILOMETERS

*Developed from: Headquarters 1st Infantry Division, "After Action Report Operation *El Paso*
II, III 2 June - 8 September 1966."

Figure 3

the rate of reinforcement of committed forces. In the battle of Mang Yang Pass, the French entered the fight with a given force. That force had to be sufficient to prevail against the enemy on its own, for it could not be assisted once it was committed deep inside guerrilla-dominated terrain. The enemy selected and prepared the battlefield. Once the battle was joined, the initiative remained with the more lightly armed Viet Minh troops, who could traverse the jungled battle area with speed and safety. The French vehicles, which gave them high-speed mobility on the roads, became major encumbrances and were highly vulner-

able when stopped and exposed to a concealed enemy. *Group Mobile* 100 represented the ultimate in technology for its day. Its failure, therefore, led Bernard Fall to conclude that only a guerrilla could defeat a guerrilla:

In the monsoon jungles of Southeast Asia, there is no cheap substitute for the most expensive commodity of them all—the well-trained combat infantryman; not the mass-produced item of the "divisional training camps" so dear to the Korean war, but the patiently trained jungle fighter who will stay in the jungle—not on the edges of it—and who will out-stay the enemy, if need be. The French had finally recognized this and their commando groups, once developed, showed surprising staying and hitting ability. But when the showdown came, there were too few of them—and they were too late.[3]

More recently Fall has been echoed by a distinguished veteran of our efforts in Vietnam, Colonel David Hackworth:

The most important lesson to be drawn from the war in Vietnam is that a lightly equipped, poorly supplied guerrilla army cannot easily be defeated by the world's most powerful and sophisticated army, using conventional tactics. To defeat the guerrilla, we must become guerrillas. Every insurgent tactic must be copied and employed against the insurgent. . . . American forces must enter the guerrilla's lair as hunters, employing skill, stealth, enterprise and cunning.[4]

These may have been appropriate conclusions for 1954, but not for today. Technology has radically changed the dynamics of the battlefield. With the helicopters available to him, given the distance of his bases from the battle, the American commander at Minh Thanh Road could reinforce at a rate of about twenty men every minute or, with the combat elements of almost an entire battalion, every thirty minutes. Furthermore, these reinforcements did not have to stay in one place. Throughout the battle, units were frequently moved by air to block enemy escape routes and to complete his encirclement. There was no intention of conducting the battle with initially committed forces. Those were used only as the "price of admission."

This operation also illustrates a remarkable alteration in the traditional relationships between assault forces, particularly the infantry, and the supporting forces or weapons, especially the artillery. The traditional form of ground combat has required that infantry troops actually close with and destroy the enemy in direct fighting—that is, wrest key terrain from him. Artillery and air strikes were clearly secondary in this effort, being used to "soften up" an enemy for the assaulting troops.

This relationship was reversed in Vietnam. To a large degree, the role of the infantry became primarily to locate and pin down the enemy in order that the *coup de grace* might

be delivered by massive application of firepower from aircraft and artillery. This was the case in the Minh Thanh Road battle.

The role of armor as a mobile striking force was also altered in battles such as this one. Here the armor was used as a holding force, while more mobile infantry moved to outflank the enemy. This is a marked change from traditional employment.

In terms of our values and resources these role transformations were logical and sensible developments, for they reduced the exposure of our troops to the enemy. The last fifty yards to the enemy positions has been the grim province of the assaulting infantryman since the beginning of military history, and all too frequently the scene of his death. Airmobile tactics, combined with heavy firepower, have meant that that last fifty yards frequently did not have to be crossed. From a purely technical standpoint, frontal assault by the infantry fails to exploit our own assets. Our great wealth and production capacity have enabled us to provide an almost incredible amount of fire support to the foot soldier in Vietnam.

This has meant that our casualties in most large engagements in Vietnam have been substantially lighter than those suffered by the enemy. While obviously the North Vietnamese and Viet Cong have been willing to expend manpower, and may have a large reservoir of able-bodied men, raw manpower alone does not constitute an army. It takes far longer to build an effective rifle battalion than to train a rifleman. Losses of the magnitude sustained by the Communists during the periods of Phase III battles must inevitably affect the quality of the enemy forces as a whole.

The alteration in the roles of supporting and assault forces constituted a serious derogation of enemy capability—one which he had not been able to foresee. The backbone of the insurgent movement in Vietnam has from the beginning been the superbly trained and motivated infantryman. But the airmobile warfare we have developed did not often permit him to be brought to bear in a direct contest with his opposite numbers—the American GI—on a conventional battlefield. There is an ironic similarity here. Many Western military leaders have decried the difficulty at "getting at" the enemy. Yet the enemy has found it even more difficult to "get at" our soldiers.

[3] *Ibid.*, p. 243.
[4] *A Distant Challenge* (Birmingham, Ala.: Birmingham Publishing Co., 1968).

It is possible that Hanoi and the Viet Cong were wrong about the prerequisites for ultimate political success. It may be that they have on their part overestimated the requirement for a military prelude to victory and underestimated the social and political momentum generated by a sustained level of violence. Certainly both sides entered the war with serious misconceptions. But it is fair to say that we have contrived a means of coping with the enemy when he seeks a conventional victory. We have done this in a way which, while very expensive in matériel, has compensated for some of the inherent defects of a largely nonprofessional Western army.

CONCLUSIONS

If our costly involvement in Vietnam is to be more than a painful memory, we must learn from it as we go about the task of building for the future. This discussion indicates that a significant conclusion to be drawn from Vietnam concerns the capabilities we developed to operate effectively at the near-conventional stage. It is in this area that we should look for guidelines for future development of Army programs and doctrine, not in attempting to build a better counterguerrilla capability as some would suggest. The principal challenge is to determine what is transferable to a conventional-type environment rather than to determine how we would do better next time in a future Vietnam-type situation.

Indeed, large-scale guerrilla or counterguerrilla operations are poor options for our use in the future because of characteristics inherent both in insurgency warfare and in ourselves— no matter how much we would wish it otherwise. As the previous discussion should indicate, the contest in Phases I and II is at least as much social and political as it is military. At issue is political power—at the local level as well as the national level. It is extremely difficult or even impossible for outsiders, especially foreigners, to operate with facility in this milieu. Precise and deep knowledge of local customs is essential. Acceptance by the local population is required, as is the ability virtually to "go native" in order to defeat the guerrilla on his own terms and in his own territory. It seems obvious that the U.S. Army is inherently ill-suited for producing substantial numbers of

soldiers with these attributes. As an Army, we are broadly representative of the general population—technically inclined, conditioned to a high standard of living, and—of greater significance—Western, largely white, and English-speaking. Only with great difficulty can many of our soldiers who are drawn from that population be given more than superficial training of the type needed to make them effective. Certainly our Special Forces personnel performed magnificently in Vietnam, but their example merely illustrates the point that a great deal of time and effort are needed to produce a competent guerrilla leader. And it is of course true that, while the Montagnard efforts were important, they were decidedly subsidiary to the overall main-force effort.

This is not a reflection on our competence, but merely an honest appraisal of our characteristics. There is no doubt that our citizens would themselves make superb guerrilla fighters if they were faced with a foreign force occupying the United States. But assisting someone else, of a different culture, to conduct internal politico-military battles among the population is an entirely different affair.

Added to these problems are thorny policy dilemmas caused by the dynamics of a revolutionary movement. A long period of Phase I and Phase II activity precedes the escalation to conventional conflict. In order to be employed at an appropriately early point in a given insurgency situation, counterguerrilla forces should be introduced long before overt hostilities develop. As a policy problem, this presents immense difficulties. Assuming that we would wish to help defeat an insurgency in its early stages, how do we know which incipient movement, of many throughout the world, carries within it the germ of growth and potential ultimate victory? Would we not be faced with the prospect of almost always being either too late in the right place or in the wrong place altogether? Even if we could correctly identify a truly dangerous movement, would it be possible to mobilize domestic support for an active U.S. role prior to the outbreak of highly visible Phase III operations? Finally, there is the problem of uniqueness. If there is anything students of revolutionary conflict agree upon (and there is not much) it is that generalization is dangerous. Each insurgency builds upon local issues and retains unique local characteristics. How, then, is one to prepare a counterguerrilla force for effective general employment? Would we have a group specifically targeted on each country or locale where a movement might develop? The alternative would be equally impractical—a group or a small number of groups trained for use in many areas—for this again confronts the problem of uniqueness. It would assume that general doctrine concerning counterguerrilla operations can be developed to train large numbers of people for use in a variety of different places.

There is another, even more complex problem associated with developing a significant counterinsurgency capability. This is the appropriateness of counterinsurgency as a major mission for the American Army itself. The great strength of American fighting forces historically has been precisely that they have exploited their uniquely American qualities and attributes. Highly mechanized and technical warfare reinforces our tendencies and talents and serves as a vehicle for evolutionary advance; counterinsurgency goes against the grain. We are a rich, industrial, urban country. Highly technical forces are compatible with our characteristics and resources.

Finally, technical conventional forces are likely to be most easily adaptable for general and rapid employment in an advanced conflict. This is important because we will in all likelihood be committed at the eleventh hour in any future conflicts, as we have been in the past. Therefore, we should design forces which can be committed with some chance of being effective in a mobile situation on short notice. Even should we become involved in insurgency-type situations, this is not likely to occur at the inception of such a conflict. We are most probably going to be called upon as a fire brigade—placed in action after a fire is in its advanced stages, as we were in Vietnam. At that point, units designed for fighting guerrillas would be too little and too late, as they would have been in 1954 and 1965. This is one of the things we should learn—not that we must condition ourselves to become guerrillas.

It can be argued—and has been—that what has been described here as a major tactical innovation in Vietnam merely illustrates the futility of the whole effort in Southeast Asia.

It is pointed out, with some justification, that concentrating on defeating Phase III concedes the perhaps more important earlier phases to the insurgents. However, in a sense, all military operations are *in extremis*—conducted as a last resort of the policymaker. In Vietnam, as elsewhere, we did, and indeed must, place primary reliance in the early stages upon indigenous forces. If they cannot deal effectively with these activities, then probably we cannot either. But this does not negate our capability of blunting the victory in its mobile-war stages. In other words, there is a residual capability of "not losing" if the enemy pursues Phase III doctrine. There is thus a dilemma for both ourselves and an insurgent force in a Vietnam-type situation: there is a ceiling on his effectiveness; there is a floor on ours. He cannot win fighting our way; we cannot defeat him fighting his way. Can he win ultimately if he limits his efforts to those activities associated with Phases I and II? We cannot answer this question from the Vietnam experience. For in the early years of our involvement the enemy chose not to conduct the war in that way, and of course the full judgment of history must wait until all the returns are in.

NO MORE VIETNAMS?

This analysis is by no means an attempt to argue that what we have gained or learned in Vietnam has been worth its cost in lives, dollars, and domestic discord. Indeed, it is clear that many Americans at this time do not believe that it has been. But we must be careful that the perspectives of our future decision-makers are not formed by the wrong or incomplete conclusions about Vietnam. We cannot tell what the future holds for us. Vietnam did more than demonstrate to us dramatically the limits of certain of our policies; it has also revealed rather clearly some of our inherent military weaknesses and strengths. We must know ourselves well enough to build upon our strengths in the future. It seems clear that Vietnam suggests a downgrading of the counterinsurgency option, and a concerted effort to capitalize upon the advanced organizational and technical developments which it produced in the conventional areas.

POLICY IMPLICATIONS

There are a number of broader features of the Vietnam experience which should bear considerably on future policy. This analysis of ground power in Vietnam has not dealt with the crucial role of air- or seapower. Both were vital to the kind of effort the U.S. Army made. Our strategic lines of communication were primarily protected by our naval forces. Our tactical lines of communication within South Vietnam were primarily protected by air, with Air Force fixed-wing aircraft providing absolutely essential support. This enabled ground forces to devote their efforts to the tactical mission without applying large resources to securing and maintaining secure supply routes. Lastly, air- and seapower provided the crucial support to the Vietnamese Army which permitted the success of Vietnamization in the 1972 offensive.

Likewise, the Army tactics described here were made possible in large degree because of air superiority, which permitted large helicopter formations and open movement on the ground, and also because of massive, close, tactical air support. Freedom of movement was restricted only by the enemy, terrain, and our own mobility assets, not by using airpower or even the threat of it.

To a remarkable extent, therefore, the Army effort was dependent on the other services—a fact which tends to be forgotten. It should not be. Army effectiveness in the future will if anything be more dependent on integrated interservice operations. The degree to which this integration was successfully achieved in Vietnam was due to great strides in command and control procedures and technical development, principally in communications. American ground power was projected, sustained, and protected thousands of miles from the United States for a period of years. The efforts and resources necessary for this cannot be taken for granted in developing strategic concepts for the future.

The implications of the Vietnam experience quite obviously extend far beyond their impact on the United States Army or on the role of ground power in the future. It has raised many issues which go to the heart of national security policy. The crucial problems raised by tenuous public support of a difficult and unpopular war effort, the difficulties of achieving sufficient national integration of effort, and many others, are beyond the capacity of the Army alone to address. They are national problems, the solutions to which cannot be provided here, if indeed solutions exist. The implications of these for the Army cannot be ignored, however.

Public discontent with the purposes to which the Army's efforts are applied in time inevitably come to include frustration and discontent with the Army itself. If the discontent is deep enough, and lasts long enough, this can affect the tactical, and thus the strategic, capabilities of the ground forces. It is hard to assess the true impact on unit morale and combat efficiency of prolonged dissent over the Army's role in Vietnam.

Termination of a large ground effort makes it possible to avoid the issue as a practical matter. Yet we know that the effect of public support, or lack of it, is crucial and must be considered in the future. Vietnam has given the Army a new awareness of its "public" nature. We cannot divorce ourselves from the public policy we are to implement. This may very well further limit the employment of Army forces in high-risk contingencies, where popular support is perhaps fragile or awaits vindication by demonstrated success.

URBAN GUERRILLA WARFARE

ROBERT MOSS

This article is a tour de force *in its description of many of the varieties of terrorism and urban militancy. It elaborates on four of the main techniques used over the last few years: (1) armed propaganda; (2) political kidnapping; (3) "stiffening" riots and strikes; and (4) subversion of the security forces. While the modern city is seen as being vulnerable to attack, the final success or failure of the terrorist is dependent on public reaction. The real goal of the urban guerrilla is to foment an erosion of consensus, a hardening of the political battle lines, and a backlash that strikes too hard and too indiscriminately. Robert Moss is on the staff of* The Economist *and writes on Latin American and Far Eastern subjects. He is a former Lecturer in History at the Australian National University, Canberra. Among his works are two research monographs,* Urban Guerrillas in Latin America *and* Uruguay: Terrorism versus Democracy, *and a forthcoming book on urban guerrillas.*

The kidnapping of ambassadors, the hijacking of aircraft, and the bombing of company offices are likely to continue to be familiar hazards of life in the 1970s. Such incidents attract headlines, but they are only part of the repertoire of urban guerrilla warfare, and not the most important part. On the face of it, the phrase "urban guerrilla" is a nonsense. From the time of Clausewitz, it has been generally agreed that guerrilla warfare can be carried on only where insurgents can range widely over the countryside and dispose of irregular, difficult terrain as a base area. Most theorists of guerrilla warfare agree with Fidel Castro that "the city is a graveyard of revolutionaries and resources."[1]

But there has been a recent upsurge of revolutionary violence in Western industrial cities; in Latin America, the heirs of Che Guevara have made the city their target; and Maoist groups in India have launched a terrorist campaign in New Delhi and Calcutta. In cities like Montevideo or Guatemala City, urban terrorism is in some ways the precise counterpart of rural guerrilla warfare—just as riots can be seen as the urban equivalent of spontaneous peasant uprisings. In military terms, the terrorists and the guerrillas are waging a campaign of harassment and attrition against superior, conventional forces. Their basic target is not control of territory but control of men's minds. They are essentially political partisans, for whom success or failure will hinge less on what happens on the battleground than on their capacity to get their message across, to erode the morale of the forces of order, and to induce a general "climate of collapse."

TERRORISM AS A POLITICAL WEAPON

Terrorism could be defined as the systematic use of intimidation for political ends; Lenin put it tersely when he said that the purpose of terror is to terrorize. In the colonial situations, the goal of political terrorists was to persuade the occupying power that it had become too costly to hold on. This was the technique successfully applied by the Irgun and the Stern Gang in Palestine, and by the

[1] See Carl von Clausewitz, *On War*, trans. J. J. Graham (London: Routledge and Kegan Paul, 1956), bk. 6, chap. 26; Peter Paret and John W. Shy, *Guerrillas in the 1960s* (New York: Praeger, 1962), pp. 11–15; Régis Debray, *Revolution in the Revolution?* (Harmondsworth, Middlesex: Penguin, 1968), p. 67.

EOKA in Cyprus. The desire to win world publicity, in the hope of enlisting outside support and of provoking a political debate inside Britain, was a key element in this strategy. The "Preparatory General Plan," drawn up by General Grivas in Athens before the start of the EOKA campaign, defined the political objective in the following terms: "The British must be continuously harried and beset until they are obliged by international diplomacy exercised through the United Nations to examine the Cyprus problem and settle it in accordance with the desires of the Cypriot people and the whole Greek nation."[2]

The strategy of the Irish Republican Army (the IRA) in Northern Ireland today has some similar features. The IRA, who see themselves as victims of a "colonial" situation, are hoping that their campaign of selective terrorism against the British troops stationed in Ulster will lead, first, to a breakdown in army discipline and morale and, second, to a failure of the will in Westminster: the political decision to hand the province over to Dublin.

Within an independent state, the use of terror is more complex. It can be employed as a defensive or an offensive weapon, to preserve the *status quo* (the original *raison d'être* of the Ku Klux Klan, the Organisation de l'Armée Secrète (OAS) in Algeria, or the *esquadrão da morte* in Brazil) or to overturn the existing system. It can be used to erode democratic institutions and clear the way for the seizure of power by an authoritarian movement (like the Nazis), as well as to resist an absolutist government or a foreign invader. The *Narodniks* in Czarist Russia regarded assassination as a means of "warning off" members of the official hierarchy who sought to abuse their powers. Unlike most present-day terrorists, the *Narodniks* were acutely conscious of the moral dilemmas involved in the systematic use of political violence. They argued that they had been forced to use terror because the Czarist regime had closed all possibilities of peaceful reform. The leaders of the *Narodnaya Volya* organization even promised that, if they ever saw signs of even "the possibility of an honest government," they would then "oppose ter-

rorism, as we are now opposed to it in free nations."[3] Nothing could be farther removed from the spirit and tactics of contemporary terrorists such as the Weathermen or Uruguay's Tupamaros. Both of those groups, with differing success, have set out to undermine their countries' democratic institutions and to create the conditions for civil war by bringing about a polarization of political forces.

Most terrorists in modern history have alienated public sympathy by adopting gangster-style techniques. A good example of that was the reaction of the crowd in an Istanbul street in June 1971 after the Turkish police had managed to rescue a fourteen-year-old girl from her kidnappers in a brilliantly executed operation. The guerrillas, members of the Turkish People's Liberation Army, shouted to the crowd "We are doing this for you" as they exchanged fire with the police from an upstairs window. But the crowd in the street broke through police barricades in an attempt to lynch the single terrorist who finally emerged alive. That is a fairly extreme example of the circumstances under which terrorist actions are purely counterproductive. A schoolgirl who is taken hostage may be expected to arouse more popular sympathy than a middle-aged banker or a *gringo* diplomat who finds himself in the same situation. But the normal response to terrorism is revulsion. That is why the more successful urban guerrillas, in Latin America in particular, have gone to considerable pains to try to rationalize their crimes and have been very selective in choosing their targets. Terrorists can never win popular support unless they can explain their actions as something more than random criminal assaults or lunatic gestures.

The need to make converts also explains the exceptional importance of marksmanship for the urban guerrilla. There has to be some discrimination in the choice of targets. At least at the outset, the urban guerrilla is less concerned with intimidating the civil population

---

[2] Reprinted as Appendix 1 in *The Memoirs of General Grivas*, ed. Charles Foley (London: Longmans, 1964), p. 204.

[3] See Feliks Gross, *The Seizure of Political Power* (New York: Philosophical Library, 1957), pp. 109–10; *idem*, "Political Violence and Terror in Nineteenth and Twentieth Century Russia and Eastern Europe," in *Assassination and Political Violence*, a staff report to the National Commission on the Causes and Prevention of Violence (New York, 1970), pp. 516–44; Stepniak, *Underground Russia* (New York: Scribners, 1892).

than with proving that the government and the forces at its disposal are vulnerable to attack. It is only when a rebel movement has *already* established a secure grip on a significant part of the civil population that it can afford to use terror as a means of extorting aid and supplies, of conscripting new recruits, and of deterring potential defectors. The Viet Cong have perfected the system of "repressive" terrorism since the late 1950s. Terrorism against neutral or anti-Communist elements in government-controlled areas has usually taken the form of preliminary warnings, followed by kidnapping or assassination. Over the four-year period between 1966 and 1969, American estimates place the total number of assassinations at 18,031. There were an estimated 25,907 kidnappings for indoctrination and other purposes. Terrorism in Communist-controlled areas has ranged from verbal intimidation through "home surveillance" and "thought reform" to execution.[4]

In Latin America, the terrorists have singled out individuals and installations that they can publicly identify with what they regard as an oppressive system. The Guatemalan terrorists, for example, have kidnapped an archbishop and a foreign minister as well as local businessmen and foreign envoys. The bombings in Montreal by the Front de Libération du Québec (FLQ) were primarily aimed at foreign enterprise and military installations. The IRA snipers in Ulster have made the British Army their prime target. Selective assaults on soldiers and policemen can bruise the morale of men who have to wear uniform (an essential precondition for any successful uprising), as well as eliminate enemies.

But indiscriminate terror also has a place in urban guerrilla warfare. The IRA bombing campaign in England that began in January 1939 was one of the most notorious examples. In the fifteen months that followed, bombs were exploded in station buildings, electricity plants, letter boxes, cinemas, post offices, public lavatories, shops, and telephone boxes. The campaign may not originally have been intended to cause injuries, but the targets chosen and the extraordinary incompetence of those

who manufactured and deposited the bombs made that inevitable. The worst incident came on August 25, 1939, when five people were killed in an explosion in Broadgate in Coventry. But the campaign was entirely counterproductive, coming at a time when the British government was wholly preoccupied with Nazi expansion in Europe, and it resulted only in effective police action to curb the IRA.[5] In Algiers in 1955, Front de Libération Nationale (FLN) terrorism progressed from actions against men in uniform to selective assaults on individual Europeans to the depositing of bombs in public places where French Algerians were known to gather (cafés, restaurants, and so on). The FLN used indiscriminate terror to dig an unbridgeable gap between the Arab and European populations and to provoke the kind of communal backlash that helped them to destroy their rivals for the Arab leadership—those they described as "the party of the lukewarm."[6] There was a period when the FLQ terrorists in Quebec went about the English-Canadian suburb of Westmount in Montreal dropping bombs into pillar boxes. That was partly an attempt to intensify the feelings of distrust and mutual dislike between the English and French communities.

In the United States, the Weathermen and the radical "bombers" set out to attack the entire capitalist system by a wave of assaults on property. There were 4,330 incendiary bombings in the fifteen months up to April 1970, and the targets included banks, company offices, high-school buildings, and military installations. Attempts to rationalize the bombings were hardly designed to convert public opinion. After the bombing of the Bank of America's Santa Barbara branch in June last year, a letter to the *San Francisco Chronicle* from a group calling itself "The Volunteers of America" likened the role of the bank to that of "the German financiers during the rise of Hitler." A letter from another group, "Revolutionary Force 9," declared that companies like IBM and Mobil Oil are "the enemies of all life," responsible not only for the prolongation

---

[4] See Stephen T. Hosmer, *Viet Cong Repression and Its Implications for the Future* (Lexington, Mass.: The RAND Corporation, 1970), pp. 63–111.

[5] See Tim Pat Coogan, *The IRA* (London: Pall Mall, 1970), pp. 150–73.

[6] See, *inter alia*, Roland Gaucher, *Les terroristes* (Paris: Albin Michel, 1965), pp. 255–77; and Edgar O'Ballance, *The Algerian Insurrection* (London: Faber, 1967), pp. 53–54.

of the Vietnam War but for such diffuse crimes as "encouraging sexism and the degradation of employees."

The American bombings are the work of a lunatic fringe, not a case of terrorism used rationally as a political weapon. But it is a central goal of all urban guerrillas to break down the existing social framework and to encourage a general feeling of insecurity and disorientation. It has been argued that the first task of the rebel is to "disrupt the inertial relationship between incumbents and the mass."[7] This terminology cannot be applied to Western pluralistic societies, where relations between government and people are complex and multifaceted. But conditions of general insecurity favor extremists in any society. The government is discredited because it cannot protect the civil population, and the people will finally be forced to side with whatever group is in a position to apply coercion or guarantee protection.

THE VARIETIES OF URBAN MILITANCY

Terrorism is only one form of urban militancy. Unlike riots, political strikes, student demonstrations, and ghetto revolts, terrorism is a minority technique, and the need to ensure security under urban conditions dictates a fairly standard form of organization: members of the terrorist group are divided into cells or "firing groups" of from three to five men, with a link man in each. This clearly limits the possibility of betrayal or of police infiltration, but it also limits the possibility of political agitation.

The terrorist has a political tool; the urban guerrilla has a strategy for revolution (however utopian it may seem). The Brazilian guerrilla leader, Carlos Marighella—who was shot dead in a police ambush in São Paulo at the end of 1969—outlined part of that strategy in his *Minimanual of the Urban Guerrilla*. Marighella wrote that "it is necessary to turn political crisis into armed conflict by performing violent actions that will force those in power to transform the political situation of the country into a military situation. That will

alienate the masses who, from then on, will revolt against the army and the police and thus blame them for this state of things."[8] That is one scenario for civil war. It might be called the strategy of militarization. Marighella's thesis, that by inviting repression the urban guerrillas will pave the way for popular revolt, seems to be working out in one part of Latin America—Uruguay. But Uruguay is an isolated case. In the rest of the continent, the urban guerrillas are learning to their cost that, if the government is sufficiently ruthless and can present a united front, effective repression is more likely than a popular uprising. The same is almost certainly true of Western societies. Modern techniques of police control rule out the possibility of a successful urban uprising unless a political crisis cripples the government or the loyalty of the security forces is in doubt.

It is dangerous to generalize about the causes of urban revolts. Clearly, the reasons why men revolt in Guatemala City or Belfast are different. It is possible to define three main contemporary forms of urban guerrilla warfare: (1) "technological terrorism" in the industrial cities; (2) ghetto revolts and separatist uprisings; and (3) urban violence in the preindustrial cities (notably Latin America). It is striking that, in the industrial countries, the groups that have resorted to urban terrorism draw their support from marginal social elements: middle-class student radicals or cultural and ethnic minorities. The increased frequency of this kind of political violence in Western societies is bound up both with a romantic or nihilistic disenchantment with existing systems and with a curious resurgence of sectional loyalties. The Basque extremists who kidnapped the West German Consul at San Sebastián in 1970, the Flemings who take to the streets to protest about the dominance of the French language in Brussels, and the Quebec terrorists who claim to be combating Anglo-Saxon imperialism are similar in their origins and the roots of their complaints. In the age of what Marshall McLuhan calls "the global village," there is a new insistence on the *patria chica*.

A hypothetical revolution in a Western

---

[7] See Thomas Perry Thornton, "Terror as a Weapon of Political Agitation," in *Internal War*, ed. Harry Eckstein (New York: Free Press of Glencoe, 1964), p. 74.

[8] See "On Principles and Strategic Questions," reprinted in *Les Temps Modernes* (Paris), November 1969; see also the Appendix of *Adelphi Paper* no. 79 (London, 1971), pp. 40–41.

country would have to be city-based; but it has come as a surprise to some observers that, since about the time of Che Guevara's death in the Bolivian hills in October 1967, his successors in Latin America have made the city their target. The reasons are fairly simple. The first was the patent failure of peasant uprisings and rural guerrilla movements in Latin America in the decade of the 1960s. Between 1965 and 1968, the Peruvian Army mopped up the remains of Hugo Blanco's peasant revolt; the rebel movements in Colombia and Venezuela melted away into insignificant frontier bands; and the Guatemalan Army waged a ruthlessly efficient campaign (including extensive resettlement and also, according to some reports, the use of napalm and defoliants) against guerrilla forces in the eastern hills. Equipped and guided by the Americans, Latin American security forces displayed a vastly increased capacity to handle rural uprisings. At the same time, it became apparent that a provincial revolt was rarely a direct threat to the government in countries where wealth and power were gravitating toward a few enormous metropolitan centers. Second, the guerrillas realized that it is much easier to win headlines by kidnapping a foreign envoy than by gunning down country gendarmes. Urban operations have an obvious attraction for an isolated extremist group bent on winning publicity, and, by the end of the 1960s, most guerrilla organizations in Latin America were cut off not only from the Moscow-line Communist parties but from Castro as well. Finally, the shift to the cities was an attempt to take advantage of the continent's phenomenal urban growth. Latin America's cities are growing faster than any in the world, but industrialization has lagged behind, creating vast and unpoliceable slums.[9]

It remains to be seen whether the special factors that have conditioned the rise of urban guerrilla warfare in Latin America will influence the future course of insurgency in Asia or Africa. It is surprising that there has so far been little urban terrorism in Asian cities, given the political instability of many of the countries in the region. The Tet offensive in South Vietnam in 1968 and the Gestapu affair

in Indonesia in 1965 (when the Indonesian Communist party, with the collusion of President Sukarno, tried to stage a *Putsch* by assassinating army leaders) might be classed among the rare attempts at urban insurrections. The Maoist groups in India recently broadened their tactics to include urban guerrilla techniques. In May 1970, one of the main organs of the Communist party of India (Marxist-Leninist) (CPI(M-L)) announced that, "while the main task of armed struggle would be in the villages, the party would not allow towns and cities to become strongholds of bourgeois terror."[10] In the same month, the Naxalites (a terrorist movement that takes its name from the Naxalbari uprising in 1967) made their first appearance in New Delhi, handing out leaflets and painting slogans on walls. One of their spokesmen promised that "the red terror activities in cities and towns have come to stay."[11] By the end of the year, the Naxalites were reported to have made 50–60 active recruits at Delhi University, and to have built up a support group on the campus of about 200.[12]

These figures, insignificant in themselves, were a sign of an attempt to transfer terrorist operations to the towns from their original bases in the rural areas of West Bengal and Andhra Pradesh. This tactic was at odds with the Maoist ideology of the groups responsible. For example, Charu Mazumdar, the leader of the CPI (M-L), has remained insistent that "the path of India's liberation is the path of people's war" and that the first step along that path is to create "small bases of armed struggle" all over the country.[13] He has also insisted that rural guerrilla warfare and agitation among the peasant poor comprise an essential apprenticeship for the young students and urban unemployed who have formed the backbone of the Maoist fighting squads.[14] A similar ideological rigidity has impeded the emergence of urban guerrilla warfare in other Asian countries.

The main thing that turned the Indian Maoists toward an urban campaign was a series of reverses in the countryside. The Naxa-

[9] See the author's *Urban Guerrillas in Latin America*, Conflict Studies, no. 8 (London: Institute for the Study of Conflict, 1970).

[10] *Times of India*, May 19, 1970.
[11] *Indian Express*, May 13, 1970.
[12] *The Hindustan Times Weekly*, January 17, 1971.
[13] *Forum* (Dacca), November 7, 1970.
[14] *Times of India*, May 19, 1970.

lites, for example, were active for many years among the Girijan tribesmen, who occupy an area of some 500 square miles of hilly uplands in Srikakulum. It is good country for guerrillas, and the Naxalites also found a popular grievance to exploit. From the early 1960s, there was considerable unrest among the Girijans, stemming from the fact that merchants and money-lenders in the towns were acquiring tribal lands through usury. But government legislation to control the transfer of land placated the Girijans, the Naxalites were divided by personal jealousies and dissension, and, by mid-July 1970, the police were confident that they had eliminated all of the six original leaders in Srikakulum. As in Latin America, urban terrorism was employed by the Indian Maoists both in the attempt to offset their rural setbacks and as a means of tying up the security forces and adding to the political crisis. The Indian Minister of Home Affairs announced on November 18, 1970, that there had been 341 murders in West Bengal since March, of which 172 were political. He added that 25 policemen had been killed during 526 attacks on individual members of the force.

Events in East Pakistan, the influx of East Bengali refugees, and the presence of the Mukti Fauj (the East Bengali resistance movement) have opened new possibilities for India's Maoists. But there is also considerable scope for urban terrorist activity in other parts of Asia. In Thailand, the failure of the Thai Communist party to develop urban guerrilla activity in Bangkok reflects the fact that the Thai insurgency is still largely bound up with the sectional grievances of ethnic minorities (encouraged, especially in the northeast, by the Chinese and North Vietnamese). But the Thai police have reported increasing activity by the Communists in Bangkok, and this could eventually lead to a campaign of selective terrorism. In Malaysia, the remnants of Chin Peng's Communist guerrillas are based in the wild country up around the Thai border, although early in 1971 there were signs of a more aggressive forward movement toward the tin-mining region around Ipoh. But the fact that a future insurgency in Malaysia would almost certainly be bound up with deteriorating race relations, and that the west coast cities are overwhelmingly Chinese, means that the possibility of a future urban guerrilla cam-

paign cannot be lightly passed over. In Singapore, some of the extremist elements associated with the *Barisan Socialis* (the main opposition to the ruling People's Action party) have been pressing for a campaign of street violence. The city-state is exceptionally well-policed, but its total dependence on trade and foreign investment might encourage extremists to try to precipitate an economic crisis through political violence.

It is possible to make three general observations about the patterns of political violence in both the industrial and the preindustrial cities.

THE DISRUPTIVE EFFECTS OF POPULATION MOVEMENTS

Internal migration has had an unsettling effect in both North America and the Third World, for rather different reasons. The cities of the Third World are like sponges, sucking in the surplus rural populations faster than they can absorb them. The visible effect of this process has been the mushroom-like spread of slums and shantytowns. Each city is encircled by its "misery belt" of huts patched together out of odd bits of cardboard, tin, and timber. In Rio de Janeiro, the *favelas* climb higgledy-piggledy up the hillsides; in Mexico City, the squatters' encampments fan out from the suburban fringes across the dusty plain.

The process has gone farthest in Latin America. More than two-thirds of the populations of Argentina, Uruguay, Venezuela, and Chile now live in towns. For Mexico, Brazil, and Colombia, the figure is over 50 percent. In southern Asia, by comparison, some 14 percent of the population of the region live in towns. The figure for black Africa is slightly lower— about 13 percent. But the static population spread matters less than the startling rate at which urbanization has been taking place. Third World cities are growing at a rate of between 3 and 8 percent a year. That means that most of them are doubling in size every ten or fifteen years.[15] The reason for this is internal migration rather than natural population growth, since there is evidence to suggest that the birth rate in most cities is below the national average.

[15] See D. J. Dwyer, "Urbanization as a Factor in the Political Development of South-East Asia," discussion paper at Pacific Conference, Viña del Mar, Chile, September 27–October 3, 1970.

There are many reasons why peasants are leaving the land. Overpopulation, or land hunger, is probably the most important, and it has been accentuated in some areas by mechanization and the application of modern techniques that have caused extra redundancies. Better roads and communications between city and countryside have facilitated population movements, and the fact that more people are going to school or listening to radios has influenced job expectations and helped to give the city a glamorous image in the minds of young villagers. It must be added that political disturbances and natural disasters (like the droughts that send hordes of starving peasants, or *retirantes,* out of northeastern Brazil toward the coastal cities every few years) have triggered the most dramatic population shifts. South Vietnam's cities doubled in size between 1963 and 1968;[16] Phnom Penh was swamped by rural refugees in the months after the fall of Prince Sihanouk in March 1970; and Calcutta's crowded streets have been swollen to bursting by the influx of Bengalis who have fled the war across the border. In Guatemala, peasant unrest and a sustained campaign of political terrorism drove the *hacenderos* (wealthy landowners) and the more affluent peasants, as well as the poor, to take the roads to the major towns in search of security in the course of the 1960s.[17]

Urbanization in the Third World is often compared with the process of urban growth in Europe and North America in the nineteenth century, but it differs from that earlier model in two vital ways. First, Third World cities are growing faster. The average rate of urban growth in Europe between 1850 and 1900 was only about 2.1 percent. Second, the rise of the European cities was related to industrialization. In most Third World countries, the Urban Revolution was not preceded by an Industrial Revolution. To take one comparison, 12 percent of India's population were living in towns in 1951, while 11 percent of the total work force were employed in industry. Austria

had reached the same stage of urbanization by 1870, but in that year 30 percent of the Austrian work force were employed in industry.[18] Failing to find jobs in industry, most of the rural migrants in Third World cities have had to scrape a living in the service sectors—a polite phrase that usually means nothing more than a daily round of boot-blacking, begging for odd jobs, or cleaning public buildings. Some 60 percent of Chile's labor force are employed in jobs that do not produce goods. Whereas in England after the Industrial Revolution, factory-owners were crying out for manpower, it seems likely that in most Third World countries the gap between the number of rural migrants looking for work and the number of new jobs being created by local industry will become bigger, not smaller.

This makes it impossible to apply the comfortable view of the link between urbanization and political violence derived from European experience to Third World conditions. According to the popular view, the life cycle of civil violence in Western societies passed through three phases in the course of urban growth and industrial development: an early phase, in which political violence was a response to the social disruption and disorientation resulting from the rise of urban industry; a transitional phase, in which a militant union movement emerged and briefly posed a serious threat to bourgeois society; and a "mature" phase, in which the organized working class was peacefully integrated into the new social system. As recent historians have demonstrated, that view of the past is inaccurate and simplistic even for Western societies.[19] It simply does not fit the very different circumstances of the Third World, where the flight of peasants to the towns has created a whole new social class that the Brazilians call *marginais* (or "marginal people") and that Marx, who had a notoriously low view of their revolutionary potential, called the *lumpenproletariat.* Friedrich Engels claimed that the members of this

[16] On Vietnam, see Samuel P. Huntington, "The Bases of Accommodation," *Foreign Affairs,* 46 (1968): 648.

[17] See Bryan Roberts, "Migration and Population Growth in Guatemala City," in Roberts and Lowder, *Urban Population Growth and Migration in Latin America* (Liverpool: University of Liverpool Press, 1970).

[18] B. F. Hoselitz, "The Role of Urbanization in Economic Development" in *India's Urban Future,* ed. Roy Turner (Berkeley: University of California Press, 1962), pp. 164–67.

[19] See, for example, Charles Tilly, "Collective Violence in European Perspective," in *Violence in America: Historical and Comparative Perspectives,* a report to the National Commission on the Causes and Prevention of Violence (New York, 1969), esp. pp. 33–37.

"underclass" were "absolutely venal and absolutely brazen," wholly concerned with the routine of eking a living by petty theft or by performing minor services.

In contrast, Frantz Fanon, the psychologist from Martinique who joined the Algerian revolution, saw them as the armies of future revolutions. He believed that this "horde of starving men, uprooted from their tribe and from their clan, constitutes one of the most spontaneous and most radically revolutionary forces."[20] Was he right? Are the people of the slums a potentially revolutionary force? It has been argued that recent migrants are too preoccupied with surviving from day to day to lend their support to a political movement; and that men who are always moving from one shack to the next without steady jobs are not easily organized by a party or a revolutionary group. It is certainly true that the "bazaar system" in Third World cities provides some kind of safety valve; unemployment is worse than underemployment, and the profusion of uneconomic service industries and petty retailing at least makes it possible for people to eat. Assuming that rural migrants have only modest expectations, the service industries are capable of absorbing new arrivals into what has been described as a "system of shared poverty": a buffer zone between the traditional and the modern economies.[21] But it seems doubtful whether this constitutes any long-term solution, both because of rising expectations and because eventually the parasitic service sector will be saturated. This means that a rising proportion of the populations of Third World cities will remain outside the modern economy and the present forms of social organization while becoming increasingly conscious of their plight.

Their political responses in the past are therefore no certain guide to the future. In Latin America, the slum-dwellers have been notoriously susceptible to the appeal of populist demagogues like Juan Perón in Argentina or Rojas Pinilla in Colombia. They have tended to vote for the man, not the party, and to be strongly influenced by promises of local improvements. A public opinion poll conducted in one slum community in Manila on the eve of the 1963 municipal elections showed that most of those interviewed wanted to reelect the existing mayor because he had made a promise to them while a candidate four years previously, to build catwalks between their stilt shanties.

One fairly sophisticated analyst has argued that the slum-dwellers are "basically conservative so long as life is barely livable" but "catapult to revolution the moment that life is no longer seen as livable for whatever reason."[22] The slum fringes of the Third World cities contain a volatile mass that may explode during periods of rapid social transition or economic recession. And the urbanization process has had other political side effects. In Southeast Asia in particular, it has heightened racial tensions, usually at the expense of the Chinese, who dominate local commerce. There have been anti-Chinese riots in several Asian cities, and it is worth noting that it was Malays who had migrated from the east coast who were responsible for the violent race riots in Kuala Lumpur in May 1969.[23] At the same time, the concentration of wealth and power in a few enormous cities means that, in Latin America in particular, a rebel movement cannot confine itself to the countryside if it hopes for success. Moises Moleiro, a former Venezuelan guerrilla leader, pointed out in a recent article: "In Venezuela, it is just not possible to start a rural uprising that will end with the countryside encircling the town. The rural areas are marginal to the life of the country. . . . A peasant revolt is impossible, in the last analysis, because we are not a peasant people."[24] It seems that a peasant revolution is no more possible in the major Latin American countries than in the industrialized West.

In the United States, internal population movements have added to social tension in

---

[20] Frantz Fanon, *The Wretched of the Earth*, trans. C. Farrington (Harmondsworth, Middlesex: Penguin, 1970), p. 103.

[21] One of the more convincing arguments along these lines is T. G. McGee and W. R. Armstrong, "Revolutionary Change and the Third World City," *Civilisations*, 18, no. 3 (1968).

[22] Martin Oppenheimer, *Urban Guerrilla* (Harmondsworth, Middlesex: Penguin, 1970), p. 42.

[23] See, for example, John Slimming, *Malaysia: Death of a Democracy* (London: Murray, 1969), pp. 25–60; and T. G. McGee, *The Urbanization Process in the Third World* (London: Bell, 1971), pp. 64–89, 149–72.

[24] Moises Moleiro, "Las Enseñanzas de la Guerra Revolucionaria en Venezuela," in V. Bambirra *et al.*, *Diez Años de Insurrección en América Latina* (Santiago: Prensa Latino-Americana, 1971), 1: 173.

subtler ways. Recent statistics from the U.S. Census Bureau show that half of the country's Negro population is now concentrated in fifty cities. Fifteen of those cities account for a third of the total. While black Americans have been moving into the city centers, middle-class whites have escaped to the suburbs, taking new industry with them. But this is not a one-way process. A recent study of the Cleveland riots of 1967 showed that Negroes with steady incomes were also moving out of the ghettos, leaving behind those at the very bottom of the social scale.[25] The black ghetto in Detroit or Chicago is not simply a racial enclave but also an island of deepening poverty. And the fact that the ghettos are often located close to the traditional centers of commerce or command key services such as railway lines or power stations makes racial unrest a threat to the normal functioning of the economy.

THE SENSE OF RELATIVE DEPRIVATION

Population movements in the Americas have sometimes added to the sense of relative deprivation. A Negro left behind in the "riot zones" of Chicago or Washington while a more enterprising neighbor moves out to a new factory job in the suburbs will feel a more acute sense of frustration and is more likely to join a rioting mob on a hot summer's night. Men do not rebel because they are deprived but because they are conscious that they are deprived. De Tocqueville's celebrated argument that the French Revolution came about because things were getting better (so that people who had formerly accepted their lot became conscious of the possibility of changing it) works equally well in reverse. Uruguay is the one country in Latin America where armed revolution seems possible in the foreseeable future. Yet it has also been one of the most enlightened societies in Latin America, with a tradition of constitutional rule and much of the apparatus of a welfare state. Uruguay is a democracy that has come upon hard times. The economic crisis that began in the late 1950s has crippled public service salaries and led to cutbacks in social spending, while the activity of an exceptionally efficient guerrilla movement has forced the government to resort

to repressive measures. The reason why the Tupamaros have been able to count upon a substantial amount of middle-class support has been that people's expectations have been disappointed.

THE CHARACTER OF THE TERRORIST

But urban guerrilla warfare is essentially the work of a tiny self-styled revolutionary elite. That makes it important to consider whether there is not something in the apparent truism that "it takes a rebel to rebel."[26] The FLQ in Quebec, the National Liberation Action (ALN) in Rio, and the Weathermen in the United States draw their recruits from similar social sectors and share not only a certain range of guerrilla techniques but a common faith in political violence and the theory of a global revolution. Frantz Fanon provided the most comprehensive version of the now-fashionable theory of violence as a liberating force. "At the level of individuals," according to Fanon, "violence is a cleansing force. It frees the native from his inferiority complex and from his despair and inaction; it makes him fearless and restores his self-respect."[27] The radical "New Left" in Western countries as well as the Guevarists in Latin America have tended to talk in similar terms.

What Fanon completely failed to analyze was the corrupting effect of the systematic use of political violence, and its reinforcement of the totalitarian impulse. He also ignored the attraction of a terrorist organization for some criminal elements. It is no accident that the IRA Provisionals in Belfast have drawn support from petty criminals in the Catholic slums and have set up their own protection rackets for extorting "party funds." The British Army has reported cases where the Provisionals have broken a man's back with an iron bar or kicked a pregnant woman in the stomach in order to compel submission or the payment of regular contributions. The FLQ in Montreal has recruited drifters and corner pickpockets from the *hangars* (or gang territories); and the Moslem FLN in Algiers enlisted the services of professional thugs like Ali-la-Pointe. The frequent confusion between criminal and political motives is bound to be accentuated when guer-

25 See Walter Williams, "Cleveland's Crisis Ghetto," in *Ghetto Revolts*, ed. Peter H. Rossi (New York: Trans-Action Books, 1970), pp. 13–30.

26 Brian Crozier, *The Rebels* (London: Chatto & Windus, 1960), p. 9.
27 Fanon, *op. cit.*, p. 74.

rilla groups rely upon "fund-raising" devices such as bank robberies for their finance—and that is why Cuban and Russian leaders have criticized this kind of operation.

The irony is that the founding impetus of many urban guerrilla groups has come from young idealists: middle-class students and intellectuals who share a belief in a global revolution aimed primarily at the United States. The Tupamaros first signed their name to a manifesto protesting the American involvement in Vietnam. The FLQ in Quebec wrote the slogan "Long Live the Cuban Revolution!" on the bottom of a kidnap note; and Pierre Vallières, their spiritual leader, has a wild-eyed vision of a worldwide revolution that would take account of the "cultural and ethnic origins" of workers as well as their "proletarian character."[28] With the American Weathermen, the idea of a global holocaust approaches sheer nihilism, an itch to tear down the class from which these middle-class rebels sprang and everything it stands for. The Weathermen are essentially derivative: they see themselves as the white auxiliaries of a revolution that would be made by colored men through a great upheaval in the Third World and an uprising by Black Power groups in the United States.

The theory of international solidarity, it must be added, has not been accompanied by much interchange of cadres or resources. The Cubans, the North Koreans and the Palestinians have all provided a certain amount of training for urban guerrilla groups. Some of the seventy Brazilian political prisoners who were freed in exchange for the life of the Swiss Ambassador in January 1971 had received training in Uruguay,[29] and there are signs that the Tupamaros have close links with guerrilla movements in Argentina and Bolivia as well. But the urban guerrillas are almost entirely self-reliant in terms of arms and supplies, and the form of cooperation that counts for most is the borrowing of ideas. The most dramatic example of that was the wildfire spread of diplomatic kidnapping as a political technique after the Brazilians used it to secure the release of fifteen prisoners in 1969. But terrorist groups have also copied methods of "armed propaganda." For example, in October 1969, on the second

anniversary of Che Guevara's death, the Tupamaros occupied the town of Pando and held it for about fifteen minutes while commando groups raided the police barracks and the banks. It was a brilliant publicity technique, and probably a decisive turning point in their campaign of political terror—although a rearguard party of Tupamaros was intercepted by the army on the way back to Pando and shot to pieces.[30] At any rate, the Argentine Revolutionary Armed Forces (FAR) were sufficiently impressed by the occupation of Pando to copy it in the following year, when they took over the town of Garín. In planning for the exercise, they even referred to Garín among themselves as "Pandito" (or "little Pando").

THE ARSENAL OF THE URBAN GUERRILLA

Four main urban guerrilla techniques have been explored over the past few years and largely explain the success of a group like the Tupamaros. They are (1) armed propaganda; (2) political kidnapping; (3) "stiffening" riots and strikes; and (4) subversion of the security forces. These will be briefly discussed in turn.

ARMED PROPAGANDA

Armed propaganda can be defined as the attempt to prove to the people, through successful military actions, that the government is weak and the guerrillas are strong. One of the central problems for all guerrilla movements is how to get their message across to the man in the street. As a Tupamaro mouthpiece put it, the problem is that, "for the urban guerrilla, discretion must take the place of the rural guerrilla's hideout in the jungle."[31] Since the possibilities for normal political agitation are restricted (and since the urban guerrillas have normally held themselves aloof from the traditional political parties, including the Communists), "armed propaganda" must take the place of polemics. A good example was the occupation of Pando by the Tupamaros, or their raid on the naval training barracks in Montevideo last year. In the face of official censorship, the

[28] Pierre Vallières, *Nègres blancs d'Amérique* (Montréal: Editions Parti Pris, 1969), pp. 66–67.
[29] See *O Jornal do Brasil*, January 12, 1971.

[30] See Maria Esther Giglio, *La guerrilla tupamara* (Havana: Caso de las Américas, 1970); and *Revolución y Cultura* (Havana), no. 21 (December 1970).
[31] *Granma* (Havana), October 8, 1970.

Tupamaros have tried to construct "counter-media," including a private radio transmitter and the use of electronics experts to break into normal broadcasts with special messages. They have also taken over public meeting places such as cinemas and workers' canteens to deliver impromptu harangues.

POLITICAL KIDNAPPING

Political kidnapping has been used to capture publicity, to free political prisoners and to extract other concessions, and to provoke controversies within governments. The government of President Pacheco Areco in Uruguay was so deeply divided after the wave of kidnappings in August 1970, for example, that he was on the point of handing in his resignation before the police captured several Tupamaro leaders in a lucky strike.[32] The Brazilian experience shows just how dangerous it is for governments to give in to kidnappers. It cost the Brazilian government fifteen political prisoners to free an American ambassador, but later the price was seventy for a Swiss ambassador—rampant inflation by anyone's standards, and a sign that for kidnappers, as for other mortals, the appetite grows with the eating. The game of bluff that is being played out between governments and guerrillas is not over. The Tupamaros held Geoffrey Jackson, the British ambassador to Uruguay, for eight months after his capture in January 1971 in what they grandiosely called a "people's prison." They also held a number of prominent Uruguayans, including a close friend of the President and a former Minister of Agriculture. The Tupamaros, secure in the knowledge that they can outfox the police, did not let themselves be panicked into murdering another hostage as they murdered the American Dan Mitrione last year. They learned that they could humiliate the government and the police more effectively by playing a waiting game.

"STIFFENING" RIOTS AND STRIKES

"Stiffening" riots and strikes is one way of establishing closer links between the terrorist organization and popular grievances. Recent experience of urban riots in Northern Ireland and the United States supports the idea that crowd disturbances can pass through several phases and can finally pass under the control of extremist organizers. Since mid-1970, for example, the rioting in Ulster has ceased to be a fairly spontaneous cycle of communal conflict and has assumed a more sinister character. The British troops, rather than members of the other religious community, became the prime targets for hostile mobs egged on and infiltrated by the IRA. Street violence was prolonged in Belfast and Londonderry for five or six nights on end. Members of the crowds were armed with fire bombs and gelignite nail bombs; snipers fired on the British troops from neighboring buildings; and there was systematic arson and destruction of property. On the night of June 27, 1970, more than 100 fires were started in Belfast, and the troops were fired on in Ballymacarett and the Crumlin Road by IRA snipers armed with machine guns. The pattern of those riots was repeated in 1971. Similarly, in the United States, from early in 1968 there was evidence of much greater organization and increased sniping in Negro riots, although many Black Power leaders were distrustful of the riot as a political weapon, and the incidence of rioting fell away after 1968.

SUBVERSION OF THE SECURITY FORCES

Subversion of the security forces was seen by Lenin as one of the essential preconditions for a successful urban uprising. "Unless the revolution assumes a mass character and affects the troops, there can be no question of a serious struggle."[33] All serious rebel movements have attempted to demoralize and subvert the army and the police, and, historically, revolution has been possible only when (for internal or external reasons) this has already succeeded. Urban guerrillas are bound to be outgunned unless they can at least manage to neutralize a majority of the security forces, and one of the reasons for the Tupamaros' remarkable capacity for survival has been that they have shaken the confidence of the men in uniform by alternately circulating propaganda and practicing selective assassination, while infiltrating their own agents at all levels. (It was the presence of a Tupamaro agent on

---

[32] *Latin America* (London), February 26, 1971; *Prensa Latina* (Havana), April 7, 1971.

[33] Lenin, "Lessons of the Moscow Uprising," in *Collected Works* (Moscow, 1967), 2: 174.

the night watch at the naval training barracks that enabled the guerrillas to occupy it last year.) Terrorists have two apparently contradictory means of subverting the armed forces: one is to appeal to individual soldiers or policemen as "fellow-workers"; the other is to issue threats and carry out selective terrorism or harassment.

The process has gone farther than is sometimes realized in some Western countries. Subversion in the American Army is obviously bound up with opposition to the Vietnam War and resistance to conscription; underground GI news sheets are primarily anti-*Vietnam* publications. Eldridge Cleaver, the man who is now contesting the leadership of the Black Panthers from his exile in Algiers, has said in his quasi-apocalyptic way that "the stockades in Babylon are full of soldiers who refuse to fight. These men are going to become some of the most valuable guerrilla fighters." Perhaps this need not be taken too seriously; but it does seem that disaffected conscripts have supplied the American underground with arms, instruction, and trained recruits. The Deputy Attorney General of California announced in April 1971, for example, that his office had recovered fifty-five grenades, ninety-four bricks of plastic explosives, ten bazookas, fifty-two rifles, and sixty-five revolvers stolen from local Army bases. The racial factor has added to the dissension in the ranks. Fighting between black and white GIs has become commonplace in Vietnam, but there have been similar incidents among the American forces stationed in Germany, as well as rioting by black soldiers at bases in the United States, including Fort Hood and the riot-control training center in Kansas. One of the prime techniques used by radical activists in the American Army has been to try to pit conscripts against professional soldiers. One of the group responsible for the bombing of a military police station in San Francisco last year, for example, declared: "We consider the GI to be a civilian, whereas we consider the lifers and the military structure to be a structure which is evolving to a more Gestapo-type experience."[34] In other contexts, terrorists have tried to isolate the "elite" units and those directly responsible for counter-insurgency operations from the armed forces as a whole.

THE LIMITS OF URBAN VIOLENCE

Are the urban guerrillas likely to achieve their goals? In Western industrial societies, to ask this question is really to ask whether revolution is possible. In the Third World, urban guerrilla warfare fits into pre-existing patterns of insurgency and political instability. The modern city is vulnerable to terrorist attack; but, in the last analysis, success or failure hinges on the public reaction.

THE VULNERABILITY OF THE INDUSTRIAL CITY

The complexity of the modern city makes it vulnerable to the forms of sabotage that might be called "technological terrorism." No extremist group has succeeded in causing serious disruption in transport and communications in a Western society, although in the United States there has been a wave of assaults on property (and in Puerto Rico this has been part of a concerted drive by the Armed Liberation Commandos to scare off outside investors).[35] But the possibility of programmatic sabotage of essential services cannot be discounted, and plans for such a campaign in the United States have been elaborated by the Revolutionary Action Movement (RAM)—an organization of black extremists founded by Robert A. Williams. One of Williams' supporters has argued: "What we must understand is that Charlie's system runs like an IBM machine. But an IBM machine has a weakness, and that weakness is complexity. Put something in the wrong place in an IBM machine and it's finished for a long time."[36] Williams pointed out that it is possible to use primitive techniques to disrupt sophisticated institutions. He advocated a black revolutionary organization divided into three sections: armed self-defense groups operating legally; underground guerrilla squads to be employed against the police during riots; and a system of autono-

[34] Warren Hinckle, *Guerrilla War in the USA*, unpublished manuscript, 1970, p. 151.

[35] See "Porto-Rico: Le Réveil en Armes," *Africasia* (Paris), April 26, 1971; and interview with Alfonso Beal, reprinted in John Gerassi, ed., *Towards Revolution* (London: Weidenfeld & Nicolson, 1971), pp. 641–44.

[36] Max Stanford, "Black Guerrilla Warfare: Strategy and Tactics," *The Black Scholar* (San Francisco), November 1970, p. 37.

mous "fire teams" that would be responsible for programmatic sabotage. The fire teams would pose as "moderates" or "patriots" in order to infiltrate high-security zones. Their first targets would be transport and communications in the major cities, followed by random attacks on corporation buildings and military installations. The saboteurs would try to create general panic and urban chaos by diverse means. For example, they might scatter tacks or boards with protruding nails on turnpikes and at major intersections during rush-hour traffic. And Williams took an unhinged arsonist's pleasure in the prospect of "strategic fires" started across the countryside by teams of roving guerrillas. The fires would be used as a diversion and "to elicit panic and a feeling of impending doom."[37] Williams, unlike most other Black Power leaders, believes in the possibility of a minority revolution in the United States. His lunatic schemes for "liberation zones" in the deep South, or his idea that American middle-class society is so soft that it would fall apart as soon as economic production fell, need not be taken seriously. But he pointed out that a marginal extremist group does have the *technical* power to cause enormous damage. The political consequences are a different matter.

Terrorism and Public Opinion

Herbert Marcuse was right to insist that the most violent political groups in Western societies are composed of marginal social elements: ethnic and cultural minorities, and middle-class radicals. That is the source of their weakness. If they push the confrontation of political forces too far through the use of violence, they will eventually be swamped by the majority groups.

The advocates of "student power" feel differently. They argue that the events of May 1968 in France demonstrated that radical students can provide the trigger for a broader movement of social unrest in an advanced industrial society. They point to the occupation of factories by French workers between 14 and 17 May and to the overnight formation of strike committees as examples of popular "spontaneity." They argue that orthodox Communists are wrong to insist that a "vanguard party" is a prerequisite for revolution. "What we need," according to Daniel Cohn-Bendit, "is not an organization with a capital O, but a host of insurrectional cells, be they ideological groups, study groups—we can even use street gangs."[38]

But in fact there has not been a follow-up to May 1968. The temporary alliance between students and workers that was achieved in France crumbled away once the government made up its mind to grant some limited economic concessions (the highest wage increase granted was about 14 percent). While student theorists were talking of revolution, most of the workers who joined the rallies and participated in strikes were merely posing bread-and-butter demands that the system was able to satisfy. The decisive factor that helped to turn the tide in Paris was the hostility and distrust shown by the leaders of the French Communist party and the trade unions toward the student movement. What made a real insurrection in France in 1968 impossible was the factor that the students had decided to neglect: the absence of a mass organization with a coherent strategy for the seizure of power. It was abundantly clear in May that the French Communists were not prepared to adopt this role. And the leaders of the Italian Communist party (PCI) have swung toward an equally reformist position more recently.

Until the Twelfth Party Congress in 1968, the Italian Communists had probably played a more militant part in political strikes and student protest than any other Moscow-line Communist party in Europe. In June 1969, the "Manifesto" group (the left-wing extremists associated with the paper *Il Manifesto*) was excluded from the party on the grounds that it had acted as a divisive force and sapped the party's strength. The present tactical goal of the party leadership, according to Luis Magri, one of the "Manifesto" rebels, "is a convergence between the working class and the 'advanced' wing of big capital, on a common economic programme for the elimination of parasitism and the development of social serv-

[37] Robert F. Williams, "The Potential of a Minority Revolution: Part 2," *The Crusader* (Havana), August 1965.

[38] Daniel Cohn-Bendit, *Obsolete Communism: The Left-Wing Alternative*, trans. A. Pomerans (Harmondsworth, Middlesex: Penguin, 1968), p. 256. See Daniel Singer, *Prelude to Revolution: France in May, 1968* (London: Cape, 1970), for an interesting attempt to use *les événements* as a basis for prediction.

ices, that will harmoniously reconcile the exigencies of productivity and the needs of the workers within the system."[39] It remains to be seen whether the new orientation of the party executive (which is being encouraged by Aldo Moro and others within the Christian Democratic party who have floated the idea of achieving an "understanding" with the PCI) will turn out to be more than a tactical ruse. The "Manifesto" group still hopes to inspire a revolt within the party ranks and argues that continuing labor unrest, student radicalism, and the resurgence of extreme right-wing groups such as the Italian Social Movement (MSI) are all leading toward the polarization of political forces, not to any lasting form of "convergence" between capitalist and Communist.

The important thing to note is that, in the two European countries with the highest incidence of political violence, the Moscow-line Communist parties seem to have placed themselves *hors de combat* as far as student rebellion and insurrectionary tactics are concerned. Something similar has happened in Japan, where student militants have remained fairly isolated from unionized workers—apart from the few thousand who have joined the Youth Committees against the War, founded in 1965, and the radical railway workers who have joined in political strikes against the Japanese-American alliance. The nationalism and devotion to duty that are built into the Japanese social system have discouraged widespread protest movements, and the fragmented character of Japanese trade unions (each corporation has its trade union) has deterred attempts at nationwide political strikes.

In the United States, student rebels are almost completely divorced from the union movement, although there was a strong faction inside the Students for a Democratic Society (SDS) group that argued that effective political action would be possible only through off-campus agitation. But that faction was outvoted by those who formed the Weathermen in 1969, and the SDS strategy was narrowed down to support for minority groups and Third World revolutionaries through a campaign of terrorist violence. "Winning state power," according to the first important Weatherman manifesto, "will occur as a result of the military forces of the US extending themselves around the world and being defeated piecemeal."[40]

The student radicals have declined in political importance because events showed that they were incapable of cementing a broad front with workers or the traditional left-wing parties. The nature of New Left protest limits its popular appeal. It is partly a *qualitative* protest against the life styles of bourgeois society and the problems of living in an advanced industrial country (centralization, urbanization, pollution, and so on); and partly a *vicarious* protest in sympathy with deprived minority groups of guerrillas and peasant rebels in the Third World. It has rarely touched upon the everyday problems of the ordinary man. It is interesting to note that as student radicals have rediscovered their basic isolation as a political force, they have become more violent and more "professional." The way that Japanese student militants have organized themselves for street-fighting is a dramatic example of that. Since 1967, they have provided themselves with helmets and gloves and sometimes gas masks; the "combat section" is armed with stones and Molotov cocktails, the "defense section" with long bamboo poles. They have also adopted more sophisticated riot tactics. Since the major protest rallies in October–November 1969 (against Mr. Sato's departure for the United States), commando squads of five or six youths have staged diversionary attacks—breaking windows, throwing fire-bombs, and so on—while the big demonstration is held in another part of the city.[41] Similar rituals of violence have become familiar in Paris, where the mass demonstrations of 1968 have given way to gladiatorial skirmishes between disciplined student gangs and riot police, who, in their turn, have become more professional and are now equipped with additional powers under the new antiriot laws. The case of the Weathermen was the supreme example of how one radical student movement, failing to strike a responsive chord within the

[39] See Lucio Magri, "Italian Communism Today," *New Left Review* (London), no. 66 (March–April 1971), p. 49.

[40] See "You Don't Need a Weatherman to Know Which Way the Wind Blows," in *Weatherman*, ed. Harold Jacobs (New York: Ramparts, 1970), p. 53.

[41] For a useful discussion of changing techniques, see Bernard Béraud, *La gauche révolutionnaire au Japon* (Paris: Editions du Seuil, 1970), pp. 131–37.

nation as a whole, took to underground violence.

It is tempting to judge these *groupuscules* and would-be guerrillas in the light of one of Lenin's more acute observations: "Serious politics begins where millions of men and women are." Popular attitudes about politics and violence in most Western societies mean that most people will tend to view a terrorist group like the Weathermen with incomprehension or anger—although it is important to note that the attitudes of minority groups are sometimes different. The "Angry Brigade" terrorists who bombed the flat of Mr. John Davies, the British Secretary for Trade and Industry, on July 31, 1971 (supposedly in sympathy with Upper Clyde Shipyards workers threatened with redundancy) were not likely to win much of a hearing in a society where the legitimacy of the private use of political violence is not generally accepted. In the United States, a country with a record of much greater civil violence, the report of a recent national commission of violence was undoubtedly right when it said: "The historical and contemporary evidence of the United States suggests that popular support tends to sanction violence in support of the *status quo*; the use of public violence to maintain public order; the use of private violence to maintain popular conceptions of social order when government cannot or will not."[42] Put in cruder terms, this means that an increase in left-wing or revolutionary political violence is likely to mobilize the "law and order" majority and drive the government to take progressively tougher measures.

In short, the failure to mobilize popular support is the weakness of most of the contemporary urban guerrilla movements. Where they can find this support, they have a chance of success; where they cannot, they fail. And failure is frequent. This stems partly from the fact that the movements are estranged from the major left-wing parties (Asia is an exception), but also from something more fundamental. The terrorist is a man who refuses to compromise, to explore the possibilities of peaceful change. It is part of his task to convince his potential supporters that there are no prospects for constitutional change or nonviolent reform. Hence we see the dilemma of a group like the

Chilean Movement of the Revolutionary Left (MIR), which advocates violent revolution, after a Marxist President, Dr. Salvador Allende, was voted into power in September 1970. It is also the dilemma of armed extremists in the Western democracies. Their common tactic is to try to erode public confidence in the constitutional system by creating disorder in the streets, economic chaos, and a polarization of political forces around the "law and order" issue. As Che Guevara observed, "Where a government has come to power through some popular vote, fraudulent or not, the guerrilla outbreak cannot be promoted since the possibilities of peaceful struggle have not yet been exhausted."[43]

That judgment might seem to have been partially invalidated by the rise of powerful urban guerrilla movements in Venezuela and Uruguay, two functioning democracies where a genuine change in society can be brought about via the ballot box. But an election was instrumental in stealing the remnants of the terrorists' support in Caracas, and the same may still prove true in Uruguay.

The Problems of Response

Experience has shown that most modern governments can contain urban terrorism, so long as they can count on the loyalty of the security forces. The question is at what cost. Experience also leads to the sorry conclusion that police states are the most efficient of all in suppressing terrorist groups. No one is anticipating a wave of urban guerrilla activity in the Soviet Union or in South Africa.

Venezuela and Brazil are good examples of strong handling. In Venezuela, this was combined with the use of an election to swing public opinion away from the guerrillas.[44] President Betancourt was very astute in handling the armed forces and in dealing out repression. By studiously cultivating his senior officers, Betancourt won back the support of the security forces (which had been notoriously faction-ridden) while crushing the 1962 mutinies ruthlessly. He took great pains to show his respect for due legal process, and excep-

---

42 *Violence in America*, pp. 813–14.

43 Che Guevara, *Guerrilla Warfare* (Harmondsworth, Middlesex: Penguin, 1969), p. 14.
44 This account largely follows Moises Moleiro, *El MIR de Venezuela* (Havana: Guaivas Instituto del Libon, 1967), and Richard Gott, *Guerrilla Movements in Latin America* (London: Nelson, 1970), pp. 93–165.

tional measures were applied only when moderate opinion was already convinced of the need for them. For example, a vicious attack by the National Liberation Front (FLN) on an excursion train in September 1963 provided the perfect justification for the tough measures and emergency laws that were applied immediately afterward. Finally, by holding a free election (where 90 percent of the voters turned out, despite the FLN instruction to boycott the polls), Betancourt imposed a shattering political defeat on the rebels. After December 1963, the insurgents were hopelessly divided and the Communists returned to the theory of "peaceful coexistence" that was formally reinstated as party policy in 1967. The Venezuelan insurgency is now confined to a few roaming guerrilla bands in the hills of a Falcón Province that have so far managed to survive but have no impact on the politics of the country as a whole.

The example of Venezuela is important because the guerrillas there came closer to realizing the conditions for a successful urban insurrection than any later movement has managed to come. Looking back on 1962, Teodoro Petkoff, a leader of the Venezuelan Communist party, still insists that "we could have won."[45] Betancourt's formula for urban counterinsurgency may not be relevant to all contemporary situations. The Brazilians, operating within a very different political framework, have tried something cruder. The military response of the Brazilian government to the urban offensive was to eliminate the terrorist bases in the cities and to force them to do battle in situations where they were bound to be outgunned. This tactic depended (as did the French operation in Algiers in the late 1950s) on the use of mass interrogation—including the frequent and often irresponsible use of torture—to track down the guerrillas. Operation *Bandeirantes,* the counterguerrilla operation launched in São Paulo in 1969, was carried out by three columns of the Second Army, each of which was subdivided into sections responsible for interrogation, analysis of intelligence, and fighting operations.[46] In the last quarter of 1970, there

were six street battles in Rio and São Paulo, from which the security forces emerged the clear victors. By the end of 1970, several urban guerrilla groups had been decisively crushed, including the Revolutionary Armed Vanguard-Palmares and the Revolutionary Communist party of Brazil, and successive leaders of the National Liberation Action (ALN) had been captured or killed. Several attempts by the People's Revolutionary Vanguard (VPR) to found a rural base had been defeated by classic methods of encirclement, and urban terrorist operations in the first half of 1971 were confined to insignificant robberies and acts of random terrorism. In the course of the campaign, it became clear that the terrorists partly succeeded in their tactic of driving President Garrastazú Medici's government toward more repressive measures, and there is no doubt that these served to alienate important sections of the Brazilian middle class as well as liberal opinion abroad. On the other hand, the cohesion of the Brazilian armed forces, the size and complexity of the country, and a period of sustained economic growth all helped the government to overpower its local opposition.

But urban guerrillas can succeed in producing a polarization of political forces in such a way that the situation cannot easily be untangled, and this is precisely what extremists of both sides are counting on. Tom Hayden, one of the founders of the SDS, gave an American version of Marighella's strategy of militarization when he wrote: "The coming of repression will speed up time, making a revolutionary situation more likely—We are creating an America where it is necessary for the government to rule behind barbed wire, for the President to speak only at military bases and, finally, where it will be necessary for the people to fight back."[47]

It is in this sense that the urban terrorist in industrial societies should be seen as a political catalyst. It is arguable that, in most cases, urban guerrillas are dangerous less for what they do than for what they inspire: the erosion of the consensus, a hardening of the political battle lines, and a backlash that strikes back too hard and too indiscriminately. Terrorism and street

[45] See interview with Petkoff in *World Marxist Review* (Moscow), April 1968.

[46] See, *inter alia,* João Quartim, "La guérilla urbaine au Brésil," *Les Temps Modernes* (Paris), November 1970, pp. 838–74.

[47] Tom Hayden, *Rebellion and Repression* (Cleveland: Meridian, 1969), pp. 14, 16.

violence were used by the Nazis to help break down the fabric of Weimar Germany; the assassination of leading moderate politicians was used by ultranationalist groups in inter-war Japan to swing government policy toward a program of military expansion. What worked for the far right between the wars is likely to have rather different consequences for the far left today, although the tactic is similar. In the advanced industrial societies, political terrorists are unlikely to win support except in conditions of extreme social and economic crisis. On the other hand, as Mr. Pierre Trudeau, the Prime Minister of Canada, observed after the Cross-Laporte kidnappings in October 1970: "It only takes a few fanatics to show us just how vulnerable a democratic society can be when democracy is not ready to defend itself."[48] The full logic of that statement seems to be working itself out in Uruguay.

The Uruguayan government of President Pacheco Areco has faced a sustained offensive from the National Liberation Movement (Tupamaros) since 1968. (The organization was founded in 1963.) The security problem and the emergency measures that Pacheco applied to deal with it have deeply divided the government, and in June 1971 there was an unsuccessful attempt to impeach the President by Congress. The Tupamaros have shown signs of having infiltrated the armed forces, the police, and the civil service. Although the relatively powerful Uruguayan Communist party and the trade union leadership have refused to declare public support for the guerrillas, they may have to revise their attitude if the left wing *Frente Amplio* is defeated in the November 1971 presidential elections. The success of the Tupamaros in winning popular support has owed something to the country's continuing economic crisis (stemming from the drop in the world price of pastoral products) and to their very selective methods. Uruguay is a small and vulnerable democratic society that has come upon hard times—a welfare state that failed. But the most important factor was that the government of President Pacheco Areco was weak and divided, while the security forces at his disposal were tiny and without experience of counterguerrilla operations. There are only about 12,000 men in the Uru-

48 *Le Monde* (Paris), October 20, 1970.

guayan armed forces and 22,000 in the police. At the same time, President Pacheco found his hands tied by public opinion when it came to dealing with the guerrillas. Congress resisted the requested reintroduction of emergency measures. The weightiest obstacle to a revolution is the possibility of military intervention by one of the giant neighbors, Brazil or Argentina.

The situation in Ulster is a special case, which might be defined as *quasi*-colonial in the sense that the IRA bases its hopes on the calculation that the British government will eventually respond to the human and economic costs of maintaining order in the province by pulling out altogether. The IRA has set out to undermine successive moderate Unionist governments in Stormont in order to provoke a right-wing Protestant backlash, or direct rule from Westminster (which has sometimes been regarded as a step toward the unification of Ireland). The IRA's strength in the current campaign has stemmed from the measure of support it can command from the Catholic part of the population rather than from any degree of military competence or ingenuity. The IRA's campaign of terror in 1970–1971 had some success, helping to precipitate the fall of the Northern Ireland Prime Minister in March 1971, and then, in August 1971, leading to the introduction of internment. From its original role of keeping the peace between the Catholic and Protestant communities, the British Army moved over to an offensive intended to root out the IRA as a fighting force. Although the new tactics produced military results, they helped to polarize opinion in Ulster and enabled Catholic critics to represent the Army as a repressive force. In this sense, IRA terrorism succeeded. It led to a situation where the British Army, which began as the referee between the two communities in Ulster, appeared as a party to the quarrel. The chaos it engendered helped to postpone the application of social reforms designed to get to the root of the problem and thus eroded Catholic faith in solutions within the existing framework.

Whatever their hopes of success, the tactics employed by the urban guerrillas pose a direct threat to the international order. The theory of global revolution that has been used in the attempt to rationalize crimes against diplomats and other foreign citizens is a flat rejection of the principles that have traditionally guided relations between sovereign states. The claim to a right to rebel under intolerable social and political conditions cannot be used to sanction this type of international crime. It is also clear that there is an indirect link between civil violence and the strategic balance.

In the United States, the immediate effect of mounting civil dissent (for which the common platform is opposition to the Vietnam War) has been to impose constraints on foreign policy. Dissent within the American armed forces has made it increasingly probable that the Army will have to dispense with the draft and "to professionalize"—which will clearly limit the country's capacity to intervene in outside conflicts and will also make it difficult to maintain current troop levels in Europe. The likelihood that dissent will continue to take violent forms in the United States adds to the possibility that the Americans will enter a new isolationist phase in their attitude toward the world. Although race relations and Black Power violence remain the most obvious threats to civil peace in America, these are unlikely to boil over into full-scale ghetto revolts. It is hard to imagine that any rational Black Power leader would expose his followers to the risks involved in an uprising in a limited area that could be easily encircled—or that any American government would fail to take vigorous action against it.

Terrorism may prove to have the most dangerous effects in Western industrial societies. A revolution in Uruguay, after all, would hardly alter the strategic balance in any significant way. On the other hand, ghetto revolts in the United States could disrupt the most powerful economy in the world and impose severe constraints on America's capacity to act as a great power. A sustained campaign of urban terrorism in Europe might undermine popular faith in the democratic system and raise the prospect of a more repressive form of government. Terrorists, of course, rarely make revolutions. In Latin America, for example, the most radical social changes in recent years have been brought about by a reformist military junta in Peru and a freely elected Marxist government in Chile. These are likely to be the patterns for future bloodless revolutions. And the Chilean formula could apply to Italy, where the prospect of a governing coalition including Communists is much more immediate, and more serious, than a revolution of the streets. This leads to the conclusion that the urban guerrilla is a political catalyst whose actions can radicalize a society and bring about the kind of social and economic confusion that will lead to a decline in popular belief in peaceful solutions. The end results may be indirect and will often take forms that neither the guerrillas nor the government anticipated.

BIBLIOGRAPHY: PART II

Bloomfield, Lincoln P., and Leiss, Amelia C. *Controlling Small Wars*. New York: Alfred A. Knopf, 1969. 421 pp.

In an age when local, limited conflicts tend to involve the superpowers and risk their confrontation, this book, through careful examination of several case studies, proposes a new strategy of conflict control that the U.S. might pursue. The proposal is designed to support U.S. interests while avoiding overreaching either those interests or U.S. power. The strategy includes multilateral pressures, insulation of the area from outside interference, promotion of internal reforms, a more rational aid policy, and the selective use of deterrent military power.

Brodie, Bernard S. *Strategy in the Missile Age*. Princeton: Princeton University Press, 1959. 423 pp. Cloth and paper.

This RAND Corporation study approaches historical and contemporary military problems and strategy from the viewpoint of the national policy planner. The author concludes that the ramifications of nuclear warfare preclude preventive war as an acceptable alternative for the United States; therefore, our strategy must be based on deterring a potential adversary from launching a first strike. The threat of nuclear devastation causes nations to prefer to settle their contests of strength in a limited, rather than an unrestricted, manner. Proper preparation for the contingency of limited war requires a balanced military force.

————. *Escalation and the Nuclear Option*. Princeton: Princeton University Press, 1966. 151 pp.

Brodie argues that the use of tactical nuclear weapons in future limited conflicts should not be entirely ruled out. Strategies which preclude the use of any weapon in our arsenal downgrade the deterrent effect of that weapon. Brodie acknowledges the often expressed danger that the use of tactical nuclear weapons could not be limited and would likely escalate to general nuclear war; however, he believes this factor alone should not eliminate their potential use. More exploration is needed in this area to determine how and when tactical nuclear weapons could be used with minimal risk of causing a wider conflict. He rules out Vietnam as a testing ground.

Bull, Hedley. *The Control of the Arms Race*. New York: Frederick A. Praeger, 1965. 235 pp.

In this study, first published in 1961, the author objectively and lucidly defines the objectives, conditions, and nature of arms control and disarmament and assesses their feasibility and desirability. He succinctly summarizes many of the arguments found elsewhere. The study still stands as one of the best available introductions to the subject.

Deitchman, Seymour J. *Limited War and American Defense Policy*. Cambridge, Mass.: M.I.T. Press, 1969. 280 pp.

This is a comprehensive study of limited war from the planner's point of view: objectives, means, and environments for limited war, and the process and techniques used in force and operations planning. Attention is paid to both conventional and unconventional limited-war planning problems.

Fall, Bernard B. *The Two Viet-Nams: A Political and Military Analysis*. New York: Praeger, 1963. 448 pp.

A classic on the roots of insurgency in Vietnam, this volume was followed by the author's *Street Without Joy* and *Vietnam Witness*. Fall examines both the similarities and differences between North Vietnam and South Vietnam and relates how the experiences of the 1950s hardened the lines between the two. He traces the political fortune of the Diem regime and the related American involvement with a skill born of intense research and scholarly analysis.

Galula, David. *Counterinsurgency Warfare: Theory and Practice*. New York: Praeger, 1964. 143 pp.

Galula concisely and clearly contrasts the phenomena of revolution, conspiracy, and civil war with insurgency in order to recognize and understand the political techniques involved. After describing a successful insurgency, Galula turns to the role of the counterinsurgent and discusses necessary tasks and common pitfalls. A broad strategy is presented along with the step-by-step tactical application necessary for the government to use its advantages to again win the allegiance of the population.

George, Alexander L.; Hall, David K.; and Simons, William E. *The Limits of Coercive Diplomacy: Laos, Cuba, Vietnam*. Boston: Little, Brown & Co., 1971. 259 pp. Cloth and paper.

A useful historical and analytical perspective is applied in this study on the use of force in international affairs. Through an intensive examination of the Cuban missile crisis, the decision to bomb North Vietnam, the Laotian crisis of 1961, and brief sketches of several other foreign policy crises in recent American history, the authors formulate a series of propositions regarding crisis management and strategies for the use of force. Particular attention is given to the strategy of coercive diplomacy—the limited, controlled use of force and threats of force to influence the opponent's will and expectations—and the special preconditions which allow for the successful adoption of this strategy.

Halperin, Morton H. *Defense Strategies for the Seventies*. Boston: Little, Brown & Co., 1971. 149 pp. Cloth and paper.

Halperin's study serves as a brief, but good, nontechnical introduction to the major strategic policy issues facing the United States in this decade. Halperin reviews the evolution of American, Soviet, and Chinese strategy since World War II, the problems of preventing general nuclear war, the problems posed by the use of tactical nuclear weapons, and the problems of escalation in limited wars. He also includes a chapter on arms control which reviews the issues involved at the Strategic Arms Limitations Talks (SALT) and the ramifications of the Nuclear Non-proliferation Treaty. A good bibliography is included.

Institute for Strategic Studies, London. *The Military Balance* and *Strategic Survey*. Annual publications of the ISS.

The Military Balance reviews the comparative military postures of nations throughout the world, placing particular emphasis on the major powers. Items covered include size and equipment of the various forces, population, gross national product, and annual defense expenditures. A comparison of the relative strengths of NATO and the Warsaw Pact is included.

Strategic Survey covers developments in strategic policy, relationships, and thought during the previous year. The studies begin with a look at the superpowers, continue with a review of each major area of the world, and conclude with some subjects of general worldwide interest. Chronologies of major events by geographic area also are included.

Kahn, Herman. *On Thermonuclear War*. Princeton: Princeton University Press, 1960. 668 pp. Cloth and paper.

This controversial book is a compilation of three lectures delivered at Princeton in 1959. Although the author is hopeful that a nuclear exchange between the two major powers can be avoided, he believes it is not enough to limit strategic thinking to deterrence. The possibility and results of nuclear warfare must be examined, and this Kahn does with what some people claim to be an exceedingly cold, calculating manner. He concludes that the United States and the Soviet Union could survive an all-out nuclear exchange, and that the societies could be rebuilt, although the losses on both sides would be staggering.

————. *On Escalation*. New York: Frederick A. Praeger, 1965. 300 pp.

Kahn's seminal work spins out in imaginative detail a conceptual model to be used in understanding the possible structure and functioning of the escalation process. The model extends from peaceful disagreement in a cold-war situation through seven thresholds, or "firebreaks," dividing forty-four rungs on an escalation ladder to spasm general nuclear war and its aftermaths.

Kissinger, Henry A. *The Necessity for Choice: Prospects of American Foreign Policy*. New York: Harper & Bros., 1961. 370 pp. Cloth and paper.

This volume updates the author's well-known book *Nuclear Weapons and Foreign Policy* (1957). At that time Kissinger advocated a nuclear strategy, believing the best deterrent against Communist aggression would be the knowledge that the United States would resort to a nuclear response at the advent of hostilities. Additional study of the problems of employment of nuclear weapons on a limited scale, plus the rapid increase in the Soviet nuclear stockpile, led the author to conclude that the use of these weapons had become too risky. As a result he advocates a defense capability which has a maximum number of alternatives through the spectrum of conventional and nuclear warfare. This book is a perceptive study of the complete range of political and military problems associated with strategy in the missile age.

Laird, Melvin R. *National Security Strategy of Realistic Deterrence (Annual Defense Department Report, FY 1973)*. Washington, D.C.: Government Printing Office, 1972. 203 pp. Paper.

The annual reports of the Secretary of Defense to Congress in support of budget requests contain considerable material on strategic planning. The Fiscal Year 1973 report discusses the implementation of the strategy of Realistic Deterrence (a deterrence system based on balanced forces) in support of the Nixon Doctrine.

Levine, Robert A. *The Arms Debate*. Cambridge, Mass.: Harvard University Press, 1963. 334 pp.

Levine describes and analyzes various schools of thought on arms policy. In order not to misinterpret their positions, he quotes at length from the original writings. He divides the schools of arms policy into five categories: systemic antiwar, marginal antiwar, marginal middle school, marginal anticommunist, and systemic anticommunist. The chief value of this book is the clarity of its classification and analysis of arms recommendations, as well as the scope of opinion which is reflected.

Liddell-Hart, Basil H. *Strategy*. 2nd ed. New York: Frederick A. Praeger, 1967. 430 pp. Cloth and paper.

The author outlines the decisive wars from 490 B.C. through the Second World War and summarizes his theories of warfare. He contends that the strategy of the indirect approach—i.e., attacks on the enemy's rear areas and lines of communication, in particular—are more effective and provide a more economical use of force than direct, frontal assaults. He holds that the dislocation of the enemy's psychological and physical balance is the critical prelude to his overthrow. Liddell-Hart believes that the strategy of the indirect approach is applicable, not only to warfare, but to all realms of life, including politics and economics. For instance, opposition to a new idea can be diminished by a flanking movement rather than by a frontal attack on a long-established position.

Mallin, Jay. *Strategy for Conquest*. Miami: University of Miami Press, 1970. 381 pp.

This volume is a compilation of writings by some of communism's leading guerrilla strategists. Contains selections by Mao Tse-tung, Vo Nguyen Giap, Che Guevara, Lin Piao, and Raul Castro. These primary sources clarify the tactics, strategies, and objectives of communist insurgencies and provide the thoughtful observer with insight into the development of insurgency theory.

McNamara, Robert S. *The Essence of Security: Reflections in Office.* New York: Harper & Row, 1968. 176 pp. Cloth and paper.

This study draws from policy statements made by Robert McNamara during his seven years as Secretary of Defense. His strategy of defense is built on two concepts, collective security and flexible response. While advocating the continuation of a strategic nuclear capability, McNamara rejects the doctrine of Massive Retaliation as being useless in meeting many threats to our security. His answer is Flexible Response, which, in essence, means having the capability of employing numerous alternatives along the spectrum of nuclear and conventional warfare. In the area of collective security, McNamara holds that our allies, particularly in Western Europe, are capable of making a greater contribution to the total effort, especially in strengthening their conventional forces.

Osgood, Robert E. *Limited War: The Challenge to American Strategy.* Chicago: The University of Chicago Press, 1957. 315 pp.

In this important book written during the period when Massive Retaliation was still the strategy relied upon to meet the threat of communist aggression, Osgood argues that the United States must be prepared to meet the challenge of limited war in the future. The author holds that the ramifications of total nuclear war are such that it cannot be a rational response to all forms of aggression; therefore, we must be prepared to meet the challenge of communist "blackmail" in thrusts which have limited objectives. In light of the Vietnam experience, the author's comments on the attitudes of the American public toward limited war are interesting, for he accurately predicted that such a strategy, which usually leads to stalemate, has little emotional or moral appeal in this country. Nevertheless, he contends that the "unconditional victory" syndrome is obsolete in the nuclear era.

Pike, Douglas. *Viet Cong.* Cambridge, Mass.: M.I.T. Press, 1966. 490 pp. Cloth and paper.

Pike opens the very archives of the Viet Cong, organizes them in a meaningful way, and gives us the most detailed and accurate portrait of the NFL/Hanoi relationship to date. The beliefs and intentions of the NFL as stated in their party directives, or by former Viet Cong in interviews, provide insight in striking contrast to the propaganda efforts which so obscure the conflict. Pike's background as a foreign service officer with six years' experience in Vietnam, coupled with the primary source material available to him, have resulted in what will very probably remain the definitive work on the subject.

Quester, George H. "Some Conceptual Problems in Nuclear Proliferation." *American Political Science Review,* 66 (June 1972): 490–97.

Assuming that the Nuclear Non-proliferation Treaty may not stop additional nations from joining the nuclear club, Quester explores the motivations that lead to weapons acquisition and the problems involved in determining a particular state's physical and political capabilities to build a bomb. The author offers some models which estimate the time-lag between a country's decision to become a nuclear power and the time when it will reach that goal. He holds that estimating nuclear proliferation may pose some of the same strategic calculation problems as does estimating deterrence capabilities once the weapons are acquired.

Rosecrance, Richard, ed. *The Future of the International Strategic System.* San Francisco: Chandler Publishing Co., 1972. 219 pp. Cloth and paper.

This reader explores the problems of nuclear proliferation. An underlying premise of the book is that the Nuclear Non-proliferation Treaty should not be cause for complacency, because some important countries are not signatories, and some others who have adhered to the treaty still possess the capability to become nuclear powers within a short period of time should they decide to renounce the agreement. Generally the contributors agree that the spread of nuclear weapons will produce a less stable international security system. Problems of strategy regarding nuclear proliferation are explored, as are systems of rewards and punishments that might deter nations from acquiring nuclear capabilities.

Schelling, Thomas C. *The Strategy of Conflict.* New York: Oxford University Press, 1960 and 1963. 303 pp. Cloth and paper.

Schelling has made a classic contribution to the theories of games, conflict, communication, bargaining, deterrence, and limited war. It contains many seminal ideas used elsewhere by scholars and practitioners alike, in both domestic and international politics.

———. *Arms and Influence.* New Haven, Conn.: Yale University Press, 1966. 293 pp. Cloth and paper.

Schelling expands some of his thoughts which appeared in *The Strategy of Conflict.* He deals primarily with the ways in which the United States can use its military resources to compel other nations to comply with its will. Schelling defines and analyzes the practice of "coercive warfare," which he defines as using our "power to hurt" to produce the desired response or behavior pattern on the part of the enemy. He examines the interplay of national purpose and military force. He has attempted to find common features in all contests of human will, especially those in which the threat of pain is present. He also asserts that modern warfare, especially since the advent of nuclear weapons, makes military strategy no longer the "science of military victory" but the "diplomacy of violence."

Schelling, Thomas C., and Halperin, Morton H. *Strategy and Arms Control.* New York: The Twentieth Century Fund, 1961. 143 pp. Cloth and paper.

This is a highly theoretical treatise which grew out of non-zero-sum game theory and bargaining that links the goals and results of arms control with those of strategy. The authors provide an original and thought-provoking analysis of the relationship of arms control to the likelihood and results of general war, limited war, and the arms race.

Waskow, Arthur I. *The Limits of Defense.* Garden City, N.Y.: Doubleday Inc., 1962. 119 pp.

A classic representative of the antideterrence school, Waskow examines counterforce deterrent, balanced deterrent (countervalue plus limited war), mixed counterforce and balanced

deterrent, and arms control theories. He rejects all four, based on concise, tightly reasoned arguments, and proposes to put in their place a gradualist policy of "disarmament-plus." Another, more recent classic of this genre is Philip Green, *The Deadly Logic* (New York: Schocken Books, 1968), 276 pp.

Wohlstetter, Albert. "The Delicate Balance of Terror." *Foreign Affairs,* 37 (January 1959): 211–34.

Wohlstetter's classic article deals with the problems defense planners faced during the 1960s. Many of the author's points remain valid today. He is concerned with the view held by most Western defense planners that general thermonuclear war is extremely unlikely because both sides have a credible deterrent that is relatively easy to maintain. The author holds that the achievement of a first-strike capability by the Soviet Union cannot be completely discounted, if the U.S.S.R. establishes such a goal, and that the temptation to use such a capability would be extremely great before an effective countermeasure could be developed. U.S. strategy should provide for a protected retaliatory capability, an increased capability for conventional warfare to deal with limited conflicts, and a better system of passive defense (shelters).

Part III · American Defense Policymaking

Introduction to Defense Policymaking

RICHARD G. HEAD

The study of defense policymaking is much like the story of the six blind men and the elephant—what one reports is often limited to what one touches. With a subject as large as defense policymaking—or an elephant—the approach is often critical, determining in advance what the outer limits of discovery may be. The approach we have chosen to take is descriptive and explanatory. Using basic data and interpretations for prediction, we approach defense policymaking through the study of three important areas: theories about how decisions are made (Chapter 6); a description of the actors and the process (Chapter 7); and a particular look at the system's response to innovation (Chapter 8).

The first of these areas is decisionmaking theory, which in political science is characterized by the study of at least six critical variables: (1) *actors*—their values and perceptions; (2) the *situation*—crisis, routine, or a mixture; (3) the *organizational system*—the general set of relatively fixed roles and relationships among the major institutions involved in the decision; (4) the *decisionmaking process*—a chronological flow of activities and events leading to the decision; (5) the *decisional unit*—the precise relationship of the major decisionmakers; and (6) *choice*—the decision—the selection of one course of action from among a list of alternatives.[1]

---

[1] The theory of decisionmaking in political science is best described by Richard C. Snyder, H. W. Bruck, and Burton Sapin, eds., *Foreign Policy Decision-Making* (New York: Free Press of Glencoe, 1962), and by Glenn D. Paige, *The Korean Decision* (New York: Free Press of Glencoe, 1968). Both volumes benefited from earlier works by Herbert A. Simon, *Administrative Behavior* (Glencoe, Ill.: Free Press, 1957) and *Organizations*, with James G. March (New York: John Wiley & Sons, 1958).

This emphasis upon "choice" is similar to the Rational Policy Model described by Allison in Chapter 6, but it introduces the valuable elements of organizational and individual actors' perceptions. Moreover, both the Rational Policy Model and decisionmaking theories tend to neglect what happens *after* the decision is made—the process variously called execution or implementation. For the purposes of this book we will use the following definition:

Defense Policymaking is a sequence of activities or a process involving authoritative governmental positions and action in the areas of national security strategy, force structure, and manpower. Analytically, it can be separated into three main parts: policy formulation, policy decision, and policy implementation. The process is characterized by the participation of a number of actors (both individual and institutional, each of whom tends to possess different definitions of the situation), uncertainty about what should be done, and high stakes in terms of the security of the nation and the interests of the various individuals and groups in a political environment.

This definition is similar to that for decisionmaking, but it places more stress on the institutional actors and includes the process of organizational implementation.

BUREAUCRACY: A THEORY OF ORGANIZATION

The focus on the institutional actors in the decisionmaking process has sparked a renewed interest in the study of bureaucracy. Richard Neustadt, Graham Allison, Morton Halperin, and others have contributed to the formulation of a Bureaucratic Politics Model which is described in Chapter 6 in "Conceptual Models and the Cuban Missile Crisis" and "Why Bureaucrats Play Games." Their main purpose is to stress that defense policymaking is *not only* a function of pure rationality—the ideas that go into the process—but also the product of organizational and bureaucratic structure. In order to understand their approach more fully, we will discuss some of the elements of a bureaucracy.

First, a bureaucracy is a large organization divided according to specialties into fixed and official jurisdictional areas that are ordered by laws, rules, and regulations. Second, a bureaucracy is organized hierarchically—that is, there are levels of graded authority with a firmly ordered system of super- and subordination. Third, bureaucratic management is based on the written documents (the "files") that are maintained. The body of officials actively engaged in a public office, their equipment, and the files constitute a "bureau." Fourth, office management presupposes thorough and expert training, and the work constitutes a career with levels of promotion. Fifth, the management of the bureau follows general rules (policy) that are relatively stable, exhaustive, and can be learned. The mastery of these rules represents a special technical learning which the officials possess. The officials decide matters in a "rational" manner—that is, they interpret "rules over the individual" in a manner of formal impersonality.

One of the early theorists of bureaucracy was Max Weber, a German sociologist who emphasized the technical functions of the bureaucracy. With his "machine model" he attempted to incorporate the advances of the Industrial Revolution into the design of organizations. The primary reason for Weber's pride in bureaucracy was that it represented a method of social organization which was superior to the personal subjugation, nepotism, emotional outbursts, and haphazard judgments that passed for management in his day. Weber saw in bureaucracy a means to institutionalize rationality—man's reasoning powers. He further specified that bureaucracy was technically the *most advanced* form of social organization known to man.

Experience tends universally to show that the purely bureaucratic type of administrative organization . . . is, from a purely technical point of view capable of attaining the highest degree of efficiency and is in this sense formally the most rational known means of carrying out imperative control over human beings.[2]

Modern theorists of organization are much less enthusiastic about the inherent technical "perfection" of bureaucracy, and are much more concerned about the social consequences of bureau operation.[3] Many of the criticisms of bureaucracy are directed at the social consequences it has on workers' lives and upon the culture of the society at large.

CRITIQUES OF BUREAUCRACY

The viable organization must meet two central criteria: (1) it must maintain an internal, human enterprise system; and (2) it must adapt to and influence the external environment. Among the criticisms in these two areas are: failure to adequately allow for personal growth and the development of mature personalities; the development of conformity and "group-think"; failure to provide adequate means for resolving differences and conflicts among the ranks, particularly between functional groups; that communication and ideas are thwarted or distorted by hierarchical divisions; that the full potential of people is not being utilized, because of mistrust, fear, etc.; and the inability to assimilate the influx of new technology or scientists into the organization.[4] Further, bureaucracy has been criticized for establishing the dominance of rules over people, for its lack of creativity, and for its resistance to innovation.

One theme that is implicit in these and many other criticisms of bureaucracy is the objection to centralized control. Indeed, for many years, bureaucratic theory was used to justify an increasing trend toward larger, more centralized organizations in both business and government. The slogans of this centralization were "economy" and "efficiency." Critics argue that the United States has passed the optimal point with centralization and that organizations should be more concerned with humanization,

---

[2] Max Weber, *The Theory of Social and Economic Organization*, trans. A. M. Henderson and Talcott Parsons (Glencoe, Ill.: Free Press, 1947), p. 337.

[3] Anthony Downs, *Inside Bureaucracy* (Boston: Little, Brown & Co., 1967), p. 40.

[4] Warren G. Bennis, "Beyond Bureaucracy," *American Bureaucracy* (New York: Aldine, 1970), p. 6.

participation, and decentralization. The latter trend, Alvin Toffler argues in *Future Shock*, is the wave of the future because "adhocracy" is the only viable organizational response to increasingly rapid technological changes.[5]

The purpose of this discussion is not to determine whether bureaucracy or its critics have the better argument; it is to set the stage for organizational and bureaucratic explanations of defense policymaking. The theory of bureaucratic decisionmaking is discussed by Allison, Halperin, Krasner, and Chayes in Chapter 6. Allison presents three conceptual models in a systematic attempt to analyze how decisionmakers approach policy problems. Halperin combines elements of Allison's models II and III and elaborates on the characteristics of Bureaucratic Politics. Chayes takes the Bureaucratic Politics perspective and applies the theory to a single area of defense policy—arms control.

This new emphasis on bureaucracy through the work of Neustadt, Allison, Halperin, and others has been widely acclaimed as a major advance in policy analysis, but three main criticisms of Bureaucratic Politics have been made: (1) it tends to undervalue the distinctive role and power of the President; (2) it focuses almost exclusively on what is happening *within* the bureaucracy and treats domestic politics, congressional relations, and other *external* matters as mere *constraints*; and (3) while invaluable for *explanation*, the model is less useful for *planning* and *prediction*.[6] Krasner combines these criticisms with some of his own and attacks Bureaucratic Politics as being inaccurate, misleading, and dangerous to democratic theory.

The theory of Bureaucratic Politics and the criticisms of it presented in Chapter 6 provide the reader with alternative conceptual approaches to the study of defense policymaking. These perspectives should allow the reader to approach the articles on the major organiza-

[5] Alvin Toffler, *Future Shock* (New York: Random House, 1970), p. 422.
[6] Allison and Halperin have attempted to increase the planning and prediction potential of the model with the publication of "Bureaucratic Politics: A Paradigm and Some Policy Implications," *World Politics*, 24, suppl. (Spring 1972): 40–79. An excellent description of Bureaucratic Politics in an intergovernmental setting is Richard E. Neustadt, *Alliance Politics* (New York: Cambridge University Press, 1970); see also the bibliography for Part III of the present volume.

tional actors (Chapter 7) with a critical viewpoint. Our primary purposes in these two chapters are to explain how policy is made and how conflict can be generated when reasonable men differ in their interpretation of what course to follow. This conflict is a part of the defense policy process, and it is caused by four basic factors: different organizational interests; different methods of perceiving reality; different information; and uncertainty. These differing perspectives of the actors have led to the development of several perpetual issues concerning the proper organization of the defense policy process. An understanding of these issues and of their underlying sources of conflict will add to the reader's grasp of the case studies presented in Chapter 8.

ISSUES IN DEFENSE ORGANIZATION

CENTRALIZATION

The most dominant trend in defense organization since the Root Reforms of the U.S. Army in 1903 has undoubtedly been *centralization*. Centralization has affected the role of each military service, the creation of an independent Air Force, the growth of the Joint Chiefs of Staff (JCS), the rise of the powerful Office of the Secretary of Defense (OSD), and the institutionalization of the National Security Council (NSC). Centralization was the issue in the World War II "unification" debates which led to the National Security Act of 1947. It was also the critical factor in the "McNamara revolution" of the 1960s. The issue briefly stated is: Should the functions of national security policymaking be centralized or decentralized? If some functions should be centralized, at what level would this be appropriate —the Secretary of Defense, the National Security Council, or some other agency? If some functions should be decentralized, which should be assigned to OSD, the services, and the combatant commands? There are no final answers to these questions, and organization theory provides no pat solutions.

The essential point is that changes in organizational structure are fundamentally political —that is, they directly affect the distribution of power, influence, and access of individuals and groups in the governing process. Defense reorganizations can be most productively analyzed as attempts to centralize or decentralize in the context of the larger political environment. Primary factors in this analysis include the perceived performance of the present structure, events in the international arena, and the distinctive operating style of the President. (See Halperin, "The President and the Military," in Chapter 7.)

Thus, being responsive to Presidents who gave him the mandate, Secretary McNamara (1961–1968) inaugurated an exceptionally centralized management system in DOD. When President Nixon was elected in 1968, one of his campaign issues was the alleged "overcentralization" of DOD decisionmaking. When Nixon appointed Dr. Henry A. Kissinger as his Presidential Assistant for National Security Affairs, a process of simultaneous centralization and decentralization of DOD functions began. Nixon and Kissinger revitalized the National Security Council and centralized many of the functions previously handled by McNamara's OSD staff. (See Leacacos, "The Nixon NSC," in Chapter 7.) At the same time Nixon and Secretary of Defense Laird *decentralized* the initiative for many other OSD functions back to the services. In a sense, what Nixon and Kissinger attempted to do was to centralize the overall, broad *policymaking* on selected defense issues, such as the DOD budget and the SALT talks, and to decentralize the detailed *management* of programs, such as field operations, requirements, and weapons acquisition. The manner in which the President arrives at these policy decisions is, itself, another issue.

Presidential Policymaking— Formalized or Pragmatic?

Beginning at the apex of policymaking in the United States, there is continuing discussion about the proper organization of the Presidency. The alternatives are roughly between the formalized National Security Council under President Eisenhower and the more loosely structured, informal system under Presidents Kennedy and Johnson. Just prior to the 1968 election the Institute for Defense Analysis in Washington compiled an interesting study on this question. The authors cited three principles that any presidential procedures should maintain:

1. They should channel major policy questions, adequately staffed, to the President.

2. They should direct most operational matters elsewhere.
3. They should provide opportunity for the President himself (at least through his staff), to keep aware of what is going on and to intervene on any matter, at any time, before it gathers a momentum of its own.[7]

The authors then made an exhaustive list of the advantages of each alternative, noting that a substantial consensus of the participants interviewed were in favor of "more systematic procedures in policymaking and guidance." After the 1968 election President Nixon structured the National Security Council as his primary defense policymaking body, but the debate continues.

Congressional Advice and Consent

At the same time that policymaking in the White House was becoming more centralized under Nixon, the critics of executive power were claiming that Congress merited a larger voice in national security. In the American governmental system of separate powers and divided responsibilities there has always been a congressional-executive debate, but it accelerated in intensity as the Vietnam War dragged on and became increasingly unpopular. Three leaders in this move to exert congressional influence were Senator Fulbright, through the Senate Foreign Relations Committee; Senator Proxmire, through the Joint Economic Committee; and Senator Mansfield, Senate Majority Leader. The specific issues where the congressional-executive relationship was prominent were the annual budget process, the Safeguard ABM deployment, the end-the-war amendments, and the SALT treaties. (See Gibson's "Congressional Attitudes Toward Defense," Chapter 7).

Role of the Secretary of Defense

The position of the Secretary of Defense with respect to the services is both critical and controversial. The first Secretary of Defense was James Forrestal, who presided over three independent service departments with only a tiny staff. The authority of OSD was formally expanded in 1949, 1953, and again in 1958, which further strengthened the centralization

---

[7] Keith C. Clark and Laurence J. Legere, *The President and the Management of National Security* (New York: Praeger, 1969), p. 29.

trend. By 1961, when Robert McNamara became Defense Secretary, the legal authority of the office was sufficient to form the base for a series of administrative, policymaking changes which has been called a "revolution." These changes were designed around the PPBS budgeting system and a centralized analytical staff, described by Enthoven and Smith in "New Concepts and New Tools to Shape the Defense Program" in Chapter 7 below. By 1968, when McNamara left office, there was widespread criticism of "overcentralization" in OSD. President Nixon appointed sixteen prominent civilians to the Blue Ribbon Defense Panel and authorized them to make a broad-scale study of the Department of Defense. Their findings were listed in a report published in 1970 and included this attack on centralization:

As a result of its examination of the Defense Department, the Panel found that: effective civilian control is impaired by a generally excessive centralization of decision-making authority at the level of the Secretary of Defense. . . .
The President and the Secretary of Defense do not presently have the opportunity to consider all viable options as background for making decisions, because differences of opinion are submerged or compromised at lower levels of the Department of Defense.[8]

President Nixon and Secretary Laird almost immediately adopted this recommendation and decentralized many OSD functions back to the services. However, the Blue Ribbon Panel went on to recommend many changes that had been discussed under the justification of centralization. These recommendations were not adopted by the Nixon Administration, but they are cited here as representative arguments for further changes in DOD organizational structure.

The panel recommended that OSD be divided into three major functional groupings: (1) Military Operations; (2) Management of Resources; and (3) Evaluation. Each of these three groups would have a Deputy Secretary (the second-ranking position in DOD). The three military departments would *not* report to the Secretary as they do now, but to the Deputy Secretary for Management of Resources. In addition, the Deputy Secretary for Operations

would assume responsibility for the vital functions of (1) military operations, (2) unified commands, (3) operational requirements, (4) intelligence, (5) communications, and (6) international security affairs. The panel also recommended the JCS be removed from the operational chain of command.

These recommendations amounted to a fundamental restructuring of the role of the Secretary of Defense and would have resulted in an extension of the centralization trend into military operations. The effect of these changes would have been to reduce severely the roles of the individual services and to question their continued viability. The panel's recommendations were controversial and show the range of discussion over the proper allocation of roles between the Secretary of Defense and the services.

INTERSERVICE RIVALRY

The issue of interservice rivalry underlies almost all criticisms of defense organization. It is closely linked to the history of roles and missions agreements among the services and to debates over unification. Huntington, a leading proponent of the advantages of independent services, coined the phrase, "Interservice rivalry was the child of unification."[9] Interservice rivalry played a major role in the B-36/flush-deck carrier debate in 1949, the Thor/Jupiter programs of 1955–1957, and the A-7/AX/Cheyenne/Harrier programs of 1965–1972. (See "Doctrinal Innovation and the A-7 Attack Aircraft Decisions," Chapter 8, and the Bibliography for Part III.)

The classic criticisms of interservice rivalry are that it is expensive and promotes duplication. Others include the charge that it motivates suboptimization at the expense of "national" policies, that it contributes to a loss of civilian (executive) control, and that it inhibits unification. These arguments are related to the issue of centralization because they essentially attempt to banish disagreement among the contending agencies by central control.

The defenders of interservice rivalry argue that disagreement is the basis for organizational

---

[8] *Blue Ribbon Defense Panel Report*, July 1, 1970, p. 1.

[9] Samuel P. Huntington, "Inter-Service Competition and the Political Roles of the Armed Services," *American Political Science Review*, 40, no. 1 (March 1961): 41.

vitality and strength. They say that competition produces better policy, better ideas, keeps the public better informed, contributes to an active role for Congress, promotes civilian control over the military, avoids doctrinal uniformity and rigidity, provides a hedge against the failure of any one doctrine, and is consistent with the American political theory of pluralism.

The causes of interservice rivalry are the subculture differences which develop when any large organization is specialized. (See the author's "Doctrinal Innovation and the A-7 Attack Aircraft Decisions," Chapter 8.) Specialization promotes professional socialization along many different lines, but the choice of *which* lines is often determined by organizational structure. Thus, if the major components are organized according to mode of transportation —air, land, and sea—the major routes of competition will parallel this organization. But, if the organization were structured along functional lines—strategic, tactical, and support, for instance—it is likely that competition would merely develop along these dimensions rather than be eliminated.

In conclusion, Part III attempts to do three things: to introduce the student to the theory of bureaucratic politics; to describe some of the major actors and institutions in the policymaking process; and to illustrate the process of innovation and change through the use of selected case studies. The strategies and concepts from Part II provide most of the issues discussed under policymaking, but the debate takes place within a structural framework and in an organizational setting described in this Part. Together, the strategies and policymaking form the basis for public evaluation of defense policy, a topic taken up in Part IV, "The Military and American Society."

CHAPTER 6

The Theory of
Bureaucratic Decisionmaking

CONCEPTUAL MODELS AND THE CUBAN MISSILE CRISIS

GRAHAM T. ALLISON

Allison challenges the traditional approach to explaining foreign policy decisionmaking and its use of a Rational Policy Model. He notes that the influence of ideas is less significant than the interplay of organizational and bureaucratic factors. Accordingly, he develops two alternative approaches: an Organizational Process Model and a Bureaucratic Politics Model. Each of the three models is explained according to its basic unit of analysis, organizing concepts, dominant inference pattern, general propositions, and specific propositions, using the Cuban missile crisis as a case study. The figure following the article presents a summary of the models and concepts. Dr. Allison is a Professor of Politics at Harvard University and teaches in the Public Policy Program of the John Fitzgerald Kennedy School of Government. This article is part of a larger study published in 1971 under the title Essence of Decision: Explaining the Cuban Missile Crisis.

The Cuban missile crisis is a seminal event. For thirteen days in October 1962, there was a higher probability that more human lives would end suddenly than ever before in history. Had the worst occurred, the death of 100 million Americans, over 100 million Russians, and millions of Europeans as well would make previous natural calamities and inhumanities appear insignificant. Given the probability of disaster —which President Kennedy estimated as "between 1 out of 3 and even"—our escape seems awesome.[1] This event symbolizes a central, if only partially thinkable, fact about our exist-

[1] Theodore Sorensen, *Kennedy* (New York, 1965), p. 705.

ence. That such consequences could follow from the choices and actions of national governments obliges students of government, as well as participants in governance, to think hard about these problems.

Improved understanding of this crisis depends in part on more information and more probing analyses of available evidence. To contribute to these efforts is part of the purpose of this study. But here the missile crisis serves primarily as grist for a more general investigation. This study proceeds from the premise that marked improvement in our understanding of such events depends critically on more self-consciousness about what observers bring to the analysis. What each analyst sees and judges

Reprinted by permission and with minor changes from the American Political Science Review, *September 1969, pp. 689–718. Copyright © 1969 by The American Political Science Association. Limitations of space have necessitated deletion of some statements that qualify the author's argument.*

A longer version of this paper was presented at the Annual Meeting of the American Political Science Association in September 1968 (reproduced by The RAND Corporation, P-3919). For support in various stages of this work I am indebted to the Institute of Politics in the John F. Kennedy School of Government and the Center for International Affairs, both at Harvard University, The RAND Corporation, and the Council on Foreign Relations. For critical stimulation and advice I am especially grateful to Richard E. Neustadt, Thomas C. Schelling, Andrew W. Marshall, and Elizabeth K. Allison.

to be important is a function not only of the evidence about what happened but also of the "conceptual lenses" through which he looks at the evidence. The principal purpose of this essay is to explore some of the fundamental assumptions and categories employed by analysts in thinking about problems of governmental behavior, especially in foreign and military affairs.

The general argument can be summarized in three propositions:

1. Analysts think about problems of foreign and military policy in terms of largely implicit conceptual models that have significant consequences for the content of their thought.[2]

. . . .

2. Most analysts explain (and predict) the behavior of national governments in terms of various forms of one basic conceptual model, here entitled the Rational Policy Model (Model I).[3]

. . . .

3. Two "alternative" conceptual models, here labeled an Organizational Process Model (Model II) and a Bureaucratic Politics Model (Model III), provide a base for improved explanation and prediction.

. . . .

MODEL I: RATIONAL POLICY

How do analysts attempt to explain the Soviet emplacement of missiles in Cuba? The most widely cited explanation of this occurrence has been produced by two RAND Sovietologists, Arnold Horelick and Myron Rush.[4] They conclude that "the introduction of strategic missiles into Cuba was motivated chiefly by the Soviet leaders' desire to overcome . . . the

existing large margin of U.S. strategic superiority."[5] How do they reach this conclusion? In Sherlock Holmes style, they seize several salient characteristics of this action and use these features as criteria against which to test alternative hypotheses about Soviet objectives. For example, the size of the Soviet deployment and the simultaneous emplacement of more expensive, more visible intermediate-range missiles as well as medium-range missiles, it is argued, exclude an explanation of the action in terms of Cuban defense, since that objective could have been secured with a much smaller number of medium-range missiles alone. Their explanation presents an argument for one objective that permits interpretation of the details of Soviet behavior as a value-maximizing choice.

How do analysts account for the coming of the First World War? According to Hans Morgenthau, "the first World War had its origin exclusively in the fear of a disturbance of the European balance of power."[6] In the period preceding World War I, the Triple Alliance precariously balanced the Triple Entente. If either power combination could gain a decisive advantage in the Balkans, it would achieve a decisive advantage in the balance of power. "It was this fear," Morgenthau asserts, "that motivated Austria in July 1914 to settle its accounts with Serbia once and for all, and that induced Germany to support Austria unconditionally. It was the same fear that brought Russia to the support of Serbia, and France to the support of Russia."[7] How is Morgenthau able to resolve this problem so confidently? By imposing on the data a "rational outline."[8] The value of this method, according to Morgenthau, is that "it provides for rational discipline in action and creates astounding continuity in foreign policy which makes American, British, or Russian foreign policy appear as an intelligent, rational continuum . . . regardless of the different motives, preferences, and intellectual and moral qualities of successive statesmen."[9]

. . . .

Deterrence is the cardinal problem of the con-

---

[2] In attempting to understand problems of foreign affairs, analysts engage in a number of related, but logically separable, enterprises: (1) description, (2) explanation, (3) prediction, (4) evaluation, and (5) recommendation. This essay focuses primarily on explanation (and, by implication, on prediction).

[3] Earlier drafts of this argument have aroused heated arguments concerning proper names for these models. To choose names from ordinary language is to court confusion as well as familiarity. Perhaps it is best to think of these models as I, II, and III.

[4] Arnold Horelick and Myron Rush, *Strategic Power and Soviet Foreign Policy* (Chicago, 1965); based on A. Horelick, "The Cuban Missile Crisis: An Analysis of Soviet Calculations and Behavior," *World Politics*, April 1964.

[5] Horelick and Rush, *Strategic Power and Soviet Foreign Policy*, p. 154.

[6] Hans Morgenthau, *Politics Among Nations*, 3rd ed. (New York, 1960), p. 191.

[7] *Ibid.*, p. 192.

[8] *Ibid.*, p. 5.

[9] *Ibid.*, pp. 5–6.

temporary strategic literature. Thomas Schelling's *Strategy of Conflict* formulates a number of propositions focused upon the dynamics of deterrence in the nuclear age. One of the major propositions concerns the stability of the balance of terror: in a situation of mutual deterrence, the probability of nuclear war is reduced not by the "balance" (the sheer equality of the situation) but rather by the *stability* of the balance—that is, the fact that neither opponent in striking first can destroy the other's ability to strike back.[10] How does Schelling support this proposition? Confidence in the contention stems not from an inductive canvass of a large number of previous cases but rather from two calculations. In a situation of "vulnerable balance" there are values for which a rational opponent could choose to strike first—for example, to destroy enemy capabilities to retaliate. In a "stable balance," where, no matter who strikes first, each has an assured capability to retaliate with unacceptable damage, no rational agent could choose such a course of action (since that choice is effectively equivalent to choosing mutual homicide). Whereas most contemporary strategic thinking is driven *implicitly* by the motor upon which this calculation depends, Schelling explicitly recognizes that strategic theory does assume a model. The foundation of a theory of strategy is, he asserts, "the assumption of rational behavior—not just of intelligent behavior, but of behavior motivated by conscious calculation of advantages, calculation that in turn is based on an explicit and internally consistent value system."[11]

What is striking about these examples from the literature of foreign policy and international relations are the similarities among analysts of various styles when they are called upon to produce explanations. Each assumes that what must be explained is an action—that is, the realization of some purpose or intention. Each assumes that the actor is the national government. Each assumes that the action is chosen as a calculated response to a strategic problem. For each, explanation consists of showing what goal the government was pursuing in committing the act and how this action was a reasonable choice, given the nation's objectives. This set of assumptions characterizes the rational policy model. . . .

Most contemporary analysts (as well as laymen) proceed predominantly—albeit most often implicitly—in terms of this model when attempting to explain happenings in foreign affairs. Indeed, that occurrences in foreign affairs are the *acts* of *nations* seems so fundamental to thinking about such problems that this underlying model has rarely been recognized: to explain an occurrence in foreign policy simply means to show how the government could have rationally chosen that action.[12] These brief examples illustrate five uses of the model. To prove that most analysts think largely in terms of the rational policy model is not possible. In this limited space it is not even possible to illustrate the range of employment of the framework. Rather, my purpose is to convey to the reader a grasp of the model and a challenge: let the reader examine the literature with which he is most familiar and make his judgment.

The general characterization can be sharpened by articulating the rational policy model as an "analytic paradigm" in the technical sense developed by Robert K. Merton for sociological analyses.[13] The systematic statement of basic assumptions, concepts, and propositions employed by Model I analysts highlights the dis-

---

[10] Thomas Schelling, *The Strategy of Conflict* (New York, 1960), p. 232. This proposition was formulated earlier by A. Wohlstetter, "The Delicate Balance of Terror," *Foreign Affairs*, January 1959.

[11] Schelling, *op. cit.*, p. 4.

[12] The larger study examines several exceptions to this generalization. Sidney Verba's excellent essay "Assumptions of Rationality and Non-Rationality in Models of the International System" is less an exception than it is an approach to a somewhat different problem. Verba focuses upon models of rationality and irrationality of *individual* statesmen; see Klaus Knorr and Sidney Verba, eds., *The International System* (Princeton, 1961).

[13] Robert K. Merton, *Social Theory and Social Structures*, rev. and enl. ed. (New York, 1957), pp. 12–16. Considerably weaker than a satisfactory theoretical model, paradigms nevertheless represent a short step in that direction from looser, implicit conceptual models. Neither the concepts nor the relations among the variables are sufficiently specified to yield propositions deductively. "Paradigmatic analysis" nevertheless has considerable promise for clarifying and codifying styles of analysis in political science. Each of the paradigms stated here can be represented rigorously in mathematical terms. For example, Model I lends itself to mathematical formulation along the lines of Herbert Simon's "Behavioral Theory of Rationality," *Models of Man* (New York, 1957). But this does not solve the most difficult problem of "measurement and estimation."

tinctive thrust of this style of analysis. To articulate a largely implicit framework is of necessity to caricature. But caricature can be instructive.

RATIONAL POLICY PARADIGM

Basic Unit of Analysis: Policy as National Choice

Happenings in foreign affairs are conceived as actions chosen by the nation or national government.[14] Governments select the action that will maximize strategic goals and objectives. These "solutions" to strategic problems are the fundamental categories in terms of which the analyst perceives what is to be explained.

Organizing Concepts

National Actor.   The nation or government, conceived as a rational, unitary decisionmaker, is the agent. This actor has one set of specified goals (the equivalent of a consistent utility function), one set of perceived options, and a single estimate of the consequences that follow from each alternative.

The Problem.   Action is chosen in response to the strategic problem which the nation faces. Threats and opportunities arising in the "international strategic market place" move the nation to act.

Static Selection.   The sum of the activity of representatives of the government relevant to a problem constitutes what the nation has chosen as its "solution." Thus the action is conceived as a steady-state choice among alternative outcomes (rather than, for example, a large number of partial choices in a dynamic stream).

Action as Rational Choice.   The components include:

1. *Goals and Objectives.* National security and national interests are the principal categories in which strategic goals are conceived.

Nations seek security and a range of further objectives. (Analysts rarely translate strategic goals and objectives into an explicit utility function; nevertheless, analysts do focus on major goals and objectives and trade off side effects in an intuitive fashion.)

2. *Options.* Various courses of action relevant to a strategic problem provide the spectrum of options.

3. *Consequences.* Enactment of each alternative course of action will produce a series of consequences. The relevant consequences constitute benefits and costs in terms of strategic goals and objectives.

4. *Choice.* Rational choice is value-maximizing. The rational agent selects the alternative whose consequences rank highest in terms of his goals and objectives.

Dominant Inference Pattern

This paradigm leads analysts to rely on the following pattern of inference: if a nation performed a particular action, that nation must have had ends toward which the action constituted an optimal means. The rational policy model's explanatory power stems from this inference pattern. Puzzlement is relieved by revealing the purposive pattern within which the occurrence can be located as a value-maximizing means.

General Propositions

The disgrace of political science is the infrequency with which propositions of any generality are formulated and tested. "Paradigmatic analysis" argues for explicitness about the terms in which analysis proceeds and for seriousness about the logic of explanation. Simply to illustrate the kind of propositions on which analysts who employ this model rely, the formulation includes several.

The basic assumption of value-maximizing behavior produces propositions central to most explanations. The general principle can be formulated as follows: the likelihood of any particular action results from a combination of the nation's relevant values and objectives, perceived alternative courses of action, estimates of various sets of consequences (which will follow from each alternative), and net valuation of each set of consequences. This yields two propositions.

1. An increase in the cost of an alternative—

---

[14] Though a variant of this model could easily be stochastic, this paradigm is stated in nonprobabilistic terms. In contemporary strategy, a stochastic version of this model is sometimes used for predictions; but it is almost impossible to find an explanation of an occurrence in foreign affairs that is consistently probabilistic.

Analogies between Model I and the concept of explanation developed by R. G. Collingwood, William Dray, and other "revisionists" among philosophers concerned with the critical philosophy of history are not accidental. For a summary of the "revisionist position" see Maurice Mandelbaum, "Historical Explanation: The Problem of Covering Laws," *History and Theory*, 1960.

that is, a reduction in the value of the set of consequences which will follow from that action, or a reduction in the probability of attaining fixed consequences, reduces the likelihood of that alternative being chosen.

2. A decrease in the costs of an alternative— that is, an increase in the value of the set of consequences which will follow from that alternative, or an increase in the probability of attaining fixed consequences, increases the likelihood of that action being chosen.[15]

Specific Propositions

Deterrence. The likelihood of any particular attack results from the factors specified in the general proposition. Combined with factual assertions, this general proposition yields the propositions of the subtheory of deterrence.

1. A stable nuclear balance reduces the likelihood of nuclear attack. This proposition is derived from the general proposition plus the asserted fact that a second-strike capability affects the potential attacker's calculations by increasing the likelihood and the costs of one particular set of consequences which might follow from attack—namely, retaliation.

2. A stable nuclear balance increases the probability of limited war. This proposition is derived from the general proposition plus the asserted fact that though it increases the costs of a nuclear exchange, a stable nuclear balance nevertheless produces a more significant reduction in the probability that such consequences would be chosen in response to a limited war. Thus this set of consequences weighs less heavily in the calculus.

Soviet Force Posture. The Soviet Union chooses its force posture (i.e., its weapons and their deployment) as a value-maximizing means of implementing Soviet strategic objectives and military doctrine. A proposition of this sort underlies Secretary of Defense Laird's inference from the fact of 200 SS-9s (large intercontinental missiles) that "the Soviets are going for a first-strike capability, and there's no question about it."[16]

. . . .

The U.S. Blockade of Cuba: A First Cut[17]

The U.S. response to the Soviet Union's emplacement of missiles in Cuba must be understood in strategic terms as simple value-maximizing escalation. American nuclear superiority could be counted on to paralyze Soviet nuclear power; Soviet transgression of the nuclear threshold in response to an American use of lower levels of violence would be wildly irrational, since it would mean virtual destruction of the Soviet Communist system and Russian nation. American local superiority was overwhelming; it could be initiated at a low level while threatening with high credibility an ascending sequence of steps short of the nuclear threshold. All that was required was for the United States to bring to bear its strategic and local superiority in such a way that American determination to see the missiles removed would be demonstrated, while at the same time allowing Moscow time and room to retreat without humiliation. The naval blockade— euphemistically named a "quarantine" in order to circumvent the niceties of international law —did just that.

The U.S. government's selection of the blockade followed this logic. Apprised of the presence of Soviet missiles in Cuba, the President assembled an Executive Committee (ExCom) of the National Security Council and directed them to "set aside all other tasks to make a prompt and intense survey of the dangers and all possible courses of action."[18] This group functioned as "fifteen individuals on our own, representing the President and not different departments."[19] As one of the participants recalls, "The remarkable aspect of those meetings was a sense of complete equality."[20] Most of the time during the week that followed was spent canvassing all the possible tracks and weighing the arguments for and against each. Six major categories of action were considered.

Do Nothing

U.S. vulnerability to Soviet missiles was no new thing. Since the U.S. already lived under

---

[15] This model is an analogue of the theory of the rational entrepreneur which has been developed extensively in economic theories of the firm and the consumer. These two propositions specify the "substitution effect." Refinement of this model and specification of additional general propositions by translating from the economic theory are straightforward.

[16] *New York Times*, March 22, 1969.

[17] As stated in the introduction, this "case snapshot" presents, without editorial commentary, a Model I analyst's explanation of the U.S. blockade. The purpose is to illustrate a strong, characteristic rational-policy-model account. This account is (roughly) consistent with prevailing explanations of these events.

[18] Sorensen, *op. cit.*, p. 675.

[19] *Ibid.*, p. 679.

[20] *Ibid.*

the gun of missiles based in Russia, a Soviet capability to strike from Cuba too made little real difference. The real danger stemmed from the possibility of U.S. overreaction. The U.S. should announce the Soviet action in a calm, casual manner thereby deflating whatever political capital Khrushchev hoped to make of the missiles.

This argument fails on two counts. First, it grossly underestimates the military importance of the Soviet move. Not only would the Soviet Union's missile capability be doubled and the U.S. early warning system outflanked. The Soviet Union would have an opportunity to reverse the strategic balance by further installations, and, indeed, in the longer run, to invest in cheaper, shorter-range missiles rather than more expensive, longer-range missiles. Second, the political importance of this move was undeniable. The Soviet Union's act challenged the American President's most solemn warning. If the U.S. failed to respond, no American commitment would be credible.

Diplomatic Pressures

Several forms were considered: an appeal to the UN or OAS for an inspection team; a secret approach to Khrushchev; and a direct approach to Khrushchev, perhaps at a summit meeting. The United States would demand that the missiles be removed, but the final settlement might include neutralization of Cuba, U.S. withdrawal from the Guantanamo base, and withdrawal of U.S. Jupiter missiles from Turkey or Italy.

Each form of the diplomatic approach had its own drawbacks. To arraign the Soviet Union before the UN Security Council held little promise, since the Russians could veto any proposed action. While the diplomats argued, the missiles would become operational. To send a secret emissary to Khrushchev with the demand that the missiles be withdrawn would be to pose untenable alternatives. On the one hand, this would invite Khrushchev to seize the diplomatic initiative, perhaps commit himself to strategic retaliation in response to an attack on Cuba. On the other hand, this would tender an ultimatum that no great power could accept. To confront Khrushchev at a summit would guarantee demands for U.S. concessions, and the analogy between U.S. missiles in Tur-

key and Russian missiles in Cuba could not be erased.

But why not trade U.S. Jupiters in Turkey and Italy, which the President had previously ordered withdrawn, for the missiles in Cuba? The U.S. had chosen to withdraw these missiles in order to replace them with superior, less vulnerable Mediterranean Polaris submarines. But the middle of the crisis was no time for concessions. The offer of such a deal might suggest to the Soviets that the West would yield and thus might tempt them to demand more. It would certainly confirm European suspicions about America's willingness to sacrifice European interests when the chips were down. Finally, the basic issue should be kept clear. As the President stated in reply to Bertrand Russell, "I think your attention might well be directed to the burglars rather than to those who have caught the burglars."[21]

A Secret Approach to Castro

The crisis provided an opportunity to separate Cuba and Soviet communism by offering Castro the alternatives "split or fall." But Soviet troops transported, constructed, guarded, and controlled the missiles. Their removal would thus depend on a Soviet decision.

Invasion

The United States could take this occasion not only to remove the missiles but also to rid itself of Castro. A naval exercise had long been scheduled in which Marines, ferried from Florida in naval vessels, would liberate the imaginary island of Vieques.[22] Why not simply shift the point of disembarkment? (The Pentagon's foresight in planning this operation would be an appropriate antidote to the CIA's Bay of Pigs!)

Preparations were made for an invasion, but as a last resort. American troops would be forced to confront 20,000 Soviets in the first Cold War case of direct contact between the troops of the superpowers. Such brinkmanship courted nuclear disaster and practically guaranteed an equivalent Soviet move against Berlin.

[21] Elie Abel, *The Missile Crisis* (New York, 1966), p. 144.
[22] *Ibid.*, p. 102.

Surgical Air Strike

The missile sites should be removed by a clean, swift, conventional attack. This was the effective counteraction the attempted deception deserved. A surgical strike would remove the missiles and thus eliminate both the danger that the missiles might become operational and the fear that the Soviets would discover the American discovery and act first.

The initial attractiveness of this alternative was dulled by several difficulties. First, could the strike really be "surgical"? The Air Force could not guarantee destruction of all the missiles.[23] Some might be fired during the attack; some might not have been identified. In order to assure destruction of Soviet and Cuban means of retaliating, what was required was not a surgical attack but rather a massive one —of at least 500 sorties. Second, a surprise air attack would of course kill Russians at the missile sites. Pressures on the Soviet Union to retaliate would be so strong that an attack on Berlin or Turkey would be highly probable. Third, the key problem with this program was that of advance warning. Could the President of the United States, with his memory of Pearl Harbor and his vision of future U.S. responsibility, order a "Pearl Harbor in reverse"? For 175 years, unannounced Sunday morning attacks had been an anathema to our tradition.[24]

Blockade

Indirect military action in the form of a blockade became more attractive as the ExCom dissected the other alternatives. An embargo on military shipments to Cuba enforced by a naval blockade was not without flaws, however. Could the U.S. blockade Cuba without inviting Soviet reprisal in Berlin? The likely solution to joint blockades would be the lifting of both blockades, restoring the new *status quo*, and allowing the Soviets additional time to complete the missiles. Second, the possible consequences of the blockade resembled the drawbacks which disqualified the air strike. If Soviet ships did not stop, the United States would be forced to fire the first shot, inviting retaliation. Third, a blockade would deny the traditional freedom of the seas demanded by several of our close allies and might be held illegal, in violation of the UN Charter and international law, unless the United States could obtain a two-thirds vote in the OAS. Finally, how could a blockade be related to the problem— namely, some seventy-five missiles on the island of Cuba, approaching operational readiness daily? A blockade offered the Soviets a spectrum of delaying tactics with which to buy time to complete the missile installations. Was a *fait accompli* not required?

In spite of these enormous difficulties the blockade had comparative advantages: (1) It was a middle course between inaction and attack, aggressive enough to communicate firmness of intention, but nevertheless not so precipitous as a strike. (2) It placed on Khrushchev the burden of choice concerning the next step. He could avoid a direct military clash by keeping his ships away. His was the last clear chance. (3) No possible military confrontation could be more acceptable to the U.S. than a naval engagement in the Caribbean. (4) This move permitted the U.S., by flexing its conventional muscle, to exploit the threat of subsequent nonnuclear steps, in each of which the U.S. would have significant superiority.

Particular arguments about advantages and disadvantages were powerful. The explanation of the American choice of the blockade lies in a more general principle, however. As President Kennedy stated in drawing the moral of the crisis:

Above all, while defending our own vital interests, nuclear powers must avert those confrontations which bring an adversary to a choice of either a humiliating retreat or a nuclear war. To adopt that kind of course in the nuclear age would be evidence only of the bankruptcy of our policy— of a collective death wish for the world.[25]

The blockade was the United States' only real option.

MODEL II: ORGANIZATIONAL PROCESS

For some purposes, governmental behavior can be usefully summarized as action chosen

---

[23] Sorensen, *op. cit.*, p. 684.

[24] *Ibid.*, p. 685. Though this was the formulation of the argument, the facts are not strictly accurate. Our tradition against surprise attack was rather younger than 175 years. For example, President Theodore Roosevelt applauded Japan's attack on Russia in 1904.

[25] *New York Times*, June, 1963.

by a unitary, rational decisionmaker: centrally controlled, completely informed, and value maximizing. But this simplification must not be allowed to conceal the fact that a "government" consists of a conglomerate of semifeudal, loosely allied organizations, each with a substantial life of its own. Governmental leaders do sit formally, and to some extent in fact, on top of this conglomerate. But governments perceive problems through organizational sensors. Governments define alternatives and estimate consequences as organizations process information. Governments act as these organizations enact routines. Governmental behavior can therefore be understood according to a second conceptual model, less as deliberate choices of leaders and more as *outputs* of large organizations functioning according to standard patterns of behavior.

To be responsive to a broad spectrum of problems, governments consist of large organizations, among which primary responsibility for particular areas is divided. Each organization attends to a special set of problems and acts in quasi independence on these problems. But few important problems fall exclusively within the domain of a single organization. Thus governmental behavior relevant to any important problem reflects the independent output of several organizations, partially coordinated by governmental leaders. Governmental leaders can substantially disturb, but not substantially control, the behavior of these organizations.

To perform complex routines, the behavior of large numbers of individuals must be coordinated. Coordination requires standard operating procedures: rules according to which things are done. An assured capability for reliable performance of action that depends upon the behavior of hundreds of persons requires established "programs." Indeed, if the eleven members of a football team are to perform adequately on any particular down, each player must not "do what he thinks needs to be done" or "do what the quarterback tells him to do." Rather, each player must perform the maneuvers specified by a previously established play which the quarterback has simply called in this situation.

At any given time, a government consists of *existing* organizations, each with a *fixed* set of standard operating procedures and programs.

The behavior of these organizations—and consequently of the government—relevant to an issue in any particular instance is therefore determined primarily by routines established in these organizations prior to that instance. But organizations do change. Learning occurs gradually, over time. Dramatic organizational change occurs in response to major crises. Both learning and change are influenced by existing organizational capabilities.

.　 .　 .　 .　 .　 .　 .　 .　 .　 .

ORGANIZATIONAL PROCESS PARADIGM[26]

Basic Unit of Analysis: Policy as Organizational Output

The happenings of international politics are, in three critical senses, outputs of organizational processes. First, the actual occurrences are organizational outputs. For example, Chinese entry into the Korean War—that is, the fact that Chinese soldiers were firing at UN soldiers south of the Yalu in 1950—is an organizational action: the action of men who are soldiers in platoons, which are in companies, which in turn are in armies, responding as privates to lieutenants, who are responsible to captains, and so on to the commander, moving into Korea, advancing against enemy troops, and firing according to fixed routines of the Chinese Army. Governmental leaders' decisions trigger organizational routines. Governmental leaders can trim the edges of this output and

---

[26] The influence of organizational studies upon the present literature of foreign affairs is minimal. Specialists in international politics are not students of organization theory. Organization theory has only recently begun to study organizations as decisionmakers and has not yet produced behavioral studies of national security organizations from a decisionmaking perspective. It seems unlikely, however, that these gaps will remain unfilled much longer. Considerable progress has been made in the study of the business firm as an organization. Scholars have begun applying these insights to governmental organizations, and interest in an organizational perspective is spreading among institutions and individuals concerned with actual governmental operations. The "decisionmaking" approach represented by Richard Snyder, R. Bruck, and B. Sapin, *Foreign Policy Decision-Making* (Glencoe, Ill., 1962), incorporates a number of insights from organizational theory.

For the formulation of this paradigm the author is indebted both to the orientation and insights of Herbert Simon and to the behavioral model of the firm stated by Richard Cyert and James March in *A Behavioral Theory of the Firm* (Englewood Cliffs, N.J., 1963). Here, however, one is forced to grapple with the less routine, less quantified functions of the less differentiated elements in governmental organizations.

exercise some choice in combining outputs. But the mass of behavior is determined by previously established procedures. Second, existing organizational routines for employing present physical capabilities constitute the effective options open to governmental leaders confronted with any problem. Only the existence of men, equipped and trained as armies and capable of being transported to North Korea, made entry into the Korean War a live option for the Chinese leaders. The fact that fixed programs (equipment, men, and routines which exist at the particular time) exhaust the range of buttons that leaders can push is not always perceived by these leaders. But in every case it is critical for an understanding of what is actually done. Third, organizational outputs structure the situation within the narrow constraints of which leaders must contribute their "decision" concerning an issue. Outputs raise the problem, provide the information, and make the initial moves that color the face of the issue which is turned to the leaders. As Theodore Sorensen has observed: "Presidents rarely, if ever, make decisions—particularly in foreign affairs—in the sense of writing their conclusions on a clean slate. . . . The basic decisions, which confine their choices, have all too often been previously made."[27] If one understands the structure of the situation and the face of the issue —which are determined by the organizational outputs—the formal choice of the leaders is frequently anticlimactic.

Organizing Concepts

Organizational Actors. The actor is not a monolithic "nation" or "government" but rather a constellation of loosely allied organizations on top of which governmental leaders sit. This constellation acts only as component organizations perform routines.[28]

Factored Problems and Fractionated Power. Surveillance of the multiple facets of foreign affairs requires that problems be cut up and parceled out to various organizations. To avoid

paralysis, primary power must accompany primary responsibility. But, if organizations are permitted to do anything, a large part of what they do will be determined within the organization. Thus each organization perceives problems, processes information, and performs a range of actions in quasi independence (within broad guidelines of national policy). Factored problems and fractionated power are two edges of the same sword. Factoring permits more specialized attention to particular facets of problems than would be possible if governmental leaders tried to cope with these problems by themselves. But this additional attention must be paid for in the coin of discretion for *what* an organization attends to, and *how* organizational responses are programmed.

Parochial Priorities, Perceptions, and Issues. Primary responsibility for a narrow set of problems encourages organizational parochialism. These tendencies are enhanced by a number of additional factors: (1) selective information available to the organization; (2) recruitment of personnel into the organization; (3) tenure of individuals in the organization; (4) small group pressures within the organization; and (5) distribution of rewards by the organization. Clients (e.g., interest groups), governmental allies (e.g., congressional committees), and extranational counterparts (e.g., the British Ministry of Defense for the Department of Defense, ISA; or the British Foreign Office for the Department of State, EUR) galvanize this parochialism. Thus organizations develop relatively stable propensities concerning operational priorities, perceptions, and issues.

Action as Organizational Output. The preeminent feature of organizational activity is its programmed character: the extent to which behavior in any particular case is an enactment of pre-established routines. In producing outputs, the activity of each organization is characterized by:

1. *Goals: Constraints Defining Acceptable Performance.* The operational goals of an organization are seldom revealed by formal mandates. Rather, each organization's operational goals emerge as a set of constraints defining acceptable performance. Central among these constraints is organizational health, defined usually in terms of bodies assigned and dollars appropriated. The set of constraints emerges from a mix of expectations and demands of

[27] Theodore Sorensen, "You Get to Walk to Work," *New York Times Magazine,* March 19, 1967.

[28] Organizations are not monolithic. The proper level of disaggregation depends upon the objectives of a piece of analysis. This paradigm is formulated with reference to the major organizations that constitute the U.S. government. Generalization to the major components of each department and agency should be relatively straightforward.

other organizations in the government, statutory authority, demands from citizens and special-interest groups, and bargaining within the organization. These constraints represent a quasi resolution of conflict—the constraints are relatively stable, so there is some resolution. But conflict among alternative goals is always latent; hence, it is quasi resolution. Typically, the constraints are formulated as imperatives to avoid roughly specified discomforts and disasters.[29]

2. *Sequential Attention to Goals.* The existence of conflict among operational constraints is resolved by the device of sequential attention. As a problem arises, the subunits of the organization most concerned with that problem deal with it in terms of the constraints they take to be most important. When the next problem arises, another cluster of subunits deals with it, focusing on a different set of constraints.

3. *Standard Operating Procedures.* Organizations perform their "higher" functions—such as attending to problem areas, monitoring information, and preparing relevant responses for likely contingencies—by doing "lower" tasks—for example, preparing budgets, producing reports, and developing hardware. Reliable performance of these tasks requires standard operating procedures (SOPs). Since procedures are "standard" they do not change quickly or easily. Without these standard procedures, it would not be possible to perform certain concerted tasks. But, because of standard procedures, organizational behavior in particular instances often appears unduly formalized, sluggish, or inappropriate.

4. *Programs and Repertoires.* Organizations must be capable of performing actions in which the behavior of large numbers of individuals is carefully coordinated. Assured performance requires clusters of rehearsed SOPs for producing specific actions—for example, fighting enemy units or answering an embassy's cable. Each cluster comprises a "program" (in the terms of both drama and computers) which the organization has available for dealing with a situation. The list of programs relevant to a type of activity—for example, fighting—constitutes an organizational repertoire. The number of programs in a repertoire is always quite limited. When properly triggered, organizations execute programs; programs cannot be substantially changed in a particular situation. The more complex the action and the greater the number of individuals involved, the more important are programs and repertoires as determinants of organizational behavior.

5. *Uncertainty Avoidance.* Organizations do not attempt to estimate the probability distribution of future occurrences. Rather, organizations avoid uncertainty. By arranging a *negotiated environment*, organizations regularize the reactions of other actors with whom they have to deal. The primary environment, relations with other organizations that comprise the government, is stabilized by such arrangements as agreed budgetary splits, accepted areas of responsibility, and established conventional practices. The secondary environment, relations with the international world, is stabilized between allies by the establishment of contracts (alliances) and "club relations" (U.S. State and U.K. Foreign Office, or U.S. Treasury and U.K. Treasury). Between enemies, contracts and accepted conventional practices perform a similar function—for example, the rules of the "precarious status quo" which President Kennedy referred to in the missile crisis. Where the international environment cannot be negotiated, organizations deal with remaining uncertainties by establishing a set of *standard scenarios* that constitute the contingencies for which they prepare. For example, the standard scenario for the Tactical Air Command of the U.S. Air Force involves combat with enemy aircraft. Planes are designed, and pilots are trained, to meet this problem. That these preparations are less relevant to more probable contingencies—for example, provision of close-in ground support in limited wars like Vietnam—has had little impact on the scenario.

6. *Problem-directed Search.* Where situations cannot be construed as standard, organizations engage in search. The style of search and the solution are largely determined by existing routines. Organizational search for alternative courses of action is problem-oriented: it focuses on the atypical discomfort that must be avoided. It is simple-minded: the neighborhood of the symptom is searched first; then, the neighborhood of the current alternative is

---

[29] The stability of these constraints is dependent on such factors as rules for promotion and reward, budgeting and accounting procedures, and mundane operating procedures.

searched. Patterns of search reveal biases, which in turn reflect such factors as specialized training or experience and patterns of communication.

7. *Organizational Learning and Change.* The parameters of organizational behavior persist for the most part. In response to nonstandard problems, organizations search and routines evolve; new situations are assimilated. Thus learning and change follow in large part from existing procedures. But marked changes in organizations do sometimes occur. Conditions in which dramatic changes are more likely include: (1) Periods of budgetary feast. Typically, organizations devour budgetary feasts by purchasing additional items on the existing shopping list. Nevertheless, if committed to change, leaders who control the budget can use extra funds to effect changes. (2) Periods of prolonged budgetary famine. Though a single year's famine typically results in few changes in organizational structure but also in a loss of effectiveness in performing some programs, prolonged famine forces major retrenchment. (3) Dramatic performance failures. Dramatic change occurs (mostly) in response to major disasters. Confronted with an undeniable failure of procedures and repertoires, authorities outside the organization demand change, existing personnel are less resistant to change, and critical members of the organization are replaced by individuals committed to change.

Central Coordination and Control. Action requires decentralization of responsibility and power. But problems overlap the jurisdictions of several organizations. Thus the necessity for decentralization runs headlong into the requirement for coordination. . . .

Intervention by governmental leaders does sometimes change the activity of an organization in an intended direction. But instances are fewer than might be expected. As Franklin Roosevelt, the master manipulator of governmental organizations, remarked:

The Treasury is so large and far-flung and ingrained in its practices that I find it is almost impossible to get the action and results I want. . . . But the Treasury is not to be compared with the State Department. You should go through the experience of trying to get any changes in the thinking, policy, and action of the career diplomats and then you'd know what a real problem was. But the Treasury and the State Department put together

are nothing compared with the Na-a-vy. . . . To change anything in the Na-a-vy is like punching a feather bed. You punch it with your right and you punch it with your left until you are finally exhausted, and then you find the damn bed just as it was before you started punching.[30]

John Kennedy's experience seems to have been similar: "The State Department," he asserted, "is a bowl full of jelly."[31] And lest the McNamara revolution in the Defense Department seem too striking a counterexample, the Navy's recent rejection of McNamara's major intervention in naval weapons procurement, the F-111B, should be studied as an antidote.

Decisions of Governmental Leaders. Organizational persistence does not exclude shifts in governmental behavior, for governmental leaders sit atop the conglomerate of organizations. Many important issues of governmental action require that these leaders decide what organizations will play out which programs where. Thus stability in the parochialisms and SOPs of individual organizations is consistent with some important shifts in the behavior of governments. The range of these shifts is defined by existing organizational programs.

Dominant Inference Pattern

If a nation performs an action of this type today, its organizational components must yesterday have been performing (or have had established routines for performing) an action only marginally different from this action. At any specific point in time, a government consists of an established conglomerate of organizations, each with existing goals, programs, and repertoires. The characteristics of a government's action in any instance follow from those established routines, and from the choice of governmental leaders—on the basis of information and estimates provided by existing routines—among existing programs. The best explanation of an organization's behavior at t is $t - 1$; the prediction of $t + 1$ is t. Model II's explanatory power is achieved by uncovering the organizational routines and repertoires that produced the outputs that comprise the puzzling occurrence.

[30] Marriner Eccles, *Beckoning Frontiers* (New York, 1951), p. 336.
[31] Arthur M. Schlesinger, Jr., *A Thousand Days* (Boston, 1965), p. 406.

General Propositions

A number of general propositions have been stated above. In order to illustrate clearly the type of proposition employed by Model II analysts, this section formulates several more precisely.

Organizational Action. Activity according to SOPs and programs does not constitute farsighted, flexible adaptation to "the issue" (as it is conceived by the analyst). Detail and nuance of actions by organizations are determined predominantly by organizational routines, not by governmental leaders' directions.

1. SOPs constitute routines for dealing with *standard* situations. Routines allow large numbers of ordinary individuals to deal with numerous instances, day after day, without considerable thought, by responding to basic stimuli. But this regularized capability for adequate performance is purchased at the price of standardization. If the SOPs are appropriate, average performance—that is, performance averaged over the range of cases—is better than it would be if each instance were approached individually (given fixed talent, timing, and resource constraints). But specific instances, particularly critical instances that typically do not have "standard" characteristics, are often handled sluggishly or inappropriately.

2. A program—that is, a complex action chosen from a short list of programs in a repertoire—is rarely tailored to the specific situation in which it is executed. Rather, the program is (at best) the most appropriate of the programs in a previously developed repertoire.

3. Since repertoires are developed by parochial organizations for standard scenarios defined by that organization, programs available for dealing with a particular situation are often ill-suited.

Limited Flexibility and Incremental Change. Major lines of organizational action are straight —that is, behavior at one time is marginally different from that behavior at $t - 1$. Simpleminded predictions work best: Behavior at $t + 1$ will be marginally different from behavior at the present time.

1. Organizational budgets change incrementally—both with respect to totals and with respect to intraorganizational splits. Though organizations could divide the money available each year by carving up the pie anew (in the light of changes in objectives or environment), in practice, organizations take last year's budget as a base and adjust incrementally. Predictions that require large budgetary shifts in a single year between organizations or between units within an organization should be hedged.

2. Once undertaken, an organizational investment is not dropped at the point where "objective" costs outweigh benefits. Organizational stakes in adopted projects carry them quite beyond the loss point.

Administrative Feasibility. Adequate explanation, analysis, and prediction must include administrative feasibility as a major dimension. A considerable gap separates what leaders choose (or might rationally have chosen) and what organizations implement.

1. Organizations are blunt instruments. Projects that require several organizations to act with high degrees of precision and coordination are not likely to succeed.

2. Projects that demand that existing organizational units depart from their accustomed functions and perform previously unprogrammed tasks are rarely accomplished in their designed form.

3. Governmental leaders can expect that each organization will do its "part" in terms of what the organization knows how to do.

4. Governmental leaders can expect incomplete and distorted information from each organization concerning its part of the problem.

5. Where an assigned piece of a problem contradicts the existing goals of an organization, resistance to implementation of that piece will be encountered.

Specific Propositions

Deterrence. The probability of nuclear attack is less sensitive to balance and imbalance, or stability and instability (as these concepts are employed by Model I strategists), than it is to a number of organizational factors. Except for the special case in which the Soviet Union acquires a credible capability to destroy the U.S. with a disarming blow, U.S. superiority or inferiority affects the probability of a nuclear attack less than do a number of organizational factors.

First, if a nuclear attack occurs, it will result from organizational activity: the firing of rockets by members of a missile group. The enemy's *control system*—that is, physical mech-

anisms and standard procedures which determine who can launch rockets when—is critical.
Second, the enemy's programs for bringing his
strategic forces to *alert status* determine probabilities of accidental firing and momentum. At
the outbreak of World War I, if the Russian
Czar had understood the organizational processes which his order of full mobilization triggered, he would have realized that he had
chosen war. Third, organizational repertoires
fix the range of effective choice open to enemy
leaders. The menu available to Czar Nicholas
in 1914 had two entrees: full mobilization and
no mobilization. Partial mobilization was not
an organizational option. Fourth, since organizational routines set the chessboard, the training and deployment of troops and nuclear
weapons are crucial. Given the fact that an
outbreak of hostilities in Berlin is more probable than most scenarios for nuclear war, facts
about deployment, training, and tactical nuclear equipment of Soviet troops stationed in
East Germany—which will influence the face
of the issue seen by Soviet leaders at the outbreak of hostilities and the manner in which
choice is implemented—are as critical as the
question of "balance."

Soviet Force Posture. Soviet force posture
—that is, the fact that certain weapons rather
than others are procured and deployed—is determined by organizational factors, such as the
goals and procedures of existing military services and the goals and processes of research
and design labs, within budgetary constraints
that emerge from the governmental leaders'
choices. The frailty of the Soviet Air Force
within the Soviet military establishment seems
to have been a crucial element in the Soviet
failure to acquire a large bomber force in the
1950s (thereby faulting American intelligence
predictions of a "bomber gap"). The fact that,
until 1960, missiles in the Soviet Union were
controlled by the Soviet Ground Forces, whose
goals and procedures reflected no interest in an
intercontinental mission, was not irrelevant to
the slow Soviet build-up of ICBMs (thereby
faulting U.S. intelligence predictions of a "missile gap"). These organizational factors (the
Soviet Ground Forces' control of missiles and
that service's fixation with European scenarios)
make the Soviet deployment of so many
MRBMs that European targets could be destroyed three times over more understandable.

Recent weapons developments—for example,
the testing of a Fractional Orbital Bombardment System (FOBS) and multiple warheads
for the SS-9—very likely reflect the activity
and interests of a cluster of Soviet research and
development organizations, rather than a decision by Soviet leaders to acquire a first-strike
weapons system. Careful attention to the organizational components of the Soviet military establishment (Strategic Rocket Forces, Navy,
Air Force, Ground Forces, and National Air
Defense), the missions and weapons systems to
which each component is wedded (an independent weapons system assists survival as an
independent service), and existing budgetary
splits (which probably are relatively stable in
the Soviet Union, as they tend to be everywhere) offers potential improvements in
medium- and longer-term predictions.

THE U.S. BLOCKADE OF CUBA: A SECOND CUT

Organizational Intelligence

At 7:00 P.M. on October 22, 1962, President
Kennedy disclosed the American discovery of
the presence of Soviet strategic missiles in
Cuba, declared a "strict quarantine on all offensive military equipment under shipment to
Cuba," and demanded that "Chairman Khrushchev halt and eliminate this clandestine,
reckless, and provocative threat to world
peace."[32] This decision was reached at the pin-
nacle of the U.S. government after a critical
week of deliberation. What initiated that precious week were photographs of Soviet missile
sites in Cuba taken on October 14. These pictures might not have been taken until a week
later. In that case, the President speculated, "I
don't think probably we would have chosen as
prudently as we finally did."[33] U.S. leaders
might have received this information three
weeks earlier—if a U-2 had flown over San
Cristobal in the last week of September.[34] What
determined the context in which American
leaders came to choose the blockade was the
discovery of missiles on October 14.

There has been considerable debate over alleged American "intelligence failures" in the

[32] U.S. Department of State, *Bulletin*, 47: 715–20.
[33] Schlesinger, *op. cit.*, p. 803.
[34] Sorensen, *Kennedy*, p. 675.

Cuban missile crisis.[35] But what both critics and defenders have neglected is the fact that the discovery took place on October 14, rather than three weeks earlier or a week later, as a consequence of the established routines and procedures of the organizations which constitute the U.S. intelligence community. These organizations were neither more nor less successful than they had been the previous month or were to be in the months to follow.[36]

The notorious "September estimate," approved by the United States Intelligence Board (USIB) on September 19, concluded that the Soviet Union would not introduce offensive missiles into Cuba.[37] No U-2 flight was directed over the western end of Cuba (after September 5) before October 4.[38] No U-2 flew over the western end of Cuba until the flight that discovered the Soviet missiles on October 14.[39] Can these "failures" be accounted for in organizational terms?

On September 19, when USIB met to consider the question of Cuba, the "system" contained the following information: (1) shipping intelligence had noted the arrival in Cuba of two large-hatch Soviet lumber ships, which were riding high in the water; (2) refugee reports of countless sightings of missiles, but also a report that Castro's private pilot, after a night of drinking in Havana, had boasted: "We will fight to the death and perhaps we can win because we have everything, including atomic weapons"; (3) a sighting by a CIA agent of the rear profile of a strategic missile; (4) U-2 photos produced by flights of August 29 and September 5 and 17 showing construction of a number of SAM and other defensive missile sites.[40] Not all of this information was on the desk of the estimators, however. Shipping intelligence experts noted the fact that large-hatch ships were riding high in the water and spelled out the inference: the ships must be carrying "space consuming" cargo.[41] These facts were carefully included in the catalogue of intelligence concerning shipping. For experts sensitive to the Soviets' shortage of ships, however, these facts carried no special signal. The refugee report of Castro's private pilot's remark had been received at Opa Locka, Florida, along with vast reams of inaccurate reports generated by the refugee community. This report and a thousand others had to be checked and compared before being sent to Washington. The two weeks required for initial processing could have been shortened by a large increase in resources, but the yield of this source was already quite marginal. The CIA agent's sighting of the rear profile of a strategic missile had occurred on September 12; transmission time from agent sighting to arrival in Washington typically was 9–12 days. Shortening this transmission time would impose severe costs in terms of danger to subagents, agents, and communication networks.

On the information available, the intelligence chiefs who predicted that the Soviet Union would not introduce offensive missiles into Cuba made a reasonable and defensible judgment.[42] Moreover, in the light of the fact that these organizations were gathering intelligence not only about Cuba but about potential occurrences in all parts of the world, the informational base available to the estimators involved nothing out of the ordinary. Nor, from an organizational perspective, is there anything startling about the gradual accumulation of evidence that led to the formulation of the hypothesis that the Soviets were installing missiles in Cuba and the decision on October 4 to direct a special flight over western Cuba.

[35] See U.S. Congress, Senate, Committee on Armed Services, Preparedness Investigation Subcommittee, *Interim Report on Cuban Military Build-up*, 88th Cong., 1st sess., 1963, p. 2 (hereafter cited as *Cuban Military Build-up*); Hanson Baldwin, "Growing Risks of Bureaucratic Intelligence," *The Reporter*, August 15, 1963, pp. 48–50; Roberta Wohlstetter, "Cuba and Pearl Harbor," *Foreign Affairs*, July 1965, p. 706.

[36] U.S. Congress, House of Representatives, Committee on Appropriations, Subcommittee on Department of Defense Appropriations, *Hearings*, 88th Cong., 1st sess., 1963, pp. 25ff. (hereafter cited as Department of Defense Appropriations, *Hearings*).

[37] R. Hilsman, *To Move a Nation* (New York, 1967), pp. 172–73.

[38] U.S. Department of Defense Appropriations, *Hearings*, p. 67.

[39] *Ibid.*, pp. 66–67.

[40] For (1) Hilsman, *op. cit.*, p. 186; (2) Abel, *op.* *cit.*, p. 24; (3) Department of Defense Appropriations, *Hearings*, p. 64; Abel, *op. cit.*, p. 24; (4) Department of Defense Appropriations, *Hearings*, pp. 1–30.

[41] The facts here are not entirely clear. This assertion is based on information from (1) "Department of Defense Briefing by the Honorable R. S. McNamara, Secretary of Defense, State Department Auditorium, 5:00 P.M., February 6, 1963" (a verbatim transcript of a presentation actually made by General Carroll's assistant, John Hughes), and (2) Hilsman's statement, *op. cit.*, p. 186. But see Wohlstetter's interpretation, "Cuba and Pearl Harbor," p. 700.

[42] See Hilsman, *op. cit.*, pp. 172–74.

The ten-day delay between that decision and the flight is another organizational story.[43] At the October 4 meeting, the Defense Department took the opportunity to raise an issue important to its concerns. Given the increased danger that a U-2 would be downed, it would be better if the pilot were an officer in uniform rather than a CIA agent. Thus the Air Force should assume responsibility for U-2 flights over Cuba. To the contrary, the CIA argued that this was an intelligence operation and thus within the CIA's jurisdiction. Moreover, CIA U-2s had been modified in certain ways which gave them advantages over Air Force U-2s in averting Soviet SAMs. Five days passed while the State Department pressed for less risky alternatives, such as drones, and the Air Force (in Department of Defense guise) and CIA engaged in territorial disputes. On October 9 a planned flight over San Cristobal was approved by COMOR, but, to the CIA's dismay, Air Force pilots rather than CIA agents would take charge of the mission. At this point details become sketchy, but several members of the intelligence community have speculated that an Air Force pilot in an Air Force U-2 attempted a high altitude overflight on October 9 that "flamed out"—that is, lost power, and thus had to descend in order to restart its engine. A second round between Air Force and CIA followed, as a result of which Air Force pilots were trained to fly CIA U-2s. A successful overflight took place on October 14.

This ten-day delay constitutes some form of "failure." In the face of well-founded suspicions concerning offensive Soviet missiles in Cuba that posed a critical threat to the United States' most vital interest, squabbling between organizations whose job it is to produce this information seems entirely inappropriate. But, for each of these organizations, the question involved the issue *Whose* job was it to be? Moreover, the issue was not simply which organization would control U-2 flights over Cuba, but rather the broader issue of ownership of U-2 intelligence activities—a very long-standing territorial dispute. Thus, though this delay was in one sense a "failure," it was also a nearly inevi-

table consequence of two facts: many jobs do not fall neatly into precisely defined organizational jurisdictions; and vigorous organizations are imperialistic.

Organizational Options

Deliberations of leaders in ExCom meetings produced broad outlines of alternatives. Details of these alternatives and blueprints for their implementation had to be specified by the organizations that would perform these tasks. These organizational outputs answered the question What, specifically, *could* be done?

Discussion in the ExCom quickly narrowed the live options to two: an air strike and a blockade. The choice of the blockade instead of the air strike turned on two points: (1) the argument from morality and tradition that the United States could not perpetrate a "Pearl Harbor in reverse"; (2) the belief that a "surgical" air strike was impossible.[44] Whether the United States *might* strike first was a question not of capability but of morality. Whether the United States *could* perform the surgical strike was a factual question concerning capabilities. The majority of the members of the ExCom, including the President, initially preferred the air strike.[45] What effectively foreclosed this option, however, was the fact that the air strike they wanted could not be chosen with high confidence of success.[46] After having tentatively chosen the course of prudence—given the decision that the surgical air strike was not an option—Kennedy reconsidered. On Sunday morning, October 21, he called the Air Force experts to a special meeting in his living quarters and probed once more for the option of a *"surgical"* air strike.[47] General Walter C. Sweeny, Commander of Tactical Air Command, asserted again that the Air Force could guarantee no higher than 90 percent effectiveness in a surgical air strike.[48] That "fact" was false.

The air-strike alternative provides a classic case of military estimates. One of the alternatives outlined by the ExCom was named "air strike." Specification of the details of this alternative was delegated to the Air Force. Starting from an existing plan for massive U.S. military

[43] Abel, *op. cit.*, pp. 26ff.; Edward A. Weintal and Charles Bartlett, *Facing the Brink* (New York, 1967), pp. 62ff.; *Cuban Military Build-up*; J. Daniel and J. Hubbell, *Strike in the West* (New York, 1963), pp. 15ff.

[44] Schlesinger, *op. cit.*, p. 804.
[45] Sorensen, *Kennedy*, p. 684.
[46] *Ibid.*, pp. 684ff.
[47] *Ibid.*, pp. 694–97.
[48] *Ibid.*, p. 697; Abel, *op. cit.*, pp. 100–101.

action against Cuba (prepared for contingencies like a response to a Soviet Berlin grab), Air Force estimators produced an attack to guarantee success.[49] This plan called for extensive bombardment of all missile sites, storage depots, airports, and, in deference to the Navy, the artillery batteries opposite the naval base at Guantanamo.[50] Members of the ExCom repeatedly expressed bewilderment at military estimates of the number of sorties required, likely casualties, and collateral damage. But the "surgical" air strike that the political leaders had in mind was never carefully examined during the first week of the crisis. Rather, this option was simply excluded on the grounds that, since the Soviet MRBMs in Cuba were classified "mobile" in U.S. manuals, extensive bombing was required. During the second week of the crisis, careful examination revealed that the missiles were mobile, in the sense that small houses are mobile: that is, they could be moved and reassembled in six days. After the missiles were reclassified "movable," and detailed plans for surgical air strikes were specified, this action was added to the list of live options for the end of the second week.

Organizational Implementation

ExCom members separated several types of blockade: offensive weapons only, all armaments, and all strategic goods, including POL (petroleum, oil, and lubricants). But the *"details"* of the operation were left to the Navy. Before the President announced the blockade on Monday evening, the first stage of the Navy's blueprint was in motion, and a problem loomed on the horizon.[51] The Navy had a detailed plan for the blockade. The President had several less precise but equally determined notions concerning what should be done, when, and how. For the Navy the issue was one of effective implementation of the Navy's blockade—without the meddling and interference of political leaders. For the President, the problem was to pace and manage events in such a way that the Soviet leaders would have time to see, think, and blink.

A careful reading of available sources uncovers an instructive incident. On Tuesday the

British Ambassador, Ormsby-Gore, after having attended a briefing on the details of the blockade, suggested to the President that the plan for intercepting Soviet ships far out of reach of Cuban jets did not facilitate Khrushchev's hard decision.[52] Why not make the interception much closer to Cuba and thus give the Russian leader more time? According to the public account and the recollection of a number of individuals involved, Kennedy "agreed immediately, called McNamara, and over emotional Navy protest, issued the appropriate instructions."[53] As Sorensen records, "in a sharp clash with the Navy, he made certain his will prevailed."[54] The Navy's plan for the blockade was thus changed by drawing the blockade much closer to Cuba.

A serious organizational orientation makes one suspicious of this account. More careful examination of the available evidence confirms these suspicions, though alternative accounts must be somewhat speculative. According to the public chronology, a quarantine drawn close to Cuba became effective on Wednesday morning, the first Soviet ship was contacted on Thursday morning, and the first boarding of a ship occurred on Friday. According to the statement by the Department of Defense, boarding of the *Marcula* by a party from the *John R. Pierce* "took place at 7:50 A.M., E.D.T., 180 miles northeast of Nassau."[55] The *Marcula* had been trailed since about 10:30 the previous evening.[56] Simple calculations suggest that the *Pierce* must have been stationed along the Navy's original arc, which extended 500 miles out to sea from Cape Magsi, Cuba's easternmost tip.[57] The blockade line was *not* moved as the President ordered and the accounts report.

What happened is not entirely clear. One can be certain, however, that Soviet ships passed through the line along which American destroyers had posted themselves before the official "first contact" with the Soviet ship. On October 26 a Soviet tanker arrived in Havana and was honored by a dockside rally for "running the blockade." Photographs of this vessel

49 Sorensen, *Kennedy*, p. 669.
50 Hilsman, *op. cit.*, p. 204.
51 See Abel, *op. cit.*, pp. 97ff.
52 Schlesinger, *op. cit.*, p. 818.
53 *Ibid.*
54 Sorensen, *Kennedy*, p. 710.
55 *New York Times*, October 27, 1962.
56 Abel, *op. cit.*, p. 171.
57 For the location of the original arc see *ibid.*, p. 141.

show the name *Vinnitsa* on the side of the vessel in Cyrillic letters.[58] But, according to the official U.S. position, the first tanker to pass through the blockade was the *Bucharest*, which was hailed by the Navy on the morning of October 25. Again, simple mathematical calculation excludes the possibility that the *Bucharest* and the *Vinnitsa* were the same ship. It seems probable that the Navy's resistance to the President's order that the blockade be drawn in closer to Cuba forced him to allow one or several Soviet ships to pass through the blockade after it was officially operative.[59]

This attempt to leash the Navy's blockade had a price. On Wednesday morning, October 24, what the President had been awaiting occurred. The eighteen dry-cargo ships heading toward the quarantine stopped dead in the water. This was the occasion of Dean Rusk's remark, "We are eyeball to eyeball and I think the other fellow just blinked."[60] But the Navy had another interpretation. The ships had simply stopped to pick up Soviet submarine escorts. The President became quite concerned lest the Navy—already riled because of Presidential meddling in its affairs—blunder into an incident. Sensing the President's fears, McNamara became suspicious of the Navy's procedures and routines for making the first interception. Calling on Chief of Naval Operations Anderson in the Navy's inner sanctum, the Navy Flag Plot, McNamara put his questions harshly.[61] Who would make the first interception? Were Russian-speaking officers on board? How would submarines be dealt with? At one point McNamara asked Anderson what he would do if a Soviet ship's captain refused to answer questions about his cargo. Picking up the *Manual of Navy Regulations*, the Navy man waved it in McNamara's face and shouted, "It's all in there." To which McNamara replied, "I don't give a damn what John Paul Jones would have done; I want to know what you are going to do, now."[62] The encounter ended with Anderson's remark: "Now, Mr. Secretary, if you and

your Deputy will go back to your office the Navy will run the blockade."[63]

MODEL III: BUREAUCRATIC POLITICS

The leaders who sit on top of organizations are not a monolithic group. Rather, each is, in his own right, a player in a central, competitive game. The name of the game is bureaucratic politics: bargaining along regularized channels among players positioned hierarchically within the government. Thus, according to a third conceptual model, governmental behavior can be understood not as organizational outputs, but as outcomes of bargaining games. In contrast to Model I, the bureaucratic-politics model sees no unitary actor but rather many actors as players who focus not on a single strategic issue but on many diverse intranational problems as well, in terms of no consistent set of strategic objectives but rather according to various conceptions of national, organizational, and personal goals, making government decisions not by rational choice but by the pulling and hauling that is politics.

The apparatus of each national government constitutes a complex arena for the intranational game. Political leaders at the top of this apparatus, plus the men who occupy positions on top of the critical organizations, form the circle of central players. Ascendancy to this circle assures some independent standing. The necessary decentralization of decisions required for action on the broad range of foreign-policy problems guarantees that each player has considerable discretion. Thus power is shared.

The nature of problems of foreign policy permits fundamental disagreement among reasonable men concerning what ought to be done. Analyses yield conflicting recommendations. Separate responsibilities laid on the shoulders of individual personalities encourage differences in perceptions and priorities. But the issues are of first-order importance. What the nation does really matters. A wrong choice could mean irreparable damage. Thus responsible men are obliged to fight for what they are convinced is right.

Men share power. Men differ concerning what must be done. The differences matter.

[58] *Facts on File*, 22 (1962): 376, published by Facts on File, Inc., New York, yearly.
[59] This hypothesis would account for the mystery surrounding Kennedy's explosion at the leak of the stopping of the *Bucharest*. See Hilsman, *op. cit.*, p. 45.
[60] Abel, *op. cit.*, p. 153.
[61] See *ibid.*, pp. 154ff.
[62] *Ibid.*, p. 156.
[63] *Ibid.*

This milieu necessitates that policy be resolved by politics. What the nation does is sometimes the result of the triumph of one group over others. More often, however, different groups pulling in different directions yield a resultant that is distinct from what anyone intended. What moves the chess pieces is not simply the reasons which support a course of action, nor the routines of organizations which enact an alternative, but the power and skill of proponents and opponents of the action in question.

This characterization captures the thrust of the bureaucratic politics orientation. If problems of foreign policy arose as discrete issues, and decisions were determined one game at a time, this account would suffice. But most "issues"—for example, Vietnam or the proliferation of nuclear weapons—emerge piecemeal, over time, one lump in one context, a second in another. Hundreds of issues compete for players' attention every day. Each player is forced to fix upon his issues for that day, fight them on their own terms, and rush on to the next. Thus the character of emerging issues and the pace at which the game is played converge to yield governmental "decisions" and "actions" as collages. Choices by one player, outcomes of minor games, outcomes of central games, and "foul-ups"—these pieces, when stuck to the same canvas, constitute governmental behavior relevant to an issue.

The concept of national security policy as political outcome contradicts both public imagery and academic orthodoxy. Issues vital to national security, it is said, are too important to be settled by political games. They must be "above" politics. To accuse someone of "playing politics with national security" is a most serious charge. What public conviction demands, the academic penchant for intellectual elegance reinforces. Internal politics is messy; moreover, according to prevailing doctrine, politicking lacks intellectual content. As such, it constitutes gossip for journalists rather than a subject for serious investigation. Occasional memoirs, anecdotes in historical accounts, and several detailed case studies to the contrary, most of the literature of foreign policy avoids bureaucratic politics. The gap between academic literature and the experience of participants in government is nowhere wider than at this point.

BUREAUCRATIC POLITICS PARADIGM[64]

Basic Unit of Analysis: Policy as Political Outcome

The decisions and actions of governments are essentially intranational political outcomes: outcomes in the sense that what happens is not chosen as a solution to a problem but rather results from compromise, coalition, competition, and confusion among governmental officials who see different faces of an issue; political in the sense that the activity from which the outcomes emerge is best characterized as bargaining. Following Wittgenstein's use of the concept of a "game," national behavior in international affairs can be conceived as outcomes of intricate and subtle, simultaneous, overlapping games among players located in positions, the hierarchical arrangement of which constitutes the government.[65] These games proceed neither

[64] This paradigm relies upon the small group of analysts who have begun to fill the gap. My primary source is the model implicit in the work of Richard E. Neustadt, though his concentration on presidential action has been generalized to a concern with policy as the outcome of political bargaining among a number of independent players, the President amounting to no more than a "superpower" among many lesser but considerable powers. As Warner Schilling argues, the substantive problems are of such inordinate difficulty that uncertainties and differences with regard to goals, alternatives, and consequences are inevitable. This necessitates what Roger Hilsman describes as the process of conflict and consensus-building. The techniques employed in this process often resemble those used in legislative assemblies, though Samuel Huntington's characterization of the process as "legislative" overemphasizes the equality of participants as opposed to the hierarchy which structures the game. Moreover, whereas for Huntington foreign policy (in contrast to military policy)· is set by the executive, this paradigm maintains that the activities which he describes as legislative are characteristic of the process by which foreign policy is made.

[65] The theatrical metaphor of stage, roles, and actors is more common than this metaphor of games, positions, and players. Nevertheless, the rigidity connoted by the concept of "role," both in the theatrical sense of actors reciting fixed lines and in the sociological sense of fixed responses to specified social situations, makes the concept of games, positions, and players more useful for this analysis of active participants in the determination of national policy. Objections to the terminology on the grounds that "game" connotes nonserious play overlook the concept's application to most serious problems both in Wittgenstein's philosophy and in contemporary game theory. Game theory typically treats structured games more precisely, but Wittgenstein's examination of the "language game," wherein men use words to communicate, is quite analogous to this analysis of the less specified game of bureaucratic politics. See Ludwig Wittgenstein, *Philosophical Investigations*, and Thomas Schell-

at random nor at leisure. Regular channels structure the game. Deadlines force issues to the attention of busy players. The moves in the chess game are thus to be explained in terms of the bargaining among players with separate and unequal power over particular pieces and with separable objectives in distinguishable subgames.

Organizing Concepts

. Players in Positions. The actor is neither a unitary nation nor a conglomerate of organizations, but is rather a number of individual players. Groups of these players constitute the agent for particular governmental decisions and actions. Players are men in jobs.

Individuals become players in the national security policy game by occupying critical positions in an administration. For example, in the U.S. government the players include "Chiefs" —the President, Secretaries of State, Defense, and Treasury, Director of the CIA, Joint Chiefs of Staff, and, since 1961, the Special Assistant for National Security Affairs;[66] "Staffers"—the immediate staff of each Chief; "Indians"—the political appointees and permanent governmental officials within each of the departments and agencies; and "*Ad Hoc* Players"—actors in the wider governmental game (especially "Congressional Influentials"), members of the press, spokesmen for important interest groups (especially the "bipartisan foreign-policy establishment" in and out of Congress), and surrogates for each of these groups. Other members of the Congress, press, interest groups, and the public form concentric circles around the central arena—circles which demarcate the permissive limits within which the game is played.

Positions define what players both may and must do. The advantages and handicaps with which each player can enter and play in vari-

ous games stems from his position. So does a cluster of obligations for the performance of certain tasks. The two sides of this coin are illustrated by the position of the modern Secretary of State.

First, in form and usually in fact, he is the primary repository of political judgment on the political-military issues that are the stuff of contemporary foreign policy; consequently, he is a senior personal adviser to the President. Second, he is the colleague of the President's other senior advisers on the problems of foreign policy, the Secretaries of Defense and Treasury, and the Special Assistant for National Security Affairs. Third, he is the ranking U.S. diplomat for serious negotiation. Fourth, he serves as an administration voice to Congress, the country, and the world. Finally, he is "Mr. State Department" or "Mr. Foreign Office," "leader of officials, spokesman for their causes, guardian of their interests, judge of their disputes, superintendent of their work, master of their careers."[67] But he is not first one and then the other. All of these obligations are his simultaneously. His performance in one affects his credit and power in the others. The perspective that stems from the daily work which he must oversee—the cable traffic by which his department maintains relations with other foreign offices—conflicts with the President's requirement that he serve as a generalist and coordinator of contrasting perspectives. The necessity that he be close to the President restricts the extent to which, and the force with which, he can front for his department. When he defers to the Secretary of Defense rather than fight for his department's position—as he often must —he strains the loyalty of his officialdom. The Secretary of State's resolution of these conflicts depends not only upon the position, but also upon the player who occupies the position.

For players are also people. Men's metabolisms differ. The core of the bureaucratic-politics mix is personality. How each man manages to stand the heat in his kitchen, each player's basic operating style, and the complementarity or contradiction among personalities and styles

ing, "What is Game Theory?" in *Contemporary Political Analysis*, ed. James Charlesworth (New York, 1967).

[66] Inclusion of the President's Special Assistant for National Security Affairs in the tier of "Chiefs" rather than among the "Staffers" involves a debatable choice. In fact he is both superstaffer and near-chief. His position has no statutory authority. He is especially dependent upon good relations with the President and the Secretaries of Defense and State. Nevertheless, he stands astride a genuine action-channel. The decision to include this position among the "Chiefs" reflects my judgment that the Bundy function is becoming institutionalized.

[67] Richard E. Neustadt, testimony, U.S. Congress, Senate, Committee on Government Operations, Subcommittee on National Security Staffing, *Administration of National Security*, 88th Cong., 1st sess., March 26, 1963, pp. 82–83.

in the inner circles are irreducible pieces of the policy blend. Moreover, each person comes to his position with baggage in tow, including sensitivities to certain issues, commitments to various programs, and personal standing and debts with groups in the society.

Parochial Priorities, Perceptions, and Issues. Answers to the questions "What is the issue?" and "What must be done?" are colored by the position from which the questions are considered. For the factors which encourage organizational parochialism also influence the players who occupy positions on top of (or within) these organizations. To motivate members of his organization, a player must be sensitive to the organization's orientation. The games into which the player can enter and the advantages with which he plays enhance these pressures. Thus the propensities of perception which stem from position permit reliable prediction about a player's stances in many cases. But these propensities are filtered through the baggage which players bring to positions. Sensitivity to both the pressures and the baggage is thus required for many predictions.

Interests, Stakes, and Power. Games are played to determine outcomes. But outcomes advance and impede each player's conception of the national interest, specific programs to which he is committed, the welfare of his friends, and his personal interests. These overlapping interests constitute the stakes for which games are played. Each player's ability to play successfully depends upon his power. Power—that is, effective influence on policy outcomes—is an elusive blend of at least three elements: bargaining advantages (drawn from formal authority and obligations, institutional backing, constituents, expertise, and status), skill and will in using bargaining advantages, and other players' perceptions of the first two ingredients. Power wisely invested yields an enhanced reputation for effectiveness. Unsuccessful investment depletes both the stock of capital and the reputation. Thus each player must pick the issues on which he can play with a reasonable probability of success. But no player's power is sufficient to guarantee satisfactory outcomes. Each player's needs and fears run to many other players. What ensues is the most intricate and subtle of games known to man.

The Problem and the Problems. "Solutions" to strategic problems are not derived by de-

tached analysts focusing coolly on *the* problem. Instead, deadlines and events raise issues in games and demand decisions of busy players in contexts that influence the face the issue wears. The problems for the players are both narrower and broader than *the* strategic problem. For each player focuses not on the total strategic problem but rather on the decision that must be made now. Yet each decision has critical consequences not only for the strategic problem but for each player's organizational, reputational, and personal stakes. Thus the gap between the problems the player was solving and the problem upon which the analyst focuses is often very wide.

Action Channels. Bargaining games do not proceed randomly. Action channels—that is, regularized ways of producing action concerning types of issues—structure the game by preselecting the major players, determining their points of entrance into the game, and distributing particular advantages and disadvantages for each game. Most critically, channels determine "who's got the action"—that is, which department's Indians actually do whatever is chosen. Weapons procurement decisions are made within the annual budgeting process; embassies' demands-for-action cables are answered according to routines of consultation and clearance from State to Defense and White House; requests for instructions from military groups (concerning assistance all the time, concerning operations during war) are composed by the military in consultation with the Office of the Secretary of Defense, that of the State, and the White House; crisis responses are debated among White House, State, Defense, CIA, and *Ad Hoc* Players; major political speeches, especially by the President, but also by other Chiefs, are cleared through established channels.

Action as Politics. Governmental decisions are made and governmental actions emerge neither as the calculated choice of a unified group nor as a formal summary of leaders' preferences. Rather, the context of shared power but separate judgments concerning important choices determines that politics is the mechanism of choice. Note the *environment* in which the game is played: inordinate uncertainty about what must be done, the necessity that something be done, and crucial consequences of whatever is done. These features force responsible men to become active players. The *pace of the game*—hundreds of issues, numerous games, and multiple channels—compels players to fight to "get others' attention," to make them "see the facts," to assure that they "take the time to think seriously about the broader issue." The *structure of the game*—power shared by individuals with separate responsibilities—validates each player's feeling that "others don't see my problem," and "others must be persuaded to look at the issue from a less parochial perspective." The *rules of the game*—he who hesitates loses his chance to play at that point, and he who is uncertain about his recommendation is overpowered by others who are sure—pressure players to come down on one side of a 51–49 issue and play. The *rewards of the game*—effectiveness, or impact on outcomes, as the immediate measure of performance—encourage hard play. Thus, most players come to fight to "make the government do what is right." The strategies and tactics employed are quite similar to those formalized by theorists of international relations.

Streams of Outcomes. Important governmental decisions or actions emerge as collages composed of individual acts, outcomes of minor and major games, and foul-ups. Outcomes which could never have been chosen by an actor and would never have emerged from bargaining in a single game over the issue are fabricated piece by piece. Understanding of the outcome requires that it be disaggregated.

Dominant Inference Pattern

If a nation performed an action, that action would be the *outcome* of bargaining among individuals and groups within the government. That outcome would include *results* achieved by groups committed to a decision or action, *resultants* which emerged from bargaining among groups with quite different positions and *foul-ups*. Model III's explanatory power is achieved by revealing the pulling and hauling of various players, with different perceptions and priorities, focusing on separate problems, which yielded the outcomes that constitute the action in question.

General Propositions

Action and Intention. Action does not presuppose intention. The sum of the behavior of representatives of a government relevant to an issue was rarely intended by any individual or group. Rather, separate individuals with different intentions contributed pieces which composed an outcome distinct from what anyone would have chosen.

Where You Stand Depends on Where You Sit.[68] Horizontally, the diverse demands upon each player shape his priorities, perceptions, and issues. For large classes of issues—for example, budgets and procurement decisions—the stance of a particular player can be predicted with high reliability from information concerning his seat. In the notorious B-36 controversy, no one was surprised by Admiral Radford's testimony that "the B-36 under any theory of war, is a bad gamble with national security," as opposed to Air Force Secretary Symington's claim that "a B-36 with an A-bomb can destroy distant objectives which might require ground armies years to take."[69]

Chiefs and Indians. The aphorism "where you stand depends on where you sit" has vertical as well as horizontal application. Vertically, the demands upon the President, Chiefs, Staffers, and Indians are quite distinct.

The foreign policy issues with which the President can deal are limited primarily by his crowded schedule: the necessity of dealing first with what comes next. His problem is to probe the special face worn by issues that come to his attention, to preserve his leeway until time has clarified the uncertainties, and to assess the relevant risks.

Foreign policy Chiefs deal most often with the hottest issue *de jour*, though they can get the attention of the President and other members of the government for other issues which they judge important. What they cannot guarantee is that "the President will pay the price" or that "the others will get on board." They must build a coalition of the relevant powers that be. They must "give the President confidence" in the right course of action.

Most problems are framed, alternatives specified, and proposals pushed, however, by Indians. Indians fight with Indians of other departments; for example, struggles between International Security Affairs of the Depart-

[68] This aphorism was stated first, I think, by Don K. Price.
[69] Paul Y. Hammond, "Super Carriers and B-36 Bombers," in *American Civil-Military Decisions*, ed. Harold Stein (Birmingham, Ala., 1963).

ment of Defense and Political-Military of the State Department are a microcosm of the action at higher levels. But the Indian's major problem is how to get the *attention* of Chiefs, how to get an issue decided, how to get the government "to do what is right."

In policymaking then, the issue looking *down* is options: how to preserve my leeway until time clarifies uncertainties. The issue looking *sideways* is commitment: how to get others committed to my coalition. The issue looking *upward* is confidence: how to give the boss confidence in doing what must be done. To paraphrase one of Neustadt's assertions which can be applied down the length of the ladder, the essence of a responsible official's task is to induce others to see that what needs to be done is what their own appraisal of their own responsibilities requires them to do in their own interests.

Specific Propositions

Deterrence. The probability of nuclear attack depends primarily on the probability of attack emerging as an outcome of the bureaucratic politics of the attacking government. First, which players can decide to launch an attack? Whether the effective power over action is controlled by an individual, a minor game, or the central game is critical. Second, though Model I's confidence in nuclear deterrence stems from an assertion that, in the end, governments will not commit suicide, Model III recalls historical precedents. Admiral Yamamoto, who designed the Japanese attack on Pearl Harbor, estimated accurately: "In the first six months to a year of war against the U.S. and England I will run wild, and I will show you an uninterrupted succession of victories; I must also tell you that, should the war be prolonged for two or three years, I have no confidence in our ultimate victory."[70] But Japan attacked. Thus three questions might be considered. First, could any member of the government solve his problem by attack? What patterns of bargaining could yield attack as an outcome? The major difference between a stable balance of terror and a questionable balance may simply be that in the first case most members of the government appreciate fully the consequences of attack and are thus on

guard against the emergence of this outcome. Second, what stream of outcomes might lead to an attack? At what point in that stream is the potential attacker's politics? If members of the U.S. government had been sensitive to the stream of decisions from which the Japanese attack on Pearl Harbor emerged, they would have been aware of a considerable probability of that attack. Third, how might miscalculation and confusion generate foul-ups that yield attack as an outcome? For example, in a crisis or after the beginning of conventional war, what happens to the information available to, and the effective power of, members of the central game.

THE U.S. BLOCKADE OF CUBA: A THIRD CUT

The Politics of Discovery

A series of overlapping bargaining games determined both the *date* of the discovery of the Soviet missiles and the *impact* of this discovery on the Administration. An explanation of the politics of the discovery is consequently a considerable piece of the explanation of the U.S. blockade.

Cuba was the Kennedy Administration's "political Achilles' heel."[71] The months preceding the crisis were also months before the congressional elections, and the Republican Senatorial and Congressional Campaign Committee had announced that Cuba would be "the dominant issue of the 1962 campaign."[72] What the administration billed as a "more positive and indirect approach of isolating Castro from developing, democratic Latin America," Senators Keating, Goldwater, Capehart, Thurmond, and others attacked as a "do-nothing" policy.[73] In statements on the floor of the House and Senate, campaign speeches across the country, and interviews and articles carried by national news media, Cuba—particularly the Soviet program of increased arms aid—served as a stick for stirring the domestic political scene.[74]

These attacks drew blood. Prudence demanded a vigorous reaction. The President decided to meet the issue head-on. The Administration mounted a forceful campaign of denial designed to discredit critics' claims. The Presi-

---

[70] Roberta Wohlstetter, *Pearl Harbor* (Stanford, 1962), p. 350.

[71] Sorensen, *Kennedy*, p. 670.
[72] *Ibid.*
[73] *Ibid.*, pp. 670ff.
[74] *New York Times*, August and September, 1962.

dent himself manned the front line of this offensive, though almost all Administration officials participated. In his news conference on
August 19, President Kennedy attacked as "irresponsible" calls for an invasion of Cuba,
stressing rather "the totality of our obligations"
and promising to "watch what happens in
Cuba with the closest attention."[75] On September 4, he issued a strong statement denying
any provocative Soviet action in Cuba.[76] On
September 13 he lashed out at "loose talk"
calling for an invasion of Cuba.[77] The day before the flight of the U-2 which discovered the
missiles, he campaigned in Capehart's Indiana
against those "self-appointed generals and admirals who want to send someone else's sons
to war."[78]

On Sunday, October 14, just as a U-2 was
taking the first pictures of Soviet missiles,
McGeorge Bundy asserted:

I *know* that there is no present evidence, and I
think that there is no present likelihood that the
Cuban government and the Soviet government
would, in combination, attempt to install a major
offensive capability.[79]

In this campaign to puncture the critics'
charges, the Administration discovered that the
public needed positive slogans. Thus, Kennedy
fell into a tenuous semantic distinction between
"offensive" and "defensive" weapons. This distinction originated in his September 4 statement that there was no evidence of "offensive
ground to ground missiles" and his warning that,
"were it to be otherwise, the gravest issues
would arise."[80] His September 13 statement
turned on this distinction between "defensive"
and "offensive" weapons and announced a firm
commitment to action if the Soviet Union attempted to introduce the latter into Cuba.[81]
Congressional committees elicited from administration officials testimony which read this distinction and the President's commitment into
the *Congressional Record*.[82]

What the President least wanted to hear, the

CIA was most hesitant to say plainly. On August 22 John McCone met privately with the
President and voiced suspicions that the Soviets were preparing to introduce offensive missiles into Cuba.[83] Kennedy heard this as what
it was: the suspicion of a hawk. McCone left
Washington for a month's honeymoon on the
Riviera. Fretting at Cap Farrat, he bombarded
his deputy, General Marshall Carter, with telegrams, but Carter, knowing that McCone had
informed the President of his suspicions and
had received a cold reception, was reluctant to
distribute these telegrams outside the CIA.[84]
On September 9 a U-2 "on loan" to the Chinese Nationalists was downed over mainland
China.[85] The Committee on Overhead Reconnaissance (COMOR) convened on September 10 with a sense of urgency.[86] Loss of
another U-2 might incite world opinion to demand cancellation of U-2 flights. The President's campaign against those who asserted
that the Soviets were acting provocatively in
Cuba had begun. To risk downing a U-2 over
Cuba was to risk chopping off the limb on
which the President was sitting. The COMOR
decided to shy away from the western end of
Cuba (where SAMs were becoming operational) and modify the flight pattern of the
U-2s in order to reduce the probability that a
U-2 would be lost.[87] USIB's unanimous approval of the September estimate reflects similar sensitivities. On September 13 the President had asserted that there were no Soviet
offensive missiles in Cuba and had committed
his Administration to act if offensive missiles
were discovered. Before congressional committees, Administration officials were denying that
there was any evidence whatever of offensive
missiles in Cuba. The implications of a National Intelligence Estimate which concluded
that the Soviets were introducing offensive missiles into Cuba were not lost on the men who
constituted America's highest intelligence assembly.

[75] *Ibid.*, August 20, 1962.
[76] *Ibid.*, September 5, 1962.
[77] *Ibid.*, September 14, 1962.
[78] *Ibid.*, October 14, 1962.
[79] Cited by Abel, *op. cit.*, p. 13.
[80] *New York Times*, September 5, 1962.
[81] *Ibid.*, September 14, 1962.
[82] Senate Foreign Relations Committee; Senate
Armed Services Committee; House Committee on Appropriations; House Select Committee on Export Control.

[83] Abel, *op. cit.*, pp. 17–18. As McCone told Kennedy, "The only construction I can put on the material going into Cuba is that the Russians are preparing
to introduce offensive missiles." See also Weintal and
Bartlett, *op. cit.*, pp. 60–61.
[84] Abel, *op. cit.*, p. 23.
[85] *New York Times*, September 10, 1962.
[86] See Abel, *op. cit.*, pp. 25–26; and Hilsman, *op.
cit.*, p. 174.
[87] Department of Defense Appropriation, *Hearings*,
p. 69.

The October 4 COMOR decision to direct a flight over the western end of Cuba in effect "overturned" the September estimate, but without officially raising that issue. The decision represented McCone's victory, for which he had lobbied with the President before the September 10 decision, in telegrams before the September 19 estimate, and in person after his return to Washington. Though the politics of the intelligence community is closely guarded, several pieces of the story can be told.[88] By September 27 Colonel Wright and others in DIA believed that the Soviet Union was placing missiles in the San Cristobal area.[89] This area was marked "suspicious" by the CIA on September 29 and "certified top priority" on October 3. By October 4 McCone had the evidence required to raise the issue officially. The members of COMOR heard McCone's argument but were reluctant to make the hard decision he demanded. The significant probability that a U-2 would be downed made overflight of western Cuba a matter of real concern.[90]

The Politics of Issues

The U-2 photographs presented incontrovertible evidence of Soviet offensive missiles in Cuba. This revelation fell upon politicized players in a complex context. As one high official recalled, Khrushchev had caught us "with our pants down." What each of the central participants saw, and what each did to cover both his own and the administration's nakedness, created the spectrum of issues and answers.

At approximately 9:00 A.M. Tuesday, October 16, McGeorge Bundy went to the President's living quarters with the message "Mr. President, there is now hard photographic evidence that the Russians have offensive missiles in Cuba."[91] Much has been made of Kennedy's "expression of surprise,"[92] but "surprise" fails to capture the character of his initial reaction. Rather, it was one of startled anger, most adequately conveyed by the exclamation: "He

can't do that to *me!*"[93] In terms of the President's attention and priorities at that moment, Khrushchev had chosen the most unhelpful act of all. Kennedy had staked his full presidential authority on the assertion that the Soviets would not place offensive weapons in Cuba. Moreover, Khrushchev had assured the President through the most direct and personal channels that he was aware of the President's domestic political problem and that nothing would be done to exacerbate this problem. The Chairman had *lied* to the President. Kennedy's initial reaction entailed action. The missiles must be removed.[94] The alternatives of "doing nothing" or "taking a diplomatic approach" could not have been less relevant to *his* problem.

These two tracks—doing nothing and taking a diplomatic approach—were the solutions advocated by two of his principal advisers. For Secretary of Defense McNamara, the missiles raised the specter of nuclear war. He first framed the issue as a straightforward strategic problem. To understand the issue, one had to grasp two obvious but difficult points. First, the missiles represented an inevitable occurrence: a narrowing of the missile gap. It simply happened sooner rather than later. Second, the United States could accept this occurrence, since its consequences were minor: "seven-to-one missile 'superiority,' one-to-one missile 'equality,' one-to-seven missile 'inferiority'—the three postures are identical." McNamara's statement of this argument at the first meeting of the ExCom was summed up in the phrase "a missile is a missile."[95] "It makes no great difference," he maintained, "whether you are killed by a missile from the Soviet Union or Cuba."[96] The implication was clear. The United States should not initiate a crisis with the Soviet Union and thereby risk a significant probability of nuclear war over an occurrence which had such small strategic implications.

The perceptions of McGeorge Bundy, the President's Assistant for National Security Affairs, are the most difficult of all to reconstruct.

---

[88] A basic, but somewhat contradictory, account of parts of this story emerges in the Department of Defense Appropriations, *Hearings*, pp. 1–70.

[89] *Ibid.*, p. 71.

[90] The details of the ten days between the October 4 decision and the October 14 flight must be held in abeyance.

[91] Abel, *op. cit.*, p. 44.

[92] *Ibid.*, pp. 44ff.

[93] See Richard Neustadt, Afterword, *Presidential Power* (New York, 1964).

[94] Sorensen, *Kennedy*, p. 676; Schlesinger, *op. cit.*, p. 801.

[95] Hilsman, *op. cit.*, p. 195.

[96] *Ibid.*

There is no question that he initially argued for a diplomatic track.[97] But was Bundy laboring under his acknowledged burden of responsibility in Cuba I? Or was he playing the role of devil's advocate in order to make the President probe his own initial reaction and consider other options?

The President's brother, Robert Kennedy, saw most clearly the political wall against which Khrushchev had backed the President. But he, like McNamara, saw the prospect of nuclear doom. Was Khrushchev going to force the President to an insane act? At the first meeting of the ExCom, he scribbled a note, "Now I know how Tojo felt when he was planning Pearl Harbor."[98] From the outset he searched for an alternative that would prevent the air strike.

The initial reaction of Theodore Sorensen, the President's Special Counsel and "alter ego," fell somewhere between that of the President and his brother. Like the President, Sorensen felt the poignancy of betrayal. If the President had been the architect of the policy which the missiles punctured, Sorensen was the draftsman. Khrushchev's deceitful move demanded a strong countermove. But, like Robert Kennedy, Sorensen feared that the shock and disgrace would lead to disaster.

To the Joint Chiefs of Staff the issue was clear. *Now* was the time to do the job for which they had prepared contingency plans. Cuba I had been badly done; Cuba II would not be. The missiles provided the *occasion* to deal with the issue: cleansing the Western Hemisphere of Castro's communism. As the President recalled on the day the crisis ended, "An invasion would have been a mistake—a wrong use of our power. But the military are mad. They wanted to do this. It's lucky for us that we have McNamara over there."[99]

McCone's perceptions flowed from his confirmed prediction. As the Cassandra of the incident, he argued forcefully that the Soviets had installed the missiles in a daring political probe which the United States must meet with force. The time for an air strike was now.[100]

The Politics of Choice

The process by which the blockade emerged is a story of the most subtle and intricate probing, pulling, and hauling; leading, guiding, and spurring. Reconstruction of this process can be only tentative. Initially the President and most of his advisers wanted the clean, surgical air strike. On the first day of the crisis, when informing Stevenson of the missiles, the President mentioned only two alternatives: "I suppose the alternatives are to go in by air and wipe them out, or to take other steps to render them inoperable."[101] At the end of the week a sizable minority still favored an air strike. As Robert Kennedy recalled: "The fourteen people involved were very significant. . . . If six of them had been President of the U.S., I think that the world might have been blown up."[102] What prevented the air strike was a fortuitous coincidence of a number of factors—the absence of any one of which might have permitted that option to prevail.

First, McNamara's vision of holocaust set him firmly against the air strike. His initial attempt to frame the issue in strategic terms struck Kennedy as particularly inappropriate. Once McNamara realized that the name of the game was a strong response, however, he and his deputy Gilpatric chose the blockade as a fallback. When the Secretary of Defense—whose department had the action, whose reputation in the Cabinet was unequaled, in whom the President demonstrated full confidence—marshaled the arguments for the blockade and refused to be moved, the blockade became a formidable alternative.

Second, Robert Kennedy—the President's closest confidant—was unwilling to see his brother become a "Tojo." His arguments against the air strike on moral grounds struck a chord in the President. Moreover, once his brother had stated these arguments so forcefully, the President could not have chosen his initially preferred course without, in effect, agreeing to become what RFK had condemned.

The President learned of the missiles on Tuesday morning. On Wednesday morning, in order to mask our discovery from the Russians,

[97] Weintal and Bartlett, *op. cit.*, p. 67; Abel, *op. cit.*, p. 53.

[98] Schlesinger, *op. cit.*, p. 803.

[99] *Ibid.*, p. 831.

[100] Abel, *op. cit.*, p. 186.

[101] *Ibid.*, p. 49.

[102] Interview, quoted by Ronald Steel, *New York Review of Books*, March 13, 1969, p. 22.

the President flew to Connecticut to keep a campaign commitment, leaving RFK as the unofficial chairman of the group. By the time the President returned on Wednesday evening, a critical third piece had been added to the picture: McNamara had presented his argument for the blockade. Robert Kennedy and Sorensen had joined McNamara. A powerful coalition of the advisers in whom the President had the greatest confidence, and with whom his style was most compatible, had emerged.

Fourth, the coalition that had formed behind the President's initial preference gave him reason to pause. *Who* supported the air strike—the Joint Chiefs, McCone, Rusk, Nitze, and Acheson—as much as *how* they supported it, counted. Fifth, a piece of inaccurate information, which no one probed, permitted the blockade advocates to fuel (potential) uncertainties in the President's mind. When the President returned to Washington Wednesday evening, RFK and Sorensen met him at the airport, Sorensen gave the President a four-page memorandum outlining the areas of agreement and disagreement. The strongest argument was that the air strike simply could not be surgical.[103] After a day of prodding and questioning, the Air Force had asserted that it could not guarantee the success of a surgical air strike limited to the missiles alone.

Thursday evening, the President convened the ExCom at the White House. He declared his tentative choice of the blockade and directed that preparations be made to put it into effect by Monday morning.[104] Though he subsequently raised a question about the possibility of a surgical air strike, he seems to have accepted the experts' opinion that this was not a live option.[105] (Acceptance of this estimate suggests that he may have learned the lesson of the Bay of Pigs—"Never rely on experts"—less well than he supposed.)[106] But this information was incorrect. That no one probed this estimate during the first week of the crisis poses an interesting question for further investigation.

A coalition, including the President, thus emerged from the President's initial decision that something had to be done; McNamara,

Robert Kennedy, and Sorensen's resistance to the air strike; incompatibility between the President and the air-strike advocates; and an inaccurate piece of information.[107]

CONCLUSION

This essay has obviously bitten off more than it has chewed. For further developments and synthesis of these arguments the reader is referred to the larger study. In spite of the limits of space, however, it would be inappropriate to stop without spelling out several implications of the argument and addressing the question of relations among the models and extensions of them to activity beyond explanation.

At a minimum, the intended implications of the argument presented here are four. First, formulation of alternative frames of reference and demonstration that different analysts, relying predominantly on different models, produce quite different explanations should encourage the analyst's self-consciousness about the nets he employs. The effect of these "spectacles" in sensitizing him to particular aspects of what is going on—framing the puzzle in one way rather than another, encouraging him to examine the problem in terms of certain categories rather than others, directing him to particular kinds of evidence, and relieving puzzlement by one procedure rather than another—must be recognized and explored.

Second, the argument implies a position on the problem of "the state of the art." While accepting the commonplace characterization of the present condition of foreign policy analysis—personalistic, noncumulative, and sometimes insightful—this essay rejects both the counsel of despair's justification of this condition as a consequence of the character of the enterprise, and the "new frontiersmen's" demand for *a priori* theorizing on the frontiers and *ad hoc* appropriation of "new techniques."[108] What is

---

103 Sorensen, *Kennedy*, p. 686.
104 *Ibid.*, p. 691.
105 *Ibid.*, pp. 691–92.
106 Schlesinger, *op. cit.*, p. 296.

107 Space will not permit an account of the path from this coalition to the formal governmental decision on Saturday and action on Monday.
108 Thus my position is quite distinct from both poles in the recent "great debate" about international relations. While many "traditionalists" of the sort Kaplan attacks adopt the first posture, and many "scientists" of the sort attacked by Bull adopt the second, this third posture is relatively neutral with respect to whatever is in substantive dispute. See Hedley Bull, "International Theory: The Case for a

Summary Outline of Models and Concepts

The Paradigm	Model I	Model II	Model III
	National government Black box → Goals (objective function), Options, Consequences, Choice	National government Leaders [A B C D E F G] → Organizations (A–G), Goals, SOPs and programs	National government Players in positions (A–F), Goals, interests, stakes, and stands (r–z), Power, Action-channels
Basic unit of analysis	Governmental action as choice	Governmental action as organizational output	Governmental action as political resultant
Organizing concepts	National actor The problem Static selection Action as rational choice Goals and objectives Options Consequences Choice	Organizational actors (constellation of which is the government) Factored problems and fractionated power Parochial priorities and perceptions Action as organizational output Goals: constraints defining acceptable performance Sequential attention to goals Standard operating procedures Programs and repertoires Uncertainty avoidance (negotiated environment, standard scenario) Problem-directed search Organizational learning and change Central coordination and control Decisons of government leaders	Players in positions Parochial priorities and perceptions Goals and interests Stakes and stands Deadlines and faces of issues Power Action-channels Rules of the game Action as political resultant
Dominant inference pattern	Governmental action = choice with regard to objectives	Governmental action (in short run) = output largely determined by present SOPs and programs Governmental action (in longer run) = output importantly affected by organizational goals, SOPs, etc.	Governmental action = resultant of bargaining
General propositions	Substitution effect	Organizational implementation Organizational options Limited flexibility and incremental change Long-range planning Goals and tradeoffs Imperialism Options and organization Administrative feasibility Directed change	Political resultants Action and intention Problems and solutions Where you stand depends on where you sit Chiefs and Indians The 51–49 principle Inter- and intra-national relations Misperception, misexpectation, miscommunication, and reticence Styles of play

Reprinted by permission from Essence of Decision: Explaining the Cuban Missile Crisis, *p. 256. Copyright © 1971 by Little, Brown & Co., Inc.*

required as a first step is noncasual examination of the present product: inspection of existing explanations, articulation of the conceptual models employed in producing them, formulation of the propositions relied upon, specification of the logic of the various intellectual enterprises, and reflection on the questions being asked. Though it is difficult to overemphasize the need for more systematic processing of more data, these preliminary matters of formulating questions with clarity and sensitivity to categories and assumptions so that fruitful acquisition of large quantities of data is possible are still a major hurdle in considering most important problems.

Third, the preliminary, partial paradigms presented here provide a basis for serious reexamination of many problems of foreign and military policy. Model II and Model III cuts at problems typically treated in Model I terms can permit significant improvements in explanation and prediction.[109] Full Model II and Model III analyses require large amounts of information. But even in cases where the information base is severely limited, improvements are possible. Consider the problem of predicting Soviet strategic forces. In the mid-1950s, Model I style calculations led to predictions that the Soviets would rapidly deploy large numbers of long-range bombers. From a Model

II perspective, both the frailty of the Air Force within the Soviet military establishment and the budgetary implications of such a build-up would have led analysts to hedge this prediction. Moreover, Model II would have pointed to a sure, visible indicator of such a build-up: noisy struggles among the services over major budgetary shifts. . . .

Fourth, the present formulation of paradigms is simply an initial step. As such, it leaves a long list of critical questions unanswered. . . . Model II's explanation of t in terms of $t - 1$ is explanation. The world is contiguous. But governments sometimes make sharp departures. Can an organizational process model be modified to suggest where change is likely? . . . Model III tells a fascinating "story." But its complexity is enormous, the information requirements are often overwhelming, and many of the details of the bargaining may be superfluous. How can such a model be made parsimonious? The three models are obviously not exclusive alternatives. Indeed, the paradigms highlight the partial emphasis of the framework—what each emphasizes and what it leaves out. Each concentrates on one class of variables, in effect, relegating other important factors to a *ceteris paribus* clause. Model I concentrates on "market factors": pressures and incentives created by the "international strategic marketplace." Models II and III focus on the internal mechanism of the government that chooses in this environment. But can these relations be more fully specified? Adequate synthesis would require a typology of decisions and actions, some of which are more amenable to treatment in terms of one model and some to another. . . .

Classical Approach," *World Politics*, April 1966; and Morton Kaplan, "The New Great Debate: Traditionalism vs. Science in International Relations," *ibid.*, October 1966.

[109] A number of problems are now being examined in these terms both in the Bureaucracy Study Group on Bureaucracy and Policy of the Institute of Politics at Harvard University and at The RAND Corporation.

WHY BUREAUCRATS PLAY GAMES

MORTON H. HALPERIN

This article is an expansion of the Bureaucratic Politics Model described in Allison's essay, but its treatment is both more informal and less complex. Specifically, the author explains that organizations with missions strive to maintain or improve their: (1) autonomy; (2) organizational morale; (3) organizational "essence"; (4) roles and missions; and (5) budgets. He suggests that Presidents need to know how organizational interests affect policy in at least four main areas: (1) information; (2) presentation of options; (3) freedom to choose options; and (4) implementation. A fuller explanation of his analysis is to be found in a forthcoming study, Bureaucratic Politics and Foreign Policy.

Charles Hitch, in the fall of 1962, was hard at work preparing the U.S. military budget for fiscal year 1964. As Comptroller of the Department of Defense, it was Hitch's responsibility to review weapons programs and make recommendations to his boss, Secretary Robert McNamara. One seemingly vulnerable item in the budget was Skybolt, an air-to-surface missile under development by the Air Force. It was designed to carry a nuclear warhead and to be fired from strategic bombers at a target up to 1,000 miles away. In 1960, at a meeting with Prime Minister Macmillan, President Eisenhower had promised to share Skybolt with Britain. Without it, or some substitute, the U.K. would no longer possess a workable nuclear force beyond the mid-1960s.[1]

But, by 1962, Skybolt was in trouble. The first five test launches were abortive, development costs had doubled, and the missile's operational date was already pushed back from 1965 to 1967. The more advanced seaborne Polaris and land-based Minuteman missile programs made a new airborne system seem all the more unnecessary. So Hitch, drawing the obvious conclusion, proposed to McNamara

[1] A fuller account appears in Richard E. Neustadt, *Alliance Politics* (New York: Columbia University Press, 1970), chap. 3. For another view, see Lord Harlech's "Suez SNAFU, Skybolt SABU," *Foreign Policy*, 1971, no. 2, pp. 38–50.

that Skybolt be canceled. Eventually it was, but only at the cost of street demonstrations in London and tumult in Parliament, strains in the NATO alliance, a summit conference between President Kennedy and Prime Minister Macmillan, an offended President de Gaulle, and a U.S. offer of Polaris submarines to Macmillan to compensate for Skybolt.

These unhappy consequences occurred despite the fact that dozens of officials, from the President down to Pentagon colonels and State Department desk officers, devoted countless man-hours, meetings, messages, and memoranda to grappling with "the Skybolt problem." Each of the main bureaucracies engaged in foreign policy in Washington became involved, but every separate organization saw the issue from its own perspective. Having different interests and perceptions, different bureaucrats took different stands on what should be done.

For *Hitch* it was primarily a budgetary matter, a question of canceling a program which he thought to be both technically difficult and strategically unnecessary. If such a program were allowed to continue, the defense budget would grow too large.

The *Air Force* saw the proposal to cancel Skybolt as a threat to the future of its strategic manned bombers, a threat which put one of its basic missions in jeopardy. It might also mean a reduction in the Air Force budget.

For the *Secretary of Defense*, this issue concerned his ability to demonstrate that defense budget decisions would be made on the basis of cost-effectiveness analysis rather than by catering to the organizational interests of the services. McNamara also recognized that, because Skybolt had been promised to the British for their bombers, the cancellation of Skybolt would create issues in U.S.–U.K. relations. But for him this was a secondary matter.

In the *State Department*, the Skybolt issue was seen largely in terms of U.S.–European relations. In the *Bureau of European Affairs*, the cancellation of Skybolt was seen as an opportunity to get the British out of the strategic-weapons business. However, these officials also sensed a danger. The President, more anxious to avoid a crisis and less concerned about the British deterrent, might offer the British a substitute system, perhaps Polaris, which would extend the life of the British independent deterrent rather than shorten it, and would jeopardize Britain's prospects for gaining entry into the Common Market.

Secretary of State Rusk seemed not to have shared the desire of the Europeanists to get the British to phase out their nuclear deterrent and primarily saw cancellation of Skybolt as a threat to close U.S.–British relations.

The *President* appears to have shared Rusk's concern, but also was concerned about his relations with his Secretary of Defense and the Air Force, and with controlling the defense budget.

Each participant saw a different face of the issue based on his own interests, and each sensed dangers, opportunities, or both. For Hitch, for example, cancellation of Skybolt was important, and the sale of Polaris to the British was a matter of indifference. For the Europeanists in the State Department, the money in the defense budget was a matter of indifference; getting the British out of the nuclear business was the important issue for them.

Skybolt was by no means unique. In seeking to understand why the U.S. government adopts a particular policy or takes a particular action, we can make no greater mistake than to assume that the participants in the process look at the issue in the same way and agree on what should be done. The reality is quite different.

THE WAY OF THE SYSTEM

When American governmental officials consider a proposed change in American foreign policy they often see and emphasize quite different things and reach different conclusions. A proposal to withdraw American troops from Europe, for example, is to the Army a threat to its budget and size; to Budget Bureau examiners a way to save money; to the Treasury a balance-of-payments gain; to the State Department Bureau of European Affairs a threat to good relations with NATO; to the President's congressional adviser an opportunity to remove a major irritant in the President's relations with Capitol Hill.

What determines what an official sees? What accounts for his stand? The examples provide some clues.

Participants in the national security policy process in the American government believe that they should, and do, take stands which advance the national security of the United States. Their problem is to determine what is in fact in the national security interest. Officials seek clues and guidelines from a variety of sources. Some hold to a set of beliefs about the world which provides strong clues—for example, the Soviet Union is expansionist and must be stopped by American military power. Others look to authorities within the government or beyond it for guidance. Many bureaucrats define what is necessary for the nation's security by a set of more specific intermediate interests. For some these may be personal: "Since, in general, I know how to protect the nation's security interests, whatever increases my influence is in the national interest." For others, the intermediate interests relate to domestic political interests: "Since a sound economy is a prerequisite to national security I must oppose policies which threaten the economy"; or "Since only my party knows how to defend the security interests of the United States I must support policies which keep my party in power."

For many participants the intermediate objectives which provide strong clues for what is in the nation's security interest are the interests of the organization to which they belong. Career officials come naturally to believe that the health of their organization is vital to the nation's security. So also do individuals who are appointed by the President to senior posts in Washington foreign-policy bureaucracies. This tendency varies depending on the individual, the strength of his prior conviction, his image of his role, and the nature of the organization he heads. On many issues a Secretary of the Air Force will be strongly guided by the organizational interests of his service. A Secretary of State, on the other hand, is likely to be less influenced by the organizational interests of his department and the Foreign Service, since these provide less clear-cut clues and in many cases conflicting guidelines to the nation's security interest. Moreover, some senior officials will seek clues less from their organizations' interests than from the interests of the President as they define them.

Despite the different interests of the participants and the different faces of an issue which they see, officials still frequently agree about what should be done. This may occur when there is strong presidential leadership or when there is a national security argument which most participants view as decisive. In many cases, however, officials reach consensus by designing an ambiguous policy which avoids substantial costs to the different interests of the participants, including the interests of the organizations involved. The compromise avoids making choices on priorities and leaves organizations free to continue operating as they have in the past and to control their own operations. Once a decision is made, the organizations themselves shape the way in which it is implemented.

Organizational interests, then, are for many participants a dominant factor in determining the face of the issue which they see and the stand which they take in pursuit of the nation's security interests. In large part they constitute U.S. foreign policy. Before there is any hope of mastering them, their mysteries—and their mystique—must be explored. What are these organizational interests? From what do they derive?

ORGANIZATIONAL INTERESTS

All organizations seek *influence*, many also have a *mission* to perform, either overseas or at home, and some organizations need to maintain expensive *capabilities* in order to perform their missions effectively.

INFLUENCE

Organizations with missions seek influence to promote the missions. Those that also have large operational capabilities—for example, the armed forces—seek influence on decisions in part to maintain the capability necessary to perform their mission. Some organizations, such as the Office of International Security Affairs in the Office of the Secretary of Defense and the Policy Planning Staff in the State Department, have neither large capabilities nor stable, organizationally defined missions. Hence their only organizational interest is in enhancing influence for its own sake; individuals in such organizations share with those in other organizations the belief that they can best judge the nation's security interests.

Stands on issues are affected by the desire to maintain influence. This could lead to support for certain policies which will require greater reliance on the organization. It can also lead officials to avoid opposing a particular policy in the belief that to do so would reduce their influence on other issues.

MISSIONS

Most organizations are charged with specific missions. Some of these can be accomplished entirely at home (such as maintaining good relations with Congress); others require actions abroad (such as deterring a Soviet attack on the United States).

Bureaucrats will examine any policy proposal from the point of view of whether or not it will increase the effectiveness with which the mission of their particular organization will be carried out. For example, in examining a proposal for a new security commitment, the Budget Bureau and the Comptroller's Office in the Pentagon will ask themselves how it will affect their ability to keep down the defense budget. Treasury will ask how it will affect its ability to maintain the U.S. balance of payments in equilibrium, while the military will be concerned with its ability to meet existing commitments. State Department officials may be concerned with the impact of the security arrangement on political relations with that country and its neighbors.

CAPABILITIES

The missions of some organizations in the national security field lead them to maintain substantial and expensive capabilities which may be employed abroad. The armed services, in particular, are responsible for creating very expensive military forces. Organizations with expensive capabilities will see the face of an issue which affects their ability to maintain what they view as the necessary capability.

Organizations with large capabilities will be particularly concerned about budgetary decisions and about the budgeting implications of policy decisions. Organizations with missions, but low-cost capabilities, will be primarily concerned with policy decisions and their implications for missions. This is an important difference between the armed services and the State Department.

Organizations with missions strive to maintain or to improve their (1) autonomy, (2) organizational morale, (3) organizational "essence," and (4) roles and missions. Organizations with high-cost capabilities are also concerned with maintaining or increasing their (5) budgets.

AUTONOMY

Members of an organization believe that they are in a better position than others to determine what capabilities they should have and how they can best fulfill their missions. They attach very high priority to controlling their own resources. They want to be in a position to spend the money allocated to them in the way that they choose, to station their manpower as they choose, and to implement policy in their own way. Organizations resist efforts by senior officials to get control of their activities by arguing that effective functioning of the organization requires freedom to determine its own procedures. The priority attached to autonomy is shown by the experiences of two recent Secretaries of Defense. Robert S. McNamara caused great consternation in the Pentagon in 1961 by instituting new decision procedures which reduced the autonomy of the services, despite the fact that he increased defense spending by six billion dollars and did not seek to alter the missions of the services. Secretary of Defense Melvin Laird, by contrast, improved Pentagon morale in 1969 by increasing service autonomy on budget matters while reducing the Defense budget by more than four billion dollars.

The quest for autonomy leads organizations to resist policies which will require them to yield their autonomy to senior officials or to work closely with another organization. The belief that autonomy is necessary in the performance of missions results in organizations informing senior officials that particular options are feasible only if full responsibility for carrying them out is delegated to the operating organization. During the 1958 Quemoy crisis, for example, the military repeatedly pressed for freedom to use nuclear weapons on their own authority. They informed the President that they could guarantee to defend this offshore island against a Chinese Communist attack only if they were granted this autonomy.[2]

ORGANIZATIONAL MORALE

An organization functions effectively only if its personnel are highly motivated. They must believe that what they are doing makes a difference and is in support of the national interest; that the organization's efforts are appreciated, and that its role in the scheme of things is not diminishing and preferably is increasing; that the organization controls its own resources; and that there is room for advancement in the organization.

Because they have learned the vital importance of morale for the effective functioning of an organization, bureaucrats give close attention to the likely effects of any change of policy or patterns of action on the morale of the organization and will resist changes which they feel will have a severe effect on morale. Officials may resist changes which even they believe would improve their organization's effectiveness in carrying out its mission if they also believe that such actions would severely affect the morale of the organization. In particular, they will be concerned about the effects on the promotion patterns of the organization. Short-run accomplishments of goals, and even increases in budgets, will be subordinated to the long-run health of the organization. Bureaucrats know that ignoring morale can have disastrous consequences.

2 Dwight D. Eisenhower, *Waging Peace* (New York: Doubleday, 1965), p. 299.

For example, almost every observer of U.S. operations in Vietnam has concluded that extending the tour of duty of commissioned Army officers from one year to two or three years would substantially improve the U.S. military performance. Yet the Army refused to make this change. This is not because the Army has differed with the assessment that there would be an improvement in effectiveness, but rather because (1) the Army has believed that there would be severe effects on morale if officers were sent to Vietnam either for an indefinite period or for a prolonged period, such as three years, and (2) particularly in the early stages of the war, Army leaders felt that there would be severe morale problems if only a small percentage of career Army officers had combat experience in Vietnam, since those officers would have an inside track on promotions. They believed it desirable, not only for morale, but also to improve the effectiveness of the force over the long run, that an opportunity be provided for as many career officers as possible to serve in Vietnam.

THE ORGANIZATION'S "ESSENCE"

Career officials generally have a clear notion of what the essence of their organization is and should be, both in terms of capabilities and in terms of missions. In some organizations the same view of the essence will be shared by all of those in the same promotional and career structure; in other cases there will be differences of view. This can be seen in the following brief discussion of the organizational essence of some of the major U.S. national security organizations.

Air Force officers agree that the essence of their program is the development of a capability for combat flying, particularly that involving the delivery of nuclear weapons. Officers whose orientation is toward the Strategic Air Command (SAC) emphasize the mission of strategic bombing; those in the Tactical Air Command (TAC) emphasize interdiction of enemy supply lines. Providing close combat support is not seen by most Air Force officers as part of the essence of their mission, nor is the development of a capability to transport Army troops and equipment.

Army officers seek to develop a capability to engage in ground combat operations employing traditional Army divisions deployed according to traditional Army doctrine. Some Army officers emphasize tank operations; others stress air mobility. Air defense, advisory missions for foreign governments, and "elite" specialized forces such as the Green Berets are not seen as part of the essence of the Army.

Navy officers agree only on the general proposition that the Navy's business is to man combat naval ships and that their mission is to maintain control of the seas. In fact, the Navy is split into three traditional groups and a fourth whose weight may be growing. Navy flyers (brown shoe) emphasize carrier-based air; others (black shoe) stress the surface Navy; the submariners focus on attack submarines. The fourth group looks to missile-firing submarines and puts emphasis on the mission of strategic deterrence (advocated in the 1940s and 1950s by the flyers). No influential group sees the transport of men and matériel as part of the Navy's essence, and most senior naval officers have tended to view the Polaris missile-firing submarines as a service to the nation but extraneous to the Navy's "essential" tasks.

Foreign Service officers see their essential functions as representation and negotiation and political reporting. Managing programs and embassies and even analyzing policy alternatives are not part of the essence of the State Department's function.

Career *CIA* officials appear to be split between those who emphasize analysis and those who view the agency's essence as its unique role of covert intelligence-gathering and operations.

The stand of bureaucrats on a policy issue is influenced by its impact on the ability of their organization to pursue its essential programs and missions. They resist most strongly efforts to take away these functions or to share them with other organizations. They also resist proposals to reduce funds for these programs or missions. Autonomy is most precious, for it affects the essence of the organization.

Conversely, bureaucrats feel less strongly about "marginal" functions, particularly those which require cooperation with other organizations or are viewed as support for them (e.g., naval and air transport for the Army). Left alone, they will devote fewer resources to such programs and missions, and ambitious career officials will ignore them. For example, during the 1950s neither the Navy nor the Air Force built air- or sealift capability. The best Army officers, to take another example, seek to avoid advisory assignments in Vietnam, seeking instead to lead troops in combat and to serve on a combat staff.

If pressed by senior officials, bureaucrats will take on new programs or missions if they believe that they can earn support which can be used on more crucial issues and if they are persuaded that the new activities will not divert funds from the essence of the organization. They resist or seek to give up functions which they believe will use up more resources than they bring in or which will require the recruitment of new personnel, with new skills and interests, who may dilute or seek to change the organization's essence. For example, the Army after World War II urged the creation of a separate Air Force in the belief that, if this was not done, flyers would come to dominate the Army. Similarly, the State Department has resisted efforts to assign to it the operational responsibility for aid, propaganda, and intelligence functions.

Organizations seek new functions only if they believe that their failure to get responsibility for them would jeopardize their sole responsibility in critical areas. Thus the Navy and Air Force insist on performing the troop-transport role, and the Air Force rejects Army efforts to perform the close-air-support role. If the Army transported its own troops by sea, they might well build ships which would enable Army troops to come ashore firing—the Marine function. By performing this mission the Navy is able, for example, to insist that the proposed Fast Deployment Logistic (FDL) ships be carefully constructed so that they cannot be used for amphibious operations, an option which in some crises a President might wish to have. The Air Force, to cite another example, fought for the medium-range missile program after it failed to kill that program, because it feared that the Army would use the missiles as a foot-in-the-door on the strategic deterrence mission.

ROLES AND MISSIONS

Few sharp dividing lines exist with regard to the responsibilities for programs and missions of various parts of the U.S. foreign-affairs bureaucracy. Some missions may be performed simultaneously by two organizations. Both the Air Force Minuteman force and the Navy Polaris force contribute to deterrence of a Soviet nuclear attack on the United States. Both the State Department and the Central Intelligence Agency evaluate the likely reaction of foreign governments to particular courses of action.

A program which at one time is shared may later be assigned to a single organization or be phased out. For example, at one time the Air Force and the Army shared responsibility for the development of medium-range missiles (MRBMs); the function was later assigned to the Air Force and still later was eliminated.

Some missions, once the exclusive province of one bureaucratic entity, may at a later date be transferred to another—either an already existing organization or a new organization. For example, intelligence functions once performed by the military and the State Department were transferred to the CIA in 1947.

Organizations are especially sensitive to this issue because of the number of disputes about roles and missions which extend back to the early postwar period, but which continue to be important now in Vietnam. The three classic disputes which divided the services in the 1940s and continue to divide them now are: the struggle between the Navy and Air Force over naval aviation; that between the Army and Air Force over combat support; and that between the Army and Marines over Marine participation in ground combat operations. The Air Force has sought authority for all combat air operations. The Navy fights hard to protect its role in air operations over the sea and has sought parity with the Air Force in tactical and strategic bombing, which it attained in Vietnam. The Army seeks control over close-combat-support air operations. The Army-Marine rivalry involves the Army effort to limit the Marines to amphibious operations and the Marine desire to participate in all ground combat.

Two other disputes have pitted the CIA against older established organizations. The CIA would like to have control over all *covert operations*. The military would also like control of all such missions, or at least those which involve combat operations. The military apparently pointed to the Bay of Pigs fiasco as proof that they and not the CIA should manage combat operations. The CIA and the Air Force have fought from the start over who should control U-2 operations.

The State Department and the CIA have never agreed where the latter's responsibility for "intelligence" *evaluation* ends and the State Department's responsibility for political reporting begins. Nor has there been agreement on the line between the CIA's functions and the military-intelligence functions of the armed services and their responsibility for evaluating Allied and U.S. military forces and operations.

New technology produces other disputes over nuclear weapons and space operations. Sensing that most of the money for aviation would be allocated to nuclear delivery, naval aviators sought to have the Navy share the nuclear-deterrence mission with the Air Force, an effort which led to the once famous but now forgotten "revolt of the admirals." With the development of missiles the Navy gained a role in strategic deterrence, as the Army did for a brief period when it had a medium-range missile under development. In a somewhat similar manner, the Army and Air Force fought for a major role in space, with the Navy showing some interest. After winning, the Air Force saw much of its function transferred to NASA, although it continues to seek a role in space.

Disputes over roles and missions affect the stands taken by organizations and the information they report to senior officials. For example, according to a former Air Force intelligence officer, both the Air Force and Navy exaggerated the effectiveness of their bombing of North Vietnam. Both recognized that the postwar dispute over the Navy's bombing role would be affected by evaluation of their bombing operations in Vietnam. Each, believing (or fearing) that the other service would exaggerate, was forced to emphasize the positive in order to protect its position.[3]

In implementing missions which they know are coveted by another organization, organizations may bend over backward to avoid the charge that they demonstrated by their behavior that the mission should be shifted. Townsend Hoopes, who was then Under Secretary of the Air Force, reports that he saw this proc-

ess at work in the Air Force request for an additional seventeen tactical fighter squadrons as part of a proposed increase in American forces in Vietnam in March 1968 following the Tet offensive:

It was a matter of some delicacy in Army–Air Force relations because it touched the boundary line between the assigned roles and missions of the two Services. If the Air Force did not provide close air support in a ratio satisfactory to the Army, that would strengthen the Army's argument for developing its own means of close support. Already, through the development of helicopter gunships of increasing power, speed, and sophistication, the Army had pressed against that boundary.[4]

In periods of crisis, bureaucrats calculate how alternative policies and patterns of action will affect future definitions of roles and missions. They do not put forward options which might lead to changes in roles and missions to their detriment. They may argue that such options are in fact infeasible. Bureaucrats may also feel obliged to distort information reported to senior officials in order to guard against the danger that it will in the future affect roles and missions. Disputes over roles and missions also affect their policy stands and the way policy decisions are implemented.

Bureaucrats have learned over time that changes in roles and missions frequently occur during crisis situations. Thus an organization concerned about its mission and desiring either to expand it or prevent others from expanding at its cost may be particularly alert to both challenges and opportunities during a crisis. Because this phenomenon is widely understood, organizations cannot trust other organizations not to take advantage of a crisis situation, and thus must be on guard. Frequently, after a crisis, an organization whose functions were expanded during the crisis will try to argue that it has now established a precedent and should continue to perform the new function.

During the Cuban missile crisis, for example, both the CIA and the military were concerned with how intelligence operations during the crisis would affect future definitions of roles and missions. A key episode is described by Graham Allison:

---

[3] Morris J. Blackman, "The Stupidity of Intelligence," in *Inside the System*, ed. Charles Peters (New York: Praeger, 1970).

[4] Townsend Hoopes, *The Limits of Intervention* (New York: David McKay, 1969), pp. 161–62.

The ten-day delay between that decision [to direct a special flight over western Cuba] and the flight is another organizational story. At the October 4 meeting, the Defense Department took the opportunity to raise an issue important to its concerns. Given the increased danger that a U-2 would be downed, it would be better if the pilot were an officer in uniform rather than a CIA agent. Thus the Air Force should assume responsibility for U-2 flights over Cuba. To the contrary, the CIA argued that this was an intelligence operation and thus within the CIA's jurisdiction. Moreover, CIA U-2s had been modified in certain ways which gave them advantages over Air Force U-2s in averting Soviet SAMs. Five days passed while the State Department pressed for less risky alternatives such as drones and the Air Force (in Department of Defense guise) and CIA engaged in territorial disputes. On October 9 a planned flight over San Cristobal was approved by COMOR [the Committee on Overhead Reconnaissance], but, to the CIA's dismay, Air Force pilots rather than CIA agents would take charge of the mission. At this point details become sketchy, but several members of the intelligence community have speculated that an Air Force pilot in an Air Force U-2 attempted a high altitude overflight on October 9 that "flamed out"—that is, lost power, and thus had to descend in order to restart its engine. A second round between Air Force and CIA followed, as a result of which Air Force pilots were trained to fly CIA U-2s. A successful overflight took place on October 14.[5]

BUDGETS

Bureaucrats examine any proposed change in policy or patterns of action for its effect on the budget of their organization. They prefer larger budgets to smaller budgets and support policy changes which they believe will lead to larger budgets.

There is, however, a substantial asymmetry between the Department of Defense and the Department of State in regard to the impact of policy issues on budgetary issues. The State Department budget is relatively small, and very few of the foreign policy matters with which the State Department deals have any direct effect on its budget. For the military services, most policy issues are likely to have important budgetary implications. For example, the question of the United States military forces in Europe does not have any implica-

tions for the State Department budget, while it could have very important consequences for the budget of the United States Army and the Defense Department as a whole.

An organization will be concerned with whether a proposed change in policy which generates a new function will in fact lead to a budgetary increase, or whether the new function may be added to its responsibilities without there being any corresponding increase in its budget. The estimate of whether a new function will lead to an increased budget will depend in part upon the nature of the budget-making process. For example, during the 1950s the budgets for the military services were largely determined by allocating fixed percentages of an over-all budgetary ceiling established by the President. Thus, in general, new responsibilities had to be financed out of existing budgetary levels. By contrast, during the 1960s there was no explicit budgetary ceiling. The budget was determined by the Secretary of Defense on the basis of functional categories and responsibilities. Thus the services believed that new functions tended to mean increased budgets.

The question of whether a new function will lead to new funds and hence should be desired, or to a reallocation of old funds, which perhaps needs to be resisted, will also depend in part on whether the new function is seen as closely related to existing functions or to substantially new ones. For example, the Army was interested in acquiring responsibility for the deployment of MRBMs in the 1950s, in part because this would give the Army a strategic nuclear role. The Army hoped that this would justify its getting an increased share of the over-all defense budget, since the existing allocation was based on the Army having no strategic function. On the other hand, the Air Force recognized that MRBMs would simply be considered another strategic weapon and that it would be forced to finance their development and deployment out of existing budgetary funds. Thus, in terms of its budgetary interests, the Army sought the MRBM role, while the Air Force was reluctant to take it on. (Concern with protecting its "essence," however, meant that, if there was to be an MRBM program, the Air Force was determined to have it.)

Organizations are concerned not only about

5 Graham T. Allison, "Conceptual Models and the Cuban Missile Crisis," p. 287 of this volume.

their absolute share of the budget but also about their relative share of a relevant, larger budget. This proposition applies particularly to each of the military services, although it may also apply to parts of the AID organization. In part, this objective seems to be based simply on the sense of competition between the services. It also apparently derives from the fear that, once established levels change in an adverse direction, they may continue to change, leading to substantial reductions in the activities of a particular service, which could have substantial effects on morale.

This objective frequently leads the services to resist proposals which may lead to increases in their own budget if they fear that it may lead to a less-than-proportionate increase in their budget as compared to other parts of the defense establishment. It also leads the services to prefer the certainty of a particular share of the budget to an unknown situation in which budgets may increase but shares may change. For example, in 1957 the Gaither Committee appointed by President Eisenhower recommended substantial increases in the budgets of all three services, arguing the need for secure second-strike retaliatory forces and for larger limited-war capabilities. However, none of the services supported these proposals, in part because they were uncertain what the implications would be for shares of the budget and thus preferred a known process with a known division of the budget to a new process which, while it might mean increased budgets for all, might involve changes in the shares of the budget.[6]

WHAT EVERY PRESIDENT
SHOULD KNOW

Organizations have interests. Career officials in these organizations believe that protecting these interests is vital to the security of the United States. They therefore take stands on issues which advance these interests and maneuver to protect these interests against other organizations and senior officials, including the President.

This process affects policy decisions and action in a number of ways and limits the power of the President and his senior associates.

[6] Morton H. Halperin, "The Gaither Committee and the Policy Process," World Politics, April 1961.

Every President needs to know how bureaucratic interests interact, in order to be the master, rather than the prisoner, of his organizations, and also in order to mold the rational interests of the bureaucracies into the national interest as he sees it. The beginning of wisdom for any chief executive is to understand that organizational interests and maneuvers affect policy in at least four main areas.

INFORMATION

Organizations focusing on acquiring the information necessary to protect their interests tend to supply to others information designed to protect their organizational interests and to lead senior officials to do what the organizations believe needs to be done. This means that the selection of information is different from what the President would like to have and many think he is getting.

PRESENTATION OF OPTIONS

Organizations construct a menu of options to meet any situation based on their notion of what the essence of their mission is. Options which involve cooperation between organizations and which would require an organization to alter its structure or perform extraneous missions are unlikely to be advanced.

FREEDOM TO CHOOSE OPTIONS

Organizations seek to prevent the President from choosing an option which runs contrary to their interests. They do so by asserting that the option is infeasible or by demanding full freedom for implementation if the option is chosen. They may leak the proposed option to the press or to congressional allies.

IMPLEMENTATION

In implementing presidential decisions, organizations feel free to vary their behavior from that required by a faithful adherence to the letter and spirit of the President's action. When organizational interests conflict with directed behavior, organizations may obey the letter rather than the spirit, they may delay, or they may simply disobey.

In seeking to mitigate the consequences of this behavior, senior officials and the President must begin by accepting the inevitability of organizational interests and maneuvers to support them. Neither appeals to patriotism nor changes in personnel will lead career officials and many of their bosses to lose their belief in the importance of the health of their organization and the need to protect it.

Awareness of organizational interests would lead senior officials to recognize that those with whom they deal see different faces of an issue and, because they have different interests, reach different stands. Abstract national security arguments usually do not change these stands. Being aware of maneuvers in support of organizational interests, senior officials learn to be skeptical of information which tends to support these interests and of analyses of options presented by organizations. They can then look to other sources for options or information. Beyond that, they can seek organizational changes to mitigate the consequences of organizational interests for high-priority objectives, and they can seek to design programs, missions, and policies to reduce their incompatibility with organizational interests.

Organizational changes can involve creating new organizations, altering the internal structure of an existing organization, or changing the rules of the game by which decisions are made. NASA is an instance of the first option, the Green Berets of the second, and the McNamara program-budgeting system of the third.

Such moves are time-consuming and their consequences are frequently difficult to predict.

Designing policies to reduce organizational opposition requires a clear understanding of the relevant interests and an ability to fashion an option which accomplishes its purpose while minimizing organizational costs. For example, proposals to withdraw forces from overseas are likely to meet less opposition if they do not appear to threaten service interests in autonomy (e.g., by delegating to the services the choice of the mix of forces to be withdrawn) or force levels and budgets (e.g., by decoupling force-level and budgetary decisions from force dispositions).

Presidents need vigorous organizations manned by highly motivated officials who believe in what they are doing. Such men cannot be expected to have the same interests as the President, to see the same face of an issue or to take the same stand. These facts limit a President's options and make it impossible for him to do some things he would like to do. If, however, the President and his senior associates are clear about their own priorities, select options with care, and understand that the name of the bureaucratic game is "organizational interests," they can lead, rather than follow, the bureaucracies. They may even be able to put them to constructive use.

ARE BUREAUCRACIES IMPORTANT?
(OR ALLISON WONDERLAND)

STEPHEN D. KRASNER

The author notes the current appeal of Bureaucratic Politics, but he argues that the bureaucratic interpretation is misleading, dangerous, and compelling. It is misleading because it undervalues the power of the President; dangerous because it relieves high officials of responsibility for their actions; and compelling because it gives policymakers an excuse for failure and scholars an opportunity for second-guessing. More important than controlling the bureaucracy, the author maintains, is the imperative for the American society to undertake a reformulation and clarification of its objectives. Krasner is an Assistant Professor in the Department of Government at Harvard University. He is currently working on a study of the political aspects of international trade in raw materials.

Who and what shapes foreign policy? In recent years, analyses have increasingly emphasized not rational calculations of the national interest or the political goals of national leaders but rather bureaucratic procedures and bureaucratic politics. Starting with Richard Neustadt's *Presidential Power*, a judicious study of leadership published in 1960, this approach has come to portray the American President as trapped by a permanent government that is more enemy than ally. Bureaucratic theorists imply that it is exceedingly difficult, if not impossible, for political leaders to control the organizational web which surrounds them. Important decisions result from numerous smaller actions taken at different levels in the bureaucracy by individuals who have partially incompatible national, bureaucratic, political, and personal objectives. They are not necessarily a reflection of the aims and values of high officials.

Presidential Power was well received by John Kennedy, who read it with interest, recommended it to his associates, and commissioned Neustadt to do a private study of the 1962 Skybolt incident. The approach has been developed and used by a number of scholars—Roger Hilsman, Morton Halperin, Arthur Schlesinger, Richard Barnet, and Graham Allison—some of whom held sub-Cabinet positions during the 1960s. It was the subject of a special conference at the RAND Corporation, a main theme of a course at the Woodrow Wilson School at Princeton, and the subject of a faculty seminar at Harvard. It is the intellectual paradigm which guides the new public policy program in the John F. Kennedy School of Government at Harvard. Analyses of bureaucratic politics have been used to explain alliance behavior during the 1956 Suez crisis and the Skybolt incident, Truman's relations with MacArthur, American policy in Vietnam, and now most thoroughly the Cuban missile crisis in Graham Allison's *Essence of Decision: Explaining the Cuban Missile Crisis*, published in 1971. Allison's volume is the elaboration of an earlier and influential article on this subject.[1] With the publication of his book this approach to foreign policy now receives its definitive statement. The bureaucratic interpretation of foreign policy has become the conventional wisdom.

My argument here is that this vision is misleading, dangerous, and compelling: misleading because it obscures the power of the President; dangerous because it undermines the assumptions of democratic politics by relieving

[1] See "Conceptual Models and the Cuban Missile Crisis," pp. 273–300 of this volume.

Reprinted by permission and with minor changes from Foreign Policy, 1972, no. 7, pp. 159–79. Copyright © 1972 by National Affairs, Inc.

high officials of responsibility; and compelling because it offers leaders an excuse for their failures and scholars an opportunity for innumerable reinterpretations and publications.

The contention that the Chief Executive is trammeled by the permanent government has disturbing implications for any effort to impute responsibility to public officials. A democratic political philosophy assumes that responsibility for the acts of governments can be attributed to elected officials. The charges of these men are embodied in legal statutes. The electorate punishes an erring official by rejecting him at the polls. Punishment is senseless unless high officials are responsible for the acts of government. Elections have some impact only if government, that most complex of modern organizations, can be controlled. If the bureaucratic machine escapes manipulation and direction even by the highest officials, then punishment is illogical. Elections are a farce not because the people suffer from false consciousness but because public officials are impotent, enmeshed in a bureaucracy so large that the actions of government are not responsive to their will. What sense is there in voting a man out of office when his successor, regardless of his values, will be trapped in the same web of only incrementally mutable standard operating procedures?

THE RATIONAL ACTOR MODEL

Conventional analyses that focus on the values and objectives of foreign policy, what Allison calls the Rational Actor Model, are perfectly coincident with the ethical assumptions of democratic politics. The state is viewed as a rational, unified actor. The behavior of states is the outcome of a rational decisionmaking process. This process has three steps. The options for a given situation are spelled out. The consequences of each option are projected. A choice is made which maximizes the values held by decisionmakers. The analyst knows what the state did. His objective is to explain why by imputing to decisionmakers a set of values which are maximized by observed behavior. These values are his explanation of foreign policy.

The citizen, like the analyst, attributes error to either inappropriate values or lack of foresight. Ideally the electorate judges the office-holder by governmental performance, which is assumed to reflect the objectives and perspicacity of political leaders. Poor policy is made by leaders who fail to foresee accurately the consequences of their decisions or attempt to maximize values not held by the electorate. Political appeals, couched in terms of aims and values, are an appropriate guide for voters. For both the analyst who adheres to the Rational Actor Model and the citizen who decides elections, values are assumed to be the primary determinant of governmental behavior.

The bureaucratic politics paradigm points to quite different determinants of policy. Political leaders can only with great difficulty overcome the inertia and self-serving interests of the permanent government. What counts is managerial skill. In *Essence of Decision*, Graham Allison maintains that "the central questions of policy analysis are quite different from the kinds of questions analysts have traditionally asked. Indeed, the crucial questions seem to be matters of planning for management." Administrative feasibility, not substance, becomes the central concern.

The paradoxical conclusion—that bureaucratic analysis, with its emphasis on policy guidance, implies political nonresponsibility—has been brought out most clearly by discussions of American policy in Vietnam. Richard Neustadt, on the concluding page of *Alliance Politics*, muses about a conversation he would have had with President Kennedy in the fall of 1963 had tragedy not intervened. "I considered asking whether, in the light of our machine's performance on a British problem, he conceived that it could cope with South Vietnam's. . . . It was a good question, better than I knew. It haunts me still." For adherents of the bureaucratic politics paradigm, Vietnam was a failure of the "machine," a war, in Arthur Schlesinger's words, "which no President . . . desired or intended."[2] The machine dictated a policy which it could not successfully terminate. The machine, not the cold war ideology and hubris of Kennedy and Johnson, determined American behavior in Vietnam. Vietnam could hardly be a tragedy, for tragedies are made by choice and character, not by fate. A knowing electorate would express sympathy,

---

[2] Quoted in Daniel Ellsberg, "The Quagmire Myth and the Stalemate Machine," *Public Policy*, Spring 1971, p. 218.

not levy blame. Machines cannot be held responsible for what they do, nor can the men caught in their workings.

The strength of the bureaucratic web has been attributed to two sources: organizational necessity and bureaucratic interest. The costs of coordination and search procedures are so high that complex organizations *must* settle for satisfactory, rather than optimal, solutions. Bureaucracies have interests defined in terms of budgetary allocation, autonomy, morale, and scope, which they defend in a game of political bargaining and compromise within the executive branch.

The imperatives of organizational behavior limit flexibility. Without a division of labor and the establishment of standard operating procedures, it would be impossible for large organizations to begin to fulfill their statutory objectives—that is, to perform tasks designed to meet societal needs rather than merely to perpetuate the organization. A division of labor among and within organizations reduces the job of each particular division to manageable proportions. Once this division is made, the complexity confronting an organization or one of its parts is further reduced through the establishment of standard operating procedures. To deal with each problem as if it were *sui generis* would be impossible, given limited resources and information-processing capacity, and would make intraorganizational coordination extremely difficult. Bureaucracies are, then, unavoidably rigid; but, without the rigidity imposed by division of labor and standard operating procedures, they could hardly begin to function at all.

However, this rigidity inevitably introduces distortions. All of the options to a given problem will not be presented with equal lucidity and conviction unless by some happenstance the organization has worked out its scenarios for that particular problem in advance. It is more likely that the organization will have addressed itself to something *like* the problem with which it is confronted. It has a set of options for such a hypothetical problem, and these options will be presented to deal with the actual issue at hand. Similarly, organizations cannot execute all policy suggestions with equal facility. The development of new standard operating procedures takes time. The procedures which would most faithfully execute a new policy are not likely to have been worked out. The clash between the rigidity of standard operating procedures which are absolutely necessary to achieve coordination among and within large organizations, and the flexibility needed to spell out the options and their consequences for a new problem and to execute new policies, is inevitable. It cannot be avoided, even with the best intentions of bureaucratic chiefs anxious to execute faithfully the desires of their leaders.

THE COSTS OF COORDINATION

The limitations imposed by the need to simplify and coordinate indicate that the great increase in governmental power accompanying industrialization has not been achieved without some costs in terms of control. Bureaucratic organizations and the material and symbolic resources which they direct have enormously increased the ability of the American President to influence the international environment. He operates, however, within limits set by organizational procedures.

A recognition of the limits imposed by bureaucratic necessities is a useful qualification of the assumption that states always maximize their interest. This does not, however, imply that the analyst should abandon a focus on values or assumptions of rationality. Standard operating procedures are rational, given the costs of search procedures and the need for coordination. The behavior of states is still determined by values, although foreign policy may reflect satisfactory, rather than optimal, outcomes.

An emphasis on the procedural limits of large organizations cannot explain nonincremental change. If governmental policy is an outcome of standard operating procedures, then behavior at time t is only incrementally different from behavior at time $t - 1$. The exceptions to this prediction leap out of events of even the last year—the Nixon visit to China, and the new economic policy. Focusing on the needs dictated by organizational complexity is adequate only during periods when policy is altered very little or not at all. To reduce policymakers to nothing more than the caretakers and minor adjustors of standard operating procedures rings hollow in an era rife with debates and changes of the most fundamental kind in

America's conception of its objectives and capabilities.

Bureaucratic analysts do not, however, place the burden of their argument on standard operating procedures, but on bureaucratic politics. The objectives of officials are dictated by their bureaucratic position. Each bureau has its own interests. The interests which bureaucratic analysts emphasize are not clientalistic ties between governmental departments and societal groups, or special relations with congressional committees. They are, rather, needs dictated by organizational survival and growth—budgetary allocations, internal morale, and autonomy. Conflicting objectives advocated by different bureau chiefs are reconciled by a political process. Policy results from compromises and bargaining. It does not necessarily reflect the values of the President, let alone those of lesser actors.

The clearest expression of the motivational aspects of the bureaucratic politics approach is the by now well-known aphorism—where you stand depends upon where you sit. Decisionmakers, however, often do not stand where they sit. Sometimes they are not sitting anywhere. This is clearly illustrated by the positions taken by members of the ExCom during the Cuban missile crisis, which Allison elucidates at some length. While the military, in Pavlovian fashion, urged the use of arms, the Secretary of Defense took a much more pacific position. The wise old men, such as Acheson, imported for the occasion, had no bureaucratic position to defend. Two of the most important members of the ExCom, Robert Kennedy and Theodore Sorensen, were loyal to the President, not to some bureaucratic barony. Similarly, in discussions of Vietnam in 1966 and 1967, it was the Secretary of Defense who advocated diplomacy and the Secretary of State who defended the prerogatives of the military. During Skybolt, McNamara was attuned to the President's budgetary concerns, not those of the Air Force.

Allison, the most recent expositor of the bureaucratic politics approach, realizes the problems which these facts present. In describing motivation, he backs off from an exclusive focus on bureaucratic position, arguing instead that decisionmakers are motivated by national, organizational, group, and personal interests. While maintaining that the "propensities and priorities that stem from position are sufficient to allow analysts to make reliable predictions about a player's stand" (a proposition violated by his own presentation), he also notes that "these propensities are filtered through the baggage that players bring to positions." For both the missile crisis and Vietnam, it was the "baggage" of culture and values, not bureaucratic position, which determined the aims of high officials.

Bureaucratic analysis is also inadequate in its description of how policy is made. Its axiomatic assumption is that politics is a game in which the preferences of players are given and independent. This is not true. The President chooses most of the important players and sets the rules. He selects the men who head the large bureaucracies. These individuals must share his values. Certainly they identify with his beliefs to a greater extent than would a randomly chosen group of candidates. They also feel some personal fealty to the President who has elevated them from positions of corporate or legal significance to ones of historic significance. While bureau chiefs are undoubtedly torn by conflicting pressures arising either from their need to protect their own bureaucracies or from personal conviction, they must remain the President's men. At some point disagreement results in dismissal. The values which bureau chiefs assign to policy outcomes are not independent. They are related through a perspective shared with the President.

The President also structures the governmental environment in which he acts through his impact on what Allison calls "action channels." These are decisionmaking processes which describe the participation of actors and their influence. The most important "action channel" in the government is the President's ear. The President has a major role in determining who whispers into it. John Kennedy's reliance on his brother, whose bureaucratic position did not afford him any claim to a decisionmaking role in the missile crisis, is merely an extreme example. By allocating tasks, selecting the White House bureaucracy, and demonstrating special affections, the President also influences "action channels" at lower levels of the government.

The President has an important impact on bureaucratic interests. Internal morale is partially determined by presidential behavior. The obscurity in which Secretary of State Rogers languished during the China trip affected both State Department morale and recruitment prospects. Through the budget the President has a direct impact on that most vital of bureaucratic interests. While a bureau may use its societal clients and congressional allies to secure desired allocations, it is surely easier with the President's support than without it. The President can delimit or redefine the scope of an organization's activities by transferring tasks or establishing new agencies. Through public statements he can affect attitudes toward members of a particular bureaucracy and their functions.

THE PRESIDENT AS "KING"

The success a bureau enjoys in furthering its interests depends on its maintaining the support and affection of the President. The implicit assumption of the bureaucratic politics approach that departmental and presidential behavior are independent and comparably important is false. Allison, for instance, vacillates between describing the President as one "chief" among several and as a "king" standing above all other men. He describes in great detail the deliberations of the ExCom, implying that Kennedy's decision was in large part determined by its recommendations, and yet he notes that during the crisis Kennedy vetoed an ExCom decision to bomb a SAM base after an American U-2 was shot down on October 27. In general, bureaucratic analysts ignore the critical effect the President has in choosing his advisers, establishing their access to decision-making, and influencing bureaucratic interests.

All of this is not to deny that bureaucratic interests may sometimes be decisive in the formulation of foreign policy. Some policy options are never presented to the President. Others he deals with only cursorily, not going beyond options presented by the bureaucracy. This will be the case only if presidential interest and attention are absent. The failure of the Chief Executive to specify policy does not mean that the government takes no action. Individual bureaucracies may initiate policies which suit their own needs and objectives. The actions of different organizations may work at cross-purposes. The behavior of the state—that is, of

some of its official organizations—in the international system appears confused or even contradictory. This, however, is a situation which develops not because of the independent power of governmental organizations but because of failures by decisionmakers to assert control.

The ability of bureaucracies to independently establish policies is a function of presidential attention. Presidential attention is a function of presidential values. The Chief Executive involves himself in those areas which he determines to be important. When the President does devote time and attention to an issue, he can compel the bureaucracy to present him with alternatives. He may do this, as Nixon apparently has, by establishing an organization under his Special Assistant for National Security Affairs, whose only bureaucratic interest is maintaining the President's confidence. The President may also rely upon several bureaucracies to secure proposals. The President may even resort to his own knowledge and sense of history to find options which his bureaucracy fails to present. Even when presidential attention is totally absent, bureaus are sensitive to his values. Policies which violate presidential objectives may bring presidential wrath.

While the President is undoubtedly constrained in the implementation of policy by existing bureaucratic procedures, he does have options in this area. As Allison points out, he can choose which agencies will perform what tasks. Programs are fungible and can be broken down into their individual standard operating procedures and recombined. Such exercises take time and effort, but the expenditure of such energies by the President is ultimately a reflection of his own values and not of those of the bureaucracy. Within the structure which he has partially created himself he can, if he chooses, further manipulate both the options presented to him and the organizational tools for implementing them.

Neither organizational necessity, nor bureaucratic interests are the fundamental determinants of policy. The limits imposed by standard operating procedures, as well as the direction of policy, are a function of the values of decisionmakers. The President creates much of the bureaucratic environment which surrounds him through his selection of bureau chiefs, determination of "action channels," and statutory powers.

THE MISSILE CRISIS

Adherents of the bureaucratic politics framework have not relied exclusively on general argument. They have attempted to substantiate their contentions with detailed investigations of particular historical events. The most painstaking is Graham Allison's analysis of the Cuban missile crisis in his *Essence of Decision*. In a superlative heuristic exercise Allison attempts to show that critical facts and relationships are ignored by conventional analysis, which assumes that states are unified, rational actors. Only by examining the missile crisis in terms of organizational necessity, and bureaucratic interests and politics, can the formulation and implementation of policy be understood.

The missile crisis, as Allison notes, is a situation in which conventional analysis would appear most appropriate. The President devoted large amounts of time to policy formulation and implementation. Regular bureaucratic channels were short-circuited by the creation of an Executive Committee which included representatives of the bipartisan foreign policy establishment, bureau chiefs, and the President's special aides. The President dealt with details which would normally be left to bureaucratic subordinates. If, under such circumstances, the President could not effectively control policy formulation and implementation, then the Rational Actor Model would be gravely suspect.

In his analysis of the missile crisis, Allison deals with three issues: the American choice of a blockade, the Soviet decision to place MRBMs and IRBMs in Cuba, and the Soviet decision to withdraw the missiles from Cuba. The American decision is given the most detailed attention. Allison notes three ways in which bureaucratic procedures and interests influenced the formulation of American policy: first, in the elimination of the nonforcible alternatives; second, through the collection of information; third, through the standard operating procedures of the Air Force.

In formulating the U.S. response, the ExCom considered six alternatives. These were: (1) do nothing; (2) diplomatic pressure; (3) a secret approach to Castro; (4) invasion; (5) a surgical air strike; and (6) a naval blockade.

The approach to Castro was abandoned because he did not have direct control of the missiles. An invasion was eliminated as a first step because it would not have been precluded by any of the other options. Bureaucratic factors were not involved.

The two nonmilitary options of doing nothing and lodging diplomatic protests were also abandoned from the outset because the President was not interested in them. In terms of both domestic and international politics this was the most important decision of the crisis. It was a decision which only the President had authority to make. Allison's case rests on proving that this decision was foreordained by bureaucratic roles. He lists several reasons for Kennedy's elimination of the nonforcible alternatives. Failure to act decisively would undermine the confidence of members of his Administration, convince the permanent government that his Administration lacked leadership, hurt the Democrats in the forthcoming election, destroy his reputation among members of Congress, create public distrust, encourage American allies and enemies to question American courage, invite a second Bay of Pigs, and feed his own doubts about himself. Allison quotes a statement by Kennedy that he feared impeachment and concludes that the "nonforcible paths —avoiding military measures, resorting instead to diplomacy—could not have been more irrelevant to *his* problems." Thus Allison argues that Kennedy had no choice.

Bureaucratic analysis, what Allison in his book calls the Governmental Politics Model [and, in his article, the Bureaucratic Politics Model], implies that any man in the same position would have had no choice. The elimination of passivity and diplomacy was ordained by the office and not by the man.

Such a judgment is essential to the Governmental Politics Model, for resorting to the "baggage" of values, culture, and psychology which the President carries with him undermines the explanatory and predictive power of the approach. To adopt, however, the view that the office determined Kennedy's action is both to underrate his power and to relieve him of responsibility. The President defines his own role. A different man could have chosen differently. Kennedy's *Profiles in Courage* had precisely dealt with men who had risked losing their political roles because of their "baggage" of values and culture.

Allison's use of the term "intragovernmental balance of power" to describe John Kennedy's elimination of diplomacy and passivity is mis-leading. The American government is not a balance-of-power system; at the very least it is a loose hierarchical one. Kennedy's judgments of the domestic, international, bureaucratic, and personal ramifications of his choice were determined by *who* he was, as well as by *what* he was. The central mystery of the crisis re-mains why Kennedy chose to risk nuclear war over missile placements which he knew did not dramatically alter the strategic balance. The answer to this puzzle can be found only through an examination of values, the central concern of conventional analysis.

The impact of bureaucratic interests and standard operating procedures is reduced, then, to the choice of the blockade instead of the surgical air strike. Allison places considerable emphasis on intelligence-gathering in the de-termination of this choice. U-2 flights were the most important source of data about Cuba; their information was supplemented by refugee reports, analyses of shipping, and other kinds of intelligence. The timing of the U-2 flights, which Allison argues was determined primarily by bureaucratic struggles, was instrumental in determining Kennedy's decision:

Had a U-2 flown over the western end of Cuba three weeks earlier, it could have discovered the missiles, giving the administration more time to consider alternatives and to act before the danger of operational missiles in Cuba became a major factor in the equation. Had the missiles not been discovered until two weeks later, the blockade would have been irrelevant, since the Soviet missile shipments would have been completed. . . . An ex-planation of the politics of the discovery is conse-quently a considerable piece of the explanation of the U.S. blockade.

The delay, however, from September 15 to October 14, when the missiles were discovered, reflected presidential values more than bureau-cratic politics. The October 14 flight took place ten days after COMOR, the interdepartmental committee which directed the activity of the U-2s, had decided the flights should be made. "This ten-day delay constitutes some form of 'failure,' " Allison contends. It was the result, he argues, of a struggle between the Central Intelligence Agency and the Air Force over who would control the flights. The Air Force maintained that the flights over Cuba were sufficiently dangerous to warrant military su-pervision; the Central Intelligence Agency, anxious to guard its own prerogatives, main-tained that its U-2s were technically superior.

However, the ten-day delay after the deci-sion to make a flight over western Cuba was not entirely attributable to bureaucratic bicker-ing. Allison reports an attempt to make a flight on October 9, which failed because the U-2 flamed out. Further delays resulted from bad weather. Thus the inactivity caused by bureau-cratic in-fighting amounted to only five days (October 4–9) once the general decision to make the flight was taken. The other five days' delay caused by engine failure and the weather must be attributed to some higher source than the machinations of the American bureaucracy.

However, there was also a long period of hesitation before October 4. John McCone, Director of the Central Intelligence Agency, had indicated to the President on August 22 that he thought there was a strong possibility that the Soviets were preparing to put offensive missiles in Cuba. He did not have firm evi-dence, and his contentions were met with skepticism in the administration.

INCREASED RISKS

On September 10, COMOR had decided to restrict further U-2 flights over western Cuba. This decision was based upon factors which closely fit the Rational Actor Model of foreign policy formulation. COMOR decided to halt the flights because the recent installation of SAMs in western Cuba, coupled with the loss of a Nationalist Chinese U-2, increased the probability and costs of a U-2 loss over Cuba. International opinion might force the cancella-tion of the flights altogether. The absence of information from U-2s would be a national, not simply a bureaucratic, cost. The President had been forcefully attacking the critics of his Cuban policy, arguing that patience and re-straint constituted the best course of action. The loss of a U-2 over Cuba would tend to undermine the President's position. Thus, COMOR's decision on September 10 reflected a sensitivity to the needs and policies of the President rather than the parochial concerns of the permanent government.

The decision on October 4 to allow further flights was taken only after consultation with the President. The timing was determined largely by the wishes of the President. His actions were not circumscribed by decisions made at lower levels of the bureaucracy of which he was not aware. The flights were delayed because of conflicting pressures and risks confronting Kennedy. He was forced to weigh the potential benefits of additional knowledge against the possible losses if a U-2 were shot down.

What if the missiles had not been discovered until after October 14? Allison argues that had the missiles been discovered two weeks later the blockade would have been irrelevant since the missile shipments would have been completed. This is true, but only to a limited extent. The blockade was irrelevant even when it was put in place, for there were missiles already on the island. As Allison points out in his Rational Actor cut at explaining the crisis, the blockade was both an act preventing the shipment of additional missiles and a signal of American firmness. The missiles already in Cuba were removed because of what the blockade meant and not because of what it did.

An inescapable dilemma confronted the United States. It could not retaliate until the missiles were on the island. Military threats or action required definitive proof. The United States could justify actions only with photographic evidence. It could take photos only after the missiles were in Cuba. The blockade could be only a demonstration of American firmness. Even if the missiles had not been discovered until they were operational, the United States might still have begun its response with a blockade.

Aside from the timing of the discovery of the missiles, Allison argues that the standard operating procedures of the Air Force affected the decision to blockade rather than to launch a surgical air strike. When the missiles were first discovered, the Air Force had no specific contingency plans for dealing with such a situation. They did, however, have a plan for a large-scale air strike carried out in conjunction with an invasion of Cuba. The plan called for the air bombardment of many targets. This led to some confusion during the first week of the ExCom's considerations because the Air Force was talking in terms of an air strike of some 500 sorties, while there were only some forty known missile sites in Cuba. Before this confu-

sion was clarified, a strong coalition of advisers was backing the blockade.

As a further example of the impact of standard operating procedures, Allison notes that the Air Force had classified the missiles as mobile. Because this classification assumed that the missiles might be moved immediately before an air strike, the commander of the Air Force would not guarantee that a surgical air strike would be completely effective. By the end of the first week of the ExCom's deliberations, when Kennedy made his decision for a blockade, the surgical air strike was presented as a "null option." The examination of the strike was not reopened until the following week, when civilian experts found that the missiles were not in fact mobile.

This incident suggests one caveat to Allison's assertion that the missile crisis is a case which discriminates against bureaucratic analysis. In crises when time is short the President may have to accept bureaucratic options that could be amended under more leisurely conditions.

NOT ANOTHER PEARL HARBOR

The impact of the Air Force's standard operating procedures on Kennedy's decision must, however, remain obscure to some extent. It is not likely that either McNamara, who initially called for a diplomatic response, or Robert Kennedy, who was partially concerned with the ethical implications of a surprise air strike, would have changed their recommendations even if the Air Force had estimated its capacities more optimistically. There were other reasons for choosing the blockade, aside from the apparent infeasibility of the air strike. John Kennedy was not anxious to have the Pearl Harbor analogy applied to the United States. At one of the early meetings of the ExCom, his brother had passed a note saying, "I now know how Tojo felt when he was planning Pearl Harbor." The air strike could still be considered even if the blockade failed. A chief executive anxious to keep his options open would find a blockade a more prudent initial course of action.

Even if the Air Force had stated that a surgical air strike was feasible, this might have been discounted by the President. Kennedy had already experienced unrealistic military estimates. The Bay of Pigs was the most notable example. The United States did not use low-flying photographic reconnaissance until after the President had made his public announcement of the blockade. Prior to the President's speech on October 22, twenty high-altitude U-2 flights were made. After the speech there were eighty-five low-level missions, which indicated that the intelligence community was not entirely confident that U-2 flights alone would reveal all of the missile sites. The Soviets might have been camouflaging some missiles in Cuba. Thus, even if the immobility of the missiles had been correctly estimated, it would have been rash to assume that an air strike would have extirpated all of the missiles. There were several reasons, aside from the Air Force's estimate, for rejecting the surgical strike.

Thus, in terms of policy formulation, it is not clear that the examples offered by Allison concerning the timing of discovery of the missiles and the standard operating procedures of the Air Force had a decisive impact on the choice of a blockade over a surgical air strike. The ultimate decisions did rest with the President. The elimination of the nonforcible options was a reflection of Kennedy's values. An explanation of the Cuban missile crisis which fails to explain policy in terms of the values of the chief decisionmaker must inevitably lose sight of the forest for the trees.

The most chilling passages in *Essence of Decision* are concerned not with the formulation of policy but with its implementation. In carrying out the blockade the limitations on the President's ability to control events become painfully clear. Kennedy did keep extraordinarily close tabs on the workings of the blockade. On direct orders from the President, the first Russian ship to reach the blockade was allowed to pass through without being intercepted. Kennedy felt it would be wise to allow Khrushchev more time. The President overrode the ExCom's decision to fire on a Cuban SAM base after a U-2 was shot down on October 27. A spy ship similar to the Pueblo was patrolling perilously close to Cuba and was ordered to move farther out to sea.

Despite concerted presidential attention, coupled with an awareness of the necessity of watching minute details which would normally be left to lower levels of the bureaucracy, the President still had exceptional difficulty in controlling events. Kennedy personally ordered the Navy to pull in the blockade from 800 miles to 500 miles to give Khrushchev additional time in which to make his decision. Allison suggests that the ships were not drawn in. The Navy, being both anxious to guard its prerogatives and confronted with the difficulty of moving large numbers of ships over millions of square miles of ocean, failed to execute promptly a presidential directive.

There were several random events which might have changed the outcome of the crisis. The Navy used the blockade to test its anti-submarine operations. It was forcing Soviet submarines to surface at a time when the President and his advisers were unaware that contact with Russian ships had been made. A U-2 accidentally strayed over Siberia on October 22. Any one of these events, and perhaps others still unknown, could have triggered escalatory actions by the Russians.

Taken together, they strongly indicate how much caution is necessary when a random event may have costly consequences. A nation, like a drunk staggering on a cliff, should stay far from the edge. The only conclusion which can be drawn from the inability of the Chief Executive to control fully the implementation of a policy in which he was intensely interested and to which he devoted virtually all of his time for an extended period is that the risks were even greater than the President knew. Allison is more convincing on the problems concerned with policy implementation than on questions relating to policy formulation. Neither bureaucratic interests nor organizational procedures explain the positions taken by members of the ExCom, the elimination of passivity and diplomacy, or the choice of a blockade instead of an air strike.

CONCLUSION

A glimpse at almost any one of the major problems confronting American society indicates that a reformulation and clarification of objectives, not better control and direction of the bureaucracy, is critical. Long-accepted conceptions of man and society are being undermined. The environmentalists present a fundamental challenge to the assumption that man can control and stand above nature, an assumption rooted both in the successes of technology and industrialization and in Judeo-Christian assertions of man's exceptionalism. The nation's failure to formulate a consistent crime policy reflects in part an inability to decide whether criminals are freely willing rational men subject to determinations of guilt or innocence or the victims of socioeconomic conditions or psychological circumstances over which they have no control. The economy manages to defy accepted economic precepts by sustaining relatively high inflation and unemployment at the same time. Public officials and economists question the wisdom of economic growth. Conflicts exist over what the objectives of the nation should be and what its capacities are. On a whole range of social issues the society is torn between attributing problems to individual inadequacies and assigning the blame to social injustice.

None of these issues can be decided just by improving managerial techniques. Before the niceties of bureaucratic implementation can be investigated, it is necessary to know what objectives are being sought. Objectives are ultimately a reflection of values, of beliefs concerning what man and society ought to be. The failure of the American government to take decisive action in a number of critical areas reflects not so much the inertia of a large bureaucratic machine as a confusion over values which afflicts the society in general and its leaders in particular. It is, in such circumstances, too comforting to attribute failure to organizational inertia, although nothing could be more convenient for political leaders who, having neither formulated any policy nor advocated bad policies, can blame their failures on the governmental structure. Both psychologically and politically, leaders may find it advantageous to have others think of them as ineffectual rather than as evil. But the facts are otherwise—particularly in foreign policy. There the choices, and the responsibility, rest squarely with the President.

AN INQUIRY INTO THE WORKINGS OF ARMS CONTROL AGREEMENTS

ABRAM CHAYES

Professor Chayes examines the prospects for compliance with arms control agreements that limit strategic weapons and finds them good. Drawing on the developing understanding of bureaucratic politics, he reviews the forces for compliance generated by the negotiation and ratification of a treaty, by the inertia and imperatives of bureaucratic operation under a treaty, and by the contemplated mechanisms for verification and enforcement. The results of this analysis are juxtaposed with those of traditional strategic theory, based on rationalistic assumptions about governmental behavior and decisionmaking, to expose the weaknesses of this approach. He concludes that, under a high-visibility strategic arms limitation agreement between the United States and the Soviet Union, the dominant factors governing compliance and termination will be political rather than strategic or technical. Abram Chayes is a Professor of Law at Harvard University and served as legal adviser to the Department of State from 1961 to 1964.

INTRODUCTION

The literature of arms control is singularly barren on the question of how a treaty or agreement actually affects the behavior of states. The premises of "strategic theory" or "strategic analysis" generally accept as a fundamental postulate "the assumption of rational behavior —not just of intelligent behavior, but of behavior motivated by a conscious calculation of advantages."[1]

A growing body of work by contemporary political scientists, of whom Graham Allison[2] and C. E. Lindblom[3] can be taken as exemplars, explicitly rejects the "assumption of rationality" as the most useful premise for understanding governmental behavior. They stress

[1] Thomas C. Schelling, *The Strategy of Conflict* (1960), p. 4.
[2] Graham T. Allison, "Conceptual Models and the Cuban Missile Crisis," *Essence of Decision: Explaining the Cuban Missile Crisis* (1971). See also pp. 273–300 of this volume.
[3] Charles Lindblom, *The Policy-Making Process* (1968) and *The Intelligence of Democracy* (1965).

instead the perception that a government is a corporate entity, and that policy decisions are the results of continuous interplay among its constituent parts. This article explores the question of compliance with arms control agreements in light of these newer theories and perspectives on state behavior.

It considers, in turn, pressures for compliance generated in the negotiating process, bureaucratic and organizational constraints against breach of a treaty that is in force, and the enforcement mechanism of the treaty itself. These are not analytically separate divisions, and many of the same issues and phenomena recur in each. Rather, they represent different perspectives from which to examine the political and bureaucratic forces that bear on treaty compliance. In this way we hope to gain an appreciation of the process of compliance and enforcement which is richer and more balanced than that provided by the one-dimensional treatments now available.

· · · · · · · · · · ·

NEGOTIATION AND RATIFICATION

Treaties are often analogized to contracts. But, unlike the voluntary exchange of promises between two individuals—itself increasingly misleading as the archetypal contract—the formulation, negotiation, and ratification of a treaty is an elaborate bureaucratic and political affair. In the field of arms control, so intimately connected with national security, the complexity of the process attains the rococo. For proponents of arms limitation, this complexity carries very high costs. It is probably fair to say that the principal reason arms control agreements take so long to negotiate and are not more far-reaching is not so much the difficulty of one side convincing the other as the need for each side to generate a broad base of agreement and acceptance within its own and allied policy-making establishments.

But there is something to be entered on the other side of the ledger. The argument of this section is that this very process of negotiation and ratification tends to generate powerful pressures for compliance, if and when the treaty is adopted. At least three interrelated phenomena contribute to these pressures: (1) by the time the treaty is adopted, a broad consensus within governmental and political circles will be arrayed in support of the decision; (2) meanwhile, principal centers of potential continuing opposition will have been neutralized or assuaged, though often by means of concessions that significantly modify the substance of the policy; and (3) many officials, leaders of the administration or regime and opponents as well, will have been personally and publicly committed to the treaty, creating a kind of political imperative for the success of the policy. After a brief description of the negotiating process as it operates in the United States and the Soviet Union, this section examines these forces in greater detail.

Dramatis Personae

The procedures of the United States government in the arms control field involve all individuals and agencies having security responsibilities.[4] Below the presidency, leading roles are played by the two great cabinet departments, State and Defense. But neither of these is a monolithic entity responding smoothly to unified policy direction from the top.

Within the State Department, the responsibilities and territories of a bewildering array of offices will be engaged: the Bureau of European Affairs, which itself will need to speak with at least two voices, one for the Soviet desk and one reflecting NATO interests; the Bureau of International Organization Affairs, which deals with UN matters; the Office of Politico-Military Affairs, which is responsible for liaison with the Pentagon; the Legal Adviser's Office, which at a minimum deals with the formal aspects of the treaty; the Bureau of Intelligence and Research; the Bureau of Public Affairs, for public statements and information; and possibly even the Policy Planning Council.

These internal entities are by no means united in institutional orientation or headed by men who share a consistent philosophical or policy outlook. Arguments within the department on arms control policies often parallel disputes in the government as a whole, both in range and in intensity.

The Department of Defense has a similar roster of concerned subunits that express a similar diversity of viewpoints: the Office of the Secretary of Defense; the Office of International Security Affairs, which is the Defense Department's Foreign Office and contains a separate section, headed by a Deputy Assistant Secretary, devoted to arms control; the General Counsel's office, if for no other reason than because the State Department's lawyers are in the act; the Defense Intelligence Agency; the Joint Chiefs of Staff, who have, in addition, an independent statutory position as military advisers to the President; and each of the services, with its separate missions and budget.

Apart from the two main departments, a number of other agencies are involved. Any agreement concerning nuclear weapons implicates the Atomic Energy Commission. Since 1961, the semi-autonomous Arms Control and Disarmament Agency, in the State Department but not of it, has had statutory responsibility for preparing and carrying out arms control negotiations. And there is the ubiquitous Central Intelligence Agency.

The luxuriantly variegated output of the

[4] The following account draws on H. Jacobson and E. Stein, *Diplomats, Scientists, and Politicians: The United States and the Nuclear Test Ban Negotiations* (1966), pp. 85–87, supplemented by my own experience from 1961 to 1964 and conversations with others who have been close to the process since then.

agencies needs a certain amount of pruning, which is known as "coordination." Until 1969, the formal repository of this function was the Committee of Principals, made up of the Secretaries of State and Defense, the Director of the CIA, the Chairman of the AEC, the Special Assistants to the President for Science and Technology and for National Security Affairs, the Chairman of the Joint Chiefs of Staff, and the Director of the USIA. Since that time, the function of working out differences among the interested agencies and refining unresolved issues for submission to the President has been performed by the Verification Panel, made up of somewhat lower-ranking officials and chaired by the President's Special Assistant for National Security Affairs. Formal review at the White House level is by the National Security Council.

This complex congeries of organizations, with a bewildering variety of formal and informal relationships, deploys hundreds of people of different roles and ranks in preparing and analyzing positions, formulating issues and arguments, sifting questions for consideration at higher levels, and hammering out the answers, evasions, or compromises by which they are resolved. This process occurs not once at the beginning or end of the negotiations but continuously, although with fluctuations in intensity, throughout their course.

In the United States, Congress is also an essential component. For a formal treaty, the requirement of bringing the Senate along is built into the Constitution.[5] Woodrow Wilson's experience with the League of Nations stands as an unhappy reminder that the process of seeking Senate advice and consent cannot begin after a treaty is signed. Even as to agreements that do not require formal concurrence, the practice of advance consultation is now standard. It is reenforced by alliances, stronger in some cases than others, between particular executive agencies and particular congressmen or committees. In this way, the process extends itself into a larger circle of concerned press and publics. Some of these—for example, defense indus-

tries, on one side, and a loose group of academic scientists, on the other—have personal and official connections within the government that assure a quasi-formal role in the decision process.

A further layer of complexity is added by United States membership in NATO. The mission at Brussels will obviously not have the same point of view as the UN delegation. But, apart from this internal problem, the necessities of alliance politics will require at least consultation with other members on major features of an arms control agreement, and a degree of support or acquiescence from the most important. This entails intra-alliance negotiations, which will trigger a similar round of bureaucratic processing activity in each of the governments involved. These features are familiar —perhaps too familiar—to United States participants in NATO affairs.

For the Soviet Union, we have not nearly so clear a picture of either the organizations or the procedures involved. And we cannot simply extrapolate from familiar models. Fundamental differences from Western policymaking processes are rooted in the authoritarian character of the system. Soviet leaders presumably have no difficulty in securing a compliant legislature. Nor is there the same need to convince broad segments of public opinion, although in recent years scientific and intellectual elites seem increasingly to be able to make themselves felt, particularly on arms control matters. On the other hand, the problem of bureaucratic coordination in the Soviet Union may be complicated by the existence of overlapping hierarchies in party, state, military, and secret police.

Recognizing these pervasive differences, we can still get some sense of a complex bureaucratic and political process of decisionmaking which is not wholly unlike that in the United States.

Final power of decision in the Soviet Union rests in the twenty-one man Politburo of the Communist Party Central Committee, which is supreme in foreign, as in domestic, affairs. Even in periods of one-man dominance, a degree of consensus has been necessary within the Politburo for major decisions. At present the best assessment is that collective leadership is still real, with the Politburo meeting once a week to discuss important matters.

---

[5] See R. Neustadt, *Alliance Politics* (1970), for a study of this consultative process and some of the results of breakdown. In addition to its allies, the United States may consult in advance other nations that have taken a prominent role in disarmament issues, particularly members of the UN Disarmament Committee.

The second most powerful institution in the Communist party hierarchy is the Secretariat of the Central Committee. It is responsible for the daily functioning of the decisionmaking apparatus and plays a key role in framing issues, preparing the agenda, and providing information, analysis, and alternatives to the Politburo. In fact, the membership of the two bodies overlaps substantially. Currently, only twenty-five men occupy the thirty-one Politburo and Secretariat positions.

Almost half of the Politburo members concern themselves with foreign affairs. Three organizations with foreign policy roles are responsible to the Secretariat—the Department of Liaison with Communist and Workers' Parties of Socialist Countries, the International Department, and the Agitprop (Ideological) Department. Organizational charts of these departments, if they were available, would undoubtedly display a complex scheme of supporting offices and staffs upon which the Secretaries and other party leaders rely. Much of Soviet foreign policy decisionmaking is the result of the pulling and hauling among these men and offices.

The personal nature of political involvement in the Soviet Union suggests that some, if not all, of the major Soviet leaders have private staffs. It is known, for instance, that Mr. Brezhnev has a "personal secretariat" headed by a man who has worked for him since 1960. These personal staffs, like their United States counterparts, will inevitably be influential.

Although the party maintains ultimate direction of Soviet international affairs, State organs also play major roles in the discussion and formulation of arms control policy. Of prime importance are the Ministries of Foreign Affairs and Defense. Indeed, the Ministers of these departments probably attend Politburo discussions on disarmament. The supporting staffs in these two ministries are as variegated as their counterparts in the United States.

In the Ministry of Foreign Affairs, the Minister, a First Deputy, seven Deputy Ministers, and a Secretary-General form the upper echelon. Below them, several departments are concerned with arms control: all five European Departments, particularly the First, Second and Third (whose major responsibilities are, respectively, France, Great Britain, and Germany); the Department of the U.S.A.; the Contractual Law Department (the Treaty and Legal Division); and the Department of International Organizations. This last has indirect supervision of the Ministry's Disarmament Section, a small staff with authority to initiate disarmament proposals within the bureaucracy but with apparently little actual power. As late as 1964, the Disarmament Section was not directly responsible to either the head of the Department of International Organizations or the U.S.S.R. Representative to the UN Disarmament Committee, who probably has an office and staff of his own.

Less is known about the organization of the Ministry of Defense. It is likely that the Minister, his two First Deputies, and several Deputy Ministers divide their responsibilities so that several of them head divisions with an interest in questions of disarmament. The Main Operational Directorate and the Military Science Administration (both headed by Deputy Chiefs of Staff) play significant roles in arms control discussions, as does the GRU (Soviet Military Intelligence), which is under the supervision of the Chief Intelligence Directorate. In addition, it has been supposed that the Ministry has a staff organ for direct consideration of disarmament policy.

Although the Minister of Defense has invariably been a uniformed officer, the Soviet armed forces, like the United States military services, have their own representation within the Ministry of Defense—the Chief of the General Staff. His office is undoubtedly involved in arms control decisionmaking, not only because of his strategic responsibility, but because the military maintains a semimonopoly on technological expertise in the weapons field. Each of the five services must have a voice in disarmament debates, particularly the Air Defense Command, which is responsible for the SAMs and the ABM, and the Strategic Rocket Forces, which control strategic offensive missiles.

There has been speculation about the existence of a Supreme Military Council, consisting of Brezhnev, Kosygin, Defense Minister Grechko, the Chief of the General Staff, the Commander of the Warsaw Pact Unified Forces, the head of the Main Political Administration of the Armed Forces, and the Chiefs of the General Staff's Operations and Intelligence Directorates. It is said to be a forum for transmitting the views of the military to the political leadership, as well as a body for the preparation of a statement of military options.

Despite its modest name, the Ministry of Medium Machine Building is responsible for the development and management of the U.S.S.R.'s atomic weapons programs. Its present leader has held his post since 1956, and it is quite likely that he has developed a power base that guarantees him a voice in disarmament matters.

Soviet governmental agencies are supposed to operate on a principle of collegiality, which requires a Minister to appoint a collegium consisting of himself, his highest-ranking subordinates, and, often, persons outside the Ministry. The collegium meets to discuss and coordinate the work and policies of the Ministry, and it may appeal a Minister's decision to the Council of Ministers.

At least three state committees impinge on the disarmament policymaking process. The Committee for State Security (the KGB) has charge of the operations of the secret police. Within that committee, the First Main Administration (the Foreign Directorate) is responsible for the collection of foreign strategic intelligence and the supervision of other Soviet intelligence organizations. It is plausible that the State Committee for Utilization of Atomic Energy, which has a Department of Foreign Relations, has some say on disarmament policy. And it has been reported that a State Committee on Questions of Disarmament exists.

Although they do not carry much political weight, Soviet scholars contribute to the disarmament debates. In 1963, the U.S.S.R. Academy of Sciences established a Commission for Scientific Problems of Disarmament. The Institute of World Economy and International Relations, and the Institutes of Law, History, and Military History also have done relevant research. It is believed that a few leading scientists and scholars are consulted by policymakers on an individual basis.

Even the problems of alliance leadership may no longer burden the United States alone. A number of observers have concluded that, in recent years, "Soviet leaders may be getting a bigger dose of coalition politics than they would like."

Consensus

The mechanics of making an arms control treaty in a modern bureaucratic state insure that the decision to adopt a treaty and to ac-

cept its obligations as legally binding is far from the calculation, will, and act of a single man and brain, or even of a small group. Instead, it tends to represent a widespread consensus among relevant power centers in each government. The more formal, explicit, and public the agreement, the more difficult it is to short-circuit normal bureaucratic channels and the more likely it will be, therefore, that the final decision is the result of a consensus-building process.

.   .   .   .

Such a consensus on both sides is an inevitable product of the successful conclusion of any major arms control agreement. It will give rise to widespread expectation and demand within each government for action in conformity with the treaty.

Concessions

Despite the consensus-building process, foci of opposition may, and probably will, remain. Treaty proponents will seek to minimize or neutralize this opposition. Important elements of the overall decision may reflect this objective and the bargains struck in its pursuit.[6]

Bargaining implies *quid pro quo*. Like the market and the price system, the political process and the voting system are two of the few available devices for comparing a great many incommensurable, and maybe even unknowable, utility and preference functions. The outcome of the policy process, like the outcome of the market process, tends to register—with very large distortions and imperfections, to be sure—not only the comparative rationality of particular positions but the political and even psychological strength of the interests that propound them.

The final United States position on the Partial Test Ban Treaty involved a good deal of this political bargaining, some of the most interesting examples of which do not appear in the treaty text. The terms and conditions upon which the treaty was submitted to the Senate included some recognition for the most important groups that might feel their interests threatened. These included senators and congressmen traditionally associated with a strong military posture, elements in the armed services and the weapons-development laboratories,

[6] See C. Lindblom, *The Policy-Making Process* (1968), p. 95, for a discussion of "bargaining as a fundamental political process."

and supporters and clients of the Plowshare program.

In submitting the treaty to the Senate for advice and consent, President Kennedy said:

Our atomic laboratories will maintain an active development program, including underground testing, and we will be ready to resume testing in the atmosphere if necessary. Continued research on developing the peaceful uses of atomic energy will be possible through underground testing.

Each of these assurances was made more specific in the course of the Senate hearings. The first two—to continue laboratory development and to maintain test readiness—were the subject of explicit undertakings made in form to the Senate leadership but in reality directed to senators known to be considering a vote against the treaty. The third—to continue peaceful-uses research—was reinforced by permitting AEC Chairman Seaborg and other administration witnesses to testify that some Plowshare testing would be possible under the treaty. The final United States decision was thus a decision not for the treaty *simpliciter* but for the treaty plus the undertakings. It was the decision in its totality which was reflected in subsequent United States action. The Soviet underground test program since August 1963 is ground for at least suspicion that similar kinds of assurances may have been made in the Soviet Union.

Were these concessions "necessary" as a practical matter? It is fairly clear that they were not needed to secure a two-thirds majority in the Senate. Their function was a different one: to minimize the possibility that powerful opposition groups, dissociated from the treaty, would be favorably positioned after its adoption to promote and exploit any failures. Some may criticize the effort to "buy off" the opposition with concessions that, to some extent, "undermined" the treaty or the "spirit of the test ban." Yet it can hardly be denied that resistance to the treaty, not only at the time of adoption, but later at the stage of operation, was damped and diverted because significant opposing interests had been partially satisfied.

Again, the point here is not whether the right balance was struck in this case. The proposition is that some such balance is struck in every case. The result is to enhance the prospects for compliance by blunting the pressures that tend in the opposite direction.

COMMITMENT

The negotiating process also influences compliance with a treaty by generating personal and political commitment. For a variety of reasons—personal, bureaucratic, political—individuals both within and without the governmental structure commit themselves to the goal of a treaty. They go out on a limb; they become advocates. Advocacy, in turn, pushes the official "to argue much more confidently than he would if he were a detached judge," and this reinforces his public or official commitment. Bureaucratic and political antennae are very sensitive to moves of the kind from influential and authoritative figures. Thus, commitment and advocacy work to bridge the gap beyond which bargaining will not carry the decision process.

Apart from its contribution to consensus, commitment operates of its own force to provide strong support for compliance after the adoption of a treaty. Within the permanent officialdom, those who actively supported the treaty will have an important stake in the success of the policy. They will become a built-in pressure group, pushing not only for strict compliance with the treaty but for avoidance of actions that would create suspicions or lead to withdrawal or violation on the other side.

More important, the chief political figures will have made public representations and created public expectations about the importance of the treaty. Indeed, there is something of an inherent tendency to exaggerate the significance of the treaty and inflate the expectations to which it gives rise. For all the incantation by both President Kennedy and Premier Khrushchev that the Test Ban Treaty was only "a first step" toward disarmament, it inevitably came to be seen as an event of immense political significance in each country and throughout the world—indeed, one that defined the political, and perhaps the historical, position of both leaders.

Commitment is not only a matter for heads of government. Leaders, big and small, in or out, from conviction or otherwise, will have to decide whether, and how far, to commit—to identify themselves publicly and politically with the treaty.

In the United States many familiar techniques are available for the expression of commitment, whether willing or reluctant: public statements, legislative debates and hearings, votes, the ethos of bipartisan foreign policy. The negotiation of the exact form and content of these commitments is an intricate if minor political art form.

Less can be said about how the Soviet government works in this respect. Certainly the concept of collective leadership is designed to insure that all major power groups are publicly identified with all major decisions. The same result may be achieved by the promulgation and elaboration of a party line through the various organizations and organs that make up Soviet society. In the case of the Test Ban, at least, there was public identification of all the chief members of the leadership group, including the military, with the adoption of the treaty. In the two months following the signing of the treaty, it was applauded by major governmental and party leaders, all of whom stressed the unanimity of approval. Public statements were reprinted in the newspapers, and speeches were made on the floor of both houses of the Supreme Soviet and in their Foreign Relations Commissions. Especially significant in the Soviet Union were the appearances of leaders at public ceremonies connected with the treaty.

Whatever their personal views, leaders who are identified with a treaty will have strong political motives for supporting strict compliance. For their own political careers and the fortunes of their party or faction will to some degree be related to the success of the treaty and the policies underlying it.

The Sum of the Parts

Consensus, concession, and commitment are all interrelated. If the required consensus has been achieved, leaders across the spectrum of parties or factions will have been brought to some degree of public commitment to the treaty. Likewise, the purpose of concessions, like those made to the Test Ban skeptics, is not only to silence opposition. They are meant to induce leaders who might be expected to oppose the treaty to crawl out on the limb of public commitment with the proponents. These forces have operated in every treatymaking exercise of recent years. It is hard to see how a major arms control agreement could be concluded between the United States and the

U.S.S.R. without allowing them full play. The consequence is that both states will embark on the treaty regime with a powerful built-in propensity toward compliance, toward making it work.

If this analysis is sound, it should quiet one of the principal fears that has dominated popular discussion of disarmament: the possibility that a party might enter into a treaty in a preconceived plan to gain advantage by secret noncompliance while the other party, its suspicions lulled, remains subject to treaty constraints. It is simply not possible to carry out a complex and extended bureaucratic and political operation of the kind described above on a foundation of pervasive dissimulation. A faction, more or less powerful, may entertain such a secret plan. Or, as in the United States under the Test Ban Treaty, a group may be charged with maintaining readiness to terminate and with re-evaluating periodically the consistency of the treaty with the national interest. But such plans or evaluations cannot be translated directly into concrete action inconsistent with the treaty. For that, a new round of bureaucratic maneuvering and political bargaining will be necessary to dismantle the old consensus, undo the old commitments, and substitute new ones. In other words, once the treaty is adopted, violation cannot occur as part of a preconceived plan, but only as a result of a new decision, itself the outcome of complicated and wide-ranging governmental interplay.

ORGANIZATIONAL CONSTRAINTS ON BREACH

Parkinsonian Virtues

Max Weber lays it down that one of the defining characteristics of bureaucracy is legalism —administration in accordance with detailed rules having either directly or mediately the force of law. It is not just that individual bureaucrats, like their fellow men, admit the obligation or indulge the habit of obedience to law. Rules are the integument that makes it possible to coordinate the fragmentary tasks and specialized functions of many people in a large organization. Admittedly, some of Weber's successors may stress the operation of rules as communications or as a basis for coordinating expectations rather than as legal or prescriptive norms. And we are learning about informal arrangements within organizations by which the strictures of prescription may be meliorated. But, when all is said and done, popular and scholarly judgments agree: rules and regulations are of the essence of bureaucracy.

When a formal arms control agreement is adopted, it becomes just such a rule for the officials of the affected agencies. It not only creates obligations internationally but acts as an internal directive (with the force of law in the United States) against certain kinds of government action. The very promulgation of a formal prohibitory rule, validated by the political processes of the state, works to unify bureaucratic views, settle old arguments, and foreclose options. "An administrative mechanism," said Henry Kissinger, "has a bias in favor of the *status quo*, however arrived at." Once the treaty goes into effect, all the classical defects of bureaucracy become virtues from the point of view of arms control. Rigidity; absence of imagination, initiative, or creativity; unwillingness to take risks; operation by the book—all are enlisted in aid of compliance with the agreement.

This general effect of the agreement as a rule of law aligning typical bureaucratic behavioral patterns in support of its provisions is reinforced by a number of more specific modifications that the agreement brings about in decisionmaking on military issues.

First, courses of action involving the violation of a significant arms control agreement ordinarily will not be on the menus of strategic options generated by military and technical planners for presentation to their superiors. This inhibition can occur even without a formal agreement. After President Eisenhower proclaimed a moratorium on nuclear testing in 1958, the AEC and Defense Department sharply reduced what had been a routine activity: cranking out test plans and programs. It was no longer very profitable, from an agency viewpoint or in terms of the career line of an official, to sit around thinking up ideas for interesting weapons tests or planning their execution. As a result, when the U.S.S.R. resumed atmospheric testing in September 1961, the United States was not ready to respond in kind. It took six months just to complete the physical preparations. But, even when the logistics were all worked out, no significant

tests and experiments had yet been developed. The tests that were actually carried out were not very productive for purposes of science or weapons technology—they were essentially political.

To make the same point in a contemporary context, under the Test Ban Treaty, it is unlikely that there has ever been a conscious decision by the United States Government on the question whether to conduct full-scale atmospheric tests. With the Treaty in effect, there is simply no occasion for gearing up the elaborate paraphernalia of national security decisionmaking to consider the issue. And, even if some zealous official were to press the point, he would stand little chance of picking up the bureaucratic support necessary even to precipitate a decision at the policy level, let alone to secure ultimate approval of action amounting to treaty violation. Absent serious indications of breach by the treaty partner or some fundamental change in the political setting, and the issue, in all probability, simply will not arise.

Second, although the treaty will be directed at a reasonably well-understood range of undesired conduct, it will tend as well to inhibit activities in a kind of penumbra surrounding that core. A zone of doubtful conduct may arise because the agreement establishes what Professor Roger Fisher calls "a precautionary rule"—that is, "a rule some distance back from the interest we are trying to protect, so that a breach of the rule does not necessarily offend that interest." Or the penumbra may result from the familiar failure to define precisely enough, either from inability or political necessity, the prohibited conduct. For example, how will an agreement prohibiting or limiting ABM deployment affect air defense systems? A new surface-to-air missile system designed to cope with high-flying, high-speed aircraft would undoubtedly have powerful, agile radars and high-performance interceptors. It would be designed to operate automatically, without human intervention. The line between such an air defense system and ABM is very thin. One could expect this particular penumbra to be of intense interest both to officials concerned with maintaining the treaty regime and to those whose main concerns were elsewhere. Similar doubtful areas might arise with respect to replacements and spares under a ceiling on strategic missiles. Examples could be multiplied.

In general, as long as the treaty regime remains viable, there will be some tendency to maintain a distance from the line which demarks the prohibited conduct. An official will have little incentive to stick his neck out by taking responsibility for an action that may become the basis for a charge of treaty violation. Political leaders will be wary of going so close to the line as to risk undermining the adversary's confidence in the treaty relationship or having to accept the onus for breakdown. There may also be a reciprocal reluctance to insist on strict compliance from the other party if the fundamentals of the treaty regime are not threatened.

However, the pressures surrounding the penumbra are not all one way. "The very meaning of a line in the law is that anyone may get as close to the line as he can if he keeps on the right side." In fact, this view finds expression in the Soviet strict constructionist doctrine, which holds that a government is bound only to the extent of its express consent. Also, the combination of a core of clearly prohibited conduct and a more doubtful surrounding penumbra may sometimes provide a tempting setting for feints and probes, and may even accelerate collapse of the treaty regime if it begins to show signs of sagging vitality.

Some of the complexity involved in the interplay of these various conflicting pressures can be seen by comparing the course of underground testing after the adoption of the Test Ban Treaty with that of the Plowshare program. The United States and the U.S.S.R. have each continued to conduct underground weapons tests. Some of these have "vented"—that is, released radioactive debris. Although the treaty prohibits any nuclear explosion causing "radioactive debris to be present outside the territorial limits of the State" conducting it, radioactive matter from some of these tests has been detected outside the boundaries of the testing state. These incidents have been the subject of only rather low-key diplomatic exchanges, largely, it would appear, for the record. Neither side has made them a serious issue, and it seems likely that, absent a comprehensive test ban, similar events will continue to occur.

The Plowshare story was somewhat different. At the time of the ratification of the treaty, the AEC had been planning an extensive series of tests designed to develop nuclear devices for excavation and earth moving. Although the devices were to be exploded well below the surface of the earth, the tests were designed to produce craters. Large quantities of radioactive debris would necessarily be released, and at least some debris would have been dispersed in the atmosphere, possibly to drift beyond the limits of national territory.

As a technical matter, there were ways of construing the treaty to permit these tests to continue. It might have been argued, for example, that "radioactive debris" meant only fallout potentially dangerous to health, and that the Plowshare experiments would involve essentially "clean" devices. And, as we have seen, AEC Chairman Seaborg testified that this aspect of Plowshare would not be completely curtailed by the treaty. In fact, however, the United States government has not taken the same attitude toward international venting from Plowshare tests as from weapons tests. Only a few of the smallest events in the series were authorized. The schedule was stretched out, and the planned test program was never completed.

Third, there will be greater caution both in evaluating and in responding to intelligence reports of military activity on the other side. Interpretations of ambiguous adversary actions relating to the subject matter of the treaty will be more careful and qualified. Absenting an agreement, we saw that there is a strong tendency to resolve these doubts on the most pessimistic basis. The essential premise of worst-case analysis is that nothing is lost by assuming the worst. Indeed, there may be no very sharp incentive to press hard for additional information that would clarify the ambiguity. With a treaty in effect, these presumptions are offset, if not reversed. Intelligence chiefs and their clients will need persuasive evidence before taking responsibility for even an internal charge that the other side has violated the agreement, especially when the top leaders are politically committed to the treaty regime.[7] In effect, the treaty has raised the signal noise threshold. This may cost something in timeli-

[7] See Allison, *op. cit.*, pp. 190–92. He argues that one of the factors in the tepid reaction of the CIA in Washington to their absent Director's suspicions about missiles in Cuba in September 1962 was that "what the President least wanted to hear, the CIA found it difficult to say plainly" (*ibid.*, p. 190).

ness of response, if it turns out on further investigation that the ambiguous activity is really signal. But if, as in the overwhelming majority of cases, it is noise, the agreement will have tempered unduly alarmist interpretations.

The elevation of the signal noise threshold affects not only the interpretation of intelligence about adversary activity but, perhaps more important, the decision whether to respond. In the absence of an agreement, it is relatively easy to move from the premise that the other side is or might be doing something to the conclusion, or at least to the argument, that some sort of response is indicated, usually in kind. It is not so easy to pursue this chain of argumentation if an agreement is in effect. At a minimum, it is much more difficult to act without asking the other side to clarify its conduct. The pressure for consultation would be almost irresistible.[8] The terms of the treaty may contain provisions to this effect. Even without them, as noted above, the United States and the Soviet Union have pursued the course of diplomatic exploration in connection with the venting incidents under the Test Ban Treaty.

Resistance will be particularly acute where the proposed response is itself an action prohibited by the agreement, for that would risk destruction of the treaty regime, which in turn would require a major readjustment of relations with the adversary. Apart from any question of sanctions that might attend such action, the existing state of affairs may be desirable on its own merits. The bureaucratic "bias in favor of the status quo" and leadership commitments will tend to overstate rather than disparage this value. A powerful combination of inertial forces will thus be arrayed against such a step, unless the evidence is pretty clear that the adversary has already taken it, or unless circumstances have changed so drastically as to induce a fundamental reappraisal of the bilateral relationship.

Fourth, each of the factors discussed above

exemplifies a more general point: any actions that raise substantial questions of compliance or treaty interpretation are likely to be referred to higher authority for decision rather than handled as a matter of organizational routine. This alone could be significant in braking what we have called technological drift in systems within the ambit of the treaty.

In general, the higher the level of decision, the wider the consultation within the government. Agencies and officials with a strong stake in treaty compliance are more likely to get an opportunity to rally their forces, to be heard, and to appeal an adverse decision. A decision at the policy level will be taken in a broader perspective, with greater likelihood of attention to political considerations and questions of values, as well as to purely military and technical factors. The chief of government and his principal associates, as we have seen, are likely to have a strong political commitment to the agreement, certainly in the early stages, when precedent and practice are being established. They will thus resist courses of action that may seem to erode or undermine the treaty regime. Decisions at these levels will in any case tend toward caution, because these officials will be more sensitive to the costs of a breakdown of the treaty and the difficulty of controlling events thereafter.[9]

Again, the Plowshare program, post–Test Ban, is illustrative. A high-level committee was organized to consider AEC proposals for Plowshare tests. The Special Assistant to the President for National Security Affairs was Chairman, and the State and Defense Departments, the AEC, the Arms Control and Disarmament Agency, the Office of Science and Technology, and perhaps others were represented. The committee acted on a case-by-case basis, taking into account not only the technical characteristics of the proposed explosion and its significance in the AEC program but a multitude of other considerations, including the prevailing winds, both climatic and political. In the end, as noted above, very few Plowshare tests were conducted.

Fifth, both the United States and the Soviet

---

[8] Even in the Cuban missile crisis, where no breach of a treaty was involved, a considerable body of respectable opinion thought the President should have confronted the Soviets privately with his evidence before taking action. See E. Abel, *The Missile Crisis* (1966), pp. 157–58; and Walter Lippmann, "Blockade Proclaimed," *Washington Post*, October 25, 1962, A25.

[9] See Allison, *op. cit.*, pp. 128–32, 212, on the sensitivity of both President Kennedy and Premier Khrushchev to the possibility of events getting out of hand in the Cuban missile crisis.

Union are operating under severe and probably intensifying budget constraints. An arms control agreement provides an easy way of identifying programs that can be eliminated as candidates for funds, not only at the stage of deployment, but for research and development as well. It is not easy to apportion limited R & D funds to systems whose prospects for deployment, even if the technical problems can be solved, are dim. And it is not easy for scientists and engineers to get overly excited about working on such projects.

Again, the history of the Test Ban Treaty may provide an illustration. It will be recalled that the President personally undertook to maintain readiness to resume atmospheric testing in the event of a Soviet breach or withdrawal. In the first fiscal year after the ratification of the treaty, there was a substantial appropriation to maintain the Pacific test areas and to keep a task force in readiness. These amounts have slowly dwindled. At present there is no substantial United States capability in existence for the resumption of atmospheric or underwater tests.

Maintenance of the weapons laboratories was the subject of an additional presidential assurance. This undertaking has fared rather better than that on testing readiness. The reason is that the underground testing program has provided a practical outlet for the work of the laboratories.

Nothing said here should be taken as a suggestion that arms control agreements can be expected to lead of their own force to substantial cuts in overall military expenditures. The iron law that every organization strives to maintain or increase its budget will continue to operate on the military establishment in both the United States and the U.S.S.R. Forces and systems outside the scope of the agreement will be worked more heavily in order to take up the slack. For example, there has been no difficulty in carrying out the presidential assurance to continue a vigorous program of underground tests. As of 1970, the rate of United States underground testing had mounted from about six per year before the treaty to thirty-three per year. Diversion of significant resources from military ends will, in all likelihood, require separate and explicit political decision.

WHITE-COLLAR CRIME

Thus far we have been considering how the structure and procedures of governmental bureaucracies constrain action in breach of an arms control agreement. These same characteristics will condition the nature and form of a departure from treaty obligations, if that should occur. In general, they tend to minimize the possibility that successful clandestine technological development will culminate in a sudden, unexpected, and quasi-decisive breakthrough.

Bureaucratic behavior is "an enactment of pre-established routines." The hardest thing for a governmental organization to do is something it has never done before. Moreover, before a new weapon can be effectively used for political or military advantage, it must gain the confidence of governmental leaders. Achieving this kind of operational system requires extensive research and development, confidence testing, the establishment of reliable production patterns, training of crews, and the like. All this requires patience, a great deal of room for trial and error, and, above all, time—running on the order of a decade or more for every new post–World War II strategic weapons system.

These requirements vastly increase the difficulty of keeping the weapons program secret, particularly with today's sophisticated surveillance technology. If the development process is foreshortened in the interest of secrecy, on the other hand, there will be heavy costs in the form of decreases in the reliability of the weapon and in the confidence that leaders will place in it.

The kinds of violation that might be within the reach of bureaucratic capacities are less fearsome. If it is hard for governments secretly to mount something really new in the weapons field, it is a good deal easier to resume activities that have been done before and stopped. Old routines and operating procedures can be revived. There may be people around who participated in and remember the earlier programs. Still, under forced draft and without the constraint of concealment, it took the United States six months from a standing start to resume atmospheric testing in 1962 after a moratorium of only four years. It is true that the Soviets were able to conceal their preparations for atmospheric testing in 1961 for what must have been at least a comparable period, but this was mostly before the advent of effective satellite reconnaissance and at a time when the U-2 was blind.

It is easiest of all to replicate existing activities at a higher rate or in a new setting. Thus, it should be possible without great organizational or bureaucratic strain to pierce an agreed ceiling on an existing weapons system. At most, what will be involved is the implementation of existing action patterns in somewhat novel ways to provide camouflage or other deceptive measures during the period in which secrecy is desired.

This reasoning suggests that there is a real difference in reliability between, to take a current instance, a zero ABM treaty and one that imposes a low ceiling of several hundred interceptors, as has apparently been proposed by the United States in the Strategic Arms Limitations Talks. A ceiling of 200–300 ABMs would provide no significant defensive capability. But it would permit either side to develop and test weapons, radars, and computers, to get production lines running and the bugs worked out, to train field crews and develop operational routines, to work on maintenance and reliability problems. Clandestine violation—or, what is a more likely eventuality, rapid expansion upon withdrawal from the treaty—is simply a matter of extrapolating the existing procedures. By contrast, it is almost impossible to conceive of either secret or speedy development of an operational ABM capability from a zero base.

The experience we have, although it is hardly more than analogous and must be treated with great caution, tends to bear out these hypotheses. Professor J. P. Ruina summarizes that experience as follows:

We have been surprised by the continued production and extent of deployment of certain Soviet weapons systems such as the SA-2 and the SS-9 though we knew of the original deployment. We have sometimes been surprised by a quick geographic redeployment of existing weapons systems, as was the case of SA-3 deployment in Egypt, SA-2 and SA-3 deployment in the Suez zone, and the IRBMs in Cuba. But it is very important to note that we have always had ample notice of the deployment of important components in the Soviet arsenal before they developed any meaningful op-

erational capability. For example, Soviet early warning radars and the Moscow ABM were known to the U.S. almost from the day construction of these weapons systems was started, and many years before any operational capability was realized. Full-scale Soviet multiple-warhead tests were observed in the Pacific before any meaningful operational capability existed for the Soviet Union. The U.S. knew of important Soviet aircraft from the time of their early flights.

THE ENFORCEMENT MACHINERY

A third set of factors which induces compliance with arms control agreements derives from the mechanisms by which it is expected that violations will be detected and sanctions applied. Both policy pronouncements and scholarly analysis have focused almost exclusively on this group. Thus, a cardinal point of United States arms control doctrine has been "no disarmament without inspection and control." This theme, first struck in 1945 in the Baruch-Lilienthal plan for international control of atomic energy, was endlessly repeated in the policy statements of the 1950s and 1960s. It has been the one point of convergence between the skeptics, who insist on copper-riveted guarantees of Soviet compliance in any agreement to be signed by the United States, and the idealists, who see the development of international institutions for verification of disarmament agreements as a first step on the road to world government.

There is an immense literature on "verification and enforcement" of arms control agreements. For the most part, it concerns itself with the technical problems of detecting violations; it contains little systematic consideration of how an inspection system, whatever its effectiveness, will work to insure compliance with treaty norms. The premise seems to be that the rational actor will disregard the agreed limitations when and as he can do so with impunity. And he can do so with impunity if he can arrange things so that he will not be found out. The operation of an arms control agreement is seen as a running duel between the "bad man" and the forces of detection, a kind of computerized game of cops and robbers.

This formulation of the verification issue dominated the disarmament and test ban debates of the 1950s and early 1960s. It created a gamesman's paradise. The onus of devising a fool-proof verification system was on the treaty proponents. The opposition's task was only to demonstrate how each proposed control scheme could be spoofed or evaded. If they could show, or even plausibly argue, that some nuclear tests could be performed without being detected by the proposed system, the round was over. The debate ground on in a series of increasingly arcane, quasi-mathematical interchanges—about the detectability of explosions in huge but hypothetical underground caverns, for example, or on the other side of the moon. No doubt all this added to the sum of human knowledge, but the effect was to stack the cards decisively against an agreement.

So obsessive was the concern with verification that basic strategic considerations were disregarded or undervalued. For example, it would seem that a fundamental question for the United States in the late 1950s was whether its lead in weapons technology would be eroded more quickly under a continuation of unrestricted testing or under a treaty banning testing that afforded some possibilities for undetected violation underground. This issue managed to escape public discussion almost entirely. As it turned out, during the five-year period of active negotiations the Soviets made significant relative gains in knowledge about high-yield weapons and weapons effects by conducting atmospheric tests that were readily detectable. If a comprehensive test ban had been in effect during this period, and if the Soviets had contrived to continue underground testing without being discovered, they still could not have made comparable gains. Thus, even on the assumption of Soviet "cheating," the United States would have been better off with a treaty than without it.

As the foregoing example shows, the preoccupation with detection is at odds with the premises of strategic analysis. The rational actor contemplating violation would have to evaluate not one, but three factors. In addition to the possibility of getting caught, he would have to assess the gains to be expected from successful violation and the losses to be expected in case of discovery. It is only by integrating all three factors in a single cost-benefit analysis that the "bad man" would reach his decision. This section first explores some of the implications of this more comprehensive rational calculus, then examines it in the real-life setting of bureaucratic and political interplay that is our principal theme.

CRIME AND PUNISHMENT

Gains

United States practice, if not doctrine, is consistent with the position that need for special verification and enforcement arrangements depends on the magnitude of the gains a violator might expect to achieve. The greater the possible gain, the greater the need for such arrangements. For example, the Non-proliferation Treaty has an elaborate safeguards program, the most highly developed verification system to be established in an arms control agreement since World War II. And properly so. The development of even a small nuclear capability by some presently nonnuclear power would represent a radical change in the local military balance, and might even afford wider opportunities for mischief. Such a capability could be readily achieved by withdrawing small amounts of nuclear material from peaceful installations.

By contrast, the Outer Space Treaty contains no special provisions for inspection and enforcement of the ban on weapons in orbit; and the United States, at least, has, no unilateral capability for reliably detecting individual violations. It is generally agreed, however, that "bombs in orbit" are not very promising from a military viewpoint. Problems of coordinating and synchronizing the attack are much greater for weapons launched from orbit than for those launched from land bases or submarines, which are fully within the physical control of the attacking forces. And there seems to be no compensating advantage. This absence of significant potential gain seems itself to have been regarded as sufficient assurance of compliance.

The relation of special verification requirements to the magnitude of the gains to be anticipated from the treaty has special significance in connection with the proposed freeze on strategic weapons and other measures that have been discussed in the Strategic Arms Limitation Talks. As has already been said, the bilateral strategic situation between the United States and the U.S.S.R. is at present one of very stable balance. Even without a treaty, there seems to be little either side can do to gain significant military advantage over the other. Thus, an agreed freeze on strategic deployments at present levels would be an agreement in which the military gains that could be expected from even large-scale undetected violations would be very small. It would seem to follow that the need for special verification arrangements is minimal and that this issue should not become a problem in the negotiations.

It may be objected that the paucity of prospective gains has not prevented competitive deployments over the past decade. As has been seen above, however, absenting a treaty limitation, normal bureaucratic and organizational forces will press for exploration and development of all possible lines of action, regardless of the immediate military advantages to be expected. The treaty operates to neutralize or reverse these forces.

The Probability of Detection

Traditional rationalistic deterrence theory in the law of crimes or torts treats the possibility of getting caught as affecting primarily the cost side of the would-be law violator's cost-benefit analysis. That is, he will first discount the absolute value of the applicable sanction by the likelihood that he can avoid detection (or at least conviction), and then weigh this result against the gains to be expected from the conduct.

Under an arms control agreement, the benefit side of the equation is affected. Ultimate discovery of violation is virtually certain. Unlike the criminal who may escape with the fruits of his crime, the state cannot avoid disclosure, however successful it may be in concealing its breach. In the end, increases in military power must be translated into political terms if the benefits are to be realized. To do so the violation must be revealed. And, unless what is revealed is an overwhelmingly decisive superiority over the adversary, whatever negative consequences are attendant on violation must ensue, tempered, perhaps, by admiration or fear of the success or daring involved.

The military benefits of violation, on the other hand, are in large part a function of the period for which it can be kept concealed. Given enough time, either party could equalize the force increases or technical advances of the other. The essence of the advantage to be gained by clandestine breach is that it gives the violator a head start. Discovery will reduce the head start. The probability of detection is

therefore a discount factor which reduces the value that can be assigned to expected gains.

If this analysis is correct, it carries an important corollary for the stability of arms control agreements in general. For any given detection system, the probability of discovery increases with the duration of the breach. Thus, the stability of a particular setting depends not only on the magnitude of the advantages to be gained by a change, but on the time needed to accomplish it. The longer it takes to achieve a *fait accompli*, the more the benefits must be discounted, and the less likely it is that the calculation will be positive. Again this view confirms the difference in verification requirements suggested above, as between a SALT-type agreement and the Non-proliferation Treaty. Whatever strategic advantages could be obtained from a massive shift in force levels would come only at the end of a long period of build-up. A small nuclear capability, on the other hand, could be obtained quite rapidly by any moderately advanced nonnuclear power with a good-sized power reactor.

The probability of detection depends not only on the duration of the breach but on the effectiveness of the verification system. As has been noted, this is the issue that has received most of the professional and scholarly attention. For most of the 1950s, it was assumed that an acceptable detection system must include some, and probably extensive, access to, and inspection of, the territory and activity of the parties. Seeing was believing. The on-site inspection issue became a sticking point in the comprehensive test ban negotiations and gave rise to debates about the comparative efficacy of three versus seven on-site inspections and the vulnerability of unmanned seismic detectors which would have delighted the heart of any medieval scholastic. And the issue has risen again to plague the renewed discussion of a comprehensive test ban.

In fact, no agreement actually in force provides for any kind of inspection on the territory of the superpowers. And, whatever the case may have been in the last two decades, the operational significance of on-site inspection will be drastically reduced for the future. The advent of sophisticated high-altitude photography—first from the U-2, and since 1961 by reconnaissance satellite—has added enormously to the volume and reliability of information about opposing deployments and developments which can be obtained by national means. Satellite reconnaissance has been tacitly accepted as a legitimate intelligence activity, at least by the United States and the U.S.S.R. Neither seems to regard it as violating the rights of the observed state in international law.

Details of the operation and performance of reconnaissance systems remain closely held secrets on both sides. But quite a bit can be learned about the state of the art from the open literature and by not very sophisticated deductions from available information. Each year since the late 1960s the Department of Defense has publicly announced an accurate count of each type of fixed, land-based missile actually deployed by the Soviets. We seem also to possess accurate knowledge of the location and dimensions of missile silos under construction. This suggests that satellite cameras may be approaching their physical limit—that is, an ability to distinguish an object on the ground six inches to one foot in diameter with good contrast. In addition, television cameras can now provide real-time visual reconnaissance, although with lesser resolution. Work is now progressing that will permit photography by moonlight, starlight, and laser illumination. Satellites carry an array of sensors in addition to visible light cameras: infrared, gamma ray, X-ray sensors, radar, electronic interceptors, and the like. Moreover, satellite reconnaissance is coordinated with a variety of other earthbound advanced systems. The battery of surveillance techniques is much more difficult to evade than any single system would be.

This greatly increased unilateral intelligence capability represents an ability to monitor performance under an arms control agreement and to detect violations. Greenwood's *Reconnaissance and Surveillance Applications to Arms Control Verification*, a recent study based entirely on the open literature, concludes:

The most important arms control issues of the moment concern the limitation of offensive and defensive strategic weapons systems. Our conclusion on this subject has been that a numerical limitation of ICBMs, IRBMs, SLBMs, submarines themselves or ABMs could be verified by observation satellites with a high degree of confidence. If mobile, land-based ICBMs exist and are to be included in the limit, the confidence of the verification would be

reduced somewhat. In order to discourage the deployment of new systems qualitatively superior to current ones, an overall ceiling could be imposed on missile tests. Such a limitation would be most useful accompanied by a proscription that tests be pre-announced and along a specific flight path. It could be verified with high confidence. A prohibition against new boosters or new re-entry vehicles could also be verified with high confidence, unless the change were so minor as to be unimportant or in the internal guidance systems. Distinguishing between MRVs and MIRVs could be difficult and perhaps not very useful. However, prohibitions against terminal maneuvering and limitations on ballistic coefficient could be verified, although probably with lower confidence than the restrictions previously mentioned.

It is no exaggeration to say that President Eisenhower's call for "open skies" has been more than fully realized.

Is there any need for more than this? As we have said, the main function of verification is to deter clandestine violations of the treaty by creating the likelihood that they will be discovered in time to deny the gains of the head start. But, even without a treaty, national intelligence establishments are charged with getting information about adversary dispositions for essentially similar purposes: to permit a timely and effective response to the other side's actions. Why is additional information thought to be necessary under an arms control regime? The operation of national intelligence is not constrained by the agreement. It may even be that, by defining and focusing what is to be looked for, the treaty will simplify the task.

The argument for more information must start from the proposition that the agreement will inhibit the party's freedom to respond to intelligence results. The very mechanism by which the treaty operates is the suppression of response to ambiguous signals. If self-help is foreclosed, so the argument runs, the party is entitled to reassurance—to clarification of the ambiguity. This must be provided by the verification mechanism of the treaty.

Can such clarification be provided by on-site inspection? What would the inspectors find? What additional information can reasonably be expected from on-site inspection? When United States experts got around to analyzing this problem in the test ban context, they concluded that the odds were very long on the inspectors being able to prove that a clandestine test had actually occurred, given the area to be searched, and reasonable constraints on time and personnel. Or, to take a more obvious example, inspection of a missile may establish that it does not carry a multiple warhead—at that moment. It would give little or no assurance for the future. Very little can be learned from visual inspection about missile accuracy, and still less can be learned about reliability.

But the question of what the inspector would find can be put differently: Would a party ever permit an inspection in circumstances where discovery of a violation was likely? United States planning proceeded on the basis that in such a case the other party would probably refuse to permit the exercise of inspection rights, *and that in itself would be the treaty breach.* In other words, inspection would operate not as an information-getting device but as a trigger mechanism.

This triggering function, however, can be performed equally well by provisions other than on-site inspection. Consider, for example, a treaty requirement that the parties make periodic declarations as to specific aspects of force levels and conditions, or that a party respond with clarifying information to queries from the other side about ambiguities generated by its national intelligence. In these cases, given presently available national surveillance capabilities, it would be hard for a party to falsify with any confidence that its statements would be consistent with all the data available to the other side, the exact contours of which would be unknown to the declarant. As with on-site inspection, a likelier result would be a refusal to honor that obligation—itself a treaty breach. An even simpler verification measure of this kind, although it presents difficult drafting problems, would be to prohibit changes in camouflage or concealment practices that would interfere with satellite observation. Breach of this obligation would call the treaty regime into question.

The position can be carried a step further. There may be little gain from specifying these kinds of requirements in the treaty. Under a withdrawal clause of the type found in the Test Ban Treaty, as we shall see, it seems entirely probable that a party would be justified in treating novel efforts to defeat its satellite observation as a justification for withdrawal. Similarly, as suggested above, ambiguous signals are likely to lead to requests for clarification, even if that procedure is not specified in the treaty. And, again, a plainly unsatisfactory response to a genuine concern could plausibly be cited as grounds for withdrawal.

Sanctions

The reasonable man, if not the rational calculator, might think that the elements already discussed are sufficient to account for the admirable record of compliance by the United States and the U.S.S.R. with extant arms control agreements. In all of them, the prospective gains from violation are small and the chances of detection high.

Yet, despite the record, there has been continuing difficulty in developing the official consensus necessary to adopt new agreements having similar characteristics—as, for example, a comprehensive test ban or limitations on strategic weapons at something like present levels. Nor has strategic analysis been unanimous in concluding that the prospects for compliance in such cases are good. These agreements, like most of those in force affect the status quo only marginally. There is still less readiness to endorse the viability of more drastic departures, where the possible gains from violation may seem proportionally larger.

The arguments in opposition to such agreements—or, as is more common, *dubitante*—continue to address the positive side of the calculation, the gains that might accrue to the violator. True to the rules of worst-case analysis, they stress the possibility, however remote, that clandestine activity could result in a decisive shift in the political or military balance.[10] In strictly rational terms, however, such a possibility could not be regarded as controlling if the likelihood of detection were high *and* the applicable sanctions were effective. Because we know ultimate discovery is not only probable but certain, the opposition's argument is defensible only if the sanctions are regarded as slight, if not negligible. In truth, although

[10] See, e.g., American Security Council, *The Changing Strategic Military Balance*, prepared for the House Committee on Armed Services (1967), pp. 11–15; and W. Kintner, *Peace and the Strategy Conflict* (1967), pp. 240–41. Much of the ABM debate revolved on the contention of the proponents that by a sophisticated combination of new weapons and new strategies the Soviets might be able to overwhelm the United States retaliatory force, or at least some components of it.

there is little careful consideration of the question, that probably represents the general evaluation.

The main sanctions underlying all arms control agreements that have been adopted or even considered by governments since World War II are political in character. They consist essentially of negative responses from the international political environment in which the violator must continue to operate. In the present state of the international system, nobody seriously argues that violation of an arms control agreement should be the occasion for punitive action against the offender, either by other parties to the treaty or by the international community as a whole.

Such attention as is given the problem of sanctions usually focuses on the sanction of political opprobrium—the unfavorable reaction of other states and peoples in the international community to the conduct of the violator. There is a strong tendency to disparage the significance of "world public opinion." Yet, it would be wrong to think that political disapproval consists primarily of newspaper editorials and protest marches somewhere "out there" that can be readily discounted by responsible officials of the acting state. In the foreign country, such expressions are domestic opinion. They must necessarily influence to some extent their government's immediate response and future policies. In a world where, even for a major power, most rational objectives—from security to economic stability to an effective communications system—require the cooperation of other states, it is not possible to disregard the probable reaction of other governments to a major breach of an arms control agreement.

Despite these caveats, one may conclude that the major powers are less sensitive to international disapproval than they were some time ago. On a number of occasions in recent years, both the United States and the Soviet Union have shown themselves willing to accept these consequences. The impact has not been negligible; nevertheless, political memories are short, and the other governments involved, like most governments, have been more pragmatic than their constituencies. On balance, the best that can be said is that international opprobrium by itself is a sanction of dubious efficacy.

Preoccupation with the sanction of international disapproval, however, diverts attention from more meaningful aspects of the sanction system. As between superpowers, the most significant constraints are bilateral. The most important responses to be taken into account are those of the treaty partner. These may conveniently be considered under two heads: (1) release of the other party from its treaty obligations; and (2) responses in areas not governed by the treaty.

Withdrawal. Under the Limited Nuclear Test Ban Treaty, a party may withdraw on three months notice "if it decides that extraordinary events, related to the subject matter of this Treaty, have jeopardized [its] supreme interests." The clause does not require any decision or action by an outside agency. The question whether events are "extraordinary," whether they are "related to the subject matter of this Treaty," and whether they "have jeopardized [its] supreme interests" are all referred exclusively to the unilateral decision of the withdrawing party.

The withdrawal clause was one of the few issues of the negotiations that caused any trouble. In the beginning, the U.S.S.R. took its traditional view that there was no need for any withdrawal provision at all. Sovereign states, it said, have an inherent right to withdraw from a treaty at any time. This version of *rebus sic stantibus* is the ultimate extension of the rigorously consensual Soviet theory of international law. The United States and Britain, on the other hand, started from a rather complicated clause in the draft they put forward in August 1962. There the right of withdrawal depended upon either a breach of the treaty or testing by a nonsignatory that would amount to a breach had it been conducted by a party. In such a case, a party would be entitled to call for a conference of the signatories to consider the evidence and to assess the situation. Regardless of the outcome of the conference, the party could withdraw from the treaty if it deemed that action "necessary for its national security." The compromise embodied in the treaty consisted of the acceptance of a formal provision for withdrawal from the agreement but a considerable expansion of the occasions for withdrawal. The procedure for trying to develop some kind of community judgment on the issues was dropped.

The Test Ban withdrawal clause is embodied

verbatim in the Non-proliferation Treaty with the addition that a party's notice of withdrawal must include "a statement of the extraordinary events it regards as having jeopardized its supereme interests." Thus it is reasonable to assume that the withdrawal formula worked out in Moscow is likely to remain for some time to come a feature of arms control agreements to which the two countries are parties.

As a legal matter, withdrawal, either under special provisions in the treaty or under general principles of international law, is freely available as a sanction against breach. Indeed, the aggrieved party may feel bound to retaliate, even if it sees little prospect of technological or military gain from doing so. The United States resumed testing in response to the Soviet atmospheric test series of September 1961, even though the technical results were relatively uninteresting.

In practice, however, this response may be less than completely effective. In the first place, to the extent that the violator has been successful in achieving a head start, withdrawal by the other party does nothing to offset it. Moreover, the existence of changed circumstances and their importance to the supreme interests of a country are not objective facts capable of authoritative determination. The adequacy of the justification for withdrawal will be largely in the eye of the beholder. A government considering the exercise of its withdrawal right must therefore take into account the probable evaluations of its rationale by other states, and these are likely to be more-or-less rather than either-or. Even in cases of breach by the other party, the evidence is rarely unambiguous, and, when it is, the breach may not be regarded as justifying, *ipso facto*, a reciprocal withdrawal. When the United States did resume atmospheric testing in April 1962, the international outcry was almost as great as that against the U.S.S.R. itself for first breaking the four-year tacit moratorium on tests.

Beyond Reprisal. The would-be violator faces more than simply the withdrawal of the other party and return to the status quo ante, probably a time of relative calm, caution, and reciprocal restraint. If the violative conduct cannot be convincingly related to factors outside the bilateral relationship, such as the need for preparations against a third power, a substantial breach, or even a withdrawal under the terms of the treaty, will in all probability be read as an unfriendly act, signaling a far-reaching shift toward a policy of hostility and confrontation. Indeed, it is likely to precipitate "a flaming crisis." Unless the breach achieves a decisive and immediately apparent military superiority, the prospective violator must anticipate a wide-ranging set of responses, many of which will be likely whether or not the other side decides to exercise its withdrawal right: the resumption of an intense, uncontrolled arms race, a worsened political climate, the strengthening of the opposing alliance.

A generalized hostile response is likely even though it may not be a "rational" counter to the breach. It will come about through shifts in power and influence brought about within the offended government. The hands of treaty opponents, who tend to be the military and hardline elements, will have been strengthened. Officials committed to the treaty, who are often those urging relaxed and accommodating bilateral relations, will have been discredited and may even overreact for political and bureaucratic self-protection.

Whatever the cause, this broad-spectrum response is likely to have a serious impact on the violator. From the Soviet standpoint, the increase in overall United States force levels and the generally hardened attitudes that resulted from the Berlin crisis of 1961 were at least as significant as any response in the immediate Berlin context. The ultimate effect was on Soviet domestic goals, always an object of the politician's tenderest solicitude. The United States actions led to the cancellation of consumer-oriented cuts in the Russian military budget.

In the context of this kind of bilateral response, the reactions of third states take on added significance. It is no longer a question of generalized disapprobation of the violator. What is involved is cooperation or support for a specific course of action being pursued by the offended state. Any response of the United States or the U.S.S.R. would be heavily dependent for its success on the energy and enthusiasm with which allies rallied round. The positive action of states beyond the immediate circle of alliance may also be required. In the Cuban missile crisis, for example, a key element was the denial of landing rights to Soviet aircraft by Senegal and Guinea, neither of which was renowned for its susceptibility to suggestions from Washington.

The Effect of Secrecy. The sanctions will be intensified in the case of clandestine breach. To look again at the Cuban missile crisis, even though no treaty was involved, the speed and secrecy of the Soviet deployment was an important constituent in the alarm of the United States leaders and in their sense of the urgent need for forceful response. It was, as well, a critical factor in mobilizing international support or acquiescence. It is an interesting speculation whether the United States could have forced a withdrawal of the missiles on the same terms if the Soviets had proceeded openly and deliberately over a considerable period, justifying their action publicly and with copious citation of NATO precedents.

Similarly, a big part of the United States chagrin and confusion at the disclosure of the U-2 incident was traceable to the secrecy of the program. The result was not only the abandonment of flights over the U.S.S.R. but the abortion of the summit conference at Paris, a centerpiece of the Eisenhower Administration's foreign policy.

In both the U-2 and Cuban missile cases, political sanctions, intensified by the clandestine character of the offending act, forced the abandonment of major military programs with self-evidently high military significance. The examples also confirm the suggestion that the key sanction is the response of the other superpower and that this may be diffused over the spectrum of bilateral relations rather than limited to the area of the objectionable conduct.

In neither case was there a breach of an agreement between the United States and the U.S.S.R. Indeed, the deployment of Soviet missiles in Cuba was entirely "legal." It could be expected that, in the usual case, the reaction would be even stronger to a deliberate, clandestine violation of an arms control agreement.

THE POLITICS OF ENFORCEMENT

To this point, we have analyzed the enforcement mechanism in fairly conventional terms. Sensitivity to the organizational and political setting has highlighted some points to which generally insufficient attention has been given. But, in the main, we have dealt with the issues of breach, withdrawal, and response as though their resolution were determined by a rational calculus of benefits and burdens. But we know that those decisions will be the products of a complex organizational structure and process in which forces of consensus, commitment, and inertia are at work. The values assigned to the terms in the calculus are not objectively fixed, but vary with the different perspectives, interests, and objectives of the participants in the process. The answers will thus differ also, even though they will be given in the utmost good faith.

Most important, the focus on relations with an external adversary will be diluted by a concern for the responses and moves of colleagues, organizations, and factions within the deciding country. The various calculations of benefit and cost will operate not as the direct determinants of decision but as elements of the internal discourse, as means of changing or rebutting the views of others. This more complex political-organizational analysis has a somewhat different bearing on breach and withdrawal than on response. These will be treated separately.

Withdrawal and Breach

Termination of the treaty relationship will necessarily have domestic political consequences. These may be larger for an outright breach than for withdrawal under the terms of the treaty. But, as suggested above, the justification for withdrawal, except perhaps in response to the adversary's breach, will never be self-validating. And, to the extent that it is not, reactions like those to breach will be generated.

In democratic societies, the opposition will express itself in normal electoral politics. In the Soviet Union, emerging elites in the scientific and intellectual areas, not completely controlled by state or party, seem to have a special influence on arms control issues. This is not to say that public opinion will always favor the treaty. In Germany after World War I, repudiation of the prohibition against rearmament imposed by the victors at Versailles became a political rallying cry. One can imagine a like syndrome emerging out of a period of generally deteriorating relations and mutual recrimination between the chief treaty partners. Often the public will simply be indifferent; and it may even applaud the appearance of energy and action conveyed by a decision to be free of irksome restraints.

Abandoning the treaty will necessarily involve resistance within the government, as well as outside it. As we have seen, the process by which the treaty comes into being insures that there will be individuals, agencies, and factions with power stakes in the agreement. They will have the incentive, and at least some are likely to have the opportunity, to fight to maintain it. Governmental structures tend to insure that repudiating a major arms control agreement cannot be the work of a few men in a few moments. Like the decision to enter the agreement, the decision to leave it must be a process which extends over time, seeking through familiar techniques of bargaining and persuasion to achieve consensus among the officers and offices whose positions and jurisdictions give them a claim to be heard.

The extension of the decisionmaking process in time and space significantly increases the impediments to successful clandestine action already discussed. The bureaucracy is no exception to the rule that the difficulty of keeping a secret grows in geometrical proportion to the number of people who know about it. Efforts are made to offset this phenomenon by limiting the number of people who are in on the decision. And there have been some successes. In general, however, bureaucratic routines for the distribution of documents, the convening of meetings, and the like are resistant to the exclusion of those whose normal bureaucratic business would involve them in the decision.

We should not speak so confidently about the Soviet Union. Governmental control over the press makes it very much easier to avoid public disclosure of secret decisions. It does not necessarily follow that control of information within the relevant bureaucracies is equally effective. Nonetheless, students have noted a high degree of compartmentalization in the Soviet bureaucratic structure, which may make it easier for the right hand to be kept in ignorance of what the left hand is doing.

The political and bureaucratic aspects of decisionmaking also affect the substantive scope of the debate. Termination of the treaty must be made to appear as the solution not only, and perhaps not even primarily, to a military problem but to a political or bureaucratic problem, and better still to a set of them. This in turn works to broaden the range of relevant considerations. It is hard to imagine a decision to terminate, say, the Test Ban Treaty or the Non-proliferation Treaty being taken strictly on the basis of considerations affecting the subject matter of the treaty itself. A decision to end such an agreement very probably would require a far-reaching realignment of the country's foreign-policy stance. This in turn most often comes about not in isolation but as an element of a wholesale policy reorientation. Thus, an attack on the treaty may very well be the cause or symptom of a major power struggle in the affected country.

A democratic system, which finds secrecy in these matters very difficult to maintain, may gain a compensating advantage in that the struggle over this kind of decision can work itself out through normal political processes. In a closed society, however, the decision to abandon a major arms control agreement seems likely to be the occasion or a consequence of a significant power shift, if not at the apex of the leadership group, then in strata immediately below. In addition to personal costs, such a struggle will exact some toll in the functioning of the state.

A political leader in any system will hesitate before assuming the burdens and risks of this kind of a contest. If he does engage, the stakes are high enough to insure that he will not easily prevail.

Response

The response to termination will also be a product of governmental decision processes rather than of rational calculation. We have already suggested that both the need and the intensity of response may be enhanced by political and organizational forces. But governmental processes can also work to inhibit response. Violations of post–World War I treaties for the disarmament of Germany were well known to the British and French cabinets. The failure to enforce the treaty requirements reflected an inability or unwillingness to accept the political responsibility for such action.

In large part as a reaction to this experience, United States policy since World War II has stressed the need for elaborate, formal, and public machinery for arms control verification and enforcement. Objective determination by a neutral entity, operated on an international basis and in a kind of adjudicative mode, has been thought necessary to put pressure on hesitant politicians to take strong counteraction. We saw that in the partial arms control measures adopted or under active discussion, international means of verification and enforcement have been substantially abandoned in favor of national means. Nevertheless, the traditional position remains an element of more general United States arms control doctrine.

There are good grounds for second thoughts about the value of international and automatic verification and response, at least in essentially bilateral strategic arms limitation agreements. On the most pragmatic level, such a requirement enormously complicates the negotiation and adoption of any treaty. It cuts against a fundamental feature of an international system still based in the main on national sovereignty —the deep unwillingness to remit international issues to third-party settlement. And it multiplies the problems of draftsmanship. Since the parties will not be in control of the verification process in operation, the tendency—a perfectly typical lawyer's reaction—is to try to pre-program the process in the agreement. This leads to a degree of detail in language which is more appropriate to a tax treaty than an arms control agreement. And it provides innumerable additional occasions for internal and external dispute.

On the merits, it is by no means clear that an automatic linkage between the verification system and response is desirable. The Test Ban–type withdrawal clause is not keyed to violations of the Treaty, but to the occurrence of extraordinary events jeopardizing the supreme interests of a party. The question of response is open even in the absence of breach; and, conversely, withdrawal is not necessarily indicated when the other party's violation seems clear. The clause makes explicit what is true in any case: the problem of response to adversary activity under an arms control agreement is a political problem which calls for judgment and discretion.

Judgment is required at two levels: (1) What is the suspected party really doing? (2) What, if anything, should be done about it? Very often the first question is not one on which additional empirical data will be particularly helpful. It may come down essentially

to interpreting and analyzing the data so as to predict the adversary's future course of conduct. The problem is classically formulated as that of divining the other party's "intentions." But by this time it should not come as a surprise that such a lapse into anthropomorphism is misleading. Consider a United States weapons program about which almost everything is public—the ABM. The configuration and location of ABM sites; the kinds, performance ratings, and probable numbers of interceptors; the types of radar; the computer requirements—all of these have been the subject of endless public hearings. The reliability of the system and the tactics that might be used against it have been publicly debated. But even an American citizen —even a governmental official—following the question closely could not confidently predict the mission of the weapon or the size of the ultimate deployment. On these questions of role and scale, whose "intentions" are the significant ones? The President's? Those of Congress? Of which congressmen? The Secretary of Defense's? The Joint Chiefs'? The Director of ACDA's? And at what point in time?

To put the question this way is to demonstrate again that the concern is not with governmental "intentions" in a psychological sense at all. The effort is to predict probable future lines of political and military policy. The difficulties of this prediction have been circumvented by resort to gross simplifying assumptions that are often highly ideological in character. In the recent Cold War period, the rubric has been that, since it was impossible to be sure of the other side's intentions, policy decisions should be based on its capabilities. But oversimplification has not always been a monopoly of the warlike. In the interwar period, an equally simplistic rule of attributing benign, or at least satiable, intentions to the adversary had catastrophic results.

Both of these methods of assuming away the problem of careful judgment about the likely course of action on the other side have proven poor guides to policy. In such a judgmental process more information about the nature, personnel, and characteristic modes of operation of the other party's governmental structure may be a great deal more helpful than more information about its weapons systems.

The very existence of the treaty may ease

the problem to some degree. If the agreement is observed, a particular set of real-life phenomena is stabilized and does not enter as a variable into the overall analysis of the other side's positions. Since the Test Ban Treaty, for example, neither United States nor Soviet intelligence has had to worry about the significance to be attributed to the other side's atmospheric, space, or underwater tests. There haven't been any. Conversely, if the Soviet Union should continue to deploy SS-9s in the absence of an agreed ceiling, the inferences to be drawn would continue to be subject to debate and speculation. But, if deployment were to proceed in violation of an express treaty prohibition, the political significance of the action would be quite plain, even though the military consequences might be rather doubtful.

This leads us to the second level of judgmental issues: What is to be done in response to evidence of an adversary's violation? Even when the evidence of violation is conclusive, it is by no means certain what the appropriate action should be. The effect of formal and public verification and enforcement procedures, especially in neutral or international hands, would most likely be to strengthen the forces within the offended government seeking a harsh or drastic reaction. Even if these forces are overcome and the violation is overlooked, the publicity tends to compromise the efficacy of the treaty restriction. In either case third-party control does not enhance the stability of the treaty regime.

The experience with the Test Ban Treaty illustrates the values of a less rigid system. Both the United States and the Soviet Union have conducted tests that vented outside their territorial limits. The language of the treaty prohibits such tests, but the restriction, as we have seen, is a precautionary rule. It is not fundamental to the purposes of the treaty, and its breach does not significantly frustrate the expectations of the parties. With informal verification by national monitoring systems, these venting incidents have received but little public attention. The parties have exchanged diplomatic correspondence to clarify their significance. In the end, both parties have been able to continue their adherence to the treaty apparently without serious internal political resistance and without formal dilution of its norms. Meanwhile the main benefits sought—the suppression of atmospheric, space, and underwater testing—have been preserved.

CONCLUSION

This excursus through the terrain of arms control agreements has consisted chiefly of the elaboration of some rather commonsensical propositions that may seem self-evident to anyone who has spent some time in government. The primitive character of these statements and the supporting documentation is testimony that we are at the very beginning of our understanding of how, when, and why states obey international law in general and comply with arms control agreements in particular. The question is a branch of a broader field of investigation which is equally virgin: how and why do states—and other large corporate aggregates—order their activities in response to law? Much more work needs to be done before we will know how to shape laws to enhance the prospects of compliance by the corporate and organizational entities on which the effectiveness of the law increasingly depends.

But despite these reservations, the analysis of arms control agreements permits us to hazard a number of conclusions that cast serious doubts on the dominant orthodoxies in the field. Recall that our principal attention has been directed at the general area of strategic arms limitation as between the United States and the Soviet Union. The set of possible agreements to which the discussion has been oriented takes some account of the constraints of political reality: it would include agreements for substantial reductions in strategic weapons, by category or overall, and significant quality controls, but nothing approaching strategic disarmament. What does the analysis suggest about this set of agreements?[11]

In the first place, we would conclude that the prospects for compliance are very high—much higher than is implicitly assumed in a public and official debate that makes the decisive issue the possibility of "cheating."

Second, verification and enforcement mechanisms do not provide the only forces operating to insure compliance, or necessarily the most important ones. An agreement that is adopted

[11] In fairness, it should be said that these conclusions are consistent with the views I held before beginning this study.

by a modern bureaucratic government will be backed by a broad official consensus generated by the negotiating process, and will carry personal and political endorsement across the spectrum of bureaucratic and political leadership. These are exceedingly hard to undo or reverse, the more so since, once the treaty goes into effect, they are reinforced by the ponderous inertia of the bureaucracy.

Third, even in the area of verification proper, the special arrangements set up by the agreement are likely to be marginal at best, given the immense capabilities for unilateral surveillance afforded by satellite reconnaissance and associated advanced techniques. The importance of on-site inspection is still more limited, and, for all practical purposes, it should be eliminated as an issue. To the extent that supplementary verification provisions are necessary, they can be "legal," relying on a variety of disclosure and declaration devices, rather than technical-scientific. This is not to say that verification questions do not deserve careful professional attention from analysts, technicians, and lawyers, in government and out. But these are second- and even third-order questions. The risks from failure of the verification mechanism—and in general they are very small—are only one category of risks to be weighed in decisions on arms control agreements. The focus on the issues of verification, detection, and on-site inspection in the debate of the last two decades has condemned arms control to the fate of Xeno's Achilles, who could never overtake the Tortoise, because, by the time he got to where the Tortoise had been, the animal was already farther on his way.

Fourth, a decision to terminate the agreement, if it comes, will be governed principally by political considerations rather than by technical or military ones. And, in fact, it is likely to be, or to accompany, a political decision of major proportions, which will have widespread ramifications in the terminating government. The Dr. Strangelove fantasy—of a superweapon, discovered and deployed in secret, and unveiled to revolutionize the relative military situation—is just that, a fantasy.

Similarly, the timing of the termination and the choice between breach and withdrawal will essentially reflect political urgencies and schedules rather than the effort to make military capital out of the decision. Once it is decided to terminate, it is possible, and perhaps probable, that there will be a period of clandestine or unacknowledged activity inconsistent with the treaty before the termination is made public. This will most likely consist of a hasty effort to resurrect abandoned projects, revive old activities, and expand existing ones. These prospects do not portend significant, much less decisive, military gains in case of breach. The analysis reinforces the healthy, commonsensical instinct that the best way to limit particular weapons systems is to stop them before they get started. Modest or token, as opposed to zero, ceilings greatly simplify the problems of expansion and deployment after breach.

These conclusions do not appear in the reassuring nimbus of quantification. But, if they are anywhere near the mark, they suggest that United States arms control policy, at least in the last decade, guided by the assumptions of strategic analysis, has erred spectacularly on the side of caution. We could have pursued a much more aggressive program, pressing for much more extensive constraints on strategic weapons, without accepting significant risks of violation or of adverse consequences in the event of termination. If we had been successful, the military and civil gains of more extensive disarmament would now be in hand.

CHAPTER 7

The Organization of
Defense Policymaking

EVOLUTION OF THE DEPARTMENT OF DEFENSE

CHARLES J. HITCH

This article traces the steady trend of centralization in organizational structure from World War I to 1961. Included are the major issues at stake in the "unification" debates during World War II and after which led to the National Security Act of 1947, and in 1949 to the creation of a Department of Defense. The Defense Reorganizations of 1953 and 1958 are also summarized. Mr. Hitch has served successively as head of the Economics Division of the RAND Corporation, Assistant Secretary of Defense (Comptroller), 1961–1965, and President of the University of California. He is the author of America's Economic Strength *(1941) and (with Roland N. McKean)* The Economics of Defense in the Nuclear Age *(1959).*

World War I was conducted without any significant instances of friction between the War and Navy Departments. As far as the United States was concerned, that war was principally a land war, and the Navy's role was limited, in the main, to protecting the lines of communication across the sea.

Yet, in the immediate post–World War I period, there was a great deal of interest in, and discussion of, unification of the armed services, a step never seriously considered before the war. There were two main reasons for this new interest: first, the high cost of the war, which called attention to the need for economy and efficiency; and, second, and far more important, the advent of a new technology—heavier-than-air flight. The airplane, by the very nature of the environment in which it operated, upset the traditional line of demarcation between the jurisdictions of the War and Navy Departments—i.e., land and sea. In addition, the early pioneers of military aviation, led by General Billy Mitchell, made a concerted drive for a separate air service.

It was this demand for a "third" service that focused the discussion on unification and made

it an important issue. As Lieutenant Commander (later Admiral) Byrd pointed out to the La Guardia Subcommittee of the House Committee on Military Affairs in the fall of 1919, a third service "may make close cooperation of the fighting branches of the country more difficult, if not impossible, by creating a third co-equal department which must effect far closer cooperation with the other two departments, than these two have ever been able to effect in the past."[1]

A separate air force was violently opposed by the Navy, and almost as violently fought by the nonflying elements of the Army. In spite of numerous congressional committee hearings in the early 1920s on a separate air force and on unification, and in spite of the introduction of at least sixty unification bills in Congress, little happened except that the old Joint Board was reconstituted with a planning staff, and two new joint committees were established—an Aeronautical Board and an Army-Navy Muni-

---

[1] *Hearings on a United Air Service before the Subcommittee of the Committee on Military Affairs, House of Representatives, December 4, 1919,* U.S. Government Printing Office, Washington, D.C., 1919.

Reprinted with minor changes from Decision-Making for Defense *(Berkeley and Los Angeles: University of California Press, 1965), pp. 12–18, by permission of The Regents of the University of California.*

tions Board. In 1926, the Army Air Corps was given a significant degree of autonomy within the War Department.[2] By then everyone was exhausted by the controversy, and further unification legislation was delayed for two decades —until 1947.

It is interesting to note that as late as 1935 the manual on "Joint Action of the Army and the Navy" still called for each service to be organized and equipped so that it could accomplish its peculiar mission independently of the other—e.g., the Army should have its own sea transports and the Navy its own land-based aircraft. And, as late as 1938, the "Joint Action" manual still declared that "operations of Army and Navy forces will normally be coordinated by mutual cooperation," reserving unified command of joint operations for special agreement between the Secretaries of the Departments or when ordered by the President.[3] Indeed, the doctrine of "mutual cooperation" survived until December 1941, when it was buried in the wreckage of Pearl Harbor.

It was the Second World War, in which combined land, sea, and air operations played such a vital role, that finally cracked the opposition to unification, at least with respect to planning and operations. The Joint Chiefs of Staff (JCS) organization was born during that war, with broader purposes than the old Joint Board, and unified commands were established, although full legislative sanction for these changes had to await the National Security Act of 1947. (A unified command has a continuing mission, a single commander and consists of elements of two or more services— e.g., the European Command, the North American Air Defense Command, etc.) The Army Air Corps was represented on the Joint Chiefs of Staff and joined with Army and Navy as a virtual equal in the formulation of joint plans. But the JCS could act only by unanimous consent, a procedure which often leads to compromises that are decidedly inferior to the views of any member. By 1943 the Army, led by General Marshall, had accepted the principle of a unified Defense establishment—although the Navy definitely had not. After much study and discussion within the

executive branch, President Truman, in December 1945, proposed to the Congress a single Department of National Defense, headed by a Secretary of Cabinet rank and supported by an Under Secretary and several Assistant Secretaries. The Department was to comprise three coordinate branches—land forces, naval forces, and air forces—each under an Assistant Secretary. Each branch was to have a military commander, and these three military commanders, together with the Chief of Staff of the Department of National Defense, were to constitute an advisory body to the Secretary of National Defense and to the President. President Truman's plan also provided for unified, centralized, common-service organizations under either civilian or military leadership in order to "ensure that real unification is ultimately obtained."

The central purpose of President Truman's proposal was to provide for "unified direction of the land, sea, and air forces at home as well as in all other parts of the world where our armed forces are serving." In order to achieve this purpose, he felt that "we should have integrated strategic plans and a unified military program and budget." In this connection he stressed a principle which I believe is only now being generally accepted in the Defense Department—namely, and I use his words, that "strategy, program, and budget are all aspects of the same basic decisions." His plan also stressed the economies that could be achieved through the unification of supply and service functions, the need for strong civilian control, and the requirement for unity of command in outlying bases.[4]

The President's plan was generally favored by the Army but was opposed by the Navy.[5] The law which finally evolved after another year and a half of discussion was very different from the one President Truman had proposed. It provided for the creation of a National Military Establishment headed by a Secretary of Defense and comprised of three separately or-

---

[2] Air Corps Act of 1926, P.L. 446, 79th Congress (44 Stat. 780).

[3] The Joint Board, *Joint Action of the Army and the Navy*, U.S. Government Printing Office, Washington, D.C., 1935, Change 2, 1938, p. 5.

[4] "Special Message to the Congress Recommending the Establishment of a Department of National Defense, December 19, 1945," *Public Papers of the Presidents, Harry S. Truman, 1945* (Washington, D.C.: Government Printing Office, 1961), p. 546.

[5] For the reaction of official Army and Navy witnesses to various unification proposals, see U.S. Senate, *Hearings before the Committee on Military Affairs on S. 84*, 79th Cong., 1st sess., 1945, and *Hearings before the Committee on Naval Affairs on S. 2044*, 79th Cong., 2nd sess., 1946.

ganized and administered executive departments—Army, Navy, and Air Force—and vested in these departments "all powers and duties relating to such Departments not specifically conferred upon the Secretary of Defense." The law also provided for the establishment of the Joint Chiefs of Staff, supported by a Joint Staff, and for various boards and committees. In effect, the National Security Act of 1947 established not a unified department, or even a federation, but a confederation of three military departments presided over by a Secretary of Defense with carefully enumerated powers.[6]

It is an irony of history that one of the men who most vehemently and effectively opposed President Truman's proposals for a truly unified Department of Defense was destined to be the first to head the new National Military Establishment. Mr. Forrestal, an extremely able and experienced public servant, destroyed his health while trying to make this loose confederation of three military departments work. Within little more than a year, Secretary Forrestal (in his first annual report) was recommending that "the statutory authority of the Secretary of Defense should be materially strengthened . . . by making it clear that the Secretary of Defense has the responsibility for exercising 'direction, authority, and control' over the departments and agencies of the National Military Establishment."[7] The 1947 act had authorized the Secretary to establish only "general" policies and programs and to exercise "general" direction, authority, and control. Secretary Forrestal also recommended that the Secretary of Defense be the only representative of the National Military Establishment to sit on the National Security Council. Under the 1947 act, the service secretaries were not only members of the National Security Council but were heads of executive departments as well.

These and other recommendations from Secretary Forrestal, the Hoover Commission, and others were incorporated into the 1949 Amendments to the National Security Act. The primacy of the Secretary of Defense as the principal assistant to the President on defense matters was stressed. The Army, the Navy, and the Air Force lost their status as executive departments and all that went with it. The Secretary of Defense was given a Deputy and three Assistant Secretaries, a Chairman was provided for the JCS, and the Joint Staff was increased from 100 to 210 officers. And, finally, Title IV was added to the act, thereby creating the Office of the Assistant Secretary of Defense, Comptroller, and providing for uniform budgetary and fiscal procedures throughout the department.[8]

On June 30, 1953, the Defense Department's top management was again reorganized. The old statutory agencies, the Munitions Board and the Research and Development Board, were abolished, and their functions were transferred to the Secretary of Defense, whose own office was expanded from three Assistant Secretaries to nine.[9] In transmitting this reorganization plan to Congress, the President made it clear that *no* function was to be carried out independently of the Secretary of Defense and that the Secretaries of the military departments were to be his "operating managers" in addition to being heads of their own respective departments.[10]

The latest chapter in the history of Defense unification legislation was written after Sputnik, in 1958, when the National Security Act was again amended to increase further the responsibilities and authority of the Secretary of Defense, especially with regard to the operational direction of the armed forces and in the research and development area.[11] The three military departments were no longer to be "separately administered" and instead were only to be "separately organized." A new post, Director of Defense Research and Engineering, was created, not only to "supervise" research and development activities, but to "direct and control" those activities needing centralized management. Also in the 1958 reorganization, the military departments which had been acting as executive agents in the operational con-

[6] National Security Act of 1947, P.L. 253, 80th Cong., July 26, 1947 (61 Stat. 495).

[7] *First Report of the Secretary of Defense, 1948* (Washington, D.C.: Government Printing Office, 1948), p. 3.

[8] National Security Act Amendments of 1949, P.L. 216, 81st Cong., August 10, 1949 (63 Stat. 578).

[9] Reorganization Plan No. 6 of 1953 (67 Stat. 638).

[10] "Special Message to the Congress Transmitting Reorganization Plan 6 of 1953 concerning the Department of Defense, April 30, 1953," *Public Papers of the Presidents, Dwight D. Eisenhower, 1958* (Washington, D.C.: Government Printing Office, 1959), pp. 225–38.

[11] Department of Defense Reorganization Act of 1958, P.L. 85-599, 85th Cong., August 6, 1958 (72 Stat. 514).

trol of the unified and specified commands were taken out of the command chain so that the line of command would run from the President to the Secretary of Defense through the Joint Chiefs of Staff to the unified commands. And, finally, to enable it to carry out its enlarged functions, the Joint Staff was further strengthened by an increase from 210 to 400 officers.

As President Eisenhower pointed out at the time:

complete unity in our strategic planning and basic operational direction [is a vital necessity]. It is therefore mandatory that the initiative for this planning and direction rest not with the separate services but directly with the Secretary of Defense and his operational advisers, the Joint Chiefs of Staff, assisted by such staff organization as they deem necessary.

No military task is of greater importance than the development of strategic plans which relate our revolutionary new weapons and force deployments to national security objectives. Genuine unity is indispensable at this starting point. No amount of subsequent coordination can eliminate duplication or doctrinal conflicts which are intruded into the first shaping of military programs.[12]

These changes greatly enhanced the authority of the Secretary of Defense as the true operating head of the Defense Department. But it was not until 1961 that the full powers of the Secretary of Defense to run the department on a unified basis were actually used.

I imply no disrespect to the predecessors of Secretary of Defense McNamara when I say that, although we have now had unification "in name" for almost eighteen years, there was little unification "in fact" until 1961, except in three areas:

1. Unified commands had been created in all overseas theaters and for continental air defense—for the first time in history, unified before the beginning of hostilities. But we still do not have a unified command for our strategic retaliatory forces.

2. Joint contingency plans for the use of existing forces had been prepared by the Joint Chiefs of Staff for many contingencies. This had been a strictly military function, with lit-

tle participation by the civilian Secretaries, but the planning was joint. However, again, there was no joint plan for the targeting of our strategic retaliatory forces until Secretary Gates in 1959–1960 established the mechanism for achieving one. And the plan that was achieved, although joint, was originally a single plan which had little in the way of options.

3. Finally, the civilian Secretaries had taken control of the over-all level of the defense budget and had brought it into line with the fiscal policy of the administration. The primary method of so bringing the defense budget into line, used by all Secretaries before the present one, was to divide a total defense budgetary ceiling among the three military departments, leaving to each department, by and large, the allocation of its ceiling among its own functions, units, and activities. The Defense Secretaries used this method because they lacked the management techniques needed to do it any other way.

In view of these shortcomings, President Kennedy before he took office was inclined to believe that some further changes in the organization of the Defense Department would be required to improve its effectiveness and make it more responsive to national security objectives and changes in technology. And his Committee on the Defense Establishment, chaired by Senator Symington and including such old defense hands as Thomas Finletter, Roswell Gilpatric, and Marx Leva, did indeed propose such changes. The committee's proposals, aimed at achieving unification in fact as well as in form, would have replaced the Secretaries of the three services with three Under Secretaries of Defense, vesting directly in the Secretary of Defense the administration of the services. The Chairman of the Joint Chiefs of Staff would have replaced the Joint Chiefs in the chain of command, and the Chiefs would have remained solely as heads of their respective services, their advisory job being assumed by a Military Advisory Council under the Chairman of the Joint Chiefs of Staff.[13] But the management innovations introduced in the Department of Defense during 1961–1962 made unnecessary so drastic an overhaul of the existing organizational structure.

---

[12] "Special Message to the Congress in Reorganization of the Defense Establishment, April 3, 1958," *Public Papers of the Presidents, Dwight D. Eisenhower, 1958*, pp. 278–79.

[13] "Report to Senator Kennedy from the Committee on the Defense Establishment," *New York Times*, December 6, 1960, p. 30.

NEW CONCEPTS AND NEW TOOLS
TO SHAPE THE DEFENSE PROGRAM

ALAIN C. ENTHOVEN AND K. WAYNE SMITH

There were several major criticisms of Defense policymaking when McNamara came to the Pentagon in 1961: (1) inadequate means for central leadership; (2) defense budgeting did not relate resources to missions and neglected multiyear planning; (3) duplication in research and development; and (4) lack of OSD staff assistance in requirements planning. McNamara, Hitch, and Enthoven attacked these areas with six major changes: (1) centralized decisionmaking under the Secretary of Defense; (2) cost-effectiveness studies; (3) explicit consideration of alternatives; (4) active use of analytical staff; (5) a multiyear force and financial plan; and (6) open and explicit analysis. Enthoven holds a doctorate in economics from M.I.T., worked with Hitch at RAND, and served from 1961 to 1965 as Deputy Comptroller and Deputy Assistant Secretary of Defense; in 1965 he became Assistant Secretary of Defense for Systems Analysis, and is currently Vice President of Litton Corporation. Smith earned a doctorate at Princeton, taught at West Point from 1963 to 1966, and then joined the Systems Analysis office as the Assistant for Draft Presidential Memorandums and as Enthoven's Special Assistant. In the Nixon Administration he has been in charge of Program Analysis in the National Security Council.

By January 1961, there was widespread recognition of the need for improvement in defense management. Through studies done at The RAND Corporation, the Harvard Business School, and elsewhere, many of the weaknesses in the current approach to defense management had been identified. Congressional leaders had expressed a desire for reforms. The 1958 act had provided the Secretary of Defense with the legal authority he needed if he was to play an active part in shaping the defense program, but it had not yet been fully used. Because of the enormous size and complexity of the defense program and the strong commitments of many to things as they were, the necessary reforms could not be made without strong leadership from the Secretary of Defense.

Secretary McNamara brought not only extraordinary managerial ability and drive but also a new concept of management to the Department of Defense. He made it clear at the

outset that he intended to exercise fully his statutory authority, that he wanted all defense problems approached in a rational and analytical way, and that he wanted them resolved on the basis of the national interest. He insisted on integrating and balancing the nation's foreign policy, military strategy, force requirements, and defense budget. In March 1961, he shocked the Department by assigning ninety-six separate projects (complete with specific questions and deadlines) to its various components for analysis and review. Many of the projects concerned items that had long been considered sacrosanct. He made clear his belief in active management from the top. As he described it:

In many aspects the role of a public manager is similar to that of a private manager. In each case he may follow one of two alternative courses. He can act rather as a judge or as a leader. As the former he waits until subordinates bring him prob-

Reprinted with minor changes from How Much Is Enough? Shaping the Defense Program, 1961–1969 *(New York: Harper & Row, 1971), pp. 31–47, by permission of Harper & Row, Publishers, Inc. Copyright © 1971 by Alain C. Enthoven and K. Wayne Smith. Footnotes have been omitted.*

lems for solution, or alternatives for choice. In the latter case, he immerses himself in his operation, leads and stimulates an examination of the objectives, the problems and the alternatives. In my own case, and specifically with regard to the Department of Defense, the responsible choice seemed clear.

The role that McNamara chose was not an inevitable one. As noted previously, the accepted role of the Secretary of Defense before 1961 was that of a referee. And there were compelling reasons for McNamara to have accepted that role: refereeing the services' struggles over limited funds is less demanding personally and less risky politically. It is also less threatening to vested service interests and more satisfactory to some members of Congress. It takes courage for the Secretary of Defense to be a leader, to become personally involved in shaping strategy and forces.

THE PLANNING-PROGRAMMING-BUDGETING SYSTEM: THE FUNDAMENTAL IDEAS

While McNamara was determined to lead, the available management information and control systems for him to do so were inadequate. He found that the Secretary of Defense had the legal authority and responsibility for defense decisions, but lacked adequate ways to exercise his authority and meet his responsibility. As McNamara described the situation:

From the beginning in January 1961, it seemed to me that the principal problem in efficient management of the Department's resources was not the lack of management authority. The problem was rather the absence of the essential management tools needed to make sound decisions on the really crucial issues of national security.

To obtain the needed information and control systems, McNamara turned to his Comptroller, Charles J. Hitch. Hitch, formerly Head of the Economics Division at RAND, was one of the nation's leading authorities on program budgeting and the application of economic analysis to defense problems. McNamara charged him with the responsibility for making a systematic analysis of all requirements and incorporating these into a five-year, program-oriented defense budget, the first of which was to be completed in nine months. Hitch met his goal. He led the establishment in DOD of

what, years later, came to be known as the Planning-Programming-Budgeting System, or simply "PPBS." In recent years, PPBS has been discussed at great length. It is not our purpose here to repeat all the arguments for and against it. It is our purpose, however, to identify the basic ideas that served as the intellectual foundation for PPBS as it operated in DOD until January 1969.

DECISIONMAKING ON THE BASIS OF THE NATIONAL INTEREST

The fundamental idea behind PPBS was decisionmaking based on explicit criteria of the national interest in defense programs, as opposed to decisionmaking by compromise among various institutional, parochial, or other vested interests in the Defense Department. The main purpose of PPBS was to develop explicit criteria, openly and thoroughly debated by all interested parties, that could be used by the Secretary of Defense, the President, and Congress as measures of the need for, and adequacy of, defense programs. In developing the defense program, it is the Secretary of Defense who is charged with ensuring that the interests of the nation take precedence over the special institutional interests of the military departments, the defense contractors, the scientists, the localities, and other groups that make up, or depend on, the Defense Department. To do so, he must examine proposals from a broader perspective than that of the organization proposing them, choose among real alternatives, and ascertain at what point further spending on a given military program results in incremental gains so small that it is no longer justified. Thus, PPBS starts with a search for plain statements of the openly defensible national purposes that each program is meant to serve, for alternative ways of achieving these purposes, and for criteria by which to judge competing alternatives. This idea provides both the goal and the rationale for PPBS.

The implementation of this idea led to a greater centralization of major-program decisionmaking in the Office of the Secretary of Defense (OSD). This led in turn to charges of overcentralization. But we are convinced that there is no viable alternative to centralization of major policy decisions regarding strategy, force, and financial planning. (This is not true of all policy decisions or execution, however.)

The revolution in military technology alone makes this almost imperative. The great technical complexity of modern weapons, their enormous cost, and their lengthy period of development place an extraordinary premium on sound choices for major weapons systems. For the top management of DOD, these choices have become the key decisions on which much of the defense program revolves. They cannot be made piecemeal by several separate and perhaps competing subordinate echelons. They must be directly related to national security objectives rather than to the tasks of any one of the services. A centralized decisionmaking authority is needed at the top to attain and exercise the over-all perspective necessary to integrate the contributing parts into a coherent whole. Finally, decentralized decisionmaking in strategy- and force-planning simply has not worked.

The success of the effort to develop criteria of the national interest in defense programs has varied widely. In some areas, good measures were developed. For example, study and reflection over the years made it clear that the overriding national interest in strategic retaliatory forces was to provide "assured destruction"—the unmistakable ability to strike back after an attack on the United States and destroy the society of the aggressor. Hopefully, if we have that power, no aggressor will choose to attack us. But that criterion was not without its controversial implications. It demanded, for example, that U.S. strategic retaliatory forces be able to survive even a surprise enemy missile attack and then retaliate by penetrating the enemy's defenses. As discussed later, the B-70 bomber and the Skybolt missile failed to meet those tests; and, despite loud and long objections from their advocates at the time, it is now generally agreed that to buy them would not have been in the national interest.

In the field of strategic mobility, it was possible to define a timetable for the rapid deployment of U.S. land and tactical air forces to reinforce allies in various theaters around the world. It was then possible to determine, under various assumptions, the best ways to provide that capability. In other areas only the first steps were taken toward defining the national interest served by major defense programs. In land forces, for example, only very crude indicators of capability were developed. No satis-factory criteria were evolved to help determine how many or what kinds of divisions were needed to support national objectives. Much the same can be said for tactical air forces. But, whether the measures were good or poor, the attempt to put defense program issues into a broader context and to search for explicit measures of national need and adequacy was a basic goal of PPBS.

CONSIDERING NEEDS AND COSTS SIMULTANEOUSLY

A second basic idea underlying PPBS was the consideration of military needs and costs together. Put another way, decisions on forces and budgets should be made together, because they cannot sensibly be made apart. Ends and means interact. What is worth trying to do depends in large part on how much it costs. If an administration is not willing or able to meet the costs implied by its foreign policy and strategic objectives, it should revise its objectives to bring them into line with the budget it is willing and able to provide. Otherwise, the consequence will be an imbalance between objectives and forces and in all probability an imbalance between planned forces and the actual budgets and programs provided to support them. As McNamara once explained it: "I do not mean to suggest that we can measure national security in terms of dollars—you cannot price what is inherently priceless. But if we are to avoid talking in generalities, we must talk about dollars: for policy decisions must sooner or later be expressed in the form of budget decisions on where to spend and how much."

The explicit acceptance of the relevance of cost in defense programs was (and still is) deeply resented by some. While the situation has changed radically now, we frequently heard charges of overemphasis on cost: "Where national security is concerned, money is no object"; "We must buy system X—we can't afford to compromise on national defense"; "Nothing is too good for our fighting men." The cries are still familiar, if somewhat less frequent. But the fact is that our total resources are always limited and must be allocated among many competing needs in our society; and the nation has always compromised on national defense, even in wartime. Benefits and costs are associated with every defense program. One cannot get effectiveness without paying a cost. The way to get the most effective total defense program is to try to put each dollar where it will add the most to total effectiveness. The emphasis is not on cost but on cost *and* effectiveness together.

Still, the idea persists among some that the United States can and should establish military requirements without serious regard for cost and then each year should meet as many of them as possible with the inevitably limited budget that the real world will dictate. All that is required is for the military experts to say what is needed. This "need only" approach to military requirements was summarized by Senator Barry Goldwater in its pure form in the hearings on air power held in 1956. "If I have any criticism of the Air Force since the Second War," he said, "it has been their seeming timidity to put down on paper what they want and then let those of us who believe in them fight for that amount, and let the money take care of itself."

One trouble with this theory as the basis for a management system—and it was prevalent before 1961—is that it produced unbalanced programs. When the defense budget had to be cut, inevitably the prestige items (carriers, divisions, air wings) were retained and the unglamorous but essential support items (ammunition, spare parts, fuel) were cut. As noted earlier, for example, in 1961 the Army had managed to hold onto fourteen divisions in its force structure, but had only a few weeks' supply of ammunition and logistic support for these divisions, and that in unbalanced amounts. Indeed, at the time, the Army's stated matériel requirement exceeded the budgeted inventory and procurement level by $24 billion.

Allocating resources among competing programs is one of the most important jobs of the Secretary of Defense. He is constantly making decisions on whether to assign more or fewer resources to this or that program. This responsibility presses even more heavily on the President. No President wishes to shortchange the defense effort. Yet he sees other priority needs and recognizes that the nation's future also depends on solving the critical problems of the cities and meeting our growing educational, health, welfare, environmental, and transportation needs. The unavoidable fact is that our society has other needs besides military power.

A main job of the Secretary of Defense is to assist the President in making judgments as to how much should be spent on military power relative to other wants. Thus, he and the President must consider cost when they consider defense needs. They may choose to delay considering it or to consider it only implicitly, but they cannot choose to ignore it.

With a defense budget as large as the one the United States now has, choices have become more and more difficult. If our national leaders were faced with a clear-cut choice between social programs and the safety of the country, there is little doubt how they would decide. But, in fact, U.S. defenses are strong, and all-or-nothing defense decisions rarely exist. The type of choices that the President, the Secretary of Defense, and Congress constantly face is not between a capability to strike back in the event of a Soviet attack and no such capability; rather, they must decide whether to spend an extra $2 billion for the ability to strike back with the goal of killing 120 million rather than 100 million Russians with retaliatory forces, or of destroying 60 percent rather than 50 percent of the Soviet attack submarines with antisubmarine warfare forces, or of moving ten divisions rather than eight to Europe in ninety days. Moreover, an extra $2 billion spent on one of these purposes might yield less in long-run security than the same amount spent on one of the others or in some totally different way.

The notion, then, that in some meaningful sense the nation's military requirements can be determined without considering costs is false. Military requirements, like all other requirements, have to be decided by judgments as to what resources will be devoted to what purposes, and what sacrifices of other purposes will be made. The nation's leaders are likely to do a much better job by explicitly recognizing this fact than by pretending that costs are not relevant. PPBS, through its emphasis on the total cost of a defense program in relationship to need, and its search for alternatives that yield the greatest military effectiveness from the resources available, has worked to enhance an awareness of the relevance of cost.

It has been suggested that PPBS has worked too well in this respect and has led to overemphasis on cost. Has this, in fact, happened? It is very hard to make a convincing case that it has, in light of the sharp increases in defense budgetary requests during 1961–1964. Even the corollary charge that the system leads to a preference for the cheapest weapon is disproved by the record. The Minuteman II and III ICBMs, the Poseidon submarine-launched ballistic missile, the F-4 and the A-7D/E attack aircraft—to name only a few—were all justified on the basis of cost-effectiveness analyses done under the PPBS. Each costs more per plane or missile, but less per unit of effectiveness, than its predecessor. In each case, however, the Secretary of Defense judged that the margin of extra effectiveness per unit was worth the extra cost, and the more expensive alternative was approved.

EXPLICIT CONSIDERATION OF ALTERNATIVES

A third basic idea of PPBS was the explicit consideration of alternatives at the top decision level. By an alternative, we mean a balanced, feasible solution to the problem, not a straw man chosen to make a course of action preferred by the originating staff look better by comparison. It could be argued that the Secretary of Defense has always considered alternatives. For example, because the JCS regularly recommend forces costing roughly 25–35 percent more than the final budget the President believes the nation should provide, a set of alternatives is offered: the JCS's force levels with their implied budget, and the administration's budget and implied force levels. But these were not even attempts at solving the problem of balancing military needs and other needs. Each looked at only one side of the coin. A basic goal of PPBS was to ensure that the Secretary of Defense could consider several alternatives in which costs, forces, and strategies had been considered together.

This search for alternatives, and their explicit consideration by top management in DOD, was a vital part of the defense decisionmaking process. Because of the many conflicting values involved, the huge costs, and the complexity and uncertainties inherent in any defense-program decision, it is not enough for the Secretary of Defense to consider only a single staff solution, no matter how well reasoned it may be. Most decisions regarding the size and mix of forces require judgments about the objec-

tives being sought and the circumstances in which the forces are to be used. These are matters of broad national security policy. The only way the Secretary of Defense can effectively translate these judgments into meaningful action is by choosing from among alternative programs. Through organized adversary proceedings, PPBS helped to identify and clarify the key issues and assumptions in these programs and to lay out the alternatives in such a way that the Secretary and other politically responsible leaders could better understand the essentials and make a reasoned choice.

Indeed, organizing information along the lines that would be useful to political leaders was a main purpose of PPBS in the Pentagon. For example, PPBS translated the defense budget from *inputs*, such as procurement and personnel, into *forces*, such as strategic retaliatory forces and airlift and sealift forces, and from forces into *outputs*, such as targets destroyed or troops deployed. It translated the detailed technical criteria produced by experts into broader criteria that would be of more significance to political leaders—weapon yield, reliability, and accuracy into target destruction, and target destruction into lives lost and lives saved in a nuclear exchange, for example.

In this way, PPBS helped correct the inherent bias in DOD toward the expert's viewpoint. We have often heard men who were running successful programs say they were unable to understand why the Secretary of Defense was not buying more of their particular system. Why stop with 41 Polaris submarines, with 14 B-52 wings, with 1,000 Minuteman missiles, with 14 C-141 squadrons—to name only a few such programs? The answer is not because they were not well-managed programs; they were. Rather, it is because the best available evidence indicated that the value to the nation would be small in relation to the cost.

Proponents of a new weapon system, particularly project managers, tend to grow enamored of their creation and sometimes lose perspective. The fact that it works or that knotty technical problems were overcome in its development becomes, in their view, sufficient reason to buy the weapon in quantity. They often lose sight of the over-all objective the weapon is supposed to help reach, and they fail to examine closely enough whether their system contributes more toward that objective than some competing system.

For example, proponents of air defense are naturally eager to buy more and better missiles, radars, and interceptors in order to shoot down more enemy bombers. Indeed, their jobs properly are based on finding ways (all of them costing money) to shoot down a larger and larger proportion of hostile aircraft. But viewed nationally from the desk of the Secretary of Defense (or the President), the air defense task looks quite different. To him, the objective of air defense is not merely to shoot down enemy aircraft but rather to limit the damage these aircraft can inflict on U.S. population, industry, and military facilities. Shooting down aircraft is merely one of several ways to achieve that objective. The Secretary may, for example, decide that he will get more effectiveness (in terms of limiting damage) by building shelters or dispersing key military facilities or buying intercontinental missiles that can strike an enemy's air bases and destroy his bombers before they can be launched. Or he may decide that it is best to rely on deterrence and not buy an active defense. PPBS aided in this decision process by organizing information into broad mission-oriented categories and by translating the technical jargon of the expert into terms that had more meaning for the generalist. Surely, the number of lives saved by the expenditure of $10 or $20 billion on an ABM system under each of various assumed circumstances is of greater significance to the generalist than the "single-shot kill probability" of a Sprint missile against a re-entering Soviet warhead. Similarly, the number of divisional forces that can be deployed to Europe within thirty or sixty days should be of more significance to him than the number of ton-miles logged by the ships or aircraft. Such broad measures, which took considerable analytical effort to develop, were presented each year between 1961 and 1969 to the President in special memorandums for that purpose and to Congress in the Secretary of Defense's statement on the program and budget.

Indeed, under the PPBS more and better information about the *broad basis* for defense decisions was made available to congressional committees than ever before. One indication of the increased volume of information being provided to Congress by the Secretary of Defense

can be seen by comparing the Secretary's annual statement to Congress before and after 1961. Secretary Gates' last presentation ran 33 pages double-spaced and ended with the apology: "Mr. Chairman and members of the Committee, I appreciate your patience and courtesy in listening to this rather lengthy statement. I felt that it was important to describe the 1961 Defense budget in some detail and show how our policies and programs related to our total national strategy." Secretary McNamara's first presentation ran 122 single-spaced pages plus 44 pages of detailed tables; his last ran 256 single-spaced pages plus 24 pages of detailed tables.

This increased volume of information was matched by an increase in quality. Carl Vinson, then Chairman of the House Armed Services Committee, told McNamara after the presentation of the first of his seven posture statements before the committee:

I want to say this. I say it from the very bottom of my heart. I have been here dealing with these problems since 1919. I want to state that this is the most comprehensive, most factual statement that it has ever been my privilege to have an opportunity to receive from any of the departments of Government.

There is more information in here than any committee in Congress has ever received along the line that it is dealing with. It is so full of information all one has to do is just study it. You dealt with both sides of the problem. When you reach a decision, you set out the reasons why you reached that decision. You point out why—it probably could have been done the other way.

These sentiments were strongly echoed by Senator Richard Russell, Chairman of the Senate Armed Services Committee.

If, then, as one Senate subcommittee has recently concluded, "Members of Congress clearly have not welcomed all the implications of PPB," it can surely not be because PPBS reduced the amount of useful information available to its members. In fact, one of the problems with PPBS from the point of view of some members was that it was providing too much information of certain kinds. By forcing open debate on explicit alternatives, PPBS was breaking up the façade of DOD internal agreement. Both sides of difficult decisions were being presented with greater frequency and in greater detail than before. As Senator Karl

Mundt expressed it in hearings on PPBS conducted in 1967:

We used to face the question, "How much should we spend for a weapons system?" Defense had a united front and asked for a certain amount of money. Now we have to make decisions . . . on which defense system and techniques we should have. . . . It is in the wrong arena at our end of the Avenue, because we are not the experts in defense, and we are not the economists and the engineers. We are here trying to make overall policy and to do what we can to keep the budget relatively sound. It is very difficult if part of [the] team says you need B-52 bombers, otherwise in the early 70s you will have no bombers at all, and other officials say, "Don't worry about that, just let the B-52 bombers go, and don't put any money in." That shouldn't be the kind of decision we have to make.

If Congress should not have to make such multibillion-dollar decisions, who should? Senator Mundt's attitude is representative of a serious problem faced by the civilian leaders of the Defense Department during the years 1961–1968. PPBS was making available more useful information to Congress, but ironically some members often did not seem to want it.

Active Use of an Analytical Staff

Few of the decisions that the Secretary of Defense must make are either simple or noncontroversial. He is constantly given conflicting views on matters of great importance. There is conflict not only in the opinions of his advisers and experts but frequently in the evidence and "facts" they present. It is imperative that the Secretary have independent staff assistance to look at problems from his point of view and to double-check the facts for him. Thus, a fourth basic idea of PPBS, at least as it was practiced in the Pentagon between 1961 and 1969, was the active use of an analytical staff at the top policymaking levels. Most large organizations, governmental or otherwise, have some kind of analytical or planning group somewhere in the organizational structure. However, these staff groups are often little more than window dressing—passive contributors to the decisionmaking process. They neither report to, nor receive guidance from, the top on what studies to undertake and for what reasons. Their continued existence depends on remaining noncontroversial, and many of them excel in this respect.

But, in the Defense Department, the active use of an analytical staff at the top levels was a key element of PPBS from the beginning. The staff we are referring to is the Systems Analysis Office. Established by Secretary McNamara early in his administration, this office was charged with the responsibility for analyzing force requirements and weapons systems. It undertook studies directly at McNamara's request. These studies were then reviewed by all interested parties and formed a major input to the decisionmaking process. The controversy surrounding the Systems Analysis Office since its inception attests to its important and active role in providing information and analysis for the Secretary of Defense.[1]

The analytical effort of the Systems Analysis Office was conducted mainly by broad mission areas, such as tactical air forces, antisubmarine warfare forces, and land forces, rather than by service. The office thus integrated the weapons, data, and ideas of the services into force packages arranged so that the Secretary could see what types of capability were proposed, what he was buying, and how the package related to over-all needs. Understandably, an office with the responsibility of looking at the entire defense program, independently of service interests, was disliked by those who felt threatened. Equally understandably, an office whose job was to question, to probe, and to challenge service proposals would be a center of controversy. At the same time, the activities of such a staff at the top levels of DOD unquestionably stimulated the development of better analytical staffs in the services and the JCS and resulted, consequently, in better staff work.

The Systems Analysis Office was frequently criticized for slowing down the decisionmaking process unnecessarily, delaying decisions to buy badly needed weapons and equipment, and stifling innovation. As one critic put it, "the systems analysis business is being used to kill ideas and to delay them. . . . I know of no study that has been made . . . by the Department of Defense which has not caused delay, or which has added one iota to our national defense, not one." This criticism rests on the false premise that all delay is bad. Some delays are inherent in defense management. When the Secretary of Defense is faced with a difficult

[1] See "Doctrinal Innovation and the A-7 Attack Aircraft Decisions," pp. 431–45 of this volume.

decision on a program costing the taxpayers millions or even billions of dollars, he must take the time to examine the issues, weighing the costs and the expected returns in effectiveness, before making a decision. The alternatives would be either to accept blindly all the recommendations that are made or to make quick decisions on some arbitrary basis. Either approach is clearly inadequate. The American people—who ultimately receive the benefits, but who also must pay the bills—have the right to expect decisions to be made on the basis of as thorough and objective an analysis as possible.

More to the point, however, the active use of analytical staff at the top policymaking level in any organization is likely to result in more time being spent on thinking through the strategic basis of a new proposal. Much of the "delay" attributed to the Systems Analysis Office was caused by the fact that new weapons systems were often proposed without adequate strategic justification. As a general rule, where the strategic basis for a new system had been thought through, decisions were relatively fast and frequently favorable. The Poseidon submarine-launched ballistic missile system, the C-5A transport, the A-7A attack aircraft and the Multiple, Independently Targetable Re-entry Vehicle (MIRV) are all examples of such prompt and favorable decisions. On the other hand, where the strategic basis had not been carefully thought through, decisions, as a rule, were slower and sometimes unfavorable. The B-70 bomber, nuclear-powered frigates, and the Nike-X ABM system are examples. In short, the major cause of delay of a proposed system was more often inadequate strategic justification than any particular action or inaction on the part of the Systems Analysis Office. Further, rather than acting as a roadblock, the office, by helping innovators do the necessary strategic thinking, provided them with criteria they could use to defend their projects, and thus aided innovation.

A Multiyear Force and Financial Plan

A fifth basic idea of PPBS was a plan combining both forces and costs which projected into the future the foreseeable implications of current decisions. Such a plan was not meant to be an inflexible blueprint for the future, or a set of goals that must be achieved. Rather, it was a projection of the implications of past decisions, a set of official planning assumptions, and a point of departure in the continuing search for improvements. Having such a plan forces a decisionmaker to look ahead to the time when today's decisions will have their most important effects and to judge programs versus needs in the light of their consequences over time. If a decisionmaker insists on seeing costs over a period of years, proponents of new programs find it harder to conceal the future cost implications of decisions made today.

Without such a plan, it is impossible to bring together at one time and place all the relevant information needed by the Secretary of Defense and his principal advisers for making sound program decisions and seeing that they are carried out. A multiyear plan that deals with forces and costs in a comprehensive manner is necessary if the Secretary of Defense is to play an active role in shaping national security policy; indeed, it is essential if there is to be a comprehensive and consistent policy.

Open and Explicit Analysis

A final basic idea underlying PPBS was that of open and explicit analysis; that is, each analysis should be made available to all interested parties, so that they can examine the calculations, data, and assumptions and retrace the steps leading to the conclusions. Indeed, all calculations, data, and assumptions *should* be described in an analysis in such a way that they can be checked, tested, criticized, debated, discussed, and possibly refuted by interested parties. The results of an analysis should not be blindly accepted simply because they appear at the end of an impressive-looking document called a study, accompanied by a sheaf of endorsements signed by high-ranking officials. The validity of a proposition should be established on the basis of some criterion other than an appeal to authority. The important element is the quality of the proof, and not the reputation or age or experience of the author. The esteem in which the originator of an analysis is held is not sufficient reason for believing the finding of the analysis.

By the end of 1968, the need for open and

explicit analysis was generally accepted in DOD. But the concept was a radical and controversial departure when McNamara introduced it in 1961. In fact, there was much debate at the time over the wisdom of requiring that all studies be made available to the Secretary of Defense and his staff. The fear was that this would lead to additional pressures for biasing studies to support predetermined conclusions. As it turned out, however, the open and explicit approach made it difficult for any group to get away with manipulating an analysis (though the attempts did not stop). The services and the JCS could check OSD studies to see if assumptions were biased to make a point; and, of course, OSD could do the same for its studies. The result was that, in most important cases, the Secretary of Defense heard all sides. In reviewing a joint analysis he got a much more precise statement of the issues, the assumptions, and the uncertainties than would otherwise have been the case.

The open and explicit approach has many important advantages. It helps protect a large organization against persisting in error over the long run. Of course, all parties might agree on an analysis containing biased or erroneous assumptions, but the chances of this happening are reduced if each party is given an opportunity to comment independently. Such an approach is also the best way of handling the uncertainties that pervade defense issues. It makes better sense to recognize explicitly that the future is uncertain and design a strategy based on uncertainty—one that includes options and gathering additional information to resolve uncertainties—than to pick a particular assumption and treat it as if it were a certainty. In addition, open and explicit analysis helps build confidence in the soundness of a study's conclusions. All sorts of mistakes can be made under the guise of analysis, just as they can under the guise of judgment and experience. There may be cases in which some people overemphasize the cost, and other cases in which they overstate the potential gains in effectiveness. But this is less likely to occur if the analyst is required to lay the whole study out, showing the estimated benefits and costs, the evidence for them, and the calculations. When this is done, others, including critics, can review and judge the analysis for themselves.

Finally, the concept of open and explicit analysis is particularly important to groups outside DOD, such as Congress, the Bureau of the Budget, and the interested public. By giving these groups a better handle on defense issues, such analyses promote more effective interrogation and debate. And, by bringing outside groups into the decisionmaking process, the chances are reduced that only parties with a pro-defense bias—a bias that it is almost impossible not to have if one works in the Pentagon—will participate in the decision.

The concept of open and explicit analysis was generally accepted in the Pentagon by the end of 1968. While some studies were still being sent to the Secretary of Defense with only their conclusions and recommendations, making it difficult to ascertain why the results came out that way and how the conclusions related to the initial statement of the problem, such events were becoming less frequent. In large part this was because the military staffs knew that their studies would be reviewed by the Systems Analysis Office.

Ironically, it was this process of open and explicit analysis that provoked much of the controversy over "downgrading military judgment." Far from being ignored, professional military judgments were subjected to thorough and rigorous review from all angles. In the debates accompanying this process, many military experts felt that their judgments should not be subjected to searching scrutiny by what they considered to be amateurs and outsiders. But the fact is that most military judgments implicitly include economic and political components as well, and it is important that the Secretary of Defense and the President be able to distinguish these.

In sum, the fundamental idea behind PPBS was decisionmaking based on explicit criteria related to the national interest in defense programs as opposed to decisionmaking by compromise among various institutional and parochial interests. PPBS also emphasized the consideration of real alternatives, the importance of evaluating needs and costs together, the need for a multiyear force and financial plan, the regular use of an analytical staff as an aid to decisionmakers at the top levels, and the importance of making analyses open and explicit. These were the basic ideas underlying PPBS and the management tools that made the system work.

PPBS never became a closed, rigid, or perfected management system. Indeed, in its broadest sense it was less a management system than a philosophy of management—a philosophy that, we believe, helped to channel the initiative, imagination, dedication, hard work, and judgment of the military and civilian leaders in DOD along more rational and objective lines than had previously been followed.

CONGRESSIONAL ATTITUDES TOWARD DEFENSE

GEORGE C. GIBSON

Two major points are made here: that Congress plays a significant role in the making of defense policy; and that a fundamental shift in the relationship has occurred since 1965. Gibson calls the pre-1965 congressional role "supportive" and the post-1965 role "critical." He cites the reasons for this shift as stemming from changes within Congress and external developments such as Vietnam, concern over domestic needs, cost overruns, My Lai, and opposition to the draft. Captain Gibson (USAF) is a 1967 graduate of the Air Force Academy, earned a master's degree from Ohio State University in 1968, and is an instructor in the Academy's Department of Political Science.

Congressional attitudes are extremely important in understanding the nature and extent of congressional influence on the Defense Department. The issue of congressional-defense relations raised explicitly in Huntington's *The Soldier and the State* in 1957 has not received adequate emphasis, despite a proliferation of research on both Congress and the executive.[1] Much of what has been written on this issue is critical of growing defense spending and argues for Congress to redress what many scholars consider to be its marginal role in the formulation of defense policy.[2] In examining congressional influence on defense matters, this paper will develop two propositions: (1) Congress does play a significant and continuing role in the defense-policy process, and (2) a fundamental shift in congressional attitudes has resulted in a change in the way Congress carries out its role in this process. In developing these propositions, the discussion will focus on the

[1] Much of the literature on congressional-defense relations was written in 1960–1962, including works by Huntington, Janowitz, Dawson, Hilsman, Dexter, Schilling, Hammond and Snyder. Very little was written during the late 1960s, but this topic is getting renewed emphasis with the recent studies by Russett, Rice, Yarmolinsky, and Kanter. These sources and others are referenced in full at the appropriate places below.

[2] These range from Huntington's observations on Congress as a "lobbyist" and the executive as the "decisionmaker" to outright indictments such as Rice's book on the C-5A. See Samuel P. Huntington, "Strategic Planning and the Political Process," *Foreign Affairs*, 38, no. 2 (January 1960): 287; and Berkeley Rice, *The C-5A Scandal* (Boston: Houghton Mifflin, 1971).

This is an original article written for this volume and the Inter-Service Conference on Defense Policy held at the Air Force Academy, May 10–12, 1972.

supportive role Congress played between the Korean War and 1965, and the emergence of a more critical attitude toward defense after 1965.

A number of studies on congressional-defense relations have emphasized the negative role Congress has played. In his explanation of "congressional negativism," Janowitz focuses on control of expenditures and the desire to eliminate waste.[3] Roger Hilsman refers to Congress's power in foreign relations as a "negative, limit-setting power—the power of deterrence and the threat of retaliation."[4] Huntington casts a more positive role for Congress in describing three major techniques it employs in "lobbying with the executive": informal representational means, investigation, and appropriation and authorization.[5] All of these points touch on crucial aspects of the congressional-defense relationship, but they tend to under-emphasize what Hilsman calls "consensus-building."[6] Consensus-building may involve either being a public critic and opposing administration policy or legitimatizing and building support for policy. Schilling observed that the "executive and Congress start their thinking about the budget with a common and very narrow range of figures in mind. The area of their choice is closely limited by the prevailing climate of opinion."[7] Congress plays a negative role to the extent that it places certain outer limits on the budget the executive believes can be enacted. Congress may also play a positive role by encouraging an overall change in these limits. Thus, Congress does play a positive role if it mobilizes support for a larger budget or for a reduction in the budget. This paper will attempt to analyze the changing climate of

opinion by looking at the consensus that existed within the government and public prior to 1965, the fragmentation of this consensus after 1965, and the diverse political factors that contributed to this change.

The various factors which most directly affect Congress's role in the policy process have been identified in the published literature. A useful approach, applied most often to studies of congressional committees, is to view the House and Senate as political systems. Richard Fenno in *The Power of the Purse* suggests that a political system has "certain identifiable, inter-dependent, internal parts, existing in an identifiable external environment, and tending to stabilize both its internal and external relationships over time."[8] Defined in this way, the House and Senate are most appropriately viewed as two similar, closely related systems. The major internal and external factors are depicted in Table 1.[9]

Table 1
Factors Affecting Congressional Attitudes on Defense

House Internal Parts	Senate Internal Parts	External Environment
Leadership	Leadership	Events
Committees	Committees	International
Membership	Membership	Domestic
		Executive
		President
		OSD
		Services
		Public Opinion
		Interest Groups/ Mass Media

This framework provides a basis from which we can organize a discussion of changing attitudes in Congress. The system calls for a stabilization of internal and external relations, and these relations will be affected by the existence or breakdown of a consensus. A firm consensus within and outside Congress will facilitate the stabilization of relations, while the breakdown of a consensus may be closely related to changing relationships.

The term "consensus" provides a meaningful, if somewhat imprecise, notion for categor-

---

[3] Morris Janowitz, *The Professional Soldier* (New York: The Free Press of Glencoe, 1960), p. 354.

[4] Roger Hilsman, *The Politics of Policy Making in Defense and Foreign Affairs* (New York: Harper & Row, 1971), p. 83.

[5] Samuel P. Huntington, *The Common Defense* (New York: Columbia University Press, 1961), pp. 135–43.

[6] In the original article he places considerable emphasis on the positive aspect, while in his book he focuses more on Congress being a public critic. Roger Hilsman, "Congressional-Executive Relations and the Foreign Policy Consensus," *American Political Science Review*, 52, no. 3 (September 1958): 732 (hereafter cited as *APSR*).

[7] Warner R. Schilling, Paul Y. Hammond, and Glenn H. Snyder, *Strategy, Politics, and Defense Budgets* (New York: Columbia University Press, 1962), p. 96.

[8] Richard Fenno, *The Power of the Purse* (Boston: Little, Brown & Co., 1966), p. xviii.

[9] The factors shown here are drawn from a review of the primary topics covered by the literature on Congress and congressional-executive relations.

izing the distribution of attitudes or opinions.[10] Consensus can be defined as shared attitudes or beliefs on certain human goals and conduct. Shared attitudes toward defense indicate a policy consensus in a specific issue area.[11] This policy consensus requires neither agreement on details nor a basic consensus on fundamental principles.[12] Attitudes on defense will probably be affected by attitudes toward foreign policy in general. And a consensus does require more than just the existence of a dominant mood or attitude; it also implies the lack of an effective or sizable opposition.

In characterizing the attitudes of Congress, one must recognize that individual members of Congress have different attitudes, depending on their committee assignments, whether they are in the House or Senate, their constituency, and their own personalities. However, certain attitudes have been widely shared within the House and Senate. Also, annual legislation and

---

[10] V. O. Key, Jr., *Public Opinion and American Democracy* (New York: Alfred A. Knopf, 1961), pp. 27–53.

[11] Dan Nimmo and Thomas D. Ungs, *American Political Patterns: Conflict and Consensus* (Boston: Little, Brown & Co., 1969), pp. 38–39; and James N. Rosenau, *Domestic Sources of Foreign Policy* (New York: The Free Press of Glencoe, 1967), pp. 11–50.

[12] Gabriel A. Almond, *The American People and Foreign Policy* (New York: Frederick A. Praeger, 1960), p. 158.

appropriations require that a majority position, if not a consensus, be established. The overwhelming number of congressmen and senators who consistently voted for passage of the defense appropriations bill (Table 2) indicates that fairly broad agreement has existed at least within Congress. A note of caution must be voiced, since justice cannot be done to any one of the individual factors being examined. Only the larger pattern of relationships can be dealt with in this article. Also, no specific period of years is totally adequate for examining congressional attitudes, because of the continual internal and external changes. These changes can be seen in the changing membership of Congress and its committees, organizational changes within the Department of Defense (DOD) and the executive, the evolution of military strategy, and, more recently, the evolutionary nature of the Vietnam issue. However, particular periods can be characterized by the variations in emphasis which Congress has given to certain issues in hearings, floor statements, and speeches.

MILITARY PREPAREDNESS

During the 1950s, Congress's major concerns were the adequacy of the nation's military preparedness and the inefficiencies and waste

---

Table 2

Vote on Passage of the Annual Defense Appropriations Bill as Presented by the Appropriations Committee

Year of Voting	House			Senate			Bill for Fiscal Year
	Yea's	Nay's	Not Voting	Yea's	Nay's	Not Voting	
1971	352	51	31	80	5	15	1972
1970	274	31	125	89	0	11	1971
1969	330	33	70	85	4	11	1970
1968	333	7	91	55	2	43	1969
1967	407	1	25	85	3	12	1968
1966	392	1	38	86	0	14	1967
1965	407	0	27	89	0	11	1966
1964	365	0	67	76	0	24	1965
1963	410	1	22	77	0	23	1964
1962	388	0	50	88	0	12	1963
1961	412	0	25	85	0	15	1962
1960	377	3	52	85	0	15	1961
1959	393	3	39	90	0	8	1960
1958	390	0	41	71	0	25	1959
1957	394	1	38	74	0	21	1958
1956	377	0	56	88	0	8	1957
1955	384	0	50	80	0	16	1956

Source: U.S. Congress, *Congressional Record*.

within the services.[13] The dual concern is evident in any number of statements made by members of Congress during this period, such as Senator Milton Young's (R-N.D.) comment in an appropriations subcommittee in 1955:

I can think of nothing more important, particularly now at a time when the United States practically stands alone in the defense of democracy in the world, [than] that we at least have the most modern type of military equipment.

The other matter that I think is awfully important . . . is . . . maintaining efficiency and economizing wherever possible.[14]

The following year, Senator Dennis Chavez (D-N.M.), Chairman of the Defense Appropriations Subcommittee, expressed these ideas even more clearly:

A year ago . . . I stated that the committee had two primary concerns. The first of these was to recommend fully adequate appropriations to provide for the national security to the United States. The second was to ascertain that for every dollar appropriated the taxpayers of the country received full value through economical administration. Today the two considerations are, if possible, more important than ever.[15]

The early 1960s (1960–1965) were in part a continuation of former issues, with the so-called missile gap and Flexible Response providing additional impetus to preparedness as the key issue.[16] Congressman George Mahon (D-Tex.), Chairman of the Defense Appropriations Subcommittee, expressed a widely shared concern in introducing the FY 1963 defense appropriations bill:

The passage of this bill will evidence to the whole world the determination of the United States Congress to stand resolute and firm in the face of the Berlin crisis, in the face of all other international crises, in the face of threats to our freedom in any area of the world.[17]

At the same time, the Defense Reorganization Act of 1958, coupled with McNamara's management innovations, created congressional concern over the limited impact of military advice and influence in defense decisionmaking.[18]

The origins of the congressional attitudes toward preparedness in the 1950s are diverse, but can to a large extent be equated with the origins of the Cold War.[19] Both the events themselves and the executive's interpretation and response to these events were primary factors which impacted on Congress. However, caution must be exercised when evaluating the impact of events. The external situation may account for the general level of the military effort, but the military budget does not necessarily respond to increases in tension.[20] Prior to 1960 President Eisenhower was trying to balance the budget, and, as a result, his administration acted as a restraining force on defense spending (even though the services were advocating increases in their own programs).[21] Both the public and Congress were more inclined than the executive to stress the communist military threat, but Eisenhower's military reputation and prestige enabled him to restrain defense spending with minimal criticism. Kennedy capitalized on this public concern, using the missile-gap issue in his 1960 campaign, and significantly increased the defense budget after he took office. Throughout this time frame, Congress either supported the increasingly large defense spending or advocated even larger expenditures. As Congressman Mahon stated in 1962:

We must have defense and we must pay, and pay in very large sums, for defense. And, insofar as I

[13] In addition to the primary sources quoted in this paper, Samuel P. Huntington, in The Common Defense, pp. 218–23, suggests that Congress usually supported increases in military spending in the 1950s compared to the executive's role of keeping defense costs down. Also, see Janowitz, The Professional Soldier, p. 354, for a commentary on Congress's concern with eliminating waste.
[14] U.S. Congress, Senate, Subcommittee of the Committee on Appropriations, Hearings, Department of Defense Appropriations for 1956, 84th Cong., 1st sess., 1955, p. 2.
[15] U.S. Congress, Senate, Subcommittee of the Committee on Appropriations, Hearings, Department of Defense Appropriations for 1957, 84th Cong., 2nd sess., 1956, p. 2.
[16] Congressional support for increased defense spending is traced through both the 1950s and early 1960s in Edward A. Kolodziej, The Uncommon Defense and Congress, 1945–1963 (Columbus: Ohio State University Press, 1966).

[17] U.S. Congress, Congressional Record, 87th Cong., 2nd sess., 1962, 108, pt. 5: 6831.
[18] U.S. Congress, House, Committee on Armed Forces, Report of Special Subcommittee on Defense Agencies, 87th Cong., 2nd sess., 1962, pp. 6631–34.
[19] For one interpretation, see Arthur Schlesinger, Jr., "Origins of the Cold War," Foreign Affairs, 46, no. 1 (October 1967).
[20] Huntington, The Common Defense, pp. 199–207.
[21] Ibid., p. 220.

know, the American people almost unanimously support a high level defense program.[22]

This observation is supported by both Huntington and the results of public opinion polls taken during those years (see Table 3).[23] The stability of public opinion suggests that it provides a basis for the prevailing mood and will not change rapidly. Its direct impact on Congress will probably vary with the saliency given to the issue in a particular year.[24]

Other environmental factors which need to be considered are interest groups and mass media. Although much of the literature states that foreign affairs tend to be affected less by interest groups than by domestic matters, aspects of military policy such as procurement have their own special interest groups. However, the impact of these groups appears to have been relatively unimportant through 1960, since the system of private interests was still uncertain and fragmentary.[25] Also, studies of 1961–1962 by Bruce Russett showed little or no relationship between Senate voting on military issues and civilian contracts awarded in various senators' states. However, these studies did show a direct relationship between a senator's voting and Department of Defense payrolls in his state.[26]

The impact of the mass media is indirect but very significant, for it provides information, interprets events, and either builds or undermines the consensus. In this regard, the media appear to have made a major contribution to strengthening and maintaining pro-defense attitudes prior to 1965.

22 U.S. Congress, *Congressional Record*, 87th Cong., 2nd sess., 1962, 108, pt. 5: 6831.
23 Huntington, *The Common Defense*, pp. 234–42.
24 Lewis A. Froman and Randall B. Ripley, "Conditions for Party Leadership: The Case of the House Democrats," *APSR*, 59, no. 1 (March 1965): 52–63; and Warren E. Miller and Donald E. Stokes, "Constituency Influence in Congress," *APSR*, 57, no. 1 (March 1963): 45–56.
25 Huntington, *The Common Defense*, pp. 175–76.
26 Bruce M. Russett, *What Price Vigilance?* (New Haven: Yale University Press, 1970), pp. 72–73; see also "The Revolt of the Masses: Public Opinion on Military Expenditures," pp. 613–25 of this volume. For a summary of research on this topic, see Carol F. Goss, "Congress and Defense Related Constituency Benefits: An Interpretation of Recent Research," a paper prepared for delivery at the Twenty-sixth Annual Meeting of the Western Political Science Association, Portland, March 23–25, 1972. Also, for a differing interpretation, see David Horowitz, *Corporations and the Cold War* (New York: Monthly Review Press, 1969).

Table 3
Opinion Polls

Question: There is much discussion as to the amount this country should spend for national defense. How do you feel about this—do you think we are spending too little, too much, or about the right amount?

	Too Little	About Right	Too Much	No Opinion
March 1950	23%	44%	15%	18%
September 1953	22	45	20	13
April 1960	21	45	18	16

Source: Gallup Poll.

If events and public opinion were the foremost environmental influences, the internal politics of Congress had their own flavor and impact. Congress provides the primary public exposure for executive decisions on defense issues. For this reason, the attitude of Congress is very important for establishing or undermining the legitimacy of these decisions. The executive may always justify its policies directly to the people, but it can seldom build a real consensus without congressional support.

Congressional committees have a longstanding reputation for being the centers of power in both houses of Congress. Informal pressure, hearings, legislation, appropriations, and investigations are the primary means they have of exerting pressure on the executive. Normally these functions have been performed by the appropriate legislative or appropriations committees; in this case the Armed Services Committees and Defense Appropriations Subcommittees. One of the criticisms of this system has been that committee members tend to identify with the military or its programs. For instance, the Air Force received strong support for its programs from Senator Stuart Symington (D-Mo.) on the Senate Armed Services Committee, especially throughout the 1956 airpower hearings.[27] The Navy had its supporter in Congressman Carl Vinson (D-Ga.), Chairman of the House Armed Services Committee.[28] The service advocates were bolstered by others on the Armed Services Committees, such as Senator Lyndon Johnson (D-Tex.),

27 Kolodziej, *op. cit.*, p. 228.
28 Bernard K. Gordon, "The Military Budget: Congressional Phase," *Journal of Politics*, 23, no. 4 (November 1961): 692; and Huntington, *The Common Defense*, p. 390. For examples of his support for the Navy, see Kolodziej, *op. cit.*, pp. 52, 104, 367.

who held subcommittee hearings to assess the impact of Sputnik.[29] The Appropriations Committees have been more searching in their committee hearings, but they have approached these hearings from the perspective of being informed rather than from that of trying to expose and publicize mismanagement or monetary waste. Even while trying to eliminate inefficiency, they have been supporters of the higher levels of defense spending. The Armed Services and Appropriations Committees provided the "expertise" in the House because of its greater emphasis on committee specialization and fragmented power, but the Senate had its own committees competing for the limelight on this topic. For instance, a major competitor was the Government Operations Committee, which conducted hearings under Senator Henry Jackson (D-Wash.) to "voice the need for a greater defense effort."[30] Johnson, as Senate Majority Leader, did much to mold a stronger consensus for defense spending in the late 1950s. This contrasted sharply with Speaker Rayburn's passive role in the House.[31]

The thrust of the committee activities in both the House and the Senate was to build an internal consensus on preparedness. The conflict which occurred between committees throughout the 1950s and early 1960s centered on committee influence and roles rather than on issues or policy.[32]

The role of the committees went unchallenged as they set the mood in the House and Senate. At best, most other members of Congress played the role of an attentive public. Studies have shown that in the 1950s the Democrats were more pro-defense than the Republicans, with support for national security programs being part of the liberal position. In the early 1960s the Republicans assumed the more hawkish position.[33] However, as evidenced by the lack of opposition in defense appropriations votes (Table 2), partisanship played a small role, particularly in the committees. As Congressman Mahon proclaimed on the House floor in 1962:

Let me say that in the matter of defense this year, as in former years, politics has played no part in the formulation of this bill. I cannot remember any occasion that members of the subcommittee divided along partisan lines on any issue which was recommended to the full committee in connection with this bill.[34]

Throughout the 1950s and early 1960s, Congress was an active participant in the defense policy process, especially in responding to, and mobilizing support for, military preparedness. Critics of Congress emphasize the small budget cuts made by the legislature during these years.[35] Between the end of the Korean War and 1959 (FY 1955–1960), Congress cut a total of less than 1 percent from the President's defense requests. In the subsequent five years (FY 1961–1966), Congress appropriated approximately 1 percent more than the executive requested (Table 4). These statistics can be

Table 4
Defense Appropriations

Fiscal Year	Appropriations above or below the President's Original Request	
	Dollars (in millions)	Percent
1972	−3,025	−4.1
1971	−2,149	−3.1
1970	−5,637	−7.5
1969	−5,204	−6.8
1968	−1,647	−2.3
1967	+ 403	+0.7
1966	+1,638	+3.6
1965	− 719	−1.5
1964	−1,794	−3.7
1963	+ 229	+0.5
1962	+3,720	+8.7
1961	+ 661	+1.7
1960	− 20	−0.005
1959	+1,405	+3.7
1958	−2,368	−6.5
1957	+ 509	+1.5
1956	− 350	−1.1
1955	−1,086	−3.6

Source: U.S. Congress, Congressional Quarterly.

[29] Kolodziej, op. cit., p. 269.
[30] Ibid., pp. 316–17.
[31] Ibid., p. 272.
[32] For a discussion of the armed services' attempts to increase their power vis-à-vis the Appropriations Committees, see Raymond H. Dawson, "Congressional Innovation and Intervention in Defense Policy: Legislative Authorization of Weapons Systems," APSR, 66 (1962): 42–57; and Herbert W. Stephens, "The Role of the Legislative Committee in the Appropriations Process: A Study Focused on the Armed Services Committees," Western Political Quarterly, 24 (1971): 146–62.
[33] Goss, op. cit., Table 2.

[34] U.S. Congress, Congressional Record, 87th Cong., 2nd sess., 1962, 108, pt. 5: 6832.
[35] For additional material, see Drew Pearson and Jack Anderson, The Case against Congress (New York: Pocket Books, 1968); and William Proxmire, Report from Wasteland (New York: Praeger, 1970).

interpreted only as an indication of congressional weakness if one ignores the attitudes existing within Congress itself and within the general public. Congress was doing what it felt was necessary and what the American people evidently wanted. And, more significant than any individual policy influence, the Armed Services and Appropriations Committees performed important functions in establishing a climate of opinion in which the executive could, and was, in fact, pressured to ask for continual increases in defense budgets.

CHANGING ATTITUDES

The earlier time period focused on the supportive role of Congress in the defense policy process. In 1966, tangible evidence of a fundamental change in attitudes began to appear. Traditionally, the Senate has acted as an appellate court in the appropriations process; the services could count on the restoration of a portion of the funds cut by the House.[36] This appellate role was followed consistently, as is borne out by the record—the Senate approved more money than the House for every Fiscal Year from 1950 through 1966. However, starting with the FY 1967 budget, the Senate has consistently reduced defense appropriations below the level of the House version of the bill.

This reversal in the long-standing role of the Senate Defense Appropriations Subcommittee, although affected by several factors, can best be understood within the context of the entire Senate. As stated in Fenno's *The Power of the Purse*, the network of interlocking memberships between committees and the leadership means that "the Senate Committee on Appropriations is expected to, and usually does, act as the Senate."[37] When viewed in this light, a more critical attitude toward appropriations would appear to reflect a changing mood within the Senate. Since the 1950s, the Senate has become increasingly more liberal. The Senate's center of power, or inner club, was destroyed under Majority Leader Johnson. Also, "younger men have come in, and liberal majorities on legislation are by no means uncom-

mon."[38] Spurred by problems in defense procurement such as the F-111, the increasing availability of information on defense, the rising cost of domestic programs, and Vietnam, many young senators adopted a more critical attitude toward the high level of defense spending. Thus, the earlier consensus began to fragment.

A subtle but important factor in these years has stemmed from the amount of information Congress has received on defense issues. Since 1959, when a law was passed requiring annual authorization for certain research and development programs, the amount of information available to Congress has increased considerably. By 1966, annual authorization was required for most research and development programs, as well as for procurement.[39] Annual authorization, which occurs prior to appropriation, means that most programs now come before Congress twice. In providing detailed and comprehensive presentations to Congress, McNamara also contributed to the wider dissemination of information. In addition, by 1966, Senator Fulbright was speaking against the "military-industrial complex," and the Joint Economic Committee released a report charging the Defense Department with wasting money as a result of "loose management."

In the following year, one begins to see occasional indications of other influences on the Senate, as shown by Senator Symington's statement to Secretary McNamara: "What worries me is that so many people are now fundamentally anti-military in this country; and I think that for some reason this is growing." Senator Stennis acknowledged the growing pressure to reorder priorities when he introduced the "largest single defense appropriations bill in the history of the Nation":

All members of the Senate must regret that the Defense bill is of this magnitude, for we are faced with the largest deficits in our history. We are also faced with nearly countless demands at home for additional outlays for domestic programs that are conceived and promoted to help solve our internal problems.[40]

---

36 The "appellate court" function has been typical for both defense and nondefense issues in the Senate. See Samuel P. Huntington, *The Soldier and the State* (New York: Vintage Books, 1957), p. 409; and Fenno, *op. cit.*, p. 615.

37 Fenno, *op. cit.*, p. 562.

38 Nelson W. Polsby, *Congress and the Presidency*, 2nd ed. (Englewood Cliffs, N.J.: Prentice-Hall, 1971), p. 69.

39 Stephens, *op. cit.*, pp. 146–52, explains how the Armed Services Committees moved from "general continuing authorizations" to annual authorizations.

40 U.S. Congress, *Congressional Record*, 90th Cong., 1st sess., 1967, 113, pt. 17: 23254.

Nineteen sixty-eight provided a real turning point, with the Tet offensive in Vietnam, President Johnson's withdrawal from the election, and a major economic crisis at home. Faced with an upcoming election and a predicted $20-billion budget deficit, Congress passed a 10 percent tax surcharge coupled with a mandatory $6-billion expenditure cut. Since over 95 percent of defense spending is controllable (appropriated on an annual basis), and only 28 percent of the civilian programs are controllable, substantial cuts had to be made in the defense budget.[41] The House has normally made a cut in the Administration's request, in keeping with its role of "guardian of the treasury," but slashing $5.1 billion out of the FY 1969 request went well beyond any routine pruning. The ability of the House Appropriations Committee, and specifically its Defense Subcommittee, to judge and conform to House expectations in making this major reduction was amply demonstrated by the overwhelming support the House gave to the bill (333 Yea's, 7 Nay's, and 91 not voting).[42] And, there was pressure to reduce military spending still further, as reflected by the June 1968 editorial a senator inserted in the *Congressional Record* under the title "Defense Budget Cuts of $10.8 Billion Seen Feasible."

The 1968 budget cut and subsequent cuts of nearly the same magnitude are only the most salient aspects in the changing relationship between Congress and the Defense Department. They do signal a major shift in Congress from concern with military preparedness to the question of domestic versus military expenditures. By 1969, Congressman Robert Sikes (D-Fla.) declared:

Those who have clamored for a reduction in defense and a buildup of other expenditures for domestic need . . . can take comfort from what is now happening to defense expenditures.[43]

An article entitled "Congress Leading Way on Military Cutbacks" explained some of this process:

George H. Mahon (D-Tex.), chairman of the House Defense Appropriations Subcommittee as well as the parent appropriations committee, himself said he could not have pushed the full Pentagon budget through the House in 1969 and was responding to what he called the "realities." He announced early in the year that he was going to cut the Pentagon's fiscal 1970 budget by $5 billion. And his old committee colleague, Defense Secretary Melvin R. Laird, scurried around and made as many of his own cuts first as he could.[44]

Since 1966, the Senate Foreign Relations Committee has also provided a different perspective. More critical of the military, it has conducted hearings on the Tonkin Gulf incident, Vietnam policy, and the *Pueblo*. Reinforcing this adverse publicity, Senator Proxmire in late 1968 and early 1969, as Chairman of the Joint Economic Committee's Subcommittee on Economy in Government, held hearings on the Air Force's C-5A cost overruns.[45] Subsequent events created more problems: continuing overruns on the C-5A and a myriad of other embarrassing disclosures or events, such as the Army's NCO Club scandal, opposition to the Sentinel System being deployed around cities, My Lai, and the growing opposition to the draft. These events reinforced the changing, more critical congressional mood.

Reasons for the more critical attitude toward the military undoubtedly rest in part on the continuing unpopularity of the Vietnam War. However, Vietnam was to a large extent merely a catalyst in heightening awareness and concern over the low priority and funding for domestic needs. It also created a more receptive audience for the Senate investigations of Lockheed's C-5A aircraft cost overruns and other problems, with their accompanying adverse publicity.

This critical mood evolved in spite of the support the Armed Services and Appropriations Committees had given the military.[46] And

---

[41] Civilian programs that are not controllable include items regulated by law, such as Medicare, public assistance grants to states, civilian retirement pay, and farm price supports. The data were taken from Secretary Laird's testimony to the House Subcommittee on Appropriations, *Department of Defense Appropriations for 1971*, 91st Cong., 2nd sess., 1970, p. 341.

[42] The relationship between the Appropriations Committee and the House is discussed extensively in Fenno, *op. cit.*

[43] U.S. Congress, *Congressional Record*, 91st Cong., 1st sess., 1961, 115, pt. 28: 37675–76.

[44] George C. Wilson, "Congress Leading Way on Military Cutback," *Washington Post*, December 8, 1969.

[45] For a well-documented, if somewhat slanted, story of this controversy, see Rice, *op. cit.*

[46] This paper does not examine whether Congress takes a fiscal (incremental) or programmatic (policy) orientation in its review of the defense budget. Wildavsky and Fenno find a fiscal orientation in nonde-

these committees have evidenced an awareness, if not sympathy, for this mood. After 1969, the interests of the liberal, anti-Vietnam groups began to converge with other groups concerned over the high level of defense spending, cost overruns and inefficiencies, and the soaring cost of manpower and weapons systems. The latter concerns were shared by liberals and conservatives both on and off the immediate committees. In addition, within the House Armed Services Committee, a group of five liberal, more openly critical members have begun to assert their own views.[47] Congressman F. Edward Hebert (D-La.), who succeeded Mendel Rivers (D-S.C.) as Chairman of the House Armed Services Committee, is as staunch a supporter of the military as his predecessor.[48] However, as Robert Leggett (D-Calif.), one of the members of the committee, commented:

I believe his [Rivers'] passing will mark the end of an era in the Department of Defense . . . there are only a few people with the charismatic power of mind that could put together the coalition he did. There is a question whether any new chairman could do it.[49]

The liberals do not seem to have affected committee decisions to any great extent, but they are a source of information and support for other members of Congress who are critical of the military or defense spending.[50]

The overriding consideration which has af-

fected Hebert's committee as well as the others is the prevailing mood within Congress. To lose a vote on the floor damages a committee's prestige and influence. For this very reason, the Senate Armed Services Committee increased its staff from nine to twenty in 1971; they are now better able to justify and defend their bill on the floor. In a similar manner, since 1969 the Joint Economic Committee and the Appropriations Committees have begun utilizing the General Accounting Office (GAO) to prepare special studies and evaluations of the development and procurement of weapons systems. As many as forty-three major weapons systems are monitored on a continuing basis to determine cost, scheduling, performance, and reasons for changes in any of these items.[51] GAO has not only increased the size of the Defense Division in Washington from 264 in 1967 to an estimated 360 in 1972, but it is devoting an increasingly large proportion of its field staff to defense activities.

Public opinion has been viewed as a major factor for understanding both the role Congress plays in building a consensus and why Congress adopts certain attitudes. Growing antiwar sentiment, concern over domestic problems, and a growing skepticism of the military have become realities within both Congress and our society. The question whether Congress influences the people or the public influences Congress diminishes in significance when the movement is in one general direction, with groups in both places reinforcing one another. This appears to have been what happened after 1965. Peace groups strengthened the Senate doves' position; adverse public reaction to a prolonged, indecisive Vietnam War created a more receptive audience for the congressional investigations of mismanagement and corruption. The end result has been a fairly widespread public desire for reduced military spending, as demonstrated by recent opinion polls (Table 5). Just as noteworthy is the very drastic change from the earlier time period.

The significance of the more critical attitudes can be interpreted in a number of ways. A

---

fense areas. Janowitz largely supports this view. Arnold Kanter argues that Congress has a programmatic orientation; however, he bases his conclusion almost entirely on policy outcomes, which appear to be program-oriented for a variety of reasons, rather than on the policy process itself. See Aaron Wildavsky, *The Politics of the Budgetary Process* (Boston: Little, Brown & Co., 1964); Fenno, *op. cit.*; Janowitz, *op. cit.*, pp. 354–58; and Arnold Kanter, "Congress and the Defense Budget: 1960–1970," *APSR*, 66, no. 1 (March 1972): 129–43.

[47] Kenneth Entin discusses the development of committee majority and minority factions in "The House Armed Services Committee: Patterns of Decision-Making during the McNamara Years," an address delivered at the Twenty-sixth Annual Meeting of the Western Political Science Association, Portland, March 23–25, 1972. For a more recent discussion of the liberals on the committee, see David E. Rosenbaum, "The Age of Hebert: Dissent Now Fostered on Key House Panel," *New York Times*, April 13, 1971, p. 26.

[48] U.S. Congress, *Congressional Quarterly Weekly Report*, 30, no. 13 (March 25, 1972): 673–77.

[49] *Ibid.*, 29, no. 1 (January 1, 1972): 25.

[50] Rosenbaum, *op. cit.*, p. 26.

[51] U.S. Congress, House, Subcommittee of the Committee on Appropriations, *Legislative Branch Appropriations for 1970*, 91st Cong., 1st sess., 1969, pp. 538–39 and 625–27; and "Status of the Acquisition of Selected Major Weapon Systems," report to the Congress by the Comptroller General, February 6, 1970.

Table 5

Opinion Polls

Question: There is much discussion as to the amount this country should spend for national defense. How do you feel about this—do you think we are spending too little, too much, or about the right amount?

	Too Little	About Right	Too Much	No Opinion
March 1950	23%	44%	15%	18%
September 1953	22	45	20	13
April 1960	21	45	18	16
July 1969	8	31	52	9
March 1971	11	31	49	9

Source: Gallup Poll.

1966 article in *Public Opinion Quarterly* concluded that the attentive public for military policy was very small—only a small part of the foreign policy attentive public.[52] One can argue that the trends discussed earlier in this paper may have reflected merely an attitude and an awareness within this very small attentive public for military policy. Evidence pointing in this direction can also be inferred from the Gallup Poll. While 91 percent of the sample had an opinion on overall defense spending (Table 3), in similar polls on Nixon's ABM program in 1969, only 40 percent of the sample had an opinion. One might conclude, therefore, that the Gallup Poll reflects the attitudes the attentive public has conveyed to the mass public. However, an alternative explanation is the possibility that a large number of individuals formerly uninvolved or uninterested in military policy are now attentive—a larger attentive public is biased against the military. The growing interest in defense issues may reflect an awareness, on the part of individuals concerned with foreign or domestic issues, that financial resources are limited, and that nondefense programs must compete with defense programs.[53] While neither explanation is totally correct, both may help explain the depth and pervasiveness of current attitudes.

The executive's pre-eminence as interpreter of international events has been partially un-

dermined in Vietnam. Nevertheless, it does retain the initiative, a tremendous information-handling capability, a wide audience, and the ability to take action. President Nixon came into office on a pledge to reorder priorities, and he has attempted to establish a new consensus somewhere between the earlier promilitary and extreme antimilitary attitudes. In many specific aspects he has been successful, but a consensus has not been established within Congress, much less in the country as a whole.

In analyzing the executive's relations with Congress, one can focus on at least three major aspects: personalities, structure, and outcomes. One might argue that Secretary Laird, with his knowledge, experience, and contacts in Congress, could have been more effective than McNamara in generating support for the military. An alternative focal point would be structure, showing how centralization initiated by McNamara has decreased congressional access to service viewpoints. A third line of reasoning would stress the outcomes of the defense policy process. Personalities and organizational structure do have a major impact, but primarily as a result of their ability to influence the actions, policies, and positions taken by the executive.

Looking briefly at personalities, Secretary Laird might have used his personal contacts to gain support on specific issues before Congress, but the good will toward him and his influence was limited by issues, events, and the individuals involved. Secretary Laird made a special effort and was more successful than most, such as on the draft-lottery plan and the ABM in 1969.[54] But since the President and Secretary of Defense have different institutional perspectives from Congress, they cannot rely on friendships to override other considerations either on important issues or on a continuing basis.

The organizational aspect raises many important questions. A number of studies indicate that interservice rivalries give Congress the opportunity to hear opposing opinions, and thus it can have a greater policy impact.[55] Such an instance can be seen in the 1958 reduction (by 20 percent) of the Bomarc and Nike-Hercules

---

[52] Bernard C. Cohen, "The Military Policy Public," *Public Opinion Quarterly*, 30, no. 2 (1966): 200–211.

[53] See also Adam Yarmolinsky, *The Military Establishment* (New York: Harper & Row, 1971), pp. 93–95.

[54] Julius Duscha, "The Political Pro Who Runs Defense," *New York Times Magazine*, June 13, 1971, pp. 19–33.

[55] See Dexter, *op. cit.*, p. 187; Huntington, *The Soldier and the State*, p. 422; and Kolodziej, *op. cit.*

missile systems.[56] Rivalries were also significant in the FY 1960 budget, where Congress appropriated 20 percent more than the President requested for limited-war forces.[57] The rivalry, and therefore Congress's opportunity to adjudicate controversies among military "experts," was lessened during McNamara's tenure as Secretary of Defense. The effect of Secretary Laird's "participatory management" was in question during his tenure as Secretary of Defense, 1969–1972.

Probably the most important means by which the executive can influence Congress is through policies themselves: how the executive interprets events, its policy statements, and budgetary proposals. Organizational changes can be important to the extent that they affect executive policies or allow these outcomes to be challenged by the services. President Kennedy was able to generate considerable support for military spending because of the publicity given to the "missile gap." President Johnson used the Gulf of Tonkin incident in 1964 to mobilize congressional and public support. In these cases, personal contacts could not have changed the mood of Congress to the same extent as the events themselves and the Administration's interpretation of these events.

The growth and impact of interest groups, particularly defense industry and research organizations, appear to have an increasingly important influence on American policy, public attitudes, and Congress. However, Russett found no correlation between Senate voting and defense contracting in 1967–1968.[58] The direct impact of the so-called military-industrial complex is questionable, but the indirect effects and adverse side effects are an explainable, if not justifiable, result of the military's involvement in the procurement, research, and development of modern weapons.[59] The impact of mass media also is ambiguous, but it has played a more important part in the breakdown of the consensus. Without the publicity it gave to controversial aspects of Vietnam and defense problems, the earlier consensus probably would have lasted much longer.

[56] Dawson, *op. cit.*, pp. 47–50.

[57] The Army had developed its case for a limited-war capability by 1956; see Kolodziej, *op. cit.*, pp. 229–51.

[58] Russett, *op. cit.*, pp. 77–86.

[59] Yarmolinsky, *op. cit.*, pp. 54–68; and Rice, *op. cit.*, pp. 178–94.

CONCLUSIONS

This paper has examined congressional-defense relations by focusing on the attitudes of Congress and how these attitudes have changed over time. Congress did in fact assume a supportive attitude toward defense prior to 1965. Subsequent to 1965, congressional and public attitudes have become more critical, even though a new consensus has not been established. During both periods, Congress provided one of the major public forums for debate on defense issues. Thus, Congress has played a significant role in the defense policy process—a role of reinforcing or undermining a climate of opinion which limits the executive's policy options.

The various factors which contributed to the maintenance of, and changes in, the congressional mood have been discussed. Changing attitudes can be tied to shifts within committees and in the committees' relations with one another and other members of Congress. External factors played a major part, with events being one of the most important considerations. Public opinion has also been an important influence on the mood of Congress. It has had an impact on congressional attitudes and has been shaped by these attitudes. The executive and, to a lesser extent, interest groups and the media have made their own particular contributions to shaping congressional attitudes.

In terms of the many aspects of congressional-defense relations, this paper has only begun to summarize a wide variety of ideas and studies. Considerable latitude exists in the interpretation of events and the congressional process. Much remains to be re-examined and studied in depth. A normative judgment as to whether Congress should have played a different role in the defense policy process at any particular time has been avoided.

The most important question raised by this paper concerns present and future trends. To what extent have relationships been stabilized within either the House or the Senate, or between these systems and their environment? This question can be addressed from two related perspectives: policy consensus and process stabilization. Is a new policy consensus emerging? And, in terms of the activities, relationships, and influence of the participants, to what extent is the process being stabilized?

Stability in either attitudes or relationships will probably contribute to stability in the other.

Attempting to predict future trends is hazardous but can be a useful exercise. Even as Vietnam fades, other very serious long-term problems confront decisionmakers in Congress and the executive. Among the most important of these is the competition for scarce resources which can only become more intense with the escalation of: (1) the cost of social programs; (2) demands for more and better government services; (3) the cost of developing and procuring modern weapons systems; (4) the cost of military manpower as the nation moves toward an all-volunteer force; and (5) the taxpayers' resistance to additional taxes. These trends will very likely continue for a good number of years, and they will most likely lead to a continuation of the present critical attitudes toward defense, even by many who are promilitary and support a strong military capability. With changes in Congress's membership, committees, committee staffs, and GAO, subtle but important modifications in the process may be institutionalized. Considerable support for the military does exist in Congress, as well as in our society, but a series of major crises would probably be necessary to revive the kind of support the military enjoyed between 1954 and 1965. Neither the prodefense consensus nor the subsequent breakdown in that consensus came about without a long series of reinforcing events and spokesmen. However, the present critical approach to defense issues must also be applied to domestic programs. In an atmosphere in which détente and Strategic Arms Limitations Talks have become an integral part of national policy, prudence and reason must prevail on both sides of the debate if a meaningful balance is to be achieved.

THE PRESIDENT AND THE MILITARY

MORTON H. HALPERIN

Halperin argues that the military poses a unique set of problems for the President because of three factors: its role in providing information; its expertise on combat operations; and its prestige and influence with Congress. Presidents have used a number of techniques to overcome the limitations of their power, including: (1) reorganization; (2) a military adviser in the White House; (3) a civilian adviser in the White House; (4) reliance on the Secretary of Defense; (5) reliance on the Secretary of State; (6) reliance on scientists; (7) reliance on the Office of Management and Budget; and (8) ad hoc techniques. Halperin recommends separating the Joint Chiefs of Staff (JCS) from the service chiefs (to make the JCS more independent) and granting the unified commanders and the service chiefs direct access to the President.

I

All Presidents are dependent on the permanent bureaucracies of government inherited from their predecessors. A President must have the information and analysis of options which the bureaucracies provide in order to anticipate problems and make educated choices. He must, in most cases, also have the cooperation of the bureaucracies to turn his decisions into governmental action. A bureaucracy can effectively defuse a presidential decision by refusing to support it with influential members of Congress or to implement it faithfully.

The President's dependence on the bureaucracy and his limited freedom to maneuver are acute in all areas. The military, however, poses a unique set of problems for him. These arise in part from the President's limitations when he is seeking military advice. When the National Security Council (NSC) or other presidential sessions are convened to discuss high-level foreign and national security matters, the President has a great deal of influence on the selection of all those who will attend, except the Chairman of the Joint Chiefs of Staff (JCS), who must be chosen from a small group of senior career military officers. Compare also the President's ability to appoint noncareer people to subcabinet and ambassadorial posts with the limitations on his range of selection for appointments to senior military positions or overseas military commands.

One dilemma for the President is finding alternative sources of military advice. The military, for example, has a virtual monopoly on providing information to the President about the readiness and capabilities of U.S., or even Allied, forces. Other groups and individuals can provide advice on many "military" questions, but their access to information is limited. The President may call for judgments from his Secretary of Defense, but the Secretary's analysis must rely on the basic factual material and field evaluations provided by the military.

Judgments about the likely effectiveness of American combat operations are also the exclusive province of the military. In assessing the potential effects of a diplomatic move, the President can turn not only to career Foreign Service Officers but also to businessmen, academics, and intelligence specialists in other agencies. On the other hand, if he wishes to know how many American divisions would be necessary to defend Laos against a Chinese attack, the legitimacy of advice from groups other than the military is distinctly reduced. The military's influence on the information and evaluation of options which reach the President is further enhanced by the important role it plays in the preparation of national intelligence estimates.

Yet another source of leverage for the military is the prestige and influence that military leaders have enjoyed, at least in the past, with leading figures in Congress. Until quite recently, this influence limited presidential effectiveness with Congress and the general public. Even now, military influence continues to be strong with the leaders of the Armed Services Committees and appropriations subcommittees. Legislation clearly gives the military the right to inform congressional committees directly of their differences with administration policy, when asked. Senior military officers frequently exercise that right. In addition, military views on matters of major concern to the services often become known to the press. Thus, Presidents have shied away from decisions that they believed the military would take to the Congress and the public, and have frequently felt obliged to negotiate with the military.

For example, both Presidents Truman and Eisenhower carried on extensive negotiations with the military to secure its support for defense reorganization programs which appeared to have little chance of getting through Congress without military acquiescence. Later Presidents have shied away from defense reorganizations requiring congressional approval, at least in part because of the difficulty of gaining military concurrence, or congressional action without the concurrence. The backing of the military has also been vital to Presidents in other important programs. Truman, for example, relied heavily on the military to endorse his Korean War policies, especially in his disagreement with General Douglas MacArthur over limiting the war. MacArthur, who then commanded the UN forces in Korea, wanted to expand the war to China and to use nuclear weapons. The Joint Chiefs were not in favor of the expansion, and Omar Bradley, Chairman of the Joint Chiefs and a much-decorated World War II hero, strengthened Truman's position enormously when he stated publicly that MacArthur's proposal would lead to "the wrong war, in the wrong place, at the wrong time."

The political influence of the military has been substantially reduced in the last few years. The fact that the Joint Chiefs favor a particular proposal is no longer a guarantee of congressional support and may in some cases be counterproductive. For example, the Joint Chiefs were not asked by the Nixon Administration to play a major role in defending the Safeguard ABM. Nevertheless, the fact that the Joint Chiefs still wield influence with certain members of Congress and with some parts of the public may inhibit the President, particularly if he fears a right-wing attack or needs a two-thirds vote to get a treaty through the Senate.

The implementation of presidential decisions by the military works both for and against the Chief Executive. The military tradition of discipline, efficiency, and a clearly delineated chain of command increases the probability that precise orders will be observed and carried out with dispatch. However, the fact that the military implements decisions according to standard procedures may cause presidential orders to be misconstrued through oversimplification. The Joint Chiefs will defer to the field commander and not monitor his compliance carefully. Moreover, Presidents find it difficult to develop alternate means to secure implementation of decisions in the military domain. For example, the President may use special envoys in place of career Foreign Service Officers to carry out delicate negotiations, while he can hardly send a retired businessman to land American forces in Lebanon or to command a nuclear missile-carrying submarine.

Presidents also have great difficulty convincing the military to create new capabilities, which they may need in the future, but which might tend to alter the traditional role of a particular branch. The services emphasize the forces which conform to their notion of the essence of their roles and resist capabilities which involve interservice cooperation (e.g., airlift), noncombat roles (e.g., advisers), and elite forces (e.g., Green Berets). At least until recently, they have also resisted the maintenance of combat-ready nonnuclear forces.

II

This is not to suggest that the President's problems with the military are greater than, for example, those with the Department of Agriculture or other agencies with strong links to domestic constituencies and congressional committees. Nor is it to suggest that the information and advice given the President by the military has over the years been less valuable than the advice of others. The point is rather that within the foreign-policy field the greatest limitations on the President's freedom of action tend to come from the military. None of our Presidents has been content with his relations with the military.

In fact, Presidents have used a number of devices to overcome limitations on their power, to get the information and advice they want, and to find support for implementing their decisions. Presidential strategies have varied, depending on the type of issue and depending on whether they were seeking (1) information or options, (2) political support, or (3) faithful implementation.

Their techniques have included the following.

REORGANIZATIONS

The Nixon National Security Council system and the appointment of the President's Blue Ribbon Panel on Defense Reorganization (Fitzhugh Panel) suggested a return to the emphasis on reorganization which tended to dominate thinking in the early postwar period and, indeed, through 1960. Reorganization efforts within the Pentagon have aimed at securing coordinated military advice rather than separate advice from each service. Presidents have in general pressed the Joint Chiefs to transcend service biases and to come up with agreed positions based on a unified perspective. Eisenhower was particularly adverse to JCS splits. But the success of these efforts has been relatively limited. Most observers conclude that JCS papers still tend to reflect particular service views, by way of either deference or compromise, rather than the unified military judgment of a "true" Joint Staff. Secretaries of Defense have not looked upon the Joint Staff as part of their own staff.

The reorganization of the National Security Council system beginning in 1969 appeared to have been designed to bring to bear a variety of different views on military problems. The evaluation of alternate military forces is centered in the Council's Verification Panel. This group first considered the Strategic Arms Limitation Talks (SALT) and then the prospects

and problems of mutual force reductions in Europe, thereby going beyond traditional military and intelligence channels. The Defense Program Review Committee was designed to apply expertise to a review of budgetary decisions from the Office of Management and Budget and the President's economic advisers, as well as the State Department and the Arms Control and Disarmament Agency. The NSC system itself was designed to take into account the views of the State Department and other governmental agencies about military commitments, bases, overseas departments, and military assistance. At the same time, these efforts assured the military of orderly consideration of its views, reflecting the judgment that the military is more willing to participate faithfully in the implementation of a decision where it has been overruled if it feels that military views have been fully taken into account.

MILITARY ADVISER IN THE WHITE HOUSE

President Franklin Roosevelt relied heavily on Admiral William Leahy as the Chief of Staff to the Commander in Chief. Truman for a brief period continued to use Leahy and then, on a part-time basis, relied on General Eisenhower for advice on budgetary issues while Eisenhower was President of Columbia University. Truman later turned to the Chairman of the Joint Chiefs.

Eisenhower, as his own military adviser in the White House, had only a junior military officer in the person of Colonel Andrew Goodpaster, who functioned in effect as a staff secretary, collecting and summarizing for the President intelligence materials from the State Department and the CIA, as well as from the military.

Kennedy, after the Bay of Pigs operation, brought General Maxwell Taylor into the White House as the military representative of the President, and Taylor advised the President on a broad range of issues involving all aspects of national security policy. When Taylor moved over to become Chairman of the Joint Chiefs, a JCS liaison office was created in the White House which worked primarily with the President's Assistant for National Security Affairs.

President Johnson relied primarily on other mechanisms but did use General Taylor as a White House consultant after his return from

Vietnam. Taylor functioned in relation to the Vietnam issue, providing an alternate source of advice and information to the President on options open to him in Vietnam operations and negotiations.

President Nixon recalled General Goodpaster briefly during the transition period and the very early days of his first Administration, but since then has not had a senior military adviser in the White House. Henry Kissinger's deputy was Army Major General Alexander Haig. He ensured, along with the JCS liaison office, that Kissinger and the President are aware of JCS concerns, but he did not serve as an alternate source of military advice.

A CIVILIAN ADVISER IN THE WHITE HOUSE

There has been a growing trend in the postwar period toward presidential reliance on White House staff assistance in both domestic and national security policy. In the national security field, civilian assistance has been used not only as a source of additional information, advice, and options but also as an aid to the President in seeing that his decisions are carried through.

Truman tended to rely on his cabinet officers and the uniformed military, but there were episodic interventions by civilians in the White House. Under Truman, Clark Clifford became heavily involved in the negotiations which led to the Defense Unification Act and the National Security Council system. Later he contributed to the creation of the Atomic Energy Commission and the continued control of atomic weapons by the commission. Averell Harriman, who became Truman's national security adviser just before the Korean War, functioned briefly during the early stages of the war as a spokesman for the President's position; his tasks included a visit to General MacArthur to explain the President's policies to him and to seek his compliance.

Eisenhower had no single national security adviser in the White House. His Assistants for National Security Council Affairs were involved only in the very limited number of issues that were handled in the rather stylized machinery of the National Security Council system as then constituted. Eisenhower brought in several advisers for specific issues, including

Nelson Rockefeller, but these advisers tended to interact and overlap with Secretary of State Dulles rather than with the Department of Defense. They were responsible for some new initiatives, such as Eisenhower's "open skies" proposal in 1954, but the instances are few.

The regularization and institutionalization of a civilian adviser in the White House on national security matters came with President Kennedy's appointment of McGeorge Bundy. Bundy, following the Bay of Pigs fiasco, moved to increase the independence of the White House in securing information by arranging to get a good deal of the raw material directly from the field, including State, Defense, and CIA cable traffic. Bundy also assumed primary responsibility for briefing the President. Despite the expanded role which involved them in many foreign policy matters with military implications, neither Bundy nor Walt Rostow, Johnson's Adviser for National Security Affairs, was heavily engaged in Defense budgetary matters. Under President Nixon, Henry Kissinger has been as active in Defense Department matters as he is in those for which the State Department has primary responsibility. Nixon appears to rely upon Kissinger as an alternative source of information and options on the broad range of military and national security matters, and as a channel for various kinds of military advice.

RELIANCE ON THE SECRETARY OF DEFENSE

Truman and Eisenhower tended to rely on their Secretaries of Defense primarily to secure the implementation of their decisions, particularly Defense budgetary decisions. They expected the Secretaries to bear the weight of military objections to ceilings on defense spending and to force the services to develop forces within those ceilings. Even in this role the Defense Secretaries were of limited value to the President, since they tended to become spokesmen for the military desire for increased spending.

The appointment of Robert S. McNamara brought to fruition a trend which had been developing gradually and which had accelerated during the brief tenure of Secretary Thomas Gates. This called for the Secretary of Defense to become, in effect, the principal military adviser to the President, superseding the Joint

Chiefs. Over time, Kennedy and then Johnson, at least until the Vietnam War accelerated in late 1965, tended to look to the Secretary of Defense for advice on commitments, bases, overseas deployments, and military aid, as well as on budgetary decisions. The Secretary's job included absorbing the advice tendered by the military and combining that in his recommendations to the President. Both Kennedy and Johnson did, of course, continue to meet with the Chairman of the Joint Chiefs in formal sessions of the National Security Council and in other meetings, but by and large they received military judgments and advice through the filter of the Secretary of Defense. As the Vietnam War heated up, JCS Chairman General Earle Wheeler was included in Johnson's regular Tuesday lunches and began to act as an independent vehicle for reporting JCS views to the President, at least on the range of issues discussed at those meetings. Defense Secretary Laird has continued the tradition of taking positions on substantive issues of military policy and operations, as well as on Defense budgetary issues, although the President seems to regard him simply as a second source of advice on military questions. The Secretary and the Joint Chiefs have a co-equal role in the National Security Council and in all of its subordinate institutions.

RELIANCE ON THE SECRETARY OF STATE

No President has given the Secretary of State a dominant role in decisions regarding combat operations or the Defense budget. Truman did call on General Marshall—when he was Secretary of State—for support in keeping the Defense budget down, and Nixon has brought the Secretary's staff into the Defense budgetary process through the Defense Program Review Committee. However, on issues concerning commitments, bases, overseas deployments, and military aid, Truman tended to rely largely on Acheson's judgment, and Eisenhower depended to a large extent on Dulles. Secretary Rusk played a major role in these issues along with Secretary McNamara.

RELIANCE ON SCIENTISTS

Although scientists have occasionally been used to evaluate combat operations, by and large their role has been limited to issues re-

flected in the Defense budget. Eisenhower depended, particularly in the later years of his Administration, on the chief scientist in the Pentagon (the Director of Defense Research and Engineering) and on his science advisers. Kennedy also looked to his science adviser, Jerome Wiesner, for alternate advice on the Defense budget, as well as on arms control matters, particularly those relating to the nuclear testing issue. The role of the science advisers seemed to decline precipitously under Johnson and Nixon, with their energies going largely to non-Defense matters.

RELIANCE ON THE BUREAU OF THE BUDGET

The role of the Budget Bureau (now Office of Management and Budget) in Defense decisions has been very limited. Truman and Eisenhower relied upon the Budget Director to help set a ceiling on Defense spending, but the Budget Bureau did not get involved in deciding how that money would be spent. Under Eisenhower, Kennedy, and Johnson it became a matter of tradition that the Budget Director would have to appeal Secretarial decisions on the Defense budget to the President, the reverse of the situation in all other departments. Press reports suggested that initially Nixon had reversed this process, but he now appears to have returned to this traditional pattern. The Budget Director sits on the Defense Program Review Committee, but the extent of Budget Bureau influence is difficult to determine.

AD HOC TECHNIQUES

Presidents have used a number of ad hoc or special techniques to secure information and options on military questions. One technique frequently used during the Truman and Eisenhower periods was the President-appointed commission. Nixon's Fitzhugh Panel may mark a return to the use of this technique, although it has thus far been limited to organizational, rather than substantive, questions.

Occasionally, Presidents have sent special representatives into the field to investigate military questions. Kennedy, for example, sent an old friend and military officer to the camp which was preparing the Cuban guerrillas for the Bay of Pigs operation, and Richard Nixon sent British guerrilla-war expert Brigadier General Thompson to Vietnam for an independent assessment.

Now and then a President has been fortunate enough to have the concurrence of the military on a particular policy without having to bargain. That the Joint Chiefs of Staff opposed expansion of the Korean War and felt that General MacArthur had indeed been insubordinate was of critical importance to Truman in securing public acceptance of this policy. However, in most cases, the President has been forced to bargain for the public support of the Joint Chiefs. Truman had to accept the case for German rearmament in order to gain JCS approval to send American forces to Europe. Kennedy and his Secretary of Defense engaged in long hours of bargaining with the Joint Chiefs before they were able to devise an acceptable safeguard program of standby preparations for nuclear testing that made it possible for the Joint Chiefs to give their reluctant support to the Nuclear Test Ban Treaty. Johnson felt obliged to have the JCS on board before he would order the cessation of the bombing of North Vietnam in 1968.

In some cases, the President has sought to use the prestige and power of his office to accomplish his objectives in the face of military opposition. This tactic has a better chance of success when the decisions involve only executive department action; when the Chiefs are split; and particularly when the decisions do not require the use of armed forces in combat operations. But it can be done in other cases. For example, on the matter of civilian control of atomic weapons and the creation of a civilian-dominated Atomic Energy Commission, Truman appealed to the public and Congress over the objections of the military, and was able to win. Eisenhower in the same way (although less successfully) enlisted the support of the American business community in his effort to reorganize the Defense Department against the judgment of the military.

Presidents have had the greatest success in bypassing the military on Defense budgetary limitations because military demands are essentially open-ended and always have to be overruled. However, the appeal to fiscal conservatism and alternative demands for resources also have tended to check Defense expenditures.

III

Techniques used to improve the information and options that reach the President can also be applied to the implementation of decisions. For example, civilian advisers in the White House have been used to monitor compliance with presidential decisions, and other Presidents have tended to rely on the Secretary of Defense to see that their decisions were carried out.

In addition, Presidents have sometimes resorted to selecting military officers whom they felt shared their views and therefore would act to implement them properly. The most dramatic case came in 1953, when Eisenhower replaced all of the Joint Chiefs of Staff and appointed Admiral Radford, a known supporter of his policy of massive nuclear retaliation, as Chairman of the Joint Chiefs and chose service chiefs who by and large were prepared to comply. After the Cuban missile crisis, Admiral George Anderson, who had not cooperated fully with the President, was not reappointed to the post of Chief of Naval Operations. However, there are severe limits to the value of such actions: General Ridgway and later General Taylor, the Army Chiefs of Staff appointed by Eisenhower, resisted the reduction in the size of the Army and the Administration's reliance on massive nuclear retaliation. When their views were ignored they resigned and protested publicly. In response to Admiral Anderson's reassignment as Ambassador to Portugal, Congress legislated statutory terms for members of the Joint Chiefs.

Another technique that has been used to increase compliance with presidential decisions is the creation of new organizations which reflect new desires. The most successful of these efforts was the creation within the Navy of a Special Projects Office to monitor the Polaris program and to alter promotion procedures so that command of a Polaris submarine would permit promotion to senior grades. The least successful effort was Kennedy's attempt in the early 1960s to give the military greater flexibility in dealing with counterinsurgency operations by creating the Green Berets.

IV

The decline of the prestige of the military over the past several years has given President Nixon greater freedom to determine how advice from the military reaches him and to accept or reject that advice. The experience of the postwar period suggests two basic changes which the President could institute now that would increase his leverage vis-à-vis the military; one involves the channel by which he receives advice from senior military officers, and the other concerns the role of civilian advisers.

The experience of the last twenty-five years suggests that the effort to reorganize the Pentagon and then to demand "unified" military advice from the Joint Chiefs of Staff has been a failure. As noted above, most observers who have had the opportunity to view the product of the Joint Chiefs would argue that unified JCS papers reflect either a compromise among the services, a form of logrolling in which the proposals of all services are endorsed, or deference to the service or field commander most concerned. As long as the function of the Joint Staff is to come up with a paper that will be endorsed by all of the Chiefs, there does not appear to be any way to alter the situation fundamentally, although some progress has been made in the last several years in increasing the flexibility and independence of the Joint Staff.

More radical changes must be effected if the President is to get good military advice. The key to improving the situation is to separate the Chairman of the Joint Chiefs of Staff and the Joint Staff from the service chiefs. The President and the Secretary of Defense would in this case solicit the separate views of each of the service chiefs and of the Chairman of the Joint Chiefs, and, where appropriate, the views of the relevant unified and specified commanders (e.g., commanders in Europe and Asia and the head of the Strategic Air Command). These latter views might be channeled to the Secretary through the Chairman of the Joint Chiefs. The Chairman would in turn be the officer in the line of command through the President and the Secretary of Defense to the commanders (by-passing the service chiefs) for carrying out operations in the field.

The basic rationale behind this change in procedure is that the service chiefs and the unified and specified commands constitute the highest level at which reliable (first-hand) information and advice are available. The Joint Staff, when it needs information, must solicit either the service staffs in Washington or the field commanders. In fact, JCS information and advice presented to the President and the Secretary usually come from the services and the

subordinate service commands in the field. For example, most of the positions taken by the Joint Chiefs of Staff on questions relating to Vietnam simply involved a JCS endorsement of the recommendations of General Westmoreland or General Abrams, the army commanders in Vietnam, and Admiral Sharp, Commander in Chief of the Pacific, who had particular responsibility for the bombing operations.

On questions of requirements for overseas bases, to take another example, the Joint Chiefs in most cases simply endorse the position of the service which utilizes the base. On budgetary issues, they tend to endorse all of the programs desired by each of the services. When forced to choose on an issue of policy, the Joint Chiefs compromise among the different service positions rather than attempt to develop a position based on a unified military point of view.

Under the proposed change of procedure the President and the Secretary of Defense would be made aware of differing positions which might otherwise be compromised. In addition, this would leave the Chairman of the Joint Chiefs and the Joint Staff free from the job of developing a compromise position and therefore able to present the Secretary of Defense with a military judgment separate from the interests of the services. If this process is to succeed, the President and the Secretary will have to choose a Chairman of the Joint Chiefs with whom they can work. Then, if the system is developed properly, the Chairman and the Joint Staff would come to be seen as part of the Office of the Secretary of Defense, providing him and the President with military advice which could be weighed against the advice of the operators—the service chiefs and the unified and specified commanders. The influence of the Chairman of the Joint Chiefs would come from his record of persuasiveness with the President and the Secretary of Defense. They will take his judgments seriously if his choice is shown to be based on a broader range of considerations than the advice of the service chiefs.

Such a procedure would increase the probability that imaginative and innovative proposals would reach the President. It would also make it more likely that the President would become aware of the wide diversity of military opinions on a question and not act on an erroneous assumption that there was a unified view.

One of the few instances on record in which the President did seek separate opinions from the Joint Chiefs came in 1961, when President Kennedy was contemplating an invasion of Laos. Partly because of the Bay of Pigs episode, in which the doubts of individual chiefs about the military feasibility of the landing in Cuba never reached him, Kennedy asked each chief separately for his views in writing and then met with them as a group. He discovered by this process that each one had a slightly different position on what should be done, what troops should be committed, and what the likely outcome of American intervention would be. Receiving this conflicting advice, it was harder for Kennedy to make a decision to intervene, but it also meant that he did not make a decision under the mistaken impression that there was a unified military view either for or against the intervention.

The proposed procedure would also increase presidential flexibility in accepting or rejecting military advice because the President would no longer be confronted with a unanimous but misleading statement of JCS views. He would be able to choose among service and command viewpoints rather than have to develop a new position which in essence would overrule all of the military, inasmuch as JCS opinions now represent all the services.

In order to increase the President's freedom to choose and the likelihood that he will get faithful implementation and political support for his actions, a procedure should be developed which provides for military access to the President on issues of importance to the military. Access should be provided not only for the Chairman of the Joint Chiefs but also for the service chiefs and the unified commanders most concerned. When he finds it necessary to overrule the military, the President should justify his decision on broad political grounds; he should be seen doing so personally; and he should do so in writing by means of a clear memorandum stating his position. All of these acts would increase military willingness to go along with presidential decisions and to implement them faithfully.

The military takes seriously the President's role as Commander in Chief and also recognizes that he has broader responsibility concerned with both domestic and international political situations. They are much more amenable to being overruled on these grounds than to being told that their military judgment is questioned. (For this reason the military resented McNamara's reliance on civilians, particularly in the Office of Systems Analysis, for judgments on what they took to be purely military questions—i.e., statements of military requirements.) They also implemented decisions faithfully when assured that their position has been heard by the President and has not been lost in the filter of Secretary of Defense memoranda.

Securing separate advice from the service chiefs and other military commanders will require that the President, or at least his White House staff, spend more time digesting the separate positions. However, this seems a price worth paying to increase the flow of new ideas or doubts about proposed courses of action to the White House.

Military compliance with presidential decisions would also be enhanced by avoiding the practice of using the military to seek public support for presidential decisions. The value of such action has become considerably reduced in recent years, and such use of the military tends to legitimize and increase the importance of their opposition when they choose to oppose policy.

V

Implicit in the new procedures as suggested is a reduced role for the Secretary of Defense from that which he assumed in the 1960s. His scope would also be affected by another proposed change—that decisionmaking on matters concerning Defense budgets and the use of military force be moved outside of the Pentagon and into a broader arena involving officials from the White House and other agencies.

The Nixon Administration has moved rather significantly, at least in form and to some extent in substance, to change the locus of decisions. The creation of the Washington Special Action Group (WSAG) brings into existence for the first time a forum in which detailed contingency planning for the actual use of military force is carried out beyond the Pentagon. WSAG is chaired by the President's Assistant for National Security and includes senior State Department and CIA officials as well as civilian and military representatives of the Pentagon. It provides a forum where the military, diplomatic, and intelligence evaluations of likely use of American military forces can be brought together in a systematic way, something which was not done in the past. This institution needs to be strengthened, probably with the addition of some White House staff assigned specifically to this task.

A second institution of significance is the Defense Program Review Committee (DPRC), which also is chaired by the President's Assistant for National Security and includes representatives not only from the State Department but also from the Arms Control and Disarmament Agency, the Council of Economic Advisers, and the Office of Management and Budget. The implications of this institution are enormous. If it functions effectively, decisions not only on the total size of the Defense budget but also on major Defense programs will be made outside the Pentagon in an inter-agency forum where White House influence is dominant. The President would receive advice on Defense budgetary issues from several different perspectives. While the institution has

been created, it does not as yet appear to have either the staff or the necessary top-level direction to get into a wide range of Defense issues.

For this purpose and also to make WSAG more effective, the President's Assistant for National Security probably needs a Senior Deputy who would take some of the responsibility for White House direction of budgetary and combat decisions, and who would be explicitly charged with bringing to bear the broader concerns of the President.

The procedures suggested here in no sense imply a downgrading of military advice. Instead they are designed to assure that the President receives the full range of the existing military opinions rather than what filters through a JCS compromise procedure or a Secretary of Defense responsible for presenting military views to the President. They also aim to give the President critical commentary on military proposals from civilian officials with a different and somewhat broader range of responsibilities. In the end, good decisions will depend on the wisdom and judgment of the President. What he decides, however, is greatly influenced by the information presented to him, as well as by his sense of freedom to choose regardless of strong military and other bureaucratic pressures.

THE NIXON NSC: KISSINGER'S APPARAT

JOHN P. LEACACOS

In 1947, by Act of Congress, a National Security Council was established "to advise the President with respect to the integration of domestic, foreign, and military policies relating to the national security so as to enable the military services and the other departments and agencies of the government to cooperate more effectively in matters involving the national security." The role of the council, or "NSC," has varied with each of the five Presidents who have used it. In the past decade its staffs, headed successively by McGeorge Bundy, Walt W. Rostow, and Henry Kissinger, have moved to the center of White House decisionmaking. As President Nixon's principal adviser, Kissinger has centralized authority in the White House which in an earlier era was wielded by Secretaries of State such as Dean Acheson and John Foster Dulles. How does the Nixon NSC staff operate, and how permanent are the innovations it has brought to policymaking? What contribution has it made to forging new policies on China, arms control, world trade, and European security? How effective has it been in organizing the work of Washington's separate military and foreign affairs departments? Mr. Leacacos is Washington Bureau Chief of the Cleveland Plain Dealer, *a position he assumed in 1958 after twelve years as the* Plain Dealer's *roving correspondent in Europe and the Middle East. He is author of* Fires in the In-Basket *(1968).*

Atop Washington's complex foreign affairs bureaucracy sits the National Security Council, a twenty-four-year-old body given new status in 1969, when President Nixon moved to make it a kind of command and control center for his foreign policy. The new Nixon NSC system, run from the White House by Henry A. Kissinger, had by 1972 existed for nearly three years, producing 138 numbered study memoranda, reaching 127 formal decisions, and employing a permanent staff of about 120 personnel (more than double the pre-Nixon figure). Though the substance of its operations are necessarily secret, interviews with officials permit tentative evaluation of the strengths and weaknesses of the Kissinger NSC. There is broad agreement on the following seven points.

1. The NSC has served President Nixon more or less as he desired—that is, in the ordered style of formal answers to detailed questionnaires. The volume of this paperwork has at times been staggering, but it has sharpened focus on the search for policy choices.

2. The answers and alternatives for action "coming up through the NSC" have produced few panaceas but have contributed greater coherence of outlook in foreign affairs management. NSC recommendations are more pragmatic than academic, reflecting Kissinger's view: "We don't make foreign policy by logical syllogism."

3. Explicit insistence on the "limited" nature of U.S. power and the need for greater restraint and cautious deliberation about its exercise have been reinforced at the highest level by Nixon's habit of withdrawing to make final decisions in solitude and of frequently deciding to take no action rather than accept advice to initiate new action.

4. By being close to the President and keeping his fingers on all aspects of the NSC process personally, Kissinger without question is

Reprinted by permission and with minor changes from Foreign Policy, *1971, no. 5, pp. 2–24. Copyright © 1971 by National Affairs, Inc.*

the prime mover in the NSC system. The question arises whether the NSC would function as effectively without Kissinger, and whether it can bequeath a heritage of accomplishment to be absorbed by the permanent machinery of government.

5. Secretary of State William P. Rogers operates within the NSC system and also utilizes it as a forum to establish whatever policy position is preferred by his State Department; but he side-steps the NSC on occasion to carry his demurrer, dissent, or alternate position to the President privately.

6. Defense Secretary Melvin R. Laird (1969–1973) was less personally involved in the NSC process, being apparently indifferent to what he believed was unnecessary NSC paperwork, which he left to his deputy, David Packard. Laird's main day-to-day operational preoccupation was with the exit of U.S. forces from Vietnam. The International Security Affairs Bureau in the Pentagon performed poorly by Washington bureaucratic standards.

7. The influence on foreign policy of the military, including the Joint Chiefs of Staff, who are usually represented in the NSC process, is at its lowest point in several years. This has been attributed to the anticlimactic winding-down atmosphere of the Vietnam War, and to the fact that the Joint Chiefs' once die-hard views and abstract argumentation on strategic nuclear superiority over the Soviet Union have been successfully emulsified into the Nixon-Kissinger basic principles for SALT negotiations with Russia. Kissinger has commented: "In my experience with the military, they are more likely to accept decisions they do not like than any other group."

From time to time, gears have clashed within the system. The State Department has complained bitterly of the "Procrustean bed" fashioned by the Kissinger staff. Meeting excessive White House demands, bureaucrats allege, robs the State and Defense Departments of manpower hours needed for day-to-day operations. After his first year, Kissinger conceded: "Making foreign policy is easy; what is difficult is its coordination and implementation."

White House NSC staffers, on the other hand, exuberant at their top-dog status, express a degree of condescension for the work of the traditional departments. In 1969 Kissinger staffers rated State-chaired studies and recommendations only "50 to 70 percent acceptable" and based on mediocre reporting which failed to sift wheat from chaff in the political cables constantly arriving from 117 U.S. embassies overseas. The Kissinger staff says that it has to hammer out the real choices on the hard issues, since a cynical and sometimes bored bureaucracy offers up too many "straw options." State Department planners, for their part, criticize the NSC staff for overdoing the options game. As senior Foreign Service officers say: "After all, what needs to be done is usually fairly obvious common sense. The crux is *how*, and *when* to do it."

COGITO ERGO IG

The NSC system in 1972 is not the tidy blueprint of January 1969. The older it has gotten, the more informal and overlapping its procedures have become. The amounts of analysis manufactured sometimes threaten to outrun the capacity of the decisionmakers to absorb. Crucial issues have been maneuvered to committees chaired by Kissinger, thence directly to the President. The frequency of full NSC meetings has diminished: 37 in 1969, 21 in 1970, and 10 in 1971 (through September).

Normally, an NSC study is jointly prepared through the IGs (Interdepartmental Groups) by all concerned agencies (State, Defense, CIA, etc.). There are six IGs—for Europe, the Far East, the Middle East, Africa, Latin America, and politico-military affairs—all of which are headed by Assistant Secretaries of State. The spread of the 138 NSC study assignments through the first thirty-three months of the Nixon Administration was: Middle East, 14; Far East, 12; Latin America, 9; Africa, 4; Europe, 11; Verification Panel, 2; Under Secretaries Committee, 1; individual departments and agencies, 13; *ad hoc* groups, 67. Due to overlapping, it is estimated that at least 30 percent of the studies contained contributions from the State Department's Bureau of European Affairs, more than 40 percent from its Bureau of East Asian and Pacific Affairs, as many as 80 percent from its Bureau of Politico-Military Affairs, and close to 90 percent from its Bureau of Intelligence and Research, which had a finger in practically every pie.

The Middle Eastern shop is one of the few to have a high degree of autonomy from "normal" procedures. Assistant Secretary Joseph J. Sisco works directly with the President, Secretary Rogers, and Kissinger, although a Kissinger staff man, Harold Saunders, monitors the paper flow.

Vietnam policy has been under close White House NSC supervision. Subsidiary NSC units at State, Defense, and CIA serve as operational checkpoints for coordination, and update and verify information required for decision via the NSC Vietnam Special Studies Group. The quality of that group's analysis is rated high by Kissinger—on a par with the exhaustive SALT inquiries. It was chaired by Wayne Smith,[1] Kissinger's systems analysis specialist, to guarantee that no White House doubt is left unanswered. Smith's staff aimed at precise intelligence on current Vietnam operations, but also tried to make projections five years ahead. A second, separate NSC *ad hoc* group on Vietnam, chaired by Deputy Assistant Secretary of State William H. Sullivan, who also works directly with the President, Rogers, and Kissinger, concentrates on the Paris negotiations.

Kissinger keeps a close eye on SALT via the NSC Verification Panel, Washington's "action center" for the Helsinki and Vienna talks with the Soviets. In the first Nixon years, for example, Wayne Smith monitored daily operations and Philip J. Farley, deputy director of the Arms Control and Disarmament Agency, acted as a coordinator within the larger bureaucracy.

What the Nixon Administration sees as its five principal areas of foreign affairs initiative —Vietnam, the Middle East, arms control, Berlin, China—have all been under more or less tight NSC White House grip—that is, direct Nixon-Kissinger overview. The NSC took special satisfaction in the August 1971 four-power Berlin accord because *there*, it felt, it had prevented the bureaucracy from rushing into a premature agreement. Progress on SALT and dramatic changes in China policy also are cited as achievements of the new NSC system, although Vietnam remains a more ambiguous test case, and most Middle Eastern peace moves have come directly from the State Department, not the NSC.

[1] See "New Concepts and New Tools to Shape the Defense Program," pp. 349–58 of this volume.

WSAG TO THE RESCUE

Between the interdepartmental groups at the base and himself and his personal staff at the apex of the NSC pyramid, Kissinger has created several special units for unique tasks. One is the Under Secretaries Committee, now chaired by Under Secretary of State John N. Irwin and originally designed as the chief implementing body to carry out many (but not all) presidential NSC directives. Its actual importance (never very great) continues to lapse.

Another is the Senior Review Group, now at the Under Secretary level and chaired by Kissinger, which usually gives final approval to the NSC study memoranda after making sure that "all realistic alternatives are presented." Kissinger also chairs the Defense Programs Review Committee, whose purpose is to keep the annual defense budget in line with foreign policy objectives. A further group, again chaired by Kissinger, though not formally part of the NSC structure, is the "40 committee" which supervises covert intelligence operations (though CIA and Green Beret commando missions in Laos and Cambodia have been transferred to a separate NSC committee, the Washington Special Actions Group).

This last-named unit, the WSAG, is the top-level operations center for sudden crises and emergencies. It watches developing situations which could gravely affect U.S. interests, such as the apparent imminence of hostilities on the Ussuri River in 1969 between the Russians and Chinese. WSAG kept tabs on Soviet submarines in Cuba in 1969, the Jordan crisis in 1970, and the East Pakistani revolt in 1971, as well as acting as the watchdog during the Cambodian sweep and the Laotian incursion. It was created in April 1969, after Nixon's surprise and embarrassment when the North Koreans shot down an American EC-121 aircraft and the normal bureaucratic mechanisms "muffed" the incident through overcaution. WSAG's chairman is Kissinger, naturally.

Regarding WSAG's work on the Jordan crisis, Kissinger recalled: "We deliberately kept options open to do enough to discourage irresponsibility, but not so much as to give a sense of irreversibility to what was going on; to restrain outside forces (Syrian) that had intervened, but not to the point where we'd trigger a whole set of other forces (Israeli), and to make sure that Soviet power would not be used." The WSAG command-and-control function in this and other crises appeared to work more smoothly than did White House controls on Vietnam in the Johnson Administration. A classic pre-WSAG snafu occurred in 1966–1967, when airpower advocates made detailed arrangements for the rendezvous of thirteen aircraft carriers, practically all those in service, to immobilize the port of Haiphong before North Vietnam's air defenses could be organized—only to be turned down at the last minute by President Johnson.

Temporary White House NSC groups have been formed from time to time for special projects such as post-mortems over Cambodia (pre-invasion intelligence had failed to pinpoint North Vietnamese supply capabilities) and Chile (the narrow election win of Socialist President Allende was a bit of a surprise, and its implications for future U.S. policy were at first unclear).

The WSAG and the Verification Panel have emerged as the President's innermost councils of war, the closest Nixon approximation to John F. Kennedy's "ExCom," which handled the Cuban missile crisis in 1962. Highlighting the importance of these two groups was the occasional attendance at their meetings of Attorney General John N. Mitchell, who played a role with Nixon not unlike Robert Kennedy's position as chief backstair adviser for his brother, President Kennedy. Mitchell, who once sardonically described Kissinger to a society reporter as an "egocentric maniac, but brilliant and indispensable," was pictured by senior Nixon aides as a man of "soundness" and sensitivity, a hard loser at giving up U.S. interests, and a counselor valued for "good, tough, hard" judgments in complicated situations, particularly in intelligence evaluations affecting the Soviets. Mitchell said relatively little at the meetings he attended, but gave his private assessments directly to the President.

Other WSAG members were CIA Director Richard C. Helms, Deputy Defense Secretary Packard, Joint Chiefs Chairman Admiral Thomas H. Moorer, and Under Secretary of State for Political Affairs U. Alexis Johnson. WSAG likes to work with as few aides as possible. As one of its members says, this eliminates kibitzers and guards against leaks.

THIRTY KEY OFFICIALS

In all this elaborate series of NSC channels and committees, only some thirty key officials are estimated to be involved in making critical decisions. Another 300, at maximum, including officials of State, Defense, and CIA, have a partial role in contributing to the decisionmaking process and in carrying out presidential directives.

Despite his perfectionist impatience with the State Department, Kissinger realizes that his unique personal role tends to weaken the institutional role of the permanent bureaucracy. He has frequently said that he would consider it a signal achievement if his NSC system goaded the State Department into "better and better" performance. The more effective State became, the less the White House staff would have to do.

In mid-1971 the State Department began to take up the Kissinger challenge. At Secretary Rogers' urging, a new system of evaluating, country by country, programs, costs, and resources, especially those controlled overseas by other agencies, is being installed within the department. The goal is to give State more weight bureaucratically vis-à-vis other agencies in the implementation of foreign policy, thus compensating in part for the ineffectiveness of the moribund NSC Under Secretaries Committee. The long-term objective is to "institutionalize" within the State Department the procedural patterns of the Nixon NSC, thus assuring that they survive beyond the Nixon presidency. The State Department, after all, starts out with a huge advantage in manpower and trained expertise—over a thousand Foreign Service Officers in Washington, compared with the White House staff of a hundred-odd, of whom only ten are currently Foreign Service Officers. But if State is to get more of the action in this Administration, it will have to revise the trade-shop slogan of its professionals, who say, "Policy is made in the cables"—that is, the actual pattern of U.S. foreign policy in the field is literally made by the spot-instructions drafted in Washington. The White House NSC's more intellectualized approach is that policy is made in Washington *after* all the incoming cables from the field have been sifted, weighed, and related to *a priori* grand strategy. Kissinger aides finally got a handle on significant outgoing cables when new LDX (Limited Distribution Xerox) communications equipment was installed in the White House basement. This gave the NSC presidential assistants enhanced technological means to enforce White House "clearance" of all important outgoing cables.

Much of Kissinger's time is spent writing memoranda to the President, compressing the summaries of lengthy NSC studies to six pages or less. Beyond these formal tasks, he has spent countless hours with the President discussing specific problems and also responding to Nixon's contrapuntal remarks and queries concerning philosophy, history, student restlessness, foreign personalities, and public opinion. Presumably Kissinger finds in Nixon a sympathetic audience for observations like this one, made after Cambodia in May 1970: "The unrest on the campus has very deep . . . maybe even metaphysical, causes, in that it is the result of the seeming purposelessness of the modern bureaucratic state, of the sense of impotence that is produced in the individual in relation to decisions that far transcend him, and that he does not know how to influence—the result of 30 years of debunking by my colleagues and myself in which now the academic community has managed to take the clock apart and doesn't know how to put it together again." To young staff members, who have sometimes argued with him about the generation gap, Kissinger has asserted that today's youth need fathers, *not* brothers.

FROM VIGOR TO RIGOR

Behind the Nixon-Kissinger table of organization lies a philosophy that is not easily articulated in public, but that nonetheless seems real. What began in mid-1969 to be called "the Nixon Doctrine" is intended, for all its ambiguity, to symbolize a fundamental shift of foreign policy. The doctrine looks to the beginnings of a more multipolar, less bipolar balance of world power, greater emphasis on military reserves at home rather than troops abroad, and a phasing-out of U.S. experiments in unilateral "social engineering" in developing nations. It is a conscious attempt to liquidate some of the vestiges (such as Vietnam) of an outworn global containment policy, but to do so in a way that does not leave gaping power

vacuums in the wake of U.S. "limited disengagement" and also does not provoke a domestic backslide into isolationism.

From the start, Kissinger has sought to make the operating bureaucracy tie specific objectives to these broader purposes. There had, he felt, been far too much instant diplomacy in the past, crisis reaction, and concentration on tactical rather than long-term strategic interests. A new bureaucratic methodology based on probing questions followed by searching and systematic analysis of every major U.S. policy was designed to provide Washington officialdom with "a new intellectual grid." To the catchword of the Kennedy Administration —"vigor"—Kissinger added "rigor." The desired end-product of a massive reanalysis of foreign policy within the NSC was to be a series of logical options, alternatives or choices consistent with long-range U.S. goals.

In the first weeks of the Nixon Administration in 1969, Kissinger installed the framework of the new NSC system, arguing that it would help stimulate "conceptualized foreign policy germination." But the structured NSC system made for an orderliness which the bureaucracy could also translate as routine, prompting Kissinger to say later: "Process itself is a boring subject. You can make awfully stupid decisions with a brilliant process. The basic question the President has asked me to produce from the bureaucracy is: where are we going, and how are we to get there? It is the question he keeps constantly before us."

Kissinger felt that the McGeorge Bundy and Walt Rostow NSC systems of 1961–1969 were too loose, had too many prima donnas, and lacked sufficient "checks and balances" to prevent factual error or premature judgments based on false assumptions. Hence we have Kissinger's passion for elaborate filters, safety valves, and controls. At a background briefing he once said rather sadly:

Anybody who has seen high officials in Washington will recognize that one of the nightmarish aspects about it is that, contrary to what I knew in academic life where, when one is identified with a problem, one could work on it as long as necessary, [here] one is forced to develop a hierarchy of priorities. . . . There are many issues that senior officials may know are coming. They may even know how they will deal with these issues— if they only had the time to get around to them.

So one of the arts of policymaking is to order your issues in such a way that the most urgent ones get solved before some that appear less urgent hit you. . . . The greater number of issues that a country takes on, the more it taxes the psychological resilience of its leadership group. It is not possible to act wisely at every moment of time in every part of the world. It isn't possible for domestic opinion to understand long-range policy in every part of the world at every moment of time.

THE 138 MEMORANDA

Now, nearly three years after the effort began, it is increasingly clear that the Kissinger method has succeeded in shifting a number of American foreign-policy assumptions. This has occurred not through any revolution-by-*Diktat* but instead through a subtler process of evolution-by-memorandum. It is in part by forcing his staff and the larger bureaucracy to answer searching questions in detailed written memoranda, and by refusing to "accept" those memos if they are not sufficiently "rigorous," that Kissinger has churned out the beginnings of new policies toward China, arms control, and European security. His cumbersome method is at its simplest a way of making the bureaucracy think harder.

The process began in January 1969, when he asked for a study that would answer twenty-six questions on Vietnam. Ten more study assignments were given out in the next ten days. The subjects were: the Middle East, U.S. military posture, foreign aid, Japan, NATO, international monetary policy, "review of the international situation," East-West relations, Nigeria, and contingency planning.

In his first 100 days, Kissinger assigned fifty-five such study memoranda, or "term papers," as they are sometimes called. A total of eighty-five were assigned in 1969, twenty-six in 1970, and twenty-seven during the first nine months of 1971. Most of the studies and many of the early efforts were returned to their bureaucratic authors for further work on further questions before they won Kissinger's approval. Some studies, complete with annexes and tables, were a foot high. These contributed to the overkill of planning by not being read by the principal NSC officials, because they were simply too long to digest. But shorter studies, prepared in a careful format to outline proposed

choices, costs, and consequences did succeed in widening the horizons of policymakers. NSC aides felt the sharpness of Kissinger's displeasure whenever they let a major policy consideration "fall between the cracks," as occurred when the issue of toxins was not mentioned in a chemical-biological warfare study assigned in May 1969. The entire study had to be reassigned and redone in December.

TITO, KHORAT, AND THE PERSIAN GULF

The contents of the 138 NSC study memoranda are classified, but a look at their subject titles discloses a fascinating variety of topics covered. Thus, a 1970 North African study explored the merit of improving U.S. relations with Algeria and Libya. Another study presented "options" as to what might happen in Yugoslavia after Tito's death. Three times in 1969, twice in 1970, and twice in 1971 there were studies of growing Soviet naval capabilities in the Persian Gulf and the Indian Ocean. The Middle East and the Arab-Israeli conflict rated six studies in 1969, four in 1970, with the trigger that prompted orders for each new study usually being some change in the military balance or a new Israeli weapons request.

Among the most prescient of Nixon decisions was the President's request of February 1, 1969, for an NSC study on China (which was followed by two more China studies in 1970 and one in 1971, along with a Japan study still underway). One problem identified and analyzed early in the China studies was the place of Thailand in any future, "neutralized" Southeast Asia, and, in particular, whether to demilitarize the $30 million U.S. command and communications complex at Khorat. This U.S. base on Thai territory, constructed in the mid-1960s with reinforced concrete for defense against nuclear attack, was conceived by the Joint Chiefs of Staff as the site of U.S. theater headquarters in the event of general war with China. A few short years later, the Khorat base looks like a very white elephant.

Among the most vital of all the studies are those relating to nuclear weapons, done in preparation for the Strategic Arms Limitation Talks (SALT) with the Soviet Union. There have been four basic and exhaustive SALT studies and at least twenty-five further collateral studies (twenty-one in 1969, four in 1970, and four in 1971), including the first review of U.S. civil defense requirements in two decades. They are Kissinger's pride. He has asserted that the SALT studies, centered in the Verification Panel, have been the most thorough and meticulous analyses ever made of the politics of nuclear strategy. He also asserts that they have virtually eliminated the narrow adversary approach to arms limitation hitherto practiced within the U.S. government, which used to provoke bitter intramural controversies leading to stultified international negotiations. Half the time used to be spent negotiating among ourselves, Kissinger says, one-quarter with our allies, and one-quarter with the Russians.

Four principles of U.S. military posture identified in the NSC studies as guidelines for SALT were: (1) the need to retain a second-strike capability; (2) the need for stable forces in a crisis—i.e., forces sufficiently safeguarded so as to be invulnerable to a sudden attack; (3) the requirement that the Russians not be allowed large leverage in the parity of inflicted damage (after all, there are more industrial and urban concentrations to destroy in the United States than in Russia); and (4) adequate defenses against threats from third countries which have nuclear weapons (France, China), or nuclear potential (Japan, India, Egypt, Israel, and Cuba, among others). The Kissinger-directed review examined the capabilities of every known weapon system and combination of systems, and the attendant risks and gains that would follow from their limitation. This analysis prepared the way for Soviet and American negotiators to seek concurrent accords on defensive and offensive arms, and for Nixon and Kosygin to exchange pledges of good faith in May 1971. There is now general agreement on the kind of mutual assurances necessary to the stability of any eventual agreement: for each side, maximum survivability of forces, adequate penetrability of weapons, and prevention of gross and tempting imbalances.

THE MAKING OF A BALANCE

Almost as important as the SALT studies have been the seven NSC study memoranda on NATO and eleven more on related concerns, such as mutual balanced force reductions (MBFR) between NATO and Warsaw Pact forces. The MBFR studies, originating in the Defense Department, are exceedingly intricate and still incomplete, but may heavily affect future U.S. policy in Europe. MBFR could be considered a spin-off from the earlier SALT studies.

When the first MBFR study was ordered in April 1970, Kissinger set strict criteria to try to jog the bureaucracy out of its habit of handling European problems in bits and pieces. The results are not yet apparent in policy changes, but a fresh look has been taken at European policies which had remained frozen for nearly two decades. For a time, the number and detail of NSC requests for new information and interpretation placed such demands on an overloaded State Department, which was screening the Defense studies, that Secretary Rogers had to appeal to the President to let up the pressure. Another inhibition was that France initially opposed the MBFR concept. The French feared that it would lead to a bloc-to-bloc negotiation between Soviets and Americans, thereby subordinating French sovereignty. MBFR also, they felt, had ominous echoes of the Soviet-supported Rapacki plan of the 1950s for an atom-free zone in central Europe that would leave a vacuum on France's eastern borders. Finally, such intangibles as the shape of a final SALT agreement, future British and French decisions on whether to retain independent nuclear forces or to merge in a common European force, and economic relations between the U.S. and the Common Market continue to affect the elaborate MBFR planning effort.

More tangible progress has been made by the NSC in another military-political field, that of defense assistance. Determination of U.S. military aid programs had been wrested by the Defense Department away from the State Department in 1961. Not until ten years later, in mid-1971, was State, at NSC insistence, given back the assignment. It is now deciding what precise amounts of aid are required to meet the five-year force levels set by the NSC Defense Programs Review Committee. As of August 1971, no five-year plan for military aid existed, but some rough priorities had been established. Aid to Vietnam, Laos, and Thailand, financed by Defense Department general service funds, would continue to be a Pentagon responsibility, with its future tied to unfolding developments in Southeast Asia. Among other countries, there were four rank-levels of military-aid priority, as follows: *first priority*, South Korea, Turkey, Cambodia; *second priority*, Greece, Taiwan, Indonesia, the Philippines; *third priority*, Spain, Ethiopia; *fourth priority*, the rest of the world.

THE RICHARDSON FACTOR

One stalwart of the Kissinger NSC system who for a time was sorely missed is Elliot Richardson, who resigned on June 23, 1970, as Under Secretary of State to become Secretary of Health, Education, and Welfare. A laconic Bostonian, Richardson impressed Kissinger (and nearly everybody else) with his incisive knowledge of how to make the bureaucracy move, combined with his air of slightly gelid insouciance. Washington wags used to compare Richardson to Sherlock Holmes' brother, Mycroft, that veritable one-man NSC staff of Edwardian Britain, whose Foreign Office assignment was to determine "how each factor would affect the other." Kissinger and Richardson lunched together every Tuesday. (The present Under Secretary of State, John Irwin, has breakfast with Kissinger every other Thursday—if both are in town.) As a fellow Harvard alumnus, Richardson had no difficulty understanding what Kissinger meant when he said that knowledge depends upon the ability to abstract generalizations from individual events, and that, the higher the level of authority, the greater the degree of abstraction necessary.

Kissinger and Richardson then (and, to a lesser degree, Kissinger and Irwin in 1971) would together decide on what NSC study memoranda to order, and would also frame an average of from ten to fifteen questions they wanted each study to answer. "You cannot get the right answers," says Kissinger, "unless you've asked the right questions." Richardson also managed to alter Kissinger's rather low opinion of the Foreign Service, just as Secretary Rogers had some effect in muting Nixon's own heavy bias against the State Department at the beginning of his Administration. Richardson is missed at the State Department not only for his decisiveness and common sense but also for his ability to exploit the talents of the career Foreign Service, whose morale has stayed generally low because its personnel have felt underutilized and distrusted by the Nixon Administration.[2]

TWO WEAK SPOTS

The Achilles' heel of the NSC system has been international economics; and its albatross has been foreign intelligence. As Kissinger is the first to admit, his reputation in diplomacy and nuclear strategy does not extend to economics, a field largely beyond his knowledge or competence. Thus the NSC has had only marginal, if not minimal, impact on economic policy.

Early efforts in 1969 to secure the staff services of a national authority in the foreign economic field lapsed under the pressure of more immediate problems. During that first year about 70 percent of the bureaucracy's contributions to NSC economic studies came from the Treasury Department, and only 30 percent from State. No senior interdepartmental group for economics was organized. Receiving little attention from Kissinger, the NSC's own economic specialists carried no bureaucratic clout. Kissinger's remedy in 1970 was to suggest formation of a Council of International Economic Policy, which was finally created in early 1971. The new body, however, has yet to get off the ground, for it is not comparable in prestige, influence, or expertise to the regular Kissinger NSC staff. The State Department, which argues that half of its work is normally economic, continues to oppose the rationale for a foreign economic council because, professional Foreign Service Officers argue, economics and politics cannot be separated. Thus it was the Treasury and the President's domestic advisers, not State or the NSC, who formulated Nixon's new economic policies of last August 15.

NSC's second weak spot, intelligence, is probably Kissinger's greatest personal disappointment. He had once said that the test of statesmanship was the ability to anticipate and evaluate threats before they occurred. His passion for objectivity and commitment to rigorous analysis appear in this case to have fallen afoul of the disorganized chaos of the multiple intelligence agencies in the U.S. government.

[2] [*Editors' note*: President Nixon, after his landslide victory in the 1972 election, appointed Richardson Secretary of Defense to replace Melvin Laird.]

One major exception to this general failure stands out. The single field in which an "agreed factual basis" for policy formulation has been more or less achieved has been SALT. Kissinger claims that "the Verification Panel has made 98 percent of intelligence disagreements disappear." The reason: policymakers and intelligence analysts sit on the same panel and directly argue out their differences over facts and policies. On most other questions, the rigid distinction between "operators" and "analysts" is maintained; it is established doctrine in the intelligence community that these two types of officials be kept separate. But Kissinger has been plainly unhappy with what he calls "the theologians of intelligence," officials more interested in advancing their particular agency interests than in seeking rigorously rational answers to difficult government-wide questions.

SIX TYPES OF AMBIGUITY IN THE MODERN CIA

Kissinger uses the euphemism "intelligence ambiguities" rather than "failures" to blunt the public thrust of his private unhappiness. Details of at least six such "ambiguities" are widely known, and one assumes there are additional cases which have not yet surfaced in public. Washington received no advance warning of the September 1969 revolutionary coup in Libya. Similarly, no notice was given of the coup against Prince Sihanouk in Cambodia in March 1970, mainly because no CIA agents had been stationed in the country, at the insistence of Senate Majority Leader Mike Mansfield. No definitive evaluation was made all through 1969 of the importance of Sihanoukville to the North Vietnamese supply build-up in the "sanctuary" provinces opposite the main population zones of South Vietnam, because of disputes over the evidence. (The Defense Intelligence Agency [DIA], it eventually turned out, had been more correct than the CIA.) Another failure, apparently one of poor coordination within the U.S. government, was the inability to act on advance knowledge that the North Vietnamese might quickly marshal 35,000 troops against the 17,000 South Vietnamese forces in the Laotian incursion of February 1971. In the blighted Defense Department operation of November 1970 to rescue U.S. prisoners of war at Sontay in North Viet-

nam, intelligence officials failed to report the obvious conclusion, on the basis of available evidence, that the prisoners were probably no longer there. The internal logic of the admittedly incomplete information on hand—credibility, verifiability, perishability—pointed clearly to that conclusion, particularly after agents on the ground failed to get close enough to Sontay in time for confirmation. Finally, there was the failure of timely aerial reconnaissance just before the August 7, 1970, Israeli-Egyptian cease-fire along the Suez Canal took effect.

In addition, NSC staffers criticize the looseness of mental discipline ("sponginess," in Kissinger's phrase) which seems to infect nearly all intelligence bodies. IG and NSC officials working on national security study memoranda have often been unable to "pry loose" from CIA basic intelligence evaluations of the subject under study; too frequently intelligence estimates have had a cautious, "cover-all-bets" quality not very useful to policymakers; and coordination between NSC studies and CIA's own internal studies has been less than complete. The quality of intelligence assessments varies widely, and the NSC has been unable to develop any agreed yardstick by which to "evaluate the evaluators" and root out hidden assumptions. Hence, intelligence estimators remain essentially their own judge and jury. Their biases, according to NSC officials, include a narrow concern for the special interests and "missions" of their particular agencies, overemphasis on foreign capabilities as opposed to intentions, and "cold war" blinders that may exaggerate both the importance of a given foreign event to the U.S. and the involvement or advantage gained by the Communists. The policymakers say they want intelligence "on tap, not on top," and sometimes show considerable impatience with the "speculative opinions" of intelligence briefers. But they have not found a method to insure against future "ambiguities" and to provide the better structure and controls now lacking.

These criticisms fall impartially on the Defense Intelligence Agency (too big, not professional enough, service-oriented) and the Central Intelligence Agency (self-serving bias on SALT judgments). In addition, the NSC is concerned about the confusion generated by mission-motivated estimates among military

G-2 intelligence sections in large subordinate theater commands overseas. In their eagerness to accomplish a mission, G-2 staffs may be more prone to wishful thinking than others without similar stakes, and they tend to slip away from effective control from the top. At the same time, there are generals who use their stars to short-circuit or unbalance G-2 procedures. There is a habitual oversell of Air Force capabilities which complicates equitable consideration of intelligence targets. There is, finally, a disposition among some generals to weigh all intelligence in the light of an ultimate nuclear war against the Soviet Union. This produces an unbalanced outlook, making most intelligence seem either inconsequential or overpoweringly important; it contributes to a national security syndrome of nuclear preoccupation which has overshadowed foreign policy for a generation. Because of these shortcomings, Defense Secretary Laird in 1972 undertook a wholesale review of the intelligence operations of the Defense Department.

A final missing element in the intelligence process is caused by the long-standing unwritten prohibition against including in intelligence evaluations any explicit consideration of U.S. policy interests or resources. Knowledge of the policy options available to the U.S. could well affect the assessment of many foreign situations. The ironclad exclusion of these policy possibilities from intelligence evaluations prevents the factor of the American presence in a foreign area, whether active or passive, from being given weight as one important element in the equation. Similarly, foreign and adversary perceptions of U.S. interests and of what the United States might do or fail to do in a given situation are frequently left out of intelligence evaluations for the NSC. These omissions work against the grain of the Kissinger method: the sorting out of every implication of an issue by close adherence to the screen of U.S. purpose, which shakes out the pattern of priorities.

THE OPTIONS GAME

How realistic are the famous "options"? Judging by the results thus far, Nixon has been better served by his more formalized national security advisory system than either Lyndon Johnson or John F. Kennedy was served by an informal system, even though it was Robert McNamara, as Defense Secretary to Nixon's two predecessors, who first made the options concept fashionable. The idea was simple enough: serve up the President a bundle of alternatives. But one sometimes wonders, while prowling the White House basement, whether often-repeated phrases like "keeping the options open" and "the President's spread of options" do not have more of a liturgical than an intellectual significance. The options mystique has even inspired some critics to accuse Kissinger of cynically circumventing the bureaucracy by hogtieing it to meaningless NSC studies while he and his staff focus on the essential issues. The charge would have more plausibility if Kissinger were indeed the Nietzschean superman his critics assume—and commanded a sufficient number of junior supermen to perform the whole job in the White House.

The path from Kissinger wish to NSC consummation has been by no means easy. President Nixon, recalling the recommendations of the Eisenhower Administration NSC, felt they had been too homogenized. In the Johnson regime, the NSC did not act as a functioning process which bound agencies together; by contrast with the Nixon system, the Johnson NSC was practically nonexistent. And Johnson staffers only infrequently and informally presented the President with options. After all, was felt, "there were only one or two sensible things to do."

So Kissinger upon entering the White House basement found little rough-and-ready argumentation among bureaucrats over alternative policy courses. He inherited, instead, the bureaucracy's time-tested habit of elaborate, negotiated "consensus" among subordinate officials and agencies (with an occasional dissenting view included as a footnote) *prior* to their submission of advice to the President. He shook this system up by passing out new kinds of study assignments. Harvard professor that he is, he made the bureaucrats write theses and proved to be a tough grader. He rated many of the early NSC studies no better than "C"— barely passing. He also came to recognize that the options game could frequently be a disguised form of special advocacy: two or three obviously untenable "straw options" served up alongside only one clearly realistic choice.

What is less clear is whether the NSC options game shades analysis toward competition within the bureaucracy for discovery of the most striking plausibility that can appeal to the holders of political power. By stimulating foreign affairs officials to engage in an adversary process, does one perhaps change the whole focus of the system toward scoring bureaucratic points on opponents, rather than defining national objectives and deciding how best to attain them?

And there may be a final dilemma, evident in the unhappiness of the Nixon NSC with the intelligence it is getting. Intelligence evaluators, by the very nature of their function, restrict options; their role is to determine likely, "reliable" outcomes, probable and feasible patterns of events. The role of the President's men, on the other hand, is to avoid being squeezed into one course, and to maintain and expand the options.

The product of all the memos and meetings, questionnaires, and options is the refined raw material of presidential decisionmaking, the identification of what opportunities and escape hatches are open to the nation's leadership. To date, Nixon's foreign policy record has indicated the seizure of opportunities, and so the NSC process that made those opportunities apparent must be judged a success.

CHAPTER 8

Case Studies in Defense Policymaking

THE POLITICS OF INNOVATION: PATTERNS IN NAVY CASES

VINCENT DAVIS

This article is drawn from a monograph of three major and several shorter case studies. From this broad base, Davis develops a theory of innovation that includes three parts: (1) characteristics of the innovation advocate; (2) the advocate's political techniques; and (3) the opponents' political techniques. Each of these parts contains several hypotheses about individual and organizational behavior patterns similar to Allison's Model III. Most interesting among the propositions are those which suggest that innovation advocates first attempt to develop a horizontal political alliance and then expand it into a vertical political alliance. Professor Davis is the Director and Patterson Chair Professor of the William Andrew Patterson School of Diplomacy and International Commerce at the University of Kentucky and formerly held the Nimitz Chair of National Security and Foreign Affairs at the Naval War College. His books include Postwar Defense Policy and the U. S. Navy, 1943–1946 *(1966) and* The Admirals Lobby *(1967).*

INTRODUCTION

An increasing number of social scientists from various scholarly disciplines in recent years have focused their study on the behavior of organizations, including the behavior of individuals within organizational roles and settings. One anticipated conclusion that has emerged from this research is that innovations proposed within an organizational setting frequently produce conflicts and disputes in that organization. Political scientists within the behavioral science community have been particularly concerned to study how such conflicts are dealt with and occasionally resolved within governmental organizations. Some of those political scientists who specialize in the study of national security policy have suggested the need for research on innovations which have

been part or all of a new weapons system for a military service. This article, written by a political scientist who has specialized in the study of national security policy, utilizes some of these converging and complementary behavioral science perspectives to focus on the behavior of individuals in the U.S. Navy in relation to a proposal by one or more such individuals that the Navy should develop a technological innovation as part or all of a weapons system.

. . . .

The term "politics" in the title of this article refers to all actions, tactics, and strategies employed by the advocates of an innovation in their efforts to get the Navy Department officially committed to its development—even if only on a pilot or experimental basis—and to all counteractions, tactics, and strategies em-

Reprinted and edited by permission of the author and publisher from The Politics of Innovation, *Monograph Series in World Affairs, vol. 4, no. 3 (Denver, Col.: The Social Science Foundation and the Graduate School of International Studies, University of Denver, 1966–1967).*

ployed by those who resisted it. This article will also attempt to outline such patterns as appeared to exist among both the advocates and the resisters in terms of their career backgrounds, their place and rank within the Navy, and other personal and personality factors.

The time period of special concern in the case to be noted here is generally that period which begins when, for the first time within the organization, some individual or individuals propose that the Navy attempt to develop a new technological innovation. This moment in time shall be regarded as t_1 for the purposes of this study. The time period ends at t_2, when the appropriate decisionmakers in the Navy decide either to go ahead and commit the Navy to the "research and development" (R&D) stage with respect to the innovative proposal or else decide not to do so. Although t_1 and t_2 are often difficult to pin-point precisely, it is believed that they may be sufficiently identified for present purposes. This manner of defining the time period of special concern here clearly implies that certain other related matters will not be included for consideration. For example, the actual conceptualization or invention of the proposed innovations will be of no concern here unless they coincide with t_1. In addition, the "politics" of the situation following t_2, although an extremely interesting subject for a separate study, lie outside the scope of this article.[1]

This article should be regarded as a tentative initial effort based on incomplete exploratory research, in part because of the several varieties of difficulty that are encountered in research of this kind. In the first place, only a very few relevant and fully developed case studies exist in the literature at the present, and virtually all of these were written for purposes other than the kind of exploratory inquiry which characterizes this article. Therefore, it was necessary to attempt crudely to adapt the case study for present purposes. In

the second place, it is difficult to develop new case studies, especially for relatively recent time periods, and especially for cases in which the innovation advocates "lost" (i.e., failed to persuade the Navy to develop their proposals). Most archival and documentary materials on recent cases still carry security classifications, and there is very little material of any kind on the "lost" cases.[2] (It should be noted that this article, insofar as the author is aware, makes no use of any classified information or materials.) The researcher is thus forced to uncover most of the relevant information through personal interviews and correspondence with knowledgeable individuals, but the inability to gain substantial access to archival and documentary materials prevents the compilation of an exhaustive list of knowledgeable individuals. When such individuals can be ascertained and contacted, some are unwilling to talk extensively; few possess complete knowledge or complete objectivity; and discrepancies often appear among the accounts obtained from individuals who presumably are equally knowledgeable. Therefore, the "historical facts" should by no means be regarded as the final authoritative record. In summary, the conclusions and generalized hypotheses reached in this article are weakened because they are drawn from too narrow an empirical base (i.e., too few cases) and from cases which in some respects are probably not altogether historically accurate as presented here.[3]

---

[1] Insofar as the author's research will allow a tentative conclusion about the politics of the post-t_2 period, it tends to follow in some respects from the politics of the t_1-to-t_2 period of special concern here, but it also appears to differ in significant respects. The differences may be largely accounted for by the different arenas in which the two kinds of politics occur. The politics of t_1-to-t_2 take place primarily within the Navy, for reasons to be suggested later, whereas the post-t_2 politics take place between the Navy and such external groups as Congress.

[2] "Losers" are difficult to identify because even their opponents within the Navy seem to join in a wall of silence to protect them from external scrutiny and perhaps publicity. And, when a loser occasionally can be located, he is usually not interested in divulging very much to an interviewer. The inability to present losing cases means an inability to present rigorously comparative conclusions that contrast winners and winning strategies with losers and losing strategies. It is also impossible, for example, to say very much of a conclusive nature about the precise degree of career risk an innovation advocate runs.

[3] A related difficulty in writing a research report such as the one in hand is that a misleading "good guys and bad guys" impression may be created. In other words, the advocates of innovation tend to be depicted as "good guys" who are "intelligent" and "progressive," whereas the opponents of innovation appear as "bad guys" who are "cautious," "conservative," even "reactionary." No such impressions are intended in the present article. It is only with the benefit of hindsight that a critic can attempt to make such invidious distinctions. At the time when a decision is made within an organization with respect to initiating R&D on a proposed technological innovation, the opponents often have very sound arguments on

In view of the limitations and reservations noted above, the chief value of the generalized conclusions with which this article concludes may be to serve as starting hypotheses for subsequent research along these same lines when more and more accurate case materials become available and when it is then possible to undertake a wide range of comparative studies.

THE DEVELOPMENT OF A CAPABILITY TO DELIVER NUCLEAR WEAPONS BY CARRIER-BASED AIRCRAFT[4]

A set of interrelated ideas became widely popular in Congress and in many other powerful places in the American government and among the American people at large in the final months of 1945 after the end of World War II. The first of these ideas was that the American monopoly on nuclear weapons could and should be used to pose a threat of devastation against any adversary, with the Soviet Union rapidly becoming the potential adversary uppermost in most people's minds. Second, it was believed that this threat would be so effective that it would deter virtually all kinds of military threats that would concern the United States, although most people at that time suffered from an extension of the Pearl Harbor syndrome which led to the conclusion that the next war that involved the United States—if such a war could not be deterred—would begin with an adversary initiating a massive surprise air attack directly against most major industrial and population centers within the United States. Third, it was therefore believed that the capability to deliver

their side. Indeed, unless one assumes that all innovative proposals are equally sound and worthy, the opponents serve the valuable function of filtering out the less worthy and less sound ideas. It is only when an innovation is in fact developed and adopted by an organization and then proves to be of great importance that one can look back and charge the opponents with having been excessively cautious, and even in these kinds of cases the charge is usually not warranted. Although the words "cautious" and "conservative" are sometimes used in this article to describe individuals, the terms are used merely as crude descriptions and carry no invidious nor pejorative implications.

[4] Most of the information presented in this case study is drawn from Vincent Davis, *Postwar Defense Policy and the U.S. Navy, 1943–1946* (Chapel Hill: University of North Carolina Press, 1966), pp. 240–59 and *passim*. For further details and documentation on this case, see Davis' book.

nuclear weapons was virtually the only military capability the United States needed. Fourth, it was believed that the U.S. Air Force was the ideal—indeed, many believed that it was the only—American military service that could and should possess this capability. Fifth, it was believed that nuclear weapons had rendered all surface military forces—i.e., armies and navies—intolerably vulnerable to attack and therefore obsolete.

A number of Navy men consequently foresaw rather quickly that the Navy would need to accomplish two goals very soon if it was to remain in existence. First, it would have to be demonstrated that ships were not excessively vulnerable to atomic attack, contrary to a rapidly growing belief in many important political quarters that they were. Second, it would have to be demonstrated that Navy carrier aircraft could be at least as useful and valuable as Air Force bombers for the delivery of nuclear weapons. Secretary of the Navy James Forrestal understood these problems very well—to be sure, he understood them before many naval officers came to these conclusions—and he took a number of steps, including the establishment of the Office of Special Weapons (Op-06, as it was called according to the number-coded system for designating the agencies within the overall Office of the Chief of Naval Operations). Forrestal gave to Op-06 broad responsibility for developing not only naval applications of atomic energy but also missiles and other foreseen new technologies.

Op-06 played a prominent role in the "Bikini tests" in the summer of 1946. The Navy men hoped that these tests would achieve the first of their two urgent goals: a demonstration that ships were not excessively or peculiarly vulnerable to atomic attack. While the tests were in many respects inconclusive, public and political pressure against the Navy eased after the tests (in large part for other reasons) to the extent that the Navy men felt that their service was at least going to be allowed to remain in existence for a while longer. This seemed to afford time—a breathing space—in which to pursue the second urgent goal: a demonstration that the Navy had the capability to deliver, as well as to endure, an atomic attack.

By the spring of 1947, however, the Navy

had appeared to win most of its points in the long-standing struggle with the Air Force in the "unification of the armed forces" dispute. Most senior naval officers were exhausted from this struggle, and they wanted to avoid anything that might further antagonize the Air Force in order to turn their full attention to a number of urgent but neglected problems within the Navy. Under the category of Navy actions that would surely antagonize the Air Force was any further effort at that moment to develop a Navy capability for delivering nuclear weapons. Accordingly, there was little sympathy in high Navy circles in the spring of 1947 for pushing ahead with such efforts, although such efforts had thus far made very little progress. On the other hand, and at somewhat lower rank levels within the Navy, there were a number of younger officers who did not share the sanguine mood of interservice disengagement and a narrow focus on internal problems that appeared to characterize the more senior officers. The younger men were more than ever convinced that the Navy's very existence remained at stake, and that the development of a nuclear delivery capability was probably the only thing that could save it. Navy appropriations were going ever downward, and the Bureau of the Budget had denied the Navy its request to initiate the so-called supercarrier building program in fiscal year 1948. At the same time, the trend of authorizations and appropriations for the Air Force seemed to foreshadow a long-range commitment by Congress and the President to make it the dominant service that it wanted to be.[5]

This interservice acrimony between the Navy and the Air Force (it did not begin in the post–World War II period—on the contrary, it had been a steady fact of life within the American armed forces from the moment Billy Mitchell returned from World War I in 1919) and the persistent feeling in the Navy for the first few post–World War II years that the Air Force was threatening the Navy's continued existence, served as a backdrop for the efforts of two younger officers between 1945 and 1949 to persuade the Navy to go all-out to develop a nuclear delivery capability with carrier aircraft. These two were Commander Frederick L. "Dick" Ashworth and Commander John T. "Chick" Hayward. The details of their story will be briefly chronicled later, but first it is necessary to suggest why the term "backdrop" has been cautiously and advisedly used here.

A stronger term than "backdrop" would be "cause," and some might think it accurate enough to suggest that the Navy's fear for its organizational life within the midst of the broader and long-standing Navy–Air Force acrimony did in fact cause Ashworth and Hayward to press their proposal regarding a carrier nuclear delivery capability. The sequence of events and other relevant details, however, do not precisely support a simple causal connection. Ashworth initiated his efforts in the early fall of 1945 as a direct continuation of his key role in the Manhattan District Project—he was one of the very few naval officers working for the Project—in which he had been significantly responsible for adapting and fitting the first atomic bombs to the large B-29 bombers of the Air Force. But, precisely because he had worked for the Project during most of the war, Ashworth was effectively isolated from most of the swirling storms of controversy between the Navy and the Air Force. Unlike many naval officers of his generation, his earlier career recorded no significant involvement in the overall "unification of the armed forces" conflict within which all Navy–Air Force disputes took place. He therefore undertook his efforts in late 1945 largely innocent of the nature and dimensions of the interservice quarrel, beginning his work with the straightforward reasoning that the first atomic bombs were fitted to Air Force rather than to Navy planes for largely coincidental rather than inherent circumstances. Given the manner in which atomic bombs could increase the offensive punch of an aircraft, Ashworth merely concluded that they now ought to be adapted and fitted to Navy planes as well as to Air Force bombers. Hayward, who initiated his efforts in the spring of 1947 and to some

[5] For further details on the high point of the Navy–Air Force dispute after World War II, see the excellent case study by Paul Y. Hammond, "Super Carriers and B-36 Bombers: Appropriations, Strategy and Politics," in *American Civil-Military Decisions*, ed. Harold Stein (Tuscaloosa: University of Alabama Press, for the Twentieth Century Fund, 1963).

degree independently of Ashworth's earlier efforts (although they proceeded from them), appeared to be primarily motivated by essentially the same kind of reasoning.

More will be said later about the motivations of Ashworth and Hayward, but at this point the arguments above still leave dangling an important question: What was the relationship between the external environment—that is, the Navy–Air Force conflict and the developing preferences for a national military strategy then emerging among most key government policymakers—and the actions of Ashworth and Hayward? The answer seems to be that this backdrop, while it did not *cause* Ashworth and Hayward to proceed as they did in the first place, served to create a climate of thinking in the Navy that made the Navy generally more receptive to proposals for innovation than might otherwise have been the case. In other words, the need to insure the Navy's survival encouraged many Navy people to look with favor on new ideas that might be of help in this cause. Looked at in a broader frame of reference and at a higher level of generalization, cutting across a number of pre– and post–World War II cases studied by this author, it may be suggested that any circumstances which have prompted Congress to legislate a build-up in the strength of any part of the armed forces—and such circumstances have generally occurred when there was a growing national perception of some other nation as an increasingly threatening adversary—have tended to encourage a heightened degree of receptivity within the Navy to proposals for innovation in weapons systems. But, returning to the case in hand, the conviction persists in this author's mind that the innovation advocates themselves—Ashworth and Hayward—would doubtless have done precisely as they did even if no Air Force had existed and the Navy was therefore the only service that could have entertained the possibility of using nuclear weapons. For Ashworth and Hayward the original and overriding stimulus was the thought that atomic bombs would give the Navy an enhanced capability for carrying out missions that the fast carrier task forces had conducted extensively during the war. In short, these two officers were mainly concerned to give the Navy an improved ability to carry out old missions that they thought had been well established for the Navy by the war, although Hayward was later one of the large number of naval officers swept into the swirling vortex of the Navy–Air Force dispute and he accordingly was not averse to using aspects of this dispute to help him sell his proposed innovation within the Navy.

The capability to deliver a nuclear weapon from carrier-based aircraft depended on a suitable combination of three basic components: a ship, a plane, and a bomb. As for the ship that would be required, the Navy Department had already initiated planning for the envisaged new "supercarriers" before World War II was over—a new class of aircraft carriers that could accommodate a range of new and much heavier carrier airplanes that the Navy also had in mind. But in the fall of 1945, when Commander Ashworth began his efforts to persuade and help the Navy to acquire this capability, the supercarriers were still little more than a gleam in the eye, the nature of atomic bombs then in existence also seemed to be a fixed factor for the short-range future, and Ashworth was not sure what kind of airplanes might be available and adaptable. The first step he took, therefore, was to visit the Navy's Bureau of Aeronautics in Washington to learn about existing or soon-to-be-available new carrier aircraft that could be adapted to carry and deliver an existing nuclear weapon.

Commander Ashworth possessed virtually unique technical qualifications in the Navy for the kind of role he was about to play. Because he had achieved a brilliant academic record as a midshipman at Annapolis with special distinction in physics, he was given opportunities in his duty assignments in the 1930s that allowed him to maintain his contact with developments in the sciences—particularly physics. Therefore, when the Manhattan District Project was created at the outset of the war as a War Department activity assigned to the Army's Corps of Engineers but actually designed to draw on the capable people in all of the armed forces, Ashworth was one of the very few naval officers who were qualified. He and Navy Captain W. S. "Deke" Parsons were thus the only two regular naval officers who were assigned to the Manhattan District for most of the war and who had important major responsibilities at Los Alamos.[6] The first crude atomic bombs had to be armed by hand immediately before release from the bombing aircraft over the target, and the man who did this job was called the "weaponeer." Parsons was the weaponeer for the first atomic bomb dropped on Hiroshima, and Ashworth performed the same role a few days later for the second atomic bomb dropped on Nagasaki. As soon as the war ended and he was released from his duties with the Manhattan District, Ashworth was assigned along with Parsons to the Navy's new Office of Special Weapons (Op-06). He immediately became the Officer in Charge of Naval Vessel Tests for the Bikini test series in 1946 as part of his responsibilities in Op-06 and, when the Atomic Energy Commission was created in 1947, he became the first Executive Secretary of the AEC's crucially important Military Liaison Committee. In short, as of the end of World War II, he was a young officer who had already enjoyed a brilliant early career, not only because of his competence in nuclear physics, but also as a naval aviator, and he seemed destined for a further career of continuing distinction. That promise was fulfilled; in 1967 he was a vice admiral serving in one of the Navy's choice sea duty billets as Commander of the U.S. Sixth Fleet in the Mediterranean. He retired from active duty in 1968. But, as a young commander in October 1945, he had been back in Washington only a few weeks following release from his duties with the Manhattan District and was just getting into his new duties with Op-06 at a time when the whole future of the development of atomic energy and weapons was uncertain, pending congressional and presidential decisions.

When Ashworth went to the Bureau of Aeronautics (BuAer) in October 1945 to inquire what kind of existing or soon-to-be-available airplanes the Navy possessed that might be suitable for a special configuration for delivering existing atomic bombs, he learned that in mid-1945 BuAer had asked the North American Aviation Company to initiate the development of a heavy new attack bomber for use aboard carriers; it was called the AJ. He met and talked with Captain Joseph N. Murphy (later Rear Admiral Murphy, in charge of the Navy's Aviation Test and Development Center at Johnstown, Pennsylvania). Murphy was BuAer's expert on planes of this type, and Ashworth recruited Murphy to his little personal project. Specifically, he persuaded Murphy to accompany him on a visit to the North American Aviation Company's main plant, then located in Los Angeles. The trip took place in early 1946, and by that time the AJ was already in the mock-up stage. Ashworth's hope was that the AJ could be sufficiently redesigned so that its bomb compartment could carry the Mark 4 "Fat Man" atomic bomb—the same primitive nuclear weapon that had been used on Nagasaki. Working only from his memory of the exact size and shape of the bomb (secrecy was still so tight at that time that Ashworth was unable to obtain the blueprints and other detailed figures on the bomb, although he himself had been a key individual in developing it and in dropping it on Nagasaki), he and Murphy quickly became convinced that the AJ could be redesigned around this requirement. With Murphy's support Ashworth sent a letter through channels intended for Secretary Forrestal's signature, asking President Truman to authorize the Navy to proceed on this. But several key officers in the channel of communications, including BuAer's Vice Admiral Arthur Radford (later a full admiral and Chairman of the Joint Chiefs of Staff in the Eisenhower Administration), had a number of reservations about the Navy's possible acquisition of a nuclear delivery capability and they stalled the Ashworth letter on its way to Forrestal. When it finally did reach the Secretary, Forrestal decided that he possessed the authority to approve the required modifications in the design of the AJ without the President's concurrence—at that stage leaving open the question whether the President would ever actually approve assigning atomic bombs to the Navy. Armed with this Secretarial endorsement, Ashworth then succeeded in getting clearance for North American to obtain the exact specifications of the Mark 4 bomb, and in June 1946 the Navy let a contract to North American to put the AJ into limited production redesigned as Ashworth wanted it.

---

[6] Parsons was promoted to rear admiral just after the war ended and was named as the first Director of Op-06, the Office of Special Weapons. He died of cancer at a relatively young age several years later, one of the most respected and well liked of the Navy's younger flag officers.

Shortly after it was created in early 1947, the AEC went to work to design and build improved atomic bombs (i.e., smaller in size but with more powerful warheads). The original Hiroshima "Little Boy" bomb yielded only 14 kilotons. The Nagasaki "Fat Man" bomb, around which the new AJ aircraft had been redesigned, was somewhat more efficient, yielding 20 kilotons, but it weighed 10,000 pounds (most Navy carrier airplanes did not themselves weigh that much at that time) and was a huge sixty inches in diameter. New weapons on the drawing boards would yield in the 100-plus kiloton range and would be as small as twenty-two inches in diameter. Such devices would be far more suitable for carrier aircraft, but they were still a substantial way from being in the operational hardware stage in early 1947.

By early 1947, however, Commander Ashworth was quickly becoming heavily involved in his duties with the Atomic Energy Commission and was therefore unable to give much more time to his personal project to help persuade the Navy to develop a nuclear delivery capability. It was at this point that Commander John T. Hayward decided to pick up the crusade and to make it his personal mission, apparently without any collusion or specific arrangement with Ashworth, although he and Ashworth were old friends with remarkably similar career patterns. Hayward, the product of a not exactly affluent family in the New York City area, had once been a bat-boy for the New York Yankees baseball team in an effort to help finance his high school education. But it was not until many years later, after he had graduated with honors from Annapolis and had largely completed his doctoral studies in nuclear physics that he was finally awarded his high school diploma on an *ex post facto* basis. In his early Navy career and during the first part of World War II he acquired a reputation as one of the Navy's most skilled (and most decorated) aviators. He was assigned to the Manhattan District Project late in the war and, although his role was not as significant as Ashworth's, he nevertheless assumed important responsibilities for the Manhattan District. Early in 1947 he was named to the key new position of Plans and Operations Director of the Armed Forces Special Weapons Project (AFSWP), an agency within the new

AEC. Thus, he and Ashworth were both in crucial AEC jobs in 1947, although Hayward apparently found more spare time to devote to the task of helping the Navy to develop a nuclear delivery capability than Ashworth could manage in the 1947–1948 period. Thus, as of the end of World War II, Hayward's early career in the Navy, like Ashworth's, was quite distinguished and seemed to portend a further career of growing distinction. As in Ashworth's case, that promise was fulfilled. By 1960 Hayward had already served as the first three-star admiral in the new position of Deputy Chief of Naval Operations for Development, with Ashworth as one of his immediate assistants, and in 1961 he was widely publicized as a leading candidate for the Navy's number one job for a uniformed officer, Chief of Naval Operations. In 1967 he was Vice Admiral Hayward in the coveted position of President of the Naval War College. Shortly thereafter, he retired and joined General Dynamics Corporation as Vice President for R&D, Vice President for Public Relations, and Vice President for Overseas Operations (all three positions simultaneously).

When Hayward picked up the ball from Ashworth in early 1947, his first action was to go see Vice Admiral Forrest Sherman, then the Deputy Chief of Naval Operations for Plans and later the Chief of Naval Operations. Sherman enjoyed a reputation in the Navy as one of the most able aviation admirals, one of the most astute thinkers, one of the most sophisticated practitioners of bureaucratic politics, and one of the few senior naval officers generally receptive and responsive to new and innovative proposals. Hayward requested that Sherman go to Congress specifically to ask for an endorsement of the Navy's plans for the AJ aircraft and more generally for approval of the Navy's overall plan for developing a nuclear delivery capability. Sherman told Hayward that this would be politically unrealistic, in view of the growing congressional faith in the Air Force's guarantee of its exclusive talents in the strategic bombing field. This, of course, had been a primary claim in the Air Force as far back as Billy Mitchell, but it was never a claim that the Navy's aviators had accepted. Although the naval aviators had not been given much opportunity to develop their capabilities in the 1920s and 1930s, when the Navy was dominated by the "battleship admirals," they nevertheless had achieved a few things. For one example, the B-17 "Flying Fortress" used so widely as an Air Force bomber during World War II had originally been designed by and for the Navy, but was then turned over to the Air Force when it proved unsuitable for naval uses. The naval aviators also recalled that, although Air Force aviators got the assignment, the first strategic bombing attack on Japan during the war was the famous "Doolittle Raid" launched from a Navy carrier. For these and other reasons the Navy fliers felt that many kinds of strategic bombing missions were just as much within the Navy's field of established competence as within the preserve of the Air Force.

Sherman and Hayward both shared these convictions that were characteristic of naval aviators, but Sherman gave Hayward a little lesson about how to do business with Congress. In response to Hayward's request that Sherman get from Congress a general endorsement of Navy plans within the area of nuclear weapons delivery systems, Sherman told him that Congress might conceivably buy the Navy idea but only after the Navy had first demonstrated on its own initiative a clear-cut capability—although perhaps quite crude at the outset—for long-range strategic bombing with airplanes that could carry then-existing atomic bombs. It was a rich-get-richer-and-poor-get-poorer theory of congressional largesse, but it was probably accurate in this case. Sherman therefore concluded that the Navy would have to use ships and planes already on hand to devise some sort of system, no matter how primitive originally, for delivering atomic bombs already in existence, before it would be realistic to ask the Congress to approve Navy plans for better ships and planes especially designed for this purpose.

Hayward accepted Sherman's advice and immediately made a request of him: assign to Hayward several of the Navy's huge P2V anti-submarine patrol bombers, which were used on land fields, and Hayward would figure out some way to fly them on and off of aircraft carriers already in existence. Sherman managed to work out a way to grant this request, and, in addition, gave Hayward permission to round up a team of top Navy men to join the project.

The P2Vs were about as much intended and designed for carrier use as were the DC-6 commercial airliners then in use, but they were nevertheless the smallest planes possessed by the Navy at that time with bomb bays large enough to hold the huge World War II atomic bombs that were still the only nuclear weapons in the nation's inventory. Hayward calculated that a P2V could take off and land on the deck of a *Midway*-class carrier (the largest carriers that the Navy then owned) with a few inches of clearance between the starboard wing tip and the superstructure "island" at the right side of the deck *if* extremely careful flying could be achieved and *if* there were no untoward circumstances. Even so, the plans would have to be greatly modified, and this was the next step in Hayward's project. Each of the twelve planes assigned to him was stripped of all expendable equipment to bring it down to a minimum weight, and tail hooks were installed for carrier landings. The bomb bays were modified to match the configuration of the "Little Boy" Hiroshima bombs. The flight decks of the three *Midway* carriers were considerably strengthened to support the vast weight of these planes and their bombs. Throughout all of this work Hayward also had to start training special assembly teams, because forty-eight hours were required to put together a "Little Boy"—and this had to be done immediately before installing the weapon in the aircraft just before sending it on its mission.

By early 1948 Hayward and his group were ready to start actual flight tests, and on April 27, with Hayward at the controls, one of the 60,000-pound P2Vs took off from the 986-foot flight deck of the U.S.S. *Coral Sea* (one of the three *Midway*-class carriers). Landing and take-off techniques were modified and practiced again and again during the rest of that year, but, by December, Hayward had proved his concepts sufficiently that the Navy Department allowed him to commission his development group under the nondescript name Composite Squadron (VC-5). He was the first commanding officer, and, appropriately, Ashworth was his executive officer. In January of 1949 a part of VC-5 was split off and formed into a second squadron, VC-6, with Ashworth as the commanding officer. Admiral Sherman meanwhile succeeded in getting the Atomic

Energy Commission to reserve one or two "Little Boy" bombs (some people have said that the national inventory of atomic bombs at that time came to a total of three) for issue to one or both of these Navy squadrons in the event of a national emergency. By the end of 1948 it was therefore possible to say that the Navy had achieved its capability—no matter, for the time being, how crude—to deliver an atomic bomb with planes from a regular operational carrier squadron. There were, it is true, a number of important episodes during the following year. For example, in September of 1949, just before the "supercarriers versus B-36 bombers" and the "revolt of the admirals" controversy reached its peak in the ever-intensifying conflict between the Navy and the Air Force, Hayward and his project team undertook an incredible publicity stunt designed to prove to Congress and other important doubters that the Navy had in fact achieved its capability. The episode featured a day on the *Midway* demonstrating the Navy's P2V capabilities for a select audience of highly prominent guests. The guests included Secretary of Defense Louis Johnson, Secretary of the Air Force Stuart Symington, Secretary of the Army Gordon Gray, Secretary of the Navy Francis Matthews, and Chairman of the Joint Chiefs of Staff Omar Bradley. At the end of the improbable day, Hayward flew these guests back to Washington from the carrier, which was located about a hundred miles off the Atlantic coast, in one of the P2Vs, with Secretary Johnson sitting in the co-pilot's seat so that he could get a close-up view of the take-off from the carrier. He would also have had a close-up view of the crash if the take-off had been unsuccessful, and, given the record of crashes during Hayward and his group's efforts to perfect the techniques for using the huge lumbering planes on the carriers, a perfect flight was by no means assured. The chances of wiping out virtually the entire high command of the U.S. military establishment in one quick moment did not appear altogether offset by the chances of making a favorable impression on this group of Navy-critical VIPs, but a flair for the dramatic gamble was a part of the Hayward style.

The events of 1949, however, were actually in the post-t_2 time period of this case, as the time period of special concern was defined in the introduction. The moment t_1 took place in October 1945, when Commander Ashworth decided to press ahead with his efforts, and the moment t_2 occurred in 1947, when Commander Hayward persuaded Admiral Sherman to let him enter what amounted to the R&D stage with the experimental group of officers and enlisted men working with the P2Vs. This was not a full-fledged t_2, because the commitment on the part of Admiral Sherman was not precisely equivalent to a formal commitment on the part of the entire Navy high command. Nevertheless, with Secretary Forrestal tacitly but strongly on the side of the Ashworth-Hayward endeavor, the Sherman commitment was sufficient to tip the balance. The effort proved successful and, accordingly, the atomic bomb could have gone to sea as early as December 1948. In February 1950, after overcoming many more political and technical problems in the post-t_2 phase of this case, the first Navy squadron—VC-5 with its new AJ airplanes—ever to be deployed on a routine carrier cruise in waters outside of the Western Hemisphere went to sea.

Several things are worth noting in this case. First, Ashworth and Hayward were relatively young officers at a middle-rank level in the Navy, senior enough to have acquired a Navy-wide perspective and concern, but not senior enough to have acquired the cautious restraint which often accompanies positions at the very top in the uniformed Navy, where perspectives and concerns cutting across the entire Washington bureaucracy may make a man more sensitive to problems than to opportunities. This attitude of cautious restraint characterized Vice Admiral Arthur Radford and a number of senior officers who emerged as a kind of high-level horizontal alliance opposing the efforts of the low-level horizontal alliance composed of Ashworth, Hayward, Murphy, and their associates. Radford and his associates had grown skeptical about the so-called flush-deck supercarrier that was a part of the vision entertained by the younger group, and Radford and the older group were also not sure that the Navy ought to press ahead with the effort to get into the atomic bombing business at a time when the Navy already had its hands full in persistent old conflicts with the Air Force.

Ashworth, Hayward, their friend Captain Murphy, and others who sided with their efforts possessed technical expertise relevant to their innovative proposal which was not generally shared by their fellow officers, and they had been fortunate in receiving duty assignments that gave them some extra leverage and additional expertise relevant to their purposes. Ashworth's and Hayward's assignments in connection with the new Atomic Energy Commission were particularly useful in keeping them abreast of developments in the overall national atomic energy policy area. Their reputations as distinguished naval aviators were also an asset in the particular cause that they were promoting. Although at the outset they did not consciously join forces to promote their shared cause—on the contrary, they first worked independently, each on his own initiative—their work converged to the extent that they and such supporters as Captain Murphy constituted a tacit horizontal political alliance at the middle-ranks level.

This middle-ranks alliance formed around Ashworth and Hayward did not make notable progress, however, until it acquired a strong vertical dimension in the form of crucial high-level support from Admiral Sherman and, behind Sherman, the tacit but strong support of Forrestal. As early as September 1945 Forrestal and other key Navy spokesmen had testified in public before a congressional committee that the Navy planned to develop a capability to deliver nuclear weapons with carrier-launched aircraft.[7] It seemed little more than political rhetoric at the time to counter Air Force claims of an exclusive mission in the field of atomic bombing, but it did coincide with Forrestal's strong determination to build the postwar Navy around carrier aviation, and everyone in the Navy knew that Forrestal was moving in this direction. It was therefore unnecessary for Forrestal to come out openly on the side of the Ashworth-Hayward alliance, because they were in effect moving to implement something that he had much earlier declared to be a Navy goal. Sherman was therefore the key man, facilitating what amounted to an end run by Ashworth and Hayward around Radford's blocking position. Radford, as the Chief of BuAer, would have been the logical man to assist the Ashworth-Hayward alliance, but, because he was playing the game

[7] See Davis, op. cit., pp. 194–95 et passim.

in the other direction, they needed Sherman to run their interference for them and to obtain for them the men and planes necessary to move ahead with their project.

It is also worth noting that the Ashworth-Hayward alliance did not attempt to justify their cause in terms of any new grand strategy. There was no great strategic vision, no talk of a revolution in naval warfare, no talk of a revolution in warfare in general. As far as Ashworth and Hayward and Sherman and Forrestal and most other naval aviators were concerned (Forrestal, too, had been a Navy flier, in World War I), the revolution in naval warfare had taken place in World War II, had been successfully won, and they were merely taking the next logical steps. The revolution in naval warfare, as the aviators saw it, was the departure during World War II from the old conviction that had dominated the Navy for decades before the war—i.e., the conviction that navies existed primarily to fight other navies—to the new view that ships at sea were merely launching platforms for projecting military force against an adversary—wherever the adversary might be located, on land or on sea—within the range of carrier aircraft.

The Ashworth-Hayward alliance did not engage in the kind of sophisticated analyses that characterized the late 1950s and the 1960s, when new weapons systems were under consideration. Those later analyses sought to predict what new weapons systems might do to international politics, power balances, and possible counterweapons produced by adversaries. Rather, these key members of the alliance justified their cause primarily in terms of simply having found a better way to perform a Navy mission they had argued for throughout a period well before World War II, a mission they felt had been clearly established within and for the Navy during the war itself. In this sense the Ashworth-Hayward alliance was primarily an action in response to factors internal to the Navy; stated more specifically, it was part of the consolidation of the naval aviators' triumph as they assumed dominance in the postwar Navy over the battleship admirals, who had dominated it for almost half a century before the war. It was in this light that the suggestion was made earlier in this article that the naval aviators would doubtless have sought a capability to deliver nuclear weapons even if the Air Force and the Navy's conflict with the Air Force had not existed. But those factors did have a bearing on the success or failure of the Ashworth-Hayward alliance, even if they were not a part of what stimulated the two men to undertake their project.

The Navy's conflict with the Air Force, as suggested earlier, helped the Ashworth-Hayward alliance in the sense that many naval officers who under other circumstances might not have favored innovative proposals were willing to tolerate these new ideas if they would help the Navy to survive in the face of the Air Force challenge. Moreover, the fact that the Air Force had attempted to embody the new "consensus" national strategy, which emphasized nuclear bombing, had assisted the Ashworth-Hayward team, not only in making the Air Force threat seem more dangerous to their fellow naval officers, but also in providing a potentially favorable climate in Congress and in the White House if these advocates could demonstrate that naval carrier planes were at least as useful as Air Force bombers in nuclear strike missions.

Little or no specific regard was given to any particular adversary in the thinking and arguments of the Ashworth-Hayward team within the Navy. Naval officers, primarily because of prodding from Secretary Forrestal, gradually came to view the Soviet Union as the main new international menace during the period beginning in early 1945 (actually late 1944) and carrying into 1947, when Hayward began his efforts in behalf of a Navy nuclear delivery capability. But neither Hayward nor other naval officers argued for this capability primarily, or even secondarily, in terms of a response to the Soviet danger. Looking back from the perspectives of the 1960s, it seems curious that this argument was not strongly used by the Ashworth-Hayward team. The Soviet Union possessed a negligible navy in the immediate post–World War II period and was not greatly dependent on maritime commerce. Therefore, if the U.S. Navy was going to play a major role in American responses to the Soviet threat, that role in the late 1940s would necessarily have to be constructed around a capability to penetrate the Soviet land mass with long-range strikes using carrier aircraft. Forrestal understood this as early as late 1944, but substantial numbers of naval officers did not really begin to understand it until several years later.[8] Members of the Ashworth-Hayward alliance accordingly based their arguments for a nuclear delivery capability mainly on the simple and broadly general proposition, derived from the far-ranging and diverse uses of carrier aircraft in World War II, that anything which improved the long-range striking power of the fleet was vitally necessary for the Navy and would be of potentially great use against almost any adversary.

In summary, only in the sense of the general proposition noted above did the Ashworth-Hayward alliance pay any explicit attention to international factors in analyzing and arguing the case for a Navy nuclear delivery capability. Their thinking and their efforts were primarily an outgrowth of the Navy's experiences in World War II, not an explicit and carefully formulated response to new threats foreseen in the postwar world. The bitter conflict between the Navy and the Air Force was neither the stimulus for, nor a major initial part of, the arguments for the Ashworth-Hayward proposal, but the conflict related to the eventual success of the Ashworth-Hayward proposal within the Navy in that it encouraged naval officers to be receptive to new ideas—especially a new idea that seemed in keeping with the major emphases in defense policymaking in Congress and in the White House. In all of these ways it seems fair to conclude that the Ashworth-Hayward proposal was far more a response to considerations internal to the Navy and internal to the national policymaking environment in Washington than a response to explicitly recognized and analyzed factors in the international political environment.

.   .   .   .

CONCLUSIONS°

To repeat a point that was emphasized at the beginning of this article, the main purpose here has not been to provide a historical case study that is complete and assuredly accurate in all details, but rather to trace some basic features of a relatively well-developed case in order to suggest some patterned aspects of individual and organizational behavior in a par-

[8] *Ibid.*, pp. 100–118, 219–25, *et passim.*

° [*Editors' note:* Once again, these generalizations were derived from a careful study of all the cases in the original work, not just the case reprinted here.]

ticular kind of setting within a fairly well-defined time frame and historical period. However, to repeat a warning that was emphasized at the outset, the case that has been used is *not* in all respects complete, and many of the conclusions to be elucidated below are based at least as much on the author's personal observations of relevant individuals as on the more conventional kinds of easily replicable hard-data research. Therefore, the behavior patterns that will be described below should be regarded as a set of hypotheses rather than as tightly demonstrated facts—hypotheses whose chief value may be to serve as a point of departure for further research of a more rigorous nature in the future. With these caveats in mind (along with other provisos stated at the outset but not repeated at this point), it is now appropriate to try to trace a number of the patterns that appear to be generally consistent and prevalent in the case considered. Some of these patterns have already been suggested at appropriate points within the case study, while others will be noted below in explicit fashion for the first time here.

CHARACTERISTICS OF THE INNOVATION ADVOCATE

1. *The innovation advocate in the Navy is usually a man in the broad middle ranks.* The three junior officer ranks in the Navy are ensign, lieutenant (junior grade), and lieutenant. The senior ranks are the flag ranks—the admirals. The middle ranks are lieutenant commander, commander, and captain. It is within these three middle ranks that the innovation advocate is most likely to be found, with commander seeming to be the most frequently observed rank level. The typical innovation advocate has usually been a commissioned officer for at least ten years, but seldom for more than eighteen, or twenty at the very most, with approximately fifteen years of commissioned service being the most frequently observed figure. Among all of the individuals considered in the case presented here, only a few of the civilian scientists had worked for the Navy for less than ten years. One may therefore offer the generalization that, if the innovation advocate is a civilian scientist rather than a uniformed officer, he will be somewhat younger in years and somewhat younger in time with the Navy than his officer counterpart. However, there

have been far more uniformed officers than civilian Navy scientists among the innovation advocates, and there have been no regular civil service Navy employees or administrators found among the innovators. The officer innovators have tended to vary in age from the early thirties to the middle forties. Those mentioned here who were flag officers were usually young rear admirals serving as the spokesmen for a group of younger officers in the middle-rank levels. The typical innovation advocate has been in the organization (i.e., the Navy) long enough to have acquired an organization-wide perspective and an affectionate concern for the welfare and the future of the whole organization. But he has not been in the organization so long that he is dull or cynical or matter-of-fact about it, nor does he have sufficient rank and responsibilities to cause him to be cautious in advocating proposals for the Navy in deference to wider perspectives at higher rank levels, where a feel for the broader implications of overall national policy problems are often found. The innovation advocate tends to identify himself very strongly with the Navy, and he tends to identify the Navy's interests with the nation's interests. He is in the full vigor of his professional years; he is energetic, hard-driving, and confident of success.

2. *The innovation advocate is seldom the inventor of the innovation that he is promoting, but he usually possesses a uniquely advanced technological knowledge pertinent to the innovation that is not generally shared within the Navy.* The innovation, in the first place, is seldom a single invention. It is almost always a combination of the newer fruits of several scientific and technical fields. The advocate, then, is the man who, having kept up with developments in these fields, sees an imaginative way in which these combined developments can be applied to a naval problem or situation. It ought to be added that in many cases the proposed innovation requires things that in fact have not yet been invented, but which the innovation advocate assumes can be brought into being if work (i.e., R&D) is performed in the urged direction.

3. *The innovation advocate is a passionate zealot.* Indeed, it may sometimes appear that he is a fanatic, so in love with his proposed innovation that he is determined to see it adopted by the Navy no matter at what cost

to other Navy programs and purposes. But this picture is almost always misleading in at least some respects. The innovation advocate is a man of strong attachments and convictions, given to expressing himself in enthusiastic and sometimes exaggerated and even emotional terms, but his real love is the organization itself (i.e., the Navy) and the nation that he tends to identify with the organization. He is a dedicated patriot, but he does not hesitate to criticize those things he loves (although he is not very charitable toward outsiders who may offer similar criticisms), because he is also a perfectionist. The characteristics of an organization or a procedure that he tolerates least well are inefficiencies of any kind, obsolete practices that can be justified only by tradition, and dull conventional thinking. If there is a better way to do it, he is determined to see it done the better way, and he is greatly annoyed by opponents who give him routine, unthoughtful replies. However, his imaginative, critical, and innovative thinking tends to focus on implementation, not on the broad goals or national strategies or social values that his proposal is presumably meant to help implement. In this sense, he takes the goals and values as unchanging givens; on these matters he is himself a dull conventional thinker who appeals to tradition. He tolerates and indeed appreciates well-reasoned rebuttal, but he does not suffer fools gladly. He has a certain intellectual arrogance because he is impatient with what he regards as dull minds. He attracts followers in part by the sheer charm of his driving dedication and his superior intellect, but he also attracts opponents from among equally intelligent people who prefer a calmer and more cautious approach, as well as from among those more conventional individuals who fear change in contrast to the comfort of established routines.

4. *The innovation advocate seldom pays any attention whatever to the way in which his crusading efforts may influence his personal career in the Navy or elsewhere.* In this sense he appears to be a most unselfish man, but this appearance is deceptive. He is not intentionally sacrificing himself, because he simply does not give himself or his career a thought when he embarks on the advocacy process. His single-minded concern is to achieve what he views as a dramatic improvement in the Navy, and he does not calculate one way or the other what his crusade may do for or against his personal advancement. He is merely a radical reformer whose momentary obsession is the reform or the innovation that he is advocating. Even if he wished to calculate in advance what his advocacy activities could do to his career, it would be most difficult for him because there are no statistics or charts to suggest to him the degree to which he is pursuing a high-risk personal career strategy. This is partly because, as was noted in the first few pages of this article, there is little evidence, even within the Navy, of "losers"—i.e., those who advocated innovations but who lost either in terms of failing to sell the innovation or in terms of deprivations in their further careers. If the typical innovation advocate considers in any manner the possible consequences for his career, he does it through an instinctive sense of what strategies tend to work within the Navy rather than through an explicit calculation. Moreover, the typical innovation advocate is a vastly self-confident person who has already enjoyed a prominent and promising career, and who is accustomed to "winning." He does not figure on losing in this case. The innovation advocates mentioned in this paper were younger officers who were later promoted to the ranks of the admirals and to extremely prominent positions in the Navy. These were all "winners," however, who not only had achieved early prominence but who also possessed the conventional qualifications for promotion along with their technical achievements. The few "losers," who have not been cited in this article, were all drawn from pre–World War II cases, and did appear to suffer for their zealous advocacies in terms of their future Navy careers. But in either case—prominent later careers or diminished later careers—the innovation advocates did not appear to calculate these possibilities in advance in any explicit sense.

Based on the inadequate and sketchy case presented here, one can at least suggest some crude generalizations about the way in which the advocacy of an innovation may relate to an individual's later career in the Navy. When an innovation advocate experiences an enhanced later career, the following conditions tend to be present: (1) he met the conventional standards for promotion; (2) his proposed innovation was rather quickly accepted and applauded within the Navy, with initial resistance being quickly overcome; (3) he acquired strong supporters in a variety of well-placed positions of seniority and power, both within and outside the Navy; (4) he avoided giving unnecessary offense to a large number of well-placed senior authorities who were not initially in favor of his proposal.

None of this is to say that there are not innovation advocates in the Navy who have carefully calculated in advance what their actions might do for or against their Navy careers, but the evidence thus far obtained by this author has not revealed any such individuals. One can conceive of the possibility of an individual who, because of factors of personal background and an undistinguished early career in the Navy, may think he has nothing to lose and everything to gain by advocating an innovation which—if successful—would give him his only chance for an enhanced later career. One knowledgeable scholar who read this article in an earlier version suggested to the author that Captain Hyman Rickover might approximate this model. However, if this is correct—and the author is not at all sure that it is correct—Rickover is the only individual known to the author who approximates this model rather than the more general model described here.

The Advocate's Political Techniques

1. *The advocate's first step is usually to try to enlist supporters from among friends and colleagues at his own rank level.* His first thought, apparently, is that if he can recruit enough supporters at approximately his rank, perhaps even within the office or bureau in which he is assigned, he may be able to get his innovation accepted at that level and some initial exploratory work underway without the need at that stage to take the matter to higher authorities. He tends frequently to be successful in gaining supporters at this lower level, resulting in what has here been called a *horizontal political alliance*, but he is seldom successful in getting the initial exploratory work underway at this level—probably because the proposed innovations are too costly and have too many far-reaching implications to be budgeted and managed at the lower levels without some form of endorsement from higher

authority. It is usually the case that the horizontal political alliance does not emerge from the work of a single individual, but from the efforts of several individuals, each of whom has the same or closely related ideas at approximately the same time, each of whom thus proceeds on his own initiative at first, and each of whom then discovers the efforts of the others, after which they combine forces. The horizontal alliance takes shape as they begin in some manner to coordinate their efforts— sometimes tacitly, sometimes in a more formal and organized manner.

2. *The advocate's second step, whether or not he achieves success in the first step, is usually to recruit supporters in key positions of authority and power at higher levels.* If he has failed in the first step, the successful achievement of the second step may be called a *vertical political alliance.* If he succeeds in both steps, the result may be called a *coordinate political alliance* with horizontal and vertical elements. In any case, a strong vertical element appears to be an absolutely essential condition for the success of the advocate's promotional efforts. This is true because, in an organization such as the Navy, which has a tight hierarchical structure and strong authoritarian patterns, things simply are not achieved by means of grass-roots movements alone, no matter how strong.

3. *The proinnovation alliance seldom seeks or even admits extraorganization supporters or allies unless and until this appears necessary as a last resort.* The author's research on the Navy's officer corps reveals a very strong value pattern against the involvement of outsiders in settling disputes or disagreements "within the family"—i.e., within the Navy. The Navy's innovation advocates have almost always seemed to be clearly aware of this, and have therefore exhibited a strong preference for settling the issues within the Navy; they have known that to bring outsiders into the discussion would most likely build resentment within the Navy against their cause. In short, extraorganization allies can be counterproductive, especially if they are admitted to the nascent alliance before it has acquired a strong vertical dimension within the Navy. In some cases where innovation advocates have suffered later in terms of their career advancement in the Navy, it appears that their premature effort to

acquire (or even their tolerance of unsolicited) extraorganization allies was part of the cause.

4. *The proinnovation coalition seldom seeks to sell its idea in terms of new conceptions of international politics, military strategy, tactics, and so on.* On the contrary, the usual gambit is to try to sell and to justify the proposed innovation as a *better way to perform some well-established Navy task or mission.* A sometimes complementary gambit is to justify this established mission in terms of whatever may be fashionable at the moment in public and high-level governmental views on national military strategy and foreign policy. The proinnovation coalition seldom succeeds in its cause unless *both* of these two related tactics are successfully employed. Two factors may in part account for the innovation advocates' tendency not to think and/or talk in terms of new conceptions of international politics and military strategy. In the first place, the advocates have usually been men with considerable technical and/or scientific training, but with very little or no training or background in the kind of intellectual operations required for political or strategic analyses. Second, the advocates may have been instinctively aware that an innovation tends to result in changes within an organization, but that it would be easier to sell the innovation to the organization if the scope and magnitude of those changes were minimized during the selling period. In short, the advocates may have understood that it would be easier to sell their proposal if it appeared that the adoption of the proposal would result in few, if any, major changes in the Navy's internal and external settings.

The Opponents' Political Techniques

1. *If and when a counteralliance comes into existence to oppose the proinnovation alliance, the counteralliance usually emerges first at senior rank levels and builds strength by acquiring members at gradually lower rank levels.* A counteralliance therefore starts with a horizontal component, like the proalliance, but the horizontal component is at the top of the rank structure rather than at middle levels. The counteralliance seldom actually needs a vertical component, in contrast to the proalliance, but it tends to acquire one in any case from among those younger officers who feel that they should respond to the cues of their superiors

who are in a part of the counteralliance. The vertical component of the counteralliance is therefore built from the top downward, whereas the vertical component of the proalliance is built from the middle ranks upward.

A counteralliance seldom has the cohesion or energetic drive of the proalliance it is attempting to thwart. It emerges from a more or less tacit understanding among senior officers and officials that a crusading procoalition must be stopped. Sometimes, however, the initial tacit understanding can evolve into more-or-less formal and concrete actions coordinated within the counteralliance with the intent of halting the proinnovation alliance.

2. *The counteralliance usually argues against the proinnovation alliance on the grounds that "it will cost too much."* The counteralliance has seldom wished to appear to be against "progress," so it typically argues merely that it would cost too much. In the earlier part of the century, the "too much" referred to the monetary cost of adopting the innovation within the Navy if it proved successful. Gradually, the "too much" began to refer to the monetary cost of finding out whether it would be successful —i.e., the R&D cost. More recently, the "too much" has referred to other kinds of costs and resource allocations. For example, after World War II, counterinnovation alliances in the Navy often agreed that the proposed innovation would at least be worth exploring in principle, but that the cost of exploring and/or adopting the innovation would be enormously disruptive of, and harmful to, other high-priority Navy goals, programs, and procedures.

3. *The counteralliance, like the proalliance, seldom argues in terms of new conceptions of international politics, grand military strategy, tactics, and the like.* To the extent that either group introduces such questions, the arguments are almost always couched in terms of presently fashionable concepts and perspectives on American military strategy and foreign policy. In short, neither side pays much explicit attention to the long-range implications and consequences for international politics, rival foreign policies, and competitive military strategies if the innovation is or is not developed and adopted within the Navy. National adversaries, real or potential, are seldom mentioned in the pro and con arguments, unless (which is not often the case) the innovation

is explicitly designed to cope with some special threat posed by an immediately perceived and widely recognized adversary. (For example, the post–World War II case outlined in this article did not feature a proalliance which based its arguments primarily on the grounds of an improved capability to cope with the main adversary envisaged during that period: the Soviet Union. On the other hand, a few innovations after World War II were proposed on the grounds of an improved capability to cope with some special aspect of the Soviet threat—e.g., the Soviet submarine threat.) This means that neither the proalliance nor the counteralliance tends to pay much heed to conceivable responses to the innovation on the part of adversaries or to what those responses might mean in broader global dimensions.

THE HORSE CAVALRY IN THE TWENTIETH CENTURY: A STUDY IN POLICY RESPONSE

EDWARD L. KATZENBACH, JR.

This study deals with one of the two major problems of technological change: obsolescence. Katzenbach points out that this problem is not narrowly technical, but broadly intellectual, involving the issue of organizational doctrine. He cites four factors in institutional survival: (1) the ambiguous role of history (the absence of a final testing agency); (2) mission justification for the future (that cavalry was necessary to fight other cavalry); (3) the concept of a balanced force ("each arm has powers and limitations"); and (4) concepts of modernization (intellectual isolation). Dr. Katzenbach was Director of the Defense Studies Program at Harvard University when this article was written.

THE PROBLEM

Lag-time, that lapsed period between innovation and a successful institutional or social response to it, is probably on the increase in military matters. Moreover, as the tempo of technological change continues to quicken, it is likely that lag-time will increase as well. This is understandable: the kind of readjustment in terms of doctrine, organization, and training that the ballistic missile will demand of those who have flown manned aircraft from land and sea simply shocks the imagination. Atomics, supersonics, and electronics of widely differentiated capabilities make the problem of successful institutional absorption most difficult.

Of course, at first there would seem to be a paradox here. As weapons systems have become more complex, the lead-time needed to bring them from the drawing board to the assembly line has become markedly longer. On the basis of the longer lead-time, one might hypothesize that the institutional lag might lessen inasmuch as prior planning would seem eminently more possible. It might even be

Reprinted by permission and with minor changes from Public Policy, 7 (1958): 120–49. *Copyright © 1958 by the Graduate School of Public Administration, Harvard University.*

surmised that the institutional response might be made to coincide with the operational readiness of new weapons. To date, however, military institutions have not been able to use this lead-time effectively, because real change has so outdistanced anticipated change. Moreover, there is not the urgency that there should be in the military to make major institutional adjustments in the face of the challenge of new weapons systems, if for no other reason than that the problem of testing is so difficult. Just as in the academic world it is well-nigh impossible to *prove* that any change in curriculum would enable future leaders to think more clearly than those with a classical education, so in the military it is quite impossible to *prove* that minor adjustments in a traditional pattern of organization and doctrine will not suffice to absorb technological innovations of genuine magnitude.

Furthermore, the absence of any final testing mechanism of the military's institutional adequacy short of war has tended to keep the pace of change to a creep in time of peace, and, conversely, has whipped it into a gallop in time of war. The military history of the past half century is studded with institutions which have managed to dodge the challenge of the obvious. The Coast Artillery continued until the middle of World War II, at least in the United States. Other such institutional anomalies will spring to mind. But the most curious of all was the horse cavalry, which maintained a capacity for survival that borders on the miraculous. The war horse survived a series of challenges, each of which was quite as great as those which today's weapons systems present to today's traditional concepts. Like the mollusk, the horse cavalry made those minor adjustments that time dictated absolutely. Then it continued to live out an expensive and decorous existence with splendor and some spirit straight into an age which thought it a memory. Indeed, it is difficult to conceive of an institution that underlines so sharply the relativity of the concept of obsolescence. In times such as these, when today's weapons are already out-of-date and there is therefore a daily need for reassessing our military institutions' response to them, the strange and wonderful survival of the horse cavalry may amount to something more than a curiously alarming anachronism.

Since the end of the nineteenth century, the horse cavalry has had to review its role in war four times, in the face of four great changes in the science of war: the development of repeating automatic and semi-automatic weapons, the introduction of gasoline and diesel-fueled engines, the invention of the airborne weapon, and the coming of the nuclear battlefield. Each new challenge to the horse has been, of necessity, seriously considered. Each has demanded a review of doctrine, a change in role and mission. And in each review, of necessity, assumptions have been made as to the relevance of experience to some pattern of future war. The role and mission of a service or branch or unit must, after all, be based on some reasoned view of men's future reactions under the circumstances of war—when man is at his most unreasonable. Indeed, the paradox of military planning is that it must be reasonably precise as to quite imprecise future contingencies.

THE WEAPONS PROBLEM

By the year 1900, or thereabouts, the clip-fed, breech-loading repeating rifle was in the hands of the troops of all the major powers. The French Lebel had been adopted in 1886 after a decade of squabbling—the most difficult weapons to adopt or to change are the simplest: sword, lance, bayonet, rifle (the improved Mauser in 1898 and the United States Springfield in 1903). The Lee-Enfield, the Ariska, the Mannlicher-Carcano, all rifles which were to become familiar to millions in two world wars, had been developed by the beginning of the century and either were in, or were about to go into, production.

Self-firing automatic weapons were also on the assembly lines of the world's armament makers. Hiram Maxim had registered the last of a famous series of machine gun patents in 1885. By the time (1904–1905) of the Russo-Japanese War, the guns of Maxim and Hotchkiss were in national arsenals everywhere, or almost everywhere, for the expense of new weapons was rapidly shrinking the ranks of those powers which could be considered "great." At roughly the same time it had been found that the use of glycerine in the recoil mechanism of artillery pieces enabled these to remain aimed after being fired. This in turn meant that the artillery piece itself would become a rapid fire (20 rounds per minute) weapon. The French "Seventy-Five," perhaps the most famous of all artillery pieces, was shortly to be in production. Firepower, in short, had a new meaning.

For the elite of the armies of the world, the cavalry, each of these developments would seem to have been nothing short of disaster. For that proud and beautiful animal, the horse, has a thin skin and a high silhouette, and its maximum rate of speed on the attack is only 30 miles per hour. Especially in conjunction with barbed wire, automatically manufactured since 1874 and in military use at the end of the century, it is difficult to imagine a target more susceptible to rapid fire.

The cavalry had always considered itself to have a variety of missions. The cavalry was the good eye of the infantry. It was taught to collect, and if necessary to fight for, information about the enemy. The cavalry protected friendly, and harried enemy, flanks and rear. It covered any necessary withdrawal. It was used in pursuit of the defeated enemy. And, above and beyond all else, the cavalry was used to charge the faltering, the weary, or the unwary, to deliver the *coup de grace* with the *arme blanche:* with cold steel, with saber or lance, to "crown victory," as the proud phrase went.

It was clear that the introduction of the automatic and the semi-automatic weapon would make some cavalry missions more difficult. But there was no doubt in any cavalryman's mind, and there was little doubt in the minds of most others, that most cavalry missions would have to continue, simply because there was no viable substitute. The horse was transport, and the horse was mobility. A group of horsemen could cover a hundred miles in twenty-four hours with a load of around 225–250 pounds each. The beast was reasonably amphibious; at least it could swim rivers.[1] To scout, to patrol, to cover flank, rear, and withdrawal, to raid— these missions remained untouched.

There remained, however, one really great problem area. Did automatic fire relegate the horse to a transport role or should it still be considered as part of a weapons system? At the time, the problem was never stated quite this simply. Indeed, it was never stated simply at all, but in essence this was the issue from roughly the end of the Boer War until World War I. The reason why the question so divided men was this: Cavalry as an arm was an integrated weapon made up of horse, man, and cold steel fighting as one. If horses were to be considered simply as transportation, and if man and horse were to be separated for the fire fight, then the cavalry as an arm would no longer exist. Only mounted infantry would remain.[2]

On the issue of the relationship between horse and man hung a number of subsidiary issues. Should the horseman be armed with the new automatic weapons? If so, he would have to be dismounted in action, for the horse, as differentiated from the elephant, is a most unsatisfactory gun platform. Yet, to deprive cavalry of the new weapons would be to deprive the weapons of mobility. And, if the horse could no longer be used to charge the new guns, then of what possible use was honed steel—e.g., lance and sword, even if one took into serious account the last-ditch defense of it—to wit, that it was "always loaded"? Finally, and here one comes to the most burning question in any issue of military policy— what would be the effect of change on morale? If the cavalry were deprived of its cold steel, would it lose that fine edge of morale, that élan without which it simply would not be "cavalry," no matter what its mission?

There should have been some way to learn through experience just what could and could not be done with the cavalry with and against the new weapons. There were, after all, two wars of some importance during the period under consideration—the Boer War (1898–1901) and the Russo-Japanese War (1904–1905). In both, cavalry and repeating and automatic weapons were used. Each fall, moreover, there were great maneuvers in each country of Europe. Present at each were foreign observers with, at least by modern standards, a free run of the field of action. Why was it, then, that no final decisions could be reached on these matters?

---

[1] This ability and the fact that the U.S. Cavalry thought more about this aspect of horsemanship than did the troops of other nations, made possible the last of the cavalry's "great raids," that across the Sabine River in the Louisiana maneuvers in 1940.

[2] Perhaps this will be better understood if a modern analogy is cited—the substitution of missiles for manned aircraft, for example.

The answer lies in the number of variables.[3] For instance, before the problem of the cavalry armament could even be tackled, the difficult question had to be answered as to what the rapid-fire weapons could do and should be doing.

There was agreement that a given weapon, *if* it was kept supplied with ammunition, could be fired for a given period of time *if* it could be kept in action (i.e., if it was *not* knocked out by, say, long-range artillery fire) at a certain rate of fire, and that the firing might or might not be worthwhile, depending on the availability of targets—i.e., enemy tactical doctrine. In short, for each demonstrable fact there was an awkwardly intangible "if" which could neither be properly accounted for nor possibly forgotten.

If into the balance of judgment concerning the machine gun was thrown the urgent problem of its resupply and its vulnerability to long-range artillery fire, the rational conclusion might be reached that the weapon was primarily defensive in character and should be dug into the earth, into a well-sandbagged bunker, there to pour forth its withering fire into an attacking force. Yet if, on the other hand, it was concluded that the withering fire of the weapon made it ideal for use on the surprise target, the target of opportunity on the enemy flank, the weapon became offensive.[4] If it was an offensive weapon, the machine gun could well be designated a cavalry weapon. If it was defensive, was it not an infantry, or even an artillery, weapon? Of course, this initial decision was a serious one, for it would most likely determine the future of the weapon. Once assigned to an organization or to a branch or arm of a service, it was at least likely that the weapon's development would be stunted, except in line with the mission of the unit to which it was assigned.

Within the military staffs of all nations the

machine gun raised many more problems than it solved—as can be expected of any new weapons system. Furthermore, these problems were broadly intellectual rather than narrowly technical. Indeed, the mechanical improvement of a given weapons system is usually less urgent and almost always less baffling than deciding a proper and fitting target for it and then solving the galaxy of problems of organization and control which hinge on this basic decision. Perhaps the fact that there are such agonizing reappraisals of organization and doctrine in the light of new invention only after what seems in retrospect the most reprehensible time-lag, whether it be a matter of horse cavalry or smallish atomic loads, may best be explained as being due to the enormous difficulty of predicting the future. For the future of war can be constructed only on the basis of enemy capabilities in unstable combination with a guestimate as to his intentions. This also explains why each nation maneuvered against itself each fall, dividing itself into Red Forces and Blue Forces, each of which was endowed with the same characteristics as the other, instead of trying another nation's tactics against itself. The latter was simply too difficult. For the cavalry to have to think about automatic weapons was understandably tortuous and time-consuming.

So in the period between 1900 and 1914 the immediate problem was to conceptualize the mission or missions of the machine gun and the tactics of the new clip-fed, bolt-action rifle and the automatic gun. The second problem was to decide the future tactics and armament of cavalry in view of the concept arrived at. What actually happened was that the new was absorbed into old organizational and tactical concepts, and nothing of the old was rejected. The reasoning from country to country, however, may be of lasting interest. The matter of the cavalry *charge* provides an excellent focal point.

THE CHARGE

It is hard to see where there was room for claim and counterclaim in so substantive an issue as this—the charge of a wave of horsemen, gaily colored (except in the United States), helmets shining, plumes flying, sabers drawn, or lances at the ready. Surely a comprehensive and conclusive study of the charge

---

[3] And it must be made quite clear that the computer, had it been available, would not have been of much greater use then than it is currently in determining the worth of the naval aircraft carrier in the supersonic age.

[4] In more recent times both tank and plane have been the subject of the offensive-defensive debate. The denouement of tank theory occurred during the course of the battle of France in the spring of 1940. For a discussion of machine gun theory, see G. S. Hutchison, *Machine Guns: Their History and Tactical Employment* (London, 1938), chap. 4, particularly p. 78.

and its role, if any, in modern war was not outside the bounds of logical possibility. Yet, just as it was impossible in the 1930s to analyze the role of the battleship in the air age, and just as it is now impossible to assess the relationship between the naval aircraft carrier and the nuclear bomber, so it was impossible to evaluate the charge—and for much the same reasons.

The reasons why the charge was continued varied from one country to another. But basically it was continued because the cavalry liked it. In virtually all countries the cavalry was a club, an exclusive one, made up at the officer level of those who could afford to ride when young, hunt, dress, and play polo when older. The impression that one absorbs from contemporary cavalry reviews, from the pictures, the social columns, the interests expressed in the less-than-serious articles, together with the portrait of the cavalryman in the contemporary novel, is one of a group of men who were at once hard-riding, hard-drinking, and hard-headed. Its leadership was derived from the countryside rather than from the city. The cavalry was the home of tradition, the seat of romance, the haven of the well-connected. New York City's Squadron A, the proud majors in the Prussian Cavalry Reserve, the French Horse Breeders' Association —all had a built-in loyalty to the cavalry, and, if the Chief of Cavalry said that the charge was still feasible, he had important backing. So it was that in Europe the charge was still considered not only feasible but a future way of war.

American cavalrymen, however, thought that the European cavalry had much to learn. And in many respects the U.S. "Red Necks" were quite the most realistic of the world's cavalries in the period just prior to World War I. To be sure, they retained the saber charge, executing it with the same straight saber, a thrust weapon, used by the Canadian cavalry. But in the years from just before World War I until just after World War II the U.S. Cavalry preferred to practice the charge with the Colt semi-automatic .45 pistol.[5] (The pistol charge

was never actually used in battle. The last battle charge of the U.S. Cavalry seems to have been in the Philippines during the insurrection of 1901.) Of course, it might be argued that to put a .45 in the hands of a man on a horse was simply to mount the inaccurate on the unstable, but, given the argument that the essence of the charge was its psychological impact, the sound of the .45 might have had an effect comparable to the sight of saber or lance.

But what the U.S. Cavalry did have that others did not was a genuine appreciation of the importance of dismounted action. It is this which is given the more elaborate treatment in the regulations, and it is this that the trooper really expected to be the rule in combat. But was this the result of a thoughtful analysis of the new weapons or something else?

Certainly the articles in the *Journal of the U.S. Cavalry Association* are the most sophisticated in regard to the new repeating arms and their impact on cavalry. In the years just after the turn of the century the great argument in U.S. Cavalry circles was whether or not the saber should be retained at all.[6] But it seems to have been generally admitted that, while "Mounted charges may yet be used on rare occasions when the enemy is demoralized, out of ammunition, or completely taken by surprise," nonetheless, "for cavalry to make a mounted charge against enemy troops who are dismounted and armed with the present magazine gun, would be to seek disaster."[7] The corollary that "the trooper must bear in mind that in fighting his carbine is his main reliance"[8] was also accepted.

Were it not that certain European cavalry groups were at the time tending to reject the thesis to which the U.S. subscribed, there would be nothing in any way remarkable about the U.S. position, so patently obvious and right does it seem in retrospect. Yet in the

---

[5] The cavalry drill regulations remain fascinating reading for those with a technical interest. See, for example, *Cavalry Drill Regulations, United States Army* (New York: Military Publishing Co., 1916). See also the 1940 edition of *Cavalry Combat* (New York, 1940).

[6] See, for example, G. H. Morgan, "Mounted Rifles," *Journal of the U.S. Cavalry Association (JUSCA)*, 13, no. 47 (January 1903); "Comment and Criticism," *ibid.*, no. 48 (April 1903); James Parker, "The Retention of the Saber as a Cavalry Weapon," *ibid.*, 14, no. 50 (July 1904); and particularly for the pros and cons on opposite sides of the page, *ibid.*, no. 52 (December 1904). This presents a particularly interesting study in conflicting expectations.

[7] "Comment and Criticism," *ibid.*, 13, no. 48 (April 1903): 720.

[8] *Ibid.*, p. 721.

early 1900s U.S. doctrine was different, and hence needs a word of explanation.

The U.S. cavalryman had a tradition quite different from that of any of the Europeans. He had always done the bulk of his fighting on his feet. Therefore there was no break in tradition for him to recognize the revolution in firepower for the great change it was. Cavalry during the Civil War most frequently fought dismounted, although clashes between cavalry were fought with the sword, and in the wars against the Indians cavalrymen also dismounted to fight with the aimed accurate fire that was quite unattainable on horseback. Horses were considered transportation, and the ground was considered a respectable substance on which to fight a battle. U.S. cavalrymen did not feel morally obligated to die on a horse— which European cavalrymen did. In short, the U.S. Cavalry reacted to the new firepower as it did because its history and its tradition made it quite natural for it to do so. In Europe the cavalry history of the U.S. Civil War was scarcely known until the very late 1900s, and hence the relevance of that war to cavalry problems was largely overlooked.[9] Or, given European experience and tradition, would a study of the Civil War have made any real difference?

Of all the cavalry arms of the world, the one which seems in retrospect to have been the furthest behind the times was that of the German Empire. The German Cavalry had adopted the lance for all ninety-three of its cavalry regiments in 1890, instead, as was true in the mid-nineteenth century, of having only one in four so armed. The lance was, of course, much more than a shaft of wood taller than a man, one tipped with steel and pennant-decked: a lance was a state of mind. And it was a reminder that those who carried it still believed that the cavalry really was an arm to be reckoned with.[10] Indeed, so committed was the German Cavalry to its use in a charge that the most vocal of the defenders of the lance and the outstanding author on cavalry matters,

General von Bernhardi, felt he had to warn the country that "in spite of the increased importance this form of fighting (i.e., with a rifle) has acquired in modern war, our cavalry has not yet paid anything like the amount of attention to the subject that it deserves." He then went on to say that "almost everywhere it is treated as of quite minor importance, and many cavalrymen still close their eyes to the view that, without a training at once as thorough and earnest for dismounted action as that bestowed on the arm to fit it for its mounted duties, modern cavalry will hardly survive the trials it will encounter in the future."[11]

Why was it that such serious students of war as the Germans are reputed to have been were in general quite so oblivious to the impact of the new firepower? There seem to have been several reasons. The first and most important was the attitude of Emperor William II toward the cavalry. A young U.S. Cavalry lieutenant who witnessed German maneuvers in the fall of 1903 was frankly appalled by it. He noted the total lack of realism in the great rolling charges of the cavalry against both rifle and artillery. And he noted too the fact that the Kaiser was so proud of his cavalry that his umpires, knowing their place, pronounced the charges successful![12] In Germany, in short, the Emperor's well-known penchant for the charge undoubtedly did much to insulate the Germans from any serious thought of change.

There was, however, another reason as well. Even after seeing machine guns fired in the late 1880s, the German General Staff refused to take them seriously.[13] Their reason lay in their misreading of their own experience with the *mitrailleuses* during the war of 1870–1871, when these were badly misused. The fact that past experience happened to be irrelevant did not make it any less important, however, and

[9] In this connection see Jay Luvass, "G. F. R. Henderson and the American Civil War," *Military Affairs*, 20, no. 3 (Fall 1956): 139ff., particularly 146.

[10] There are a number of articles on the lance which are of much more than antiquarian interest. See, for example, Charles Ffoulkes, "The Lance," *Army Quarterly*, 17, no. 2 (January 1929): 91ff.

[11] Lt. Gen. Frederick von Bernhardi, *Cavalry in Future Wars* (London, 1909), p. 248. For a comment on German dismounted cavalry in the Franco-Prussian War see G. T. Denison, *A History of Cavalry*, 2nd ed. (London, 1913). Denison was one of the earliest of those who recognized the meaning of the new firepower for the future of cavalry.

[12] Frank R. McCoy, "Notes of the German Maneuvers," *JUSCA*, 14, no. 49 (January 1904): 27. Although he denied it, Hindenburg was rumored to have retired early because in 1908 he let the corps which the Kaiser commanded lose the battle. John W. Wheeler-Bennet, *Wooden Titan* (New York, 1936), p. 5.

[13] Hutchison, *op. cit.*, p. 55.

it was not until 1908 that the machine gun was given the serious attention in Germany that it so obviously deserved.[14] Even then it was only the infantry that recognized the importance of the new automatic weapons. Cavalry units, although armed with them, did not take them very seriously. German cavalry went trotting off to war in 1914, pennons flying from their lances, just as units of French infantry went off to war in red trousers, and for much the same reason: psychological effect. For the real effect of cavalry when on the charge was a psychological one, and was generally admitted as such. It was the role of the charge to break the enemy's will, and what could do this more effectively than a charge by lancers? The same argument was used by those who wanted to keep the infantry in red pants. They advanced the proposition that the sense of belonging was the essence of group spirit, and group spirit in turn was the touchstone of the will to fight, the ingredient that won battles. They added the corollary that nothing gave units the sense of oneness that red trousers did, and that, therefore, camouflaged material would actually sabotage national security. Red pants and lances were both subject to this unshakable *quod erat demonstrandum*.

So tradition, personal predilection, and misinterpreted past experience kept the cavalry charge alive in Germany. The experiences of the British after the Boer War likewise suggest how difficult it is to test the relevance of one's own experience in war.

THE RELEVANCE OF EXPERIENCE

From the end of the Boer War to the beginning of World War I the great debate in the British Cavalry, as in other countries, dealt with the retention of the lance and the charge. The arguments put forward for their retention inevitably raise the question of whether faith was not interfering with reason. The charge is a heroic gesture, and its success depends on each cavalryman's faith that he is invincible. Indeed, the problem of faith is present in all military affairs: the soldier has to believe that he *can* in order to *do*. He must be taught to believe that there are no limitations. By his very training, then, the military man finds it

hard to perceive limitations when such there are, let alone acknowledge them. Experience should be a valuable teacher, yet experience is not always relevant.

A U.S. Cavalry officer noted on a trip to Aldershot in 1903 that "every change is made entirely with reference to the Boer War and the Boer country, as though future wars would be fought under the same conditions."[15] But what this observer should also have noted was that there was a wide division of opinion as to just what that war proved and how genuinely relevant it really was. This problem of the interpretation of experience was not a new one in the historiography of military operations, and is a continuing one. When, after all, is a war or even a battle an aberration from an established norm? And who is to say with any precision just what a "norm" is? When war is won in a battle rather than in a series of battles, such a norm could be established with some semblance of reality. But by its very nature modern war is made up of a series of battles, a cumulative effect. Battles, if not war itself, are decisive in only a limited sense.[16] Furthermore, it has been increasingly true in wars from the Civil War to the Korean episode that what is the correct doctrinal application of force in one area at one time is not always correct for some different time and place. But the very urgency of having a doctrine to teach, of having to write regulations to insure that degree of unity of approach without which no hierarchy can be fully effective, has militated against that flexibility of thought which is only realistic given the differing circumstances under which battles are fought in modern war.[17]

Like other modern wars, the Boer War was made up of a series of actions, no one of which was decisive. The Boers, fine shots and fine horsemen, used their horses as transportation. In effect, they fought as mounted infantry, employing the mobility of the horse in combination with the aimed firepower of infantry. They

[14] *Ibid.*, p. 120.

[15] McCoy, *op. cit.*, pp. 30, 31.
[16] See the suggestive essay on the indecisiveness of war in John Holland Rose, *The Indecisiveness of Modern War and Other Essays* (London, 1927).
[17] Thus German air-tank doctrine won the battle of France and made it possible for Hitler to dance his jig at Réthondes. But this same doctrine never took the Nazis to Omsk and was irrelevant to the problem of taking London.

possessed all the advantages of great space and a friendly and embattled population, and the British were hard put to bring them to terms. But these were virtually the only points on which there was any agreement whatsoever. What did the facts mean, if anything?

Two of Great Britain's best-known military figures, Lord Roberts, the British Chief of Staff, and Field Marshal Sir John D. P. French, Cavalry Commander in Africa and, in 1914, Commander in Chief of the British Expeditionary Forces, led two factions within the army whose views of the future of cavalry were in direct opposition.

The Right Honorable Field Marshal Earl Roberts placed the *imprimatur* of his authority on a book called *War and the Arme Blanche* by one Erskine Childers. In his introduction to this book Lord Roberts set forth his basic beliefs. Thenceforth Mr. Childers supplied the footnotes, so to speak, for those who thought as Lord Roberts did and opposed Sir John. Mr. Childers was a man who led a curiously romantic life—running guns into Southern Ireland, winning the D.S.C. with the Royal Naval Air Service, becoming a Sinn Feiner, and dying before a firing squad. But in his time he was quite an able historian. He wrote a volume of *The Times History of the War in South Africa,* and his *The Riddle of the Sands* is still read. But it is as one of those very rare people, the military critic who proved right, that Mr. Childers deserves a generously dimensioned niche in history.

Lord Roberts believed simply that the "main lesson" to be learned from the Boer War and the Russo-Japanese War was that, "knee to knee, close order charging is practically a thing of the past." He qualified his opinion somewhat. "There may be, there probably will be, mounted attacks, preferably in open order against Cavalry caught unawares, or against broken Infantry," he wrote. But even these mounted attacks, he said, should be carried out with the rifle, rather than with steel.[18] These ideas he actually wrote into the British regulations, *Cavalry Training,* in 1904.

In Childers' *German Influence on British*

Cavalry and in his *War and the Arme Blanche* the details can be found which, from his point of view and Lord Roberts', justified their position against the charge and the lance and in favor of the rifle. The general argument, as one can imagine, was first that lances and sabers were not killing men in war, and second that infantry and mounted infantry were killing, when dismounted, cavalrymen. Three wars —the U.S. Civil War, the Boer War, and the Russo-Japanese War—were cited as proof of the contention. In retrospect this point of view hardly needs explanation. It seems quite obvious to think that the armaments which took the warrior off his feet and put him on his belly would by the same token take him off his charger and put him on the ground.

For a time Lord Roberts was Commander in Chief of the British Army, and his views were thus imposed for a brief moment on the generals. What this meant in effect was that the lance disappeared in Britain between 1903 and 1906. But Lord Roberts proved unpopular, and, as is the way with unpopular leaders, was gently eased out of office in quite short order to become a disturbing shadow among their eminences in the House of Lords. The lance came back into use in 1906 and remained for better than two decades—until 1927, to be precise.

Sir John French, an officer whom one of the most distinguished of Great Britain's War Secretaries, Lord Haldane, called "a real soldier of the modern type,"[19] was an old Hussar. He had entered the army through the militia and had thus avoided Sandhurst and the mental training this would have involved. For Sir John the experience of the Boer War was disturbing only because a number of his colleagues had been disturbed by it. As he thought over this experience, his final assessment as of the very eve of World War I was that "it passes comprehension that some critics in England should gravely assure us that the war in South Africa should be our chief source of inspiration and guidance, and that it was not normal."[20]

---

[18] Erskine Childers, *War and the Arme Blanche* (London, 1910), with an introduction by the Right Honorable Field Marshal Earl Roberts, V.C., K.G., p. xii.

[19] Richard Burdon Haldane, *An Autobiography* (London, 1929), p. 295.

[20] Gen. Friedrich von Bernhardi, *Cavalry* (New York, 1914), with a preface by Field Marshal Sir J. D. P. French, p. 9.

The field marshal's reasoning was very simple. First, he said, "The composition and tactics of the Boer forces were as dissimilar from those of European armies as possible," and he added, "Such tactics in Europe would lead to the disruption and disbandment of any army that attempted them."[21] Second, he noted that in South Africa both unlimited space and the objective of complete submission of the enemy made it a most unusual war. Third, he maintained that the British had not at the time developed proper means for remounting the cavalry with trained horses.[22] But to say this is really to say nothing at all. It is only by uncovering Sir John's basic premises that there is really any possibility of understanding his view of his own experience.

Perhaps Sir John summarized his own thinking best when he wrote sometime during the course of 1908 that "the Boers did all that could be expected of Mounted Infantry, but were powerless to crown victory as only the dash of Cavalry can do."[23] It was the "dash of Cavalry" of which Sir John was thinking. There is ample evidence to document the point. If cold steel were thrown away as "useless lumber," he wrote, "we should invert the role of cavalry, turn it into a defensive arm, and make it a prey to the first foreign cavalry that it meets, for good cavalry can always compel a dismounted force of mounted riflemen to mount and ride away, and when such riflemen are caught on their horses they have power neither of offence nor of defence and are lost."[24] On the basis of this analysis of the effect of rapid fire on mounted cavalry action, he deduced that the proper role of cavalry was first to fight the battlefield's greatest threat— i.e., the enemy cavalry. "The successful cavalry fight confers upon the victor command of the ground."[25] This, he said, was a job for cold steel. Only when the enemy cavalry was out of action did he think that the cavalry would rely more on the rifle than on steel— which is not to say that he ruled "out as impossible, or even unlikely, attacks by great bodies of mounted men against other arms on the battlefield."[26]

So it was that Sir John and his followers decided that the experience of recent wars was irrelevant. The Boer War was not relevant, because it had not been fought in Europe and because the Boers had not been armed with steel as were cavalries in Europe. The war in Manchuria between the Russians and the Japanese was irrelevant, not only because it had not been fought in Europe, but also because the cavalry used there had been badly mounted, rode indifferently, and, above all, was poorly trained—i.e., in dismounted principles. "They were," wrote Sir John, "devoid of real Cavalry training, they thought of nothing but of getting off their horses and shooting."[27] From one principle, note, Sir John never deviated: *Unless the enemy cavalry was defeated, the cavalry could not carry out its other responsibilities.* And there was a corollary of this: *"Only cavalry can defeat cavalry,"* cavalry being defined, of course, as "a body of horsemen armed with steel."

Sir John, however wrong he may have been in his estimate of the firepower revolution of his day, made one point of real consequence when he insisted that the cavalry should keep its mind on a war likely to be fought—which a war in Manchuria, the United States, or South Africa was not. To talk about wars which are likely seems eminently sensible, although there are times when the unlikely ones are given rather more attention than they warrant, depending on what set of premises is in search of some wider acceptance.[28] To cite a recent example, the war in Korea in 1950–1953 provided what seemed to the U.S. Air Force to be irrelevant experience because bombers were not effectively used. To the U.S. Navy and Marine Corps, on the other hand, it seemed very relevant indeed because Korea was a peninsula admirably suited to the projection of naval power. To the U.S. Army it presented a whole new way of thinking: that limited war involving ground troops might well

---

[21] *Ibid.*

[22] *Ibid.*, pp. 10ff.

[23] From his introduction to the English edition of Bernhardi, *Cavalry in Future Wars*, p. x.

[24] Bernhardi, *Cavalry*, p. 11.

[25] *Ibid.*, p. 13.

[26] *Ibid.*, p. 15. See also A. P. Ryan, *Mutiny at the Curragh* (London, 1956), pp. 97–100, for a further elaboration of Sir John's views.

[27] Bernhardi, *Cavalry in Future Wars*, p. xxiii.

[28] The difficulty is readily admitted that wars seem either "likely" or "unlikely" depending upon whether the perspective is past or future.

be the way of the future, despite and because of the horrors of nuclear exchange.

THE LIMITS OF A WEAPONS SYSTEM EVALUATION

But, even if history in terms of recent war experience seemed irrelevant for one reason or another to the problem of the charge, it is hard to believe that war is a science so limited that means could not be found to test in practice the effectiveness of the charge, that a conclusive study could not be made of charges made in a variety of patterns, in different formations, and with different weapons against simulated "enemy formations." But the simple truth is that nothing is more difficult to test than a weapon's effectiveness. (This should be patently obvious to anyone who, during the late 1950s, troubled himself to inquire into the missile development claims of the several U.S. armed services.) Maneuvers, like wars, take place, after all, under certain sets of conditions, and who is to say, therefore, what their meaning is?

There are a grievously large number of intellectual stumbling blocks in first setting up and later evaluating any test experience. For example, during the summer of 1936[29] the U.S. Infantry maneuvered against the U.S. Cavalry at Fort Benning, Georgia. As the problem started, the cavalry rode and the infantry trucked to the given maneuver area. The motor vehicles being rather faster than the horses, the infantry had ample time to get into position first. This proved a most frightening advantage. The infantry, well camouflaged, waited with some excitement while the cavalry was allowed to pass concealed forward infantry units. Only when the advance units of cavalry hit the main units of infantry did the infantry's stratagem become apparent. It was at that moment that the infantrymen rose shouting from entrenched positions waving bed sheets. The horses thought their Day of Judgment had arrived as ghosts rose over the battlefield, and what followed is best left to the imagination.

To infantrymen the maneuver proved conclusively that trucks gave the infantry a mo-bility with which the cavalry could not hope to compete, and that, when minus multicolored uniforms and not drawn up in drill formation, the infantry made an unsatisfactory cavalry target. Yet, to the cavalrymen—and this raised a furor that still stays in men's minds—the whole exercise proved only that infantrymen were practical jokers. The problem of "proving out" doctrine in the field of maneuver is distressingly difficult.

Essentially the problem lies in one's estimate of that appalling obscurity, "the nature of man."[30] The cavalryman knows, as he charges "the enemy designate," that, if this were really the enemy, he would be quite too frightened to fire accurately. And he knows this because it is part of a credo without which he could never be induced to charge in the first place. Therefore the "effect of fire" becomes a subjective, instead of an objective, judgment, mitigated by one's belief in a concatenation of other effects—of surprise, of fear, of the use of the defilade. So, while all will call for more realism in testing,[31] getting a consensus as to what "realism" is, more frequently than not, is quite outside the realm of possibility.

FACTORS IN INSTITUTIONAL SURVIVAL

THE ROLE OF HISTORY

On the morrow of victory in World War I, a member of the House of Commons rose to criticize the Secretary of War, Winston Churchill. He noted that the cavalry was at "practically the same figure as before the war, and yet if I should have thought anything had been proved by the War, it was that cavalry was less useful (than) we had previously thought it was going to be."[32]

Shortly thereafter, in 1930 to be precise, there appeared a history of the French Cavalry in the World War by a Professor of Tactics at

[29] The story is from eye-witness reports and there is a date problem.

[30] Compare, for example, the U.S. airman's view of the Russian's will to resist, as demonstrated in testimony before Congress, in the journals, and elsewhere, with that of the U.S. infantryman.

[31] As, for example, Sir John French's plea in an appendix on "Cavalry at Peace Maneuvers": "It is in my opinion impossible to go too far in the direction of making conditions resemble as much as possible those of actual warfare." Bernhardi, *Cavalry*, p. 233.

[32] 125 *H.C. Deb.* 25, pp. 1366ff.

l'École Militaire et d'Application du Génie, a most prolific writer by the name of Capitaine F. Gazin. The next to the last paragraph reads as follows:

Today, really more than yesterday, if the cavalry is to have power and flexibility, following along with technical progress, it must have horses with better blood lines, cadres filled with burning faith, and above all well trained troops conscious of the heavy weight of past glory.[33]

There would seem to be no reasonable doubt but that in the minds of the doughboy, the *poilu*, or Tommy Atkins, the day of the horse was over. The cavalryman had been called a number of things during the war— "Pigsticker," the "Rocking Horseman," and the like—which indicated what the infantry thought of his contribution. But to the cavalryman himself the cavalry was not dead, and the history of the Great War was never written in really meaningful terms. To him the role of the horseman in the victory became swollen with the yeast of time. Indeed, in cavalry historiography, the role of the horse in World War I was most emphasized at that moment in time when the cavalry was most threatened in army reorganization plans, between 1934 and 1939.[34]

The cavalry had been used in World War I. The Germans used it extensively on that last stronghold of the cavalryman, the eastern frontier. The British and French used it extensively in 1914 during the retreat from Le Mans in late August and early September. Indeed, the largest item of export from Great Britain to its forces on the Continent for the war as a whole was horse fodder[35]—which goes to show that the expression "eat like a horse" is a simile of substance! For the most part the cavalry fought dismounted, but it did fight mounted as well. It did charge machine guns. In one case the Canadians charged a group of German machine guns and came out unscathed, so great was the surprise achieved when the horsemen charged, blades bared. And it was used mounted as late as 1918. Indeed, this claim has been made for its work at that time—by a cavalryman: "It may or may not be true to say that we (the allies) should have defeated the Germans just the same in the autumn of 1918, even without our cavalry. But it is certainly true that, had it not been for that same cavalry, there would have been no autumn advance at all for the Germans would have defeated us in the spring."[36]

But the campaign which did more to save the horse cavalry than any other was not fought in Europe at all. It was fought on the sands of Palestine, at Gaza, at Beersheba, at Jerusalem, and it was fought in part, indeed in large part, with the lance. It was as dashingly romantic as anything that happened during that singularly drab war, and it was strong drink to the cavalry.[37] In a sense it kept the cavalry going for another quarter-century. There was irony in this, for the most eager of the cavalrymen, men of the stamp of Sir John French, had for a decade defended the cavalry regulations on the basis of the forecast of their utility for the big war on the Continent, only to have the cavalry successfully used only on the periphery of the great battlefields.

So experience, the most revered of teachers, continued to couch the "lessons" of war in a certain studied ambiguity. The horse retained that place in warfare which it had had for a thousand years—in the minds of its military riders.

MISSION JUSTIFICATION FOR THE FUTURE, 1920–1940

On the eve of World War II the general officers of the U.S. Army were, next to those of Poland, Rumania, and possibly the U.S.S.R., most convinced of the continuing utility of the horse. The French had four divisions of mixed horse and mechanized cavalry. The Germans had a debated number of horses and mechanized cavalry, for use largely as reconnaissance. The British were converting from oats to oil as rapidly as possible.

---

[33] F. Gazin, *La cavalerie dans la guerre mondiale* (Paris, 1930), p. 325.

[34] To illustrate see Lt. Col. T. Preston, "Cavalry in France," *Cavalry Journal* (Britain), no. 24 (1934), pp. 167ff., 338ff., 496ff.; no. 25 (1935), pp. 7ff., 165ff., 332ff., 489ff.; no. 26 (1936), pp. 1ff. See also Général Requichot, "La 4e Brigade Légère du 30 juillet au 5 octobre 1914," *Revue de Cavalerie*, no. 49 (1939), pp. 159, 261; Lt. Col. A. G. Martin, "Cavalry in the Great War," *Cavalry Journal* (Britain), no. 29 (1939), pp. 131ff., 264ff., 437ff.

[35] G. C. Shaw, *Supply in Modern War* (London, 1938), p. 133.

[36] Preston, *op. cit.*, no. 26, p. 19.

[37] For a description see Sir Archibald Wavell, *Allenby: A Study in Greatness* (New York and London, 1941), pp. 186ff.

A number of problems immediately present themselves. First, a very general question must be asked of the cavalrymen themselves: What did they consider their mission to be in the period between 1920 and roughly 1935, when the development of both plane and tank had reached the stage at which their future development could be foreseen with some clarity, and at which, therefore, some reasonable readjustment of forces to the fact of their existence could be expected. How can one account for those great differences in thinking among the responsible staffs of the larger nations during the years between 1935 and the outbreak of war in 1939?

With the introduction of each new weapon into the arsenal of any power the future is more difficult to see than it was previously. Each of the four revolutions in warfare which have occurred in this century has made policy determination that much more difficult. One of the reasons for this is that each new weapons system is so quickly idealized by those who control it. Those situations which frustrate its usefulness are left for those out of control to exaggerate. The bomber pilot remembers that he can destroy the hub of industry and forgets that he has only a very limited capacity to win a war against a self-sustaining countryside. He thinks of Germany rather than of China. The tankman remembers the plains cut by roads and forgets the jungles cut by rivers. The anti-whatever-it-is man thinks of the power of the defense over that of the offense. The crystal ball has been shattered by technology. It was fractured by 1900, but this became quite evident only after World War I.

The basic argument of the cavalrymen in their journals and in their manuals in the period between the great wars was an absolutely sound one. They argued in essence that new weapons obviated only those with like characteristics. They argued that, while a better tank scrapped a worse one, the tank as a weapons system could not replace the horse until such time as it could perform all the missions of a horse. Whether these missions were worthwhile was seldom considered.

Many of the arguments which cavalrymen of all nations advanced to substantiate their claims as to their future role in war will be recognized by any student of recent military

history as a version of what one can describe only as standardized clap-trap. One was the argument that, since most of the world was roadless, "To base our transportation needs solely upon conditions existent in the comparatively tiny proportion of the earth's surface containing roads . . . is putting too many eggs in the same basket."[38] This will be recognized as a cavalry variant on the navy contention that "since the world is 60 per cent water . . ." and the air contention that "since air surrounds the earth and the shortest distance between two points . . . ." Another argument familiar to all military historians came up again and again in the journals. This one was to the effect that mechanical aids and auxiliaries end by neutralizing each other, an argument which in its most outrageous form had the antitank weapon returning the battlefield to the horse.[39] "It is quite within the bounds of possibility that an infantry anti-tank weapon may be produced which will make tanks useless as weapons of attack," wrote one enthusiast[40] in a vein not unlike that used by airmen against seamen at roughly the same moment in time. The difficulty of supplying tanks was brought up as the supply problem is brought up as a limitation on each new weapons system.[41] And, of course, the essentially experimental nature of tanks— "as yet untried" is the term—raised its head perennially and everywhere.

But there were other problems and more serious ones. If the tank could be made to replace the cavalry on the charge, did that mean that the tank could take over all the other cavalry missions: reconnaissance, raids, flank protection in rough country? Could the plane be made to supplement the tank in such a way that the two used in combination could effectuate a complete substitution for the horse? Or would some kind of combination of horse and tank, and plane and tank, be a future necessity? And, if this were so, with whom would the control lie, with tankmen or horsemen or pilots? And, finally, if this was a prob-

[38] Major Malcolm Wheeler-Nicholson, *Modern Cavalry* (New York, 1922), p. vii.
[39] Anon., "Oil and Oats," *Cavalry Journal* (Britain), no. 28 (1938), p. 31; Col. Sir Hereward Wake, "The Infantry Anti-Tank Weapon," *Army Quarterly*, 17, no. 2 (January 1929).
[40] Wake, *op. cit.*, p. 349.
[41] Lt. F. A. S. Clark, "Some Further Problems of Mechanical Warfare," *Army Quarterly*, 6, no. 2 (July 1923): 379.

lem of phasing out the horse, what factors should govern the timing of this phasing?

These questions do not seem to have been asked with any precision, largely perhaps because they edged too closely on the emotion-packed matter of prestige, on the one hand, and on an essentially insoluble organizational problem on the other. Naturally armor wanted maximum independence as do those who service and fire any weapon. The tankman wanted a command of his own, just as the machine gunner wanted his own battalion, the artillery its own regiment, the horse cavalry its own division, and the airman his own service. And this is logical, for in a decentralized structure growth is faster because imagination is given a freer rein. But the difficulty is that, war being all of one cloth, each weapon component also wishes to control elements of the others. And this is why the sparks flew between arms in the period between the World Wars, and before the First and after the Second. Where, as in Germany and Great Britain, armor was given its independence, it thrived. Where, as in the United States and Poland, the cavalry (horse) remained in control, tank doctrine never grew roots. But where, as in France, tank and horse were joined together in what at first blush seemed to be a happy marriage, a unity was forced which was pitifully inadequate from every standpoint.

For the man on the horse there was much greater difficulty in understanding the tank than in understanding the rapid-fire weapon. Perhaps this could be expected since tank and horse were competitors for the same missions. Certainly the limpid eye and high spirit of the one and the crass impersonal power of the other were enough to render partisans of the one quite helpless when it came to understanding the military views of the other,[42] indeed, quite as helpless as the sea-based fighter is to understand the land-based or air-based fighter and his view of world geography.

PRACTICALITY AND THE CONCEPT OF THE BALANCED FORCE

One finds the horse cavalryman making the same points over and over again. He stressed the tanks' need for spare parts, without taking into consideration that one of the greatest difficulties of the cavalry was that horses do not have spare parts.[43] He stressed the lack of mobility of the tank along mountain trails without mentioning the appalling problem of getting horses overseas—they have a tendency to pneumonia, together with a soft breast, which becomes raw and infected with the roll and pitch of the ship.[44] Whereas the point was occasionally made that the Lord took care of the resupply of horses—i.e., that, while factories could be bombed out, sex could not— no mention was ever made that in wartime, as in peace, the Lord still took four or five years to produce each animal. And, finally, although the horse was claimed to have certain immunities to gas warfare,[45] the peculiar problems of getting gas masks on the poor beasts were omitted.[46]

[42] This was not always so. U.S. Gen. George S. Patton is on record as wanting to add a division of horse cavalry to an army as late as 1944. "In almost any conceivable theater of operations, situations arise where the presence of horse cavalry . . . will be of vital moment." Maj. P. D. Eldred, "Are Horses Essential in Modern War?" *JUSCA*, 53, no. 3 (May–June 1944): 3. Compare this attitude to Marshal Weygand's in his *Mémoires: Idéal Vécu* (Paris, 1953), p. 80. How much did his filly, La Houzard, and the remembrance of his days as an instructor at the French Cavalry School have to do with the French Army's inability to understand the role of tanks? Gen. Gamelin called him the "natural defender of cavalry." *Servir* (Paris 1946–1947), 1: 254.

[43] Gen. Riley of Missouri managed to get a good many of the ailments of a horse into what is believed to be the most defamatory military judgment on the politician presently extant. "The people," he said, "have been fed on buncombe, while a lot of spavined, ringboned, ham-strung, wind-galled, swine-eyed, split-hoofed, distempered, poll-eviled, pot-bellied politicians have had their noses in the public crib and there ain't enough fodder left to make gruel for a sick grasshopper."

[44] During the conflict in Korea in 1950–1951 there was an uproar for cavalry by those who envisioned their usefulness there and forgot the problem of transportation—an item which frequently is the last remembered.

[45] Capt. H. Barrowcliff Ellis, "The Horse in Chemical Warfare," *Cavalry Journal* (Britain), no. 25 (1935), pp. 615ff.

[46] In the author's opinion the most complete, which is not to say the most rational, defense of horse cavalry will be found in Col. H. S. Stewart, "Mechanization and Motorization: The Final Chapter Has Not Been Written," *JUSCA*, 49, no. 1 (January–February 1940): 35ff.; "General Hawkins' Notes: Conclusions Drawn from the First Army Maneuvers," *ibid.*, p. 162. But see also H. V. S. Charrington, *Where Cavalry Stands Today* (London, 1927); V. W. Germains (foreword by Sir F. Maurice), *The Mechanization of War* (London, 1928); and although the author has been able to see only reviews of it, Gen. Von Poseks' *Reflections on Modern Cavalry*. For details see the review in *Cavalry Journal* (Britain), no. 25 (1935), p. 351.

Yet, whether partisans were ankle deep in the sands of prejudice or not, certain aspects of the relationship between horses and planes, and between horses and tanks, were so obvious that they could hardly be missed. However low and slow it flew, the plane would not be a substitute for a still lower and still slower man on a horse. And the plane could not penetrate forests; neither, within limits, could tanks. So there was, and indeed there still is, a gap between what the horse can do and what the plane and the tank can do. But, admitting the gap, there still remained the most vexing problem of all—to wit, whether that gap was worth filling and, if so, how. And this was something which each general staff decided somewhat differently and for itself.

In retrospect, the U.S. Cavalry was as retrogressive in 1940 as it had been progressive in the years before World War I. Due to transportation difficulties,[47] it had never crossed the sea during World War I; it had spent the war chasing Mexicans. But it shared every confidence that its future role would be everything that it had not been in the recent past. As of 1940 it labored under the most embarrassing of illusions. The U.S. Cavalry believed that it had modernized itself. And it defended its horse cavalry on the sacred ground of "balanced force." "Each arm has powers and limitations," explained Major General John K. Herr, Chief of Cavalry, before the Subcommittee on Military Affairs of the House Committee on Appropriations on March 11, 1940. "The proper combination is that which arranges the whole so that the powers of each offset the limitations of the others." It was because the Poles did not have that balance that they were, said General Herr, overrun by the Germans.

Judging from Spain, had Poland's cavalry possessed modern armament in every respect and been united in one big cavalry command with adequate mechanized forces included, and supported by adequate aviation, the German light and mechanized forces might have been defeated.

Then General Herr went on to add these words of comfort:

Mechanized cavalry is valuable and an important adjunct but is not the main part of the cavalry and cannot be. Our cavalry is not the medieval cavalry of popular imagination but is cavalry which is modernized and keeping pace with all developments.[48]

Yet it certainly does not seem that the U.S. Cavalry was "keeping pace with all developments." Putting horses in trucks to give them mobility (this was the so-called *portée* cavalry) and adding inadequate antitank batteries can hardly be called modernizing. Is there any reasonable explanation for the illusion?

CONCEPTS OF MODERNIZATION

One cannot help but be impressed with the intellectual isolation in which the U.S. armed forces operated in the 1930s. The *Journal of the U.S. Cavalry Association* paid almost no attention to mechanization throughout the period. Compared to the military periodicals on the Continent, this U.S. journal seems curiously antiquated. And because there was so little critical thinking going on within the service, it is not surprising that there was virtually no thinking going on in Army ordnance either, for ordnance, after all, works on a demand basis and, if there is no demand, there is likely to be no new hardware. In the United States there was, in short, no intellectual challenge.[49]

Not only were there no pressures to change cavalry thinking from inside the arm; there were no pressures from outside either. United States industry was not anxious to sell to the services during the Depression years or before. They were no more willing to put money into military research and development than were the services or Congress.[50] The few Secretaries of War who can be considered adequate were interested in the managerial aspects of their office and not in matters which they considered "purely military." And finally there was considerable pressure for the *status quo* in Con-

---

[47] See Frederick Palmer, *Newton D. Baker: America at War*, vol. 2 (New York, 1931), pp. 338ff.

[48] The text of General Herr's testimony before Congress may be found reprinted in *JUSCA*, 49, no. 3 (May–June 1940); see p. 206. The point which General Herr made concerning the "one big cavalry command" was part of a vicious fight then going on in the War Department as to how much control the Chief of Cavalry should have over armored units. The relevant correspondence may be found in *ibid.*, 55, no. 3 (May–June 1946): 35ff.

[49] For the really shocking story of U.S. tank development see Constance L. Green, H. B. Thompson, and P. C. Roots, *The Ordnance Department* (Washington, D.C., 1955), chaps. 7–10.

[50] *Ibid.*

gress. The U.S. had some ten million horses, and government spending in this direction, little though it was, was a chief source of revenue to all the many horse breeders, hay growers, and saddle makers.[51]

In Great Britain, the situation was markedly different. Although the British had their branch journals—the tankers founded their own in 1937—they also had a great advantage in having two journals which were more generally read. The first was the *Army Quarterly*, which published on all topics of concern to the army as a whole, and the other was *The Journal of the Royal United Service Institution*, which crossed service lines. Into these journals articles poured from a singularly able and remarkably prolific and dedicated group of publicists, of whom J. F. C. Fuller and Captain Basil H. Liddell-Hart are merely the best known. Officers in the British Empire, unlike U.S. officers, were simply unable to escape from challenge. Thus from 1936 onward there was an increasingly strong movement in favor of conversion to oil. Furthermore, this was helped rather than hindered by the stand taken by many in Parliament. For Parliament was at least conscious of *The Times* military correspondent Liddell-Hart and of the battle he was waging for mechanized warfare, a form of warfare which would, so he thought, limit and shorten future wars by making them more rapid, and hence shorter and cheaper than the war of the trenches. To be sure there were those who, like Admiral of the Fleet Sir Roger Keyes, took a position against the reduction of cavalry.[52] But they were in the minority. Most felt that the Household Cavalry and two mounted regiments still left in Egypt in 1939 were probably two too many. On the very eve of the war a statement made by Mr. Duff Cooper while defending the conversion of the army to mechanization may also explain Britain's willingness to change. Duff Cooper mentioned the lack of horses which would be subject to wartime draft.[53]

After World War II the French, as is the wont of democracies, held an inquiry into the military disasters of some five years before. But the questions which were put to the generals and the questions which they wanted to answer were all in terms of why they had not understood and appreciated the role of the tank and the plane. Never does the question seem to have been asked in the converse—i.e., why was the horse thought to have been so useful *circa* 1939? It would have been interesting to know, too, what thinking had been done as to the circumstances under which cavalry divisions, offensive forces, were to be used in conjunction with the Maginot Line, a defensive ideal. Perhaps they were to have been used in the second phase of the struggle in a counteroffensive after the enemy had partially defeated himself by throwing his troops against the defensive fires of the line. Unfortunately, the scholars who have put their minds to the matter have not come up with any answer. The French cavalry regulations follow old formulas and include all possible uses to which cavalry might be put, but they do not concentrate on the one to which, in the minds of the planners, it would be put.[54]

However, the overall development of French cavalry thinking between the wars is plain enough. What they did was to absorb the new machines of war into old doctrine. Instead of allowing the characteristics of new weapons to create new doctrine, the French General Staff simply gave them missions to fulfill that were within the old framework. Thus tanks were made subordinate and supporting weapons to the infantry, and subordinate and supporting weapons to the cavalry.[55] In a sense the French achieved what General Herr of the U.S. Cavalry wanted to achieve, except that the French did look forward to complete mechanization at some future date, which Herr did not. And the *Revue de Cavalerie*, a strange hodge-podge of oats, history, and oil, reflects this point of view.

The German experience was somewhat different again. Whereas the French looked back

---

[51] Pendleton Herring, *The Impact of War* (New York, 1941), p. 119.
[52] "I have seldom met a good horseman . . . not . . . well able to lead a destroyer attack." 344 *H.C. Deb.* 5s, p. 2250. The date was March 8, 1939.
[53] 321 *H.C. Deb.* 5s, p. 1890. In the decade 1928–1938 there had been a decline of three-quarters of a million horses in England. To what extent was the lack of horses the real reason for change?

[54] There is an excellent review of French regulations in *Cavalry Journal* (Britain), no. 29 (1939), pp. 513ff.
[55] Donald J. Harvey, *French Concepts of Military Strategy, 1919–1939* (New York, 1953), p. 153. See also Alvin D. Coox, "French Military Doctrine, 1919–1939" (Ph.D. diss., Harvard University, 1951), pp. 116ff.

to the stalemate at Verdun, the great achievement of defensive weapons, the Germans looked back to the great offensives of 1918 and to the very near miss of the Schlieffen plan in 1914. Particularly in the case of the younger officers, the great objective was to regain the lost means of offensive. A defeated army, the Germans were in a position to start once more from the beginning. To be sure there was a very difficult period of struggle with German horse cavalrymen, but those in Germany with an interest in tanks had an advantage which those in the democracies did not. They had the interest of the Chief of State. When Hitler saw Panzer units in action, he said repeatedly: "That's what I need! That's what I want to have!"[56] To Hitler they were the keystone in a concept of total war.

The *Revue de Cavalerie* stopped publication during World War II and never appeared again. The British *Cavalry Journal* disappeared forever as well. Only the *Journal of the U.S. Cavalry Association* continued to appear. Its heroes were the horse-drawn artillery which landed on Guadalcanal, the animals flown over the Burma "Hump" into China, the U.S. units which were remounted on Italian Cavalry horses in Italy and German horses in Germany; the great heroes were the only real cavalry left—the Cossacks.[57] Duly noted was how greatly needed were horse cavalries during the battles in Normandy and elsewhere.[58]

In the closing chapter of *He's in the Cavalry Now*, Brigadier General Rufus S. Ramey, a former commander of the U.S. Cavalry School, concluded in 1944, "Currently we are organizing and training adequate mechanized horse cavalry for field employment."[59] His was the final testament. The last old Army mule, except for the West Point Mascot, was retired in 1956. The horse cavalry had been disbanded five years before.

NEW ITEM

In 1956 the Belgian General Staff suggested that, for the kind of dispersed war which low-yield atomic weapons necessarily create, the horse, which in Europe could be independent of depots, should be reintroduced into the weapons system.[60]

CONCLUSION

The military profession, dealing as it does with life and death, should be utterly realistic, ruthless in discarding the old for the new, forward-thinking in the adoption of new means of violence. But equally needed is a romanticism which, while it perhaps stultifies realistic thought, gives a man that belief in the value of the weapons system he is operating that is so necessary to his willingness to use it in battle. Whether a man rides a horse, a plane, or a battleship into war, he cannot be expected to operate without faith in his weapons system. But faith breeds distrust of change. Furthermore, there is need for discipline, for hierarchy, for standardization within the military structure. These things create pressures for conformity, and conformity, too, is the enemy of change. Nor is there generally the pressure for the adoption of the new which is found in other walks of life. There is no profit motive, and the challenge of actual practice, in the ultimate sense of war, is very intermittent. Finally, change is expensive, and some part of the civilian population has to agree that the change is worth the expense before it can take place. What factors, then, make for change in situations short of war?

Surely the greatest instigation of new weapons development has in the past come from civilian interest plus industrial pressure. The civilian governors get the weapons system *they* want. Hitler gets his tanks, the French public its line of forts. When society shows an interest in things military, weapons are adopted —apparently in great part because of the appeal they make to a set of social values and economic necessities. The abolition of the horse cavalry came about first in those countries which could not afford to raise the horses and in which there were those with a hungry in-

[56] Gen. Heinz Guderian, *Panzer Leader* (New York, 1952), p. 30.

[57] The uses of the cavalry of the U.S.S.R. are described in B. H. Liddell-Hart, ed., *The Russian Army* (New York, 1956), pp. 337ff.

[58] "General Hawkins' Notes," *JUSCA*, 54, no. 1 (January–February 1945): 42ff.

[59] Brig. Gen. Rufus S. Ramey, *He's in the Cavalry Now* (New York, 1944), p. 190. There were 60,170 animals in the U.S. forces on December 31, 1943.

[60] "Belgians Hit U.S. Concept of Atomic War," *Christian Science Monitor*, August 25, 1956.

tellectual interest in the ways of war. When there was no interest in the military, as in the United States, there was no pressure to change, and the professional was given tacit leave to romanticize an untenable situation. Thus the U.S. Horse Cavalry remained a sort of monument to public irresponsibility in this, the most mechanized nation on earth.

THE ROLE OF DOCTRINE

PERRY M. SMITH

Doctrine is the life blood of a military service. In combination with roles and missions, doctrine gives the service a justification for its very existence as a separate and distinct part of the national security establishment. In this article, Perry Smith describes succinctly and critically how the Air Corps combined the ideas of Douhet and Mahan to formulate a strategic doctrine which, in turn, helped to make the Air Corps case for autonomy. During the period 1943–1945, the postwar planners, using the doctrinal arguments developed at the Air Corps Tactical School in the 1930s, helped the Air Corps leadership win its case for a separate service in the immediate postwar period. Colonel Perry M. Smith (USAF) is a West Point graduate and has a Ph.D. from Columbia University. Presently serving as Deputy Head, Department of Political Science, United States Air Force Academy, Colonel Smith served on the faculty of the National War College during the 1970–1971 academic year. His operational background is in F-100 and F-4 aircraft.

Air Corps doctrine in the 1930s and during World War II was basically the same, and it was based primarily on the concept of the decisiveness of strategic bombardment in war. Although there may be some question as to whether, in the thirties, this doctrine was used to justify the Army Air Corps case for autonomy or whether autonomy was a means the Army Air Corps leadership tried to use to insure that American military airpower would be heavily weighted in favor of the strategic bombing mission, the evidence indicates that in the 1943–1945 period the former was the case. Since their goal could best be supported if the efficacy and decisiveness of strategic airpower in war could be fully demonstrated, any arguments concerning the necessity for tactical aviation in support of ground warfare would undermine their case. Therefore, the doctrine and the decisiveness of strategic bombardment in future warfare were inextricably tied to the AAF case for autonomy. If strategic bombardment could not be decisive in warfare, and if victory could be obtained only by having an army actually meet and defeat the enemy on the battlefield, then it would be difficult to refute the case for maintaining within the United States Army the Army Air Corps (with

Reprinted by permission and with minor changes from The Air Force Plans for Peace: 1943–1945 *(Baltimore: The Johns Hopkins Press, 1970), pp. 27–38.*

its missions of close support of ground troops and interdiction of lines of communication) in order to support the majority of this nation's forces.

If the AAF postwar planners had had as their primary goal the independence of the strategic element of military airpower, the value of tactical aviation could still have been acknowledged by them without undermining their position that strategic bombardment was a mission distinct from the mission of the ground army. However, since they wanted to place all land-based military airpower in the autonomous postwar Air Force, acknowledgment of any tactical aviation doctrine would have weakened their case. The relationship between doctrine and force structure within the prewar Air Corps had caused its leadership to neglect some important technological breakthroughs in pursuit aviation. The narrow doctrinal focus which the postwar planners felt obliged to maintain to achieve autonomy was no more than a continuation of rather inflexible prewar thinking.

A long-time student of airpower, Professor William R. Emerson, has observed: "Making all due allowances for the difficulties and the genuine accomplishments of our strategists, it should, nevertheless, be perfectly clear that every salient belief of prewar American air doctrine was either overthrown or drastically modified by the experience of war."[1] What Emerson fails to mention is that the lessons learned about the limitations of strategic aviation were not applied to the formulation of the postwar Air Force. Instead of making the common mistake of planning to fight the next war with weapons and techniques that had been effective in the last, the Air Corps planners were laying plans to conduct the next war using weapons and techniques that had been proven largely ineffective in the present war. The reason is quite obvious: the planners were not making detailed plans for fighting the next war, but rather were planning for a force that could provide the justification for autonomy. The doctrinal dedication to strategic bombardment at the expense of close air support and interdiction led to difficulties, among them lack

of adequate support of ground forces during the Korean conflict, de-emphasis of tactical training, and lack of development of tactical weapons systems and tactical munitions (much of the development in these areas was done by the Navy in the first two decades following World War II).

To understand the assumptions made, and the doctrine upon which the postwar force structure was based, it is useful to trace the doctrinal development of the United States military strategic bombardment theory. This theory, developed in the twenties and thirties and fully incorporated in the major Army Air Corps prewar plan, AWPD/1, can best be described as modified Douhet. Recent evidence confirms the direct Douhetan input into the Tactical School as early as 1923, but the doctrine that was fully developed by 1940 was Douhetan, modified in a number of significant areas.[2] Douhet's tenets that the air weapon was strongly offensive, that technology favored the defensive on land and sea, and that airpower alone could bring victory were fully accepted Army Air Corps doctrine.[3] Not all of Douhet was incorporated; his gross exaggeration of bomb damage was rejected by the Tactical School by 1938,[4] and by 1939 the school no longer recognized as valid his belief that enemy morale was an effective target. The abandonment of the undermining of civilian morale as a useful aim of bombardment was a

[1] William R. Emerson, "Operation Pointblank: A Tale of Bombers and Fighters," United States Air Force Academy, The Harmon Memorial Lectures in Military History, no. 4, 1962, p. 40.

[2] Raymond R. Flugel, "United States Air Power Doctrine: A Study of the Influence of William Mitchell and Giulio Douhet at the Air Corps Tactical School, 1921–1935" (Ph.D. diss., University of Oklahoma, 1965), p. 20.

[3] AWPD/1 gives the best indication of Army Air Corps doctrine just prior to the commencement of World War II (it must be noted that Army Air Corps doctrine was not Army doctrine). "AWPD-1 was almost straight Pre-War Tactical School doctrine." H. S. Hansell, "The Development of the U.S. Concept of Bombardment Operations," lecture to Air War College, November 12, 1953, p. 502.

[4] Kuter, in a lecture entitled "American Air Power—School Theories vs. World War Facts," which he wrote and delivered in 1938 to the students of the Air Corps Tactical School, acknowledged some limitations in strategic aviation.
"The Mystery Bomber may have come 10,000 miles through the stratosphere at the velocity of sound . . . but the power it can apply to the bridge is absolutely unchanged and many defensive measures must now be overcome. . . . Let us start with the honest admission that the bomb of today is no more powerful than similar bombs of the World War." Papers of General Lawrence S. Kuter, USAF (Retired), vol. 2, p. 13, Special Collections Office, USAF Academy Library.

result of a 1939 lecture presented at the Tactical School, which made the point that Chinese morale and the will to resist increased as a result of Japanese bombardment.[5]

In addition to these differences, Douhet's vagueness on target selection had been replaced by an explicit doctrine of bombardment based on the thesis that precision bombardment would allow specific targets to be attacked and that a nation's economy could be totally incapacitated by the careful selection and elimination of a few essential industries. Captain (later Major General) Donald Wilson is usually credited with establishing this theory of economic vulnerability, which by the late 1930s was fully accepted as Air Corps doctrine.[6] The theory had a certain validity but was expressed in such a generalized form that the economic principle of "substitution" was ignored. In a 1933 lecture at the Tactical School, Wilson stated that transportation and electric generator manufacturing plants were considered key components of a nation's economy, and that "it would seem obvious that any air force worthy of the name should be able to destroy faster than replacement could be effected."[7] By considering a nation's economy a "structure" rather than a set of activities which could be undertaken in a wide variety of ways, the instructors at the Tactical School demonstrated an unsophisticated grasp of macroeconomics. "The fault was one of economics, not airmanship."[8] I. B. Holley points out that without "a doctrine regarding the use of weapons"[9] there has been a great reluctance on the part of both military and civilian leaders in many states to develop and use new and superior weapons. "New weapons when not accompanied by correspondingly new adjustments in doctrine are just so many external accretions in the body of an army."[10]

The Army Air Corps leadership firmly believed that superior arms favor victory; they recognized the relationship between doctrine and weaponry; and they understood the need for effective techniques for recognizing and evaluating potential weapons.[11] Unfortunately, their focus both before and during World War II was narrow, so that only ideas and weaponry which favored the offensive role of aviation were given thorough consideration. The doctrine developed in the Air Corps Tactical School (ACTS) from 1926 through 1940 was not airpower doctrine in the broadest sense of the word "airpower." It was strategic, daylight, precision bombardment, a very important part, but only a part, of military aviation. The emphasis on bombardment made the Tactical School instructors acutely aware of technological advances in this area, such as the development of bomb-sight equipment which permitted bombing accuracy from altitudes over 25,000 feet, and improvements in engine and airframe construction which permitted considerable advancement in bomber range, speed, and altitude capabilities during the 1930s. The familiarity with the technological developments in bombardment aviation within the Tactical School in the twenties and thirties, among the AAF leadership prior to and during the war, and among the AAF planners during the war was exceptional (though the PWD was unaware of atomic developments prior to August 6, 1945).[12] Yet the narrow focus of prewar Air Corps planners and leaders made these officers unaware of aircraft developments outside the strategic mission. Although throughout the thirties the retarded development within the Army Air Corps of radar, the air-cooled engine, and the long-range fighter is beyond the scope of this article, it should be pointed out that the narrow doctrinal focus, which inhibited these developments, continued throughout the entire war within the Air Force operational and postwar planning offices.[13]

[5] Joe Gray Taylor, "They Taught Tactics," *Aerospace Historian*, 13 (Summer 1966): 68.

[6] Wilson takes credit for initiating this theory into the Air Corps Tactical School. Donald Wilson, "Origin of a Theory for Air Strategy," typewritten study, 1962, p. 3. See also Robert T. Finney, *History of the Air Corps Tactical School, 1920–1940* (Maxwell Air Force Base, Montgomery, Ala.: USAF Historical Study no. 100, 1955), pp. 31–32.

[7] Wilson, "Origin of a Theory," p. 2.

[8] Mancur Olson, Jr., "The Economics of Strategic Bombing in World War II," *Airpower Historian*, 9 (April 1962): 123.

[9] I. B. Holley, *Ideas and Weapons* (New Haven: Yale University Press, 1953), p. 10.

[10] *Ibid.*, p. 14.

[11] Holley indicates that throughout history there have been three specific shortcomings in the procedure for developing new weapons: "a failure to adapt, actively and positively, the thesis that superior arms favor victory; a failure to recognize the importance of establishing a doctrine regarding the use of weapons; and a failure to devise effective techniques for recognizing and evaluating potential weapons in the advances of science and technology." *Ibid.*, p. 10.

[12] Interviews with Kuter, Norstad, Smith, and Cabell.

[13] For some interesting insights into the relationship between doctrine and weaponry, see Bernard Boylan,

Once a military doctrine is established, it is difficult to change, especially if technological advancements in weaponry seriously bring into question a doctrine upon which a specific military service is based. Like policy, doctrine has a gyroscopic effect. And, if service doctrine is questioned by members of that service, there is a tendency for the leadership to brand the critics heretics, especially if the doctrine is the basis upon which the primary goals of a service are constructed. In addition, the formulation and articulation of the doctrine is ordinarily designed to justify fully the service's attempt to obtain or maintain exclusive control over certain missions. Criticism usually results in an undermining of the case the service has so carefully made for certain roles and missions in national defense. Dissent is therefore discouraged, and breakthroughs in technology which might bring established doctrine into question are often ignored.

It is unfair to say that Arnold and other Air Force leaders completely ignored the vulnerability of long-range bombardment aircraft to defensive fighter attack, or that they were totally unaware of the lessons of the Battle of Britain regarding the technological advances in pursuit aviation. What was ignored or overlooked was the possibility of building a long-range escort fighter which would be essentially a pursuit aircraft and not a heavily armed bomber.[14] While the Air Force leaders understood the value of the four-engine bomber and its advantages in range, capacity, reliability, and defensive firepower over the two-engine bomber (in the words of two eminent students of the AAF, "The Army airman thereafter was, above all else, an advocate of the big bomber, and around the potentialities of that type of plane he built his most cherished hopes."[15]), these same leaders almost totally ignored the advances being made in pursuit aviation— advances that were even greater than those made in bombardment aviation.[16] Among these

were the increased speed, altitude, and range capabilities of projected fighter aircraft. The neglect by the Air Corps leaders of technological developments in pursuit aviation, from 1935 to 1943, provides an interesting case study of the relationship between doctrine and force structure. The postwar planners made a similar error for the same basic reason. They neglected tactical aviation in their postwar force structure because of their doctrinal focus upon strategic aviation. The story of the retarded development of the long-range fighter escort mission will be briefly traced to illustrate the continuity of the Air Corps planners' focus from 1935 through 1945, as well as to illustrate how doctrine affects force structure and can undermine objectivity.

Air Corps leaders had reached a doctrinal decision by 1935 as to the efficacy of unescorted long-range strategic bombardment and were unwilling either to question that decision or even to observe technological advances that might cause them to modify this doctrine until 1943, when the whole concept of strategic bombardment was endangered by the horrendous losses over Germany. It is paradoxical that their total acceptance of the doctrine prevented them from observing the technological advances that would have been the salvation of the very concept they were proclaiming. From 1931 until 1938 the bombardment advocates denied pursuit aviation any role other than the harassment of enemy bombers. The more radical even advocated the discontinuation of all pursuit procurement. The official Air Force history on the development of air doctrine during this period states that, "coupled with the apparent authority in performance of the new bombers over existing pursuit, acceptance of Douhet led the bombardment enthusiasts to an extreme position. Some instructors at the ACTS believed that pursuit could be abolished altogether, and OCAC [Office of Chief of Air Corps] adopted the slogan, 'Fighters are obsolete.' "[17] By 1938, however,

---

Development of the Long-Range Escort Fighter (Maxwell AFB, Montgomery, Ala.: USAF Historical Study no. 136, 1955). The classified nature of radar research probably impaired the transfer of information from the Army Signal Corps to the Army Air Corps on radar developments.

[14] *Ibid.*, pp. 33–35.

[15] Wesley F. Craven and James L. Cate, eds., *The Army Air Forces in World War II* (Chicago: University of Chicago Press, 1948), 1: 67.

[16] In the fall of 1941 General Kuter wrote a memorandum entitled "Reference Data on Heavy Bombers,"

in which he pointed out seventeen reasons why "big bombardment airplanes are better than little bombardment airplanes." Some of Kuter's reasons are of interest. For example: "6. The big bomber can defend itself"; "8. The big bomber can work alone." Army Air Corps files, 168.80-1, 5-2405-2, Air Force Archives, Maxwell AFB, Alabama.

[17] Thomas H. Greer, *The Development of Air Doctrine in the Army Air Arm, 1917–1941* (Maxwell Air Force Base, Montgomery, Ala.: USAF Historical Study no. 89, 1955), p. 45.

the bombardment men were willing to admit that, through proper early warning, pursuit aircraft could not only harass but, if properly massed, might even disrupt the bombardment formation. "Major Harold L. George, on 26 December 1937, advised Maj. Gen. Delos C. Emmons, Commander of GHQ Air Force, that there was no question in his mind that American bombardment units were defenseless against American pursuit groups."[18]

An interesting facet of this realization of the increasing danger presented by defensive fighters is the solutions that were sought. Instead of checking with the aircraft companies or with the Air Corps development center at Dayton, Ohio, the Army Air Corps leaders became their own amateur aeronautical engineers and arrived at the idea of a heavily armored bomber aircraft with enormous defensive firepower. (In fact, Douhet's idea of a combat plane was quite similar to the Air Corps idea of a heavily armored plane of bomber size designed to provide the defensive firepower needed to protect bomber formations.)[19] The Air Corps leaders advocated the use of very large masses of bombers, which would force the enemy to split his defensive efforts and face as many as a thousand bombers in formation with coordinated defensive firepower. They also advocated better and more turrets, high-caliber machine guns, and other changes in the craft.

The idea of increasing the range of fighter aircraft to the point that it would approach that of the bomber was quickly rejected as impractical, without a systematic inquiry into the possibility. The Air Corps leaders were certainly technologically oriented (Arnold himself was the leader in his appreciation of the technological impact upon aviation), but their orientation was narrow in scope in that the questions asked were not how could the strategic mission be improved but what improvements could be made in the strategic aircraft. In this case, Arnold's grasp of technology, in conjunction with his doctrinal preconceptions, prevented him in 1939 from asking some key questions. Once aware of the improvements in defensive fighter capability, he should have asked two questions: Is the doctrine of strategic bombardment valid in light of the difficulties involved in delivering bombs against well-defended targets? In what way can the strategic bombardment mission be improved in order to insure its efficacy despite the defensive improvements previously observed?

This doctrinal commitment to strategic bombardment made the first question a difficult one for Arnold to ask, but the second question should have been much easier to examine in light of his admitted realization of the dangers bombers might expect to face. Yet there is no evidence, in the form of any systematic analysis of the various possibilities, that the second question was ever asked by Arnold or his immediate staff.

A recent study of the Tactical School concludes: "Attachment to this commitment [strategic bombardment] was, however, so inflexible that it inhibited the development of tactics for escort, for air defense, for support of ground forces and for reconnaissance and transport aviation. Thus the school's greatest achievement as a laboratory for Air Corps thought prevented the full accomplishment of the purpose designated by the name, the Air Corps Tactical School."[20] Even to ask whether fighter range could be increased to the point at which escort would be feasible was to indicate some questioning of the earlier statements about the need to abolish the pursuit mission. Overstatements made to sell bombardment in the 1935–1938 period committed Air Corps leaders to a fixed view on how to execute the strategic mission.

The lack of a voice for pursuit aviation in the higher echelons of the Air Corps made the questioning of doctrine unlikely. Interestingly, every Air Corps leader had been a pursuit pilot, yet by the late 1930s the commitment to bombardment was almost complete. This is curious only in that these same men ignored the advances in the pursuit mission made in

---

[18] Boylan, *Long-Range Escort Fighter*, p. 33.

[19] Giulio Douhet, *The Command of the Air*, trans. Sheila Fischer (Rome: Rivista Aeronautica, 1958), p. 97. For a discussion of the inadequacies of bombers modified to provide increased firepower as a means of protecting bomber formations, see Stephen P. Birdsall, "The Destroyer Escorts," *Airpower Historian*, 12 (July 1965): 92–94. See also Boylan, *Long-Range Escort Fighter*, pp. 136–46.

[20] Taylor, "They Taught Tactics," p. 72. Taylor might have added liaison aviation also. I. B. Holley points out the neglect by the Army Air Corps of liaison aviation from 1920 to 1940 in *Evolution of the Liaison-Type Airplane: 1917–1944* (Washington, D.C.: AAF Historical Study no. 44, 1946).

the late 1930s. Since there was no real bombardment mission in the Air Corps until the late 1920s, due to the lack of an aircraft that had the range, speed, and bomb-carrying capability to be called a bomber, the pursuit mission was the only mission the American Air Service had prior to the advent of the B-9 and B-10 bombers.[21]

The outspoken exponent of pursuit aviation during the crucial years of the 1930s, when the Army Air Corps was searching for a doctrine, was Claire Chennault. Holding a number of responsible positions at the Air Corps Tactical School, he provided both written and verbal opposition to prevalent ideas that pursuit aviation was obsolete. When Chennault retired as a Captain in 1937, the Army Air Corps lost its only articulate, albeit polemical, voice for fighter aviation. His career was a signal to the pursuit enthusiasts that advances in the Air Corps were not likely to be most rapid in those channels, and ambitious officers were quick to select the bombardment side of military flying.

There was enough outside emphasis from the ground Army officers that the attack mission was never completely overlooked, but the pursuit mission had no real interest group to support it from 1931 to 1935, when bomber technology advanced more rapidly than did pursuit technology. Attack aviation had infantry support, and bombardment aviation had the support of all Air Corps men interested in autonomy. Pursuit aviation had a kind of negative support, since to support it doctrinally was to point out the vulnerabilities of bombardment aviation. If pursuit aviation enthusiasts could have supported their case by pointing out its value without explicitly or implicitly infringing on the sacred doctrine of bombardment aviation, perhaps their voice would have survived the technologically lean years.

To point out the vulnerabilities of strategic bombardment was to jeopardize the Air Corps case for autonomy, for, if strategic bombardment was proved ineffective as the element of warfare which alone might prove to be decisive in battle, then its case would be seriously undermined. If flights of bombardment aircraft could be turned back, or if the defensive fighters could inflict unacceptable losses upon the bombing formation, then the whole concept of strategic bombardment would be proved erroneous, and the Air Corps would then be expected to accomplish only close support, air superiority, and interdiction, none of which (nor all in combination) could justify complete autonomy. In the history of military aviation (from 1907 until the present, except for the brief period from 1931 to 1935), pursuit aircraft have held an advantage over bombers in combat, where the latter have sustained heavier losses. Although the reasons for fighter superiority vary, the combination of higher altitude and speed capability, in addition to greater maneuverability, have usually given the advantage.

The quest for autonomy led to the advocacy of strategic bombardment, which led, in turn, to the deprecation of not only defensive pursuit aircraft but all pursuit aircraft. Bombardment and autonomy were so inextricably bound together that the questioning of bombardment by an Air Corps officer was not only impolitic but unwise. Chennault's memoirs, though definitely lacking objectivity, give some idea of the problems pursuit enthusiasts encountered in the 1930s.[22]

In the 1943–1945 period, the postwar planners did not consider that the case for autonomy had been won. Although the wartime arrangements gave credence to the strong probability of obtaining autonomy in the immediate postwar world, the AAF planners were unwilling to assume that it was a certainty. First of all, the prewar laws which placed the Air Corps in a subordinate position to the Army were suspended for the duration of the war plus six months, and, unless Congress acted quickly at the termination of hostilities, it appeared to the planners that the Air Corps might revert to its pre–World War II status. Second, there was a suspicion on the part of many of the leaders that the Army and the War Department were neither committed to, nor enthusiastic about, a separate Air Force. The commitment to bombardment was therefore just as strong in the 1943–1945 period as it had been

[21] Greer, *Air Doctrine*, p. 45.

[22] *Way of a Fighter: The Memoirs of Claire Lee Chennault*, ed. Robert Hartz (New York: G. P. Putnam's, 1949), pp. 3–31. See also Greer, *Air Doctrine*, pp. 58–65. At the Tactical School there were a few other officers who were pursuit enthusiasts, including Millard L. Harmon and A. H. Gilkeson. Their impact on air doctrine was even less than that of the more flamboyant and outspoken Chennault.

previously, and the only evident variation was the commitment to long-range escort. The air-power lesson of the war up until August 6, 1945, was the efficacy of tactical aviation in its threefold mission of air superiority, interdiction, and close support of ground troops. Yet postwar planning was aimed at the strategic bombardment mission, with fighters provided primarily in the escort mission.[23] Walter Millis, an eminent student of the U.S. military, said:

The one great, determining factor which shaped the course of the Second War was not, as is so often said and so generally believed, independent air power. It was the mechanization of the ground battlefield with automatic transport, with the "tactical" airplane and above all with the tank. Air power in its independent form was, in sober fact, relatively ineffective. It was the teaming of the internal combustion engine in the air and on the surface, in order to take the traditional objectives of surface warfare which, together with the remarkable development of electronic communications, really determined the history of the Second World War.[24]

Since the aim of the postwar planners was to plan for and justify an autonomous Air Force, and since this was the reason that Arnold "tolerated" the planners, it is understandable that they based their plans on theories of war causation, potential enemies, and base requirements which would best justify autonomy. (General Kuter believes that Arnold's attitude toward the planners was one of toleration rather than enthusiastic support.)[25] This is not to imply that the Air Force planners were cynics who were searching for ways to justify their existence. These men believed that airpower was the most effective way to maintain national security, but they did not come to this belief by a scholarly weighing of a number of alternatives.

Although there is no evidence that the postwar planners relied on the strategic and politi-cal concepts of Alfred Thayer Mahan, the conceptual similarities between some of his ideas and their assumptions invite a hypothesis: a selective use of Mahan, adapted to justify not naval power but airpower, was the basis for many of the planners' assumptions concerning the economic causes of conflict and the causes of actual war.

With the substitution of the word "airpower" for the word "seapower," much of Mahan's writing becomes quite similar to AAF doctrine. Mahan skillfully used a theoretical construct to justify the building of a large navy and to prove that navies would be decisive in warfare. The AAF planners wished to accomplish what Mahan had succeeded in doing for the Navy; they wanted to prove not only that the Air Force should be a separate, autonomous force but that it was America's first line of defense and *the* decisive element of the American military. Mahan, though a reluctant imperialist, was nevertheless an imperialist when it came to the acquisition of overseas bases.[26] The Air Force planners likewise evidenced imperialistic qualities when it came to acquiring overseas air bases. The commercial aspects of naval and air bases were often emphasized, but military importance was always the primary consideration in their selection. Mahan's interpretation of history, in which he linked seapower with national greatness, and imperialism with seapower, affected the thinking of the wartime AAF planners, who wanted to secure bases in the Western Pacific, Alaska, Newfoundland, Iceland, Western Africa, and the Western Hemisphere. Like Mahan, the postwar planners were not unwilling to use coercion to acquire permanent bases.

Mahan's "principles" of naval strategy, which were largely based on Jomini's principles of war,[27] but modified to fit the peculiar problems of seapower, included the principle of concentration of force, a principle which the Air Force planners incorporated in all but one of their postwar plans.[28] These plans included a large reservoir of strategic aviation located

---

23 "Our most persuasive and articulate people are almost without exception bomber minded." "I think it is self-evident that heavy bomber thinking continues to dominate the Air Force." "If the experience of the European air war means anything, we have not provided sufficient fighters in the post war air force." Colonel S. F. Giffin, "Future Trends in Air Fighting" (memorandum), November 25, 1944.

24 Walter Millis, *Arms and Men: A Study in American Military History* (New York: G. P. Putnam's, 1956), p. 283.

25 Interview with General Kuter.

26 Margaret Tuttle Sprout, "Mahan: Evangelist of Sea Power," in *Makers of Modern Strategy: Military Thought from Machiavelli to Hitler*, ed. Edward Mead Earle (Princeton: Princeton University Press, 1952), p. 429.

27 *Ibid.*, p. 431.

28 The exception was the Initial Post War Air Force Plan (105 groups).

within the United States. Mahan criticized the French for using their fleet as a defensive force and praised the British for using theirs to seek out the enemy or to trap his fleet in port, where it could not protect its commercial vessels or control the sea. Mahan was contemptuous of the *guerre de course* and considered cruiser and commerce raiding operations the province of land warfare and hence a grave error in naval strategy.[29] Again a parallel is evident, for the AAF leaders and planners were reluctant to divert airpower to the close support of troops or to the defensive role of interception.

When Mahan described the dominant characteristic required of a war fleet as not speed but "the power of offensive action,"[30] his approach was similar to the arguments in favor of the long-range superfortress in great formations warding off the ineffective defensive forces with concentrated firepower and heavy armament. Douhet's combat plane and Kuter's battleplane were both somewhat similar to Mahan's heavy ships-of-the-line (the battleship or the capital ship). The similarity between Mahan's political defense of the nation through offensive use of the fleet and the proposed AAF defense through strategic bombardment also is evident.

Mahan was unwilling to consider that the submarine or the airplane might be an effective defense against the battle fleet; and AAF postwar planners were unwilling to see air defense —aircraft, guided missile, or anti-aircraft—as an effective defense against the escorted bomber formation. Mahan had shown how, in naval warfare, the best defense against attack was concentrated offensive naval fleet. The airpower enthusiasts were quick to utilize this most logical argument to make a case for a preponderant offensive air-force-in-being as the first line of defense.

Even the tendency of Mahan to ignore technology was evident in the thinking of the AAF planners, except where it applied directly to the strategic bombing mission. Whereas Mahan ignored the impact of technology on overland travel, and the effect of rapid overland travel on the importance of seapower, the Air Corps planners neglected to study the changing impact that overland transportation of armies by use of the tank and truck, and even the airplane, was to have on the relative advantages of the offensive over the defensive in warfare. The parallel between Mahan and his airpower counterparts is striking; the great American naval strategist seems to have provided the theoretical bases for the usurpation by the Air Force of the primary means of ensuring national security.

A major difference between the airpower enthusiasts and Mahan was that, while the latter lived in a period when the British fleet was the largest in the world, the former faced a postwar world situation in which no other state would possess the strategic bombardment capability with which the United States would end the war. The U.S. and Great Britain alone had developed a strategic bombardment capability, and, in the 1943–1945 period, the planners foresaw that with the B-29, B-32, and B-36 the United States' qualitative and quantitative lead over Great Britain in the postwar world would be appreciable. The AAF planners thus anticipated an enviable situation which in turn presented a dilemma. The dilemma, of course, was the difficulty of justifying a large Air Force when no country in the world presented a real threat to the United States.

Two factors helped the Air Corps planners as they looked for justification. First, they anticipated that the impending international organization would have a military force based largely on airpower. Second, the expeditious build-up of airpower within Nazi Germany was indicative of the rapidity with which any industrial state might close the airpower gap through concentration on airpower development. Even taking these two factors into consideration, the planners' case for a large air-force-in-being was weak. The sneak attack on Pearl Harbor presented another case for a strong Air Force, but not necessarily a strategic one.

The arguments for strategic bombardment had evolved from the early 1930s to the period 1943–1945. Destruction of enemy fleets on the high seas had been used as a justification for bombers when the range of bombers was short and the dangers from Western Hemisphere states appeared nonexistent. As the United States Navy developed an effective carrier-

[29] Sprout, "Mahan," p. 433.
[30] *Ibid.*

borne air arm which could effectively intercept and disrupt an invading fleet, the Army Air Forces had difficulty justifying the strategic bombardment mission, since even the B-17 did not have the combat radius to reach the heartland of any potential enemy in the middle and late thirties. The possibility that the Axis powers might establish bases in the Western Hemisphere was used in the late thirties as an argument to warrant the development and expansion of strategic bombardment to destroy these bases before an attack from them could be launched against the United States. The AAF postwar planners had a precedent in assuming that a danger lay in the south, and therefore they planned for a large deployed force in the Caribbean, with additional bases in South America.

Another fundamental difference between the beliefs of Mahan and AAF planners was that the latter were convinced that the encounter between opposing air forces would not take place within the operating medium (that is, in the air). They believed that victory would go to the state which could destroy first the enemy's offensive air capabilities and then his defensive air capabilities, followed by the demolition of his industries and the undermining of his will to continue the war.

The doctrine of Douhet, modified by the Tactical School in the thirties and generally accepted throughout AAF Headquarters, had an important effect upon all the postwar AAF plans. Douhet provided the basic military theory of strategic bombardment, while Mahan apparently provided some of the political and economic, as well as strategic, bases for the assumptions that would justify the Douhetan approach to national security. The marriage of modified Mahan to modified Douhet provided the doctrinal structure upon which most of the postwar Air Force would be built.

DOCTRINAL INNOVATION AND THE A-7 ATTACK AIRCRAFT DECISIONS

RICHARD G. HEAD

Defense decisionmaking on major weapons acquisition programs is inherently controversial because it involves the security of the nation, large budgets, and organizational missions for the future. This article develops a generalized model of such decisionmaking and applies it to the Air Force decision to buy the A-7 attack aircraft. The conclusion of the author is that the A-7 represents a doctrinal innovation, with the advocates of a specialized close air support aircraft winning at least a partial victory over the advocates of multipurpose tactical aircraft. Major Head (USAF) is an Assistant Professor of Political Science at the U.S. Air Force Academy, from which he graduated in 1960. He holds a master's and doctorate in Public Administration from Syracuse University. His operational experience includes four years in F-100s, two years as an instructor in F-4s, and 325 combat missions in the A-1 attack aircraft.

Doctrine has been described as the "life blood of a military service,"[1] but very little has been written on how doctrine affects (and is affected by) specific decisions on weapons systems. Doctrine is an "authoritative statement of principles," a "set of shared values that give direction and purpose to organizational activity."[2]

The doctrine or principle involved here is an Air Force preference for *multipurpose* aircraft to perform the three central missions of tactical air superiority, interdiction, and close air support. This principle evolved out of World War II and by 1961 had become a central issue in Air Force–Army debates over roles and missions. The Army insisted the Air Force should develop a *specialized* close air support aircraft; the Air Force steadfastly argued that only multipurpose aircraft could provide the flexibility that the overall tactical mission required. The puzzle posed by the A-7 decisions is simply this: Why did the Air Force reverse its doctrine of multipurpose tactical aircraft and decide in 1965 to buy a specialized A-7?

The first purpose of this article is to explain how the Air Force A-7 program was initiated and to examine what it shows us about the defense policymaking process. A second pur-

[1] See the previous selection in this chapter, Perry M. Smith, "The Role of Doctrine."
[2] For a more complex discussion of Air Force doctrine, see the author's larger study, *Decision Making on the A-7 Attack Aircraft Program* (D.P.A. diss., Syracuse University, 1971). Limitations of space have necessitated the omission of several reservations concerning the author's argument.

This is an original article written for this volume. Its completion would have been impossible without the assistance, advice, and cooperation of countless individuals in the Department of Defense, Ling-Temco-Vought, Inc., the Institute for Defense Analysis, and The RAND Corporation. I owe a special debt to two former Air Force officials: Chief of Staff General John P. McConnell, and Secretary of the Air Force Dr. Harold Brown. Acknowledgments are also due to General Gabriel P. Disosway, Lt. General Gordon M. Graham, Maj. General Robert E. Hails, Brig. General Howard Fish, Colonel Harold W. Stoneberger, Captain Robert F. Doss, Dr. Alain C. Enthoven, Mr. Russell Murray II, and many unnamed individuals who contributed to this research. The decisions I discuss are their decisions, made not in the cool detachment of academic reflection but in the daily fire of political controversy. I am indebted as well to Graham Allison, Robert Coulam, Barry Horton, and Ted Warner for comments on previous drafts. The views expressed herein are the author's and do not necessarily reflect the views of the United States Air Force or the Department of Defense.

pose is to illustrate how a Professional Organizational Model can be developed to help explain weapons decisions. The third purpose is to focus on the individual actors in the decision process, to examine their perspectives as they relate to their organizational roles.

The traditional method of research into a major weapons decision like the A-7 has been to analyze perceived international threats, interpreted in the light of broad national strategy. The accuracy of this approach can be enhanced, however, by additional research into organizational and individual actors. The most rigorous of recent efforts to examine these bureaucratic factors is Graham Allison's three conceptual models for policy analysis—a Rational Policy Model, an Organizational Process Model, and a Bureaucratic Politics Model.[3]

Allison's main argument is that the important "actors" in the development of a nation's foreign or defense policy are not unitary "nations," making policy on the basis of some rational, universally accepted plan. On the contrary, the central concept in the Organizational Process Model is the observation that the national actor can be best analyzed as a set of large organizations and prominent individuals, and that "a 'government' consists of a conglomerate of semifeudal, loosely allied organizations, each with a substantial life of its own."[4] Allison goes on to describe *how* the many organizations in the Cuban missile crisis differed in their approach, but he neglects some of the *why* of their differences. The main hypothesis of this paper is that organizations differ in their perspectives and approaches to problems largely because of the professional socialization of their members.

A PROFESSIONAL ORGANIZATIONAL MODEL

"Professional" in this study is used to mean those individuals who perceive themselves to be part of a distinctive group based on a proven body of knowledge with a tradition of service. One aspect of organizational professionalism is corporateness—a sense of organic

unity—gained through lengthy training, discipline, and experience. Corporateness also creates a system of shared values through professional socialization, the result of selective recruitment, common training, common career experience, and group pressures for conformity.[5] This common perspective is so strong that the individuals seldom realize they are conforming; they are merely doing what is "right" according to their professional standards. These professional perspectives are often expressed in organizational doctrine and in a conception of what the organization's core mission is and what it should be—the organization's "essence."[6] The purpose of developing a Professional Organizational Model in this article is to explain why the actors in the A-7 decisions saw different sides of the issue.

There are five main components to the Professional Organizational Model as presented here: (1) *professions*, which provide the basis for education, training, and standards of performance; (2) *organizational actors*, who tend to specialize in their use of certain professional skills; (3) *professional perspectives*, derived from expertise and socialization; (4) *organizational essence*, a conception of organizational needs and "core" missions; and (5) the *decisionmaking process*, the events and interactions that combine to throw relatively more influence to one or more of the organizational actors on a specific issue. An important part of the policymaking process—implementation—will be left for discussion in another article.

THE ACTORS AND THEIR PROFESSIONAL PERSPECTIVES

There were two central, and three peripheral, organizational actors in the A-7 decision process. Systems Analysis in the Office of the Secretary of Defense (OSD) and the U.S. Air Force were the central actors; other participants included the Office of the Director of Defense Research and Engineering, the Navy, and the

---

[3] See Graham T. Allison, "Conceptual Models and the Cuban Missile Crisis," pp. 273–300 of this volume.

[4] *Ibid.*, p. 280.

[5] A more complete development of the causes and effects of organizational perspectives was communicated to the editors by Edward L. Warner III in "Bureaucratic Politics: a Thematic Outline" (unpublished paper).

[6] The concept of organizational "essence" is described further in Morton H. Halperin, "Why Bureaucrats Play Games," pp. 301–10 of this volume.

Army. These organizations took positions on the A-7 that highlight two substantive themes. First, the A-7 issue represents a debate between advocates of "state of the art" technology and those advocates who favored advancing technology with each successive weapons program. Second, the A-7 issue shows how the executive of a large governmental organization can create incentives for innovation in a subordinate agency.

OSD Systems Analysis

First organized in the office of the Comptroller in 1961, Systems Analysis became the single most powerful office in the determination of military force structure during the Kennedy and Johnson Administrations. Secretary McNamara's use of this small analytical staff was seen as a deliberate tool to centralize DOD decisionmaking and to increase the influence of the Secretary of Defense over the services.[7] The professional expertise most closely identified with Systems Analysis was economics. A 1967 study revealed that economists represented 32 percent of the professional staff, over twice the percentage of the next largest group, the physical scientists.[8] The organizational "essence" of Systems Analysis included the advocacy of three concepts: quantitative methodology, centralized management, and the importance of cost as a decision criterion. This led to "cost-effectiveness" studies becoming a primary factor in defense decisionmaking. That Systems Analysis was very much interested in the cost side of the equation was emphasized by the office's orgins in the Comptroller's shop. A more subtle factor that will be discussed later was the office's tendency to prefer weapons systems that were "in hand" and that did not require extensive research and development. At a minimum, Systems Analysis felt no obligation to buy "effectiveness" for its own sake and was critical of advocates of advanced technology. In other words, Systems Analysis

professionals were generally convinced that with lower-cost weapons, a service could have a larger force. This larger force in turn would have more total effectiveness than a small force of expensive weapons. The professional perspective of Systems Analysis was cogently expressed by Charles J. Hitch, McNamara's Comptroller:

It should always be our policy to spend whatever is necessary for defense, but to spend whatever is spent in such a way as to achieve the greatest possible military capability—not to buy quality when the same amount spent on quantity will purchase greater effectiveness, and vice versa. Sometimes a weapon system with less than the maximum unit cost and effectiveness does win out as in the case of the new Navy attack aircraft, the A-7, which is far slower than many other aircraft now in the forces—and also much cheaper. The A-7 program promises to be not only satisfactory for the missions it is intended to perform, but superior in those missions to alternatives which cost more per aircraft.[9]

The Air Force

Two major components of the Air Force influenced the A-7 program: the Tactical Air Command (TAC) and the Air Staff. TAC was representative of the combat air operations subprofession in the Air Force, while the Air Staff was directly responsible for running cost-effectiveness studies and advising on new weapons programs.

The most common educational background for Air Force officers is engineering, but the unifying professional specialty is the "management and application of military resources" in deterrent and combat roles. To perform this specialty the Air Force needs weapons, and, especially since World War II, technically superior weapons have been seen as the key to victory. Some writers have even gone so far as to call this tendency the "Doctrine of Quality" —the view that the effectiveness of a modern military force depends largely, if not wholly, on the perfection of its equipment.[10] For the Air Force, advancing technology has become a part of the professional ethic, and the op-

---

[7] Alain C. Enthoven and K. Wayne Smith, *How Much Is Enough? Shaping the Defense Program, 1961–1969* (New York: Harper & Row, 1971); see also the excerpt reprinted on pp. 349–57 of the present volume.

[8] Brig. General Arnold W. Braswell, *The Role of the Systems Analysis Staff in Defense Decision Making* (Master's thesis, George Washington University, 1967), p. 22.

[9] Charles J. Hitch, *Decision Making for Defense* (Berkeley and Los Angeles: University of California Press, 1965), p. 50.

[10] M. M. Postan, D. Hay, and J. D. Scott, *Design and Development of Weapons* (London: Her Majesty's Stationery Office, 1964), p. 1.

erationalized form of "quality" was primarily defined as speed and survivability.

Although there are many similarities between tactical pilots in the Air Force and those in the Navy, there is one difference that relates to professional socialization. That is the fact that the Air Force trains its tactical fighter pilots to be generalists, to perform all three missions of air superiority, interdiction, and close air support. The Navy, on the other hand, tends to specialize its tactical pilots into two groups: fighter pilots, who train for the air superiority role; and attack pilots, who train for the missions of interdiction and close air support.

The reason for this divergence between the two services stems from differences in tactical doctrine. The Air Force developed a doctrine favoring *multipurpose* aircraft capable of performing air superiority, interdiction, and close air support. Navy tactical doctrine stresses the advantages of *specialized* fighter and attack aircraft. The significance of these doctrinal differences is that they stem from differing organizational experiences (many during World War II) and have over the years been incorporated into professional perspectives. The services seldom challenged each other's professional perspectives, because there existed a common commitment to the combat role, and each service focused on a slightly different operational environment.

Within the Air Force these two professional characteristics were reinforcing—multipurpose aircraft required the use of advanced technology because they were technically more difficult to design and required a larger operating envelope than did specialized aircraft. Further, within TAC the mission of air superiority (and the fighter pilots who were good at it) tended to have more prestige than the close air support mission. Air superiority was closer to the "essence" of the Air Force.

OSD DDR&E

The office of the Director of Defense Research and Engineering (DDR&E) was established in its present form in 1958 after Sputnik I. Its role was to advise the Secretary of Defense on matters of a scientific or technical nature, and specifically to monitor the development of new combat aircraft for the military services. Whereas only about 17 percent of the

Systems Analysis staff were engineers or physical scientists, one survey of DDR&E indicated 86 percent of its personnel had been educated in these skills.[11] In addition, most DDR&E personnel had had engineering experience with the aerospace industry before joining DOD. The dominant shared value in DDR&E was a commitment to advancing technology and to technical excellence—again, the "Doctrine of Quality."

The Navy

The A-7 was first developed for the U.S. Navy in 1963 to replace the A-4 and to perform the missions of interdiction and close air support. It was developed around a technological innovation (the turbofan engine) to provide greatly increased range; it was flown by attack pilots who considered it superior in its mission of long-range weapons delivery. It was not designed for, nor did the attack pilots demand that it be capable of attaining, air superiority through fighting other aircraft in the skies. The Navy, in the A-7 case, was mainly represented by professionals in attack combat operations, and their shared values included a common belief in the value of large numbers of load-carrying, low-cost aircraft to increase the cost-effectiveness of the attack carrier task force.

The Army

The combat profession was also represented in the Army, but its pressures on the A-7 program took a different form. The Army has always been interested in increasing the amount of firepower available in support of ground forces, but in 1962–1963 this took the form of Army requests for its own weapon-carrying aircraft—both fixed and rotary wing. Although the requests for Army development of fixed-wing, close support aircraft were consistently denied by the Secretary of Defense, Army pressure for a load-carrying specialized aircraft increased.

In summary, as the A-7 issue arose, the professional organizations' values could be differentiated according to the following general outline:

---

[11] DDR&E, Office of the Assistant Director for Laboratory Management, Personnel Files, 1966.

Organizations/ Professions	Dominant Value*	Specific Impact on A-7 Program
Systems Analysis/ Economics	Cost- effectiveness	Proposed AF buy A-7
DDR&E/ Engineering	Doctrine of Quality	Neutral
Navy/Operations Fighter Pilots	Supersonic performance	Negligible
Attack Pilots	Low cost, large numbers	Liked A-7 in Navy
Army/Operations	Responsive close air support	Wanted specialized attack aircraft
Air Force/ Operations	Supersonic performance	Preferred F-4

* The concept of a Professional Organizational Model is not sufficiently developed to make this outline definitive. The association of specific organizations with professions, and especially the attribution of a single "dominant value," is recognized as being slightly perfidious. Individuals in each organization held many different values. The outline is meant only to be a suggestive simplification of the organizations as they appeared to the author.

THE FIRST DECISION: THE NAVY INITIATES THE A-7 PROGRAM

The A-7 was first developed by the U.S. Navy in the aftermath of turmoil over the OSD decision to have *joint* Air Force–Navy development of the TFX/F-111 aircraft. In light of the difficulty and the prolonged period of the F-111's initiation, many observers were amazed that the almost concurrent Navy development of the A-7 was ever approved by Systems Analysis or McNamara. A later member of Systems Analysis related how the A-7 decision was made, and the significance of a Systems Analysis official, Mr. Russell Murray II, who had previously become acquainted with Navy attack doctrine while working for Grumman.

The Navy convinced Russ Murray that we needed a new airplane, and that the appropriate criterion was to build the cheapest possible airplane to deliver a large amount of ton-miles. . . . I think that is the most important institutional factor, because Russ Murray was directly responsible for convincing Alain Enthoven, who, in turn, was directly responsible for convincing McNamara to go ahead with the whole thing. And, of course, the way they got Enthoven and McNamara to go ahead with the whole idea was that they were going to have cheap airplanes. That whole competition was just going to be cost to deliver ton-miles.[12]

The Navy recommendation to develop a new attack aircraft as a follow-on to the A-4 came out of a 1963 cost-effectiveness analysis, the Sea-Based Air Strike Forces Study. The competition for the new attack aircraft contract was intense, with Grumman, Douglas, North American and Ling-Temco-Vought (LTV) submitting designs and bids. At this point, comparison with the F-111 competition is intriguing. The OSD decision to award the F-111 contract to General Dynamics was in the policy process for over thirteen months; the award of the A-7 contract to LTV took less than three weeks!

The reasons for this are many, but among them is an unusual relationship of personalities —Russell Murray in Systems Analysis and George Spangenberg in the Navy's Bureau of Naval Weapons. The Navy's decision to award the A-7 contract to LTV was made primarily on the basis of Spangenberg's analysis of the competing designs, but the F-111 controversy had cast some doubt on the ability of the services to convince OSD of the integrity of service-based evaluations. Russell Murray II was the primary OSD Systems Analysis representative assigned to monitor the A-7 evaluation, and his view of the process is enlightening. When asked how Systems Analysis viewed the Bureau of Naval Weapons procedure, he said, "George Spangenberg did his usual, first-rate, excellent job on the competition."[13] When asked if he respected Spangenberg's professional competence, he responded philosophically:

It's the only one like it I've ever heard of. He's just in a class by himself. He is extremely knowledgeable and absolutely the soul of integrity. Unfortunately he got on McNamara's list for what he said about the F-111, but I have known George for a long time, and I have the highest respect for him. He is first rate from a technical sense and with a sense of integrity. He's done great service for the country. As far as evaluating the competition, Systems Analysis was there really to sort of monitor what the evaluation was. Nobody in our shop was competent and nobody in DDR&E was competent to second-guess George on what the

[12] Interview with Pierre M. Sprey, OSD Systems Analysis, October 16, 1969.
[13] Interview with Russell Murray II, April 28, 1970.

airplane was going to do and how much the contractors' estimates should be changed. From my point of view, having known George for a long time, I figured that anything he said was the most knowledgeable, authoritative source on performance. I took that at face value. Then we ran some relatively simple tests of the airplane to see if it lived up to what the Sea-Based Air Strike Forces Study had claimed such an airplane would. We presented that to McNamara, and he agreed. He said "OK, let's go ahead with it," and that was that. There was the Navy's new attack aircraft program.[14]

DDR&E was not intimately involved with the selection of the prime contractor for the A-7. The Director of DDR&E, Dr. Harold Brown, was consulted on the selection of LTV and approved, but he reported that, since advanced technology was not involved, DDR&E really had no large role.[15]

Five brief conclusions can be drawn from this sketch of the Navy's decision to develop the A-7. (1) The professional influence of Navy attack pilots and naval attack experience tended to argue for the development of another Navy attack aircraft program, even while the F-111 was being developed. (2) The same attack professionalism influenced the characteristics required in the new A-7. These characteristics were simplicity, reliability, maintainability, light weight, small size, and low cost. (3) There was a certain congruence—a coordination of expectations—between Navy attack advocates and Systems Analysis on the desirable characteristics of a new aircraft. (4) The difficulty OSD experienced in getting the Navy to agree to *joint* development of the F-111 increased the probability that the *next* Navy proposal for a weapons program would meet with OSD approval. (5) The fortuitous professional relationship between George Spangenberg and Russell Murray aided greatly in the Navy's attempt to get the A-7 program off the ground.

THE SECOND DECISION: THE AIR FORCE BUYS THE A-7

At the time the Navy was developing the initial A-7 in 1963–1964, the Air Force was coming under increasing pressure from the Army and OSD to develop a close air support aircraft. This pressure was the result of a series of close air support boards, with the Army requesting the development of a "specialized" aircraft and the Air Force countering with the thesis that high-performance (supersonic), multipurpose aircraft were better able to conduct *all* the missions of tactical air superiority, interdiction, and close air support.

Although Systems Analysis had at other times advocated multipurpose aircraft and commonalty, the office at this point was firmly on the side of the specialized A-7. There were many reasons for this, including the lower cost of the A-7 and a philosophical agreement with professional Navy attack doctrine, in which the specialized aircraft was held in high esteem.

As the Air Force–Army controversy grew, DDR&E came to take a larger role in the debate. Dr. Harold Brown wrote to McNamara in June 1964 that the Army and Air Force positions were in fundamental disagreement, and that it appeared to him they could not be made compatible by quantitative analysis. Brown indicated his thoughts that the multipurpose aircraft had advantages, but that at some point a lower-cost aircraft might improve the quality of the tactical air forces. This ratio, he wrote, could be around one-third the cost of the F-111 ($8 million).[16] In 1964 the A-7 aircraft were estimated to cost about $1 million each.

THE AIR FORCE PRINCIPLE OF MULTIPURPOSE AIRCRAFT

The Air Force continued to maintain its professional position that multipurpose aircraft like the F-4 Phantom were superior in the tactical support role because of their high speed, large thrust-to-weight ratio, and low vulnerability to enemy action. Within the Air Force the operations professionals specifically rejected the Navy doctrine on the survivability of the subsonic attack aircraft. The Air Force doctrine on supersonic tactical fighters was expressed strongly by the officers in TAC and the Plans and Operations section of the Air Staff. One of the most respected of these professionals was triple-ace Lt. General Gordon M. Graham,

14 *Ibid.*
15 Interviews with Dr. Harold Brown, April 8, 1970, and Mr. George Spangenberg, August 17, 1970.

16 Interview with Dr. Harold Brown, April 8, 1970.

who later expressed the general feelings of TAC pilots:

We hadn't bought an attack airplane since World War II. The general doctrine and philosophy in the tactical area is that those (A-7 attack) aircraft are not the kinds of machines that would survive in a sophisticated environment, and that is the kind of war that we have to be prepared to fight. So we don't want to encumber ourselves and fill our force structure up with them.[17]

Similarly, General LeMay, Air Force Chief of Staff, replied tersely to a 1964 congressional proposition that the Air Force buy the A-7. "I am very unenthusiastic" about the A-7; "preliminary investigations that we have made so far indicate, cost-analysis-wise, it is not much good."[18] As the events of the 1960s unfolded, this position was increasingly difficult to maintain.

The pressures on the Air Force to re-examine its requirements for close air support accumulated from the Army Close Air Support Board's report, the formulation of a new Army air assault division, the Army's initiation of an attack helicopter program (the Cheyenne), and Dr. Brown's memo of June 1964. In addition, Systems Analysis was encouraging the Air Force to look at the A-7 and specifically requested a study of alternative mixes of tactical aircraft during the summer of 1964.

THE BOHN STUDY

Such a study was initiated under the auspices of the Air Staff Directorate of Plans in 1964. It was entitled *Force Options for Tactical Air,* but became known informally as the Bohn Study, after the project leader. The basic approach of the study group was to analyze the cost-effectiveness of various force mixes with F-111s, F-4s, F-105s, and two lower-cost aircraft, the LTV A-7 and the supersonic Northrop F-5 Freedom Fighter. At that time the costs of the F-5 were estimated to be about $700,000 apiece, and that of the A-7 was slightly over $1 million.

It is significant to note that LTV representatives had been trying to interest the Air Force in the A-7 for some time. They made their first contact with the Air Staff only three weeks after the award of the Navy contract. During the Bohn Study they continued to supply the Air Staff information as to the A-7's capabilities and performance. They received some sympathy but very little encouragement from lower-ranking Air Staff officers.[19]

Systems Analysis monitored the Bohn Study with an intention expressed by its head, Dr. Alain C. Enthoven:

We asked the Air Force to do studies of alternative force mixes, and we in Systems Analysis were *definitely* trying to encourage the Air Force to buy the A-7. Why were we trying to do that? Because first of all we believed that for the kind of wars the tactical air forces were likely to fight that the A-7 would simply be substantially better. It would have a longer range and better payload and the payload could be translated into all sorts of things. . . . It would be a lot more effective in relation to cost, and in fact, there was even good reason to believe that it was just more effective— that a subsonic design would be positively advantageous because it would be more maneuverable; you could have a better (steeper) dive angle for bombing which would mean more accuracy and less vulnerability.[20]

As noted in the study, the differences between the A-7 and the F-5 were pronounced, but their characteristics were not strictly comparable. The turbofan engine and the large fuel capacity of the A-7 gave it advantages in range, loiter time, and bomb load. With six wing bomb racks and two fuselage missile racks, it could carry a varied, 15,000-pound load of ordnance. The F-5 was generally limited to about 3,000 pounds of ordnance. Thus, if the decision criterion was low cost per ton-mile, the A-7 showed a significant comparative advantage. On the other hand, the twin engines of the F-5 and its overall small size gave it a high degree of survivability against enemy ground fire; its supersonic speed gave it definite advantages in air-to-air combat with enemy fighters, and it was cheaper. The F-5 was supersonic and multipurpose and thus consistent with Air Force doctrine and pilot preferences.

The conclusions of the Bohn study were that some lower-cost aircraft would improve the overall effectiveness of the force, and the im-

---

[17] Interview with Lt. General Gordon M. Graham, Vice Commander, TAC, February 11, 1970.
[18] "USAF Snubs VAL (A-7)," *Aviation Week and Space Technology,* March 23, 1964, p. 15.

[19] Interview with Mr. J. W. Lankford, LTV Marketing Director, April 1, 1970.
[20] Interview with Dr. Alain C. Enthoven, April 8, 1970.

plied recommendation was for the F-5 to be that aircraft. Systems Analysis found some fault with these conclusions. Russell Murray expressed the Systems Analysis position:

In the first one (the Bohn Study) the Air Force's predilection for supersonic airplanes just came through everything. One of the airplanes that they wanted was the F-5 for an attack airplane. I think it was just generally the feeling of the Air Staff that we should have a supersonic aircraft, and the idea was to look for a little less expensive airplane. They didn't want something big like the F-111 because they already had that.[21]

Systems Analysis was still interested in getting the Air Force to adopt the Navy A-7, and Enthoven and Murray recommended that the Air Force run another study, this time with full Systems Analysis participation. The method of their recommendation was a memorandum from Secretary McNamara to the Secretary of the Air Force in January 1965 requesting a study of tactical aircraft in production and "optimized for close air support," assuming that air superiority or air cover was available in all cases. The first response to the McNamara memo was an Air Force request for two wings of F-5s.

The position of TAC during this period was quite clear. TAC pilots wanted more F-4s and F-105s, not A-7s or F-5s. But TAC was being approached by Systems Analysis with proposals for the A-7. As Lt. General Graham described it:

In December 1964, Vic Heyman, who was one of the exponents of the A-7 in Systems Analysis, told me personally that we were going to be given that airplane, and I laughed at him. In fact, I didn't really know what it was. That spring of 1965, we got the first specific piece of paper that said, "We are considering giving you the A-7."[22]

Heyman asked the TAC pilots if the A-7 would be acceptable if more of them were available on a three-to-two ratio with the F-4. The TAC pilots emphatically said "No!" Heyman later recalled his conversations with General Graham and the TAC staff.

I was taking the devil's advocate point of view there and pushing the A-7 to see what the reac-

tion was, and why, and how strongly the view was held. They really considered the A-7 a dog. There is something about being supersonic that the pilots love; I don't know what it is.[23]

At this point it is imperative to clarify one issue. The debate over the A-7's performance was *not* strictly a matter of its being subsonic. *All* tactical fighter aircraft in 1965 were subsonic when loaded with bombs; a more important criterion was the aircraft's reserve thrust—its thrust-to-weight ratio, which is a critical factor in estimating an aircraft's maneuvering ability, acceleration, and thus its survivability.

Thrust-to-Weight Ratios

	F-4 Phantom	A-4A Skyhawk	A-7A Corsair II
Thrust	34,000 lbs.	7,700 lbs.	11,000 lbs.
Weight with bombs	56,000 lbs.	20,000 lbs.	40,000 lbs.
Thrust-to-Weight ratio	1:2	1:3	1:4

The Navy A-7A, which was still on the drawing boards in 1965, had approximately one-half the thrust-to-weight ratio of the Air Force–Navy F-4, and was even significantly lower than the A-4, which the A-7 was to replace in the Fleet. Thus, it was not just the subsonic characteristic of the A-7 that bothered Air Force pilots; it was the aircraft's overall low ceiling limitation (about 15,000 feet with bombs) and its attack speed (slower than that of the F-4).

The commander of Tactical Air Command during this period was General Gabriel P. Disosway. In a later interview General Disosway described the general sentiments of the air operations profession and related them to the need for advanced technology in weapons systems.

As soon as you get a better machine you can take on all those low performing aircraft (and shoot them all down). You've got historic examples of that that are just as applicable today as when they happened. Look at the German Stuka; it was a great airplane (for attacks on ground forces) as long as it didn't run into anything that could shoot it down. As soon as they

[21] Interview with Russell Murray II, April 28, 1970.
[22] Interview with Lt. General Graham, February 11, 1970.

[23] Interview with Dr. Victor K. Heyman, March 12, 1970.

started using it in the air where British Spitfires and P-40's were available to fight it, it disappeared off the battlefield. The Me-109 and FW-190 were a similar example because they set their production on those two aircraft prior to the time we set the production on ours, and ours were superior aircraft. And we beat them. Now, if they had come out with the Me-262 (jet fighter) sooner, they would have beaten us. I don't think there is any question about it, in the air-to-air business you've got to have a superior aircraft.[24]

The Secretary of Defense and OSD, on the other hand, were still not convinced that the Air Force was making a full effort to develop a true close air support capability as envisioned in the national strategy of Flexible Response. OSD doubled its disapproval of the Bohn Study and denied (by postponing) the Air Force request for F-5s! With this disapproval and the Army's continued development of the Cheyenne helicopter, the Air Force was having its alternatives limited. In May, the new Chief of Staff, General John P. McConnell, sent a formal request to the Secretary of the Air Force and OSD, recommending the development of a completely new attack aircraft.[25] The recommendation was never acted upon.

THE FISH STUDY

OSD Systems Analysis pressure for a new study continued, and in July 1965 a large computer study entitled *Joint Air Force/OSD FX Effort* was begun. In the Air Staff the project was given to a most forceful and dynamic officer, Colonel Howard M. Fish. The Fish Study, as it was soon called, was to compare the A-7 with the F-5, a stripped F-4 with an internal gun, and two other aircraft. The study boiled down to another evaluation of the F-4 versus the A-7 and the F-5, although the F-4 was recognized as being more expensive, even in a stripped-down version.

The computer study became an *extremely* complex analytical effort and was a real learning experience for the participants. This was one of the first efforts to model the air-to-air battle and to integrate it with the air-to-ground situation. The magnitude of the problem was indicated by the Systems Analysis representative, Russell Murray.

The activity that I can remember best is sitting in Harold Brown's conference room, day after day, having these meetings with generals and DDR&E. We would have these great discussions. Then the Air Force computer was just going like mad; it was grinding out pages and pages of data. They built this gigantic model which simulated a whole air war. . . .

There was a lot of this (discussion) going on, and I didn't feel we were getting to any particular conclusion. Naturally Systems Analysis was pushing for an A-7 or an airplane like that. By pushing I mean we were there to see that it at least got a fair shake. The calculations were not done by us; they were done by the Air Force. But the Air Force model was (complex). . . . I spent some time running through these pages and pages of data, and I can still recall a couple of things that came out of this war. We had a situation where the F-4 was just shooting down everything in sight. It was wonderful what the F-4 could do. . . .

It was so complicated that nobody could figure out really what was going on in the model, that was the problem. It was a gigantic set-up that put forth reams and reams of data, and there wasn't anybody that could analyze the thing and understand it.[26]

As the Fish Study evolved, the cost of the A-7 continued to be a prominent factor. General Graham commented from his perspective as the TAC representative on the study's Steering Group:

Although that study never came out and said, "Buy the A-7," of course it was used that way. I'll give you another very concrete and specific reason on why it came out the way it did. The single most important item in that Fish study was the cost quote on the A-7. . . . (LTV and Systems Analysis) validated the cost, the unit flyaway cost, at 1.4 million dollars a copy. This made the A-7 come out shining because of the price. We had an exact price of the F-4 because of the history of production, but the A-7 was mushy enough that you could call it whatever you wanted and get away with it. . . . (LTV) people in furnishing the cost came up with this, and the Systems Analysis guys popped on that and insisted that be used, although we in the panel objected to it because we knew what it involved.[27]

---

[24] Interview with General Gabriel P. Disosway, April 3, 1970.

[25] This was the first recorded request for what was much later to become the A-10 (AX) program. Interview with General John P. McConnell, Air Force Chief of Staff, May 6, 1970.

[26] Interview with Russell Murray II, April 28, 1970.

[27] Interview with Lt. General Graham, February 11, 1970.

Before the Fish Study was completed, four external events intervened. The first was the initial test flight of the Navy A-7 at the Dallas plant of LTV on September 27, 1965. Less than a week later the Secretary of the Air Force retired, and McNamara appointed his head of DDR&E, Dr. Harold Brown, to the new position. Brown, at thirty-eight years of age, was to be the youngest Air Force Secretary; he took over on October 1, 1965. The third factor was the steadily increasing American military effort in Vietnam, which only highlighted the need for more close air support. The fourth factor, representing the interplay between international and domestic forces, was a set of congressional hearings on close air support by the Special Subcommittee on Tactical Air Support of the House Armed Services Committee under the chairmanship of Congressman Pike. Pike was critical of the Air Force performance in Vietnam and specifically charged the Air Force with neglecting to develop a specialized close air support aircraft.

The Positions of the Actors

The Systems Analysis representatives in the Fish Study group were of the opinion that the A-7 suited the needs of the nation and the Air Force better than any of the alternatives. They preferred the A-7 because of its load-carrying capability, low cost, and the fact that it was already in production for the Navy. The fact that the Air Force considered the aircraft to possess fewer capabilities than advanced technology offered did not deter Systems Analysis.

DDR&E, which normally would have taken a strong stand in favor of an advanced weapon system, did not assume that role. This was due to the obvious intention of the Fish Study to select between the A-7 and the F-5; advanced systems were not even seriously considered. DDR&E did, however, advocate putting an internal gun in the F-4.

The Air Staff was split. Colonel Fish was asked if there were differences in professional perspectives within the Air Staff. He answered:

Oh yes, I think the best way to point that out was the fact that the Operations people strongly emphasized a supersonic capability (the F-4 and F-5). Our Requirements people were that way, and TAC people were that way. But when we finished all of our simulations I would say the Requirements people . . . had come around to the fact that it made sense to have some small part of the force able to carry large loads of bombs, like the A-7 showed up in the studies. You couldn't have the whole force doing that, but you would always have some portion of it doing close air support.

The Plans position was that we wanted a *decision*. Here's an interesting thing. The Plans position was that we wanted an airplane that we could put into that force structure and get on with the problem. We needed a decision in November for the December budget cycle. So the Plans position was whichever airplane comes out best, that's the one we want, but we needed a decision.[28]

Colonel Fish's remarks regarding the change of attitudes during the study are instructive. What, in fact, was occurring was a process of organizational learning, an alteration of the "core of shared concepts" that contributes so importantly to doctrine. Previous studies had taught the Air Staff that the "most rational" strategy for winning a limited war was to establish air superiority over the battlefield *before* committing air resources to the interdiction and close air support missions. Although there is little doubt the majority of tactical professionals would have preferred to maintain the emphasis on an air superiority capability in *all* tactical aircraft, the results of these two studies indicated that the optimum strategy would probably not be politically feasible. That is, the Air Force would be committed to provide *some* close air support right from the start of any hostilities, and for this mission a specialized aircraft would be acceptable, maybe even superior in some respects. This conceptual change was the beginning of the doctrinal innovation.

Finally, the results of the study came into form. They were summarized in a memo written by Colonel Fish which said: "Let's buy the A-7, and put bigger engines and a gun in the F-4 to fill in for an air-to-air fighting capability in the near term to compensate us for the fact that the A-7 would not have an air-to-air fighting capability, and start a crash development program for the FX, the F-15, a superior air-to-air aircraft that would be able to withstand the enemy threat in 1975 plus 20%."[29]

---

[28] Colonel Howard M. Fish to the author, January 7, 1971.

[29] *Ibid.*

THE AIR FORCE'S DECISION

Colonel Fish went on to describe the events which led to the critical decision point on November 5, 1965:

I thought it would be better if we didn't come up with "Buy the A-7" or "Buy the F-5." One night about two in the morning I said the way we should present this thing is to list all the characteristics in two columns and say, "Buy the A-7 if you believe in these things," and "Buy the F-5 if you believe in these things." Because even within my own group there was a division of opinion as to what we should do; there was no consensus.

We briefed it to the OSD/Air Force Steering Group, and arranged a meeting for the Chief of Staff, and he said he'd take the briefing with the Secretary. This thing got on a real fast train. I've spent six years on the Air Staff, and I don't think in all the days I've been here that I remember anything like this going quite as fast as this. We took it in to the Chief of Staff and the Secretary at about six o'clock at night.

I gave the briefing, and I ended up with these two slides: "Buy the F-5 if you believe these things," and "Buy the A-7 if you believe these things." One of the Air Staff officers indicated that there were a lot of things wrong with the A-7 list. General McConnell indicated that there were a lot of things wrong with the F-5 list. And I knew right then where we were! Up to that minute we really didn't know which way the Chief was coming down.

The Chief of Staff indicated to Dr. Brown that he thought we ought to buy the A-7. The Secretary indicated his agreement and directed an appropriate paper to be prepared. I prepared a letter to the Secretary of Defense immediately the next day with direct guidance from General McConnell and Secretary Brown.[30]

What were General McConnell's thoughts as he listened to the briefing and balanced it against the other factors he had to consider as the Chief of Staff? General McConnell later related his decision to the long history of roles and missions disputes between the Air Force and the Army:

Ever since World War II the Air Force began dedicating all of its funds gradually towards the build-up of a strategic offensive capability and continental defense capability, and therefore didn't have enough money to go into a tactical air capability the way they should have. But that was the philosophy of the government at that time—Massive Retaliation, at places of our own selection with weapons of our own choosing. So we got behind the eight-ball in tactical aviation. And naturally the Army attempted to move into the tactical aviation area with organizational aircraft. . . .

The thing that was pushing (in 1965) was that we *had* to get something to give the Army close air support. First, it was our job. Second, if we didn't do it, somebody else was going to do it for us. Every once in awhile that would come up on the Hill, especially with Representative Pike. Pike wanted to turn the Army into another Marine Corps since he was an old Marine. . . .

The thrust of the whole thing was that if the Air Force was going to meet its responsibilities, it *had to* go to a tactical weapons system that would drop iron bombs in close support and *specialize it* for close support. That is what drove it. . . .

We didn't pay too much attention to the briefings and the computer study; we knew we had to have an airplane, and this one we thought we were going to get for $1.4 million. . . .

Secretary Brown and I practically lived together on these things; he and I were very close. We never came up with a split decision between us; we'd work it out. Not one time did we ever go downstairs with a split. Through Secretarial channels he always went the same that I went through JCS channels.[31]

This decision on a new tactical aircraft had been weighing on the minds of General McConnell and Secretary Brown for some time. Dr. Brown later reflected on his perspective of the professional and doctrinal aspects of the decision.

It was perfectly clear by late 1965 and early 1966 that the Air Force was going to be put to the test both by the existence of the Vietnam War and its nature—however representative or unrepresentative they would be of a war somewhere else—and by congressional interest and by OSD interest in the question of how could the close support role—however defined—be handled as part of the area intrinsic to the ground battlefield.

The Air Force was going to be put to the test by all these things, and therefore it had to look at the question of close support specifically, and not just say as had been part of doctrine of organizations within the Air Force for many years, that whatever can fight the air battle can then go ahead and do the close support role. I think there was coming to be an awareness in the Air Force that, as a result of constraints inherent in limited war, you might not be able to fight the air battle. You

---

[30] Interview with Colonel Howard M. Fish, August 15, 1970.

[31] Interview with General McConnell, May 6, 1970.

might be forced to a close support situation where you hadn't won the air battle; you might have complete air superiority, but there might be other constraints as well. . . . This I think was reinforced by the political view that lacking *some* close support aircraft the Army would inevitably have a better argument for developing its armed helicopters to do the close support role. . . .

It really narrowed down to the F-5 and the A-7. By then enough information had come in from Vietnam on how important it was to have a big payload—both because of the bombs you could carry and because it gave you room to put in all kinds of targeting equipment which would allow you to get accuracy. People didn't yet realize the importance of this, at headquarters at least, but were beginning to. So a decision was made to go with the A-7.[32]

The assumptions behind the decision to buy the A-7 were: (1) the F-4 was needed in the gun version for air superiority; (2) the A-7 was the most cost-effective of the candidates; (3) only minimum changes in the Navy A-7 would be needed to meet Air Force needs; (4) it would be possible to divert part of the early Navy production to the Air Force; (5) the A-7 would be available to participate in the Vietnam War; and (6) the cost of the A-7 would be about $1.4 million per aircraft.[33]

With these assumptions the Air Force decision was to request three separate weapons acquisition programs: (1) to immediately begin development of a new air superiority fighter, the F-X (later to be the F-15 Eagle); (2) to put a larger engine and a gun in the F-4 (F-4E); and (3) to purchase 387 A-7 aircraft.

Secretary Brown later reflected on his view of the memorandum of November 5, 1965, as it went to McNamara and then to Systems Analysis:

We then sent down this recommendation to the Office of the Secretary of Defense, which was well received at the time partly because some of the people in Systems Analysis considered this was their airplane.

I'm sure they had some reservations about the question of future growth. They were trying to keep the price down, again because it was their airplane; if you kept the price down it would look better.[34]

Secretary McNamara consulted with Systems Analysis, who advised against the F-X and the F-4E, largely on the basis of their cost and uncertainties about their effectiveness. McNamara quickly, on November 19, sent his answer. He denied the request for an F-X program, denied approval to put an internal gun in the F-4, and *increased* the Air Force recommendation of 387 to 561 A-7's!

Epilogue

The Air Force A-7D program was placed under the management of Colonel Robert E. Hails, who skillfully guided it through a maze of interservice influences. Despite his best efforts, many of the assumptions of the original Brown-McConnell decision began to erode. TAC requested many changes in the Navy A-7A to make it suitable for Air Force use; it proved impossible to obtain early diversion of part of the Navy production line; the A-7D was not sent to Indochina until October 1972; and the cost rose from $1.4 million to over $3.0 million each. The original proposal for only a 387-aircraft program remained an Air Staff goal, although the reduction was not approved by OSD until 1969, after Mr. McNamara had left the Pentagon.

The major changes in the program after 1965 were the switch to a more powerful engine, the substitution of an Air Force gun, and an extremely significant addition of a computerized weapons delivery system. These changes, however, added to the price, and by 1969 the A-7 cost almost as much as the F-4. There was even a moment after the Army cancelled the production contract for the Cheyenne helicopter in 1969 that the interservice and cost factors caused General McConnell to recommend, and the Senate to cancel, the Air Force A-7D program. The cancellation proved not to be feasible, however, and by 1972 the Air Force was nearing the end of production for the 387-aircraft program. The aircraft itself performed well and drew praise from TAC pilots for its range, payload, and extremely accurate weapons delivery system introduced by Colonel Hails and Navy Captain Robert Doss. In 1972 an A-7D wing was de-

---

[32] Interview with Dr. Harold Brown, April 8, 1970.
[33] These assumptions were brought to my attention by Lt. Colonel Donald Clelland, USAF, and were subsequently confirmed by other participants in the A-7 decision process.

[34] Interview with Dr. Harold Brown, April 8, 1970.

ployed to Thailand to replace the A-1 in search and rescue, interdiction, and close air support missions.

The other two research and development programs were only temporarily delayed by McNamara's decision on the A-7. The internal gun for the F-4 was approved eight months later in July 1966 and became the basis for the F-4E. The F-X underwent further examination and was approved as a 729-aircraft F-15 program shortly after Secretary McNamara left DOD. With the eventual implementation of all three of the Fish Study's recommendations, the outcome had, and still is having, far-reaching effects on Air Force force structure.

CONCLUSIONS

The data surrounding the Air Force decision to buy the A-7 support some general conclusions about the policy process.

1. *The Importance of Situational Factors.* Systems Analysis and the Air Force were the two central organizational actors, each with resources and commitments to professional values. These values were in conflict on the A-7 program, with Systems Analysis advocating that the Air Force buy the aircraft and the Air Force preferring the multipurpose F-4. Why did the Air Force reverse its position? The answer can be explained in terms of situational factors—Vietnam, Army pressures, congressional interest, and the fact that the Navy already had the aircraft in production. These factors operated in the 1963–1965 time period to swing relatively more influence toward the Systems Analysis position on the A-7 issue.

2. *The Location Principle—the Advantages of Having Influence Near the Approval Authority.* Systems Analysis was significantly smaller than the Air Staff, yet it was located near, and had influence with, the Secretary of Defense (SecDef). This gave Systems Analysis a disadvantage in certain aspects of policy-making (e.g., implementation) but resulted in advantages when the issue needed SecDef approval. Thus, Systems Analysis was able to *withhold* a decision on the Air Force recommendation for two wings of F-5s and for the research and development program for a new attack aircraft until the Air Force requested the A-7.

3. *The Role of Interservice Competition.* The most critical factor in the statements of both Dr. Brown and General McConnell was the credibility of the Army threat to move into the mission of close air support. The Air Force's response to this threat to one of its assigned missions was not, however, directed only toward the Army in an internal struggle over different professional perspectives. It was also directed toward an external goal—the improvement of close air support capability—in the light of Vietnam experience. The two goals are essentially inseparable. One important conclusion is that interservice competition provides a powerful incentive to develop better, more efficient, more capable forces.

4. *The Ability of the Secretary of Defense to Create Incentives for Innovation in the Services.* The Secretary of Defense did not order the Air Force to buy the A-7, just as he did not order the Navy to develop the aircraft two years previously. What he and Systems Analysis did, however, was to create an incentive structure that led indirectly to the desired result.

The first policy change that McNamara made to start this process was to notify the Army in 1962 that it should take an innovative approach to aircraft technology and not be bound by traditional viewpoints and past policies in DOD roles and missions agreements. Similarly, McNamara wrote to the Air Force and threatened to remove the close air support mission from its responsibility unless it developed a better capability for Army support.[35] Thus, by 1965, when the Army was moving ahead with the Cheyenne attack helicopter program, the threat had credibility. The Secretary of Defense did not challenge professional Air Force doctrine, but he allowed the Army to create a situation in which the Air Force was forced to question its own doctrine on tactical aircraft, as explained by Dr. Brown. He also used his direct authority to terminate the F-105 program, withheld a decision on the F-5 request, and was reluctant to authorize the purchase of any additional F-4s above the approved level. The success of these direct and indirect incentives for innovation can be measured by the fact that the decision to purchase a specialized, rather than a multipurpose, air-

---

[35] *Aviation Week and Space Technology,* January 14, 1963, p. 27.

craft (a doctrinal innovation) was accomplished virtually without innovation advocates in the Air Force. There were Air Force officers who thought the A-7 might be a good close air support aircraft, but they were few in number, and none conducted themselves in a manner that would be called advocacy.

5. *The Critical Importance of Certain Key Individuals.* Organizations factor problems and provide opportunities for lower-ranking personnel to establish organizational positions on certain issues. Certainly this was the case in Systems Analysis, where Dr. Enthoven considered Russell Murray his expert on tactical matters and largely left the A-7 issue in his hands. For his part, Murray had been associated with subsonic attack aircraft while at Grumman, felt a deep professional respect for the Navy Chief of Evaluation, George Spangenberg, and pressed the Air Force to buy the Navy A-7. When Murray left Systems Analysis in 1969, that organization's view of the A-7 changed to a more critical attitude. On the Air Force side, it is significant that Dr. Brown had been Secretary of the Air Force for only five weeks when he made the A-7 decision, and his first association with the issue had been as McNamara's Director of DDR&E. General McConnell was still in his first year as the Air Force Chief of Staff at the time of the decision. The conclusion is that, when new policy is to be made, it is more likely to be accomplished by new people.

6. *Doctrinal Innovation.* The experiences of an organization are embodied in doctrine, which provides a unifying core for the development of a professional organization; decisions that require a change in doctrine will take longer and will require a greater accumulation of forces than nondoctrinal decisions. Accomplishment of the A-7 decision required over two years and a multitude of forces.

The Air Force decision to buy the A-7 was only a modification—not a complete rejection —of organizational doctrine because the direction of the change was consistent with professional standards of performance—improvement within the close air support mission. In addition, Dr. Brown and General McConnell said they did not want to change all Air Force tactical aircraft to specialized ones, but only to specialize a portion of the force. The overwhelming majority were still to be multi-

purpose aircraft, and *the decision stressed the value of the F-4E and the F-15.*

However, even incremental modifications are significant policy changes. The decision to buy the A-7 did several things that initiated a doctrinal innovation. (1) It ratified the learning process that had occurred during the Fish Study—that some specialized attack aircraft increased the total mission capability of the tactical forces. (2) It broke the back of the Air Force's insistence on multipurpose fighters across the board. (3) It paved the way for a more specialized air superiority fighter, the F-15. (4) It focused attention on the close air support mission. (5) It gave added influence to those few low-ranking TAC pilots who had been arguing for more aircraft like the prop-driven A-1. (6) It provided organizational incentive to develop the A-10 (AX) program. And (7) it opened the door for a further process of organizational learning which was to occur when Air Force pilots began flying the A-7D.

What began as a cost-effectiveness simulation has been reinforced by test-pilot reports and, by 1972, combat experience. Thus, the A-7 initiated a doctrinal shift, an alteration over time of the "core of shared concepts" of the profession. As the A-7 becomes obsolete, the innovation will approach a critical point; for it to be sustained, a follow-on specialized aircraft will have to be recognized. At the present time the A-10 appears to be a likely candidate, but it will have to prevail over other institutional and situational factors to gain its position and sustain the doctrinal innovation.

7. *The Influence of Professional Socialization.* The actors in the A-7 decision not only were individuals but were players in organizational positions. The organizations had clearly discernible organizational interests, developed over years of specialization and professional socialization. The effect of this process was that the organizational actors developed unique attitudes and perspectives relative to the core profession and the mission of the organization. Systems Analysis was committed to the methodology of economic analysis, where the salience of cost was a shared value. Systems Analysis also developed a collective attitude that advanced technology was expensive and filled with uncertainty; many advantages were

seen to derive from having the Air Force buy the A-7 aircraft that was already in production. One of these advantages to Systems Analysis was the reduction of the overall DOD-wide cost per unit aircraft of the A-7 program; another hope was that the low-cost A-7 would somehow replace some of the multimillion dollar F-111s in the Air Force force structure.

The Air Force, on the other hand, rejected the professional economic viewpoint that selecting weapons programs was "primarily" an economic problem. The Air Force commitment to a professional ethic of advancing technology saw weapons development as primarily a technological problem (with economic overtones) of meeting strategic goals. Experience in wartime had convinced Air Force leaders that technological superiority was essential, and if the A-7 did not possess sufficient performance to survive, the Air Force did not want to buy it, no matter what the cost.

The practical effect of these belief systems was professional socialization, the shaping of individuals' views of the environment and the establishment of policy preferences for specific kinds of aircraft. The significant point is that decisions on major weapons programs and other defense policy issues appear to be the outcome or resultant of political disagreement. The sources of the disagreements are genuine and stem from different interpretations of the problem. In the environment of defense decisions the organizations are extremely important because they define the problems and design the alternatives. The organizations differ in many respects, some of them in professional perspective. The A-7 case has provided an analysis of these differences, and, if the concept of a Professional Organizational Model has helped to clarify the complexity of the policy process, this article has fulfilled its purpose.

RAND CASE STUDY: SELECTION AND USE OF STRATEGIC AIR BASES

BRUCE L. R. SMITH

This study of policy innovation lends itself to an application of the Davis model for developing horizontal and vertical alliances. The article's thesis is that it is useful to do empirical research on policy issues facing decision-makers. One conclusion of the study is that the manner and technique of communicating results is almost as critical as the research itself. RAND's position of being close to, but not within, government is seen as an asset in effectively communicating policy advice. This is part of a larger study published in 1966 under the title The RAND Corporation: Case Study of a Nonprofit Advisory Corporation. *Dr. Smith completed his Ph.D. in the Department of Government, Harvard University, and has served in the Department of Defense and in the Social Science Department of The RAND Corporation.*

One of the most striking phenomena in postwar defense organization in the United States is the growth of the nonprofit research or advisory corporation. The "nonprofits" form a significant portion of the small but influential community of scientific strategists, made up to a considerable degree of civilian researchers and advisers, that has come to play a role in defense policy formation scarcely imaginable as recently as several decades ago.[1] Struck by the phenomenon, one foreign observer reportedly remarked that "representatives of certain U.S. research organizations stalk the Pentagon like the Jesuits in the chancelleries of 18th century Europe." Each of the three military services has at least one of the novel advisory corporations performing policy and operations research or systems analysis for it on a contractual basis. The Navy has the Center for Naval Analysis, administered by the Franklin Institute of Philadelphia, with several specialized advisory groups as component parts. The Army has sponsored the creation of a number of such organizations: the Research Analysis Corporation (RAC),[2] the Human Relations Research Office (HumRRO), and the Special Operations Research Organization (SORO). In addition, the Army has a contract research group furnished by the Stanford Research Institute (SRI) and a contract research operation also in effect with Technical Operations, Inc. The Air Force has The RAND Corporation and Analytic Services, Inc. (ANSER), as well as a number of other nonprofit institutions whose functions differ rather sharply from the "paper-pure" research mission of RAND and ANSER. At the Department of Defense level, the Weapons System Evaluation Group (WSEG), the Institute for Defense Analyses (IDA), and the Logistics Manage-

[1] For a general description of the community of "scientific strategists," see the essay by Wesley W. Posvar, "The Impact of Strategy Expertise on the National Security Policy of the U.S.," *Public Policy*, 13 (1964): 36–68. Other useful studies are: Bernard Brodie, "The Scientific Strategists," in *Administration of National Security: Selected Papers*, Committee Print, Subcommittee of National Security Staffing and Operations, Committee on Government Operations, U.S. Senate, 87th Cong., 2nd sess., pp. 190–201: Joseph Kraft, "The War Thinkers," *Esquire*, September 1962, pp. 102–4; and Kathleen Archibald, "Social Science Approaches to Peace: Problems and Issues," *Social Problems*, 11 (Summer 1963).

[2] Formerly the Operations Research Office (ORO).

Reprinted by permission and with minor changes from "Strategic Expertise and National Security Policy: A Case Study," Public Policy, 13 (1964): 69–106. Copyright © 1964 by the Graduate School of Public Administration, Harvard University.

ment Institute (LMI) perform various advisory services for defense policymakers.

What are the implications of this development for the process of national security policy formation in the United States? Is the nonprofit corporation an answer to the ills of bureaucracy? A form of governmental organization particularly well adapted to an era of science and technology? Or a threat to the established executive agencies and to orderliness and accountability in the conduct of public policy? Will there be, as one ardent operations researcher urges, a "necessity for some modification in the political structure of the democracies of the world [required] . . . by the ultimate success of operations research techniques for solving broad problems?"[3] Questions such as these have received scant attention in the scholarly literature. Like Rabbit, we seem to have awakened one morning and found a Strange Animal among us. Something of a revolution in government organization has taken place, yet we have hardly begun to develop the intellectual basis for understanding what has happened, much less to deal intelligently with the many practical issues that have resulted. Indeed, the whole subject of the scientists' role in national policymaking generally is little understood at present. It is therefore hardly surprising that the role of the advisory corporations, one part of the scientific advisory culture, should remain unclear. As Robert Gilpin has remarked, "the study of the political participation of natural scientists has lagged far behind the activities of scientists. . . . the literature which seeks to comprehend and evaluate scientists as participants in government still leaves the field of inquiry largely unexploited."[4] There is a great need, in brief, for a body of empirically grounded theory to explain the role of scientists in the processes of national policy formation.

The objective of this study is to contribute to a broad understanding of the scientific adviser's role in national policy formation through a

careful look at the operations of one of the chief advisory corporations working in the defense area: The RAND Corporation. I will approach the task by undertaking a case study of the origins, execution, and eventual communication to Air Force policymakers of one of the most significant studies ever done at RAND: the Strategic Bases study (RAND Report 266).[5] An incidental advantage of selecting the basing study (R-266) for analysis is the fact that most of the relevant materials are now free from security restrictions and can be discussed in the open literature. More important, the study offers an excellent illustration of what a useful RAND systems analysis is and how it can influence public policy. Tracing the study's evolution also throws important light on the nature of RAND and how it has operated.

A particular virtue of the case approach used here is the degree of realism and specificity it can give to our analysis of the policymaking process and the advisory group's role in that process. Generalized discussions of decision-making with little empirical content often have an air of unreality about them. It is perhaps due in part to the absence of detailed studies specifying the adviser's role in actual decisions that some misleading and even fanciful notions have arisen concerning the relationship between the scientific adviser and the policymaker. The view presented here sees the scientific adviser as playing a vital, yet subordinate, part in the policy formation process. In a complex technical age, the task of the defense policymaker can be enormously facilitated by analytic advice. Yet no amount of research or advice can absolve the policymaker from making a painful choice at some point: he must synthesize various technical and analytical considerations into a policy context which also includes value judgments, imprecise knowledge gained through experience, and intuitive estimates about such elusive entities as "human nature" or the "intent" of another nation. Rare is the research or piece of advice that can be translated directly into policy in some simple and straightforward fashion. Useful policy advice, especially at the broad strategic level, has increasingly become an effort to define the major alternatives confronting the policymaker in

---

[3] W. L. Whitson, "The Growth of the Operations Research Office in the U.S. Army," *Journal of the Operations Research Society of America*, 8, no. 6 (November–December 1960): 824.

[4] "Introduction: Natural Scientists in Policy-Making," in *Scientists and National Policy Making*, ed. Robert Gilpin and Christopher Wright (New York, 1964), p. 2. The pioneering work is Don K. Price, *Government and Science* (New York, 1954), and the best general treatment of the subject is Don K. Price, *The Scientific Estate* (Cambridge, Mass., 1966).

[5] A. J. Wohlstetter, F. S. Hoffman, R. J. Lutz, and H. S. Rowen, *Selection and Use of Strategic Air Bases*, RAND R-266, April 1, 1954; declassified in 1962.

a situation of choice involving great uncertainty.[6]

As a corollary to the above, it should be stressed that the notion of "scientific adviser" used here suggests much more than the traditional physical or natural scientists giving technical advice to policymakers on the performance of some missile, bomb, or other item of military hardware. Corresponding to the changes in the nature of effective systems analysis work in the years since World War II there have been noticeable changes in the skill group composition of the staffs of various advisory corporations. Whereas once mathematicians and physical scientists were the dominant skill groups represented, social scientists (and particularly the economists) have increasingly gained in numbers and importance and today play a leading role in effective systems analysis work.[7] What has resulted, as the basing study will illustrate, is the emergence of a new group of "generalist experts" which serves as something of a bridge between the worlds of science and technology and the world of policy. This is not to suggest that the traditional scientist or technologist or other expert with specialized knowledge has been, or will be, totally supplanted in the process of national policy formation. Certainly they will remain important participants in policymaking in a complex, technical age. Not the least of their tasks will be to participate extensively in the making of na-

tional policy *for* science—e.g., in the development of policies for the management and support of the national scientific enterprise, the strengthening of the country's basic scientific potential, and the selection and evaluation of substantive scientific programs. But, on the issues of science *in* policy—basically political or administrative issues, but issues strongly influenced by technical considerations—the kind of expertise that seems more and more useful to national policymakers is the generalizing variety that integrates the work of a number of separate disciplines into a generalized policy framework. The RAND systems analysis work, with its marked interdisciplinary flavor, provides a good example of this generalist-type expertise.

There are several reasons why it is particularly important to recognize the infusion of economists and other social scientists into the scientific advisory culture. For one thing, this awareness serves as a healthy corrective to the view, popularized by Sir Charles Snow and others, that scientists in the strict sense (meaning physical and natural scientists and engineers) are possessed of some special gift of foresight in dealing with the "cardinal choices" facing the advanced industrial societies today.[8] Such views apparently die hard, despite much critical commentary. Witness the following recent observation by a leading statesman of science: "Especially on matters of military technology, scientists are often in a position to exercise their political and ethical judgments as citizens in a more realistic and balanced manner than other citizens."[9] The danger of such views is that, on the one hand, they lead to a search for certainty—for intellectually pure solutions to enormously complex problems which admit of no certainty and no precise solutions deduced from a few simple initial premises. And, on the other hand, they foster an anti-intellectualism which undervalues the contribu-

---

[6] In contrast, operations researchers in World War II sought principally to provide simple solutions to low-level problems that could be stated precisely and treated in exact quantitative terms. Much confusion has resulted from a failure to distinguish these two different components of the broad term "operations research." The differences between traditional operations research techniques applied to low-order choices and the broad-gauged systems approach to strategic issues are ably expounded in James R. Schlesinger, "Quantitative Analysis and National Security," *World Politics*, 15, no. 2 (January 1963): 295–315.

[7] Interestingly, this development seems to have occurred principally in the United States. In Britain and Canada, operations researchers continue to be trained predominantly in mathematics and the physical sciences. Their work remains oriented toward the more narrow range of problems characteristic of World War II operations research. The fact that the British and Canadian operations research groups are located organizationally within the governmental hierarchy is perhaps significant in explaining why they have for the most part avoided a concern with the broader policy questions and have concentrated their attention on solving low-level problems within a "given" policy framework.

[8] C. P. Snow, *Science and Government* (Cambridge, Mass., 1961). For an effective critique of Snow, see Albert Wohlstetter, "Strategy and the Natural Scientists," in *Scientists and National Policy Making*, ed. Gilpin and Wright, pp. 174–239.

[9] Harvey Brooks, "The Scientific Adviser," in *Scientists and National Policy Making*, ed. Gilpin and Wright, p. 80. Brooks insists on the value and importance of the scientist's advice in reaching a balanced decision in matters involving the use of scientific results, "even when the scientist is speaking primarily as a citizen outside his area of special competence."

tion of behavioral research and analysis to rational policy choices in the nuclear age. The cardinal choices of today are simply too complex, involve too many considerations beyond the competence of one trained in a particular scientific discipline, and are too beset with large uncertainties to be resolved by an almost preternatural insight possessed by an elect of scientists and engineers.

Pretensions to unique insights and to scientific exactitude in the making of broad defense decisions often lead to insupportable hypotheses about political phenomena and to simpleminded policy prescriptions. These pretensions also help account for the extraordinarily bitter intrascience wrangles over such issues as fallout and the test ban. Some scientists have carried over into the muddy normative world of high policy their traditional quest for objective and readily acceptable solutions to clearly defined problems. Accordingly, if scientist X disagrees with scientist Y's conclusions, it is easy for one to conclude that the other lacks the necessary mental equipment or goodwill or both to be regarded as a respectable member of the brotherhood. It is only a short step from here to denigrating the work of those who proceed by tentative and empirical methods to analyze the broad choices facing defense policymakers. Thus, paradoxically, a chief criticism of scientists in politics is that in a sense they are not scientific enough. They often operate on a basis of dogma and revealed truth, are careless in the manipulation of new types of data, and look down on those who deal with political phenomena in a serious professional way as being merely apologists for the politicians or purveyors of common-sense notions dressed up in pretentious language. A recent study sums up the point well:

But it may also be that the scientists' greatest failing has been that to date they have not actually applied their skills competently and seriously to an analysis and manipulation of the political process. They have not paused to become versed in new types of data or bothered to observe seriously the phenomena with which they are now concerned. They have encountered trouble by being casual or careless, or even diffident, in their study of the political world not because they function as poor politicians, but because they function as poor scientists. Perhaps those who now best represent the scientific and the revolutionary tradition in policy-making are that small but growing number of experts variously dubbed civilian strategists working seriously at the business of applying the techniques of empirical investigation and controlled experimentation to political aspects of human behavior.[10]

What the basing study shows above all is that it is possible to do useful empirical research on the cardinal choices which can be of great assistance to defense decisionmakers. The results of this work are not merely trivial; they are more reliable guides to decision than simple intuition, and they are vastly superior to either the civilian or military conventional wisdom.

A related reason why it is important to recognize the infusion of economists and other social scientists into the scientific advisory culture concerns how one views the relationship between scientific adviser and policymaker. Led astray by his assumption that the bases for making cardinal choices are accessible only to a chosen few, Sir Charles Snow could naturally conclude that the policymaker is almost helplessly dependent upon his scientific advisers. A very different view of the scientific adviser's role is suggested, however, if the community of scientific advisers is understood to include a broader base of professional skills than simply the physical and natural sciences. Many more persons, then, have something useful to say about the cardinal choices, and they can say it in a language likely to be more intelligible and comprehensible to the policymaker. This is one of the salient differences between our present cold war situation and the circumstances in which decisions had to be made in World War II—a difference which I believe the basing study discussion will bring clearly to light. The policymaker, civilian and military, is in a better position today to understand and to evaluate the advice he receives from his scientific advisers. His ability to make sophisticated decisions is enhanced by the filtering layer of generalist experts who help him to define the relevant policy alternatives that spring from scientific and technological developments. Moreover, he frequently has the time to acquaint himself with the data and the kind of reasoning required to give him a "first-hand knowledge of what those choices depend upon

[10] Robert C. Wood, "Scientists and Politics: The Rise of an Apolitical Elite," in *Scientists and National Policy Making*, ed. Gilpin and Wright, p. 71.

or what their result might be."[11] In a wartime situation, we would probably have a good deal more reason to fear that cardinal decisions would be made hastily and on the basis of unusual deference to scientists and other experts.[12] But in the present circumstances there is ample opportunity for debate, study, discussion, and review of advisory recommendations at a number of different policy levels. This has an important bearing on the question of how the scientific adviser figures in the policy process, and invites revision in elitist notions that the cardinal choices are steadily slipping out of the hands of accountable officials. The real problem we face in this area more and more becomes one of organizing our scientific advisory apparatus in such a way as to assure policymakers at various levels a broad base of scientific advice—while at the same time avoiding an extreme diffusion of influence and expertise and a fragmentation in our decisionmaking machinery that would make it difficult to develop a framework for coherent, unified, and sustained national policies.

ORIGINS AND EARLY HISTORY OF THE STRATEGIC BASES STUDY

The origins of R-266 go back to May 1951, when the Air Force addressed a request to RAND for a study of the selection of overseas air bases.[13] Military construction authorized by Congress for the fiscal year 1952 included some $3\frac{1}{2}$ billion dollars for air base construction, almost half of which was for overseas base construction, and the prospect was that a much larger volume of new construction would be planned in the next several years. It appeared to the Air Force officer responsible for the request that RAND might make a useful contribution by studying the most effective ways of acquiring, constructing, and using air base facilities in foreign countries. The criterion then

in use for guiding decisions on basing questions was a very crude one, having to do principally with minimum cost for given facilities. No concern was shown to total systems costs, which, as it turned out, were markedly different under alternative basing policies. The request was referred to Charles J. Hitch, head of RAND's Economics Division.

In keeping with the general RAND practice, Hitch sought to interest some of his staff in researching the area rather than attempt to thrust the project on anyone. The interest or lack of interest shown in a proposed study by the research staff would be an important factor in determining whether or not RAND would accept the Air Force's request. One of the men approached by Hitch was Albert Wohlstetter, a consultant of diverse background and interests newly added to the RAND Economics Division. Wohlstetter was not very interested in working on the project. "It did not look to me at the time," Wohlstetter recalls, "like a very interesting or challenging study . . . dull, full of nuts-and-bolts, the kind of thing one normally associates with logistics."[14] For a time, it appeared that the request for the base study would be one of those Air Force requests that RAND turned down. However, before giving a definite "no," Wohlstetter asked for a week or two to think about the matter. The week's reflection brought Wohlstetter to the conclusion that some potentially major problems might be raised by such a study. He opted to work on the study, and RAND informed the Air Force that it was willing to undertake the project.

Throughout the spring and summer of 1951, Wohlstetter was the only one formally working on the project. At this stage, Wohlstetter spent most of his time trying to formulate what exactly was the problem. He asked questions of himself and others constantly, and spent long hours familiarizing himself with Air Force procedures and current basing policies. He became convinced that the real task lay in discovering

[11] Snow, *Science and Government*, p. 1. For an extended discussion of the importance of the time factor, see Wohlstetter, "Strategy and the Natural Scientists," pp. 181–83.

[12] For the effect of crises on decision making, see Charles F. Hermann, "Crisis and Organizational Viability," *Administrative Science Quarterly*, 8, no. 1 (June 1963): 61–82.

[13] The request came from Col. L. C. Coddington, Deputy to General Maddux, Assistant for Air Bases. The original request for the study included a tentative formulation of the problem and posed a number of questions for analysis in a short supporting staff paper.

[14] All direct quotations used in this study that are not otherwise documented are based on personal interviews. My special thanks are due to Albert Wohlstetter, formerly of The RAND Corporation and currently Ford Research Professor at the University of California, for giving generously of his time and cooperating fully in this case study's preparation. I also benefited greatly from interviews with Henry S. Rowen, Fred S. Hoffman, Robert Belzer, Frederick Sallaghar, and L. J. Henderson, Jr., of The RAND Corporation.

what were the right questions to ask instead of accepting the client's tentative formulation of the problem and providing answers to ready-made questions. Conversations with Henry S. Rowen, a RAND economist with engineering training, were particularly helpful at this stage. Rowen was then engaged in several RAND projects related to Wohlstetter's field of interests, which made him a particularly valuable collaborator in the research. Later, another economist, Fred S. Hoffman, and an aeronautical engineer, Robert J. Lutz, joined Wohlstetter and Rowen.

While acknowledging Wohlstetter's and his team's primary responsibility for R-266, it should at the same time be stressed that they benefited throughout from functioning in a research environment that enabled them to draw on the skills and knowledge of others. The Wohlstetter team was able to solicit brief memoranda from RAND colleagues in the Electronics, Cost Analysis, and Mathematics areas on selected aspects of the basing problem and to interest some engineering people in making various calculations. Complementary studies in progress also provided a fund of data without which it would have been difficult to carry out the basing study.

INDIVIDUAL RESPONSIBILITY FOR STUDIES

The final report R-266, incidentally, bears the names of these four men as authors. The fact of individual authorship credit is significant, for it underscores an important point about RAND studies—namely, that they are the efforts of *individuals* and not the products of an abstract corporate personality. It is also important to note that the RAND practice of individual authorship credit contrasts sharply with the tradition of anonymity in governmental staff papers and reports. This is a consequential factor in considering how to create conditions for attracting and keeping research talent. A traditional feature of scholarly inquiry of all sorts is a strong desire on the author's part for recognition of his work.[15]

Yet RAND is not without its own problems

in this regard. The fact that much of RAND's work is classified poses some difficult problems. For one thing, the "audience" with access to a classified report or study is typically much smaller than what one would reach in unclassified work. Since it is not always possible to prepare an unclassified version of a classified study for publication in the open literature, this can mean that on occasion an important study will be unknown outside a small community of cleared individuals. Second, a source of much irritation to people working on classified studies is the practice of outsiders occasionally publishing in the open literature, and receiving credit for, ideas developed earlier by others in classified work. For this reason the academic strategist with access to classified materials is particularly resented by some strategists working primarily in the classified arena. Finally, classified research often tends to be more ephemeral than research published in the open literature, and is poorly indexed and difficult to gain access to, with the net result that a thoroughly professional tradition is lacking in classified research.

A DRAFT OF THE STUDY APPEARS: THE HARD JOB OF FILLING IN THE GAPS AND CHECKING THE ANALYSIS

By the late fall of 1951, Wohlstetter's thinking had crystallized to a point where he felt able to put some ideas down on paper. With Rowen he drafted a "D"—or internal working paper —for internal RAND consumption which was completed on December 29, 1951—D-1114 "Economic and Strategic Considerations in Air Base Location: a Preliminary Review." This paper, though a document some 100 pages long and containing 40 pages of graphs and tables, represented only a sketchy summary of some useful approaches to the basing problem. But it did lay down in preliminary form what were to become the central concerns of R-266. Among the most important of these was the question of the vulnerability of aircraft on the ground to surprise atomic attack. It occurred to Wohlstetter that the past thinking on strategic bombing and basing posture had not given adequate attention to a question that could become of vital importance in the future: what would happen if the enemy struck first, hitting U.S. bombers on the ground before they

---

[15] Robert K. Merton, "Priorities in Scientific Discovery: A Chapter in the Sociology of Science," in *The Sociology of Science*, ed. Bernard Barber and Walter Hirsch (Glencoe, Ill., 1962), pp. 447–85.

reached enemy air space? The full importance of this question was seen only vaguely at this point, but certain uncomfortable conclusions emerged even from the preliminary analysis. It was found, for example, that Air Force regulations on base installation called for the concentration of facilities to minimize the costs of utilities, pipelines, roads, and normal peacetime operational costs. Wohlstetter and Rowen discovered that such a system was highly vulnerable to enemy nuclear attack and suggested tentatively that a policy of dispersing facilities on bases would be preferable.

D-1114 contained many gaps and was inconclusive at points, but it had at least raised some significant questions and suggested new approaches to the problem of basing policy. For a variety of reasons, the study encountered considerable opposition and skepticism within RAND. Earlier RAND strategic bombing studies had dealt with such questions as What is the best way to penetrate enemy fighter defenses? How high should bomber aircraft fly? What kind of aircraft, turboprop or turbojet, should be used? The question of where the strategic strike force should be based was not considered a very important issue. The offensive capability the Soviet Union had at the time was considered likely to be used only against cities, not bases, and this could be taken care of by appropriate air defense measures. It was assumed that we could base U.S. aircraft at a variety of points within range of enemy targets at minimum risk. Because of this assumption many RAND people did not consider D-1114 to be dealing with a very significant or vital problem. Some at RAND even believed the project was a waste of time and money, and should be discontinued. On the other hand, a few RAND staff members were impressed by D-1114, and thought the matter important enough to be briefed at the Pentagon without delay.

At this juncture, RAND's permissive and decentralized management policies played an important role in preventing either a premature cutoff of the project or a hasty effort to bring the findings to the Air Force without adequate verification. The decision was made at the divisional level by Economics chief Hitch that the study raised enough interesting possibilities to warrant further investigation. Top RAND management served a useful function in not in-

tervening and forcing a decision on the research staff at this early point. The decision of when to bring the results of the research to the attention of the Air Force was left to Wohlstetter himself for the time being. Wohlstetter opposed any effort to communicate the findings of D-1114 to the Air Force at this point on the grounds that further work was needed before any firm policy recommendations could be drawn from the research.

For the next several months, Wohlstetter and his small team (by now Rowen and Lutz were working more or less full time on the study) spent long hours rechecking the assumptions of D-1114; calculating the effectiveness and costs of alternative basing postures under a variety of different conditions; injecting new variables into the analysis and estimating their effect on the data; and determining which base systems would be most affected by errors in assessments of uncertainties (e.g., if enemy capabilities were greater than anticipated by a factor of 10, or if mechanical failures were to cause a much higher rate of aborts than expected). Throughout, the RAND team was concerned only with *gross differences* in system cost and system performance—i.e., differences that would still be important despite large elements of uncertainty in the analysis.

By the end of the spring of 1952, Wohlstetter and Rowen had completed a draft of the study. The 400-plus pages of the draft, and the numerous supporting papers used in its preparation, attest to the extensive detailed and empirical work required to carry out a complex study. This time the results of the work appeared to be conclusive and to contain far-reaching policy implications. The analysis pointed toward the shattering conclusion that in the last half of the 1950s the Strategic Air Command, the world's most powerful striking force, faced the danger of obliteration from enemy surprise attack under the then-programmed strategic basing system.

Meanwhile, concern had gradually begun to grow in the Air Force over the implications of the Soviet A-bomb for the security of U.S. forces, and problems such as air defense were receiving increased attention. A group around Secretary of the Air Force Thomas Finletter was particularly active in calling attention to the potential dangers of the Soviet Union's acquisition of a nuclear capability and in urging that the United States begin planning for the time when the Soviet Union would have developed a substantial force of long-range bombers. In late 1951 Secretary Finletter wrote to Air Force Chief of Staff Hoyt S. Vandenberg suggesting that the Air Force undertake a major study of the vulnerability of SAC bases to enemy nuclear attack. In May 1952, a request came to RAND from General Craigie (which carried the imprimatur of the Air Force Chief of Staff) for RAND to study the problem of SAC base vulnerability. Like the original request for a study of basing policies, the Air Force request only vaguely groped to define the issues. But, as in the basing study case, the request showed the responsible governmental official's genuine concern and sense for what is important, which often generates significant problems for detailed study. A special RAND study team on vulnerability was thereupon formed under the direction of mathematician Igor Ansoff. Although this team's work was eclipsed by the base study, and no final report was ever published or issued to the Air Force, some of its work provided useful data for integration into the final version of the basing study. One of the researchers active in the other project also proved useful in the process of communicating the base study's findings to the Air Force.

It is also important to point out here the occurrence of a natural disaster in the fall of 1952 that indirectly had a bearing on the basing study's fate.[16] As often only disaster can, the event aroused high-level concern and dramatized the importance of a problem that had hitherto been only dimly recognized. The event in question was a tornado that ripped through a major U.S. military air base, completely destroying 12 B-36 heavy bombers. Since the bombers were thought to be secure, the disaster added to the worry over aircraft vulnerability that was already present in some Air Force circles and helped fashion a frame of mind receptive to the basing study's suggestions.

The last phase of work on the study marked the beginnings of the stage of communicating the research results to the client (and also the beginning of the sizable feedback of questions for further study). In talking to large numbers of Air Force officers during the middle and late months of 1952, Wohlstetter and his associates began injecting the ideas of the study into the Air Force hierarchy and, through personal contact, forming allies who were later to prove important in getting the results of the study incorporated into Air Force policy. Before turning to that part of the story, however, let us take a close look at the study itself.

THE STRUCTURE AND CONTENT OF THE STUDY

As well as having broad implications for national security policy, the strategic bases study marked an important step in the evolution of RAND systems analysis. It involved less elaborate mathematics than previous RAND systems analyses, which typically featured impressive methodologies and analytic techniques, combined with a large number of machine computations, aimed at finding the optimum solution to a specific problem. Instead, R-266 proceeded from the assumption that the elaborateness of the analytic techniques was not as important in policy-oriented analysis as the consideration, based on extensive use of empirical data, of all the major factors and contingencies which affect the problem under investigation. While the RAND systems analysis became henceforth ostensibly less precise in method, at the same time it became perhaps more relevant to the policymaker's actual concerns.[17] Further, in broadening the scope of the inquiry to include consideration of U.S. strategic objectives and such factors as political conditions of overseas base choice, R-266 figured prominently in the development of a "strategic sense" at RAND. Also, R-266 did not strive so much for an optimum solution[18]—the best of all possible systems —as it did for a proximate approach that would

16 The historical records at SAC headquarters report that the disaster occurred at Carswell Air Force Base on September 1, 1952. Personal correspondence, R. L. Belzer, The RAND Corporation.

17 For an elaboration of this point, see R. D. Specht, "Rand—A Personal View of Its History," *Journal of the Operations Research Society of America*, 8 (November–December 1960): 825–39.

18 Many systems analysts believe that the concept of an "optimum" solution to complex choice problems under conditions of great uncertainty has no operational meaning. It is impossible to identify a "best possible" system to cope with a "worst possible" contingency. It is possible to say that one system is "better" than another and is able to function satisfactorily under a range of differing conditions. See E. S. Quade, ed., *Analysis for Military Decisions* (Chicago, 1964), chap. 7.

identify a satisfactory system capable of functioning well under widely divergent conditions and even giving some satisfactory performance in a major catastrophe.

The objective of the study was to provide an analysis of how to select and use air bases for the strategic Air Force for the 1951–1961 period. Note that the time period with which the analysis was concerned extended nearly a decade into the future. The study involved considerations of the basing and use of weapons systems *which were not yet in operation* (and, in the case of the B-52, *not yet even in existence*).[19] At the time the study was started, the U.S. strategic bombing force consisted of B-29s, B-36s, and B-50s. The focus of the study was to be the basing and deployment of the B-36, B-52, and especially the medium-range B-47; the latter was to be phased into the combat fleet beginning in 1953 and was destined to constitute the bulk of the strike force for the 1950s and sometime thereafter.[20]

The research strategy involved an exhaustive examination of four alternative basing systems in terms of their costs and their effectiveness in destroying enemy targets: (1) as a point of departure, the then-programmed system of bombers based in time of war on advanced overseas operating bases; (2) bombers based on intermediate overseas operating bases in wartime; (3) United States–based bombers operating intercontinentally with the aid of air-refueling; and (4) United States–based bombers operating intercontinentally with the help of ground-refueling at overseas staging areas. The examination of each of these four alternative systems was carried out by taking certain principal factors which are important determinants of system cost and effectiveness and applying them to each system. These principal factors were the distances the bombers must fly from base to targets, to favorable entry points into enemy defenses, to the source of base supply, and to the points from which the enemy could attack these bases. The analysis was concerned with the joint effects of these respective factors on the costs of extending bomber radius; on how the enemy might deploy his defenses, and the number of our bombers lost to these defenses; on logistics costs; and on base vulnerability and our probable loss of bombers on the ground. The analytical treatment of the four critical base location distances presented intricate problems and required skillful handling. On its face the problem appeared to involve contradictory elements. Considerations of logistics costs and ease of penetrating enemy defenses argue for locating bases close to the Soviet Union. Nearness to the source of supply and reduced vulnerability to enemy attack, on the other hand, argue for locating bases in or near the United States and away from the Soviet Union.

The results of the study showed that the preferred system was alternative (4): United States operating bases for the strike force with the assistance of overseas refueling bases.

The then-programmed system of advanced overseas operating bases proved to be decidedly inferior to the U.S.-operated system with overseas bases used only for staging and refueling purposes.[21] R-266 demonstrated that this system would be extremely vulnerable to enemy attack in 1956 (even under very conservative estimates of Soviet forces). It would, in consequence, have the least destruction potential of enemy targets of any of the systems. Most of the projected overseas bases would be easily within the range of Soviet bombers. Moreover, warning time prior to an enemy attack would not be sufficient to permit evac-

---

[19] The first prototype of the B-47 appeared in October 1951, and the B-47 was not included in SAC war plans until after 1953. Contrary to what is often supposed, however, the fact that a weapons system is not operational does not mean that there are no empirical data on which to base a systems analysis of a future period. Flight tests and weapons performance data are examples of the numerous quantitative indices available for carrying out a rigorous analysis grounded in empirical data rather than pure speculation or deductive reasoning. For an extended discussion of this point, see Wohlsetter, "Strategy and the Natural Scientists," pp. 208–12.

[20] The force was to be composed of approximately 1,600 B-47s and RB-47s. While R-266 recognized that base availability had a bearing on R&D policy and the desirability of developing bombers with certain range and performance features, it avoided, for the most part, any attempt to choose among the types of bombers programmed for the force. It accepted as "given," in other words, the state of bomber technology and the types of bombers available to perform the mission.

[21] The then-programmed system envisaged the bulk of the U.S. strategic force being located in thirty bases in the continental United States in peacetime and then, upon the outbreak of war or a sharpening of international tension which presaged war, being moved overseas to operate from a base system consisting of about seventy bases. Fighter defense and anti-aircraft battalions would be provided, but relatively little emphasis was given to the passive defense of this system.

uation of our aircraft in time to escape destruction. Furthermore, even under favorable assumptions about the size of enemy stockpiles of atomic weapons and the yield of the weapons and the state of U.S. base-defense capabilities, it was found that, in a first strike, the enemy could destroy almost our entire combat force while it was still on the ground. And the attack would make it unlikely that the small surviving part of our force could respond effectively and penetrate enemy defenses in a retaliatory strike. The cornerstone of U.S. policy at the time—deterrence of aggression through the nuclear striking power of the Strategic Air Command and destruction of enemy industrial targets if deterrence failed—was thus seen to be jeopardized by the projected basing system. Indeed, the whole concept of deterrence as it was then conceived seemed in need of revision. "Deterrence" was thought of largely as deterring a massive assault on Europe. R-266 showed that a vital part of any viable deterrence policy had to be deterrence of an attack on the deterrent forces themselves through the provision of a second-strike strategic capability. Thus the basing study contributed to important changes in U.S. strategic thought and doctrine.

The alternative of intercontinental operation with the aid of air-refueling (which had some strong advocates in the Air Force) was shown to buy lower base vulnerability at so high a cost that total striking power would be drastically reduced. Air-refueling, the study demonstrated, was much more expensive than conventional ground-refueling for any one of a number of different possible air campaigns. Here one sees what is meant by *gross differences* in system cost and system performance. The differences in cost between the air- and ground-refueling systems were not of a marginal nature—they were of the order of magnitude of 10–15 billion dollars over the life of the system.

The alternative of intermediate overseas operating bases proved to be the worst of all the systems in that it combined some of the major disadvantages of the advanced overseas operating system and the air-refueling system. It would be almost as vulnerable as the former because even intermediate-distance operating bases would be within range of enemy attack and not within the warning network that permitted evacuation of our aircraft in time to escape destruction. And, like the air-refueling system, it would be costly to operate because supplies and personnel would have to be moved overseas and expensive facilities constructed at the bases to accommodate the maintenance, bomb-loading, and manifold other functions of an operating base.

The system relying on overseas bases for staging and refueling purposes was shown to be the "best" system, on the grounds, first, that it was relatively invulnerable to enemy attack either before or after the strike against the enemy: U.S. bombers would be on the ground for refueling for only a short time before and/or after striking their targets, thus making it very difficult for the enemy to destroy them on the ground. Routes could be varied so that the enemy would never be sure which base the U.S. bomber force would use. Moreover, the bases would not need the large-scale construction of expensive and vulnerable facilities that would be necessary on an operating base. Modest expenditures on underground storage for fuel would radically reduce vulnerability to almost any atomic attack within the enemy's capabilities at that time. This conclusion was not sensitive to unfavorable resolution of some of the uncertainties of the analysis. The results would hold true even if, for example, the estimates of the number of A-bombs in the enemy's stockpile were underestimated by a factor of 10 or if the bombs were of a larger yield than anticipated. Further, the overall costs of the system were lower than those of the other three systems, thus freeing additional resources for the performance of the mission. Considered in all its complex aspects, the overseas staging-base system appeared to be markedly superior to the other three systems.

COMMUNICATING THE RESEARCH RESULTS TO THE FOCAL POINTS OF DECISIONS

In policy-oriented research the communication of results is almost as important a task as the research—and sometimes hardly less difficult and demanding. Paradoxically, the client agency may be strongly motivated not to use the research that it has sponsored. As a recent study comments:

Offhand, it might be expected that the client, by virtue of his role, would function wholly to foster utilization. Having commissioned a research project, he, among all the parties concerned, would be the most highly motivated to use its results. Where utilization does not occur, therefore, one would be tempted to look elsewhere for an explanation. However, an examination of the record suggests, perhaps surprisingly, that the client is very often directly responsible for the nonutilization of the results of research which he sponsors.[22]

At the outset it is important to recall that decisionmaking in the defense establishment (as elsewhere in the government) is a *process*. Phrases like the "decisionmaking process" and the "process of policy formation" are not mere incantation: they refer to the continuous flow of decisions, large and small, that make up the seamless web of policy formation and administrative action in our federal government. The dynamic flux of the process makes the job of the adviser particularly difficult. It means that there is no orderly procedure whereby the adviser can state his views or explain his research and then retire from the scene confident that his advice will receive systematic consideration. Once made, decisions can become unmade a week later. *Continuity* is thus an essential attribute of effective communication of policy-oriented research.

A corollary of this is that the advice cannot be given simply to the top levels if favorable decision and effective implementation of the advice is desired. Take the case of a high-level decisionmaker accepting the recommendation of an advisory group and making a "policy" decision designed to implement the advice. Unless the subordinates carry out the decision effectively, the whole intent of the policy decision can be defeated.[23] Comprehension of the basis for the decision reached at the higher level can be a vital factor in winning the con-

sent and enthusiasm of those who must execute the decision and, in doing so, make myriad other decisions which can determine the success or failure of the original decision. It follows, therefore, that it is often desirable to communicate the research or advice to the working levels of an organization as well as to the higher policy levels.

In the case of R-266, the task of communicating the findings of the analysis to the Air Force lasted from about the fall of 1952 through most of 1953. By the end of 1952, the study had begun to assume final form. For some months, Wohlstetter and his colleagues had been in close contact with Air Force officers, checking out the assumptions of the study and beginning to circulate its potentially revolutionary conclusions. In January of 1953, the research had progressed to the point where Wohlstetter now felt confident that RAND should present the findings formally to the Air Force. At the division-head level Hitch agreed, and so did the top RAND management. Pressure also began building up within the Air Force from sympathetic officers for an early release of the findings. The question then became one largely of tactics.

A first concern felt by RAND management was the need for some special device or tactic to dramatize the study's importance so as to maximize its impact on Air Force policy. Accordingly, it was decided that the results of the study, by now nearly completed, would be disseminated to the client in preliminary form. This staff report (R-244-S) amounted to a condensed version which summarized the essential findings and policy recommendations of the larger study, and would be distributed solely to the Air Force.

With the publication and distribution of 75 copies of R-244-S throughout the Air Force on March 1, 1953, the dissemination of the basing research findings entered into its most intensive phase. This phase lasted until approximately November of the same year.

Wohlstetter had made several trips to Washington in January and February 1953 in preparation for the report's release, but after the March 1 date of publication he was almost constantly in Washington. A large portion of that time was consumed in briefings. The briefing can often be a very effective technique of communication because it permits interaction be-

[22] Charles Y. Glock, "Applied Social Research: Some Conditions Affecting Its Utilization," in *Case Studies in Bringing Behavioral Science into Use*, Studies in the Utilization of Behavioral Science, Institute for Communications Research, Stanford University, vol. 1, 1961, p. 7 (hereafter cited as *Case Studies*).

[23] Good discussions of this theme include: Henry Wriston, "The Secretary and the Management of the Department," and Don K. Price, "The Secretary and Our Unwritten Constitution," in *The Secretary of State*, ed. Don K. Price (New York, 1961), pp. 76–112 and 166–190; Seymour Martin Lipset, *Agrarian Socialism: A Cooperative Commonwealth Federation in Saskatchewan* (Berkeley and Los Angeles, 1959); Peter M. Blau, *Bureaucracy in Modern Society* (New York, 1956), pp. 85–101; and Paul Appleby, *Policy and Administration* (University, Ala., 1949).

tween the researcher and the decisionmaker, and the researcher can answer objections to the study that the decisionmaker might raise. In the present case, the importance of the subject meant an extraordinarily large number of briefings, and its startling conclusion foretold a vigorous interchange of views.

In fact, Wohlstetter gave ninety-two briefings (most of them during the period from March to the end of October). Some idea of the considerable interaction between briefer and audience is suggested by the fact that sixteen charts were used for the main briefing, whereas it was found necessary to prepare seventy charts for use during the question period. The question period also typically lasted longer than the main briefing.

The initial briefing began with the Strategic Air Command (SAC), the functional command most directly affected by the study's recommendations. The immediate response was enthusiastic. The briefing (and report) came as a "shocker" and aroused great interest within SAC. Increased support was added to the initial group of sympathetic officers who shared Wohlstetter's conclusion that the vulnerability of SAC under the programmed base system was a serious threat to the nation's security. Surprisingly, at this point very little opposition to the study was encountered on the basis of its being done by civilians without "military experience." Next Wohlstetter and his team went to the Pentagon to brief a group of about forty senior colonels representing various directorates of the Air Staff. The reception was generally favorable. It was determined that a "saturation" campaign of briefings should be undertaken throughout various commands and major components of the main Air Force directorates with a view to testing the research findings and generating the momentum to bring them eventually to the Air Force Council.[24] The satura-

tion campaign of briefings continued through the end of May. Then, in early June, a significant briefing was arranged with officers of general rank. This was the highest-ranking group that Wohlstetter had briefed thus far, and it was at this briefing that an important decision was taken. The generals decided to create a special *Ad Hoc* Committee of the Air Staff to check out the component parts of the study in terms of their accuracy, reasonableness of assumptions, and feasibility of implementation.[25] The general intention was that the *Ad Hoc* Committee would examine the study in depth and prepare a report for submission to the Air Force Council. If the *Ad Hoc* Committee submitted a favorable report, the prospects looked bright for favorable decision and action on the study's recommendations.

A number of factors, however, cautioned against any easy optimism. As happens frequently with review committees, the *Ad Hoc* Committee decided to operate on the basis of parceling out specific areas of interest to particular committee members. This meant that something of a system of "concurrent majorities" would obtain, with the Wohlstetter team having to persuade each committee member (and the directorate or functional command he represented) to endorse the study. It was important to persuade each committee member (and each directorate) because separate "concurrences" were to be solicited from each directorate to form a major part of the *Ad Hoc* Committee's Report. In effect, each member to some extent could exercise a check or veto on the committee's recommendations.

Meanwhile, the momentum that had developed toward a rapid decision on the study's recommendations at this point had begun to slow down. Jurisdictional questions arose, for example, which presented new obstacles to early decision on the study. SAC, as a specified command, was responsible to the Joint Chiefs of Staff (JCS) for policy guidance. But at the same time it was still tied closely to the Air Force and had certain ill-defined responsibili-

[24] In the Air Force hierarchy the Air Force Council was attached to the Vice Chief of Staff's office; it acted as a staff arm and decisionmaking aid to the Vice Chief of Staff. The Chief of Staff had the final authority to act or not to act on Air Force Council advice. Typically, however, a recommendation by the Air Force Council met with the Chief of Staff's approval and where possible the Chief of Staff encouraged consideration of important issues by the Council. It might be noted, parenthetically, that it was at this briefing of senior colonels that Wohlstetter encountered his only serious objection to civilians proffering advice to military professionals. But several officers

with extensive combat experience successfully rebutted their colleagues' objections to civilian assistance of this kind.

[25] The *Ad Hoc* Committee was also to absorb another Air Staff *Ad Hoc* Committee which had been organized separately in March 1953 to analyze the vulnerability question.

ties to the Air Staff. This divided responsibility between JCS and the Air Staff raised difficult questions as to the exact nature of SAC's relationship to the Air Staff. Elements within SAC began to fear that the study could be used as an opening wedge for the Air Staff to interfere with internal SAC operations and responsibilities.

Elsewhere pockets of resistance developed as it was realized that acting on the study would involve drastic changes in programmed activity.[26] The inertia of established programs proved difficult to overcome, even in the face of strong evidence arguing for innovation. A point of concern also was the prospect that substantial changes might be interpreted by rivals as an admission of error on a vast scale. The RAND team as well encountered opposition from a number of Air Force officers who genuinely feared that the drastic revision in policy suggested by the study could undermine the confidence and morale of their units. Conceivably the Air Force could also be embarrassed before Congress and might even become involved in a congressional investigation. Thus even some Air Force officers who agreed with the RAND study's recommendations felt it desirable to straighten out the error as unobtrusively as possible at some future date. In this general atmosphere, critics saw the special *Ad Hoc* Committee as a convenient vehicle for delaying action. Studying the study, it should be noted, often affords the decisionmaker a min-

imum-risk course of action: he can thereby avoid or postpone action that might create enemies and at the same time appear to be doing something to satisfy critics. Hence those who, for one reason or another, did not favor adopting the study's recommendations now largely adopted the tactic of delay and attrition and opposition to any immediate action or decision on the study's main recommendations.

The delaying tactics had notable success in July and August of 1953. Wohlstetter had the feeling that his "wheels were spinning" during this period. "It looked as though we would convince everybody intellectually," he recalls, "but that nothing would get done." Some of the sense of urgency had departed, and the RAND team found that something of a reverse "bandwagon effect" was beginning to take effect. A number of original Air Force supporters reversed themselves and either lined up with the opposition or adopted a noncommittal position.

In the face of these setbacks, the RAND team and the Air Force group favoring the study intensified their efforts to communicate the research results. A planning exercise was even carried through which tested the recommended system's capacity to handle a complex strike. Despite redoubled efforts, the fortunes of the study continued in doubt. By the end of the summer, Wohlstetter was convinced that some drastic step was necessary to assure that the study reached the Air Force Council for consideration. Consequently, he proposed to RAND Vice President Henderson that a special visit be made to General Thomas S. White, acting Chief of Staff of the Air Force,[27] to focus high-level attention on the study and to guard against a permanent tie-up in delays and jockeying at lower levels. Henderson agreed, and an interview was arranged between General White and a delegation from RAND consisting of Wohlstetter plus the top echelon of RAND's management (President Collbohm, Vice President Henderson, and Vice President J. R. Golstein). This interview proved to be an important turning point.

The RAND team was now assured of consideration of the study by the Air Force Council; and in any event they could now count on an appeal to the highest decisionmaking level in the Air Force. From this point on, the prospects

---

[26] This is consistent with the March-Simon contention that organizational innovation will occur more easily if the proposed changes are of a gradual incremental nature—"when the carrot is just a *little* way ahead of the donkey—when aspirations exceed achievement by a small amount." If the proposed innovation is too drastic a departure from current doctrine or procedure, frustration results and "neurotic reactions interfere with effective innovation." James G. March and Herbert A. Simon, *Organizations* (New York, 1958), p. 184. To allay doubts, the Wohlstetter team on occasion sought to underplay the novelty of their recommendations. The subject of organizational change and innovation has recently attracted increasing scholarly interest. It is widely recognized that organizations, and especially large organizations, have great difficulty in effecting change in their policies and procedures. For a good theoretical discussion of organizational innovation, see *ibid.*, chap. 5. For an application of the March-Simon conceptual schema to strategic program innovation in defense agencies, see Samuel P. Huntington, *The Common Defense* (New York, 1961), chap. 5, "Innovation of Strategic Programs." A comprehensive general treatment of innovation is Everett M. Rogers, *Diffusion of Innovations* (New York, 1962).

[27] General Hoyt S. Vandenberg, Chief of Staff, was ill with cancer.

for favorable decision brightened and the opponents of the study were placed on the defensive. Ironically, Wohlstetter and his colleagues also received a fortuitous assist from an unexpected quarter: Premier Malenkov's announcement that the Soviet Union had detonated a hydrogen bomb.[28] Though intelligence estimates at this time were uncertain, there was little disposition in the Air Force after the Malenkov announcement to doubt that the Soviet Union had a substantial nuclear capability. Wohlstetter and his colleagues capitalized on this announcement in the late summer briefings to dramatize the dangers of an enemy first strike against vulnerable overseas staging bases.

Several aspects of the interview with General White deserve additional comment. First, White was influenced in his decision to place consideration of R-244-S on the Air Force Council agenda in part by the pressure of the budgetary cycle. For the advisory group interested in timing the release of reports and briefing campaigns to maximize their impact on policy, this is an important factor. Though the decisionmaking process is diffuse and tends to be geared to crises which are by their nature unpredictable, there is always the assurance that the pressure of budget preparation will pose important policy choices and in general serve as a stimulus to decision.

Second, the fact that it was even possible to approach General White, when they had been seemingly blocked or delayed at lower echelons, deserves notice. RAND's existence *outside* the Air Force hierarchy, and its reputation for independence and objectivity, is seen as having played an important role. It is doubtful whether an Air Force officer, an "in-house" advisory group made up of Air Force career personnel, or even a civilian advisory group attached to a unit within the normal chain of command, would have the same opportunity or incentive to bypass immediate superiors and press for the adoption of controversial ideas at higher levels. The data here thus support the tentative hypothesis of Merton and others that the utilization of expert advice in the behavioral sciences will be positively influenced by

location of the adviser outside the organization for whose procedures or policies he is suggesting innovation.[29]

In this connection it should also be stressed that location of the research or advisory unit outside the organizational framework of the decisionmaking agency allows greater scope for truly original and creative ideas to emerge in policy-oriented research. Within an agency responsible for policymaking and operations, there are strong and understandable pressures to ensure agency-wide policy coordination and orientation of the work effort toward clearly defined and shared objectives. It is difficult for anything but "symbolic" research—i.e., research that is innocuous, does not reflect unfavorably on agency policies or procedures, and raises no disruptive problems to be conducted in such an organizational setting.[30] Thus it would appear both on grounds of accessibility to the various points of decision scattered throughout the client organization and on grounds of effective use of scarce creative research talent that a strong case can be made for contracting many policy research and advisory functions to an outside organization.

This conclusion has an important bearing on questions of government organization in the scientific age. As the business of government becomes ever more complex and governmental agencies increasingly require various research and advisory services, it may be that experimentation with novel and decentralized organizational forms like The RAND Corporation (which are well adapted to research activities) will extend to a growing number of nondefense agencies.[31] The traditional Weberian notions of

[28] The Malenkov announcement more than offset the negative effect of former President Truman's famous comment after he had left the White House that he doubted whether the Russians really had the A-bomb.

[29] Robert K. Merton, "The Role of Applied Social Science in the Formation of Policy," *Philosophy of Science*, 16, no. 3 (July 1949): 168; and Ronald Lippit, "Two Case Studies in the Utilization of Behavioral Research," in *Case Studies*, pp. 34ff. See also Posvar, "The Impact of Strategy Expertise."

[30] Joseph W. Eaton, "Symbolic and Substantive Evaluative Research," *Administrative Science Quarterly*, 6, no. 4 (March 1962); and Ashley L. Schiff, *Fire and Water: Scientific Heresy in the Forest Service* (Cambridge, Mass., 1962). Schiff, overstating his case considerably, even goes so far as to suggest at one point that research should be entirely divorced from an action agency. A useful commentary on the Schiff study is W. Eric Gustafson, "Science vs. Administrative Evangelism," *Public Administration Review*, 22 (Spring 1962): 84–88.

[31] NASA has recently developed a "think" corporate entity which works by contract and bears a striking affinity to RAND's relationship with the Air Force. There is, however, a notable difference. The NASA

the bureaucracy as a hierarchy of fixed offices may then seem antiquarian as a loose-jointed and flexible system of administration-by-contract emerges and makes the business of government resemble in many ways the management of a giant research establishment.

Last, it should be noted that there was no "end run" of the sponsor in this case. Clearly, problems of a fundamentally different and more complex nature would have been presented had RAND sought to bypass the Air Force in the present case and bring the study results directly to the Secretary of Defense's attention. A striking feature of this incident, indeed, is the fact that strategic decisions of enormous importance were made solely by a military service. Now that more and more the OSD level is assuming primary responsibility for strategic policy it is doubtful that such decisions could be made without involving OSD agencies and personnel.

A McNamara memorandum of April 12, 1962, has had a somewhat ill-defined, though potentially important, bearing on the question of "end runs" around a military service client to a higher policy echelon. Secretary of Defense McNamara directed the Secretaries of the Air Force, Army, and Navy to forward to his office copies of "each report of study received by your Department from Rand [sic] Corporation, Operations Research Office, Operations Evaluation Group, Institute for Defense Analyses, similar research or analysis groups under contract with your Department . . . concurrently with receipt by your Department."[32] For a time, this McNamara order caused great alarm and shock throughout the military services and the contract research organizations.

organization—Bellcomm, Inc.—is a subsidiary corporation of a profit-making firm, the American Telephone and Telegraph Company. The State Department, an agency that parallels the Defense Department in needing long-range thinking to perform its mission effectively, has had almost no tradition of support for outside research activities. Recently, however, the affiliated Agency for International Development (AID) has embarked on a substantial program of supporting analytical research of various kinds with a number of contract research organizations, including RAND. In part, this has probably been inspired by the growing complexity of foreign affairs and the intricate technical-political problems involved in managing the foreign aid program. For a brilliant general discussion of this subject, see Don K. Price, "Creativity in the Public Service," *Public Policy*, 9 (1959): 4–17.

[32] Copy of the McNamara memorandum obtained from the Office of the Secretary of Defense.

The military services particularly were concerned that there might no longer be scope for private and confidential exchanges of information and analytical advice between the service and its advisory institution. As yet, however, the April 12 memorandum appears not to have been applied strictly and not to have had the expected far-reaching consequences. Secretary McNamara seems to have been more interested in informing himself and keeping abreast of the latest research on important defense problems than he was in exercising control over the military services' policies respecting the distribution of reports and studies coming from the service advisory institutions. Nevertheless, the problem of "end runs" around a service sponsor has become a more real and troublesome one for the service-affiliated advisory institution. The researcher faces particularly difficult problems of professional ethics on rare occasions when conflicts develop between loyalties to a service sponsor and loyalties to the larger national interest.

THE IMPACT: R-266 REFLECTED IN AIR FORCE POLICY CHANGES

Distinguishing between the stage of communicating the research results and the stage of their actual reflection in Air Force policy is somewhat arbitrary. One could say that in a sense the study began to have an "impact" even before the RAND team distributed copies of the special staff report R-244-S and initiated the program of formal briefings. Numerous informal contacts existed between the RAND team and various parts of the Air Force, and the thinking of many Air Force officers had already been affected by contact with the ideas contained in the study. While the mental set of the policymaker doubtless may have important implications for policy, it does not follow that a "policy" change will necessarily result from a change in attitude or outlook.

The fact that a policy change follows in a temporal sequence the submission of advice does not, of course, necessarily imply a causal relationship between the two. It is also evident that influential advice often may come from different sources. Witness, for example, the decision to accelerate plans for the development of the ICBM as a military weapon. A RAND scientist, Bruno Augenstein, and scientists of the Von Neumann Committee independently arrived at the conclusion that smaller-weight warheads could make such a weapon system feasible. In such a case, it clearly becomes difficult to assign weights to the relative impact of the different advisers.

Added to these general considerations is the fact that the effective advisory group usually goes to great pains to conceal its impact on policy. It is not a sensible tactic to claim credit for particular decisions, since this will likely irritate, annoy, and even frighten those who must assume final responsibility for decisions. On the contrary, one of the most important tasks of the advisors is to elicit the decisionmaker's involvement in the study's fate. Clearly, this can be accomplished more readily in most circumstances by making the decisionmaker feel the ideas are really reflections of his own thinking than by making him appear obtuse and intransigent. In the present case, the final publication of R-266 was held up until April 1, 1954, in part to permit the Air Force to implement some of the suggested changes on its own, prior to the report's formal release. An opportunity was thus afforded for the decisionmakers to have already initiated policy changes at the time R-266 was being circulated generally within the defense establishment. The final wording of the report also reflects this concern with the sensitivities of the decisionmakers. Phrases like "the *formerly*-programmed" and "the *then*-programmed system" were used to refer to the base system originally planned for the 1956–1961 period, and care was taken to note the efforts made by the Air Force to revise the original plans.

Nonetheless, despite these difficulties, which must accompany any effort to identify the policy impact of a research product or item of advice, the evidence in the present case clearly indicates that the RAND base study was the catalyst to major Air Force policy changes.

A chain of personal interaction establishes beyond doubt that the ideas developed in the base study were brought to the attention of Air Force decisionmakers. Furthermore, an unmistakable causal relationship seems to exist in this case between the advice and the policy changes. The evidence suggests that the distinction between a first-strike and a second-strike capability—perhaps *the* central contribution of R-266—originated with the Wohlstetter

team. The concept was essentially a novel one. No other study or other group had so clearly recognized its importance and spelled out its implications for U.S. policy. Several previous studies had dealt generally with the problem of vulnerability, but none had drawn explicit attention to the need for developing a deterrent force capable of surviving an initial enemy atomic assault and still inflicting unacceptable damage on the enemy. Nor had the operating procedures and strategic doctrines of the defense agencies reflected a clear appreciation, prior to the base study, of the need to achieve a secure deterrent capability. Some indication of how firmly entrenched were the traditional World War II categories of thinking and discourse on strategic air attack is given by the fact that, in the bitter controversy with the Air Force over the B-36 in the late 1940s, even the Navy showed no awareness of the potentially revolutionary implications of the vulnerability of aircraft on the ground to atomic attack. Striving to find ways to embarrass and discredit the Air Force, the Navy employed a wide variety of arguments against a further build-up of the strategic Air Force, but never raised the question of the vulnerability of aircraft on the ground to surprise atomic attack.[33] It is of course possible that the Air Force at some later date might have generated the policy changes on its own in the absence of the basing study, but unquestionably the costs (both in monetary terms and in terms of a lessened security of the deterrent) would have been much greater. It is also clear that it can become more and more difficult to reverse a policy course once vast sums of money have been committed and a program becomes firmly entrenched as part of the agency's mission.

Let us now complete the story of the basing study's impact on Air Force policy. In September 1953 an important breakthrough occurred when the Air Staff *Ad Hoc* Committee reached agreement and endorsed the study's broad policy suggestions. Its report concurred with the RAND findings that the programmed base system would be extremely vulnerable in the 1956–1961 period, and found the RAND-proposed overseas refueling-base concept gener-

33 See U.S. Congress, House, Committee on Armed Services, *Investigation of the B-36 Bomber Program*, Hearings on H. Res. 234, 81st Cong., 1st sess., August–October 1949.

ally the most feasible approach to maintaining a high strike capability with reduced vulnerability. Of particular importance in the *Ad Hoc* Committee's report was the estimate in the Installations Section of the report that the overseas refueling-base system would save at least $1 billion over the programmed system in construction costs alone. This augured well for the disposition of the RAND study. For it held up to the top Air Force decisionmakers the prospect of achieving a more secure capability *and actually saving money in the process.*

In October, the issues went to the Air Force Council as General White had promised. There the *Ad Hoc* Committee appointed to evaluate the RAND study presented its report, after which Wohlstetter briefed the council for an hour and a half.

The Air Force Council continued its deliberations for some three weeks. Quite properly, only Air Force officers participated in these final deliberations of exactly how the RAND research would be translated into Air Force policy. In late October 1953, the council reached a decision on the following essential points: (1) that the vulnerability of air base facilities be recognized in all Air Staff planning and action; (2) that a hardening program be initiated on critical facilities in overseas bases; (3) that new overseas bases be constructed to the specifications of ground-refueling functions; (4) that exceptions to these instructions will require special justification; and (5) that vulnerable stocks of matériel on overseas bases be reduced. Shortly thereafter, in early November, the Air Force Chief of Staff ratified the council's action.

Changes were quick to follow. The Air Force's plans no longer called for deployment of the bulk of the strike force from overseas bases at the outbreak of hostilities. Instead, Operation Full-House, a new system employing the RAND proposed overseas staging-base concept, was adopted. The construction program on overseas bases was modified significantly; some critical facilities were dispersed and hardened. Runways at some new bases were made narrower so as to reduce construction costs and make possible the addition of more bases to the system (in keeping with the RAND suggestion that a larger number of cheaper bases would complicate the enemy's problem in launching a surprise attack). Meas-

ures designed to safeguard key personnel at overseas bases were put into effect. And plans for an expensive major depot in Alaska, on which it would be possible to do long-term maintenance of SAC bombers, were canceled.

In all, the basing study had made several dozen specific suggestions. Some of these were adopted *in toto* by the Air Force, some were partially adopted, and some were never adopted. In addition, the Air Force initiated certain changes on its own that did not relate to any specific RAND suggestion, but that indirectly grew out of the Air Force's consideration of the problem raised by the basing study. The changes affected many parts of the Air Force hierarchy, including the functional command level and the Air Staff units responsible for war plans, logistics, installations, personnel and even the Directorate for Medical Requirements. The changes were also distributed over a time span: some went into effect almost immediately, while others were adopted only at various later points. Follow-up research to the basing study by Wohlstetter and Hoffman led to further specific changes in Air Force policies and procedure. The "fail-safe" procedure now employed by SAC, whereby SAC bombers are sent winging toward enemy targets on receipt of even ambiguous warning only to return automatically to their bases unless given an explicit presidential order to proceed to target, was recommended in the next major study. The concept of the airborne alert and increased readiness of SAC forces also originated from later RAND research. RAND suggestions on the importance of warning of enemy nuclear and thermonuclear attack, too, contributed to important changes in Air Force policies. Later RAND studies which influenced Air Force policies pointed out certain problems of command and control under wartime conditions and the need for hardening ICBM sites.

In the end, the Air Force does not come out badly as a user of advice in the present case. It was neither uncritically receptive nor hostile to the suggestions. Though made uncomfortable by the findings of the RAND study, the Air Force recognized the need for innovation. And it acted with discretion and reasonable expedition in taking the steps necessary to guard against the dangers brought to light in the study, even though this involved substantial changes in its plans and operating procedures.

The delay and opposition that developed were hardly surprising in view of the magnitude of some of the proposed changes.

Finally, we see an important role for a "RAND-type" advisory corporation in facilitating organizational innovation in the client agency. From its position as friendly critic, RAND injected heretical ideas into the Air Force hierarchy which stimulated needed change. The concept of an institutionalized critic, sufficiently independent to be really provocative and useful, yet closely related so as to have access to information and the points of decision within the sponsor organization, will likely gain increasing acceptance and usage in the government in the years ahead. If we are to survive in an age of organization and rapid change, it is clear that our organizations will have to be flexible and adaptable enough to cope with rapidly changing conditions and social needs.[34] This is most visible at present in the area of national defense, where science and technology have had their most immediate and dramatic impact on public policy. But, as the "social fallout" from developments in science and technology increasingly affect the operation of other governmental agencies, we shall likely see more value attached to innovative abilities and growing stress put on institutional arrangements designed to promote organizational flexibility and adaptability.

CONCLUSION

We have traced here the evolution of a significant RAND study through its genesis in an Air Force request down to its reflection in Air Force policy changes some three years later. It is seen that the freedom of the researcher to reformulate the problem under investigation and to pursue a novel line of inquiry can give an important "payoff" for the policymaker. The example of the basing study also illustrates some interesting aspects of the question of how an interdisciplinary research effort like the RAND analysis is carried out. A large and amorphous "team" is not necessarily involved in the creation of a good systems analysis

(though it may be on occasion). On the contrary, the present case suggests that small groups headed by one individual responsible for the end result, and operating informally to secure assistance from others when needed, more nearly represent a paradigm of the successful RAND systems analysis project.

Further, this case study provides some useful glimpses into the intricate task of communicating the research product or advice to the client. Our analysis suggests that the position of the researcher or adviser outside the immediate governmental framework and his reputation for objectivity may be an important factor in increasing the likelihood of effective utilization of the research or advice. In the present case, this factor operated to allow Wohlstetter to present his findings directly to General White, thus avoiding a permanent tieup in the consideration of the analytic findings at a lower level. It further served to dissociate the RAND study from intra-agency conflict. This made it difficult to discredit the study on the basis that it sought to further the institutional and personal interests of a special group or subunit within the Air Force.

The decisionmaking process in "closed politics" is seen in the present case as containing certain built-in safeguards against arbitrary action based on uncritical deference to the scientific adviser. The RAND advisers faced a long and arduous struggle to bring their ideas to the attention of Air Force officers and to keep the ideas alive in the face of inertia and skepticism and careful scrutiny at numerous points in the Air Force hierarchy. The decisionmaker does not emerge here in the passive and largely reactive role that Sir Charles Snow portrays in *Science and Government*. Nor is it evident, if the present case is at all typical, that the cardinal decisions are always, or even usually, made by a "handful of men." There is opportunity for laborious dissection of advisory recommendations at various policy levels. As in "open politics," the fragmentation of power and influence throughout many parts of the decisionmaking machinery means that action can be delayed or blocked or vetoed at a number of points. A handful of men can block action or decision with relative ease, but it is doubtful whether they can initiate it with the same ease. For favorable action on an advisory recommendation to occur, the adviser must normally

---

[34] For the role of the behavioral sciences in effecting organizational change, see Warren G. Bennis, "A New Role for the Behavioral Sciences: Effecting Organizational Change," *Administrative Science Quarterly*, 8 (September 1963): 125–65.

persuade large numbers of people throughout the decisionmaking organization and foster something of a consensus among the interests affected by the recommendations. In short, "closed politics" seems to resemble "open politics" in a number of important respects.

Indeed, a last vital role we can discern for the advisory corporation like RAND is precisely to provide a link between the realm of "closed politics" and that broader public discussion of national security issues which is essential to a flourishing democracy.[35] Allowing RAND and similar advisory institutions a semiautonomous status outside the framework of the government keeps open channels of communication for debate and discussion of broad policy issues, and encourages exchanges of ideas and information between the "insiders" and the wider attentive public of journalists, publicists, academic scholars, and informed citizens. This type of institutional arrangement thus substantially reduces the danger that great issues will be decided by closed scientific politics or that the free play of policy debate will be choked off within a narrow, self-contained elite.

As defense policy choices become ever more complex, there can only be a growing need for some set of institutions to help serve as a bridge between the realm of "closed politics" and the larger public. This is needed not only on grounds of democratic theory—i.e., to help counteract the tendencies toward technocracy inherent in the politics of the nuclear age. It is also needed because the formation and exelution of a broad national security policy adequate to the challenges of the nuclear age will require a high level of public understanding and will have to exploit a wide share of society's creative energies. The advisory corporation like RAND can serve a vital function in tapping the intellectual capabilities of people outside the government for work on public problems and in generally promoting the public understanding necessary for the successful functioning of modern democratic government. In sum, the point is that

education of the wider public in questions of fundamental strategy seems particularly desirable, not only on grounds of democratic theory during an age when technology increasingly demands delegation of fateful decisions, but also because so many of the government's problems revolve around the question of what the public can be induced to support. . . . Though there must be decision, it should be decision tempered by the freest possible flow of thought in the widest market compatible with national security: a limit likely to be generous on the more fundamental questions of strategy.[36]

In sum, the device of the RAND-type advisory corporation seems to reflect both the strengths and weaknesses of American pluralism. The presence of a number of advisory corporations like RAND helps to assure decisionmakers of a broad base of scientific advice and to guard against the dangers of a closed system, in which men in power are cut off from the healthy effect of criticism and advice from a number of different points. There is very little danger that anything like a monolithic statism will emerge, given a system which decentralizes expertise and influence throughout many different institutions in society. Such a system also serves to maintain the dynamism of American government and to facilitate the adaptation of governmental organization to changing social needs. The real dangers of this system may not be what is commonly supposed. There is probably little reason to fear that the cardinal choices will have to be made by a handful of men who do not understand the bases for decision, or that a small body of anonymous advisers will insidiously come to dominate policy formation. Rather, the chief danger may well be that familiar problem of American politics: keeping organizational pluralism within some sort of bounds so that a framework for coherent, unified, and sustained national policies can be maintained. If there is a growing need for professionalism in our generalist advisory ranks, there is surely an even greater need for professionalism among

---

[35] For a discussion of some of the difficulties occasioned in Great Britain by the lack of adequate linkage between the formal governmental establishment and outside critics and lay strategists as well as informed citizens, see Laurence W. Martin, "The Market for Strategic Ideas in Britain," *American Political Science Review*, 56 (March 1962): 23–41. Martin concludes (p. 41): "It thus seems possible that, paradoxically, one of the more promising areas in which to look for improving the British defense machinery may lie outside the machine itself, in the encouragement of closer attention to questions of national security both by officially countenanced, specialized consultants, and by a wider attentive public."

[36] *Ibid.*, p. 41.

our generalist policymakers (both career and political). For it is these men who must make sense of different analyses of a problem and come up with a coherent policy and action program. No amount of analysis, even of the broad synthesizing variety, can exhaust all the possibilities or definitively treat all the variables with which the policymaker must be concerned. Consequently, a system which drains off a large share of society's intellectual talents to nongovernmental institutions cannot help but have some impact on the government's ability to keep a steady and controlling hand on its advisory apparatus and to maintain a clear central direction in policy. This suggests that it will be important to enhance the attractiveness of the government as an employer so that a fair share of the individuals with scarce technical and intellectual talents will seek a public career. It also suggests that we will have to make much more discriminating use of various institutional arrangements that now exist in the broad partnership between science and government. It may be unwise, for example, to extend the use of the nonprofit corporation beyond the area of "paper pure" policy research and advisory services. The use of the nonprofit corporation for technical direction of the work of other contractors, for example, might be contracting for a range of functions that properly belong with responsible governmental officials. Considered judgments on this sort of question, however, must await a much greater understanding than we now possess of the various component parts of the contract-out system for scientific advice and other technical services. What is clear, at least, is that we must avoid such a diffusion of power and influence that consistent and effective public action becomes impossible. The formal government must remain the political center of gravity, or else, in making our governing system complex, we will have made it unmanageable. Perhaps, as Sheldon S. Wolin has suggested, the real "task of non-totalitarian societies is to temper the excesses of pluralism."[37]

[37] Sheldon S. Wolin, *Politics and Vision* (Boston, 1960), p. 434.

THE DECISION TO DEPLOY THE ABM:
BUREAUCRATIC AND DOMESTIC POLITICS
IN THE JOHNSON ADMINISTRATION

MORTON H. HALPERIN

Halperin uses the Bureaucratic Politics Model to analyze this critical policy decision. He examines the organizational stakes of the major participants, the rules of the game, shared images, and the arguments for and against deployment. In doing so he provides a fascinating account of the private decisionmaking process among the President, the Secretary of Defense, and the Joint Chiefs of Staff. This article has been expanded and enriched in Halperin's larger work, Bureaucratic Politics and Foreign Policy *(forthcoming).*

Why did the Johnson Administration decide in the late 1960s to deploy a ballistic missile defense system in the United States?

In attempting to answer this question we need to seek an understanding of several distinct decisions and actions.[1] The most puzzling event occurred in San Francisco on September 18, 1967, when Secretary of Defense Robert McNamara delivered an address to the editors and publishers of United Press International.[2] McNamara devoted the first fourteen pages of his talk to a general discussion of the strategic arms race, emphasizing the limited utility of nuclear weapons and the fact that neither the United States nor the Soviet Union had gained any increased security from the arms race. With this as background, he turned to a specific discussion of the ABM issue:

. . . Now let me come to the issue that has received so much attention recently: the question of whether or not we should deploy an ABM system against the Soviet nuclear threat.

To begin with, this is not in any sense a new

[1] The framework of analysis used here is drawn from the author's ongoing study of bureaucratic politics and foreign policy.

[2] Robert S. McNamara, "The Dynamics of Nuclear Strategy," *Department of State Bulletin*, October 9, 1967, pp. 443–51.

issue. We have had both the technical possibility and the strategic desirability of an American ABM deployment under constant review since the late 1950s.

While we have substantially improved our technology in the field, it is important to understand that none of the systems at the present or foreseeable state of the art would provide an impenetrable shield over the United States. Were such a shield possible, we would certainly want it—and we would certainly build it. . . .

Every ABM system that is now feasible involves firing defensive missiles at incoming offensive warheads in an effort to destroy them.

But what many commentators on this issue overlook is that any such system can rather obviously be defeated by an enemy simply sending more offensive warheads, or dummy warheads, than there are defensive missiles capable of disposing of them.

And this is the whole crux of the nuclear action-reaction phenomenon.

Were we to deploy a heavy ABM system throughout the United States, the Soviets would clearly be strongly motivated to so increase their offensive capability as to cancel out our defensive advantage.

It is futile for each of us to spend $4 billion, $40 billion, or $400 billion—and at the end of all the spending, and at the end of all the deployment, and at the end of all the effort, to be rela-

Reprinted by permission and with minor changes from World Politics, *25, no. 1 (October 1972): 62–95. Copyright © 1972 by Princeton University Press. An earlier version of this paper was prepared for delivery at the Sixty-sixth Annual Meeting of the American Political Science Association, September 8–12, 1970. I have benefited from comments from a number of readers of previous drafts, including Graham Allison, William Capron, Leslie Gelb, Arnold Kanter, Herbert Kaufman, and Jerome Kahan.*

tively at the same point of balance on the security scale that we are now. . . .

If we in turn opt for heavy ABM deployment —at whatever price—we can be certain that the Soviets will react to offset the advantage we would hope to gain.

Many listeners undoubtedly expected the speech to end with the Secretary of Defense committing the United States firmly against an ABM deployment. Instead, McNamara immediately turned to another tack:

. . . Having said that, it is important to distinguish between an ABM system designed to protect against a Soviet attack on our cities, and ABM systems which have other objectives.

One of the other uses of an ABM system which we should seriously consider is the greater protection of our strategic offensive forces.

Another is in relation to the emerging nuclear capability of Communist China.

There is evidence that the Chinese are devoting very substantial resources to the development of both nuclear warheads, and missile delivery systems. As I stated last January, indications are that they will have medium-range ballistic missiles within a year or so, an initial intercontinental ballistic missile capability in the early 1970s, and a modest force in the mid-70s.

Up to now, the lead-time factor has allowed us to postpone a decision on whether or not a light ABM deployment might be advantageous as a countermeasure to Communist China's nuclear development.

But the time will shortly be right for us to initiate production if we desire such a system. . . .

Is there any possibility, then, that by the mid-1970s China might become so incautious as to attempt a nuclear attack on the United States or our allies.

It would be insane and suicidal for her to do so, but one can conceive conditions under which China might miscalculate. We wish to reduce such possibilities to a minimum.

And since, as I have noted, our strategic planning must always be conservative, and take into consideration even the possible irrational behavior of potential adversaries, there are marginal grounds for concluding that a light deployment of U.S. ABMs against this possibility is prudent.

The system would be relatively inexpensive— preliminary estimates place the cost at about $5 billion—and would have a much higher degree of reliability against a Chinese attack, than the much more massive and complicated system that some have recommended against a possible Soviet attack. . . .

After a detailed review of all these considerations, we have decided to go forward with this Chinese-oriented ABM deployment, and we will begin actual production of such a system at the end of this year.

Before concluding, the Secretary of Defense returned to his earlier theme and warned of the danger in the deployment he had just announced:

. . . There is a kind of mad momentum intrinsic to the development of all new nuclear weaponry. If a weapon system works—and works well—there is strong pressure from many directions to procure and deploy the weapon out of all proportion to the prudent level required.

The danger in deploying this relatively light and reliable Chinese-oriented ABM system is going to be that pressures will develop to expand it into a heavy Soviet-oriented ABM system.

We must resist that temptation firmly—not because we can for a moment afford to relax our vigilance against a possible Soviet first-strike—but precisely because our greatest deterrent against such a strike is not a massive, costly, but highly penetrable ABM shield, but rather a fully credible offensive assured destruction capability.

The so-called heavy ABM shield—at the present state of technology—would in effect be no adequate shield at all against a Soviet attack, but rather a strong inducement for the Soviets to vastly increase their own offensive forces. That, as I have pointed out, would make it necessary for us to respond in turn—and so the arms race would rush hopelessly on to no sensible purpose on either side.

The apparent contradictions in the speech were a puzzlement to the audience. Some speculated that McNamara had planned to give an anti-ABM speech and was instructed by the President at the last minute to add a deployment decision. However, an examination of the following questions will show us that the speech was planned from the first as it was delivered.

1. Why, in January 1967, did President Johnson ask Congress to appropriate the funds to deploy an ABM, but state that he would defer a decision to initiate the deployment pending an effort to get the Soviet Union to engage in talks on limiting the arms race?[3]

3 Lyndon Baines Johnson, "Annual Budget Message to the Congress, Fiscal Year 1968, January 24, 1967," *Public Papers of the President of the United States, 1967: Book I* (Washington, D.C., 1968), p. 48. "In 1968, we will: continue intensive development of Nike-X but take no action now to deploy an anti-

2. Why was the decision to deploy an ABM announced at the end of a speech whose whole structure and purpose was to explain why an ABM defense against the Soviet Union was impossible?

3. Why did the Secretary of Defense describe the system as being directed against China, while the Joint Chiefs of Staff and their congressional allies described it as a first step toward a full-scale defense against the Soviet Union?

4. Why was the system that was finally authorized for deployment one which was designed and deployed as if its purpose was to protect American cities against a large Soviet attack?

Having stated the questions, we must postpone attempting to provide the answers until we have examined in some detail the nature of the process by which the decisions were made. We must ask who the participants in the process were. We must examine the personal and organizational interests that defined their stakes in the ABM debate. We must determine the constraints operating on the process in terms of the decisionmakers' shared images of the world, the rules of the game by which decisions were made, and the participation of large organizations. We must also ask what arguments were advanced on each side to secure the outcome desired, and what the consequences were. After thus analyzing the process we will be better prepared to find answers to our puzzling questions.

In seeking to understand why the United States government makes a particular decision or takes a particular action, we can make no greater mistake than to assume that all the participants in the process looked at the issue in the same way and agreed on what should be done. The reality is quite different.

When individuals in the American government consider a proposed change in American foreign policy, they often see and emphasize quite different things and reach different conclusions. A proposal to withdraw American troops from Europe, for example, is to the Army a threat to its budget and size; to Budget Bureau examiners a way to save money; to the Treasury Department a gain in balance of payments; to the State Department's Bureau of European Affairs a threat to good relations with NATO; and to the President's congressional advisers an opportunity to remove a major irritant in the President's relations with the Hill.

The differences stem from the differing faces of the issue which they see; they depend in part on whether their interests lead them to perceive a threat or an opportunity.

What determines which face an individual sees? What accounts for his stand?

Participants in the process of national security policy in the American government believe that they should take stands which advance the national security of the United States. Their problem is to determine what is in fact in the interest of national security; they must seek clues and guidelines from a variety of sources. Some hold to a set of beliefs about the world (e.g., the Soviet Union is expansionist and must be stopped by American military power). Others look to authorities within the government or beyond it for guidance. For many participants, what is necessary for the nation's security comes to be defined as a set of more specific intermediate interests. For some, these may be personal (e.g., since, in general, I know how to protect the nation's security interests, whatever increases my influence is in the national interest). For others, the intermediate interests relate to domestic political interests (e.g., since a sound economy is a prerequisite to national security, I must oppose policies which threaten the economy).

Many participants define national security according to the interests of the organization to which they belong. Career officials naturally come to believe that the health of their organization is vital to the nation's security. Organizational commitments on the part of outsiders appointed to senior posts vary depending on the individual, the strength of his prior convictions, his image of his role, and the nature of the organization he heads. Some senior officials seek clues less from their organization's interests than from the interests of the President, as they define them.

---

ballistic missile (ABM) defense; initiate discussions with the Soviet Union on the limitation of ABM deployment; in the event these discussions prove unsuccessful, we will reconsider our deployment decisions. To provide for actions that may be required at that time, approximately $375 million has been included in the 1968 budget for the production of Nike-X for such purposes as defense of our offensive weapons systems."

The proposal to deploy an ABM was seen in different ways by different people and posed different threats and opportunities to their perception of the national interest as well as domestic, organizational, and personal interests. A look at the faces of the issue as seen by the participants, and their calculation of the stakes, is the place to begin to seek a solution to our puzzles.[4]

We will start with the organizations that were exerting pressure upward on the Secretary of Defense and the President. In doing so we will oversimplify: we will talk about the Army, the Directorate for Defense Research and Engineering, and the like. Just as the United States government can be broken down into major departments, and these departments in turn into smaller components, these smaller components themselves have parts with differences of interest, objectives, and perspective. For our purposes in explaining the ABM decision, it is sufficient to go no lower than the main components of the Defense Department, such as the Army and the Directorate of Defense Research and Engineering.

ORGANIZATIONAL STAKES[5]

THE ARMY[6]

Throughout the 1950s the Army fought for a role in the preparations for strategic nuclear war. It did so because it recognized that budget funds were moving toward strategic nuclear programs and because it believed that these programs were critical to the security interests of the United States. Most of the Army's efforts, however, were unsuccessful. It did re-

[4] The discussion of the interests of the participants is based in part on knowledge gained by the author as a participant in the process, as Deputy Assistant Secretary of Defense (ISA). Some of the observations are based on guesses about positions taken. Many of the same insights can be derived from a reading of congressional testimony, speeches, etc. See also Edward Randolph Jayne II, "The ABM Debate: Strategic Defense and National Security," M.I.T. Center for International Studies, Center Paper no. C/69-12, 1969, pp. 669–712. This study, based largely on interviews, confirms many of the stands described here. To be fair to the reader (and to add to his confusion), it should be noted that the present author was one of those interviewed by Jayne.

[5] On Service interests, see Morton H. Halperin, "Why Bureaucrats Play Games," pp. 301–10 of this volume.

[6] On the Army's interest in ABM in particular, see Herbert York, *Race to Oblivion* (New York, 1970), p. 214.

ceive partial responsibility for air defense, that involving warning systems and surface-to-air missiles, but it did not have the tactical fighter component of the air defense system, and it failed to get involved in strategic offensive forces. The Army did receive permission to work on the R&D of medium-range ballistic missiles, but in the end the responsibility for deployment went to the Air Force. Thus, by the late 1950s the Army realized that its role in strategic nuclear forces would be restricted to defense. Because of the limited role of anti-aircraft defenses, those in the Army who were responsible for developing, deploying and operating air defense systems turned to missile defense. For them it was simply the next step in the same direction.

One of the most publicized aspects of the program-budgeting system installed in the Pentagon by McNamara and his Comptroller, Charles Hitch, was the so-called program package. Under this concept, strategic forces would compete for defense funds with one another, rather than with other programs in the budget of each service. Insofar as this procedure really affected budgets, the funds for the ballistic missile defense program would come out of the budget for strategic offensive and defensive systems and not out of the Army budget, as it would probably have in the 1950s, when budgeting was explicitly done on the basis of service shares of the budget. Some in the Army undoubtedly opposed the ABM, arguing that in fact each service still had a limited budget which, in the case of the Army, should be used for its main purpose—namely, ground combat forces. However, this was also a period of rising defense expenditures, with the services competing vigorously for the larger funds. Thus, the opposition within the Army to seeking a major ballistic missile defense was weakened: proponents could argue that the means would come, not from the existing Army budget, but from new funds which would otherwise go to Air Force and Navy strategic programs.

THE NAVY

In the post–World War II period, the United States Navy developed a broader participation in the various roles and missions of the United States armed forces than either the Army or the Air Force. The Navy has its own ground troops in the form of Marines, and its own air capability, both for tactical air support of Marine operations and for strategic bombing missions from carriers. In the late 1950s it staked out a major role in strategic offensive missions when it got permission to proceed with Polaris submarines, with their nuclear missiles. Strategic defense was the only area in which the Navy was not yet active.

The Navy's attitude toward ABM was determined in part by a search for a share in the responsibility. By the early 1960s the Navy had a program aimed at developing a ship-based ballistic missile defense. Naval officials recognized that they could not hope to get exclusive responsibility for ballistic missile defense, since the Army had primary responsibility. The Navy therefore sought to justify its system as a supplement to the Army's land-based system. Consequently, the Navy recognized that the only hope of getting permission for deployment was to have the Army go forward first. The Navy, then, wished to proceed with the ABM in a way which kept open the possibility that later additions to this system would include a Navy-controlled, sea-based system.

In return for Army support of continuing development of the Navy sea-based ballistic missile system, the Navy was prepared to support an Army land-based system.

Moreover, the Navy was concerned, as was the Air Force, with maintaining the system of unanimous support by the Joint Chiefs of Staff for service procurement programs. This issue is discussed in detail below in considering the rules of the game.

THE AIR FORCE

The Air Force–Army rivalry in the field of defense has always been intense because of the lack of a clear division of roles in air defense. Both the Army and the Air Force have sought total control over the air defense role, the Air Force viewing it as part of the strategic mission and the Army seeing it as related to battlefield defense. In the late 1950s, when the Air Force got exclusive authority for medium-range ballistic missiles, an uneasy truce was worked out on air defense, under which the Air Force would be responsible for air defense fighters and the Army for surface-to-air missiles. The Air Force did not, up to the end of

1968, make any effort to challenge this division by seeking a role in deploying ballistic missile defense.

Some Air Force officials, particularly those in SAC, were concerned about the proposals from the Office of the Secretary of Defense (OSD) for defending Minuteman silos with the Army ballistic missile defense system. In part this was a reflex reaction, a desire not to have Air Force missiles protected by "Army" ABMs. In part there was concern that the Air Force would not be funded for a new offensive missile if billions were spent defending the Minuteman missiles with an ABM system. The Air Force clearly preferred that the funds for missile defense be used by the Air Force to develop new hard rock silos or mobile systems.

However, as long as the ABM was an area defense, competing (as the Air Force saw it) with Army funds for air defense and for civil defense, the Air Force was prepared to go along. Area defense did not challenge any Air Force missions or appear to pose competition for funds for new strategic offensive forces.

Although each of the three services saw a different face of the ABM issue, in the end they all were prepared to support it. There was no such unanimity within the Office of the Secretary of Defense, to which the Secretary looked for advice and support on this matter. The three offices involved were the Office of the Director of Defense Research and Engineering, headed during this period by John S. Foster; the Office of Systems Analysis, headed by Alain Enthoven; and the Office of International Security Affairs, headed by John McNaughton and then by Paul Warnke. Each of these offices saw a different face of ABM and reached different conclusions.

DEFENSE RESEARCH AND ENGINEERING (DDR&E)

The Director of Defense Research and Engineering is the Secretary of Defense's principal adviser on scientific and technical matters. He is also the manager of R&D programs. Foster, therefore, was responsible for monitoring the progress of ballistic missile defense, both in the Army and in the Advanced Research Projects Agency, which was a part of his office. He had previously been head of an AEC nuclear laboratory, and viewed his role as representing within the higher councils of the Pentagon and within the White House the perspective of the research scientist. Foster took it for granted that technology should be pushed as hard as possible, although he recognized the need to choose from the wide variety of different possible new technologies. He also believed that, when technology reached the state of military effectiveness, it should be deployed.

For Foster, the ABM issue was relatively simple and straightforward. At stake was the continued effectiveness of the weapons laboratory and the scientific research teams of American industry. Having developed an ABM system that was technically well designed, that community would expect it to be deployed. Its morale would be adversely affected by a decision not to deploy a system considered technologically "sweet." As the decision to deploy the ballistic missile defense system was delayed far beyond the time Foster thought to be justifiable on scientific and technical grounds, he began to fear that the laboratories involved would break up as the scientists became convinced that the United States would under no circumstances deploy a ballistic missile defense. He also feared that rising costs due to the delay in opening production lines would make it harder to justify a later decision to deploy. Furthermore, Foster believed that the Russians, in deploying an ABM while we did not, could develop a technologically more efficient system. As far as he was concerned, national security required that we maintain the vigor of our R&D establishment in order to maintain military superiority.[7]

Thus, Foster was for deployment of the ABM. The move from research and development to deployment was more important to him than how the decision was rationalized publicly.

[7] Industrial groups and contractors shared these concerns, as did research organizations such as the Stanford Research Institute, which worked on the ABM for the Army. However, the influence of these groups was limited to supplying arguments for ABM supporters in the Administration and helping to arouse congressional concern. AT&T, the prime contractor, is much less dependent on defense contracts than the prime contractors of most large systems; nevertheless, AT&T was eager for the contract because it used its involvement in air defense and missile defense to help prevent an antitrust suit to split Bell Labs, the research group, and Western Electric, the manufacturing unit, from the Bell system.

SYSTEMS ANALYSIS (SA)

Systems analysis was perhaps McNamara's major innovation in Pentagon organization and decisionmaking. Organized by Enthoven in 1961, the SA office was responsible for preparing for McNamara a series of Draft Presidential Memoranda (DPM), including one on strategic offensive and defensive forces. This document laid out McNamara's rationale for procuring strategic forces and indicated his decisions on particular force-posture issues.

Enthoven believed that we were spending too much on strategic forces and strongly resisted service-proposed programs to build a new bomber, a new missile, a new submarine, or to increase expenditures vastly on strategic forces. He doubted whether strategic superiority gave the United States any significant advantage.

In deciding whether an ABM system should be deployed, Enthoven and his colleagues examined the possible role of the system as compared to other methods of accomplishing the same objectives. With regard to city defense they expressed doubts about whether the system would function effectively; they pointed out that the Russians could respond at much less cost and negate the value of any larger ABM system. Defense against China was difficult to evaluate in terms of systems analysis. SA could only calculate the cost of the system relative to the possible savings in lives in the event of a Chinese attack; it could not judge whether the cost was justified. For the defense of Minuteman silos, SA calculated the cost of ABM protection by comparing it to the cost of moving into much harder rock silos or to that of a mobile land-based missile. In terms of these comparisons, the choice of whether or not to proceed with a ballistic missile defense was always a marginal one. In the end, however, the advantage of heading off service pressures for new strategic offensive systems tipped the balance in Enthoven's mind toward support of ABM defense for Minuteman silos.

INTERNATIONAL SECURITY AFFAIRS (ISA)

ISA has no budget, no relations with outside laboratories, industry, or foreign governments, and is committed to no specific method of analysis. Hence, the approach it takes tends to be dominated by the views of the Assistant Secretary. John McNaughton and Paul Warnke brought to this position a strong commitment to arms control, in terms of both a United States–Soviet agreement on strategic forces and a nuclear nonproliferation treaty. Both saw American ABM deployment as a threat to these interests and opposed it.[8]

SECRETARY OF DEFENSE ROBERT S. McNAMARA

During the course of his seven years as Secretary of Defense, McNamara became more and more concerned with the problems of getting the strategic arms race under control. By 1965 he came to believe that, early in the Kennedy Administration, the United States had bought a far larger strategic force than was necessary for deterrence of the Soviet Union, which in turn had stimulated a Soviet build-up which was now threatening to force the United States to step up the arms race once again. He believed that what he called the "mad momentum of the arms race" had to be brought under control in order to prevent nuclear war and to create a climate in which political relations between the United States and the Soviet Union might be improved. McNamara appears to have viewed the ABM as in some sense a symbol of the arms race. If the United States could take the decision not to deploy an ABM, then it might be possible to negotiate an agreement with the Russians or to reach a tacit understanding with them which would permit a leveling off of the strategic expenditures on both sides and, ultimately, their reduction. On the other hand, the decision to deploy the ABM— a system which McNamara, unlike Foster, believed was technologically unlikely to work— would symbolize our determination to buy whatever was available and to continue the

[8] The Arms Control and Disarmament Agency, the State Department, and the President's Science Advisory Committee shared many of these concerns. None of these organizations played a major role in the decisions. Cf. the comment of Herbert Scoville, who at the time was an Assistant Director of ACDA: "ACDA was at no time a participant in any of the senior-level discussions leading up to it [McNamara's speech]." Herbert Scoville, Jr., "The Politics of the ABM Debate: The View from the A.C. & D.A.," paper prepared for the Sixty-sixth Annual Meeting of the American Political Science Association, September 8–12, 1970, p. 4. The rules of the game, as explained below, limited the involvement of these organizations as well as that of the Budget Bureau. Secretary of State Rusk's role involved direct and private communication with the President.

search for a superiority which McNamara felt was unattainable and much less useful than many believed. Perhaps more than any other participant in the process, McNamara saw very high stakes for the national interest in the decision whether or not to deploy an ABM system; and he had no doubt that the correct decision, on grounds of national security, was *not* to deploy.

As Secretary of Defense, McNamara was keenly conscious of his accounts both with the military and with the President. He believed that he could overrule the Joint Chiefs of Staff on matters about which they felt strongly on only a limited number of occasions, and he carefully chose the issues. He recognized that on such occasions the Chiefs might go directly to the President, and that they would almost certainly go to the Hill to seek to enlist their supporters in bringing pressure to bear on the President to overturn his decision. Nevertheless, he expected to get (as he did on most occasions) the President's backing, but this depended on not seeking presidential support too often, and never on issues on which the President was strongly committed to the other side.

ABM was for McNamara a vital issue, and he was prepared to overrule the Chiefs and to seek the President's support. At the same time, he was not prepared to push the issue to the point of a break with the President.

WALT W. ROSTOW

Serving as the President's National Security Assistant, Walt W. Rostow was potentially in a position to play a major role. However, Rostow never had the mandate (which both Bundy and Kissinger have had) to involve himself heavily in the substance of all major foreign policy issues, particularly those pertaining to defense. Furthermore, McNamara tended to deal directly with the President, and to get involved in between on an issue concerning McNamara and Johnson would have meant a substantial cost to Rostow. Since the two apparently were in disagreement on the issue, he could only lose by stating a position. In this relationship, Rostow tended to save his own influence for Vietnam and a few other issues about which he felt very strongly.

Rostow's own stakes in the decision were not very high compared to the cost of involvement. He thus remained outside and did not play a key role, either in providing information for the President or in seeking to influence his decision directly.

CONGRESSIONAL LEADERS

Under the rules of the game in the United States, military leaders have not only the right but the obligation to state their personal views on defense issues to Congress when asked by members of the Armed Services or Appropriations Committees. Thus, it was routine for Congress to be informed that the Joint Chiefs of Staff were unanimously in favor of a ballistic missile defense system and to hear the arguments for such a deployment from senior military officers. In addition, there may well have been private discussions between military leaders and senior senators and congressmen.

Congressmen tend to defer to expertise, and the leaders of these committees viewed the military, rather than the civilians in the Pentagon, as the experts on national security. They were prepared to support programs which the military believed were vital to the improvement of America's military capability. In particular, they found it difficult to understand why we should not deploy something which would save American lives in the event of a war. As Richard Russell said in explaining his position, if only two human beings were to survive a nuclear war, he wanted them to be Americans; as he saw matters, an ABM would clearly increase this possibility. In general, the legislators were suspicious of Soviet motives and believed that the United States should maintain strategic superiority. Many of them also derived advantages, in terms of defense industries in their states and districts, from increased defense spending. Finally, they felt that the Secretary of Defense was seeking to substitute his judgment for that of the military, and that this was dangerous. For congressional leaders like Russell, Stennis, Jackson, and Thurmond, the stakes were the national interest as defined by the military.

PRESIDENT LYNDON B. JOHNSON

President Johnson assumed the presidency of the United States without any strong commitments to particular foreign policy positions. His own concerns and interests were tied up mainly with domestic issues.

Johnson does not appear to have seen any major national security stakes in the decision whether or not to deploy the ABM. Because it was an issue that generated intense passion in others, he was concerned, but he did not ascribe to it any intrinsic importance in terms of his conception of American security or America's role in the world. He was apparently wary of possible Chinese irrationality, having recently received a number of reports that the Russians believed the Chinese to be dangerous. Therefore an ABM against China, while not imperative, made sense to him. As will be discussed below, Johnson was interested in Strategic Arms Limitation Talks (SALT) with the Russians, but evidently did not share McNamara's fear that an American ABM deployment would impede agreement.

The issue for Johnson tended to be defined in terms of his relations with the other participants, including the Secretary of Defense, the Joint Chiefs of Staff, and congressional leaders concerned with defense matters—particularly those on the Senate Armed Services, Joint Atomic Energy, and Appropriations Committees. He was also, of course, sensitive to the implications that any decision might have for the 1968 presidential election.

Johnson's relations with McNamara had become uneasy during this period because of their growing disagreements about the conduct of the Vietnam War. Though prepared to overrule McNamara on Vietnam issues, Johnson was—at least until he made the decision to move him to the World Bank—interested in keeping McNamara on board, and he recognized that this meant supporting him on a number of other issues. Johnson could have had no doubt that McNamara felt strongly that a ballistic missile defense system should not be deployed, certainly not a large area defense system against the Soviet Union.

If the Chiefs' assertion of vital interests was not enough to settle the issue, neither was it something to be dismissed out of hand. Johnson clearly viewed the Joint Chiefs of Staff as a separate entity. He did not believe that he could leave the job of managing them to the Secretary of Defense. In general, he was reluctant to overrule the military; he viewed them as a group to be bargained with, in large part because of their power and influence on the Hill. He also was not prepared totally to discount their views on issues of national security. If the Chiefs said that an ABM was vital to the security of the United States, Johnson was not prepared to dismiss that as the rhetoric of the military, which always wants every new system.

For Johnson, certain of his former colleagues in the Senate constituted a major reference group on national security matters. He had had a close relation with Richard Russell, who was then Chairman of the Senate Armed Services Committee, as well as with such men as John Stennis and Henry Jackson. Johnson did not like to challenge their positions. He also took their views on national security seriously, and knew that they all felt very strongly that the United States should deploy a ballistic missile defense designed to deal with a Soviet attack against the United States.

The domestic political stakes could not be ignored by the President. There could have been little doubt in his mind that the Republican nominee, whether Richard Nixon or Nelson Rockefeller, could well make defense a major issue in the campaign. At the urging of his Secretary of Defense and under intense budgetary pressures, Johnson had permitted the non-Vietnam portion of the defense budget to decline, at least in real terms, and he was regularly rejecting proposals from the Joint Chiefs to develop and deploy a whole array of new strategic systems (e.g., a new manned strategic bomber) and new general-purpose systems. Opposition to his defense program was building, particularly among leaders of the Senate and House, and the Republicans were beginning to sense the possibility of a defense issue in the next presidential election. The ABM was rapidly becoming a symbol of defense preparedness. Johnson had to recognize that, if he did not deploy an ABM, he was open to the charge that he had failed to take a step which would save American lives in the event of a war. Although political scientists may point out that issues of defense procurement rarely swing votes in an election, Presidents are not so certain. Kennedy had apparently scored effectively against Nixon in 1960 on the missile-gap issue, and Johnson was reluctant to run the risk that the "defense-gap" issue would be used effectively against him.

Thus, Johnson saw the stakes largely in terms of his relations with the Secretary of Defense, with the military, and with the senior members of Congress who were concerned with defense, especially inasmuch as implications for the 1968 election were involved. As the President saw it, McNamara was strongly against deployment of the ABM (as was Secretary of State Dean Rusk), while congressional leaders and the military strongly favored it. All claimed to be reasoning from the point of view of national security. Johnson's own instincts would have led him to search for a compromise which would minimize the damage to his relations with his advisers.

The other participants were maneuvering and putting forward arguments in an effort to alter his perception of domestic or international consequences. The way in which they struggled to define an issue for the President and to seek the outcome they desired was biased by the images that are taken for granted in the top hierarchy of the United States government, the rules of the game, and the fact that deployment of the ABM could be carried out only by the United States Army and only by the use of existing procedures.

RULES OF THE GAME

The most important rule of the game which affected the nature of the ABM debate in the executive branch was the one requiring the President to make budgetary decisions once a year and to defend his decision publicly. This is a rule that derives from our system of government and applies to any President. Since the ABM had aroused great congressional and public interest, the President could not duck the issue in his budgetary messages. Instead, he had to discuss the subject and state clearly why he was for or against an ABM. This meant that the option of trying to keep the issue away from the President was not open to the opponents of the ABM. Because it was an annual budgetary issue, proponents of the deployment of an ABM system had no difficulty reaching the President, and opponents had to persuade the President not only to rule against deployment but to take a public stand. Thus, at each budgetary cycle McNamara had to devote considerable effort and energy to developing a rationale against deployment which the President would be prepared to accept and to embrace publicly as his own.

Other rules of the game were peculiar to the

Johnson Administration. The nature of the President's relationship with his Secretary of Defense affected the outcome of the ABM debate. McNamara tended to deal privately with the President on issues of major concern to him. Formal memoranda, which he would clear throughout the Defense Department and send to the President, were prepared only after he and the President had privately agreed on a position. The President's meeting with the Joint Chiefs on the budget tended to be a routine and formalistic opportunity for the Chiefs to appeal the Secretary of Defense's decisions. McNamara's annual meeting with the President's National Security Adviser, Science Adviser, and Budget Director was equally formalistic. Although this procedure eventually broke down on Vietnam, it did not do so on defense budgetary issues. This meant that there was no open debate within the Administration. Because of the private nature of McNamara's relation with the President, other agencies such as the State Department, ACDA, and the President's Science Adviser were not able to make inputs to the decision in an orderly way before McNamara and the President had reached tentative agreement.

The rules of the game under which the Joint Chiefs of Staff operated also influenced the outcome of the ABM question. During the 1950s the Joint Chiefs of Staff tended to split on major issues, particularly on those affecting the deployment of systems for one service. Each service tended to support its own deployment, and except where specific deals were made, to oppose controversial deployments for the other services—particularly expensive ones which might upset the existing arrangement for allocating shares of the defense budget. Because they did not see any threat to their autonomy from the Secretary of Defense in the 1950s, the Chiefs were prepared to deal separately with the Secretary and the President. Robert McNamara's approach changed their procedures dramatically.

Unlike his predecessors, McNamara saw himself as a decisionmaker on strategic issues and not simply as a business manager who left policy to the military. The Joint Chiefs discovered that, when they split, McNamara would use their disagreements to reject programs supported by just one of the services. In order to counterbalance this influence, the Joint Chiefs

developed a policy of compromise—to unite in support of each service. Thus, by 1965 the Army was able to make a strong enough case for ABM to get the support of the other Chiefs. The Navy was apparently brought along by the Army's support for development of the concept of a ship-based ABM system and some other Navy programs. The Air Force appears to have been brought along by the Army's support for Air Force strategic programs, and by the Army's willingness to forgo ABM protection of Minuteman silos. As a result of these arrangements, the Secretary of Defense and the President were confronted by the Joint Chiefs' unanimous position that ballistic missile defense was vital to the security of the United States, even though really only the Army favored it strongly. Congress was informed that the Chiefs unanimously supported deployment.

SHARED IMAGES

The debate within the executive branch was founded on a set of widely shared images about the role of the United States in the world and about the nature of the threats to its security. All participants in the debate accepted the notion that the Soviet Union and China were potential enemies of the United States who would engage in military threats and who might use military force, if not against the United States, at least against our allies, unless the military power of these countries was counterbalanced by that of the United States.

It was also widely believed that nuclear power was an important component of national power. It was widely accepted that the United States had to maintain strategic superiority over the Soviet Union and China because these countries were aggressive and expansionist and the United States was defensive and peaceful. It was also assumed that any military capability which would enhance the ability of the United States to survive a nuclear war should be procured; many believed that the United States should procure any weapons system the Russians had.

Although McNamara began to argue against some of these beliefs beginning in the mid-1960s, they were by and large accepted by most of the participants, and the debate was carried out within these terms. McNamara was forced to construct his arguments largely within the framework of the images held by the rest of the participants. The proponents of ABM deployment found that the shared images biased the debate in their direction.

ARGUMENTS

Within these constraints, proponents and opponents of ABM deployment put forward arguments designed either to convince other participants or to demonstrate that a decision reached because of organizational or political interests could effectively be defended before domestic audiences.

ARGUMENTS IN SUPPORT OF DEPLOYMENT[9]

This Will Save American Lives

Supporters of the ABM argued that in the event of a nuclear war the ABM system would shoot down incoming Soviet missiles and hence would save American lives. The extreme form of this argument, as had already been mentioned, was presented by Senator Richard Russell. Others pointed out that even if 60 million Americans were killed in a nuclear attack, the expenditure on ABM would be worth saving a possible 120 million other Americans.

The Russians Have It

Throughout the post–World War II period the United States has felt obligated to match Soviet deployments. It has been argued that, if we let the Russians have something that we do not have, they would gain a psychological or political advantage in dealing with us. Similarly, if the Russians were to develop something while we did not, they would gain a technological lead. Thus, in the public debate, and even within the bureaucracy, the argument that "we need it because the Russians have it" has carried great weight.

It Works

Proponents of the ABM sought to counteract technological arguments against deployment by asserting its effectiveness. They pointed to tests in which a single ABM had in-

tercepted a single incoming warhead, and they expressed confidence that the entire system would in fact work in the event of a nuclear attack. If it worked, it should be deployed.

ARGUMENTS AGAINST DEPLOYMENT

It was more difficult to find clear and simple arguments against deployment of the ABM system that would appeal to the President and be persuasive in dealing with Congress and the public. Over time, the Secretary of Defense developed a series of arguments against ABM deployment, and specifically against a large-scale deployment directed against the Soviet Union, which was the system the Joint Chiefs of Staff and the senior congressional leaders were proposing.

The System Is Not Technologically Ready

Up to 1963, McNamara was able to argue, with wide support from the technological community, that the Army-proposed Nike-Zeus system simply could not be effective against the kind of decoys and other penetration aids that the Soviets were fully capable of producing.[10] If we went ahead with a deployment, he argued, we would wind up with a second-rate system. On the other hand, if we waited, we had hopes of developing a new and more effective system. By 1963 this argument was no longer valid, because a new and more technologically efficient system had been developed, and it appeared unlikely that additional breakthroughs would occur in the foreseeable future.

Expenditures on This System Will Bring Less Return Than Expenditures on Other Systems

After 1963, the Secretary of Defense introduced arguments of cost effectiveness. He pointed out that a large ABM system designed to protect American cities would be aimed at reducing American casualties in a nuclear war. He suggested that one had to examine alternative ways of reducing casualties and determine which would be the most effective for any

---

[9] See U.S. Senate Debates, *Congressional Record*, 90th Cong., 2nd sess., 1968, 114, pt. 22: 529169–90; and testimony of General Earle Wheeler, Chairman, Joint Chiefs of Staff, *Hearings before the Preparedness Investigating Subcommittee of the Senate Committee on Armed Services*, 90th Cong., 2nd sess., April 23, 1968.

[10] Robert S. McNamara, *Testimony before the Subcommittee of the House Committee on Appropriations*, 87th Cong., 1st sess., April 6, 1961, p. 17. For a summary of McNamara's arguments against deployment as presented to various congressional committees from 1961 to 1967, see Benson D. Adams, "McNamara's ABM Policy, 1961–67," *Orbis*, 12 (Spring 1968): 200–225.

given sum of money. McNamara examined a number of alternative ways of reducing casualties, including air defense and civil defense. He argued that the studies made clear that the installation of a nationwide system of fallout shelters would produce the largest saving. Thus, if the United States were to commit itself to a "damage-limiting" program designed to save lives in the event of a nuclear war, it should build a shelter system. Only after the shelters were completed should one consider spending money on other measures, such as ballistic missile defense.[11] The civil defense argument was a complicated one. It depended on people understanding marginal utility and accepting that one should always proceed in the most efficient way. McNamara appears to have put this argument forward not to make a case for civil defense but to make one against ballistic missile defense.

An Equal and Opposite Reaction Will Occur Which Will Negate the Value of the System

McNamara next turned to the argument of the equal and opposite reaction.[12] As he explained it to Congress, if the United States deployed a large ABM system which would cost between $20 and $40 billion, it would, against the *currently expected* Soviet threat, save a number of American lives in the event of a nuclear war. McNamara then proceeded to show that the Russians could offset our ABM deployment at substantially smaller cost, and casualties would return to the previous level. Thus, he argued, our ABM system would bring an equal and opposite reaction from the Soviet Union which would totally negate the value of the ABM system—which would be capable of producing the same number of casualties at a higher expense to us. Although sophisticated critics were able to point out that there was nothing in the history of the arms race to sug-

gest that in fact an equal and opposite reaction was inevitable or even likely, McNamara's argument was a simple and effective one. It summarized in a crude way the truth that over time the Soviets would build decoys and MIRVs if the United States built an ABM system, and that in the end there would not be the savings in lives that ABM proponents suggested.

We Must Resist "the Mad Momentum of the Arms Race"

In his speech announcing that the United States would deploy a light area defense directed against China, McNamara introduced a new argument against an ABM deployment directed at a large Soviet attack. He talked about the history of the arms race and argued that the United States on a number of occasions had built a larger force than it needed for deterrence. He suggested that in turn this had stimulated the Soviets to build more. Such an interaction, which he called "the mad momentum of the arms race," was, he said, a danger to the security of the United States, and therefore the United States should take the initiative in exercising restraint.

We Must Negotiate Arms Limitation with the Soviet Union

Encouraged by Johnson's interest in strategic arms limitation talks, McNamara sought to utilize this presidential concern to delay the decision to deploy ABM. He argued that a public call for talks would serve as a reasonable rationale for delaying deployment. He also argued that an American commitment to deploy ABMs would decrease the likelihood of Soviet agreement.

PUZZLES AND TENTATIVE SOLUTIONS

Having examined the stakes as the participants saw them, as well as the constraints and the arguments that were used, we can now consider in detail the questions we posed at the outset.

1. Why, in January 1967, did President Johnson ask Congress to appropriate the funds to deploy an ABM system, but state that he would defer initiating the deployment pending an effort to get the Soviet Union to engage in talks on limiting the arms race?

As preparations for the budget for the fiscal

---

[11] Robert S. McNamara, "Statement of the Secretary of Defense before a Joint Session of the Senate Armed Services Committee and the Senate Subcommittee on the Department of Defense Appropriations on the Fiscal Years 1965–69 Defense Program and the 1965 Defense Budget" (multilith), p. 42.

[12] Robert S. McNamara, "Statement of the Secretary of Defense before a Joint Session of the Senate Armed Services Committee and the Senate Subcommittee on the Department of Defense Appropriations on the Fiscal Years 1968–72 Defense Program and the 1968 Defense Budget" (multilith), pp. 39, 40.

year 1968 neared completion in the closing months of 1966, time appeared to be running out on McNamara's efforts to prevent deployment of a Soviet-oriented ABM system. A number of pressures seemed to be coming to a head, including the following:[13]

TECHNOLOGICAL IMPROVEMENT

The technology of ballistic missile defense had improved drastically in the preceding few years. Those responsible for the program in the scientific community, in DDR&E and its operating arm, the Advanced Research Projects Agency (ARPA), as well as in the Army, were now arguing that an effective ABM system could be built and could ultimately be improved to handle even a large Soviet attack. In previous years, the testimony of these scientists had effectively served to offset the pressure exercised by the Joint Chiefs of Staff and had enabled McNamara to persuade the President and Congress that the technology was not yet ripe for an ABM deployment. They were no longer prepared to play this role.[14]

SOVIET ABM DEPLOYMENT

There was growing evidence that the Soviet Union was beginning to deploy an ABM system around Moscow. In the past the intelligence community had been split as to whether the so-called Tallinn system being deployed across the northern part of the Soviet Union was in fact an ABM system. (Although some military intelligence agencies were pressing the view that Tallinn was an ABM system, the majority of the intelligence community believed that it was an air defense system.) However, there was no dispute at all that the system being deployed around Moscow was an ABM. This added to pressures to begin an American deployment in order to avoid an ABM gap.

JCS PRESSURE

In part because of the changes in technology and the Soviet ABM deployment, the Joint Chiefs of Staff were no longer willing to concur in delaying ABM deployment; they were determined to go firmly on record before Congress in favor of deployment *now*, and in par-

ticular for a deployment that would develop into a large anti-Soviet system.

SENATE PRESSURE

Pressure was also mounting from Senate leaders for an initial ABM deployment. Among others, Russell, Jackson, and Thurmond had spoken out in favor of an early ABM deployment. The general expectation in the executive branch was that Congress would put great pressure on the President to agree to a deployment if he did not include it in his budgetary message.[15]

REPUBLICAN PRESSURE

It was also becoming evident that the Republican party planned to make a campaign issue out of an alleged ABM gap. Governor George Romney of Michigan, then believed to be a leading Republican candidate for the presidential nomination in 1968, had, on a "Meet the Press" broadcast in November, talked of an ABM gap and made it clear that this would be an issue in the campaign. Moreover, the GOP Congressional Policy Committee, led by Melvin Laird, had decided to make the ABM a vehicle by which to challenge Lyndon Johnson's strategic policies. Senator Strom Thurmond, a leading Republican expert on defense matters, had also attacked the failure to deploy the ABM.[16]

There was no doubt that JCS demands for an immediate ABM deployment would be made known to leaders on the Hill, as would the growing evidence of a Soviet ABM deployment around Moscow. Congress had in the previous year included funds for the ABM deployment which the President had not requested; the stage was set for a confrontation should Johnson again accept the advice of his Secretary of Defense and delay an ABM deployment.

The President's choices seemed to be rather narrow. He could reject ballistic missile defense, embrace McNamara's arguments against deployment, and prepare to take his case to congressional leaders and the public. Alternatively, he could proceed with a ballistic missile

---

[13] The documentation for this section is drawn from Jayne, *op. cit.*
[14] *Ibid.*, p. 309.

[15] See, e.g., *Baltimore Sun*, November 21, 1966, and December 3, 1966; *Washington Post*, November 24, 1966.
[16] Jayne, *op. cit.*, p. 346.

defense deployment at the cost of overruling his Secretary of Defense. The odds were high that the President would proceed with the ballistic missile defense deployment being pressed on him by the Joint Chiefs and the Senate leaders. Only if he could find another option did McNamara stand any chance of again delaying a presidential commitment to ballistic missile defense.

It appears that McNamara first discussed the subject with the President at meetings held on his Texas ranch on November 3 and 10. These discussions reportedly focused on the ABM and the question of extending the bombing to additional targets in North Vietnam.[17]

Following the meeting with the President on November 10, McNamara reported at a press conference that the Soviets were now believed to be deploying an ABM system around Moscow. McNamara's initiative in releasing this information made it possible for him to pre-empt an inevitable news leak and, at the same time, to air his view that the Soviet ABM deployment required improvements in American offensive capability rather than a matching deployment. McNamara noted that the United States was moving ahead with Minuteman III and Poseidon, and therefore was fully confident of its ability to deter this Soviet ABM. He declared that it was too early to begin deployment of an anti-Chinese system, and that no decision had been made on other possible reasons for a deployment.[18]

The decisive meeting with the President appears to have been held on December 6. At this meeting—attended by McNamara, his Deputy Secretary, Cyrus Vance, all the members of the Joint Chiefs, and the President's Special Assistant Walt Rostow—the Joint Chiefs were given the opportunity to put forward their argument for what was then called Posture A, a full coverage of the United States with a system designed for defense against more than a Chinese attack. The Joint Chiefs made it clear that they intended to see that Posture A would develop into Posture B, a larger anti-Soviet system designed to reduce casualties in the United States in the event of a large Soviet attack, and that they would accept nothing less. McNamara countered by presenting the argu-

ments against an anti-Soviet system, emphasizing that the Soviets would eventually have an offensive capability which would fully offset the value of the ABM. At this point he appears to have presented the President with two possible compromises. The first, which he was ultimately able to persuade the President to accept, called for the procurement of production items requiring a long lead-time, with no specific decision as to what system, if any, would be deployed; this was to be accompanied by an effort to begin arms limitation talks with the Soviet Union. The second option was to begin deployment of a small anti-Chinese system. The meeting ended with Johnson agreeing that the State Department should begin to probe the Soviets on the possibility of talks, but apparently withholding any decision on ABM deployment.

The State Department thus proceeded to explore the possibilities of arms limitation talks with the Soviets. At the same time, McNamara wrote up and presented to the President a DPM summarizing his arguments against an anti-Soviet system, but suggesting that an ABM defense against China might prove useful.

To demonstrate that he was not the only opponent of a large Soviet-oriented ABM system, McNamara arranged for the President and the Joint Chiefs of Staff to meet early in January 1967 with past and current Special Assistants to the President for Science and Technology and Directors of Defense Research and Engineering. None of the scientists present dissented from the view that an ABM to defend the American people against a Soviet missile attack was not feasible and should not be built. There was some discussion of a Chinese-oriented system and some divergence of views, but a majority was opposed to deployment.[19]

Following this meeting, McNamara was apparently able to persuade Johnson to delay any deployment, whether anti-Russian or anti-Chinese, to pursue the option of procuring long lead-time items, and to concentrate on the

---

[17] These meetings are described by Jayne, *op. cit.*

[18] *New York Times*, November 13, 1966.

[19] The scientists present were Science Advisers James R. Killian, Jr., George B. Kistiakowsky, Jerome B. Wiesner, and Donald F. Hornig; the Directors of Defense Research were Herbert York, Harold Brown, and John S. Foster, Jr. The meeting is described in York, *op. cit.*, pp. 194–95.

effort to open arms limitation talks with the Soviet Union.

The proposal for such talks seemed to be a vehicle for the pursuit of a number of presidential objectives. Johnson was haunted, as all of his postwar predecessors had been, by the specter of nuclear war. He was anxious to try to do something to bring nuclear weapons under control. Moreover, here was an issue on which the President could appeal to the desire of the general public for peace, and specifically to the left wing of the Democratic party, which was becoming increasingly disaffected on Vietnam. It was also an issue that could make history for Johnson as the man who made the decisive move to end the nuclear arms race which threatened mankind's doom. Johnson was quick to sense these possibilities.

McNamara argued that a decision to proceed with ballistic missile defense would hamper arms limitation talks with the Russians, since one of the main purposes of such talks would be to seek an agreement by both sides to avoid any ballistic missile defense deployments. Further, he argued that a dramatic act of restraint by the United States would increase the probability that the Russians would respond favorably, and that the talks would begin. In any case, a bold gesture for peace on the part of the President would undercut much of the opposition to his decision not to proceed right away with a ballistic missile defense deployment.

At the same time, by asking for funds for ballistic missile defense and implying that he would be prepared to spend them if talks did not get under way, the President was able to avoid making the argument that the United States should unilaterally forgo deployment of a ballistic missile defense. Johnson would be able to tell the Joint Chiefs and the senior congressional leaders that he had certainly not ruled out a ballistic missile defense; that in fact he had taken a major step toward such a deployment, but that he was postponing the actual deployment pending an effort to get an arms control agreement with the Soviet Union. Though the military and congressional leaders might be somewhat uneasy about the further delay, they could not effectively mount a campaign against an effort to seek agreement with the Soviet Union, given the widespread popularity of such efforts.

Thus, the proposal to link the two issues enabled McNamara to gain a further delay, which he hoped would last indefinitely as the talks continued. The President could avoid paying any major price in his relations with McNamara, the Joint Chiefs, or the congressional leaders who favored an ABM deployment. He could put off a hard choice and open up the possibility of arms control negotiations, which would substantially enhance his domestic position and solidify his prospects for a favorable place in the history books.[20]

2. Why was the decision to deploy an ABM announced at the tail end of a speech whose whole structure and purpose was to explain why an ABM defense against the Soviet Union was impossible?

3. Why did the Secretary of Defense describe the system as being directed against China, while the Joint Chiefs of Staff and their congressional allies described it as a first step toward a full-scale defense against the Soviet Union?

What has been said thus far should make it clear that the answers lie in the bargaining between McNamara and Johnson, with each taking account of the positions of the Joint Chiefs and the congressional leaders.

The effort to get the Soviets to agree to set a date for arms limitation talks was unsuccessful. When President Johnson met with Soviet Premier Kosygin at a hastily arranged summit conference at Glassboro, New Jersey, on June 23 and 25, there was still no Soviet agreement to enter into arms limitation talks. Johnson brought McNamara along; while the two leaders ate lunch, the Secretary of Defense gave them a lecture on nuclear strategy, previewing his San Francisco speech and emphasizing the value of an agreement to both sides. The Soviet leader was unyielding; he described ABM as defensive and unobjectionable and was not prepared to agree to talks.[21]

Following the Glassboro conference there could be little doubt that talks would not be under way before the President's next budgetary message in January 1968. Almost im-

[20] On the tendency to make the minimum decision necessary, see Warner Schilling, "The H-Bomb Decision," *Political Science Quarterly*, 76 (March 1961): 24–46.

[21] Jayne, *op. cit.*, pp. 366–69.

mediately Johnson informed McNamara that some kind of ABM deployment would have to be announced by January at the latest.[22] At that time the President would have to account for the disposition of the ABM contingency funds he had requested and state whether he was seeking additional sums for deployment of an ABM system. Given his stakes as we have defined them, and given the implicit commitment that he had made in January of 1967 to go forward in the absence of arms limitation talks, the President's decision was not difficult to predict. January of 1968 would be Johnson's last chance to announce the deployment in a budgetary message before the presidential elections in November. To hedge again, stating that he was still seeking talks, would have seemed unconvincing, since Johnson had been unable to secure Kosygin's agreement to talks at the Glassboro meeting. The intermediate options had run out. The President was determined to go ahead, even if it meant paying a price in his relations with the Secretary of Defense. Apparently, Johnson also felt that by beginning to deploy the ABM he might convince the Soviets to enter into arms limitation talks.[23]

Having decided to proceed with an ABM deployment, Johnson was obviously concerned about reducing the cost in terms of his relations with McNamara. He was willing to let the Secretary announce the deployment in any way he chose. For the sake of military and congressional acceptance, the President may have insisted that the deployment be such that others could describe it as the first step toward an anti-Soviet system.

McNamara's primary goal remained to prevent deployment of a large system directed at the Soviet Union. If the United States were to go forward with any ABM deployment, it was important to do whatever possible to create in the public mind a clear distinction between the system being deployed and a large system, while at the same time vigorously putting forward the case for not deploying a large system against the Soviet Union. It was therefore in McNamara's interest to be able to explain his view of the arms race, explain his opposition to a large anti-Soviet system, and *then* announce an ABM deployment. The apparent contradic-

tion in the speech was designed by McNamara as a way of emphasizing that this was not a large ABM deployment against the Soviet Union. He may also have hoped that his speech would generate substantial public opposition to an ABM deployment.

McNamara had recognized several years earlier that he might lose the battle against deploying any kind of ABM system and had begun laying the groundwork for a fallback position in the form of a small ABM system directed against China. In February 1965, he publicly raised the possibility of ABM protection against a small nuclear attack from China, but argued that even on those grounds the decision was not then needed, because "the lead-time for additional nations to develop and deploy an effective ballistic missile system capable of reaching the United States is greater than we require to deploy the defense."[24] In the following year McNamara indicated that the ABM system now being developed would not be effective against a larger attack, but could deal with a small Chinese threat.[25]

Thus, in September 1967, McNamara announced that the lead-time for an ABM deployment was now about the same as the lead-time for the Chinese deployment of an ICBM system of significant size. Therefore, it was now prudent to proceed with this deployment which he had been discussing for several years. And McNamara appears to have been convinced that, in its own terms, ABM defense against China was, as he described it in his speech, "marginal" but nevertheless "prudent." In announcing the decision to deploy an ABM system against China, McNamara was putting forward arguments which he believed.

Even more important was the fact that McNamara's major concern was to try to prevent a large deployment directed at the Soviet Union, which would force the Soviets to respond, thereby setting off another round of

---

[22] *Ibid.*, p. 372.
[23] *Ibid.*, p. 373.

[24] Robert S. McNamara, "Statement of the Secretary of Defense before a Joint Session of the Senate Armed Services Committee and the Senate Subcommittee on the Department of Defense Appropriations on the Fiscal Years 1966–70 Defense Program and the 1966 Defense Budget" (multilith), p. 49.
[25] Robert S. McNamara, "Statement of the Secretary of Defense before a Joint Session of the Senate Armed Services Committee and the Senate Subcommittee on the Department of Defense Appropriations on the Fiscal Years 1967–71 Defense Program and the 1967 Defense Budget" (multilith), p. 70.

the arms race. An anti-Chinese system could be limited more easily than a small system directed against the Soviet Union. One alternative was to describe the system as one designed for protection for Minuteman installations, although it would be difficult to justify on grounds of cost effectiveness. Moreover, a system deployed only around missile sites would have been resisted by the Joint Chiefs and the Senate leaders; it would not have paved the way for a larger system against the Soviet Union and could not be described as the beginning of one. It is not clear whether McNamara himself or the President ruled out this alternative.[26]

4. Why was the system authorized for deployment one which was designed and deployed as if its purpose were to protect American cities against a large Soviet attack?

Once a presidential decision is made on a policy issue, the details of implementation must be turned over to an individual or organization. In the case of the ABM, there was no choice but to assign responsibility to the Army. Although McNamara could and did attempt to monitor how the Army would deploy the system, he was unable or unwilling to direct that the system be designed and deployed so as to minimize the possibility of growth. The Army's freedom may have been enhanced by the fact that McNamara's scientific and technical advisers themselves tended to favor keeping open the option for growth into a large ABM system. Deputy Secretary of Defense Paul Nitze, to whom general responsibility for much of the day-to-day administration of the Pentagon fell as McNamara devoted more and more of his time to Vietnam, also tended to favor keeping open the option for a large system.

But there was a more fundamental problem. Once the decision had been made to proceed

with a ballistic missile defense directed against China, there was strong pressure to move forward quickly. The President could not admit at that point that we had no hardware for such a system and that three or four years of research and development would be necessary before deployment could begin; one had to start by deploying the components that were already developed, even though they were not the optimum ones for a defense system against China which could be kept from growing into a large ABM system against the Soviet Union.

Geography also worked against a limited system. Both Russian and Chinese ICBMs approach the United States through the same corridor over the pole. The same radar could be used for an anti-Chinese system and an anti-Russian system, and long-range missile launchers would be useful against both threats.

DDR&E, which favored a large Soviet-oriented system, had no incentive for using its ingenuity to develop components that could be effective against China but that had little potential for a large anti-Russian system. And, in making precise decisions about the location of radar and missile-launching sites, the Army in fact opted for sites close to cities, in order to permit the eventual deployment of a large anti-Russian system.

McNamara's control over the implementation of this decision was simply not great enough to prevent these developments. His attention was increasingly absorbed by Vietnam, and he was clearly on his way out. He did not have the support of the President in seeking to limit the system. His principal assistant did not share his desire to reduce the possibility of growth, and the Army, charged with deployment, favored a large anti-Soviet system. Thus, despite McNamara's efforts in his statements to distinguish sharply between an anti-Chinese and an anti-Russian system, the Army was able to tell Congress that actual deployment was not different in any significant way from the projected first stages of an anti-Russian system, and that the system being deployed was expected to grow.

CONCLUSIONS

The decision of the Johnson Administration to deploy an ABM system, the way in which it was announced, and the preparations for de-

26 In his San Francisco speech McNamara stated, with regard to Minuteman defense, that "the Chinese-oriented ABM deployment would enable us to add— as a concurrent benefit—a further defense of our Minuteman sites against Soviet attack, which means that at modest cost we would in fact be adding even greater effectiveness to our offensive missile force and avoiding a much more costly expansion of that force." A short time later, in an article in *Life* (September 29, 1967, pp. 28A–C) which elaborated on the speech, McNamara stated unequivocally that the Minuteman defense would be deployed. However, following a trip to Europe for a meeting of the NATO Nuclear Planning Group, he declared that no decision had been made as to whether the option to defend Minuteman sites would be exercised.

ployment which followed illustrate the pulling and hauling of many different players with different interests that is characteristic of the foreign policy process in the United States. No single player's views—including those of the President—of what should be done dominated, although the President's views played a major role in shaping the general direction in which American actions moved.

Two independent decisions were involved, and different actors influenced the course of each. The first decision was simply whether or not to deploy the ABM at all. This was necessarily a presidential decision; there was no "end run" around him. As the ABM decision illustrates, the President is qualitatively different—not simply a very powerful player among less powerful players.

The second decision related to the timing, substance, and shape of deployment, given the previous decision that there was to be an ABM of some kind. In this latter decision the President played a much less central role, and other players were somewhat more influential. Johnson was both less interested and less in control.

The decision to announce some sort of deployment by January of 1968 can thus best be explained by exploring the multiple constituencies and interests that the President had to balance. The foreign policy interests of all postwar Presidents have come to focus on relations with the Soviet Union as they affect the nuclear balance and the need to avoid nuclear war. While from time to time these concerns have stimulated interest in arms control, they have mainly led to support for defense efforts. At the same time, the Presidents have all been concerned with their image in history and have developed a desire to go down as men who contributed to a peaceful international environment. All of them felt, as Johnson did, the responsibility to avoid a nuclear holocaust that would destroy civilization.

Moreover, no President can ignore the pressures exerted by the bureaucracy—especially the military and the senior cabinet officers—or by senior congressional leaders and the public when a presidential campaign is around the corner. All of these pressures came to bear on Lyndon Johnson as he faced the ABM decisions during the course of 1967. Johnson appears here in the characteristic presidential role of conciliator: a man who attempts to give as much as he can to each of a number of his principal subordinates and the permanent bureaucracies while seeking a position that avoids any conflict between his own various interests and constituencies beyond the government. The limited ABM which Johnson ultimately directed be deployed could be described by Robert McNamara as anti-Chinese and therefore not a danger to Soviet-American relations in general, or to future arms talks in particular. At the same time, the Joint Chiefs and Senate leaders had their own payoffs. Despite McNamara's statement, they could describe it as a first step toward an anti-Soviet system. Moreover, the small anti-Chinese system which Johnson approved was much larger than the system the Soviet Union was deploying around Moscow. Given these ambiguities and the simplified nature with which the public views such questions, the Republican party had effectively been deprived of a missile-gap issue. That was the President's payoff.

Johnson was also able to reconcile his own concern to seek an end to the nuclear arms race with the Soviet Union with the need to maintain American military strength. Early in 1967 he was prepared to go along with McNamara's proposal that arms talks with the Soviet Union be sought before a firm, final decision was made to proceed with an ABM deployment. After talking with Kosygin, he concluded that the Soviets would not enter talks under the current circumstances. He believed that perhaps the pressure that would be put upon the Soviet leaders by the beginnings of an American deployment would constitute a leverage on the Russians to agree to talks. In ordering the deployment, Johnson was not abandoning his efforts for arms talks and an arms agreement with the Soviet Union; rather, he was structuring the issue, making the American ABM deployment a way to get the very talks that both he and McNamara desired.

If the decision to order a deployment can be most clearly understood in terms of the conflicting pressures on the President, the precise nature of the deployment can be understood largely in terms of pressures within the bureaucracy below the President, pressures constrained by the operating procedures of the Army and of the Pentagon as a whole. Although McNamara himself favored no deployment or a limited deployment, the staffs on which he had to depend to monitor and implement the President's decision were unanimous in their belief that an ABM system should be built that could grow into a large anti-Soviet system. Science Adviser John S. Foster, who would have to have the major role in monitoring both the research on the ABM system and its development and production, believed strongly that the option for a large system should be left open, as did Paul Nitze, McNamara's Deputy Secretary of Defense (following the departure of Cyrus Vance, who more closely shared McNamara's views). The Army itself favored a big system. No imaginative thought had gone into the design of components for a specifically anti-Chinese system. In fact, the implementers were straining as hard as they could to design and deploy a system that could be expanded as far as possible. As suggested above, McNamara's power was weak in this game; he lacked a strong presidential directive as well as strong staff support to keep the system small. His primary attention was focused on Vietnam, and his days as Secretary of Defense were obviously numbered.

One of the truisms of bureaucracy is that it resists change. Innovation, when it occurs, must generally be explained. The history of the ABM appears to be an anomaly. McNamara, the defender of the status quo, had to take the initiative to prevent an ABM deployment, since the system seemed to be grinding inevitably toward it. The explanation for this lies in the fact that the system was heavily biased toward the deployment of new weapons systems under certain conditions; ABM deployment was not seen as change. A number of components of the rules of the game, the shared images, and the organizational procedures of the American government produced a situation from the time of the Korean War through the end of the 1960s in which the procurement of new systems was part of the routine.

As has already been noted, the budgetary process itself creates a unique set of pressures. The fact that ABM decisions had to be recorded in the budget meant that the issue would reach the President without any effort on the part of its proponents. This was particularly true because of the rule which gives the JCS the right to appeal to the President any decision of the Secretary of Defense or the Budget Director. No other career service enjoys this right. Moreover, the President had to make a decision and announce it publicly, in keeping with a deadline brought about by the budget. To urge him to delay was equivalent to urging him to take a public stand against the deployment of ABM at that time.

The operating rules of the Joint Chiefs of Staff, as well as their access to congressional leaders and congressional committees, also produced a bias toward deployment of weapons systems that were favored strongly by one of the services. Given strong Army support for an ABM system, and given the judgment of scientists that it was technically feasible, unanimous JCS support for the system was forthcoming under the logrolling rules which the Chiefs had begun to use in the McNamara period. The fact that they would report their views to Congress when asked meant that the President could not keep differences hidden and, in order to prevent a deployment, would have to challenge the JCS in public.

The sequence of the private decisionmaking process involving negotiations of the President and the Secretary of Defense with the Joint Chiefs also biased decisions toward deployment; the normal desires of the Budget Bureau to avoid expensive weapons systems, the skepticism of the scientists on the President's Science Advisory Committee, and the opposition of some parts of the State Department to deployment could not be brought into play early enough in the process to affect presidential decisions.

Shared images, which, according to official belief, dominated American society, also biased the system toward ABM deployment. It was widely accepted that the United States needed to have strategic superiority over the Soviet Union and that the United States needed to match any system the Soviets deployed. The general view was that the United States should deploy any strategic system which worked well and which appeared to have the prospect of reducing damage if war should occur. The existence of these shared views made it difficult to put forward arguments within the bureaucracy against ABM deployment, and even more difficult to shape arguments which the President would consider to be effective with Congress and the public. Given this situation, the President had to be concerned with the domestic political effects—particularly on his prospects for re-election in 1968—if he appeared to be opening an ABM gap, failing to match the Soviet system, and giving up American nuclear superiority.

The organizational procedures of the Pentagon also tended to be biased toward a decision to deploy. Research, both in the Army and in the Advanced Research Projects Agency, was dominated by scientists who believed that any feasible system should be deployed. Moreover, the focus tended to be on the greatest conceivable threat, and hence on designing a system against a large Soviet attack. In addition, the desire to make an effective case for deployment led to underestimates of cost and overestimates of feasibility.

McNamara seemed to recognize that, because of the constraints within the system, success was unlikely. Thus his effort had to be directed as much toward changing the long-standing strategic nuclear biases as toward devising a delaying action against deployment. Although he lost the short-run battle to prevent deployment or to deploy a system that could not grow into a large anti-Soviet system, his efforts to change the terms of the debate within the bureaucracy, with Congress, and with the public were considerably more successful.

By 1969 President Nixon had accepted nuclear sufficiency rather than superiority as the American goal. He had also embraced, as his own, McNamara's arguments against an anti-Soviet system. He announced that the United States had no intention of deploying such a system, not only because it was technically infeasible, but also because such a system would threaten the Soviet deterrent. While he proceeded with a system that was deployed against China and in defense of Minuteman sites, Nixon directed that it be designed so that it could not grow—nor appear to the Soviets that it could grow—into a large anti-Russian system. In part as a result of the arguments McNamara had made in his speech announcing the deployment, as well as his posture statements, the attitude of the Senate changed dramatically on this range of issues.

Perhaps the most successful conversion was that of the Russians. Kosygin had argued at Glassboro that ABMs were purely defensive weapons and that the American effort to prevent their deployment was immoral. However, by 1971 the Russians were pressing for an agreement at the strategic arms talks simply to limit ABMs. The fact that the talks were under way at all can be attributed to McNamara's efforts to prevent an ABM deployment.

Changes in the rules of the game and in the shared images of the bureaucracy, Congress, and the public have altered the biases of the system. However, the actions of the Nixon Administration can be explained only by considering the new set of players and their interests. It is a new tale, but one not unaffected by this one.

NEGATIVE MARGINAL RETURNS IN WEAPONS ACQUISITION

JACK N. MERRITT AND PIERRE M. SPREY

This article examines one of the central issues facing defense policymakers today—weapons acquisition. Its thrust is different from the previous articles because the authors' primary purpose is not to describe, explain, or predict policy; it is to advocate a solution to the problem of the increasing unit-cost of weapons. Using empirical data, the authors analyze the "quantity" versus "quality" debate and come down on the side of quantity— with reservations. They recommend changes in the DOD budgeting system, congressional appropriations, and a renewed emphasis on three critical areas—weapons simplification, tactics, and training. Colonel Merritt (USA) has a M.B.A. from George Washington University and has served as a battalion commander in Vietnam, on the Army General Staff, and in OSD Systems Analysis. At the time this article was written he was Deputy Director of Program Analysis, National Security Council Staff. Pierre Sprey holds a B.E. in mechanical engineering and a M.S. in statistics. He was an analyst in OSD Systems Analysis from 1965 to 1970 and is currently Manager of the Systems Division of Enviro Control, Inc.

Over the last fifteen years, increasing emphasis has been placed on the "management" of the Department of Defense. While the management problem encompasses a broad range of issues, many, if not all, are subordinate to the major issues surrounding weapons acquisition. These decisions on weapons systems influence the structure of our forces, their specific mission capabilities, and future manpower levels for the services. In a broad sense these decisions determine the kind of armed forces we will have.

With the introduction of the systems analysis theology in weapons acquisition, it became fashionable to pose weapons acquisition decisions in terms of the trade-off between *quality* and *quantity* in weapon hardware. The analysts, the cost-cutters, and a minority group of military tacticians have argued strongly, and often on false premises, for the *quantity* side of the debate; by and large, the majority of senior officers and R&D officials have argued that neither the threat technology nor the dominant importance of saving American lives permits any compromise with *quality*. Needless to say, the latter approach has enjoyed considerable success on Capitol Hill for the last twenty or thirty years. The analytical side of the *quality* argument has been shored up by the popular belief and the economist's dogma that, if you pay more, you must be getting at least a little more capability.

It is on this axiomatic cornerstone that the whole *quantity* versus *quality* issue founders. If, in the real world, you get less capability (or performance or effectiveness) when you pay more, then the whole debate will have missed the mark entirely. Unfortunately, it is becoming clear that there are very few weapons indeed for which we can relate technical configuration to actual combat usefulness in any credible quantitative way—neither field experimentation nor a combat data base exists to tell us the real value of low profile in a tank, high speed in a submarine, or maneuverability in a fighter.

This is an original article written for this book and the Inter-Service Conference on Defense Policy held at the Air Force Academy, May 10–12, 1972. The views are those of the authors only and do not represent the official policies of the Department of Defense or the United States government.

And, at the same time, despite the nearly infinite number of war-gaming models and simulations, we know very little about the effect of increasing numbers or force ratio on the outcomes of battles or wars. All we can reliably say in this area is that the most fashionable models and war games (i.e., the Lanchesterian or "concentration of firepower" models) consistently overestimate the effect of force ratio.

The original Lanchester formulation consists of a pair of differential equations that describe the rate of attrition for each side during a battle. Lanchester actually posed three alternative hypotheses as follows: (1) the attrition rate (e.g., force units lost per hour or day) for a side throughout a battle is constant (linear law). (2) The attrition rate for a side is a constant percentage of the surviving strength for *that* side, regardless of the opposing strength (logarithmic law). (3) The attrition rate for a side, regardless of its size, is a constant multiplied by the surviving strength of the *other* side (square law or "concentration of firepower" effect).

The last of these, the square law, is the only one widely used (as is, or modified) in modeling today.[1]

Despite the fact that there are a number of implausible assumptions in such a model (e.g., only attrition determines battle outcome and losses inflicted per force unit are completely independent of the size of the target force), the Lanchester square law and its myriad computerized offspring are the only widely used tools for analyses of the benefits of larger force levels. The much simpler (and in our opinion more scientifically reputable) tool of direct empirical plots of historical win-loss results has been almost totally ignored, even though almost every published historical analysis[2] has

shown the Lanchesterian predictions to be inconsistent with actual battle outcomes—always in the direction of markedly overestimating the certainty of battle outcomes and the effect of force ratio. We will return to the evidence and reasons for this perverse behavior of history after discussing the cost side of the *quantity* versus *quality* issue.

It is certainly useful to review the historical cost trends that correspond to the allegedly great increases in individual weapon "quality" since World War II. Figures 1–3 show the trends in constant dollars for three major systems: the tank, the air-to-air munition, and the fighter. Several interesting points can be observed. First of all, the tank and the fighter cost about the same in World War II—about $100,000 (FY 1970 dollars).[3] The cost of the tank in constant dollars has increased by about a factor of 10 since then (if we count the ill-fated MBT-70 as the most modern example of the technology trend in tanks); the cost of the fighter has increased by a factor of 100.[4] Note that we have no direct evidence on the increase in effectiveness of either weapon over the same time period, though it is unlikely that anyone seriously believes that tanks are 10 times better than they were or that fighter aircraft are 100 times as lethal as they used to be. Looking at indirect evidence, the Israeli armored forces made extensive use of an up-gunned World War II M-3 tank in 1967 and achieved decisive victories over the technically dominant T-54 and T-55.[5] Similarly, the pre-Korea prop-driven A-1 Skyraider has demonstrated vastly

---

Theory, Munich, Germany, July 3–7, 1967; H. K. Weiss, "Systems Analysis Problems of Limited War," *Annals of Reliability and Maintainability*, 5 (July 1966); and D. Willard, RAC Technical Paper no. 74, November 1962.

[3] See U.S. Congress, Senate, Committee on Armed Services, *Weapons System Acquisition Process*, Hearings, 92nd Cong., 1st sess., December 3, 6, 7, 8, 9, 1971, pp. 239–89.

[4] As an aside, this certainly has some relevance to the issue of whether it is more attractive to chase tanks with aircraft today than it was in World War II.

[5] As everyone knows, these victories are really based on the great advantage in skill and training of Israeli tank crews; what is normally overlooked is the fact that we have the option of spending as large a percentage of our defense budget on crew selection and training as the Israelis do. There is some evidence and a great deal of experience to support the hypothesis that the skill and combat training level of personnel has a much greater effect on combat outcomes than any normal differences in weapons hardware; this will be discussed later in the present article.

---

[1] The square law is expressed as follows:

$$\frac{d\,x(t)}{dt} = -K_y\,y(t)$$

$$\frac{d\,y(t)}{dt} = -K_x\,x(t)$$

where $x(t)$ and $y(t)$ = the surviving force units for each side as a function of time, and K_y and K_x = the attrition rate per surviving force unit inflicted on the other side; the constants are normally computed from manipulations of firepower "indices."

[2] E.g., Robert L. Helmbold, "Some Observations on Validating Combat Models," paper read at the NATO Conference on Recent Developments in Lanchester

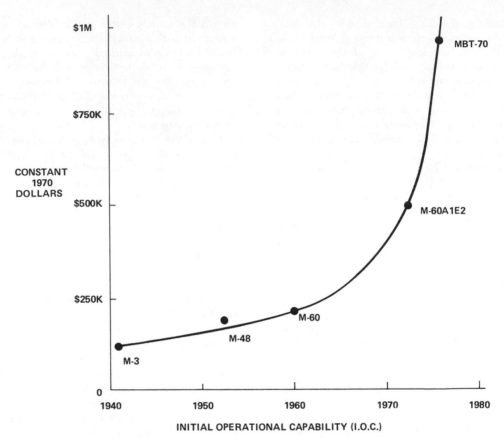

Figure 1
Symptom: Cost of the Tank

more utility in the close support role in Southeast Asia (SEA) than modern $3.5 million F-4 Phantoms, F-105 Thunderchiefs, or A-7 Corsair IIs, according to the documented preferences of forward air controllers, pilot after-action reports, and numerous articles in the open literature.

In Figure 2 we have one of the few direct measurements of combat effectiveness available in the weapons business—namely, the number of kills per trigger squeeze for air-to-air munitions using Korean and SEA combat data.[6] It can be seen that as we proceeded from guns to AIM-9 Sidewinder infrared missiles to AIM-7 Sparrow radar missiles, we reduced our lethality per firing attempt by half with each development. Combining cost and

kills, munitions cost per air-to-air kill has gone up by a factor of 8,000 since the Korean War.

One other interesting insight gained from this set of figures is the difference in institutional response to technology on the part of the Army as opposed to the air components of the Navy and Air Force. Note that the aircraft and aircraft munitions cost curves start to accelerate seriously in the mid-fifties, while the tank cost trend does not turn strongly upward until some ten years later.

The tank, the air-to-air munition, and the fighter are not isolated examples; the steepness of the cost trends given here can be reproduced in almost every major weapons area from infantry anti-tank weapons through bombers, submarines, and destroyers. Unfortunately, credible trends in combat effectiveness corresponding to the cost trends for these weapons are generally unavailable because of the lack of field-effectiveness testing.

[6] The Korean kill data are taken from the Institute of Air Warfare's excellent series of analyses of all reported air-to-air engagements from 1950 to 1953; the SEA data are from the Institute for Defense Analysis RED BARON series.

It is possible, however, to get data on the reliability of new systems, which, in almost every case, has declined precipitously. For instance, destroyers fifteen years old and older experience one-fifth as many major combat systems failures as destroyers less than five years old do (despite the traditional annual testimony on the decrepit condition of the superannuated destroyer fleet).[7]

Perhaps the most interesting aspect of analyzing cost-trend acceleration (or, more accurately, cost-trend explosion) is estimating the potential performance and cost of austere alternatives to the complex weapons we have actually developed and deployed. One area in which these alternatives have been extensively studied is the fighter area. Here, detailed de-

sign studies[8] have been performed showing that small, lightweight fighters ranging from 15,000 to 25,000 pounds can be built for from one-third to one-sixth the investment and operating cost of current development fighters (of 40,000–55,000 pound size) and with more than double the maneuvering and accelerating performance of the last generation of fighters —an unprecedented leap forward in combat performance. These advantages have been obtained not by technological break-throughs in aerodynamics, structures, and propulsion but simply by carefully eliminating "nice-to-have" features in equipment, avionics, and specifications wherever these features were not demonstrably related to combat effectiveness in the visual air battle. In this particular case, the austere alternative design studies were ex-

[7] We recognize that there is a maintenance "learning" period with new systems, but this period is normally considerably less than five years. Moreover, the severity of a "learning" period reflects inadequate operational testing.

[8] P. M. Sprey, "Austere, Low-Cost, High-Performance Alternatives: The F-XX and the VF-XX," Staff Study, Office of the Assistant Secretary of Defense (Systems Analysis), 1969 (secret).

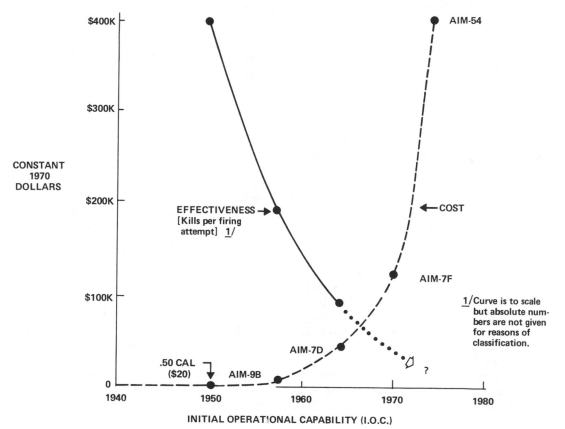

Figure 2
Symptom: Cost of the Air-to-Air Munition

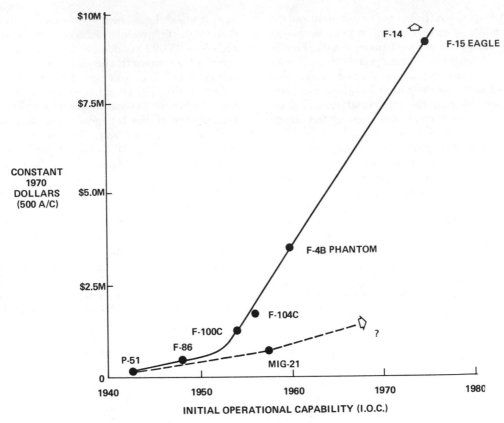

Figure 3
Symptom: Cost of the Fighter

tended and improved upon by the USAF and have actually culminated in at least a funded prototype program (i.e., the Lightweight Fighter Program) that confirms the possibility of spectacular advances in performance at low cost and without relying on technological breakthroughs.

Similar savings of factors of from three to ten are available in the great majority of tactical weapons systems when emphasis is placed on minimum complexity for achieving a single, well-defined combat mission capability. In all cases, these austere alternatives will achieve greatly improved reliability; in many cases, significantly improved performance and combat effectiveness also will result.

Without going into the design and performance details of austere bombers, austere submarines, austere carriers, or austere tactical missiles, it is clear that at current budgetary levels such systems offer the possibility of very significant increases over current force levels

and probably even greater increases in the combat capability of U.S. forces. Unfortunately, it seems equally clear that most incentives in the acquisition process are operating in such a way as to hinder the exploration, much less the development, of such austere alternative weapons concepts—despite the marked emphasis on low cost in recent public statements by senior Defense officials. Without proceeding into a full investigation of these motivational obstacles, it can be said that the primary hindrance in applying traditional military cost consciousness in weapons development is the Department of Defense budgetary process and the incremental line-item budgetary system practiced by Congress itself. From the point of view of any of today's services, it appears that proposing new, massive, complex, and poorly understood weapons acquisition programs is a relatively successful way of increasing the annual service budget (both in terms of immediate R&D-procurement and with a view toward subsequent Operations and Maintenance [O&M] and personnel), albeit often at the expense of another service. On the other hand, the service that proposes an austere, simple, low-cost weapon to replace one twice as expensive is likely to receive no commensurate force increase—it faces the prospect of one-for-one replacement and a cut in budget.[9]

Under these circumstances, our almost unbelievable weapons cost increases since World War II can be seen as rational institutional responses to the type of management imposed by the executive and legislative branches. On the other hand, it means that the prospects for better, more usable weapons and more adequate force levels are dim until the current system of budgeting and requirements-determination is significantly changed.

What, then, of the *quantity* versus *quality* issue—does the foregoing clearly argue that "more is better"? If the reader insists on real combat or field test measurements of effectiveness that could pass the test of serious scientific scrutiny, we must admit that there is no way of knowing. If, on the other hand, the reader is willing to accept such evidence as competent engineering analyses from outside the R&D community, the incomplete historical combat data available, and the combat experience of professionals other than technologists, the answer is almost certainly "yes." If our more complex, newer weapon systems have demonstrated little proven relevance to success in combat, but serious deficiencies in reliability and countermeasures-susceptibility, then larger numbers of simpler, *testable* systems of demonstrated reliability, with fewer demands on supporting troops, are likely to prove more useful. But, even here, we should be cautious because it is easy to overestimate the value of more forces.

As noted earlier, historical samples of combat are remarkably non-Lanchesterian. That is, historically, battle outcomes are relatively insensitive to the prevailing force ratios, despite the fact that almost all currently used predictive models show great sensitivity to force ratios—i.e., 2:1 or 3:1 superiority practically guarantees success according to these models.

Figure 4 shows a comparison of the empirical variation of battle outcomes according to the usual theoretical square-law type of prediction. Note that the Lanchesterian prediction (which behaves quite similarly to most of the more recent computerized battle models) does not even come close to reproducing the historical trend. Even more interesting is the fact that the historical numbers demonstrate that even an overwhelming force-ratio advantage such as 5:1 is far from a guarantee of victory (as an aside, think of the economic impossibility of our buying enough forces to achieve a 5:1 superiority in Central Europe).

Further analysis of the historical data quickly illuminates why additional forces add so little to the probability of victory. Whereas simple intuitive thinking (as well as most battle models since Lanchester) assumes that the relative kill effectiveness per force unit for both sides is a constant which depends on weapons characteristics (as expressed through the well-known but unverifiable firepower indices), historical data for infantry, armor, and air show consistently that, *the more outnumbered a force is, the better its exchange ratio will be.* Needless to say, the fact that increasing force inferiority increases relative kills per force unit does *not* mean that smaller forces win more often. It simply means that there is no "concentration of firepower" effect and that small forces can extract a favorable enough exchange ratio to make victory highly uncertain for large forces. How powerful this effect can be is seen in the historical loss data of Figure 5, which show that doubling the superior force improves the inferior force's exchange ratio by at least *four*, on the average. This should make it clear why large forces cannot be certain of defeating small forces.

In sum, there are no simple force-structure answers as to how to "win the war." Unfortunately, we often fail to consider some of the most important alternatives available for achieving this goal.

---

[9] In fairness, the Department of Defense has tried to move away from the McNamara system of force ceilings (as opposed to budgetary ceilings) toward a system which gives the services an annual budgetary goal and some freedom to plan within that goal. However, it appears that the services do not yet perceive that they are being offered the opportunity for realistic equal-cost force trades. The fact that there have been severe pressures on the budget since 1968 makes them even more certain that reducing force unit costs will result in further cuts in the budget rather than in increased force levels. Moreover, the proper line between giving adequate guidance to insure reasonable integration of Defense programs and allowing appropriate service autonomy is not easy to determine.

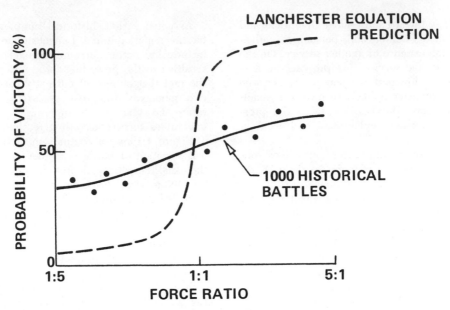

Figure 4
(From D. Willard, Research Analysis Corporation, Technical Paper no. 74, November 1972)

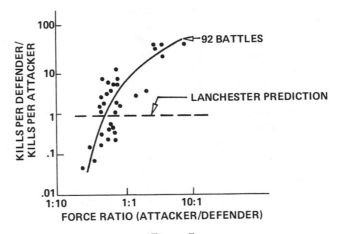

Figure 5
(From Robert L. Helmbold, paper presented at the NATO Conference on Recent Developments in Lanchester Theory, July 3–7, 1967)

Given the fact that battle outcomes are quite insensitive to force ratio, we must look elsewhere for the important factors within our control that can, in fact, significantly influence combat outcomes. The available historical evidence indicates that, short of huge force disparities, the dominant aspects of combat capability are training and tactics. Serious and detailed historical investigations of individual air and ground actions almost invariably point to the conclusion that sound training, well-considered tactics, and individual competence overwhelm most other aspects of the battle. While quantitative evidence in this area is scanty (due mostly to lack of emphasis), some examples are discussed below.

1. A remarkably innovative analysis of pilot ability has been published by H. K. Weiss.[10] Using data from both World War I and World War II, Weiss plotted the probability of being killed versus the number of *decisive* combats experienced by a pilot and showed that after

10 Weiss, *op. cit.*

the first five decisive encounters a pilot's chance of surviving the next has improved by a factor of *twenty*. This means that the less capable and less well trained are quickly lost, and that rigorous pilot selection and training can have an extraordinarily high payoff. (This finding is reinforced by the fact that a very small number of men dominate the air-to-air results of an entire war: a simple check by the authors showed that 4 percent of the pilots have contributed about 40 percent of the total kills in every war since World War I.) By an elegant application of moment-generating functions, Weiss derives the distribution of pilot skill for these populations of World War I and World War II pilots on the assumption that skill does not change much in five combats. He concludes that *there are almost no average air-to-air pilots* (i.e., the distribution of ability is ∪-shaped rather than bell-shaped), and that only 15 percent of the pilots have a better-than-even chance of surviving a decisive combat. In other words, very few pilots are good at air-to-air combat, and they tend to run up high scores, almost exclusively at the expense of the large number of pilots on the opposing side who have low skills. The implications are clear: with intensive pilot training and selection, an air force could develop a pilot group capable of sustaining 5:1 or 10:1 exchange ratios against any air force that simply produces pilots on a standardized production line curriculum.

2. In the Army's brilliant 1965 Fort Ord Combat Development Command field experiments, which compared squads equipped with M-14, M-16, and AK-47 rifles, the differences among the rifles were swamped by the differences among squads. Although the M-16 showed up to 50 percent superiority over the M-14, depending on the measure of effectiveness, individual squads showed differences of from 50 to 300 percent.[11] Careful review by the observers revealed that individual, highly skilled riflemen were improving the results for their entire squads. If true, these findings would make it possible to double the rifle effectiveness of the Army by placing one of these individuals in every rifle squad.

3. For tactics, the experience is equally compelling. For example, in small-unit tank engagements (historically notorious for being independent of force ratios *or* equipment characteristics), the large range of tactical advantages accruing to the side that is in a position to fire the first round is dominant. Figure 6, which is taken from an unpublished staff study (based on approximately 300 World War II platoon-to-company-size armor engagements in France), shows the importance of first-round tactical position. It can be seen that an attacking unit outnumbered 2:1, but firing first, will do considerably better than an attacker with 5:1 superiority, but firing second.

(Advocates of the "quality" side of the argument frequently use the importance of first-round kills—as opposed to first-round tactics—to support a variety of devices—e.g., laser range finders, shoot-on-the-move, guided mis-

[11] *Small Arms Weapons Systems*, Combat Development Command Experimentation Command (CDCEC), 65-4, May 1966.

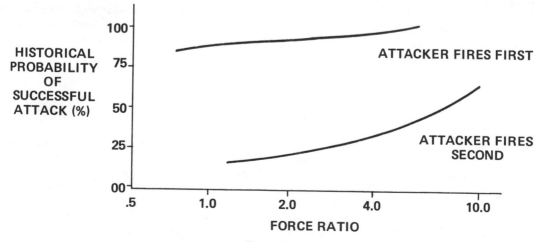

Figure 6

siles, and so on. Unfortunately, these devices have not *proven* to be technological substitutes for sound tactical judgment; even worse, because of their expense, they exact severe opportunity costs in force size and in tactical training.)

CONCLUSION

The search for *quality*—for the "technological threshold"—has dominated U.S. force posture for at least a dozen years. This is not surprising, since the acquisition system provides many incentives for taking this route. And, of course, the general faith in technology and in getting more when you pay more has contributed to this emphasis.

The McNamara era greatly accelerated the unfortunate DOD management tendency to control force quantities while exercising little control over the *quality and cost* aspects of requirements. The services were (and are) unlikely to act against self-interest by emphasizing austere weapons, tactics, and training, because (1) in practice, most budgeting is incremental; (2) while there may be an implied ceiling on the Defense budget, there are no really fixed service ceilings; (3) any major hardware program which is actually "sold" is perceived to be either an add-on or a decision made at the expense of another service; and (4) any service which considers developing a cheaper tank, ship, or airplane must face the possibility that it is proposing a decrement to its budget and consequently to its overall manpower, influence, and the like.

If DOD and Congress could agree to give budgetary allocations (based on rational objectives) to the services and insure the inviolability of these grants, there might be incentives to get more with less. However, line-item budgets and decisions on specific systems are a source of power. Offering "equal-cost trades" to the services to provide incentives for more rational decisions is a major change in the philosophy of defense management in both DOD and Congress.

As a consequence, we continue to have systems which are at the same time less capable and more expensive than their predecessors. Test programs do not identify problems, because there are no budgetary incentives for identifying failures; on the contrary, major program failures identified through testing result

in budgetary decreases due to program cancellations. Thus, operational testing is oriented toward learning to live with problems rather than toward determining operational suitability versus unsuitability.

The unfortunate result is that effects are compounded. Not only do new systems *not* give us true qualitative advantage, but they impact adversely on quantity and even more on the tactics and training that our historical analysis shows to be so central to "winning the war." The list of adverse effects of *quality* weapons systems on our tactics and training is almost endless; a few examples follow:

1. The high cost of new systems inevitably produces a plethora of "safety" rules which inhibit essential *realistic* training, for the loss or damage of a unit of equipment is prohibitively expensive.

2. The very high cost per operational hour limits the amount of training time because peacetime pressures are always in the direction of cutting O&M budgets to pay for procurement.

3. The net availability of manpower is sharply reduced by the complexity of the equipment, which requires more time in technical schools *and* more manpower in maintenance, particularly for the high skill levels, where we have the greatest shortages.

4. More people are required throughout the entire supporting structure, thus decreasing our already low ratio of combat manpower to logistics personnel (the "tooth-to-tail" ratio).

5. Training is further drastically curtailed by the much greater cost of associated munitions, particularly guided weapons (many pilots and soldiers are already familiar with the problems of being allowed less than one live firing of their principal weapon per year).

In summary, we resolve the argument between *quality* and *quantity* on the side of *quantity*—with reservations. Given the opportunity for an equal-cost trade-off between a new piece of equipment representing a "breakthrough in sophistication" and just a "better," simpler item, we would take the "better"—and *more* of them and with *more* training. Furthermore, we believe that an increasing number of military professionals are coming to agree with this point of view.

This raises a key question: Is it in fact possible to modify the adverse effects of incremental budgeting? The reluctance of Congress to relinquish line-item review authority is natural, and, indeed, this authority is important to Congress in fulfilling its proper role. However, there may be practical solutions which preserve congressional prerogatives while greatly enhancing the possibility of realistic, equal-cost force trade-offs within the Department of Defense. The following sketch of a legislative procedure is an approach which might be feasible and which would ameliorate the perverse incentives fostered by our current budgetary process.

1. The budgetary cycle could begin with DOD's submission to Congress of budgetary totals for each service (or, even better, major-mission category totals within each service). The Armed Services committees would consider and make recommendations on these totals. These recommendations would then be voted on by both houses of Congress and established as binding appropriation totals. This step would precede any consideration of line items and would be based on considerations of the overall need for, and relative weaknesses in, the various military missions, *in the context of national foreign policy.* Admittedly, translating foreign policy into service totals is not a simple task—nor can it be done precisely. In fact, it is not clear that elegant quantitative techniques are of much use in addressing such large issues. Allowing these decisions to be settled explicitly by the competing demands for the federal dollar, comparisons with last year's budget, and presidential and congressional judgment may not be as intellectually satisfying as analytical "optimization" of force levels. On the other hand, the resulting defense posture is more likely to reflect our broad policy objectives.

2. Given the agreed-upon totals, the Armed Services committees would then review the individual line items of the budget, changing only one current procedure—namely, that any addition or reduction to a given line item would be accompanied by equal dollar decreases or increases in other line items within the same total.

Some approach of this type would have a profound effect in changing the motivations of the services. It would greatly reduce the attractiveness of proposing high-risk, massive new programs; at the same time, it would provide an equitable framework for serious trade-offs between *quantity* and *quality* that would eliminate the possibility of low-cost weapons proposals leading to budgetary cuts.

However, reversing the trend of the last twenty years—that toward progressively increasing weapons complexity and cost—will be a slow process. Like other large organizations, military services in peacetime tend to reward those who enhance the organization—i.e., those who contribute to expanding its budget and manpower. Even if Congress and the executive branch could decide partially to relinquish the power of line-item incremental budgeting, traditional service perceptions, reinforced by declining budgets, will continue to militate against simpler, lower-cost weapons for fear of attendant budgetary losses.

It is unlikely that dramatic changes will come about. But more people in Congress, the executive, and the uniformed services are beginning to recognize the problem. We hope that they will be able to reverse our seemingly inexorable trend toward costlier weapons and decreased military capability—i.e., our unwitting progress toward unilateral disarmament at an ever-increasing cost.

BIBLIOGRAPHY: PART III

Armacost, Michael H. *The Politics of Weapons Innovation: The Thor-Jupiter Controversy.* New York: Columbia University Press, 1969. 304 pp.

This is an excellent account of research and development "prototyping" in the pre-McNamara era. It shows how the political process can affect weapons acquisition programs. In studying the impact which interservice rivalry had on the development, production, and deployment of the intermediate-range ballistic missile, Armacost focuses on the lobbying activities of the competing services and their industrial contractors.

Art, Robert J. *The TFX Decision: McNamara and the Military.* Boston: Little, Brown & Co., 1968. 202 pp. Cloth and paper.

This case study provides both a narrative and an analysis of two of McNamara's controversial decisions on the TFX: (1) to develop the TFX to meet both Navy and Air Force requirements; and (2) to award the contract to General Dynamics Corporation. Different institutional roles and analytical approaches are given as the reasons why the civilian leaders were united in overriding the unanimous advice of the top military leaders on these decisions.

Clark, Keith C., and Legere, Laurence J. *The President and the Management of National Security.* New York: Frederick A. Praeger, 1969. 274 pp.

Clark and Legere provide an overview of the National Security Council, State Department, and Defense Department and of their roles in the formulation of national security policy. They set forth major issues and problems that are encountered in the management of the policymaking structure from the single perspective of the presidency.

Davis, Vincent. *The Admirals Lobby.* Chapel Hill: University of North Carolina Press, 1967. 329 pp.

This is the definitive work on the role played by naval officers in politics and policymaking from the late 1800s to the present. Davis' primary conclusion is that the officer corps of each of the military services is a distinctive political subculture. Thus, subculture differences often explain both interservice differences and political activity. Davis identifies the factors which reduced the naval officer corps' traditional aversion to politics and moved it to participate both indirectly and directly in the political process. Two of these factors were increased organizational centralization and the argument that aircraft (and later missiles) had rendered surface fleets obsolete. The Navy's response to these two threats explains much about interservice relationships and Navy-OSD controversies.

Enthoven, Alain C., and Smith, K. Wayne. *How Much is Enough? Shaping the Defense Program, 1961–1969.* New York: Harper & Row, 1971. 337 pp.

This study makes a major contribution to an understanding of the controversial issues of defense management: centralization, roles and missions, weapons acquisition, and the role of analysis. As leaders of the Systems Analysis Office under Secretary McNamara, the authors make an impressive case for McNamara's style of management. The work is not, however, a detailed "insider's history" of the McNamara years. It *does* provide the Systems Analysis perspective on such policy issues as NATO, nuclear strategy, the B-70 bomber, Skybolt, the TFX/F-111, and Vietnam. Its major limitation is its relative neglect of arguments on the other side of these controversial issues and a tendency toward overstatement.

Hammond, Paul Y. *Organizing for Defense: The American Military Establishment in the Twentieth Century.* Princeton: Princeton University Press, 1961. 403 pp.

Hammond examines the formal administrative structure in a historical perspective. He deals with the experience of War and Navy Department administration from 1900 until 1960, and Defense Department administration from 1947 until 1960. Emphasis is placed on the organizational changes which evolved to meet the demands of modern warfare and how these changes occurred within the context of the entire American governmental structure.

———. *Super Carriers and B-36 Bombers: Appropriations, Strategy, and Politics.* Inter-University Case Program, no. 97. Indianapolis: Bobbs-Merrill Co., Inc., 1963. 101 pp.

Hammond examines the Air Force–Navy rivalry in 1949 and 1950 as a controversy over roles and missions. He shows the rivalry over budget, strategy, and defense organization. He also analyzes the role Congress played through congressional hearings.

Hitch, Charles J., and McKean, Roland N. *The Economics of Defense in the Nuclear Age.* New York: Atheneum, 1965. 405 pp. Cloth and paper.

Originally published as a RAND Corporation study in 1960, this is the classic and extremely influential blueprint for revolutionizing defense decisionmaking that one of the authors, Dr. Hitch, had a large part in implementing when Robert McNamara became Secretary of Defense. It anticipates and explicitly deals with many of the problems and criticisms that arose when cost-benefit analysis was applied in McNamara's time and since. It remains perhaps the most lucid statement of the application of economic reasoning to defense problems.

Huntington, Samuel P. *The Common Defense: Strategic Programs in National Politics.* New York: Columbia University Press, 1961. 500 pp.

Strategic programs are viewed as responses of the government to conflicting pressures from the foreign and domestic environments. Huntington treats congressional and executive involvement in strategic policy decisions and the politics of the budgetary process.

Kolodziej, Edward A. *The Uncommon Defense and Congress, 1945–1963.* Columbus: Ohio State University Press, 1966. 630 pp.

Kolodziej investigates Congress' use of the power of the purse to influence military force levels, weapons systems, and strategic policy between 1945 and 1963. He provides an extremely detailed, well-documented account of Congress' role in defense policy during these years.

Millis, Walter, ed. *The Forrestal Diaries.* New York: The Viking Press, 1951. 581 pp.

This collection of personal files and papers provides insight into the activities and concerns of James Forrestal from 1944, shortly after his appointment as Secretary of the Navy, until 1949, when he resigned as Secretary of Defense. The authenticity of the collection makes it a valuable source of information about the "unification" debate and Forrestal's evolving conception of the role of the Secretary of Defense.

Neustadt, Richard E. *Alliance Politics.* New York: Columbia University Press, 1970. 167 pp.

Neustadt makes a major breakthrough in the use of a bureaucratic politics perspective to explain defense and foreign policy. He uses the 1956 Suez crisis and the 1962 American cancellation of the Skybolt missile to illustrate how the British and U.S. governments failed to perceive each other's positions. He cites differences in political accountability, operating procedures, lines of authority, and institutional perspectives as causes of misperception.

Paige, Glenn D. *The Korean Decision: June 24–30, 1950.* New York: Free Press, 1968. 375 pp. Cloth and paper.

Paige presents an important analytical framework for decisionmaking and explains the multitude of factors that influenced the U.S. decision to intervene in Korea. Its focus resembles Robert F. Kennedy's *Thirteen Days,* and its rigor is similar to Graham F. Allison's *Essence of Decision,* both of which are explanations of the Cuban missile crisis.

Rice, Berkeley. *The C-5A Scandal: An Inside Story of the Military-Industrial Complex.* Bos-

ton: Houghton Mifflin Co., 1971. 238 pp.

This is a useful, although biased, insight into the politics of weapons acquisition, specifically the C-5A cargo plane. In recounting the attempts to cover up cost overruns, Rice examines the interrelationships among contractors, Congress, and the military.

Ries, John C. *The Management of Defense: Organization and Control of the U.S. Armed Services.* Baltimore: The Johns Hopkins Press, 1964. 228 pp.

Ries provides a concise description of the formal defense organizational structure. He examines the proposed and actual organizational structure during World War II, the initial attempts to keep the Defense Department decentralized in the National Security Act of 1947, and the subsequent trend toward centralization in the reorganizations of 1949, 1953, and 1958. He is strongly critical of increased centralization in DOD.

Roherty, James M. *Decisions of Robert S. McNamara: A Study of the Role of the Secretary of Defense.* Coral Gables, Fla.: University of Miami Press, 1970. 223 pp.

Roherty provides a valuable comparative analysis of six Secretaries of Defense through 1968. His major contribution is theoretical, for he posits two distinctive role conceptions. He argues that Forrestal, Lovett, and Gates were "generalists"—that is, concerned mainly with overall policy and convinced that there was an integral relationship between military policy and national policy. On the other hand, Wilson and McElroy were "functionalists" who saw a sharp line between policy and administration and attempted to be management specialists. Roherty is critical of McNamara's attempt to fuse these two roles because of his alleged rejection of the political process, "which alone can be productive of policy."

Schilling, Warner R.; Hammond, Paul Y.; and Snyder, Glenn H. *Strategy, Politics, and Defense Budgets.* New York: Columbia University Press, 1962. 532 pp.

This first-rate compendium of three lengthy case studies demonstrates admirably both policymaking and the civil-military relationship. The Washington decisionmaking milieu is the focus of all three of these studies: "Fiscal 1950," "NSC-68," and "The 'New Look' of 1953." The themes of the studies include strategy, executive-congressional relations, interservice rivalry, and bureaucratic politics. The tension between domestic and national security priorities makes this book a particularly relevant one for the 1970s.

Part IV · The Military and American Society

Introduction

PERRY M. SMITH

A VIEW OF THE RELATIONSHIP BETWEEN THE MILITARY AND SOCIETY

The relationship of the military to society is important in all states and crucial in many. As experts in the techniques of violence with considerable control over the warmaking capabilities of a nation, military professionals have become—individually at the higher ranks, and collectively as a structured, bureaucratic organization—a force that national decision-makers must contend with constantly in the formulation of domestic and foreign policy.

The phrase "civil-military relations" is often used to describe the conflictual and consensual relationships between the military and society. However, this phrase is not wholly satisfactory, for it connotes to many the conflictual relationships alone. The phrase used more often in recent years is perhaps more appropriate and less confusing; it is "the military and society."

There are two basic ways of viewing the relationship between the military and society. These two typologies are useful conceptual starting points, though neither exists in pure form. The first typology focuses on the military as a separate and distinct subculture of society with its own norms and value structure to which all members must conform. The second typology suggests a military that is simply a microcosm of the greater society, a military that cannot create a lasting value system which is appreciably different from the value system of the greater society.

THE SIZE VARIABLE

One important variable that impacts on this relationship is the size of the military structure. If the number of men under arms and the budgetary impact of the military are large, the probability of having a military significantly isolated from society is minimal. Since 1950, the American military has been of such size (both in manpower and budget) that isolation has been impossible. In rough terms, 1 percent of the population and 5 percent of the Gross National Product are useful thresholds between a military that may, if its leaders and the national political leaders so choose, isolate itself to an appreciable degree and a military that cannot. A military of smaller dimensions than those described above, if it is able to obtain posts, stations, and bases of sufficient size and reasonable isolation from major urban areas, may be able to cause its soldiers and their dependents to live exclusively on base and to restrict (by regulation or by geographical isolation) the contacts between the military community and the larger society. Over a period of time, this isolation can become a way of life, with friendships, church affiliations, sports teams (both military and dependent), and social contacts being predominantly intramilitary. Inbreeding can occur, with sons of military men forming a large portion of the enlisted and officer ranks. With a small officer corps, the service academies can also provide a larger portion of the officer corps, which may exceed 50 percent of the annual input into the officer ranks. A similar situation developed in the 1920s and 1930s, but has not occurred since.

There are, however, many military professionals who would like to form a distinct subculture for the military and who would press hard for this course if military size diminished sufficiently. During the political campaign of 1972, George McGovern proposed a considerably reduced American military force with a budget of approximately $54 billion and less than two million men. If his proposal were to

become reality, a serious debate would probably take place within and without the military
concerning the isolation or nonisolation of the
military from the society.

THE MILITARY'S ATTITUDINAL
VARIABLE

Of course, size is not the only variable in
this equation. Attitudes are also important. By
no means do all military leaders wish to see the
military become a separate subculture, nor is
there any consensus on this issue among political leaders. A major underlying philosophical
and practical issue is the danger that an isolated military subculture presents to the government and value system of the society. Although much literature suggests that the
military is a reactionary influence in any
society, is authoritarian by nature, and, if given
a chance, would choose tyranny and stability
over democracy and confusion, there is little
historical data to substantiate the thesis that
the military profession is dangerous to the
American system of government. The analogy
of the *coup d'état* in Latin America or Africa
being readily transferable to the American or
Canadian (or for that matter to most West
European) political systems can be made persuasively in conceptual and theoretical terms,
but becomes much more difficult to substantiate in fact. The Douglas MacArthurs, Edwin
Walkers, and John Lavelles may be useful examples of individuals who chafed under the
restrictions of civilian controls, but each man
was handled rather easily by Truman, Kennedy,
and Nixon, respectively; what was claimed to
be a grave threat to our democracy turned out
to be an unfortunate aberration in a long tradition of unquestioning dedication of military
leaders to civilian supremacy.

THE SOCIETY'S ATTITUDES
TOWARD THE MILITARY

Societal attitudes toward the military are, of
course, important, if not crucial, in this relationship. After a century and a half of disdain
for the military (except in periods of war) by
most of society, a fundamental change occurred
in the late 1940s. The American society accepted a large military; it accepted administration leadership on proposed military budgets,
and it showed a greater acceptance of military
professionals than at any other peacetime
period. (See Russett's article in Chapter 10.)
This promilitary attitude, engendered by the
reasonably effective way in which the United
States military organized for and fought World
War II and by the fear of communist aggression, lasted until the late 1960s. The dislike
and distrust of the hierarchical quality of military life, coupled with a fear of the political
and economic power of high-ranking military
officers, have been parts of the American political culture for centuries. Although some residual promilitary feeling remains throughout
society, this basic antimilitarism has returned.
Antimilitarism was particularly evident among
the youth in the late 1960s and early 1970s;
however, there are some indications that amilitarism—that is, apathy toward the military and
all things connected with it—may be replacing
antimilitarism among the youth of this country.
Unfortunately, apathy is not a strong basis
upon which to build a positive civil-military
relationship. (See Rosser's article in Chapter 10.)

THE STUDY OF THE
MILITARY PROFESSION

If one is to understand the relationship of
the military to society, both the military and
the society should be studied separately. Subsequently, a study of this relationship should
be undertaken. In this way, the student can
fully understand the two cultures, their values,
and attitudes before he tries to understand how
they interact. Space limitations, together with
the assumption that most readers will have a
solid grasp of the American society, caused the
editors to decide not to include any specific
articles on the American society. However,
articles on the military profession are included
before discussion of the relationships of the
military and society. What is a military professional? What are his fundamental values? What
unique qualities allow him to fit the conceptual
category of professional? Huntington's short,
classic essay should be read in conjunction with
the superb critique of the Huntington analysis
by Bradford and Murphy.

The Huntington analysis is basically traditional, while the Bradford-Murphy piece is a
fusionist critique of the traditional approach. As

the boundaries between "military" and "civilian" have become blurred, Huntington's thesis about the separations of the military profession has become questionable.

From conceptualization about the military professional, the editors move to a sociological explanation and extrapolation of recent trends in the military profession. Charles Moskos represents a group of highly competent and prolific sociologists who compose the Inter-University Seminar on the Armed Forces and Society, which has, in recent years, made significant contributions to the understanding of this relationship. As he suggests, there may be a pluralistic "middle ground" between the traditional and fusionist positions toward which the military profession is moving in the aftermath of the long and traumatic Vietnam experience.

THE DILEMMA OF COMPETING VALUES

There is, inevitably, a competition among democratic values such as popular control, political equality, and individual liberty and national security values (some examples are the internment of Japanese-Americans during World War II, greater restrictions on dissent, and greater secrecy in times of national emergency or war) which is less a "how to control the military" problem and more a "how to allocate values" problem in a society interested in both preserving democratic values and providing for national security. As John Lovell has argued elsewhere, there may be agreement in goal values among certain individuals but fundamental disagreement on instrumental values. Therefore, two individuals may highly value political equality, with one favoring the all-volunteer military because of his belief that it is more equitable than the draft, and the other opposing the all-volunteer scheme because it will lead to greater inequities.

Another underlying question concerning the relationship between the military and society is what controls should be put on those civilians who control the military. Should the President and Secretary of Defense be more limited by Congress or the Supreme Court, or both, in what actions it can take in the national security field? A plethora of congressional amendments and resolutions were proposed to curtail the power of the President in the conduct of the

Vietnam War, and continued attempts to limit the power of the executive by Congress must be anticipated. Much empirical research remains to be done on a whole range of questions concerning the relationship between the national security establishment and society.

Case studies in civil-military relations often give useful insights into the basic dilemma of antithetical values held by national leaders. The Truman-MacArthur controversy remains a classic case of civil-military conflict at the highest leadership levels and has been included to demonstrate vividly the problems of civilian control of the military.

SOCIALIZATION OF THE MILITARY

The political socialization of the professional military officer is most relevant to studies of the military. Because socialization and education are inextricably related, the study of ROTC and Academy educations and their impact on military attitudes and ideas are the subjects of three articles in Chapter 9. Two of the articles are concerned with the largest source of military officers, ROTC. The third, by Charles Cochran, provides a fascinating study of service academy midshipmen and cadet profiles. The last article in Chapter 9 evaluates the entire professional educational system from pre-commissioning education to the War Colleges. The impact of these various educational institutions on the plans, policies, and attitudes of military leaders make this evaluation useful if one is to understand the various "minds" of the military.

THE RELATIONSHIP OF THE MILITARY TO SOCIETY

The editors chose to leave out articles on the American society and to begin Chapter 10 with a discussion of the relationship between the military and society. Those readers who feel that their background in the American societal milieu is weak should spend some time on articles or books such as Toffler's *Future Shock* (1970), Brzezinski's *Between Two Ages* (1970), and Ravel's *Neither Jesus nor Marx* (1971) prior to dealing with the articles in Chapter 10.

The military-industrial complex (MIC) looms large in the perceptions of many observers of the American political system. A great deal of rhetoric about the MIC is countered by thorough and objective discussions of the relationship between the military and industry (Kurth and Wolf). Public attitudes toward defense spending (Russett), the impact of social programs on military effectiveness (Brown), and the bureaucratic, corporate, and strategic imperatives in weapons procurement (Kurth) all are treated in an attempt to give a well-rounded view of the relationship between the military and society.

The impact of the military on society and the impact of society on the military are dealt with in all of the articles in Chapter 10. For instance, in the late 1940s, the 1950s, and the early 1960s, the military led the way in racial integration, and the experience of many blacks in integrated communities on posts and bases caused them to develop expectations of greater integration when they returned to society. Today the military's progressiveness in the area of racial harmony is under serious question. Despite twenty years of leadership in this area, the armed forces have failed to integrate their officer corps effectively. There has been greater racial strife within the military in the late 1960s and early 1970s than at any time in history. How the military is adapting to changing societal attitudes toward race is dealt with in the final chapter (Yarmolinsky).

A CRITIQUE OF PART IV

What, then, has been slighted in Part IV? There are no articles on professional socialization in the post-college or service academy experience. Lack of space precluded articles on the use of federal troops in domestic disorders; the American enlisted men; the social values of the American military; the system of military justice; and the military public relations networks.

Part IV is a comprehensive view of the relationship between the military and the American society. It addresses issues across the broad spectrum of that relationship. It not only should acquaint the reader with important issues but also should raise questions in his mind and cause him to look further into this vital relationship. Unless, or until, the millennium should come and the nation-state should fade from the international scene, national security will remain a basic concern of all nation-states. Although military forces are only a part of the national security equation, they are, and will be, present on the national scene of any nation-state that perceives threats to its national security. Each state must work out a relationship between the military and society which fits its political culture. This relationship is dynamic in the United States and is certainly worthy of a major portion of a book on American defense policy. Part IV attempts to open the door of inquiry; I believe the attempt has been successful. I commend the reader to further research and suggest the bibliography to Part IV as the next step in his scholarly inquiry.

CHAPTER 9

The Military as a
Socializing Institution

OFFICERSHIP AS A PROFESSION

SAMUEL P. HUNTINGTON

In what has become the classic essay on the military profession, Samuel Huntington defines professionalism in terms of expertise, responsibility, and corporateness and then uses these categories to further define the military profession. By excluding active duty enlisted men and women, reserves and national guard personnel, and certain specialists within the active duty officer corps, Huntington defines a military professional as someone who has the intellectual skills and professional responsibilities to carry out "the management of violence." This brilliant essay is a useful conceptual starting point in the study of the military profession and the relationship between that profession and the larger society. Samuel Huntington is Professor of Government at Harvard University. His interests are eclectic, varying from the military to problems of development. His more recent works include Authoritarian Politics in Modern Society: The Dynamics of Established One-Party Systems *(1970) and* Political Order in Changing Societies *(1968).*

PROFESSIONALISM AND THE MILITARY

The modern officer corps is a professional body and the modern military officer a professional man. This is, perhaps, the most fundamental thesis of this article. A profession is a peculiar type of functional group with highly specialized characteristics. Sculptors, stenographers, entrepreneurs, and advertising copywriters all have distinct functions, but no one of these functions is professional in nature. Professionalism is, however, characteristic of the modern officer, in the same sense in which it is characteristic of the physician or lawyer. Professionalism distinguishes the military officer of today from the warriors of previous ages. The existence of the officer corps as a professional body gives a unique cast to the modern problem of civil-military relations.

The nature and history of other professions as professions have been thoroughly discussed. Yet the professional character of the modern officer corps has been neglected. In our society, the businessman many command more income; the politician may command more power; but the professional man commands more respect. Yet the public, as well as the scholar, hardly conceives of the officer in the same way that it does the lawyer or doctor, and it certainly does not accord to the officer the deference which it gives to the civilian professionals. Even the military itself is influenced by its image in the public mind and at times has refused to accept the implications of its own professional status. When the term "professional" has been used in connection with the military, it normally has been in the sense of "professional" as contrasted with "amateur" rather than in the sense of "profession" as contrasted with "trade" or "craft." The phrases "professional army" and "professional soldier" have obscured the difference between the career enlisted man, who is professional in the sense of one who works for monetary gain, and the career officer, who is professional in the very different sense of one who pursues a "higher calling" in the service of society.

THE CONCEPT OF PROFESSION

The first step in analyzing the professional character of the modern officer corps is to define professionalism. The distinguishing characteristics of a profession as a special type of vocation are its expertise, responsibility, and corporateness.

EXPERTISE

The professional man is an expert with specialized knowledge and skill in a significant field of human endeavor. His expertise is acquired only by prolonged education and experience. It is the basis of objective standards of professional competence for separating the profession from laymen and for measuring the relative competence of members of the profession. Such standards are universal. They inhere in knowledge and skill and are capable of general application irrespective of time and place. The ordinary skill or craft exists only in the present and is mastered by learning an existing technique without reference to what has gone before. Professional knowledge, however, is intellectual in nature and capable of preservation in writing. Professional knowledge has a history, and some knowledge of that history is essential to professional competence. Institutions of research and education are required for the extension and transmission of professional knowledge and skill. Contact is maintained between the academic and practical sides of a profession through journals, conferences, and the circulation of personnel between practice and teaching.

Professional expertise also has a dimension in breadth which is lacking in the normal trade. It is a segment of the total cultural tradition of society. The professional man can successfully apply his skill only when he is aware of this broader tradition of which he is a part. Learned professions are "learned" simply because they are an integral part of the total body of learning of society. Consequently, professional education consists of two phases: the first imparts a broad, liberal, cultural background; the second imparts the specialized skills and knowledge of the profession. The liberal education of the professional man is normally handled by the general educational institutions of society devoted to this purpose. The second, or technical, phase of professional education, on the other hand, is given in special institutions operated by, or affiliated with, the profession itself.

RESPONSIBILITY

The professional man is a practicing expert, working in a social context, and performing a service, such as the promotion of health, education, or justice, which is essential to the functioning of society. The client of every profession is society, individually or collectively. A research chemist, for instance, is not a professional man, because the service he renders, while beneficial to society, is not essential to its immediate existence and functioning: only Du Pont and the Bureau of Standards have a direct and immediate interest in what he has to offer. The essential and general character of his service and his monopoly of his skill impose upon the professional man the responsibility to perform the service when required by society. This social responsibility distinguishes the professional man from other experts who possess only intellectual skills. The research chemist, for instance, is still a research chemist if he uses his skills in a manner harmful to society. But the professional man can no longer practice if he refuses to accept his social responsibility: a physician ceases to be a physician if he uses his skills for antisocial purposes. The responsibility to serve and devotion to his skill furnish the professional motive. Financial remuneration cannot be the primary aim of the professional man *qua* professional man. Consequently, professional compensation normally is only partly determined by bargaining on the open market and is regulated by professional custom and law.

The performance of an essential service not regulated by the normal expectation of financial rewards requires some statement that will govern the relations of the profession to the rest of society. Conflicts between the professional man and his clients, or among members of the profession, normally furnish the immediate impetus to the formulation of such a statement. The profession thus becomes a moral unit positing certain values and ideals which guide its members in their dealings with laymen. This guide may be a set of unwritten norms transmitted through the professional educational system or it may be codified into written canons of professional ethics.

CORPORATENESS

The members of a profession share a sense of organic unity and consciousness of themselves as a group apart from laymen. This collective sense has its origins in the lengthy discipline and training necessary for professional competence, the common bond of work, and the sharing of a unique social responsibility. The sense of unity manifests itself in a professional organization which formalizes and applies the standards of professional competence and establishes and enforces the standards of professional responsibility. Membership in the professional organization, along with the possession of special expertise and the acceptance of special responsibility, thus becomes a criterion of professional status and publicly distinguishes the professional man from the layman. The interest of the profession requires it to bar its members from capitalizing upon professional competence in areas where that competence has no relevance and likewise to protect itself against outsiders who would claim professional competence because of achievements or attributes in other fields. Professional organizations are generally either associations or bureaucracies. In the associational professions such as medicine and law, the practitioner typically functions independently and has a direct personal relationship with his client. The bureaucratic professions, such as the diplomatic service, possess a high degree of specialization of labor and responsibilities within the profession, and the profession as a whole renders a collective service to society as a whole. These two categories are not mutually exclusive: bureaucratic elements exist in most associational professions, and associations frequently supplement the formal structure of bureaucratic professions. The associational professions usually possess written codes of ethics, since each practitioner is individually confronted with the problem of proper conduct toward clients and colleagues. The bureaucratic professions, on the other hand, tend to develop a more general sense of collective professional responsibility and the proper role of the profession in society.

THE MILITARY PROFESSION

The vocation of officership meets the principal criteria of professionalism. In practice, no vocation, not even medicine or law, has all the characteristics of the ideal professional type. Officership probably falls somewhat farther short of the ideal than either of these. Yet its fundamental character as a profession is undeniable. In practice, officership is strongest and most effective when it most closely approaches the professional idea; it is weakest and most defective when it falls short of that ideal.

THE EXPERTISE OF OFFICERSHIP

What is the specialized expertise of the military officer? Is there any skill common to all military officers and yet not shared with any civilian groups? At first glance this hardly seems to be the case. The officer corps appears to contain many varieties of specialists, including large numbers which have their counterparts in civilian life. Engineers, doctors, pilots, ordnance experts, personnel experts, intelligence experts, communications experts—all these are found both within and without the modern officer corps. Even ignoring these technical specialists, each absorbed in his own branch of knowledge, just the broad division of the corps into land, sea, and air officers appears to create vast differences in the functions performed and the skills required. The captain of a cruiser and the commander of an infantry division appear to be faced with highly different problems requiring highly different abilities.

Yet a distinct sphere of military competence does exist which is common to all, or almost all, officers and which distinguishes them from all, or almost all, civilians. This central skill is perhaps best summed up in Harold Lasswell's phrase "the management of violence." The function of a military force is successful armed combat. The duties of the military officer include: (1) the organizing, equipping, and training of this force; (2) the planning of its activities; and (3) the direction of its operation in and out of combat. The direction, operation, and control of a human organization whose primary function is the application of violence is the peculiar skill of the officer. It is common to the activities of the air, land, and sea officers. It distinguishes the military officer *qua* military officer from the other specialists which exist in the modern armed services. The skills of these experts may be necessary to the achievement of the objectives of the military force. But they are basically auxiliary vocations, having the same relation to the expertise of the officer as the skills of the nurse, chemist, laboratory technician, dietician, pharmacist, and X-ray technician have to the expertise of the doctor. None of the auxiliary specialists contained within or serving the military profession is capable of the "management of violence," just as none of the specialists aiding the medical profession is capable of the diagnosis and treatment of illness. The essence of officership is embodied in the traditional admonition to Annapolis men that their duty will be to "fight the fleet." Individuals, such as doctors, who are not competent to manage violence but who are members of the officer corps are normally distinguished by special titles and insignia and are excluded from positions of military command. They belong to the officer corps in its capacity as an administrative organization of the state, but not in its capacity as a professional body.

Within the profession itself there are specialists in the management of violence on sea, on land, and in the air, just as there are heart, stomach, and eye specialists within medicine. A military specialist is an officer who is peculiarly expert at directing the application of violence under certain prescribed conditions. The variety of conditions under which violence may be employed and the different forms in which it may be applied form the basis for subprofessional specialization. They also form the basis for evaluating relative technical competence. The larger and more complex the organizations of violence which an officer is capable of directing, and the greater the number of situations and conditions under which he can be employed, the higher is his professional competence. A man who is capable of directing only the activities of an infantry squad has such a low level of professional ability as to be almost on the border line. A man who can manage the operations of an airborne division or a carrier task force is a highly competent professional. The officer who can direct the complex activities of a combined operation involving large-scale sea, air, and land forces is at the top of his vocation.

It is readily apparent that the military function requires a high order of expertise. No individual, whatever his inherent intellectual ability and qualities of character and leadership, could perform these functions efficiently without considerable training and experience. In emergencies an untrained civilian may be capable of acting as a military officer at a low level for a brief period of time, just as in emergencies the intelligent layman may fill in until the doctor arrives. Before the management of violence became the extremely complex task that it is in modern civilization, it was possible for someone without specialized training to practice officership. Now, however, only the person who completely devotes his working hours to this task can hope to develop a reasonable level of professional competence. The skill of the officer is neither a craft (which is primarily mechanical) nor an art (which requires unique and nontransferable talent). It is instead an extraordinarily complex intellectual skill requiring comprehensive study and training. It must be remembered that the peculiar skill of the officer is the management of violence, not the act of violence itself. Firing a rifle, for instance, is basically a mechanical craft; directing the operations of a rifle company requires an entirely different type of ability, which may in part be learned from books and in part from practice and experience. The intellectual content of the military profession requires the modern officer to devote about one-third of his professional life to formal schooling, probably a higher ratio of educational time to practice time than in any other profession. In part this reflects the limited opportunities of the officer to acquire practical experience in the most important elements of his vocation. But to a large degree it also reflects the extreme complexity of the military expertise.

The peculiar skill of the military officer is universal in the sense that its essence is not affected by changes in time or location. Just as the qualifications of a good surgeon are the same in Zurich as they are in New York, the same standards of professional military competence apply in Russia as in America, and in the nineteenth century as in the twentieth. The possession of a common professional skill is a bond among military officers which cuts across other differences. The vocation of the officer also possesses a history. The management of violence is not a skill which can be mastered simply by learning existing techniques. It is in a continuous process of development, and it is necessary for the officer to understand this development and to be aware of its main tendencies and trends. Only if he is aware of the historical development of the techniques of organizing and directing military forces can the officer expect to stay on top of his profession. The importance of the history of war and military affairs receives sustained emphasis throughout military writings and military education.

The military skill requires a broad background of general culture for its mastery. The methods of organizing and applying violence at any one stage in history are intimately related to the entire cultural pattern of society. Just as law at its borders merges into history, politics, economics, sociology, and psychology, so also does the military skill. Even more, military knowledge also has frontiers in the natural sciences of chemistry, physics, and biology. To understand his trade properly, the officer must have some idea of its relation to these other fields and of the ways in which these other areas of knowledge may contribute to his own purposes. In addition, he cannot really develop his analytical skill, insight, imagination, and judgment if he is trained simply in vocational duties. The abilities and habits of mind which he requires within his professional field can in large part be acquired only through the broader avenues of learning outside his profession. The fact that, like the lawyer and the physician, he is continuously dealing with human beings requires him to have the deeper understanding of human attitudes, motivations, and behavior which a liberal education stimulates. Just as a general education has become the prerequisite for entry into the professions of law and medicine, it is now also almost universally recognized as a desirable qualification for the professional officer.

The Responsibility of Officership

The expertise of the officer imposes upon him a special social responsibility. The employment of his expertise promiscuously for his own advantage would wreck the fabric of society. As with the practice of medicine, society insists that the management of violence be utilized only for socially approved purposes. Society has a direct, continuing, and general interest in the employment of this skill for the enhancement of its own military security. While all professions are to some extent regulated by the state, the military profession is monopolized by the state. The skill of the physician is diagnosis and treatment; his responsibility is the health of his clients. The skill of the officer is the management of violence; his responsibility is the military security of his client, society. The discharge of the responsibility requires mastery of the skill; mastery of the skill entails acceptance of the responsibility. Both responsibility and skill distinguish the officer from other social types. All members of society have an interest in its security; the state has a direct concern for the achievement of this along with other social values; but the officer corps alone is responsible for military security to the exclusion of all other ends.

Does the officer have a professional motivation? Clearly he does not act primarily from economic incentives. In Western society the vocation of officership is not well rewarded monetarily. Nor is the officer's behavior within his profession governed by economic rewards and punishments. The officer is not a mercenary who transfers his services wherever they are best rewarded, nor is he the temporary citizen-soldier inspired by intense momentary patriotism and duty but with no steadying and permanent desire to perfect himself in the management of violence. The motivations of the officer are a technical love for his craft and the sense of social obligation to utilize this craft for the benefit of society. The combination of these drives constitutes professional motivation. Society, on the other hand, can assure this motivation only if it offers its officers continuing and sufficient pay both while on active duty and when retired.

The officer possesses intellectualized skill, the mastery of which requires intense study. But, like the lawyer and doctor, he is not primarily a man of the closet; he deals continuously with people. The test of his professional ability is the application of technical knowledge in a human context. Since this application is not regulated by economic means, however, the officer requires positive guidelines that spell out his responsibilities to his fellow officers, his subordinates, his superiors, and the state which he serves. His behavior within the military structure is governed by a complex mass of regulations, customs, and traditions. His behavior in relation to society is guided by an awareness that his skill can be utilized only for purposes approved by society through its political agent, the state. While the primary responsibility of the physician is to his patient, and of the lawyer to his client, the principal responsibility of the military officer is to the state. His responsibility to the state is the responsibility of the expert adviser. Like the lawyer and physician, he is concerned with only one segment of the activities of his client. Consequently, he cannot impose decisions upon his client which have implications beyond his field of special competence. He can only explain to his client his needs in this area, advise him as to how to meet these needs, and then, when the client has made his decisions, aid him in implementing them. To some extent, the officer's behavior toward the state is guided by an explicit code expressed in law and comparable to the canons of professional ethics of the physician and lawyer. To a larger extent, the officer's code is expressed in custom, tradition, and the continuing spirit of the profession.

THE CORPORATE CHARACTER OF OFFICERSHIP

Officership is a public bureaucratized profession. The legal right to practice the profession is limited to members of a carefully defined body. The commission is to the officer what the license is to a doctor. Organically, however, the officer corps is much more than simply a creature of the state. The functional imperatives of security give rise to complex vocational institutions which mold the officer corps into an autonomous social unit. Entrance into this unit is restricted to those with the requisite education and training and is usually permitted only at the lowest level of professional competence. The corporate structure of the officer corps includes not just the official bureaucracy but also societies, associations, schools, journals, customs, and traditions. The professional world of the officer tends to encompass an unusually high proportion of his activities. He normally lives and works apart from the rest of society; physically and socially he probably has fewer nonprofessional contacts than most other professional men. The line between him and the layman or civilian is publicly symbolized by uniforms and insignia of rank.

The officer corps is both a bureaucratic profession and a bureaucratic organization. Within the profession, levels of competence are distinguished by a hierarchy of ranks; within the organization, duties are distinguished by a hierarchy of office. Rank inheres in the individual and reflects his professional achievement measured in terms of experience, seniority, education, and ability. Appointments to rank are normally made by the officer corps itself applying general principles established by the state. Assignments to office are normally somewhat more subject to outside influence. In all bureaucracies, authority derives from office; in a professional bureaucracy, eligibility for office derives from rank. An officer is permitted to perform certain types of duties and functions by virtue of his rank; he does not receive rank because he has been assigned to an office. Although in practice there are exceptions to this principle, the professional character of the officer corps rests upon the priority of the hierarchy of rank over the hierarchy of office.

The officer corps normally includes a number of nonprofessional "reservists." This is due to the fluctuating need for officers and the impossibility of the state maintaining continuously an officer corps of the size required in emergencies. The reservists are a temporary supplement to the officer corps and qualify for military rank by education and training. While members of the corps, they normally possess all the prerogatives and responsibilities of the professional in the same rank. The legal distinction between them and the professional is preserved, however, and entrance into the permanent corps of officers is much more restricted than entrance into the reserve corps. The reservists seldom achieve the level of professional skill open to the career officers; consequently, the bulk of the reservists are in the lower ranks of the professional bureaucracy while the higher ranks are monopolized by the career professionals. The latter, as the continuing element in the military structure and because of their superior professional competence as a body, are normally charged with the education and indoctrination of the reservists in the skills and the traditions of the vocation. The reservist only temporarily assumes professional responsibility. His principal functions in society lie elsewhere. As a result, his motivations, values, and behavior frequently differ greatly from those of the career professional.

The enlisted men subordinate to the officer corps are a part of the organizational bureaucracy but not of the professional bureaucracy. The enlisted personnel have neither the intellectual skills nor the professional responsibility of the officer. They are specialists in the application of violence, not in the management of violence. Their vocation is a trade, not a profession. This fundamental difference between the officer corps and the enlisted corps is reflected in the sharp line which is universally drawn between the two in all the military forces of the world. If this cleavage did not exist, there could be a single military hierarchy extending from the lowest enlisted man to the highest officer. But the differing character of the two vocations makes the organizational hierarchy discontinuous. The ranks which exist in the enlisted corps do not constitute a professional hierarchy. They reflect varying aptitudes, abilities, and offices within the trade of soldier, and movement up and down them is much more fluid than movement in the officer corps. The difference between the officer and enlisted vocations precludes any general progression from one to the other. Individual enlisted men do become officers, but this is the exception rather than the rule. The education and training necessary for officership are normally incompatible with prolonged service as an enlisted man.

A NEW LOOK AT THE MILITARY PROFESSION

ZEB B. BRADFORD, JR., AND JAMES R. MURPHY

The present authors criticize the Huntington thesis as well as the use and misuse of this thesis by both military and civilian authors. Colonels Bradford and Murphy find Huntington's "management of violence" concept too restricive as an explanation of military expertise. They also quarrel with Huntington's two other characteristics, responsibility and corporateness. The result is a thoughtful criticism of Huntington's ideal type. Bradford and Murphy may be criticized, in turn, for expanding the concept of military professionalism too far and therefore losing the conceptual unity that Huntington presents. Both graduates of the United States Military Academy, Colonels Bradford and Murphy have pursued different, albeit somewhat parallel, courses. Colonel Bradford is an Army officer, while Colonel Murphy chose the Air Force upon graduation from USMA. Both have taught in the Social Science Department of their alma mater and have attended their respective Command and Staff Schools. Colonel Bradford has served in a number of operational assignments, including tours in Vietnam and Korea. He spent the 1971–1972 academic year at the Woodrow Wilson International Center for Scholars. Colonel Murphy, after two years on the National Security Council Staff, has returned to the operational Air Force as a strategic missile squadron commander.

The military estbablishment today occupies a very prominent and controversial place in American national life. The prominence is readily understandable—$84 billion of the federal budget, more than three million Americans in the armed forces, an extensive draft, worldwide defense commitments, and a large-scale war in Vietnam. These facts, of course, generate considerable public controversy over national policies, priorities, costs, and alternatives. But more fundamental is the controversy in the minds of many soldiers and the thoughtful public over the very nature and purpose of their profession in America. Is there some truth in the emotion-charged allegation of "a huge, powerful and somewhat autonomous military establishment whose influence reaches into almost every aspect of our national life"? What is the military profession's reason for existing? What is the character of personal military professionalism?

Most of the general assumptions and concepts which define the role of the soldier in our society are inaccurate and misleading. Simply stated, our prevailing notions concerning the military profession rest upon a narrow concept of specialized function. A unique expertise is asserted as the distinguishing characteristic which justifies a place for the professional officer in the councils of government, and gives him a claim to the support and respect of our society. This explanation tends to narrow the perspective of our career officers, and fails to provide a basis from which American society can gain a rational understanding of its military establishment.

The officer corps must accept most of the responsibility for these faulty conceptions that dominate the thinking about its basic character, for it has failed to question its own assumptions or to state its own case. The military has been too willing to leave theorizing about the profession of arms to civilian intellectuals, who, although often talented, have failed to grasp its

Reprinted by permission and with minor changes from Army, *February 1969, pp. 58–64. Copyright © 1969 by Association of the U.S. Army.*

essentials, simply because their viewpoint from outside the military prevents sufficient insight. The result is an artificial conceptualization in terms of conventional social theory which distorts the perspective of both the military and the public, creating confusion and obstruction.

Many Americans find it difficult to explain a large professional military establishment in a democratic society. Most social theory asserts an anomaly created by a group specializing in the techniques of violence and serving an essentially liberal society which deplores force as an affront to man's assumed rational nature. The American historical experience of long periods of refraining from involvement in international power politics, interrupted only by sporadic forays, has reinforced the assumption that the military is at best a necessary but unnatural evil. Indeed, the standing army of yesteryear was a cadre, and postwar demobilizations insured that it remained out of sight and mind. This condition helps to explain an unending search on the part of the American military for self-justification and its willingness to embrace theses of legitimacy advanced by civilian intellectuals in terms of a highly specialized and unique purpose. This quest for meaning involves establishing a respectable conceptual basis for making claims upon society—in part for resources, but primarily for acceptance.

To deal with the military as an institution, we may start with the definition of the profession given by Samuel P. Huntington in *The Soldier and the State*—perhaps the best-known, most widely accepted, and certainly the most methodically developed conceptualization.

Dr. Huntington states that the military is a profession because it possesses three characteristics common to all generally acknowledged professions and essential to professional status: expertise, responsibility, and corporateness. For the unique expertise of the military, he adopts from Harold Lasswell the "management of violence." This is distinct from the mere application of violence, such as physically firing weapons, for the latter ability gives only technical competence or tradesman status. All activities conducted within the military establishment, Dr. Huntington says, are related to the management of violence. This peculiar expertise is the hallmark of the profession as a whole and distinguishes the professional officer. Fur-

thermore, the military holds a monopoly on this particular expertise. No one else may both possess and apply it.

The second characteristic Dr. Huntington cites is social responsibility. The nature of military expertise imposes an obligation upon the military to execute its function not for selfish ends but only in the service of society. The military profession does not exist for self-interest, profit, or personal motives.

Corporateness, the final characteristic, means that there is a shared sense of organic unity and group consciousness which manifests itself in a particular professional organization. The organization formalizes, applies, and enforces the standards of professional competence. For the individual, membership in the organization is a criterion of professional status; laymen are excluded. In the case of the military, Dr. Huntington designates the officer corps as the professional organization. Not all officers are considered professionals in his view, however, since some lack functional competence in the peculiar military expertise of management of violence. Those only temporarily serving, with no thought of a military career, are only amateurs. Enlisted men, as a group, are considered tradesmen and are outside the professional corps, although many career soldiers may qualify for the higher status—most frequently those in the upper noncommissioned ranks.

Dr. Huntington's model is attractive in its consistency and logic, and it is true that the military does share in some measure the characteristics of other professional groups such as law and medicine. But the analogy is insufficient to describe the military as a profession. The error is due to the attempt to find characteristics in the military which allow it to fall within a conventional definition of profession which is better fitted to other recognized groups. Rather than being defined by its own distinguishing characteristics, the military is interpreted in accordance with a socially standardized definition. This approach leads to the search for a particular expertise upon which the military can peg its professional status.

There are two basic objections to this approach. First, "management of violence" (or similar formulations for the same thing, such as "the ordered application of force to the resolution of a social problem") is insufficient to describe what is actually required of the

American military establishment in our contemporary global security commitments. Second, the military profession cannot be defined sufficiently in terms of any functional expertise.

Military expertise is not a constant; it is contingent and relative. Military expertise will vary according to whatever is required of the profession to support the policies of the state. The range of possibilities includes "management of violence," "peace-keeping," "deterrence," "nation-building," "revolutionary development," "civic action," or "pacification." There are many examples of military establishments being required to do all sorts of "nonmilitary" tasks. To name only a few in the American experience, we can point to the construction of the Panama Canal, the building of railroads to the West, the rehabilitation of domestic social groups, conservation of natural resources, work projects for the unemployed, and even polar and space exploration.

We may look at our experience in Vietnam for further examples. The "pacification" effort required a whole range of skills that were not related to "management of violence." Should that conflict end, it is conceivable that a major portion of our military there would turn to tasks related more to economics and social psychology than to the employment of arms. Professional "expertise" might then be something as unheroic as crop irrigation, village development, or vocational education.

Within our defense establishment, the past decade has seen a great transformation in the skills required of the military. The widespread use of systems analysis and our mushrooming technology have created whole new dimensions of military expertise necessary for national security. Quite obviously, any attempt to decide who is a professional, based upon the relationship of his occupational skill to management of violence or combat role, is arbitrary and too restricted. It also can be self-denying, in terms of doing what is required by the country, if the military does not comprehend a broader role and develop the necessary skills as part of professional expertise. Combat expertise, of course, is the single most vital skill of the soldier, and one which is uniquely his to develop and use. Hopefully, however, this would not be to the exclusion of all other— perhaps more desirable or socially productive

—employment of the military establishment. Indeed, a military created or existing solely for the purpose of war may be dangerous to the values and goals of a democracy. Furthermore, the facts simply contradict such a narrow concept of the function of the military profession. In times of national security crises, the historical American approach has been to augment a small permanent military cadre with a vast mobilization of "citizen soldiers." The resulting successful management of violence has not seemed to depend upon qualities or expertise exclusive to the "military professionals."

As Morris Janowitz points out in *The Professional Soldier*, there is a narrowing skill differential between military and civilian elites. No particular skill, including management of violence, is restricted to the military profession. To take an extreme case, are not the Secretary of Defense and his top aides "managers of violence"? Of course they are; indeed, these civilian leaders brought the managerial revolution to the Pentagon, but that does not make them a part of the military profession, as they themselves would be the first to insist. We could say that those outside the uniformed officer corps fail to qualify as professionals, but this reduces professionalism simply to being a member of a group. Yet there are officers who are not considered professionals, and there are those in uniform who are considered professionals but who contribute only indirectly to "managing violence." The military profession is more than a uniformed structure incorporating a functional expertise.

The other two characteristics which Huntington cites—responsibility and corporateness —do exist in the military, and are important. But they lack real meaning in the way he relates them to expertise. In explaining the responsibility of officership, Dr. Huntington says that "the expertise of the officer imposes upon him a special social responsibility." Here again we see the crucial importance placed upon expertise as the essential qualification of the profession. Responsibility is said to be a function of the peculiar military expertise. This is putting the cart before the horse, for responsibility must come first. A more accurate wording would turn the phrase around. "The special social responsibility of the officer requires of him an expertise." As explained earlier, the varying demands of state service may prescribe that the officer possess skills unrelated to "management of violence." Responsibility is more than a means of insuring that the military exercise its expertise in the service of the state. Far more essential to military professionalism is an internalized *sense* of responsibility, of allegiance to duly constituted authority.

The third characteristic—corporateness—is, as Dr. Huntington states, a mark of the military profession and helps to describe it. Yet the significance of corporateness is missed, due to two errors. One is a faulty interpretation of the role of management of violence in defining the rank structure. The other is a failure to emphasize the primary role of the professional organization as that of institutionalizing essential values and formalizing these legally.

The first point is expressed in this way by Dr. Huntington: "The larger and more complex the organization of violence which an officer is capable of directing, . . . the higher is his professional competence." We come full circle and are contradicted once more by the example of the Secretary of Defense, who is *not* a member of the military profession. More disturbing is the focus on the size and complexity of the organization directed as the measure of professional competence. Degrees of competence, of course, are reflected and rewarded by rank; and the higher the rank, the higher the position in any corporate hierarchy. But the forms of competence are so diverse that the corporate structure becomes a way of organizing large numbers of people with many different functions for a common purpose, as in any other bureaucracy. Beyond certain minimum standards of competence, in the military service, seniority and career-development patterns largely determine the rise through echelons of command. Certainly the size of the organization does not define personal professional competence.

It is evident that the concept of the military profession described by Dr. Huntington rests fundamentally upon the attribution of a particular expertise, and that other characteristics, such as responsibility and corporateness, are defined in terms of this expertise. Without a unique skill the edifice falls.

Huntington's model has been discussed at some length because it has come to dominate thinking about the military and provides a widely used vocabulary. The military itself has attempted to rationalize its position and to solicit support in Dr. Huntington's terms—terms which are inadequate. For example, Brig. General Robert N. Ginsburgh wrote in *Foreign Affairs* in January 1964:

> The maintenance of a high degree of military professionalism is essential to the preservation of our nation's security without a sacrifice of basic American values. The challenge to military professionalism is reflected in each of what Samuel P. Huntington calls the essential characteristics of a profession: corporateness, responsibility and—especially—expertise. . . .
>
> The challenge to military expertise is the most important aspect of the challenge to military professionalism, because expertise is, after all, the very basis of any profession.

General Ginsburgh then went on to state that in order to salvage the profession we must achieve "the abandonment of the fusionist theory whereby military and non-military factors are so entwined that a separate expertise in the military aspects of national security is simply impossible."

This is a self-defeating split. If the military insists on such an artificial compartmentalization of security policy issues to defend some hypothetical military preserve, the profession does not deserve to be taken seriously. One thing has been clearly established in recent years: there is no "purely military" sphere in security policy. The military has a responsibility for participation in both the formulation and the execution of policy. At the same time, there is a continuing effort to integrate at all levels, in both formulation and execution, every aspect of policy—economic, political, and military. If he is to be termed a professional and entitled to a place in the councils of government, the soldier's horizons must be broad enough to encompass all of these factors as they apply to national security policy.

The narrow concept of the profession described by Dr. Huntington and exemplified by General Ginsburgh fails to encourage the career officer to develop his knowledge in fields such as economics and politics, which give meaning and purpose to the use of military power. This restricted approach is illustrated by the statement of retired Brig. General Lynn D. Smith in *Army Digest:*

> As a professional soldier, you must understand the difference between national strategy and mili-

tary strategy. Military strategy is defined in the *Dictionary for Joint Usage* as: "The art and science of employing the armed forces of a nation to secure the objectives of national policy by the application of force, or the threat of force."

If you master this art and science, you will earn all the stars and decorations your country can bestow. You will be so occupied that you will not have time to concern yourself with the debates on the fine points of the political, economic, and psychological aspects of national strategy.

If the military's own conception of the profession leads to the kind of narrowness evidenced above, we will forfeit our responsibility. National security policy is directed at protecting the essential values of our nation. If the U.S. military is to contribute fully to that purpose, it must have the ability and the inclination to relate the objectives of military power and alternative means of achieving these objectives to other aspects of public policy.

If the analysis is correct thus far, it is clear that Dr. Huntington has failed to describe the truly unique and distinguishing characteristics of the military profession. The military is not a profession in the way that certain other groups are, such as law or medicine. The term has to mean something different in the military case. Expertise, corporateness, responsibility—all are applicable in describing the functioning and organization of the military institution, but they do not of themselves define the distinctive quality of professionalism in the military context. We may continue to refer to the military as a profession only if it can be established that the military is a unique social group, and that its uniqueness gives content to the meaning of "profession."

The military profession can be properly defined only in terms of *both* its purpose and the conditions placed upon the fulfillment of that purpose. The military exists only for the service of the state, regardless of the skills required or the functions performed. As a profession, the military does not condition this commitment, for, in the words of Lt. General Sir John Hackett, a distinguished British soldier-scholar, the contract for service includes an "unlimited liability clause."

The military's obligation of unconditional service to the lawful authority of the state is unique. From time to time, changes in the nature of expertise are required for this service.

There may even be changes in the meaning of national security itself when viewed in terms of policies and programs. But these do not alter the basic character of the military profession. Many people outside the profession may have a self-imposed commitment to unconditional service to the state, but only the military possesses the obligation *collectively* as a defining characteristic. Certainly, in this respect, it is far different from any other profession.

A military establishment cannot confer upon itself professional status. This is the prerogative of the state. The status of the profession is bound irrevocably to that of the governing authority which it serves. When, for any reason, a military group challenges the governing authority of the state, it loses its professional character and becomes an armed political force. As history illustrates through numerous examples, a professional military organization goes through a severe crisis when, for one reason or another, it cannot identify either an effective governing authority or one to which it can concede legitimacy.

Crucial to the character of a professional military group is the existence of a lawful and effective state authority to which the military owes allegiance. A professional military is impossible without such authority. It is pointless to attempt to define abstractly the conditions under which a military group should renounce its professional status. One's own values will determine how the legitimacy of authority should be judged. As a *profession*, however, if that term is to be grounded in reality, a national military establishment must share the destiny and moral stature of its governing master. No state can deny the morality of its own policies or its own legitimacy. The military profession is a creature of the state. The military's status as a profession, therefore, can be defined only in terms of its unique, unconditional obligation to serve the lawful authority of the state. It will develop whatever expertise is required to fulfill its unlimited contract for public service.

Up to this point our analysis has dealt with the meaning of the military establishment as a profession, and has deferred a discussion of the meaning of professionalism in individual terms. Obviously, the line between the two is not distinct. The nature of the profession dictates the basis of personal professionalism. If the profession is to survive on the basis defined above, it will do so because of the personal commitment of the professional soldiers. The basis for this commitment must now be studied.

What *is* military professionalism? Unfortunately, here also a substantial mass of undergrowth must be cleared away before the forest becomes visible. It is common but inaccurate to conceive of military professionalism in terms of beliefs which a person must hold in order to be a professional soldier. Dr. Huntington offers an example of this tendency. In his view, the "military ethic" is "a constant standard by which it is possible to judge the professionalization of any officer corps anywhere, any time." Even if a particular ethic is not a prerequisite to professional status, it is nevertheless assumed that the typical officer will have a predictable set of social and political concepts, thus stereotyping the "military man."

The professional ethic, according to Dr. Huntington, "emphasizes the permanence, irrationality, weakness and evil in human nature . . . is pessimistic, collectivist, historically inclined, power oriented, nationalistic, pacifistic and instrumentalist in its view of the military profession. It is in brief, realistic and conservative." This sort of standard ideology is incorrect at best and can be dangerous in its support of stereotyped thinking by and about the military. Yet the possession of this view of man and society is widely assumed to be both true and necessary. The root of the problem here lies in setting down as reality what would seem in the abstract to be a compatible outlook for a warrior, and one which would theoretically support the role of a fighting group as a social organism. This error is in part caused by the incorrect explanation of the profession as resting on functions of violence. But neither careful study nor a walk through the Pentagon supports an argument that this set of norms is required for military professionalism.

In the first place, this set of beliefs simply does not pervade the officer corps with anything resembling universality. Morris Janowitz, in his sociological study *The Professional Soldier*, concludes that, actually, "the political beliefs of the military are not distinct from those that operate in civilian society." This reflects the diverse origins and representative nature of the officer corps. The U.S. officer corps has neither social class nor dynastic origins. Coming randomly from across the range of a pluralistic society, it has a pluralism in attitudes within its ranks.

Even if the argument against a "professional ethic" is accepted, it is generally assumed that the military professional must be unique on one point at least: his acceptance of the use of force in the pursuit of national objectives makes him an inherently different type of person from his average fellow citizen.

This is incorrect. If the soldier is apparently willing to solve problems by military means, it is only when so ordered by competent authority. He has been taught to see the military implications of problems and is charged with the responsibility of providing a military instrument to civilian policymakers. But, even given this, there is no sharp line dividing the soldier from society at large. There are "hawks" and "doves" on all branches of the social tree. As history and contemporary affairs amply illustrate, both the soldier and his civilian fellow share a willingness, although sometimes reluctant, to bear and use arms in common cause. There are higher values which even the dedicated liberal holds which justify to him the use of force. Civilians and professional soldiers alike have found themselves in the service of the state in all of our wars. While the soldier may find it easier to resort to force than some of his civilian fellows, in most cases it is only a matter of degree. It is not a matter of values, but one of acquired and required perspective. As a product and dedicated servant of his society, the professional officer shares the core values of the nation. He is not a mercenary.

It must be realized that one can be a professional officer while holding any number of political and social beliefs, some of which contradict "conservative realism." As the tasks of the profession are dictated by the state, so are the imperatives of professionalism. The officer may believe what he likes and may view the world as he chooses, so long as he can find it within himself to serve the state on its terms. And there are many diverse motivations. One may serve because he wants glory, loves patriotism, seeks social advancement or needs the work. One may fight the enemy with bloodthirsty joy or sadness in his heart. All that matters is that he do it well enough to fulfill his obligations. Liberal and conservative, idealist and realist, can and do share the profession of arms. A fixed and elaborate set of social beliefs is a false basis upon which to define professionalism. Archetypes are abstractions; soldiers are not.

Much effort has been expended thus far in attempting to demolish false notions about a military ethic. There is a hard core of truth, however, which does serve as a common denominator. If a particular ethic is not basic to professionalism, there must be something else. What is basic is related to the unlimited obligation of the military as a corporate professional community and functional organism. What is it? In individual terms it has often been termed personal commitment. But a better way of phrasing it is a "sense of duty."

Commitment implies less than duty. Whereas commitment may indicate what one must do in terms of a consciously made obligation, duty has personal moral value content. A sense of duty is a feeling of what one *ought* to do and must do in terms of one's values. Robert E. Lee called duty "the sublimest word in the English language." Here we come again to a point made earlier concerning the nature of a profession: that a sense of belonging and a professional organization are required. It was argued that a corporate unconditional obligation distinguishes the military. In more subjective terms, it can be called a "collective sense of duty."

The officer cannot be a respected member of his profession without subscribing to the operating norms of his professional community. These norms are in fact a necessity for the success of the group in fulfilling its tasks. Without a collective sense of duty the military could not function and certainly could not be trusted. Military professionals must share a sense of duty to the nation. The professional officer must be an unconditional servant of state policy; he must have a deep normative sense of duty to do this. The rigorous demands made upon the profession by this sense of duty, and the tasks required of it, explain the premium placed upon other "soldierly" qualities. One cannot do his duty unless he has courage, selflessness, and integrity. The military profession must have these group values as a functional necessity.

A sense of duty is necessary, but not sufficient, for professional status. The person must also have competence to perform the service required to fulfill his obligations. As described earlier, this may require one or more of a number of skills. Finally, he must be a member of the officer corps of the armed forces. By joining the officer corps he makes his professional commitment and adopts the community values as his own.

Apart from belonging to the officer corps, professionalism is, then, a status determined jointly by the officer and his government. Neither the state nor the officer corps will grant professional standing to the man who lacks the necessary competence or who will not agree to make a commitment to duty which on the part of the state is assumed to be unconditional. The unconditional quality of this commitment is signified by the career length and a life of selfless sacrifice, ranging from Melville Goodwin's "genteel poverty" to the Gettysburg "last full measure of devotion."

Professionalism thus has both *objective* and *subjective* content. It is objective in that professional status is granted by the state if certain performance criteria are met by the officer. It is subjective in that the officer must feel a sense of duty to serve the lawful government "for the full distance," even at the risk of his life. Mentally, he does not condition this obligation.

This analysis has attempted to deal with the difficult problems of the ideas which provide a frame of reference for the military professional in our society. Narrow concepts of the meaning of professionalism, especially those which are dependent on an exclusive expertise, have been rejected as inadequate to describe the uniqueness of the U.S. military profession. We have merely stated what should be obvious: that the military profession is an unconditional servant of lawful state authority and that its collective sense of duty makes the role possible. A particular skill is not basic. Also rejected is any rigid pattern of social and political beliefs as being necessary for a professional ethic for the individual. Only a sense of duty which somehow justifies sacrifice to the officer himself is required.

Some officers may feel that the denial of a professional expertise akin to that of law or medicine is a self-inflicted wound. We would urge, on the contrary, that acceptance of what we have tried to argue as the real meaning of professionalism will enable officers to accept a more demanding role in national security policy. As a profession of unlimited service, no considerations are taboo in formulating military advice, and no skill which is necessary to the nation conflicts with the professional status of the officer.

This analysis should not be misinterpreted as a suggestion for an expanded mandate for the military. What is suggested is that we recognize the profession for what it is—a profession of unconditional service to the nation, but one engaged in a multitude of tasks. For more than two decades the military has been required to

participate in the formulation of national security policy and to assist in executing it. This has required broad knowledge and competence in many diverse branches of public affairs. False notions concerning the meaning of military professionalism must not be allowed to prevent the officer corps from equipping itself mentally for its required duty. The military professional has no vested interest save that of the health and security of the nation itself. We must not forfeit this trust by adopting a self-conception which unwittingly betrays our duty.

THE EMERGENT MILITARY:
CIVIL, TRADITIONAL, OR PLURAL

CHARLES C. MOSKOS, JR.

A future-oriented and conceptually innovative essay sets the stage for a look into the future of the military profession. With the important changes in military education and attitudes which were inspired in part by the McNamara revolution in the Pentagon, by innovations at the service academies, by the cauldron of Vietnam, and by outside forces which have impacted on the military, the military of the future may be quite different from that of the recent past. Professor Moskos develops three typologies for analysis which are not only thought-provoking but also may inspire empirical research into a profession that has not been studied very systematically. Charles Moskos, a sociologist with an eye on the future, poses three possible emergent militaries. His analysis comes from both a long interest in military affairs and solid research. Moskos, chairman of the Sociology Department of Northwestern University, is the author of The American Enlisted Man: The Rank and File in Today's Military *(1970) and editor of* Public Opinion and the Military Establishment *(1971).*

Academic definitions, as well as ideological attitudes, of the American armed forces fluctuate between two poles. At one end are those who see the military as a reflection of dominant societal values and an instrument entirely de-

pendent upon the lead of civilian decision-makers. Conversely, others stress how much military values differ from the larger society and the independent influence the military has come to exert in civil society. In a real sense,

Reprinted by permission of the author and the Pacific Sociological Association. Minor editorial changes have been made.

these two emphases differ over whether the armed forces or society is primary. Yet, neither conception is wholly wrong nor wholly accurate. Rather, the issue is one of the simultaneous interpenetration and institutional autonomy of the military and civilian spheres.

At the outset, nevertheless, it should be made clear that the conceptual question of the independent versus dependent relationship of the military and civilian orders is not intrinsically a value judgment. Indeed, we find diverse viewpoints on the conceptual question crisscrossing political positions. Thus, supporters of the military organization have argued both for and against greater congruence between military and civilian structures. Likewise, the harshest critics of the armed forces have variously claimed the military establishment to be either too isolated or too overlapping with civil society. The point here is that at some level a sociological understanding of the armed forces and American society can be analytically distinguished from a political position. In fact, of course, this is not always so readily apparent when one gets down to concrete cases. But it is my personal statement that an ideological position must ultimately lead to social science analyses. This is especially mandatory in the present period, when the American military establishment is undergoing profound changes both in its internal organization and in its relationship to the larger society.

ARMED FORCES AND AMERICAN SOCIETY IN RECENT RETROSPECT

Even in the single generation which has elapsed since the start of World War II one can readily observe that the American military establishment has passed through several distinctive and successive phases. Prior to World War II the military forces of this country constituted less than 1 percent of the male labor force. Armed forces personnel were exclusively volunteers, most of whom were making a career out of military service. Enlisted men were almost entirely of working-class or rural origin, and officers were overproportionately drawn from Southern, Protestant, middle-class families. Within the military organization itself, the vast majority of servicemen were assigned to combat or manual-labor positions. Socially, the pre–World War II military was a self-contained institution markedly separated from civilian society. In its essential qualities, the "From Here to Eternity" Army was a garrison force predicated upon military tradition, ceremony, and hierarchy.

World War II was a period of mass mobilization. By 1945 close to 12 million persons were in uniform. Although technical specialization proceeded apace during the war, the large majority of ground forces were still assigned to combat and service units. Even in the Navy and Air Corps—services in which specialization was most pronounced—only about one-third of their personnel were in technical or administrative specialties. The membership of the World War II forces consisted largely of conscripts or draft-induced volunteers. To put it another way, the military of World War II, while socially representative of American society, was still an institution whose internal organization contrasted sharply with that of civilian structures. At home, nevertheless, there was popular support of the war, and criticism of the military establishment was virtually nonexistent.

Following World War II, there was a sixteen-month period when there was no conscription at all. By the time of the outbreak of the Korean War in 1950, however, the draft had been reinstituted. The conflict in Korea was a war of partial mobilization, with slightly over 3.6 million men serving at the peak of hostilities. Organizationally and materially, the armed forces of the Korean War closely resembled those of World War II. Unlike World War II, however, the war in Korea ended in stalemate, which in turn contributed to adverse accounts of soldiers' behavior: prisoner-of-war collaboration, the lack of troop motivation, and the deterioration of military discipline.

The Cold War military which took shape after Korea averaged around 2.5 million men, again relying in great part on the pressures of the draft for manpower. Significantly, technical specialization became a pervasive trend throughout the military during the 1950s and early 1960s.[1] The proportion of men assigned to combat or service units declined markedly with the corresponding increase in electronic and technical specialists. These trends were

[1] Kurt Lang, "Technology and Career Management in the Military Establishment," in *The New Military*, ed. Morris Janowitz (New York: Russell Sage Foundation, 1964), pp. 39–81.

most obvious in the Air Force, somewhat less so in the Navy, and least of all in the Army and Marine Corps. Moreover, because of the post-Korean doctrine of nuclear deterrence and massive retaliation, the Air Force experienced the greatest proportional growth during the 1950s.

Although Cold War policies were generally unquestioned during the 1950s and early 1960s, the military did not escape embroilment in political controversy during the Cold War period. Such controversy was centered on issues of military leadership and the institutional role of the military. Command policies at the highest level were subjected to conservative charges in two major Senate hearings. The military establishment found itself on the defensive in countering charges of being soft on communism in both the McCarthy-Army hearings of 1954 and the 1962 hearings resulting from the *cause célèbre* following Maj. General Edwin Walker's relief from command (for sponsoring troop information programs with extreme conservative content). During the same period, intellectuals on the Left emerged from their quiescent stance and began critically to attack the military establishment from another direction. Deep concerns about the military-industrial complex in American society were raised—an issue which was to achieve fruition of sorts more than a decade later. By and large, however, the Cold War criticisms of the military were relatively weak, and in basic respects the armed forces maintained the high regard of the American public.

The war in Vietnam ushered in another phase of the armed forces in American society. There was the obvious increase in troop strength—to a high of 3.5 million in 1970. At the same time, the role of the Air Force and Navy went into relative descendancy as the Army and Marine Corps came to bear the brunt of the conflict in Indochina. The Vietnam War also led to deviations from the Cold War policies of manpower recruitment. In 1966, entrance standards were lowered to allow the induction of persons coming from heretofore disqualified mental levels—overproportionately lower-class and black. In 1968 the manpower pool was again enlarged; this time by terminating draft deferments for recent college graduates—largely middle-class whites. For the first time since the Korean conflict, the membership of the armed forces again bore some resemblance to the social composition of the larger society.

If the debates concerning the military establishment were generally muted in peacetime, this was not to be the case once America intervened massively in Indochina. Although a brief spate of glory attached to the Green Berets, opposition to the war soon led to negative portrayals of the armed forces. As the antiwar movement gained momentum it began to generalize into a frontal attack on the military system itself—particularly within elite cultural and intellectual circles. The 1967 march on the Pentagon crossed a symbolic threshold. Not only was the war in Vietnam opposed, but for a growing number the basic legitimacy of military service was brought into open question. Adding to the passion of the antimilitarists were the revelations of American atrocities in Vietnam and the physical and ecological devastation being perpetuated throughout Indochina. To compound matters, a host of other factors somewhat independent of Vietnam served to tarnish the image of the American military: the capture of the *Pueblo*, the inequities of the draft, reports of widespread drug abuse among troops, corruption in the operation of post exchanges and service clubs, astounding cost overruns in defense contracts, and military spying on civilian political activists.

Even more telling, there were undeniable signs in the late Vietnam period of disintegration within the military itself. Some numbers of men in uniform—white radicals, disgruntled enlisted men, antiwar officers—were increasingly communicating their feelings to other servicemen, as well as to groups in the larger society. Moreover, throughout all locales where U.S. servicemen were stationed, racial strife was becoming endemic. The possibility that black troops might owe higher fealty to the black community than to the United States military began to haunt commanders. In Vietnam, the American military force by 1971 was plagued by breakdowns in discipline, including violent reprisals against unpopular officers and noncoms. Although much of the malaise in the ranks was attributed to changes in youth styles —as manifested in the widespread use of drugs —it was more likely that the military's disciplinary problems reflected in larger part that general weakening of morale which seems always to accompany an army coming to an end of a war. Even the use of sheer coercive power on the part of commanders has limitations once the *esprit* of an armed force has been so sapped.

The contrast in ideological and public evaluations of the American military establishment over three wars is revealing. In World War II, the American military was almost universally held in high esteem in a popularly supported war. Conservative and isolationist sectors of American public opinion were quick to fall in line behind a liberal and interventionist national leadership. In the wake of the Korean War, defamatory images of the American serviceman were propagated by right-wing spokesmen. Liberal commentators, on the other hand, generally defended the qualities of the American armed forces. In the war in Southeast Asia a still different image has emerged. Although initially an outcome of a liberal Administration, the war has come to be primarily defended by political conservatives, while the severest attacks on both the behavior of American soldiers and the military establishment now emanate from the Left.

But, even beyond Vietnam and factors unique to armed forces and society in the United States, the decline in status of the American military establishment may well be part of a more pervasive pattern occurring throughout Western parliamentary democracies. Observers of contemporary armed forces in Western Europe, the United Kingdom, Canada, and Australia, have all noted the sharp depreciation in the military's standing in these societies. Indeed, although it seems somewhat far afield, the possibility suggests itself that Vietnam may be a minor factor in explaining the lessened prestige of the American military establishment. This is to say that the American military, like its counterparts in other Western post-industrialized societies, is experiencing a historical turning point with regard to its societal legitimacy and public acceptance.

THE SOCIAL COMPOSITION OF AN ALL-VOLUNTEER FORCE

A stated goal of the Nixon Administration is the establishment of an all-volunteer force. Shortly after assuming the presidency, Nixon appointed a commission to study the implementation of the all-volunteer force. This panel —referred to by the name of its chairman, Thomas S. Gates—published its report in February 1970. It was the unanimous recommendation of the Gates Commission to establish an all-volunteer force with a stand-by draft. In July 1970, legislation was introduced in the U.S. Senate which would put into effect the recommendations of the Gates Commission. The breadth of support for this legislation was revealed in its sponsorship, which included political figures as diverse as Barry Goldwater and George McGovern. Moreover, a bill was passed and signed by the President in 1971 which substantially increased military salaries, especially those for servicemen on their first tours. The Department of Defense has set July 1, 1973, as the goal for achieving a "zero draft." According to this plan, it is expected that all entering servicemen will by that date be volunteers, but Congress will retain a two-year extension of induction authority and stand-by authority thereafter.

It seems fairly certain, then, that, sooner rather than later, this country's generation-old reliance on the draft for military manpower will come to an end. Before looking at some probable consequences of this change, however, some background data are in order on military procurement and retention rates in the modern era. Over the past two decades, with some variation, about one-third of all age-eligible men have failed to meet the mental test standards required for military entrance; this group has been disproportionately poor and/or black. About a quarter of the age-eligible men have obtained draft deferments (primarily educational) which result in de facto exemptions; this group is greatly over-representative of upper-middle-class youth. (In the most recent period, upper-middle-class youth have also decreased their draft liability by utilizing liberalized conscientious objection procedures and by obtaining medical documentation of ersatz physical disabilities.) Thus, only about 40 percent of age-eligible young men actually have served in the military in recent years; and these men were overproportionately drawn from the American stable working and lower-middle classes.

Between the wars in Korea and Vietnam, about one-fourth of all incoming military personnel were draftees (in almost all cases these were Army entrants). About another quarter were draft-motivated volunteers—that is, men who joined the military to exercise a choice in time of entry or branch of service. Therefore, only about half of all entering servicemen in peacetime were "true" volunteers—that is, men who would have presumably joined the service without the impetus of the draft. During both the Korean and Vietnam wars the number of draftees and draft-motivated volunteers increased sharply. It was estimated that in 1970 less than 25 percent of incoming servicemen were "true" volunteers.

The military's retention rates vary by manner of service entry. In peacetime years, about 20–25 percent of volunteers re-enlist for a second term; among draftees the proportion going on to a second term averages about 10 percent. In the later years of the Vietnam War, however, volunteer re-enlistments dropped to 15–20 percent, and draftee re-enlistments were less than 5 percent. Once a serviceman has made the transition from first to second term, however, he has usually decided upon a military career. With remarkable consistency, about four out of five second-term servicemen remain in the military to complete at least twenty years' service (the minimum time required for retirement benefits).

What lessons does the experience of the recent past offer for an understanding of the military establishment that will emerge from the institution of an all-volunteer force? Will the armed forces maintain a membership which resembles in basic respects that which existed prior to the Vietnam War, or will the social composition of the military undergo a fundamental transformation? Not too surprising, as in most controversial issues, social science data have been quoted to assert contrary predictions and conclusions.

Changes in the Enlisted Ranks

One of the most telling arguments against the establishment of an all-volunteer force is that such a force will have an enlisted membership which is overwhelmingly black and poor.[2] Yet the Gates Commission counters: "The frequently heard claim that a volunteer force will be all black or all this or all that simply has no basis in fact. Our research indicates

that the composition of the armed forces will not fundamentally change by ending conscription. . . . Maintenance of current mental, physical, and moral standards for enlistment will ensure that a better paid, volunteer force will not recruit an undue proportion of youths from disadvantaged backgrounds."[3]

Another study, contracted by the Institute of Defense Analyses, differs on virtually all counts from the findings of the Gates Commission.[4] Based on a detailed statistical comparison of civilian and military employment earning potential, the Defense Analyses report concludes: (1) non–high school graduates suffer a financial loss if they choose civilian employment over continued military service; (2) enlisted men who have attended college experience a financial loss if they remain in military service; (3) military and civilian earnings for high school graduates are roughly the same; and (4) military earnings for blacks with a high school education or less will far exceed the blacks' earnings in the civilian labor force. In other words, on the assumption that social groups will generally behave in their own economic self-interest, an all-volunteer force would significantly overdraw its membership from the less educated and minority groups of American society.

Reference to the experience of all-volunteer forces in other nations is also inconsistent. Again, in support of the all-volunteer force, the Gates Commission finds: "The recent experience of the British, Australian, and Canadian Armed Forces suggest[s] that competitive wages will attract an adequate quantity and quality of volunteers."[5] Yet, an account of the British experience notes that typical recruits are "untrained school-leavers" coming from older and impoverished urban areas.[6] Indeed, over a third of British volunteers now join the armed forces *before* their seventeenth birthday

[2] Harry A. Marmion, *The Case against a Volunteer Army* (Chicago: Quadrangle Books, 1971).

[3] *The Report of the President's Commission on an All-Volunteer Armed Force* (New York: Macmillan, 1970), pp. 15–16.

[4] Gary R. Nelson and Catherine Armington, *Military and Civilian Earnings Alternatives for Enlisted Men in the Army*, Research Paper P-662 (Arlington, Va.: Institute for Defense Analyses, 1970). See also K. H. Kim, Susan Farrell, and Ewan Clague, *The All-Volunteer Army: An Analysis of Demand and Supply* (New York: Praeger, 1971).

[5] *Report of the President's Commission*, p. 168.

[6] Gordon Lee, "Britain's Professionals," *Army*, July 1971, pp. 28–33.

(20 percent of all British volunteers being only fifteen years old!).[7]

With such contradictory findings, what are we to conclude as to the probable future social composition of the enlisted ranks? In all probability an all-volunteer force will be less socially representative than the present military establishment, but, with pay raises, nowhere near exclusively dependent on the lowest social and economic classes. That is, a reasonable expectation is that the rank and file of a nonconscripted military will fall somewhere between the claims of the Gates Commission and the dire predictions of an "all black" or "all poor" force.[8] Which of the two extremes an all-volunteer force will tend toward will largely be determined by the eventual total manpower strength of the armed services. A smaller force —say, close to 2 million persons—will be able to afford higher entrance standards, thus precluding overrecruitment from America's under classes. Conversely, a larger force will have to draw more deeply from previously unqualified groups.

Changes in the Officer Corps

The movement toward an all-volunteer force will be accompanied by significant changes in the social bases of officer recruitment.[9] The ROTC units from which the bulk of the officer corps is now drawn will almost certainly decrease in number and narrow in range. Partly as a result of anti-ROTC agitation at prestigious colleges and universities, ROTC recruitment will increasingly be found in educational institutions located in regions where the status of the military profession is highest—in rural areas, in the South, and in the mountain states. It must be candidly acknowledged that such ROTC units will often be located at colleges and universities which have modest academic standards. Within the larger urban areas themselves there is a possibility that ROTC units may be removed from campuses and instituted instead on a metropolitan basis. This eventuality would most likely further restrict recruitment of ROTC cadets coming from upper-middle-class backgrounds.

Moreover, the armed forces will obtain a growing proportion of its officers from the service academies, a step which has already been taken by substantially increasing the size of the student body at these institutions. Although the system of selection into the service academies is broadly based, there is a strong possibility that military family background will become even more prevalent among academy entrants. Because of the expansion of the armed forces over the past twenty years, the number of such military families and their offspring has increased markedly. Such excessive selection from military families—officers and enlisted men—would result in a separation of the officer corps from civilian society by narrowing the basis of social recruitment. Likewise, any increased reliance on government-sponsored military preparatory (or even privately-sponsored preparatory) schools would similarly narrow the social and geographical background of future officers.

Finally, there is the probability that recruitment from the ranks into the officer corps will decline. With the greater and greater emphasis on a college degree, there will be an acceleration of the trend to recruit from college graduates rather than to promote from the ranks. Such a decline in the proportion of commissioned officers coming from the ranks has already been experienced by European all-volunteer forces.[10] A countervailing factor, however, may be a stepping up of military programs which offer college educations to highly motivated enlisted personnel.

DEVELOPMENTAL MODELS OF THE EMERGENT MILITARY

Underlying much of social change theory are developmental constructs which are implicit

---

[7] *Ibid.*, p. 31.

[8] In this regard, a 1969 survey based on a representative national sample of high school male students found an amazingly high 16–25 percent who said they would volunteer for the armed forces, given no draft and no war. Jerome Johnston and Jerald G. Bachman, *Young Men Look at Military Service* (Ann Arbor, Mich.: Institute for Social Research, 1970).

[9] Most of the discussion presented here on the probable changes in the social background of the officer corps in an all-volunteer force is a paraphrase of Morris Janowitz, "The Emergent Military," in *Public Opinion and the Military Establishment*, ed. Charles C. Moskos, Jr. (Beverly Hills, Calif.: Sage Publications, 1971), pp. 261–62.

[10] Erwin Häckel, "Military Manpower and Political Purpose," *Adelphi Papers*, no. 72 (London: Institute for Strategic Studies, 1970). This is an excellent comparative analysis of recruitment and retention policies in Western military systems.

predictions of an emerging social order (for example, a classless society, a bureaucratic society, a garrison state). Most simply, developmental constructs are modes of analyses which
entail historical reconstruction, trend specification, and, most especially, a model of a future
state of affairs toward which actual events are
heading.[11] Developmental analysis, that is, emphasizes the "from here to there" sequence of
present and hypothetical events. Put in a
slightly different way, a developmental construct is an "ideal" or "pure" type placed at
some future point by which we may ascertain
and order the emergent reality of contemporary
social phenomena. Models derived from developmental analysis bridge the empirical world
of today and the social forms of the future. It
follows that one's reading of current and past
reality will vary depending upon which developmental model is constructed.

Our purpose here is to apply developmental
analysis to the emergent form of the military
establishment in American society. Put plainly,
what is the shape of the armed forces likely to
be in the foreseeable future? Initially, two opposing developmental models are presented,
each of which has currency in military sociological thought. A third model is then introduced which both synthesizes and differs from
the two previous models. All three models,
however, have in common a reference to a
continuum ranging from a military organization
highly differentiated from civilian society to a
military system highly convergent with civilian
structures.

Concretely, of course, America's military
forces have never been entirely separate from,
or entirely coterminous with, civilian society.
But conceiving of a scale along which the military has been more or less overlapping with
civilian society serves the heuristic purpose of
highlighting the ever-changing interphase between the armed forces and American society.
It is also in this way that we can be alerted to
emergent trends within the military establishment, trends that appear to augur a fundamental change in the social organization of the
armed forces within the near future.

The convergent-divergent formulation of
armed forces and society, however, must account for several levels of variation. One variable centers on the way in which the *membership* of the armed forces is representative of
the broader society. A second variation is the
degree to which there are *institutional* parallels
(or discontinuities) in the social organization
of military and civilian structures. Differences
in required *skills* between military and civilian
occupations are a third aspect. A fourth variable refers to *ideological* (dis)similarities between civilians and military men. Furthermore,
internal distinctions within the armed forces
cut across each of the preceding variables: differences between officers and enlisted men;
differences among the services; differences
among branches within the services; differences
among echelons within branches.

Needless to add, formidable problems are
encountered in ascertaining meaningful evidence on the degree of convergence or divergence between the armed forces and society.[12]
In dealing with this issue, some of the more
important findings of previous researchers,
along with the introduction of new materials,
are given in the developmental models presented below.

MODEL I: THE CONVERGENT, OR CIVILIANIZED, MILITARY

A leitmotiv in studies of the military establishment between the wars in Korea and Vietnam was the growing convergence between
military and civilian forms of social organization. In large part this convergence was a consequence of changes induced by sophisticated
weapons systems. These new technological advances had ramifications on military organization which were particularly manifest in the
officer corps. For weapons development gave
rise to a need not just for increased technical
proficiency but also for men trained in managerial and modern decisionmaking skills. This
is to say that the broader trend toward technological complexity and an increase in organizational scale which was engendering more
rationalized and bureaucratic structures
throughout American society was also having

---

[11] Heinz Eulau, "H. D. Lasswell's Developmental
Analysis," *The Western Political Quarterly*, 11 (June
1958): 229–42.

[12] For a somewhat different formulation of the
variables involved in a convergent-divergent model of
the armed forces and society, see Albert D. Biderman
and Laure M. Sharp, "The Convergence of Military
and Civilian Occupational Structures Evidence from
Studies of Military Retired Employment," *American
Journal of Sociology*, 73 (January 1968): 383.

profound consequences within the military establishment. In the military, as in civilian institutions, such a trend involved changes in both the qualifications and sources of leadership.

These changes in military leadership were examined in several landmark studies dealing with the Cold War military establishment. Ironically enough, both sympathetic and hostile observers of the changing military establishment were in accord that there was a convergence in the managerial skills required in both civilian and military organizations. In a highly critical and perceptive appraisal of these trends, C. Wright Mills described the "military warlords" as constituent members of the power elite in American society.[13] Mills highlighted the increasing lateral access of military professionals to top economic and political positions. From a different perspective, other writers—most notably, Gene Lyons and John Masland in *Education and Military Leadership*, and Samuel P. Huntington in *The Soldier and the State*—argued that the complexities of modern warfare and international politics required new formulations of officer professionalization and civil-military relations.[14]

The most comprehensive study of American military leadership in the Cold War era was *The Professional Soldier* by Morris Janowitz.[15] Documentation was given of the broadening of the social origins of officers to include a more representative sampling of America's regions and religious groups, and of the increase in the number of nonacademy graduates at the highest levels of the military establishment. Moreover, the military of that period was seen as increasingly sharing the characteristics typical of any large-scale bureaucracy. In effect, Janowitz stated that the military was characterized by a trend away from authority based on "domination" and toward a managerial philosophy which placed greater stress on persuasion and individual initiative.

The trend toward convergence has in some respects become even more pronounced in the contemporary period of the early 1970s. Significantly different from the pre-Vietnam military, where convergence was most pronounced at the elite levels, the more recent changes were largely focused—with the accompaniment of much mass media coverage—on the enlisted ranks. Partly as a result of internal disciplinary problems occurring toward the end of the Vietnam War, and partly in anticipation of an all-volunteer force after Vietnam, the military command inaugurated a series of programs designed to accommodate civilian youth values and to make the authority structure more responsive to enlisted needs.

Starting in late 1969, VOLAR (Volunteer Army) programs were instituted on a growing number of Army posts.[16] VOLAR reforms included such changes as a greater margin in hair styles, abolition of reveille, minimal personal inspections, and more privacy in the barracks. Much of the changed Army outlook was captured in its new recruiting slogan "The Army Wants to Join You." The "Z-grams" of Chief of Naval Operations Admiral Zumwalt similarly alerted commissioned and petty officers to concern themselves with enlisted wants and to show more latitude in dealing with the personal life styles of sailors. The Air Force, which has always been the most civilianized of the armed services, issued a new regulation in July 1971 (AFR 30-1) specifying a broad set of standards (ranging from haircuts to political protest) which was unprecedented in applying equally to officers and airmen.

Whether changes such as these are really fundamental or are merely cosmetic only time

[13] C. Wright Mills, *The Power Elite* (New York: Oxford University Press, 1956). Similar analyses are found in Fred Cook, *The Warfare State* (New York: Macmillan, 1962); and Tristram Coffin, *The Armed Society* (Baltimore: Penguin Books, 1964). See also the more recent: John Kenneth Galbraith, *How to Control the Military* (New York: Signet, 1969); Sidney Lens, *The Military-Industrial Complex* (Philadelphia: Pilgrim Press, 1970); and Seymour Melman, *Pentagon Capitalism* (New York: McGraw-Hill, 1970).

[14] Samuel P. Huntington, *The Soldier and the State*, (Cambridge, Mass.: Harvard University Press, 1957); and Gene M. Lyons and John W. Masland, *Education and Military Leadership* (Princeton: Princeton University Press, 1959). For more recent statements on changing military roles, see Ritchie P. Lowry, "To Arms: Changing Military Roles and the Military-Industrial Complex," *Social Problems*, 18 (Summer 1970): 3–16; Robert G. Gard, Jr., "The Military and American Society," *Foreign Affairs*, 49 (July 1971): 698–710; and Sam C. Sarkesian, "Political Soldiers: Perspectives on Professionalism in the U.S. Military," paper presented at the annual meetings of the American Political Science Association, 1970, Los Angeles.

[15] Morris Janowitz, *The Professional Soldier* (New York: Free Press, 1960).

[16] U.S. Department of the Army, *Project Volunteer in Defense of the Nation*, executive summary (Washington, D.C.: Office of the Deputy Chief of Staff for Personnel, 1969).

will tell. But something more than just "beer-in-the-barracks" innovations does seem to be occurring. Human relations councils consisting of black and white servicemen are coming to play an increasing role in the military's attempt to cope with racial strife. Even more novel are the officially sanctioned councils of junior officers and enlisted men which now exist on a number of bases. The formal purpose of such councils is to serve as communication channels between the ranks and the command structure. But a precedent has been established which could be an omen of a major reordering of the traditional chain-of-command authority structure.

Perhaps the *sine qua non* of a civilian labor force in advanced industrialized societies is the collective bargaining of workers. Although trade unionism is hardly more than a cloud on the horizon, there are indirect signs that such an eventuality may someday come to pass. The growing labor militancy of heretofore quiescent public employees at municipal, state, and federal levels may be a precursor of like activity within a future military. Already, union membership and military careerism have proved compatible in the military establishments of several West European countries—notably, Germany and Sweden. Even in the United States a precedent of sorts has been set by the assignment of full-time National Guardsmen, who are members of state employee unions, to antimissile installations. There is also the Trotskyist-influenced American Serviceman's Union (ASU), which was founded in 1967.[17] In 1971 the ASU claimed an enlisted membership of 10,000 and representation on all major military posts. Extremely ideological and violently hostile toward career servicemen ("off the lifers" is an ASU slogan), the ASU's viability as a genuine trade union is beset by internal contradictions. Nevertheless, the very existence of an organization such as the ASU is indicative of the incipient potential for unionization of the military.

At the professional level, the trend toward civilianization is even more apparent. Among active-duty doctors and lawyers there are manifold indications of greater identity with civilian professional standards than with those consonant with military values. (That the chaplain corps seems less likely to use its civilian clerical counterparts as a reference group is worthy of note, however.) Most notable, at the service academies the long-term trend has definitely been away from traditional military instruction and toward civilianization of both student bodies and faculties—for example, less hazing, reduction of military discipline, more "academic" courses, and civilian professionalization of the teaching staff.[18]

In brief, there is ample evidence to support the model of the military moving toward convergence with the structures and values of civilian society.[19] This developmental model anticipates a military establishment which will be sharply different from the traditional armed forces. An all-volunteer membership will be attracted to the services largely on the grounds of monetary inducements and work selection on the pattern of what is now found in the civilian market place. Some form of democratization of the armed forces will occur, and the life styles of military personnel will basically be those of like civilian groups. The military mystique will diminish as the armed services come to resemble other large-scale bureaucracies. The model of the convergent military foresees the culmination of a civilianizing trend that began at least as early as World War II and that was given added impetus by the domestic turbulence of the Vietnam War years.

MODEL II: THE DIVERGENT, OR TRADITIONAL, MILITARY

The conceptual antithesis of the convergent-military model is the developmental construct which emphasizes the increasing differentiation between military and civilian social organization in American society.[20] Although the consequences of the military build-up caused by the

[17] An account of the founding of the ASU by its chairman is Andy Stapp, *Up against the Brass* (New York: Simon & Schuster, 1970).

[18] Laurence I. Radway, "Recent Trends at American Service Academies," in *Public Opinion and the Military Establishment*, ed. Moskos, pp. 3–35.

[19] For additional references to the thesis that the military system will increasingly converge with civilian society, see Anthony L. Wermuth, *The Impact of Changing Values on Military Organization and Personnel* (Waltham, Mass.: Westinghouse Electric Corp., Advanced Studies Group, 1970).

[20] Among sociologists of the military, the view stressing the divergence of the emergent military from civilian society has perhaps been most forcefully argued in my own previous writings. See Charles C. Moskos, Jr., *The American Enlisted Man* (New York: Russell Sage Foundation, 1970), pp. 166–82. As is apparent in the conclusions of this paper, this is a position I have now abandoned.

war in Vietnam somewhat obscure the issue, persuasive evidence can be presented that the generation-long institutional convergence of the armed forces and American society has begun to reverse itself. It appears highly likely that the military in the post-Vietnam era will markedly diverge along a variety of dimensions from the mainstream of developments in the general society. This emerging apartness of the military will reflect society-wide trends as well as indigenous efforts toward institutional autonomy on the part of the armed forces. Some of the more significant indicators of this growing divergence are summarized immediately below.

First, recent evidence shows that starting around the early 1960s the long-term trend toward recruitment of the officer corps from a representative sample of the American population has been reversed. Three measures of the narrowing social base of the officer corps in the past decade are: (1) the overproportionate number of newly commissioned officers coming from rural and small-town backgrounds,[21] (2) the pronounced increase in the number of cadets at service academies who come from career military families,[22] and (3) an increasing monopolization of military elite positions by academy graduates.[23]

Second, although the enlisted ranks have always been overrepresentative of working-class youth, the fact remains that the selective service system, directly or indirectly, infused a component of privileged youth into the military's rank and file. The institution of an all-volunteer force will serve to reduce significantly the degree of upper- and middle-class participation in the enlisted ranks. Since the end of World War II, moreover, there has been a discernible and growing discrepancy between the educational levels of officers and enlisted men.[24] (The 1968 decision to draft a higher proportion of college graduates to meet the manpower needs of the Vietnam War can be regarded as only a temporary fluctuation in this trend.) Very likely, an all-volunteer enlisted membership, coupled with an almost entirely college-educated officer corps, will contribute to a more rigid and sharp definition of the castelike distinction between officers and enlisted men within the military organization of the 1970s.

Third, the transformation of the armed forces from a racially segregated institution (through World War II) into an integrated organization (around the time of the Korean War) was an impressive achievement in directed social change. Although the military did not become a panacea for race relations, it was remarkably free from racial turmoil from the early 1950s through the middle 1960s.[25] It is also the case that the armed forces—like other areas of American life—are increasingly subject to the new challenges of black separatism as well as the persistence of white racism. Interracial embroilments have become more frequent in recent years and will almost certainly continue to plague the military. Nevertheless, whatever the racial turn of events within the military, the very integration of the armed forces can be viewed as a kind of divergence from a quasi-apartheid civilian society. The military establishment, albeit with internal strife, will for the indefinite future remain the most racially integrated institution in American society.

Fourth, the well-known trend toward increasing technical specialization within the military has already reached its maximal point. The end of this trend clearly implies a lessened transferability between military and civilian skills. Harold Wool's careful and detailed analysis of military occupational trends reveals that the most pronounced shift away from combat and manual-labor occupations occurred between 1945 and 1957.[26] Since that time there has been relative stability in the occupational requirements of the armed forces. Moreover, as Wool points out, it is often the technical jobs (e.g., specialized radio operators, warning systems personnel) that are most likely to be automated, and that thereby would indirectly increase the proportions of combat personnel. The use of civilians in support-type positions can be expected to increase with the advent of an all-volunteer force, and again would thereby increase the proportion of traditional military occupations within the regular military organization.

Fifth, there are indications of an emerging

---

21 Radway, *op. cit.*

22 Janowitz, "The Emergent Military," pp. 261–62.

23 David R. Segal, "Selective Promotion in Officer Cohorts," *Sociological Quarterly*, 8 (Spring 1967): 199–206.

24 Moskos, *The American Enlisted Man*, p. 196.

25 *Ibid.*, pp. 108–33.

26 Harold Wool, *The Military Specialist* (Baltimore: The Johns Hopkins Press. 1968).

divergence between the family patterns of military personnel and those of civilians. Before World War II, the military at the enlisted levels was glaringly indifferent to family needs. In World War II, except for allotment checks, families of servicemen more or less fended for themselves. Starting with the Cold War, however, the military began to take steps to deal with some of the practical problems faced by married servicemen. An array of on-post privileges (e.g., free medical care, PX and commissary privileges, government quarters for married noncoms) were established or expanded to meet the needs of military families. This greater concern for service families on the part of the military became especially evident in the late 1960s. Activities such as the Army's Community Service and the Air Force's Dependents Assistance Program are recent efforts to make available a wide range of services for military families: legal and real-estate advice, family counseling, baby-sitting services, employment opportunities for wives, and the loan of infant furnishings, linen, china, and the like. At the risk of some overstatement, the pre–World War II military might be seen as a total institution encapsulating bachelors, while the post-Vietnam military may well encapsulate the family along with the serviceman-husband-father.

The above five factors are only a partial list of the indicators that support the developmental model of a divergent military. Mention can also be made of other parallel indicators. Thus, charging the armed forces with welfare and job-training programs—along the lines of Project 100,000 and Project Transition—can lead only to greater social distance between officers and the ranks. The continued downgrading of the National Guard and reserve components implies the final demise of the citizen-soldier concept. The further employment of foreign troops under direct American command—such as the South Korean troops who today constitute one-sixth of the "American" Eighth Army —would be a paramount indicator of a military force divergent from civilian society.

Perhaps the ultimate indicator of divergence lies in the ideological dimension. There is a widespread mood among career officers and noncoms that the armed forces have been made the convenient scapegoat for the war in Vietnam. The mass media, seaboard intelligentsia,

and professors at our leading universities are seen as undermining the honor of military service and fostering dissent within the ranks. Although documentation is elusive, the consequence of this has been a spreading defensive reaction within the military community against the nation's cultural elite.[27]

Suffice it to say, there are convincing indicators that the military is undergoing a fundamental turning inward in its relations with the civilian structures and values of American society. With the arrival of an all-volunteer force, the military will find its enlisted membership more compliant to established procedures and its self-selected officer corps more supportive of traditional forms. Without broadly based civilian representation, the leavening effect of recalcitrant servicemen—drafted enlisted men and ROTC officers from prestigious campuses—will no longer exist. It appears that, while our civilian institutions are heading toward more participatory definition and control, the post-Vietnam military will follow a more conventional and authoritarian social organization. This reversion to tradition may well be the paradoxical quality of the "new" military of the 1970s.

MODEL III: THE SEGMENTED, OR PLURALISTIC, MILITARY

In somewhat dialectical fashion the two contradictory developmental constructs of the civilianized versus the traditional military can be incorporated into a third formulation—a model of the emergent military as segmented or pluralistic. Such a pluralistic model of the military establishment accommodates and orders the otherwise opposing set of empirical indicators associated with the civilianized or traditional models. Simply put, the pluralistic military will be both convergent and divergent with civilian society; it will simultaneously display organizational trends which are civilianized and traditional.

It must be stressed, however, that the pluralistic military will not be an alloy of opposing trends; rather, it will be a compartmentalization of these trends. The pluralistic develop-

[27] For perceptive journalistic accounts of growing military estrangement from civilian political and social attitudes, see Ward Just, *Military Men* (New York: Knopf, 1970); and H. Paul Jeffers and Dick Levitan, *See Parris and Die: Brutality in the U.S. Marines* (New York: Hawthorn, 1971).

mental model, that is, does not foresee a homogeneous military somewhere between the civilianized and traditional poles. Rather, the emergent military will be internally segmented into areas which will be either more convergent or more divergent than the present organization of the armed forces. Such a development already characterizes trends among the services. Thus, while the Air Force continues to move toward civilianization and participatory control, the Marine Corps announces that it will uphold traditional training procedures and regimentation of personnel. What will be novel in the emergent military, however, is that developments toward segmentation will increasingly characterize intra- as well as intermilitary organization.

Traditional and divergent features in the military will become most pronounced in combat forces, labor-intensive support units, and perhaps at senior command levels. Those in the traditional military will continue to cultivate the ideals of soldierly honor and the mystique of the armed forces. A predilection toward noncivilian values will result from the self-recruitment of the junior membership reinforced by the dominant conservatism of career officers and noncoms. Once beyond the first tour of duty, personnel turnover will be very low. The social isolation of such a traditional military will be compounded by its composition, which will be overrepresentative of rural and southern regions, men coming from the more deprived groups of American society, and sons of military men.

Contrarily, the civilianized, or convergent, features in the military system will accelerate where functions deal with clerical administration, education, medical care, logistics, transportation, construction, and other technical tasks. Those with specialized education or training will be attracted to the service in a civilian capacity rather than in a military one and will gauge military employment in terms of market place standards. Terms of employment will increasingly correspond to those of strictly civilian enterprises. Lateral entry into the military system, already the case for professionals, will gradually extend to skilled workers and even menial laborers. Concomitantly, there will be a relaxation of the procedures required to leave the military. The social composition of such a civilianized military will

resemble that of those organizations which perform equivalent roles in the larger economy. In all likelihood the present less than 2 percent female membership in the armed forces will increase substantially.

From an institutional standpoint, the segmented, or pluralistic, military will require new organizational forms. The range of such alternative forms can only be sketched here. But as a minimal requirement there must be some structure which will embrace variegated personnel policies, diverse sytems of military justice and discipline, and differing work ethos. Indeed, the antinomies between the civilianized and traditional conceptions of the military may be so great as to prohibit a conventional armed forces establishment. "Two militaries" may develop, each organized along entirely different premises. In this format the civilianized military might come to encompass a host of nonmilitary goals—for example, job training, restoring ecologically devasted resources, performing services of health care.[28] Another possible alternative would follow the Canadian pattern, where unification of the armed forces has resulted in a complete separation of support and administrative functions from combat arms (now referred to as "land, sea, and air environments" in Canadian nomenclature).

Our task here, however, is not to forecast the precise shape of the pluralistic military, but rather to define the constants which will determine the emergent military establishment. Most likely, the armed forces of the United States will keep their overall present framework, but bifurcate internally along civilianized and traditional lines.[29] The traditional or divergent sector will stress customary modes of military organization. In the case of the Army this could entail a revival of the old regimental system. At the same time there will be a convergent sector which operates on principles common to civil administration and corporate

[28] Such a role expansion of the armed services into nonmilitary endeavors is outlined in Albert D. Biderman, "Transforming Military Forces for Broad National Service," paper presented at the Russell Sage Foundation Conference on Youth and National Service, New York, March 1971.

[29] In August 1971, the Department of the Army announced that soldiers will henceforth be unable to "hopscotch" across military occupational specialties. *Army Times*, August 11, 1971, p. 4. Policies such as these are direct indicators of the move toward a more segmented military.

structures. Contemporary examples of such organization are metropolitan police forces, the Army Corps of Engineers, and the Coast Guard.

THE EMERGENT MILITARY AND AMERICAN SOCIETY

Developmental analysis serves to steer the social researcher between the Charybdis of unordered data and the Scylla of unsubstantiated conjecture as to future social reality. It was with this purpose that three alternative developmental constructs of the military were presented—civilianized, traditional, and pluralistic. And it was the pluralistic or segmented model which seemed to correspond most closely with contemporary trends in emergent military organization.

Ultimately, the implications of each of these models must be assessed for the civil polity and the internal viability of the armed forces. A predominantly civilianized military could easily lose that élan so necessary for the functioning of a military organization. A military force uniformly moving toward more recognition of individual rights and less rigidity in social control would in all likelihood seriously disaffect career personnel while making military service only marginally more palatable to its resistant members. A predominantly traditional military, on the other hand, would most likely be incapable of either maintaining the organization at its required complexity or attracting the kind of membership necessary for effective performance. More ominous, a traditional military in a rapidly changing society could develop anti-civilian values which would tear the basic fabric of democratic ideology.

It is the pluralistic model—with its compartmentalized segments—which seems to offer the best promise of an armed force which will maintain organizational effectiveness while in the main being consonant with civilian values. Indeed, the model of an emergent military with intrainstitutional pluralism may have broader applicability to the framework of the larger social system. Our American society seems to be moving toward a future which is not a rigid maintenance of the old order or an all-encompassing bureaucracy or a "greening" of the country. Rather, new forms of voluntarism and counterculture will coexist with persisting large-scale organizations and established values. In the last analysis, the developmental model of a kind of split-level pluralism may well be the defining quality of the emergent American society.

TRUMAN AND MacARTHUR

WALTER MILLIS

The "man on horseback" fear has gripped the Anglo-Saxon consciousness since the Cromwellian experience of the seventeenth century. The Walter Millis treatment of the famous Truman-MacArthur controversy provides insights into the kinds of dilemmas a democratic society faces when a major military figure chooses to question the civilian leadership openly. MacArthur, a powerful military leader with a significant political following within the United States, challenged a tough, pragmatic President. The ensuing controversy is an excellent case study of conflictual civil-military relations which gives insights into many important interrelationships in national security decisionmaking groups. The late Walter Millis was a journalist and historian. Among his more prominent works, in addition to Arms and the State *(1958), are* The Forrestal Diaries, *which he edited (1951), and* Arms and Men: A Study in American Military History *(1956).*

THE BEGINNING OF THE KOREAN WAR

The Korean War was to bring the most dramatic, most complex, and most illuminating issue of civil-military relationships since the end of World War II. It was not often clearly argued in these terms, and the central episode, the relief of General MacArthur, never in fact represented a direct clash between the military and the civil power in the state. It was in part a clash between the traditionally independent field general and the Washington top military command. But mainly it was a clash between personalities and partisan political interests. Had any other of the leading American generals of the time been in command in Tokyo, or had another President—particularly another President of a different party—been in office, it could hardly have arisen. Turning as largely as it did upon the individual men and the particular political situation involved, it was not typical of American military-civil development; it would be somewhat idle to base institutional or organizational changes upon this almost unique episode.

Yet it is still instructive in the basic principles of civil and military authority in the modern democratic state. All elements which go to make up total national policy were involved in it—the troops, who must be prepared to die in support of great national ends; the theater commander, who not only directs them but is responsible for them; the high command at the center, which is anxiously aware of its responsibility for the broader political and economic consequences of its military decisions; the diplomats, whose political achievements must justify and make good the expenditure of military force; the Chief Executive, who must see that military and political means are kept in consonance toward viable national ends; the Congress and the people, who are supposed to be the final regulators of the entire process. The events of late 1949 and early 1950 were a case history in the reaction of a modern democracy to a revolutionary, but long-range, shift in the international power balances. Korea was a case history in its reaction to an immediate military crisis.

. . . .

MacArthur

Douglas MacArthur was a "political soldier" —a phenomenon comparatively rare in American experience, though by no means previously unknown. Because of the difference in backgrounds, the American political soldier has differed considerably from his European counterparts. We have never had a Cromwell to turn out a Parliament with bayonets or a Boulanger to act the man "on horseback." Because the military interest has never been a major institution in our state, we have never had a Waldersee or Ludendorff or Schleicher to assert the paramountcy of "the army" in political or diplomatic affairs. MacArthur never had "the Army" (much less the Navy or the Marines) behind him; he never spoke for a military interest as such, even though many military men were to agree with his positions, and there was never a time when he could be fairly compared to the European or Latin American political soldiers.

Yet he was a military politician. From an early date he had taken a close interest in partisan politics; he was prepared to use his prestige as a soldier to influence civil policy decisions, and the arguments of military necessity to override the diplomatic or political objectives of his civilian superiors. As Samuel P. Huntington put it:

MacArthur had been a brilliant soldier but always something more than a soldier; a controversial, ambitious, transcendent figure, too able, too assured, too talented to be confined within the limits of professional function and responsibility. As early as 1929 his name was mentioned in connection with the Presidency, and in 1944, 1948, and 1952 he was on the fringes of the presidential political arena.[1]

His was a complex, arrogant, and forceful character. He was a military leader of indisputable ability, yet in his enormous reputation there was an element of propaganda myth, dating from the dark days of early 1942, when the American people had desperately needed a hero and MacArthur, defending Bataan, was the only figure available for the role. It can only have been galling to that proud personality. It may have intensified the natural egotism and sensitivity; his constant insistence upon the importance of the Far East as opposed to the European theater (where much less brilliant men, like Eisenhower or Bradley, were to earn greater laurels); his scorn of the politicians;

and his almost compulsive drive to be always alone, supreme and unfettered.

This was the remarkable personality who presented what Forrestal, in the later stages of the Pacific war, once described as "the MacArthur problem." It was a problem with which most Washington staffs and administrators had long been familiar. Everybody knew that it had to be handled with gloves. Franklin Roosevelt had been adept at managing it, while the Truman State Department, alike under Marshall and Acheson, had experienced comparatively little difficulty with it during the long proconsulship in Japan. But fate now decreed that General MacArthur should become the chief executive agent of policies with which he did not agree, laid down by a Commander in Chief to whom he was politically opposed and whom he appears to have regarded with contempt. Something of the same kind had happened in the days of Lincoln and McClellan.

At the beginning, all went well so far as command relationships were concerned. The two divisions first deployed in Korea were swept back; but by late July a position was stabilized in the Pusan perimeter in the extreme southeast corner of the peninsula; reinforcements arrived; MacArthur reported that he now held "a secure base," and by August he was planning the brilliant counterstroke at Inchon. MacArthur had to argue the Joint Chiefs into accepting this military gamble, but it seems fair to say that, so far, national policy, diplomacy, grand strategy, and tactics in the theater had run in close harness. But now, with the immediate crisis apparently under control, issues of policy and politics raised an ugly head.

In the UN resolution of July 7, which had called upon members to assist in repelling the aggression and to place their forces under the American UN commander, Chiang Kai-shek had seen an opportunity. The Generalissimo had offered 33,000 Chinese Nationalist troops to the common cause. MacArthur had agreed with the Joint Chiefs that it would be unwise to accept the offer. It was unlikely that these poorly trained and worse-equipped formations would be "effective" in Korea; besides, they were needed to hold Formosa against a possible descent by the Chinese Communists. There were other considerations, of which the State Department was particularly aware. One

---

[1] *The Soldier and the State* (Cambridge, Mass.: Harvard University Press, 1957), pp. 369–70.

of the first decisions taken in the Blair House conferences was that Formosa should be neutralized. The United States had never before committed itself to defend Formosa against an attack from the mainland; now that it was about to do so by sending the Seventh Fleet into Formosa Strait, it seemed essential to make it clear that we would not permit Formosa to be used as a base for a descent upon Communist China. To introduce Chinese Nationalist troops into Korea, where they would have a direct land approach into Manchuria, would vitiate this policy. The Chinese Communists were known to be extremely sensitive about Manchuria, where their position vis-à-vis the Russians was none too secure. Even in these early days, the possibility of a Chinese Communist intervention in the Korean War could not be disregarded. Nothing seemed more likely to invite it than the arrival of large Chinese Nationalist forces in the peninsula.

THE VISIT TO FORMOSA

But the decisions of June 25 and 26 in Washington had made MacArthur, for the first time, responsible for the whole Far Eastern defense, including Formosa as well as Japan and Korea. Toward the end of July MacArthur informed Washington that he intended to inspect the Formosan addition to his command. JCS tried tactfully to suggest that, since the State Department was dealing with the sensitive international problems of Formosa, MacArthur might prefer to send a senior staff officer to make the military survey rather than go himself. MacArthur brushed this idea aside and visited the island on July 31.

According to his faithful aide, General Courtney Whitney, "It did not dawn on MacArthur that his visit to Formosa would be construed as being sinister in any way."[2] Unfortunately, it dawned on nearly everybody else, and the world press immediately took the visit as an effort by MacArthur, if not by the United States, to revive the Chinese Nationalist forces as an instrument for a full-scale attack on Red China. This was not at all what our allies had had in mind in supporting our resistance to North Korean Communist aggression within the confines of Korea. MacArthur may have been as naive in this instance as Whitney represents him; but MacArthur was never a naive character. The reaction of the world press was fairly violent, and on August 5 Louis Johnson dispatched a directive instructing MacArthur once more that United States policy was both to protect Formosa against Communist attack and to prevent any attack upon the mainland by the Generalissimo. MacArthur answered that he "understood" and would be governed "meticulously" by the directive. But the Administration was uneasy. It dispatched Averell Harriman, as special representative of the President, in the hope of arriving at a better understanding.

Harriman reached Tokyo on August 6 and had several long sessions with the Commander in Chief Far East (CINCFE). He reported:

For reasons which are rather difficult to explain, I did not feel that we came to a full agreement on the way we believed things should be handled on Formosa and with the Generalissimo. He accepted the President's position and will act accordingly, but without full conviction. He has a strange idea that we should back anybody who will fight communism, even though he could not give an argument why the Generalissimo's fighting Communists would be a contribution towards the effective dealing with the Communists in China.

MacArthur made the rather pointed suggestion that he was "prepared to deal with the policy problems," but added that he would "conscientiously deal only with the military side unless he is given further orders from the President." It was an early sign of a dangerous ambiguity in the situation. Through the four and a half years of his rule in Japan, MacArthur had combined the functions of a five-star general with those of the principal American political officer in the Far East. His experience and position entitled him to "deal with the policy problems"; what it did not entitle him to do was to control policy issues in the guise of giving "purely military" advice.

The newspapers were now interpreting MacArthur's visit to Formosa as a sign that the general had "rejected" the President's policy of neutralizing the island. Since MacArthur had privately agreed to be good and go along, Truman issued a statement that he and the general "saw eye to eye on the Formosa problem." Naturally, this only created more hostility between two forceful personalities who were actually seeing eye to eye on almost nothing.

[2] Courtney Whitney, *MacArthur: His Rendezvous with History* (New York: Knopf, 1956), p. 372.

On August 10 MacArthur issued a scorching declaration on his visit to Formosa:

This visit has been maliciously misrepresented to the public by those who invariably in the past have propagandized a policy of defeatism and appeasement in the Pacific. I hope the American people will not be misled by sly insinuations, brash speculations and bold misstatements invariably attributed to anonymous sources, so insidiously fed them both nationally and internationally by persons 10,000 miles away from the actual events, if they are not indeed designed, to promote disunity and destroy faith and confidence in American purposes and institutions and American representatives at this time of great world peril.[3]

Though elusively worded, like so many MacArthur statements, it sounded very much like an accusation of defeatism and appeasement against the Truman Administration; at the very least, it seemed to represent a claim by MacArthur to comparable authority with Truman's in the development of Far Eastern policy. Clearly, there were rifts ahead.

THE VFW MESSAGE

The military position, on the other hand, seemed increasingly hopeful. While UN forces had been compressed into a perilously narrow perimeter around Taegu and Pusan (in the extreme southeastern corner of the peninsula), they were holding, and reinforcements were arriving. The Twenty-fourth, Twenty-fifth, and First Cavalry Divisions from Japan were in Korea; the First Marine Division, representing the initial reinforcement from the United States, had begun to arrive on August 2. By mid-August MacArthur was concerting his plans for a counterattack. At this moment an invitation arrived in the Tokyo headquarters to prepare a message for the annual convention of the Veterans of Foreign Wars. A theater commander in the full tide of dangerous action is scarcely required to respond to such requests. But "MacArthur decided," in the somewhat incredible words of Whitney, "that this was an excellent opportunity to place himself on record as being squarely behind the President."[4]

His method of doing so was curious. The message to the VFW carried several implied barbs for Administration policy. "Nothing could be more fallacious than the threadbare argument by those who advocate appeasement and defeatism in the Pacific that if we defend Formosa we alienate continental Asia." At the moment, Tokyo dispatches were quoting "reliable sources" to the effect that MacArthur felt that the United States should "take more aggressive action against communism not only in Korea but elsewhere in Asia." Our UN allies were already nervous over the idea that the Korean police action might be expanded into a general crusade against communism in the Far East that would precipitate the third world war. Before the United Nations, the Soviet Union was resoundingly accusing us of "aggression," not only in Korea but because of our alleged designs on Formosa; the MacArthur message could be (as later it was) used as powerful ammunition in this propaganda war. Truman first saw it on August 26, two days before its intended release. He later said that he thought then of relieving the general. The matter was so serious that he summoned the Secretaries of State and Defense, the Joint Chiefs, and Secretary of the Treasury John W. Snyder. They were all "shocked," but apparently none dared at that point to suggest the relief of the towering figure of the Commander in Chief Far East. Instead, the President instructed Johnson to send him a message directing that he "withdraw" the statement. Truman knew that it was already in type (in the *U.S. News and World Report*) and so could not be suppressed; the withdrawal order was intended simply to limit the damage, so far as possible, by making it clear that MacArthur was not speaking for the Administration.[5]

According to Whitney, MacArthur was "utterly astonished." He withdrew the statement in an abrupt telegram of acquiescence; but began to see himself the victim of conspiracy. In the eyes of the Tokyo headquarters it seemed "logical," again according to Whitney, that the VFW statement had "innocently" run afoul of "plans being hatched in the State Department to succumb to British pressure and desert the Nationalist Government on Formosa. . . . in the event that the State Department was conspiring with the British to hand over For-

---

[3] *Ibid.*, p. 375.
[4] *Ibid.*, p. 377.

[5] Harry S. Truman, *Memoirs*, vol. 2: *Years of Trial and Hope* (Garden City, N.Y.: Doubleday & Co., 1956), pp. 354–56.

mosa to the Communists, it is easy to see how the statement to the VFW would cause consternation."[6] Here, as elsewhere, it is difficult to know how accurately General Whitney, writing after the event, represents the state of mind obtaining in Tokyo at the time. If his report is trustworthy, it would seem to indicate that already an impossible situation had developed between the Commander in Chief Far East and his superiors, both military and political, in Washington. The episode, says Whitney,[7] gave MacArthur "his first clear illustration of the devious workings of the Washington-London team." A theater commander in wartime who really believed that the civil authorities were "conspiring" against him with a foreign power would surely be compelled to resign. But MacArthur did not resign; and the issue passed.

WAR OBJECTIVES IN KOREA

In mid-August, General Collins and Admiral Sherman, representing the Joint Chiefs, were in Tokyo to discuss the planned offensive. MacArthur's proposal of an "end-run" amphibious landing at Inchon seemed bold to them, but they were persuaded to accept it and the planning went rapidly forward with a target date of September 15. But, though accepted by the military, it was a plan which raised new worries for the civil policymakers. If successful, it would bring the fighting back to the neighborhood of the 38th parallel, thus forcing a policy question which had so far gone unanswered and raising a threat which had so far not received much consideration. In reaching the great decisions on June 25 and 26, it had been assumed by all parties that the objective was simply to push the Communists back again behind the 38th parallel boundary—in Truman's words, "to restore peace there and to restore the border." This was certainly the State Department's view at the time and apparently that of the soldiers. However, the UN Security Council resolutions (as drafted, of course, in the State Department), not only calling for the repulse of "aggression" and the restoration of "peace," but also noting the long-standing purpose of the UN to bring about "the complete independence and unity of Korea," were at best ambiguous. Did these license not merely the

restoration of the parallel boundary but also the destruction of the North Korean regime and the reunification of the country?

If the latter was now to be taken as the objective, it would obviously heighten the interest of the Chinese Communist government in the struggle. So far, the North Koreans had apparently been deriving their support only from the Soviet Union. But as early as August 20 the Chinese Communist Foreign Minister, Chou En-lai, telegraphed the UN Secretary-General, Trygve Lie, that "the Chinese people cannot but be most concerned about the solution of the Korean question."[8] He had been following this up with similar hints. The threat of a Red Chinese intervention was at least menacing enough to lead Truman, in his statement of war aims on September 1, to include a hope "that the people of China will not be misled or forced into fighting against the United Nations and against the American people." Both the policy problem and the threat were submitted to the National Security Council; it came up with a paper, approved by Truman on September 11, which seems (from the former President's paraphrase) to have been something of an evasion:

General MacArthur was to conduct the necessary military operations either to force the North Koreans behind the 38th parallel or to destroy their forces. If there was no indication or threat of entry of Soviet or Chinese Communist elements in force, the National Security Council recommended that General MacArthur was to extend his operations north of the parallel and to make plans for the occupation of North Korea. However, no ground operations were to take place north of the 38th parallel in the event of Soviet or Chinese Communist entry.[9]

This really begged the question; and Johnson's later testimony, to the effect that up to the time he left the Defense Department (in mid-September) "there was no definite policy lined out as to what our action should be and how we were going to end this thing," would seem to have been well justified. The NSC finding placed upon MacArthur responsibility for decisions which should have been faced by the high command in Washington. If Washington was to commit our troops to the "occu-

---

[6] Whitney, *MacArthur*, pp. 380–81.
[7] *Ibid.*, p. 384.

[8] Leland Matthew Goodrich, *Korea: A Study of U.S. Policy in the United Nations* (New York: Council on Foreign Relations, 1956), p. 138.
[9] *Memoirs*, 2: 359.

pation of North Korea," then it should have been prepared to accept the possible consequences, already foreseen; if the risks were too great, then the commitment should not have been authorized. The finding quite failed to provide against the highly likely contingency which in fact materialized—that only after MacArthur had been allowed fully to commit himself would there occur the intervention which was the condition on which the commitment was not to take place. MacArthur's later complaints of his inability to secure clear policy directives from Washington were not without substance.

At the time there were no complaints; MacArthur was fully prepared to accept whatever responsibility was left to him. The JCS directive embodying the NSC finding was dispatched on September 15, the day of the brilliantly successful Inchon landing. Ten days later the military situation had been transformed. Seoul had been liberated by the Tenth Corps; the Eighth Army, breaking out of the Pusan perimeter, had destroyed or dissipated most of the North Korean army and joined up with the Tenth Corps to establish an irregular line (still at most points well south of the parallel) across the Korean peninsula. The war to rescue South Korea from aggression seemed virtually won. But the question whether to go on and capture North Korea from the Communists was now acute, and was being debated in every capital of the non-Communist world.

To MacArthur it was no question. He had assumed from the beginning that the UN resolutions of June and July had authorized the reunification of the country. In the September 15 directive JCS had authorized him to "plan for the possible occupation of North Korea, but to execute such plans only with the approval of the President." On September 26 this was enlarged; JCS gave him as his military objective "the destruction of the North Korean armed forces," and in attaining it authorized him to "conduct military operations north of the 38th Parallel." But this was accompanied by the most strict injunctions not to permit any of his forces to cross the Manchurian or Russian borders. In no circumstances were air units to be allowed to pass the frontiers, and it was suggested "as a matter of policy" that only Republic of Korea ground troops should be employed in areas near the border. MacArthur replied

two days later with a brief outline of his plan: the Eighth Army was to advance on the west and capture Pyongyang, the North Korean capital; the Tenth Corps was to be withdrawn from Inchon for another amphibious landing, this time at Wonsan, on the east coast, whence it would advance through North Korea in a wide sweep to a "juncture" with the Eighth Army. The plan was approved, but there was a good deal of uneasiness in Washington.

It was known that the Chinese Communist government, beginning at about the time of the Inchon landing, had been concentrating its best army units along the Yalu frontier. On September 30 Chou En-lai, in a broadcast from Peiping, announced that Communist China could not "supinely tolerate" a crossing of the parallel, and warned that she "would not stand aside" if North Korea were invaded by the UN forces.[10] On the same day MacArthur reported to Washington that he intended to issue a public directive to the Eighth Army's commander, declaring that the parallel was no longer a factor—"to accomplish the enemy's complete defeat, your troops may cross this parallel at any time." Nervously, JCS instructed him to "proceed with your operations without any further explanation or announcement. . . . Our government desires to avoid having to make an issue of the 38th Parallel."

.   .   .   .

But to Washington the adventure was already looking more and more dubious. The North Koreans did not respond to the demand for surrender; but the Chinese did. On October 9 there was a broadcast from Peiping: the American invasion of North Korea was a serious menace to the security of China. "We cannot stand idly by. . . . The Chinese people love peace, but, in order to defend peace, they never will be afraid to oppose aggressive war."[11] And it was in these days that they began secretly to pass their divisions across the Yalu to build up for the counterstroke. Washington, like Tokyo, was in complete ignorance of this movement, but Washington was disturbed. By this time Truman appears to have trusted MacArthur as little as MacArthur trusted Truman. On the day of the Peiping broadcast another JCS directive went off, again strictly enjoining the general against any "mili-

[10] Goodrich, *Korea*, p. 139.
[11] *Ibid.*

tary action against objectives in Chinese territory." According to Acheson, the preponderant
view in Washington was still that a Chinese
Communist intervention, while possible, was
"not a probability," though some, like Kennan,
were prophesying trouble. And the President
felt that he must have a personal interview
with the great military figure whom, despite
several invitations, he had never met face to
face.

The Wake Island Meeting

The meeting at Wake Island was outwardly
cordial. In their first (and private) conversation the President found the general "very
friendly—I might say much more so than I had
expected." Just what he had expected, Truman
does not explain. The general said he was sorry
if the VFW statement had caused embarrassment; the President assured him it was a closed
incident, and the general declared "that he was
not in politics." Later, at the conference table,
the general assured the President that the war
in Korea was all but won; that he did not believe that either the Russians or the Chinese
would intervene; and that even if the Chinese
tried to do so they could not get more than
fifty or sixty thousand troops across the Yalu.
"General MacArthur stated his firm belief that
all resistance would end, in both North and
South Korea, by Thanksgiving. This, he said,
would enable him to withdraw the Eighth
Army to Japan by Christmas."[12]

The two men separated with no apparent
rift between them, and, in fact, up to this
point the command relationship had been correct and effective. MacArthur had voiced his
policy differences with the Commander in
Chief on the matter of Formosa (as well as a
barely concealed contempt for the Administration), but he had not put these on military
grounds. He had been restless under the restrictions placed upon his operations in Korea
by what he thought was a timid and pro-British
State Department; he felt that Washington had
been unduly parsimonious with reinforcements
in the Far East, apportioning too much to
NATO and to Europe, where there was no
war. But the great victory at Inchon had cured
most of these discontents. Despite all of Washington's irritating failings, the end was now in

sight; and MacArthur alone had done it. According to Whitney,[13] the general saw no sense
in the mid-Pacific conference with the President, could not understand why Truman
should have wasted MacArthur's time, and
flew back to Tokyo believing that the whole
thing had been merely a "political ambush" designed to appropriate something of the Mac-
Arthur glory for Truman and the Democrats,
who were facing the November congressional
elections. Outwardly, the meeting had been
cordial, but it left further dangerous rifts
within the American policy and command
structure.

THE CHINESE ATTACK

Meanwhile, Washington was preoccupied
with a great deal more than the congressional
elections or even the Korean War. It was obviously necessary to support and reinforce Mac-
Arthur; but the overriding fear of that summer
and fall was that Korea simply foreshadowed a
Soviet attack upon the Western world. Korea
could be, and apparently was being, held with
the available bits and pieces of the World War
II military machine. But to hold the free world
itself it seemed suddenly urgent to convert the
new NATO alliance into an effective instrument of defense—to raise and re-equip American military forces for its support, and, even
more, to raise the American military production
potential to a point at which we would be reasonably prepared to face the possibility of a
third general war.

Marshall as Secretary of Defense

The American reaction to this global problem will be discussed later. But it was obvious
from the onset of the Korean crisis that the
days of Louis Johnson as Secretary of Defense
were numbered. Johnson's relations with Acheson were already dangerously strained, and it
was plain that the man who had been so assiduously economizing the services into incapacity was not the one to preside over the
major rearmament effort now demanded.
Under presidential pressure, Johnson resigned
on September 15, as the Marines were going
ashore at Inchon; and Truman turned again to

---

[12] Truman, *Memoirs*, 2: 365–66.

[13] *MacArthur*, p. 395.

George C. Marshall, the one public servant whose abilities he most respected and whose integrity he most deeply trusted. The provision of the Security Act excluding professional soldiers from the office of Secretary of Defense had to be hastily amended to permit the nomination; this produced some partisan by-play, but the amendment was adopted without real difficulty and confirmation was immediate. Marshall took office on September 18.

It was a singularly suitable appointment. During World War II Marshall had been the country's outstanding military statesman; and the success of the Joint Chiefs (as also of the Anglo-American Combined Chiefs) as a corporate director of that conflict was certainly in large measure due to his wisdom and influence. In 1950 Marshall had his civilian experience as Secretary of State behind him. At the same time, he had not lost the respect of his former military colleagues nor the touch of his old command authority over them. Under him a harmonious relationship between Defense, State, NSC, and their staffs was established. This was, no doubt, facilitated by the fact that in August the President had strengthened NSC with a "Senior Staff" composed of some of the ablest men from State, Defense, Treasury, JCS, the National Security Resources Board, and the Central Intelligence Agency.

In the subsequent congressional hearings, Marshall was to describe the mechanism of policy formation as it operated in late 1950 and in 1951. Beginning with UN resolutions, JCS would prepare precise military directives (of course with the assistance of its own Joint Staff, with its complex structure of joint planning committees). If of a minor nature, they were approved by the Secretary of Defense and then carried directly to the White House by Bradley, who regularly met with the President at 10:00 in the morning. The Chairman of the Joint Chiefs got the President's approval and the directives were sent. If, however, the matter "involved precise political consideration it was discussed as a rule with members of the State Department or sent them and their reaction awaited." After formulation between State and Defense, the policy paper would go to NSC, where the new Senior Staff, including high-level representatives of all interested agencies, would study the question and "final action would be taken." (Legally, NSC was only advisory, and there could be no "final" action except upon approval by the President; here Marshall may have been telescoping a bit.) In transmitting the resultant directive to the theater commander (MacArthur), General Collins, the Army Chief of Staff, acted as the executive agent of JCS, and the channel through whom all communications passed. The men who operated within this system testified later as to its efficiency. Marshall and the individual Chiefs of Staff were to say several times that it produced smooth and agreed military solutions, and that they were never overborne by the civilian diplomatists of the State Department. Acheson was to say, in response to a question, "Yes, sir, it has been a very satisfactory relationship throughout."

The record would appear to bear out these statements. The Joint Chiefs of Staff, under the sensitive hand of the Secretary of Defense, were consistently to support the civil-political direction; the State Department was consistently responsive to the military considerations presented by JCS, and there was a warm personal relationship between Acheson and Marshall. In regard to Korea, the Joint Chiefs were to show themselves keenly aware of the larger policy problems which led the Truman Administration to insist upon a limited war—much more so, it is interesting to note, than MacArthur and most of the field commanders. In the MacArthur crisis in the coming spring, these professional soldiers not only loyally supported the civilian Commander in Chief (as the Constitution required them to do) but indicated rather strongly their personal agreement with Truman. At the same time, they worked out and brought in the massive estimates for new military spending and for foreign military aid required to buttress the NATO system—estimates which were in large measure dictated by political rather than immediate military considerations, and for which the State Department rather than the Department of Defense carried the immediate responsibility. Issues between rearming ourselves or rearming our allies—of a kind that was rather prominent in the year before Pearl Harbor—were not wholly absent in 1950–1951, but were to play a minor role. Except for the partial and peculiar exception of the MacArthur crisis, civil-military relations in the difficult Korean period were to operate with remarkable harmony and success.

Appearance of the Chinese Troops

Unforeseen by any of the parties, that crisis was now in the making. The Eighth Army had crossed the 38th parallel on October 7 and were headed generally northwestward along the more or less open valleys of the "invasion route" leading to Pyongyang, the North Korean capital.

.   .   .   .

For a week or so UN troops had been meeting with only occasional skirmishes as they ranged freely across North Korea. But on October 24, when the advance element of the Sixth ROK Division had been filling its canteens in the Yalu, another element of the same division, some fifty miles behind them to the southeast, had run into a trap at Unsan, on the upper reaches of the Chongchon. The American First Cavalry Division started northward in relief. On the night of October 26, it, likewise, ran into an ambush. One squadron lost a great part of its men. "Both traps," says S. L. A. Marshall,[14] "had been sprung by Chinese troops in superior strength," but of the prisoners taken at Unsan only two were Chinese. Their stories were like those of the earlier prisoners. They were forced "volunteers" in the North Korean armies. But they said that the units with which they had crossed the border were not mere regimental groups; they were full-sized Chinese divisions.

.   .   .   .

Evaluating Chinese Intervention

That there was at least some Chinese intervention was now obvious to all. On November 5, the day after the inconclusive report to the President and JCS, MacArthur addressed an angry "special report" to the UN Security Council: "It is apparent to our fighting forces, and our intelligence agencies have confirmed the fact, that the United Nations are presently in hostile contact with Chinese Communist military units deployed for action against the United Nations." To support this, a whole series of incidents was summarized, beginning on August 22, when anti-aircraft fire from the Manchurian side of the Yalu had attacked our aircraft; including instances in which enemy aircraft had retreated across the Yalu to receive

sanctuary on the Chinese airfields; including the identification of small Chinese "volunteer" units, up to regimental size, in the North Korean forces. By November 4, this report stated, thirty-five Chinese Communist prisoners had been taken.

More than this, a "special communiqué" was issued to the world on November 6.[15] It announced that the war had been won; with the capture of Pyongyang and the invasion of northeastern Korea, "the defeat of the North Koreans and destruction of their armies" had become "decisive." But at this point the Chinese had intervened:

. . . the communists committed one of the most offensive acts of international lawlessness of historic record by moving, without any notice of belligerence, elements of alien Communist forces across the Yalu River into North Korea and massing a great concentration of possible reinforcing divisions with adequate supply behind the privileged sanctuary of the adjacent Manchurian border. A possible trap was thereby surreptitiously laid, calculated to encompass the destruction of the United Nations forces. . . . This potential danger was avoided with minimum losses only by the timely detection and skillful maneuvering of the United Nations commander responsible for that sector, who with great perspicacity and skill completely reversed the movement of his forces in order to achieve the greater integration of tactical power necessitated by the new situation and avert any possibility of a great military reversal.

The last sonorous sentence sounded a great deal better than the time-worn "our troops affected a strategic withdrawal" or "our lines were rectified to improve the tactical position," but it meant exactly the same thing. In short, it covered Walton Walker's retreat to the Chongchon. But the whole communiqué suggests today that the general was losing his touch with reality. The Chinese concentrations were still only a "possible" reinforcing group beyond the Yalu; MacArthur obviously did not know that they had passed the Yalu many days before and were actually massing in the midst of his own forces. The "trap" had not been avoided; the real trap had not yet even been detected.

The Yalu Bridges

The sequence is rather striking. On November 4 MacArthur reported to his government

---

[14] *The River and the Gauntlet* (New York: Morrow, 1953), p. 10.

[15] The following report of this communiqué is from Whitney, *MacArthur*, p. 405.

and his military superiors that it was "impossible to appraise" the danger of an all-out Chinese intervention, and that "many logical reasons" were against it. On November 5 he appealed to the United Nations, and on November 6 to world opinion, on the assumption that such an intervention was about to take place. It was also on November 6 that MacArthur ordered his air commander, Lieutenant General George E. Stratemeyer, to mount a strike of ninety "strategic" B-29 bombers on the Yalu bridges at Sinuiju, and advised Washington of the order. In Washington it caused consternation. The President was in Missouri, casting his ballot in the congressional election. Acheson got him on the telephone; Under Secretary of Defense Lovett was in Acheson's office with MacArthur's message.[16]

It was then about 10:00 in the morning, and the bombers were to take off in three hours. Lovett said that "from an operational standpoint he doubted whether the results to be achieved would be important enough to outweigh the danger of [accidentally] bombing Antung or other points on the Manchurian side of the river." There were other considerations. "Dean Rusk pointed out that we had a commitment with the British not to take action which might involve attacks on the Manchurian side of the river without consultation with them." On the basis of the MacArthur report of November 5, the State Department had already requested an "urgent" meeting of the UN Security Council to consider the Chinese intervention; if a bombing attack meanwhile hit Manchuria, it might wreck further chances of progress through the United Nations. Acheson said that he and Lovett were agreed that "this air action ought to be postponed until we had more facts about the situation there"; Truman's reply over the telephone was that he would not approve the strike unless "there was an immediate and serious threat to the security of our troops," of which MacArthur had given no indication. At 11:40 A.M., JCS, in conformity with this instruction, dispatched a directive to MacArthur, ordering the postponement of all bombing of targets within five miles of the Yalu and asking his reasons for mounting the attack.

This evoked a sizzling, and somewhat curious, reply:

Men and material in large force are pouring across all bridges over the Yalu from Manchuria. This movement not only jeopardizes but threatens the ultimate destruction of the forces under my command. . . . The only way to stop this reinforcement of the enemy is the destruction of these bridges and *the subjection of all installations in the north area supporting the enemy advance to the maximum of our air destruction.* Every hour that this is postponed will be paid for dearly in American and other United Nations blood. . . . I am suspending this strike and carrying out your instructions. . . . [But] I cannot overemphasize the disastrous effect, both physical and *psychological,* that will result from the restrictions which you are imposing. I trust that the matter be immediately brought to the attention of the President as I believe your instructions may well result in a calamity of major proportion for which I cannot accept the responsibility without his personal and direct understanding of the situation.[17]

This seems to have baffled both the President and the Joint Chiefs, as well it might have done. Two days before, the general had reported that logic was against any large-scale Chinese intervention; now, two days later, "men and material in large force" were "pouring across" the Yalu bridges, and he had already ordered a major transformation in the whole character of the war to meet not only the new military problem but also the "psychological" factors it involved. The MacArthur reply violated a fundamental canon of command relations by using a sudden threat of the destruction of his forces as a lever to compel a change of orders. (On an occasion in World War II George Patton met a similar maneuver on the part of a division commander by asking him, first, if he had any recommendation as to his successor.) It implied an effort by MacArthur to go over the heads of his superiors, JCS, to the President. Worst of all, it sought to justify a new strategy and tactics, which he had already ordered, by an appeal to a change in the situation which he had not reported, and which he did not now explain. Had MacArthur really foreseen "a calamity of major proportion," he would have done much more than order a bombing strike at Sinuiju. He would, first, have advised Washington of the facts; he

---

[16] The report of the telephone conversation which follows is from Truman, *Memoirs,* 2: 374.

[17] *Ibid.,* p. 375 (italics added).

would then have formed a defensive position along the Chongchon and put the Tenth Corps into a posture of defense to the eastward. He would immediately have adjusted his military strategy to State Department and UN policy. But he did none of these things. Both JCS and the President were not unwarranted in believing (as apparently they did) that MacArthur was trying to impose his own political policies upon the government of the United States under the guise of a "military necessity" which the general had failed to establish.

The conduct of civil-military policy as regards Korea had reached a serious breakdown. Perhaps this was the point at which the problem should have been faced. The actual decision was less heroic. Since MacArthur "felt so strongly," Truman told the Joint Chiefs to give him "the go-ahead."[18] In the resultant directive JCS noted somewhat pointedly the discrepancy between the November 4 message ("impossible . . . to . . . appraise the actualities of Chinese Communist intervention") and the November 6 message ("Men . . . are pouring across all bridges over the Yalu"), but nevertheless authorized MacArthur to bomb Sinuiju and the bridges up to the middle of the river. The previous restriction of air action to a limit five miles within Korea was removed.

But Washington also had to consider where this new situation was to end. If the Chinese Communists were really "pouring" troops across the Yalu, the policy would obviously have to be readjusted. Assuming that the new attack (if in fact there was to be a new attack) could be held by the UN lines now established along the Chongchon and in the Chosin Reservoir area, the United Nations would be in a strong position to offer a peace which, while leaving to the Communists a "buffer" area, the hydroelectric plants, and the barren expanses of northern and northeastern Korea, would preserve to the Republic of Korea almost all the productive parts of the country. Proposals in this sense were already being advanced in London, at Lake Success, and in Washington. But this was precisely the outcome which MacArthur believed should be prevented. About this time he discharged an emphatic "warning" against "the widely reported British desire to appease the Chinese Communists by giving

them a strip of Northern Korea." The warning (according to Whitney, who does not give date or addressee) continued:

To give up a portion of North Korea to the aggression of the Chinese Communists would be the greatest defeat of the free world in recent times. Indeed, to yield to so immoral a proposition would bankrupt our leadership and influence in Asia and render untenable our position, both politically and militarily. . . . From a military standpoint, I believe that the United States should press for a resolution in the United Nations condemning the Chinese Communists for their defiance of the United Nations' orders . . . calling upon the Communists to withdraw forthwith . . . on pain of military sanctions . . . should they fail to do so. I recommend with all the earnestness that I possess that there be no weakening at this critical moment and that we press on to complete victory which I believe can be achieved if our determination and our indomitable will do not desert us.[19]

MacArthur Resumes the Offensive

MacArthur here appealed to the "military standpoint"; yet this seems clearly a political, rather than a military, recommendation. He was asking not for support for his military command against a new threat (which he still did not seem to take seriously) but for an alteration of national policy to permit "sanctions" against Communist China, essentially political in character, which his government had not theretofore contemplated. Washington had reason to feel that it was MacArthur, rather than the Chinese, who was trying to start a "new war" in Asia, and that the order to bomb Sinuiju may have been motivated as much by this desire as by a military need to interdict Chinese reinforcements. Such feelings cannot have been lessened when on the next day, November 7, the general reported that he had been confirmed in his belief that the Chinese were not launching a full-scale intervention, and that he proposed to resume the offensive, in order to take "accurate measure . . . of enemy strength."[20]

---

[18] *Ibid.*, p. 376.

[19] *MacArthur*, pp. 411–12.

[20] It was also on November 7 that MacArthur reported that hostile planes were operating in increasing numbers from the inviolate Manchurian airfields and asked that our pilots be authorized, under the long-established international law rule of "hot pursuit," to follow these hit-and-run enemies for two or three minutes' flying time across the border. To Washington, this seemed only reasonable: Marshall "urgently" approved, Acheson agreed, and the President directed

In Tokyo, MacArthur was still supremely confident, and urged Walker, who remained dissatisfied with the condition of his army and supply, to hurry on with the planned offensive. There had been no significant change in the intelligence picture. The Tenth Corps was beginning its march northward from the east coast ports into the unknown; and its Seventh Division was in fact to reach the headwaters of the Yalu itself. But Washington in mid-November was extremely anxious; and there seemed an increasing opacity between the planners in the State Department and the Pentagon and the executants in Tokyo and Korea.

While Tokyo was boldly committing itself to the offensive, the discussion in Washington seems to have been almost wholly in defensive terms. JCS advised the President that "every effort should be expended as a matter of urgency to settle the problem of Chinese Communist intervention in Korea by political means, preferably through the United Nations, to include reassurances to the Chinese Communists with respect to our intent, direct negotiations through our Allies and the Interim Committee with the Chinese Communist Government, and by any other available means." Meanwhile, there should be no immediate change in MacArthur's directive, but all planning should proceed "on the basis that the risk of global war is increased." At a National Security Council meeting on November 9, Bradley speculated on the three possible purposes of the Chinese: simply to hold a buffer area along the Yalu; to force us into a war of attrition that would commit us so deeply in Asia as to assure a Soviet victory in a global war; to drive us completely off the Korean peninsula. If the last was the purpose, it would mean a third global war, since the Chinese could not do it alone and would have to bring Russia into the conflict. Bradley gave it as the Joint Chiefs' opinion that we could probably hold in the existing Korean positions, though, if the pressure increased, we might well have to attack the Manchurian bases. Acheson thought that, while the primary interest of the Chinese was "to keep us

involved," they also had a strong secondary interest in holding the border area and its power plants. He thought we ought to "explore privately" the possibility of securing a settlement on the basis of a twenty-mile demilitarized zone along both sides of the Yalu, under a UN commission. But he recognized, as a major difficulty here, the fact that we had so few means of making direct contact with the Chinese Communists.[21]

MacArthur was not a party either to these deliberations or to these doubts. He was committed to the offensive; and it had been agreed that there should be no change in his directive. This introduced another factor. There was now a firmly established tradition (dating mainly from Pershing's independence in World War I) that, once a field commander had been assigned his mission, there must be no interference with his method of carrying it out. If he bungled it, he could be relieved; but, until he was relieved, there could be no back-seat driving from the Pentagon or the White House. This, coupled with MacArthur's tremendous military prestige, made JCS extremely reluctant to intervene in the events which were now to transpire.

On November 20 Walton Walker issued to the Eighth Army his directive for the offensive, set for the twenty-fifth. On the next day, November 21, JCS did go so far as to "request information" from MacArthur about the coordination of the Eighth Army and the Tenth Corps, which were being separately commanded from Tokyo. Under the etiquette, a "request for information" was an indication from the high command that it thought the field commander was going wrong. An answering "request for clarification" was the field commander's indication that he thought his superiors were being silly. In this case, MacArthur did not immediately reply. Instead, on November 24, he flew to the Chongchon to launch Walker and the Eighth Army on their way with a resounding communiqué which he was later to regret:

The United Nations massive compression envelopment in North Korea against the new Red armies operating there is now approaching its decisive effort. The isolating component of the pincer, our Air Forces of all types, have for the last

---

the State Department to inform our allies of the intended authorization. Our allies reacted so strenuously in the negative that the plan was held in abeyance; and within a few weeks our forces were driven so far from the border that the matter was reduced to the academic.

[21] Truman, *Memoirs*, 2: 378–79.

three weeks . . . successfully interdicted enemy
lines of support from the north so that further
reinforcement therefrom has been sharply curtailed
and essential supplies markedly limited. The eastern sector of the pincer . . . has steadily advanced
in a brilliant tactical movement and has now
reached a commanding enveloping position, cutting in two the northern reaches of the enemy's
geographical potential. This morning the western
sector of the pincer moves forward in general
assault in an effort to complete the compression
and close the vise. If successful, this should for
all practical purposes end the war.

Visiting one of the forward headquarters, he
told the corps commander, General John B.
Coulter: "If this operation is successful, I hope
we can get the boys home by Christmas."[22]
Emplaning for his return to Tokyo, he ordered
the pilot to take him on a personal reconnaissance along the Yalu frontier. On the snow-
covered roads and bridges and fields he saw no
signs of military activity, no indication that
troops had passed the river or were intending
to do so. It was the day after Thanksgiving.

But in Tokyo that evening the general found
another "disquieting"[23] message from JCS. The
gist was that there was "growing concern" in
the United Nations and in Washington over
the possibility of another general war; the top
command felt that they must close out the
Korean War, and that this might be accomplished if MacArthur would halt "short of the
border," taking only the approaches to the Yalu
and holding these only with ROK troops. Mac-
Arthur replied immediately and (as usual) at
length, indicating that he had no such intention. He advanced the military argument that
the hills overlooking the Yalu were unsuited to
defense. To this he added the political argument that a failure to recover the entire body
of Korea "would be . . . regarded by the Korean people as a betrayal . . . and by the Chinese and all of the other peoples of Asia as
weakness reflected from the appeasement of
Communist aggression." He informed JCS that
"it is my plan" to consolidate along the Yalu,
and only thereafter to replace "as far as possible" American with ROK troops. When this
had been done, it was "my plan" publicly to
announce the return of American forces to
Japan and the parole of all prisoners of war,
leaving the question of the unification of Korea
to its own people, with the advice and assistance of the United Nations. In the context of
Washington's problems at the moment, this
outgiving was not, it must be granted, very
helpful. But it made no difference. Two days
later all the plans were abruptly vetoed—by
the Chinese Communists.

Walker had barely started forward on November 25 when his right flank was heavily
hit by strong Chinese units; by the next day
he was under the heaviest kind of pressure,
and the grim truth was soon apparent. Before
it had got off the ground the Eighth Army offensive had collided with a Communist offensive carrying the weight of at least six Chinese
armies behind it. By November 28 Walker's
right was collapsing; retreat had become inevitable; the crisis was extreme; and Mac-
Arthur issued a communiqué in terms very
different from those used only four days before.
It was now recognized and proclaimed that
there were as many as 200,000 organized
Chinese Communist troops already in Korea;
the United Nations was facing "an entirely
new war." The general concluded: "This situation, repugnant as it may be, poses issues beyond the authority of the United Nations military council—issues which must find their
solution within the councils of the United
Nations and the chancelleries of the world."

THE NEW WAR

Here was a crisis not only of war but of
policy, and one unquestionably complicated by
MacArthur's remarkable personality. "Within a
matter of four days," Truman observes,[24]
MacArthur "found time to publicize in four
different ways his view that the only reason for
his troubles was the order from Washington to
limit the hostilities to Korea. . . . This," the
former President adds with some justice, "was
simply not true." Indeed, up to this point the
general himself, while expressing his resentment of the "extraordinary inhibitions" imposed
on him, had done so primarily on political
grounds, regarding them as evidence of appeasement and weakness. He had made no
great issue of them as military limitations. Despite the cancellation, in early November, of

---

[22] Whitney, *MacArthur*, p. 416. Other versions of
the remark make it less conditional.
[23] *Ibid.*, p. 417.

[24] *Memoirs*, 2: 382, 384.

his order to bomb the Yalu bridges, he had declared in the November 24 communiqué that his air forces had "successfully" interdicted the enemy lines of communication. Collins, searching the record afterward, could find no instance either before the disaster or after it in which MacArthur had specifically asked for authority to carry the strategic air war into Manchuria. Until November 28 MacArthur's pressures toward enlarging the war had been political rather than strategic in motivation; it was only after the debacle that the "extraordinary inhibitions" became prominent as an excuse for the military failure. The element of self-justification which now entered the correspondence did not lessen the corrosive want of confidence between Washington and Tokyo, nor did it ease the problem of devising a new policy and strategy.

The first interchanges were not helpful. On November 29, later described by MacArthur as the day of "the highest crisis," when "it was not certain just what losses I would sustain in my strategic withdrawal," the Commander in Chief Far East appealed to JCS to accept Chiang Kai-shek's offer (made at the beginning of the war) of 33,000 Chinese Nationalist troops. The Joint Chiefs seemed surprised. MacArthur himself had agreed that such troops would be "ineffective" in Korea; and JCS now had the report of the survey party which the general had sent to Formosa after his own visit and which strongly confirmed this opinion. JCS replied that they were "considering" the proposal, but that "world-wide consequences may be involved." The next day, November 30, another communication was received from CINCFE. Prior to the debacle the Joint Chiefs had "requested information" as to the lack of coordination between the Eighth Army and the Tenth Corps. MacArthur now brusquely replied that it was "quite impractical to have a continuous line across the neck" of the peninsula; and that, while his forces might seem to be overextended, the nature of the terrain made it "extremely difficult for an enemy to take any material advantage thereof." This was too much for JCS, and they replied, not with hints but with a flat directive: the advanced elements of the Tenth Corps "must be extricated from their exposed position," while the entire region northeast of the waist of the peninsula was henceforth to be "ignored" save for strictly military considerations. At this time, the Tenth Corps had not yet been hit, and illusion still reigned in Tokyo. At a command conference on December 1 they were still "optimistic" and even thought (according to Whitney[25]) that they could send the First Marines right across the peninsula to fall on the rear of the forces attacking the Army. That day they were disabused. The Chinese delivered their ambush blow at the Marines in the Chosin Reservoir area, and the Tenth Corps' tragedy began.

THE NEW HISTORY

In Tokyo two operations were going on. It was necessary, on the one hand, to rewrite the history—which had been so largely provided by MacArthur himself—and, on the other, to rewrite the policy and strategy with which to meet the "new war." Apparently, these two operations became to a certain extent confused. The new history began to issue forth in communiqués and public statements from December 1 onward. The "massive compression envelopment" of the November 24 communiqué became only a "reconnaissance in force" to "develop" Communist strength; the "successful" air interdiction became an example of the "extraordinary inhibitions . . . without precedent in military history" under which MacArthur had been laboring; the Tenth Corps' "pincer" movement into a "commanding enveloping position" became its "fortunate presence" on the enemy's flank, which "forced" him to "divide his forces and thus weaken his offensive capabilities"; the advance into the Chinese trap which was to end the war by Christmas became a "fortunate premature disclosure of enemy build-up operations." Before the month was out CINCFE had convinced himself that, as he officially assured the United Nations in his report of December 26, the operations initiated with the November 24 offensive were "possibly in general result the most significant and fortunate of any conducted during the course of the Korean campaign." And, in the spring, when he appeared before the congressional committees, he declared with every appearance of sincerity that "the disposition of those troops, in my opinion, could not have been improved upon, had I known the Chinese

[25] *MacArthur*, p. 423.

were going to attack. . . . Had I been permitted to use my air, when those Chinese forces came in there, I haven't the faintest doubt that we would have thrown them back."

THE NEW STRATEGY

If the history had to be rewritten, the rewriting of the strategy to preserve the Eighth Army was somewhat more urgent. Washington was arguing for a general retreat and regroupment of the Eighth Army and the Tenth Corps on some defensible line across the peninsula. In a long message on December 3 MacArthur rejected this idea—which would, of course, have reflected upon the wisdom of dividing the two in the first place. He advanced technical reasons; the junction of the two forces would "jeopardize the free flow of movement that arises from the two separate logistical lines of naval supply and maneuver." But, when he added that he refused to accept such a "defensive" concept, this suggested that self-justification was getting involved with strategy. He went on:

I do not believe that full comprehension exists of the basic changes which have been wrought by the undisguised entrance of the Chinese Army into the combat. . . . This small command actually . . . is facing the entire Chinese nation in an undeclared war, and unless some positive and immediate action is taken, hope for success cannot be justified and steady attrition leading to final destruction can reasonably be contemplated.

This last was serious. It was also puzzling. Did MacArthur actually foresee the "final destruction" of his forces, or was he merely using this as a threat, possibly in an effort to cover his own military defeat, to force the all-out war with Communist China at which he had so often hinted? Collins, again in Tokyo, had a long conversation with MacArthur which he reported to Washington:

[MacArthur's] basic position was that the United Nations should not fail to accept the new challenge of Communist China's aggression and that the full power of the United Nations should be mounted at once. If reinforcements could arrive in time, the most advantageous action would be a withdrawal in successive positions, if necessary, to the Pusan area; otherwise, the command should be evacuated.

Collins was back in Washington on December 7 with a more detailed report. It was a delicate moment. The President, at his press conference on November 30, had been trapped into an intimation that the use of the atomic bomb in Korea had been considered. This created a worldwide sensation, and so violent a reaction in Great Britain that the Prime Minister, Clement Attlee, flew to Washington. He arrived on December 4. He was reassured as to the atomic bomb, but the dramatic trip only emphasized the mounting distrust in the Free World of American policies, particularly as executed by the UN Commander in Tokyo. Collins returned as the conferences with the British were ending, and Truman called him in to brief the combined group of British and American statesmen. According to Truman,[26] Collins (not unnaturally) gave a comforting picture: "the situation in Korea was serious but no longer critical." Collins was confident that the Tenth Corps could be evacuated by sea and added to the Eighth Army. He reported that Walton Walker was convinced that he could hold "a sizable part of Korea for an indefinite time," that MacArthur "shared this confidence," and that Collins himself agreed with them.

But Collins' report to the JCS on MacArthur's attitude was in slightly different terms. Fundamentally, CINCFE's view was that, if he was to continue under the "restrictions" which had been imposed upon him, the war was lost, evacuation was inevitable, and there was no point in seeking an armistice with the Chinese, for our troops could be got off without one. If, however, the United States and the United Nations would accept all-out war with China—including naval blockade, the bombardment of the Chinese mainland, the maximum use of the Chinese Nationalists, and air reconnaissance over Chinese territory—MacArthur would be willing to recombine the Tenth Corps with the Eighth Army and "hold a position across the peninsula as far north as possible." For men in responsible charge of global military-political decisions, this was at best ambiguous. CINCFE was apparently saying that, if his views as to enlarging the war against China were accepted, he would be able to re-form a line—something which had seemed to him "quite impractical" on November 30. Would the removal of the "inhibitions" so completely alter the military situation in Korea? Was the "final destruction"

[26] *Memoirs*, 2: 410.

or evacuation of the Eighth Army otherwise in fact inevitable? MacArthur, as he was afterward to claim, was never technically "insubordinate"—indeed, he was to tell the congressmen that he was probably the "most subordinate" soldier in history—but he was resistant. As Chief of Naval Operations Forrest Sherman was to testify, "Throughout this period the conduct of affairs was made difficult by a lack of responsiveness to the obvious intentions of the directives which were transmitted out there and a tendency to debate and in certain cases to criticize."

THE RIFT WIDENS

At the moment when CINCFE was maneuvering for an all-out war on China as the response to the disaster into which he had run, the high civil and diplomatic command was taking the opposite direction. As has been said, Attlee reached Washington on December 4. On December 5 Lester Pearson, the Canadian Foreign Minister, stressed the need for negotiating a peace with Asian communism. Nehru continued urgently to advocate a cease-fire in Korea and a settlement. At the same time, "The attacks currently being made on the Administration's China policy by its domestic critics suggested that within the United States powerful forces were bent on pushing the country into open and all-out conflict with Communist China."[27] MacArthur's statements and communiqués, though always carefully veiled, were a prominent cause of this impression. A serious issue of high policy—between a probably major war on China or a cease-fire and settlement which would necessarily accept more or less the status quo—had been joined. How far was it appropriate to allow a military commander to employ his military prestige in weighting the decision?

On December 6 JCS dispatched to all theater commanders a directive ordering them to exercise "extreme caution" in their public utterances and to clear all speeches, press releases, or statements concerning foreign or military policy with the Department of the Army before publication. It was, of course, for MacArthur's benefit, but was given a common address in order not to make this too obvious. CINCFE indicated both his understanding of the intent and his contempt for the order by elaborately submitting his next routine communiqué for clearance. Naturally, he was told that this was not required; and he was to use this reply as justification for his freedom with later statements which, unlike the communiqué, did directly concern foreign and military policy.

Meanwhile, the policy decision was being taken. On December 8 the Truman-Attlee conference ended with a communiqué announcing complete agreement: "There can be no thought of appeasement or of rewarding aggression in the Far East or elsewhere." But "we are ready, as we have always been, to seek an end to the hostilities by means of negotiation." It added that every effort would be made to achieve the UN purposes of a free and independent Korea by "peaceful" means. This was the critical point. The aim of clearing all Communists out of North Korea and reuniting the country, which had been embodied in the UN resolution of October 7, was here tacitly abandoned. The United States, with its UN partners, was now willing to end hostilities not by "victory" but by "negotiation." In effect, this meant a settlement on whatever lines the armies might have reached when "negotiation" became effective. Attlee had suggested that "perhaps we could limit our negotiations to the question of keeping the Communists on the 38th parallel," and the Americans had not seriously rebutted the idea.[28] Meanwhile, the unification and democratization of Korea would have to wait upon "peaceful" means. In essence, this was a decision to settle for the status quo ante. When on December 12 India brought into the General Assembly a resolution, supported by thirteen Arab and Asian states, to set up a three-man committee to explore the basis for a cease-fire in Korea, the United States supported it.

In his initial announcement of the "new war" MacArthur had declared that it posed issues beyond the competence of the military command—"issues which must find their solution within the councils of the United Nations and the chancelleries of the world." The solution which had now in effect been returned by the United Nations and the chancelleries of the world was not in the least what MacArthur had in mind. Through the next month or so an ex-

27 Goodrich, Korea, pp. 157–58.

28 Truman, Memoirs, 2: 407.

traordinary and baffling correspondence flowed back and forth between Washington and Tokyo as Washington sought to translate the new policy and the new military strategy into directives which MacArthur would carry out, and as MacArthur sought to use his military recommendations as a means of changing policies with which he did not agree.

It was during the last two or three weeks in December that the Administration, on the one hand, stiffened its new policy, while the Commander in Chief Far East, on the other hand, developed the policy and strategy which he was to advance, after his relief, as his justification. The military situation at this time was significant for both processes. The initial Chinese onslaught had expended its force, and there was something of a lull on the battle lines which everyone knew to be only temporary. The Eighth Army had lost Pyongyang, but it had formed a position of sorts above the parallel and covering Seoul. The Tenth Corps was making its bloody and bitter retreat into the Hungnam perimeter, losing much of its equipment on the way. Its evacuation had not yet been accepted as inevitable, but the possibility that the UN armies might be driven completely from the peninsula was acute in every mind. "Bug-out fever" was epidemic, not only on the fighting fronts, but in many headquarters. As early as November 28 the Joint Chiefs had initiated a staff study of what could be done in case the armies were expelled from Korea.

MacArthur's message of December 3 and Collins' glosses upon it had left Washington in a quandary. The problem, according to Acheson, "led to discussions between the Secretary of Defense and Chiefs of Staff and myself during the latter part of December." Marshall was to provide a vivid little sketch of civil-military relations in this difficult period:

We had a great many discussions. It has been a rather common procedure for the Secretary of State and one or two of his principal men, Mr. Lovett [Under Secretary of Defense] and myself and the Chiefs of Staff to meet in the Chiefs of Staff room and hold discussions of two and three hours over these various matters, generally with some specific document. . . . Then we would investigate it, or the Chiefs of Staff had, through their lower working levels, and then their reply had gone back informally [to State], and then this meeting would occur. . . .

We always reached agreement, and it was an agreement where the Chiefs of Staff sat on one side of the table, and Secretary of State Acheson, with his people, and Lovett and myself sat on the other; in other words, the civilian discussing it from our point of view, as nearly as I was civilian, and the military across from us.

Now those were carried either to the Security Council or direct to the President. . . . and I do not recall a case where the President overrode the Secretary of Defense or the Chiefs of Staff . . . to the advantage of the State Department.

On December 22 Walton Walker, commanding the Eighth Army, was killed in a jeep accident. General Matthew B. Ridgway was snatched from his family's Christmas observances and rushed to Korea to replace him. Conferring with MacArthur in Tokyo on Christmas Day, Ridgway was approached by CINCFE with the idea that the Chinese Nationalists on Formosa should be "used" as a diversionary force in "mainland China"—something of a new suggestion, much as the previous (and rejected) proposals had been for the employment of such troops in Korea. Ridgway, new to the theater and to the Far East, sent a cautious personal memorandum to Collins, explaining that he accepted "the logic" of this proposal, considered "entirely as related to my responsibilities . . . for ground operations." He made it rather plain that the memorandum was sent only to insure that silence would not be construed as opposition to his new theater commander. But, whatever Ridgway thought, the incident shows that a new buttress was being established for the MacArthur strategy.

The New Directive

The directive of September 15 (issued on the now far-distant day of the Inchon landing) had instructed CINCFE that the United States "would not permit itself to become engaged in a general war with Communist China" and, in the event of Chinese intervention, had authorized MacArthur only "to continue military action as long as it offered a reasonable chance of successful resistance." This, if not completely out of date, at least seemed no longer to be controlling in CINCFE's mind. On December 27 Marshall completed a draft directive to meet the new situation. It was discussed among Truman, Acheson, Bradley, Rusk, and Marshall during the following day. It was put into final form and dispatched on December 29:

It appears from all estimates available [these, it must be noted, were mainly MacArthur's estimates] that the Chinese Communists possess the capability of forcing United Nations forces out of Korea if they choose to exercise it. The execution of this capability might be prevented by making the effort so costly to the enemy that they would abandon it [was this a reference to the strategic atomic bombing of China?], or by committing substantial additional United States forces to that theater, thus seriously jeopardizing other commitments including the safety of Japan.

We believe that Korea is not the place to fight a major war. Further, we believe that we should not commit our remaining available ground forces to action against Chinese Communist forces in Korea in face of the increased threat of general war. However, a successful resistance to Chinese–North Korean aggression at some position in Korea and a deflation of the military and political prestige of the Chinese Communists would be of great importance to our national interest, if they could be accomplished without incurring serious losses.

Your basic directive [to assist the Republic of Korea and restore peace and security] . . . requires modification in the light of the present situation. You are now directed to defend in successive positions [subject to safety of your troops as your primary consideration*], subject to the primary consideration of the continued threat to Japan, to determine in advance our last reasonable opportunity for an orderly evacuation. It seems to us that if you are forced back to position in the vicinity of the Kum River . . . and if thereafter the Chinese Communists mass large forces . . . with an evident capability of forcing us out of Korea, it then would be necessary under these conditions to direct you to commence a withdrawal to Japan.[29]

The directive concluded with a request for CINCFE's views and a statement, which Tokyo thought "ominous," that "definite direction on conditions for initiation of evacuation will be provided when your views are received."

[29] Whitney, *MacArthur*, pp. 429–30. There are two versions of this directive. One was a paraphrase read into the record of the MacArthur hearings (*The Military Situation in the Far East*, Hearings, 82nd Cong., 1st sess., 1951, p. 2179), the other that given (without source) by General Whitney. Since the Whitney version reads much more clearly and intelligibly, it is presumably the original, and has been used here. But the starred phrase, in brackets here, does not appear in the Whitney version, where there are three dots. It has been inserted from the paraphrase of the hearings.

MacArthur's Counterproposal

MacArthur, according to Whitney,[30] received this directive "in utter dismay." It declared that Korea was not the place to fight a major war. "Was it, then," in Whitney's words, "a policy that we would meet Communist aggression in Asia only if we could do it without too much trouble?" MacArthur, reading this formal directive from his superiors, made two deductions: first, that the Administration had "completely lost the 'will to win' in Korea"; second, that it was trying to offload upon the general's shoulders its responsibility for the "shameful decision" to evacuate the peninsula. The Commander in Chief Far East sat down late on the night of December 30 to compose an excoriating reply:

It is quite clear now that the entire military resource of the Chinese nation, with logistic support from the Soviet, is committed to a maximum effort against the United Nations command. . . . Meanwhile, under existing restrictions, our naval and air potential are being only partially utilized and the great potential of Chinese Nationalist force on Formosa and guerrilla action on the mainland are being ignored. . . .

Should a policy determination be reached . . . to recognize the state of war which had been forced upon us by the Chinese authorities . . . we could: (1) blockade the coast of China; (2) destroy through naval gunfire and air bombardment China's industrial capacity to wage war; (3) secure reinforcements from the Nationalist garrison in Formosa to strengthen our position in Korea *if we decide to continue the fight for that peninsula*; and (4) release . . . the Formosan garrison for diversionary action (possibly leading to counterinvasion) against vulnerable areas of the Chinese mainland.

I believe that by the foregoing measures we could severely cripple and largely neutralize China's capability to wage aggressive war and thus save Asia from the engulfment otherwise facing it. [Italics added.]

The general went on to intimate that once this general war had been opened upon Communist China, we could evacuate Korea and "effect a strategic displacement of our forces [to] . . . the littoral island chain" without embarrassment. The same officer had hotly insisted only a few weeks before that to leave even a five-mile buffer strip along the Yalu

[30] *MacArthur*, pp. 430–31.

would be "appeasement" and "so immoral a proposition" as to bankrupt our influence in Asia. As to whether the proposed retaliation on China would bring on Soviet intervention, CINCFE felt that to be a matter purely "of speculation." He believed that a Russian decision for or against a general war would depend solely on the Russians' own estimates of relative strength; that it would, in other words, in no way be affected by anything that we did. Yet he had just seen the full force of the Red Chinese army thrown against him because of an American advance which had changed the Chinese calculations of strength and interest.

MacArthur ended by giving what Whitney, inaccurately, calls a "cold, professional estimate": Unless the "restrictions" were removed and the proposed all-out war on China were accepted, then the plan of a successive retreat into the Pusan beachhead was "tactically sound." In execution of this plan it would be unnecessary for JCS to make an "anticipatory decision for evacuation"; the implication was that, when they had been forced to the beachhead, evacuation would be inevitable anyway.

Ridgway Takes Command in Korea

This, surely, was a remarkable reply by a field general to his higher military and civil command. What not only Truman but the Joint Chiefs of Staff wanted, and desperately needed, to know was whether MacArthur could and would hold on in Korea under the conditions—or "restrictions"—which had been imposed upon him for what were believed to be the most compelling reasons of high policy. What they got was not a "cold, professional" answer to this question; it was in effect an announcement that MacArthur would not play unless both the policy and the strategy were transformed in accordance with his liking. Ridgway was in these hours touring the front lines of the Eighth Army. It is not surprising that he was shocked by the state of morale which he encountered. It was an army of beaten, apprehensive men who had lost not only their aggressiveness but their alertness. They were "not patrolling as they should"; they knew nothing about the enemy before them; they did not know the terrain; they were not preparing rear lines of defense against the attack which everyone expected to come, and

they did not know what they were fighting for or why they should be expected to continue.

Ridgway flung himself into the task of infusing a new spirit. When he met President Syngman Rhee his first words were: "Mr. President, I am glad to be here. And I've come to stay."[31] It was not the mood in Tokyo, where they were considering the abandonment of the peninsula and a retreat to "the littoral islands."

Shortly after dark on New Year's Eve (the day after MacArthur's reply to JCS) the Chinese delivered the expected attack. Despite Ridgway's efforts, the Eighth Army was still spread too thin and was too dispirited to stem it; on January 2 the hard decision to evacuate Seoul had to be taken; the UN forces retreated south of the Han into central Korea, but the prepared lines which Ridgway had urged were enough to hold against the diminishing enemy attack. The Hungnam perimeter was abandoned and the Tenth Corps rejoined the Eighth Army. A position was reconstituted across the peninsula. It was far south of the 38th parallel, but it was also far north of the Pusan beachhead into which CINCFE had intimated that he must inevitably be driven. Temporarily the situation had been stabilized. No one knew whether or how long it could be maintained.

REJECTION OF THE MacARTHUR PROGRAM

For MacArthur's superiors in Washington, both military and civilian, his message of December 30 posed a formidable problem. They were being compelled to deal in these days with issues of rearmament, of NATO, of global defense and global policy, in which Korea was only a part, yet into which Korean policy had to be fitted with care if the whole was to succeed. Yet they had to deal with the Korean aspects through this unusual man who had access to strong popular and political forces, the workings of whose subtle mind they did not easily follow, and whose motivations they had been taught by experience to distrust. CINCFE's demand for an all-out war on China (accompanied by the hint that under cover of such a war they might evacuate Korea altogether, thus reducing the American casualties)

[31] Matthew B. Ridgway, *Soldier* (New York: Harper, 1956), p. 204.

clearly raised two major questions. One, which was to be endlessly discussed after MacArthur's recall, concerned the danger of bringing on Soviet intervention and a third world war, or, at the very least, of fragmenting the UN and NATO alliances and leaving the United States naked to a Soviet-dominated world. The other, which received comparatively little public attention, concerned the effectiveness of MacArthur's strategy as regarded strictly from a military viewpoint.

In his message of December 30 MacArthur had advanced four specific proposals. The first, a naval blockade of China, could not interrupt the main line of Chinese military supply, which was overland from the Soviet Union, and could add little to the embargo which we were already organizing. The second, destruction of China's industrial capacity by air bombardment, could have had only a long-delayed effect upon the operations in Korea. It might ultimately have put so much pressure upon the Mao regime as to lead it to abandon the Korean War and retire behind the Yalu in order to escape further punishment; but all World War II experience with "strategic" and "population" bombing combined to suggest that such a result, if attained at all, could be attained only at the cost of a slaughter of Chinese civilians and a devastation of the country so vast that our own people would rebel at the horror while our name would become anathema throughout the world.

It is interesting that, when MacArthur returned to lay his program before Congress and the country, he suppressed this proposal for the destruction of China's "industrial capacity to wage war," doubtless because its real implications were too obvious. On the other hand, in his December 30 message to JCS he wasted no words over the demand for an attack upon the "sanctuary" bases in Manchuria, of which so much was afterward to be made. Doubtless this was because it would be apparent to the experienced military men in JCS that, with his air demonstrably unable to interdict the 200-mile enemy communication line now running from the Yalu to the military frontier, the extension of the air attack across the river, while it could have helped, would hardly have been decisive.

As to the third and fourth points in the MacArthur program, the "use" of Chinese National-

ist troops in Korea had been rejected by everyone on the grounds that they would be "ineffective," while it required a belief in military miracles to imagine that they could create any significant diversion by guerrilla operations in South China. "We are not prolonging this war," as Bradley was later to put it, "just for the fun of it. The only difference is General MacArthur thinks that to do certain additional operations would be decisive, and we do not think they would be decisive. They might help a little bit, but to offset that you must run the risk of opening up World War III." But enmeshed as they were in "security," the Joint Chiefs were never able to get this point of view over clearly to the public. The military-technical aspects of the MacArthur program (if it can be called a "program") were always its most obscure facet.

In Washington, as the new year came in, the public was not yet a factor in the argument, and the Joint Chiefs had no difficulty in appraising the MacArthur recommendations. What they could not clearly judge, through the fluent prose of CINCFE's telegrams, was the extent to which they might be risking the destruction of the Eighth Army by following their own policy—which was, essentially, to hang on in Korea as long as possible with the means available in the hope of securing an acceptable cease-fire. They were not on the ground; and the great tradition of independence for the theater commander forbade them from questioning his reports. Their uncertainty about the real position of the Eighth Army was MacArthur's greatest weapon against them; and it is hard to doubt that CINCFE at least tried to use it to secure the policies he believed were necessary.

KOREA, 1951—THE PHILIPPINES, 1942

On January 9 the Joint Chiefs of Staff, with the approval of the President and the Secretary of State, produced another official directive. CINCFE was told that his proposed retaliatory measures against China could not be permitted, and was again directed to "defend in successive positions" subject to "the safety of his troops and his basic mission of protecting Japan." But it added: "Should it become evident in the judgment of CINCFE that evacuation was essential to avoid severe losses of men and material, CINCFE was at that time to withdraw from Korea to Japan." The reception of this message in Tokyo reflects the curious state of mind now ruling in that proud, defeated, and withdrawn headquarters. What they saw in it was not an order but, in Whitney's words, a "booby-trap"! The pro-British, if not pro-Communist, conspirators in Washington were trying to throw on MacArthur the onus for the Korean debacle and the evacuation which, as a result of it, might become inevitable. "MacArthur refused to be so easily taken in,"[32] and on January 10 sent an angry, yet subtle, reply:

There is no doubt but that a beachhead line can be held by our existing forces for a limited time in Korea, but this could not be accomplished without losses. . . . The troops are tired from a long and difficult campaign, embittered by the shameful propaganda which has falsely condemned their courage and fighting quality in misunderstood retrograde maneuver, and their morale will become a serious threat to their battle efficiency unless the political basis on which they are asked to trade life for time is quickly delineated, fully understood and so impelling that the hazards of battle are cheerfully accepted.

One cannot help contrasting Ridgway's efforts to restore morale and fighting spirit at the front with this attempt by the theater commander to use the alleged dissatisfactions of his troops to achieve his political ends. CINCFE went on to tell JCS that he was in full agreement with "their" estimate that the limitations imposed on him would eventually render evacuation unavoidable. "In the absence of overriding political considerations, under these conditions the command should be withdrawn from the peninsula just as rapidly as it is feasible to do so." There was a final turn of the screw:

Under the extraordinary limitations and conditions imposed upon the command in Korea . . . its military position is untenable, but it can hold, if over-riding political considerations so dictate, for any length of time up to its complete destruction. Your clarification requested.

This threw Washington into a consternation comparable to that which had been caused nearly a decade before by a similar message from the same officer under similar circum-

32 Whitney, *MacArthur*, p. 435.

stances. In February 1942, at the height of the defense of Bataan, MacArthur had shocked Washington by supporting a proposal from President Quezon that the Philippines be neutralized and the American troops evacuated. Then, as in 1951, the apparent purpose was to compel the dispatch of reinforcements (which were not yet in existence) and force a reversal of high policy, from the strategy of "Europe first," which had at that time already been adopted, to one of "the Far East first." In 1942 MacArthur was told, immediately and emphatically, that "American forces will continue to keep our flag flying in the Philippines so long as there remains any possibility of resistance"; and that put an end to the maneuver. Under the political and psychological conditions of 1951 it was difficult for Washington to be so forthright.[33]

According to Admiral Sherman, the Chief of Naval Operations, "the character of that reply of the 10th January was such as to precipitate an immediate meeting of the Joint Chiefs on the 11th, a further meeting on the 12th; the preparation of a new military directive which was then dispatched, and then the Department of State . . . arranged to send their message.

33 The parallel between the two episodes is so close that it deserves elaboration for the light it throws on MacArthur's attitude in Korea. In 1942, as in 1951, the general was careful to evade any direct responsibility for the proposed evacuation. He encouraged and assisted Quezon to make the proposal, to which he merely appended his own "comments." In these he said: "Since I have no air or sea protection, you must be prepared at any time to figure on the complete destruction of this command. . . . The temper of the Filipinos is one of almost violent resentment against the United States. Every one of them expected help and when it has not been forthcoming they believe they have been betrayed in favor of others. . . . the plan of President Quezon might offer the best possible solution of what is about to be a disastrous debacle. It would not affect the ultimate situation in the Philippines for that would be determined by results in other theaters. . . . Please instruct me." The instructions were prompt; and the "violent resentment" of the Filipinos, which he had used as an argument, just as he used the low morale of the Eighth Army a decade later, evaporated. The military debacle which he prophesied was unavoidable (as it proved not to be in Korea), but few would hold today that either the national interest or his own reputation would have been served by adopting the proposal which, for whatever reason, he abetted and supported. (Henry L. Stimson and McGeorge Bundy, *On Active Service in Peace and War* [New York: Harper, 1948], pp. 397–404; Richard H. Rovere and Arthur M. Schlesinger, Jr., *The General and the President and the Future of American Foreign Policy* [New York: Farrar, Straus & Young, 1951], pp. 58–59.)

That period of January 9, 10, 11, 12 and 13 was a very difficult one." Washington was not interested in "booby-trapping" General MacArthur. These high military and civilian officials were carrying a tremendous responsibility, trying desperately to reach correct solutions for desperately serious issues of national policy and strategy. At this juncture the Commander in Chief Far East had presented them with the deadliest threat which a military commander— in a democratic society at least—can raise against his military and civil superiors: the threat of the "complete" and useless "destruction" of the armies under his command. That the Joint Chiefs' position was indeed "difficult" is plain. MacArthur's motivations, on the other hand, are more obscure. But, whether his real purpose was to force an enlargement of the war or to force an immediate evacuation, one cannot help noting another obvious consequence of his recommendations. Whatever Washington might do, they would have the effect of putting MacArthur in a position in which he would be free of responsibility and free of blame.

Should Washington enlarge the war, this would validate MacArthur's contention that his defeat had been due solely to the inhibitions under which he had suffered, while, since this would be a "political" decision which the general had insisted was beyond his "military" competence, any resultant disasters would be the fault of the politicians. Should Washington elect for an immediate evacuation, that would equally exonerate him of the military reverse and prove him right in maintaining that Korea could not be held under the limitations imposed upon him by the politicians. But, since he had expressed his willingness to fight to "destruction" if the politicians so ordered, he could not be blamed for the evacuation. If Washington ordered him to stay on the restricted basis, then MacArthur would be free to wash his hands of the consequences. Whatever disasters might ensue could not be blamed on him; but neither—as this brilliant mind only tardily realized—could subsequent successes be laid to his credit. It may seem invidious to imply that General MacArthur made so personal and egoistic a calculation of the immense responsibilities of his office; yet we have the faithful Whitney's word for it that MacArthur saw in the January 9 directive only a personal "booby-trap" and that the January 10 response which caused such alarm in Washington was dictated by a refusal "to be so easily taken in." When Admiral Sherman was later asked whether there had not been at this time a "failure of teamwork" between MacArthur and the Joint Chiefs, his reply, emphatic as it was, must seem an understatement: "At this period, possibly better than any other indication [sic], the normal relationships which are desirable between one echelon of command and another had been seriously impaired."

THE NEW INSTRUCTIONS

The crisis produced three documents. The first was another directive, sent on January 11, which repeated the previous instructions, or, "in other words," as Bradley later put it, told MacArthur "to stay in Korea." The second was a JCS "memorandum," dated January 12, on possible courses to be followed in case the United States should be forced back into the Pusan beachhead or compelled to evacuate. This paper had its source in the staff studies which JCS had ordered on November 28, a month and a half before; as finally evolved and approved (after two revisions), it clearly reflected some of MacArthur's ideas. It was submitted to the National Security Council, but a copy went to CINCFE. The third was a message direct from the President to MacArthur, sent on January 13. MacArthur had repeatedly insisted that he must have "political" decisions. "In the absence of over-riding political considerations, . . . the command should be withdrawn," and so on. It had been intended to explain the political considerations to him in the military directive, but to the purists in the Pentagon this was a forbidden commingling of the two spheres. After anxious discussion between the President, the State Department, and the Joint Chiefs, the "military part" was "pulled out" and sent as a directive; the political part was embodied in Truman's message of January 13, which sought to expound to the general the serious political considerations which underlay his military orders. But no one by that time could have supposed that what MacArthur really wanted was explanations, or that he would be materially affected by any given him. The really critical question was no longer CINCFE: it was the Eighth Army—its morale, its capabilities, its adequacy as an in-

strument of the policy not of General Mac-
Arthur but of the United States. As Truman's
message was dispatched, General Collins em-
planed for another visit to the Far East to find
out what was really going on.

It seems not too much to say that, with
Collins' arrival in the Far East, MacArthur's
influence was largely finished. Perhaps this was
the real end of that overshadowing career. Collins is represented by MacArthur's supporters
as having been under the impression when he
landed in Tokyo that evacuation was inevitable. If so, he realized by the time he reached
the front in Korea that the peril had been
grossly exaggerated. Ridgway had restored the
Eighth Army to a fighting outfit, while Mac-
Arthur had been sitting withdrawn in Tokyo,
knowing really very little about the armies he
commanded, nursing his personal grievances
against an Administration which he detested.
From the moment of the retirement in early
January to the prepared lines below the Han,
Ridgway had started his people on aggressive
patrolling. The Chinese at the same time had
spent their drive and outrun their communications. Ridgway had felt out the opposition
against him, first with platoon and company
units, then with battalions and regimental combat teams. On January 25, only ten days after
Collins' arrival in the Far East, Ridgway
launched a full-scale attack on a two-corps
front that "was never stopped until it had
driven the enemy back across the Parallel."[34]
MacArthur had provided for every contingency
save one—the contingency of success.

Belatedly, MacArthur appeared to realize
that he was in an untenable position, just as
he had in the case of his maneuver in the Philippines a decade before. In 1942 he had
quickly shifted his stance; he had carried on
the great defense of Bataan, and, although disaster was inevitable, he had emerged from it as
the hero of the Pacific war. In 1951 a similar
shift was attempted. With the messages from
Washington and Collins' arrival it was clear
that the MacArthur program of evacuation
under cover of an expanded war against China
had no future; with the growing success of the
Eighth Army it was clear that the Washington
policy was promising. MacArthur seized upon
the President's "political" message of Janu-

ary 13 as his avenue of retreat. As Whitney
maintained then and thereafter, this was the
"first" indication the Tokyo command had received that Washington intended for them to
stay in Korea—something which Washington
had for weeks been urgently desiring that they
should do if possible. Whitney even put an
added twist on this contention. During the
controversy later in the spring he was quoted
in the newspapers:

> General MacArthur's spokesman said today that
> until January 13 this year, MacArthur believed
> Washington officials wanted our forces evacuated
> from Korea and made a scapegoat for some politi-
> cal advantage. Major General Courtney Whitney,
> MacArthur's aide, said a January 13 message from
> President Truman was the Government's first clear
> statement to MacArthur to hold in Korea.

But it was too late by that time. The general
could no longer emerge as the hero of policies
which he had so persistently obstructed; and
the further course of the Korean War passed
beyond the influence of the Tokyo headquarters. The controlling factors thenceforth were
to be, after the President, the State Department, JCS, and Ridgway.

KOREAN OBJECTIVES RECONSIDERED

In mid-December the United Nations had
adopted the resolution looking toward a cease-
fire in Korea; in mid-January it was considering the "five principles" submitted by the
Canadian Foreign Minister, Lester Pearson,
looking toward an immediate cease-fire with a
"united Korea" to be established later by diplomatic negotiation. The Canadian resolution
was adopted on January 13 and immediately
rejected by the Chinese Communists. "Now,"
said Acheson, "we must face . . . the fact that
the Chinese Communists have no intention of
ceasing their defiance of the United Nations";
the United States demanded a UN resolution
formally declaring Red China, as well as North
Korea, an aggressor.[35] But this was not a declaration of war; and it was a reluctant General
Assembly which in early February adopted
even this much. According to the *New York
Times* report, "The aggression was undeniable,
but most of the Asian and Arab countries held
back to the last, and the Western European
nations accepted it only with the reservation

---

[34] Ridgway, *Soldier*, p. 216.

[35] Goodrich, *Korea*, pp. 160–62.

that they would oppose almost any further action."

Under the circumstances, the condemnation had little meaning. MacArthur continued to issue statements or inspire newspaper stories demanding the "use" of the Chinese Nationalists, complaining of his "inhibitions," or calling for "decisions far beyond the scope of the authority vested in me as the military commander, . . . but which must provide on the highest international levels an answer to the obscurities which now becloud the unsolved problems raised by Red China's undeclared war in Korea." But, as the nightmare of forced evacuation receded, as the Eighth Army under Ridgway continued to forge ahead, despite the "inhibitions" and "obscurities," it seemed increasingly probable that the United States could bring the Chinese Communists to negotiate for a cease-fire on terms relatively favorable to the United Nations.

Beginning on February 6, there were informal meetings once a week between representatives of the State Department and JCS to consider ultimate objectives in Korea. As the battle once more approached the 38th parallel it was realized that serious decisions would once more have to be made; but the soldiers and the diplomats were agreed that they could not be made until the real balances of power became clearer. MacArthur was already publicly implying that, despite Ridgway's successes, the best that could be hoped for was simply an endless military stalemate and an endless drain of blood. Both the civilians and the soldiers in Washington thought it better to wait and see. The State Department could not define rational political objectives until it knew what were the military capabilities on which it would have to rely; JCS could not determine a "suitable" course of military action until it knew what political objectives would be adopted. This did not represent a conflict between the civilian and the military viewpoints, but a mutual understanding that decisions, for each, would have to be kept in abeyance until the situation, in Korea and on the global stage, was clearer.

THE RELIEF OF MacARTHUR

By the middle of March, Seoul was being retaken and the armies were again close to the 38th parallel. Our UN allies felt that we should not again invade North Korea without attempting a settlement; and the State Department, with the concurrence of the Department of Defense, recommended another effort to secure a cease-fire approximately on the parallel. On March 20 General MacArthur was advised that a presidential announcement was being planned to the effect that the United Nations was prepared to discuss "the conditions of settlement" in Korea. It was explained to CINCFE that this would be done because of the UN belief that a diplomatic effort should be made before another military crossing of the parallel, but that Washington, on the other hand, recognized that the parallel had no military significance and did not want unduly to restrict MacArthur's military operations in the interests of this essentially diplomatic move. The State Department desired MacArthur's recommendations as to how much freedom of military action it should preserve for him over the next few weeks in respect to this artificial boundary. CINCFE replied at once that, since he could not clear North Korea in any event with his existing force, his directives required no modification.

MacARTHUR DEMANDS SURRENDER

A draft of the presidential statement was thereupon prepared; and it was still being elaborately discussed among the State Department, the Department of Defense, and the Allied representatives in Washington when on March 24 General MacArthur in Tokyo issued his own public demand for a cease-fire. It was very different from that being debated in Washington:

Even under the inhibitions which now restrict the activity of the United Nations forces . . . Red China . . . has been shown its complete inability to accomplish by force of arms the conquest of Korea. The enemy, therefore, must by now be painfully aware that a decision of the United Nations to depart from its tolerant effort to contain the war to the area of Korea, through an expansion of our military operations to its coastal areas and interior bases, would doom Red China to the risk of imminent military collapse. These basic facts being established, there should be no insuperable difficulty in arriving at decisions on the Korean problems if the issues are resolved on their own merits, without being burdened by extraneous matters not directly related to Korea, such as Formosa or China's seat in the United Nations.

The Korean nation and its people . . . must not

be sacrificed. This is a paramount concern. . . .
I stand ready at any time to confer in the field
with the commander-in-chief of the enemy forces
in the earnest effort to find any military means
whereby realization of the political objectives of
the United Nations in Korea . . . might be accomplished without further bloodshed.

Thus did CINCFE adroitly torpedo the
Washington political initiative of which he had
been privately advised. Unable or unwilling to
climb back upon the Washington policy, he
was apparently determined to destroy it. With
this statement, he transformed what had been
intended as an offer to negotiate into what
could only come as a demand for surrender,
on pain of sanctions which neither Washington
nor the United Nations had any intention of
applying and in the interest of an objective
(the military unification of Korea) which both
Washington and the United Nations had long
since abandoned. Perforce, the draft of the
presidential statement had to be laid aside. In
his *Memoirs*[36] the former President recalled the
anecdote which Lincoln produced when confronted by a somewhat similar move on the
part of General McClellan: "it made me think
of the man whose horse kicked up and stuck
his foot through the stirrup. He said to the
horse: 'If you are going to get on, I will get
off.' " Like Lincoln, Truman was in no doubt
as to who was going to get on and who would
get off. "By this act," he writes, "MacArthur
left me no choice—I could no longer tolerate
his insubordination."

Acheson, Lovett, and the Joint Chiefs met
immediately to consider this latest MacArthur
crisis; later on the same afternoon they discussed it with Truman. The only immediate
result was an icy message from JCS: "The
President has directed that your attention be
called" to the order of December 6 requiring
clearance for statements dealing with policy. In
view of the private information given him on
March 20, "any" further statements by the general "must be coordinated" as therein prescribed. Truman had not yet fully decided on
his course, but within a day or two his mind
was made up: MacArthur would have to be relieved. There is some reason to believe that
Marshall may have arrived independently at

[36] 2: 442, 443.

the same conclusion, also well before the next
incident, which was to provide the opportunity.

THE LETTER TO MARTIN

In February the House Minority Leader,
Representative Joseph W. Martin, Jr., had delivered a violently and explicitly partisan attack
on the Truman foreign policy, turning mainly on
a demand for the employment of "the anti-Communist forces of the Republic of China"—
forces which the Minority Leader put somewhat extravagantly at "800,000 trained men."
There was, he said, "good reason to believe"
that MacArthur favored their use, and that
there were "people in the Pentagon" who favored it likewise. Martin shipped his speech to
the general with a request for comment. On
March 20 (the day he was advised of Truman's proposed offer to negotiate) MacArthur
responded with his usual fluency. The congressman's views on the "utilization" of the
Chinese Nationalists were in conflict neither
with "logic" nor the "tradition" of invariably
"meeting force with maximum counterforce."
He continued:

It seems strangely difficult for some to realize
that here in Asia is where the Communist conspirators have elected to make their play for
global conquest, and that we have joined the issue
thus raised on the battlefield; that here we fight
Europe's war with arms while the diplomats there
still fight it with words; that if we lose this war
to Communism in Asia the fall of Europe is inevitable, win it and Europe most probably would
avoid war and yet preserve freedom. As you point
out, we must win. There is no substitute for victory.

The general did not ask that these views be
held in confidence; he did not add such a request after he had read the message about the
forthcoming offer to negotiate. Nor did he follow the letter with such a request when, a few
days later, he received the peremptory directive, ordering him to clear all policy statements.
Martin read the letter on the floor of the House
on April 5, 1951, and the next morning, a Friday, it was headlined throughout the country
and the world. MacArthur, as the *New York
Times*' report put it, "struck at the very basis
of the Administration's concept of how the tide
of Communist imperialism is to be rolled back.
With barbed words he asserted that he was

fighting Europe's war with arms." The President moved to take action.

THE DECISION IS MADE

Bradley had been alerted, he could not remember by whom, on Thursday afternoon, and had held a brief meeting of the Joint Chiefs to warn them that they had better begin studying "the military aspects." Before the Cabinet meeting on Friday morning, Truman conferred with Acheson, Marshall, Bradley, and his own special assistant, Averell Harriman. All apparently agreed that MacArthur ought to be relieved, though Marshall expressed caution and the arresting thought that, if the general were dismissed, "it might be difficult to get the military appropriations through Congress." These were, of course, the huge appropriations for rearmament and NATO. Acheson foresaw "the biggest fight of your administration." After the Cabinet meeting these same men had a further discussion. Truman was "careful not to disclose that I had already reached a decision"; and it was determined that he would seek the views of the Joint Chiefs on "the military aspects."[37] The rituals had to be meticulously observed. It was not military usurpation which was the danger at the moment; the danger was that any assertion of civilian control in seeming disregard of military advice would be used by opposition politicians to attack the civil Administration.

The same group met again briefly on Saturday, April 7. According to Truman,[38] Marshall, who had been reading the files, now said that MacArthur should have been fired two years before. They discussed the possibility of giving the command in Korea to Ridgway while retaining MacArthur in his essentially political post in Tokyo; but this they rejected as impracticable. Truman sent them away to think it over, while Bradley got the Joint Chiefs together Sunday afternoon. They were, he reported, unanimous in the opinion that, from a strictly "military" point of view, MacArthur should be relieved. It was necessary to have a theater commander who was "more responsive" to JCS control from Washington; besides, they thought the general had been insubordinate in failing to comply with the directive to clear his

[37] *Ibid.*, p. 447.
[38] *Ibid.*, p. 448.

statements, and they believed that "the military must be controlled by civilian authority in this country." Truman called the original group back to the White House on Monday; Bradley reported the views of JCS; all declared their conclusion that the general should be relieved, and the President announced his decision to relieve him.

On Tuesday afternoon, April 10, they discussed the drafts of the messages and announcements. To soften the blow as much as possible, they arranged for its delivery through Frank Pace, Secretary of the Army, who was then in Korea. But there was a foul-up of communications; Pace, visiting the front lines, could not be reached; Washington feared that there had been a leak, and the announcement was given to the press at 1:00 A.M. Wednesday, April 11. In Tokyo, it was about 3:00 in the afternoon of the same day. The news reached MacArthur, rather brutally, by way of the commercial news broadcasts, which were brought to him as he sat at the end of a luncheon. The famous general had been summarily dismissed.

If this had never really represented a conflict between the "civilian" and "military" elements in the control of national policy, it at least threw considerable light upon the actual (as distinct from the theoretical or rhetorical) relationships between them. Whether or not they dealt wisely, Truman and his advisers, in uniform and out of it, had at least dealt firmly and effectively with a complicated problem of policy, politics, and personality which affected civil-military considerations of great difficulty and delicacy. As far as the Administration was concerned, the "MacArthur problem" had been solved, for good or ill. But the Administration, of course, represents but one element in the formulation and control of American military and foreign policy. Congress, the political party system, the press, and the public remained. Not the least instructive aspect of the MacArthur episode is the manner in which these other great instruments of policy formulation responded to it.

THE MacARTHUR HEARINGS

Douglas MacArthur returned to the United States in an enormous fanfare of publicity in which partisan political pressures—which the

general had seldom sought to discourage—
were prominent. IIe was invited to appear on
April 19 before a joint session of the two
houses of Congress, where he was received
with the utmost deference, and where he delivered a self-justification (in some respects
rather less than frank) and an attack upon the
Administration's conduct of a foreign war of a
kind not often permitted to top generals just
relieved for insubordination to the civil authority.

Had the American people believed themselves to be engaged (as in fact they were) in
a large-scale war effort for the attainment of
vital national objectives, the MacArthur address to Congress could hardly have been
given. But because Korea represented a struggle which the Administration was trying to
keep within the bounds of limited warfare; because there was no grasp of the fact that even
limited warfare might produce major political
results; because there was almost no understanding of the real nature of the enemy's
strength and, consequently, almost no appreciation of the advantages which our internal
dissensions were daily providing him; because
there seemed to be no overriding national peril
to silence the petty bickerings of personal or
party interest, it was possible both for the general to make the address and for it to be received as a major contribution to statesmanship.

.   .   .   .

To most of the Republican senators the hearings were chiefly a means through which they
might exploit MacArthur's relief to the maximum damage of the Truman Administration,
while the cautious Democrats were mainly conducting a kind of delaying action. They dared
not seem too critical of the great military figure who enjoyed so enormous a public reputation; the most they could do was to turn some
of his and the Republicans' shafts. The skill
with which Senator Richard B. Russell (of
Georgia), the chairman of the hearings, managed this has often been noted, and it undoubtedly helped to preserve the nation from courses
which might have been disastrous. But the
Democrats evidently felt it inadvisable to enter

a positive and challenging support of the Truman foreign policies or of MacArthur's dismissal—some of them probably did not want to.
In consequence, although the great majority of
the witnesses were favorable to the Administration, the Administration's case was seldom
clearly or effectively brought out, nor were the
underlying issues of civil-military relationships
with which nearly everyone struggled in one
way or another in the course of the hearings.

.   .   .   .

On June 23, four days before the MacArthur
hearings reached their tortured and, by this
time, tiresome and neglected end, Jacob Malik,
the Soviet delegate to the United Nations,
threw out the suggestion in a UN radio talk
that a truce in Korea was possible. A week
later, Ridgway broadcast an offer to the Chinese commander to consider a truce. The
United Nations and United States command
had in effect asked for peace. It was to take
another two years to get it, and many lives
were to be sacrificed in the interim, but the
whole character of the Korean War was now
altered.

From this point on, the American national
objective was no longer either "victory" or a
reunification of Korea; it was simply and solely
a cessation of hostilities. Against this simple
desire, MacArthur and his supporters could
make no headway. The hearings had generated
enormous amounts of political ammunition for
discharge against the Democratic Administration; what they had quite failed to generate
was any significant public pressure for reversing the course which that Administration was
following. The salient fact is that the American
people did not accept the veiled MacArthur
prescription for "victory"; they did acquiesce
in the Truman policy of a limited war for
limited ends, and were grateful for Eisenhower's conclusion of the war on these terms.
They had listened to General MacArthur with
the enormous respect claimed by his character,
his career, and his achievements; but they
hardly lifted a finger to promote the courses
which he appeared to recommend. "Victory,"
in the terrible modern contexts, had become
too barren a goal to pursue.

MIDSHIPMAN AND CADET PROFILES AND NATIONAL NORMS: A COMPARISON

CHARLES L. COCHRAN

Since service academy graduates continue to predominate in the higher ranks of the military, the individuals who are entering the service academies today will have a great impact on the strategy, doctrine, and policy of the military from twenty to forty years from now. By comparing entering freshmen at the service academies, four-year colleges, technical institutes, and private universities, Professor Cochran is able to formulate some interesting hypotheses concerning academy students, their attitudes, and their impact on the military services. Professor Charles L. Cochran is serving on the faculty of the U.S. Naval Academy; he earned his master's degree from Niagara University and his Ph.D. in political science from Tufts University. He has served as a consultant in international law at the U.S. Naval War College.

INTRODUCTION

This paper is based on the growing recognition of the political impact of the military. The military not only transmits its codes and mores to those who join its ranks, but also attracts people whose images, habits, motives, and values appear to have the greatest chance of fulfillment in the military service. Although the service academies are relatively small institutions, they produce an overwhelming majority of the officers who attain flag rank. Therefore, they have an influence out of proportion to their numbers in determining military policy as well as in giving direction to the military's overall orientation toward the rest of society.

This study examines national normative data of students entering colleges as first-time freshmen during the summer and fall of 1970. The test, designed and scored by the American Council on Education (ACE), is based on responses from 180,684 freshmen entering some 275 different institutions.[1] The data were collected by administering the 1970 Student In-

formation Form to freshmen no later than the first 2 weeks of classes. Data meeting the ACE's quality control requirements were then differentially weighted to be representative of the population of entering freshmen students at all higher educational institutions in the United States.[2]

The 275 institutions that were included in the national norms were then divided into subpopulations consisting of two-year colleges, four-year colleges, and universities. The institutions have been further divided into nine other categories—namely two-year public colleges, two-year private colleges, technological institutions, four-year public colleges, four-year private, nonsectarian colleges, four-year Protestant colleges, four-year Roman Catholic colleges, public universities, and private universities. Responses were also broken down into male and female categories. In this study the ACE-weighted norms for freshmen men at pri-

---

[1] *National Norms for Entering College Freshman: Fall 1970* (Washington, D.C.: American Council on Education, Office of Research, 1970), vol. 5.

[2] For technical details about the sampling design and the weighting procedures which have been used to correct for the disproportionate sampling of institutions in each cell, see John A. Creager *et al.*, *National Norms for Entering College Freshmen: Fall 1968* (Washington, D.C.: American Council on Education, Office of Research, 1968), vol. 3.

Reprinted by permission of the author and publisher from the Naval War College Review, *May 1972, pp. 37–47. Minor editorial changes have been made.*

vate universities will be used in comparing the academies with the university set. Other categories will be used when the contrast or comparison proves useful.

The U.S. Air Force Academy (USAFA) and the U.S. Military Academy (USMA) also took part in the ACE test, and their results are included in this study. Therefore, unless otherwise identified, figures for the academies will refer to the Air, Naval, and Military Academies combined.

BACKGROUND CHARACTERISTICS

Before examining the beliefs and attitudes of midshipmen and cadets, it is worthwhile to consider briefly some background characteristics that might affect their outlook and behavior.

Entering plebes at the academies reported a higher average grade in secondary schools than did males in any other group. Technical institutions, a category in which the three academies are included, had the next highest grade distribution, followed by private universities. Table 1 indicates the dispersion. The difference between the academy students and the non-academy students at four-year colleges is statistically significant at all levels. It is also signifi-

cantly higher than private universities in at least the three highest categories.

The responses to the question concerning grades were supported by cross-checking them with the question concerning class standing. (See Table 2.) Once again the academies reported the highest class rankings, followed by technical institutions, while private universities virtually tied with public universities as the third highest respondent. The academy students compiled this impressive record while attending, for the most part, schools in which an unusually high percentage of the students were college bound[3] and where the scholastic competition was keen.

The achievements of academy students while in high school, when compared with students of other colleges, suggest that Military and Naval Academy students as a whole not only have excellent academic potential but are high achievers as well. Plebes were more likely to have excelled in areas where excellence can be measured by the individual's performance, such

---

[3] Academy students estimated that 75 percent of their classmates were going to college 35 percent of the time, while 32 percent of college males estimated that such a high percentage of their classmates were college bound. Forty-eight percent of those attending private universities estimated that about 75 percent of their classmates were college bound.

Table 1
Average Grade in High School (Males)

Average Grade	Academies	Four-Year Colleges	Technical Institutions	Private Universities
A or A+	17.5%	4.7%	14.0%	10.1%
A−	24.7	8.7	20.9	13.3
B+	28.2	17.1	29.9	19.6
B	18.1	24.2	22.0	23.8
B−	7.1	18.3	8.5	16.6
C+	2.6	16.5	3.4	11.8
C	0.3	10.0	1.2	4.6
D	0.0	0.6	0.1	0.1

Sources: National Norms for Entering College Freshmen: Fall 1970; and Gerald W. Medsger, *A Comparison of New Cadets at USMA with Entering Freshmen at Other Colleges, Class of 1974* (West Point: Office of Institutional Research, 1971), p. 9. Data were also supplied by USAFA and USNA Student Information Form responses. Four-year colleges include all public and private institutions granting a bachelor's degree. Private universities are those colleges under private control that are parts of universities, as opposed to public universities, which fall under state or local governmental control. Both technical institutions and private university-related colleges provide a selective base for comparison because of their generally more selective admissions policy and because they probably draw on much the same population of high school graduates as the service academies.

Table 2
Academic Rank in High School (Males)

Rank	Academies	Four-Year Colleges	Technical Institutions	Private Universities
Top quarter	85.3%	43.0%	80.4%	56.6%
Second quarter	12.1	35.4	15.9	29.8
Third quarter	2.3	18.7	3.2	12.2
Fourth quarter	0.3	2.9	0.5	1.4

Sources: National Norms for Entering College Freshmen: Fall 1970, p. 24; Medsger, *op. cit.,* p. 10; and responses from the Student Information Form of the Air Force Academy and the Naval Academy. The American Council on Education has included the U.S. Air Force Academy, the U.S. Coast Guard Academy, the U.S. Military Academy, the U.S. Naval Academy, the Virginia Military Institute, and seven other institutions in the category of technical institutions. Since the service academies make up such a large part of the institutions in the category, extreme caution must be exercised in interpreting comparative data between the academies and the category of technical institutions. The similarity between this category and the service academies may be due in large measure to the "contamination" of the technical institutions by the high portion of academy representation.

as in earning a varsity letter or by being elected president of an organization. Plebes were not particularly outstanding in areas where it is more difficult to measure success, such as in art, forensics, music, or drama. The significance of Table 3 lies in the high correlation shown by academy students in these achievement areas. Those who were not letter winners or honor society members, unlike the situation even at the private universities, were the exception rather than the rule. Plebes performed better in these areas than did students in any other institutional category. The percentages for the academies correlate closely with the statistics from those institutions for the last five years. Plebes come to the academies with a record of having excelled in competitive areas.

While the service academies undoubtedly attract students who are unusually competitive and have a high academic potential, it also must be noted that the academies actively recruit this type of student. For example, those students who win National Merit Recognition are routinely sent invitations to investigate the possibilities of attending the service academies, as are students who receive awards in state or regional science contests. Military recruiters throughout the country seek out the unusual student through guidance counselors and articles in local newspapers with the purpose of putting the promising prospects in touch with their respective service academies. Through this active recruitment policy each academy ultimately accepts approximately 1,300 plebes of unusual ability each year. In contrast, pri-

Table 3
Secondary School Achievement (Males)

Achievement	Academies	Private Universities	Four-Year Colleges
Elected president of a student organization	39.5%	23.4%	19.1%
Varsity letter (sports)	77.7	45.2	44.7
Scholastic honor society	61.2	33.4	20.2
National merit recognition	18.8	17.8	7.5

Sources: National Norms for Entering College Freshmen: Fall 1970, p. 24; Medsger, *op. cit.,* p. 12; and responses from the Student Information Form of the Air Force Academy and the Naval Academy. It should be noted that academy students were at least average in participation in the categories of art, music, and drama.

vate universities embark on smaller-scale re-cruitment campaigns and, for the most part, wait passively for applications.

SOCIOECONOMIC CHARACTERISTICS

The statistics from each of the institutional categories reflect the fact that blacks make up a smaller percentage of the student population than they do of the nation as a whole. In the fall of 1970 the black freshman population varied from a high of 13.8 percent at two-year public colleges to a low of 2.0 percent at technical institutions. If the academies are compared with the same categories that most closely approached their student body in terms of high school achievements, the statistics reveal the following. (See Table 4.) Excluding two-year colleges and technical institutions, public universities most closely resemble the academies, with 95.9 percent of the students in the category being white and 2.5 percent black. The dispersion does not depart appreciably from what would have been expected given the data from the previous tables.

These figures are particularly relevant in considering the linkage with attitudes. The expectation is that whites would tend to be more conservative and nonwhites would be more liberal. This was borne out by a cross-tabulation which revealed that at the Naval Academy 34 percent of the white plebes identified themselves as having moderate political attitudes and 26 percent characterized themselves as liberal, while 50 percent of the black plebes characterized themselves as moderate and 43 percent identified themselves as liberal.

The fact that there are fewer nonwhites at the service academies stems from many factors. The discriminatory bias that once prevailed within the officer corps continues to make it difficult to attract racial minority groups, despite service efforts to eliminate racism and attract more nonwhites. While all legal discrimination has been removed, social discrimination is perhaps as widespread within the military as in the civilian world. The discrimination that forced many blacks into inferior secondary schools has made it more difficult for the academies to find qualified black students, even when they actively recruit them. Nonetheless, there have been significant increases in the number of black plebes in each freshman class at the academies in the last five years.

The parents of academy students tend to be more highly educated and earn higher incomes than might be expected from the national statistics. The figures indicate, for example, that approximately 40 percent of the parents of these students have college degrees, while another 20 percent have had some college education. Private university students reported, on the whole, higher parental education than did any other category. West Point and Annapolis students do not vary significantly in the reported father's educational achievement. (See Table 5.) The Air Force Academy's returns, however, show a departure from the norm expected from the other academies. The norms for most categories of institutions participating tended to cluster around the figures for four-year colleges.

Predictably, academy and private university students were less likely to report that their fathers' occupations were those of unskilled, semiskilled, or skilled workers. The only major distinction between the occupations of the parents of academy students and private university students lies in the area of business and a military career. Thirty-nine percent of the fathers of students going to private universities were businessmen, while 29.1 percent of the

Table 4
Racial Background of Freshmen, Class of 1974

Racial Background	Academies	Four-Year Colleges	Technical Institutions	Private Universities
Caucasian/White	96.3%	91.1%	96.4%	93.7%
Negro/Black	2.1	7.2	2.0	4.1
American Indian	0.1	0.1	0.0	0.1
Oriental	0.5	0.7	1.2	1.4
Other	0.3	0.8	0.4	0.7

Sources: National Norms for Entering College Freshmen: Fall 1970, p. 21; Medsger, *op. cit.,* p. 2; and responses from the Student Information Form of the Air Force Academy and the Naval Academy.

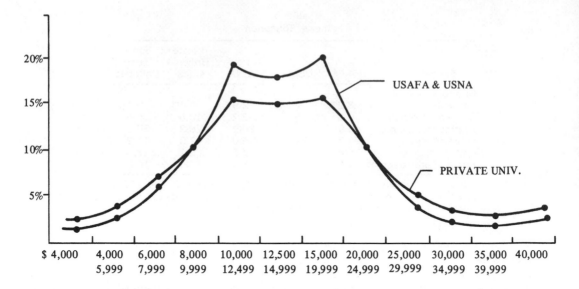

Figure 1
Estimated Parental Income: USNA and USAFA Compared with Private Universities

which a high percentage of academy students are recruited. Also, most private universities are located in the large urban areas, which explains their much higher percentage of Jewish students. The higher retention of religious preference at the academies may be due in part to the military stress on religious belief which the cadets accept as part of the life they chose upon entering.

POLITICAL ATTITUDES

Conservatism has been a traditional hallmark of the officer corps, both in terms of military routine as well as in the military's approach to politics. Career officers usually accept the conservative ethic of the military through the general socialization process if they were not conservative at the time they joined the military. The military ethos also attracts many who already have a conservative bias to make the service a career.

It is not surprising, then, that plebes entering each of the three academies in the summer of 1970 tended already to perceive themselves as being more conservative in political preferences than the national norms. Academy students' political identification compares most closely to the category of technical institutions, which tends to have the most conservative

identity. The most liberal categories were private universities, followed very closely by Catholic four-year colleges. Many students of private universities expect that their political preferences will be more liberal at the end of four years. Cadets and midshipmen expect to shift to the right, however.[5] Apparently, students in both categories expect to be politicized during their college careers because in both instances fewer freshmen expect to identify as a moderate by the end of their college career. There is a projected net loss of 6.5 percent of the plebes and 8.6 percent of the university freshmen who expect to identify themselves as moderates in four years. The inference could be drawn that polarization is a concomitant aspect of politicization.

The academies attract significantly fewer liberal and leftist students and more conservative students than would be expected due to chance. At the end of four years the disparity is expected to be even greater, with relatively

[5] There is good evidence that the college experience socializes but does not "necessarily" liberalize the student. See Philip Jacob, *Changing Values in College: An Exploratory Study of the Impact of College Teaching* (New York: Harper & Bro., 1957), pp. 38–54. Professor Jacob suggests that freshmen become "seniorized" during their college career. That is, imitation and emulation of upperclassmen by underclassmen result in the latter adopting the attitudes of the former and winning respect in the process.

fewer liberals and more conservatives at the academies than we might expect at private universities.[6] (See Figure 2.)

It should be emphasized that the academies are being compared here with the private university category, which responded as the most liberal group. Every other category was closer to the norm of the academies.

Interesting results were obtained by cross-tabulating religious preference and political characterization at the Naval Academy for the class of 1974. Table 7 contains a cross-tabulation of some of the most significant religions for our consideration. A higher percentage of Catholics characterized themselves as liberal, and fewer identified themselves as conservative, than any other religious group. No one identifying himself with a Protestant religion indicated he would characterize his attitudes as far left. The results are as we might have expected since the American Council on Education reported that, next to the private universities, students attending four-year Catholic colleges identified themselves as being the most liberal of all the categories. Protestant four-year colleges were, next to technical institutions, the most conservative of those institutions giving at least the bachelor's degree.

[6] The importance of expectations in affecting the outcome of an experience has been well documented elsewhere. See R. Rosenthal and L. Jacobson, *Pygmalion in the Classroom: Teacher Expectation and Pupil's Intellectual Development* (New York: Holt, Rinehart & Winston, 1968); see also R. Rosenthal and R. Lawson, "A Longitudinal Study of the Effects of Experimenter Bias on the Operant Learning of Laboratory Rats," unpublished manuscript, Harvard University, 1961.

No statistically significant results were obtained by cross-tabulating political identification with parental income, which indicates that religion is more important in determining political attitudes than is income.[7]

The divergence of attitudes that might be expected on the basis of political preference is borne out when plebes are compared to freshmen entering private universities concerning views that generally separate liberals and conservatives. (See Table 8.) In almost every category plebes are more likely to agree with the general conservative philosophy which would restrict the role the federal government plays in daily domestic affairs while supporting a strong governmental position in areas related to foreign policy. In some areas self-interest, or lack of it, affects the response. For example, fewer plebes favor compensatory education for the disadvantaged, and fewer still would support any financial aid for the disadvantaged, although 41.8 percent of the academy students would support greater governmental involve-

[7] Both Catholics and Protestants attending the Naval Academy were from the more conservative segments of their religious groups since those attending Catholic colleges tended to be more liberal than Catholics attending the Academy, and Protestants attending the Academy were more conservative than the norm of those attending Protestant four-year colleges. Catholics attending Catholic colleges identified their political preferences as being far left, 3.4 percent; liberal, 43.0 percent; middle of the road, 36.9 percent; conservative, 15.9 percent; and far right, 0.9 percent. Protestants attending four-year Protestant colleges gave their political preferences as follows: far left, 3.3 percent; liberal, 33.9 percent; middle of the road, 41.3 percent; conservative, 20.4 percent; and far right, 1.2 percent.

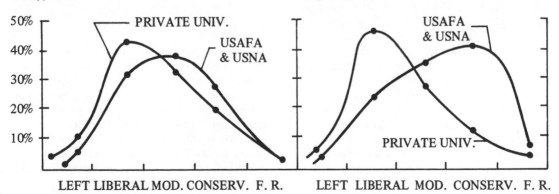

Figure 2
Current and Expected Political Preferences: USAFA and USNA Students Compared with Private University Students

Table 7
Cross-Tabulation of Religion and Political Characterization

Religion	Far Left	Liberal	Middle of the Road	Conservative	Far Right
Baptist	0%	27.9%	31.3%	38.3%	2.3%
Episcopal	0	30.5	24.5	43.5	1.5
Lutheran	0	32.5	41.2	25.0	1.2
Methodist	0	18.0	40.3	39.8	1.2
Presbyterian	0	19.4	44.9	33.9	1.6
Roman Catholic	0.3	34.1	37.9	26.0	1.7

Table 8
Opinions Concerning the Role of Government

Percent who feel the Federal Govt. should increase its commitment or initiate a crash program in:	Service Academies	Private Universities
Compensatory education for disadvantaged	51.9%	65.4%
Elimination of poverty	68.0	82.2
School desegregation	42.8	54.5
Financial aid for the disadvantaged	32.7	49.4
Military involvement in Southeast Asia	34.1	11.1
Development of ABM	62.1	20.9
Control of TV and newspapers	12.7	8.3
Space program	59.9	33.8
Control of firearms	30.8	55.2
Consumer protection	58.8	69.8

ment in giving special benefits to veterans while only 28 percent of the private university students would do so.

One final area of interest in considering the attitudes of academy students and how they compare with others concerns the objectives in life that the students consider to be important. Table 9 confirms the observations made earlier concerning the drive for achievement by academy students. Academy plebes reported goals and objectives in life that have a competitive aspect (particularly items 1, 2, 7, 10, and 11) more frequently than did students from private universities. In fact, academy students scored higher in those areas than did any other category. While academy plebes thought objectives where authority and respect are a major part of the reward were very important, they scored lower than any other category in concern over financial rewards.

One other area of significant divergence from the pattern of responses at private universities was that the Naval Academy plebe thought it more important to keep up with political affairs than did other students. Thirty-four percent of the plebes at the Naval Acad-

emy agreed that the individual cannot change society, while 40 percent of the students of the private universities agreed with the proposition. The indication is that the plebe is less likely to feel powerless in the face of society. Finally, only 5.7 percent of the Naval Academy plebes agreed strongly that there was a generation gap with their parents, while 18.7 percent of the students at the private universities agreed.

CONCLUSIONS

Academy students occupy a unique position upon entering the officer corps in that they are viewed as being the elite in the military profession, much as the graduate of the private university is viewed in the civilian world. Some very interesting similarities and differences surface when the military academy student is compared with his nonmilitary counterpart.

First of all, the students entering the military academies have demonstrated high potential. They have outperformed every other group in terms of their class rank in high school and average grades received while in high school.

Table 9
Objectives Considered to be Essential or Very Important

Objectives	USNA Plebes	Private Universities
1. Be an authority in my field	83.4%	71.2%
2. Obtain recognition from peers	51.6	44.8
3. Influence political structure	22.8	26.8
4. Raise a family	75.0	61.8
5. Have an active social life	56.6	56.3
6. Have friends different from me	56.0	59.9
7. Be administratively responsible	53.2	23.4
8. Be very well off financially	34.9	43.1
9. Help others in difficulty	63.1	61.6
10. Become a community leader	30.3	19.1
11. Contribute to scientific theory	19.7	17.3
12. Not be obligated to people	20.4	22.4
13. Keep up with political affairs	73.1	62.2
14. Succeed in my own business	34.5	47.4
15. Develop a philosophy of life	76.8	77.4

Second, the academy plebe has received recognition for secondary school achievements in competitive areas such as winning varsity letters, being elected president of student organizations, or being a member of a scholastic honor society in greater measure than has his private university colleague.

Economically and socially there are many similarities between students at the academies and the private universities. They both come from families having much higher incomes, on the average, than students in any other category. Parental education for both these categories is higher than for any other category, further indicating a secure financial and social background. The student enrolling at a private university is more likely to have lived in a large city while growing up, however, while the academy student is more likely to have lived in a moderate-sized town. Both the private universities and the academies tend to have fewer nonwhites than most of the other categories.

Religiously, there are more Protestants and fewer Jews at the academies. The higher number of Protestants correlates to a significant degree with the conservative political attitude. Catholics at the academies are more liberal than any Protestant denomination.

Students entering private universities are more liberal than students entering the academies, and they expect to become more liberal, while plebes expect to become more conservative.

Two points should be made here. First, there is a general consensus among academicians in the social sciences that political liberalism provides the framework through which political problems can best be solved; this is a view shared by the writer. However, it is not necessarily true that the military should also represent or accept the same view. That is, perhaps academy graduates and the military should be skewed in a direction inappropriate for the rest of the population.

Second, the academies themselves are undergoing significant changes that will bring them more closely in line with private universities in terms of attitudes. Every attempt is being made to recruit more blacks, for example. The social sciences and humanities have recently expanded their curricula and now offer majors in their respective disciplines.

The hypothesis that academy students tend to be high achievers with high potential appears to be substantiated by the evidence available at this time. Academy plebes have outperformed their closest competitors in the private university category in secondary schools in the areas of scholastic, athletic, and student leadership. This also correlates with the objectives they feel to be very important in life, such as becoming a community leader, obtaining recognition from peers, and becoming an authority in a career field.

This study would appear to have provided considerable evidence to support a second working hypothesis—that is, that academy students have a high need for social approval.

This hypothesis is related to the first and is not unexpected. One goal of achievement, after all, is to be recognized and approved socially. This is also posited on the academy students' need to be recognized by their peers and to be community leaders.

A great deal of uniformity is reflected in the background of the academy students in terms of race, religion, socioeconomic status, and attitudes. The attitudes are probably uniform because of the uniformity of other factors. But "uniformity" is not the same as "conformity." A study that would untangle the threads of social approval, high achievement, and its relationship to uniformity and conformity would be most useful at the academies. It is true that, when the emphasis is on group affiliation, such as in the military, there tends to be more social conformity than occurs when the group is task oriented. However, it is also true that a higher achiever feels less need to fit in[8] unless he has a strong affiliative motivation, in which case he might be even more susceptible to group pressures, at least in certain circumstances.[9]

This leads to a third working hypothesis. On the basis of the demonstrated high potential and competitiveness of the academy student, we might expect that academy graduates would fill the flag ranks out of proportion to their numbers. On the strength of their greater capability and ambition, their desire to be administratively responsible, and their desire to lead, one could expect the academy graduate to work harder in the military to achieve rank. It would appear that the academy graduate may get ahead for reasons other than merely preferential treatment as critics charge. More investigation of the performance of service academy graduates compared with nonacademy officers in the career service is needed, however, before any definitive conclusions can be reached in this regard.

---

[8] See D. C. McClelland *et al.*, *The Achievement Motive* (New York: Appleton-Century-Crofts, 1953).

[9] See John W. McDavid and Frank Sistrunk, "Personality Correlates of Two Kinds of Conforming Behavior," *Journal of Personality*, 32 (1964): 420–35.

ROTC, MY LAI, AND THE VOLUNTEER ARMY

PETER KARSTEN, ED BERGER, LARRY FLATLEY, JOHN FRISCH, MAYDA GOTTLIEB, JUDY HAISLEY, LARRY PEXTON, AND WILLIAM WORREST

Despite serious attacks on many campuses during much of the Vietnam War, ROTC remains the major source of officer procurement for the military services. By comparing attitudes held by ROTC and Academy cadets, the authors have found important differences, which, in turn, have caused them to ask a fundamental question. Will two "liberal" causes of recent times, the volunteer army and the end of ROTC, produce illiberal results? The authors are associates at the University of Pittsburgh.

Voluntary professionals may replace citizen-soldiers in the American armed forces of the 1970s. Apart from the question of draft reform and plans to end conscription entirely after Vietnam, plans that are widely discussed in Washington today, the Reserve Officers Training Corps (ROTC) is under attack on many of the nation's campuses. ROTC has been asked to leave a number of universities, while falling enrollments, broken windows, burned-out offices, and a hostile student environment have led the three armed services to cancel some of their programs. Still, ROTC currently provides a majority of the career officers in the military services as well as in the reserve system.

ROTC has made an inviting target for critics of the Vietnam War. Those seeking ROTC's demise have also made much of the indoctrinary nature of its curriculum, the presence of external, governmental control of the program, and the militarization they feel the ROTC student experiences—all of which occurs within an academic setting with the contrary goal of liberating and stimulating the students' powers of inquiry.

Defenders of ROTC have warned that its removal from the nation's campuses would severely injure the efficiency of a military that has increasingly come to depend on the technical and managerial skills that the ROTC graduate can offer. Such an argument is not a very telling blow to the case of the critics. Indeed, many of these critics are quite satisfied with an arrangement which may weaken the ability of the government to prosecute its policies in Southeast Asia while at the same time ridding the campuses of an alien spirit. But several ROTC defenders have offered an argument that does alarm some of the critics.

ROTC VERSUS THE PROS

These defenders have argued that dismantling ROTC would result in an increase in the number of officers recruited from the enlisted ranks and in the size or number of the service academies. In the former case—recruitment from the ranks—tests have established that the average enlisted man, with less than a college education, scores higher on psychological attitude scales measuring authoritarianism, acceptance of military ideology, and aggression than does the average college-bred officer candidate.[1] These same ROTC defenders have then claimed (without verifying the claim)

[1] R. W. Gage, "Patriotism and Military Discipline as a Function of the Degree of Military Training," *Journal of Social Psychology*, 64 (1964): 101–11; E. G. French and R. R. Ernst, "The Relationship between Authoritarianism and the Acceptance of Military Ideology," *Journal of Personality*, 24 (1955): 181–91; William A. Lucas, "The American Lieutenant: An Empirical Investigation of Normative Theories of Civil-Military Relations" (Ph.D. diss., University of North Carolina, 1967), *passim*.

Reprinted by permission and with minor changes from Foreign Policy, *no. 2 (Spring 1971), pp. 135–60.* Copyright © 1971 by National Affairs, Inc.

that the latter case—an increase in the number of service academy graduates—would have the same effect. The average West Pointer or Annapolis graduate, they argue, is less flexible and able to think for himself than the average ROTC or Officer Candidate School (OCS) officer. Thus ROTC and OCS officers may provide a desirable "leavening," a counterbalance to the more aggressive values of academy graduates and "rankers." The Association of State Universities and Land-Grant Colleges put it this way in a recent report: "The continued presence in substantial numbers in the Armed Forces of officers from a wide variety of civilian educational institutions and backgrounds is one of the best guarantees against the establishment in this country of a military caste or clique."[2]

For those critical of the presence of formally accredited ROTC programs on campus, the suggestion that the death of ROTC would result in expansion of service academies and enlisted-oriented OCS programs should provoke serious reflection. If the citizen-officer defenders are correct, any changes in present recruitment that would result in a significant increase in the flow of professional soldiers from the enlisted and academy ranks might be counterproductive. That is, the demise of ROTC would only temporarily dislocate military leadership plans. And any increase in the percentage of authoritarian, aggressive "leaders" would, we submit, be undesirable. But are the citizen-officer defenders correct?

The question concerns the nature of citizen-officers—ROTC and college-grad OCS types who serve for two or three years as platoon and company grade officers or pilots and then either stay on as careerists or (in most cases) resign. Some citizen-officers rise to high command, but all, whether they stay on or not, may as lieutenants, due to the nature of modern, dispersed military deployment, be faced with awesome on-the-spot decisions. For the inhabitants of many a Vietnamese hamlet or river village, survival may well depend on the attitude of the platoon leader, gunboat skipper, or helicopter gunship pilot approaching, guns trained on their homes.

We know that the average ROTC or college grad OCS student scores lower on F-scale (au-

[2] Cited in *Harvard Bulletin*, May 25, 1970, p. 26.

thoritarianism) psychological measurements than the average enlisted man or noncollege peer.[3] Thus, for those concerned about the attitudes and values of individuals placed in positions of military authority and responsibility, the ROTC or college grad OCS officer would appear to be a safer bet than one who acquired his commission without first acquiring a college degree. It is probably not simply the fact of the college experience that makes the difference. Less advantaged youths, after all, receive a different moral education in their environments than do the college-bound, suburban children of the middle and upper-middle classes. But, for whatever reasons, the difference between the two potential military leader groups is a known, significant quantity.

What is *un*known is just how such ROTC students compare with their service academy counterparts. Are the ROTC types more "flexible" than the academy types, as claimed? One leader of the anti-ROTC movement at Harvard thinks not: "An officer trained at Princeton kills on orders as quickly as an officer trained at the Point."[4] Is there any significant attitudinal distinction between the two types at all?

MEASURING ATTITUDES

The best way of answering such a question would be to measure the attitudes of the two groups in the field a year or two after graduation or commissioning. But the Defense Department does not appear ever to have conducted such an investigation; and our own research capacities did not allow for such an analysis. We had to be satisfied with administering an attitude questionnaire (with a near 100 percent response) in the spring and fall of 1970 to 90 randomly selected service academy (Annapolis) students, 177 ROTC students (110 Air Force and Army ROTC students from the University of Pittsburgh and 67 Naval ROTC students from Ohio State University), and 117 male non-ROTC college undergraduates.[5] Such a comparison may be of limited

[3] *I.e.*, Gage, *op. cit.*
[4] *Harvard Bulletin*, May 25, 1970, p. 29.
[5] We asked the Military Academy and the Air Force Academy for permission to survey random samples of their cadets, but neither academy authorized the study. We recognize that Annapolis students may differ from their peers at the other two academies on some scores, but we have discovered virtually no statistically sig-

value if earlier researchers are correct when they claim that ROTC graduates quickly adjust and adapt to the codes and mores of the professional military. But such a claim is highly moot, and, even if a certain amount of adjustment and adaptation does occur, if significant differences between ROTC and academy types exist upon entry into the officer corps, it seems reasonable to expect that *some* of those differences would persist.[6]

Over the years, a number of studies have been made using attitude questionnaires to analyze service academy students, and to compare ROTC undergrads to non-ROTC undergrads. But, to the best of our knowledge, service academy and ROTC students have never been systematically compared. C. J. Lammers has compared the development of values and attitudes—that is, the "socialization"—of Royal Netherlands Naval College midshipmen and Candidate Reserve Officers, but the circumstances of that socialization process are not altogether the same as those we are dealing with. Furthermore, Lammers was concerned only with "the socialization process," not with attitudes. John Lovell, in his study of "the professional socialization of the West Point cadet," compared West Pointers to a sampling of Dartmouth students, 82 percent of whom expected to perform military service upon graduation, but the sample did not appear to be exclusively composed of ROTC students, and Lovell did not pursue the attitudinal comparison very far. R. W. Gage and William A. Lucas have compared the attitudes of ROTC and non-ROTC students, and both have concluded that ROTC students are significantly more accepting of authority and military ideology than non-ROTC students; but neither study included a sampling of service academy students.[7] Thus the need for our own study.

THREE GROUPS

Our three sample groups do not spring from precisely the same social background. In terms of family income, parents' level of education, and father's occupation, our Annapolis respondents come from families with slightly higher incomes, better educated parents, and more professional fathers than either the non-ROTC students, who were next, or the ROTC students, whose social origins were slightly more humble than either of the other groups. But these differences in social origins are not relevant to the differences we found in the attitudes of members of our three groups— that is, *there was no difference in the response of representatives of one level of social origin from those of any other level.*

This surprised us, since one would expect lower-class respondents to be somewhat more authoritarian than those whose parents were college graduates and professional people. And this would probably have been the case if our respondents had been sampled at random from the public at large. But Annapolis students were overrepresented in the upper economic echelons. And since these same Annapolis students were consistently more authoritarian, absolutistic, and militaristic than either of the other two groups, the "class differentials" were neutralized.

R. W. Gage, in his earlier study, found that ROTC students were more "patriotic" and accepting of military discipline than non-ROTC college students,[8] and we found that ranking

---

nificant differences among the three ROTC groups; we feel that the "service academy" label is appropriate. (In any event, we do not claim that our analysis is any more than suggestive. None of us has any special training in social psychology or statistics. But we suspect that we are on to something significant. We would be pleased if our study were to provoke a more thorough and sophisticated analysis.)

[6] Gene Lyons and John Masland, *Education and Military Leadership* (Princeton, 1959), p. 169. Major Gilbert L. Whiteman has engaged in such research. Whiteman hypothesizes that "civilian college-trained officers [do not] retain their liberal views for very long after entering active duty . . . they sooner-or-later adopt the philosophies of power, influence, and authority which those not trained on college campuses might display." (Personal communication, Whiteman to Peter Karsten, October 1, 1970.) He may be right, Arthur Niederhoffer argues that "police authoritarianism does not come into the force along with the recruits, but rather is inculcated in the men through strenuous socialization." (*Behind the Shield* [New York, 1967], p. 160.) But Whiteman's "sooner-or-later" will have to be precise; if it takes two or three years to sour the "liberalism" of college graduate officers, then many may function in an unsocialized fashion during that important first (and, for many, only) tour of duty. Moreover, Whiteman may be wrong.

[7] C. J. Lammers, "Midshipmen and Candidate Reserve Officers at the Royal Netherlands Naval College: A Comparative Study of a Socialization Process," *Sociologia Neerlandica*, 2 (1965): 98–122; John Lovell, "The Professional Socialization of the West Point Cadet," in *The New Military*, ed. Morris Janowitz (New York: Norton, 1964); Gage, *op. cit.*; Lucas, *op. cit.*

[8] Gage, *op. cit.*, pp. 101–11.

to apply with every aspect of aggressiveness, absolutism, "patriotism," and military discipline tested. *But our service academy students were consistently more aggressive and absolutistic than our ROTC sample.* When asked what their reaction might be if, while walking with their girl friend, someone were to make "a vulgar, obscene comment about her," nearly half (49 percent) of our sample of Annapolis officers-and-gentlemen-to-be indicated that they would offer some form of physical response, typically: "I'd kick his teeth in." Only 31 percent of the ROTC sample, and only 23 percent of the non-ROTC group, gave similar responses (see Table 1). No less than 60 of the 90 Annapolis respondents indicated that, if given the choice, they would prefer to serve in a "combat" capacity, while only 32 percent of ROTC students preferred "combat" duty to the alternatives offered: administrative or technical work.[9] The question was more hypothetical for the non-ROTC male undergraduates, many of whom will see no service at all, but, for what it is worth, predictably, only 8 percent indicated that they would prefer combat service to the other less belligerent options.

John Lovell long ago noted that West Point students "tend to be more 'absolutistic' in their

strategic perspectives than their Dartmouth peers."[10] Our study revealed the same distinction between our Annapolis and our Pittsburgh–Ohio State sample (see Table 2). Seventy-seven percent of the Annapolis sample agreed with the statement "war is the inevitable result of man's nature," while only 55.3 percent of the ROTC, and 39 percent of the non-ROTC, sample agreed. And twice as many Annapolis students (24 percent), as Pittsburgh–Ohio State students agreed *strongly* with that statement. No less than one in every three midshipmen could conceive of circumstances in which a takeover of the U.S. government by the military would be justified, while only 19.5 percent of ROTC, and 18 percent of non-ROTC, students were of the same mind. Only 8 percent of the non-ROTC "control" sample felt that the U.S. should ever use nuclear weapons in situations other than retaliation. A larger percentage (16 percent) of ROTC students, and a still larger percentage (28 percent) of Annapolis students, were "first-strikers."

"MY COUNTRY, RIGHT OR WRONG"

While only 39 percent of our *combined* sample of academy and ROTC officer candidates indicated that they would obey orders morally repugnant to them (see Table 3), nearly half (48 percent) of all our officer candidates who indicated a preference for combat duty, and 44 percent of those who indicated that they would offer physical violence to one who insulted their girl friend, would

---

[9] Since many Naval Academy midshipmen expect to be assigned to men-of-war, comparison of the percentage of those preferring "combat" service at the Academy with those preferring "combat" service in ROTC (only a third of whom are Navy-bound) may be unfair to the Academy, since the options are somewhat different. Shipboard "combat" service is, of late, considerably safer than airborne or ground "combat" duty. On the other hand, many Annapolis graduates will serve on river gunboats, in combat-area aircraft, or in Marine infantry units—that is, in posts equally perilous to those preferred by our "combat" ROTC sample.

[10] Lovell, *op. cit.,* p. 129.

Table 1

	Offer Physical Response to Insult to Girl Friend (%)	Offer Verbal Response or Ignore Insult (%)	Prefer Combat Duty (%)	Prefer Administrative or Technical Service (%)
Annapolis (90)	49.9 (44)	16.1 (29)	66.7 (60)	25.5 (23)
ROTC (177)	31.6 (56)	57.6 (102)	32.0 (57)	64.0 (113)
Non-ROTC "Control" Group (117)	23.0 (27)	62.4 (73)	7.7 (9)	69.0 (81)

Note: Figures do not always total 100 percent because some respondents had "no opinion" or "no preference."

Table 2

	Agree that "War is the Inevitable Result of Man's Nature" (%)	Disagree (%)	Military Takeover Might be Justified (%)	Regard "First-Strike" Use as Acceptable (%)
Annapolis	77.0 (68)	22.0 (20)	33.3 (30)	28.0 (25)
ROTC	55.3 (98)	37.0 (65)	19.5 (34)	16.0 (28)
Non-ROTC "Control" Group	39.0 (46)	47.8 (56)	18.0 (20)	8.0 (10)

obey such orders. The same positive correlation between aggressive propensities and what we regard as undesirable behavior exists with regard to our questions about the use of nuclear weapons. Less than one in every five (19.5 percent) of our *combined* samples of officer candidates felt that the U.S. should ever strike first with nuclear weapons. But 27.3 percent of those showing a preference for combat duty, and 28 percent of our "physical force" group, were nuclear "first-strikers."

Our heroic fighters were not the only ones to correlate positively to "first-strikers." We asked our subjects whether or not they agreed that "the practice of war is a science best left to professionals." Of those who agreed, 28 percent were also "first-strikers" (Table 3). One West Point cadet may have spoken for this group when he recently observed that "small tac nukes" could be of considerable value in suppressing revolution in Latin America: "Well, you have got to hold the spread of Communism [which he defined as "sedition, and so forth"] down, and keep whoever is in government *there*. That's what's important." Lieutenant William Calley says that he went to Vietnam "with the absolute philosophy that the U.S.A.'s right. And there was no grey . . . there was just black or white." In another interview he told John Sack: "I'll do as I'm told to do. I won't revolt. I'll put the will of America above my own conscience, always."[11]

[11] Cited in Ward Just, "Soldiers," *Atlantic*, October 1970, p. 66; Calley, interviewed by Sack, "The Confessions of Lieutenant Calley," *Esquire*, November 1970, p. 229.

Table 3

	% Who Would Obey Morally Repugnant Orders	% Who Consider "First Strike" to be Acceptable	% Who Agree with "My Country, Right or Wrong"
Combined Officer Candidates (267)	39.0 (105)	19.5 (52)	52.0 (138)
Officer Candidates Preferring Combat (117)	48.0 (56)	27.3 (32)	63.2 (74)
Officer Candidates Offering Physical Force Response (100)	44.0 (44)	28.0 (28)	69.0 (69)
Officer Candidates Feeling War a Science for Professionals (125)	53.6 (67)	28.0 (35)	67.2 (84)
Annapolis Sample (90)	41.0 (67)	28.0 (25)	74.0 (67) ROTC 40.0 (71) Non-ROTC 19.5 (23)

Moreover, as in the case of our fighter group, no less than 53.6 percent of those who agreed that war was a science best left to the control of pros indicated that they would obey morally repugnant orders. Over half (51.7 percent) of all officer candidates agreed with that pre-Nuremberg canon of the ardent statist, "My country, right or wrong," but no less than 67.2 percent of those feeling war to be a science best left to professionals, and approximately the same percentage of "fighter" types, found this conscience-evading dogma attractive.

For one familiar with Morris Janowitz's distinction between "heroic" and "managerial" professional military officers,[12] this high correlation between "fighters," "professionals," service academy students (see Table 3), and undesirable propensities may be somewhat surprising, unless one is also familiar with John Lovell's research. Lovell could find no statistically significant difference at West Point between "heroic" fighter types and "managerial" types (our "pros") in terms of absolutism.[13] "Pros" are just as dangerous to have around as "fighters."

THE SCIENCE OF WAR

How did our three categories of students like the "pro" and "statist" tenets? No less than 72 percent of Annapolis respondents agreed with the remark that war was a science best left to professionals (with 33.3 percent agreeing *strongly*), whereas only 47.5 percent of our ROTC "citizen" officer candidates, and only 18 percent of the non-ROTC "control" group,

[12] Morris Janowitz, *The Professional Soldier* (Glencoe, Ill., 1960), and "Changing Patterns of Organizational Authority: The Military Establishment," *Administrative Science Quarterly*, 3 (March 1959): 473–93.
[13] Lovell, *op. cit.*

agreed. And the same pattern held for the dogma found to be so attractive to our "pros." Almost three of every four Annapolis students sampled (74 percent) found the adage of Captain Stephen Decatur, U.S.N., "My country, right or wrong," to be attractive, whereas only 40 percent of the ROTC and 19.5 percent of the non-ROTC, students approved of this pre-Nuremberg code of conduct.

These attitudinal distinctions occurred again when our subjects were asked their opinions about the military budget and the war in Vietnam. Only a few non-ROTC students and only a handful of the ROTC sample felt the military budget was too small (Table 4), but 39 percent of the Annapolis sample thought the budget inadequate. On questions relating to the Vietnam War, however, ROTC students were closer to their fellow officer candidates than they were to their non-officer-bound peers. Four of every five non-ROTC students objected to the war in Vietnam, while only 36.7 percent of ROTC, and 28 percent of the Annapolis, students found the war objectionable. Only 10 percent of our sample of non-ROTC students expressed a willingness to volunteer for service in Vietnam, while 40 percent of the ROTC, and 60 percent of the Annapolis, sample indicated they would volunteer for that war. Only one of every four non–officer candidate respondents imagined that he would obey a direct order morally repugnant to him; no less than 38 percent of the ROTC sample and 41 percent of the Annapolis sample indicated that they would obey such an order. Only 18.7 percent of non-ROTC students felt that the atrocities committed at My Lai were "extremely rare" in Vietnam, but the same percentage (37 percent) of the ROTC and Annapolis samples considered My Lai "extremely rare."

Table 4

	Military Budget Too Small (%)	Object to Presence of U.S. Troops in Vietnam (%)	Would Volunteer for Vietnam (%)	Consider My Lai "Extremely Rare" (%)
Annapolis	39.0 (35)	28.0 (25)	60.0 (54)	37.0 (32)
ROTC	10.0 (18)	36.7 (65)	40.0 (71)	37.0 (67)
Non-ROTC "Control" Group	4.0 (5)	78.5 (92)	10.0 (12)	18.7 (22)

It could be argued that our officer candidate groups, having once committed themselves to military service, find Vietnam tolerable and My Lai exceptional largely because they recognize that they must live with a decision to serve that may one day thrust them into a Southeast Asian rice paddy or river delta. They may have come to accept the validity of "morally repugnant orders" as a result of their introduction to the military's traditions, mores, and missions—the military's point of view.

However, we think it more likely that they were *always* more positive toward the war and the military than those who avoided the officer candidate programs. We suspect that the reasons for the persistent attitudinal differences between those who are officer candidates and those who are not lie primarily in the process of self-recruitment, by which means they selected military futures in the first place, and less in the process of military "socialization" which takes place as they prepare for command. Our reasons are twofold, having to do with (1) self-selection and (2) the impotence of "militarization."

The research of William Lucas and C. J. Lammers shows that there is a self-selection process at work in both the American ROTC and the Dutch naval officer corps. "Militaristic" young men elect at age seventeen or eighteen to pursue a course that will make them officers.[14] Moreover, Lammers notes that the regular academy midshipmen, many the sons of naval officers, are considerably more accepting of military ideology than their reserve officer candidate counterparts.[15] That seems to be the case with our service academy

14 Lucas, *op. cit.*, p. 53; Lammers, *op. cit.*, p. 109.
15 Lammers, *op. cit.*, p. 106.

and ROTC samples, and the reason may well be related to the reasons they gave for selecting Annapolis or ROTC. Nearly half of the Annapolis sample (48 percent) indicated that one of their reasons for seeking appointment was a desire to "be a career officer." Only 17 percent of the ROTC sample indicated that such ambitions had motivated them (Table 5). Nearly three in every four (73 percent) of the ROTC sample confessed that a prime motive for joining the program was a "preference to serve as an officer versus an enlisted man" (a few wrote in "to dodge the draft"). Slightly more Annapolis students (26 percent) than ROTC (19.2 percent) students indicated that an important reason for joining was a "belief in military traditions and methods." Conversely, nearly half (47.5 percent) of the ROTC sample said that an important reason for seeking a commission was a desire to secure "training for assuming positions of responsibility in civilian life," while only 36.5 percent of career-bound Annapolis midshipmen gave a similar response. In short, the ROTC students appear to have more limited and "practical" reasons for service than the professional-minded middies. As one anonymous Annapolis ditty puts it:

Some join for the love of the Service,
Some join for the love of the Sea,
But I know a guy who's in Rotcie;
He joined for a college degree.

Similarly, just as Lammers found disproportionate numbers of naval officers' parents in his sample of Royal Netherlands Naval College midshipmen, we found that the fathers of 33.3 percent of our Annapolis, 12.4 percent of our ROTC, and only 2.3 percent of our non-ROTC samples had been commissioned officers.

Table 5

	Desire to Make a Career of Military (%)	Due to Belief in Military Traditions and Methods (%)	Desire Training for Responsibilities in Future Civilian Life (%)	Prefer to be Officer Rather than Enlisted Man (%)
Annapolis	48.0 (43)	26.0 (23)	36.5 (31)	56.0 (49)
ROTC	17.0 (29)	19.2 (34)	47.5 (84)	73.0 (130)

Moreover, when we added those whose fathers had served in a non-commissioned status we got similar results (see Table 6). Apparently many of the sons of military officers seek programs that will allow them to emulate their fathers.

Table 6

	Father a Commissioned Officer (%)	Father Served in Military in Some Capacity (%)
Annapolis	33.3 (30)	89.0 (80)
ROTC	12.4 (22)	81.7 (145)
Non-ROTC "Control" Group	2.3 (3)	68.2 (80)

THE IMPOTENCE OF MILITARIZATION

Once in the programs, a buttressing of pre-judgments, values, and goals may occur. C. J. Lammers and William Lucas both maintain that officer candidates "socialize" one another over time, and Lammers hypothesizes that, where initial motivation is low, such "socialization" may actually serve to drive the student out of the program.[16] But, when we asked respondents to recall views held on entering college, or created an *ersatz* time-lapse by comparing various school years, *we did not find evidence of any significant shifts on the part of either officer candidate group in a direction away from that which the non-officer candidate group might be taking.* All three groups, for example, showed a slight increase, from freshmen to seniors, in opposition to the war in Vietnam, a slight shift from conservative to moderate, or from moderate to liberal views, and a slight move toward a more critical view of the size of the military budget. In the case of immoral orders, to offer one illustration (see Table 7), fewer and fewer officer candidates indicated a willingness to obey immoral orders with each succeeding class. Not all of these differences were statistically significant, but they all point in the same direction as John Lovell's study of West Pointers, the Feldman-Newcomb study of college under-

grads, and the Campbell-McCormack study of Air Force Academy classes.[17] Thus we feel that, while there may be some reinforcing of previously held values taking place within the officer candidate programs that we did not detect, we doubt that there are many new values being created. Surely some traditions, mores, and attitudes are "learned" by officer candidates—particularly by those at the "closed-circuit" service academies—but our data lead us to claim that the differences between our three subject samples are less a function of in-house "militarization" or "humanization" than they are a function of a self-selection (or joint-selection) process which occurs when young men of seventeen decide whether to seek a professional military career, or a program that offers leadership training for future civilian life and a chance to serve as an officer rather than an enlisted man, or no voluntary military service at all. It is this decision that separates the "fighters" and "pros" from the "citizen-soldiers" and "civilian types." The liberal arts environment of academe may have *something* to do with the fact that ROTC students are less absolutistic, less aggressive, less militaristic than service academy students, but *our* data could not prove it. Furthermore *if ROTC units on campus do not significantly "militarize" any of those who volunteer to take their programs, neither do we find any evidence suggesting that the "liberal arts" environment of academe does any "liberalizing" of ROTC students.* The responses of freshmen ROTC students fall between those of their Annapolis and non-ROTC peers, and so do those of sophomores, juniors, and seniors. College education, four years of relative insulation from the school of hard knocks, apparently "humanizes" *all three* groups at approximately the same pace. If pre-college self-recruitment is the key factor, then the *particular* college environment may make very little difference, since our evidence, as well as the Lovell and Campbell-McCormack studies, suggests that there may be a progressive softening of many of the "hard-line" views held as freshmen by members of all three groups.

[16] Lammers, *op. cit.*, p. 119; Lucas, *op. cit.*, pp. 75–77, 120–27.

[17] Lovell, *op. cit.*, p. 129; Kenneth Feldman and Theodore Newcomb, *The Impact of College on Students* (San Francisco, 1969), 1: 31; Donald Campbell and Thelma McCormack, "Military Experience and Attitudes Toward Authority," *American Journal of Sociology*, 62 (1957).

Table 7

	Would Obey Orders Morally Repugnant (%)
Combined Officer Candidate Freshmen (78)	48.5 (38)
Combined Officer Candidate Sophomores (55)	42.0 (23)
Combined Officer Candidate Juniors (62)	35.5 (22)
Combined Officer Candidate Seniors (70)	30.0 (21)

THE MY LAI MENTALITY

In the spring of 1969, Ronald Ridenhour, a college-bound Vietnam veteran, precipitated an investigation into the March 1968 massacre of the villagers of My Lai. Before the dust had settled, two generals, three colonels, nine other officers, and six enlisted personnel faced courts martial.

Of the twenty men (fourteen officers and six enlisted men) involved, who faced charges ranging from mass murder to suppressing evidence, one (Major General Samuel Koster) was a West Pointer. One (Brigadier General George Young) was a graduate of Columbia Military Academy and The Citadel ("the West Point of the South"). Twelve, including six of the officers, had entered the Army as enlisted personnel with high school educations. These included Captain Ernest Medina (charged with murder), Captain Eugene Kotouc (charged with murder), Captain Kenneth Boatman, Captain Dennis Johnson, Major Robert McKnight, Colonel Robert Luper (all charged with suppressing evidence or making false official statements), and six enlisted personnel, four of whom were charged with murder. Of the remaining six officers all had attended colleges in the South, several for only a year or two. These were First Lieutenant William Calley (charged with murder), who had attended one year of junior college; Captain Thomas Willingham (charged with murder), a graduate of Murray State College, Kentucky; Major Charles Calhoun, a Clemson graduate; Lieutenant Colonel William Guinn, who had attended the University of Tennessee and the University of Alabama; Lieutenant

Colonel David Gavin, a graduate of Mississippi Southern College; and Colonel Oran Henderson, who attended military base extension centers of the University of Maryland and George Washington University. Captain Willingham, the Murray State graduate, was the only one of the eight charged as principals in the massacre who was a college graduate.

Members of one platoon, Lieutenant Calley's, were accused of committing the vast majority of the murders. The platoon appears to have developed the impression (as one of its members put it) that, "if they wanted to do something wrong, it was always all right with Calley. He didn't try to stop them." Calley impressed one soldier as "a kid trying to play war."

A few weeks before My Lai, Calley ordered one of his men, PFC Michael Bernhardt, to shoot a woman running from them. Bernhardt called in Vietnamese for the woman to stop, but did not fire on her when she continued to run. Bernhardt was convinced that the woman was a noncombatant, but Calley was furious. Thereafter, Bernhardt explained, "I would just fire and miss on purpose." Bernhardt had been a junior and an ROTC honor student at the University of Miami before he enlisted "to test [his] courage under fire." Consequently he was only a private when his platoon entered My Lai. Bernhardt was the last of his platoon to enter the village. He was appalled by the indiscriminate killing going on. When he spoke of reporting the massacre to his congressman, Captain Medina warned him to keep silent. Bernhardt was the key source of Ronald Ridenhour's information about My Lai, and was a willing witness before the two non–West Pointers, Colonel William Wilson and General William Peers, who pressed home the overdue investigation.

When it appeared possible that the White House or the Army was prepared to allow Lieutenant Calley to leave the service before being formally charged with any crime, Captain William Hill, a reservist and thoroughly "civilianist" legal officer at Fort Benning (to which post Calley had been transferred during the course of the investigation), urged his careerist superior to overcome his reluctance to offend higher-ups and "to go ahead with the trial even if he had to defy the Pentagon [or the White House]." Hill was instrumental in precipitating the lodging of formal charges against Calley a day before Calley's separation from the service would have withdrawn him from the Army's jurisdiction.

When word reached West Point of the charges against General Koster, head of the Americal in 1968 and Superintendent of the Academy in 1969, the Corps of Cadets was assembled to hear Koster speak. He told them that "throughout my military career the cherished principles of [our Academy's] motto—Duty, Honor, Country—have served as a constant guide to me." The corps gave Koster a ninety-second ovation. As one plebe put it, "everybody [here] seemed to sympathize with the general."[18]

Simultaneous with news of Koster's implication came word of the first recorded case of a West Point graduate ever to request a discharge on the basis of selective conscientious objection to a war. First Lieutenant Louis Font, twenty-three, had been attending Harvard Graduate School in government at the time.[19]

While our first data were being assembled, in late May 1970, the Army charged two officers, Captain Vincent Hartmann and First Lieutenant Robert G. Lee, Jr., with attempted murder and manslaughter for ordering their men to conduct "target practice" on a number of Vietnamese huts in 1969. One woman eventually died of wounds inflicted during this "target practice"; her nephew was wounded. Neither officer had ever attended college.[20]

In early 1968 Lieutenant Commander Marcus Aurelius Arnheiter, a graduate of the Naval Academy, was relieved of command of the U.S.S. *Vance.* Several junior officers of Arnheiter's command, Lieutenant (j.g.) William Generous (an ROTC honor graduate, Phi Beta Kappa, from Brown University), Lieutenant (j.g.) Edward Mason (an OCS college graduate), and Ensign Luis Belmonte (another OCS college grad), had complained that Arnheiter had hazarded his vessel, falsified its

location while entering prohibited areas, sought to draw enemy fire on his ship, and generally had taken the vessel, as Arnheiter put it, "where the action is."

At one point, the junior officers claimed, he ordered Lieutenant (j.g.) Mason, in an armed motor whaleboat, to fire at a number of Vietnamese ashore. Mason refused. "I can't see shooting a bunch of civilians or even shooting at them," he told Arnheiter. Mason says he feared that Arnheiter would "interpret my shooting as somebody else's shooting and start shooting himself." The Vietnamese turned out to be refugees from a coastal village bombed out by American air strikes. As one crewman put it, "that kind of guy [Arnheiter] could start World War III."

Arnheiter's executive officer, Lieutenant Ray Hardy, another product of the Naval Academy, remained loyal to his chief and enforced Arnheiter's often bizarre orders. (Hardy acquired an ulcer in the process.) All of those who came to Arnheiter's defense (Rear Admiral Walter Baumberger, Rear Admiral Daniel Gallery, and Captain Richard Alexander) were Academy graduates. Admiral Gallery referred to the non-Annapolis critics of our veritable Captain Queeg as "oddball officers who should have been wearing beads and picketing the White House." Arnheiter himself called them a "bunch of dissident malcontents . . . a Berkeley-campus type of Vietnik/beatnik."[21]

Would that there had been a Mason at My Lai.

THE RESPONSIBILITIES OF "HARVARD BASTARDS"

What are the lessons of our experiment in attitude-behavior analysis and our excursion into the backgrounds of officers involved in "alleged misconduct" in Vietnam?

Certainly one conclusion is that *those critics of ROTC who have suggested that "an officer trained at Princeton kills as quickly on orders as an officer trained at the Point" are probably incorrect.* ROTC (and probably college-grad OCS officers) appear to be less belligerent and

18 *New York Times*, November 25, 1969, p. 16; and March 18, 1970, pp. 1ff. See also U.S., Department of Army, *U.S. Army Register*, vol. 2 (Washington, D.C., 1969), pp. 157, 742, *passim;* Seymour Hersh, *Mylai 4* (New York, 1970), pp. 20, 26, 32, 124, *passim;* Joseph Lelyveld, "The Story of a Soldier Who Refused to Fire at Songmy," *New York Times Magazine*, December 14, 1969, pp. 32ff.

19 *New York Times*, March 18, 1970, p. 17.

20 *New York Times*, May 29, 1970, p. 1.

21 *New York Times*, May 8, 1968, p. 12; May 10, 1968, pp. 1ff. See also U.S. Department of Navy, *Register of Commissioned Officers* (NavPers, 1966); Neil Sheehan, "The 99 Days of Captain Arnheiter," *New York Times Magazine*, August 11, 1968, pp. 7–9, 69–75.

less militaristic then either noncollege or service academy officers. (Indeed, one Ohio State NROTC student went so far as to note that he had joined ROTC to "work constructively to 'pacify' the military.") This is not to say that the ROTC student is the ideal officer candidate. We would prefer officers from a still more humanistic mold, but we are not likely to get a lottery drafting of college graduates for Officers Candidate School for some time, and meanwhile, the apparent contrast of service academy and ROTC student values suggested by our analysis ought to provoke those intent on driving ROTC from the liberal arts campus to give the matter some serious second thoughts.

We do not feel it proper that there be any formal relationship between the military and the academic community. ROTC, like OCS and the Marine Corps' summer training program for officer candidates, could well go "off campus." But it should be allowed—indeed, it should be encouraged—to "stick around." Since we are of the opinion that the military is going to be with the U.S. for some time, we feel that any "reform" that makes it difficult for a Princeton English major or a Pittsburgh philosophy major to become an officer is most undesirable. Major William Muhlenfeld recently put it nicely when he argued that it was

of utmost importance that [our] armies be led by just and compassionate men—men who understand that as leaders they are also public servants who have a profound responsibility to minister to the welfare of those they command, to serve with . . . the wisdom to see beyond their actions to the effects their actions wreak. This kind of leadership must come from the university . . . The paradox is that we must wait for the professors to learn.

One senior officer was more explicit: "[Lieutenant] Calley never would have become an officer if we were not so short-handed. Why are we short-handed? Because the bastards at Harvard wouldn't . . . step up to their responsibilities."[22]

Our own notion of the "responsibilities" of "Harvard bastards" may differ somewhat from the Army's, but, in any event, for the benefit of the American GI, as well as the Vietnamese villager, we hope that college graduates continue to serve as officers.

THE HUMANIST AS OFFICER?

This leads us to our second conclusion. We feel that English, philosophy—the "humanities" —majors should be encouraged to become military officers (and probably, for that matter, policemen, social workers, and governmental officials as well). Why humanities majors? Because these were the types who consistently gave the "best" responses to our questionnaire. Those who indicated that they were humanities majors[23] were *less* willing to obey immoral orders than were social science, natural science, or engineering majors (Table 8). They were the *least* willing to use nuclear weapons; they were the *least* likely to respond physically to insult; they were the *least* capable of imagining a situation in which a military takeover of the U.S. government would be justified; they were the *least* interested in endorsing "My country, right or wrong"; and they were the *most* critical of the size of the military budget.[24]

The trouble is that humanities majors do not seem very enthusiastic about joining the military, nor are they the bemedaled recruiting officer's dream-come-true. Isabella Williams has found them to be less interested than any of the other majors in joining ROTC, and more insistent than others on "the right of the soldier to criticize his superior officer and/or government policies without facing sanctions for his dissent."[25] Very few (less than 5 percent) of our ROTC sample were humanities majors. But they were disproportionately represented in that group of respondents who feel that the military, as an organization, constitutes one of the "most dangerous" threats to the American system of government (see Table 8).

Many military men, concerned as they are with "leadership," body counts, power, and discipline, are probably quite satisfied with any system that allows Yosarians, Pete Seegers, and Staughton Lynds to stay clear of the military. The advocates of a volunteer professional

22 Muhlenfeld, "Our Embattled ROTC," pp. 581–89 of this volume.

23 There was no statistically significant difference among choice of major in our universe of respondents on grounds of family income, father's level of education, or any other criteria.

24 Cf. Feldman and Newcomb, *op. cit.*, 1: 167.

25 Isabella Williams, "The Other West Points," unpublished paper, August 1969, in the possession of Professor Peter Karsten, History Department, University of Pittsburgh.

Table 8

College Major	Willing to Obey Morally Repugnant Order (%)	Willing to Respond Physically to Insult to Girl (%)	Willing to Use Nuclear Weapons (%)	Military Takeover Might be Justified Some Day (%)	Agreed with "My Country, Right or Wrong" (%)	Disagreed with "My Country, Right or Wrong" (%)	Felt Military Budget too High (%)	Felt Military Budget too Low (%)	Felt Military "Most Dangerous" to U.S. Gov't (%)
Humanities (29)	14.0	14.0	37	14	14	72.5	72.5	6.7	55
Social Science (100)	30.0	33.0	65	23	39	46.0	51.0	16.0	14
Natural Science (102)	37.0	40.0	75	26	37	43.0	41.0	19.0	8
Engineering (117)	42.5	30.5	76	22	48	38.5	24.0	17.0	2

army argue the virtues of such a self-selection process. We are not as convinced of the advantages of any system that can do without the citizen-officer or, for that matter, the citizen-soldier.

THE CITIZEN-OFFICER

That brings us to our third conclusion. *If you do not like the way the military functions, you cannot expect it to improve by insulating yourself from it.* William Lucas feels that ROTC is undesirable because it "does not reflect the composition and attitudes of society,"[26] and thus serves as no check on service academy Arnheiters and "up-through-the-ranks" Medinas. But Lucas did not *compare* ROTC people to the other types of officer candidates. Had he done so, we feel that he would have discovered significant differences. Moreover, we are a little uneasy with the way Lucas has phrased his hypothesis. We are not at all certain that officers *should* reflect the "attitudes of society," as society is presently structured. The "up-through-the-ranks" and service academy officers probably *do* reflect such attitudes. What Lucas may have intended to say and, in any event, what we feel ourselves, is that the citizen-officer should represent the noblest attitudes and values in American society— values which, we maintain, would include a refusal to obey immoral orders, a reluctance to sling nuclear weapons around, and a strong

[26] Lucas, *op. cit.*, p. 52; but see his more recent views in "Anticipatory Professional Military Socialization and the ROTC," in *Public Opinion and the Military Establishment*, ed. Charles C. Moskos, Jr. (Beverly Hills, Calif., 1971), pp. 99–134.

disinclination for any military coup or other invasion of the political process.

Some will say that we are naive—that one officer is as powerless as the next to effect any significant check on the ways of a military which, after all, takes its orders from civilians in Washington. We admit that having "good" officers does not mean that they will receive "good" orders. We concede that, if a sensitive officer distinguishes between combatants and non-combatants, moral and immoral orders, he may still kill the combatants, may still obey the "moral" orders. But we have seen infantry lieutenants in Cambodia wearing peace symbols on the TV news, telling reporters of how they had deliberately led their men clear of the combat zone. We have seen young Army doctors refusing to collaborate, young Army lawyers demanding justice, and young junior officers protesting the war. A volunteer army would end all of that.

It is true that the most significant changes must occur higher up the ladder of authority (which is why we suggested politics and governmental service for humanities majors). But the vicissitudes of the antiwar movement have demonstrated the difficulties that dissenters will have in penetrating the political process. The military and the police are more accessible. We must all work toward the day when war and inequity no longer exist, but, in the meantime, for the villagers at My Lai and those under the guns of Arnheiter, Mason, and the *Vance*, the presence of a "good" officer counts.

That is why we were chagrined to find that 84 percent (31 of 37) of those who felt the military is "most dangerous" also favored a volunteer army! A volunteer army of "pros," void of citizen-officers coming in out of the draft, *would* be dangerous. As Peter Barnes recently put it:

an end to the draft would shield the army from the influx of citizen-soldiers who are the yeast of internal change. The army *needs* Yosarians, Ronald Ridenhours, independent-minded ROTC junior officers and J.A.G. lawyers—soldiers who do their jobs but who are not committed to the cover-your-ass system, whose loyalties are to civilian, not careerist values.[27]

Critics of ROTC, ironically, the Army needs you!

[27] Peter Barnes, "All-Volunteer Army?" *The New Republic*, May 9, 1970, p. 23. See also Peter Karsten, "The American Citizen Soldier: Triumph or Disaster?" *Military Affairs*, 30 (1966): 34–40.

OUR EMBATTLED ROTC

WILLIAM F. MUHLENFELD

Carrying on the analysis of ROTC by a number of scholars in the previous article, the perspective here shifts to an insider's view of the Reserve Officer Training Corps. While the alternatives to ROTC are considered, a general restructuring, rather than abandonment, is suggested. In addition, the author appeals for some thought on what kind of officer corps the United States wants in the years ahead. Major William F. Muhlenfeld is a career officer (artillery) in the United States Army. He was commissioned from ROTC at Western Maryland College and served in the late 1960s as an instructor with the Army ROTC at Rutgers University.

On a cold, blustery Monday morning in early November 1967, members of the Department of Military Science at Rutgers University found their office building surrounded by students from the campus chapter of the Students for a Democratic Society (SDS). The students would not permit the military staff to enter their building, and a spokesman said they intended to stay where they were until ROTC left the Rutgers campus. For three days and nights they stood their ground. To every effort to breach the cordon they responded, and they made it clear that the building could be entered only at the cost of some kind of violence.

Finally, it all ended. The university administration acted in the interests of order. The students were required to desist. Hearings were held, punishments meted out, and disciplinary probations were imposed. But ROTC had become a celebrated cause. Crowds of hecklers had gathered. National news networks had come with microphones and TV cameras. The campus newspaper had had a field day. Most important, the administration had set up a faculty-student committee to evaluate the ROTC program. From its recommendations and the ensuing faculty debate came certain reforms—too mild to satisfy the protesters, but strong enough to cast doubts about ROTC's future.

A year has passed since the now famous siege. After a furious faculty debate—notable

Reprinted by permission and with minor changes from Army, February 1969, pp. 21–29. Copyright © 1969 *by the Association of the U.S. Army.*

primarily for the latent hostilities and misunder-standings it revealed—the character of ROTC at Rutgers has been altered slightly. The overall credit for participation has been reduced by 14 percent. Procedures for withdrawal have been simplified. Portions of the ROTC cur-riculum which nominally fall outside the area of military expertise are to be taught by the civilian faculty. Academic credit for drill has been abolished. Incoming officers are to be appointed in the same way as are other faculty —that is, in terms of the breadth of their edu-cational backgrounds and professional achieve-ments—and the faculty committee on appoint-ments is to have veto power over nominations. Generally speaking, the Department of Military Science is to function precisely as does any other department of Rutgers College, and to the extent that this may interfere with fulfill-ment of the military mission, the professor of military science has a delicate problem. He must not, for example, condone an intensive recruiting campaign, as this is presumed to be an incursion upon the student's free choice.

The net effect of these reforms has been to erode—some might say emasculate—ROTC at Rutgers. Cadet activities, which once indirectly offered academic credit because they were part of the drill program, now are wholly extra-curricular, since leadership laboratory itself is a zero credit course. The band, rangers, color guard, drill team, and other groups can get operating funds from the student activities committee only if they demonstrate autonomy from ROTC. The department itself, bastion of the "military mind" as it is, survives as a kind of leper colony whose inhabitants are pre-sumed to be a collection of saber-rattling, missile-toting madmen. The student newspaper fulminates with vitriolic passages at the slight-est provocation. And, through it all, freshman enrollment has declined steadily: from 491 in 1966, to 242 in 1967, to 170 in 1968. Why?

The answer to this question is a long one indeed. An objective analysis is especially diffi-cult for anyone with strong feelings about the worth of ROTC, its importance to the military services, and its consequent importance to the national interests of the United States.

To begin with, it is specious to suppose that opposition to ROTC stems exclusively or even primarily from liberal opposition to the Viet-nam War. That opposition might be a catalyst,

a kind of fuse to the Molotov cocktail, as it were, but it is hardly the principal cause. The argument is pleasantly seductive because it suggests that, when the war goes away, so will opposition to ROTC. Unfortunately, it seems more probable that when the war goes away opposition to ROTC may grow, since in the minds of critics the need for military leaders will have declined. ROTC is quietly tolerated by many academics because they pragmatically realize that the national interest demands it. To discern this unhappy truth, one need only ask a cross section of the silent majority who de-cline to join the debate.

Next, it is incorrect to suppose that opposi-tion to ROTC is regional. This understandably myopic assessment usually comes from the Northeast, where those in the eye of the storm believe that, since they inhabit the liberal's traditional domain, they are the sole victims of wild-eyed attacks against "militarism" on the campus. It is a fact, however, that ROTC has taken its knocks rather generally in the last year and a half. At Michigan State, opponents of ROTC infiltrated "spies" into the program. At Tulane, hooded demonstrators fell into ranks with marching Naval ROTC cadets. At the Chicago Circle campus of Illinois Univer-sity, pickets appeared at an ROTC review. At Stanford, thirteen students (six of them girls) enrolled in ROTC deliberately to ridicule the program. At Howard, students "sat in" upon the president to protest compulsory ROTC. At Boston University, students complained about military "propaganda." The Yale *Daily News* led a campaign to abolish credit for ROTC participation. Objections to compulsory ROTC were in part responsible for demonstrations at Tuskegee Institute, where students locked the trustees in a campus guest house. These ex-amples are only a few of those significant enough to attract attention in the public press.

Finally, the standard arguments against ROTC—now repeated so often—are not the real arguments.

Argument number one is that military officers are unfit to join a university faculty, since they do not have doctoral degrees and are not by temperament scholars. This does not, however, preclude the appointment of a selected few others to full faculty status, including full pro-fessorships, when they similarly lack formal qualification. Nor does it preclude the referral of teaching duties to "teaching assistants"— young men not yet twenty-five who themselves only recently have been granted a bachelor's degree.

The next argument attacks the "intellectual content" of ROTC courses. Here one makes the nice distinction between "education" and "training," and between what is basically "intellectual" and what is basically "professional." The implication is that academic credit should be offered for the one and not for the other. Yet the distinction—and its implications concerning academic credit—is apparently inapplicable to courses concerning piano playing, practice teaching, physical education, and the control of weeds.

Another argument, only slightly more sophisticated, holds that it is contrary to the philosophy of higher education to teach the techniques of violence if, in fact, it truly is devoted to enlightenment and reason. Carried to its logical extension, however, holders of this view finally must agree that it is better for the ignorant and brutal to wage war than for the educated and compassionate.

The last major argument deals with the invidious character of "outside influences." Here, in one's mind's eye, he sees himself locked in a bare room while a poisonous black fluid slowly rolls in under the door. The fluid of the metaphor, of course, is the "military mind," with all of its right-wing conservatism, its unfashionable red-white-and-blue patriotism, its loyalty to the Establishment, its propaganda, its simple-minded solutions to complex problems, its threat to scholarly iconoclasm. What is unclear, however, is that the only outside influence sufficiently threatening to provoke reaction is that of the military—not government generally, not the foundations, not business, just the military. Once one pokes through the vitriolic haze and grasps this kernel of truth, the whole melancholy litany stands revealed for what it is: an elaborate apparatus to justify a prejudice against the military and its ways. What, after all, is more antithetical to free and reasoned dissent than the chain of command, or to the freedom which must characterize creativity and scholarly inquiry than the regimen of a military organization? And what personal conflict is more inevitable than that between those committed to the former and those committed to the latter?

In terms of faculty opposition to ROTC, what we are seeing is this long-latent but fundamental cleavage in full flower, goaded into the open by students who are neither as inhibited nor as prudent as their mentors, and who are untroubled by the injustice of it all because they do not perceive it. Some years ago, Morris Janowitz, the prominent sociologist, recognized the academician's peculiar aversion to military matters when, in his preface to *The New Military*, he felt constrained to justify to his peers the object of his scholarship. By implication, many considered the military unworthy of scholarly attention, just as a vocal minority considers the military unworthy of a place on the campus. Somehow, that minority will have to decide how it can favor university involvement in the great issues of our time while concurrently attempting to expel from its midst those who need its help; how it can be concerned about social institutions generally but not particularly; how it can seek an enlightened military while seeking to deprive the military of its enlightened leadership; how it can favor participatory democracy while participating itself only selectively.

Yet, one realizes that the untapped reservoir of faculty opposition had been quiescent for years and that it could have been catalyzed into activity only by dissident students. It is to the phenomenon of student activism in the 1960s, then, to which we must turn if we are to speculate further upon the extraordinary confluence of two minorities which, for their separate reasons, jointly seek to undermine ROTC. One finds considerably more cause for charity on behalf of students than for their faculties, but here, too, there is a substantial measure of error.

All who are close to higher education recognize the advent of a new era. It is not clear whether the change has been gradual or abrupt, but there is no question that today's student is much more sensitive to his society and concerned about its direction. Moreover, the phenomenon is worldwide in scope and therefore beyond, in the causative sense, national manifestations. Student reaction to national policies is a symptom of student activism and not a cause of it. It is not clear why the wave of student concern should have occurred in the decade of the 1960s, rather than, let us say, the 1930s. The expansion of higher education, its mass extension across class lines, improved communications, the vexing problems of the twentieth century, our more mobile society—probably all have something to do with it. But, for whatever reason, as students probe their environment and see starvation in Appalachia, the despair of the underprivileged and poverty-stricken, the ofttimes futile striving of the ethnic minorities, the butchery of modern warfare, the predatory machinations of organized crime, it is understandable that they dissent from the *status quo*. To many sensitive people, the blunt conclusions of the Kerner report on civil disturbances accurately assess America in the twentieth century. For them, it has become a rude, ever-growing split, driven toward divisiveness in the final analysis by its own political and social systems, gone plunging toward destruction like a runaway locomotive. For some, arrest of this rush to oblivion—by the violent overthrow of government if necessary—is the crucial objective. Such people comprise the radical student left, the left wing of which is the Students for a Democratic Society.

On the ROTC issue the SDS is, of course, livid. The Army, in its roles of foreign and domestic "enforcer" for the Establishment, protector of "decadent" government, and practitioner of "genocide," lies beyond the pale. Little wonder, then, that the ROTC program should face the spearhead of their attack and that the guilty university administrations, "enslaved by the Washington–Wall Street axis," should finish a close second. The SDS parrots the same anti-ROTC arguments solemnly advanced by their collaborators on the faculty, and to a large extent shares their fundamental antipathy to, and revulsion toward, things military. But the SDS, in ascribing to the military the intention to preserve by force the *status quo*, injects a new and quite different purpose for opposition. Presumably, if the Army were committed to altering the *status quo*, if by some wild turn of events it were of use to the SDS, the ROTC might become a very satisfactory institution indeed. This would not help the professors, however, for the military mind is the military mind, and it would still be around to "contaminate" the campus.

What has happened is that two sources of opposition—one student and one faculty—and two sets of reasons—one largely ideological and the other largely emotional—have fallen into coincidence and interacted. The students could not have survived without faculty support. The faculty would not have come around without student agitation. The concerted opposition of these two minorities has succeeded in driving from ROTC many of the uncommitted and uncertain majority. Instinctively, one realizes, however, that this is by no means the whole story. No one is more inclined toward his own self-interest than the adolescent freshman. Anyone who has counseled a freshman knows well that freshmen do what they wish to do, what fits their system of values. After years of parental restraint, the atmosphere of college is headily permissive. We can be assured that, if, in the mind of the entering freshman, ROTC were not in the first place a questionable option, attacks upon it would be futile. Clearly, ROTC is an option with important pros and cons. Since the freshman enrolls in the program, one must view it through his eyes and adopt his values in order to understand his decisions. If that is possible, if Chief Justice Earl Warren is wrong in his estimate of the generation gap, within these eighteen-year-old heads we shall find some important answers. The freshmen control the fate of ROTC; occasionally their organized opposition exercises a frail and fleeting balance of power.

Freshmen entertain some rather ambivalent notions about military service. By and large, they are uninterested in it, not because they are unpatriotic, but because, vocationally speaking they are motivated in other directions. They accept their responsibility to serve in the armed forces if called upon to do so, but many are quite unwilling to *guarantee* that they will do so by joining ROTC—and almost all are uncomfortable at being confronted with the decision during their first week at college, at a time when they have barely registered with the Selective Service System.

In addition, freshmen are inveterate dreamers. Until they come rudely to earth at the end of their first semester, nearly all are going to graduate schools, there to become physicians, lawyers, public administrators, and captains of industry. Military service therefore remains comfortably beyond the horizon. Much can happen over five or more years and, for the undergraduate years at the very least, the walls of ivy keep the predatory minions of Selective Service locked securely outside. Only two varieties of frosh enroll in ROTC: the comparatively few who genuinely want to get a commission, and the relatively many who have decided that sooner or later, one way or the other, they would otherwise be drafted.

The number in the latter group has been shrinking as the anti-ROTC campaign has developed. Because they wish to defer the inevitable decision about military service, they are prey for dissuaders who argue that joining the ROTC is neither necessary nor desirable, and who portray the ROTC cadet as a square and a jerk. That image is not, of course, fully credible; but it is somewhat credible, given the freshman's adolescent values. When it is seen as additive to other factors which in his mind are important, it assumes its significance. Those other factors have been part of ROTC for some time and are a commentary on the Army's failure to move with the times. Some are truly significant and some are not, but all are important, since it is not what is real, but what students perceive to be real, that is important.

First among these is drill—what is euphemistically termed "leadership laboratory." It is very hard to find anything good about this anachronism. Surely it cannot be required: ROTC cadets methodically plod through the same close-order rituals each week for four years, in order to master what basic trainees are taught in the first days of their service. Yet, drill has survived for nearly fifty years as the most immutable aspect of ROTC. All the while it has become progressively less relevant and more annoying. Today, since ROTC instructors have exhausted the even remotely conceivable justifications for it, they usually merely dismiss it as undesirable but necessary. This demonstrates to friend and foe alike that the military is in fact unprogressive, inflexible, and dogmatic. Moreover, to the cadet it is extremely boring, demeaning because it is mindless, and embarrassing because it is public. And, if that were not enough, because drill entails the inconvenience of shining brass and shoes, drawing a rifle, putting on a uniform and taking it off, traveling to and from a parade ground, it requires a good deal of time—usually the better part of an afternoon, which sometimes results in schedule conflicts or lateness to other classes. In sum, "leadership laboratory" may well be the program's worst enemy.

The second factor is the uniform. Many cadets apparently do not like to wear their uniforms, and for those of us who have chosen military careers this is difficult to understand. But it is true. One need only observe that, without exception, cadets change clothes at the end of ROTC class whenever they can do so. The cadets give a variety of reasons for this. They say their uniforms fit poorly and are out of style; in particular, some basic-course cadets abhor the green garrison cap, which somehow they compare to a freshman beanie. They say the uniforms are uncomfortable and complicated when compared, for example, to the leisurely ease of a simple coat and tie. But the most important reason is that the uniform attracts attention. College students, moving through the self-conscious transition to adulthood, do not wish to be the focus of attention. What they wish more than anything is a position of esteem in the body collegiate, to fit in the warp and woof of the collegiate ethos, to mirror the easy sophistication perceived as the mark of the educated man. At the present time, Army green simply is not part of this image.

The third factor is ROTC instruction itself. It is apparently true that ROTC classes do not enjoy high marks in terms of either interest or relevance. Instructors, by and large, do not—and cannot—bring to the classroom the kind of scholarship which is the norm among their civilian colleagues. The Army provides every conceivable instructional aid, many of which are expensive and elaborate, but that cannot overcome the fundamental contrast. The cadets, after all, judge ROTC instruction in terms of the university environment, because that is *their* environment. The course work is entirely new to them; it involves material with which they ofttimes do not relate. The well-greased class, replete with viewgraph projector and working models—the kind that wins approval in the military service schools—probably contributes to the estrangement. To many students, ROTC classes have about them an unreal, mechanical feature which mitigates against the rapport between instructor and student which is so vital to the educational process. In all events, these are the criticisms that lend credence to unconscionable attacks upon the fundamental worth of the instruction and support the related attempts to remove or reduce academic credit. They are also criticisms that have been voiced on the campus for a long time and that today constitute a kind of folk-lore which freshmen quickly assimilate.

It is no wonder, really, that the axis welded together among faculty and students by the SDS is having an apparent effect. The program has some real faults in the student mind, and it it surprising that these in themselves have not provoked a deleterious effect much sooner and of their own accord. The demands and opportunities in higher education are steadily expanding. Each year more and more interests compete for the student's attention. University life is becoming more dynamic and exciting, for the activism is pervasive. Unless the Army can draw apace of this trend and join it, there will be no hope to infuse ROTC with new vitality. Policy people throughout the Army realize that ROTC must succeed, for the "Reserve" part of "Reserve Officers' Training Corps" has become a misnomer in the last twenty years. The Army depends upon the university to provide the bulk of its commissioned leaders. One need only observe that if West Point were to graduate 1,000 officers a year for thirty years and not one of them resigned, that figure would constitute 20 percent of a 150,000-man officer corps.

The Army has begun to react. The process of reform has begun, but so far the progress has been slow and unsure. It is undoubtedly true that, at the policy level, traditionalists and revisionists have collided over the choice of options. And it is clearly true that soldiers in academe cannot move with celerity and self-confidence as they do on the battlefield. This necessitates some time-consuming poking around to "get the feel of the problem." The ungodly tedium of the bureaucracy, the staffing process, practical questions of money and resources, the necessity for pilot projects—all these contribute to further delays. It may well be that the element of urgency has also been absent, since declining freshman enrollments do not affect officer production for at least four years. Nonetheless, the four-year Army ROTC program that began in 1919 and remained fundamentally unchanged for forty-five years now exhibits some new wrinkles. These date largely from the Revitalization Act of 1964 and generally predate the current ROTC controversy. They also present a new set of conceptual inconsistencies and operational problems. But they are change.

The two-year program, offered at the option of the institution, was designed to accommodate primarily juniors who would be transferring from two-year junior colleges where there had been no ROTC. It has the drawback of requiring an additional summer camp (prior to the start of the junior year), but it does afford for some a second chance at ROTC and it does open up the junior colleges for recruiting. Unfortunately, in 1967 only 14 percent of the enrollees came from the junior colleges. The rest were late-starters from the four-year colleges and graduate students. When Selective Service last year announced its intention to draft graduate students, the applications from this group jumped sharply. All of this raises some interesting problems. Certainly the Army desires officers who possess graduate degrees, but it does not want the two-year program to become a device for evading induction. The Army wants the two-year program to supplement, not compete with, the traditional four-year program, but there is at least impressionistic evidence that the latter is occurring. Finally, implicit with the two-year concept is the assumption that the additional camp can do in a few weeks what the basic course does in two years; indeed, there is little difference in the performance of the two groups at the regular summer camp. This, then, brings into question the need for a four-year program; and *that* forces a study of whether the Army's training base could support the expansion of the two-year program's basic camp should the four-year plan be eliminated.

Another innovation of the current decade is the Army's scholarship program, whose main purpose is to attract undergraduates interested in a military career. There are options for both four and two years, which make it possible for college sophomores as well as high school seniors to apply. Generally speaking, the scholarship idea has worked well, but with certain hurdles along the way. One of these has been a shortage of applicants. While the four-year program is drawing only about 30 percent of the desired number, so far this seems not to have affected the quality of the recipients, 92 percent of whom in 1968 were in the top 20 percent of their graduating class. The more vexing (but predictable) problem is that the scholarships attract only the students who were interested to begin with. They apparently further exploit the same group which is applying, for example, to West Point, but do not stimulate appreciably the much larger group which in the past had not seriously considered a military career. Indicators of this are the 20 percent who are sons of Army families and the more than 50 percent who decline scholarship assistance because they had been appointed to service academies. Thus, the scholarship scheme accomplishes its principal purpose, which is to increase the number of young men nominally committed to careers as commissioned officers, but it does not stimulate any special interest among the others. Consequently, although it may expand the number of careerists produced by ROTC, it has little effect on ROTC enrollment.

The matter of curriculum reform—the heart of student criticism—also has been given attention in recent years. Step one was Curriculum B, an optional course of study which eliminates some of the standard ROTC topics and substitutes in their places certain university electives. Undeniably, this affords the student more flexibility in devising his own program, satiates the apoplectic professors, lightens the military teaching load, and eases scheduling. It also weakens the opportunity to evaluate the cadets, creates semester-long gaps when the cadets more or less disappear from view, and therefore raises another important question: can it be that the length, scope, and content of the ROTC courses have little to do with how good a commissioned officer the program produces? This question, after all, is not so very different from the one raised by the two-year program and the implicit assumptions about the compensatory value of the basic camp compared to that of the basic course.

The answer to that question is likely to be found among the results garnered from step two, an interesting exercise in curriculum tinkering—some might say curriculum elimination—now going on experimentally at eleven volunteer institutions. The experiment, called Curriculum C, is a result of a proposal drawn up in 1964 by the Mershon Committee at Ohio State University. The committee sought to assess Army ROTC in contemporary terms and to propose revisions which would be more relevant—and consequently more valuable—to all concerned. Hopefully, the results of the experiment will make the program more vital

and therefore more attractive for students, more intellectual and therefore more satisfactory to the institutions, more qualitative and therefore more productive for the Army. The experiment is encumbered by no sacred cows. Importantly, the Army has designated a control group of other institutions to provide the basis for comparative analysis, and it intends to evaluate its results empirically, so that what turns out to be incorrect may prove as valuable as what is correct. Everyone hopes, of course, that student acceptance will be high and that curriculum reform in and of itself will prove sufficient to infuse Army ROTC with the new vitality it seeks.

Afoot also is an effort to raise the academic qualifications of the military officers assigned as instructors with ROTC units. This effort is a reaction to attacks upon the men who teach (which accompany attacks upon the substance of their teaching). Earnestly concerned that there may be truth in such drivel, the Army has set out to send to the campus as many master's degrees as possible. It has formally designated the degree of master of arts as a prerequisite for the position of professor of military science (PMS) and has succeeded in so assigning 34 percent of the incumbents. It is true, of course, that the PMS—like any other departmental chairman—is seldom a full-time teacher, and it is therefore also true that, degree in hand, the PMS does little to enhance classroom instruction. What he does do is climb a little closer to parity with his colleagues, who ascribe quite the same significance to degrees that military men ascribe to rank, but who ignore rank-degree differentiations as completely as they ignore the excellence of the Army service schools system. Fortunately, the intrinsic values of higher education have their own justification (as the Army well knows and has repeatedly demonstrated by its general educational policies). The master's degree project will surely have its own beneficial fallout, but it likely will do little to pacify critics who want a doctor of philosophy in every classroom. Indeed, one wonders whether the trappings of academia are to be desired; the differences between academicians and soldiers in many ways are so profound as to be irreconcilable. What is needed is mutual respect.

The present decade has brought one other

change: a gradual expansion of the Army's ROTC recruiting effort. The increase is strikingly obvious when one realizes that the recruiting effort now demands—and gets—the undivided attention of special divisions in the public information offices of regional Army headquarters. These information staffs engage in extensive promotional activities which include direct mailings to area high schools, the preparation of recruiting literature, the placing of professionally prepared advertising, and the administration of an annual enrollment campaign—through the offices of institutional ROTC units—among entering college freshmen. Seldom subtle and at times heavy-handed, often a source of friction with college administrators, who justifiably deplore pressure tactics of any sort, the recruiting effort is a dubious blessing. It has aroused the resentment of freshmen, who, constantly bombarded with mailings and campus courtships, resist the coercion and doubt the motives of its practitioners. It has angered otherwise sympathetic faculty, who properly insist that students have their own self-interests which must be defined and served in the larger context of undergraduate education, of which ROTC is merely a peripheral part. And it has embarrassed Army officers, who regard the "hard sell" and image-making as the special provinces of hucksters from Madison Avenue, as unworthy techniques for procuring officers and demeaning to the concepts associated with commissioned service. The very use of the word "recruit," suggesting as it does that students must be "sold," again drives into focus the fundamental and recurring question: If the ROTC were all that it should be, why should solicitation be necessary? It is an inquiry that by inference embraces all the other questions, the passions of moderate and militant alike, and it raises doubts in the minds of the uncommitted. In the last analysis, only one other question is more important: What can be done to improve the program so as to make solicitation unnecessary?

It is hoped that evaluation of Curriculum C will provide many of these answers. The Mershon Committee saw officer development in the professional context so brilliantly articulated by Samuel Huntington in *The Soldier and the State* and has attempted to divide Army ROTC into professional and pre-professional phases. This sort of conceptualization is especially valuable in the operational sense because it does permit collaboration with civilian faculty in pre-professional preparation and it does permit a reordering of the purely military curriculum so that close-order drill, for example, will cease to be the program's most pervasive and persistent feature. This, in turn, will relax tensions over matters concerning academic credit, since curriculum reform has the overall effect of improving the quality of "professional" phase instruction. Will Curriculum C stimulate student interest to the same degree that it gains faculty approbation? Whether it does or not, the general restructuring of ROTC that appears on the horizon offers an important opportunity to affirm some necessary fundamentals concerning *any* ROTC program.

First, what is most important about ROTC instruction is that it provides a vehicle for evaluating cadets in terms of their commission potential. This is a highly subjective decision which depends for its accuracy on the judgment of commissioned officers. Stated in another way, it is far more important to assure that commissions go to the best potential leaders, not necessarily to the best scholars or the best athletes, and not necessarily to any other sort of student. Since this is true, any "new look" must preserve the evaluation opportunity. It must not weaken that opportunity by seriously curtailing the contact between military instructor and cadet, by reducing the number of semesters during which the evaluation is made, or by transferring part of the evaluation responsibility to civilian faculty (who demonstrate by their behavior that they have a poor appreciation of the special demands of officership). One of the weaknesses of the two-year program is that it introduces to the advanced course students of whom the PMS has no prior knowledge and halves his opportunity to evaluate their fitness for commissioned service.

Next, ROTC, because of the way it is structured, must not conflict with other student interests. For example, it must not conflict with the graduation requirements of the institution; in the past it has caused scheduling conflicts, academic overloads, credit imbalances which are difficult to adjust, and difficulties with the sequential alignment of courses in the student's major field. ROTC must be *convenient*—and this again evokes the complaints about leadership laboratory, uniform regulations, and other trappings of the military which the cadets do not understand and continually object to. The professor of military science clearly needs a great deal of autonomy in this area, since conditions at institutions vary greatly.

Third, ROTC must be worthwhile in terms of student perceptions just as clearly as commissioned service is worthwhile in terms of officer perceptions. Since only a few students perceive officership in a mature and balanced way, since during college years they themselves are grappling with private identity crises, since it is fundamentally impossible for freshmen to feel strongly about a matter with which they cannot relate, the incentives must be immediate, practical, and sufficiently compelling to override doubts. In other words, the incentives must be an end in themselves while the students are learning the meaning of their purpose. Clearly, fear of the draft is the worst sort of incentive. It is unattractive, suggests that an Army commission is the best of poor alternatives, breeds cynicism about the military and its purposes, and therefore attracts many of the wrong people. In the area of attractive incentives, there are a number of possibilities—including substantially higher pay, pay to freshmen, and extension of at least some active duty privileges (such as space-available travel). Such ideas at the very least require major policy decisions because of their cost and implications about membership in the Army Reserve, but they are worth considering.

Finally, ROTC must be supported by institutional administrations and faculty. If, after curriculum reform, efforts to send officers with advanced degrees, and every conceivable accommodation in the area of scheduling, the hostility of an implacable and persistent minority continues to impede the ROTC at every turn while administrators maintain an Olympian silence, the incentives will be strong, indeed, if they alone are to sustain a healthy program. A principal value of academic credit is that it serves as tangible testimony of the program's worth in the eyes of an institution, and it is that stamp of approval which must pervade the spirit of the relationship as well as its letter. Even though it is true that academic credit has surprisingly little connection with ROTC enrollment, it is equally true that a program without it is likely to subsist on the fringe of the academic community, held in contempt by some, ignored by many, and with a small voice in the institutional affairs which are its legitimate concern. This is an ignominious situation which places the Army in the position of groveling for officers, an unworthy role which it ought not to countenance.

There is a sad ambiguity about the ROTC controversy. In terms of dissident sentiment the ambiguity is a paradox. Only the naive seriously argue that armies can be eliminated from this unsettled world. But who would not wish it so? In the unhappy interim, while free nations secure themselves with the materials of war, it is of utmost importance that their armies be led by just and compassionate men —men who understand that as leaders they are also public servants who have a profound responsibility to minister to the welfare of those they command, to serve with fidelity, integrity, and the wisdom to see beyond their actions to the effects their actions wreak. This kind of leadership must come from the university, where the fundamental humanism undergirding the very concepts of a liberal education thrive and infect those who come to learn. It can come from nowhere else, because there is nowhere else. The Army has only a minor influence on the university. The influence of the university on the Army is very great, and its importance is urgent. Among the contributions of the universities to the professions, few are more important than this. The paradox is that we must wait for the professors to learn.

THE MILITARY MAN IN ACADEMIA

AMOS A. JORDAN AND WILLIAM J. TAYLOR, JR.

The officer educational system is in a period of overdue, dynamic change in military curricular substance and approach. The challenge to the officer educational system is to produce the required numbers of officers with expertise in the management and application of military resources in deterrent, peace-keeping, advisory, and combat roles in the context of rapid technological, social, and political change. This educational system must provide "training" to develop specific skills and military professionalism; it must also develop broadly applicable analytical skills and critical judgment. The officer educational system can define the parameters of the former far more easily than the latter. Jordan and Taylor provide an overall assessment of training requirements for the future as well as an assessment of the values which the nation wishes its military officers to hold. Their evaluation of the little-known and little-understood post-service academy educational system provides some useful insights into the continuous socialization process of the officer corps. Amos Jordan is Director of the Aspen Institute of Humanistic Studies. Recently retired as a brigadier general, Dr. Jordan was Professor of Social Sciences at the United States Military Academy for over seventeen years. He is the author of several books and numerous articles on national security policy and on officer education. Lt. Colonel William J. Taylor, Jr., Ph.D., is the Permanent Associate Professor for National Security Policy Studies and Director of the Debate Council and Forum at the Military Academy. Dr. Jordan and Colonel Taylor are co-authors of The Elements of National Security Policy *(forthcoming).*

THE MILITARY PROFESSION

Professional education can be discussed sensibly only in terms of how and how well it prepares those being educated for roles in that profession. Accordingly, we begin with a sketchy description of the profession of arms and the roles and skills essential to its practitioners.

The military has many of the same characteristics as the other professions—namely, a specialized body of knowledge acquired through advanced training and experience, a mutually defined and sustained set of standards, and a sense of group identity and corporateness.[1] In addition, the military profession has several characteristics not shared by such other professions as law, education, or medicine; it is, for example, bureaucratized, with a hierarchy of offices and a legally defined structure;[2] it is a uniquely public profession marked by its members' commitment to unlimited service, which extends to the risk of life itself; it is singular, too, as a profession which trains its members to perform many tasks that one hopes it will never have to perform.[3] These charac-

[1] Morris Janowitz, *The Professional Soldier* (New York: The Free Press, 1960), pp. 5–7.

[2] Samuel P. Huntington, *The Soldier and the State* (New York: Random House, 1957), p. 16. See also pp. 505–11 of this volume.

[3] Morris Janowitz, "The Emergent Military," in *Public Opinion and the Military Establishment*, ed. Charles C. Moskos, Jr. (Beverly Hills, Calif.: Sage Publications, 1971), p. 258.

teristics have important implications for military education, as we shall see later.

The particular expertise of the military profession has been defined in various ways. Traditional definitions, such as Harold Lasswell's familiar formulation of it as the "management of violence," will no longer suffice. In the context of the likely national security environment of the 1970s and beyond, a better definition of the expertise which the military education system should develop is "the management and application of military resources in deterrent, peacekeeping, and combat roles in the context of rapid technological, social, and political change."[4]

Military expertise, so defined, necessarily implies a broader set of roles for the military officer than has traditionally been expected of him. Included are (1) helping to define the nature of the nation's security tasks, especially their politico-military dimension; (2) applying scientific and technological knowledge to military matters; (3) advising foreign military establishments as required; and (4) training, supplying, deploying and—if necessary—employing the fighting capability of military units in complex changing environments. The model of a modern major general (or a major for that matter) must not only master the broader dimensions of this fourth, traditional role but also develop a competence in one or more of the other roles as well. He must do so, that is, if he expects to rise in his profession, for the politico-military and scientific-technological dimensions of security problems interact with the narrowly tactical-technical ones in a complex and continuing way. Mastery of the traditional role alone is not adequate to the increasingly broad range of tasks required of the military professional since World War II. This multiple role requirement has, of course, been based upon the assumption that the traditional military system of professional development which produced the Marshalls, Eisenhowers, and Taylors—generalists *par excellence*—was adequate for the nation's future security requirements.

Fundamental changes in recent years have increasingly called that assumption into question.

THE DYNAMICS OF CHANGE

First, the traditional linkages between military force and political objectives were cast into doubt by the implications of the nuclear balance of terror and the painful lessons of revolutionary warfare. A growing awareness of the practical limitations of American power and a shift in emphasis to domestic priorities (the dimensions of which are yet to be clearly defined) have—for example—de-emphasized the military's role in intervention and focused instead upon its security assistance task.[5] Second, the continuing sociological revolution in the United States, one manifestation of which has been a reappearance of virulent antimilitarism, has expanded significantly the number and difficulty of the problems with which the professional military officer is confronted. Drugs, racism, and dissent have impacted upon the military, raising challenges on moral, philosophical, and ideological grounds to established traditions, policies, and practices.[6] Third, the continued technological advance that has been reshaping American society has had its impact upon the military services. The highly technical economy of the United States, and its shift from production of goods to production of services, has had important implications for the skill composition and educational requirements of the society from which the military services draw their manpower. The computer and information-processing revolutions have multiplied the potential for weapons and communications systems, logistics systems, and organization and management techniques. And, as nature would have it, the new potentials have led to an almost inexorable drive in defense research and development to realize those potentials.[7] Technological advance has inevitably

---

[4] Amos A. Jordon, "Officer Education," in *Handbook of Military Institutions*, ed. Roger W. Little (Beverly Hills, Calif.: Sage Publications, 1971), p. 212. One should add the advisory role, the objectives of which may be other than deterrence, peacekeeping or combat—e.g., "civic action" and "pacification support."

[5] Richard M. Nixon, *United States Foreign Policy for the 1970s: Building for Peace* (Washington, D.C.: Government Printing Office, 1971), pp. 5, 14, 16, 183–85. See also pp. 74–76 of this volume.

[6] Sam C. Sarkesian, "Political Soldiers: Perspectives on Professionalism in the U.S. Military," *Midwest Journal of Political Science*, 16, no. 2 (May 1972): 241–42.

[7] See Jack N. Merritt and Pierre M. Sprey, "Negative Marginal Returns in Weapons Acquisition," pp. 486–95 of this volume.

increased the number of professional specialties and subspecialties required to handle new bodies of knowledge. This, in turn, means that the military services must turn toward greater specialization to develop and maintain essential officer expertise.[8] Increasingly, these considerations have derogated the traditional concept that every officer must be a generalist, and, to the extent that this is true, necessitate fundamental changes in officer education, career patterns, and management.

THE MILITARY'S RESPONSE TO CHANGE

The facts of technological and societal change have indeed been perceived within the military services, the former more clearly and more rapidly than the latter. Given the inherent tendencies of large bureaucratic organizations to respond slowly to fundamental change, the services have been surprisingly quick to recognize the potentials of technology. Qualitative "improvements" abound in the hardware associated with weapons systems, logistical support systems, and communications and management techniques. The services' educational programs required to provide the skills needed to keep pace with technological innovation are broad indeed.

The assumption of an increased requirement for officer involvement in the politico-military dimension of the nation's security tasks and the trauma of the nation's social revolution, as it has manifested itself both within the military and in civil-military relations, have led to an increasing emphasis upon officer education in liberal arts fields.[9] In the 1960s, for example, the number of positions in the services defined as "requiring" civilian graduate school preparation in the social sciences nearly quadrupled.

Projecting officer educational requirements for the various services years into the future has always been difficult; it is particularly so

now. What will be the tasks the nation will call upon the military services to perform in the late 1970s and the 1980s? What will be the geographical and substantive parameters of U.S. interests which will require military resources in deterrent, peace-keeping, advisory, or combat roles? What will be the nature and scope of the threat to the security of the United States? How can answers to these questions be applied in military budget and force-level figures in Five-Year Defense Programs? What will be the educational level, educational potential, and retention rate of the officers attracted to serve in an all-volunteer force?

OFFICER EDUCATIONAL SYSTEMS IN THE 1970s

The armed forces have become the world's largest educators. By 1968 the Army alone was operating thirty-seven schools with 500 separate curricula.[10] Another gauge of the scope of the services' educational efforts is the Department of Defense estimate that about 40,000 resident officer students were enrolled in service and joint school educational courses in FY 1967. By FY 1972 there were about 12,000 cadets in the three service academies and over 7,000 military officers enrolled full time in postgraduate programs, either fully funded in civilian institutions or in the Navy's and Air Force's own equivalent postgraduate schools.[11] Tens of thousands of other officers were enrolled in off-duty programs and nonresident courses at the various military schools and colleges or through correspondence school centers throughout the world, which offer hundreds of college and postgraduate courses.

As they have evolved, the services' educational systems can be described structurally as a combination of generalist and specialist subsystems, the former category comprising three types—preprofessional, entry, and professional levels—and the latter category consisting of courses offered in both military and civilian educational institutions in managerial, politico-military, scientific, and technological fields, as well as in more narrowly military subjects such as procurement and intelligence.

[8] For an opposite view related primarily to trends in the enlisted ranks, see Charles C. Moskos, Jr., "Armed Forces and American Society: Convergence or Divergence," in *Public Opinion and the Military Establishment*, ed. Moskos, pp. 283–84.
[9] See Morris Janowitz, "The Emergent Military," p. 265. President Kennedy was explicit about the growth of politico-military tasks for military officers in his June 1962 speech to the graduating class at West Point.

[10] Amos A. Jordan, "Army Service Schools," *Encyclopedia Americana*, 1971, pp. 362–63.
[11] Office of the Secretary of Defense (Manpower and Reserve Affairs).

PRECOMMISSIONING EDUCATION

The first precommissioning rung of the military education ladder is occupied primarily by two educational programs: the service academies and ROTC. Each service also draws on various Officer Candidate School or Officer Training Program sources for commissioned recruits. Although these other sources tend to be more significant and expand when wartime needs necessitate a large-scale, rapid force build-up, they decline in significance and contract during postwar force reductions. They focus essentially on short-term training and indoctrination and are not basically educational in character. Although officers from the latter sources tend to be highly committed to the services, they generally have considerably lower educational qualifications.[12]

THE SERVICE ACADEMIES

Although numerically far from the dominant source of newly commissioned officers, the service academies are generally viewed as a key source of career officers because of the relatively high degree of career commitment by their graduates and the distinctive ethos inculcated by them. In 1970 the three academies furnished only about 5 percent of all new officers entering the services (2,300 out of 58,000).[13] When both the Military (Army) and Air Force Academies complete expanding their student bodies in the early 1970s to the 4,417 strength figure long authorized for the Naval Academy, the annual output of all three will still be only about 3,000.

The academies have been criticized occasionally for too much of a "lock-step" approach to education, with too little attention being given to individual cadets' interests and abilities and too great an emphasis being placed on conformity and uniformity.[14] Certainly, it is true that by retaining the view that they are responsible for character development as well as for intellectual growth, the academies maintain a controlled environment more akin to the nineteenth-century college than the modern university. It is also true that this climate has extended to curriculum. Perhaps it is natural that institutions which prepare men explicitly for a profession charged with defending society should not leave the form of preparation purely, or even mainly, to chance or individual choice.

In recent years all three academies have increased the proportion of electives in their curricula, the Air Force Academy having gone somewhat further than its sister academies in this respect, so that the lock-step charges of the past are less true now.[15] Moreover, the rapid evolution of the profession, stemming from scientific advances and the deepening complexity of the politico-military environment, assures that the curricular trend toward diversity and adaptation to student abilities and interests will continue.[16] The trend, too, in major academic extracurricular activities at the academies is toward recognition of diverse interests and views on contemporary public policy issues.[17] Even so, the academies will not become typical liberal arts or engineering colleges—nor is it clear that, in view of their mission, they should do so. Their educational climate will undoubtedly remain too "directed" for the tastes of many, though their products measure up well when compared with other college graduates—not only in performance in the profession, but by such educational yardsticks as graduate record examination scores, scholarship and fellowship competition, and achievement in postgraduate studies.[18]

RESERVE OFFICERS' TRAINING CORPS

Recently, the services have experienced difficulty in attracting through ROTC a fair share of the nation's talent into a military career, particularly in a climate of economic boom and social and political disaffection. The ROTC

[12] Mayer N. Zald and William Simon, "Career Opportunities and Commitments Among Officers," in *The New Military*, ed. Morris Janowitz (New York: Russell Sage Foundation, 1964), p. 264.

[13] Richard F. Rosser, "American Civil-Military Relations in the 1980s," pp. 667–81 of this volume.

[14] David Boroff, "West Point: Ancient Incubator for a New Breed," *Harper's Magazine*, December 1962, p. 56; "Air Force Academy: A Slight Gain in Attitude," *ibid.*, February 1963, p. 92; and "Annapolis: Teaching Young Sea Dogs Old Tricks," *ibid.*, January 1963, p. 49.

[15] Laurence I. Radway, "Recent Trends at American Service Academies," in *Public Opinion and the Military Establishment*, ed. Moskos, pp. 14–18.

[16] W. E. Simons, *Liberal Education in the Service Academies* (New York: Bureau of Publications, Teachers College, Columbia University, 1965), p. 148.

[17] Radway *op. cit.*, pp. 26–27 and n. 54.

[18] U.S. Congress, House Committee on Armed Services Special Subcommittee on Service Academies, *Report and Hearings*, 90th Cong., 1st and 2nd sess., 1967–1968, pp. 10261, 10297.

Vitalization Act of 1964 has helped, for it enabled the Army and Air Force to match the Navy's already attractive program with 5,500 competitive, full-tuition, fees, books, and allowance scholarships. Partly as a consequence of the Vitalization Act's stimulus, and even more because they furnished college students an alternative to the Vietnam draft, the service ROTC programs were apparently flourishing as recently as the late 1960s. In 1971, the statistics were still impressive. In that year the Navy commissioned 1,330 officers from NROTC units at 57 colleges; the Air Force figures were 4,411 from more than 170 institutions; and the Army figures were 13,970 from over 280 campuses.[19] Two new measures approved by Congress in 1972 to induce larger ROTC student enrollments increased the amount of subsistence from $50 to $100 per month and increased the number of scholarships that each service can offer (6,500 each for the Army and Air Force and 6,000 for the Navy).

Despite this evidence of apparent health, the ROTC programs have been the subject of increasingly sharp questioning as to their necessity, curricula, faculty, and relationship to the college and university community. From 1966 to 1972, enrollment in Army ROTC programs dropped from 177,422 to 50,234, and several of the Ivy League colleges dropped ROTC altogether.[20] To some degree the problem stems from the critics' failure to realize how important the programs are to national defense. Yet the facts are clear: since the academies provide only a minor part of the new officers needed each year, and since only about 60 percent of the short-term officer candidate school graduates are college-educated, even in "normal times" the bulk of second lieutenants —including half or more of the regulars—must come from the ROTC or something like it.*

Although the services have sought to make ROTC curricula challenging, they have had great difficulty in bringing many of the subjects to an intellectual level comparable with many other college courses. Since the military background and skills needed by a *new* officer do not have a high intellectual content, the services have developed courses with less immediate applicability to postcommissioning service but with more mental challenge, such as the Army's "American Military History" or the Air Force's "World Military Systems," or have permitted substitution of related normal college courses for part of the ROTC program. Both of these broad approaches call into question the viability of the ROTC goal of preparing a new officer for active duty; the former also raises the subject of the competence of the military faculty to handle such courses.

In the more narrowly military courses the uniformed instructors typically assigned to ROTCs by the services are undoubtedly competent. But broader courses, such as military history or "The Role of the United States in World Affairs," require a background and sophistication that are often lacking in the military instructor. The Army, for instance, while increasingly appointing only highly rated and experienced officers to the most senior ROTC posts, has found that it can supply men with advanced degrees for less than half of these positions. The Army's problem is common to all the services; by the time higher priority needs have been met, there are not enough officers with the proper credentials for ROTC faculties.[21] It is likely that the customary priority given the ROTCs in a quieter era, when their mission was to prepare reserve officers, will have to be upgraded in light of their new situation and responsibilities. Recruiting for the ROTC in the absence of a draft will be a formidable challenge. Educating sufficient numbers of good officers who accept extended ROTC assignments, and ensuring that these officers as a group are competitive for promotion, will constitute in the 1970s and 1980s one of the foremost challenges to be faced by the services' personnel managers.

19 U.S. Department of Defense, "The Status of the Reserve Officers Training Corps," *Commanders Digest*, December 23, 1971, pp. 6–7.

20 See "Army Seeks Halt in ROTC Decline," *New York Times*, September 14, 1972, p. 21.

* [*Editors' note*: Since the Air Force requires all of its officers to have bachelor's degrees, its three-month Officer School of Military Sciences (formerly Officer Training School) accepts only college graduates.]

21 The Army Education Requirements Board for 1972 concluded that not all ROTC instructor positions require advanced degrees fully funded by the Army; that the Army's Advanced Degree Program for ROTC Instructor Duty (under which an officer on ROTC duty could enroll in courses at the university part-time) is providing a significant number of ROTC instructors with advanced degrees and that the number will increase to approximately 500 annually by 1976. *Army Educational Requirements Board Proceedings*, 1972, pp. 5–6.

ENTRY LEVEL

Virtually all new Air Force, Army, and Marine Corps officers, and, in a few cases, Navy officers, attend "basic" or "technical" schools immediately after their commissioning. The emphasis in the relatively brief (generally two-to-four month) courses taught at the basic schools is on training, but they also contribute importantly to the indoctrination and socialization functions of military education. Apart from the significant but too-brief association with his ROTC instructors and the glimpse of military life afforded by summer camp, the typical new officer, other than the academy graduate, gets his first sustained exposure to the profession and to his fellow officers at basic schools which vary in length from nine weeks (Army) to twenty-six weeks (Marine Corps). The Air Force relies primarily on technical schools; the Navy relies on "on-the-job training" and does not generally use basic schools. At these entry-level schools, instruction is chopped into small blocks and given at rapid-fire tempo in lectures and demonstrations; there is little time or inclination for students to philosophize about "why," for attention is centered on their engaging in practical exercises devoted to "what" and "how."

To the degree that "military training" in ROTC is reduced in the search for a *modus vivendi* on campus between the services and university administrations, the tasks of the basic schools will become more difficult and even more important.

PROFESSIONAL LEVEL

The next step in officer education brings us to a multitiered system of "general military professional" education. At all levels, professional courses are a mixture of training and education, with the former tending to predominate at the lower levels. Even the higher professional schools devote some attention to developing skills and techniques and to imparting doctrine, but the higher up the ladder one goes, the more dominant the educational content of the courses becomes.

First Professional Level

After from three to eight years of line and staff duties, career officers in three of the four services (the Navy generally excepted) return to school for "advanced" or "career" courses. These courses are designed to prepare their relatively junior students for duties at the intermediate level in the military hierarchy—e.g., command of a battalion or squadron—and for staff work at the next two or three higher headquarters. They seek to deepen the officer's competence in his career field, to bring him up to date, to widen his understanding of his own service's roles, missions, and doctrines, and to introduce him to subjects that transcend his own service. Although instruction of this last type is limited, explicit attention is often paid, generally for the first time in a typical officer's schooling, to the other services and the armed forces as a whole.

While the contribution of these first professional-level courses to developing military expertise is important, their focus tends to be more on training than on education. Instruction tends, as in the basic courses, to be rapid-fire and the subjects are numerous and compressed. The emphasis at this level is again clearly on imparting techniques and military doctrine rather than on generating independent thinking and analysis. The Army is a partial exception, for, in the wake of the Haines Board criticism that students were not being sufficiently challenged at this level,[22] increasing numbers of elective courses have been introduced into the curricula in such fields as systems analysis, logistics management, military history, and international relations.

Second Professional Level: Command and Staff Colleges

Sometime between their ninth and fifteenth year of service about one-half of all eligible Army and Marine officers, one-quarter of eligible Air Force officers, and one-sixth of eligible Navy officers are selected for the Command and Staff College of their service, for the integrated Armed Forces Staff College, or for one of the other services' schools at the same level. These college programs are about ten months in length, except for that at the Armed Forces Staff College (Norfolk, Va.), which is half as long. Since this will be the highest general military educational experience for most of these officers, the colleges have traditionally focused attention on bringing all of them to a

---

[22] Haines Board, *Report of the Department of the Army to Review Officer Schools*, February, 1966.

uniform level of staff competence and to a common understanding of the principles of military leadership and command of forces in the field. Inevitably, this "leveling" objective has resulted in instruction below the potential of the abler students; it has also necessitated a stultifying attention to drill in doctrine and techniques and stress on the "approved solution." Many students are "turned off" by this approach after the first few weeks and learn to coast through the remainder of the course.

The Army's Command and General Staff College (CGSC) at Fort Leavenworth, the oldest and best known of these second professional-level colleges, has moved to meet these problems,[23] most of which were identified in two recent, major studies of the Army officer educational system.[24] For the 1,102 students in the class of 1973, the common professional curriculum and one "associate" elective course have been compressed into the first of two semesters. The student is then given a choice of four (of twenty-three) professional electives and at least one (of thirty-one) other associate elective offering in the second semester. Some of the associate electives are taught at Fort Leavenworth by CGSC military faculty and some by contract civilian professors; others may be taken on civilian campuses through cooperative programs with three local universities. The number of classroom hours has been reduced to meet justified complaints of "overstuffing." Clearly, the Army is attempting to make the CGSC a challenging, intellectually stimulating, and exciting experience for its officers at mid-career and, simultaneously, to adapt its curriculum through elective offerings to the Army's career areas of specialization. Whether or not these objectives are achieved will depend largely on the quality of the teaching faculty. (But, as of August 1972, only 30 percent of the CGSC faculty had graduate degrees, although many others were at various stages of progress toward such degrees.)

Third Professional Level: War Colleges

At the peak of the military educational system stand five co-equal institutions: two joint colleges—the National War College and the Industrial College of the Armed Forces—and the Army, Navy, and Air war colleges. Their goals are roughly the same: to prepare carefully selected officers for the highest-level command and staff positions within their own services and with national and international forces and headquarters. The Industrial College of the Armed Forces (ICAF) has a somewhat different mission and curricular emphasis; it focuses on the economic and industrial aspects of national security and resource management in the context of both national and world affairs.

All the colleges have students from each service; additionally, civilian agencies with defense-related responsibilities, such as the Department of State and CIA, send students to them. All have traditionally examined the military and international environment, the strategic threats to the nation, Allied and U.S. capabilities to meet those threats, and optimal strategies and programs to use those capabilities. In addition, all have shared a number of problems. The typical war college faculty member has been a highly qualified military professional, but he was not tenured, often lacked any formal academic preparation or sometimes even wide experience in the politico-military or resource management fields on which the college curricula center, and he was frequently serving a terminal tour of duty (immediately prior to retirement).

A related problem has been overreliance on guest lectures, which force the student into a largely passive role. Only limited use has been made of the few highly qualified civilian professors on the faculty who could provide continuity to lecture programs. Also, the "self-teaching," student committee (seminar) approach of all the colleges, which seeks to capitalize on the diversity of backgrounds among senior professional officer-students, has frequently resulted in superficial treatment of complex issues. Perhaps the range of problems was best summarized by Admiral Stansfield Turner, new President of the Naval War College, at the college's first academic convocation on August 24, 1972:

There has been a creeping intellectual devitalization in all of our War Colleges since World War II. Rarely does one meet a graduate of any War

---

[23] Ivan J. Birrer, "The New CGSC Curriculum," *Military Review*, 52, no. 6 (June 1972): pp. 20–26.

[24] Haines Board, *Report*; and Norris Study Group, *Review of the Army Officer Educational System*, December 1, 1971.

College who said that he had been intellectually taxed by a War College course of instruction.

The basis for these familiar criticisms of the past may soon disappear, for the senior colleges have moved into a period of rapid transition. Based upon a series of in-depth studies and a college commandant who is determined to place the institution at the center of politico-military doctrinal development, the Army War College envisions a number of important changes.[25] The college will adopt a trisemester curriculum involving a greatly expanded electives program. Guest lectures will be kept to a minimum; the most qualified of the senior faculty will move from a coordinating-monitoring role to a teaching role; and, to the extent that military expertise is not available, civilian professors under contract will teach the expanded electives program.

The National War College (NWC) in Washington, D.C., long the most prestigious of all the war colleges, has launched a three-year program to adapt its curriculum to the changing times. The essential ingredient of the program is the faculty; the NWC intends to enter in earnest the competition for the services' most scarce resources—relatively young and highly competitive-for-promotion lieutenant colonels or colonels with sound academic credentials and expertise in certain subjects who will share the teaching task with the faculty. Although electives will remain within the realm of U.S. national security policy studies, they will be increased and guest lectures will be decreased. The more technically oriented electives, such as operations research, systems analysis, or economics of national security, will be left to the Industrial College of the Armed Forces. There is an aura of excitement and momentum at the National War College.

In the summer of 1972 the new president of the Naval War College at Newport, R.I., abruptly scrapped the planned curriculum for academic year 1972–1973 and turned to reform, somewhat along the lines of the Army and National war colleges—except that he was determined to accomplish the task *now* rather than over a three-year period. He largely abandoned the contemporary issues approach for one which focuses largely on recurrent, historical politico-military lessons. No longer will the student leisurely saunter through concept-oriented collections of articles; instead, he will read (and be tested on) complete volumes—Thucydides, Napoleon, Bismarck. Guest lectures (over 200 in AY 1971–1972) have been drastically reduced to 4 or 5 per month. All three major portions of the course—strategy, management, and tactics—share a common thread: resource allocation, with emphasis on marginal analysis.

Though in some ways different, all three approaches are designed to provide a greater intellectual challenge for the student, broaden his perspectives, and stretch his imagination in politico-military affairs. One must conclude that the winds of change at the senior colleges are blowing very strong—and, perhaps prematurely, that they are favorable winds. However, quality faculty is a major short-term limiting factor at all the war colleges, as well as at the command and staff colleges. One obvious solution for removing this constraint is to expand the services' graduate-level civil schooling programs; another may be found in implementing new educational technology. Expanded use of television, computer-based programmed instruction, and other multimedia methods are possible alternatives.[26] Perhaps these methods could be linked to a variation of the "university without walls," one geared to officer "self-study" programs in which "comprehensive" examinations would be given at various stages of officers' careers to measure achievement.

SPECIALIST MILITARY EDUCATION AND TRAINING

When confronted with a major development for the profession, such as a scientific breakthrough or a significant shift in strategy, the services have tended both to orient *all* professionals around the new development through the general military educational schooling system and to prepare a smaller number of officers to focus directly upon the development

---

[25] U.S. Department of the Army, *Board to Review Army Officer Schools Report*, vols. 1–3 (Washington, D.C., February 1966); "Mission Curriculum Study" (1970); and "Long Range Development Concept Study" (1972).

[26] See, e.g., Edward B. Roberts and Henry B. Weil, "Implementing New Educational Methodology for the Military," *Naval War College Review*, 23, no. 8 (April 1971): 12–28.

through more intensive and specialized schooling arrangements. Thus, the development of battlefield nuclear weapons necessitated the introduction of material on nuclear warfare throughout the basic, advanced, and professional schools of the Army in the late 1940s and, in addition, resulted in intensive courses on nuclear weapons and their application at certain of the specialist schools—the latter of which led to "military occupational specialty" designations as "Nuclear Weapons Officer" for any one completing them.

Similarly, by the late 1960s, the Army had concluded, largely from its experience in Vietnam, that it needed to improve its ability to deal with insurgency and "stability operations" in less developed areas. Consequently, it not only increased the amount of attention given to such subjects throughout its general military educational courses but also instituted in 1969 a new career field, the "Military Assistance Officer Program" (MAOP), to develop officers in civil affairs, psychological operations, and related politico-military affairs. As it became apparent that some of the educational requirements and many of the functions of MAOP officers were related to those of officers in another program, The Foreign Area Specialist Program (FASP), the Army decided in the spring of 1972 to merge the two. Selected officers will prepare for this specialty field by doing graduate work in one of the social science disciplines at a civilian university and by attending specialized military courses yet to be spelled out in an Army regulation.

In addition to service-conducted specialist courses, there are also a number of joint or "defense" schools for specialist training and education—e.g., the Defense Language Institute, the Defense Information School, the Defense Computer Institute, Defense Intelligence School, Defense Race Relations Institute, and so on. Both the Office of the Secretary of Defense (OSD) and the Joint Chiefs of Staff (JCS) have responsibilities for joint training and education in areas of specialization which affect more than one service. But, despite the expanding reach of OSD and the statutory responsibility of the JCS to "formulate policies for the joint training of the armed forces and . . . for coordinating the military education of members of the armed forces," the services retain the bulk of the responsibility for specialist, as well as generalist, education. In fact, the

individual services usually operate the joint or defense specialist schools with only broad guidance from OSD or JCS. Given the different personnel management systems of the services, this appears to be a necessity.

CIVILIAN HIGHER EDUCATION

Impelled by the deepening complexity of the tasks facing the profession, the services have steadily enlarged their programs for sending military officers to civilian institutions for postgraduate courses ranging in length from a few months to three or four years. Prior to the 1960s, service interest in civilian schooling focused on scientific and engineering studies. However, the services now prepare their officers in political science, economics, international relations, psychology, sociology, business administration, and so on. By 1971 the number of "validated" (approved) positions requiring graduate or professional degrees had grown to over 27,000—12,472 for the Air Force, 9,421 for the Army, 4,844 for the Navy, and 471 for the Marine Corps.[27]

The Army, in particular, turned increasingly to social science–type graduate specialization, as it became interested in "stability operations" in less-developed countries and as its resource management tasks grew more complex. The number of positions throughout the Army structure designated as requiring graduate preparation grew from 4,461 in 1964 to 8,628 in 1967; of these, the physical and biological sciences and engineering positions grew by roughly 70 percent, the business figures more than tripled, and the social sciences positions nearly quadrupled.

Assignment to graduate school—probably sometime in the first decade of service—is becoming part of the expectations of large numbers of career officers. Projections are not available across the services, but the fact that about two-thirds of the Military Academy's graduates of the past two decades have gone to graduate school is one indication of the pattern. The West Point figure will probably grow to three-fourths or five-sixths in the next few years.

The Navy and Air Force offer graduate-level academic programs in their own fully accredited institutions as well as in civilian universities. The Naval Postgraduate School fo-

27 Norris Study Group, *Review*, pp. 1–4; figures include positions for medical schooling.

cuses primarily on scientific, engineering, and management fields, but also offers limited work in such social science subjects as economics and political science. In contrast to the Navy, which leans heavily on its own postgraduate training facilities, the Air Force depends essentially on civilian institutions for the postgraduate education of its officers. But the Air Force Institute of Technology (AFIT) does conduct a limited postgraduate program (in addition to undergraduate and nondegree programs) in such subjects as engineering, systems management, and business administration.[28] The Army does not have a postgraduate institution which is authorized to grant advanced degrees.[29]

Each service also provides tuition assistance for personnel pursuing higher education on an off-duty basis. Any university near a military post will have dozens, perhaps hundreds, of officers so enrolled on a part-time basis. Another form of off-duty study—namely, correspondence courses—should be noted. Whether out of a desire for self-improvement, hopes for quicker promotion, preparation for a second career, or sheer boredom, thousands of officers are among the hundreds of thousands of servicemen enrolled at any one time in correspondence courses. The services have their own voluntary programs in addition to the correspondence and group study of the U.S. Armed Forces Institute, an enterprise directed by the Assistant Secretary of Defense for Manpower and Reserve Affairs.

The Army's Degree Completion Program ("Bootstrap") provides an eighteen-month leave of absence with pay and varying degrees of financial assistance to officers and enlisted men who can complete the requirements for a bachelor's degree. In 1971, 325 officers received baccalaureates under the program. Although statistics are not available across the services, it is well known that officers perform well in civilian higher education. As mature

professionals, they look upon civilian education as an important aspect of their duty commitment and treat their courses accordingly. For Army officers the academic failure rate in civilian education is extremely low.

Judgments differ as to whether so much civilian higher education is necessary or desirable. In addition to the antimilitary critics who would prefer to see professional military men fenced off from all civilian contact in their own enclaves, there are military traditionalists who fear the contaminating effect of too much graduate education and who are concerned lest soldiers be seduced thereby to stray from the paths of duty. It is hard to take this view seriously. For one thing, military men are universally skeptical of the intellectual community with its characteristic antimilitary values. For another, military officers are fully aware of the perpetual tension between "thinkers" and "doers," between the academician's "Why?" and the military man's need to make and act on decisions, even when judgments differ and all the facts are not available.

Although widespread military graduate schooling is only about two decades old, there is already substantial evidence that traditionalist fears are simply unwarranted. Apparently the roles of "military executive," with its attendant civilian graduate school preparation, and "combat leader," with the usual generalist and specialist military schooling, are not generally antithetical; for, in terms of combat record, retention in the service, promotion to high rank, and selection for senior service schools, officers with higher educational backgrounds are proving to be outstanding professionals. Thus, the Navy has discovered that an astonishingly small fraction of the 8,000 naval officers who have completed postgraduate training since 1948 have resigned before completing twenty years of service;[30] the Army has noted that the resignation rate among its Regular Army officers with advanced degrees is low and that a large share of its officers currently being selected for the ranks of colonel and general and roughly half of those being chosen to attend the Army War College have graduate degrees.[31] Almost half the officers selected for

---

[28] Office of the Secretary of Defense (Manpower), *Officer Education Study*, July 1966, vol. 3, chap. 6.

[29] In 1963 the Army instituted a master's degree program at the Command and General Staff College at Fort Leavenworth. The program was duly endorsed by the necessary accrediting organizations, but failed to secure from Congress the authorizing legislation needed by federal institutions before they can grant degrees. Accreditation was withdrawn temporarily in 1966. By 1972 over 150 officers had completed the college's stringent requirements, but the institution was still awaiting authority to grant its first "Master of Military Art and Sciences."

[30] Haines Board, *Report*, p. 342.

[31] On the Army's 1971 promotion list to the rank of general, 62 of 80, or 75 percent, of those selected had a graduate degree. Norris Study Group, *Review*, pp. 1–10.

the National War College also have graduate degrees.

Yet, the services' civil schooling programs have been subject to recurrent challenge by members of Congress and the General Accounting Office over the years.[32] The Department of Defense is eventually going to have to prove the case for higher civilian education for its officers through a comprehensive assessment. The case for higher education will have to rest on three pillars. The first of these is the *technical component* of officer education, which develops scientific and management skills to keep pace with technological advances. The second pillar is the *critical component* of officer education, which develops the capability for human judgment on difficult questions of priorities and trade-offs among resources and values. There is not only a need to develop this capability in officers but also a crying need for personnel management systems which identify those officers who are best at making such judgments and promote them rapidly to the higher positions of military responsibility and authority. In some cases this may mean bypassing one or more assignments considered integral to "normal career progression." The third pillar must be an *assessment of values and attitudes* which the nation wants its officers to hold. The values held by officers have recently been called into question.[33] This is an important issue which needs broader airing in American society.

Quantitatively, officer education has im-

proved significantly. Department of Defense estimates show that in 1956 only 56 percent of all commissioned officers on active duty had baccalaureate degrees; by the end of 1971 the figure was over 76 percent. Similarly, the percentages of commissioned officers with graduate degrees had grown high by 1970 (see Table 1).[34]

What the increased exposure to higher civilian education means qualitatively in terms of officer values is another matter—one that has for some time deserved serious study.[35]

A PERSPECTIVE ON OFFICER EDUCATION

Judged by overall results, the military's educational and training system has, by and large, continued since World War II to serve the profession well. The leaders, managers, and specialists flowing from it have played a major role in deterring nuclear war and in safeguarding other national interests through the training, equipping, deploying, and—as needed—employing the fighting of military units of unprecedented complexity and power. As required, they have also served other national goals, been loaned to other governmental departments, trained foreign forces, administered military aid programs, and so on. It is not self-evident, of course, that the educational system has always contributed to these accomplishments as effectively and efficiently as it might have; indeed, it would be surprising if schooling patterns which have emerged through evolution

---

[32] U.S. Comptroller General, Report to Congress, *Improvement Needed in Determining Graduate Education Requirements for Military Career Positions*, August 28, 1970, *passim*.

[33] See, e.g., Peter Karsten et al., "ROTC, My Lai, and the Volunteer Army," pp. 569–81 of this volume.

[34] U.S. Department of Defense, *Selected Manpower Statistics*, April 15, 1972, p. 41.

[35] See John W. Masland and Laurence L. Radway, *Soldiers and Scholars* (Princeton: Princeton University Press, 1957), pp. 508–10.

Table 1
Active-Duty Commissioned Officers with Graduate (or Professional) Degrees

	2nd Lt./ Ens. (%)	1st Lt./ Lt. (jg.) (%)	Capt./Lt. (%)	Maj./Lt. Cmdr. (%)	Lt. Col./ Cmdr. (%)	Col./Capt. (%)	Gen./Adm. (%)	Total (%)
Army	3	6	14	24	33	47	59	16
Navy	3	6	21	27	37	52	47	21
Air Force	6	10	20	26	31	36	39	21
Marines	1	1	2	9	16	23	37	4
All Services	4	6	17	25	32	43	48	18

Source: Percentages aggregated from separate service data for end-1970 were provided by the Office of the Assistant Secretary of Defense (Comptroller), Directorate for Information Operations.

and accretion, as well as by overall design, were ideally fitted to the needs of the past, let alone to those of the future.

Aware of concern within the profession on this point, President Johnson, in 1964, announced that he was "directing the Secretary of Defense to review the educational systems and major schools within the services—and the opportunities now offered for continued civilian education while in service—to broaden and strengthen these programs." That Defense-wide analysis, shoved aside by Vietnam's mounting demands on top officials' attention, has yet to be undertaken, although a partial, small-scale review of current programs was made in 1965 as a direct consequence of the President's initiative, and a similar review has recently been undertaken by OSD. The various services and their schools review their own programs periodically, with 1971 being a vintage year in this respect. However, the military profession still awaits its Flexner or Conant.

Any total "systems" study of professional schooling must inevitably ask whether, in the interests of service cooperation and efficiency, there should not be more common, joint, or interservice education—perhaps starting with the academies and ROTCs. The lack of enthusiasm within the services for this approach (or even for centrally directed studies of the question) is rooted in the virtually unanimous view among professionals that schooling should be keyed directly to service personnel systems, which are themselves based directly upon service tasks. Thus the question is not merely one of service or joint schools but of the very existence of the services themselves.

Yet the increasing interdependence of the services, which necessitated the first joint school—the Army-Navy Staff School—in 1943 and which has gained impetus in the quarter-century since, shows no sign of lessening. In fact, the trend has picked up momentum in the last decade, especially in combat support activities, as exemplified by the creation of the Defense-wide agencies. In view of this trend, it may well prove impossible in the future, in contrast to the past and present, for an officer to rise to positions of high rank and responsibility without schooling or experience outside his own service.

Achieving the service integration needed in some functional fields may necessitate increasing the number of joint or defense schools. In many cases, however, a better approach may be "interservice" schools—i.e., schools in which one service provides facilities, faculty, and curriculum for students from all the services. The respective roles and responsibilities of the services, the Joint Chiefs, and the Office of the Secretary of Defense will undoubtedly need further sorting out and clearer delineation if any of these approaches to the challenge of interdependence is to proceed further.

In addition to adapting to increasing service interdependence, future military schooling patterns will also have to cope with still more specialization. More schooling for more officers may be part of the answer; but part may also lie in the Army's approach of strengthening the line between specialists and generalists so that the latter need not try to be part-time specialists and the former need not forgo high rank and responsibility unless they also try to be part-time generalists. Whatever the personnel management approach to the specialization dilemma, the question of whether an increasingly complex profession necessitates officers' spending still more time in school must be faced.

Distillation of past experience and/or straight-line projections from military doctrine will continue to form an important part of military schooling in the future, but the military educational system of the future must also take responsibility for creating the kind of environment which will generate innovative and creative thinking among its students. The Army, cognizant of the important trade-off between service requirements and officer interest, appears headed in the right direction. But it remains to be seen whether the services' personnel management systems will indeed identify and advance to high positions of responsibility and authority significant numbers of officer specialists and functionalists whose educational experience has conditioned them to the kinds of imaginative and critical thinking increasingly required of the military profession. Indications are that the services have recognized the problem. But, lacking a comprehensive assessment of the purposes and objectives of the entire officer educational system, one hopes that there will not be too many missteps in the right direction.

CHAPTER 10

The Professional Soldier in a Democratic Society

THE ARMY AND SOCIETY

FREDERIC J. BROWN

The United States Army has in recent years become very involved in social programs such as domestic action, alcohol and drug abuse prevention, Project One Hundred Thousand, Project Transition, and many others. Although the positive aspects of these programs are generally well known, the negative aspects, especially in terms of the readiness of military forces, are often overlooked. In this chapter, Frederic Brown addresses himself to each of these programs and constructs criteria for evaluation of present and future programs. Lt. Colonel Frederic J. Brown is a career Army (Infantry) officer who has served in numerous command and staff positions. He is a graduate of the United States Military Academy, the National War College, and the Graduate Institute of International Studies in Geneva, Switzerland. He holds a Ph.D. in international relations and is the author of Chemical Warfare: A Study in Restraints *(1968).*

These are difficult days for the military establishment and particularly for the Army. Faced with the need to readjust after a long enervating commitment to a complex, confusing, and frustrating war in Vietnam, the Army is seemingly assailed from all sides. Public animosity exceeds that in the previous experience of any of those soldiers presently serving. The fiber of units is stretched by racial stress, drug excess, and an environment of hyperactive inquiry, if not hostile dissent. In the view of critical observers, the Army not only serves an increasingly questionable social purpose—the use of force in defending the nation—but also is dysfunctional in that it constitutes a nonproductive, inefficient drain of resources which could be better used to meet pressing social problems.

Critical public sentiment often strikes a responsive chord in the Army. The assertion has been made, within the professional ranks, that the Army must become "meaningful" if it is to continue to exist. The proposition is most often stated to buttress arguments favoring the development of noncombat-related "socially productive" roles which not only will keep the Army active and committed to the mainstream of American life but also, because of their utility to the nation, will serve as added justification for the continued existence of the Army.

This proposition is wrong. The greatest current danger to the Army is the stimulus to overinvolvement in efforts to maintain social "relevance," not any isolation stimulated by underinvolvement. The evolving nature of the American society constitutes a reasonable guarantee that the problem for the military profession is not lack of social integration; the character of our postindustrial society will insure that the necessary ties continue to be maintained, even in an all-volunteer force. The Army is already deeply committed to a broad range of social welfare programs. Further,

Reprinted by permission of the author and publisher from Military Review, *March 1972, pp. 3–17. Minor editorial changes have been made.* Military Review *is published by the U.S. Army Command and General Staff College.*

there has been a trend of continually increasing involvement. Isolation is not the problem.

The real challenge to the Army today is to conduct responsible and necessary social welfare programs while preserving those core values of the military which combine to produce units and men who willingly serve the national defense with "unlimited liability"—to and including the ultimate price. The danger is overcommitment to social welfare programs which can erode the core values and capabilities of unit readiness.

The concern is not that the Army exercises social responsibilities. Many are absolutely necessary for management of the armed forces or to perform an essential public service such as disaster assistance or civil defense planning. The problem is to subordinate, in a responsible manner, the aggregate of such efforts to the maintenance of adequate defense readiness.

HISTORICAL PRECEDENT

The Army is engaged today in a broad series of social programs developed over the years in response to general acceptance of an increasing governmental role in providing for the social welfare of individuals and in taking direct responsibility for many other important areas of public life. Current social programs in which the Army is involved have historical precedent in a general tradition of civic assistance provided by the Army over the years.

In the past, however, the Army did not see itself, nor was it seen by others, as possessing enduring responsibilities to conduct programs to improve the lot of any particular individuals in society or to correct social ills which plagued the nation.

Since World War II, there has been increasing pressure to commit the Army to social programs involving improvement of the individual. Some programs were necessary for better management of the armed forces; others were intended to improve community relations by providing useful public services.

CURRENT EFFORTS

The rhetoric of leadership has led to the development of a broad set of social welfare programs, most of which are desirable for improvement of personnel management. Yet some programs directly affect the environment and life style of the individual citizen both in and out of military service. Major current efforts are: Domestic Action, Equal Opportunity (minority relations), General Educational Development (education), Alcohol and Drug Abuse Prevention and Control, Project One Hundred Thousand, and Project Transition.

DOMESTIC ACTION

This is a recent Department of Defense (DOD) "carrier" program for most externally oriented social welfare activities conducted by the military services under the guidance of a DOD Domestic Action Council. The program includes manpower efforts such as Project Referral, intended to assist in securing jobs for retirees; Project Value, designed to provide jobs in DOD for over 1,000 of the hard-core unemployed per year; and the Youth Employment Program, an effort to provide summer jobs for over 40,000 youths per year.

Military procurement is also channeled to minority small business enterprises. Physical resources (equipment, facilities, services, and property) are made available on a reimbursable basis where possible. Over 275,000 disadvantaged youths were provided recreational, cultural, educational, and training activities during the summer of 1969 in the community relations effort. Lastly, technical knowledge, such as low-cost modular housing, aeromedical evacuation, and environmental improvement, is provided to civilian communities. The sixth element of the program is equal rights, which continues long-standing efforts in minority relations.

EQUAL OPPORTUNITY

Beginning with desegregation in 1948, the services have led the national effort in minority relations. Secretary Robert S. McNamara saw the services as "a powerful fulcrum in removing the barriers to racial justice not merely in the military, but in the country at large." Consistent with this philosophy, the DOD open housing policy predated the comparable provisions of the Civil Rights Act of 1968. In further extension of this activist social role, places of local entertainment practicing segregation have been placed off limits by the Secretary of the Army. Formal education in minority relations is being expanded for all service personnel. The level of involvement has increased each year.

GENERAL EDUCATIONAL DEVELOPMENT

The military is the largest vocational training institution in the United States. The rate of turnover of personnel—an estimated 24 million veterans since 1940—and the physical plant required have resulted in a major and expanding national educational system within the services.

Prior to Vietnam, of the approximately 500,000 individuals who left the military services annually for civilian life, an estimated 50 percent had received post–high school occupational and professional education and training. Such Army programs continue to increase dramatically. A $22.6 million program in 1968 to increase high school, college, and postgraduate qualifications of all enlisted and officer grades may expand to over $40 million.

Recently, the Modern Volunteer Army Program envisaged "an educational system which provides each soldier the opportunity to acquire, on duty time, civilian-recognized skills or education" so that the soldiers will see the Army "as an avenue and not as an alternative, to their personal and educational development."[1] A policy of providing veteran benefits to insure that an individual not suffer as a result of governmental service has become a program of providing personal benefits through governmental aid and assistance while serving and during duty hours—a new horizon of social responsibility for the Army.

ALCOHOL AND DRUG ABUSE PREVENTION AND CONTROL

Although it is too early to gauge the resource implications of this new program, the principle is clear: the military services are expected to provide professional rehabilitation for individuals discovered to be suffering from addiction during their period of national service. As is the case with educational programs, national service will, through rehabilitation, benefit the individual whether he acquired the disorder before or during service.

In its embryonic stages, the drug abuse program will require over 2,900 specialized personnel and over $32 million in direct costs for FY 1972, according to the DOD FY 1973 budget hearings in October 1971. Unsupported estimates of true costs, which include salaries of addicts, guards for facilities, and so forth, range up to $100 million per year for the Army. All that seems certain at this point is that the military has entered into a new and uncharted area of social responsibility.

PROJECT ONE HUNDRED THOUSAND

This project was developed by Secretary McNamara to broaden the manpower base and to make the marginally productive civilian into a successful, competitive citizen. He saw the challenge as

a ghetto of the spirit. Chronic failures in school throughout their childhood, they were destined to a sense of defeat and decay in a skill-oriented nation that requires from its manpower pool an increasing index of competence, discipline and self-confidence. Many of these men, we decided, could be saved.[2]

From October 1, 1966, to September 30, 1971, the Army accepted over 200,000 of these individuals; the estimated cost for FY 1970 was under $3 million.

PROJECT TRANSITION

The objective of Project Transition is to assist the soldier in securing a job upon completion of service. Begun in 1968, the program consists of job counseling, vocational training, and job placement assistance. By 1970, 240,000 men had been counseled and 69,000 had been trained at fifty-five installations in the United States. Due to the high veteran unemployment rate, a major expansion of Project Transition is now underway. The program is being enlarged in the United States and extended overseas to include Vietnam. Specific job training installations are now being established to provide sixty days of training for combat soldiers without civilian skills. Thus expanded, the program could cost some $200 million per year.

Broad guidance is evident in the varying objectives, techniques, and beneficiaries of these six programs. The range of variation is so broad as to preclude establishment of un-

[1] U.S. Department of the Army, *The Army's Master Program for the Modern Volunteer Army*, September 1971, p. 17.

[2] Robert S. McNamara, *The Essence of Security: Reflection in Office* (New York: Harper & Row, 1968), p. 131.

equivocal general criteria for evaluation of the suitability of programs. Of these programs, two—Minority Relations and Drug Abuse—address problems which directly affect the military readiness of units and demonstrate acceptance of federal responsibility to state and local governments. Two other programs—General Educational Development and Project One Hundred Thousand—improve individual skills for both service and postservice activity. A third—Project Transition—addresses only veteran activity.

Several of the Domestic Action and technical knowledge programs would cost very little and could make useful and necessary contributions to the improvement of life in the United States. Examples would be use of military posts to develop new techniques of low-cost housing construction, mass transit systems, or pollution abatement. Other programs merely serve to open military resources to the ghetto or rural poor, much as service children have been accommodated in the past—for example, scouting and club activities. Some programs, such as disaster relief, are purely humanitarian. In the face of such diversity, program objective seems an inadequate criterion.

The case for Army acceptance of increased social responsibilities rests upon five arguments:

1. There are major national social welfare tasks to be accomplished.

2. The Army is capable of assisting in their accomplishment through the amelioration of social ills.

3. Acceptance of social responsibilities by the military will assist in assuring the availability of resources with which to maintain operational readiness to fulfill conventional defense responsibilities.

4. Social involvement will serve to disarm traditional critics of military programs.

5. Social involvement will help to attract and retain quality personnel.

SOCIAL WELFARE TASKS

The first premise appears self-evident. There are major social welfare tasks to be undertaken. As income levels rise, education and communication create greater awareness of the need for action. This has been the pattern of the last decade.

The premise that the Army can undertake major new social responsibilities is more controversial. The Secretary of the Army has strongly supported current Army Domestic Action projects. In fact, after stating that the Army must maintain mission readiness, he called for major expansion:

> We must do more, much more. . . . As long as we limit it to something that will help the soldier in his training mission; as long as we can accomplish our other goals without adding more men or dollars, I see no limitation . . . domestic action has to become more and more important.[3]

The activist case appears to rest on two premises: availability of sufficient quality personnel to carry out the programs within the service; and presumed ability to institutionalize successful social action programs. The Army does possess extraordinarily capable and dedicated managers. Attracted to public service by the professional nature of military service, the officer and senior noncommissioned officer corps are precisely the action-oriented managers called for by John W. Gardner as he bemoaned the "chasm between the worlds of reflection and action" and called for "leaders who can move beyond their special fields to deal with problems of the total community."[4]

Quality alone will not solve the problem. First-rate management talent is limited. There may not be sufficient top-flight managerial capability within the Army to maintain ready combat capability while supporting complex social programs. With normal distribution, most of the Army's social welfare projects would be administered by "average" officers and noncommissioned officers.

COMPLEX PROGRAMS

If a program is too complex or too innovative to be understood and honestly accepted by average men and women, it may fail, despite the most optimistic prognostications of central authority. Racial attitude conditioning and establishment of the environment of discipline

---

[3] "Civic Action: Army's New Battlefield," *Washington Post*, September 19, 1971, p. A14.

[4] John W. Gardner, *The Recovery of Confidence* (New York: W. W. Norton & Co., 1970), pp. 93ff.

based upon mutual trust called for by the Modern Volunteer Army Program are current attempts to institutionalize sophisticated social programs. It is not certain that these programs can be implemented by "average" Army managers.

Requirements for quality personnel, sheer size, and the bureaucratic nature of the Army combine to make social action programs difficult to run properly. The Army, as a bureaucracy, may be a blunt instrument incapable of institutionalizing the finesse required to deal with complex social problems at the federal level. This inability is not unique to the Army; it is a characteristic of large organizations.

The third argument supporting increased social responsibilities is more conjectural. Increased social action may or may not justify the allocation of additional resources to the Army. It is conceivable that there could be major increases in program responsibility without parallel increases in funds or personnel. For example, the real burden of expanded Project Transition training is borne by the unit which must support the project while continuing other missions.

Additionally, even if added resources were provided, they might not be suitable for improved defense readiness. Potential missions in the inner city would provide ill-suited justification for additional maneuver battalions configured and trained for combat operations.

DISARM THE CRITICS

The fourth premise is that increased social responsibilities would help in disarming the most voluble critics of the military—that is, the "liberal establishment" representing the latest in a tradition of liberal hostility toward, and suspicion of, military affairs. Presumably, by its efforts at social improvement, the Army would convince its arch critics that it performs a useful and necessary social function. This seems a problematical *non sequitur* at best. Gardner, John Kenneth Galbraith, Goldberg, and others would appear more likely to insist that the resources be administered by another federal department.

In any event, Army activity in such areas would be subjected to intense critical review by a skeptical audience. There is scant prospect of changing a basic philosophical view of

the nature of force in a democratic society by volunteering to accept, or willingly accepting, peacetime social responsibilities. By blurring the limits of its functional responsibilities as the possessor of legitimate force, the Army could well exacerbate the conventional criticism.

ATTRACT QUALITY PERSONNEL

The fifth premise is that extensive social involvement will attract and retain quality personnel who might not otherwise serve in the Army. Underlying this premise is a belief that, to attract and retain, the Army should have the image of a compassionate, understanding organization which accepts and develops the individual as a means of contributing to the resolution of pressing domestic problems. Inferentially, the social value of securing the nation provides insufficient attraction. This view is evident in the Modern Volunteer Army master program, which infers that the citizen's contribution to society comes after his period of military service:

to fulfill his needs and those of the nation, the Army today must be an institution in which men grow . . . and from which they emerge, having served as proud competent soldiers better prepared to contribute to our society.[5]

For the soldier, the basic contribution to society is his period of military service—a socially acceptable end in itself. The latter attitude appears to be shared by many young Americans. Current national sample opinion polls reveal the essential traditionalism of most young Americans. Performance of "socially relevant" responsibilities does not appear to motivate young Americans to service in the enlisted ranks as much as basic acceptance of patriotic service—the notion that somebody must defend the nation. They expect reasonable income, personal improvement, and job satisfaction derived from being a serving participant in military preparedness.

The young college graduate officer may well expect a more active social role based upon the activist environment on today's campuses. The opportunity to contribute to the resolution of ecological or inner-city problems may be necessary to retain quality officers, but such activism

[5] Department of the Army, *Master Program*, p. 23.

need not involve military units. One-to-two-year sabbaticals permitting a limited number of officers to assist state or local governments would permit individual "activist" roles without committing unit resources.

The myth of the necessity of "meaningful" social involvement throughout the Army may be more real to some of the educated leaders of the Army who are influenced daily by the values of the elite establishment—represented by the *New York Times* and the *Washington Post*—than it is to the Army as an organization composed of average people, with traditional motivations, who stem from middle America.

Conversely, there are substantial reasons for Army concern about acceptance of extensive social action responsibilities. The case rests on four arguments:

1. The Army exists to provide military security to the Nation; hence, resources should be focused on this purpose.

2. Challenged by external criticism and internal review, the Army today is ill-suited to address nonmilitary problems.

3. Current social welfare programs are difficult to manage; hence, expansion of these programs would compound the problem.

4. Domestic social action may stimulate overinvolvement by well-meaning nation-building experts.

MILITARY SECURITY

It is a basic proposition that the Army exists to defend the nation. The Army must be skilled, tough, and ready to perform its mission in defending the country, and it must be seen as such by the American people, who have a right to expect that several billion dollars per year will produce the necessary units with fully capable fighting troops. If such resources also produce some form of social benefit, so much the better, but the funds are appropriated to provide the basic military preparedness expected by Congress and the public.

Until recently, the Army has been assigned increased social welfare responsibilities during a period of increasing defense budgets. Today, the situation has changed; budgets are steadily declining in real and absolute terms.

The major stimulus for allocation of national resources to the Army is, and must remain, basic congressional acceptance of the need for a reasonable level of general defense readiness roughly divided to meet the land, sea, and air threats. It appears unlikely that social welfare projects could become a convincing rationale for allocation of additional military resources. More fundamentally, increased social welfare responsibilities could serve to dilute, rather than create, basic military readiness.

The problem is more basic than just diversion of resources. It is possible that assignment of social responsibilities to combat units may blur their role. A diminution or masking of this role could deprive the Army of the purpose, direction, and pride which are the roots of combat capability. However, certain combat service support units—medical, transportation, communication, and maintenance—might effectively perform limited social roles which, by their similarity to wartime missions, could truly enhance combat readiness.

EXTERNAL CRITICISM AND INTERNAL REVIEW

The Army is under serious attack—partially due to Vietnam and partially due to its role as a competitor for resources which might otherwise be available to civilian agencies for social welfare. Seen as "lax and fat" by such responsible national spokesmen as Gardner,[6] the image becomes far more damaging when changed to that of some youths who view the Army "as a wicked greedy aggressor conspiring with other vested interests to subvert the American dream."[7]

Disturbing as they are, views such as this will moderate as time and events moderate the current disillusionment caused by Vietnam. Far more serious is the widespread questioning by responsible decisionmakers. Capable and dedicated Americans are in profound disagreement about the nature of the threat to the United States and the size and composition its defense establishment should have.

The external debate has stimulated a searching internal review of policies and practices. The Army is undergoing a serious "questioning

---

[6] Gardner, *op. cit.*, p. 154.

[7] Adam Yarmolinsky, *The Military Establishment: Its Impact on American Society* (New York: Harper & Row, 1971), p. 406.

of confidence" precipitated by Vietnam. There is a lurking sentiment within the Army that the nation could have been better served.

It is a simple yet fundamental truth that the mission of the Army is to control the land and people who inhabit it. The Army, as an institution, concerns and derives its strength from people—the challenge of the diversity of man —as compared with the attractions of machines (of the sea or air), which are the lifeblood of the other military services. Due to its intimate relationship with people, the Army must believe that it is accepted as a necessary, if not always popular, profession. This atmosphere of acceptance is lacking in many quarters.

Today, as in the past, the key to external acceptance and internal satisfaction is proud, capable, confident units prepared to perform traditional missions. The re-establishment of traditional capabilities must take precedence over initiation of beneficial and useful career-attracting programs such as on-duty educational opportunities for the soldier serving in operational units. Until there are fully manned, truly trained and maintained units, hours devoted to on-duty education must detract from the development of honest mission readiness. Particularly at a time of concerned introspection, those tasks which divert resources from unit readiness and job satisfaction within the small unit should be avoided.

CURRENT SOCIAL WELFARE PROGRAMS

Current social welfare programs have been difficult for the military to manage. The normal diversity of situations and requirements faced by the Army, combined with the temporary but vexing problems of Vietnam—such as personnel instability—have required that local commanders manage many social programs.

In many cases, however, local authorities have neither the knowledge nor the resources to deal with complex social phenomena. Conditioning racial attitudes, applying techniques of out-patient drug rehabilitation, and skill training of the marginally productive are examples of challenging problems which strain the limits of current social knowledge, but which are essentially problems that local military commanders have been forced to solve.

In many cases, local commanders have had to address these expanded responsibilities with neither a lessening of existing responsibilities nor an increase in resources. Most commanders are understandably cautious about releasing men from military training to attend civilian skill training or expanded educational programs unless there is an explicit change in directed missions or priorities. Yet acceptance of such responsibilities has seldom provided a persuasive rationale for a reduced level of unit readiness. The time and effort is often "out of the hide" of already taxed commanders and units. Under these conditions, expanded personnel activities can become a disturbing stimulant for a hypocrisy of "statistical" performance.

Lastly, the local commander is the cutting edge, innovating at the local level social change which was proposed at the theoretical level. To the average American, the innovator is not Secretary McNamara or any other Secretary of Defense. It is the Army. As Adam Yarmolinsky has observed,

> The establishment has assumed a certain responsibility for stimulating social change and has ceased to be contented solely with maintaining the status quo of the society it serves.[8]

He is correct, but the burden is not borne by the "establishment," which comes and goes from public service; it is borne by the average captain and sergeant in the Army year after year.

OVERINVOLVEMENT

Another effect of Vietnam has been to make many within the military profession chary of civic action responsibilities. One of the real issues of involvement in Vietnam was the process of overcoming institutional reluctance to commit the Army to the resolution of problems that were primarily social, economic, and political. The jump from Special Forces to Regular Army participation in civic action, nation-building, and counterinsurgency was significant. It symbolized the acceptance of social and economic action as a conventional, primary Army responsibility. For a myriad of reasons, the transition was done poorly.

---

[8] *Ibid.*, p. 353. See also Adam Yarmolinsky, "Military Service and Race," pp. 658–67 of this volume.

Dismayed by the Vietnam experience in social endeavors, many officers do not want to permit a similar experience in the United States. The Army has thousands of capable advocates who have invested a decade of service in counterinsurgency. Doctrines of nation-building forged in Vietnam are often assumed to be transferable and applicable to the improvement of domestic poverty conditions.

To some, domestic social action projects will at last permit the nation to gain full value from the special capabilities developed for Vietnam. These advocates see increased social involvement in the United States as a way to maintain the capability, and thus the readiness, for some future contingency while simultaneously serving to alleviate the conditions of the ghetto or rural poor. This rationale was evident in a recent study of Army personnel policies for the mid-1970s:

A deeper Army involvement will improve our understanding of the causes of insurgency and the means needed for countering them.[9]

A more indirect and disturbing assumption of domestic education and security responsibilities is also inferred in the same document:

The Army social action role is thoroughly anchored in doctrine which dictates that rear areas must be kept secure so as not to divert or weaken the effort at the front.[10]

ALLOCATION OF RESOURCES

Another vexing but oft-forgotten aspect of domestic action is the problem of allocation of resources at the local level. While Army motives may be humanitarian and pure, the allocation of resources is a function of political power. Politics is the process of resolving conflicting values and wants. When the Army provides resources to any civilian community, it becomes enmeshed in political processes. It cannot escape a role of direct or indirect influence. For example, are resources to be distributed through Republicans or Democrats? The Army can be placed in a difficult, untenable position.

Special Forces are out today conducting

imaginative civic action operations in the poverty-stricken communities of the mountainous areas of North Carolina. The danger of unfortunate involvement is real.

The major and abiding determinant of the proper level and nature of social responsibilities of the Army is the basic relationship of the military profession to the social and political system it exists to defend. This relationship is dynamic—highly dependent upon the perceived needs of the society as a whole and defense requirements placed on the Army.

THE CHANGING AMERICAN SOCIETY

One of the more mundane truisms today is acknowledgment that American society is changing at a rapid, if not accelerating, pace. Various descriptions of the change have been advanced, and the more adventurous of the theoreticians have attempted to chart the future—Daniel Bell's postindustrial state, Herman Kahn's sensate society, Zbigniew Brzezinski's technetronic age (the third revolution), Charles Reich's consciousness III, and the accelerating change of Alvin Toffler's future shock.

Each attempts to chart the dimensions of major change underway in American society, including our sense of values. Each work overwhelms with statistics of change, but is understandably vague about probable institutional responsibilities and relationships in the future. Perhaps the frankest admission of uncertainty comes from Gardner: "We're like a man driving eighty miles per hour in a fog that permits him to see only thirty feet ahead."[11]

The potential impact of such rapid change may be more pronounced for the military than it is for the rest of society. It jars the conservative bias of the military profession and erodes the traditional isolation which has served to preserve the professional ethic. During such a period of change, the challenge to the Army is to modify its policies and procedures to accommodate change while retaining that essence of order and discipline which enables a unit to succeed in battle. The Army has often met this challenge; but, in the past, change was effected behind the protective barrier of isolation. Samuel P. Huntington has noted that the

---

[9] U.S. Department of the Army, Deputy Chief of Staff for Personnel, DPSR, *Army 75: Personnel Concept*, vol. 2 (draft), 1968, pp. 1–25.
    [10] *Ibid.*, pp. 1–22.

[11] Gardner, *op. cit.*, p. 84.

military profession is "probably unique among significant social institutions in the United States in the extent to which it was created independent of American society."[12]

EFFECTS OF CHANGE

Change in the past was accomplished at a relatively leisurely pace. The Army had ample time to adjust to the new values stimulated by the Industrial Revolution as it dropped from public view in the late nineteenth and early twentieth centuries.

Today, the military appears to be no longer permitted the luxury of such self-paced, isolated change. One effect of the "technetronic age" has been to place the Army squarely in the center of the arena of rapid change. The effects of these changes upon the Army's relationship with American society are manifested in numerous ways.

1. National concern for the welfare of the individual has focused critical attention on the military justice system. Military justice has become a subject of critical public attention to the extent of severely restricting the authority of the commander.

2. The mass communications media have maintained an unblinking eye on military activities. Griping and grousing by disgruntled servicemen consequently have become nationally advertised dissent.

3. National concern for equal opportunities for minorities has encouraged creation of racial organizations within, and existing apart from, the military chain of command.

4. The scourge of drug abuse has tied the military unit inexorably closer to the local community. Drug abuse can be met only through the closest coordination of policy and activity between adjacent military and civilian communities.

CIVILIAN ISOLATION

The problem of the moment does not appear to be military isolation from the civilian community. It is precisely the reverse. Given the apparent tendency of man in the postindustrial

state toward increased social involvement and concern, the danger to national security and the military profession is that the unique characteristics and capabilities of the profession may become eroded beyond repair by over-immersion in such a rapidly changing value system.

The Army must seek ways to promote a gradual adjustment to new American post-industrial values which will retain good order and discipline.

The path and rate of institutional change will be difficult to determine. There are numerous detours along the way. Two pitfalls are: (1) a search for national acceptance by redirecting readiness resources to social welfare purposes; and (2) presenting the false image of an institution actively supporting natural social welfare activities in order to gain the transitory support of the "liberal establishment."

Others may suggest such paths in the honest belief that the only way to maintain an Army in the future will be to deliberately blur its functional role in an array of increased general social welfare responsibilities. Such sentiment reflects the implicit fear that an army which retains its traditional image and structure is not supportable in postindustrial America.

FLEXIBLE POSTURE

Yarmolinsky argues that, if the Army is to survive, it must "assume a lower and more flexible posture." To Yarmolinsky, such a posture would cause a desirable and necessary erosion of military values:

As the military character of the military establishment becomes less distinctive, absolutist perceptions may be replaced by more realistic ones. The military may come to be regarded as any other part of government.[13]

The military character of the military establishment is precisely what has been found to be essential to develop the order and discipline necessary to successful performance in war.

The Army must view with caution the understandable pressures for acceptance of greater general social welfare responsibilities. The current Department of Defense and Army action

[12] Samuel P. Huntington, *The Soldier and the State: The Theory and Politics of Civil Military Relations* (Cambridge, Mass.: Harvard University Press, Belknap, 1957), p. 233.

[13] Yarmolinsky, *op. cit.*, p. 406.

policy is excellent. It is basically conservative of Army resources today because of the unknowns of Vietnam withdrawal and the reduced defense budget.

Unfortunately, the policy may be fragile after Vietnam is resolved. For example, it will be subject to substantial erosion if the Army aspires to increased social welfare responsibilities in an attempt to "be liked" and thereby attract volunteers. Furthermore, the guidance may be sufficiently broad to permit well-intentioned erosion by those within and above the Army who believe it necessary to stimulate additional convergence between the Army and society at large.

Several actions or policy guidelines could serve to reinforce the conservatism of present policy:

1. To display the range and costs of involvement, aggregate and publicize the current level of Army participation in social welfare programs. Where possible, include both dollar and personnel costs, with particular reference to the impact on the tactical unit.

2. Evaluate ongoing or proposed programs on the basis of their impact on the readiness for combat of tactical units.

a. Programs which directly and substantially contribute to the tactical readiness, morale, good order, and discipline of combat, combat support, and combat service support units should be encouraged and increased. Examples of programs which could be increased are those to reduce racial and drug abuse problems in all units, off-duty educational and training improvement programs for soldiers, and social infrastructure assistance to the civilian community, such as aeromedical evacuation or engineer construction projects, which are unequivocal, direct applications of wartime combat service support skills.

b. Programs which serve to reduce directly the combat readiness of units should be reduced to the essential minimum. Examples of such programs are Project Transition—which could be accomplished by the Veterans Administration after the individual is no longer expected to be militarily ready—and Project One Hundred Thousand—which could be replaced with nonmilitary pretraining before an individual is expected to be prepared to accept national defense responsibilities.

Decisions on personnel programs with uncertain impact upon unit readiness should be decentralized to the local commander with decision guidance to plan, budget, and conduct projects which he believes will contribute to improved unit readiness. Projects impacting on civilian communities would be encouraged after detailed coordination and approval by the local political, business, and labor leadership. Examples of projects for decentralized leadership could be Special Forces operations, social action–oriented adventure training, or community relations projects such as summer camps. Other, more extensive programs could be undertaken by the Reserve establishment.

This guidance would permit continuation, if not expansion, of a wide range of current projects that are shown to be demonstrably neutral politically, useful socially, and not detrimental to unit readiness. The Army's policy theme must be willing acceptance of socially useful tasks insofar as they contribute to the building of proud, capable units—as perceived by the local commander responsible for unit readiness.

Centrally administered and publicized complex major programs such as training for integration and drug rehabilitation must be aggressively supported; they genuinely increase unit readiness. Decentralization of other projects to the local commander who is directly and immediately responsible will continue the essential pre-eminence of the traditional roles and responsibilities of the Army. At that level, maintenance of the capability to fight is an instinctive response.

Policies such as these would reflect necessary, positive acceptance of responsibility to meet and solve challenging social issues yet would preserve the unique nature of the profession. These policies and programs would be strictly subordinated to maintenance of combat readiness. However unpopular or "reactionary" these policies might be, the Army must persevere.

Upon the soldiers, the defenders of order, rests a heavy responsibility. The greatest service they can render is to remain true to themselves, to serve with silence and courage in the military way. If they abjure the military spirit, they destroy themselves first and their nation ultimately.[14]

14 Huntington, op. cit., p. 466.

THE REVOLT OF THE MASSES: PUBLIC OPINION ON MILITARY EXPENDITURES

BRUCE M. RUSSETT

From the beginning of scientific opinion sampling until the 1960s, popular attitudes toward military spending in the United States were very permissive. Only a small minority ever favored reducing the armed forces. A somewhat larger minority rather consistently advocated expanding the military, but at most times a majority of the population either expressed satisfaction with the existing defense effort or was indifferent to the question. By the late 1960s, however, this situation had changed markedly. In recent soundings a near-majority of the entire populace has regularly advocated a reduction in military spending. Several possible explanations for changing attitudes toward defense are considered here. No relationship emerges between popular attitudes and actual levels of military spending. Long wars do seem to generate some opposition to defense spending, but that explanation is incomplete. Mass attitudes and those of the political elite (in this case senators) rather closely coincide, but it is not obvious which is leading which. Insofar as the current high, and apparently fairly stable, level of mass opposition to the military is politically effective, there will be important pressures for a reduction in arms levels and perhaps in the likelihood of war. Bruce M. Russett is a Professor in the Department of Political Science at Yale University and is the author of Trends in World Politics *(1965) and* What Price Vigilance? The Burdens of National Defense *(1970).*

MYTHS ABOUT POPULAR CONCERN

Many theories about the sources of national security and foreign policy stress the limiting, and occasionally the initiating, effect of public opinion. Certainly explanations solely in terms of external stimuli are inadequate, even for such phenomena as military expenditures and arms races. A search for determinants within a nation's domestic political system may concentrate upon governmental or interest elites, as is done in the variants of theories about a "military-industrial complex," or it may probe deeper to include mass attitudes. Among analysts who have considered the question, there are a number of conflicting views. Some formerly well-regarded beliefs have been shown to belong largely in the category of mythology; others were probably correct in their time, but need sharp revision under conditions of the new politics of the 1970s.

Political leaders have sometimes assumed that mass opinion constituted a major constraint on the choice of military policy, and

Reprinted from Peace, War, and Numbers *(Beverly Hills, Calif.: Sage Publications, 1972), pp. 299–319, by permission of the publisher. Footnotes have been omitted, and minor editorial changes have been made.*

Author's Note: *This article was written while I was a Visiting Professor at the University of Brussels on Fulbright-Hays and Guggenheim awards, and the research was supported in part by Grant No. 2635 from the National Science Foundation. I am indebted to Philip K. Hastings of the Roper Public Opinion Research Center, Williams College, for providing me with most of the survey material cited here, and to Alfred O. Hero for bringing some of it to my attention. Philip Converse made available material from an SRC survey made under his direction. H. W. Moyer provided valuable assistance in a seminar paper at Yale. Moyer, Arnold Kanter, Michael Sullivan, and H. Bradford Westerfield offered useful comments. Of course, no person or agency is responsible for anything I express here.*

have hesitated, for fear of popular reaction, to pursue policies they thought desirable. But, in the past, public opposition to military spending really was not widespread. At the beginning of World War II President Roosevelt led very cautiously toward intervention because he thought the majority of the people were not initially ready to support a large defense program and aid to the Allies. Yet, in fact, a program of rearmament, at least, was very widely desired in the late 1930s. In other periods differing arms policies have been pursued within the context of fairly stable mass opinion. For example, during the entire cold war period from 1946 to 1960, repeated national surveys always found a substantial majority of the population in favor of a large army and navy. Despite this relative constancy of preference on the mass level, national policy varied from initial disarmament, through the beginnings of a cautious build-up, the exertions of the Korean War, and the cutbacks associated with the "new look" of the Eisenhower Administration, to the makings of a new build-up at the beginning of the Kennedy years. The pattern of mass preference on military spending, however, has changed drastically very recently. For the first time in more than thirty years a majority of the population has come to advocate reduction in military expenditures, and has become, as never before, a serious potential constraint on national security policy. This article examines relevant data on several assertions concerning the state of public opinion toward defense spending over the last four decades.

The myth of public constraint was expressed clearly by Walter Lippmann in 1955:

At critical junctures, when the stakes are high, the prevailing mass opinion will impose what amounts to a veto upon changing the course on which a government is at the time proceeding. Prepare for war in time of peace? No. It is bad to raise taxes, to unbalance the budget, to take men away from their schools or their jobs, to provoke the enemy.

Two specific propositions are embedded here. First, governmental decisions, including military policy, are shaped and limited by public opinion. Second, at most times ("time of peace") public opinion serves to restrict and reduce the level of defense spending. The public is allegedly insensitive to the requirements of national security and requires that the de-

fense budget be curtailed in favor of tax reductions or popular domestic programs.

Senator J. William Fulbright, on the other hand, more recently typified the view that mass opinion serves as a primary impetus to military spending and a barrier to its reduction. In 1964 he castigated

the readiness with which the American people have consented to defer programs for their welfare and happiness in favor of costly military and space programs. Indeed, if the Congress accurately reflects the temper of the country, then the American people are not only willing, they are eager to sacrifice education and urban renewal and public health programs—to say nothing of foreign aid— to the requirements of the armed forces and the space agency.

Although there is some ambiguity about whether popular opinion is correctly perceived ("if the Congress accurately reflects the temper of the country"), this is nevertheless a fairly clear statement of a widely held view. Moreover, while the systematic literature on arms races considers various sorts of possible restraints on expenditures, mass attitudes are seldom among them.

EARLY PERMISSIVENESS AND PRO-PREPAREDNESS

The first careful study of the survey data on this matter very firmly and convincingly rejected the proposition that public opinion restricts military spending. According to Samuel P. Huntington, Lippmann and others of like mind attributed to the mass public "a view which it did not possess and an attitude it did not hold." Huntington found in the surveys that on military programs and the defense budget the public tended to follow the lead of the Administration when the Administration took a definite position. In situations where the Administration did not take a strong stand, public opinion was, at the least, passive and permissive, and, at the most, very favorably disposed to stronger defense. A similar view, but one which stressed the general preference for a large defense establishment, emerged from a more recent review by Alfred O. Hero.

The general public acquiescence in heavy defense spending up to the late 1960s, with occasional but not common heavy pressures for increases, is also documented clearly below, in Figures 1 and 2 and Tables 1 and 2. Only the percentages favoring a reduction in defense spending are given in the tables, since that will be our primary interest, but those favoring an increase are shown graphically in Figure 2. The solid lines in both figures show responses over time to somewhat differing questions in a variety of AIPO, NORC, and Roper national surveys from Table 1; the broken lines between December 1950 and June 1953 indicate, from Table 2, responses to an identical question asked in ten NORC surveys.

First and most obviously, except for the most recent years, mass opinion certainly never really constituted a constraint on the level of military spending or the size of the armed forces. Except in the responses to a couple of questions seriously biased against military spending, in Figure 1 we see that those in favor of reducing the resources going to defense always numbered less than 30 percent of the population, with the remainder wishing an increase, expressing satisfaction with current levels, or indifferent and uninvolved (do not

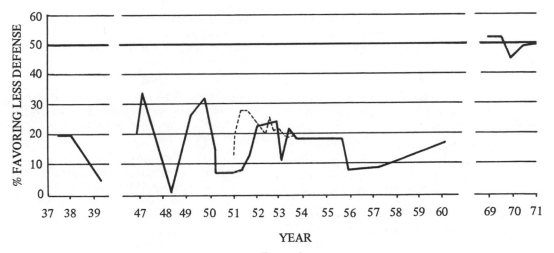

Figure 1
Percentage of Respondents Favoring Less Defense Spending

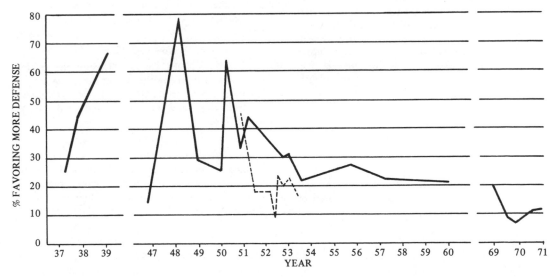

Figure 2
Percentage of Respondents Favoring More Defense Spending

Table 1
National Surveys on Defense Spending, 1937–1971

May 1937 (AIPO 82): "Do you think the amount of money we are now spending on the Army and Navy is too much, too little, or about right?"

Too much, 20%

*October 1937 (AIPO 101): "Do you think government expenditures should be increased or decreased for the Army and Navy?" ("Remain same" not offered, but coded.)

Decreased, 20%

*January 1939 (AIPO 143): "Do you think government spending should be increased or decreased for national defense?" ("Remain same" not offered, but coded.)

Decreased, 8%

January 1939 (AIPO 145): "Should government spending for national defense be increased, decreased, or remain about the same?"

Decreased, 3%

*November 1946 (AIPO 385): "About half the cost of our government today goes to support the Army and Navy. Which of these do you think should be done—
   "Reduce taxes by cutting down our Army and Navy/Keep our Army and Navy as they are for another 3 years?" ("Increase" not offered or coded.)

Reduce taxes by cutting, 20%

November 1946 (NORC 146): "This year the United States is spending about thirteen billion dollars on our armed forces. Which of these things do you think Congress should do next year—
   "Reduce the size of our armed forces, in order to save money?/Keep them at their present size, or *increase* the size of our armed forces, regardless of cost?"

Reduce, 21%

**February 1947 (AIPO 391): "Have you followed the arguments in Congress for and against cutting down on the money for the Army and Navy?" If yes: "Do you think Congress should reduce the amount of money which the Army and Navy have asked for?" ("Increase" not offered or coded.)

Yes, 35%

Note: This response is very unusual, because the respondents with a college education are much more likely (by about 13 percent) to favor reduction than are those with only a grammar school education. Ordinarily there is a slight *negative* relationship between education and favoring reductions. Since those with a higher education are more likely to answer

yes to the first part of the question, it is clear there is in this formulation a bias toward reduction.

March 1948 (Roper Fortune 64): "Do you think our military strength should be increased at the present time, left about the same as it is now, or do you think it should be cut down?"

Cut down, 1%

January 1949 (NORC 163): "Last year the United States spent about thirteen billion dollars on our armed forces. During the coming year, do you think we should spend more than this amount, or less, on our armed forces?"

Less, 26%

**September 1949 (AIPO 447): "Do you think it is a good idea or a poor idea to cut down on expenses in the U.S. military defense setup at this time?" ("Increase" not offered or coded.)

Good, 33%

February 1950 (AIPO 453): "Do you think the amount of money we are now spending on the Army, Navy, and Air Force is too much, too little, or about right?"

Too much, 15%

March 1950 (AIPO 454): "Do you think U.S. Government spending should be increased, decreased, or remain about the same on the following: National Defense?"

Decreased, 7%

*November 1950 (AIPO 467): "When the Korean War began, the United States had about one and a half million men in the armed forces. It has been decided to increase this number to three million men. Do you think this number is too high or too low?" ("About right" not offered, but coded.)

Too high, 7%

April 1951 (NORC 303): "During the coming year, do you think we should cut down the amount we are spending on our rearmament program, keep it about the same, or spend even more on our armed forces?"

Cut down, 8%

*July 1951 (AIPO 447): "If the Korean War is brought to an end soon, do you think the United States should continue our defense program as planned, or do you think the defense program should be reduced?" ("Increase" not offered or coded.)

Reduced, 11%

*December 1951 (NORC 315): "Do you think our government should keep on building up our defenses and helping our allies, even if it means continued high taxes for you?" ("Keep on building" is ambiguous.)

No, 22%

*November 1952 (AIPO 508): "Do you think the government should spend more money or less money for defense purposes?" ("Same" not offered, but coded. Includes a qualified "less.")

Less, 25%

December 1952 (NORC 334): As in April 1951

Cut down, 11%

*April 1953 (AIPO 514): "At present there are about 3½ million men in our armed forces, both in the United States and overseas. If a truce is reached in Korea, do you think we should cut down the size of our armed forces, or not?" ("Increase" not offered or coded. Includes qualified "should.")

Should, 22%

*August 1953 (AIPO 519): "Do you think too much of the taxes you pay is being spent for defense, or is too little being spent for defense?" ("About right" not offered, but coded.)

Too much, 19%

*September 1955 (AIPO 553): "Do you think we should keep on spending as much as we do now for our defense program, or should we cut down on the amount we spend for defense?" ("Increase" not offered or coded.)

Cut down, 19%

October 1955 (NORC 378): "During the coming year, do you think we should cut down the amount we are spending on our arms program, keep it about the same, or spend even more on our armed forces?"

Cut down, 8%

February 1957 (AIPO 579): "The biggest part of government spending goes for defense. Do you think this sum should be increased, decreased, or kept about the same as it was last year?"

Decreased, 9%

February 1960 (AIPO 625): "There is much discussion as to the amount this country should spend for national defense. How do you feel about this —do you think we are spending too little, too much, or about the right amount?"

Too much, 18%

*December 1968 (AIPO 773): "More than half of the money spent by the U.S. government goes for military defense. Looking ahead the next two or three years, would you like to see this amount increased or decreased?" ("Same" not offered, but coded.)

Decreased, 53%

July 1969 (AIPO 784): "There is much discussion as to the amount of money the government in Washington should spend for national defense and

military purposes. How do you feel about this: do you think we are spending too little, too much, or about the right amount?"

Too much, 53%

November 1969 (AIPO 793): As in July 1969

Too much, 46%

September 1970 (AIPO): "Congress is currently debating how much money should be spent for military purposes. Would you like to have your congressman vote to keep spending for military purposes at the present level, increase the amount, or reduce the amount?"

Reduce, 49%

March 1971 (AIPO): As in July 1969

Too much, 50%

Note: * or ** indicates bias in question wording.

Table 2
NORC Surveys on Defense
Spending, 1950–1953

"Do you think the people in this country have been asked to make too many sacrifices to support the defense program, not enough sacrifices, or about the right amount?"

Too Many	%
#295, December 1950	13
#298, January 1951	22
#300, March 1951	29
#312, August 1951	28
#323, April 1952	20
#327, June 1952	25
#329, August 1952	21
#333, November 1952	23
#337, February 1953	19
#341, June 1953	21

know). At times the percentage wanting less military spending fell very low indeed, below 10 percent—and this was usually precisely at times when the political leadership considered external threats to be especially serious and the need for a military build-up to be greatest —e.g., 1939, the beginning of the cold war in 1948, and the first year of the Korean War. (The 1939 case is perhaps especially poignant, given President Roosevelt's difficulties with Congress in pushing Selective Service and rearmament. Similarly, the lack of actual constraint in March 1950, before the Korean War, is noteworthy. That was about the time of NSC-68, the conviction of many in the government that American defense forces should be dramatically expanded, and a great fear that the populace would be unwilling to bear the burden. For many of these leaders the Korean War, despite its costs and dangers, at least had the virtue of providing an occasion for the build-up they wanted and hesitated—probably unnecessarily—to embark upon.)

Figure 2 shows the proportion of the population which favored an increase in the military establishment. This percentage was always—again, except for the late 1960s—higher than the corresponding percentage who wished for a reduction, but it, too, normally held at a level of well under half the population. The only exceptions to this last statement are clear external threats: 1939, March 1948 (immediately after the Communist coup in Czechoslovakia, and at the time of increasing threat to Berlin—but before the blockade), and, more surprisingly, March 1950, before the Korean War.

This characterization is further supported by the only series we have of identical questions asked over a number of surveys to the same kind of sample: the NORC material from Table 2. Again the proportions favoring a change in the *status quo*, either for an increase or a decrease in defense spending, remain well under half—typically about 20 percent for each. The only serious exceptions are the number in the first two surveys (45 and 36 percent) who favored more defense in the first months of the Korean War. After 1951 the figures fluctuate within a very narrow range, and the differences from one survey to the next are usually not statistically significant.

Thus, regardless of political leaders' perceptions, we have a picture of a public that was generally ready to rely on the judgment of the political leadership, to acquiesce in existing or planned levels of military strength. Only a minority of the populace favored change in either direction. This is true generally across the population by income and educational level. For example, comparing the college-educated and those with only a grammar school education, there was at most a difference of about 15 percent between those who wished defense spending to be cut, virtually always with the better-educated being more favorable toward the military. (That is, 20 percent of the college-educated might favor a reduction whereas 35 percent of those with a grade school education held that opinion.) To the degree that popular dissatisfaction with arms levels existed, pressures for increases were more widespread than those for decreases. *Hence, when spending did go up, there was greater resistance to cutting it back to its original level than there had been to the initial boost.*

Some other evidence that supports an image of public permissiveness is as follows:

1. When asked generally whether they were "satisfied with the way" America's military strength was being handled, the overwhelming majority usually expressed substantial contentment. For example, even in May 1966, during the Vietnam War, in an AIPO survey 88 percent declared themselves "extremely well," "considerably well," or "somewhat," satisfied.

2. The low salience of the defense spending issue is shown in the responses to open-ended questions asking whether, without suggesting items, there was any category of governmental spending that the respondent thought ought to be increased or decreased. Military expenditures were rarely mentioned. For instance, in AIPO surveys in January 1959, April 1963, and October 1963 neither the percentage for increase, nor that for decrease, in defense spending ever reached 7 percent. By contrast, typically one-third of the respondents volunteered foreign aid as a candidate for the ax, and, in April 1963, 15 percent of the sample wanted public spending for education to be increased.

3. Over the years, congressmen have reported relatively little correspondence on the issue of military expenditures.

4. There is substantial, if perhaps shallow, support for mutual disarmament. In response to repeated AIPO and NORC questions between 1946 and 1963 asking whether the United States should agree to reduce its armed forces if other countries (or specifically the Russians) cut down theirs, typically about half the sample, and almost always a majority of those with opinions, approved. The level was almost entirely independent of changes in opinion about the desirability of building or reducing the American armed forces taken alone, and was particularly strong even in 1951 and 1952, when our data in Figure 2 showed more than 30 percent of the respondents in favor of greater American military spending.

This state of affairs gave political leaders a good deal of freedom to promote disarmament, perhaps even at the same time that they advocated increased military expenditures.

POSSIBLE CAUSES OF VARIATION

A second important element in these data concerns the fact that, after wide swings in attitudes toward military spending in the early years, the fluctuations evened out and opinion became quite stable during the 1950s. For the entire 1947–1960 period both the highs and the deepest lows in both graphs come before 1951; after that the entire range of fluctuation is only about 20 percent, despite substantial variation in the form of the question. The only later fluctuations that are that big involve the lows of December 1952 and October 1955, each of which has an unbiased question preceded and/or followed by biased ones. This is what we would expect with an issue that is at first new, or seen in a new context—the emerging cold war—but later becomes embedded in a structured set of attitudes toward the new situation. The early oscillations in attitude toward military spending perhaps reflect the great swings in the mood and salience of foreign policy noted in Gabriel Almond's classic study, swings which also seem largely to have settled down and to respond less to dramatic external events.

Much of the variation that does exist must be due to substantial changes in the way the question about military spending or preparedness is phrased. I have noted with asterisks those questions in Table 1 which seem to me to be seriously biased—always, incidentally, against high levels of military spending. Types of biases at issue include:

1. Bias in question wording—i.e., offering only increase or decrease, not retaining the current level. ("Remain the same" is always coded, even if not offered explicitly.) This tends to inflate answers in both the increase and decrease categories, perhaps by about 5 percent in each. Two AIPO surveys in January 1939 asked quite similar questions except that one did not offer "remain the same" explicitly. The one offering only change produced percentages of 8 for decrease and 67 for increase; where the status quo was offered the percentages were 3 and 62 for change respectively.

2. Offering only decrease or status quo, not offering or coding increase. With "increase" not offered, "keep about the same" may lose some of the attractiveness it would have as a middle course, and some people may then choose "decrease" instead.

3. Explicit reference to the possibility of reducing taxes, or to the desirability of "cutting down on expenses," can be expected to prejudice many answers against high spending levels.

4. One survey, that by AIPO in February 1947, asked a two-part question in which the attitude portion was addressed only to those who acknowledged paying attention to the congressional debate about defense spending. This survey, and another (AIPO in September 1949) which both failed to offer "increase" and asked simply whether the respondent thought it a good idea "to cut down on expenses in the U.S. defense setup," mark the pre-1968 high points of opposition to military spending. It is very possible that the bias there is so serious that the responses should be removed from the trend study, though I have left them in with cautions.

5. Explicit reference to the current or planned size of the armed forces or military spending might, at least relative to the stripped-down question, impress the respondent particularly with the burden at issue. Relevant phrasing includes references to "about half the cost of our government today," "thirteen billion dollars," "the biggest part of government spending," and "3½ million men." This seems, however, not to be a notable biasing factor if adjacent surveys November 1950/April 1951, October 1955/February 1957/February 1960, and December 1968/July 1969 are compared. Hence, such phrasing alone is not sufficient for the award of an asterisk.

Because of the relatively few data points available, and, much more important, because of the variation in question wording, it is impossible to apply a very sophisticated trend analysis. Nevertheless, some hypotheses can be suggested and some points made. Two hypotheses about the possible effects of war occur. One is that, at the inception of war or severe external crisis, the popular response is one of patriotic rallying round the flag, with an immediate jump in the opinion that is very favorable toward expanding the military to deal with the threat, and a drop in the number of people wishing to curtail defense spending. While we must be very careful about post hoc attribution of the label "severe crisis" to those events corresponding to increased public sentiment for military spending, some of this phenomenon seems to be present in 1939 and at the time of the Czechoslovak coup in 1948.

The effect of the Korean War is harder to pin down. As manifested by both the February and March 1950 surveys in Figure 1, and the March 1950 survey in Figure 2, opposition to military spending had *already* dropped very sharply just before the onset of the war, perhaps in reaction to the announcement of the first Russian atom bomb test in late 1949, and then remained low for more than a year thereafter. The war probably helped retain a climate of opinion very favorable toward greatly expanding the military, but preceding lows are more puzzling. Here, however, it is essential to pay close attention to the questions' wording. The February and March 1950 questions are essentially unbiased, and again are preceded and followed by surveys using queries which tend to exaggerate opposition to the military. The preceding survey (September 1949) is a particularly grave offender. Thus, the immediate pre-Korean lows are probably deceptive, and it is likely that the war really did create a substantial change in opinion— that the November 1950 low, on a question that might be expected to inflate the proportion favoring a smaller army by perhaps 5 percent, is a true low in large part induced by earlier wartime conditions. This would be predicted by most of what we now know about popular response to international crises. A similar situation seems to have arisen in the enormous—and short-lived—upsurge in preparedness sentiment early in 1948.

A second war-related hypothesis, which especially reflects the apparent building of public distrust and hostility toward the military over the course of the long-current conflict in Indochina, is that, as any war (in this case the Korean conflict) drags on, public opposition to the military will mount. The evidence supporting this hypothesis is nevertheless extremely slim. Antimilitary sentiments did seem to build up over the course of the latter half of 1951, but there is no apparent change thereafter. Even the rise in antimilitary feeling

in 1951 is dubious because much of the shift in the solid line in Figure 1 may be accounted for by the insertion of important bias in all but one of the questions from July 1951 through September 1955. The one unbiased question in this set appears in December 1952, and the percentage then expressing a desire for a smaller army is markedly lower than before and after. About all that is clear is that in Figure 2, measuring the proportion who want a larger army, there is indeed a substantial and pretty steady drop which cannot be attributed to question bias.

Thus, the effect of the war was to produce a popular frame of mind that neither supported further expansion in the armed forces nor generated sentiments for reducing the army. And the latter cannot be simply attributed to wartime patriotism ("Do not cry out against the armed forces while a war is going on") either, since no new antimilitary sentiments surfaced after the war, despite the efforts of the Eisenhower Administration to cut the military budget and reduce military manpower.

The failure of opposition to the military to emerge in mass opinion is especially striking since presidential popularity is generally considered to be a victim of extended wars. Harry Truman's popularity rating dropped from over 40 percent at the beginning of the Korean war to 23 percent in early 1952 (though it then rose again into the low 30s), and Lyndon Johnson's fell from about 70 percent just after his election to under 40 percent in 1968. This last should not be taken too seriously, however, because domestic events and a "normal" decline in a president's esteem greatly compound and confuse the effects of war. Our impressions that long wars severely damage leaders' popularity are actually very hard to document convincingly.

Another plausible set of hypotheses concerns the relation of actual levels of military spending to the publicly desired level. One might suppose (1) that there is a close positive association between actual and desired levels, probably because mass opinion perceives and responds to the same external events that cause political decisionmakers to raise or lower the military budget; or (2) that actual and desired levels are negatively related, as mass opinion holds a fairly stable image of a desirable level of military spending and reacts against sharp changes in either direction. Further, the above hypotheses might apply to a more or less simultaneous association, or to a lagged one either way. Mass opinion might follow after the elite's change in response to threat, or, in a political system very sensitive to mass opinion, it might first be necessary to have change in mass opinion before the political leadership would be willing to vary military spending importantly.

Figure 3 shows the level of military spending as a percentage of Gross National Product (GNP) over the period 1946–1970. Precise tests of the above hypotheses are impossible because of variation in the questions and the incomparability of data points for the two variables—survey responses perhaps two or three times a year, expenditure data on an annual basis. But even on inspection it is apparent that there is little support for any of the above hypotheses. A simple sign test for a concurrent relationship in the direction, up or down, of annual changes in each variable (correlation of the magnitudes of changes would be too powerful for these data) also shows no relationship. For the eleven years where one

can match changes in the two variables, they are positively related in five and vary in opposite directions in the other six. Introduction of a one-year lag either way does little better. Nor does it improve matters to use the total military budget, or the military proportion of governmental spending, instead of the military share of GNP. No simple explanation of public attitudes toward defense expenditures is adequate, and the puzzle becomes even more perplexing as we look at more recent events.

THE SLEEPER AWAKES

The general image we have now built up—of a public usually rather indifferent to the size of the armed forces and the level of military spending, uninvolved and basically prepared to follow the political leadership, and, if anything, more disposed toward building a larger army than toward reducing it—makes very strange reading in light of the data for mass opinion since 1968. Recent antimilitary feeling is absolutely unprecedented from the beginning of scientific opinion-sampling. What had been a less than 20 percent minority who

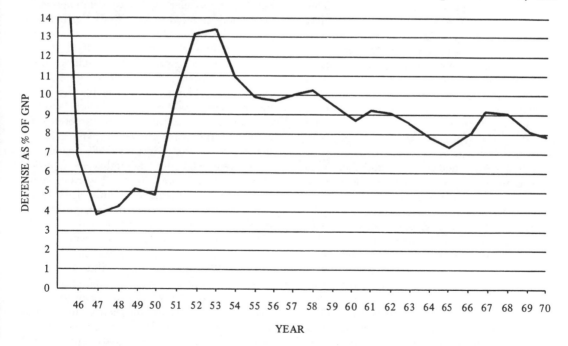

Figure 3

Defense as a Percentage of GNP, 1946–1970. Figures for 1946–1967 are taken from Bruce M. Russett, *What Price Vigilance?* (New Haven: Yale University Press, 1970), p. 132; those for 1968–1970 are from *Survey of Current Business.*

wanted to reduce the defense budget has become approximately half the populace; whereas two decades ago nearly a quarter of the population could always be counted on to support increased military spending, those ranks have shrunk to only one American in ten. The recent questions are essentially "perfectly straight," without any notable biases. Also remarkable is the fact that this happened at a time when military expenditures were decreasing slightly and, though higher than they had been since the early 1960s, were far below the exertions characteristic of the Korean War and even lower than those of 1954–1959. (See Figure 3.) And opposition has remained at a stable high level for more than two years—a striking divergence from earlier patterns.

Moreover, popular disenchantment with the military currently permeates all sections and levels. In the AIPO survey of July 1969, for instance, none of the standard major population categories—sex, race, education, occupation, age, religion, politics, region, income, or community size—shows fewer than 45 percent of its members responding that too much of government's money goes to national defense, and none shows greater than 60 percent. This is a remarkably even distribution. The widest differential is for education, with 60 percent of the college-educated group declaring that too much money went to defense, as compared with only 46 percent of the population with only a grade school education holding that opinion. This spread increased in September 1970 to 60 percent among the college-educated and 40 percent among those with only elementary schooling.

Such a clear association of education with opposition to defense spending is also new: it suggests that *antimilitarism is now strongest in the attentive public*, where it is likely to be politically effective, and that the salience of military spending as a political issue has become very high. Supporting evidence can be found in a Survey Research Center study of October 1968. Respondents were asked to indicate their generalized sentiments toward "the military" on a 0 to 100 scale called a "feeling thermometer." Of those with only a grade school or high school education, 39 percent placed their sentiments in the "warmest" or most favorable decile of the scale, but only 18 percent of those with some college education

did so. Similarly, favorable attitudes toward the military were negatively associated with information on the extent of military spending. Another question on the SRC survey asked respondents what proportion of the national government's budget they thought went to defense. The correct answer was just under 40 percent; the median answer was 50 percent. Of those who thought less than 20 percent of the budget was devoted to defense, a full 40 percent scored themselves in the warmest decile of the feeling scale toward the military. Even those who thought defense took between 80 and 99 percent of the budget tended to have favorable attitudes toward the military—37 percent of those put themselves in the top decile. But only 29 percent of respondents with an at least remotely accurate image of the military establishment's true size (placing it from 20 to 79 percent of the budget) were in the most approving decile.

It seems very unlikely that this astonishing shift, especially among the attentive public, can be attributed solely to the Indochina War. We have just seen how the Korean War, though it was also—in lesser degree—drawn out and unpopular, failed to stimulate major opposition to military spending. Furthermore, despite the regrettable absence of survey material for the early and middle 1960s, there is some reason to suspect that antimilitary sentiments have been building for a long time. In the last three surveys we have for the Eisenhower years, question bias is slight or nonexistent. Yet a clear increase in preference for a smaller army is nonetheless apparent. The 18 percent figure for February 1960 marked an eleven-year high for an unbiased question. President Eisenhower's farewell warning about the "military-industrial complex" came in the context of growing, if still modest, public concern. By the end of the 1950s and the 1960s the cold war had become less salient to many Americans; particularly after the Cuban missile crisis of 1962, images of stability, parity, and low threat became generally accepted. The lower salience of the cold war may well have made possible a re-examination of its assumptions, thus providing the basis for very different opinions at the end of the 1960s, when defense and foreign policy questions once more seemed pressing.

It might be hypothesized that popular sentiment either produces or follows high-level political antimilitarism. Figure 4 graphs the ups and downs of one measure of legislative opposition to defense spending over the period 1946–1970. It shows the highest percentage of the Senate recorded in favor of any reduction in military authorizations or appropriations below the level requested by the executive branch, as manifested in each session of Congress.

As with the graph of actual military spending, there is no consistent relationship between year-to-year changes in congressional resistance to defense spending and such resistance in the mass public. An increase in Senate votes to cut the defense budget was about as likely to coincide with a decline in popular preference for such a move as with a similar increase. The search for a lagged relationship, however, turns up something a bit more promising. In six out of eight cases where one can match an increase or decrease in Senate antimilitarism with subsequent popular changes, the two correspond. Nevertheless, the number of cases is too small to allow us to take the finding very seriously.

More impressive is the overall similarity in pattern between Figure 4 and the relevant portions of Figure 1. Both the masses and the political elite showed some opposition (stronger in the latter case) as the Korean War continued, and both reached their peak at the end of the 1960s as the Indochina War dragged on. Whereas in the initial post–World War II decade it was common practice for not a single senator to be recorded in favor of reducing the defense budget, from 1966 onward more than a quarter of the legislators took such a position. Ignoring the wide fluctuations in mass opinion as registered in the polls of the 1940s (due in substantial measure to changes in question wording), the only important divergence between the elite and popular patterns probably occurred in 1963, when considerable sentiment emerged in Congress for reducing military spending. Even here we cannot be sure that such a divergence occurred, because we lack proper measures of popular sentiment for that period. But the fact that Senate opposition quickly fell off again until several years later suggests that the legislative doves failed to strike an immediate chord of popular resistance.

Yet, by the end of the 1960s, opposition to defense expenditures had become widespread at all levels of the political system, and it is by no means obvious who was leading whom. It seems quite likely that in the recent phase congressional antimilitarists were responding to public opinion as much as they were molding it. While the senatorial doves doubtless made opposition to the military respectable in a number of less-exalted quarters, it is also true that many of those solons either took up an already popular issue or used the new sentiment as an opportunity to express some latent feelings about defense spending that they previously feared to speak about. The precise mechanism triggered by this mass sentiment is unclear and doubtless varies for different politicians.

If the new attitude toward the military cannot be attributed solely to political leadership from the top or to simple fatigue with war or opposition to extraordinarily high military budgets (compared with past budgets, either as a share of total governmental spending or as part of the GNP, those of 1968–1970 are not extraordinary), where does it come from? Here one can only speculate. We should not, from mere temporal distance, forget that the Korean War was an unpopular conflict which produced a good deal of skepticism at home about American political and military leaders. But the Indochina War has almost certainly reached much lower depths of public esteem. It has dragged on twice as long, brought more casualties, and resulted in a much less favorable gain/loss balance for American foreign policy than did the Korean conflict. Despite some ambiguities and hopes for reunifying Korea, the war of the 1950s did achieve the minimal goals of the government and of most Americans—the repulsion of communist aggression. The same cannot be said for the 1960s' war in Indochina; whatever the ultimate outcome, the communists almost certainly will play a major role in the government or in much of the territory of each of the three Indochinese states, and the avowed aim of the American government—establishment of a democratic regime in South Vietnam—seems very distant. The Indochina War is the clearest failure of American foreign and military policy in 150 years. A special casualty perhaps has been popular respect and awe for the efficiency of the American professional military, and

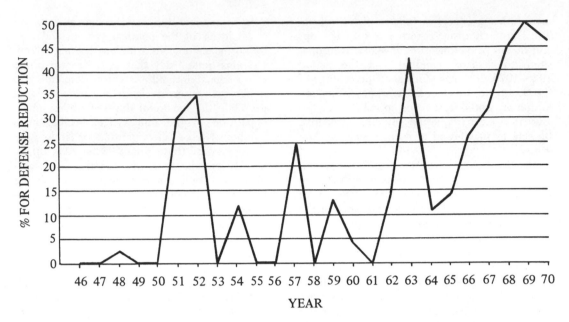

Figure 4
Highest Senate Votes for Cutting DOD Expenditures, 1946–1970

1946, 1947 No negative votes.

1948   Supplemental Defense appropriation; adopted 74–2.

1949, 1950 No negative votes.

1951   Flanders motion to recommit DOD appropriation with instructions to cut total to $55 billion; rejected 29–49.

1952   Morse amendment to reduce Air Force appropriation by $200 million; rejected 33–43.

1953   No negative votes.

1954   Long amendment to reduce by $45 million funds for barracks program; rejected 12–63.

1955, 1956 No negative votes.

1957   Dworshak amendment reducing DOD funds by $182 million; rejected 24–49.

1958   No negative votes.

1959   Young motion that Senate recede from its amendment to increase by $15 million House-approved funds for civil defense; rejected 12–72. Senate increase merely restored House cut; did not exceed original executive request[a].

1960   Appropriate $40 billion to DOD for fiscal 1961; adopted 83–3.

1961   No negative votes.

1962   Young amendment to delete $94 million appropriated for civil defense; rejected 14–68.

1963   Saltonstall amendment to cut DOD procurement appropriation by 1 percent; rejected 43–45[b].

1964   Nelson amendment to reduce DOD appropriation by 2 percent; rejected 11–62.

1965   Young amendment to reduce civil defense funds by $35 million; rejected 13–72.

1966   Young amendment to reduce by $15 million appropriation for civil defense; rejected 27–59.

1967   Young amendment to reduce civil defense allotment by $20 million; rejected 32–55.

1968   Williams amendment to reduce defense authorization by $700 million; adopted 45–13.

1969   Smith amendment to delete funds for Safeguard ABM system while allowing development of other ABM systems; rejected 50–50.

1970   Hart-Cooper amendment deleting $322 million for deployment of Safeguard ABM system in Missouri and Wyoming; rejected 47–52.

---

a 1959: I did not consider Thurmond's motion to reduce MATS funds by $20 million, since his primary motivation was not a reduction in defense spending. Rather, Thurmond was against spending the money in the civilian sector, which he felt would impair the development of military air transport capabilities. See U.S. Congress, *Congressional Record*, July 13, 1959, pp. 13202–8, esp. p. 13202; and July 14, 1959, pp. 13291–316, esp. p. 13315.

b 1963: Another motion that showed fairly strong antidefense feelings was Young's motion to reduce civil defense funds by $47 million; it was rejected 24–48.

hence there is a new willingness to cut military funds. The McNamara years of new-style civilian analysis of military budgetary proposals may also have contributed somewhat to a general skepticism concerning military demands.

Furthermore, disillusionment with the military arises at a time of domestic crisis and new needs for governmental spending. The 1950s in large part constituted a period of reaction against big public expenditure programs, of fears of big civilian government. Thus, at least on the public expenditure level, there were few popular competitors for the defense budget. But, with current requirements for better health, better cities, pollution control, and a fight against hunger, new demands, widely considered legitimate, are being made for public funds. Some programs initiated or expanded in the Eisenhower Administration—e.g., the great post-Sputnik inputs into education and research—now contribute to this climate.

Another probable contributing factor is the presence in the electorate of a whole generation with no adult memory of intervention in World War II or even of the beginnings of the cold war. This new cohort of voters is thus less ready to accept the standard arguments for an interventionist foreign policy or the need for large armed forces. In the September 1970 survey 60 percent of the voters under the age of thirty wanted to reduce military spending, whereas only 46 percent of those who were thirty and over gave such an answer. And, in an article published in 1952, Frank Klingberg presented some fascinating evidence for generation-long cycles of involvement-withdrawal in American foreign affairs—a cycle which he predicted would move into its withdrawal phase in the late 1960s.

In any case, what is clear is that the former popular permissiveness toward military spending is gone. Should the new climate of mass opinion be politically influential, we will have to revise our conceptions about the determinants of military and foreign policy. Implications for the likelihood of violent international conflict are not hard to draw. Research is increasingly establishing a causal link from high arms levels to war. If politically effective, popular resistance to military spending may therefore help avoid not just wasteful arms races but war itself.

AEROSPACE PRODUCTION LINES AND AMERICAN DEFENSE SPENDING

JAMES R. KURTH

What are the imperatives which impact upon American weapons procurement? The author outlines two important, but not always overriding, economic imperatives, the "follow-on imperative" and the "bail-out imperative." An even more important imperative may be the "bureaucratic imperative," which helps explain how McNamara bought more missiles than he thought necessary in order to kill the B-70, which he believed was totally obsolete. In addition, there are cases, such as ULMS, where economic and bureaucratic factors may be less important than strategic factors. By examining specific cases of procurement and nonprocurement, James R. Kurth vividly demonstrates the effect of various imperatives on executive decisionmaking and executive-congressional relationships.
Dr. Kurth is Associate Professor of Government at Harvard University. He received his B.A. degree from Stanford University and his Ph.D. from Harvard.

COMPETING EXPLANATIONS OF WEAPONS PROCUREMENT

How can the major cases of American weapons procurement be explained? Why, for example, does the United States buy multiple, independently targeted re-entry vehicles (MIRV), despite expert testimony about the grave dangers that they will bring? With their high accuracy in targeting, their high number of warheads, and their high immunity to aerial surveillance, MIRVs could provoke a Soviet fear of an American first strike against Soviet land-based missiles and thereby provoke the Soviets into acquiring their own MIRVs, perhaps leading again to "the reciprocal fear of surprise attack" and "the delicate balance of terror" of the 1950s. Why does the United States buy a costly ABM system, despite expert testimony that it will not work, given the ease with which the Soviets could overload the system with a dense attack? And why does the United States buy such costly aircraft as the F-111, with its frequent crashes and repeated groundings; the C-5A, with its mechanical and structural failures; and the B-1, said to be obsolete even before the first prototype is built?

The problem with such questions about weapons procurement is not that there are no answers but that there are too many answers. Around MIRV, or around ABM, or around many cases of aircraft procurement, there has grown up a cluster of competing explanations, a thicket of theories. Does MIRV, for example, result from rational calculations about Soviet threats, or from reckless pursuit by weapons scientists and military bureaucrats of technological progress for its own sake, or from resourceful efforts by weapons manufacturers and their allies in Congress to maintain production and profits, or from some combination of these factors? More generally, we can distinguish in the academic and journalistic literature on military policy four broad, major, competing explanations of weapons procurement: the strategic, the bureaucratic, the democratic, and the economic.

Strategic explanations are familiar enough; they argue that weapons procurement results from rational calculations about foreign threats or from the reciprocal dynamics of arms races. Not surprisingly, policymakers and officials offer strategic explanations. They are less fa-

This article was prepared for delivery at the Annual Convention of the International Studies Association, Dallas, Texas, March 14–18, 1972, and was revised in October 1972.

vored, however, outside official circles. *Bureaucratic explanations* see weapons procurement as the outcome of bureaucratic politics, competition between bureaucracies, especially the Army, Navy, and Air Force; or as the output of bureaucratic processes, standard operating procedures within bureaucracies. Many liberals favor bureaucratic explanations; for them, the problem is, as the title of a book by John Kenneth Galbraith puts it, "how to control the military."[1] *Democratic explanations* see weapons procurement as the outcome of electoral politics—e.g., a President's efforts to avoid being vulnerable to campaign charges that he has neglected the nation's security and permitted a "missile gap." Some liberals are drawn to this kind of explanation. *Economic explanations* see weapons procurement as the result of aggregate economics, the needs of the capitalist system; or, in a less sweeping formulation, as the result of corporate economics, the needs of particular corporations in the aerospace industry. Radicals favor such explanations; for them, the problem is not how to control the military but how to control the economy. The bureaucratic and economic explanations in combination yield, of course, the theory of the military-industrial complex, which in its pure form argues that the military and industry are roughly equal in their influence on policy outcomes.

This essay is an effort to cut away at the thicket of theories. In it we will examine the major cases of aircraft, missile, and antimissile procurement by the U.S. government during the 1960s and 1970s—i.e., during the period of the Kennedy, Johnson, and Nixon Administrations. These are: (1) the F-111 tactical fighter; (2) the C-5A jumbo transport; (3) the B-1 strategic bomber; (4) the massive build-up of Minuteman and Polaris missiles from 1961 to 1964; (5) MIRV; and (6) ABM. Each of the six can be defined as a major case because of the large sums ($5 billion or more) that have been, or will be, spent on procurement of the system. All but the missile build-up can be defined as major cases because of the intense political debate over the program. And each of the last three can be defined as a major case because of its impact on the strategic balance between the superpowers. We will also examine the major cases of nonprocurement—i.e., the B-70 bomber and the Skybolt air-to-surface missile.[2]

AIRCRAFT PROCUREMENT AND ECONOMIC EXPLANATIONS

The two most debated cases of manned aircraft procurement in the 1960s were the F-111 tactical fighter and the C-5A jumbo transport. Both aircraft became famous, even notorious, because of "cost overruns," mechanical failures, prolonged groundings, and congressional investigations.[3] Further, in June 1970 the Air Force awarded a contract to produce prototypes of a new, large, manned bomber, the B-1, which begins anew the numbering of the bomber series and which would go into operational deployment in the late 1970s. By that time, given the efficiency of strategic missiles and anti-aircraft missiles, the new B-1 would seem to be about as useful and about as obsolete as the first B-1 of the 1920s.

Why does the United States buy such aircraft? There are, of course, the official, strategic explanations: The F-111 is needed for a variety of tasks, such as tactical bombing, strategic bombing, and air defense; the C-5A is needed for massive airlifts of troops and supplies; and the B-1 is needed for strategic bombing and postattack reconnaissance. But these explanations neglect the fact that the respective tasks can be performed by a variety of ways and weapons, and that these particular manned aircraft are not clearly the most cost-effective (to use the proclaimed criterion of Robert McNamara) way to do so.

Bureaucratic explanations also are possible: The F-111 is needed by the Tactical Air Command to preserve its power and prestige within the over-all balance of the military bureaucracies; similarly, the C-5A is needed by the Mili-

---

[1] John Kenneth Galbraith, *How to Control the Military* (New York: New American Library, 1969).

[2] For a study of earlier cases of weapons procurement, see Merton J. Peck and Frederic M. Scherer, *The Weapons Acquisition Process: An Economic Analysis* (Boston: Harvard Business School, 1962).

[3] For a detailed analysis of the early F-111 case, see Robert J. Art, *The TFX Decision: McNamara and the Military* (Boston: Little, Brown & Co., 1968). For a critical account of the C-5A case, see Berkeley Rice, *The C-5A Scandal* (Boston: Houghton Mifflin, 1971); a more sympathetic account is Harold B. Meyers, "For Lockheed, Everything's Coming Up Unk-Unks," *Fortune*, August 1, 1969, pp. 71–81, 131–34.

tary Airlift Command; and the B-1 is desired by the aging commanders of the Air Force, and of the Strategic Air Command within it, who look back with nostalgia to their youth and to the manned bomber in which they rode first to heroic purpose and then to bureaucratic power. But these explanations are not fully satisfactory. Neither the Tactical Air Command nor the Military Airlift Command is the strongest organization within the Air Force (the strongest is the Strategic Air Command), and probably neither of them could achieve such expensive programs as the F-111 and C-5A without allies. And even the powerful commanders of the Air Force and the Strategic Air Command could not achieve the B-1 on the basis of nostalgia alone, especially in a period of unusually sharp criticism of military spending and after the predecessor of the B-1, the B-70, had been canceled as obsolescent by Mc-Namara several years before. Nor would a democratic explanation which focused on public fears of an "aircraft gap" be persuasive, simply because the public has had no such fears.

An alternative explanation, more economic in emphasis and more general in scope, can be constructed, for these aircraft and perhaps for some other weapons systems also, by drawing some relations between two variables for the period since 1960: (1) aerospace systems which are military or military-related (i.e., military aircraft, missiles, and space systems); and (2) aerospace corporations which produce such systems.

AEROSPACE SYSTEMS

The major military aerospace systems produced at some time during the period since 1960 have been the following: the B-52, B-58, and B-70 bombers;[4] the F-111 and F-4 tactical fighters; the C-130, C-141, and C-5A transports; the Minuteman and Polaris missiles and their MIRV successors or "follow-ons," Minuteman III and Poseidon; and the ABM system, including the Spartan and Sprint missiles. In addition, there has been the military-related Apollo moon program. Major military aerospace systems presently planned for production in the mid- or late 1970s are the B-1, which can be seen as a long-delayed follow-on to the

canceled B-70; the F-14 and F-15, which will follow the F-4; a lightweight fighter; a STOL transport; the Trident Undersea Long-Range Missile System (ULMS), which will be a follow-on to Poseidon, and perhaps a super-MIRV, which will follow Minuteman III; and the military-related space shuttle program. These add up to twenty-two major military or military-related aerospace systems for the 1960s and 1970s.[5]

These various aerospace systems can be grouped into six functional categories or production sectors: (1) strategic bombers, (2) air defense and tactical fighters, (3) military transports, (4) missile systems, (5) antimissile systems, and (6) space systems.

AEROSPACE CORPORATIONS

At the beginning of the period studied here, in 1960, a large number of aerospace corporations produced military aircraft, missiles, or space systems. Four stood out, however, in the sense that each received in FY 1961 military and space "prime contract awards" of some $1 billion or more: General Dynamics, North American, Lockheed, and Boeing.[6]

During the decade after 1960, each of these four corporations normally continued to receive each year $1 billion or more in military and space contracts, although Boeing's awards occasionally dropped below that amount. Mc-Donnell, a minor contractor at the beginning of the decade, with contracts of $295 million in FY 1961, greatly expanded its military sales, primarily with the F-4 Phantom. In 1967, Mc-Donnell merged with Douglas, another minor contractor. In FY 1961, Douglas was awarded contracts of $341 million, much of which went to research and development programs for Skybolt, an air-to-surface missile canceled in 1962, and for Nike Zeus, the first antimissile missile; in FY 1966, the last year before the merger, Douglas was awarded contracts of $539 mil-

---

[4] The B-70 was produced only in the sense that two prototypes were built.

[5] For descriptions of the aerospace systems and contract awards since 1960, see various annual editions of Aerospace Industries of America, *The Aerospace Year Book* (Washington, D.C., Books), and *Jane's All the World's Aircraft* (New York, McGraw-Hill). For information on recent systems and awards, see recent issues of *Aviation Week and Space Technology*.

[6] See *Aviation Week and Space Technology*, November 13, 1961, p. 30, and December 25, 1961, p. 66. Annual figures for Department of Defense and NASA prime contract awards are normally published by *Aviation Week and Space Technology* each November or December.

lion. Since 1967, the merged corporation of McDonnell Douglas has normally received contracts of $1 billion or more each year. Grumman, another minor contractor in FY 1961, with contracts of $249 million, also greatly expanded its military and space sales, primarily with two large subcontracts awarded in the early 1960s, one for the aft fuselage of the F-111 and one for elements of the Apollo moon program. There are now six aerospace corporations which produce military aircraft, missiles, or space systems and which each normally receive some $1 billion or more in military and space contracts each year; in FY 1971, Lockheed, General Dynamics, Grumman, McDonnell Douglas, and North American Rockwell[7] each were awarded contracts amounting to almost $1 billion or more; Boeing was awarded some $800 million.[8]

We can analytically split Lockheed, which is normally the largest military contractor, into its two main military divisions, Lockheed–Missiles and Space, located in California, and Lockheed-Georgia. Similarly, we can split McDonnell Douglas into its McDonnell division in Missouri and its Douglas division in California. There are thus eight major production lines.

Given these aerospace systems and aerospace corporations, two related but different economic explanations can be constructed, which we shall call the follow-on and the bail-out imperatives.

THE FOLLOW-ON IMPERATIVE

We can chart the major military aerospace systems according to the production line to which the U.S. government awarded the contract and according to the years when major development or production was phased in or out or was (is) scheduled to do so.[9] Some interesting patterns result. (See Table 1.)

About the time a production line phases out production of one major governmental con-

[7] North American merged with a nonaerospace company, Rockwell-Standard, in 1967.

[8] These six aerospace corporations are also major corporations in terms of another, related, indicator: total annual sales (commercial as well as governmental). With the exception of Grumman, each in 1971 had sales of more than $1 billion; Grumman had sales of $800 million. See the *Fortune* directory of the 500 largest U.S. industrial corporations, *Fortune*, 85 (May 1972).

[9] See various editions of *The Aerospace Year Book* and *Jane's All the World's Aircraft* and recent issues of *Aviation Week and Space Technology*.

tract, it phases in production of a new one, usually within a year. In the case of new aircraft, which usually require a development phase of about three years, the production line normally is awarded the contract for the new system about three years before production of the old one is scheduled to phase out. In the case of new missiles, the development phase usually is about two years. Furthermore, in most cases, the new contract is for a system which is structurally similar while technically superior to the system being phased out—i.e., the new contract is a follow-on contract. (An exception is Apollo, but even here North American was NASA's largest contractor before the Apollo contract was awarded; in the case of the B-1, the follow-on is one step removed from the B-70.)

A large and established aerospace production line is a national resource—or so it seems to many high officers in the armed services. The corporation's managers, shareholders, bankers, engineers, and workers, of course, will enthusiastically agree, as will the area's congressmen and senators. The Defense Department would find it risky and even reckless to allow one of only eight or less large production lines to wither and die for lack of a large production contract. This is especially so because, for each of the aircraft production sectors (strategic bombers, fighters, and military transports), there are actually only four or five potential production lines out of the eight major lines we have listed. Strategic bombers are likely to be competed for and produced only by General Dynamics, North American Rockwell, Boeing, and perhaps Lockheed-Georgia; air defense and tactical fighters only by General Dynamics, North American Rockwell, Boeing, McDonnell division, and Grumman; and military transports only by Boeing, Lockheed-Georgia, Douglas division, and, for small transports, Grumman. Thus, there is at least latent pressure upon the Defense Department from many sources to award a new, major contract to a production line when an old major contract is phasing out. Furthermore, the disruption of the production line will be least and the efficiency of the product would seem highest if the new contract is structurally similar to the old, in the same functional category or production sector—i.e., is a follow-on contract. Such a contract renovates both the large

Table 1

The Follow-on Imperative: Major Production Lines and Military Aerospace Systems

Year	General Dynamics	North American Rockwell	Boeing	Lockheed–M & S	Lockheed-Georgia	McDonnell	Douglas	Grumman
1960	B-58	B-70	B-52 Minuteman	Polaris	C-130	F-4	Nike Zeus d.	Misc.
1961		Apollo d. in	Minuteman build-up	Polaris build-up	C-141 d. in			
1962	B-58 out F-111 d. in		B-52 out					F-111 sub. d. in
1963								Apollo sub. d. in
1964		B-70 out			C-141 p. in			
1965					C-5A d. in		Nike Zeus out Spartan d. in	
1966	F-111 p. in	Apollo p. in	Minuteman III d. in	Poseidon d. in				F-111 sub. p. in Apollo sub. p. in
1967								
1968			Minuteman out Minuteman III p. in	Polaris out Poseidon p. in	C-141 out C-5A p. in			
1969						F-15 d. in		F-14 d. in
1970		B-1 d. in						
1971				ULMS d. in				
1972		Apollo out Shuttle d. in			C-5A out	F-4 out	Spartan p. in	F-111 sub. out Apollo sub. out F-14 p. in
1973	F-111 out Lightweight fighter in ?	B-1 p. in	Minuteman III out Super-MIRV or SST in ?	Poseidon out ULMS p. in	STOL transport in ?	F-15 p. in		

Note: d. = development; p. = production; sub. = subcontract.

and established aerospace corporation that produces the weapons system and the large and established military organization that deploys it.

This latent constraint, or rather compulsion, imposed on weapons procurement by industrial structure might be called the follow-on imperative and contrasted with the official imperative. The *official imperative* for weapons procurement might be phrased as follows: If a military service needs a new weapon system, it will solicit bids from several competing companies; ordinarily, the service will award the contract to the company with the most cost-effective design. The *follow-on imperative* is rather different: If one of the eight production lines is opening up, it will receive a new major contract from a military service (or from NASA); ordinarily, the new contract will be structurally similar to the old—i.e., a follow-on contract. Relatedly, the design competition among production lines is only a peripheral factor in the award.

The follow-on imperative would have predicted, and perhaps can explain, the production line and the product structure of eleven of the twelve major contracts awarded from 1960 through 1972: (1) Minuteman III follow-on to Minuteman; (2) Poseidon follow-on to Polaris; (3) ULMS follow-on to Poseidon; (4) C-141 follow-on to C-130; (5) C-5A follow-on to C-141; (6) F-14 follow-on to F-111 major subcontract; (7) F-15 follow-on to F-4; (8) Spartan follow-on to Nike Zeus; (9) space shuttle follow-on to Apollo; (10) F-111 after B-58 (superficially a less certain case, but the two planes are structurally similar, with the F-111 being a relatively large tactical fighter and the B-58 being a relatively small bomber); and (11) B-1 delayed follow-on to B-70. In regard to the twelfth contract, Apollo, North American might have been predicted to receive the award, because it was already NASA's largest contractor.

Not surprisingly, the imperatives of the industrial structure are reinforced by the imperatives of the political system, as would be suggested by a democratic explanation. Five of the production lines are located in states which loom large in the Electoral College: California (Lockheed–Missiles and Space, North American Rockwell, and Douglas division of McDonnell Douglas), Texas (General Dynamics),

and New York (Grumman). The three others are located in states which in the 1960s had a senator who ranked high on the Senate Armed Services Committee or Appropriations Committee: Washington (Boeing, Henry Jackson), Georgia (Lockheed-Georgia, Richard Russell), and Missouri (McDonnell division of McDonnell Douglas, Stuart Symington).

It might be said, however, that one should expect most contracts to be follow-on contracts. Production of the original system should give an aerospace corporation a competitive edge in technical experience and expertise which will win for it the next system awarded in the same production sector. But, in at least three major cases, the Source Selection Board on technical grounds chose a different corporation than the one already producing a similar system; the contract became a follow-on contract only when the board was overruled by higher officials. With the F-111, the original, technical choice was Boeing rather than General Dynamics; with the C-5A, it was Boeing rather than Lockheed; and, with Apollo, it was Martin rather than North American. More important, it is not always obvious that there should be any new system at all in an old production sector. This is especially the case because of the recent evolution of the six functional categories or production sectors. The aerospace systems within them or follow-on contracts are of course becoming progressively more complex and expensive, but they are also becoming progressively more dangerous strategically (MIRV) or operationally (F-111, F-14, and C-5A), or at best dubious (B-1, F-15, ABM, and the space shuttle).

THE BAIL-OUT IMPERATIVE

A related but inferior economic explanation can be constructed by looking at the annual sales, income, and employment figures for all six (originally seven) aerospace corporations for the period 1960 to 1971. Again, we can chart the major military aerospace systems according to the corporation to which the U.S. government awarded the contract and according to the years in which it did so. But this time we will also include in the table those years in which the corporation suffered either (1) a drop in sales of almost 10 percent or more from the previous year, (2) a deficit in income, or (3) a drop in employment of almost

10 percent or more from the previous year.[10] (See Table 2.)

There have been many occasions when an aerospace corporation has experienced one or more of these three difficulties. In twelve cases the U.S. government within the next year has awarded the corporation a new, major, military contract: (1) General Dynamics and the F-111 in 1962; (2) North American Rockwell and the B-1 in 1970; (3) North American Rockwell and the space shuttle in 1972; (4) Boeing and the Minuteman build-up in 1961; (5) Lockheed and the Polaris build-up and the C-141 in 1961; (6) Lockheed and the C-5A in 1965; (7) Lockheed and the development of ULMS in 1971 (as well as the government's guarantee of $250 million in bank loans); (8) McDonnell and the Air Force version of the F-4 in 1962; (9) Douglas and Skybolt in 1960; (10) McDonnell Douglas and the Johnson Administration's approval of the Sentinel ABM system, including Spartan, in 1967; (11) McDonnell Douglas and the Nixon Administration's approval of the Safeguard ABM system, including Spartan, in 1969; and (12) McDonnell Douglas and the F-15 in 1969. These observations suggest that the government comes to the aid of corporations in deep financial trouble, that there is what might be called a bail-out imperative.

In two cases the government has not awarded any new, major contract to the afflicted corporation. General Dynamics did not immediately receive contract aid after its bad year of 1970, but it is in a good position to receive a contract for the Air Force lightweight fighter and a large subcontract for the space shuttle in 1972 or 1973. (Similarly, General Dynamics did not immediately receive aid after 1960, but was awarded the F-111 in 1962.) Boeing did not immediately receive aid after 1969, but perhaps this was because the government planned for the SST to fill the gap in 1971; instead the SST was canceled by Congress. In three other cases the government has awarded

the corporation a contract for the development of a major weapons system which could be expected to shortly revive the corporation as the system moved toward production (General Dynamics in 1963, McDonnell Douglas in 1970, and Grumman in 1970). Over-all, however, the bail-out imperative is a less general explanation than its follow-on counterpart: three major weapons systems have been awarded without an immediately preceding corporate crisis (Minuteman III, Poseidon, and the F-14).

At first glance, the follow-on and bail-out imperatives might seem to explain cases not only of aircraft procurement but also of missile procurement (the Minuteman and Polaris build-up of 1961–1964 and, with the follow-on imperative, their MIRV successors, Minuteman III and Poseidon) and antimissile procurement (the Spartan missile of the ABM). But such an extension of the two imperatives is not without problems.

First, a general point: the mere fact that a condition is present in many cases does not in itself demonstrate that it is important or salient in each of them. Alternative explanations may be less general but more real.

Second, in regard to the missile build-up of 1961–1964, the two imperatives are flawed by *overcomplication*. A complex array of economic considerations may not be necessary to explain the outcome; a simpler model may serve just as well.

Third, in regard to MIRV, the two imperatives are flawed by *underprecision*. Neither explains why highly accurate warheads, as opposed to merely multiple ones (MIRV as opposed to MRV), were procured; economic needs would have been met equally well by a missile carrying either kind of warhead, and, therefore, economic needs alone do not explain the most important part, the "I," of MIRV.

Fourth, in regard to ABM, the two imperatives are flawed by *overprediction*. Each predicts large-scale procurement of Spartan; neither explains why the Nixon Administration moved in the Strategic Arms Limitation Talks (SALT) with the Soviet Union to limit deployment of Spartan and Sprint together to only 200 missiles.

Given these problems with the extension of economic explanations into the major cases of missile procurement and antimissile procure-

---

[10] These figures are calculated from the annual editions of the *Fortune* directory of the 500 largest U.S. industrial corporations, normally published in *Fortune* each May or June. Sales and earnings figures can also be found in annual editions of *Moody's Industrial Manual* (New York: Moody's Investor Service) and quarterly editions of *Moody's Handbook of Common Stocks* (New York: Moody's Investor Service).

Table 2
The Bail-Out Imperative: Corporate Financial Troubles and Military Aerospace Systems

Year	General Dynamics	North American Rockwell	Boeing	Lockheed	McDonnell	Douglas	Grumman
1960	$27 mil. deficit		9% emp. drop	$43 mil. deficit		$19 mil. deficit 25% emp. drop Skybolt in	
1961	$143 mil. deficit	Apollo in	Minuteman build-up	Polaris build-up C-141 in	21% sales drop 13% emp. drop	32% sales drop 22% emp. drop	
1962	20% emp. drop F-111 in				Air Force F-4 in		F-111 sub. in
1963	25% sales drop						Apollo sub. in
1964				17% sales drop			
1965				C-5A in		Spartan in	
1966			Minuteman III in	Poseidon in		$28 mil. deficit	
1967					McDonnell Douglas merger Johnson ABM decision		
1968					11% emp. drop		
1969		9% emp. drop	13% sales drop 15% emp. drop	$33 mil. deficit	Nixon ABM decision 16% sales drop 13% emp. drop F-15 in		F-14 in
1970	12% sales drop $7 mil. deficit 22% emp. drop	10% sales drop 22% emp. drop B-1 in	34% emp. drop	$86 mil. deficit 13% emp. drop	31% sales drop 14% emp. drop		16% sales drop 21% emp. drop
1971	16% sales drop 17% emp. drop	10% emp. drop	17% sales drop 16% emp. drop	12% emp. drop $250 mil. gov't loan guarantee ULMS in			20% sales drop $18 mil. deficit
1972		Space shuttle in					

Note: emp. = employment; mil. = million; sub. = subcontract.

ment, we should examine these cases on their own and in search of alternative explanations.

MISSILE PROCUREMENT AND BUREAUCRATIC EXPLANATIONS

The first case of missile procurement during the period since 1960 was the massive build-up of Minuteman and Polaris missiles from 1961 to 1964. This is also the simplest case of weapons procurement to examine and explain: a decision was made during a relatively limited time for a merely quantitative change.[11]

Because Minuteman and Polaris were invulnerable and thus second-strike weapons, they had a generally stabilizing impact on the strategic balance between the Soviet Union and the United States. As such, a strategic explanation of the U.S. build-up, focusing on international stability, might seem quite sufficient. However, even Secretary of Defense McNamara in 1967 retrospectively criticized as excessive the *degree* of the U.S. expansion and its effect on the Soviets:

Our current numerical superiority over the Soviet Union in reliable, accurate and effective warheads is both greater than we had originally planned and more than we require. . . . Clearly, the Soviet build-up is in part a reaction to our own build-up since the beginning of the 1960s.[12]

Why did the United States deploy as many missiles as it did? McNamara's own explanation, like almost all official explanations, is a strategic one, but it stresses his lack of accurate information.

. . . In 1961 when I became Secretary of Defense, the Soviet Union possessed a very small operational arsenal of intercontinental missiles. However, they did possess the technological and industrial capacity to enlarge that arsenal very substantially over the succeeding several years. We had no evidence that the Soviets did plan, in fact, fully to use that capability. But, as I have pointed out, a strategic planner must be conservative in his calculations; that is, he must prepare for the worst plausible case and not be content to hope and prepare merely for the most probable.

Since we could not be certain of Soviet inten-

tions, since we could not be sure that they would not undertake a massive build-up, we had to insure against such an eventuality by undertaking ourselves a major build-up of the Minuteman and Polaris forces. Thus, in the course of hedging against what was then only a theoretically possible Soviet build-up, we took decisions which have resulted in our current superiority in numbers of warheads and deliverable megatons. But the blunt fact remains that if we had had more accurate information about planned Soviet strategic forces, we simply would not have needed to build as large a nuclear arsenal as we have today.

Let me be absolutely clear. I am not saying that our decision in 1961 was unjustified; I am saying that it was necessitated by a lack of accurate information.[13]

But McNamara's account does not explain why the U.S. ordered a massive build-up all at once instead of ordering part of the build-up at first and delaying the rest of it until more information became available.

An alternative explanation emphasizing bureaucratic politics is given by Schlesinger in his account of the drawing up of the Kennedy Administration's first full defense budget in the fall of 1961.

The budget . . . contemplated a sizable increase in missiles; and the White House staff, while favoring a larger Minuteman force than the original Eisenhower proposal, wondered whether the new budget was not providing for more missiles than national security required. But the President, though intimating a certain sympathy for this view, was not prepared to overrule McNamara's recommendation. As for the Secretary, he did not believe that doubling or even tripling our striking power would enable us to destroy the hardened missile sites or missile-launching submarines of our adversary. But he was already engaged in a bitter fight with the Air Force over his effort to disengage from the B-70, a costly, high-altitude manned bomber rendered obsolescent by the improvement in Soviet ground-to-air missiles. After cutting down the original Air Force demands considerably, he perhaps felt that he could not do more without risking public conflict with the Joint Chiefs and the vociferous B-70 lobby in Congress. As a result, the President went along with the policy of multiplying Polaris and Minuteman missiles.[14]

A similar account is given by David Hal-

---

[11] The following discussion of the missile build-up is taken from my "A Widening Gyre: The Logic of American Weapons Procurement," *Public Policy*, 19 (Summer 1971): 380–83.

[12] Robert S. McNamara, *The Essence of Security* (New York: Harper & Row, 1968), pp. 57–60.

[13] *Ibid.*, pp. 57–58.

[14] Arthur M. Schlesinger, Jr., *A Thousand Days* (Boston: Houghton Mifflin, 1965), pp. 499, 500.

berstam, but it is one which emphasizes more the power of Congress.

In 1961 some White House aides were trying to slow the arms race. At that point the U.S. had 450 missiles, and McNamara was asking for 950, and the Chiefs were asking for 3,000. The White House people had quietly checked around and found that in effectiveness the 450 were the same as McNamara's 950.

"What about it, Bob?" Kennedy asked.

"Well, they're right," he answered.

"Well, then, why the 950, Bob?" Kennedy asked.

"Because that's the smallest number we can take up on the Hill without getting murdered," he answered.[15]

In summary, the massive build-up of Minuteman and Polaris missiles resulted from a decision made during a relatively limited time for a merely quantitative change. It is best explained by bureaucratic politics: bargaining among different actors within the executive branch over the share and degree of incremental change, with allies in Congress playing a supporting role. Although the missile build-up can also be fitted into the broader economic frameworks formed by the follow-on and bail-out imperatives, it is neither easy nor necessary to do so. Bureaucratic factors were the salient consideration for policymakers at the time, and they are a sufficient explanation for policy analysts looking back.

More generally, the particular quantity of any weapons system bought will ordinarily be the outcome of bureaucratic politics, of a complex bargaining process of negotiating, logrolling, and trading. Each military service wants more of what it already has or is scheduled to get. The services compete with one another and with other bureaucracies over their share of the budget. Quantitative disputes, being about merely numerical changes and generally familiar weapons, are especially amenable to bargaining and to precise compromises and trade-offs. The bargaining ordinarily takes place among actors within the executive branch; it is, as Samuel Huntington long ago

pointed out, "executive legislation."[16] Although each service has its own allies in Congress and among the corporations beyond, these normally play only a supporting role.

The Minuteman and Polaris build-up was the first important case of American missile procurement during the period since 1960. But the most important case, because of its potentially destabilizing impact on the strategic balance between the Soviet Union and the United States, was MIRV.[17]

Why did the United States develop and deploy MIRV? The official explanation is again a strategic one, and the usual argument has been that MIRV is needed to penetrate Soviet ABM systems. But this, like the economic explanations, does not explain why highly accurate, as opposed to merely multiple, warheads (MIRV instead of MRV) are needed. Nor does it explain why the U.S. continued to develop MIRV in the mid-1960s after the Soviets limited their development of ABM. A more accurate strategic explanation, suggested by the following censored congressional testimony, would argue that MIRV was developed in order to increase the U.S. capability to destroy Soviet missiles, and, in effect, to give the U.S. a first-strike capability.

Question (by Senator Mike Mansfield, D-Mont.):

Is it not true that the U.S. response to the discovery that the Soviets had made an initial deployment of an ABM system around Moscow and probably elsewhere was to develop the MIRV system for Minuteman and Polaris?

Answer (by Dr. John S. Foster, Director of Defense Research and Engineering):

Not entirely. The MIRV concept was originally generated to increase our targeting capability rather than to penetrate ABM defenses. In 1961–62 planning for targeting the Minuteman force it was found that the total number of aim points exceeded the number of Minuteman missiles. By splitting up the payload of a single missile (deleted) each (deleted) could be programmed (de-

---

[15] David Halberstam, "The Programming of Robert McNamara," *Harpers*, February 1971, p. 54. A similar account is given by Jerome B. Wiesner, President Kennedy's Special Assistant for Science and Technology, in his "Arms Control: Current Prospects and Problems," *Bulletin of the Atomic Scientists*, 26 (May 1970): 6.

[16] Samuel P. Huntington, *The Common Defense* (New York: Columbia University Press, 1961), pp. 146–66.

[17] For a detailed discussion of the MIRV case, see Herbert York, *Race to Oblivion: A Participant's View of the Arms Race* (New York: Simon & Schuster, 1970), pp. 173–87; and Ralph E. Lapp, *Arms beyond Doubt: The Tyranny of Weapons Technology* (New York: Cowles Book Co., 1970), pp. 17–34.

leted) allowing us to cover these targets with (deleted) fewer missiles. (Deleted.) MIRV was originally born to implement this payload split up (deleted). It was found that the previously generated MIRV concept could equally well be used against ABM (deleted).[18]

Although Secretary of Defense McNamara had rejected a first-strike targeting doctrine, the Air Force commanders, formally his subordinates, had not. They preferred a first-strike doctrine, with its double implication that the United States could win a war with the Soviet Union and that the Air Force would have the prime role in doing so, to a second-strike doctrine, which implied that the United States could only deter a war and that the Air Force would be only an equal of the Navy in the task. Against McNamara, the Air Force commanders could not achieve an official first-strike targeting doctrine for the United States; with MIRV, however, they could achieve a real first-strike targeting capability for the Air Force.[19] The initiation of MIRV in 1961–1962, then, can be explained by bureaucratic politics.

Furthermore, the research and development of MIRV in the mid-1960s was of course highly classified, so that knowledge of it would be kept from the Soviets. But the effect was also to keep knowledge of MIRV from Congress and the public.[20] In the early phases of the program, Defense officials did not have any need to build support in Congress and the public for large expenditures of funds. As a result, the MIRV program faced no political opposition, and it quietly progressed in accordance with technical and bureaucratic procedures of research and development internal to different organizations within the Defense Department.

The MIRV program may have been reinforced by another round of bureaucratic politics in late 1966. McNamara was attempting to prevent the procurement of ABM but was

meeting with the united opposition of the Joint Chiefs of Staff, who were supported by leading members of Congress. One of the main arguments of the proponents of ABM was that the Soviets were going ahead with their own ABM system. One way for McNamara to neutralize this argument was to go ahead with an American offensive system which had high penetration capabilities—i.e., MIRV.[21] Thus, in late 1966, MIRV procurement may have been the price for ABM postponement, just as, in late 1961, missile procurement was the price for manned bomber postponement. In each case, of course, the price bought only a delay: in the case of the manned bomber, almost a decade; in the case of ABM, less than a year.

The MIRV program continued to progress quietly in accordance with technical and bureaucratic procedures of research and development through 1967 and 1968. By the time the strategic implications of MIRV became public knowledge, it had already been tested, the production of Minuteman III and Poseidon missiles had already commenced and the conversion of Polaris-launching submarines into Poseidon ones had already begun.[22] Given this momentum generated by bureaucratic processes, the MIRV program could have been brought to a halt in 1969 or after only if the President or leading members of Congress had been willing to expend an extraordinary amount of political capital. And thus MIRV finally reached the point where bureaucratic pressures were reinforced by economic ones, where Dr. Foster, the Director of Defense Research and Engineering, could make before a congressional committee in 1970 an economic argument against stopping the MIRV program which was much like our earlier argument about production lines:

Another consequence of our stopping at this time would be financial. These programs I am discussing now have a number of years of research

---

[18] Quoted in Lapp, op. cit., p. 21.

[19] On the nuclear strategies of McNamara and the Air Force, see Alain C. Enthoven and K. Wayne Smith, How Much is Enough? Shaping the Defense Program, 1961–1969 (New York: Harper and Row, 1971), pp. 163–96; and William W. Kaufmann, The McNamara Strategy (New York: Harper & Row, 1964), chap. 2, an excerpt of which is reprinted in the present volume (pp. 67–74).

[20] F. A. Long, Science and the Military, Cornell University Peace Studies Program, Occasional Papers, no. 1 (Ithaca, N.Y.: Cornell University), pp. 11–12.

[21] See Morton H. Halperin, "The Decision to Deploy the ABM: Bureaucratic and Domestic Politics in the Johnson Administration," pp. 466–85 of this volume.

[22] See the discussion of MIRV before the Congressional Conference on the Military Budget and National Priorities (March 28 and 29, 1969), especially the statements by Jeremy J. Stone, George W. Rathjens, Leonard Rodberg, and Representative Robert L. Leggett (D-Calif.), in Erwin Knoll and Judith Nies McFadden, eds. American Militarism, 1970 (New York: Viking Press, 1969), pp. 70–82.

and development behind them and have also developed a significant production capability. . . . I do not see how we can justify the added expense that would be incurred as a result of keeping production capability on standby.[23]

Furthermore, once the United States had successfully tested MIRV, the Soviets could not be sure that the United States had not also deployed it. The Soviets then probably felt compelled to develop, test, and deploy their own MIRV; the Soviet program, in turn, reinforces the pressures behind the American one.

In summary, the procurement of MIRV, of highly accurate, as well as multiple, warheads, resulted from a developmental process over a relatively lengthy time. It is best explained by a combination of bureaucratic politics and bureaucratic processes: bargaining among different actors within the executive branch and standard operating procedures for research and development. Although the Minuteman III and Poseidon missile programs can be fitted into the broader economic framework formed by the follow-on imperative (but not by its bail-out counterpart), economic explanations do not capture the most important part of MIRV.

Bureaucratic politics may have structured another aspect of American missile procurement—i.e., the close parallelism of the Air Force and Navy programs. As Table 1 indicates, each service took the same steps at the same time: Minuteman and Polaris build-up in 1961; Minuteman III and Poseidon development in 1966; and production in 1968. Indeed, the first flight tests for Minuteman III and Poseidon occurred on the same day, August 16, 1968. It is as if the two services had reached an agreement on rough equality, a "minimax" solution, in regard to their respective progress in the prestigious mission of strategic offense. If so, the recent funding for development of the Navy's ULMS has imposed a considerable strain on the Air Force to achieve comparable funding for development of a super-MIRV or a mobile missile system.

The ULMS program is important in another sense. Given the necessity to maintain an invulnerable nuclear deterrent, a long-range, submarine-launched missile system is clearly

the most rational way to do so; for the next decade at least, its vulnerability to Soviet attack will be much less than that of land-based missiles, even with such Air Force gimmicks as ever-more-hardened silos or putting missiles on railroad cars. The present development and eventual procurement of ULMS, therefore, can readily be explained in strategic terms; ULMS is one of the few American weapons systems initiated since 1960 for which the best explanation is the strategic one. Bureaucratic and economic interests are present, of course, and many insure that the rational, strategic choice will in fact result. But, over-all, ULMS is a salutary reminder that not all cases of American weapons procurement can be reduced to bureaucratic and economic factors.

ANTIMISSILE PROCUREMENT AND DEMOCRATIC EXPLANATIONS

The ABM is, in many ways, the superlative case of weapons procurement in the period since 1960. In regard to the probable cost of a completed system, it would be the most expensive. In regard to the length of time that the system has been an issue (programs date back to 1955), it is the most extensive. In regard to the scope of actors participating in the decisionmaking process, it has been the most inclusive. And, in regard to the heat of the public debate over procurement, it has been the most intensive.[24]

Why did the United States buy the ABM? More specifically, why did the Johnson Administration in September 1967 propose the Sentinel ABM, and why did the Nixon Administration in March 1969 and later propose the Safeguard ABM? The official, strategic explanations have been many and varied. McNamara in 1967 argued that the ABM was needed to protect cities from China. Nixon and Laird in 1969 argued that it was needed to protect Minutemen from the Soviet Union. Later, they extended the proposed protection to some cities again. All of the justifications have been questioned by many strategists, sci-

---

[23] U.S. Congress, Senate, Committee on Foreign Relations, *ABM, MIRV, SALT, and the Nuclear Arms Race: Hearings before the Subcommittee on Arms Control*, 91st Cong., 2nd sess., 1970, p. 428.

[24] For detailed analyses of the ABM case, see Halperin, *op. cit.*; Aaron Wildavsky, "The Politics of ABM," *Commentary*, 48 (November 1969): pp. 53–63; and Abram Chayes and Jerome B. Wiesner, eds., *ABM: An Evaluation of the Decision to Deploy an Anti-ballistic Missile System* (New York: New American Library, 1969).

entists, and congressmen; the most decisive refutation is simply the argument that the ABM will not work, especially given the ease with which the Soviets could overload the system with a dense attack.

Bureaucratic explanations are more helpful. The Army saw the ABM as its way to get back into strategic missile programs, from which it had been excluded while the Air Force had Minuteman and the Navy had Polaris and Poseidon, and thus as its way to restore the bureaucratic balance of power. But, as long as the Army was alone in its support of ABM, not much happened. Furthermore, within the Army the air defense and missile defense organizations were not the dominant organizations (these were the ground combat forces); the large-scale deployment of ABM would redistribute bureaucratic power within the Army.

By 1966, however, the Air Force and the Navy each came to see the Army's ABM as the opening wedge and necessary condition for its own entry into the ABM field, and the Joint Chiefs of Staff adopted a unified position in support of ABM procurement. The Joint Chiefs, in turn, were supported by leading members of Congress. This confronted Secretary of Defense McNamara, who was opposed to ABM, with a difficult problem in November 1966, when he was due to make decisions about the next defense budget.[25] But, as we have suggested above, one of McNamara's responses was to trade the procurement of MIRV for the postponement of ABM. Another response was to place a great deal of emphasis on the prospects for successful arms control negotiations with the Soviet Union as grounds on which to justify postponement. What, then, brought about the decision in September 1967, less than a year later, to procure and deploy ABM?

At this point, a democratic explanation becomes most persuasive. President Johnson feared being vulnerable in the approaching election to charges from the Republicans that he had neglected the nation's security. John Kennedy in 1960 charged a "missile gap"; Lyndon Johnson in 1967 feared an "ABM gap."[26] One possible antidote to the image of gap-maker in a Soviet-American arms race was the image of

peacemaker in a Soviet-American arms control agreement. But, just as Khrushchev eliminated that possibility for Eisenhower and the Republicans in 1960, when he broke up the Paris summit meeting, so did Kosygin eliminate that possibility for Johnson and the Democrats in 1967, when he was totally unreceptive to American proposals concerning ABM limitation at the Glassboro summit meeting in June 1967. In September, McNamara announced the decision to procure and deploy ABM.

For the Nixon Administration's affirmative decision in March 1969 and later, a democratic explanation is plausible, but less so. Congress had to be pressured by the Administration to approve ABM, the reverse of the situation two years before (in the Senate in 1969, an amendment to prevent deployment was defeated by only two votes), and within the public there was much more criticism of ABM. But Nixon may have reasoned that by 1972 his political situation would resemble Johnson's in 1967 more than his own in 1969, and he may have feared being vulnerable to charges not only of having neglected the nation's security but of having wasted the military assets which he inherited from the Democrats.

By the time 1972 came around, however, even more political advantage was to be found in the image of peacemaker. The Nixon trip to China was the most dramatic result, but an arms control agreement with the Soviet Union also offered political advantage in the forthcoming presidential election. Why ABM, rather than some other weapons system, was the object of a cutback in planned procurement can be explained in several different ways. Perhaps the major factor was bureaucratic: it is easier to cut back the major system of a subordinate organization within a service (e.g., the missile defense forces within the Army) than to cut back the major system of the dominant organizations within a service (e.g., the bomber and missile forces within the Air Force and the carrier and missile submarine forces within the Navy).

In summary, the procurement of ABM and the limitation imposed on that procurement resulted from a political process involving an unusually wide scope of actors over an unusually great length of time. The major milestones in that process (1967, 1969, and 1972) are best explained by electoral politics, by the

25 See Halperin, op. cit.
26 See ibid. and Ralph E. Lapp, The Weapons Culture (Baltimore: Penguin, 1969), pp. 150, 151.

efforts of Presidents to satisfy the electorate and to win the next election. Although the Spartan missile portion of the ABM program can be fitted into the broader economic frameworks formed by the follow-on and bail-out imperatives, economic explanations would have predicted procurement of somewhat more Spartans than will probably occur in fact.

CANCELED PROCUREMENT AND ECLECTIC EXPLANATIONS

Any satisfactory analysis of policy outcomes within an issue area must account not only for those outcomes which did occur but also for those which, despite similar conditions, did not. In regard to aerospace weapons systems, an analysis must account for the two major cases of nonprocurement or canceled procurement in the period since 1960. These were the B-70 heavy bomber and the Skybolt air-to-surface missile, designed to be launched from heavy bombers.[27] Superficially, at least, economic explanations, such as the follow-on and bail-out imperatives, and bureaucratic explanations stressing the dominant role of the bomber generals within the Air Force would have predicted large-scale production of the B-70 and Skybolt.

Why did the United States cancel the B-70 and Skybolt? A strategic explanation, focusing on the vulnerability of the manned bomber and on its low cost-effectiveness versus Minuteman and Polaris, might seem quite sufficient (although similar strategic considerations have not been sufficient to bring about the cancellation of the B-1). Such strategic factors may have been reinforced by bureaucratic politics—i.e., McNamara's determination to establish his authority over the military services and over the traditional autonomy of their procurement practices. A similar argument has been made to explain McNamara's insistence on commonality between the Air Force and Navy versions of the F-111, another case which occurred at the same time, 1961–1962.[28] Together, strategic and bureaucratic factors seem to account for the cancellations.

[27] On these two cases, see Enthoven and Smith, *op. cit.*, pp. 243–62. On Skybolt, see also Richard E. Neustadt, *Alliance Politics* (New York: Columbia University Press, 1970).
[28] Art, *op. cit.*

In the case of the B-70, however, cancellation came at the cost of compensation. First, as the account by Schlesinger suggests, the Air Force and its allies in Congress had to be compensated for the cancellation of the B-70 with a massive missile build-up, with its attendant costs of a Soviet build-up and an arms race. Second, as the follow-on imperative suggests, North American had to be compensated for the cancellation of the B-70 with another major contract, in this case the Apollo moon program.

The cancellation of Skybolt a year later does not seem to have exacted such a price. The Air Force and its allies in Congress did not receive any obvious compensation (although one could imagine the continuation of the Minuteman build-up and of the MIRV program as part of an over-all compromise). Douglas, which was a minor contractor at the time, did not immediately receive another major contract comparable to Skybolt. This suggests that the compensation pattern for minor contractors (less than $500 million in military and space contracts per year) may be different from the pattern for major ones (more than $1 billion in military and space contracts per year), and that there may be a sort of class system for weapons contractors.

In summary, then, canceled procurement is best explained by eclectic accounts. Strategic analysis and bureaucratic politics can enact a cancellation, but when a dominant military organization and a major aerospace corporation are involved, bureaucratic politics and economic imperatives will also exact a compensation. Such considerations would predict, for example, that any successful effort in the mid-1970s to cancel the B-1 would be confronted on the morrow of victory with a super-MIRV for the Strategic Air Command and more space shuttles for North American Rockwell.

THE FUTURE OF AMERICAN WEAPONS PROCUREMENT

The analysis of weapons procurement presented in this essay may have other implications for the future. Table 1 indicates that recently the pressure on the U.S. government has become especially intense. In 1972 the Nixon Administration was confronted with the impending phase-out of the F-111 program of General Dynamics and the C-5A program of

Lockheed-Georgia, and thus with the impending opening up of two major production lines. The first was in an important state in the Electoral College, Texas; the second was the largest industrial enterprise in the southeastern United States.[29] The Administration temporarily resolved its dilemmas with a contract to General Dynamics for twelve additional F-111s and a contract to Lockheed-Georgia for twenty additional C-130s. But, unless the Administration decides to buy yet additional numbers of these older aircraft, it will again be confronted with the same dilemmas in 1973. At the same time, a third production line, Boeing, will open up. How will the Administration fill the contract gap?

One answer might seem to lie in conversion of production to commercial aircraft. But here past experience suggests that the cure would be worse than the disease. Thus, General Dynamics in the early 1960s entered the commercial aircraft market with the Convair 880, only to lose so much money that the F-111 contract was needed to save the corporation from bankruptcy. Similarly, Lockheed in the early 1970s entered the market with the L-1011, only to drive Rolls Royce into bankruptcy and consequently Lockheed itself into a position in which only governmental guarantees of bank

[29] Berkeley Rice, "What Price Lockheed?" *New York Times Magazine*, May 9, 1971, p. 24.

loans saved it from bankruptcy. Even the government's extraordinary effort to save the L-1011 will not solve the problem of Lockheed-Georgia, to say nothing of any distant problem of Lockheed–Missiles and Space, which is located in northern California. For the L-1011 is produced at a third, mainly commercial, Lockheed division, Lockheed-California, which is located in southern California. Conversion might seem more plausible for Boeing, already an established producer of superior commercial aircraft. But its major candidate for a new commercial aircraft, the SST, was canceled by Congress in 1971. Nor is conversion of production away from aerospace to other sections, such as mass urban transportation or waste disposal systems, promising or likely.

The follow-on imperative, however, would suggest other answers. For General Dynamics in the next year or two, it would predict a major contract for the Air Force lightweight fighter, now [1972] only being planned. For Lockheed-Georgia, it would predict a major contract for the STOL transport, also now being planned. And for Boeing, it would predict a super-MIRV, if there is no revival of the SST. Then, at last, with each of the eight major production lines safely supported by a major governmental contract for the remainder of the 1970s, the follow-on imperative will have done its work and can be laid to rest.

MILITARY-INDUSTRIAL SIMPLICITIES, COMPLEXITIES, AND REALITIES

CHARLES WOLF, JR.

Much of the literature on the "military-industrial complex" has been simplistic, laden with conspiracy theories, and deficient in scholarly analysis. In reality, the military-industrial complex is more pluralistic than monolithic, is often ineffective and impotent, and is probably as motivated by concern for national interests as are its critics. The limited political potency of the MIC has been demonstrated in recent years by high unemployment rates in the aerospace industry, a sharp reduction in military procurement since the late 1960s, and reduced defense budgets in real dollars and in the percentage of the Gross National Product. By forming a framework for analysis and by examining the underlying premises of previous discussion of the MIC, Wolf demonstrates the complexities of the issues that face our nation. Charles Wolf, Jr., is a senior economist at The RAND Corporation. His publications include United States Policy and the Third World: Problems and Analysis *(1967) and* Rebellion and Authority: An Analytic Essay on Insurgent Conflicts *(with Nathan Leites, 1970).*

I

One of the central questions to which this article is addressed is whether and to what extent the military-industrial complex (MIC) is an obstacle to arms control. As posed, the question assumes that there *is* something that can accurately be referred to as a "military-industrial complex," and that the term connotes something clearly (and similarly) understood by readers. The first assumption is at least debatable; the second assumption is much less debatable because it is much more assuredly wrong.

Consider three different meanings frequently ascribed to the term, tacitly or explicitly.

The first I will characterize as a *primitive monolithic* (PM) view of the MIC. A typical formulation of this view is advanced in a re-

cent book on the MIC.[1] According to its author, the MIC is "an outgrowth of a new . . . concept of national purpose—global expansion," whose effect has been "to *weld together* those elitist elements at home which have a stake in militarism—the Armed Forces, a group of legislators, industrialists, government officials, the labor hierarchy, an important segment of academia—into . . . the military-industrial complex." In its behavior, the MIC seeks to "manufacture a public stance of hard-line anti-communism." It also "withholds information and misinforms the public . . . [and]

[1] Sidney Lens, *The Military-Industrial Complex* (Philadelphia and Kansas City, 1970). All quotations are from pp. 99–100; italics have been added. Other books of the same genre include Richard J. Barnet, *The Economy of Death* (New York, 1969), and Erwin Knoll and J. N. McFadden, eds., *American Militarism, 1970* (New York, 1969).

Reprinted from The Military Industrial Complex: A Reassessment, *ed. Sam C. Sarkesian (Beverly Hills, Calif.: Sage Publications, 1972), pp. 3–23, by permission of the publisher. Minor editorial changes have been made.*

Author's Note: *Any views expressed in this paper are those of the author. They should not be interpreted as reflecting the views of The RAND Corporation or the official opinion or policy of any of its governmental or private research sponsors.*

This paper was prepared as an invited contribution to the University of Chicago's seminar series on Arms Control and Foreign Policy, Chicago, December 3, 1971.

inhibits the process of dissent." The MIC, "far from assuring peace, . . . develops a momentum for war. The very preparation for war has become an independent factor in promoting it."

A milder version of the same view is advanced, though not uniformly, in Adam Yarmolinsky's recent study, which speaks of "the coincidence of self-interest, in regard to military expansion, between Congress and the military-industrial establishment."[2]

A second meaning, which I will characterize as a *primitive pluralistic* (PP) view of the MIC, was recently advanced by Soviet writers in the *Literaturnaya Gazeta* to explain publication of the Pentagon Papers by certain American newspapers. According to this view, the MIC's industrial arm has two components: one principally concerned with producing conventional arms used in Indochina; the other consisting of the chief suppliers of strategic weapons. The two components have differing interests, which are notably reflected in the competition between them for defense expenditures. This conflict within the MIC, combined with a further split between the conventional-weapons part of the MIC and the "civilian-industrial complex," led to publication of the Pentagon Papers, according to the PP view.[3] The aspect of PP that is germane to the subject of this article is the perception that the MIC is divided, that it has splits within it, and that there are some (in this case, the "civilian" complex) effective counterweights against it.

I do not mean to caricature these views. They are held, and quite firmly, by a number of people. Yet they seem to me to be quite wide of the mark, simplistic and misleading formulations of phenomena which are more complex and diffuse. Let me suggest some of the complexities, embodying them in a third view that seems to me more nearly correct.

The so-called MIC consists of many different "turfs," with differing and often conflicting interests, indicators, perceptions, managers, and behavioral patterns. Three turfs are occupied by the *military services*. Their primary focus is on national security, among the country's na-tional goals. The services are also concerned with preserving and, if possible, raising their budgets, and their budgetary *shares* relative to the other services. Thus there is competition, sometimes excessive, among them, not only for budgets, but for roles and missions which get reflected in budgetary shares: competition between the Air Force and the Navy for strategic missions as well as for tactical air missions; between the Army and the Air Force for close air support; and between the Army and the Marines for air mobile *versus* amphibious forces, respectively. This rivalry can be perverse in various ways, not excluding logrolling. It can also be benign, a source of discipline which tends to keep each of the services from overstating a position or making an excessive claim on resources for research and development or weapons systems acquisition. Both the perversities and the benefactions are part of the complex reality of the MIC. Concentrating on either one to the exclusion of the other is simplistic and misleading.

Another part of the so-called MIC, *defense industry*, is itself differentiated along lines that do not exclude, but are not confined to, those suggested by PP. The defense industry includes aerospace industrial firms, for which a major share of total sales is to the Defense Department; large conglomerates, often also in high-technology fields, but usually with only a minority of their total sales going to the DOD; and various other firms, including small suppliers of components, manufacturers of small arms, and segments of the automotive industry for whom defense procurement is a negligible part of total business. The occupants and management of the industrial "turf" are assuredly concerned with contracts, sales, and profits (although, as the recent example of Lockheed suggests, and from other data we will discuss later, their concerns often yield quite mixed and discouraging results). Their interests also include pushing technology forward, particularly where spillover benefits may be realized in the civilian sector, as in the case of computers and jumbo-jet aircraft technology.

The interests encompassed within the defense industrial turf are often in sharp competition with one another. Competitive bidding is evident on developmental contracts, but less evident on procurement contracts. Lockheed's

[2] Adam Yarmolinsky, *The Military Establishment* (New York, 1971), p. 6.
[3] *New York Times*, July 15, 1971, p. 6; and *Time*, July 26, 1971.

recently precarious financial predicament provides other examples. Several competing firms in the aerospace industry publicly urged that the government *not* provide financial assistance to bail Lockheed out. At least one offered to provide a comparable aircraft for those airlines that had placed orders for the L-1011, if Lockheed went under; it hoped to remove this part of the Lockheed case for emergency governmental assistance and thus to remove Lockheed as a competitor!

Another of the MIC's turfs is occupied by those senators and congressmen who exercise a major influence in the congressional authorization and appropriations committees responsible for military affairs. That many of them are keenly mindful of the interests of their local constituencies, as well as of the power that they themselves exercise, does not gainsay the genuine concern they feel for the security and well-being of the country or the considerable knowledge and expertise they have acquired concerning national security matters. Their concerns and motives are, in other words, mixed, though not necessarily more so than those of the rest of us. Sometimes the interests and concerns of these legislative leaders accord with those of the military services and of the defense industries. And sometimes divergences arise. Examples of divergences between the congressional leadership and some of the military services include the F-111, the Fast Deployment Logistics Ships, the recently accelerated rate of military pay increases, and the allocation of resources for the maintenance of local military bases rather than for procurement or other uses.

One can adumbrate other turfs that are usually closely associated with the MIC, notably various private research institutions and individual members of the scientific and academic communities. (As a slight digression, it may be worth mentioning that, among the individual and scientific experts who testified in connection with the Safeguard ABM system, as many consultants of the Department of Defense were opponents as were supporters of the Administration's 1969 proposal!)

In any event, even this brief sketch is sufficient to support a few central points about the complexity of the MIC.

1. Its structure is highly pluralistic. The MIC abounds with separate turfs that frequently conflict with one another and provide rivalry and competition as well as convergence or collusion.

2. Occupants and managers of these turfs are concerned with national welfare and national security interests as well as with local and constituent interests, and they do not perceive any serious conflict between the two.

The reality of the MIC is complex, not simple; pluralistic, not monolithic; sometimes effective and potent, sometimes ineffective and impotent; no less motivated by concern for national interests than its critics, and no less motivated by a mixture of other motives than its critics.

II

In support of these complexities about the MIC, let me cite a few numerical realities by way of further refutation of the simplistic views, PM and PP, about the MIC.

Consider three major public issues of the last few years that were conceived of as involving the deepest interests and commitments of the MIC: (1) the Safeguard ABM deployment in 1969; (2) the Cooper-Church amendment barring funds for military operations in Cambodia in June 1970; and (3) appropriations for development of the supersonic transport in December 1970. All three were regarded as symbolic of the interests and influence of the MIC. With respect to two of the three issues, the position putatively favored by the MIC won in the congressional voting. An interesting question arises as to what one would have predicted about the voting by state congressional delegations, assuming the adoption as a prior hypothesis of either the Primitive Monolithic or the Primitive Pluralistic view of the MIC?

It seems reasonable that one would have predicted, on the basis of these views, that the proportion of Senate and House votes in support of the putative MIC position on each of these issues would have been closely associated with the relative size of Defense Department contracts by state. This prediction would assuredly follow from the PM view for all three issues. It would also seem to follow from the PP view, at least in the case of the SST.

What do the data show?

If one ranks the states in order of dollars of defense contract awards per capita (for 1969), and compares that ranking with separate rankings of the states in accordance with the percentage of their combined House and Senate votes (a) *for* the Safeguard deployment, (b) *against* Cooper-Church, and (c) *for* the SST appropriation, one finds that the rank-order correlation coefficients are −0.12, 0.1 and 0.1, respectively. None of these correlation coefficients is significantly different from 0![4] The results provide no evidence of a relationship between defense expenditures by states and congressional voting on these key issues.

A second set of quantitative data, also inconsistent with the simplistic views of the MIC discussed earlier and with the exaggerated rhetoric that is sometimes bandied about concerning the arms "race," relates to U.S. defense budgetary expenditures.

In FY 1961, the last year of tight Eisenhower defense budgets, U.S. defense outlays were about $45 billion, which was approximately 8.8 percent of the GNP and a little over 44 percent of total federal governmental expenditures. In 1969, defense expenditures had risen to nearly $79 billion, about 8.7 percent of the GNP and nearly 42 percent of total federal outlays. For FY 1971, defense expenditures were down to $72 billion, about 7 percent of the GNP and less than 36 percent of total federal budgetary expenditures. Moreover, in constant 1961 prices, defense expenditures in fiscal 1971 were about $55 billion, or just $10 billion more than they were in 1961. And the budget for *strategic* offensive and defensive forces in 1971 was only *half* the 1961 amount, in constant dollars.

For FY 1973, defense outlays rose to about $76.5 billion. The increase was equivalent to the extent of inflation in the economy as a whole. Hence, in constant prices the real value of FY 1973 outlays was about the same as that of FY 1971 outlays, and the proportion of the GNP was slightly *below* that of the preceding two years.

Thus, while the level of defense expenditures in 1971 was still extremely large, it represented the smallest percentage of total governmental expenditures and the smallest percentage of GNP since the start of the Korean War in 1950. Even more important, the rates of change are negative and substantial. The military share of governmental and total resources has gone dramatically *downward* at the same time as the amount and the shares devoted to health and education have gone dramatically upward, from less than $2.5 billion, or 2.5 percent of federal governmental expenditures, in 1961 to $23 billion, or 11.5 percent of total governmental expenditures, in 1971.

To say, as some do, that military expenditures are "out of control," or that the MIC is a powerful and effective obstacle to limiting arms expenditures, is inconsistent with these data.

A third set of data, which refutes some of the popular imagery about the MIC, is contained in a recent report to Congress by the General Accounting Office (GAO) on defense industry profits.[5] The GAO study showed that profit rates, before federal income taxes, realized on equity capital investment (which excludes facilities contributed by the government) were almost exactly the same for thirty-two randomly selected large defense contractors doing *more* than 10 percent of their total business with the Defense Department as for thirteen randomly selected contractors doing *less* than 10 percent of their total business with the Defense Department. The weighted averages for the 1966–1969 period were 22.7 percent and 23.1 percent, respectively.[6] The result nicely accords with what economic theory would suggest, and is sharply at variance with exaggerated rhetoric about high profits realized in defense contracting.

---

[4] I am indebted for these computations to Timothy V. Wolf. The computations are based on pooling House and Senate votes for each state delegation on each of the three issues. The legislation on the ABM Safeguard system was S.2546 and H.R. 14000 (*Congressional Quarterly*, August 8, 1969, and October 10, 1969); for Cooper-Church, H.R. 15628 (*ibid.*, July 17, 1970, and January 15, 1971); and for the SST, H.R. 17755 (*ibid.*, December 11, 1970, and January 15, 1971). The figures on defense expenditures per capita by state are taken from the *Statistical Abstract of the United States for 1969*.

The significance of the rank-order correlation coefficient, r_s, was tested by the value of t, where

$$t = r_s \sqrt{(n-2)/(1-r_s^2)},$$

with $n-2$ degrees of freedom, and $n = 50$.

[5] U.S. General Accounting Office, *Defense Industry Profits Study*, report to Congress by the Comptroller General of the United States, 92nd Cong., 1st sess., March 17, 1971.

[6] *Ibid.*, pp. 66 and 67.

III

I have so far considered some simplicities, several complexities, and a few numerical realities pertaining to the MIC. Let me now turn to the question of obstacles in the way of arms control and the MIC's role among these obstacles. The position I am going to advance has three components.

1. First, some degree of arms limitation is already in operation—the data on defense expenditures presented in the preceding section strongly suggest that "arms race" metaphors are far from the reality that has obtained in the last half-dozen or ten years.

2. There are numerous and substantial obstacles in the way of more stringent arms limitations—not infinite and not insuperable, just numerous and large.

3. Among these obstacles, the role of the MIC is distinctly limited. Emphasizing it with colorful rhetoric and slogans does a disservice to arms limitations because it turns attention away from the major obstacles, on which serious work and effort are needed, including the Soviet Union's own MIC and the question of whether and how it can be influenced. In fact, one of the extraordinary aspects of the MIC issue is the extent to which sloganeering and invective about it provide an escape from, and a substitute for, careful work on arms limitations problems.

What are some of these major issues and problems?

At the core of the arms limitation problem is the relationship between U.S. behavior with respect to weapons development, deployment, operations, and budgets, and that of the Soviet Union and the Chinese. Consider three fundamentally different models.[7] One model postulates positive interaction: the more the U.S. does with respect to one or more of these variables, the more the Soviets or/and the Chinese are likely to do; and the less, the less. (Furthermore, the interactions may be contemporaneous or lagged.)

The second model is autonomous: what the Soviets or/and the Chinese do in the military field depends largely on technological oppor-

tunities, organizational and bureaucratic continuity, competing resource claims at home, and the scale and composition of economic growth. Consequently, changes in U.S. defense efforts will have little or no effect.

A third model implies negative interaction: if the United States does too little, with respect to offensive or defensive capabilities, or strategic or general-purpose forces, the Soviets may be stimulated to expand their own efforts so as to move from "parity" or "sufficiency" to "superiority," perhaps for reasons of political advantage as much as military advantage.

Other possible formulations involve elements of all three of these models, and there is some degree of simultaneous interaction between U.S. behavior and that of the Soviets, the Chinese, or both. The issue is still further complicated by the fact that differing relationships may apply to different military activities. For example, a different relationship may apply to R&D activities and outlays, from that which applies to the deployment of strategic offensive or defensive systems, to general-purpose forces, or to defense budgets as a whole. Choosing among the different relationships requires a great deal of serious study and analysis, although in fact very little analytical effort has been devoted to this problem. It seems to be the case that some evidence can be cited in support of several of these quite different models, especially with respect to different parts of our own military efforts and those of the Soviet Union.

The important point to make is that, without a better understanding of these relationships, as well as more accurate and timely information-gathering and analysis to keep constant track of whether and how these relationships may change, we are ill-prepared to pursue arms limitations very far. In the absence of understanding, good intentions may have no effects, or even perverse effects. Critics of the American MIC seldom ponder whether and how the Soviet MIC might be influenced, especially if it has the characteristics they attribute to our own.

A second major problem concerns the pairing or sequencing of limitations on strategic offensive and defensive systems. Should an effort be made to obtain a limitation agreement with respect to ABM, with or without limitations on strategic offensive weapons, or

---

[7] In characterizing these models, I am indebted to analytical work under way by my colleague, John Despres. I have also drawn from an earlier paper of mine, "Military-Industrial Complexities," *Bulletin of the Atomic Scientists*, February 1971.

in what proportions? This is one of those para-doxical situations where stricter *limitations* may or may not be equivalent to more effec-tive arms *control*. For example, in a crisis sit-uation, it can be argued that there is greater stability (and hence "control") if both sides' offensive forces are reasonably well protected, either actively or passively, so that neither side is tempted to strike first. A situation in which both sides have some defensive, as well as offensive, forces may thus be more stable and "controlled" than one in which both sides have only offensive forces. And a situation in which one side has *both* offensive and defensive forces, and the other side has *only* offensive forces, may be risky for both, as well as acutely un-comfortable for that "other" side.

Furthermore, the incentives toward nuclear proliferation—which is a major potential source of arms *de*control—by other countries (for example, India, and/or Pakistan or Japan) might be increased if the United States and the Soviets were to confine their strategic capa-bilities to offensive forces only. Again, the risks entailed may be worth taking, particularly if one is reasonably convinced of the positive interaction model described earlier. But at least one would like to be fully aware of what the risks and the benefits of moving in this direc-tion are. And a clearer awareness requires a lot of hard work and careful study.

Many other difficult substantive problems affect the type and extent of arms control that should be sought in the strategic area. For ex-ample, should the United States, by joint agreement or even unilaterally, place less re-liance on a three-pronged strategic force (the so-called triad, which consists of land-based missiles, strategic bombers, and missile-carry-ing submarines) and instead limit the U.S. strategic force to only one of these compo-nents?

Enthusiastic advocates of arms control some-times answer this question by advocating a one-pronged force on the grounds that this would be more "limited," and hence presum-ably better. But would it? Each component of the triad has different system characteristics. Each differs in the accuracy with which it can hit targets and in its vulnerability to attack. Moreover, each component of the triad pre-sents different problems and uncertainties for an attacking force, thereby complicating the

attacker's task and reducing the incentive to attack. Furthermore, a "monad" instead of the triad would be more vulnerable to the risk of a technological breakthrough that might criti-cally diminish the effective deterrence that such a stripped force could provide. Indeed, the incentive for one side to strive for a tech-nological breakthrough would be enhanced if the other side's force were confined to a single component.

So the single-pronged force, though in one sense more "limited," might be distinctly more destabilizing to the balance of military forces.

Or consider other questions outside the stra-tegic area, which also require careful study and analysis if progress is to be made. Con-sider the proposal that has recently been ad-vanced of withdrawing both Soviet and U.S. naval forces from the Mediterranean. Currently the United States has its Sixth Fleet in the Mediterranean with backup provided by the Second Fleet in the Atlantic. The Soviet Union now maintains an almost equal number of naval vessels in the Mediterranean, with backup provided from its Black Sea fleet. Whereas the U.S. Mediterranean fleet is built around attack-carrier task forces, the Soviet Mediterranean fleet has no attack aircraft carriers, but em-phasizes missile cruisers, destroyers, and attack submarines. The Soviet navy relies for its air support on land-based aircraft in the Mediter-ranean area. This land-based force has grown appreciably in recent years, and is larger than U.S. land-based air forces in the area.[8]

Under these circumstances, would an ar-rangement in which Soviet naval forces with-drew inside the Bosporus to the Black Sea, and U.S. forces withdrew west of Gibraltar, tend to ease tensions and increase prospects for peace in the Middle East? Or would such a move have the reverse effect? Either of these effects could ensue, depending on a number of other circumstances: the further deployment of land-based aircraft by the Soviets or the United States; the expansion or diminution of military assistance to Israel and to the Arab countries; and the pattern of over-all relation-ships between the United States and the Soviet Union outside the Middle Eastern area.

All of these examples support one central

[8] See *The Military Balance, 1970–71* (London, 1971); and Lawrence L. Whetten, *The Soviet Pres-ence in the Eastern Mediterranean* (New York, 1971).

point. The difficulties and obstacles that lie in the way of arms control are not governed, or in most cases heavily influenced, by the military-industrial complex. The problems are just hard and complex, and the constraints often numerous and severe, quite apart from the putative role of the MIC as an organized pressure group. To say that the MIC prevents or hinders government action toward controlling arms in these fields is both to exaggerate its influence and to underestimate the fundamental complexities of the problems themselves. Slogans blaming the MIC for our failure to move farther in the direction of arms control not only do the military an unwarranted disservice but hinder, rather than help, in finding solutions by diverting attention and effort from the real problems.

While difficult substantive problems unrelated to the MIC complicate the achievement of meaningful arms control, there also are circumstances in the international environment that warrant considerable caution in reducing our military strength, if damaging consequences for international peace are to be avoided. What are some of these circumstances?

As the United States moves toward accelerated withdrawal of its forces from Vietnam and diminished deployment and basing overseas, what we find in the international arena is an expanding Soviet presence in the Middle East, as well as increasing evidence of such expansion (in bases and in influence) in the Asian area as well. In congressional testimony, a group of leading British and American students of the Soviet Union emphasized the high likelihood that a more aggressive and expansionist Soviet policy would be applied throughout the world as the U.S.S.R.'s strategic military capabilities reach equality or superiority compared with those of the United States.[9]

Another serious hazard lies in the prospect of nuclear proliferation, which does not seem to be receding. Nor can we say that the possibilities of conventional conflict (for example, between North and South Korea), let alone of insurgent wars in the Third World, are negligible. In light of the Nixon Doctrine and for

other reasons, the likelihood of our involvement in such conflicts is much less than it formerly was. We are committed, and wisely so, to placing greater reliance on the capacities of friendly and allied countries for their *self*-defense. And the threshold of provocation that would involve us in direct military support of their efforts is likely to be much higher in the future than it has been. Nevertheless, we should not adopt an ostrich policy if we want to contribute to progress in international peace-keeping and stability.

For all of these reasons, military considerations and substantial military capabilities remain important ingredients of responsible policy and conduct by the United States.

In summary, the main obstacles to arms control seem to me to be twofold: the difficulty and complexity of specific arms control issues and opportunities themselves (not insuperable, but difficult and complex and requiring serious study and analysis); and the realities of the international arena, including the growth of Soviet military capabilities in general-purpose, as well as in strategic, forces. Neither of these real impediments to arms control is illuminated or indeed significantly influenced by the imagery and rhetoric that accompanies clichés about the "military-industrial complex."

I recently had an opportunity to discuss certain general problems pertaining to arms control with a Soviet official who expressed concern about the power and influence of the industrial part of the U.S. military-industrial complex. He acknowledged that the military establishment in the Soviet Union, like that in the United States, presents opposition to arms control, and he felt that this opposition is similar in the two systems. The contrast, he said, lies in the opposition that is provided by the industrial part of the U.S. MIC, which does not correspond to any such opposition in the Soviet Union. As far as the U.S. defense industry is concerned, he went on, it differs from that of the Soviet Union because of the profits that it might stand to lose, and because it is not subject to governmental discipline and control. On the other hand, in the Soviet Union, he asserted, the defense industry is secure in knowing that it will be fully employed in any event, and so does not have the powerful incentive to persist in military production once the government decides otherwise.

---

[9] U.S. Congress, Senate, Committee on Government Operations, *Hearings before the Subcommittee on National Security and International Operations*, 91st Cong., December 1969–May 1970.

Since variants of this view are current in the United States as well, it is well worth examining. The argument does not stand up to critical examination. For example, in the United States, the distinctly limited political potency of the defense industry is indicated by a number of glaring facts: over 100,000 engineers and technologists are currently unemployed; the high rate of general unemployment in the aerospace industry is well above that in the nation as a whole; especially sharp reductions have been made in defense budgetary expenditures for strategic offensive and defensive forces, as noted earlier; the stock market has heavily discounted the market prices of defense industry stocks; and two U.S. senators from the state of California, where the aerospace industry is concentrated, are vociferous opponents of the MIC and advocates of arms control!

On the other hand, if one inquires about similar sorts of indicators of the limited influence of the high-technology defense industry in the Soviet Union, it is much harder to come by. Instead, what one finds in recent years is buoyant expansion (prosperity) in these sectors of the Soviet economy, an expansion amply fueled by large and growing outlays for research and development and procurement. In fact, given the profound inertial momentum of large organizations under *any* system, one may well be skeptical that the public sector defense industry in the Soviet Union will be nearly as docile in accepting reduced arms expenditures as the private sector defense industry has been in the United States.

IV

In conclusion, I would not want to leave the impression that the military establishment and industrial firms in the United States are likely to be other than cautious, reserved, and skeptical toward arms control. Furthermore, the previous discussion has already suggested a number of reasons why such caution and skepticism are warranted. But there is a more important point to be stressed. If and as the basis for such caution and skepticism diminishes— e.g., by more careful attention and better answers to the serious issues and problems noted earlier, and by the progress of improved understanding and increased contacts between the

Soviets and ourselves—it seems to me evident that opposition by the MIC to further arms limitations would be minor and ineffectual.

In an effort to keep matters in perspective, I would make a still stronger argument. The MIC is a much *weaker* source of opposition to lower defense budgets and increased arms limitations than are "other industrial complexes" (OICs)[10] to the reduction of costs and increases in efficiency in their own special domains. Let me be specific.

Both education and health care are "industrial complexes" whose scale is of the same magnitude as that of the entire defense sector. The educational-industrial complex involves annual outlays of about $65 billion, and health care expenditures are somewhat above that figure. If one looks inside the large black box that is the educational-industrial complex, one finds a most impressive and depressing result from the considerable research undertaken in the last ten years: cognitive measures of educational effectiveness are not consistently influenced by increased resource allocations for education. The result seems to apply at primary, secondary, and higher educational levels, and applies whether the increased resource allocations are in the form of teachers, buildings, or technological aids of one sort or another. Evidently, social, family, and environmental factors are the main factors affecting cognitive performance, not educational inputs.

An obvious inference follows from this depressing result: some, perhaps substantial, *reductions* in resource inputs and costs should be possible without incurring any loss of educational outputs, at least as concerns the cognitive dimensions of educational performance. And there is no clear evidence to suggest that *non*cognitive measures, fuzzy and primitive though they be, are reliably linked with the formal educational process. One source of substantial savings would be to differentiate among teachers' salaries according to their relative market values. Mathematics and science teachers in high schools, for example, would get higher pay, and teachers of physical education, home economics, and history, with comparable seniority, would get lower pay.

I dare say that the power of teachers' unions and school administrators to resist this or other

[10] See "Military-Industrial Complexities," *Bulletin of the Atomic Scientists*, February 1971, pp. 20–22.

means of lowering costs and increasing efficiency in education is vastly greater than the power of the military-industrial complex to resist arms limitations!

Turning to health care, one finds a similarly depressing picture of high costs and limited effectiveness. For example, if one compares the performance of the health industry in Great Britain under its National Health Service with the health industry in the United States, the picture that emerges is severely prejudicial to the United States. Infant mortality and maternal death rates are appreciably lower in Britain than in the United States; twenty-five years ago the discrepancy was substantial and in the opposite direction, with Britain's rates appreciably above those in the United States. As Anthony Lewis has pointed out in a striking series of articles in the *New York Times*, if one looks at seven leading causes of death in the United States and Great Britain over the past two and a half decades (respiratory tuberculosis, diabetes, arteriosclerotic disease, heart disease [including coronary, hypertensive heart disease] influenza, pneumonia, and bronchitis), in every case the death rate has risen less, or fallen farther, in Great Britain than in the United States.[11]

At the same time, the costs of health care in the United States have been rising much faster than those in Great Britain. Currently nearly 7 percent of the GNP is expended on health care in the United States; in Great Britain the figure is less than 5 percent. How might costs be lowered and efficiency improved in the health industry? One possibility surely lies in the substitution of paramedical for medical personnel, an innovation which has progressed much more rapidly in the military than in civilian medical care. In this connection, it is worth noting that Horton's recent study of medical productivity in the Navy showed a much higher rate of increase (measured in terms of patient care per physician day) than that which occurred in the private medical economy as a whole.[12] Another possibility lies in allowing the capacity of existing medical schools for producing doctors to expand more rapidly, as well as in allowing greater freedom of entry into the field.

Once again, opposition by the health-industrial complex—in this case, the American Medical Association, the County Medical Associations throughout the country, the American Hospital Association, and so on—is a much more potent obstacle to innovation and change than is the MIC in relation to arms limitation.

The point is not just *tu quoque*. When we talk about the MIC, arms limitations, and obstacles to arms control, it is important to maintain perspective and balance if simplicities are to be avoided and realities appreciated. A reminder about the "other-industrial complexes" can contribute to such a perspective, as well as to a lessening of the shrill rhetoric that abounds these days.

[11] *New York Times*, October 2, 1971.

[12] Melvin E. Horton, *"An Economic Analysis of Progress in the Medical Care of the U.S. Navy and Marine Corps Personnel"* (Ph.D. diss., University of Washington, 1966).

TOWARD AN ALL-VOLUNTEER MILITARY

MORRIS JANOWITZ

A volunteer military of large size (1.5 million men and women) is almost totally alien to American historical experience. When the United States has had large active-duty military forces, there has been the draft. When it has had small military forces, the recruitment system has been a voluntary one. Janowitz deals with the problems of the large all-volunteer force, and his discussion of ten-year retirement, pension transfer, general officer force-outs, inefficiency in military education, and, most important, the requirements to redefine the profession provide valuable food for thought. Can the United States learn from the Israeli experience, or the British or the Swedish? These and other issues make this article relevant to the problems facing the military and the general society in the era of voluntarism. Morris Janowitz is a Professor of Sociology at the University of Chicago. His major works include The Professional Soldier *(1959),* The New Military: Changing Patterns of Organization *(1964), and* The Military in the Political Development of New Nations *(1964).*

For over twenty-five years, the United States relied on Selective Service as the means of obtaining military manpower. By July 1973, this system is scheduled to be terminated by Congress.

Thus far the chief means of realizing an all-volunteer armed force has been an economic incentive. The revised schedules will raise the basic pay of a recruit to $268 a month, and, if we add allowances, the effective total will come to $4,872 a year, or close to the symbolic $5,000 pay that many analysts have thought necessary to achieve an all-volunteer armed force. But a substantial pay raise without a more thorough-going reorganization of the armed forces, and, indeed, a rethinking of the entire meaning of the military profession, may leave us far from the intended objective.

So far, the steps to adapt the armed forces to an all-volunteer system have been limited. There has been some improvement in the physical character of barracks facilities for enlisted personnel, a wider latitude in the rules about personal appearance, and an alteration of the daily routine of garrison life. In the area of race relations, there have been extensive training programs and group discussions, which take into account the new self-consciousness of black personnel. But on the crucial question of the relationship of the military to a *career* pattern, a relationship which links the military to later civilian life, there has been little thought, particularly as it affects officers. Many of the younger military personnel are committed to the success of the all-volunteer system, which they see as an opportunity to institute needed reforms, but the exodus of some of the most intelligent and innovative officers from the ground forces—in part because of the reduction of the military total—squeezes out some of the men who could have taken the lead in the necessary rethinking and reorganization.

On balance, it appears that the United States military will be reduced, by 1975, to an overall total of 1,750,000 men;[1] in fact, the

[1] President Nixon's Commission on an All-Volunteer Armed Force projected, after the end of the draft, an all-volunteer force of approximately 2.6 million, or slightly less than the total before the pre-Vietnam build-up. In retrospect, this appears a major miscalculation, if not a form of self-deception. In the spring of 1971, civilian officials in the Department of Defense were speaking publicly of a post–Selective Service force of approximately 2.25 million, while privately they predicted a more realistic level of 2.0 million. However, it now seems likely that the total will be 1.75 million by 1975.

Reprinted by permission and with minor changes from The Public Interest, *no. 27 (Spring 1972), pp. 104–17. Copyright © 1972 by National Affairs Inc.*

possibility of a force of 1,500,000 men thereafter cannot be ruled out. The reduction in personnel reflects national policy to limit the overall size of the armed forces and the number of troops stationed abroad. The cost of military equipment will rise at a steady rate because of the new machinery that military authorities believe they require; so will personnel costs. To keep the military budget within limits, the trend will be to reduce the number of active-duty personnel. Following the experience of Great Britain, the United States forces will most likely fail (but by a lesser margin) to meet the authorized requirements. An American equivalent of that most descriptive British term, "shortfall," will come into vogue. No doubt a range of factors will account for the failure of the military to meet its recruitment quotas: low prestige of the military profession, family dissatisfaction, excessive job rotation, underemployment during early assignments. However, it is clear that the decline in career prospects will operate as the most powerful negative incentive. Why enter a profession whose career and promotion opportunities are highly uncertain and declining? A powerful element of a self-fulfilling prophecy is already at work; each reduction in forces serves only to dampen new recruitment, especially officer recruitment. Paradoxically, the faster the initial reduction to a long-run troop level, the more readily the adaptation to a volunteer force can be made.

But all of this obscures the fact that an all-volunteer force for the first time will be a professional force, and the United States will have to confront an issue which it has not had to face before—how a full-time professional military fits into the larger framework of a democratic society. Until now, under Selective Service, there was an admixture of civilians for whom military service was an excursus in their lives; because of this large leavening the army was not walled off from the society. At the same time, the armed services always thought of the officers as a cadre which could be quickly expanded, on the outbreak of war, to include large numbers of reservists and newly inducted officers from civilian life. But, given our present doctrine of deterrence, the army that is being created will be a "force-in-being," a self-contained, technically trained

force which presumably will be adequate to maintain the "balance of terror" in nuclear war.

The problem before us, then, is what *kind* of armed forces does a modern democratic society need, and how does professional service in the army, for officers and enlisted men, mesh with civilian life. In short, the military is no longer the distinctive, isolated, "heroic" *calling* of the past, that of maintaining the "honor" of the society, but is now a *profession* and *occupation* subject to all the vicissitudes which life is exposed to in a bureaucratic setting. Given this changeover, major reorganizations are necessary in the areas of education, career system, deployment, and participation of the military in civilian life, if the men of the quality that is necessary are to be attracted to the service and if the military is to be compatible with the standards of a democratic society. It is to these problems that this essay is addressed.

THE REDEFINITION OF CAREER

The all-volunteer service requires a fundamental redefinition of the content and duration of the military career. A significant number of both officers and enlisted men will continue to serve for six years or less; for them, military experience is an interlude in an essentially civilian existence. But, for another segment, military service will cover an expanded period of time, often up to twenty years. But where do they go after that? For this group, military service must be redefined as one stage in a two-step career in public service, military service being the first step, and entry into the civil service the second. In this way the idea of a career can be shaped.

For enlisted men and women the successful completion of a specified period of service, such as two or three periods of enlistment, would constitute effective entrance into civil service employment. The United States Civil Service or the Department of Labor would have the responsibility for placing these people in the federal service or, by negotiation, with state or local governments. Such an approach would make recruitment manageable and insure a higher quality of personnel. It would also make reform of the pension system possible and would reduce costs. When an enlisted man transferred to the civil establishment, his pension benefits would be incorporated in his new job and paid upon retirement from civil employment. Or he could, if he wished, opt for private employment and take a military-type pension. Such a system is operating today in the Federal Republic of Germany with considerable effectiveness.

The pattern of the officer career would be restructured to permit a more flexible system of exit from active duty. Today, most officers leave either after short-term duty (from two to five years of obligatory service) or after twenty years of service. But an exit with appropriate pension protection after from ten to twelve years is essential for a flow of personnel which takes advantage of the newer skills of the younger men. As in the case of enlisted personnel, after a specified number of years of service, officers should have the option of joining the civilian governmental establishment or have some vested, transferable pension rights. While such an approach could be fully applied only after the present reduction in the size of the officer corps is accomplished, it could be implemented immediately for new officers entering the system.

The armed forces today face the trauma of reduction in force and at the same time the need to retain the most able personnel during a period of contracting opportunities. The impact falls most heavily on the Army, and particularly on its officers, the young captains and majors who must anticipate a slow and limited rate of advancement. This is the so-called "hump in rank" which develops during a contraction after a period of rapid expansion. The negative effects are already being felt in the high proportion of able young officers who are planning to leave after their short-term obligatory service.

A system which permits retirement after from ten to twelve years of service is an essential step to enable the armed forces to retire with dignity those of less competence and, at the same time, to reduce the hump-in-rank problem.

However, it is equally essential to deal with the more serious problems posed by the presently expanded number of general officers. The ratio of general officers to total military personnel has grown steadily since the mid-1950s, yet, despite the overall reduction of personnel, the Pentagon is reluctant to force out general officers. The excessive number of such officers has a very negative effect as the military strug-

gles to adapt to a new environment. The ground force, in particular, is sharply divided between its junior and mid-career officers, who actually fought in Vietnam, and the cadre of senior officers who flew over the battlefield or were in command management positions.

The incorporation of men in their forties into the general officer group is essential to heal the breach and to offer an incentive for able mid-career officers to remain in the service. But existing retirement procedures are only partially adequate to deal with this problem because of the large numbers involved. A special commission of the Secretary of Defense is necessary to handle the major reduction (as much as 50 or 60 percent) in the number of active-duty general officers.

PROVIDING A HOME

Over the years the United States armed forces have evolved a deployment system which reassigns manpower through the continuous movement of personnel. The pattern is justified in the name of preventing stagnation, training personnel for higher command, and adapting the organization to change. During the period between World War I and World War II, the necessity of training a small cadre which could be expanded readily during wartime gave validity to such a service-wide reassignment system. In the post-Vietnam period, as we move toward an all-volunteer force of less than two million, these procedures are outmoded.

The practice is needlessly expensive, it is disruptive of military effectiveness and solidarity, and it serves as one of the major sources of discontent with the conditions of military life. The frequent fluctuations of manpower strength since 1945 to some extent made these patterns of rotation necessary, but the all-volunteer force will have a more stable level of manpower, thus making possible a more stable system of personnel deployment.

In the case of the Army a modified version of the British regimental structure is required. Each enlisted man and each officer would be attached to a basic unit, and a significant portion of his military career would be spent within that brigade, and in rotation of assignments within the brigade. When rotated out of his basic unit for staff duty and advanced schooling, he could be expected to return to his original unit. Overseas assignments and rotation home would be within the brigade system. For the Navy a home port concept, and for the Air Force a home base, would be the equivalent of an Army brigade. These are not novelties but regular practices in other armies.

One of the most powerful sources of negative attitudes toward career military service, especially among young officers, is the feeling that their talents are underutilized. In the past, military personnel were less sensitive to their immediate assignment, since there was always the assumption that some future war would "break out" and they would be effectively engaged. But in the present political context, officers want to establish a linkage between their immediate assignment and the military purpose. The reliance of the military on short-term officers and the emergence of the concept of deterrence make the issue of boredom and the day-to-day job especially relevant.

One of the changes urgently required is that operational units be given some degree of responsibility for military training. The current practice is to centralize training in specialized training units, a practice which was justified during a period of rapid mobilization and expansion. The allocation of training functions to operational units would make it possible for personnel, especially junior officers, to be more fully engaged; it would also produce important fiscal savings. In many support, technical, and even educational units, underutilization is less a matter of inadequate daily work loads. Here the morale problem derives from the failure of military personnel to be incorporated into the life of the larger military establishment; they feel excluded from the basic mission and purpose. In such units personnel could be organized into the equivalent of fully alerted reserve units with monthly evening assignments and annual field training operations.

The armed forces have developed extensive educational programs as means of upgrading their personnel, such as programs of basic literacy and the completion of high school and even college-level work. These programs generally make use of civilian personnel and civilian institutions. While such arrangements are generally appropriate, there is considerable room for the employment of qualified active-duty military personnel. Such assignments would not interfere with regular active-duty tasks since they would be secondary and after-duty assignments.

A NEW KIND OF EDUCATION

In all the services, an officer's career is linked to an elaborate system of professional education—initial academy or ROTC schooling plus a three-stage, professional, in-service educational stepladder, to which specialized courses are added. For an important minority, there is also an advanced degree at a civilian institution. The successful officer following the prescribed career will spend as much as 25–30 percent of his career in a classroom. Military officers require extensive education; moreover, some of this education is a fringe benefit, in that it assists them in the transition to civilian employment after retirement. But the present system is wasteful; it is often mechanical and repetitive, and it involves costly logistical support and a change of duty station. Also, it is generally true that the higher the level of in-service schooling, the more the training becomes merely a form of indoctrination in official policy. Consequently, much military education is resented by military officers as a waste of time of effective portions of their professional career.

Military education, like the reassignment system, is based on the traditional notion of the "outbreak" of war and the need for rapid mobilization of a mass armed force. The services believe that they require a large pool of highly trained professional officers who have been exposed to higher professional schools, so that, if the military had to expand rapidly, enough trained officers would be available for rapid promotion. But, with the advent of nuclear weapons and the doctrine of deterrence, the military has become more a force-in-being and less a cadre for mobilization; consequently, the existing notions of military education need to be revised.

With the termination of Selective Service, the number of officer recruits who will enter the active service will decline, their academic quality will be lower, and they will be much less representative of the nation as a whole, being drawn largely from the South and Southwest and from rural and small-town areas. In order to maintain the number, quality, representativeness, and vitality of short-term, active-duty reserve officers, two basic changes are required.

First, the military services need to place a stronger emphasis on Officer Candidate Schools for recruitment and training of new officers. Young men who have successfully completed two years of college should be eligible. Many men in the middle of their college careers seek a break in their education, and can be expected to return to college after from two to four years of military service; others will be expected to work toward the completion of their college degree while on active duty.

Second, any college student in the United States—either on entrance into college or when he becomes a junior—should have access to a collegiate ROTC program. In addition to the existing and modified ROTC programs in each of the ten major metropolitan areas, there should be a composite ROTC program which would enroll students from any accredited college in the vicinity. In a particular metropolitan area, one of the existing ROTC units should be responsible for the administration and conduct of the program, but the program should be available to all colleges in the area. In many metropolitan centers, this arrangement is being carried out informally, but it needs to be formalized and publicized.

Basic changes in the nature of officer education are required. First, the format of service academy training needs to be modified in order to insure the maximum integration of the new officer into civilian society. Two paths (or a combination of the two) are possible. One would be to permit all or a portion of the junior class to study at a civilian university in the United States or abroad. Another would be to extend the academy program to five years, one of which would be devoted to a work experience with the Peace Corps or Vista or to some other form of community or business employment.

Second, the three-step, in-service schooling system needs to be consolidated. At a minimum, it should be converted into a two-level system. The most direct approach would be to eliminate the National War College and increase the *interservice* component of the colleges of the three services. Much of the National War College curriculum repeats that of the service war colleges; its atmosphere is doctrinaire and, since it is located in Washington, it places an undue emphasis on current events. The services should make more use of intensive short courses of one or two weeks duration to deal with new organizational and strategic doctrine. These courses would not involve costly logistical support or change of station, and they would be more flexible as to content and timing. Equally, there should be more alternatives to attendance at the service schools, and their importance in the system of promotion should be reduced. Instead of attendance at a service school, attendance at a civilian institution or participation in a short, intensive military course would be an acceptable substitute. This would increase the diversity of skills, backgrounds, and experience in the armed forces.

THE QUESTION OF AUTHORITY

The military must face openly and candidly the question of authority. The United States Marine Corps may be able, as its top commanders hope, to maintain its traditional organizational code of repressive basic training and formal ritual and protocol. This may be possible since the Marine Corps requires only a small number of men, and any advanced industrialized society produces a sufficient number of young men who are attracted to the aggressive symbolism and "killer" imagery of its enlisted ranks. The United States Marine Corps is a carry-over from nineteenth-century gentlemen-type officers with an admixture of toughs in the ranks. The Marines will persist, but they are more and more incompatible with the emerging political and social values of the larger society—especially in a period in which United States foreign policy operates under the banner "no more Vietnams" or its equivalents, and the purpose of the military is to maintain a defensive posture of deterrent force, operating under the conception of a constabulary.

There is sufficient experience to show that a combat-ready force, fully sensitive to its "heroic" traditions and under the closest operational control, can be trained and maintained without brutality, personal degradation, or "Mickey Mouse" discipline. The armed forces must review their routines, for they do not fully realize the extent to which, in comparison with other highly effective forces, they are maintaining outmoded procedures. (Thus, for example, saluting on base serves no purpose other than to degrade the act; saluting must be reserved for crucial and selected formations.) Military traditions, military ceremonies, and *esprit de corps* are even more essential in an all-volunteer force. Moreover, these changes will have to be generated by the military itself within the context of standards set by the civilian society. In order to modify and modernize military discipline, an all-service commission on these issues needs to be established and a comparison made with the experiences of our allies.

RELATION TO CIVILIAN LIFE

The amenities supplied by the military base are essential for the well-being of the military officer and his family. The military establishment is more of a welfare state than civilian society, and these benefits are important for the retention of personnel. Nevertheless, there is considerable evidence that the military base tends to isolate the military professional from the larger civilian society. In recent years, the Department of Defense has sought to expand off-base housing under the assumption that such facilities are less expensive, or that they relieve the military of the complex of overhead activities associated with military community housing.

Yet there is no reason to believe that off-base housing enhances recruitment or effectively integrates the military into civilian society. Relocation of residence into a civilian community does not necessarily produce social integration into civilian society. It may, in fact, produce an off-base ghetto of military families. Off-base housing tends to separate military families from military base facilities, and exposes the family to disruptive pressures as long as high rates of rotation are maintained, especially under conditions where the male head of the household must frequently be away on duty assignments. A delicate balance needs to be maintained. The opportunity for base housing, in particular and appropriate areas, should be expanded. However, the essential issue is that military personnel should have some choice between residing on base or off base. But, if the question is one of integration into civilian society, the issue of civic participation is more important than location of residence. What is involved is participation in the voluntary associations which are characteristic of the larger society.

The vitality of the military profession depends on a delicate balance between a special sense of inner-group loyalty and participation in the larger society. Rather than residence per se, the quality of integration in civilian society depends on personal initiative and membership in voluntary religious and community associations. Military regulations and practice encourage participation within the format of nonpartisanship—i.e., without direct affiliation to political party groups. But rotation from one assignment to another limits the ability of a military man and his family to make contact with their community. Some research studies indicate that the level of community participation of military personnel is similar to that of persons in other occupations which have a high degree of job rotation. One would hope, therefore, that the introduction of a modified regimental system with less job rotation would increase the possibilities for more meaningful community integration.

However, new perspectives on civic participation are required if the military profession, under an all-volunteer force, is not to become socially isolated and if it is to maintain and enhance its self-respect. In West Germany the idea that an army man is a civilian in uniform has been pressed to the point that regular personnel—both officer and enlisted—are permitted to stand for political elections while on active duty. In the American context, the need to avoid a political party affiliation probably is essential. However, military personnel should be permitted to serve on local school boards, run in nonpartisan local elections, and be members of governmental advisory boards and public panels wherever they have the essential qualifications, competencies, and interest.

But the issue goes deeper. It is not the responsibility of military personnel to defend and publicize the official military policies of the United States. This is the responsibility of the elected national officials who make policy. However, in the contemporary scene, as the volunteer service becomes more and more a reality, military personnel are highly sensitive to the charge that they are mere "mercenaries." Military personnel who wish to articulate the goals and purposes of the military in a democratic society cannot be deprived of participation in community and public affairs.

By law, and particularly by judicial decree, military personnel now exercise an element of free speech and citizen petition. In a truly pluralistic society, military personnel on active duty should be able to attend educational, community, and public affairs meetings and to state their definition of the legitimacy of their profession. In short, new definitions of civic participation need to emerge, definitions which are broader than the existing ones but still compatible with the nonpartisan stance of American military law and traditions.

REDEFINING THE PROFESSION

Men select a profession or occupation for a variety of motives, and in part by accident or the sheer force of immediate circumstances. The military in the future, as in the past, will recruit from among the sons of military families —the same pattern also holds for other professions. But, because of the overriding importance of the military, it is essential that there be no concentration of military families (difficult though it may be to define that level). In fact, it is doubtful whether the military could be managed without the particular input of the sons of military families.

The military has distinctive characteristics as to the style of life it offers. In the years ahead, under a volunteer force, some of this distinctiveness will no doubt be maintained. There is also an element of activism in the military life of movement and outdoor living. Even foreign travel attracts some, and leads them to remain. Yet the scope for travel and residence abroad will decline, and again the British experience indicates that this limitation operates to inhibit recruitment and retention.

The issues of professional morale and self-respect, of course, are vital and involve the background of prolonged hostilities in Indochina and their aftermath. First, there is the issue of atrocities: their origin and character, their extent, and their appropriate punishment. From the point of view of the military profession, the orderly process of military investigation and military justice constitutes the essential mechanism for coming to terms with these grave issues. But this problem is more complex; it involves an examination of the training and outlook of the United States military in Vietnam, including an understanding of the impact of that particular environment on the behavior of Americans under combat conditions. It is not an issue that can be avoided.

Second, the conduct of the war in Vietnam brings into question the role of military advice and the adequacy of military planning. In the post–Korean War period, the military expressed the "never again" concept, and strongly resisted the idea of a land force commitment on the mainland of Asia. This strategic perspective was embodied in the person of General Matthew Ridgway, even though other views were found in the military. In Indochina, basic decisionmaking has been managed in all three Administrations by the small group in the office of the President. Vietnam has been a President's war. Whatever may have been the initial opposition (or more accurately, reluctance to become involved), it gave way, and the military displayed its traditional dedication once the decision was made by civilians. However, many military issues and failures need to be clarified. Once it became engaged in the war, the United States military accepted the notion of "victory through air power"; the limitations of that doctrine which were evident in World War II and Korea were ignored. How does one explain this extraordinary shift in military doctrine, and why was it accepted by the Joint Chiefs? These are issues for professional self-clarification.

But the purpose and goals of military institutions are the key elements in the quality of an all-volunteer force. Much has been written about the changing role of the military in contemporary society. The military profession is divided and unclear as to how much of the emerging doctrines it will accept. The notion that the military is mainly in the "killing business" dies slowly. It is difficult for any profession, and especially for the military, to see its function alter and change.

TOWARD A NEW MILITARY ROLE

Basically, the goal of effective deterrence requires a break in military traditions for the United States, although important steps have already been taken in this direction. The military will face real organizational problems in attempting to maintain its viability. A variety of tailor-made suggestions supplies no realistic basis for change. For example, while there may be specific lessons to be learned from the Israeli model, differences both in military tasks and in political settings render such an approach irrelevant to the American context. The same can be said for the Swedish format. If analogies with foreign armies are to be drawn, the experience of Great Britain with its volunteer force is the closest. Likewise, monumental schemes for giving the military new functions tend to be more ideological than practical. The tasks of the American military remain, in the first instance, military.

There is a second instance, however, and the military can and should have multiple functions. The deterrent force will have vast stand-by resources. To reconstruct the American military it will be necessary that these resources be utilized for a wide range of national emergency functions. A force-in-being of one and a half million, with only a ground force element stationed in Western Europe for NATO, will present considerable available manpower. The basic issue is not (as traditionalists see it) one of diverting the military from its fundamental mission. In fact, the military has traditionally been engaged in a variety of tasks, but the nature and content of such work changes. Not to make use of its stand-by capacity would weaken the vitality of the military, unduly isolate it from civilian society, and represent a vast waste of valuable resources.

Clearly, the military cannot engage in activities or programs which are better performed by civilian agencies. The armed forces cannot make up for the failure of civilian education and welfare, although they can and do make their contributions in these areas as a result of their routine activities. Moreover, in a democratic society the military must be removed from domestic police activities except in rare and grave crises. But a military committed to deterrence will have considerable ability to respond to emergencies, broadly defined, and to improvise. The armed forces are already involved in the control of natural disasters. Floods, hurricanes, and the like pose emergency situations which require the military's flexible resources. To natural disasters can be added the increasing number of "man-made" emergencies: oil spills, power failures, and chemical and atomic disasters. The armed forces are already indispensable in a vast array of air and sea rescue work, to which is being added, on an experimental basis, medical evacuation. But the major frontier facing the military in the years ahead rests in environmental control and in the handling of particular aspects of pollution and the destruction of resources.

The armed forces of the future will have to understand and participate in arms control arrangements. A case can be made for renaming them national emergency forces (as suggested by Albert Biderman) in order to emphasize their evolving character. I have made use of the term constabulary forces. But it makes little sense to argue about new labels. It is more important that civilian society assume an active role in directing the military to redefine its professional outlook so that it will understand that peace-keeping through a military presence, deterrence, and participation in the control of national emergencies constitute the modern definition of the heroic role.

MILITARY SERVICE AND RACE

ADAM YARMOLINSKY

The crisis of race relations is one of the most crucial issues facing the military establishment. In this article Adam Yarmolinsky traces the evolution of defense policies toward minorities and identifies several unresolved issues. Chief among these questions are the low black participation in the National Guard, the acceleration of racial unrest, and threats to minority identity within the military structure. Despite these problems, Yarmolinsky concludes that the military has accepted a certain responsibility for social change and should remain committed to the goal of total equality of opportunity. Adam Yarmolinsky has served as Special Assistant to former Secretary of Defense Robert S. McNamara and has held the position of Deputy Assistant Secretary of Defense for International Security Affairs. He is currently Chief Executive Officer, Welfare Island Development Corporation, New York.

The role of the military establishment in the status of racial minorities in American life has been important throughout the nation's history. At various times the military has followed, and at other times has led, civilian institutions in the implementation of racial policy.

Negroes fought in all of the nation's wars, but until recently—ironically enough, in a widely unpopular war—their services were usually unwanted, unwelcomed, and restricted. Negroes struggled to be included in military service from the beginning, but won only limited gains. A degree of integration occurred in the War of 1812, but Negro troops were essentially segregated until after World War II. On December 1, 1941, six days before the Japanese attack on Pearl Harbor brought the United States into that war, General George C. Marshall declared that "the settlement of vexing racial problems cannot be permitted to complicate the tremendous task of the War Department."[1] With isolated exceptions, that view prevailed throughout the war, despite the urgent need for manpower. The controversy over the fighting qualities of the Negro combat soldier, which occurred in World War I, was revived in World War II. The armed forces, in effect, followed the restrictive racial practices of civilian society. Not only were military units segregated, but Negro personnel were assigned to noncombat units with limited responsibilities. In the prestige system of the military, Negroes were placed in lower-status positions, duplicating their place in the civilian social structure. Some efforts were made to upgrade Negro personnel and to develop all-Negro combat units, but Negro soldiers were systematically underutilized, and segregated units often had low effectiveness. Negro military and civilian morale suffered in response. Only toward the end of World War II were steps taken to develop integrated combat units in the European theater; these units performed with distinction.

The first major step toward integration came on February 27, 1946, when the late Secretary of the Navy, James V. Forrestal, ordered all naval ratings open to all sailors, regardless of race. Three years later, in response to a 1948 executive order by President Truman calling for "equality of treatment and opportunity in

[1] Cited in Ulysses Lee, *The Employment of Negro Troops*, one of a series of special studies of the U.S. Army in World War II (Washington, D.C.: Office of the Chief of Military History, United States Army, 1966), p. 140.

the armed services," the Air Force implemented a program of total integration. In 1949, the Army also began to integrate—there were 220 all-black Army units in 1949—and accelerated its efforts in mid-1950 under pressure of the manpower needs of the Korean War.[2] Combat units, in particular, were rapidly integrated. But it was not until 1954 that the Army abolished its last all-Negro units.[3]

As a result of these measures, the military establishment as an institution was more racially integrated than most civilian institutions. The degree of integration varied. Enlisted ranks were integrated more rapidly and thoroughly than the officer corps. Only three blacks had been graduated from West Point prior to 1936, and the first black midshipman did not graduate from Annapolis until 1949.[4] Today [1970] West Point has sixty-two black undergraduates, Annapolis has forty, and the Air Force Academy has fifty-two. By 1969, only 2.1 percent of all officers—8,335 in the Army, Navy, Marine Corps, and Air Force—were black, though blacks are 11.2 percent of the total population.[5] There are two black brigadier generals in the Army, and one black lieutenant general in the Air Force, but there are no black admirals. A second black Air Force general recently resigned at the end of his normal career period.

The Vietnam War changed the racial profile of the armed forces dramatically. By mid-1968, Negroes made up 10.5 percent of American troops in the war zone, including those in Thailand and on naval vessels off Vietnam. The Negro has been warmly welcomed into the armed forces during the Vietnam War. General Westmoreland singled out the Negro for commendation for valor in a speech to the South Carolina legislature, a posture consistently maintained throughout his command.

Many have expressed concern about the social class basis of United States induction and

battle deaths. Deferments of middle-class students and the drafting of lower-status youths have until recently proceeded side by side, and the pressure for equalization has arisen only as the war has dragged on. It was assumed that the risks of modern war were unequally distributed and, therefore, that the casualty rate as well would fall most severely on the lower socioeconomic classes, on Negroes in particular. The argument of unequal casualties is linked to the technology of war. The heaviest casualties are to be found in the infantry, and, since its educational and skill requirements are the most limited, the infantry is expected to recruit the greatest concentrations of lower-status personnel. Research conducted on the casualties of the Korean conflict had, in effect, indicated such a heavier concentration of the battle casualties among the lower socioeconomic groups.[6] In the Vietnam War, therefore, a similar concern was raised. Of the 6,644 deaths in Vietnam for 1961–1966, 14.6 percent were Negro. During 1967, of the 9,378 men killed by enemy action, the Negro percentage was 13.5 percent. In 1970, roughly 9.9 percent of the troops in Vietnam were Negro; but Negro deaths in April 1970 stood at roughly 14 percent of the total deaths.[7]

In the Army and Marine Corps, as a whole, however, Negroes amounted to 13.3 percent of total personnel, approximately the same as the Negro component of the United States population. The proportions of Negroes in the Navy and Air Force were smaller than in the total population. Negro involvement in Vietnam combat has been disproportionately higher for a combination of reasons. According to Thomas A. Johnson, Negroes made up an estimated 20 percent of combat troops and more than 25 percent of high-risk, elite Army units such as paratroops. He reported: "Estimates of Negro participation in some airborne units have been as high as 45 percent, and up to 60 percent of some airborne rifle platoons."[8]

The acceptance—even the seeking—of dan-

[2] Charles C. Moskos, Jr., "Racial Relations in the Armed Forces," *The American Enlisted Man* (New York: Russell Sage Foundation, 1970); pp. 108–33.

[3] The Defense Department announced on October 30, 1954, that there were no longer any all-Negro units. Defense Secretary Clark Clifford said on July 25, 1968: "By 1955 all formal racial discrimination had been eliminated, although vestiges lingered into the early 1960's."

[4] Richard Bardolph, *The Negro Vanguard* (New York: Vintage Books, 1961), p. 448.

[5] *New York Times*, January 4, 1969, p. 11.

[6] A. J. Mayer and T. F. Hoult, "Social Stratification and Combat Survival," *Social Forces*, 34 (December 1955): 155–59.

[7] Thomas A. Johnson, *New York Times*, April 29, 30, and May 1, 1968. Johnson, a Negro reporter, described his findings on a trip to Vietnam in a series of three articles.

[8] *Ibid.*; see also *New York Times*, August 17, 1969, p. 54.

ger and high risk is itself related to the in-
sidious damage of racial injustice. As a white
junior infantry officer told Johnson in Vietnam:
"It's an awful indictment of America that many
young Negroes must go into the military for
fulfillment, for status—and that they prefer
service overseas to their homeland."[9] The *esprit
de corps*, prestige, and additional pay of combat arms and elite combat units are spurs to
acceptance of the possibility of death among
soldiers, many of whom have felt that life in
"the real world"—GI slang for the United
States—offers far less.

Substantial numbers of blacks have chosen
to make the military a career, attracted by the
opportunity for advancement, job security,
pay, the absence of overt discrimination, and
the sense of manhood that the military tends
to inspire. Re-enlistment rates for blacks are
double those for whites, and the percentage of
black noncommissioned officers is higher than
the percentage of blacks in the national population.[10] In the Army, one out of four middle-
level sergeants in combat occupation specialties
is black, though black soldiers in Vietnam
maintain that the number of black junior officers is decreasing.[11]

In a 1964 study of servicemen, veterans, and
nonveterans, in the sixteen to thirty-four age
bracket, sociologist Charles C. Moskos, Jr.,
found that Negro enlisted men were more inclined to like military life than were whites.
Negro civilians—both veterans and nonveterans—were more favorably disposed toward
the military than their white counterparts, and
Negro veterans placed a higher value on military training than did whites (53.9 percent
compared to 29.9 percent).[12]

But the pattern is quite the reverse in the
National Guard, where Negro membership is
disproportionately low. The *Report of the National Advisory Commission on Civil Disorders*
found that the higher percentages of Negroes
in Army units, compared with the small numbers in the National Guard, "contributed substantially to [the Army's] better performance"
on riot duty; the commission recommended an
increase in Negroes in the Guard. In response
to such recommendations, the commander of

the National Guard Bureau, Air Force Major
General Winston P. Wilson, commissioned
analysts to conduct attitude surveys, instituted
reforms in accordance with reports of the special boards, and inaugurated an experimental
test of Negro recruitment in New Jersey, where
the Guard was authorized a temporary over-
strength of 5 percent—865 extra vacancies. By
July 31, 1968, these positions had been filled,
88.7 percent of them by Negroes, and the
statewide proportion of black Guardsmen rose
from 2.5 to 6.4 percent. The Guard then
sought to increase Negro recruitment nationally, but Congress rejected a version of the
New Jersey plan because it appeared to smack
of "discrimination in reverse." By the end of
1969, the low rate of Negro enlistment had
shown no change; indeed, fewer Negroes were
in the Guard than had been at the end of
1968—5,487 in 1969, fewer than in 1968,
when 5,541 were in service, which was fewer
than in 1967, when 5,802 were in service. A
perplexed General Wilson commented: "For
some reason we haven't been able to get a handle on why they haven't wanted to enlist in
the National Guard."[13]

There is little evidence to explain low black
involvement in the National Guard. But a variety of such explanations have been given,
centering primarily on two related and racially
defined reasons: first, the black conception of
the Guard as a white institution, which they
see as related more to the states, which are
seen as socially limited, than to the federal
government, which is seen, under liberal administrations, at least, as more cosmopolitan;
and, second, the black fear that Guard duty
will require them to confront black civilians in
an adversary situation. For example, several
Negroes on riot details at Fort Knox told in-
terviewers they would not shoot Negroes, even
if ordered to do so; some said they might even
join insurrectionists. (Some whites at Fort
Knox also expressed dislike of riot duty, but
on grounds of dislike of racial rioting and personal inconvenience.) And a group of Negro
soldiers at Fort Hood, Texas, balked at the
prospect of going to Chicago for riot duty during the 1968 Democratic Convention; of the
dissidents, forty-three were ordered to the
guardhouse.

[9] Johnson, *New York Times* series.
[10] *Christian Science Monitor*, May 18, 1968, p. 1.
[11] *New York Times*, January 25, 1970.
[12] Moskos, *op. cit.*, p. 118.

[13] *New York Times*, February 26, 1970.

Despite the many positive signs of Negro involvement in the armed services, racial unrest in the armed services, paradoxically, has accelerated. Disruptions have occurred at military bases in the United States and in Vietnam. For example, at Camp Lejeune in North Carolina, in the summer of 1969, a cross was burned on the lawn of a Negro civilian employee of the base. The riot at Longbinh stockade outside Saigon in September 1968 was another serious racial incident. One white soldier was killed and several wounded after a black "takeover" of the stockade.

The most serious tensions exist in the Marine Corps, which has a higher percentage of blacks than the other services, and where iron discipline and uncompromising rules are a matter of tradition and pride. Although they have not been widely publicized, there have been numerous racial clashes at Marine bases and stockades since 1965. These outbreaks often led to harsher rules aimed at preventing communication among blacks, and stronger measures to stamp out what was considered alien black-power influence. The situation became so tense in the spring of 1969 at Camp Lejeune, North Carolina, where 3,500 Marines were stationed, that the commanding general appointed a committee of seven officers, several of them black, to study the situation. The committee reported that "a racial problem of considerable magnitude continues to exist and, in fact, may be expected to increase," and that Marines, both black and white, were being returned to civilian society "with more deeply seated prejudices than were individually possessed upon entrance to service."[14] They found "complete disillusionment of the young black Marine with progress toward the realization of equal treatment and opportunity," and noted racial prejudices in many white officers and NCOs often manifested in stories, jokes, and references; continued segregation of many local community facilities; discrimination against blacks by the MPs; failure of the "mast procedure" to provide effective redress for grievances of blacks; and increased "polarity of white to white and black to black." The command took no action on the report; on July 20, 1969, a white Marine was killed in a fight, according to charges, begun in an attack by

thirty black and Puerto Rican Marines on fourteen white Marines. The division commanding officer, Major General Michael P. Ryan, said there were "indications" that members of the Black Panthers were involved because some had been seen giving the clenched fist salute. The battalion involved was suddenly sent to the Mediterranean for training.[15]

In August there were large racial brawls at Kaneohe Marine Air Station in Honolulu and Fort Bragg, North Carolina. When the Marine Corps commandant, General Leonard F. Chapman, flew to Honolulu, a number of ranking black enlisted men presented more than a dozen complaints about bias in promotions, harsher punishment of blacks, lack of black toiletries in the post exchange, and absence of soul music in the enlisted clubs. On September 3, 1969, General Chapman issued a message to all Marine commands calling for an end to racial violence and renewed attempts to eliminate discrimination against blacks.[16] The message contained concessions to the rights of blacks to cultural diversity and racial identity. The Afro haircut would be permitted if neatly trimmed and not more than three inches on top. Blacks would not be forbidden from giving the black-power clenched fist salute to greet one another as long as it was not given "in a manner suggesting direct defiance of duly constituted authority." Soul music would be provided in the service clubs. Commanders were ordered to review their promotion and mast procedures to insure that there was no discrimination and that blacks' needs were being attended to, and to be available "after hours" to hear grievances.

After General Chapman's order, the Army and Air Force also announced that they considered Afro haircuts within regulations.[17] Secretary of the Army Stanley Resor released a directive to army commanders on racial problems which was similar to General Chapman's.[18] Thus, at a time when it appeared that

[14] *Ibid.*, August 10, 1969, p. 67.

[15] *Ibid.*, July 29, 1969, p. 19.
[16] *Ibid.*, September 4, 1969, p. 39.
[17] *Army Times*, September 17, 1969, p. 1. New Army regulations permit three-inch haircuts and neatly trimmed mustaches (goatees and beards are still banned), and decree that hair cannot be cut less than one inch without the soldier's permission. The shaving of heads or excessively short haircuts are described as "degrading or depersonalizing." *New York Times*, June 1, 1970.
[18] *New York Times*, October 14, 1969, p. 1.

official military policies and black nationalism were so far apart that no room could be made for black cultural identity, the services gave ground.

Nevertheless, a few concessions on dress will not remove many of the deep-seated antagonisms of blacks in the military or the various practices of subtle or flagrant persecution against black servicemen on and off the base. Two staff writers on the *Los Angeles Times* reporting on racial tensions in California military installations in November 1969 observed that "the troublemaker often cited is the young, single, black serviceman . . . a product of a society increasingly aware of minority civil rights, impatient and assertive in the presence of discrimination," who frequently wears an Afro haircut and reads militant black literature. They quoted a black sergeant's comments on young black recruits: "They resent taking orders from whites. First of all they see me as a brother. Right away they get me in trouble."[19] Military demands for conformity seem to the racially conscious black a reflection of white institutional authority generally and an affront to his new sense of cultural racial identity. It remains to be seen whether the militant and the military styles can be reconciled.

An Army study of race relations in United States Army bases throughout the world reported in January 1970 that "an increase in racial tensions" was widespread, and warned that, "unless immediate action is taken to identify problem areas at the squad and platoon level, increased racial confrontations can be expected." Racial problems had been ignored or covered up in the past and, therefore, "Negro soldiers seem to have lost faith in the Army."[20]

A briefing of commanders in South Vietnam on the study's findings produced some significant comments, as recorded on tape and replayed for newsmen; a sampling from the official briefing follows:

We have found that the potential and the ingredients for widespread racial violence in the Army appeared to be present.

[19] William Endicott and Stanley Williford, "Color and Mayhem: Uptight in the Armed Forces," *The Nation*, November 3, 1969.
[20] The study, reported in the *New York Times* of January 25, 1970, had been commissioned in the summer of 1969 by Army Chief of Staff General William C. Westmoreland.

The assessments of the degree of danger vary, but several different individuals of various grades said that if nothing is done there are likely to be widespread disruptions in a year or less. . . .

. . . to take an ostrichlike approach to racial fear, hostility and misunderstanding is indefensible, especially when the signs can be read in the racial obscenities written by both groups on latrine walls and can be heard from an alarming number of black soldiers who readily complain they suffer injustice in the Army solely because of their race. . . .

. . . the cries of the Negro soldiers—enlisted men and even officers—have never been so loud.

The location of a large number of sizable military installations in the South has encouraged the adoption of discriminatory attitudes among some career military personnel and has increased the tension for the black recruit. Incidents such as the burning of a wooden cross and the flying of a Confederate flag over the base at Camranh Bay in Vietnam on the day Martin Luther King was assassinated attest to continuing affronts to black racial pride. The Concerned Veterans of Vietnam, formed after the Camranh incident, now has a $65,000 grant from the Office of Economic Opportunity, offices in three states, and a veteran's assistance program. To take another example, the Moormen have organized at Quantico Marine Base in Virginia; they wear black berets and dashikis off duty and give each other the clenched fist black-power salute. Initially such actions were subjected to Marine discipline, but in an unusual departure from traditional practices, the Corps regulations have been relaxed to permit them.

Most blacks have the common problem of establishing and maintaining identity within the military structure, and, although identity is a problem confronting all servicemen, it affects blacks more deeply because the officially sanctioned military ideology rejects attempts by groups, and particularly blacks, to establish their own separate identity within the system. This highly structured way of life is considered by the military to transcend all separate identities, but it is seen by blacks as heavily dependent on traditional white attitudes and cultural identifications. Furthermore, many white officers are still unable to regard the proud young black as other than arrogant, as one who does not know his place, and needs to be brought into line for the good of the service. They see this as the legitimate military approach, while angry young blacks see it as racism.

Black anger and black separatism are correspondingly on the increase. A number of black military groups now segregate themselves in clubs and dining halls. In Vietnam it is reported that all major United States enclaves have Negro-only clubs on their fringes, "from combination whore-house and truck-wash emporiums outside Danang, to bars on Saigon's waterfront,"[21] just as whites have their favorite off-post meeting places. Jack Moskowitz, then Deputy Assistant Secretary of Defense for Civil Rights, has predicted that Negro protests would increase in Vietnam as the fighting decreased. "The young Negro serviceman is expressing his black awareness and wants to be respected."[22]

Alfred B. Fitt, Assistant Secretary of Defense for Manpower under President Johnson, has pointed out that military integration has been mainly institutional: "In all significant respects and all ways that can yield to objective analysis, in all matters over which we have any control, integration works. I would not suggest that in social, nonofficial conduct there is absence of all prejudice. In off-duty associations there is not necessarily the same kind of companionship of the duty period."[23]

According to Charles Moskos, sanctions imposed by military authorities keep on-duty racial incidents at a minimum and most "confrontations" occur off duty, and many, off base. He found—in 1966—greater integration in basic training and maneuvers than on garrison duty, in sea versus shore duty, in combat rather than in noncombat service.

If these suggestions are correct, a slowdown or cease-fire reducing combat and sea duty, but increasing noncombat garrison duty, could seriously heighten racial tension in the years to come. The acknowledged progress of Negroes in the armed services could bear the same relationship to present racial unrest as the rising expectations in civilian life probably bear to the urban rebellions. As a deprived group breaks out of confinement and sees the possibility of hope, its members become more impatient and angry.

Despite the rising and ominous signs of racial polarization in the services, there are certain indications of positive attitudinal changes among whites, and these reflect a similar paradox in the civilian society. Also paradoxical is the tendency of whites to perceive Negro progress more affirmatively than blacks do, a gap in perspective that, in itself, tends toward further alienation.

Young whites who have served in integrated units have, usually for the first time in their lives, had prolonged contact with Negroes under conditions of relative equality. According to studies of the impact of service in integrated combat units at the close of World War II, such service reduced racial prejudice among white soldiers.[24] Social contact is not enough to change attitudes; but social contact under conditions of mutual interdependence, which combat is, may lead to unit cohesion, self-esteem, and reduced prejudice.

A 1963 survey[25] indicated white and Negro agreement that an integrated military system was more efficient and more effective than a segregated one. But, while whites generally felt that Negroes were their equals in combat effectiveness and that Negroes were afforded equal opportunities, Negroes, on the other hand, were skeptical about promotional practices and believed white officers discriminated against them. White soldiers felt, almost unanimously (except for those interviewed in an "alien culture"—e.g., Korea or Hawaii), that social activities between the races should be kept to a minimum; they attributed lack of interaction between the races to "self-segregation."

Of fifty-five white GIs interviewed in the summer of 1968 while awaiting discharge at Fort Knox, Kentucky, almost one-third said they "learned something [presumably positive] about Negroes in the Army." More than one-

[21] "The Other War: Whites against Blacks in Vietnam," *The New Republic*, January 18, 1968.

[22] *Washington Post*, November 15, 1968.

[23] Interview, August 19, 1968.

[24] "Opinions about Negro Infantry Platoons in White Companies of Seven Divisions," in Guy E. Swanson *et al.*, *Readings in Social Psychology* (New York: Henry Holt, 1952), pp. 502–6.

[25] Based on interviews with seventy-eight Negro and white enlisted men and officers in four service branches and a range of ranks in Europe, the Philippines, and Korea, and interpreted by Robert F. Holz, Boston University sociology professor. Robert F. Holz, "Negro-White Relationships in the Armed Forces" (unpublished paper).

fourth indicated that they engaged in non-military "social" activities with Negroes—drinking (45 percent), attending post dances (22 percent), accompanying Negroes on leave in town (42 percent). When closer social relationships are explored, however, the color line is sharply drawn. Only 3 percent approved interracial sex and/or marriage. Of a small sample of eighteen Southern white veterans responding to a third survey,[26] one-third indicated that they had become *more* prejudiced as a result of military experience; another third reported that their racial views had not changed; and slightly less than one-third said the military experience had made them less prejudiced. Questioned about interracial sex and marriage, a surprising number manifested modifications of once-rigid views. In this regard, Whitney M. Young, Jr., executive director of the National Urban League, quotes other white soldiers from the South as saying:

they would never again be the victims of the most stupefying myths on which they were brought up. . . . It was an unusual experience to hear white men criticize a society which permitted them to grow up with superstitious notions about the Negro. These men will represent a strong and positive force for the kind of legislation and local action that will be needed when they return to their communities.[27]

Nevertheless, the majority of the small sample cited said their contacts with Negroes in the military had come primarily through compliance with orders and did not necessarily reflect "free choices," and the group tended to react with fear or hard-line attitudes toward recent civil disturbances—both of which are indications that positive attitudinal change may not be sustained in civilian life. When white veterans come home, they return to segregated institutions, and most of them readily adapt to racially defined civilian patterns, especially in housing. The conditions for maintaining interracial adhesion—mutual interdependence in a common cause—are no longer in force.

Service in an integrated unit appears to have a greater impact on Negro service members. The style of life of the armed forces between Korea and Vietnam represented to the Negro a partial achievement of the demands of the civil rights movement. At first, hostility toward whites often decreased. However, military experience contributes to rising expectations and, therefore, to more clear-cut demands among Negro veterans. At least one study indicates that black veterans experience greater difficulty in transition to civilian employment than do white veterans.[28] The long-term consequences on the civilian social structure appear to be in the direction of increased militancy in the black community. But the impact of racial integration in the armed forces extends beyond the experiences of the whites and blacks who served in the armed forces. The accomplishments of the armed forces—in particular the achievement of racial integration without violence or undue social stress—have provided a social experiment that has strengthened and validated the demands of both Negro and white civil rights leaders.

In the final months of the Johnson Administration, Assistant Secretary of Defense Fitt appraised the impact of military integration. First, military integration has served as a model indicating to the civilian society that Negroes and whites can live and work together successfully; second, it has changed racial attitudes of white servicemen; third, Negro servicemen return to civilian life prouder, more self-reliant, better able to make their way in civilian society—and less willing to tolerate unfair treatment; and, fourth, affirmative efforts to assure equal treatment for Negroes while off duty have altered attitudes in communities near military posts, even in Deep South communities.

The military, which originally followed the

---

[26] The personal experiences were obtained through interviews with veterans, most of them in Georgia, who are members of the American Legion. They were conducted "with the hope of shedding some light on the effects of the military at changing the attitudes of whites toward Negroes among a sample of whites who had been discharged from the military and had experienced some interracial contact in the military." Holz, "Negro-White Relationships in the Armed Forces."

[27] National Urban League news release, July 27, 1966.

[28] James M. Fendrich and Michael Pearson, "Are Black Veterans Making It? A Study of Veterans' Readjustment to Civil Life in a Southern Metropolis" (unpublished manuscript, Florida State University, 1969).

lead of the civilian society on racial matters, has in recent years assumed the initiative, comparatively speaking, and has served as a powerful stimulus for change in civilian practices. This process has been under way for roughly twenty years. In the early 1950s, before the Supreme Court handed down its landmark school desegregation decision, desegregation of schools for dependent children on Southern military bases had already begun; it was completed long before any Southern state began even token compliance with the 1954 Brown decision. Justice Department attorneys arguing the school integration case cited a book tracing the early military experience with desegregation, and chapters of the book in manuscript form were submitted for Supreme Court review.[29] In 1953, Judge Charles Fahy of the U.S. Court of Appeals for the District of Columbia cited the armed forces movement toward equal treatment in his minority opinion arguing for integration of Washington, D.C., restaurants. The armed forces' efforts to secure equal treatment in restaurants, in airports, and in bus and train stations for troops in transit undoubtedly affected segregation nationally in a visible way. An order banning segregation was signed by the Interstate Commerce Commission in 1961.

Until the 1960s, however, post commanders generally maintained *laissez-faire* policies toward the communities near or surrounding military bases. But, in 1963, the U.S. Commission on Civil Rights reported that off-base discrimination had a detrimental effect on the morale and efficiency of "significant numbers of military personnel."[30] Similar findings were reported by the committee appointed by President Kennedy to investigate racial conditions in the armed forces.[31] Those reports were followed by a directive of July 26, 1963, from Secretary Robert McNamara, stating that every commander "has the responsibility to oppose discriminatory practices affecting his men and their dependents and to foster equal opportunity for them, not only in areas under his immediate control, but also in nearby communities where they may live or gather in off-duty hours." The Pentagon followed up the new order by requiring commanders of bases with 500 or more personnel to submit quarterly "Off-Base Equal Opportunity Inventories" (now reduced to annual reports), and a new office of Deputy Assistant Secretary of Defense for Civil Rights and Industrial Relations sent survey teams to check on progress and single out problem areas for further attention. Restaurants, bars, taxi services, and even bathing beaches near military bases were desegregated after military intervention, usually brought about by complaints of Negro servicemen.

After sporadic attacks on the problem of equal access to off-base housing, the Defense Department in 1963, spurred by the Civil Rights Commission and the Gesell Committee, also ordered all leases for family housing to include a nondiscrimination clause. Base housing offices were directed to refuse any listings not available to all servicemen, but this policy proved difficult to enforce—a 1967 survey indicated that only 31 percent of the housing near bases was certified in writing by owners or base commanders as open to occupants of all races. In April of that year, the Defense Department ordered commanders to take a census of multiple dwelling units in their areas and to submit monthly reports on their efforts to end discriminatory practices. Metropolitan Washington was designated a "model area" for intensified efforts, and meetings were arranged between the service secretaries, civil leaders, and real-estate agents.

On February 28, 1967, the Maryland General Assembly passed a resolution calling on the Secretary of Defense to end housing discrimination for all military personnel in Maryland. On June 22 the Defense Department declared multiple-family rental facilities (apartments and trailer courts) within a prescribed radius of four main Maryland bases off limits to military personnel unless equally available

[29] Lee Nichols, *Breakthrough on the Color Front* (New York: Random House, 1954). This is an account of the development of policies of military integration.

[30] U.S. Commission on Civil Rights, *Overall Evaluation and Comments on the Department of Defense Study: The Services and Their Relations with the Community*, June 17, 1963.

[31] The Gesell Committee, appointed by President Kennedy in 1962 and headed by Washington lawyer Gerhard Gesell, found that, while within the formal framework of the military, "substantial progress . . . [has been made] toward equality of treatment and opportunity," there was a serious pattern of off-base discrimination that needed urgent attention.

to *all* military personnel. By September 1 the number of "open" facilities in Maryland had increased by 270 percent (175 facilities) and the number of units by 195 percent (13,603), which prompted the Department to step up a nationwide campaign for voluntary compliance. In 1968, after Congress passed a new civil rights act containing a fair housing provision, the Supreme Court in *Jones* v. *Mayer*, in effect, held housing discrimination to be unconstitutional; Defense Secretary Clark Clifford extended military housing sanctions to all United States bases. In June 1969, Secretary Clifford reported that 96 percent of rental units nationwide were "open" to all servicemen.[32] Still, dwellings housing fewer than four families are excluded from the statistics, and there are indications that areas designated as covered by the sanctions have excluded sections near some bases in which prospects for compliance seemed limited. A member of the American Veterans Committee, surveying the area near a South Dakota base, for example, found only about half as many nondiscriminatory units as a Defense Department inventory. By August 31, however, the Defense Department reported that 91 percent of facilities surveyed in forty-seven states were listed as "open," compared with 31 percent a year earlier, a gain of 727,400 units to a total of 1,107,100.[33]

Several military programs designed to transform former rejects into effective soldiers, including Project Transition, also have long-range implications for civilian institutions, primarily in education and employment patterns. The original Project Transition was much expanded in 1968 by order of President Johnson. About the same time, the Veterans Administration established Veterans Assistance Centers to give special aid to the "disadvantaged" in job placement and other benefits in cooperation with eight federal agencies. Names of all discharged servicemen are forwarded to the U.S. Employment Service of the Department of Labor, assuring postservice contact. Moreover, the National Urban League operates an ambitious program of postservice counseling, financed by grants from the Rockefeller Brothers Fund and a number of private firms. The Urban League job counselors, who have access to the names of discharged Negroes (apparently the first nongovernmental group accorded this privilege), report that most Negro veterans are highly employable and actively recruited by government and industry, although some are disappointed at their opportunities. Joseph Cannon, Assistant Director of the League's veterans' program, said industry is interested in the returned black veteran "because we have a salable product; besides skills, the Negro has obtained responsibility, developed leadership skills—he has been a squad leader, has done his share of decision-making under tension." A tank unit commander, for example, who has handled $40–$60 million worth of equipment commented: "It's big business; these people are managers."

Clarence Mitchell, head of the Washington Bureau of the National Association for the Advancement of Colored People, has said he found that large numbers of Negroes had obtained a further impetus from military service to enter public life, particularly politics. Their experience in the military had taught them not to be afraid of their environment.

Racial integration of military life has not served to increase the general prestige of the military. In fact, the reverse may be the case. Those in the white society who are liberals in racial matters are already the least sympathetic to the problems of the military. Instead, the military has traditionally drawn prestige and respect from Southern and rural civilians, who are the least sympathetic to racial integration. But the military establishment, whatever the unsolved problems that remain within or without its boundaries, has undoubtedly gone too far along the road to full integration and total equality of opportunity for all, regardless of class or race, to turn back. The establishment has assumed a certain responsibility for stimulating social change and has ceased to be contented solely with maintaining the *status quo* of the society it serves.

[32] Defense Department figures include two categories: "Open" and "Listed." The former are apartments or trailer courts declared "open" by management upon personal inquiry by a base commander or his senior representative. To be "listed" in the base housing referral listing, a facility must have either a signed assurance of "open" policy by management or a signed certificate by the base commander that adequate assurances have been received.

[33] The figures for housing that was "open" but not "listed" were 92 percent as of August 31, 1968, compared with 62 percent a year earlier. By this calculation the gain in "open" units was about half that shown on Pentagon records—from 747,900 to 1,117,200, an increase of 369,300 units.

In his book *The Essence of Security*, published shortly after he resigned as Defense Secretary, Robert McNamara made clear that social change was his conscious goal.

During my seven years in the Department it seemed to me that those vast resources could contribute to the attack on our tormenting social problems, both supporting our basic mission and adding to the quality of our national life. For, in the end, poverty and social injustice may endanger our national security so much as any military threat.[34]

A continuing tension between that goal and the bureaucratic reality is characteristic of the role of the military establishment in the contemporary crisis of race relations.

[34] Robert S. McNamara, *The Essence of Security* (New York: Harper & Row, 1968), pp. 122–23.

AMERICAN CIVIL-MILITARY RELATIONS IN THE 1980s

RICHARD F. ROSSER

The future of civil-military relations is a vital part of a course in American defense policy. In fact, the structure of national security policy and force levels is built on the foundation of civil-military relations. Rosser argues that the antimilitarism of the late 1960s and early 1970s will be replaced gradually by three basic factors: a restricted role for the military; the primacy of domestic politics; and amilitarism among the young. The development of his concept of amilitarism is particularly relevant to both the future of the military and its relationship with society. Colonel Richard F. Rosser is Professor and Head of the Department of Political Science at the U.S. Air Force Academy. A graduate of Ohio Wesleyan University (B.A.), he earned a master's degree in public administration and a Ph.D. in political science from Syracuse University. He is the author of An Introduction to Soviet Foreign Policy (1969) *and is presently working on a book on Soviet relations with Southeast Asia.*

A common concern in the United States is the supposed drift of American society toward militarism. Observers claim to see persuasive evidence of a foreign policy dominated by military considerations; of the armed forces of the United States essentially beyond the control of the people, Congress, and even the executive branch; of a major segment of American industry dependent upon the "war machine." The result of this "military-industrial

This paper was originally prepared in October 1970 at the Imperial Defense College, and was published in Seaford House Papers, *ed. Alastair Buchan, in 1970. It was subsequently reprinted in* Military Review, *March 1972,* Naval War College Review, *June 1972, and, in an abbreviated form, in* Air Force and Space Digest, *June 1972.*

Author's Note: *My views on civil-military relations in no way represent the official position of the Department of Defense or any other agency of the U.S. government.*

complex" is a complete distortion of American priorities at a time when America's internal problems cry out for immediate attention.[1]

My theme is that such a view of civil-military relations in the United States is wrong. The drift, I will maintain, is away from "militarism." It will be argued that the United States is experiencing a trend which is already common in other advanced nations of the West.

The factors which probably will affect American civil-military relations in the 1980s can be arbitrarily grouped under three headings: a restricted role for the military; the primacy of domestic politics; and amilitarism among the young. These factors obviously are interrelated and interdependent. For purposes of analysis, I will examine them separately.

A RESTRICTED ROLE FOR THE MILITARY

The American soldier before World War II served mainly in the continental United States. American society considered the armed forces a haven for misfits, and frowned on interchange between civilian and military society. Isolated on posts in the southern and western United States, the military turned inward.

Life for the American military changed dramatically after World War II. The United States helped occupy the defeated Axis powers, and attempted to preserve the stability of Europe and Asia to "contain communism." This fundamental revolution in peacetime American defense policy brought a fundamental change in the mission of the American armed forces. Most postwar soldiers could expect to serve half or more of their careers abroad. Moreover, American society respected the American serviceman. It believed that the military performed a vital function in protecting the "Free World" from communism.

The Nixon Doctrine indicates that the mission of the American military again may change. Vietnam surely has been a major factor in forcing a basic re-examination of the limits of America's ability to influence the course of

events in a foreign nation, and of the nature and extent of the defense commitment which America should give an ally. But a reduced role for the American armed forces probably would have come about in any case because of certain long-range trends.

The "threat" is different. There is no apparent danger today from "monolithic communism." The Soviets and the Chinese can agree on very little, certainly not on any coordinated thrust against the West. The Soviets, moreover, are changing their tactics. They finally appear to have learned the folly of attempting to engineer revolution from afar. The Kremlin continues to aid some revolutionary groups because it competes with the Chinese People's Republic. But the U.S.S.R. obviously prefers to help legitimate, anti-Western governments.

The potentially most explosive conflicts today are not between the West and the communist states, but between the two major communist powers, Russia and China, and between Israel and the Arab world. The least likely conflict of all, provided each side respects the vital interests of the other, is a general war between the West and the communist world.

The danger lies in assuming that there is no threat whatsoever from the Soviet Union or China. And this assumption could become an article of faith among Western political elites and the electorate by the next decade. Many influential and informed West Europeans already are said to believe that the Soviets are not interested in military aggression in Europe. A sudden thrust from Russia against the United States seems even more remote. We must look to military planners, who have to assume the worst possible case, to find any serious concern over a surprise attack from the Warsaw Pact Powers. Western specialists on China also claim to see little danger from the Chinese People's Republic, noting her generally restrained and defensive approach to international politics in the past several decades.

What the layman tends to forget is the cause-and-effect relationship between military preparedness and national security. Europe, for example, must be at least partly secure because of the very existence of NATO. Yet such an elementary fact appears to be poorly understood. A polling organization in West Germany

---

[1] The term "militarism" is used with considerable imprecision today, partly because it has meanings on a variety of levels—regarding foreign policy, societal value systems, style of life, and an elevated status for certain occupational groups. I will use it to mean primarily the predominance of the military over civilian factors in the internal and external relations of society.

recently found that only 7 percent of a sample group of young people could explain that NATO is an alliance which links America and Western Europe in defense against the Soviet Union. Twenty-four percent knew that NATO had something to do with defense; 52 percent had no idea what NATO was; 17 percent indulged in bizarre guesses as to its meaning.[2]

Not only the threat has changed. America's allies no longer seem to need her military aid to the degree once required. Western Europe may be several decades from political unity, but it already appears to be an economic superpower. Japan, with the third largest Gross National Product (GNP) in the world and one of the smallest defense expenditures in relation to GNP (0.8 percent in 1970), clearly could carry a greater share of her defense burden.

As America's allies grow stronger, an understandable dislike can arise for reliance on the American nuclear umbrella. General de Gaulle was the first to carry this to its logical extreme —the development of a truly independent nuclear deterrent. It is too soon to determine whether a more closely integrated Europe or a more independent Japan will follow the same path.

Barring some dramatic reversal of Soviet or Chinese policy, American public opinion may dictate a greatly reduced American presence in Europe and Asia by the 1980s, and inadvertently spur the development of independent nuclear deterrents. A Louis Harris poll commissioned by *Time* in 1969 could not find a majority of Americans who would use nuclear weapons to defend any other country. The high runner was Canada, but only 17 percent would risk the use of America's nuclear armory to defend that intimate neighbor. In the case of Italy, a staunch NATO ally, 27 percent would opt for the use of American military (*not* nuclear) force, 15 percent would offer help short of force, 37 percent would refuse to aid Italy at all, while 21 percent were not sure.[3]

Inevitably, the utility of conventional forces is being questioned. Perhaps the sharpest test will come if the American ground troop contribution to NATO is reduced in the next few years. Conventional forces in NATO already are officially declared to be at a minimum. West European NATO defense ministers reportedly have agreed in principle on "strengthening the European pillar within NATO" to try to stave off or reduce the prospective American troop withdrawal. The implementation of this agreement, however, will not be easy. The West Germans have refused for "political" reasons even to consider increasing their NATO forces, preferring instead to raise their financial contribution. Britain, according to official sources in London, could at the most supply one or two extra battalions to her army on the Rhine.[4]

If it is difficult to find enthusiasm in Europe for maintaining conventional forces in 1970, it may be even more difficult in the United States in 1980. The utility of ground forces for the protection of North America will seem even less relevant than their utility in Western Europe. NATO forces in that area at least have faced communist armies along a tangible Iron Curtain.

One factor may mitigate the trend to reduce the conventional ground forces in the advanced countries of the West—the appearance of domestic violence on a large scale and the use of armies for internal security. Most armies have done similar duty at some time in their history. But the necessity today is still a shock to the advanced societies; they supposedly had progressed to a state of internal harmony where even the police function might eventually be reduced.

Internal security duty may be a normal military duty in the advanced countries by the 1980s. When announcing the French government's 1971–1975 program for defense spending, President Pompidou singled out for special praise the *gendarmerie*,—the army branch which acts as a police force in the country and includes mobile units for riot control. He indicated that there would be especially high expenditures on the *gendarmerie* because of "the multiplication of the burdens which are imposed on it."[5] In the United States, a Directorate of Civil Disturbance Planning and Operations now functions in the Pentagon. In Britain, only a rash man would predict when

[2] *Baltimore Sun*, August 30, 1970.
[3] *Time*, May 2, 1969. It could be argued that Senator Mansfield's resolution to withdraw part of the American troops in Europe reflects an optimistic view of the commitment to defend Europe felt by the American people.

[4] *Daily Telegraph*, October 2, 1970.
[5] *The Times* (London), July 30, 1970.

troops could be withdrawn from Northern Ireland.

In short, military forces in the Western democracies will still exist in the 1980s. The question will be their size and effectiveness. There does not seem to be any particular minimum force level for national defense in an era of declining missions.

THE PRIMACY OF DOMESTIC POLITICS

A second major factor affecting civil-military relations in the 1980s in the United States— and in all Western democracies—probably will be the primacy of internal political, economic, and social issues in the minds of the public, and the relative lack of interest in international problems. One could argue that such is the natural tendency in the political process of a democracy. The individual understandably feels strongest about those things which directly affect him: the cost of living, wages, taxes, social services, law, and order. This natural tendency in politics is interrupted by war, which focuses attention on the external threat to the nation. It also is interrupted by international crises, such as the Cuban missile confrontation in 1962.

With the end of the dramatic encounters characteristic of the Cold War years, it probably was inevitable that people in the West again should think primarily about their personal well-being. And this factor in turn made the Vietnam conflict seem such an anachronism to many in the United States and Europe. They could not see a grave danger to the West in a coalition, or even a communist, government in South Vietnam. The domino effect of an all-communist Vietnam seemed an even more remote threat.

But more than the end of the Cold War is responsible for the primacy of internal questions and, particularly in the case of the United States, their urgency. The relatively prosperous Western nations now have the economic means to eliminate poverty in their societies. The contradiction between the economically possible and the political and social reality is increasingly obvious.

Affluent democratic societies also are especially vulnerable targets for minority group grievances. In the absence of threats to national

security or of internal economic crises, such groups see no reason to hold back claims on the majority for equality of political, economic, and social rights and benefits.

Elections in the Western nations are a particularly significant indicator of public concentration on domestic issues. In the British election of June 1970, the question of continuing the pullback "East of Suez" was hardly mentioned. Even the Common Market issue was ignored. This was partly because all major party leaders had agreed that Britain should join EEC. But, if debate had broken out, it probably would have centered on the kind of impact Britain's entry into EEC would have on local food prices. The longer-range political implications of joining EEC, clearly seen by political leaders, would have received little attention.

A foreign policy issue did play a major role in the United States presidential and congressional elections of 1968—Vietnam. But here the question was how to pull out—immediately or with varying degrees of "honor." No presidential aspirant suggested that this was the kind of war Americans might have to fight again in some other, distant country.[6] In contrast, the question of the adequacy of the defense budget—the supposed "missile gap"— had played an important part in the 1960 presidential election.

The most suggestive evidence of the increasing primacy of domestic concerns in the Western democracies is found in the relative share of their national resources allocated to defense, and in the manner by which they allocate that share. Because the budget and the budgetary process are so significant, I will discuss them in some detail. I also will need to distinguish among the countries of Europe and North America in this respect because the various Western democracies are at different stages in shifting priorities from international issues to domestic issues.

Defense budgets in Western Europe appear

[6] Forty percent of the electorate cited Vietnam as the most important problem facing the government on the eve of the presidential election. Black voters when taken alone, however, cited civil rights as the paramount issue. The other major issues for the white majority were "the racial crisis" and "law and order." Philip E. Converse et al., "Continuity and Change in American Politics: Parties and Issues in the 1968 Election," *American Political Science Review*, December 1969, pp. 1086–90.

to be determined primarily by domestic political considerations. The critical criterion is what the legislature and public will stand, not strategic need. The common yardstick is a given percentage of the Gross National Product. A high official of the British Ministry of Defence, for example, remarked recently that 5.5 percent of the GNP of the United Kingdom was a "reasonable" figure for annual defense expenditures.

This was not always so in Europe. During the two world wars, no one in the Western democracies worried about the percentage of the GNP spent on defense. The only limit on military spending was the national capability to produce weapons. Even in the Korean War, defense expenditures in Britain rose from 7 to 10 percent of the GNP over a two-year period.

But, as the memory of World War II faded and the visible threat from Soviet Russia appeared to decrease, West European nations seemed to reach a point where domestic concerns began to take priority over military needs. Naturally, political leaders were reluctant to admit that the defense of the state might have been compromised by another budgetary cut. They carefully assured legislators and electors that the nation was still secure. They were most convincing when a dramatic reduction in national commitments could be shown to justify an arms cut.

The primacy of internal considerations was put bluntly by Prime Minister Wilson to the House of Commons in January 1968:

There is no military strength, whether for Britain or for our alliances, except on the basis of economic strength; and it is on this basis that we best insure the security of this country. We, therefore, intend to make to the alliances of which we are members a contribution related to our economic capability.

British Defence Minister Denis Healey was especially candid about the reason for the defense cuts when speaking to the House of Commons in March 1969: Britain had to rely on the nuclear deterrent for defense because the cost of conventional forces was too great, bringing conscription, controls on trade, catastrophe for social services, and continued economic difficulties for the whole nation. This line of thinking, however, had begun much earlier in Britain. The 1957 Defence White

Paper of Duncan Sandys initiated the series of defense cuts justified on the basis that Britain's economic health had to come first. That paper envisaged that by 1962 the British Army would be reduced to 165,000 men. The figure reportedly was set according to the number of men who could be recruited, given the level of pay the Treasury would support.

In France, President de Gaulle was attempting the costly luxury of going it alone. But his nuclear deterrent was being financed at the expense of the conventional forces. The French government had never permitted military expenditure to jeopardize investment in the social and educational field. Indeed, the deployment of the deterrent force itself was delayed after the French economic crisis of 1968. Public spending for industrial and educational reform demanded first priority. In July 1970, President Pompidou announced a five-year program (1971–1975) for defense expenditures and promised more drastic cuts. For the first time, the French government will spend more annually on education than on defense. By 1975, the French defense budget will be reduced to 3 percent of the GNP (from 5.6 percent in 1965).

Perhaps the most dramatic shift in national priorities has come in Canada. Prime Minister Trudeau revealed on April 3, 1969, that his government would withdraw all of the 10,000 Canadian troops stationed in Europe. First priority would be given to the protection of Canadian sovereignty, second to the joint defense of the North American continent; NATO and United Nations commitments were well down the list. The defense budget would be frozen at $1.8 billion. Trudeau's decision to withdraw all Canadian troops from NATO subsequently was softened, but there was little doubt about his intention to forge ahead with the plan to cut the Canadian armed forces by some 15 percent in the next several years.[7]

I will now be blamed for charging that the political leaders of the Western nations have neglected the defense needs of their countries. This is not my intention. These leaders are merely reacting to public opinion as they interpret it.

Naturally, West European political leaders play a very important role in forming the pub-

[7] *The Times* (London), September 29, 1970.

lic's image of the threat. But any politician from that area who attempts to increase defense expenditures today, let alone merely maintain them at their present level, faces major roadblocks. He has great difficulty in convincing the public of a possible frontal attack by the Warsaw Pact powers on NATO. The real dangers are more subtle and thus more difficult to explain; they are the complexities of escalatory politics or nebulous future confrontations in the Third World.

The West European politician has a further problem. NATO has come to rely increasingly on the American nuclear deterrent for Europe's defense. Even the credibility of the French *Force de Frappe* depends in the last analysis on the American deterrent. How will a West European political leader in the coming decade justify even a "reasonable" figure of his country's GNP for defense needs, particularly if these funds are to pay for conventional forces which seem to the public to be increasingly irrelevant for the defense of Europe—or the North American continent? A given percentage of a GNP for defense expenditure is hardly sacrosanct. Indeed, most NATO countries are gradually decreasing the percentage of their GNP spent on defense.[8]

The ratio between defense expenditure and GNP, of course, is hardly an exact guide. The actual amount spent on defense can increase, although the percentage of GNP declines where an economy is experiencing high economic growth. West Germany in 1963 spent almost DM22 billion on defense, 6.7 percent of her GNP; in 1969, defense expenditures rose to almost DM24 billion, 4.7 percent of the GNP. Nevertheless, there would seem to be a danger in the increasing tendency to think of defense expenditure primarily in terms of a percentage of a nation's GNP. An appropriate defense effort can be soundly constructed only if it is based on a fairly realistic assessment of the present and future threats to national security.

The defense budget in the United States is not yet subordinated to domestic political or economic considerations, but there are signs that this may come about long before 1980.

[8] From 1965 to 1969, Britain decreased her defense expenditures from 6.3 to 5.1; West Germany from 4.4 to 3.5; Italy from 3.4 to 2.9; Canada from 3.2 to 2.5. See *The Military Balance, 1969–1970*, and *The Military Balance, 1970–1971*, by the Institute for Strategic Studies (London, 1969 and 1970).

Such a development has been retarded by a number of factors: the great economic wealth of the United States and the relatively light strain on the U.S. economy of defense expenditures during the postwar years; the leading role of the United States in the noncommunist world and the dependence of this sector on the American deterrent; the preoccupation of leading American political figures in the executive branch and Congress with the communist threat or international politics (witness John F. Kennedy's lack of action on civil rights until militant blacks forced the issue); and, finally, the involvement in Vietnam in the latter part of the 1960s.

The military, on the other hand, was hardly given a blank check. The growing costs of weapons systems in the 1950s, especially systems for nuclear deterrence, meant that some limit had to be placed on defense spending. This need was buttressed by the philosophical political principles of the new Republican Administration in 1952, which pledged to reduce expenditures, lower taxes, and balance the budget.

Secretary of Defense McNamara introduced the major revolution in defense budgeting in the early 1960s. For the first time, the services had to relate their force structures to specific foreign policy objectives. The capabilities of Polaris submarines were compared directly with land-based ICBMs and bomber aircraft. The Secretary of Defense then selected those systems which were politically relevant and economically feasible.

Yet the new budgetary approach did not lead to lower defense expenditures. President Kennedy found that the Eisenhower Administration had continued to place all of its eggs in the nuclear basket: the basic defense plans rested on the assumption of total nuclear war. Conventional weapons and ground forces were at a dangerously low level. Kennedy was told a few weeks after his inauguration that dispatching 10,000 men to Southeast Asia would deplete the strategic reserve. His administration went to Congress in March 1961 with a request to raise the defense budget. "Flexible Response" was to replace "Massive Retaliation."

The defense budget and the armed forces expanded greatly after 1965 to meet the costs of the Vietnam War (from 8 percent of the GNP in 1965 to 9.4 percent in 1968). And this expansion to pay for probably the most unpopular war in American history triggered the first serious debate in the United States since World War II about foreign and domestic priorities. Fuel was thrown on the fire with the signs of a new and extremely costly escalation of the strategic arms race, specifically the proposal to install an ABM system. America's internal problems with her cities, her black minority, poverty, crime, and education also appeared to be reaching a crisis stage. These pressures coincided with President Nixon's election in 1968.

The Nixon Administration seems to have abandoned McNamara's search for a "rational" calculation of the proper level of defense spending. The defense budgetary ceiling is now determined by calculating the expected revenue and subtracting the money needed for necessary domestic programs. This has resulted in a planned $5 billion reduction in defense expenditures for 1971, primarily by cutting manpower and weapons for the conventional forces. Contingency planning in the Pentagon will be based on maintaining a capability to fight one and a half wars at any given moment rather than two and a half wars (McNamara's famous planning figure). The goal for the deterrent forces will be nuclear sufficiency rather than parity or superiority.

But defense planning runs up against stubborn domestic problems, such as inflation and the pressure to end the draft. The President's target for 1972 appeared to be a $70 billion defense budget, $7 billion less than the estimate for 1970 and $10 billion less than the Vietnam high. When the budget actually went to Congress, it was around $75 billion. Eight hundred million dollars was added to the $7 billion research and development budget for new weapons. But most of the increase went for soaring manpower costs, while the general decline continued in the number of ships, planes, and men in the armed forces.

The Administration requested $83.4 billion in new, obligational authority for 1973, with an anticipated expenditure during that year of $76.5 billion. However, this will continue to give us less defense for the dollar.

In summary, Department of Defense manpower, military and civilian, is down by 1,440,000 from 1968. Purchases from industry have been cut by 40 percent in real terms.

Such reductions should have produced a massive slash in defense spending. But pay increases for military and civilian personnel totaling $16.3 billion since 1968, and price inflation for goods and services from industry totaling $6.2 billion in the same period, have wiped out any expected savings. Meanwhile, the Defense budget has fallen from 9.4 percent of the GNP in 1968 to 6.4 percent in 1973.[9] The trend experienced by other Western democracies of declining military budgets in terms of GNP now appears to be evident in the United States.

Increasing emphasis on solving domestic problems also is evident in the United States federal budget. As in Western Europe, there has been a steady increase in the proportion of tax money spent, in particular, on social services. For example, the percentage of the federal budget allocated to defense had declined steadily from 58.7 percent in 1955 to 31.8 percent in 1973. Expenditures on "human resources"—education and manpower, health, income security, and veterans' benefits—have risen during the same period from 21.1 percent to 45.0 percent.

Major reductions in defense spending of this scale, however, may not satisfy the growing group of congressional critics of the military and of the "military-industrial complex." This group is a new phenomenon in postwar American politics, and probably will play a highly significant role in American defense policy in the next decade. It is important to investigate its origins.

The executive branch initiated budgetary cuts for the armed forces in the first two decades after World War II. There was no significant congressional pressure for lowering the military budget and no critical scrutiny of weapons programs. Legislators considered such questions highly technical, and national security seemed clearly at stake.

The rise of serious congressional criticism of the defense budget in the later 1960s resulted from a number of factors, some of which were mentioned earlier: the attempt to redefine America's role in the world as a result of

[9] The United States was spending 8.3 percent of its GNP on defense in 1964, the last "peacetime" year. The American presence in Southeast Asia, therefore, was only partially responsible for the high figure of 9.4 percent in 1968.

the frustration of Vietnam; and certain long-range trends—the economic growth of Western Europe and Japan, the increasing severity of America's internal problems and an awareness of their existence. There were additional factors which have not been noted. The Vietnam War, for example, severely tarnished the prestige of the American military. It was charged with inefficiency, indecisiveness, "body count" psychology, brutality, and heavy-handed methods in dealing with conscientious objectors and dissenters within the services.[10]

The military was even challenged on questions of tactics—a subject on which it should be the recognized expert. Some observers, basically sympathetic to the military, claimed that the armed forces did not understand the essential nature of the Vietnam War itself.[11] Other recent events have not helped the military image: a congressional report saw the North Koreans' capture of the *Pueblo* as an example of a bureaucratic structure that had grown so vast and complex that it was "unable" to respond swiftly to a major crisis.

Criticism of the military extended to the civilian leadership of the Department of Defense. Former Secretary of Defense McNamara's overly optimistic judgments in the middle 1960s on the probable course of the Vietnam War were ridiculed. But his managerial streamlining of the Department of Defense also was criticized. Forty-five Congressmen published a report in 1969 demanding that Congress reassert control over the "military bureaucracy," and blaming McNamara's rationalization of the defense structure in part for what they consider the undue influence of the military in American society. The former Secretary declared that he had lost only two percent of his battles with the military-industrial complex, but antimilitarists saw only that the armed forces were far stronger and better financed than they had been in 1960.

Equally damaging to the image of all military and civilian members of the Department of Defense and of the defense industries have been investigations into contracting and procurement practices. Senator Proxmire's subcommittee on "Economy in Government" charged that the C-5A was costing some $2 billion more than originally estimated. Proxmire claimed that it was a normal practice for most major weapons systems to cost at least twice their original estimate.

It is hard to escape the conclusion that American defense expenditures will be increasingly determined by general economic considerations, and will come into competition with what are thought to be equally compelling, if not overriding, domestic needs. The American military is entering an era experienced by the militaries of other Western nations for a decade or more.

There is a final development which underlies all that I have been saying about the primacy of domestic politics, and which may have profound implications for the future conduct of foreign and defense policy by the Western democracies. For the first time in recorded history, the elite's essential monopoly of the formulation of foreign and defense policy is being seriously challenged. The mature industrial states were democratized in theory during the nineteenth and early twentieth centuries; today they are being democratized in fact. Populations are becoming mobilized politically as a result of mass education, universal and rapid communication, leisure to consider political questions, and, most of all, a feeling of competence to handle such questions.

The elite of the past, largely through their control of the socialization process, were able to indoctrinate young and old with the desired foreign and defense policy goals. The careful attention now given by the American presidency and Congress to public rumblings regarding Vietnam shows dramatically that the attempts of the policymaking elite to form public opinion face increasing difficulty. The British government of 1956 perhaps had a taste of the new phenomenon of an aroused public over Suez; the French government faced the phenomenon over Algeria. Today, lack of the credibility of the Soviet threat in the eyes of Western Europeans certainly has an impact on the ability of West European leaders to maintain their NATO contributions.[12]

---

[10] Compare these charges with similar criticism leveled against the French army for its conduct of the war in Indochina, and especially for its conduct in Algeria.

[11] See Herman Kahn *et al.*, *Can We Win in Vietnam?* (New York: Praeger, 1968); see also Robert Thompson, "What Went Wrong? The Failure of American Strategy in Vietnam," *Interplay*, April 1969.

[12] On the process of democratization in the mature industrial states, see Karl de Schweinitz, Jr., "Growth, Development, and Political Modernization," *World Politics*, 22 (July 1970): 518–40.

We are not yet at the point where every voter has an intelligent and informed opinion about all issues. There are also exceedingly difficult mechanical problems in translating public opinion into any kind of useful and accurate guide for policymakers. Nevertheless, the impact of a potentially concerned and mobilized public on policy implementation should be carefully considered by a Western statesman before he commits his nation in the future to a foreign venture which might prove unpopular. He almost certainly will be more selective about the use of military power—at home as well as abroad. He will be particularly wary of expensive weapons systems, which tend to multiply in cost with every technological generation. The danger is that mobilized public opinion may frustrate foreign and defense policy decisions which, though unpopular, are important to national security. Increased interest by an informed public may not always be in the public interest. As de Tocqueville wrote long ago about the American experiment, "Foreign politics demand scarcely any of those qualities which are peculiar to a democracy; they require, on the contrary, the perfect use of almost all those in which it is deficient."[13]

AMILITARISM AMONG THE YOUNG

The third major factor which will affect civil-military relations in the United States in the 1980s is the attitude of contemporary youth toward the military in general, the military as a profession, the concept of military service, the use of force in international relations—in effect, toward those concepts summarized in the West Point code of behavior: "duty, honor, country." I will crudely characterize the predominant attitude of American youth toward the military in the next decade as "amilitarism." I define "amilitarism" as apathy toward the military and all things connected with it.

Amilitarism is not the normal description of the current attitude of many American young people toward the military. We generally see the phrase "antimilitarism." And there is no doubt that this attitude exists. The young men who have made the headlines by burning draft

cards, storming the Pentagon, and distributing underground newspapers on Army posts have not been indifferent to the military.

Because antimilitarism occurred earlier in this century, the older generation in America tends to brush it off as transitory. This is largely true. Antimilitarism is never static. It seems to be greater in a given Western society: (1) the higher the rate of technological advance and sociological upheaval; (2) the more unpopular the functions the armed forces perform, externally and internally; and (3) the larger, more obvious, and more expensive the military establishment. Starting from these assumptions, the United States qualifies as the society experiencing the greatest degree of antimilitarism today.

But the vital question is what replaces antimilitarism when the above variables change, when anti-militarism is defused, as it probably will be in the United States after Vietnam. Here we must draw on the experiences of the other advanced Western nations. They appear to be over the hump as far as violent antimilitarism is concerned. They largely avoided or defused it earlier by reducing their armed forces, by opting for a volunteer army (in Britain and Canada), and by eliminating unpopular foreign commitments. Increasing use of armies for internal security may counteract this earlier achievement. Moreover, these societies have not yet caught up with the United States in regard to the state of social and technological change. Yet the antimilitarism which did exist seems to have been replaced by amilitarism among the youth.

Amilitarism among young people, of course, makes it particularly difficult to recruit for the armed forces. If a nation has universal military training or selective service, it will find a sufficient number of young men. But it may import into its ranks amilitarism, which can change to antimilitarism. If a nation has a volunteer armed force, amilitarism may make a successful recruiting campaign difficult, if not impossible.

Too little is known about the attitudes toward the military of the various social, educational, and racial groupings among American youth to determine whether antimilitarism is being displaced by amilitarism. We are dealing with a complex phenomenon in a complex society. Strains of antimilitarism, amilitarism, and *pro*militarism exist side by side among

<hr>

[13] Alexis de Tocqueville, *Democracy in America* (New York: Knopf, 1960), 1: 234.

white and black youth, college-educated men and high school dropouts, sons of middle-class parents and of "hard-hats." But I suggest that amilitarism will become dominant in the United States by 1980. I would like to give my reasons for this assumption.

The most fundamental long-range trend in the West as a whole which is affecting the attitudes of contemporary youth toward the military is the extraordinary rate of change in the twentieth century. Any major change in a society—war, revolution, economic depression —places a great strain on traditional customs and mores. And no century has witnessed such upheavals as our own. These social changes have been compounded by unprecedented developments in technology and their impact on the economic system, the political structure, and all aspects of society.

The cumulative effect of these changes is clearly profound and deep—the very nature of the authority of the "establishment" is in question. The leaders of political, religious, educational, and economic institutions are under pressure, not just to make changes, but to explain why their rule should be considered legitimate. The military, that most "establishment" of organizations in the advanced West, inevitably is called into question. How could it have been otherwise? The American armed forces, as noted earlier, are now labeled unnecessary, brutal, inhuman, irresponsible, wasteful, and, at the very least, inefficient.

The leaders of the fight for social change in the United States come from all strata and age groups, but most of all from the college youth.[14] Their generation is the first to suffer the full impact of the accumulated changes in society; they are affluent students, supported by affluent parents or state scholarships, with time to think—and demonstrate; they have learned how to dramatize their cause. Columbia University's president-elect, William J. McGill, testified before the President's Commission on Campus Unrest in August 1970 that

as many as 50 percent of all collegians now belong to an "alienated culture, hostile to science and technology, which is growing at a very rapid pace."[15] Most of the "alienated" students, incidentally, appear to be studying in the liberal arts.

America's college population does not represent all of America's youth. But a higher percentage of young people go to college in the United States than in any other country. Perhaps 40 percent of those of college age, some seven million, enter institutions of higher learning. Almost all future political and business leaders will have gone to a university, as will, by requirement of the armed forces, most officers. (The military academies, four-year degree-granting institutions, must be counted as universities in this respect.)

It has been suggested that the students pressing for change are largely the children of left or liberal parents.[16] Yet a significant development is the number of young people from impeccable WASP establishment families who now are questioning the system, in particular the Vietnam War. After talking with his children, Conservative Secretary of the Interior Walter J. Hickel wrote a famous letter to President Nixon pleading for more understanding of the antiwar attitudes of the young. Ohio Republican Senator William B. Saxbe viewed most antiwar dissenters as "crazies" until he received a jolting letter in June 1970 from his "most conservative" son—a Marine lieutenant—asking his father to help end "a war that is contrary to everything I've been taught to believe about America."[17]

The actual number of true radicals in the college population who espouse violent change is very small—perhaps no more than 1 or 2 percent of all college students. The striking thing, however, is the large number of students who are opting for withdrawal from Vietnam, a reordering of national priorities, and a change in life style.

We have yet to discuss the students concentrated in the engineering sciences, medicine, agriculture, and other technical fields who are not "turned off" by the establishment. They

---

[14] James A. Johnson notes, for example, that the greatest number of isolationists today in the United States are in the under-thirty generation. Although in no sense xenophobic and unsympathetic to the problems of foreign countries, they believe the United States would be better off tending to its more immediate domestic problems. See Johnson's article "The New Generation of Isolationists," *Foreign Affairs*, October 1970, pp. 137–46.

[15] Quoted in the feature article "When the Young Teach and the Old Learn," *Time*, August 17, 1970.
[16] Seymour Martin Lipset, "American Student Activism," The RAND Corporation, n.d.
[17] Quoted in *Time*, August 17, 1970.

combine with the blue-collar children, who go straight from high school to work or to war, to form some 80 percent of their generation. This majority tends to follow parental politics. Yet it is hardly quiescent, for it has joined the disaffected college group in diverging from parental guidelines on hair, dress, and drugs.

Here we turn to the central problem of this section: what will be the impact of the attitude of youth toward the military on armed forces recruiting in the 1980s? I will examine this question from the assumption that the present system of selective military service (the "draft") will be phased out, as planned, sometime in 1973. The armed forces then will rely completely on volunteers.

Establishment college youth may provide a sufficient reservoir of officer manpower. Having balanced the loss of Reserve Officer Training Corps (ROTC) units at prestigious Ivy League universities with the other schools on the waiting list for units, and drawing hope from the increasing number of ROTC graduates, military recruiters seem to think so. The critical imponderable is what happens to this major source of officer recruitment when a volunteer army becomes a reality?

Young men appear to join ROTC primarily so that they may avoid the draft, finish college, and later serve as an officer rather than as an enlisted man. This motivation is graphically demonstrated by the small percentage of ROTC graduates who continue in the service after their initial obligation.[18] A somewhat higher percentage of officers from the various officer candidate schools, the second most important commissioning source, remain in the service. A majority of academy graduates remain, but even that percentage may be declining. Moreover, the academies have provided only a small fraction of the new officers entering the services each year.

There is a further question, rarely asked, about officer recruiting in the absence of the draft: What kind of young men will volunteer

for the officer ranks? There will not be the broad spectrum which now exists in the service at this level. We have just noted the loss of ROTC units at Ivy League schools and the disaffection of the liberal arts students from the establishment. In short, there is the prospect of an officer corps which is increasingly unrepresentative of society as a whole. I am not concerned, however, with the supposed danger of an isolated "military caste" backed by an out-of-control military-industrial complex.[19] The problem is that a modern armed force needs highly intelligent officers with training in all the disciplines. Moreover, the military would seem to have much more sympathetic support for its needs if it were broadly representative of society.

The recruiting situation as far as enlisted men are concerned is even less encouraging. Draftees comprise only 20–25 percent of the Army's strength, but Pentagon studies show that 38 percent of the enlistees in all the services would not have volunteered without the pressure of the draft. The Air Force, for example, admits that it has had young men with high IQs waiting in line to volunteer in order to avoid the Army.

How then do we man the armed forces, and procure the right kind of personnel? The President's Commission on an All-Volunteer Armed Force, the "Gates Commission," believed the primary answer to be better pay, especially for first-term officers and enlisted men. However, there is considerable doubt as to whether a mere pay raise is sufficient inducement to procure the required number of men, with the proper skills, and to keep them in the service after their initial commitment. For in the coming decade the United States will see the further development of trends which will make even the young man who is essentially pro-military think twice before joining the armed forces, regardless of pay.

I described one of these trends in the first section of this paper—the declining world role of the American military. The American armed forces have yet to enter the era of a drastically altered mission. Yet we can gain some idea of the impact of the change in the nature and

---

[18] Only 11 percent of Army ROTC-source officers, 27 percent of regular Navy ROTC-source officers, and 38 percent of Air Force ROTC-source officers extended beyond their minimum obligation in 1970. Moreover, the retention rate for each service appears to be steadily declining. In 1961, the Army retained 32 percent of a comparable group; in 1965, 21 percent. Brooks Nihart, "Why Junior Officers Get Out," *Armed Forces Journal*, August 3, 1970.

[19] This disturbing possibility is argued in an article by Blair Clark (Senator Eugene McCarthy's national campaign manager in 1968), "The Question is What Kind of Army?" *Harper's*, September 1969.

scope of an armed forces mission or recruiting by noting the British experience.

Young British gentlemen in former years joined the army or its colonial offshoots for travel, excitement, leisure, sport, and congenial companionship. Coming from families where military service was hereditary, many thought that this was the only way of life.[20] The lure of adventure in distant lands was a powerful motivation for enlistment—not service in Britain. Even the enlisted ranks, largely composed of Irish peasants and urban poor, must have been attempting to escape a confining environment at home.[21]

Life for a British soldier today is quite different. He probably will spend most of his career in Europe, primarily in his home country. Unfortunately, the densely populated areas of Europe are not conducive to active soldiering. Moreover, the standard of living in Britain, and of the officer corps in particular, is considerably below that which had been typical of imperial postings. The British soldier is part of a deterrent force which we all hope will never be used. But what happens to armies when they never fight? The populace begins to question whether they are really necessary, and a young man inevitably asks whether service in the armed forces is worthwhile. He may see "combat," but only in performing internal security duty. And there is no more distasteful and frustrating assignment for a military man in Western society. This is not the enemy he expected.[22]

The changing role of the armed forces in major Western industrial societies such as Britain undoubtedly is having an effect on recruiting. Boys who once joined the British Army to see the Middle East, says one British school-

master, now go into middle management. They believe that they can see more of the world with an oil company than with the Army. Others suspect that the recruiting problem has deeper roots. A public school teacher who has been closely associated with the British military academy at Sandhurst and with officer recruiting comments:

There is a general failing among boys to appreciate why we need an army, a feeling that "the army is not for me." They are searching for something which they feel is more purposeful, rather than what seems to many to be a negative, unproductive policing job at the present time.[23]

There is a second trend which will make the services less attractive. I refer to the increasing contrast between life in the military and life as a civilian in the mature industrial state. A man can be patriotic, satisfied with the pay, and still not enlist or extend, because of the relative hardship of life in the military compared with a similar job in the civilian economy.

Polaris nuclear submarine officers are a case in point. They are hand-picked, highly trained and motivated seamen. Yet such men are leaving the service in increasing numbers. In the U.S. Navy, they spend sixty days under water, then ninety days in port—sixty of these ninety days involve intensive training. Many officers have been assigned to submarine sea duty for up to seventeen years. If they leave the Navy and join private industry, they earn more money, spend every night with their families, and still are doing a task which is considered a service to the community. The seriousness of the retention problem is demonstrated by the unprecedented bonus of $15,000 the Navy gives promising Polaris officers with eight years of service who volunteer to remain on duty for an additional four-year period.

The contrast between other positions in the civilian and military communities may not be as great, but it is there. For there are relatively few jobs left in a modern military organization which are completely unskilled or lack a civilian equivalent. The services need computer programmers, missile repairmen, electronic technicians, jet-engine mechanics, pilots—the list of skilled occupations is almost endless. Ad-

---

[20] See C. B. Otley, "Militarism and the Social Affiliations of the British Army Elite," in *Armed Forces and Society*, ed. Jacques Van Doorn (The Hague: Mouton, 1968), p. 105. Cf. Correlli Barnett, *Britain and Her Army* (London: The Penguin Press, 1970), pp. 343–46 and 410–13.

[21] Barnett, *op. cit.*, pp. 240–42, 280–82, 429.

[22] The desire of most career military men to be doing what they are trained for is a motivation that is often unappreciated. British recruiters have found, for example, that one variable which seems to have an immediate and beneficial impact on recruiting is for the British forces to be in action. Moreover, any kind of action ups the recruiting numbers—even duty in Ulster. Canadian officers have told me that a considerable number of young men who in other times would have joined the Canadian Army have enlisted in the United States Army to see battle in Vietnam.

[23] Henry Stanhope, "Shortfall in Sandhurst Recruiting," *The Times* (London) September 21, 1970.

vanced societies have an equal need for such valuable skills, and soon will probably offer thirty-five-hour working weeks with considerably higher pay for almost exactly the same kind of work. The former enlisted man is particularly relieved to be through with the "Mickey Mouse" annoyances of KP (Kitchen Police), reveille, barracks life, and inspections.[24]

A third trend militating against recruiting for the enlisted ranks is hard to quantify, but definitely exists. Societal values are shifting in the United States toward increased individualism, equality, and cultural and educational uniformity. The average young recruit entering the service today is likely to be at least a high school graduate who expects to earn $600–$800 a month and have his own car in civilian life; a decade ago he rarely would have graduated from high school, and his earning expectations were much more modest. Yet this young man still goes through the traditional derogatory and harsh recruit indoctrination procedures.[25]

The significance of the egalitarian ethic for the enlisted man does not necessarily diminish after basic training. Indeed, it may grow as he comes into closer contact with the officer ranks. Based on personal experience, I can testify that a considerable number of enlisted men no longer accept the armed forces' definition of an officer. They do not believe a college education is a sufficient distinction, since many enlisted men have a college education or gain it while in service. (Enlisted men who enter the service with college degrees are primarily draftees.) Moreover, Air Force enlisted men do not believe that a pilot is automatically qualified to be an officer.

It may be that in many service specialties the traditional distinction between officer and enlisted man is no longer relevant, and indeed is a needless irritant. Discipline and rank certainly must be maintained, but there could be equal opportunity for all to advance through the ranks. Police forces have operated on this principle for decades.[26]

The officer structure itself is no longer free from the egalitarian trend in American society. The "Concerned Officers' Movement," consisting of some 250 active-duty junior officers mainly educated in northeastern schools, has made national headlines by speaking out against the war in Vietnam. But even more extraordinary is the fact that some of the leaders of this movement initially were considered to be excellent young naval officers with impeccable academic and military records in ROTC or Officers' Candidate School. One of these men commented, "The Navy has no questioning, and I'd just spent four years questioning things." Establishment youth cannot totally escape wondering about the "system" while at a university. What is more natural than to question the first organization they join—the military?[27]

A fourth trend in the advanced societies also impacts on both the officer and enlisted ranks: the nature of the commitment to the organization. In mature Western societies, an individual with a skill is highly mobile. He does not feel the same degree of loyalty as did his father to a given company, industrial concern, or educational institution. The professional man supposedly is loyal to at least his profession. But even this may breaking down. Medical doctors, for example, are charged with having forgotten their Hippocratic oath; professors, their students.

This trend finds its inevitable reflection in the service. Older officers cannot understand why younger officers are not philosophically and psychologically committed to a thirty-year career when they receive their commissions. In part, military professionalism, like professional-

---

[24] See, in particular, the excellent study by Harold Wool, *The Military Specialist* (Baltimore: The Johns Hopkins Press, 1968). By 1974, only 10 percent of the enlisted men in the U.S. armed forces will be in ground combat jobs; significantly, 11 percent will be in electronics; 17 percent in other technical jobs; 18 percent in administration; 24 percent will be mechanics; 7 percent will be craftsmen, and so on. Data from the Gates Commission, *Report*, p. 44, which is based in turn on Wool's study.

[25] See the critique by Colonel Samuel H. Hays, "What is Wrong with Induction Procedures," *Military Review*, May 1970, pp. 3–7. It should be noted that the U.S. Army is now carefully reviewing its basic training program in respect to such criticisms.

[26] Shortly after World War II, the so-called Doolittle Committee (headed by Air Force General James Doolittle) attempted to narrow the differences between officer and enlisted man in the U.S. armed forces. The postwar British Labour government, philosophically committed to egalitarianism, made a serious —but unsuccessful—effort to establish a "one-ladder" system of promotion. Philip Abrams, "Democracy, Technology, and the Retired British Officer," in *Changing Patterns of Military Politics*, ed. Samuel P. Huntington (Glencoe, Ill.: The Free Press, 1962), p. 154.

[27] See Robert B. Rigg, "How the Navy Radicalized Three Young Officers," *Washington Post*, September 13, 1970.

ism in other areas, is weakening. Why should an officer make sacrifices for an ideal, a young captain asks, when few others in society are prepared to forgo the good life?[28]

Perhaps the biggest challenge to the concept of military professionalism is the need for specialization in all ranks. Young men in the service increasingly think of themselves as meteorologists, economists, electrical engineers, political scientists, nuclear physicists. If they have a commitment, it is primarily to their particular profession or discipline, and secondarily to the military profession.[29]

The officer today who has a professional skill may be most concerned about his opportunities to practice his particular specialty and to advance in that specialty. He will stay in the service if he considers that his opportunities in this regard are equal to, or better than, those in the civilian community. To put it bluntly, his basic question is what can the organization offer him—not what can he offer the organization.[30] Recent surveys indicate this trend. In a motivation survey of 400 junior officers in the U.S. Air Force in 1970, job dissatisfaction, the promotion system, and family separation were listed as the prime deterrents to an Air Force career. Pay and living conditions were the last concerns.

The American soldier is much better off today in regard to pay, training, and living conditions than his predecessor. But the attractiveness of his job always is relative. And the armed forces demand a degree of commitment, of professionalism, of sacrifice, of hardship, which increasingly diverges from that demanded by other sectors of an advanced, democratic society. Above all, the American soldier will be asked in the coming decades to accomplish tasks which probably will be both more difficult and less popular.

CONCLUSION

The dangers of prediction are well known, especially when forecasting political and social aspects of society. Alfred Vagts wrote some years ago that we all would soon live in militarist societies; Harold Lasswell, that we would move toward the garrison state. I am attempting to demonstrate that this has not happened, and will be even less probable in the advanced, democratic societies of the West—specifically the United States—by the next decade. Instead of an era of militarism, these states may be entering an era of "civilianism."[31]

I may be wrong. Certain of the trends I describe could be reversed or modified. For example, changes in leadership in the Soviet Union or China could lead to much more bellicose policies against the West. If the threat were clear, the worst days of the Cold War might be repeated. There also could be changes in the internal political climate in the United States. The so-called "silent majority" might find its voice. On the other hand, I am not sure exactly what it would say. An emphasis on law and order internally would not necessarily lead to more money for the armed forces.

If "civilianism" does come to prevail, I will not quarrel with such a state, provided the timing is right. Like most professional soldiers, I hope that the military eventually will be an anachronism. My concern is that Western societies may downgrade the necessity of having to rely on force before such action is warranted. For there is no indication yet that national security in the last analysis can depend on

[28] I recognize that this hypothesis conflicts with a study done in the early 1960s which suggested that U.S. Air Force officers had a stronger commitment to their organization than did a comparable group of business executives to their firm. The difference was thought to be in the underlying professional attitudes of the Air Force officers. See Oscar Grusky, "The Effects of Succession: A Comparative Study of Military and Business Organization," in *The New Military*, ed. Morris Janowitz (New York: Norton, 1964), pp. 83–108.

[29] A decade ago, Morris Janowitz noted the inherent tension in the military between the "heroic leader" and the "manager." The tension I am referring to is the conflict between the specialty the young officer has studied at his university and both of the types Janowitz describes. He also referred to a third type—the military technologist. There appears to be less tension between academic training and service position in this third category as long as the man is properly assigned. See Janowitz, *The Professional Soldier* (Glencoe, Ill.: The Free Press, 1960), p. 21.

[30] *Air Force Times*, October 21, 1970.

[31] Harold Lasswell defines "civilianism" as "the absorption of the military by the multivalued orientation of a society in which violent coercion is deglamorized as an end in itself and is perceived as a regrettable concession to the persistence of variables whose magnitudes we have not been able to control without paying what appears to be an excessive cost in terms of such autonomy as is possible under the cloud of chronic peril." See Lasswell's essay "The Garrison-State Hypothesis Today," in *Changing Patterns of Military Politics*, ed. Huntington, p. 65.

other than national defense forces and solidly constructed alliances.

Once a society begins to downgrade its armed forces, a descending spiral seems to take hold. The less the military function is valued by the public, the fewer good men will join the military. The fewer good men there are in the military, the more derogatory the opinion of the public about the armed forces will become—and the less money will be appropriated. At some point, the spiral will stop. Few in the West are ready for unilateral disarmament. The unanswerable question is whether the resulting armed force will be sufficient to support a society's foreign and defense policy. For it is doubtful whether any general war in the future between the major powers will permit leisurely mobilization. Even minor crises between major powers require forces-in-being. Once torn asunder, an armed force will not be easily or quickly rebuilt in the last decades of the twentieth century.

A MEDAL FOR·HORATIUS

W. C. HALL

Rome. II Calends, April, CCCLX

SUBJECT: Recommendation for Senate Medal of Honor

TO: Department of War, Republic of Rome

I. Recommend Gaius Horatius, Captain of Foot, OMCMXIV, for the Senate Medal of Honor.

II. Captain Horatius has served XVI years, all honorably.

III. On the III day of March, during the attack on the city by Lars Porsena of Clusium and his Tuscan army of CXM men, Captain Horatius voluntarily, with Sergeant Spurius Lartius and Corporal Julius Herminius, held the entire Tuscan army at the far end of the bridge until the structure could be destroyed, thereby saving the city.

IV. Captain Horatius did valiantly fight and kill one Major Picus of Clusium in individual combat.

V. The exemplary courage and the outstanding leadership of Captain Horatius are in the highest tradition of the Roman Army.

JULIUS LUCULLUS,
Commander, II Foot Legion

Ist Ind. AG. IV Calends, April, CCCLX
TO: G-III
For comment.

G. C.

Reprinted by permission and with minor changes from Army Combat Forces Journal, *January 1955, p. 18. Copyright © 1954 by the Association of the U.S. Army. Artwork is reproduced by permission from* Leatherneck, *magazine of the U.S. Marines.*

IId Ind. G-III. IX Calends, May, CCCLX
TO: G-II

I. For comment and forwarding.

II. Change paragraph III, line VIII, from
"saving the city" to "lessened the effectiveness
of the enemy attack." The Roman Army was
well dispersed tactically; the reserve had not
been committed. The phrase as written might
be construed to cast aspersions on our fine
Army.

III. Change paragraph V, lines I and II,
from "outstanding leadership" to read "com-
mendable initiative." Captain Horatius' command was II men—only I/IV of a squad.

J. C.

IIId. Ind. G-II. II Ides, June, CCCLX
TO: G-I

I. Omit strength of Tuscan forces in paragraph III. This information is classified.

II. A report evaluated as B-II states that the
officer was a Captain Pincus of Tifernum. Recommend change "Major Picus of Clusium" to
"an officer of the enemy forces."

T. J.

IVth Ind. G-I. IX Ides, January, CCCLXI
TO: JAG

I. Full name is Gaius Caius Horatius.

II. Change service from XVI to XV years.
One year in Romulus Chapter, Cub Scouts, has
been given credit for military service in error.

E. J.

Vth Ind. JAG. IId of February, CCCLXI
TO: AG

I. The Porsena raid was not during wartime; the temple of Janus was closed.

II. The action against the Porsena raid, ipso
facto, was police action.

III. The Senate Medal of Honor cannot be
awarded in peacetime. (AR CVIIIXXV, paragraph XII, c.)

IV. Suggest consideration for Soldier's
Medal.

P. B.

VIth Ind. AG. IV Calends, April CCCLXI
TO: G-I

Concur in paragraph IV, Vth Ind.

L. J.

VIIth Ind. G-I. I day of May, CCCLXI
TO: AG

I. Soldier's Medal is given for saving lives;
suggest Star of Bronze as appropriate.

E. J.

VIIIth Ind. AG. III day of June, CCCLXI
TO: JAG

For opinion.

G. C.

IXth Ind. JAG. II Calends, September,
CCCLXI
TO: AG

I. XVII months have elapsed since event
described in basic letter. Star of Bronze cannot
be awarded after XV months have elapsed.

II. Officer is eligible for Papyrus Scroll with
Metal Pendant.

P. B.

Xth Ind. AG. I Ide of October, CCCLXI
TO: G-I

For draft of citation for Papyrus Scroll with
Metal Pendant.

G. C.

XIth Ind. G-I. III Calends, October, CCCLXI
TO: G-II

I. Do not concur.

II. Our currently fine relations with Tus-
cany would suffer and current delicate negotiations might be jeopardized if publicity were
given to Captain Horatius' actions at the present time.

T. J.

XIIth Ind. G-II. VI day of November, CCCLXI
TO: G-I

A report (rated D-IV), partially verified,
states that Lars Porsena is very sensitive about
the Horatius affair.

E. T.

XIIIth Ind. G-I. X day of November, CCCLXI
TO: AG

I. In view of information contained in preceding XIth and XIIth Indorsements, you will
prepare immediate orders for Captain G. C.
Horatius to one of our overseas stations.

II. His attention will be directed to paragraph XII, POM, which prohibits interviews

or conversations with newsmen prior to arrival at final destination.

L. T.

Rome. II Calends, April I, CCCLXII

SUBJECT: Survey, Report of DEPARTMENT OF WAR

TO: Captain Gaius Caius Horatius, III Legion, V Phalanx, APO XIX, c/o Postmaster, Rome

I. Your statements concerning the loss of your shield and sword in the Tiber River on III March, CCCLX, have been carefully considered.

II. It is admitted that you were briefly in action against certain unfriendly elements on that day. However, Sergeant Spurius Lartius and Corporal Julius Herminius were in the same action and did not lose any government property.

III. The Finance Officer has been directed to reduce your next pay by II I/II talents (I III/V talents cost of one, each, sword, officers; III/IV talent cost of one, each, shield, M-II).

IV. You are enjoined and admonished to pay strict attention to conservation of government funds and property. The budget must be balanced next year.

H. HOCUS POCUS,
Lieutenant of Horse, Survey Officer

BIBLIOGRAPHY: PART IV

Ambler, John Stewart. *Soldiers against the State: The French Army in Politics*. Columbus: Ohio State University Press, 1966. 464 pp. Cloth and paper.

This is the best of a number of books on the relationship between the French military and the French society. It presents an excellent opportunity for the American student to break with a natural ethnocentricity and observe how this important relationship has existed in another cultural milieu. The chapters on post–World War II France are particularly useful. Other books on this interesting relationship in France include George A. Kelly, *Lost Soldiers: The French Army and Empire in Crisis, 1947–1962* (Cambridge, Mass.: M.I.T. Press, 1965); Orville D. Menard, *The Army and the Fifth Republic* (Lincoln: University of Nebraska Press, 1967); Henri Alleq, *The Question* (New York: George Braziller, 1958); Jean Lartequy, *Les Pretoriens* (Paris: Les Presses de la Cité, 1961).

Donovan, James A. *Militarism, U.S.A.* New York: Scribner's, 1970. 265 pp. Cloth and paper.

Militarism, U.S.A., is one of many books that try to explain the pervasiveness of the military in America today. Other books of this nature include *The Warfare State*, by Fred Cook; *Pentagon Capitalism: The Political Economy of War*, by Seymour Melman; *The War Profiteers*, by Richard F. Kaufman; *The Armed Society: Militarism in Modern America*, by Tristram Coffin; *The Economy of Death*, by Richard J. Barnet; *The Military-Industrial Complex*, by Sidney Lens; and *How to Control the Military*, by John Kenneth Galbraith. Students of the relationship between the military and society should read at least one of these books to understand a point of view which is widely held in academia and among many people within the attentive American public. The Donovan book was chosen because, as an insider's view (Donovan is a retired Marine colonel), it has greater credibility than some of the others mentioned. The military-industrial complex, a polemical phrase in itself, has inspired a great deal of writing that has only recently been subjected to serious academic criticism.

Finer, S. E. *The Man on Horseback: The Role of the Military in Politics*. New York: Praeger, 1962. 268 pp.

A study by a well-known British political scientist, this book tries to take a world view of the role of the military in politics. Finer's brief chapter entitled "The Political Weaknesses of the Military" is a useful rebuttal of much of the current literature on the pervasiveness and perniciousness of the military in politics in the United States. Conceptually sound and tightly reasoned, Finer's book shows a depth of scholarship which is often lacking in books of this kind. His knowledge of political systems throughout the world and the role of the military in these systems is encyclopedic.

Hickman, Martin B., ed. *The Military and American Society*. Beverly Hills, Calif.: Glencoe, 1971. 167 pp. Cloth and paper.

This small but useful collection of articles deals with the U.S. military's relationship with the American society. A number of excellent articles combine with a nice balance of selections to make this an extremely useful reader. The articles cover such topics as militarism, the military-industrial complex, the military and the campus, and controlling the military.

Huntington, Samuel P. *The Soldier and the State: The Theory and Politics of Civil-Military Relations*. Cambridge, Mass.: Harvard University Press, 1957. 534 pp. Cloth and paper.

This classic work is a must for all students of civil-military relations. Professor Huntington combines historical and philosophical approaches in order to educate the reader on the American military profession. Huntington feels that the military must retain its particularistic value system, its severity, regularity, and discipline. This is a thoughtful, conservative study which stands in contrast to a number of studies (including Yarmolinsky's) which discuss and salute the civilianization of the military.

———, ed. *Changing Patterns of Military Politics*. New York: Free Press, 1962. 266 pp.

This excellent collection of essays is an early attempt in a growing field, comparative civil-military relations. Huntington has selected carefully; some of the better articles include "The Garrison State Hypothesis Today," by Harold D. Lasswell; "A Comparative Theory of Military and Political Types," by David C. Rapoport; "Civil and Military Power in the Fourth Republic," by Raoul Girardet; and "Recent Writings in Military Politics—Foci and Corpora," by Huntington.

Janowitz, Morris. *The Professional Soldier. A Social and Political Portrait*. New York: The Free Press, 1972. 464 pp. Cloth and paper.

A pioneering sociological study of the officer corps of the United States military, this 1959 study still has great relevance, though some of its data need updating. For instance, the pervasive influence of service academy graduates in the higher ranks has been reduced somewhat since the mid-1950s. A recent paperback edition (1972) includes an introductory chapter which helps to bring Janowitz's earlier analysis up to date.

King, Edward L. *The Death of the Army: A Pre-Mortem*. New York: Saturday Review Press, 1972. 244 pp.

This book, written by a disgruntled, retired Army officer, is a scathing criticism of the military profession. Nevertheless, it presents a point of view that should be considered by students of American defense policy. King feels that the United States Army needs a fundamental restructuring, which would include closing down West Point, reforming the system of military justice, withdrawing most of our troops from overseas, ending most officer privileges, and purging most of the top general officers in the Army.

Little, Roger W., ed. *Handbook of Military Institutions.* Beverly Hills, Calif.: Sage Publications, 1971. 607 pp.

This is a major reference book with generally excellent, though at times outdated, articles on military organization. The emphasis is fundamentally sociological and evidences the interests of the Inter-University Seminar on Armed Forces and Society. Extensive appendixes, as well as a detailed bibliography, add to the book's value.

Masland, John W., and Radway, Laurence I. *Soldiers and Scholars: Military Education and National Policy.* Princeton: Princeton University Press, 1957. 530 pp.

The best work available on a vital, but largely overlooked, part of the military subculture: its complex educational system. Part 1 of this book is particularly useful, and Chapter 2, "Qualifications for High Level Policy Roles," presents an outstanding conceptual framework. Parts 3–5 are quite dated, and scholars interested in the specifics of military education should read the more current, but less conceptually sound, Roger W. Little, ed., *Handbook of Military Institutions.*

Moskos, Charles C., Jr., ed. *Public Opinion and the Military Establishment.* Beverly Hills, Calif.: Sage Publications, 1971. 294 pp. Cloth and paper.

This collection of papers from the ongoing Inter-University Seminar on Armed Forces and Society includes some very useful insights into a number of topical issues. The section on military education, which includes articles on trends at service academies, a comparison of attitudes between academy and ROTC students, and the socialization process in ROTC, is balanced and relevant. The section on the civilian response to military roles is also an outstanding collection of articles.

Russett, Bruce M. *What Price Vigilance? The Burdens of National Defense.* New Haven: Yale University Press, 1970. 261 pp.

Russett attempts to go beyond the traditional intuitive and anecdotal discussions of the "military-industrial complex" through the use of quantitative research. He examines the growing defense budget, finds little or no correlation between defense spending and Senate voting, shows defense spending by other nations, and discusses the "opportunity cost" of America's defense budget. The book, as an initial step toward the use of quantitative material, challenges us to be more substantive in our examination of defense issues.

Sarkesian, Sam C., ed. *The Military-Industrial Complex: A Reassessment.* Beverly Hills, Calif.: Sage Publications, 1972. 340 pp. Cloth and paper.

An excellent collection of articles, this book centers on, but is not restricted to, the military-industrial complex. Read in its entirety, it demonstrates the real complexities of the relationship between the military and industry and can, if read critically, destroy some myths which have permeated the American society for many years. The contributors include Charles Moskos, Charles Wolf, Morris Janowitz, Seymour Melman, Bruce Russett, Wayne Smith, and Adam Yarmolinsky, among others, so the approach is both eclectic and interesting.

Shiller, Herbert I., and Phillips, Joseph D., eds. *Super-State: Readings in the Military-Industrial Complex.* Urbana: University of Illinois Press, 1971. 353 pp.

A collection of twenty-three articles on the military-industrial complex, this book includes both excellent and polemical pieces. Unfortunately, it lacks balance and does not include any really first-class articles that question the premises underlying the military-industrial complex hypothesis. Nevertheless, the better articles are absolutely first-rate, and the general conspiracy tone of much of the writing on this issue is missing from most of the articles.

Stein, Harold, ed. *American Civil-Military Decisions: A Book of Case Studies.* Birmingham: University of Alabama Press, 1963. 705 pp.

This edited book of case studies by the Twentieth Century Fund should be used in conjunction with the historical study of civil-military relations, *Arms and the State.* These case studies demonstrate individually and collectively the close interaction that exists among military and civilian decisionmaking, the press, the attentive public, and mass attitudes. Some of the more interesting studies include "The Far Eastern Crisis of 1931–1932: Stimson, Hoover, and the Armed Services," by Michael Reagan; "Super Carriers and B-36 Bombers: Appropriations, Strategy, and Politics," by Paul Y. Hammond; "The American Decision to Rearm Germany," by Laurence W. Martin; and "Birth and Death of the M-Day Plan," by Albert A. Blum.

Vagts, Alfred. *A History of Militarism: Civilian and Military.* New York: Meridian Books, 1959. 542 pp.

Vagts' classic is useful not only as a historical study but also as a conceptual tool for understanding the differences between militarism and the military way, between civilian and military militarism, between traditional and modern militarism, and between totalitarian and non-totalitarian militarism.

Wolfe, J. N., and Erickson, John, eds. *The Armed Services and Society: Alteration, Management, and Integration.* Edinburgh: Edinburgh University Press, 1970. 170 pp.

A number of topical essays are presented in this volume, and each is critiqued by one or more discussants. The international flavor, as well as the interdisciplinary approach, makes this small reader particularly useful, especially in a course that includes comparative civil-military relations.

Van Doorn, Jacques, ed. *Armed Forces and Society: Sociological Essays.* The Hague: Mouton, 1968. 386 pp.

This reader covers a broad range of issues within the general framework of comparative civil-military relations. The military profession, the military and societal change, the military in developing nations, and peace-keeping military forces are the subject areas addressed by seventeen authors. The nations covered include Sweden, Britain, Ireland, Australia, the Soviet Union, the Federal Republic of Germany, France, Poland, Pakistan, Argentina, and South Korea.

Van Gils, M. R.; Janowitz, Morris; and Van Doorn, Jacques, eds. *The Perceived Role of the Military,* vols. 1–3. Rotterdam: Rotterdam University Press, 1971. Vol. 1, 390 pp.; vol. 2, 520 pp.; vol. 3, 272 pp.

This three-volume series is a first-class collection of both conceptual articles and case studies in comparative civil-military relations. Unfortunately, these volumes are available only in cloth and are expensive. Anyone interested in designing a course in civil-military relations and wishing to take a comparative approach will find this series quite helpful. Volume 1 deals with military education, organization, leadership, morale, and management, as well as with the military and public order. Volume 2 consists exclusively of case studies from Europe, Africa, Asia, the Middle East, and Latin America. Volume 3 also consists mostly of case studies; however, these studies are arranged topically rather than geographically.

Walzer, Michael. *Obligations: Essays on Disobedience, War, and Citizenship.* Cambridge, Mass.: Harvard University Press, 1970. 244 pp. Cloth and paper.

The relationship between the military and society concerns a citizen's obligations, what they are, and when he incurs them. The issue of military service depends, in part, on a theory of obligation. Using vigorous analysis, this study in modern political theory addresses a vital and topical concern and includes such issues as civil disobedience, the obligation to die for the state, conscientious objections, and the obligations of prisoners of war.

Yarmolinsky, Adam. *The Military Establishment: Its Impacts on American Society.* New York: Harper & Row, 1971. 434 pp. Cloth and paper.

This first-rate study credits the work of numerous scholars associated with the Twentieth Century Fund. Of the more recent major studies of the United States military, it is the most thorough and most balanced. In addition, this book can serve as a useful text in an undergraduate course in national security affairs or defense policy.

SECRETARIES OF DEFENSE

JAMES V. FORRESTAL, September 1947–March 1949

LOUIS A. JOHNSON, March 1949–September 1950

GEORGE C. MARSHALL, September 1950–September 1951

ROBERT A. LOVETT, September 1951–January 1953

CHARLES E. WILSON, January 1953–October 1957

NEIL H. MCELROY, October 1957–December 1959

THOMAS S. GATES, JR., December 1959–January 1961

ROBERT S. MCNAMARA, January 1961–February 1968

CLARK M. CLIFFORD, March 1968–January 1969

MELVIN R. LAIRD, January 1969–January 1973

ELLIOT L. RICHARDSON, January 1973–

Index